Socio-Economic Approach to Management Treatise

This page intentionally left blank.

Socio-Economic Approach to Management Treatise

Theory and Practices

edited by

Henri Savall

Institute of Socio Economic Approach to Management of Companies and Organizations (ISEOR) and Jean Moulin University

Véronique Zardet

Institute of Socio Economic Approach to Management of Companies and Organizations (ISEOR) and Jean Moulin University

IAP

INFORMATION AGE PUBLISHING, INC.

Charlotte, NC • www.infoagepub.com

Library of Congress Cataloging-in-Publication Data

A CIP record for this book is available from the Library of Congress
http://www.loc.gov

ISBN: 979-8-88730-262-1 (Paperback)
979-8-88730-263-8 (Hardcover)
979-8-88730-264-5 (E-Book)

Printed and bound by CPI Group (UK) Ltd, Croydon, CR0 4YY

In memory of Professors
Germán Bernácer
François Perroux
Pierre Tabatoni
Michel Péron
Gilbert Blardone

In tribute to Roger Delay Termoz

This page intentionally left blank.

CONTENTS

PART I

SOCIO-ECONOMIC MANAGEMENT: PURPOSE AND APPLICATIONS

PART II

THE ORGANIZATION OF THE ISEOR RESEARCH CENTER, PIVOT OF AN INTERNATIONAL NETWORK (CAPITALIZATION, VALIDATION, AND DIFFUSION OF SCIENTIFIC AND PRACTICAL KNOWLEDGE IN MANAGEMENT)

PART V

LEADING PUBLIC AND PARA-PUBLIC SERVICE ORGANIZATIONS: HEALTH, EDUCATION, LOCAL AUTHORITIES, ETC.

PART VI

SOCIO-ECONOMIC STRATEGIES: ORGANIZATIONAL DEVELOPMENT, CORPORATE SOCIAL RESPONSIBILITY, "TETRANORMALIZATION," BUSINESS TRANSFERS, MERGERS AND ACQUISITIONS...

PART VII

SOCIO-ECONOMIC MANAGEMENT OF HUMAN RESOURCES AND HUMAN POTENTIAL

PART VIII

SOCIO-ECONOMIC MANAGEMENT CONTROL

PART IX

ECONOMICS AND MANAGEMENT: ARTICULATION AND CONTINUUM

PART X

EPISTEMOLOGY AND RESEARCH METHODOLOGY

PREFACE TO ENGLISH EDITION

Using the Socio-Economic Approach to Management to Tackle Societal Grand Challenges

Herman Aguinis

I am delighted to write a preface for this definitive tome on socio-economic theory and the socio-economic approach to management (SEAM) co-edited by Henri Savall and Véronique Zardet. Since 1973, when he earned his PhD in economics, Professor Henri Savall has been an indefatigable researcher, educator, leader, and change-maker on a global scale. His journey regarding the creation and development of SEAM began with the publication of his 1975 book *Enriching Work, Economic Evaluation.* Since then, he founded the Institute of Socio-Economics of Enterprises and Organizations (ISEOR) in Lyon, which I had the privilege to visit on several occasions, disseminated SEAM through more than 40 trips to North America and 80 to Latin America, and developed numerous partnerships with universities, non-for-profit, and for-profit organizations. The success of his ISEOR team is no doubt also related to the fact that he has adopted a trilingual approach (i.e., French, English, and Spanish) in his publications as well in his educational and organizational applications and interventions.

I first learned about SEAM in the early 2000s. In a nutshell, SEAM has a dual and simultaneous focus on people *and* financial results. In addition, SEAM highlights the critical role of employee engagement and the need to develop the potential of all employees. This dual approach results in increased efficiency and profitability, sustainable organizational development, and higher levels of employee engagement.

The SEAM approach taught us, long ago, that we must focus on both people and profits. But, when it was first proposed, it was ahead of its time. Today, we see how needed and useful the SEAM approach can be for addressing many of today's societal grand challenges (Kunisch et al., 2023). Although I could refer to several, I will describe just three such grand

SEAM Treatise, pages xvii–xx

challenges and an admittedly selected set of chapters in this book illustrating the usefulness of the SEAM approach to tackle each of them.

SEAM AND ENCOURAGING CORPORATE SOCIAL RESPONSIBILITY

Arguably, the concept of corporate social responsibility (CSR) was launched by Howard Bowen in his 1953 book *Social Responsibilities of the Businessman.* Bowen wrote that organizational leaders have an obligation to make decisions and implement actions that are desirable in terms of the objectives and values of our society. In other words, leaders have an obligation to consider both the people and profit aspects of their organizations. SEAM is entirely consistent with this approach and therefore very well positioned to address grand challenges related to CSR, as illustrated in the chapter by Eva Conraud Koellner and Martha Ríos Manríquez titled "Impact of the socio-economic model on corporate social responsibility."

In addition to people and profit, CSR is also conceptualized to include a third "planet" dimension and hence CSR is usually referred to as addressing the "three ps:" People, profit, and planet (Aguinis & Glavas, 2012). The SEAM approach is also ideally suited to address grand challenges related to climate change as well as environmental and business sustainability, as described in the chapter by Raymond Saner and Lichia Yiu titled "Successful sustainable development goals transformation through socio-economic co-creation," the chapter by Christophe Combaudon and Helga Fouré-Joopen titled "The creation of sustainable enterprises: Contributions of the socio-economic approach to management," the chapter "An original and evaluated experiment to stimulate the sustainable development of socio-economic productivity" by Philippe Lacroix, Frantz Datry and Rodolphe Bachaud, and the one titled "Environmental change and strategic management of Universities. Towards a paradigm shift?" by Claude Jameux.

SEAM AND PROMOTING EQUITY, INCLUSION, SOCIAL JUSTICE, AND HEALTH

Equity, inclusion, social justice, and health are also considered societal grand challenges of the 21st-century. What is the role of organizations in promoting opportunities for all? What can and should organizations do to promote employee mental and physical wellbeing?

Because of SEAM's emphasis on employee development and engagement, it is an ideal approach for encouraging organizations to be more equitable and inclusive in the allocation of opportunities and resources. Good examples of this point are the chapters by Henri Savall, Michel Péron, Véronique Zardet and Marc Bonnet titled "Socially responsible capitalism" and Pierre-Alain Raphan's chapter titled "Socially responsible policy does exist."

On a related note, the SEAM approach has been applied successfully in health organizations, whose obvious goal is to promote both mental and physical wellbeing. Examples of the successful application of the SEAM approach include the chapter titled "The socio-economic approach to management and hospital organizations" by Anne Thiébaut-Bertrand and Denis Fière, the chapter "Interaction between regulation and organization: The case of the hospital system" by Frédéric Kletz and Jean-Claude Moisdon, and the chapter titled "The socio-economic improvement project, a source of quality and performance in hospitals" by Chantal Thouverez.

SEAM AND ALLEVIATING POVERTY AND PROMOTING ECONOMIC DEVELOPMENT

As a third example of societal grand challenges that can be tacked successfully by applying the SEAM approach, consider the issues of poverty and economic development. Small and family-owned business are the engine of the economy in most countries worldwide. For example, in Latin America, family businesses account for about 60% of the gross national product and over 80 % of total employment (Gomez-Mejia et al., 2023).

The SEAM approach is also ideally positioned to address the grand challenge of how to alleviate poverty and accelerate economic development, especially with a focus on small and medium enterprises—including family-owned businesses. Good examples of this point are the chapter by Gérard Desmaison and Thomas Rouveure titled "Survival-development of very small enterprises," and the chapter by Victor Frontera and Victor Caumeil titled "Professionalization of a family business through human support in order to sustain value creation."

In closing, I have been fortunate to have been exposed to the SEAM approach years ago. I certainly hope this tome will serve as a catalyst for the further dissemination of this approach worldwide.

—Herman Aguinis
The George Washington University
Washington, DC
Immediate Past President, Academy of Management
http://www.hermanaguinis.com/

REFERENCES

Aguinis, H., & Glavas, A. 2012. What we know and don't know about corporate social responsibility: A review and research agenda. *Journal of Management, 38*(4), 932–968.

Bowen, H. R. 1953. *Social responsibility of the businessman.* Harper & Row.

Gomez-Mejia, L., Mendoza López, A., Cruz Serrano, C., Duran, P., & Aguinis, H. 2023. Socioemotional wealth in volatile, uncertain, complex, and ambiguous contexts: The case of family firms in Latin America and the Caribbean. *Journal of Family Business Strategy.* https://doi.org/10.1016/j.jfbs.2022.100551

Kunisch, S., zu Knyphausen-Aufsess, D., Bapuji, H., Aguinis, H., Bansal, T., Tsui, A. S., & Pinto, J. 2023. Using review articles to address societal grand challenges. *International Journal of Management Reviews.* https://doi.org/10.1111/ijmr.12335

This page intentionally left blank.

PREFACE TO THE 1ST EDITION

René Ricol[1]

This *Treatise on Socio-Economic Approach to Management* (SEAM) will be a major reference work for a long time to come, not only for companies but also, and more globally, for the definition of public policies and in our understanding of "living together." This treatise would not have been possible and would not have brought together so many eminent contributors without the determined and absolute commitment of Professor Henri Savall, joined by Professor Véronique Zardet, to put the human dimension at the center of economic and social activity.

They began by focusing on economic and accounting data, only to quickly realize that these could lead to misinterpreting situations, making bad decisions, and choosing the wrong direction, because these figures are too often examined and used only in the light of financial performance and immediate gain. However, this Treatise aims at a Socially Responsible Capitalism, i.e., at the service of women and men who live together not only in the same company but, more globally, in the same environment and on the same planet. The work of Henri Savall, Véronique Zardet and their teams goes far beyond the search for performance in the workplace, far beyond personal fulfillment. It gives serious and concrete elements to respond to the malaise in developed societies and to poverty in developing societies.

The basic postulate is the refusal of financial capitalism, i.e., capitalism that aims to make money on money, to manage "people", a term so often used, and not "talents", to make the rich richer and the poor poorer. This postulate, clearly and distinctly expressed, is in line with the anguish revealed by all these popular movements that are taking place all over the world, and that the political powers, even before having difficulty accepting them, have difficulty to understand them because, in a way, the right words are not put on the placards brandished by the demonstrators. For example, we are going to demonstrate against an increase in the price of gasoline, the financial impact of which on the household budget, however real it may be, is often not very significant. But what this demonstration will reveal is much

SEAM Treatise, pages xxi–xxiv

deeper and more radical, it is first the incomprehension in front of the information where one will give the feeling that the society is economically well if the stock exchange prices are up, and economically badly if the prices are down. When, reasonably, one can think that the health of an economy is judged, first, by the number of jobs and the capacity to pay decent salaries and pensions that allow people to live. There is a kind of disconnection between the consensus of analysis of the elites and the daily life of citizens.

It would be possible to multiply the examples, but they all lead to the conclusion that entrepreneurial capitalism is the only way to build a model in which, naturally, the values of performance and sharing will find their place. There will be no wealth to distribute if there is no performance, and the major interest of this Treatise is to demonstrate, through an approach that is both qualitative and quantitative, that "socially responsible" favors performance, because it will allow each woman and each man at work to give the best of themselves, by being recruited in a position that matches their talents, by being trained "with patience", which means with confidence on the part of the employer, by being fully integrated because they have the right to make proposals, by having the capacity to evolve in their positions, and finally by improving their financial situation because they are entitled to receive a share of the profits. Indeed, without sharing, there can be no adherence to any economic model.

Sharing does not simply mean paying, sharing means first of all being transparent about what works and what does not, about what makes money and what does not, and in what does not make money, what is nevertheless essential to the proper functioning of the company, the association or the service. Sharing also means having clear and known rules for fixed and variable remuneration, as well as profit sharing for a company or performance-based remuneration for a public service. Finally, sharing means being concerned about those who work and knowing, when possible, how to help them in the difficulties they may face. This is a new vision of management and of the role of human resources managers when the function exists. This is not a return to a form of paternalism, which has not always been detestable. It is the simple fact that a woman or a man whose spouse is ill, whose child is disabled or, more simply, whose commuting time is unbearable is not able to do his or her job with full efficiency.

The models and examples in this book go far beyond the application of a new approach to corporate management, as all sectors of activity, public and private, are concerned. It is, in fact, a new social pact in which each person is a stakeholder in the life of the community, which is why the Treatise introduces an innovative concept by making "entrepreneurship" and "intrapreneurship" co-exist, which is the recognition of the right to act within the company, association or service. And this concept of "intrapreneurship" is very essential because it carries many consequences described in the different contributions, even if the reference to "intrapreneurship" is not explicit. For example, it is necessary to encourage dialogue, not to hide reality or to avoid allowing situations of latent conflict to develop. But beyond that, "intrapreneurship" imposes clarity on entrepreneurship because, for the concept to work, the final objectives must be clear and the most important of these objectives is the satisfaction of the client or the end user.

Is there anything revolutionary about this? Is it a desire to return to the communism that has not withstood the test of history? Is it a desire to create a form of co-management where everyone would have the same responsibilities, the same rights and same income? Is it a utopian vision carried for more than 50 years by Henri Savall? Nothing of the sort, quite the contrary. The reading of this Treatise and more generally of all the writings of the contributors, first and foremost Henri Savall, Véronique Zardet and their teams, shows that the starting point of their analyses and their models is an objective observation of situations as they are, without any preconceived ideas. I would like to refer to my father, one of the founders of the *Institut d'Administration des Entreprises* (IAE) in Lyon, who taught that, too often, we start discussing solutions before we have even examined the problem and made sure that it is properly understood.

Well, that's exactly what the contributors did. At no point did they say or write "nothing is right, we have to break everything." Nor did they propose a return to communism, which was shattered by the consequences of a bureaucracy that no one understood any more, including those who ran it. They did not propose to create a form of co-management, on the contrary, their proposals are all in the direction of improving management which, by definition, supposes that there are "managers" and therefore a hierarchy. They simply considered that the hierarchy had to be open-minded and that, consequently, management had to ensure that all those working together were well "on board", which means that they were both aware of the reasons for being and the objectives of the activity, and that each one could contribute to it in his or her own place, well trained and in his or her role. Finally, the vision of the world and of the company underpinned by this Treatise is not a utopia carried by Henri Savall, it is, and I am one of the many witnesses to it, his refusal of the misfortune, of the disinheritance of human societies that are losing their values to the point of making money "God" and the richest "gods." It is also his observation that the reconciliation between money and fulfillment at work is possible and even necessary. In fact, it is the simple observation that fulfillment at work is a key element of performance.

Henri Savall, Véronique Zardet, their teams and the many contributors to this Treatise have not only observed and proposed, but they also have in fact, as we say in the hard sciences, "proved the concept." This model works, it is effective and efficient, and the economic or social entities that use it are fully satisfied. This Treatise, which, as I said at the beginning of this preface, will be a milestone and will remain a reference work for a long time to come, is not an end but a beginning. The Treatise will allow a wider dissemination of the concepts developed, in several languages, in many countries. It is up to all of us to make it known and recognized, to promote it so that all its proposals, all its models and the underlying vision of a Socially Responsible Capitalism are used and implemented as widely as possible. We are all in a position of duty regarding this incredible amount of work, successful experimentation, and permanent implementation in many activities. And our duty is to ensure that the use of this know-how becomes widespread everywhere and in all areas of human activity because it is a concrete response to the expectations of our fellow citizens in all countries. Let there be no mistake about it, what I am saying is neither circumstantial nor grandiloquent. It is the simple observation of a man who has had to manage the consequences of a financial crisis on employment and companies, a man who has seen the crazy risks for society of financial capitalism, its risks of drifting away from democracy, and at the same time the incredible capacity to recover from situations considered lost, as soon as one trusts the women and men in charge and gives them confidence. In 2009 alone, I was able to see that with the help of the banks, restored to their historic role of supporting the real economy, we were able to save more than 140,000 jobs in France over the long term.

Before concluding, I would like to draw the attention of readers to an element developed in the Treatise and in my opinion quite essential, even beyond the subject of the Treatise itself. It indicates the usefulness, not to say the necessity, of the external view. This obviously concerns the interest of calling on consultants from outside the company, the not-for profit organization or a given public service. Those in charge of the activity have "their hands on the handlebars" and "their eyes fixed on the road, if possible, a little far away, as one learns in driving on snowy roads." But no matter how talented one is, no one has the gift of ubiquity, and the first consequence is that one cannot watch oneself in action. During a long professional life, I have noticed that all successes, without exception, are based on the quality of the men and women working on a given project, but also on the contribution of external consultants who have the double advantage of an external viewpoint but also of specialized skills. This is true for the company but also for the States. It should be added, for the sake of complete honesty, that the first to forget this rule are often the consulting actors themselves.

My conclusion could be to congratulate and thank all the contributors to the book, and in the first place Professor Véronique Zardet, for the quality of their contributions. But in fact, I would like to pay tribute to a man and to a professional life that is still far from over. I have known Professor Savall since 1970 when he was teaching accounting and I was one of his students. We lost touch and then found each other again, then lost touch and then found each other again, and finally we never left each other. Of course, I am grateful to him for having taught me accounting, and even more so for not having turned me away from it because no one can say that the subject, at first approach, gives a young student the feeling that he will be able to blossom. But, during all these years, what he has shown me and taught me are the virtues of determination and intellectual honesty. Determination is what Henri Savall needed to arrive at this Treatise. He has weathered all the headwinds, and there have been many. I don't think it's a question of jealousy, but rather the fact that his ideas and innovative research were disturbing. And that's where the second cardinal virtue of honesty came in. At no time, without acrimony, without anger, without bitterness, nor without refusing to discuss, did Henri Savall accept to make compromises that would have made his life much easier. He serenely pursued his activity as a teacher, researcher, and field man because he had proven the concept. And at no time did he stray into pride, accepting all useful external contributions, even if this led him to revise some of his approaches. May he receive here the expression of a sincere homage from his former student.

NOTE

1. President of Ricol-Lasteyrie, chartered accountant and auditor; former President of IFAC (International Federation of Accountants), and former General Commissioner for Investment appointed by French Government.

FOREWORD TO THE ENGLISH VERSION

Our thanks go first of all to Marc Bonnet for translating this work into English. Marc Bonnet joined ISEOR in 1978, after studying at the École supérieure de commerce (now E.M.Lyon). He prepared his post-graduate thesis, then his doctoral thesis in management sciences, under the direction of Henri Savall, which he defended at the Université Lumière Lyon 2. He was appointed lecturer and then professor. Since 2003, he has taught at the Institute of Business Administration (IAE Lyon) of the University Jean Moulin Lyon 3.

In 1973, Henri Savall defended his doctoral thesis in economics on a great Spanish author, a precursor of contemporary economics: Germán Bernácer. The analysis of Bernácer's heterodox work was at the origin of Henri Savall's creation of the socio-economic theory (SEAM). He then undertook research in management sciences, founded the Institute of Socio-Economics of Enterprises and Organizations (ISEOR) and published the beginnings of this theory in the seminal work *Enriching Human Work, Economic Evaluation*, published in 1975 (Dunod, Paris).

In 1998, the editors of this Treatise made their first trip to the United States.

Subsequently, more than 40 trips by Henri Savall and Véronique Zardet to the United States and Canada, plus 80 trips to Mexico and various Latin American countries, have intensified the dissemination of Socio-Economic Approach to Management (SEAM), the development of higher education and research programs, as well as socio-economic interventions in companies and organizations, with the support of institutional partners in these countries.

The first book in English on socio-economic theory was published in 1981 by Oxford University Press in New York; it is a translation of the book published in French six years earlier. Ten more of our SEAM books have been published in the United States since then.

In 2000, the International Labor Office published an educational presentation of SEAM in three languages (French, English, and Spanish) for distribution to the 180 ILO member countries.

The publication in 2003 of a special issue of the *Journal of Change Management* dedicated to SEAM, at the initiative of its editor, David Boje, stimulated the dissemination of our work in the United States, as well as the publication of our books in English, under the leadership

SEAM Treatise, pages xxv–xxvi

of Anthony Buono, editor and founder of the Research in Management Consulting book series (Information Age Publishing, Charlotte, NC).

Throughout this period, numerous academic symposia and professional conferences have presented the work of ISEOR in North America, in the United States, Canada and Mexico, as well as in Latin America, in Argentina, Uruguay, Brazil and Colombia. For over 30 years, ISEOR has developed a systematic strategy of trilingual publication in French, English and Spanish. For nearly three decades, important partnerships have been patiently built and developed with institutions of higher education, academic networks, and 50 companies and organizations that have implemented SEAM.

ISEOR has developed an important partnership with the *Academy of Management* since 1998. This renowned international institution aims to promote high quality management research worldwide and has nearly 20,000 members. ISEOR has organized 23 groundbreaking Conferences with the Academy of Management (AOM) in Lyon, France, including the partnership of Peter Sorensen and Therese Yaeger of Benedictine University and the ODC division.

In addition, more than 200 papers by ISEOR researchers have been presented at the Academy of Management (AOM) Annual Meeting since 1998: in San Diego, Chicago, Toronto, Seattle, Denver, New Orleans, Honolulu, Atlanta, Philadelphia, Anaheim, Boston, and Vancouver, among others.

ISEOR researchers have received several AOM awards and honors, including an award for cross-divisional research conducted within the Academy involving the Management Consulting, Organizational Development and Change, Research Method, Social Issues in Management divisions as well as the AOM Cross-Divisional Colloquium on CSR and Environmental Performance Measures. Institutional responsibilities have been assumed by ISEOR faculty members, including Marc Bonnet, Rickie Moore, Amandine Savall, Laurent Cappelletti, and Jérémy Salmeron.

Every year since 2013, a conference dedicated to the Socio-Economic Approach to Management (SEAM) has been organized in Duluth (Minnesota, USA) by John Conbere and Alla Heorhiadi at Saint Scholastica College, in which ISEOR's work is presented as well as papers from scholars from the United States and English-speaking countries on SEAM model.

In the United States, SEAM is taught at Benedictine University in Chicago, Bentley University in Boston, Central Michigan University, New Mexico State University in Las Cruces, Western Carolina University, and Pepperdine University in Los Angeles. Students are conducting SEAM application work in U.S. companies and organizations, with the participation of their professors, trained at the ISEOR Research Center.

We would like to thank our English-speaking colleagues for the stimulating discussions we have had over the years. Several of them agreed to contribute an interesting chapter to this treatise, in particular Herman Aguinis (Preface), Charles Richard Baker, Rana Barazi, Dolly Bassil, David Boje, Anthony Buono, Bruno Cohanier, John Conbere, Thomas Cummings, Éric Davoine, Dave Dobosenski, Jocelyne Eid, Pierre El Haddad, George El Rahbani, Robert Gephart, Tonya Henderson, Alla Heorhiadi, Yue Cai & Mark Hillon, Lara Khabbaz, Omaya Kuran, Murray Lindsay (Afterword), Emmanuel Monod, Rickie Moore, Joanne Preston, Grace Ann Rosile, Debra Salsi, Eric Sanders, Raymond Saner, Peter Sorensen, Christopher Worley, Therese Yaeger, and Lichia Yiu.

Without forgetting our late colleague and friend Michel Péron who guided us so well in our adventure in the United States and without whom it would not have been so fruitful.

—**Henri Savall** and **Véronique Zardet.**

ABSTRACTS

PART II

The organization of the ISEOR research center, pivot of an international network (capitalization, validation, and diffusion of scientific and practical knowledge in management)

La organización del centro de investigación ISEOR, eje de una red internacional (capitalización, validación y difusión de los conocimientos científicos y prácticos en materia de gestión)

L'organisation du centre de recherche ISEOR, pivot d'un réseau international (capitalisation, validation & diffusion des connaissances scientifiques et pratiques en management)

2 Junior Intervener Researchers at the ISEOR Research Center: Discovery and Integration Process

Pierrick Govart and Suzon Roche

Abstract

This chapter presents a four-handed testimony from two researchers newly integrated by the ISEOR research center after respectively 20 months and 6 months of internship. They present the story of their first months of integration, their surprises and the specificities of the working methods of the research center. In particular, they describe how they learned to set an example, how they sought to strike a balance between autonomy and cooperation, and how they analyzed the induction process and its impact.

Resumen

Este capítulo ofrece un testimonio "de cuatro manos" de dos investigadores que se han incorporado recientemente al centro de investigación ISEOR tras 20 y 6 meses de prácticas respectivamente. Nos

SEAM Treatise, pages xxvii–xcvi

cuentan la historia de sus primeros meses de integración, sus sorpresas y las peculiaridades de los métodos de trabajo del centro de investigación. En particular, describen cómo aprendieron la ejemplaridad, cómo buscaron el equilibrio entre la autonomía y la concertación, y cómo analizaron el proceso de integración y sus efectos.

Résumé

Ce chapitre propose un témoignage à quatre mains de deux intervenants-chercheurs nouvellement intégrés par le centre de recherche ISEOR après respectivement 20 mois et 6 mois de stage. Ils nous proposent le récit des premiers mois de leurs intégrations, leurs surprises et les spécificités des méthodes de travail du centre de recherche. Il y est détaillé en particulier l'apprentissage de l'exemplarité, la recherche du point d'équilibre entre l'autonomie et la concertation ainsi que leur analyse du processus d'intégration et de ses effets.

3 A Tamed Digitalization Process to Support the Development of the Socio-Economic Approach to Management

Nouria Harbi, Henri Savall, Véronique Zardet, Ridha Ziani

Abstract

SEGESE software is a major IT application designed at ISEOR since 1987 to support the socio-economic diagnoses operations. The design method of this application and the key role of the users in the initial development and in the ongoing enrichment of the knowledge base for 35 years are key and original characteristics. This tool illustrates the principle of a "tamed" digitalization, the adaptations of roles and working methods of computer experts and user-experts in socio-economic management.

Resumen

SEGESE es una importante aplicación informática diseñada dentro del ISEOR en 1987 para apoyar la realización de diagnósticos socioeconómicos. El método de diseño de esta aplicación y el papel clave de los usuarios en el desarrollo inicial y en el enriquecimiento continuo durante 35 años de la base de conocimientos son características importantes y originales. Esta herramienta ilustra el principio de la digitalización "domesticada," las adaptaciones de roles y métodos de trabajo de los expertos en informática y los usuarios-expertos en la gestión socioeconómica.

Résumé

SEGESE est une application informatique majeure conçue au sein de l'ISEOR en 1987 pour supporter la réalisation de diagnostics socio-économiques. La méthode de conception de cette application et le rôle clé des utilisateurs dans le développement initial et dans l'enrichissement permanent depuis 35 ans de la base de connaissances sont des caractéristiques majeures et originales. Cet outil illustre le principe d'une numérisation «apprivoisée», les adaptations de rôles et de méthodes de travail des experts informatiques et des utilisateurs-experts en management socio-économique.

4 Executive Education Seminars: A Scientific and Pedagogical System Complementary to Intervention-Research

Véronique Zardet and Karile Morel

Abstract

Since 1987, inter-company executive seminars have been created at the ISEOR research center. Many executives, managers and employees of the companies where intervention-research projects take place have signed up to these seminars. A variety of seminars have been developed overtime. They are specialized by theme, audience or foreign language. These seminars create scientific and pedagogical impacts by consolidating a core of generic knowledge, alongside the specific knowledge of each intervention-research. They also enhance learning and changes in managerial and professional practices thanks to the diversity of the participants.

Resumen

Desde 1987, el ISEOR ha creado cursos de formación profesional inter-empresarial, a los que asisten principalmente directores, ejecutivos, gerentes y empleados de las empresas donde se realizan las investigaciones-intervenciones. A lo largo de los años se han diseñado distintos cursos, especializados en diferentes temas, públicos o idiomas. Estos cursos producen efectos científicos y pedagógicos al consolidar un núcleo de conocimientos genéricos, junto a los conocimientos específicos de cada investigación-intervención, y al mejorar el aprendizaje y los cambios en las prácticas directivas y profesionales. La diversidad de los participantes en los cursos desempeña un papel fundamental en este sentido.

Résumé

À partir de 1987, l'ISEOR a créé des stages inter-entreprises de formation professionnelle, auxquels participent pour l'essentiel des dirigeants, cadres, managers et employés des entreprises où se déroulent les recherches-interventions. Différents stages ont été conçus au fil du temps, spécialisés par thèmes, publics ou langues étrangères. Ces stages produisent des effets scientifiques et pédagogiques, en consolidant un noyau dur de connaissances génériques, à côté des connaissances spécifiques à chaque recherche-intervention, et améliorent les apprentissages et les changements de pratiques managériales et professionnelles. La diversité des participants aux stages y joue un rôle clé.

5 Consolidating Intervention-Research Through Communication and Dissemination Mechanisms: Annual Conferences and the Journal *Recherches En Sciences De Gestion–Management Sciences–Ciencias De Gestión*

Véronique Zardet and Michelle Bonnard

Abstract

To consolidate its intervention-research activities, the ISEOR research center has deployed three complementary mechanisms, largely self-financed, to produce and disseminate innovative knowledge in management: an annual conference with a professional focus that allows for the co-evaluation of research results and is extended by the publication of conference proceedings, and an annual international academic conference that aims for openness and multi-linguistic exchanges, and finally, a trilingual academic journal, *Recherches en Sciences de Gestion–Management Sciences–Ciencias de Gestión,* that advocates diversity, tolerance, and scientific rigor, and that has been developed since 1978 with a high level of ethics.

Resumen

Para consolidar sus actividades de investigación-intervención, el centro de investigación ISEOR ha desplegado tres mecanismos complementarios autofinanciados para producir y difundir conocimientos innovadores en materia de gestión: (a) un coloquio anual mixto, con un enfoque profesional, que permite la coevaluación de los resultados de la investigación y se amplía con la publicación de las actas de la conferencia; (b) un coloquio anual internacional mixto, con un enfoque académico, que tiene como objetivo la apertura y los intercambios multilingües; (c) una revista académica trilingüe Recherches en sciences de gestion, que aboga por la diversidad, la tolerancia y el rigor científico, creada y desarrollada desde 1978 con gran ética.

Résumé

Pour consolider ses activités de recherche-intervention, le centre de recherche ISEOR a déployé trois dispositifs complémentaires autofinancés, pour produire et diffuser des connaissances innovantes en management: a) un colloque annuel mixte, à dominante professionnelle qui permet la co-évaluation des résultats de la recherche et se prolonge par la publication d'actes de congrès ; b) un colloque annuel international mixte, à dominante académique qui vise l'ouverture et les échanges multi-linguistiques ; c) une revue académique trilingue Recherches en sciences de gestion qui prône la diversité, la tolérance et la rigueur scientifique, créée et développée depuis 1978 avec une grande éthique.

---

6 The Socio-Economic Approach to Management (SEAM): A Fruitful Theory and Method: Contributions to the Collective Work and Specificities of Doctoral Theses
Alexis Roche

Abstract

This chapter presents the contribution of the doctoral theses prepared in the ISEOR international research center over the past 46 years. It highlights the contributions of theses and intervention-research for a citizen science, at the service of practitioners and not only of researchers. It shows the variety of companies and organizations in which the intervention-research have been carried out, as well as the diversity of the issues addressed according to the systemic approach of the research center. Finally, it presents a wide variety of themes of interest to companies and organizations.

Resumen

Este capítulo presenta la contribución de las tesis doctorales elaboradas en el ISEOR durante los últimos 46 años. Destaca las aportaciones de las tesis y de la investigación-intervención para una ciencia ciudadana, al servicio de los profesionales y no sólo de los investigadores. Muestra la variedad de empresas y organizaciones en las que se han llevado a cabo investigaciones-intervenciones, así como la variedad de temas abordados según el enfoque sistémico del centro de investigación. Por último, presenta una gran variedad de temas de interés para las empresas y organizaciones.

Résumé

Ce chapitre présente l'apport des thèses de doctorat préparées dans le centre de recherche international ISEOR depuis 46 ans. Il met en avant les contributions des thèses et de la recherche-intervention pour une science citoyenne, au service des praticiens et pas seulement des chercheurs. Il montre la variété des entreprises et organisations dans lesquelles ont été réalisées les recherches-interventions, ainsi que la diversité des problématiques traitées selon l'approche systémique du centre de recherche. Il présente enfin une grande de variété de thématiques qui intéressent les entreprises et les organisations.

---

7 The "Henri Savall-ISEOR Foundation"
Michel Grivel and René Charmasson

Abstract

Organizations are discovering that their performance can't be exclusively financial and short-termist. The time to reconcile economic, social, societal and environmental requirements is coming. Capitalism has to be more human to succeed. Some business leaders recognizing the relevance of ISEOR's research works have decided with its leaders to create the Henri Savall-ISEOR Foundation to reward virtuous practices of overall performance management and bring their contribution by inviting managers who wish to go further, thanks to the results of Socio-Economic research and its field methods proven for half a century.

Resumen

Las organizaciones están descubriendo que su desempeño no puede ser exclusivamente financiero y de corto plazo. Ha llegado el momento de reconciliar los imperativos económicos, sociales y medioambientales y el capitalismo se está volviendo más humano. Los líderes empresariales reconociendo la relevancia del trabajo de investigación de ISEOR, han decidido con sus gerentes crear la Fundación Henri Savall-ISEOR para recompensar las prácticas de gestión virtuosas con un desempeño global y hacer su contribución invitando a quienes deseen ir más allá, gracias a los resultados de la investigación socioeconómica y a los métodos probados en el campo durante medio siglo.

Résumé

Les organisations, découvrent que leur performance ne peut pas être exclusivement financière et court-termiste. Le temps de la conciliation des impératifs économiques, sociaux, sociétaux et environnementaux est arrivé et le capitalisme s'humanise. Des chefs d'entreprise reconnaissant la pertinence des travaux de recherche de l'ISEOR, ont décidé avec ses responsables de créer la Fondation Henri Savall-ISEOR pour récompenser les pratiques vertueuses du management à performance globale et apporter leur contribution en invitant ceux qui le souhaitent à aller plus loin, grâce aux résultats de recherche Socio-Economique et aux méthodes éprouvées sur le terrain depuis un demi-siècle.

---

8 School of Thought in the Humanities and Social Sciences and More Specifically in Economics and Management: Application to the ISEOR Research Center

Roland Pérez

Abstract

This contribution tries to answer the following questions: what is a school of thought in the humanities and social sciences in general and in the field of economics and management more particularly? How are they constructed? How do they develop? What do they become? Using this analysis grid, how can we situate ISEOR as a school of thought in the socio-economic field? The conditions of its creation, its development over several decades, its activities and products, its institutional recognition are presented.

Resumen

Esta contribución intenta responder a las siguientes preguntas: ¿Qué es una escuela de pensamiento en las humanidades y las ciencias sociales en general y en el campo de la economía y la gestión en particular? ¿Cómo se construyen? ¿Cómo se desarrollan? ¿En qué se convierten? Utilizando este cuadro de análisis, ¿Cómo podemos situar a ISEOR como escuela de pensamiento en el ámbito socioeconómico? Presentamos las condiciones de su creación, su desarrollo durante varias décadas, sus actividades y productos, su reconocimiento institucional.

Résumé

Cette contribution tente de répondre aux questions suivantes: qu'est-ce qu'une école de pensée en sciences humaines et sociales en général et dans le champ des sciences économiques et de gestion plus particulièrement ? Comment se construisent-elles ? Comment se développent-elles ? Que deviennent-elles ? En utilisant cette grille d'analyse, comment situer l'ISEOR comme école de pensée dans le domaine socio-économique ? Pour celle-ci sont rappelées les conditions de sa création, son développement sur plusieurs décennies, ses activités et produits, sa reconnaissance institutionnelle.

PART III

Stimulating the development of SMEs, very small and medium-sized enterprises (business creation, family business, cultural . . .)

Estimular el desarrollo de las PYMES, las micro y medianas empresas (empresas de nueva creación, empresas familiares, empresas culturales, etc.)

Stimuler le développement des PME, très petites et moyennes entreprises (création d'entreprise, entreprise familiale, culturelle . . .)

9 The Restaurant That Didn't Exist Yet

Barbara Filippazzo

Abstract

This chapter explains in which way and with which method the socio-economic management and the ISEOR team accompanied me in order to realize my project of creation of company: "the restaurant which did not exist." Indeed, we co-constructed with the ISEOR team a tailor-made intervention program to reduce as much as possible the dysfunctions and to recycle hidden costs in a preventive approach by using the method of scenarios.

Resumen

Este capítulo presenta de qué manera y con qué método, la gestión socioeconómica y el equipo del ISEOR me acompañaron para llevar a cabo mi proyecto de creación de empresa: "el restaurante que no existía." De hecho, hemos co-construido con el equipo de ISEOR un programa de intervención a medida para reducir al máximo los disfuncionamientos y los costos ocultos en un enfoque preventivo utilizando el método de los escenarios.

Résumé

Ce chapitre expose de quelles manières et avec quelle méthode le management socio-économique et l'équipe d'ISEOR m'ont accompagnée afin de réaliser mon projet de création d'entreprise: «le restaurant qui n'existait pas». En effet, nous avons co-construit avec l'équipe d'ISEOR un programme d'intervention sur mesure pour réduire au maximum les dysfonctionnements et coûts cachés dans une démarche préventive en utilisant la méthode des scénarii.

10 The Creation of Sustainable Enterprises: Contributions of the Socio-Economic Approach to Management (SEAM)

Christophe Combaudon and Helga Fouré-Joopen

Abstract

The improvement of interactions between the structures and behaviors of actors during the start-up phase of an enterprise is an important factor to take into account in terms of consolidating its survival and development. This contribution analyzes the results and impacts of a process of setting up a socio-economic approach on the performance of a company in the creation phase based on 12 scientific observation fields.

Resumen

La mejora de las interacciones entre las estructuras y los comportamientos de los actores durante la fase de creación de una empresa es un factor importante a tener en cuenta para consolidar su supervivencia y desarrollo. Esta contribución analiza los resultados e impactos de un proceso de implantación de un enfoque socioeconómico en el desempeño de una empresa en fase de creación, a partir de 12 campos de observación científica.

Résumé

L'amélioration des interactions entre les structures et les comportements des acteurs lors de la phase de démarrage d'une entreprise est un facteur important à prendre en compte en termes de consolidation de sa survie et de son développement. Cette contribution analyse les résultats et les impacts d'un processus de mise en place d'une démarche socio-économique sur la performance d'une entreprise en phase de création, basée sur 12 terrains d'observation scientifique

11 Internal Stucturing and External Development: The Challenges of the Second Generation of a Family

François Filippazzo

Abstract

The transition between two generations of SME owner-managers is always a very sensitive stage in the life of family businesses, between continuities and ruptures. This chapter shows how this transition was managed with the support of the socio-economic method of change management. The new generation of managers invented the second generation-organization in the service of a strategy of diversification of its products.

Resumen

La transición entre dos generaciones de propietarios-gestores de PYMES es siempre una etapa muy delicada en la vida de las empresas familiares, entre continuidad y ruptura. Este capítulo muestra cómo se gestionó esta transición con el apoyo del método socioeconómico de gestión del cambio. La nueva generación de directivos ha inventado la organización de segunda generación al servicio de una estrategia de diversificación de sus productos.

Résumé

La transition entre deux générations de dirigeants propriétaires de PME constitue toujours une étape très sensible dans la vie des entreprises familiales, entre continuité et rupture. Ce chapitre montre comment cette transition a été gérée avec l'appui de la méthode socio-économique de conduite du changement. La nouvelle génération de dirigeant a inventé l'organisation de seconde génération au service d'une stratégie de diversification de ses produits.

12 Learning to be a Leader

Julien Vinay, Muriel Legendre, Laura Bondin, and Olivier Voyant

Abstract

What is a leader? A human being? Unquestionably. This chapter is the story of a man who embodies this idea. The transmission of a family business is the setting; the father, the son and the employees are the main characters.

Resumen

¿Qué es un líder? ¿Un ser humano? Sin duda alguna. Este capítulo es la historia de un hombre que encarna esta idea. La transmisión de una empresa familiar es el escenario; el padre, el hijo y los empleados son los protagonistas.

Résumé

C'est quoi, un être dirigeant ? Un être humain ? Incontestablement. Ce chapitre est le récit d'un homme qui incarne cette idée. La transmission d'une entreprise familiale est le décor ; le père, le fils et les collaborateurs en sont les personnages principaux.

---

13 Survival-Development of Very Small Enterprises (VSE): Support for VSE Managers

Gérard Desmaison and Thomas Rouveure

Abstract

In France, Small Business Companies (SBC) represent 96% of companies but 50% disappear before their sixth year, mainly because of a lack of strategic anticipation. This chapter highlights the decisive character of the structure/behavior relationship at several phases of the entrepreneurial process. The strategic skills of the entrepreneur are a key dimension to increase the survival and development of the company. The entrepreneur's beliefs about each area of the Entrepreneur's Activity Nomenclature (EAN) change his behavior and, ultimately, the structure of the company. The HCVAVC is a synthetic indicator for measuring overall and sustainable performance of SBC.

Resumen

En Francia, las micro-Pymes representan el 96% de las empresas pero el 50% desaparecen antes de su sexto año, principalmente por falta de anticipación estratégica. Este capítulo destaca el carácter determinante de la relación estructura/comportamiento en varias fases del proceso empresarial: incubación, supervivencia y desarrollo. Las competencias estratégicas del empresario constituyen una dimensión clave para aumentar la supervivencia y el desarrollo de la empresa. Las creencias del empresario en cada campo de la Nomenclatura de Actividades del Empresario (NAE) modifican su comportamiento y, en última instancia, la estructura de la empresa. La CHVACV es un indicador sintético para medir el desempeño global y sostenible.

Résumé

En France, les TPE représentent 96% des entreprises mais 50% disparaissent avant leur sixième année, principalement par manque d'anticipation stratégique. Ce chapitre présente le caractère déterminant de la relation structure/comportement à plusieurs phases du processus entrepreneurial. Les compétences stratégiques de l'entrepreneur constituent une dimension clé pour accroitre la survie-développement de l'entreprise. Les croyances de l'entrepreneur sur chaque domaine de la Nomenclature d'Activités de l'Entrepreneur (NAE) modifient son comportement et, in fine, la structure de l'entreprise. La CHVACV est un indicateur synthétique de mesure de la performance globale et durable des TPE.

---

14 Organizational Decoding in the 21st Century

María Elizabeth Canllo de Montoto and Juan Matías Montoto Canllo

Abstract

The objective of this chapter is to demonstrate the depth of our language when we relate to each other in the workplace and thus be able to determine the dysfunctions that are generated by lack of understanding or concealment of certain data and information on a daily basis.

The study was based on a family company with 130 employees in Argentina, which is dedicated to the distribution of mass consumption products. The socio-economic approach to management was applied in this company.

Through sterring meetings, a proximity to the managers of the different areas was implemented and it was possible to identify some meanings of the internal language. This then helped to work on the actual strategic path.

Resumen

El objetivo de este capítulo es demostrar la profundidad de nuestro lenguaje a la hora de relacionarnos unos con otros en el ámbito laboral y así poder determinar los disfuncionamientos que se generan por falta de comprensión u ocultamiento de ciertos datos e informaciones en el día a día.

Se tomó como base el estudio en una empresa familiar de 130 empleados en Argentina, que se dedica a la distribución de productos de consumo masivo. En esta empresa se aplicó la metodología socioeconómica.

A través de reuniones de pilotaje, se implementó una proximidad a los managers de las diferentes áreas y se pudo identificar algunos significados del lenguaje interno. Luego esto ayudo a trabajar en el verdadero camino estratégico.

Résumé

L'objectif de ce chapitre est de démontrer la profondeur de notre langage lors des interactions les uns et les autres dans la vie professionnelle, et ainsi être en mesure de déterminer les dysfonctionnements générés par l'incompréhension ou la dissimulation de certaines données et informations au quotidien.

La recherche-intervention socio-économique s'est déroulée dans une entreprise familiale en Argentine de 130 employés, qui se consacre à la distribution de produits de grande consommation.

Grâce à des réunions pilotes, une proximité avec les managers des différents services a été mise en place et il a été possible d'identifier certaines significations du langage interne. Cela a ensuite servi à travailler dans la voie de la stratégie et sa mise en œuvre.

---

15 Earning More by Working Better is Feasible
Laurent Paysac, Bertrand Paysac, and Mélissa Sanchez

Abstract

According to the Marxist theory, the search for profit leads to capitalist exploitation and class struggle. Socio-economic theory shows on the contrary that the search for economic performance is inseparable from social performance. In this chapter, we present the case of a Lyon-based SME, SLB Médical, which designs and markets medical devices and articles for overpackaging medical products. ISEOR has been supporting this SME since 2016 in improving working life conditions and cleaning up its internal operations. Its outstanding achievements illustrate that it is indeed possible to earn more by working better.

Resumen

Según la teoría marxista, la búsqueda de utilidades conduce a la explotación capitalista y a la lucha de clases. Por el contrario, la teoría socioeconómica demuestra que la búsqueda de resultados económicos es inseparable de los resultados sociales. Este capítulo presenta el caso de una PYME en Lyon, SLB Médical, que diseña y comercializa dispositivos y artículos médicos para el sobre-embalaje de productos médicos. ISEOR lleva apoyando a esta pyme desde 2016 en la mejora de las condiciones de vida profesional y el aseo de su funcionamiento interno. Sus destacados logros ilustran que sí es posible ganar más trabajando mejor.

Résumé

Si l'on en croit la théorie marxiste, la recherche de profits conduit à l'exploitation capitaliste et à la lutte des classes. La théorie socio-économique montre au contraire que la recherche de performance économique est indissociable de la performance sociale. Ce chapitre présente le cas d'une PME lyonnaise, SLB Médical, qui conçoit et commercialise des dispositifs médicaux et articles de suremballage de produits médicaux. L'ISEOR accompagne cette PME depuis 2016 dans l'amélioration des conditions de vie professionnelle et le toilettage du fonctionnement interne. Ses réalisations marquantes illustrent qu'il est effectivement possible de gagner plus en travaillant mieux.

16 How to Professionalize Managerial Practices in Family Businesses?

Éric Pernoud, Gilles Pernoud, and Françoise Goter

Abstract

In this chapter we explore how the socio-economic management model allows family firms (FFs) to professionalize their managerial practices and increase their performance. Based on a intervention-research initiated in 2017, we highlight the managerial specificities of these firms, their main dysfunctions as well as the proven improvement actions. This chapter also makes explicit the characteristics of the methods and tools of socio-economic management that play a decisive role in resolving the difficulties encountered by family businesses

Resumen

En este capítulo exploramos cómo el modelo de gestión socioeconómica permite a las empresas familiares (FBE) profesionalizar sus prácticas de gestión y aumentar su rendimiento. A partir de una investigación-intervención iniciada en 2017, destacamos las especificidades de gestión de estas empresas, sus principales disfunciones así como las acciones de mejora probadas. Este capítulo también explica las características de los métodos y las herramientas de gestión socioeconómica que desempeñan un papel decisivo en la resolución de las dificultades encontradas por las FBE.

Résumé

Dans ce chapitre nous explorons comment le modèle de management socio-économique permet aux entreprises familiales (EF) de professionnaliser leurs pratiques managériales et d'accroître leurs performances. À partir d'une recherche-intervention initiée en 2017, nous mettons en évidence les spécificités managériales de ces entreprises, leurs principaux dysfonctionnements ainsi que les actions d'amélioration éprouvées. Ce chapitre permet également d'expliciter les caractéristiques des méthodes et des outils du management socio-économique jouant un rôle déterminant dans la résolution des difficultés rencontrées par les EF.

17 From a Small Traditional Company to an International Group: Structuring the Growth of the Aganova Group

María Ángeles Rastrollo Horrillo, Marisa Rastrollo Horrillo, and Agustín Ramírez

Abstract

This research shows how the socio-economic model developed by ISEOR has contributed to overcome the internal barriers that made it difficult for a Spanish business group to take advantage of national and international markets. The findings reveal how organizational deficiencies are accentuated when penetrating international markets, due to the added difficulties of physical, psychological and cultural distance. And this occurs even in companies that have important competitive advantages, such as international patents. These results enrich the literature on firm growth and have important practical managerial implications.

Resumen

Esta investigación muestra cómo el modelo socio-económico desarrollado por el ISEOR ha contribuido a superar las barreras internas que dificultaban el aprovechamiento de los mercados nacionales e internacionales de un grupo empresarial español. Los hallazgos revelan como las deficiencias organizativas se acentúan al penetrar en mercados internacionales, por las dificultades añadidas de la distancia física, psíquica y cultural. Y esto ocurre incluso en empresas que cuentan con importantes ventajas competitivas, como patentes internacionales. Estos resultados enriquecen la literatura sobre crecimiento de las empresas y tienen importantes implicaciones prácticas de gestión.

Résumé

Cette recherche montre comment le modèle socio-économique développé par l'ISEOR a contribué à surmonter les barrières internes au sein d'un groupe d'entreprises espagnol qui rendaient difficile de tirer profit des marchés nationaux et internationaux. Les résultats révèlent comment les déficiences organisationnelles sont accentuées lors de la pénétration des marchés internationaux, en raison des difficultés supplémentaires liées à la distance physique, psychologique et culturelle. Et cela se produit même dans des entreprises qui disposent d'avantages concurrentiels importants, tels que des brevets internationaux. Ces résultats enrichissent la littérature sur la croissance des entreprises et ont des implications managériales pratiques importantes.

18 SEAM in Cross-Cultural Context

Omaya Kuran, Dolly Bassil, and Lara Khabbaz

Abstract

The mosaic contextual profile of the MENA countries requires the adoption of innovative consulting approaches to reach the desirable change results. The three authors of this chapter being SEAM interveners in 3 different sectors: Public Sector, Private Higher Education, and SME-Performing Arts, in addition to their over 20 years compiled experience in working in different professional settings within the MENA region discuss the region cultural dimensions, the consulting tools and the intercultural communication skills adopted as part of organizational development and change (ODC) initiatives.

Through their proven effectiveness, SEAM adopted tools, methods and concepts play a substantial role in making it the innovative approach of choice to overcome cross-cultural challenges that might be hindering ODC.

Resumen

El perfil de mosaico de los países del Oriente Medio y África del Norte requiere la adopción de enfoques de consultoría innovadores para alcanzar los resultados de cambio deseados. Los tres autores de este capítulo son intervinientes en el Management socioeconómico en tres sectores diferentes: el sector público, la educación superior privada y las pymes de artes escénicas, además de su experiencia acumulada de más de 20 años trabajando en diferentes entornos profesionales dentro de la región Oriente Medio y África del Norte, debaten las dimensiones culturales de la región, las herramientas de consultoría y las habilidades de comunicación intercultural adoptadas como iniciativas de desarrollo y cambio organizacional.

A través de su eficacia probada, las herramientas, los métodos y los conceptos elaborados por el Management socio-económico desempeñan un papel importante para convertirlo en el enfoque innovador elegido para superar los desafíos interculturales que podrían obstaculizar la ODC.

Résumé

Le profil en "mosaïque" des pays du Moyen Orient et Afrique du Nord nécessite d'adopter des approches de conseil innovantes pour atteindre les résultats de changement souhaités. Les trois auteurs de ce chapitre étant des intervenants SEAM dans trois secteurs différents: Le secteur public, l'enseignement supérieur privé et les PME-arts du spectacle, en plus de leurs plus de 20 ans d'expérience accumulée dans différents contextes professionnels au sein de la région du Moyen Orient et Afrique du Nord, discutent des dimensions culturelles de la région, des outils de conseil et des compétences en communication interculturelle adoptés comme initiatives de développement et changement organisationnels (ODC).

Par leur efficacité prouvée, les outils, méthodes et concepts du management socio-économique jouent un rôle important en faisant de lui l'approche innovante pour surmonter les défis interculturels qui pourraient entraver l'ODC.

---

19 From the Artist-Director to the Director-Artist: The Case of Very Small Performing Art Organizations in France

Isabelle Horvath and Caroline Adoumbou

Abstract

In a context of budgetary constraints, artistic organizations must resolve the equation between economic performance and creation. But they often come up against an image conflict between art and business. From an intervention-research, we show in this chapter how an artist-manager of a Very Small Performing Arts Organization (VSPO) can develop managerial skills in order to perpetuate his activity and deploy his artistic project. This experiment highlights the improvements in the management of the organization and the need for intra-organizational learning to build a dialectical relationship between art and management.

Resumen

En un contexto de restricciones presupuestarias, las organizaciones artísticas deben resolver la ecuación entre desempeño económico y creación. Pero se enfrentan a menudo a un conflicto de imagen entre arte y empresa. A partir de una investigación-intervención, mostramos en este capítulo como un artista-dirigente de una Organización Muy Pequeña de Espectáculo en Vivo puede desarrollar competencias de gestión con el fin de mantener su actividad y desarrollar su proyecto artístico. Esta experimentación pone de manifiesto las mejoras en la dirección de la organización y la necesidad de aprendizaje intra-organizativo para construir una relación dialéctica entre arte y gestión.

Résumé

Dans un contexte de contraintes budgétaires, les organisations artistiques doivent résoudre l'équation entre performance économique et création. Mais elles se heurtent souvent à un conflit d'image entre l'art et l'entreprise. A partir d'une recherche-intervention, nous montrons comment un artiste-dirigeant d'une Très Petite Organisation de Spectacle Vivant (TPOSV) peut développer des compétences managériales afin de pérenniser son activité et déployer son projet artistique. Cette expérimentation met en évidence les améliorations du pilotage de l'organisation et la nécessité de l'apprentissage intra organisationnel pour construire une relation dialectique entre l'art et le management.

---

20 Development of Managerial Skills and Sustainable Performance of Small Businesses in The Liberal Professions

Renaud Petit and Véronique Zardet

Abstract

The results of socio-economic management implementations, conducted in 200 small companies in the liberal professions, illustrate the main consequences of managerial deficiencies. The qualimetric data obtained made it possible to determine the generic and contingency elements of the four major sectors of regulated liberal activity accompanied: medical, paramedical, legal and real estate professions. But the most remarkable result of this intervention-research is to highlight the capacity as well as the speed of these companies to recycle their important hidden cost-performance deposits.

Resumen

Los resultados de las implantaciones de gestión socioeconómica, realizadas en 200 pequeñas empresas de profesiones liberales, ilustran las principales consecuencias de las deficiencias de gestión. Los datos cualimétricos obtenidos permiten determinar los elementos genéricos y contingentes de los cuatro grandes sectores de actividad liberal regulada acompañados: profesiones médicas, paramédicas, jurídicas e inmobiliarias. Sin embargo, el resultado más destacable de esta investigación-intervención es poner de manifiesto la capacidad y la rapidez de estas empresas para reciclar sus importantes reservas ocultas de costes-desempeños.

Résumé

Les résultats des implantations du management socio-économique, conduites dans 200 petites entreprises en profession libérale, illustrent les principales conséquences des carences managériales. Les données qualimétriques obtenues ont permis de déterminer les éléments génériques et de contingence des quatre grands secteurs d'activité libérale réglementée accompagnés: médicaux, paramédicaux, métiers du droit et de l'immobilier. Mais le résultat le plus remarquable de ces recherches-interventions est de mettre en évidence la capacité ainsi que la rapidité de ces entreprises pour recycler leurs importants gisements de coûts-performances cachés.

21 Management and Training of French Notaires: Results of 20 Years of Transformation of a Profession

Xavier Daudé and Laurent Cappelletti

Abstract

For more than 20 years, ISEOR has conducted transformative intervention-researches with the notarial profession, its offices, its departmental chambers, its regional councils and its Superior Council. The main transformations observed in the management of notarial professionals, in their training and in the functioning of the offices are described in this chapter, as well as the perspectives they generate and the progress that remains to be made.

Resumen

Desde hace más de 20 años, ISEOR lleva a cabo investigaciones-intervenciones transformadoras con la profesión notarial francesa, sus oficinas, cámaras departamentales, consejos regionales y su Consejo Superior. En este capítulo se describen los principales cambios observados en la gestión de los profesionales notariales, su formación y el funcionamiento de las empresas, así como las perspectivas que generan y los avances que quedan por realizar.

Résumé

Depuis plus de 20 ans, l'ISEOR a mené des recherches-interventions transformatives auprès de la profession notariale française, ses offices, ses chambres départementales, ses conseils régionaux et son Conseil supérieur. Les principales transformations observées de management des professionnels du notariat, de leur formation et du fonctionnement des offices sont décrites dans ce chapitre, ainsi que les perspectives qu'elles engendrent et les progrès restant à accomplir.

PART IV

Supporting the development of mid-sized and large companies

Apoyar el desarrollo de las medianas y grandes empresas

Accompagner le développement des entreprises de taille intermédiaire (ETI) et des grandes entreprises

22 Nearly 40 Years of Socio-Economic Approach to Management: Lessons Learned Regarding the Notion of Dynamic Equilibrium

Pascal Pasquier and Amandine Savall

Abstract

This chapter presents the results of nearly 40 years of application of the socio-economic approach to management in the Brioche Pasquier company, from the point of view of a key managerial concept: "balance," which is both a compass and a deliberate policy for running the company and managing the 3,440 people who work there. The concept of balance is detailed in various forms: external strategy, internal organization and structure, people management, human resources...

Resumen

Este capítulo presenta los resultados de casi 40 años de aplicación de la gestión socioeconómica en la empresa Brioche Pasquier, desde la perspectiva de un concepto clave de gestión: "equilibrio," tanto brújula como política deliberada para dirigir la empresa y gestionar las 3,440 personas que trabajan allí. El concepto de equilibrio se detalla en diversas formas: estrategia externa, organización y estructura interna, gestión de personas, recursos humanos...

Résumé

Ce chapitre présente les résultats de près de 40 ans d'application du management socio-économique dans l'entreprise Brioche Pasquier, sous l'angle d'un concept managérial clé: «l'équilibre», à la fois boussole et politique délibérée pour diriger l'entreprise et manager les 3,440 personnes qui y travaillent. Le concept d'équilibre est détaillé sous diverses formes: stratégie externe, organisation et structure interne, management des personnes, ressources humaines...

23 Professionalization of a Family Business Through Human Support in Order to Sustain Value Creation

Victor Frontera and Victor Caumeil

Abstract

The family business model is not only very particular, but also singular from one company to another. This paper aims to demonstrate that it is possible to maintain a family model in a fast-growing company, by professionalizing it. By relying on all the internal potential that will be put to use, by clarifying the role and prerogatives of management and finally by harmonizing practices and vision through a common language, the family business can be an extremely successful model both socially and economically.

Resumen

El modelo de empresa familiar no sólo es muy particular, sino también singular de una empresa a otra. Este documento pretende demostrar que es posible mantener un modelo familiar en una empresa de rápido crecimiento, profesionalizándolo. Apoyándose en todo el potencial interno que se va a aprovechar, aclarando el papel y las prerrogativas de la dirección y, por último, armonizando las prácticas y la visión a través de un lenguaje común, la empresa familiar puede ser un modelo sumamente eficaz tanto social como económicamente.

Résumé

Le modèle des entreprises familiales est non seulement très particulier, mais aussi singulier d'une entreprise à l'autre. Il est question ici de démontrer qu'il est possible de conserver un modèle familial dans une entreprise en forte croissance, en le professionnalisant. En s'appuyant sur tout le potentiel interne qui est mis à contribution, en clarifiant le rôle et les prérogatives du management et finalement en harmonisant les pratiques et la vision par un langage commun, l'entreprise familiale peut être un modèle extrêmement performant socialement et économiquement.

24 Independent Leadership and Shared Governance

Jean Claude Pénicaud-Tesson, Mireille Tesson-Pénicaud, and Yann Goudy

Abstract

The managerial transformation of a company in the retail sector, in a movement of independent leaders, resulting from co-optation and linked together by professional sponsorship, is a complex and exciting process. It obliges the volunteer leaders to make a lasting commitment, in particular, to new management practices and to a change in the way the hierarchy works. The virtues of this transformation (a less solitary experience of management, an increase in the "competence - autonomy" of the different levels of the hierarchy and a measured and relevant acceleration of decision-making) are quite quickly perceptible and sustainably consolidate the company.

Resumen

La transformación directiva de una empresa de gran distribución, en un movimiento de líderes independientes, fruto de la cooptación y vinculados entre sí por el patrocinio profesional, es un proceso complejo y apasionante. Obliga a los dirigentes voluntarios a comprometerse de forma duradera, en particular, con nuevas prácticas de gestión y con un cambio en el funcionamiento de la jerarquía. Las virtudes de esta transformación (una experiencia menos solitaria de la gestión, un aumento de la "competencia-autonomía" de los diferentes niveles de la jerarquía y una aceleración mesurada y pertinente de la toma de decisiones) se perciben con bastante rapidez y consolidan de forma sostenible la empresa.

Résumé

La transformation managériale d'une entreprise de la grande distribution, dans un mouvement de dirigeants indépendants, issus de la cooptation et reliés entre eux par un parrainage professionnel, est une démarche complexe et passionnante. Elle oblige les dirigeants volontaires à un engagement durable, en particulier sur de nouvelles pratiques du pouvoir de direction et sur une mutation du fonctionnement hiérarchique. Les vertus de cette transformation (une expérience moins solitaire de la direction, une montée en «compétence–autonomie» des différents niveaux hiérarchiques et une accélération dosée et pertinente des prises de décisions) sont assez vite perceptibles et consolident durablement l'entreprise.

25 Mastering Growth While Sustaining Both Profitability and Human Potential: The Successful Challenge of an Agro-Indutrial SME in Mexico

Isaac Sanchez, Arturo Guerrero Lizardi, and Véronique Zardet

Abstract

Since 2005, Sánchez Aguacate Hass has relentlessly pursued a growth strategy based on the diversification of its products and markets, and the development of its human potential. The principles and tools of socio-economic management served as tutors to structure this growth, organize the concerted delegation, establish operational and strategic management indicators.

Resumen

Desde 2005 Sánchez Aguacate Hass ha perseguido sin descanso una estrategia de crecimiento basada en la diversificación de sus productos y mercados, y en el desarrollo de su potencial humano. Los principios y herramientas de la gestión socioeconómica sirvieron como tutores para estructurar este crecimiento, organizar la delegación concertada, establecer indicadores operativos y de gestión estratégica.

Résumé

Sánchez Aguacate Hass a conduit sans relâche depuis 2005 une stratégie de croissance basée sur la diversification de ses produits et de ses marchés, et sur le développement de son potentiel humain. Les principes et outils du management socio-économique ont servi de tuteurs pour structurer cette croissance, organiser la délégation concertée, mettre en place des indicateurs de pilotage opérationnel et stratégique.

---

26 How to Succeed a Post-Downsizing Large-Scale Economic Recovery?

Françoise Goter

Abstract

In the face of economic crises, the use of the Employment Protection Plan (EPS) is frequent but not very conclusive, both on the social and economic levels. Through the study of an intervention-research conducted within a middle size company, this chapter shows that the external environment alone does not explain the economic difficulties of companies and that a large part of the socio-economic performance is internal. This case study also shows how a proactive strategy, focused on hidden costs-performance, constitutes the "foundation" of a deep and sustainable restructuring, and allows for a large-scale economic recovery.

Resumen

Ante las crisis económicas, el recurso al "Plan de Salvaguardia del Empleo" es frecuente pero poco concluyente, tanto a nivel social como económico. A través del estudio de una investigación-intervención realizada en el seno de una PYME, este capítulo muestra que el entorno exterior no explica por sí solo las dificultades económicas de las empresas y que una gran parte de los resultados socioeconómicos se juega a nivel interno. Este estudio de caso también muestra cómo una estrategia proactiva, centrada en la conversión de los costos ocultos en valor agregado, es la "base" de una reestructuración profunda y sostenible y permite un giro económico a gran escala.

Résumé

Face aux crises économiques, le recours au Plan de Sauvegarde de l'Emploi (PSE) est fréquent mais peu concluant, tant sur le plan social que sur le plan économique. À travers l'étude d'une recherche-intervention conduite au sein d'une PME, ce chapitre montre que l'environnement externe n'explique pas à lui seul les difficultés économiques des entreprises et qu'une grande partie des performances socio-économiques se jouent en interne. Cette étude de cas montre également comment une stratégie proactive, centrée sur la conversion des coûts-performances cachés en valeur ajoutée, constitue le «socle» d'une restructuration profonde et durable, et permet un redressement économique de grande ampleur.

27 An Original and Evaluated Experiment to Stimulate the Sustainable Development of Socio-Economic Productivity

Philippe Lacroix, Frantz Datry, and Rodolphe Bachaud

Abstact

This chapter presents a concrete application of socio-economic intervention within the Belux subsidiary of the Manpower Group, whose objective is to improve the socio-economic productivity of teams by means of a methodology called "5 stars." This testimonial, co-written with the head of Manpower Group Belux, explains the construction of this method to improve the company's profitability and the involvement of its people.

Resumen

Este capítulo presenta una aplicación concreta de intervención socioeconómica en la filial Belux del grupo Manpower, cuyo objetivo es mejorar la productividad socioeconómica de los equipos mediante una metodología denominada "5 estrellas." Este testimonio, coescrito con el dirigente de Manpower Group Belux, explica cómo se desarrolló y se implementó este método para mejorar la rentabilidad de la empresa y la implicación de su personal.

Résumé

Ce chapitre présente une application concrète de l'intervention socio-économique au sein de la filiale Belux du Groupe Manpower, dont l'objectif est d'améliorer la productivité socio-économique des équipes au moyen d'une méthodologie dénommée «5 étoiles». Ce témoignage, co-écrit avec le dirigeant de Manpower Group Belux, explique la construction et le déploiement de cette méthode pour améliorer la rentabilité de l'entreprise et l'implication des personnes.

28 Learning from the Implementation of the Socio-Economic Approach to Management at La Poste

Joseph Gauchard

Abstract

The economic and political evolution led to the evolution of La Poste and its structures in 1990. This led to a reform of the personnel management to take into account the constraints of the environment. The Institute of Socio-Economic Management was chosen to accompany this evolution under the conditions described below.

Resumen

Los acontecimientos económicos y políticos han provocado cambios en La Poste y sus estructuras en 1990. Esto condujo a una reforma de la gestión del personal para tener en cuenta limitaciones ambientales. El Instituto de Socio economía de las Empresas y Organizaciones (ISEOR) fue seleccionado para apoyar este desarrollo en las condiciones que se mencionan a continuación.

Résumé

L'évolution économique et politique a conduit à faire évoluer La Poste et ses structures en 1990. Cela entrainait une réforme du management du Personnel pour tenir compte des contraintes de l'environnement. L'Institut de Socio-Economie des Entreprises et des Organisations (ISEOR) fut retenu pour accompagner cette évolution dans les conditions évoquées ci-après.

29 Developing Organization Agility

Thomas G. Cummings, Christopher G. Worley, and Rickie Moore

Abstract

In rapidly changing environments, organization agility can be a source of survival and also competitive advantage. In this chapter, we demonstrate how two methods developed in the USA and in Europe—Self Design and SEAM—helped organizations to continually develop and reinforce their agile performance either by keeping pace with changing conditions or by identifying and reducing organizational dysfunctions and the ensuing hidden costs. Using two mini case studies, we illustrate how the two methods were applied and outline the results that were obtained and sustained.

Resumen

En entornos que cambian rápidamente, la agilidad organizativa puede ser una fuente de supervivencia o incluso de ventaja competitiva. En este capítulo, demostramos cómo dos métodos desarrollados en Estados Unidos y Europa—el autodiseño y el modelo socioeconómico—han ayudado a las organizaciones a desarrollar y reforzar continuamente su desempeño ágil, ya sea manteniendo el ritmo de las condiciones cambiantes o identificando y reduciendo las disfunciones organizativas y los costos ocultos. A través de dos mini-estudios de caso, ilustramos cómo se aplicaron los dos métodos, resumimos los resultados obtenidos y cómo se mantuvieron.

Résumé

Dans des environnements en évolution rapide, l'agilité organisationnelle peut être une source de survie voire d'avantage concurrentiel. Dans ce chapitre, nous démontrons comment deux méthodes développées aux États-Unis et en Europe—Self Design et SEAM—ont aidé les organisations à développer et à renforcer continuellement leur performance agile soit en suivant le rythme de l'évolution des conditions, soit en identifiant et en réduisant les dysfonctionnements organisationnels et les couts cachés. En s'appuyant sur deux mini études de cas, nous illustrons comment les deux méthodes ont été appliquées et exposons les résultats obtenus durablement.

30 Contextualizing Seam in the Broad Milieu of Consulting Methodologies

Eric J. Sanders and Tonya L. Henderson

Abstract

There is a broad milieu of consulting methodologies available to the well-trained scholar-practitioner. General categories include expert (topic-specific technical guidance), doctor-patient (a variant of expert stressing the client's symptoms and perspective), and process consulting (helping an organization develop fundamental capabilities to sustain and expand near-term improvements). The Academy of Management's Management Consulting Division embraces all responsible, theory-supported consulting methodologies, and as past chairs of the Division, the authors explore the contribution of Socio-Economic Management (SEAM) to the field, with special attention to its action research implications.

Resumen

Hay una amplia variedad de metodologías de consultoría responsable disponibles para el académico-practicante bien capacitado. Categorías generales incluyen experto (orientación técnica sobre un tema específico), médico-paciente (una variante del experto que enfatiza los síntomas y la perspectiva del cliente) y consultor de procesos (quien ayuda a una organización a desarrollar capacidades fundamentales para mantener y expandir las mejoras a corto plazo). La División de Consultoría de Gestión (Management Consulting Division) de la Academy of Management abarca todas las metodologías de consultoría responsables y basadas en teorías, y como ex presidentes de la División, los autores exploran la contribución de la Gestión Socioeconómica al campo, con una especial atención a sus implicaciones de investigación-acción.

Résumé

Il existe un large éventail de méthodologies de conseil à la disposition des universitaires et des praticiens bien formés. Les catégories générales comprennent l'expert (conseils techniques spécifiques à un sujet), le médecin-patient (une variante de l'expert mettant l'accent sur les symptômes et la perspective du client) et le consultant en processus (aider une organisation à développer des capacités fondamentales pour soutenir et étendre des améliorations à court terme). La division Conseil en Management (Management Consulting Division) de l'Academy of Management englobe toutes les méthodologies de conseil responsables et fondées sur des théories. En tant qu'anciens présidents de la division, les auteurs explorent la contribution du management socio-économique (SEAM) au domaine, en accordant une attention particulière aux implications de la recherche-action.

PART V

Livening public and para-public service organizations: healthcare, education, local authorities, etc.

Animar a las organizaciones de servicios públicos y semipúblicos: sanidad, educación, autoridades locales, etc.

Animer les organisations de service public et parapublic: santé, éducation, collectivités territoriales...

31 Socially Responsible Policies Do Exist

Pierre-Alain Raphan

Abstract

It is by planting seeds that we can hope to admire the forest one day. In politics, thoughts, ideas and projects are the seeds that allow us to target the root causes of our problems, to free up energies, to understand the major transitions (ecological, technological, economic, managerial), to prepare the future and to be able to envisage a sustainable world.

This is the meaning of each of its actions in the service of sustainable development objectives. This daily political life demonstrates the complexity of a system built by humans, which could prevent them, in the long run, from assuming their responsibilities towards future generations. I hope that this experience will inspire others.

Resumen

Es mediante la plantación de semillas que uno puede esperar admirar el bosque algún día. En política, las reflexiones, las ideas, los proyectos son las semillas que permiten apuntar a las causas profundas de nuestros males, liberar energías, aprehender las transiciones importantes (ecológica, tecnológica, económica, de management), prepararnos para el futuro y ser capaz de imaginar un mundo sostenible.

Este es el significado de cada una de sus acciones al servicio de los objetivos de desarrollo sostenible. Este diario político muestra la complejidad de un sistema construido por el ser humano que, en última instancia, podría impedirles asumir sus responsabilidades para con las generaciones futuras. Espero que esta experiencia inspire a otros.

Résumé

C'est en plantant des graines que l'on peut espérer admirer un jour la forêt. En politique, les réflexions, les idées, les projets sont ces graines qui permettent de cibler les causes racines de nos maux, de libérer les énergies, d'appréhender les grandes transitions (écologique, technologique, économique, managériale), de préparer le futur et de pouvoir envisager un monde durable.

C'est tout le sens de chacune de ces actions au service des objectifs de développement durable. Ce quotidien politique démontre la complexité d'un système construit par les humains, qui pourrait les empêcher, à terme, d'assumer leurs responsabilités vis-à-vis des générations futures. J'espère que cette expérience en inspirera d'autres.

---

32 The Socio-Economic Approach to Management and Hospital Organizations

Anne Thiébaut-Bertrand and Denis Fière

Abstract

This chapter exposes the similarities between medical and socio-economic diagnosis approaches and between experimental research in medicine and intervention-research in management sciences. Two cases of socio-economic approaches illustrate the point, one conducted in the hematology department of the Lyon University Hospital and the other relating to the organization of blood transfusion. The similarity between these two methodologies is such that the socio-economic theory appears to be understandable to health care professionals. It should facilitate the identification and understanding of dysfunctions in hospital structures, to enable the definition of new practices in order to promote innovative strategic projects.

Resumen

Este capítulo expone las similitudes entre los enfoques de diagnóstico médico y socioeconómico y entre la investigación experimental en medicina y la investigación-intervención en ciencias de gestión. Dos casos de enfoque socioeconómico ilustran el tema, uno realizado en el servicio de hematología del Hospital Universitario de Lyon y el otro relativo a la organización de la transfusión de sangre. La similitud entre ambas metodologías es tal que la teoría socioeconómica parece comprensible por parte de los profesionales de la salud. Debe facilitar la identificación y la comprensión de los disfuncionamientos de las estructuras hospitalarias, para permitir la definición de nuevas prácticas; con el fin de favorecer los proyectos estratégicos innovadores.

Résumé

Ce chapitre expose les similitudes entre démarche diagnostique médicale et socio-économique et entre recherche expérimentale en médecine et recherche-intervention en sciences de gestion. Deux cas de démarches socio-économiques illustrent le propos, l'une conduite dans le service d'hématologie du CHU de Lyon et l'autre relative à l'organisation de la transfusion sanguine. La parenté entre ces deux méthodologies est telle que la théorie socio-économique apparait compréhensible pour les acteurs de santé. Elle doit faciliter l'identification et la compréhension des dysfonctionnements des structures hospitalières, pour permettre la définition de nouvelles pratiques afin de favoriser des projets stratégiques innovants.

---

33 Complexity, Magical Thinking, and SEAM

John Conbere, Alla Heorhiadi, and Dave Dobosenski

Abstract

Complex problems require a different mode of problem solving than simple problems. Magical thinking is a delusional management issue, and it is rooted in the TFW virus. Using a SEAM intervention in a rural medical center in the United States S, the authors describe how SEAM lessened magical thinking and prepared employees to manage complex problems.

Resumen

Los problemas complejos requieren un modo diferente de resolución de problemas que los problemas simples. El pensamiento mágico es un problema delirante de gestión, que tiene sus raíces en el virus TFW. Usando una intervención socioeconómica en un centro médico rural en los Estados Unidos, los autores describen cómo el management socio-económico disminuyó el pensamiento mágico y preparó a los empleados para manejar problemas complejos.

Résumé

Les problèmes complexes nécessitent un mode de résolution de problèmes différent de celui des problèmes simples. La pensée magique est un problème délirant du management, elle est enracinée dans le virus TFW. À l'aide d'une intervention socio-économique dans un hôpital rural aux États-Unis, les auteurs décrivent comment le management socio-économique a atténué la pensée magique et préparé les salariés à gérer des problèmes complexes.

34 Improving Managerial Skills Through the Implementation of the Socio-Economic Approach to Management: An Approach for the Survival and Development of the Hospital

Patrick Tabchoury, Donabelle Zakkour, and Rocks Mazraani

Abstract

The services provided in Health Organizations need continuous improvement. Managers of the Healthcare Institutions have to be able to respond quickly to the increasing demands of the community they are serving. In other way, the leaders of health establishments must be trained and have the tools that allow them to monitor and to master the introduction of change and to help their organizations to overcome challenges especially in times of health or economic crises.

In this chapter, the aim is to present the socio-economic approach to management (SEAM) applied in three hospitals in the Middle East as well as the impact of this approach on the result and the development of managerial skills.

Resumen

Las organizaciones sanitarias necesitan un desarrollo y una mejora continuos de los servicios prestados. En otras palabras, los directivos de las instituciones sanitarias deben estar formados y disponer de herramientas que les permitan dominar el cambio y superar los retos, especialmente en tiempos de crisis sanitaria o económica.

Este capítulo presenta el enfoque de gestión socioeconómica aplicado en tres hospitales de Oriente Medio, así como el impacto de este enfoque en los resultados y el desarrollo de las competencias de gestión.

Résumé

Les organisations sanitaires ont besoin d'un développement et d'une amélioration continue des services rendus. Elles ont besoin d'une réponse rapide aux exigences de la communauté, en d'autres termes, les dirigeants des établissements de santé doivent être formés et avoir des outils qui leur permettent de bien maitriser la conduite de changements et de surmonter les défis surtout en période de crises sanitaires ou économiques.

Il s'agit dans ce chapitre de présenter la démarche du Management socio-économique appliquée dans trois hôpitaux au Moyen Orient ainsi que l'impact de cette démarche sur le résultat et le développement des compétences managériales.

35 Interaction Between Regulation and Organization: The Case of the Hospital System

Frédéric Kletz and Jean-Claude Moisdon

Abstract

The history of the implementation of activity-based pricing in the French hospital system reveals the difficulties encountered by the State in changing hospital organization, which is highly inertial given the complexity of this organization. Thus, the State has recently decided to test another intervention policy, by letting the actors in the field propose and experiment with changes in organization and financing. We can thus see a new form of articulation between regulation and organization taking shape. It is also a way of opening up the field of organization, no longer seen in the narrow sense of the hospital, but integrating the other health actors.

Resumen

La historia de la implantación de la tarificación por actividades en el sistema hospitalario francés pone de manifiesto las dificultades que encuentra el Estado para modificar la organización hospitalaria, que es muy inercial dada la complejidad de esta organización. Por ello, el Estado ha decidido recientemente poner a prueba otra política de intervención, dejando que los agentes en el terreno propongan y experimenten cambios en la organización y la financiación. De este modo, podemos ver cómo se perfila una nueva forma de articulación entre regulación y organización. También es una forma de abrir el campo de la organización, que ya no se ve en el sentido estricto del hospital, sino que integra a los demás agentes sanitarios.

Résumé

L'histoire de la mise en place de la tarification à l'activité dans le système hospitalier français révèle les difficultés rencontrées par l'État pour faire évoluer l'organisation hospitalière, dotée d'une grande inertie compte tenu de la complexité de cette organisation. C'est ainsi que récemment, l'Etat a décidé de tester une autre politique d'intervention, en laissant les acteurs de terrain proposer et expérimenter des changements d'organisation et de financement. On voit ainsi se profiler une nouvelle forme d'articulation entre régulation et organisation. Une façon également d'ouvrir le champ de l'organisation, vu non plus au sens étroit de l'intérieur de l'hôpital, mais intégrant les autres acteurs de santé.

36 The Socio-Economic Improvement Project, a Source of Quality and Performance in Hospitals

Chantal Thouverez

Abstract

Following an audit carried out in three departments of a hospital, the author identifies, in the first part, the dysfunctions and hidden costs affecting the patients, the health professionals themselves, but also the finances and the reputation of the establishment. The author then presents the socio-economic project and describes the improvement actions that were created during the first year to improve working conditions and services. Finally, the paper describes the socio-economic tools used. The competency grids and the priority action plan, for example, are high value-added tools in an environment that demands quality, efficiency, safety and serenity.

Resumen

Basándose en las conclusiones de una auditoría realizada en tres servicios de un centro hospitalario, el capítulo lista, en una primera parte, los disfuncionamientos y costos ocultos que perjudicaban a los pacientes, a los profesionales de la sanidad, a las finanzas y a la reputación del establecimiento. A continuación, se presentan el proyecto socioeconómico y las acciones llevadas a cabo para mejorar las condiciones de trabajo y los servicios durante el primer año de seguimiento. Se describen finalmente las herramientas socioeconómicas utilizadas (matriz de competencias, plan de acciones prioritarias).

Constituyen recursos con un fuerte valor añadido en un entorno que exige calidad, eficacia, seguridad y serenidad.

Résumé

À la suite d'un audit réalisé dans trois services d'un centre hospitalier, ce chapitre recense, dans une première partie, les dysfonctionnements et coûts cachés portant atteinte aux malades, aux professionnels de la santé eux-mêmes, mais également aux finances et à la renommée de l'établissement. Il présente ensuite le projet socio-économique et décline les actions d'amélioration qui furent créées, au cours de la première année, pour améliorer les conditions de travail et les services. Il décrit enfin les outils socio-économiques utilisés. Les grilles de compétences ou le plan d'actions prioritaires constituent, par exemple, des outils à forte valeur ajoutée dans un milieu qui exige qualité, efficacité, sécurité et sérénité.

---

37 Ramping Up Public Policies: The Case of the General Labor Inspectorate in Angola
Kianvu Tamo

Abstract

The cardinal virtue of public policy is the translation of the political authority's will into economic, social and environmental welfare of the national community. To this end, with regard to public management, especially in relation to working conditions in the civil construction sector, this empirical work, carried out in accordance with the theory and socio-economic analysis, proves that it is possible to accompany the achievement, by private and public companies, of overall performance. In fact, the detection of symptoms that hide high costs can open up avenues for an effective management of the General Labor Inspection.

Resumen

La virtud cardinal de la acción pública consiste en traducir la voluntad de la autoridad política en bienestar económico, social y medioambiental de la comunidad nacional. En este sentido, en lo que respecta a la gestión pública, especialmente en lo que se refiere a las condiciones de trabajo en el sector de la construcción civil, este trabajo empírico, realizado de acuerdo con la teoría y el análisis socioeconómico, demuestra que es posible acompañar la consecución, por parte de las empresas privadas y públicas, de un desempeno global. De hecho, la detección de los síntomas que ocultan los altos costos puede abrir el camino para una gestión eficiente de la Inspección General del Trabajo.

Résumé

La vertu cardinale de l'action publique consiste à la traduction de la volonté de l'autorité politique en bien-être économique, social et environnemental de la collectivité nationale. Pour ce faire, en ce qui concerne la gestion publique relative notamment aux conditions de travail dans le secteur de Construction civile, ce travail empirique mené en adéquation avec la théorie et l'analyse socio-économique prouve qu'il est possible d'accompagner la réalisation, par les entreprises privées et publiques, la performance globale. En effet, le dépistage des symptômes occultant des coûts élevés peut ouvrir les pistes pour une gestion efficace de l'Inspection Générale du Travail.

---

38 How to Involve Employees to Write the History of the Company
Norbert Deville and Olivier Voyant

Abstract

A crisis is a useful pretext to activate the real, not to say unique, source of differentiation of the company, namely the Human Potential. Ten years ago, CETAF was confronted with an institutional, social and economic crisis. It made the choice of Human Potential. This chapter traces its journey and how the transformation allowed employees to write the company's history rather than undergo it.

Resumen

Una crisis es un pretexto útil para activar la verdadera, si no la única, fuente de diferenciación de la empresa, es decir el Potencial Humano. Hace diez años, el CETAF se enfrentó a una crisis institucional, social y económica. Hizo la elección de lo Humano. Este capítulo repasa su trayectoria y cómo la transformación permitió a los empleados escribir la historia de la empresa en lugar de sufrirla.

Résumé

Une crise est un prétexte utile pour activer la réelle, pour ne pas dire unique, source de différenciation de l'entreprise, à savoir le Potentiel Humain. Il y a 10 ans, le CETAF a été confronté à une crise institutionnelle, sociale et économique. Il a fait le choix de l'Humain. Ce chapitre retrace son parcours et la manière dont la transformation a permis aux collaborateurs d'écrire l'histoire de l'entreprise plutôt que de la subir.

39 Necessary Communication-Coordination-Cooperation to Fight Against the Blockages of Locked Organizations: Cases of Hospitals

Isabelle Barth and Marc Frachette

Abstract

Hospitals have always been places of complicated interactions between physicians, nurses and management. Hospital organizations have reached a level of blockage and "lock-in" that is rarely reached, and that only a more "clinical" management approach combining a controlled level of communication-coordination-cooperation (3Cs) between its stakeholders can achieve. An in-depth diagnosis of the functioning of each structure, followed by a socio-economic project, a real "care plan" conducted with method, can help unlock the mechanisms of cooperation that are essential to hospital performance.

Resumen

Los hospitales siempre han sido lugares de complicadas interacciones entre médicos, enfermeras y directivos. Las organizaciones hospitalarias han llegado a un nivel de bloqueo y "encierro" que rara vez se alcanza, y que sólo una gestión más "clínica" que combine un nivel finalmente dominado de comunicación-coordinación-concertación (3C) entre sus actores puede lograr. Un diagnóstico profundo del funcionamiento de cada estructura, seguido de un proyecto socioeconómico, un verdadero "plan de cuidados" realizado con método, puede contribuir a desbloquear los mecanismos de cooperación esenciales para el desempeño del hospital.

Résumé

Les hôpitaux ont toujours été des lieux d'interactions compliquées entre médecins, soignants et directions. Les organisations hospitalières sont arrivées à un niveau de blocage et de «verrouillage» rarement atteints, que seul un management plus «clinique» alliant un niveau enfin maîtrisé de communication-coordination-concertation (3C) entre ses parties prenantes. Un diagnostic approfondi du fonctionnement de chaque structure, suivi d'un projet socio-économique, véritable «plan de soins» conduit avec méthode, peut contribuer à déverrouiller les mécanismes de coopération indispensable à la performance hospitalière.

40 Listening and Mediation as a Lever for Transforming a Conflictual State Into a Cooperative State

Laurent Bertrand and Renaud Petit

Abstract

Listening and mediation are powerful levers of success for organizational change management. The transformation of the numerous individual conflicts and resistances, natural phenomena in organizations, into cooperation is the main managerial response to obtain collective performance. The remarkable qualitative, quantitative and financial results of the combined implementation of socio-economic management and the Non-Violent Communication approach, within an institution in the health and social sector, attest to this. The right mix of methodologist/mediator/therapist roles for managers is crucial for the sustainable and continuous success of cooperation in the workplace.

Resumen

La escucha y la mediación son poderosas palancas de éxito para liderar el cambio organizativo. La transformación de los numerosos conflictos y resistencias individuales, fenómenos naturales en las organizaciones, en cooperación es la principal respuesta directiva para obtener un rendimiento colectivo. Los notables resultados cualitativos, cuantitativos y financieros de la aplicación combinada de la gestión socioeconómica y el enfoque de la comunicación no violenta, dentro de una institución del sector sanitario y social, dan fe de ello. La combinación adecuada de los papeles de metodólogo/mediador/terapeuta de los directivos es decisiva para el éxito sostenible y continuo de la cooperación en el entorno profesional.

Résumé

L'écoute et la médiation sont des puissants leviers de succès pour la conduite de changement organisationnel. La transformation des nombreux conflits et résistances individuels, phénomènes naturels dans les organisations, en coopération est la principale réponse managériale pour obtenir la performance collective. Les résultats qualitatifs, quantitatifs et financiers remarquables de la mise en œuvre combinée du management socio-économique et de l'approche de la Communication NonViolente, au sein d'une institution du secteur sanitaire et social, en attestent. Le bon dosage des rôles de méthodologue/médiateur/thérapeute des managers est déterminant pour la réussite durable et continue de la coopération en milieu professionnel.

41 Modernizing the Associative Model in the Medico-Social Sector in France

Frédéric Gloro and Denis Hamayon

Abstract

The associative model in the medico-social sector is not outdated. It remains relevant for the development of social missions, particularly in the field of disability. However, it is necessary to recognize the existence of increasing difficulties in the management of these institutions, which constitute as many challenges for the modernization of their management. At least two areas could be the subject of a transformation of the associations: their governance and the implementation of a decentralized and synchronized management of their activities at the territorial level.

Resumen

El modelo asociativo en el sector médico-social no está superado. Sigue siendo pertinente para el desarrollo de las misiones sociales, especialmente en el ámbito de la discapacidad. Sin embargo, hay que reconocer que existen crecientes dificultades en la gestión de estas instituciones, que suponen un reto para la modernización de su gestión. Dos ámbitos podrían ser objeto de una transformación de las asociaciones: su gobernanza y la implantación de una gestión descentralizada y sincronizada de sus actividades a nivel territorial.

Résumé

Le modèle associatif dans le secteur médico-social n'est pas dépassé. Il demeure pertinent pour porter le développement des missions sociales, notamment dans le domaine du handicap. Cependant, il faut reconnaître l'existence de difficultés croissantes dans la gestion de ces institutions qui constituent autant d'enjeux de modernisation de leur management. Deux domaines au moins pourraient faire l'objet d'une transformation des associations: leur gouvernance et la mise en place d'un pilotage décentralisé et synchronisé de leurs activités à l'échelle des territoires.

---

42 The Socio-Economic Drive to Transformation From Non-Governmental Organization Into Social Enterprise

Pierre EL Haddad & Rana Barazi

Abstract

Increasing societal needs and receding resources are driving NGOs to transform from funding dependency into social entrepreneurship. This comparative study undertaken within three different organizations demonstrated the effectiveness of SEAM to guide the transformations. The interventions protruded the need for inclusivity, strategic clarity, aligned competencies, and adequate management control, and guided the constituents into working symbiotically towards concerted objectives.

Resumen

El aumento de las necesidades de la sociedad y la disminución de los recursos están impulsando a las ONG a pasar de la dependencia de la financiación al emprendimiento social. Este estudio comparativo realizado en tres organizaciones diferentes demostró la eficacia del modelo de gestión socioeconómica para guiar las transformaciones. Las intervenciones pusieron de manifiesto la necesidad de inclusión, claridad estratégica, alineación de competencias y control adecuado de la gestión, y guiaron a los integrantes para que trabajaran simbióticamente hacia objetivos concertados.

Résumé

Les besoins sociétaux croissants et la raréfaction des ressources emmènent les ONG à se transformer en entreprises sociales. Cette étude comparative menée au sein de trois organisations différentes a démontré l'efficacité de SEAM pour guider cette transformation. Les interventions ont fait ressortir le besoin d'inclusivité, de clarté stratégique, de compétences alignées et de contrôle de gestion adéquat, et ont guidé les acteurs à travailler en symbiose vers des objectifs concertés.

---

43 SEAM in America: Cultural Compatibility for Teaching and Diffusion

Yue Cai Hillon, Debra Salsi, and Mark E. Hillon

Abstract

The culture of an enterprise reflects beliefs about action. Values guide our actions and management tools are created to represent causal assumptions about how performance variables are connected. This cultural logic constrains how people act at work, but remains hidden because American management is so pervasive throughout the world. Alternatives are blocked. Authentically teaching SEAM forces the cultural self-reflection needed to unearth the barriers to adoption of innovative management. Our study draws on 13 years of data from American MBA students learning and doing SEAM in an intervention research course. Student reflections offered insight into the hidden cultural barriers to adoption of SEAM in America.

Resumen

La cultura de una empresa refleja creencias sobre la acción. Los valores guían nuestras acciones y las herramientas de gestión se crean para representar supuestos causales sobre cómo se conectan las variables de desempeño. Esta lógica cultural limita la forma en que las personas actúan en el trabajo, pero permanece oculta porque la gestión estadounidense está muy extendida en todo el mundo. Las alternativas están bloqueadas. La enseñanza auténtica de SEAM obliga a la autorreflexión cultural necesaria para descubrir las barreras a la adopción de una gestión innovadora. Nuestro estudio se basa en

13 años de datos de estudiantes estadounidenses de MBA que están aprendiendo y haciendo SEAM en un curso de investigación de intervención. Las reflexiones de los estudiantes ofrecieron información sobre las barreras culturales ocultas para la adopción de SEAM en Estados Unidos.

Résumé

La culture d'une entreprise reflète les croyances sur l'action. Les valeurs guident nos actions et les outils de gestion sont créés pour représenter les hypothèses causales sur la façon dont les variables de performance sont connectées. Cette logique culturelle contraint la façon dont les gens agissent au travail, mais reste cachée parce que la gestion américaine est si omniprésente dans le monde entier. Les alternatives sont bloquées. L'enseignement authentique de SEAM force l'auto-réflexion culturelle nécessaire pour dénicher les barrières à l'adoption d'une gestion innovante. Notre étude s'appuie sur 13 ans de données d'étudiants américains en MBA apprenant et faisant SEAM dans un cours de recherche interventionnelle. Les réflexions des étudiants ont permis de mieux comprendre les barrières culturelles cachées à l'adoption de SEAM en Amérique.

44 Long-Term Organizational Change Processes in Mexico
Martha M. Fernández Ruvalcaba and Graciela Carrillo González

Abstract

The objective is to analyze the project of a group of professors-researchers of the UAM whose purpose was to adopt and adapt the ISEOR methodology to Mexican organizations, in order to explain the processes of long-term change in dynamic and highly institutionalized contexts. For this purpose, proposals of: E. Morin (Complex systems); H. Maturana (Organizations as human social systems); and Powell & DiMaggio (Organizational change from neoinstitutionalism). It is concluded that the evolution of the institutions generated a decoupling between the interests of the professors and the objectives of the project. Nevertheless, the application of socioeconomic theory and management is preserved in teaching and research.

Resumen

El objetivo es analizar el proyecto de un grupo de profesores-investigadores de la UAM cuyo propósito fue adoptar y adaptar la metodología del ISEOR a organizaciones mexicanas, para explicar los procesos de cambio de largo aliento en contextos dinámicos y altamente institucionalizados. Para ello se abordan propuestas de: E. Morin (Sistemas complejos); H. Maturana (Organizaciones como sistema social humano); y Powell & DiMaggio (Cambio organizacional desde el neoinstitucionalismo). Se concluye que la evolución de las instituciones generó un desacoplamiento entre los intereses de los profesores y los objetivos del proyecto. No obstante, se conserva en la docencia y la investigación la aplicación de la teoría y de la gestión socioeconómica.

Résumé

L'objectif du chapitre est d'analyser le projet d'un groupe de professeurs-chercheurs de la UAM dont le but était d'adopter et d'adapter la méthodologie ISEOR aux organisations mexicaines, pour expliquer les processus de changement à long terme dans des contextes dynamiques et fortement institutionnalisés. Nous étudions les apports de: E. Morin (Systèmes complexes); H. Maturana (Les organisations en tant que système social humain); et Powell & DiMaggio (Changement organisationnel selon le néo-institutionnalisme). On en conclut que l'évolution des institutions a généré un découplage entre les intérêts des professeurs et les objectifs du projet. Cependant, l'application de la théorie et du management socio-économiques a été préservée dans leurs recherches et cours.

45 Evolution of Business School's Business Model

Gilles Guyot and Marc Bonnet

Abstract

Business schools have developed since the second half of the 19th century and most of them have adopted the Wharton model, inspired by a scientist approach that neglects Human Potential. This model became widespread throughout the world under the pressure of accreditation systems, with the defect that the theories disseminated were not relevant. However, there is currently an evolution towards an innovative approach, as in the case of the qualimetrics intervention-research model implemented by ISEOR.

Resumen

Las escuelas de gestión se han desarrollado desde la segunda parte del siglo XIX y la mayoría de ellas han adoptado el modelo de Wharton, inspirado en un enfoque científico que descuida el potencial humano. Este modelo se generalizó en todo el mundo bajo la presión de los sistemas de acreditación, con el defecto de que las teorías difundidas no eran pertinentes. Sin embargo, actualmente existe una evolución hacia un enfoque innovador, como es el caso del modelo de investigación-intervención cualimétrica implantado en ISEOR.

Résumé

Les écoles de management se sont développées depuis la deuxième partie du 19ème siècle et elles ont adopté pour la plupart le modèle de Wharton, inspiré par une approche scientiste qui néglige le Potentiel Humain. Ce modèle s'est généralisé dans le monde sous la pression des systèmes d'accréditation, avec pour défaut le manque de pertinence des théories diffusées. On observe toutefois actuellement une évolution vers une approche innovatrice, comme dans le cas du modèle de recherche-intervention qualimétrique mis en œuvre à l'ISEOR.

46 Changes in the Environment of Universities Impact in Their Strategy: Towards a Paradigm Shift?

Claude Jameux

Abstract

For the past twenty years, French universities have been facing three major changes in their environment: the globalization of higher education and research activities; public policy responses in terms of the autonomy of actors and the reorganization of the system; and a budgetary environment that has been constrained for a long time. This chapter argues that under the combined effects of these changes, a paradigm shift is taking place in favor of a strategic management approach. Universities must now respond to a strategic positioning constraint, develop their capacity for self-organization and revise the criterion of the sustainability of their projects.

Resumen

Desde hace veinte años, las universidades francesas se enfrentan a tres grandes cambios en su entorno: la globalización de la enseñanza superior y de las actividades de investigación; las respuestas de las políticas públicas en términos de autonomía de los actores y de reorganización del sistema; y un entorno presupuestario constreñido desde hace tiempo. Este capítulo sostiene que, bajo los efectos combinados de estos cambios, se está produciendo un cambio de paradigma hacia un enfoque de gestión estratégica. Las universidades deben responder ahora a una restricción de posicionamiento estratégico, desarrollar su capacidad de auto organización y revisar los criterios de sostenibilidad de sus proyectos.

Résumé

Depuis une vingtaine d'années, les universités françaises font face à trois mutations d'envergure de leur environnement: la globalisation des activités d'enseignement supérieur et de recherche; les réponses des politiques publiques en termes d'autonomie des acteurs et de recomposition du système; un environnement budgétaire durablement contraint. Ce chapitre soutient que sous les effets conjugués de ces mutations, un changement de paradigme s'opère au profit d'une démarche de management stratégique. Les universités doivent désormais répondre à une contrainte stratégique de positionnement, développer leur capacité d'auto-organisation et réviser le critère de soutenabilité de leurs projets.

---

47 Knowing and Being Able to Build One's Path in an Increasingly Complex and Uncertain World: The Challenge of Knowing How to Become

Paul Rousset and Michel Grivel

Abstract

In an increasingly complex and uncertain world, where most of tomorrow's jobs are still unknown, knowing and being able to build one's career path is becoming an essential skill, encompassing and exceeding professional skills and the triptych of knowledge/know-how/know-how to be. This skill, the ability to become, can be learned and trained through and for the experience processed and then integrated into new experiences.

Resumen

En un mundo cada vez más complejo e incierto, donde aún se desconocen la mayoría de las profesiones y trabajos del mañana, conocer y ser capaz de construir la propia carrera se convierte en una habilidad imprescindible, que abarca y va más allá de las competencias profesionales y el tríptico saber/saber-hacer/saber-ser. Esta habilidad, saber llegar a ser, se puede aprender y entrenar a través de la experiencia adquirida que luego se puede incorporar a nuevas experiencias

Résumé

Dans un monde de plus en plus complexe et incertain, où la plupart des métiers et emplois de demain sont encore inconnus, savoir et pouvoir construire son parcours devient une compétence essentielle, englobant et dépassant les compétences professionnelles et le triptyque savoir/savoir-faire/savoir-être. Cette compétence, le savoir devenir, s'apprend et on peut y et s'y former par et pour l'expérience traitée puis intégrée à de nouvelles expériences.

---

48 Enhancing the Managerial Impact of Management Research Towards Doctoral Training in Management Associating Academics and Practitioners

Michel Kalika, Jérôme Chabanne-Rive and Marc Bonnet

Abstract

As management research must increasingly make its managerial and societal impacts explicit, doctoral programs in management are now opening up to corporate practitioners and collaborative research. This chapter shows the example of two doctoral programs that contribute to this evolution: the DBA of the Business Science Institute, the EDEN program of EIASM and the hundreds of theses prepared at ISEOR.

Resumen

Dado que la investigación en gestión debe explicar cada vez más sus repercusiones en la gestión y la sociedad, la formación doctoral en gestión está ahora abierta a los profesionales de la empresa y a la investigación en colaboración.. Este capítulo muestra el ejemplo de dos programas de doctorado que contribuyen a esta evolución: el DBA del Instituto de Ciencias Empresariales y el programa EDEN de EIASM y los centenares de tesis doctorales elaboradas en el centro de investigación ISEOR.

Résumé

La recherche en management devant de plus en plus expliciter ses impacts managériaux et sociétaux, les formations doctorales en gestion s'ouvrent désormais aux praticiens d'entreprises et à des recherches collaboratives. Ce chapitre montre l'exemple de deux formations doctorales qui contribuent à cette évolution: le DBA du Business Science Institute, le programme EDEN de l'EIASM et les centaines de thèses préparées à l'ISEOR.

---

49 Socio-Economic Theory at the Heart of Student Entrepreneurship Support
Sylvie Mira-Bonnardel and Isabelle Géniaux

Abstract

Socio-economic theory constitutes a praxeology of entrepreneurial support, and more specifically of student entrepreneurship. Both a framework and a substrate for transformative coaching, socio-economic theory makes it possible to articulate the cognitive transformation of the student entrepreneur with the achievement of economic objectives. This chapter specifies the specificities of entrepreneurial cognition and the practices of coaching students in business creation projects, in order to explain how socio-economic theory offers an epistemological, methodological and operational framework for a renewal of these practices.

Resumen

La teoría socioeconómica constituye una praxeología relevante para el acompañamiento empresarial y, más particularmente, para el emprendimiento estudiantil. Marco y sustrato del acompañamiento con objetivó de transformación cognitiva, la teoría socioeconómica permite vincular el desarrollo cognitivo del emprendedor con el cumplimiento de objetivos económicos. Explicaremos las especificidades del acompañamiento de los proyectos empresariales de los estudiantes y destacaremos cómo la teoría socioeconómica permite una renovación de estas prácticas de acompañamiento.

Résumé

La théorie socio-économique constitue une praxéologie de l'accompagnement entrepreneurial et plus particulièrement de l'entrepreneuriat des étudiants. A la fois le cadre et le substrat d'un accompagnement à visée transformative, la théorie socio-économique permet d'articuler la transformation cognitive de l'étudiant.e entrepreneur.e avec la réalisation d'objectifs économiques. Ce chapitre précise les spécificités de la cognition entrepreneuriale et des pratiques d'accompagnement des projets de création d'entreprise chez les étudiant.e.s afin d'expliciter en quoi la théorie socio-économique offre le cadre épistémologique, méthodologique et opérationnel, permettant un renouveau de ces pratiques.

---

50 The Role of Management Schools in Accompanying the Transformation of a Profession and Society
Marc Bonnet and Réda Gourine

Abstract

The purpose of this chapter is to present the case of a school that shares with ISEOR an Aristotelian conception of science and teaching. This is the École des Hautes Études en Assurances in Algiers, with which ISEOR is linked, whose director prepared and defended his doctoral thesis in management within the framework of the ISEOR laboratory. This chapter also shows the importance of this type of school in contributing to the evolution of the professions and the prosperity of a country.

Resumen

El propósito de este capítulo es presentar el caso de una escuela que comparte con ISEOR una concepción aristotélica de la ciencia y la enseñanza. Se trata de la École des Hautes Études en Assurances de Argel, con la que ISEOR está en contacto y cuyo director elaboró y defendió su tesis doctoral en el marco del laboratorio ISEOR. Este capítulo también muestra la importancia de este tipo de escuelas para contribuir a la evolución de las profesiones y a la prosperidad de un país.

Résumé

Ce chapitre a pour objet de présenter le cas d'une école qui partage avec l'ISEOR une conception aristotélicienne de la science et de l'enseignement. Il s'agit de l'École des Hautes Études en Assurances d'Alger, avec laquelle l'ISEOR est en relation dont le directeur a préparé et soutenu sa thèse de doctorat de gestion dans le cadre du laboratoire ISEOR. Ce chapitre montre aussi l'importance de ce type d'école pour contribuer à l'évolution des professions et à la prospérité d'un pays.

51 Contribution of the Socio-Economic Approach to Management to Steering Action Plans in a Changing World

Samia Khenniche and Sébastien Podevyn-Menant

Abstract

Our society is faced with a profound change resulting from techno-scientific, economic and political transformations, which is particularly challenging for public action. At the same time, the multiplicity of its stakeholders and the increase in their demands reinforce the paradoxical nature of its performance. Socioeconomic approach to management, because it takes an overall approach to performance, understands short- and long-term results, and gives central importance to steering, contributes to the management of public action in times of change. By placing the principle of contradictory intersubjectivity at the heart of management, it makes it possible to overcome these paradoxes.

Resumen

Nuestra sociedad se enfrenta a un profundo cambio derivado de las transformaciones tecnocientíficas, económicas y políticas, que supone un reto especial para la acción pública. Al mismo tiempo, la multiplicidad de sus partes interesadas y el aumento de sus exigencias refuerzan el carácter paradójico de su actuación. La gestión socioeconómica, al adoptar un enfoque global de la actuación, comprender los resultados a corto y largo plazo y conceder una importancia central al pilotaje, contribuye a la gestión de la acción pública en un periodo de cambio. Al situar el principio de intersubjetividad contradictoria en el centro de la gestión, permite superar estas paradojas.

Résumé

Notre société se trouve confrontée à une profonde mutation issue de transformations technoscientifiques, économiques et politiques, qui réinterroge tout particulièrement l'action publique. Concomitamment, la multiplicité de ses parties prenantes et l'accroissement de leurs exigences renforcent le caractère paradoxal de sa performance. Le management socio-économique, parce qu'il approche la performance dans sa globalité, qu'il appréhende les résultats à court et à long termes et qu'il accorde une importance centrale au pilotage, contribue à la conduite de l'action publique en période de mutation. En inscrivant au cœur du pilotage le principe d'intersubjectivité contradictoire, il permet de dépasser ces paradoxes.

52 Local Authorities and Monitoring

Philippe Sauvannet and Marie-Christine Chalus-Sauvannet

Abstract

The legislator, through three successive "acts" from 1982 to the present day, has profoundly modified the functioning of local authorities and drawn a new panorama of the organization of the French administration. Local communities have consequently become major players in economic, social and cultural life. Territorial monitoring was gradually put in place, with the aim of better adapting public services to the needs of citizens.

Resumen

El legislador, a través de tres "actos" sucesivos desde 1982 hasta la actualidad, ha modificado profundamente el funcionamiento de las autoridades locales y ha trazado un nuevo panorama de la organización de la administración francesa. En consecuencia, las comunidades locales se han convertido en protagonistas importantes de la vida económica, social y cultural. La vigilancia territorial se fue implantando gradualmente, con el objetivo de adaptar mejor los servicios públicos a las necesidades de los ciudadanos.

Résumé

Le législateur, au travers de trois "actes" successifs de 1982 à nos jours, a profondément modifié le fonctionnement des collectivités territoriales et dessiné un nouveau panorama de l'organisation de l'administration française. Les collectivités locales sont devenues en conséquence des acteurs majeurs de la vie économique, sociale et culturelle. La veille territoriale s'est mise en place progressivement, dans l'objectif de mieux adapter les services publics aux besoins des citoyens.

53 An Original Experiment in Evaluating the Impacts of Networking Through Socio-Economic Analysis: Case of the Lyon Health and City Workshops

Pascal Brenot and Michaël Baska

Abstract

Current methods of evaluating public systems underestimate the creation of value generated by these approaches, thereby jeopardizing the quality of the resulting public policies. The concept of socio-economic evaluation, derived from the socio-economic theory, provides methodological keys to better evaluate public systems. Using the case of the Ateliers Santé Ville (ASV), this chapter shows the hidden socio-economic performance of this scheme and describes the methodology used to achieve it. The results show that the ASV scheme, which is relevant from the point of view of public health, is economically viable.

Resumen

Los métodos actuales de evaluación de los sistemas públicos infravaloran la creación de valor generada por estos planteamientos, poniendo en peligro la calidad de las políticas públicas que de ellos se derivan. El concepto de evaluación socioeconómica, que procede de la teoría socioeconómica, proporciona las claves metodológicas para evaluar mejor los sistemas públicos. Utilizando el caso de los Ateliers Santé Ville (ASV- Talleres de salud en la ciudad), este capítulo muestra el rendimiento socioeconómico oculto de este plan y describe la metodología utilizada para conseguirlo. Los resultados demuestran que el sistema ASV, relevante desde el punto de vista de la salud pública, es económicamente viable.

Résumé

Les méthodes actuelles d'évaluation des dispositifs publics sous-évaluent la création de valeur générée par ces démarches, mettant en danger la qualité des orientations publiques qui en découlent. Le concept d'évaluation socio-économique issu de la théorie socio-économique apporte des clés méthodologiques permettant de mieux évaluer les dispositifs publics. À partir du cas des Ateliers Santé Ville, ce chapitre montre les performances socio-économiques cachées de ce dispositif et décrit la méthodologie utilisée pour y parvenir. Les résultats montrent que le dispositif ASV, pertinent du point de vue de la santé publique, est économiquement viable.

54 Strategic Planning and Change Management in Public Organizations: Integration of Socio-Economic Tools in Belgian Local Governments

Henri Talaszka and Xavier Pierre

Abstract

Public organizations, in particular municipalities, need strategic planning and change management in a context of evolution of their strategic environment and a need to control public finances. Public managers need methods that allow them to set a course, identify efficiency gains and lead transformations while obtaining the support of their teams. Based on the case of 12 Belgian municipalities, this chapter shows how socio-economic tools (Internal and External Strategic plans, Priority Action Plans, Competency Grids, Time Management) meet the needs of managers.

Resumen

Las organizaciones públicas, especialmente los municipios, tienen necesidades de planificación estratégica y gestión del cambio que se expresan en un contexto de cambios en su entorno estratégico y en la necesidad de controlar las finanzas públicas. Los directivos públicos necesitan métodos que les permitan fijar el rumbo, identificar las fuentes de eficiencia y liderar las transformaciones obteniendo el apoyo de sus equipos. Basándose en el caso de 12 municipios belgas, este capítulo muestra cómo las herramientas socioeconómicas (PAEINTEX, PAP, matriz de competencias, gestión del tiempo) responden a las necesidades de los directivos.

Résumé

Les organisations publiques, en particulier les communes, ont des besoins de planification stratégique et de conduite du changement s'exprimant dans un contexte d'évolution de leur environnement stratégique et d'un besoin de maitrise des finances publiques. Les managers publics ont besoin de méthodes leur permettant de fixer un cap, d'identifier des gisements d'efficience et de conduire des transformations en obtenant l'adhésion des équipes. S'appuyant sur le cas de 12 communes belges, ce chapitre montre comment les outils socioéconomiques (PASINTEX, PAP, grille de compétences, gestion du temps) répondent aux besoins des managers.

55 Strategic Development and Implementation: Managing Rythms and Relationships With Time—Case of a Congregation

François Du Penhoat and Maïté Rateau

Abstract

In a multigenerational and multicultural religious organization, the relationship to time is not the same as in a company and is not the same for everyone. While everyone would like to see strategic projects move forward more or less quickly, the lack of a common methodology for building and implementing these projects makes it difficult to develop or even successfully accomplish the public interest mission. This chapter presents the results of a socio-economic intervention carried out within a religious congregation that enabled the emergence of a common strategic project for the community while managing the biological rhythms of each person.

Resumen

En una entidad religiosa multigeneracional y multicultural, la relación con el tiempo no es la misma que en una empresa y no es igual para todos. Aunque a todos les gustaría que los proyectos estratégicos salieran adelante con mayor o menor rapidez, la falta de metodología común para la construcción y ejecución de estos proyectos dificulta su desarrollo e incluso el cumplimiento de la misión de interés público. El capítulo presenta la intervención socioeconómica llevada a cabo en el seno de una congregación religiosa que permitió la emergencia de un proyecto estratégico común a la comunidad, gestionando al mismo tiempo los ritmos biológicos de cada uno.

Résumé

Dans une organisation multigénérationnelle et multiculturelle religieuse, le rapport au temps n'est pas le même que dans une entreprise et n'est pas le même pour tous. Alors que chacun aimerait voir avancer plus ou moins vite les projets stratégiques, l'absence de méthodologie commune pour construire et mettre en œuvre ces projets rend difficile le développement voire le bon accomplissement de la mission d'intérêt public. Le chapitre présente les résultats d'une intervention socio-économique menée au sein d'une congrégation religieuse qui a permis de faire émerger un projet stratégique commun à la communauté tout en gérant les rythmes biologiques de chacun.

PART VI

Socio-economic strategies: Organizational development, corporate social responsibility, "tetranormalization," business transfers, mergers and acquisitions...

Estrategias socioeconómicas: desarrollo organizativo, responsabilidad social de las empresas, "tetranormalización," transferencia de negocios, fusiones y adquisiciones...

Stratégies socio-économiques: développement organisationnel, responsabilité sociale de l'entreprise, «tétranormalisation», transmission d'entreprise, fusions et acquisitions...

56 SEAM as an Organization Development Intervention: Fifty Years of Common Ground

Peter F. Sorensen and Therese F. Yaeger

Abstract

This paper reviews SEAM within the context of Organization Development (OD) and Change. It compares the foundation and basic principles of SEAM with the origins and classic OD work of Beckhard and Blake, the two early contributors to whom the term Organization Development is attributed. We also address the parallels between recent developments in the field—Appreciative Inquiry, Agile concepts, and Strategic OD. The common ground of SEAM principles originated by Henri Savall in 1973 and 1974, almost 50 years ago, parallel concepts in Organization Development.

Resumen

En este capítulo se examina la gestión socioeconómica (GSE) en relación con el desarrollo organizativo (DO) y el cambio. Compara el fundamento y los principios básicos de la GSE con los orígenes y el trabajo clásico de DO de Beckhard y Blake, los dos primeros que contribuyeron al término "desarrollo organizativo." También discutimos los paralelismos entre los recientes desarrollos en el campo:

"Appreciative Inquiry," los conceptos de agilidad y el DO estratégico. La base común de los principios de la GSE, iniciados por Henri Savall en 1973 y 1974, hace casi 50 años, es paralela a los conceptos de desarrollo organizativo (DO).

Résumé

Ce chapitre examine le management socio-économique (MASE) au regard du développement organisationnel (DO) et du changement. Il compare le fondement et les principes de base du MASE avec les origines et le travail classique du DO de Beckhard et Blake, les deux premiers contributeurs à qui l'on attribue le terme de développement organisationnel. Nous abordons également les parallèles entre les développements récents dans le domaine: "Appreciative Inquiry," les concepts d'agilité, et le DO stratégique. Le terrain d'entente des principes du MASE, initiés par Henri Savall en 1973 et 1974, il y a presque 50 ans, est parallèle aux concepts du développement organisationnel (DO).

---

57 A Powerful Organization Development Resource That Remains Overlooked

Joanne C. Preston

Abstract

This chapter looks at the major alignments that SEAM and the values of ODJ have in common and the resource potential that this methodology has for change leaders. The topics covered are the importance of people's contribution to change, inclusion of the entire system, systems thinking, listening to all the stories about the organization, tying change to the bottom line, social responsibility, and hybrid consulting. All elements together make a powerful resource that has been overlooked in the change field. The goal is to make readers globally aware of the importance of this methodology and the usefulness that it has as a tool for change.

Resumen

En este capítulo se examinan las principales alineaciones que tienen en común el modelo socioeconómico y los valores del Desarrollo Organizacional, y el potencial de recursos que tiene esta metodología para los líderes del cambio. Los temas tratados son la importancia de la contribución de las personas al cambio, la inclusión de todo el sistema, el pensamiento sistémico, la escucha de todas las historias de la organización, la vinculación del cambio a los resultados, la responsabilidad social y la consultoría híbrida. Todos los elementos juntos constituyen un poderoso recurso que se ha pasado por alto en el campo del cambio. El objetivo es que los lectores de todo el mundo sean conscientes de la importancia de esta metodología y de la utilidad que tiene como herramienta para el cambio.

Résumé

Ce chapitre examine les principales proximités entre le management socioéconomique et les valeurs de l'ODJ, ainsi que le potentiel de ressources que cette méthodologie offre aux responsables du changement. Les sujets abordés sont l'importance de la contribution des personnes au changement, l'inclusion de l'ensemble du système, la pensée systémique, l'écoute de toutes les histoires concernant l'organisation, le lien entre le changement et les résultats, la responsabilité sociale et le conseil hybride. Tous ces éléments réunis constituent une ressource puissante qui a été négligée dans le domaine du changement. L'objectif est de sensibiliser les lecteurs du monde entier à l'importance de cette méthodologie et à l'utilité qu'elle présente en tant qu'outil de changement.

58 Organizational Theory Early Developments: Locating the Seeds of Socio-Economic Approach to Management (SEAM)

Richard Baker and Bruno Cohanier

Abstract

Using an organization theory historic approach, the purpose of this chapter is to provide evidence that the seeds of the Socio-Economic Approach to Management (SEAM) were laid as early as the seminal work on motivation at the workplace of the Human Relations School in the 1920's. The main objective of this chapter is to show that SEAM contributes to tackle the reconciliation problem of the social and economic sides of business management which the Human Relations School failed to address properly and was subsequently criticized for.

Resumen

Utilizando un enfoque histórico de la teoría de las organizaciones, el propósito de este capítulo es mostrar que en los fundamentos del Enfoque Socioeconómico de la Gestión se pueden vislumbrar desde el trabajo seminal sobre de motivación en el trabajo de la Escuela de las Relaciones Humanas en la década de 1920. El objetivo principal de este capítulo es mostrar que la teoría socioeconómica contribuye a reconciliar los aspectos sociales y económicos de la gestión empresarial que la Escuela de las Relaciones Humanas no ha abordado adecuadamente y por el que ha sido criticada.

Résumé

En utilisant une approche historique de la théorie des organisations, le but de ce chapitre est de montrer que les germes de l'Approche Socio-Économique du Management (SEAM) peuvent être repérés dès les travaux fondateurs sur la motivation au travail de l'Ecole des Relations Humaines dans les années 1920. L'objectif principal de ce chapitre est de montrer que la théorie socio-économique contribue à gérer le problème de la réconciliation des aspects sociaux et économiques du management des entreprises que l'Ecole des Relations Humaines n'a pas correctement traité et pour laquelle elle a été critiquée.

59 Negotiated Commitment, a Key to Continous Improvement in the Chinese Companies That Have Adopted Lean Management

Jean Ruffier and Ziyuan Tang

Abstract

Ignorance of the defect of the socio-technical approach causes a general failure of Human Resources Management practices in Chinese companies. The submission paradigm is a real hindrance to increasing the performance of enterprises. Based on a case of socio-economic intervention-research carried out in a Chinese factory that has adopted LEAN, this chapter aims to highlight the relevance of the paradigm of negotiated commitment in the development of employee motivation in the search for continuous improvement and to confirm the motivational effect of the Periodically Negotiable Activity Contract.

Resumen

El desconocimiento de las debilidades en el enfoque socio técnico provoca un fracaso general de las prácticas de gestión de recursos humanos dentro de las empresas chinas. El paradigma de la obediencia y la subordinación es un freno real para mejorar el rendimiento empresarial. Basado en un caso de investigación-intervención socioeconómica llevado a cabo en una fábrica china que ha adoptado LEAN, este capítulo tiene como objetivo resaltar la relevancia del paradigma del compromiso negociado en el desarrollo de la motivación de los empleados. Así verificamos el efecto motivacional del Contrato de Actividad Periódicamente Negociable.

Résumé

L'ignorance du défaut de l'approche sociotechnique provoque une défaillance générale des pratiques de GRH au sein des entreprises chinoises. Le paradigme de la soumission constitue un véritable frein à l'accroissement des performances des entreprises. En s'appuyant sur un cas de recherche-intervention socio-économique effectuée au sein d'une usine chinoise ayant adopté le LEAN, ce chapitre vise à mettre en évidence la pertinence du paradigme de l'engagement négocié dans le développement de la motivation des salariés à la recherche d'amélioration continue et confirmer l'effet motivationnel du Contrat d'Activité Périodiquement Négociable.

---

60 The Impact of Socio-Economic Intervention on the Development of Ambition and Strategic Implementation in a Medium Size and in a Small Company

Jérémy Salmeron and Carole Bousquet

Abstract

The objective of this chapter is to show the effect induced by the implementation of a socio-economic intervention on the ambition, on the design and on the strategic implementation as well as on the development of strategic competences of very small and small businesses. Based on two intervention-research case studies, the chapter highlights a methodology and systems that make it possible to reduce dysfunctions linked to strategy and improve the performance of these companies.

Resumen

Este capítulo pretende mostrar el efecto inducido por la implementación de una intervención socio-económica en la ambición, la definición y la implementación estratégica, así como en el desarrollo de las competencias estratégicas de la VSE/PYME. A partir de dos estudios de caso de investigación-intervención, destacamos una metodología y unos dispositivos para reducir las disfunciones relacionadas con la estrategia y mejorar los resultados de estas empresas.

Résumé

Ce chapitre a pour objectif de montrer l'effet induit par la mise en place d'une intervention socio-économique sur l'ambition, la définition et la mise en œuvre stratégique ainsi que sur développement des compétences stratégiques des TPE/PME. En nous appuyant sur deux cas d'études de recherche-intervention, nous mettons en évidence une méthodologie et des dispositifs permettant de diminuer les dysfonctionnements liés à la stratégie et d'améliorer les performances de ces entreprises.

---

61 The Technord Group: An Industrial Adventure and Advanced Social Responsibility

Michel Foucart

Abstract

The Technord industrial group has experienced an exceptional strategic and human trajectory, based on humanist values and the deployment of socio-economic management, which has accelerated the implementation of strategic vigilance practices that have fostered the development of new activities based on listening to customers and their expectations. This chapter also presents the singular trajectory of its historical leader, who decided to return to higher education in management at the age of 60, and organized the succession of the management with his son.

Resumen

El grupo industrial Technord ha experimentado una trayectoria estratégica y humana excepcional, basada en los valores humanistas y el despliegue de la gestión socioeconómica, que ha acelerado la implementación de prácticas de vigilancia estratégica que han propiciado el desarrollo de nuevas actividades desde escuchar a clientes y sus expectativas. En este capítulo también se expone la trayectoria singular de su líder histórico, decidiendo retomar los estudios de postgrado en administración a los 60 años, y organizando la sucesión de la administración a su hijo.

Résumé

Le groupe industriel Technord a vécu une trajectoire stratégique et humaine exceptionnelle, basée sur des valeurs humanistes et le déploiement du management socio-économique, qui a accéléré la mise en place de pratiques de vigilance stratégique qui ont favorisé le développement de nouvelles activités à partir d'une écoute des clients et de leurs attentes. Ce chapitre expose aussi la trajectoire singulière de son dirigeant historique, décidant de reprendre des études supérieures en management à 60 ans, et organisant la succession de la direction auprès de son fils.

62 Corporate Citizenship, a Common Good and the Search for Sustainable Performance
Christophe Fargier and Frantz Datry

Abstract

Is the idea of corporate citizenship a simple slogan or, on the contrary, a strong principle that can guide the actions of the entrepreneur-manager? The experience of the Ninkasi group, a small business created in Lyon in 1997, shows that this concept exists, guides strategic choices and is embodied in the professional behavior of the company's managers and employees. We propose to give a meaning and a definition to this proposal of corporate citizenship.

Resumen

¿Es la idea de ciudadanía corporativa un simple eslogan o, por el contrario, un principio sólido que puede guiar las acciones del directivo-empresario? La experiencia del grupo Ninkasi, una pequeña empresa creada en Lyon en 1997, muestra que este concepto existe, orienta las decisiones estratégicas y se plasma en el comportamiento profesional del director y los empleados de la empresa. Proponemos dar un significado y una definición a esta propuesta de ciudadanía corporativa.

Résumé

L'idée d'entreprise citoyenne est-elle un simple slogan ou au contraire un principe fort qui peut guider l'action du dirigeant-entrepreneur ? L'expérience du groupe Ninkasi, PME créée à Lyon en 1997, montre que ce concept existe, guide les choix stratégiques et s'incarne dans les comportements professionnels du dirigeant et des collaborateurs de l'entreprise. Nous proposons de donner un sens et une définition à cette proposition d'entreprise citoyenne.

63 Pro-Actively Reacting to the Tetranormalized Business Environment: Cases of a Lebanese Bank and a Small Family Insurance Brokerage Firm
Jocelyne B. Eid and George N. EL-Rahbani

Abstract

The notion of compliance and conformance with laws and regulations has gained the recognition in the market place to be not a simple back-office function but something that must be embedded into the fabric of the organization, in alignment with performance objectives, in a way that the organization as a whole can meet the obligations of various stakeholders: from the customers to suppliers, employees, investors regulators and others (Simons, 1994). The foundation of this work is based on two socio-economic intervention research projects undertaken in a Lebanese private Bank and a Small Family Insurance Brokerage Firm (SFIBF) aiming to enhance the management of complex norms and standards. The purpose of this work is to present the common mechanisms put in place via two socio-economic innovative projects. Within the context of this research projects, two interveners researchers one is internal (assuming an additional function as an Operational Risk Manager in the Bank) and the other is a consultant which are classmates share the common process and learning experience. This dual role enriched the outcomes of the intervention and the overall process as detailed in the different sections of the Chapter.

Resumen

La noción de cumplimiento y conformidad con las leyes y los reglamentos ha ganado el reconocimiento en el mercado de no ser una simple función de back-office, sino algo que debe estar incrustado en el tejido de la organización, en consonancia con los objetivos de rendimiento, de manera que la organización en su conjunto puede cumplir con las obligaciones de las diversas partes interesadas: desde los clientes a los proveedores, empleados, inversores reguladores y otros (Simons, 1994). El fundamento de este trabajo se basa en dos proyectos de investigación de intervención socioeconómica llevados a cabo en un banco privado libanés y en una pequeña empresa familiar de corretaje de seguros (SFIBF) con el objetivo de mejorar la gestión de normas y estándares complejos. El objetivo de este trabajo es presentar los mecanismos comunes puestos en marcha a través de dos proyectos socioeconómicos innovadores. En el contexto de estos proyectos de investigación, dos investigadores intervinientes, uno interno (asumiendo una función adicional como gestor de riesgos operacionales en el Banco) y otro consultor, que son compañeros de clase, comparten el proceso común y la experiencia de aprendizaje. Este doble papel enriqueció los resultados de la intervención y el proceso general, como se detalla en las diferentes secciones del capítulo.

Résumé

La notion de conformité et de respect des lois et des règlements a été reconnue sur le marché comme n'étant pas une simple fonction de back-office, mais comme quelque chose qui doit être intégré dans le tissu de l'organisation, en alignement avec les objectifs de performance, de manière à ce que l'organisation dans son ensemble puisse répondre aux obligations des différentes parties prenantes: des clients aux fournisseurs, en passant par les employés, les investisseurs, les régulateurs et autres (Simons, 1994). Le fondement de ce travail est basé sur deux projets de recherche d'intervention socio-économique entrepris dans une banque privée libanaise et une petite société de courtage d'assurance familiale (SFIBF) visant à améliorer la gestion de normes et de standards complexes. L'objectif de ce travail est de présenter les mécanismes communs mis en place via deux projets socio-économiques innovants. Dans le cadre de ces projets de recherche, deux intervenants chercheurs, l'un interne (assumant une fonction supplémentaire de gestionnaire des risques opérationnels dans la banque) et l'autre consultant, camarades de classe, partagent le même processus et l'expérience d'apprentissage. Ce double rôle a enrichi les résultats de l'intervention et le processus global comme détaillé dans les différentes sections du chapitre.

---

64 Rigor and Relevance of "Responsible" Strategic Management Contributions of the Socio-Economic Theory

Alexandre Asselineau

Abstract

Faced with current societal issues, integrating social and environmental considerations alongside the economic dimension has become as imperative as it is urgent. But some questions remain. First, considering social aspects is still often seen as a constraint on companies. Second, the operational execution of "responsible" strategies often deviates significantly from the initial intentions, due to the deficiency of strategic management in proposing methods that embrace the complexity of organizations. On the contrary, Socio-Economic Theory seems to provide a fruitful framework for creating the conditions for efficient, responsible, and humanistic management.

Resumen

Ante los actuales retos de la sociedad, integrar las consideraciones sociales y medioambientales junto a la dimensión económica se ha convertido en algo imperativo y urgente. Pero siguen existiendo dudas.. En primer lugar, la toma en consideración de los aspectos sociales sigue siendo a menudo un obstáculo para las empresas. En segundo lugar, la implementación operativa de las estrategias "responsables" suele desviarse considerablemente de las intenciones iniciales, debido a la deficiencia de la gestión estratégica a la hora de proponer métodos que abarquen la complejidad de las organizaciones. Por el contrario, la teoría socioeconómica parece proporcionar precisamente un marco fructífero para crear las condiciones de una gestión exitosa, responsable y humanista.

Résumé

Face aux enjeux sociétaux actuels, intégrer des considérations sociales et environnementales aux côtés de la dimension économique est devenu aussi impératif qu'urgent. Mais des questions subsistent. D'abord, la prise en compte d'aspects soci(ét)aux est encore souvent vécue comme une contrainte pesant sur les entreprises. Ensuite, l'exécution opérationnelle des stratégies «responsables» s'écarte souvent significativement des intentions initiales, en raison de de la déficience du management stratégique à proposer des méthodes embrassant la complexité des organisations. Au contraire, la Théorie Socio-Économique semble précisément fournir un cadre fécond pour créer les conditions d'un management performant, responsable et humaniste.

---

65 Impact of the Socio-Economic Model on Corporate Social Responsibility

Eva Conraud Koellner and Martha Ríos Manríquez

Abstract

This chapter analyzes the impact of the ISEOR socioeconomic model on the corporate social responsibility developed by a company. It will address the intervention and delegation tools of the socioeconomic model as a particularly relevant strategy to involve employees in social responsibility actions. A case study of a self-diagnosis applied to the human capital of a primary sector company in Mexico, which has been implementing the socioeconomic management model for more than fifteen years, is presented to measure its perception of the achievements in corporate social responsibility.

Resumen

Este capítulo analiza el impacto del modelo socioeconómico del ISEOR sobre la responsabilidad social empresarial que desarrolla una empresa. Se abordarán las herramientas de intervención y de delegación del modelo socioeconómico como una estrategia de especial relevancia para involucrar a los empleados en acciones de responsabilidad social. Se presenta un estudio de caso de un autodiagnóstico aplicado al capital humano de una empresa del sector primario de México, que cuenta con más de quince años de implementación del modelo de gestión socioeconómica, para medir su percepción de los logros alcanzados en responsabilidad social empresarial.

Résumé

Ce chapitre traite de l'impact du modèle socio-économique de l'ISEOR sur la responsabilité sociale des entreprises développée par une entreprise. Les outils d'intervention et de délégation du modèle socio-économique seront abordés comme une stratégie d'une importance particulière pour impliquer les employés dans les actions de responsabilité sociale. Une étude de cas d'un autodiagnostic appliqué au capital humain d'une entreprise du secteur primaire mexicain, qui a plus de quinze ans de mise en œuvre du modèle de gestion socio-économique, est présentée pour mesurer sa perception des réalisations réalisées en matière de responsabilité sociale des entreprises.

66 Towards a General Model of Hidden Costs Integrating Ecological Issues

Stéphane Trébucq and Jocelyn Husser

Abstract

The purpose of this chapter is to associate the integration of ecology to the hidden cost model following the recent evolutions of the standards and the management tools. An integrated model of global performance is proposed and then associated with the hidden cost method. This model is essential for companies that must learn to integrate data related to their environmental impacts into their evaluation and management tools. The theory of hidden costs can thus be deployed in complex informational environments enriched with new social and environmental standards

Resumen

El proposito de este capítulo es associar la integración de la ecologia con el modelo de costos ocultos siguiendo desarrollos recientes en estandares y herramientas de gestion. Se propone un modelo de desempeño global integrado y luego se asocia con el método de costos ocultos. Este modelo es fundamental para las empresas que deben aprender a integrar datos relacionados con sus impactos ambientales en sus herramientas de evaluación y gestión. La teoría de los costos ocultos puede así desplegarse en entornos de información complejos enriquecidos con nuevos estándares sociales y ambientales.

Résumé

L'objet de ce chapitre est d'associer l'intégration de l'écologie au modèle des coûts cachés suite aux évolutions récentes des normes et des outils de gestion. Un modèle intégré de performance globale est proposé puis associé à la méthode des coûts cachés. Ce modèle est essentiel pour les entreprises qui doivent apprendre à intégrer dans leurs outils d'évaluation et de pilotage des données relatives à leurs incidences environnementales. La théorie des coûts cachés peut ainsi se déployer dans des environnements informationnels complexes enrichis de nouvelles normes sociales et environnementales.

67 From the Territory as a Territory of Standards to ISO Standards Without Territories

Yvon Pesqueux and Benoît Pigé

Abstract

Normative conflict is a tangle of norms that places people at odds with that they must live with in the society around them. The failure to take into-account the possible conflicting nature of standards is explained by the process of a-territorialization of international standards. The reference to "interested stakeholders" marks the shift from a status of a-territorial standard (ISOs were "industrial" standards) to that of political standards. This passage opens the question of multi-level governance art the level of territory by consensus with the more distant levels.

Resumen

El conflicto normativo es una maraña de normas que pone a las personas en desacuerdo con lo que tienen que vivir en la sociedad que les rodea. La falta de consideración del posible carácter conflictivo de las normas se explica por el proceso de a-territorialización de las normas internacionales. La referencia a "partes interesadas" marca el cambio de un estado de normas técnicas a-territoriales (las ISO eran normas "industriales") a la de normas políticas. Este pasaje abre la cuestión de la gobernanza multinivel a nivel del territorio por consenso con los niveles más distantes.

Résumé

Le conflit normatif est un enchevêtrement de normes qui place les personnes en situation de contradiction avec ce qu'elles ont à vivre avec la société qui les entoure. La non-prise-en-compte de la conflictualité possible des normes s'explique par le processus d'a-territorialisation des normes internationales. La référence à des «parties intéressées» marque le passage d'un statut de normes techniques a-territoriales (les ISO étaient des normes «industrielles») à celui de normes politiques. Ce passage ouvre la question d'une gouvernance multi-niveaux au niveau du territoire par consensus avec les niveaux plus éloignés.

68 The Management of Normative Inflation by Control and Management Functions: Case of the French Financial Sector

Nicolas Dufour And Imen Abdou

Abstract

This chapter deals with the issue of the complex management of standards and regulations in the financial sector. Our objective is to illustrate the fact that standards can be anticipated, managed and negotiated. They require a clear positioning of the governance of financial institutions, but also a real and daily involvement of management and operational staff. The chapter addresses this issue through case studies in the French financial sector.

Resumen

Este capítulo aborda de manera ilustrativa el reto de la compleja gestión de las normas y reglamentaciones en el sector financiero Nuestro objetivo es ilustrar el hecho de que los estándares se anticipan, gestionan y negocian. Requieren un posicionamiento claro de la gobernanza de las instituciones financieras, pero también una implicación real y diaria del personal directivo y operativo. El capítulo aborda este tema a través de estudios de casos en el sector financiero francés.

Résumé

Ce chapitre aborde de manière illustrée l'enjeu de la gestion complexe des normes et réglementations dans le secteur financier. Notre objectif est d'illustrer le fait que les normes s'anticipent, se gèrent, se négocient. Elles nécessitent un positionnement clair de la gouvernance des institutions financières, mais aussi une implication réelle et quotidienne du management et des opérationnels. Le chapitre aborde cet enjeu au travers de cas de mise en situation dans le secteur financier français.

69 Digital Transformation: The Human–Digital Competitiveness (HDC). Framework From Technological Determinism to a Socio-Economic Perspective

Emmanuel Monod

Abstract

The high failure rate of digital transformation projects might be lowered by socio-economic approach to management. SEAM is not only holistic performance measurement system, but also an organizational transformation method encompassing workforce differentiation and business process innovation. However, SEAM shall develop digital dimensions such as development methods, technological infrastructure and enterprise architecture in consistence with the "Human–Digital Competitiveness" (HDC) framework. Combined with HDC framework, the SEAM stands as a customer-driven, people-driven performance management for improving the odds of digital transformation in companies.

Resumen

El alto nivel de fracaso en los proyectos de transformación digital puede reducirse mediante el enfoque de gestión socioeconómica, que no es sólo un sistema de gestión del desempeño integral, sino también un método de transformación organizativa. No obstante, las dimensiones digitales de la gestión socio-económica merecen un mayor desarrollo, especialmente los métodos de desarrollo, la infraestructura tecnológica y la arquitectura empresarial, en coherencia con el enfoque de Competitividad Humano-Digital (CHD). Llevado a cabo en coherencia con la CHD, la gestión socioeconómica tiene el potencial de ser un enfoque de gestión del desempeño orientado al cliente y al ser humano, que aumentaría el éxito de las transformaciones digitales en las empresas.

Résumé

Le haut niveau d'échec des projets de transformation numérique est susceptible d'être réduit par l'approche socio-économique du management (SEAM), qui n'est pas seulement un système holistique de management de la performance, mais également une méthode de transformation organisationnelle. Néanmoins, les dimensions numériques de SEAM mériteraient un développement, en particulier les méthodes de développement, l'infrastructure technologique et l'architecture d'entreprise, en cohérence avec l'approche "Human-Digital Competitiveness" (HDC). Mené en cohérence avec HDC, SEAM a le potentiel d'être une approche de management de la performance orientée client et humaine, qui accroîtrait le succès des transformations numériques en entreprise.

70 Managerial Engineering at the Service of Robotics-Vision

Amandine Savall, Hervé Henry, and Nylème Chettih

Abstract

This chapter presents the case of a robotics-vision company that employs about 80 engineers. Engineers represent a very specific population to manage. It is therefore up to the company, which needs managerial skills to run its organization, to identify and train these young engineers in management. By intervening at the heart of this robotics-vision company, the ISEOR team of researchers was confronted with a high level of resistance to change in managerial and organizational practices. The local managers were more "flexible" and saw their resistance to change diminish as the intervention progressed.

Resumen

Este capítulo presenta el caso de una empresa de robótica-visión que emplea a unos 80 ingenieros. Los ingenieros representan una población muy especial para manejar. Por lo tanto, depende de la empresa, que necesita competencias de gestión para dirigir su organización, identificar y capacitar en la gestión a estos jóvenes ingenieros. Al intervenir en el corazón de esta empresa de robótica-visión, el equipo del ISEOR se ha enfrentado a un alto nivel de resistencia al cambio de las prácticas organizativas y de gestión. Más "flexibles," los gerentes locales han visto disminuir su resistencia al cambio a medida que avanza la intervención.

Résumé

Ce chapitre présente le cas d'une entreprise de robotique-vision qui emploie environ 80 ingénieurs. Les ingénieurs représentent une population très particulière à manager. C'est donc à l'entreprise, qui a besoin de compétences managériales pour faire fonctionner son organisation, d'identifier et de former ces jeunes ingénieurs au management. En intervenant au cœur de cette entreprise de robotique-vision, l'équipe d'intervenants-chercheurs de l'ISEOR a été confrontée à un haut niveau de résistance au changement de pratiques managériales et organisationnelles. Plus «souples», les managers de proximité ont vu leur résistance au changement s'atténuer au fur et à mesure de l'intervention.

71 SEAM's Role in Merger and Acquisition Integration

Anthony F. Buono

Abstract

Most merger and acquisition strategies continue to be dominated by financial analyses, legal considerations, and power plays by dominant groups as individuals jockey for position and influence. Rather than focusing on the inherent dysfunctions that can emerge in the combined organization due to the informal power held by organizational members—from low productivity, poor quality and reduced commitment, to voluntary turnover and related hidden costs and untapped potential—far too many companies seem to meander through post-combination integration. Drawing on an intervention in a US hospital merger, the chapter illustrates how SEAM can facilitate the challenge of merger integration.

Resumen

La mayoría de las estrategias de fusión y adquisición siguen estando dominadas por los análisis financieros, las consideraciones legales y los juegos de poder de los grupos dominantes, ya que los individuos compiten por su posición e influencia. En lugar de centrarse en los disfuncionamientos inherentes, que pueden surgir en la organización combinada debido al poder informal que ostentan los miembros de la organización—desde la baja productividad, la mala calidad y la reducción del compromiso, hasta la rotación del personal voluntaria, los costos ocultos relacionados y el potencial desaprovechado—demasiadas empresas parecen dar tumbos en la integración posterior a la fusión-adquisición. A partir de una intervención en la fusión de un hospital noret-americano, el capítulo ilustra cómo el modelo socioeconómico puede facilitar el reto de la integración después de la fusión.

Résumé

La plupart des stratégies de fusion et d'acquisition continuent d'être dominées par les analyses financières, les considérations juridiques et les jeux de pouvoir des groupes dominants, les individus se disputant la position et l'influence. Plutôt que de se concentrer sur les dysfonctionnements inhérents qui peuvent émerger dans l'organisation fusionnée du fait des pouvoirs informels détenus par les membres de l'organisation—de la faible productivité, la mauvaise qualité et la réduction de l'engagement, de la rotation du personnel volontaire, des coûts cachés associés et du potentiel inexploité—Beaucoup trop d'entreprises semblent errer dans les méandres de l'intégration post-fusion-acquisition. En s'appuyant sur une intervention dans le cadre de la fusion d'un hôpital nord-américain, le chapitre illustre comment le management socio-économique peut faciliter le défi de l'intégration après fusion.

---

72 Considerations on the Socio-Economic Approach to Management in the Context of a Merger Between Two Competitors
Jean Caghassi

Abstract

The industrial group GIFA has implemented socio-economic management since the year 2000. The main contributions were the creation of a strategic base common to two sites, the improvement of economic performances, the valorization of intangible activities and human potential, the implementation of an original management control system compared to the traditional accounting system. The contribution of socio-economic management was decisive in consolidating the merger of human and economic potential and ensuring the success of the merger of two sites with different cultures.

Resumen

El grupo GIFA ha implantado el método de Management socioeconómico a principios de los años 2000. Las mayores contribuciones fueron la creación de un sólido zócalo estratégico compartido entre dos sitios, el mejoramiento de sus desempeños económicos, la valorización de sus activos inmateriales y potencial humano, y la implementación de un sistema de control de gestión original, diferente de sistemas contables clásicos. La contribución del Management socioeconómico ha sido un factor decisivo para asegurar la consolidación del potencial humano y económico de los dos equipos, superando las reluctancias de dos sitios con culturas diferentes.

Résumé

Le groupe industriel GIFA a implanté le management socio-économique à partir des années 2000. Les principaux apports ont été la création d'un socle stratégique commun à deux sites, l'amélioration des performances économiques, la valorisation des activités immatérielles et du potentiel humain, l'implantation d'un système de contrôle de gestion original par rapport au système comptable classique. La contribution du management socio-économique a été décisive pour consolider la fusion du potentiel humain et économique et assurer le succès de la fusion de deux sites imprégnés de cultures différentes.

73 International Communication in an Intercultural Environment: Illustrations

Jeannette Rencoret and Georges Peillon

Abstract

Communication has proven to be a powerful lever for the Socio-Economic Approach to management of international companies. This chapter shows, thanks to three concrete examples, how the development and implementation of internal and external communication contribute both to the performance of the company and to the development of its reputation.

Resumen

La comunicación está demostrando ser una poderosa palanca en la gestión socioeconómica de las empresas a escala internacional. Este capítulo demuestra, a través de 3 ejemplos concretos, cómo el desarrollo, así como la implementación de la comunicación interna y externa contribuyen al desempeño de la empresa, y al aumento de su notoriedad y reputación. Lo esencial reside en la anticipación estratégica de la comunicación en el funcionamiento global de la empresa u organización.

Résumé

La communication se révèle comme un puissant levier participant au management socio-économique des entreprises à l'international. Ce chapitre montre, grâce à trois exemples concrets, comment le développement puis la mise en œuvre de la communication interne et externe, contribuent tant à la performance de l'entreprise qu'au développement de sa notoriété et de sa réputation, l'essentiel étant l'anticipation stratégique de la communication dans le fonctionnement globale de l'entreprise.

74 The Socio-Economic Approach to Management: A Metaphor From the Panarchy

Pedro Constantino Solis Perez and Juan Castaingts Teillery

Abstract

This chapter studies the ISEOR Socio-economic Model from the metaphor of panarchy and resilience to offer a new look at the cornerstone theory of ISEOR strategy, where the success of a firm's external strategy depends on the degree of internal cohesion. On the other hand, the individual and collective behavior of conflict and cooperation and their impacts on the internal cohesion of the firm are observed from another plane. The aim is to argue that the metaphor of panarchy and the postulates of the cornerstone of socioeconomic theory are consistent with each other for the study of current organizations.

Resumen

En este capítulo se estudia el Modelo Socioeconómico del ISEOR a partir de la metáfora de la panarquía y la resiliencia para ofrecer una nueva mirada a la teoría de la piedra angular de la estrategia del ISEOR, donde el éxito de la estrategia externa de una empresa depende del grado de cohesión interna. Por otra parte, se observa desde otro plano la conducta individual y colectiva de conflicto y cooperación y sus impactos sobre la cohesión interna de la empresa. Se pretende plantear que la metáfora de la panarquía y los postulados de la piedra angular de la teoría socioeconómica son consistentes entre sí para estudiar las organizaciones actuales.

Résumé

Ce chapitre étudie le modèle socio-économique ISEOR basé sur la métaphore de la panarchie et de la résilience pour offrir un nouveau regard sur la théorie fondamentale de la stratégie ISEOR, où le succès de la stratégie externe d'une entreprise dépend du degré de cohésion interne. D'autre part, le comportement individuel et collectif de conflit et de coopération et ses impacts sur la cohésion interne de l'entreprise sont observés sous un autre plan. Il s'agit de faire valoir que la métaphore de la panarchie et les postulats de la pierre angulaire de la théorie socio-économique sont cohérents les uns avec les autres pour étudier les organisations actuelles.

PART VII

Socio-economic management of human resources and human potential

Gestión socioeconómica de los recursos humanos y del potencial humano

Gestion socio-économique des ressources humaines et du potentiel humain

75 Crossed Reflections on Transdisciplinarity in Maritime Expeditions: Entrepreneurship and Crew Spirit: In Memory of the Dedication of a Father to His Son
Serge Péron

Abstract

The complexity and the danger of the maritime expedition led very early to develop specific forms of association between partners. A contract between "merchant adventurers" and emigrants financed the voyage of the Mayflower. Trans-disciplinarity is a necessary dimension of these high seas, scientific, commercial, or political enterprises. Trust and solidarity are conditions of their efficiency. Despite technical progress, they remain and are embodied in the crew, both a living cohesive structure and a management tool. The French Navy has developed a discourse and practices around the crew spirit, in companionship with the entrepreneurial spirit.

Resumen

La complejidad y el peligro de la expedición marítima hicieron que se desarrollaran pronto formas específicas de asociación entre los socios. A contrato entre aventureros mercantiles y emigrantes financió el viaje del Mayflower. La transdisciplinariedad es una dimensión necesaria de estas empresas oceánicas, científicas, comerciales o políticas. Confidence and solidarity are the conditions for its effectiveness. A pesar de los avances técnicos, siguen siendo y se encarnan en la tripulación, tanto una estructura cohesionada viva como una herramienta de gestión. La Marina francesa ha desarrollado un discurso y unas prácticas en torno al espíritu de la tripulación, en compañía del espíritu empresarial.

Résumé

La complexité et la dangerosité de l'expédition maritime conduisirent très tôt à développer des formes spécifiques d'association entre partenaires. Un contrat entre «merchant adventurers» et émigrants finança le voyage du Mayflower. La transdisciplinarité est une dimension nécessaire de ces entreprises hauturières, scientifiques, commerciales ou politiques. Confiance et solidarité sont des conditions de leur efficacité. Malgré les progrès techniques, elles demeurent et s'incarnent dans l'équipage, à la fois structure cohésive vivante et outil de management. La Marine nationale a développé un discours et des pratiques autour de l'esprit d'équipage, en compagnonnage avec l'esprit d'entreprise.

76 Giving Meaning to Work and Reducing Psychosocial Risks

Nathalie Ombelets and Sandra Fattorutto

Abstract

In companies with a social purpose, the emotional and mental load is high, which increases psychosocial risk, can affect the quality of life at work and even the health of workers, and deteriorates the company's socio-economic performance. In this context, the meaning that employees give to their work plays a fundamental role in containing psychosocial risk. The different tools of socio-economic management have specific effects on the meaning of work, in particular the tools of strategic multiplication and management self-control. The definition of the company's vision and the choice of its values also have an impact on meaning.

Resumen

En las empresas con objeto social, la carga emocional y mental es elevada, lo que aumenta el riesgo psicosocial, puede afectar a la calidad de vida laboral e incluso a la salud de los trabajadores y deteriora los resultados socioeconómicos de la empresa. En este contexto, el sentido que los empleados dan a su trabajo juega un papel fundamental al contener el riesgo psicosocial. Las distintas herramientas de gestión socioeconómica tienen efectos específicos sobre el sentido del trabajo, en particular las herramientas de desglose estratégico y de autocontrol de gestión. La definición de la visión de la empresa y la elección de sus valores también son significativas.

Résumé

Dans les entreprises à finalité sociale, la charge émotionnelle et la charge mentale sont élevées, ce qui augmente le risque psychosocial, peut porter atteinte à la qualité de vie au travail, voire à la santé des travailleurs et détériore la performance socio-économique de l'entreprise. Dans ce contexte, le sens que les salariés donnent à leur travail joue un rôle fondamental pour contenir le risque psychosocial. Les différents outils du management socio-économique ont des effets spécifiques sur le sens au travail, en particulier les outils de la démultiplication stratégique et d'autocontrôle de gestion. La définition de la vision de l'entreprise et le choix de ses valeurs sont également porteurs de sens.

77 How to Contribute to the Development of Managerial Skills in SMEs?

Sébastien Payre and Aline Scouarnec

Abstract

The mastery of the managerial function, although essential in terms of survival-development of SMEs, is only rarely mentioned in the literature and in the professional world. We consider that it is necessary to go beyond the difficulties that are regularly encountered in the exercise of the manager's job, to implement a support approach that will support it. In this respect, the mobilization of the skills grid contributes to de-dramatizing situations, but also and above all to initiating a dialogue between members of the management and supervisory staff to make the professionalization of managers possible.

Resumen

El dominio de la función de management, aunque es esencial en términos de supervivencia-desarrollo de las PYMEs, sólo se evoca poco en publicaciones así como en el mundo profesional. Consideramos que es necesario ir más allá de las dificultades que se encuentran habitualmente en el ejercicio del trabajo del directivo y mando, para aplicar un enfoque de apoyo que lo respalde. En este sentido, el uso de la matriz de competencias ayuda a relativizar las situaciones, pero también y sobre todo a iniciar un diálogo entre los miembros de la dirección y los mandos superiores e intermediarios, para hacer posible su profesionalización.

Résumé

La maîtrise de la fonction d'encadrement, bien que primordiale en termes de survie-développement des PME, n'est qu'assez peu évoquée dans les publications comme dans le monde professionnel. Nous considérons qu'il faut dépasser les difficultés qui sont régulièrement rencontrées dans l'exercice du métier de manager, pour mettre en œuvre une démarche d'accompagnement venant le soutenir. A ce titre, la mobilisation de la grille de compétences contribue à dédramatiser les situations, mais aussi et surtout à engager un dialogue entre membres de la Direction et de l'encadrement pour rendre possible la professionnalisation des managers.

78 Recycling Hidden Costs: Importance of the "Serial Learner"

Jean Marie Peretti and Soufyane Frimousse

Abstract

In the current context of accelerating transformations, organizations must become agile and set up a learning ecosystem to continuously develop new skills and make their employees talented. This requires that each employee becomes a "Serial Learner." A Serial Learner is someone who can learn and develop outside the box. The key is to create the conditions for everyone to learn. The question is no longer what to learn, but how to create a permanent learning dynamic. How can we ensure that each work situation becomes a learning situation and reduce hidden costs? There are many similarities between learning and integrated training developed by the ISEOR team under the leadership of professor Savall.

Resumen

En el contexto actual de aceleración de las transformaciones, las organizaciones deben ser ágiles y establecer un ecosistema de aprendizaje para desarrollar continuamente nuevas competencias y hacer que sus empleados tengan talento. Para ello, cada empleado debe convertirse en un "aprendiz en serie." El aprendiz en serie es aquel que tiene la capacidad de formarse y aprender pensando de forma innovadora. Lo más importante es crear las condiciones para que todos aprendan. The question is not how to learn, but how to create a permanent learning process. How can we ensure that every work situation becomes a learning situation and reduce the costs involved? Hay muchas similitudes entre el aprendizaje y la formación integrada desarrollada por el equipo del ISEOR bajo la dirección del profesor Savall.

Résumé

Dans le contexte actuel d'accélération des transformations, les organisations doivent devenir agiles et mettre en place un écosystème d'apprenance, pour développer continuellement de nouvelles compétences de leurs collaborateurs et de les rendre talentueux. Il faut pour cela que chaque collaborateur devienne un «Serial Learner». Le Serial Learner est celui qui possède la capacité de se former et d'apprendre en sortant des sentiers battus. L'essentiel est de créer les conditions pour que chacun apprenne. La question n'est plus de savoir quoi apprendre, mais comment susciter une dynamique d'apprentissage permanent. Comment faire pour que chaque situation de travail devienne apprenante et réduise les coûts cachés ? Il y a de nombreuses proximités entre l'apprenance et la formation intégrée développée par l'équipe de l'ISEOR sous la conduite du Professeur Savall.

79 Contribution of the Socio-Economic Approach To Management (SEAM) to the Renewal of the Territorial Human Ressource Management Model (HRM)

Anne Loubès and Florence Noguera

Abstract

Although many experiments in territorial HRM were undertaken, about ten years ago, within various territories, through employer groups, regional mobility poles, provision agreements and territorialized networks of organizations, the results today seem mixed. After analyzing the causes of the difficulties in implementing territorial HRM, this contribution proposes ways to rethink territorial HRM, using the concept of socio-economic management.

Resumen

Si hace diez años se iniciaron muchas experiencias territoriales de gestión de recursos humanos en varios territorios, a través de grupos de empleadores, polos de movilidad regional, acuerdos de provisión y redes de organizaciones territorializadas, los resultados hoy parecen mixtos. Después de haber analizado las causas de las dificultades en la implementación de la GRH territorial, este aporte sugiere formas de repensar la GRH territorial, movilizando el concepto de gestión socioeconómica.

Résumé

Si de nombreuses expériences de GRH territoriale ont été engagées, il y a une dizaine d'années, au sein de divers territoires, au travers de groupements d'employeurs, de pôles de mobilité régionaux, de convention de mise à disposition ainsi que de réseaux territorialisés d'organisations, le bilan aujourd'hui semble mitigé. Après avoir analysé les causes des difficultés de mise en œuvre de la GRH territoriale, cette contribution propose des pistes pour repenser la GRH territoriale, en mobilisant le concept de management socio-économique.

80 Exploration of Convergence and Normative Articulation in the Field of Professional Training

Arnaud Muret

Abstract

This chapter explores two possible and desirable avenues of evolution in the vocational training sector in France, through normative convergence and articulation of norms:

- The first is in a systemic plan apprehending a long time, which would make it possible to reconcile the life course of an employee,
- The second is in a more operational level based on an engineering recombination articulating "human capital" and economic capital.

The coherence of the life-course could be improved by converging the professions of skills operators (Opco) and social protection groups (GPS) by imagining the creation of groups operating on the life-course (GPV).

Then it is a matter of designing a Region/Opco experiment aimed at exploring the simultaneous unification of economic and "human capital."

Resumen

Este capítulo explora dos posibles y deseables vías de desarrollo en el sector de la formación profesional en Francia, mediante la convergencia normativa y la articulación de normas:

- El primero está en un plan sistémico de larga duración, que permitiría conciliar la trayectoria vital de un empleado,
- La segunda se sitúa en un nivel más operativo, basado en una recombinación de ingeniería que

articula el "capital humano" y el capital económico.

La coherencia del curso de la vida podría mejorarse reuniendo las profesiones de los operadores de competencias (Opco) y los grupos de protección social (GPS), imaginando la creación de grupos que operen en el curso de la vida (GPV).

Se trata entonces de diseñar un experimento Región/Opco destinado a explorar la unificación simultánea del capital económico y humano.

Résumé

Ce chapitre explore deux pistes d'évolution possible et souhaitable dans le secteur de la formation professionnelle en France, par des convergences normatives et des articulations de normes:

- La première se situe dans un plan systémique appréhendant un temps long, ce qui permettrait de concilier le parcours de vie d'un salarié,
- La seconde est dans un niveau plus opérationnel se fondant sur une recombinaison d'ingénierie articulant le "capital humain" et le capital économique.

La cohérence du parcours de vie pourrait être améliorée en faisant converger les métiers des Opérateurs de compétences (Opco) et des Groupes de protection sociale (GPS) en imaginant créer des Groupes opérant sur le Parcours de Vie (GPV).

Puis il s'agit de concevoir une expérimentation Région/Opco visant à explorer l'unification simultanée du capital économique et du "capital humain."

PART VIII

Socio-economic management control

Control de gestión socioeconómico

Contrôle de gestion socio-économique

81 Overcoming the Poverty of Conventional Management Control Philosophy Through SEAM
Murray Lindsay and Henri Savall

Abstract

Management control in the Anglo-Saxon world has largely followed a cybernetic philosophy since the turn of the 20th century, with Robert Anthony's (1965) conceptual framework having had a profound influence. The dominance of this philosophy has made it difficult to conceive of control in an alternative way, hampering a wider audience from appreciating what SEAM has to offer. However, Anthony's (1988) comments regarding his framework's shortcomings, which have been largely overlooked, provide exceptional clarity in signposting the key issues underlying what Hofstede (1978) refers to as "the poverty of management control philosophy." They also serve as a lens for viewing SEAM in a new and compelling light.

Resumen

El control de gestión en el mundo anglosajón ha seguido en gran medida una filosofía cibernética desde principios del siglo XX, habiendo tenido una profunda influencia el marco conceptual de Robert Anthony (1965). El predominio de esta filosofía ha dificultado la concepción del control de forma alternativa, impidiendo que un público más amplio aprecie lo que la gestión socioeconómica Sin embargo, los comentarios de Anthony (1988) sobre las deficiencias de su marco, que en gran medida se han pasado por alto, aportan una claridad excepcional al señalar las cuestiones clave que subyacen a lo que Hofstede (1978) denomina "la pobreza de la filosofía del control de la gestión." También sirven como lente para ver la gestión socioeconómica bajo una luz nueva y convincente.

Résumé

Le contrôle de gestion dans le monde anglo-saxon a largement suivi une philosophie cybernétique depuis le début du 20ème siècle, le cadre conceptuel de Robert Anthony (1965) ayant eu une profonde influence. La domination de cette philosophie a rendu difficile une conception alternative du contrôle, empêchant un public plus large d'apprécier ce qu'offre le management socio-économique. Cependant, les commentaires d'Anthony (1988) concernant les lacunes de son cadre, qui ont été largement négligées, apportent une clarté exceptionnelle en signalant les questions clés qui sous-tendent ce que Hofstede (1978) appelle "la pauvreté de la philosophie du contrôle de gestion." Ils permettent également de considérer le management socio-économique sous un jour nouveau et convaincant.

---

82 Management Control as a Paradoxical Speciality

Yves Dupuy, Gérald Naro, Denis Travaillé

Abstract

The contribution questions the edge of management specializations, and more particularly that of management control. The latter is in fact the result of a paradoxical convergence between multiple technical imperatives and a global organizational vision. This paradox could be extended to the whole of management and, consequently, invite a decompartmentalized conception of research, teaching, and practices in this field.

Resumen

La contribución cuestiona los contornos de las especializaciones de la gestión, y más concretamente la del control de gestión. Esta última es, de hecho, una convergencia paradójica entre múltiples imperativos técnicos y una visión organizativa global. Esta paradoja podría extenderse al conjunto de la gestión y, en consecuencia, invitar a una concepción descompartimentada de la investigación, la enseñanza y las prácticas en este ámbito.

Résumé

La contribution interroge les contours des spécialisations en gestion, et plus particulièrement celle en contrôle de gestion. Cette dernière relève en effet d'une convergence paradoxale entre impératifs techniques multiples et vision organisationnelle globale. Ce paradoxe pourrait s'étendre à l'ensemble de la gestion et, par suite, inviter à une conception décloisonnée des recherches, enseignements et pratiques en la matière.

---

83 The Socio-Economic Approach to Management as a Conceptual Framework for Strategic Cost Management

Miguel Juan Bacic

Abstract

Strategic cost management (SCM) uses a set of tools to increase the value of products and reduce costs with the objective of improving the competitiveness of companies. However, it lacks a broader conceptual framework that discusses and understands organizational complexity and the interaction of human and technical structures that lead to dysfunctions and hidden costs. Socioeconomic management offers such a conceptual framework, which allows for a better interpretation of organizational reality and better results when applying SCM tools.

Resumen

La gestión estratégica de costos (GEC) usa un conjunto de herramientas para aumentar el valor de los productos y reducir costos con el objetivo de mejorar la competitividad de las empresas. Sin embargo, le falta un marco conceptual más amplio que discuta y entienda la complejidad organizacional y la interacción de las estructuras humanas y técnicas que llevan a disfuncionamientos y costos ocultos. La gestión socioeconómica ofrece ese marco conceptual, lo que permite una mejor interpretación de la realidad organizacional y obtención de mejores resultados al aplicar las herramientas de la GEC.

Résumé

La gestion stratégique des coûts (GSC) utilise un ensemble d'outils pour augmenter la valeur des produits et réduire les coûts afin d'améliorer la compétitivité des entreprises. Cependant, il manque un cadre conceptuel plus large qui discute et comprenne la complexité organisationnelle et l'interaction des structures humaines et techniques qui entraînent des dysfonctionnements et des coûts cachés. Le management socio-économique propose ce cadre conceptuel, qui permet une meilleure interprétation de la réalité organisationnelle et l'obtention de meilleurs résultats lors de l'application des outils de Gestion Stratégique des Coûts

---

84 Entrepreneurial Risk as a Hidden Cost
Daniel Farré and Susana T. Máspero

Abstract

The influence of the Stakeholder Theory on Financial Accounting is notorious at the moment of not considering the Cost of Entrepreneurial Risk. The chapter analyzes the hypothesis of incorporating the sacrifice for such risk as an economic cost, except for considering it together with the added value within the hybrid concept of accounting profit, and expressing it in all the analytical processes of the socio-economic theory in order to optimize the sustainable surplus value. When made visible, it makes it possible to identify other strategies such as prevention, value chain management, association to the business, replacement of shareholder structures and reinvestment of surpluses, among others, improving the holistic management of Risk.

Resumen

Es notoria la influencia de la Teoría de los Stakeholders sobre la Contabilidad Financiera al momento de no considerar el Costo del Riesgo Empresario. El capítulo analiza la hipótesis de incorporar el sacrificio por dicho riesgo como costo económico, exceptuando de considerarlo junto con el valor agregado dentro del concepto híbrido de utilidad contable, y expresándolo en todos los procesos analíticos de la TSE en pos de optimizar la Plusvalía sustentable. Visibilizado, posibilita identificar otras estrategias como prevención, gestión de cadena de valor, asociación al negocio, reemplazo de estructuras de accionistas y reinversión de excedentes, entre otras, mejorando la gestión holística del Riesgo.

Résumé

L'influence de la théorie des parties prenantes sur la comptabilité financière est notoire dès l'instant où l'on ne tient pas compte du coût du risque commercial. Le chapitre analyse l'hypothèse consistant à intégrer dans le coût économique le sacrifice généré par ce risque, sauf à le considérer, avec la valeur ajoutée, dans le concept hybride de bénéfice comptable, et à l'exprimer dans tous les processus analytiques de la théorie socio-économique (TSE), afin d'optimiser la plus-value durable. Ainsi rendue visible, cela permet d'identifier d'autres stratégies telles que la prévention, la gestion de la chaîne de valeur, l'association à l'entreprise, le remplacement des structures d'actionnariat et le réinvestissement des excédents, entre autres, améliorant ainsi la gestion globale du risque.

85 Socio-Economic Management Control, a Lever for Changing Organizational Standards: The Case of Operating Norms and Occupational Health

Thierry Nobre and Laurent Cappelletti

Abstract

This chapter presents how the socio-economic approach (SEA) contributes to giving management control its dimension as a lever for change to improve the medium- and long-term performance of organizations. This analysis focuses more specifically on the theme of health. First, a synthesis of research-intervention shows how ESA implements change in a health organization based on the different stages of socio-economic intervention. Then, a second approach shows how ESA tools through standardization integrate the concern for occupational health to transform the organization.

Resumen

En este capítulo se presenta cómo el modelo socioeconómico contribuye a dar al control de gestión su dimensión como palanca de cambio para mejorar el desempeño de las organizaciones a mediano y largo plazo. Este análisis se centra más específicamente en el tema de la salud. Primero, una síntesis de investigación-intervención muestra cómo el modelo socioeconómico implementa el cambio en una organización de salud desde las diferentes etapas de la intervención socioeconómica. Luego, un segundo enfoque muestra cómo las herramientas del modelo socioeconómico a través de la estandarización integran la preocupación de la salud ocupacional para transformar la organización.

Résumé

Ce chapitre présente comment l'approche socio-économique (ASE) contribue à donner au contrôle de gestion sa dimension de levier de changement pour améliorer la performance de moyen et long terme des organisations. Cette analyse porte plus spécifiquement sur thème de la santé. Dans un premier temps une synthèse de recherche-intervention montre comment l'ASE implémente le changement dans une organisation de santé à partir des différentes étapes de l'intervention socio-économique. Ensuite, une deuxième approche montre comment les outils de l'ASE par le biais de la normalisation intègre la préoccupation de la santé au travail pour transformer l'organisation.

86 Hourly Contribution to Value-Added on Variable Costs (HCVAVC) as a Concept and Tool to Manage the Creation of Added Value

Cécile Ennajem and Mohammed Ennajem

Abstract

The HCVAVC makes it possible to measure the economic value generated by a unit of work time. In normal operation, when a solvent product (good or service) is generated, it generates an assessable value based on the hourly contribution to value-added over variable costs. The opposite reasoning leads to a non-contribution to the added value when a dysfunction appears and produces ipso facto a hidden cost.

The HCVAVC, coupled with the six areas of dysfunction, makes it possible to raise the awareness of the company's actors to the notion of wealth creation and to make the strategic and operational management of the creation of socio-economic added value tangible.

Resumen

La CHVACV permite medir el valor económico generado por una unidad de tiempo de trabajo. En funcionamiento normal, cuando se genera un producto solvente (bien o servicio), genera un valor tasable en función de la contribución horaria al valor agregado sobre costos variables. El razonamiento contrario conduce a una no contribución al valor agregado, cuando aparece un disfuncionamiento y éste produce ipso facto un costo oculto.

La CHVACV, sumada a las seis áreas de disfunción, permite sensibilizar a los grupos de interés de la empresa sobre el concepto de creación de riqueza y hacer tangible la gestión estratégica y operativa de la creación de valor añadido socioeconómico.

Résumé

La CHVACV permet de mesurer la valeur économique engendrée par une unité de temps de travail. Dans un fonctionnement normal, lorsqu'un produit (bien ou service) solvable est généré, il génère une valeur évaluable sur base de la contribution horaire à la valeur ajoutée sur coûts variables. Le raisonnement inverse débouche sur une non-contribution à la valeur ajoutée, lorsqu'un dysfonctionnement apparait et qu'il produit ipso facto un coût caché.

La CHVACV, couplée aux six domaines de dysfonctionnements permet de sensibiliser les acteurs de l'entreprise à la notion de création de richesse et de rendre tangible le pilotage stratégique et opérationnel de la création de valeur ajoutée socio-économique.

87 Analysis of the Socio-Economic Risks of Organizations: A Current Vision

Francisco Javier Quesada Sánchez and Mª Ángela Jiménez Montañés

Abstract

At present, organizations are linked to and subjected to a set of changes and threats that condition their socioeconomic behavior. This set of threats translates into business risks, which must be identified and assessed in order to mitigate the negative effects they can have on the economic and social performance of organizations. This chapter presents and analyzes the importance of the study of risks at present and their management, under the perspective of the COSO Model and the ISO 31000 Standard, considering the different classifications of risks that can and should be identified. Finally, we conclude with a brief description of the risks that should be identified in the audit activity, applying the Risk Model identified in the International Standard on Auditing ISA-ES 315.

Resumen

En los momentos actuales, las organizaciones se encuentran vinculadas y sometidas a un conjunto de cambios y amenazas que condicionan su comportamiento socioeconómico. Este conjunto de amenazas se traduce en riesgos empresariales, los cuales deben ser identificados y valorados, al objeto de mitigar los efectos negativos que pueden causar en el desempeño económico y social de las organizaciones. Este capítulo expone y analiza la importancia del estudio de los riesgos en los momentos actuales y su gestión, bajo la óptica del Modelo COSO y de la Norma ISO 31000, considerando las distintas clasificaciones de riesgos que pueden y deben ser identificados. Por último, concluimos con una breve exposición de los riesgos que deben identificarse en la actividad de la auditoría de cuentas, aplicando el Modelo de Riesgos identificado en la Norma Internacional de Auditoria NIA-ES 315.

Résumé

Les organisations sont liées et soumises à un ensemble de changements et de menaces qui conditionnent leur comportement socio-économique. Cet ensemble de menaces se traduit par des risques commerciaux, qui doivent être identifiés et valorisés, afin d'atténuer les effets négatifs qu'elles peuvent avoir sur la performance économique et sociale des organisations. Ce chapitre expose et analyse l'importance de l'étude des risques à l'heure actuelle et leur gestion, dans la perspective du modèle COSO et de l'ISO 31000, compte tenu des différentes classifications de risque qui doivent être identifiées. Enfin, nous concluons par une brève présentation des risques à identifier dans l'activité de vérification des comptes, en appliquant le modèle de risque identifié dans la Norme internationale d'audit NIA-ES 315.

88 Cost Calculation, Management Indicators, "Business Intelligence" and "Business Analytics" for Urban and Metropolitan Transport Services

Daniel Carrasco and Daniel Sánchez Toledano

Abstract

Nowadays, companies and organizations have at their disposal a wide range of transversal technological possibilities, which constitute an opportunity to improve their management. Our study is oriented to the analysis of the information systems and the exploitation of the data of a public transport company, on the totality of the global dimensional matrix of the organization, for the definition of management indicators and scorecards, which allow the generation of adequate information to know the reality of the organization and to support the decision-making processes at different levels of responsibility.

Resumen

En la actualidad, empresas y organizaciones disponen de un amplio abanico de posibilidades tecnológicas de carácter transversal, que constituyen una oportunidad para la mejora de su gestión. Nuestro estudio se orienta al análisis de los sistemas de información y la explotación de los datos de una empresa de transporte colectivo, sobre la totalidad de la matriz dimensional global de la organización, para la definición de indicadores de gestión y cuadros de mando, que permitan generar información adecuada para conocer la realidad de la organización y apoyar los procesos de toma de decisiones a sus diferentes niveles de responsabilidad.

Résumé

Actuellement, les entreprises et les organisations disposent d'un large éventail de possibilités technologiques transversales qui constituent une opportunité d'améliorer leur gestion. Notre étude est orientée vers l'analyse des systèmes d'information et l'exploitation des données d'une entreprise de transport collectif, sur l'ensemble de la matrice dimensionnelle de l'organisation, pour la définition d'indicateurs de gestion et de tableaux de bord, qui permettent de générer des informations adéquates pour connaître la réalité de l'organisation et soutenir les processus décisionnels à différents niveaux de responsabilité.

89 The Chartered Accountant and the Decision Support of Managers

André Rostan and Marc Rostan

Abstract

Beyond his interventions in accounting matters in companies and organizations, the chartered accountant is frequently asked by the manager to assist him in certain decisions. He is also led, in view of his own observations, to propose improvements or corrections of anomalies, to improve an operation or limit a risk. He will be even more effective in his proposals if his approach is structured by a method and tools, while adapting to the personality of the manager, the final decision maker. But he will also have a key role to play in ensuring that a decision taken becomes a reality.

Resumen

Además de su labor contable en las empresas y organizaciones, el contador público suele ser requerido por el directivo para que le ayude en determinadas decisiones. También se ve llevado, a la luz de sus propias observaciones, a proponer mejoras o correcciones de anomalías, con el fin de mejorar una operación o limitar un riesgo. Será tanto más eficaz en sus propuestas si su enfoque está estructurado por un método y unas herramientas, al tiempo que se adapta a la personalidad del directivo, el responsable final de las decisiones. Pero también tendrá un papel clave para que la decisión tomada se convierta en realidad.

Résumé

Au-delà de ses interventions en matière comptable dans les entreprises et organisations, l'expert-comptable est fréquemment sollicité par le dirigeant pour l'assister dans certaines décisions. Il est amené également, au vu de ses propres observations, à proposer des améliorations ou des corrections d'anomalies, de manière à améliorer un fonctionnement ou à limiter un risque. Il sera d'autant plus efficace dans ses propositions que sa démarche sera structurée par une méthode et des outils, tout en s'adaptant à la personnalité du dirigeant, décideur final. Mais il aura également un rôle-clé à jouer pour faire en sorte qu'une décision prise devienne une réalité.

PART IX

Economics and management: articulation and continuum

Economía y gestión: articulación y continuidad

Économie et gestion: articulation et continuum

90 Towards a Participative Management of Companies and the Economy

Gilbert Blardone

Abstract

The socio-economic theory is based on responsible and sustainable economic foundations inscribed in a socially responsible capitalism. Financial capitalism leads to crises whose origins were exposed as early as 1922 by the Spanish economist Bernácer. The ultraliberal ideology attributes to the market the capacity to regulate itself. A two-level strategy, the firm and the general economy, is needed to move from traditional management to participatory management by all actors involved. The author advocates the social and solidarity market economy, built from the enterprise and based on the substitution of a humanist ideology for ultraliberalism, in order to improve the living conditions of the population. Socio-economic theory shows that the existence of considerable reserves of productivity delays or prevents the creation of jobs.

Resumen

La teoría socioeconómica se basa en fundamentos económices responsables y sostenibles dentro de un capitalismo socialmente responsable. El capitalismo financiero conduce a las crisis, cuyos orígenes fueron expuestos ya en 1922 por el economista español Bernácer. La ideología ultraliberal atribuye al mercado la capacidad de autorregularse. Para pasar de la gestión tradicional a la gestión participativa por parte de todos los agentes implicados, es necesaria una estrategia a dos niveles, la empresa y la economía general. El autor aboga por la economía de mercado social y solidaria, construida desde la empresa y basada en sustituir una ideología humanista al ultraliberalismo, para mejorar las condiciones de vida de la población. La teoría socioeconómica demuestra que la existencia de considerables reservas de productividad retrasa o impide la creación de puestos de trabajo.

Résumé

La théorie socio-économique s'inscrit dans des fondements économiques responsables et durables inscrite dans un capitalisme socialement responsable. Le capitalisme financier mène à des crises dont les origines étaient exposées dès 1922 par l'économiste espagnol Bernácer. L'idéologie ultralibérale attribue au marché la capacité de s'autoréguler. Une stratégie à deux niveaux, l'entreprise et l'économie générale, est nécessaire pour passer de la gestion traditionnelle à une gestion participative par tous les acteurs concernés. L'auteur préconise l'économie sociale et solidaire de marché, construite à partir de l'entreprise et fondée sur la substitution d'une idéologie humaniste à l'ultralibéralisme, afin d'améliorer les conditions de vie de la population. La théorie socio-économique montre que l'existence de réserves de productivité considérables retarde ou empêche la création d'emploi.

91 For a Europe of Organized Exchange Zones: A Socio-Economic Approach to Decentralization

Jean-Simon Tabournel

Abstract

To fight against the disparities that weaken the European Union, it is necessary to transform it into an Organized Trade Area (OTA), in the words of François Perroux and Maurice Allais. An OTA brings together states with the same culture, with comparable levels of economic and social development, with a common project that they decide to implement in a concerted and flexible manner. The OTA project is imperative for a Union that wants to be a force of proposition in world regulation

Resumen

Para combatir las disparidades que debilitan a la Unión Europea, ésta debería transformarse en una Zona de Comercio Organizado (ZCO), en palabras de François Perroux y Maurice Allais. Una ACLO reúne a Estados con la misma cultura y niveles comparables de desarrollo económico y social, con un proyecto común que deciden poner en marcha de forma concertada y flexible. El proyecto ZEO es imperativo para una Unión que quiere ser una fuerza de propuesta en la regulación mundial.

Résumé

Pour lutter contre les disparités qui affaiblissent l'Union Européenne, il convient de la transformer en Zone d'Echanges Organisés (ZEO), selon les termes de François Perroux et Maurice Allais. Une ZEO rassemble des États de même culture, de niveaux de développement économique et social comparables, ayant un projet commun qu'ils décident de mettre en œuvre de manière concertée et souple. Le projet de ZEO est impératif pour une Union qui veut peser comme force de proposition dans la régulation mondiale.

92 The Socio-Economic Approach to Management: A Lever for Action in Organizations of the Southern Countries

Geneviève Causse and Pierre Hidalgo

Abstract

In the 1980s, the reforms implemented by international donors in sub-Saharan countries generally consisted of transplanting management methods considered universal. The use of the socio-economic method, by considering the specificities of the context, made the reforms more appropriate and acceptable. After examining the problems posed by the reforms, the presentation of a few activities implemented in accordance with values very similar to those of ISEOR shows how socioeconomic management can be a lever for action for countries in the South.

Resumen

En los años 80, las reformas aplicadas por los donantes internacionales en los países subsaharianos consistían generalmente en trasplantar métodos de gestión considerados universales. El uso del método socioeconómico, al tener en cuenta las especificidades del contexto, hizo que las reformas fueran más adecuadas y aceptables. Tras examinar los problemas que plantean las reformas, la presentación de algunas actividades realizadas de acuerdo con valores muy similares a los del ISEOR muestra cómo la gestión socioeconómica puede ser una palanca de acción en los países del Sur.

Résumé

Dans la décennie 80 les réformes mises en œuvre par les bailleurs de fonds internationaux dans les pays subsahariens ont consisté généralement à transplanter des méthodes de management considérées comme universelles. Le recours à la méthode socioéconomique, par la prise en compte des spécificités du contexte, a permis de rendre les réformes plus appropriées et plus acceptables. Après l'examen des problèmes posés par les réformes, la présentation de quelques activités mises en œuvre dans le respect des valeurs très proches de celles de l'ISEOR montre comment le management socioéconomique peut être un levier d'action pour les pays du Sud.

93 Hidden Risk: Socio-Economic Theory and Crises

Robert Gephart

Abstract

Hidden risk involves potential threats to organizations that are neglected or tacitly accepted. These risks create hidden costs unaddressed in formal accounting reports and information systems. They undermine revenue, impede organizational performance, and engender crises. SEAM processes can recover some these costs. But when unaddressed, the costs can accumulate and evolve into crises. The current chapter addresses the nature of hidden risk, how it emerges in organizations, how hidden costs produce dysfunctions that make society more risk-prone, and how SEAM's six new management tools, along with Ethnostatistics, can help manage hidden risks and prevent organizational crises.

Resumen

El riesgo oculto implica amenazas potenciales para las organizaciones que se descuidan o se aceptan tácitamente. Estos riesgos crean costes ocultos que no se abordan en los informes contables y sistemas de información formales. Minan los ingresos, impiden el rendimiento de la organización y generan crisis. El modelo de gestión socioeconómica puede recuperar algunos de estos costos. Pero cuando no se abordan, los costes pueden acumularse y convertirse en crisis. El presente capítulo aborda la naturaleza del riesgo oculto, cómo surge en las organizaciones, cómo los costes ocultos producen disfunciones que hacen que la sociedad sea más propensa al riesgo, y cómo las seis nuevas herramientas de gestión socioeconómica, junto con la Etnoestadística, pueden ayudar a gestionar los riesgos ocultos y prevenir las crisis organizativas.

Résumé

Le risque caché implique des menaces potentielles pour les organisations qui sont négligées ou tacitement acceptées. Ces risques créent des coûts cachés qui ne sont pas pris en compte dans les rapports comptables et les systèmes d'information officiels. Ils sapent les revenus, entravent les performances des organisations et engendrent des crises. La méthode socio-économique permet de récupérer certains de ces coûts. Mais lorsqu'ils ne sont pas traités, les coûts peuvent s'accumuler et se transformer en crises. Le présent chapitre traite de la nature du risque caché, de la manière dont il émerge dans les organisations, de la façon dont les coûts cachés produisent des dysfonctionnements qui rendent la société plus vulnérable aux risques, et de la manière dont les six nouveaux outils de gestion du management socio-économique, ainsi que l'ethnostatistique, peuvent aider à gérer les risques cachés et à prévenir les crises organisationnelles.

94 Hidden Costs Stemming From Situations of Uncertainty: The Case of Cyberattacks

Philippe Laurier

Abstract

The company is a social body concerned with its survival, even before aiming for profitability or growth. Its organization and its choices will be influenced by this imperative. Threats to this survival, such as the growing risk of computer attacks, are not easily measurable ex ante by decision-makers and create uncertainty that hinders the optimal allocation of resources, and thus cause hidden costs. Moreover, the mere possibility of such an attack, weighing on the processes and decision-making function of the company in a diffuse manner, lowers its performance and cohesion.

Resumen

La empresa es un ente social preocupado por su supervivencia, incluso antes de aspirar a la rentabilidad o al crecimiento. Su organización y sus decisiones se verán influidas por este imperativo. Las amenazas a esta supervivencia, como el creciente riesgo de ataques informáticos, son difíciles de medir ex ante por los responsables de la toma de decisiones, y crean una incertidumbre que dificulta la asignación óptima de los recursos y, por tanto, provoca costes ocultos. Además, la mera posibilidad de un ataque de este tipo, que pesa sobre los procesos y la función de toma de decisiones de la empresa de forma difusa, disminuye su desempeño y cohesión.

Résumé

L'entreprise est un corps social soucieux de sa survie, avant même de viser une rentabilité ou une croissance. Son organisation comme ses choix seront influencés par cet impératif. Les menaces contre cette survie, telles que le risque croissant d'attaque informatique, étant peu mesurables ex ante par les décideurs, engendrent une incertitude qui nuit à une allocation optimale des ressources, et causent en cela des coûts cachés. Au surplus, la simple éventualité d'une telle attaque, pesant de manière diffuse sur les processus et la fonction décisionnelle de l'entreprise, abaisse sa performance et sa cohésion.

95 Successful SDG Transformation Through Socio-Economic Co-Creation

Raymond Saner and Lichia Yiu

Abstract

The 2030 Agenda represents unprecedented opportunities for doing well and doing good. To leverage this historical momentum and succeed in overcoming the Covid-19 pandemic, communities, businesses and governments together need to identify innovative ideas, products, services and processes for new wealth creation in a sustainable and inclusive manner. According to WBCSD, 12 trillion US$ of value creation and employment could be realized. The three dimensions are conceived as forming an interdependent whole, requiring policies that are inter sectorial, multi-stakeholder, inclusive, participatory and transparent. This chapter proposes ways to implement such a holistic sustainable and partnership-based development strategy.

Resumen

La Agenda 2030 representa oportunidades sin precedentes para hacer el bien y hacer el bien. Para aprovechar este impulso histórico y lograr superar la pandemia de Covid-19, las comunidades, las empresas y los gobiernos deben identificar conjuntamente ideas, productos, servicios y procesos innovadores para la creación de nueva riqueza de forma sostenible e inclusiva. Según el WBCSD, podrían realizarse 12 billones de dólares de creación de valor y empleo. Las tres dimensiones se conciben como un todo interdependiente que requiere políticas intersectoriales, multipares titas, inclusivas, participativas y transparentes. En este capítulo se proponen formas de aplicar esa estrategia holística de desarrollo sostenible y basada en la asociación.

Résumé

L'Agenda 2030 représente des opportunités sans précédent pour bien faire et faire le bien. Pour tirer parti de cet élan historique et réussir à vaincre la pandémie de Covid-19, les communautés, les entreprises et les gouvernements doivent identifier ensemble des idées, des produits, des services et des processus innovants pour créer de nouvelles richesses de manière durable et inclusive. Selon le WBCSD,

12 000 milliards de dollars US de création de valeur et d'emplois pourraient être réalisés. Les trois dimensions sont conçues comme formant un tout interdépendant, nécessitant des politiques intersectorielles, multipartites, inclusives, participatives et transparentes. Ce chapitre propose des moyens de mettre en œuvre une telle stratégie holistique de développement durable et fondée sur le partenariat.

96 Saving Companies, Entrepreneurs and Jobs
Robert Louis MEYNET

Abstract

The amicable and judicial treatment of companies in difficulty is in France a field that is little known in the world of socio-economic analysis. However, there is a time when the search for hidden costs is prioritized, first by a social restructuring that is always urgent, inevitable and indispensable (article L 631-17 of the Commercial Code), and then by an enrichment of the tasks of the employees who remain to lead to very important gains in productivity (+30% on average).

Resumen

El trato amistoso y judicial de las empresas en crisis es en Francia un ámbito muy poco conocido en el mundo del análisis socioeconómico. Sin embargo, hay un momento en el que priorizamos la búsqueda de costes ocultos, primero por una reestructuración social siempre urgente, inevitable y esencial (artículo L 631-17 del Código de Comercio) y luego por un enriquecimiento de las tareas de los empleados que siguen conduciendo a ganancias de productividad muy significativas (+30% de media).

Résumé

Le traitement amiable et judiciaire des entreprises en difficultés est en France un domaine très peu connu dans le monde de l'analyse socio-économique. Pourtant, il est un moment où l'on priorise la recherche des coûts cachés tout d'abord par une restructuration sociale toujours urgente, inévitable et indispensable (article L 631-17 du Code de Commerce) puis ensuite par un enrichissement des tâches des salariés qui restent pour conduire à des gains très importants de productivité (+30% en moyenne) .

97 Contractual Efficiency: Socio-Economic Approach to Management Versus Agency Theory: The Case of an IT Services Company in Morocco
Tariq Zidi

Abstract

The contractual approach of the firm presents the firm as a node of contracts between its stakeholders. The divergence of interests between the parties generates tensions and conflicts and pushes each party to the contract to adopt various strategies to preserve its interests. To resolve this dilemma, socio-economic theory has shown that replacing subordination in the relationship between the stakeholders of the firm by the establishment of a contractual relationship based on recognition, negotiation and discussion makes it possible to minimize the risks inherent in the agency relationship and thus to generate a greater commitment of the agents to the objectives of the organization.

Resumen

El enfoque contractual de la organización presenta la empresa como un nudo de contratos entre sus partes interesadas. La divergencia de intereses del conjunto genera tensiones y conflictos y empuja a cada parte del contrato a adoptar diversas estrategias para preservar sus intereses.

Para resolver este dilema, la teoría socioeconómica ha demostrado que la sustitución, en la relación entre los grupos de interés de la empresa, de la subordinación por el establecimiento de una relación contractual basada en el reconocimiento, negociación y la discusión permite minimizar los riesgos inherentes a la relación de agencia y así generar un mayor compromiso de los agentes, a favor de los objetivos de la organización en su conjunto.

Résumé

L'approche contractuelle de la firme présente l'entreprise comme un nœud de contrats entre ses parties prenantes. La divergence des intérêts de l'ensemble génère des tensions et des conflits et pousse chaque partie du contrat à adopter diverses stratégies pour préserver ses intérêts. Pour résoudre ce dilemme, la théorie socio-économique a montré que la substitution, dans la relation entre les parties prenantes de l'entreprise, de la subordination par l'instauration d'une relation de contractualisation basée sur la reconnaissance, la négociation et la discussion permet de minimiser les risques inhérents à la relation d'agence et ainsi susciter un engagement plus important des agents, en faveur des objectifs de l'organisation dans son ensemble.

98 The Global Heritage Value Chain: Technological and Social Innovation

Claudia Rocío González Pérez and Pedro Constantino Solís Pérez

Abstract

The management of cultural heritage is analyzed from the interactive networks of the global heritage value chain, using the scope defined by the relationships between stakeholders in the tetranormalization at global, regional and territorial levels. The processes of technological innovation, public management and social innovation are referred to from the concept of territory as the space where socio-economic activities are carried out, as a meta-organization, to manage the actors involved in cultural heritage projects. The case of cultural heritage management in Tepeyahualco (Puebla) is presented.

Resumen

La gestión del patrimonio cultural se analiza a partir de las redes interactivas de la cadena valor global del patrimonio, utilizando el ámbito definido por las relaciones entre las partes interesadas en la tetranormalización a nivel global, regional y territorial. Los procesos de innovación tecnológica, de gestión pública y de innovación social son referidos a partir del concepto de territorio como el espacio donde se realizan actividades socioeconómicas, como una meta-organización, para administrar a los actores implicados en proyectos de patrimonio cultural. Se presenta el caso de gestión del patrimonio cultural en Tepeyahualco (Puebla).

Résumé

La gestion du patrimoine culturel est analysée à partir des réseaux interactifs de la chaîne de valeur du patrimoine mondial, en utilisant l'approche définie par les relations entre les parties prenantes de la tétra-normalisation aux niveaux mondial, régional et territorial. Les processus d'innovation technologique, de management public et d'innovation sociale sont définis à partir du concept de territoire, vu comme l'espace où se déroulent les activités socio-économiques, en tant que méta-organisation, pour gérer les acteurs impliqués dans les projets de patrimoine culturel. Le cas de la gestion du patrimoine culturel à Tepeyahualco (Puebla) est présenté.

99 The Importance of the Role of Intermediaries in the Creation and Maintenance of Collaborative Networks

Laura P. Peñalva Rosales and Silvia Pomar Fernández

Abstract

The research is approached from a descriptive and explanatory perspective of the role of intermediary organizations as generators of trust and governance, facilitators of communication and readers of reality; hence their relevance for the conformation of organizational networks. For this purpose, a documentary analysis is carried out. The importance of these organizations is exemplified with the presentation of the case of the Instituto Nacional del Emprendedor (INADEM), an organization created by the Mexican federal government that supports entrepreneurship and micro, small and medium-sized enterprises that have the potential for growth.

Resumen

La investigación se aborda desde una perspectiva descriptiva y explicativa del papel de las organizaciones intermedias como generadoras de confianza y gobernabilidad, facilitadores de la comunicación y lectores de la realidad; de ahí su relevancia para la conformación de redes organizacionales. Para ello se realiza un análisis documental. Se ejemplifica la importancia de estas organizaciones con la presentación del caso del Instituto Nacional del Emprendedor (INADEM) una organización generada por el gobierno federal mexicano que apoya el emprendimiento y a las micro, pequeñas y medianas empresas que tienen posibilidades de crecimiento.

Résumé

La recherche est abordée dans une perspective descriptive et explicative du rôle des organisations intermédiaires en tant que générateurs de confiance et de gouvernance, facilitateurs de communication et lecteurs de la réalité; d'où leur pertinence pour la formation de réseaux organisationnels. Pour cela, une analyse documentaire est réalisée. L'importance de ces organisations est illustrée par la présentation du cas de l'Institut national des entrepreneurs (INADEM), une organisation créée par le gouvernement fédéral mexicain qui soutient l'entrepreneuriat et les micro, petites et moyennes entreprises qui ont un potentiel de croissance.

---

100 Is Today's Management Science Up to the Task?

Guy Devillebichot

Abstract

For half a century, "scientific and technical knowledge" has been of a rare abundance. However, humanity has come to jeopardize its real conditions of survival!

Do economic and management thoughts have something to do with this fiasco? Or with such a serious absence of general policy? How can we discern tracks of renewed relevance, to be elaborated in common?

Resumen

Durante medio siglo los "conocimientos científicos y técnicos" fueron de una rara abundancia. Sin embargo, ¡la humanidad ha llegado a poner en peligro sus condiciones reales de supervivencia!

¿Tuvo el pensamiento económico y de gestión algo que ver con este fiasco? ¿O con una falta de política general tan grave? ¿Cómo podemos discernir caminos de renovada relevancia, para ser trabajados en común?

Résumé

Depuis un demi-siècle, les "connaissances scientifiques et techniques" sont d'une rare abondance. Pourtant, l'humanité en est arrivée à mettre en péril ses conditions réelles de survie!

Les réflexions économiques et de gestion ont-elles quelque chose à voir avec ce fiasco ? Ou avec une absence aussi grave de politique générale ? Comment discerner des pistes de pertinence renouvelée, à élaborer en commun ?

PART X

Epistemology and research methodology
Epistemología y metodología de la investigación
Épistémologie et méthodologie de la recherche

101 The Socio-Economic Approach to Management (SEAM) Uses Ensemble Storytelling, Abduction-Induction-Deduction and Self-Correcting Methods for Highly Rigorous, Effective and Ethical Organizational Interventions

Grace Ann Rosile and David M. Boje

Abstract

We contend that the Socio-Economic Approach to Management (SEAM) is so extraordinarily effective in improving organizational performance in large part due to its collaborative strategies coupled with highly rigorous organizational research methods. We view SEAM's collaborative methods through our own lens of Ensemble Storytelling. Using this lens, we find evidence of five (5) forms of Ensemble Storytelling relevant to SEAM.

Resumen

Sostenemos que el Enfoque Socioeconómico de la Gestión (SEAM) es extraordinariamente eficaz para mejorar el rendimiento de las organizaciones, en gran parte gracias a sus estrategias de colaboración junto con métodos de investigación organizativa altamente rigurosos. Consideramos los métodos de colaboración de intervención socioeconómica a través de nuestra propia lente de «Narración Conjunta» (Ensemble Storytelling). Utilizando esta lente, encontramos evidencia de cinco (5) formas de Narración Conjunta relevantes para la intervención socioeconómica.

Résumé

Nous soutenons que l'approche socio-économique de la gestion (SEAM) est extraordinairement efficace pour améliorer la performance organisationnelle, en grande partie grâce à ses stratégies de collaboration couplées à des méthodes de recherche organisationnelle hautement rigoureuses. Nous analysons les méthodes de collaboration de l'intervention socio-économique à travers notre propre vision du «storytelling d'ensemble». En utilisant cette grille de lecture, nous trouvons des preuves de cinq (5) formes de storytelling d'ensemble pertinentes pour l'intervention socio-économique.

102 The Socio-Economic Theory of Firms and Organizations: Heterodoxy in Management Science

Laurent Cappelletti

Abstract

The socio-economic theory of firms and organizations presents important fractures with the dominant theories in management sciences, which structure its orthodoxy. These fractures, which are explained and discussed in the chapter, are particularly noteworthy in terms of epistemology, methodology and the societal utility of science. They thus form the basis of a singular heterodoxy in management science, a powerful lever for disruptive knowledge.

Resumen

La teoría socioeconómica de las empresas y organizaciones presenta importantes fracturas con las teorías dominantes en las ciencias de la gestión que estructuran su ortodoxia. Estas fracturas, aclaradas y discutidas en el capítulo, son particularmente notables en los niveles epistemológico, metodológico y utilidad social de la ciencia. De este modo, crean una heterodoxia singular en las ciencias de la gestión, una poderosa palanca para el conocimiento disruptivo.

Résumé

La théorie socio-économique des entreprises et des organisations présente des fractures importantes avec les théories dominantes en sciences de gestion, qui en structurent l'orthodoxie. Ces fractures explicitées et discutées dans le chapitre sont particulièrement remarquables aux plans épistémologique, méthodologique et de l'utilité sociétale de la science. Elles fondent ainsi une hétérodoxie singulière en sciences de gestion, levier puissant de connaissances disruptives.

---

103 An Aristotelian Archeology: CSR and the Socio-Management Paradigm

Jean-Jacques Rosé

Abstract

The singular strength of socio-management is to resolve the contradictions inherent to CSR and its implementation. The path follows the work of A. Smith, often misunderstood because the complementarity of the Wealth of Nations and Moral Sentiments expresses the same necessity. This complementarity is illustrated by two presidents of the Society for Business Ethics who adopt a similar Aristotelian response, borrowed by D. Bonnet, for whom socio-management, by going from hidden costs to hidden meaning, reveals the deep Aristotelian basis of socio-management.

Resumen

La fuerza singular de la sociogestión es que resuelve las contradicciones inherentes a la responsabilidad social de las empresas y su aplicaciónEl camino sigue la obra de A. Smith, a menudo mal entendida porque la complementariedad de la Riqueza de las Naciones y los Sentimientos Morales expresa la misma necesidad. Complementariedad ilustrada por dos presidentes de la Sociedad de Ética Empresarial que adoptan una respuesta aristotélica similar, tomada por D. Bonnet para quien la sociogestión, al pasar de los costes ocultos al sentido oculto, desvela la base aristotélica profunda de la sociogestión.

Résumé

La force singulière du socio-management est de résoudre les contradictions inhérentes à la Responsabilité Sociale de l'Entreprise et à sa mise en œuvre. Le chemin emprunte l'œuvre d'A. Smith, souvent mal comprise parce que la complémentarité de la Richesse des Nations et des Sentiments Moraux exprime la même nécessité. Complémentarité illustrée par deux présidents de la Society for Business Ethics qui adoptent une réponse similaire et aristotélicienne, empruntée par D. Bonnet pour qui le socio-management, en allant des coûts cachés au sens caché, dévoile le socle aristotélicien profond du socio-management.

---

104 Three Elements for Positioning Intervention-Research in the Epistemological Debate of Plato and Aristotle

Manuel Garcia and Emmanuel Beck

Abstract

The reading of Plato and Aristotle still shows today epistemological convergences which question us. Plato develops an analytical approach and rigorous reasoning, while Aristotle invests in a global and systemic approach of an object in evolution thanks to its potential: "the being." The socio-economic theory applies a similar approach to organizations. Significant epistemological improvements have been made, on the one hand, to clarify the abductive process of analysis of the evolving organization, and, on the other, to make explicit the relations between contingency factors and invariants in a form of generic constructivism.

Resumen

La lectura de Platón y Aristóteles siempre muestra convergencias epistemológicas que nos cuestionan. Platón desarrolla un enfoque analítico y un razonamiento riguroso, mientras que Aristóteles se invierte en un enfoque global y sistémico, de un objeto que evoluciona gracias a su potencial: "el ser." Sin embargo, se han realizado importantes mejoras epistemológicas, por un lado para aclarar el proceso abductivo de análisis de la organización en evolución y, por otro lado, para aclarar las relaciones entre los factores de contingencia y las invariantes, en una forma de constructivismo genérico.

Résumé

La lecture de Platon et d'Aristote montre encore de nos jours des convergences épistémologiques qui nous interrogent. Platon développe une démarche analytique et des raisonnements rigoureux, alors qu'Aristote s'investit dans l'approche globale et systémique d'un objet en évolution grâce à son potentiel: «l'étant». La théorie socio-économique applique aux organisations une approche similaire. Des améliorations épistémologiques sensibles ont été apportées, d'une part pour clarifier le processus abductif de l'analyse de l'organisation en évolution, et, d'autre part, pour expliciter les relations entre les facteurs de contingence et les invariants dans une forme de constructivisme générique.

---

105 Transforming the Mental Structures of Organizaitons: A Clinical Approach to Socio-Economic Intervention

Daniel Bonnet and Emmanuel Beck

Abstract

This chapter puts into perspective the clinical dimension of Socio-Economic Intervention Research. The clinical dimension of the Socio-Economic Intervention-Research allows for an in-depth search for the root causes of the dysfunctions at the origin of Hidden Costs-Performances. Socio-Economic Intervention-Research leads the actors to carry out an intellectual and psychological work to collectively implement the actions of change to be envisaged to "repair" the dysfunctions and convert the hidden costs into added value for the company. In certain contexts, it is a matter of dealing with major problems. The work of the actors is guided by a research device accompanying the transformation of mental structures.

Resumen

Este capítulo pone en perspectiva la dimensión clínica de la Investigatión-Intervención Socioeconómica (RISE). La dimensión clínica de la RISE permite una investigación en profundidad de las causas fundamentales de los disfuncionamientos en el origen de los costos-desempeños ocultos. The RISE lleva a los actores a realizar un trabajo intelectual y psicológico para implementar colectivamente las acciones de cambio a considerar con el fin de "reparar" las disfunciones y convertir los costos ocultos en valor agregado para la empresa. In some contexts, it is necessary to address serious problems. El trabajo de los actores está guiado por un dispositivo de investigación que apoya la transformación de las estructuras mentales.

Résumé

Ce chapitre met en perspective la dimension clinique de la Recherche Intervention Socio-Économique (RISE). La dimension clinique de la RISE permet une recherche approfondie des causes-racines des dysfonctionnements à l'origine des Coûts-Performances Cachés. La RISE conduit les acteurs à réaliser un travail intellectuel et psychologique pour mettre en œuvre collectivement les actions du changement à envisager pour «réparer» les dysfonctionnements et convertir les coûts cachés en valeur ajoutée pour l'entreprise. Dans certains contextes, il s'agit de traiter des problématiques lourdes. Le travail des acteurs est orienté par un dispositif de recherche accompagnant la transformation des structures mentales.

106 The Mirror-Effect: A Self-Image for Change

Éric Davoine

Abstract

This chapter focusses on the mirror-effect session which is a crucial stage in the SEAM approach of the organizational change process. Through the validation of a (dysfunctional) "self-image" of the organization, this stage initiates a learning process that encourages the action of organizational actors. Using conceptual frameworks of Lacan (1949) and Argyris (2004), we analyze the impacts of the mirror (-effect) stage in two audit cases carried out in Switzerland within two industrial firms, and we discuss the contributions of different types of information used during mirror-effect sessions.

Resumen

Este capítulo trata del efecto espejo, que es un paso crucial en el proceso de cambio organizativo según el análisis socioeconómico. A través de la validación de una "autoimagen" (disfuncional) de la organización, este paso permite iniciar un proceso de aprendizaje en los actores de la organización. Utilizando los marcos conceptuales de Lacan (1949) y Argyris (2004), analizamos los impactos de la etapa de espejo en dos casos de auditoría realizados en Suiza en dos empresas industriales, y discutimos las contribuciones de los diferentes tipos de información utilizados durante las sesiones de espejo.

Résumé

Ce chapitre aborde l'effet-miroir qui est une étape cruciale dans le processus de changement organisationnel selon l'analyse socio-économique. A travers la validation d'une "image de soi" (dysfonctionnelle) de l'organisation, cette étape permet d'initier un processus d'apprentissage et donc un changement chez les acteurs organisationnels. En utilisant les cadres conceptuels de Lacan (1949) et d'Argyris (2004), nous analysons les impacts de l'étape de l'effet-miroir dans deux cas d'audit réalisés en Suisse au sein de deux entreprises industrielles, et nous discutons les contributions des différents types d'informations utilisées lors des sessions d'effet-miroir.

107 Lifting the Veil of a Managerial Illusion Through the Contribution of the Humanly Integrated Operational and Functional Information System: Saying What We Do and Doing What We Say

Miguel Delattre and Rodolphe Ocler

Abstract

Organization and information are inseparable in management science. However, the lack of clarity in the hypotheses used sometimes leads to vagueness about the nature of the link between them, as well as to biased representations for decision-making. The notion of a humanly integrated and stimulating Operational and Functional Information System offers a fruitful perspective to avoid giving in to the ease of an overly normative managerial discourse.

Resumen

La organización y la información son inseparables en las ciencias de la gestión, pero la falta de claridad en las hipótesis utilizadas conduce a veces a la vaguedad sobre la naturaleza del vínculo entre ellas, así como a sesgos en las representaciones para la toma de decisiones. La noción de un Sistema de Información Operativa y Funcional humanamente integrada y estimulante ofrece una perspectiva fructífera para evitar ceder a la facilidad de un discurso directivo demasiado normativo.

Résumé

Organisation et information sont indissociables en sciences de gestion, pour autant, le manque d'explicitation des hypothèses mobilisées conduit parfois à entretenir un flou sur la nature du lien concernant leur rapprochement ainsi que des biais de représentations pour la prise de décisions. La notion de Système d'informations opérationnelles et fonctionnelles humainement intégrées et stimulantes propose une perspective féconde pour ne pas céder à la facilité d'un discours managérial trop normatif.

---

108 Intervention in Socio-Economic Management: Epistemci and Methodological Elements and Principles of Action

Jean-Michel Plane and Florence Noguera

Abstract

This text is devoted to the question of management intervention in organizations. It raises several epistemological, methodological, and axiomatic problems of various kinds. Most of these difficulties are beginning to be well known by the scientific community, and some answers and perspectives for action have been developed for several years now.) The reflections and the works devoted to the methods of intervention in management are certainly structured in an unequal but also constant way.

Resumen

La intervención en la gestión de las organizaciones, aunque es una aventura apasionante y a veces fascinante, no deja de plantear una serie de problemas de distinta índole. La mayoría de estas dificultades están comenzando a ser bien conocidas por la comunidad científica e incluso desde hace algunos años se han formado elementos de respuesta y perspectivas de acción (Buono, Savall, Cappelletti, 2018). Las reflexiones y el trabajo dedicado a los métodos de intervención en la gestión se estructuran ciertamente de manera desigual pero también constante.

Résumé

Ce texte est consacré à la question de l'intervention en gestion dans les organisations. Celle-ci n'est pas sans soulever nombre de problèmes épistémologiques, méthodologiques et axiomatiques de différentes natures. La plupart de ces difficultés commence à être bien connue par la communauté scientifique et des éléments de réponse ainsi que des perspectives d'action se sont même constitués depuis quelques années déjà). Les réflexions et les travaux consacrés aux méthodes d'intervention en management se structurent certes de façon inégale mais aussi constante.

---

109 Intervention-Research and Team Management: Epistemological Reflections and Proposal of a Heuristic and Transformative Methodological Device

Antoine Masingue

Abstract

This chapter aims to better understand the complexity of intervention-research applied to team management. It questions the epistemological framework of this type of intervention and presents an engineering device likely to help us better understand the functioning of teams to improve their performance.

Resumen

Este capítulo pretende comprender mejor la complejidad de la investigación de intervención aplicada a la gestión de equipos. Cuestiona el marco epistemológico de este tipo de intervención y esboza un dispositivo de ingeniería que puede utilizarse para comprender mejor el funcionamiento de los equipos con el fin de mejorar su rendimiento.

Résumé

Le présent chapitre vise à mieux cerner la complexité des recherches-interventions appliquées au management des équipes. Il questionne la cadre épistémologique de ce type d'interventions et expose un dispositif ingéniérique susceptible de mieux comprendre le fonctionnement des équipes afin d'en améliorer la performance.

PART XI

Connections: philosophical, sociological, geographical

Conexiones: filosóficas, sociológicas, geográficas

Connexités: philosophique, sociologique, géographique

110 Socio-Economic Management of Urban Spaces: From Urban Planning to "Urbanology"

Jacques Bonnet and Nathaël Torrès

Abstract

Urban planning reflects society defined by experts and elites. Urbanology is oriented by the society of users. The latter places the question of housing at the heart of its concerns, not as a simple commercial product, but as a center of social life for living together.

Resumen

El urbanismo es un reflejo de la sociedad definido por los expertos y las élites. La "urbano-logía" está orientada por la sociedad de usuarios. Esta última sitúa la cuestión de la vivien-da en el centro de sus preocupaciones, no como un simple producto comercial sino como un centro de vida social para la convivencia.

Résumé

L'urbanisme est un reflet de la société défini par des experts et des élites. L'urbanologie est orientée par la société des usagers. Celle-ci place la question du logement au cœur de ses préoccupations, non comme un simple produit marchand, mais comme un centre de vie sociale pour vivre ensemble.

111 From the Socio-Economic Model to Organizational Ability: A Human-Centered Path

Consuelo García de La Torre, Osmar Arandia, and Luis Portales

Abstract

This chapter analyzes the current organizational ecosystem in which human beings operate. It places the human being at the center of the action, under the assumption that, if he/she works in conditions of trust, freedom to act and is empowered, he/she will become the agent of change that the company needs to face today's challenges. The most important finding is that the socioeconomic management model, as well as organizational agility, are management concepts that are born and developed in volatile, uncertain, complex and ambiguous contexts.

Resumen

Este capítulo analiza el ecosistema organizacional actual en que se desenvuelven los seres humanos. Sitúa al ser humano en el centro de la acción, bajo el supuesto de que, si se trabaja en condiciones de confianza, libertad de actuar y se le empodera se convertirá en el agente de cambio que la empresa necesita para afrontar los retos de hoy. El hallazgo más importante es que el modelo de gestión socioeconómico, al igual que la agilidad organizacional, son conceptos de gestión que nacen y se desarrollan en contextos volátiles, inciertos, complejos y ambiguos.

Résumé

Ce chapitre analyse l'écosystème organisationnel actuel dans lequel les êtres humains opèrent. Elle place l'être humain au centre de l'action, sous l'hypothèse que s'il travaille dans des conditions de confiance, de liberté d'agir et de pouvoir, il deviendra l'agent de changement dont l'entreprise a besoin pour faire face aux défis d'aujourd'hui. La conclusion la plus importante est que le modèle de gestion socio-économique, comme l'agilité organisationnelle, est constitué de concepts de gestion nés et développés dans des contextes volatils, incertains, complexes et ambigus.

112 The Golden Triangle of the Socio-Economic Approach to Management (SEAM)

Philippe Trouvé

Abstract

Starting from a pictorial triangular representation of the Socio-Economic Management Model, the sides of which represent three of its main dimensions and the inner surface of which represents sustainable socio-economic performance as a general objective, this chapter attempts to show that the approach modeled and tested for nearly five decades by ISEOR provides a radical departure from mainstream management technologies, the most accomplished forms of which in contemporary companies and organizations have today entered into crisis. The game is not won in advance, since the innovations brought about by the socio-economic approach are at odds with the dominant currents, both in business practices and in the academic world.

Resumen

Partiendo de una representación pictórica triangular del modelo de gestión socioeconómica, cuyos lados representan tres de sus principales dimensiones y la superficie interior el rendimiento socioeconómico sostenible como objetivo general, este capítulo muestra que el enfoque modelado y experimentado durante casi cinco décadas por el ISEOR representa un alejamiento radical de las tecnologías de gestión dominantes, cuyas formas más consumadas en las empresas y organizaciones contemporáneas han entrado ahora en crisis. La partida no está ganada de antemano, ya que las innovaciones aportadas por el enfoque socioeconómico están en desacuerdo con las tendencias dominantes, tanto en las prácticas empresariales como en el mundo académico.

Résumé

Partant d'une représentation triangulaire imagée du Modèle de Management Socio-Économique dont les côtés figureraient trois de ses principales dimensions et la surface interne la performance socio-économique durable comme visée générale, ce chapitre s'efforce de montrer que l'approche modélisée et expérimentée depuis près de cinq décennies par ISEOR opère une sortie radicale des technologies mainstream de management, dont les formes les plus accomplies dans les entreprises et les organisations contemporaines sont aujourd'hui entrées en crise. La partie n'est pas gagnée d'avance, tant les innovations apportées par la démarche socio-économique sont en rupture avec les courants dominants, tant dans les pratiques d'entreprises que dans le monde académique.

113 Socially Responsible Capitalism: A Relevant Setting for the Socio-Economic Approach to Management (SEAM)

Henri Savall, Michel Péron (†), Véronique Zardet & Marc Bonnet

Abstract

Socially Responsible Capitalism (SRC) is based on entrepreneurship, promotes exemplary behavior that is effective, efficient and ethical, and encourages the assumption of social responsibility by companies and organizations, combined with the development of economic empowerment and the legitimate efforts of each citizen, considered as actor in the economy. SRC does not confuse financial capitalism with entrepreneurial capitalism. The former cultivates the creation of fake value that leads to financial bubbles and ruins the real economy. On the contrary, entrepreneurial capitalism creates robust economic value and jobs, justified by production activity that responds to the legitimate needs of citizen-consumers. SRC is not a utopia; it is already part of the history of economic and social facts and covers a set of good practices, described as socio-economic management, which has been successfully experimented.

Resumen

El Capitalismo Socialmente Responsable (CSR) se basa en el espíritu de empresa, fomenta comportamientos ejemplares, eficaces, eficientes y éticos, y promueve la asunción de la responsabilidad social por parte de las empresas y organizaciones, combinada con el desarrollo de la responsabilidad económica y el esfuerzo legítimo de cada ciudadano, actor de la economía. El CSR no confunde el capitalismo financiero con el capitalismo empresarial. El primero cultiva la creación de valor falso que conduce a burbujas financieras y arruina la economía real. Por el contrario, el capitalismo empresarial es un creador de valor económico robusto y de puestos de trabajo, justificado por la actividad productiva que responde a las necesidades legítimas de los ciudadanos-consumidores. El CSR no es una utopía; ya forma parte de la historia de los hechos económicos y sociales y abarca un conjunto de buenas prácticas, calificadas de gestión socioeconómica, que ha sido probado con éxito.

Résumé

Le Capitalisme Socialement Responsable (CSR) est fondé sur l'esprit d'entreprise, favorise les comportements exemplaires, à la fois efficaces, efficients et éthiques, et encourage la prise de responsabilité sociale des entreprises et des organisations, conjuguée au développement de la responsabilisation économique et des efforts légitimes de chaque citoyen, acteur de l'économie. Le CSR ne confond pas capitalisme financier et capitalisme entrepreneurial. Le premier cultive la création de valeur factice qui conduit à des bulles financières et ruinent l'économie réelle. Au contraire, le capitalisme entrepreneurial est créateur de valeur économique robuste et d'emplois, justifiés par l'activité de production qui répond à des besoins légitimes des citoyens-consommateurs. Le CSR n'est pas une utopie, il s'est déjà inscrit dans l'histoire des faits économiques et sociaux et recouvre un ensemble de bonnes pratiques, qualifiées de management socio-économique, qui a été expérimenté avec succès.

ACKNOWLEDGMENTS

Since the beginning of our research in management sciences in 1973,[1] the socio-economic theory of organizations and the Socio-Economic Approach to Management (SEAM) method have acquired their credentials in the national and international spheres. Our meeting with Jacques Delors in 1972, then with the sociologist Jean-Daniel Reynaud at the Royaumont Seminar in March 1974 was decisive in orienting our work on hidden costs. The main marks of recognition of our work are the Rossi Prize Medal of the Academy of Moral and Political Sciences (Institute of France) in 2001, the Legion of Honor in 2017; the publication by ILO (International Labor Organization) in 2000, of our book in English, French and Spanish (co-authored with our colleague Marc Bonnet), as well as the special issue (March 2003) of the *Journal of Organizational Change Management* (United States) entrusted to us by David Boje, entirely devoted to the work of ISEOR. The books coordinated with Anthony Buono, published by Information Age Publishing (IAP), in the United States in 2007 and in 2015, as well as the publication in English of 10 of our books. In addition, the *Academy of Management* in the United States (Organizational Development and Change, Management Consulting and Research Methods Divisions) has entrusted ISEOR with the organization of 23 delocalized conferences from 2001 to 2023 in Lyon. In a world dominated by Anglo-Saxon managerial thought, these events are signs of recognition of the innovative, original, and robust nature of the research conducted by ISEOR over the past 48 years. Our action in the United States (named *La Fayette Operation*), during the numerous presentations of our work at the annual Conferences of the Academy of Management since 1998, would not have been as rapid and effective without the support of our American colleagues, authors of this treatise, as well as Monique Péron-Bois, Herman Aguinis & Georges Trépo (HEC).

The ISEOR (*Institut de Socio-Économie des Entreprises et des Organisations/* Institute of Socio-Economic Approach to Management of companies and organizations), created by Henri Savall in 1975, is an international networked team of more than 125 active researchers, one of the most important poles of research in management.

This Treatise disseminates the research results that the ISEOR think-tank has been accumulating for half a century. It is based on numerous and varied pilot actions, carried out in 72 sectors of activity, 48 countries on 4 continents. We are grateful to the 2,150 companies and organizations that, for several years, have agreed to partner with ISEOR to experiment with new modes of strategic and operational management, perfectly suited to our times. Leaders, managers,

SEAM Treatise, pages xcvii–xxiii

executives, supervisors, workers, employees, and employee representative bodies have accepted the requirements of a rigorous external intervention, in a word: *scientific. These companies and organizations have entirely financed our research, which was deliberately carried out without public subsidies:* very small companies, SMEs, large industrial and service groups, public companies, administrations, hospitals, health, and social establishments. Most of these *intervention-researches* were conducted in Belgium, France, Morocco, Mexico, Portugal, Lebanon, and Switzerland.

This book is the result of considerable and persevering teamwork. 193 authors have contributed to this Treatise, in the perspective of what we call *citizen science* or *socially responsible research.* These contributions are both theoretical and practical and are the result of an open conception of cooperation between universities and companies, between professors and management practitioners. Let us also thank the 207 PhDs and DBAs who prepared their doctoral thesis at ISEOR. Many young researchers and doctoral students who spent a few years of their career at ISEOR now have responsibilities as professor-researchers, company managers, experts, or consultants in many countries.

Other important potential authors would have had their place in this Treatise, had it been more voluminous. In particular, we would like to thank Jacques Morin, Marc-André Lanselle and Maurice Sardier, of the Péchiney Ugine Kuhlmann group; Yves Chaigneau and Pierre Louis Rémy, directors of ANACT (National Agency for the Improvement of Working Conditions/*Agence nationale pour l'amélioration des conditions de travail*); Serge & Louis-Marie Pasquier of the Brioche Pasquier Group; Jean Pichon, Loïc Daniel of La Poste; Olivier Sagot of Banque Populaire; Gérard Pigaglio of URSSAF; Jean-Pierre Méan of Le Forem; Raúl Arceo, of the Government of the State of Yucatán, Mexico; and Michel de Trogoff and Thierry Girard of the Morbihan Chamber of Commerce. Among the authors of this Treatise, we would like to emphasize the key role in the development of the socio-economic theory and of the Socio-Economic Approach to Management of certain intervention-researches, such as Brioche Pasquier (for 39 years) ; Technord in Belgium (27 years); Aguacates Sánchez in Mexico & Ninkasi (17 years); Manpower Belgium and Luxembourg (12 years); Fondation Aigues Vertes in Switzerland (12 years); as well as the Autonomous Metropolitan University of Mexico, Mermet, Hospices civils de Lyon; the companies of the "E. Leclerc Movement", as well as the competency operator OPCO EP of local businesses.

The FNEGE, under the leadership of J.-M. Doublet, then P.-L. Dubois, M. Thévenet and J. Caby, has regularly encouraged us. The Order of Chartered Accountants (*Ordre des Experts-Comptables),* the Supreme Council of Notaries (*Conseil Supérieur du Notariat*) and the Order of Architects (*Ordre des Architectes)* have recommended this management method to their members. M. Bernadet, P. Lucas, M. Cusin and B. Gelas, Presidents of the University Lumière Lyon 2 as well as Dean Paul Rousset, have actively supported our work and the development of the innovative degrees we have created. Finally, *last but not least,* we would like to thank the Presidents of the University Jean Moulin Lyon 3, Gilles Guyot, Guy Lavorel, as well as Jérôme Rive, General Director of IAE Lyon and his successor Christian Varinard, for welcoming us in 2003 and allowing us to pursue our innovative action in favor of management training and research, sources of an intensified international development. The support of Olivier Faron, General Administrator, has led to the establishment of ISEOR's partnership with CNAM and its continuation with the support of the current General Administrator, Bénédicte Fauverque-Cosson.

Henri Savall — Professor Emeritus
Véronique Zardet — University Professor

IAE Lyon, Université Jean Moulin Lyon 3

President and Founder of ISEOR — General Director of ISEOR

Award Recipients of the French Academy of Moral and Political Sciences
(Institute of France)
(Académie des Sciences Morales et Politiques, Institut de France)

NOTE

1. Savall H. (1974), *Enrichir le travail humain dans les entreprises et les organisations,* doctoral thesis, University of Paris-Dauphine, awarded with the I.A.E. Management Prize, published with the title *Enrichir le travail humain: l'évaluation économique,* by Dunod: Paris in 1975 and prefaced by Jacques Delors; 4th edition 1989, Economica: Paris. Translated into English: (1981) *Work and People. An economic evaluation of job enrichment,* Prefaced by H. Igor Ansoff, London: Oxford University Press. Translated into Spanish (1977), *Por un trabajo más humano,* Techniban, Madrid; 2nd edition in 2010, IAP, Charlotte (NC) and Dutch.

PART I

SOCIO-ECONOMIC MANAGEMENT: PURPOSE AND APPLICATIONS

CHAPTER 1

UPDATED SYNTHESIS OF THE SOCIO-ECONOMIC THEORY AND OF THE SOCIO-ECONOMIC APPROACH TO MANAGEMENT (SEAM)

Henri Savall and Véronique Zardet

1 THE SOCIO-ECONOMIC APPROACH TO MANAGEMENT: A CONTRIBUTION TO THE DYNAMICS OF CHANGE AND ORGANIZATIONAL METAMORPHOSIS

The Socio-Economic Theory is a theoretical, empirical and operational contribution to the problem of change and organizational development. The key concepts and foundations of the Socio Economic Approach to Management (SEAM) are presented in this chapter. Then, we summarize the essential implications of the Socio-Economic Approach to Management on strategic management practices, management control, sales and marketing strategy, human resource management, etc. Many chapters of this treatise explain in detail and with numerous concrete applications, how internal practices evolve in a company that has chosen the Socio-Economic Approach to Management, as well as their performance.

An Experienced and Sustainable Response: The Socio-Economic Management of Organizations

The Socio-Economic Approach to Management is a tool equipped thinking method. Indeed, the proposed itinerary is to move from the cult of the object, characterized by abstraction and disembodiment, to the accompaniment of the subject-person, which restores all its

SEAM Treatise, pages 3–44

importance to the personalization of management and its elements. As a matter of fact, any idea appears as a simple ingredient of the action. It is when ideas lead to an action, a set of micro-decisions, that they produce a result or a performance. The implementation of ideas is therefore of the utmost importance for the management and performance of companies and organizations.

1.1 Origin, Genesis, Foundations, and Essential Characteristics of the Socio-Economic Approach To Management (SEAM)

A theory that can be used in the long term deserves that we *define* the key concepts. Strictly speaking, each key word conveys a different content according to theories and contexts, by virtue of the linguistic principle of *polysemy*. Likewise, access to the fundamental principles that constitute it requires that the *keys* be made explicit.

1.1.1 Introductory Definitions

In connivance with the reader and by simple convention, this Treatise will use the word *company* and the word *organization* interchangeably to designate any human group, whatever its size and legal status, bringing together individuals to produce goods and services, whatever their nature, from the most material to the most spiritual.

1.1.1.1 Social performance, economic performance, socio-economic performance. The *social performance* of an organization is a production of value that allows the satisfaction of the qualitative needs of a person, a group or a population. These needs are physiological, psychological, sociological, economical and political.

The *economic performance* of an organization is a production of value in the form of resources allowing the acquisition of goods or services likely to satisfy the qualitative needs. It combines the criteria of the *effectiveness* of an action, which consists of succeeding in reaching an objective, and the *efficiency* of this action, which consists of using limited resources to achieve a result. The combination of effectiveness and efficiency is a factor of economic success. *Sustainable economic performance* depends on the level of competitiveness of the company or organization. It is composed of two elements: *immediate results*, identified by the creation of resources available in the short term, and the *creation of potential*. The latter consists of the value of time invested by human potential in the short term to produce later on sustainable results in the medium and long terms. The actors involved in the creation of potential are numerous and spread throughout the company or organization.

Socio-Economic performance refers to social performance that is compatible with economic performance and vice versa. The dichotomy between economic performance and social performance is considered a sham in Socio-Economic Theory. Indeed, economic performance is social performance and vice versa. We are faced with an apparent paradox, that of the altruistic nature, i.e., intended for others, of economic activity and performance, whether it be staff, customers or shareholders, compared with the egoistic nature of so-called social activity and performance, which, in French, is intended to satisfy individual people, primarily staff.

1.1.1.2 Qualimetrics, or the problem of measurement in space and time. Talking about economic and social performance immediately raises the question of their measurement, because this performance has two facets, one visible, the other hidden. Thus, visible performance, as measured by the usual classical indicators, conceals hidden costs, some of which are borne by the company itself, while others are externalized. In Socio-Economic Theory, the importance of the hidden costs of *externalities*, in space and time, has long been emphasized (Savall, 1978b), recommending that firms pilot a strategic ratio of external costs/internal costs.[1]

Qualimetrics, a concept that we proposed in our seminal book *The Qualimetrics Approach, Observing the complex object* (Savall, Zardet, 2004; Boje, 2004). It expresses the principle of a continuum between qualitative-quantitative-financial indicators with complementary forms of measurement of all kinds of phenomena of organizational life, in particular, the evaluation of economic and social performance contributing to the same "fight" for sustainable quality of life and prosperity. Qualimetrics is a response to the unnatural separatism that has led, since the first years of education, to separate the literary from the "mathematical" persons, whereas the human being is a qualimetric being who combines these two essential qualities.

In the qualimetric approach, the *qualitative* form, expressed by key words, shapes or colors, makes it possible to restore the intrinsic richness of the complex object that one studies in management or social sciences and to make explicit the deep meaning of the knowledge thus produced. The *quantitative* form is expressed by key numbers that allow for mathematical processing. It provides measurement indicators that support meaning, by reducing subjectivity, and facilitate the operations of aggregation and comparison of the elements of the object studied. A qualimetric model refers to a set of variables and links described with qualitative, quantitative and financial measurement indicators. Thus: "*A word needs numbers to make sense; a number needs words to make sense.*"

The *qualimetric* approach in research activities consists in recognizing that the *essence* of the information processed during the scientific process of knowledge elaboration is simultaneously qualitative (expressed by key words) and quantitative (key numbers and mathematical processing). Among the key numbers, Socio-Economic Theory emphasizes the importance of financial indicators. Indeed, a care protocol that costs an exorbitant amount does not have the same societal value as one that costs a modest amount and can treat millions of people. A model can therefore take a form that is either simply *qualitative*, simply numerical, or qualimetric.

1.1.1.3 Socio-economic rationality. The plural dimension of performance and the qualimetric dimension of its measurement make it possible to revisit rationality in management science. Socio-Economic rationality is the basis of Socio-Economic calculation. Socio-Economic decisions are subject to a qualimetric calculation, which incorporates qualitative, quantitative and financial indicators to measure their social, societal and economic impacts.

We propose a broadened definition of rationality to integrate multiple decision-making criteria. It differentiates from management literature where not prioritizing short-term economic performance is considered irrational. Numerous practical applications stem from socio-economic rationality, such as: a *qualimetric* model of investment choice (Savall, 1979a), the concept of *cost-value* in management analysis (Savall, Zardet, 2008), and the critique of the "T-account" dear to accountants, which creates a barrier between expenses and revenues, costs and performance. Socio-Economic Theory recognizes the eminently systemic dimension of the firm or organization, a complex human system in which many variables interact. It includes an *ergonomic* or psycho-physiological dimension of socio-economic management. This consists, in simplifying, in saving gestures and human energy to achieve a performance. According to the *systemic* approach, the smallest element has a significant value. We could thus consider that the romantic poet Lamartine (19th century) was an early *systemic thinker*, when he wrote "one being is missing and everything is depopulated", in his *Poetic Meditations*, "Isolation", 1820.

1.1.1.4 How can we succinctly summarize the socio-economic approach to management? It is a mode of operation of a human group that favors sustainable socio-economic performance. The *management of persons* is at the heart of the theory and practice of Socio-Economic management. Dysfunctions and hidden costs (cf. 1.1.3.) constitute an expenditure of human energy, an evasion of the actors, often resigned to the repetition of dysfunctions. To overcome resistance to change, *levers* must be found to trigger and maintain individual and collective energies, in order to modify the behaviors that, in interaction with the structures, generate the dysfunctions. One of these levers consists of periodically renegotiating commitments to more active, more effective and more efficient behaviors, to transform negative energies devoted to regulating dysfunctions into positive energies, in order to *create value added.* This transformation also implies modifying activity structures, improving horizontal and vertical cross-functionality, and encouraging each actor to develop his or her personal value added. The appropriate *multi-skilling, synchronized decentralization* and *concerted delegation* make it possible to improve the combination of contributions and rewards for each individual. Participative forms of management are more effective and generate sustainable value added, provided that they are accompanied by vigilance and steering, primarily by the manager in charge of the *orchestration.*

1.1.2 The Keys and Principles of the Socio-Economic Functioning of the Company or Organization

ISEOR's Intervention-Research projects in 2,015 companies and organizations of all kinds have made it possible to identify *generic knowledge* about the functioning of companies or organizations, regardless of their size, activity, status or country. This generic knowledge characterizes The Socio-Economic Theory and the Socio-Economic Approach to Management. They are summarized below.

1.1.2.1 Learning curve and strategic patience. Professional and personal life appears as a *learning process.* Learning is a gradual process of acquiring the information and knowledge necessary to perform some action. It is very effective and efficient when it recognizes and acknowledges that the memorization of the information and knowledge necessary for a person or a team to carry out an activity can only be done *very gradually,* in order to allow each person to connect *one's memory* with the needs of the activity to be carried out. The explanation is ergonomic. Indeed, the *mental load* that inhabits the mind of any person, at any time, prevents him or her from focusing fully on the "new" activity to be performed. Learning is individual, but it is even more effective and efficient when a group of people must learn to synchronize in order to perform an operation, since experience shows that an individual cannot perform an action in its entirety without the help of other individuals.

The *learning curve* (Figure 1.1) represents this phenomenon and applies equally well to ensuring the effectiveness and efficiency of a short meeting, an action over several weeks or a project over three years. It is broken down into *three distinct periods.* During the *first period of patience and quality preparation,* the individual or team must not overreact, which is harmful to sustainable effectiveness and efficiency. This is followed by a second period where the performance of the individual or group increases *exponentially.* The third period "caps" at the maximum result as sought. In short, achieving a result within a given time frame (an hour, a month, a year) requires a *very progressive approach* to the start of the meeting, activity or project. Such a reflex of *strategic patience* on the part of people, and managers in particular, allows for a quality of preparation and start-up of activities, avoiding defects, accidents, and the backtracking of a too hasty start-up. The learning curve is therefore an important factor in *sustainable socio-economic productivity.* The respect of the learning curve is more and more threatened, even flouted, by the excessive speed of modern life and the pressure of

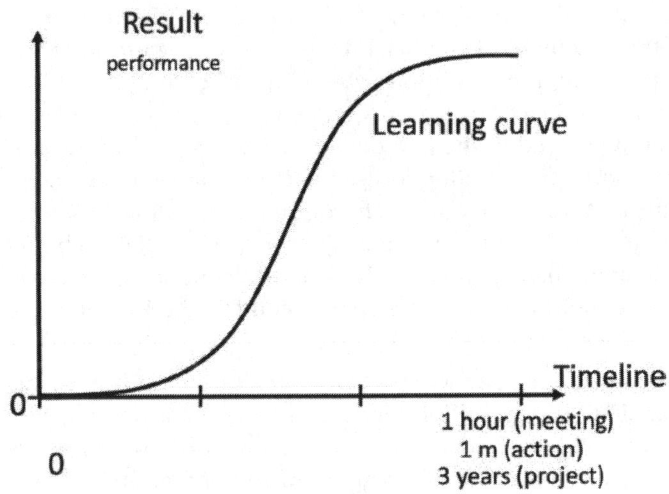

Figure 1.1 Applications of the learning curve and "strategic patience," sources of sustainable effectiveness and efficiency.

the impatient environment, especially professional. The demands made by some people of a technology that is poorly mastered and even diverted from its purpose, offer an additional pretext for hasty and impatient behavior, which is the source of many daily dysfunctions.

1.1.2.2 Human potential: energy, competence, behavior. *Human potential* reveals the particularity of the human being and emphasizes the set of human *capacities* to create value, by means of energy, *skills* and *behavior.* These human capacities are most often underused or misused. Socio-economic approach to management (SEAM) suggests *activating the development of human potential* to improve the socio-economic performance of the company or organization. Socio-Economic Theory differentiates from other economic theories by the pre-eminent and determining place it gives to the human factor in economic activity and value creation (see below 1.1.3.2).

1.1.2.3 The discovery of the TFW virus. The TFW virus metaphor (taylorism-fayolism-weberism) refers to the anachronistic application by contemporary actors of the principles of the Classical School of Organization, proposed by Taylor (1911, 1957), Fayol (1916) and Weber (1924). In their time, they contributed to economic and social progress in a completely different context than in the present day (Savall, Zardet, 2005). It is indeed unfortunate that a century later, theorists, experts and practitioners continue to propagate three principles that have become obsolete: the maximum *division* of labor, the *dichotomy between conception, decision and realization* of activities (Savall, 1974, 1975a, 1979a), as well as the *depersonalization* of workstations, organization charts, processes, methods and rules. These principles no longer contribute to sustainable overall performance, given the changes in behavior and skills in the social, economic and political environment.

A virus is a small infection agent, which reproduces inside animal, human or plant cells. Most viruses are pathogenic. A team or an organization is infected by the TFW virus, as soon as a lasting lack of cooperation between the participants in the activity is detected: individuals, teams, operation sites, subsidiaries of a company. The dynamics of the human organizational system are then driven by external pressures. E.g., According to Taylor (1911), it is the specialist in the methods department who prescribes the concrete work methods.

The traditional organization of work, which is based on the notion of individual workstations and the measurement of standard times for carrying out tasks, does not take-into-account the quality of working conditions which interfere with productivity. Thus, the time needed for communication, coordination, cooperation, and permanent integrated training is minimized or even ignored in the codified organization of work. As a result, cooperative arrangements are poorly structured, poorly encouraged or even neglected.

The evils of the TFW virus are effectively countered by intensified practices of cooperation, integration and synchronized decentralization (see 1.1.2.5). The *TFW antivirus* that inhabits socio-economic management, calls upon the consciousness of the individual who acts and the implementation of his/her human potential, thanks to the activation of his/her energy, his skills and his behavior.

1.1.2.4 The five natural and recurrent characteristics of the human being, observed in many situations of change. ISEOR's intervention-research projects have led to the identification of five natural characteristics of the human being, observed in professional situations of metamorphosis of work situations in companies and organizations. These characteristics are important for understanding dysfunctions and behaviors in situations of change, in order to take them into account in the conduct of socio-economic innovation processes that result in *"working differently."* They are ignored or strongly underestimated by the classical school of organization. Thus, every person:

a. is endowed with a significant dose of *intelligence*, i.e., a potential capacity to understand his or her immediate environment in order to find ways to survive and achieve his or her objectives, whatever his or her level of education, hierarchical level and responsibility in the company;
b. has *comedian skills* that encourage him/her to adapt his/her behavior to the situations and people with whom he/she interacts. Indeed, a very useful metaphor in change management is to consider any professional situation as a theater play;
c. can be considered as a *strategist*, with one or more mobilizing objectives, following a certain path to achieve them, using the resources at his/her disposal or that he/she obtains;
d. has a natural ability and propensity for *disobedience*, that is to say, he/she spontaneously finds it difficult to carry out instructions or orders from others;
e. is *amnesiac*, having a limited capacity for memory at any given moment and a natural propensity to forget, which is unlimited and recurrent.

When these five natural characteristics are taken-into-account in the management of change, they allow for robust and relatively sustainable results. The socio-economic management tools (see below 2.1.4.) make it possible to "exploit" these five characteristics for the benefit of socio-economic innovation actions, both for the benefit of the individuals and for the company or organization where they carry out their professional activity.

In summary, observation shows that humans are not spontaneously obedient, submissive or even subordinate, contrary to the presuppositions of the TFW virus. He or she is an agent driven by his/her contradictory impulses: conflict/cooperation, individualism/team solidarity, autonomy/cooperation. Human and social performance is the result of this system of numerous and eminently dialectical, complex and fluctuating behaviors.

1.1.2.5 Socio-economic integration, cooperation and proximity. The concept of *proximity* expresses the short distance in *space*, between people and teams, and in *time*, between the sequences of an action process. It is a factor of sustainable effectiveness and efficiency. The concept of *socio-economic productivity* refers to productivity that is compatible with the quality of life in professional, lucrative or voluntary activity.

One may wonder why humans, who are naturally disobedient, accept to be integrated into the "symphonic discipline" of a team. Probably because socio-economic integration expresses the situation where the satisfaction of human needs is greater than the cost of the effort involved. Socio-economic *integration* is based on the practice and intensification of inter-individual *cooperation* as a factor of sustainable performance. Indeed, it simultaneously produces mutually compatible social and economic performance.

Cooperation is a mechanism and a behavioral model based on the organized complementarity of skills as well as communication-coordination-cooperation between individuals and groups (teams, entities, establishments, subsidiaries). The level of performance of an organization depends on the capacity of its members to *cooperate in a sustainable* way, i.e., on their know-how to *negotiate* productive, effective and efficient relationships, which are inevitably deconstructed and must be rebuilt, tirelessly.

Cooperation is part of a chain of behaviors and actions: communication – *negotiation* – cooperation – coordination – concertation. Communication refers to the exchange of information flows between one or more transmitting actors and one or more receiving actors. Communication is a necessary but not sufficient condition for effective and efficient cooperation. This condition and a negotiation stage are necessary to move from simple communication to cooperation that is truly productive of *socio-economic value*, i.e., mutually compatible social and economic performance. Negotiation implies the recurrent creation of common ground between the partners in order to carry out the action effectively and efficiently.

1.1.2.6 Synchronized decentralization and individual and collective commitment. Synchronized decentralization combines the principle of *decentralization* of productive initiatives and the resulting responsibilities with that of *synchronization*, defined as coordination in real time, or with very short time lags, according to the model of the orchestration of a symphony concert.

Synchronized decentralization presupposes that the individual and collective commitment of people is realized. The *theory of individual and collective commitment* refers to commitment through actions, not just words, which are both a signal and a factor of socio-economic integration. Commitment is itself influenced by the "intangible system of production" characterized by the level of infection of the TFW virus and the intensity of steering, particularly by managers (Savall, Zardet, 2011b, 2013). Thus, in a highly virus infected system with little steering, individual and collective commitment is low. In a less virus infected organization, or at least a better piloted one, people's commitment increases due to greater individual satisfaction at work and a more satisfying work environment, produced by the quality and intensity of the piloting of people and activities.

1.1.2.7 Role and mode of action of the "socio-economic" manager: interactive pedagogy. The manager or supervisor plays the role of *conductor*, surrounded by musicians with their human potential, i.e., energy, skills and more or less disciplined collaborative behavior.

The manager uses *interactive pedagogy*, a concept that we have created and experimented with for five decades, based on the Freinet's method. This consists of inculcating knowledge by *making the learners-collaborators talk*, so that they rediscover the relevant knowledge to be transmitted, prepared by the manager. This method of animation is based more on doing than on saying. The principle is that *it is by doing that we learn* ("Learning by doing").

Interactive pedagogy is a powerful engine of change. It is based on the principle of *multidimensional, multiform and stochastic determinism* that characterizes socio-economic management. Multidimensional, because a result never depends on a single cause (systemic approach); multiform, because learning is achieved through writing, speaking, experimenting, listening…; and stochastic or random, because learners evolve according to their encounters and experiences with other people and teams.

1.1.3 The Major Problem to Solve: Caring Organizational Pathologies, i.e., Dysfunctions and Their Hidden Costs

The functioning of companies and organizations includes a specific subset composed of anomalies, disturbances, and gaps between the desired functioning, or "*orthofunctioning*", and the observed functioning, affected by *dysfunctions*. These are classified into six families: *working conditions, work organization, communication-coordination-cooperation, time management, integrated training and strategic implementation*. These families constitute both explanatory variables of the actual functioning of the company and areas for improvement, aimed at reducing the dysfunctions identified in the socio-economic diagnoses of companies and organizations.

1.1.3.1 Dysfunction: a socio-economic phenomenon. Dysfunctions have a double facet. They deteriorate social performance, the satisfaction of actors (producers, clients, suppliers, shareholders, etc.) and have an economic impact. Indeed, the *regulations* generated by dysfunctions cause costs for the organization which are, for the most part, hidden costs, i.e., costs not identified in the usual information, monitoring and decision-making systems of the company. The relevant concept is the *hidden cost–performance* duo. Hidden cost refers to the loss of economic value caused by dysfunctions. When dysfunctions are reduced through sustainable improvement actions, the loss of value that was experienced in the form of hidden costs is reduced. It is not common to measure the performance that this recovery of value added represents, which is why it is called *hidden performance*. Hidden cost and hidden performance are therefore in a *dialectical relationship*: a reduction in hidden costs constitutes a hidden performance and a reduction in hidden performance constitutes a hidden cost. By metaphor, we can consider that dysfunctions constitute *organizational waste*, hidden costs are analogous to the cost of waste, and the *recycling of hidden costs*, obtained by reducing dysfunctions, allows the recovery of value added, an economic resource.

The hidden cost analysis method created and developed through successive experiments in 2,150 companies and organizations includes five hidden cost indicators. Three of them are social or behavioral: absenteeism, work-related accidents and work-related illnesses, and staff turnover. Two are economic: the non-quality of products (goods and services) and direct under-productivity (quantities produced). Hidden costs constitute a *destruction of actual and potential value added.*

These hidden costs affect the overall economic performance of the company. Indeed, hidden costs have six components. The first three are costs that the company or organization could avoid, at least partially, if its level of dysfunction were lower: *over-salaries, over-time* and *over-consumption*. The fourth, fifth and sixth components do not constitute an expense, but a non-production in the accounting sense, i.e., a loss of production or activity generated by the dysfunctions, a loss of profit, an opportunity cost that is never accounted for. It is a question of *non-production, non-creation of potential* and *risks* suffered by the company due to recurrent dysfunctions.

Hidden costs–performance therefore affect the two components of economic performance: the company's *immediate results* and its creation of potential. The latter is generated by actions taken today to ensure immediate results tomorrow. Hidden costs-performance thus constitute budgetary leeway, a self-financing reserve for improving the company's sustainable economic performance.

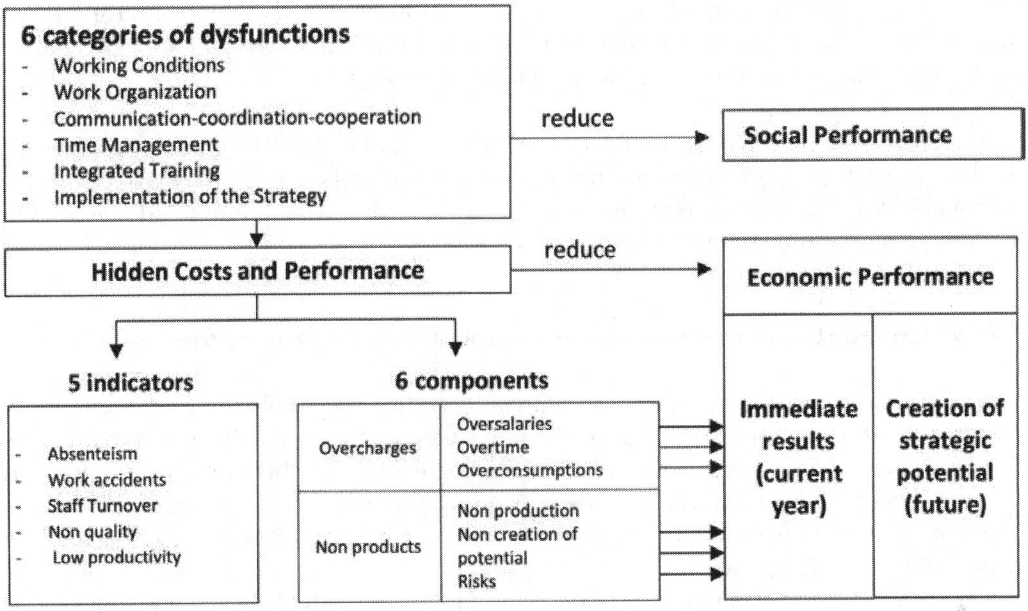

Figure 1.2 Dysfunctions and hidden costs–performance

1.1.3.2 The place of humans and machines in value creation. In traditional economic theory, the value of production is assumed to depend on two main factors, capital and labor. These two factors can be complementary or, on the contrary, in competition. Thus, many business decisions and macro-economic policies, at the level of public authorities, have led to automation, with the objective of replacing the labor factor (humans) by the capital factor (machines and technologies), thus favoring the "*substitution* of factors" over their complementarity.

According to the Socio-Economic Theory, there is an *intangible performance factor*: the capacity of the company or organization to recycle the hidden costs of its dysfunctions into value added. Indeed, without intangible investment, technological automation does not produce the expected profitability, because the dysfunctions and hidden costs cancel out or reduce the potential performance expected from the material investment.

The intangible investment in human potential has proven to be very profitable. Coupled with material investment, it increases the profitability of technological investments. *Intangible investment in the qualitative development of human potential (IIQDHP)* consists mainly of training integrated into professional practices, adaptation of work organization, intensification of communication and learning, etc. Thus this deliberate and organized complementarity of factors ensures a better overall profitability of the investment.

The Socio-Economic Theory includes the concept of *socio-economic rationality*, which proposes a more effective and sustainable qualimetric model for assisting decision-making than traditional economic rationality (Savall, 1979a). Indeed, the latter mobilizes only the visible costs and performances of classical accounting and ignores the loss of resources caused by dysfunctions.

The two factors, capital and labor, are not of the same nature. Capital is important for improving productivity, reducing drudgery.... As for human potential, carried by the labor factor, it is crucial for better ensuring the expected performance. In socio-economic theory, human potential is the only *active factor* in the creation of value added, technical and/or financial capital being a precious but sterile tool, when it is not activated and directed by human potential to install the machine, to adjust it, to use it, to maintain it, to program it, to perfect it or to repair it...

At a time when the risks of "ferocious" technological hegemony or of technology being diverted from its purpose are major, it is essential to remember the crucial role of human potential in the creation of value added, and to work so that digitalization and automation are *tamed* and that human beings take *ownership* on them.

1.2 Permanent Management of the Company or Organization

An important purpose of theories is to provide a comprehensible representation of observable phenomena, and then to inspire actions to generate sustainable performance. Socio-Economic Theory constitutes a constructive critique of established theories and decision support models in economics and management. It proposes an overall approach to the functioning of a company and its performance, as well as a socio-economic approach to the classical fields of management.

The numerous experiments in Socio-Economic Approach to Management (SEAM) as experimented in 2,150 companies and organizations, 48 countries, 72 sectors of activity have given rise to Socio-Economic concepts in the main fields of action of companies and organizations: strategy, marketing and sales, management control, organization and human resources management (Savall, 1974, 1979a; Savall and Zardet, 1987, 1992, 1995, 2005).

1.2.1 Concept of Socio-Economic Strategy

The dominant theory and practice emphasize *strategic intent* and *strategy definition.* However, long-term observation of organizations shows the central role of the implementation, or staging, of the strategic plan.

The strategy of a company or an organization is made up of all the actions that have lasting effects in the short, medium and long term. It is applied to a "*relevant environment*", taking into account the internal characteristics of the company or organization and those of its external environment. According to socio-economic theory, the boundary that delimits the inside and outside of the company is *porous,* as it allows flows to pass from the inside to the outside and vice versa. These flows are carried by customers, suppliers, institutions as well as by staff members, because these actors enter and leave the company or organization on a recurring basis and carry the *seeds of dysfunctions,* in both directions.

The outcome (success or failure) of the strategy is measured by the joint level of social performance and economic performance resulting from the countless interactions between the actors in the relevant environment, both internal and external to the company or organization. Rigorous and long-term observation shows that the result obtained in the external environment depends on the intensity and quality of the *internal action.* The latter is less costly than external action because it is more concentrated and produces a *leverage effect.*

Socio-Economic Strategy is a mix of economic and social objectives, simultaneously compatible, carried by a coalition of actors led by a strategist (the active unit) (Savall, 1979a; Savall, Zardet, 1995, 2013). It should be emphasized that, from this perspective, social objectives such as maintaining employment, developing qualifications, and improving working conditions can drive the strategy in the same way as traditional economic objectives. Socio-Economic Strategy encompasses both internal strategy, i.e., the definition of projects for and by the company's staff, and external strategy, i.e., the definition of projects for the company aimed at its stakeholders, in its external environment.

1.2.1.1 The place of the external environment. Socio-Economic Strategy (Savall, 1974, 1975a, 1979a; Savall, Zardet, 1987, 1995) is part of a *continuum* between the internal and external perimeters of the firm, considering that the boundary between the firm and its economic, social and ecological environment is porous. This internal-external dialectic relationship determines the degree of competitiveness of the organization.

Competitiveness refers to the ability of a company or organization to survive and develop. It implies a suitable level of socio-economic performance, resulting from multiple interactions with its main external and internal stakeholders:

- customers, suppliers, normative institutions, professional and trade union organizations, competitors;
- governance structure, shareholders or supervisory body, management, salaried or volunteer staff;

Competitiveness governs relations in the different spheres, private, but also public or associative. Competitiveness is the source of sustainable value creation that allows all stakeholders to be remunerated, by distributing the resources thus created.

Adaptation to the environment can be regressive or progressive. Indeed, when the company adapts "passively" to the pressures of its environment exerted by its stakeholders, it tends to shrink and risks disappearing through liquidation or absorption. *Progressive* adaptation corresponds to an increase in its competitiveness and implies an "*integral innovation*" strategy that successively activates the main components of the strategy.

1.2.1.2 Attributes of the socio-economic strategy. Integral innovation is an effective and efficient lever for sustainable socio-economic competitiveness, stimulating effective *differentiation* strategies. Integral innovation is socio-economic in nature. It concerns all the components of the strategy: products, markets, technologies, human potential, and their combination: the organization. Innovation requires *internal creativity* and consists in provoking a deliberate action of recurrent change affecting products, goods or services, the quality of service and the relationship with the customer or user, the conquest of solvent markets or new user segments, the integration of technologies by learning new know-how. This implies the *stimulation, constantly renewed,* of the company's human potential and its level of commitment, as well as the permanent evolution of skills and the periodic readjustment of teams and processes.

Integral innovation therefore constitutes a progressive and *proactive* adaptation of the organization to the changes in its relevant environment.

1.2.1.3 The tetranormalization phenomenon. The concept of tetranormalization refers to a complex phenomenon that increases the difficulty of decision-making, and then of the action of the company or organization in its dual environment, internal and external. The main components of this increased complexity are the *proliferation* of norms and the *contradiction* between norms, as well as their subjectivity, which make it impossible, in rigor, to perfectly respect the innumerable norms.

At the level of the national and global economy, tetranormalization appears to be a new source of growth of hidden macro-costs that hinder the economic and social development of nations.

Citizens, consumers, producers and employees express a growing need for standards and norms. Public and private institutions are increasingly increasing their competitive supply of standards in the economic and social environment. However, standards and norms are not only sound *rules of the game*, a factor of equity, they also have a dark side. They constitute *barriers to entry* into the competitive game within the public and private spheres, and are accompanied by practices of interference and even espionage.

The theory of tetranormalization (Savall, Zardet, 2005; Cappelletti, Pigé & Zardet, 2015) describes and explains the impacts of the proliferation of standards and contradictions between the four poles of standards and norms: social, environmental, accounting and trade. These phenomena cause dysfunctions, create distortions in the rules of the game on markets and within organizations and territories. They generate an additional and growing layer of hidden costs. The management of companies must integrate these multiple and often contradictory standards and norms, without jeopardizing their raison d'être, their economic performance and their ability to survive and develop.

1.2.1.4 The theory of the strategic bedrock. This theory (Savall, Zardet, 1995, 2005) has three "theorems":

- The success of an organization's external strategy is a function of the intensity of its internal strategy.
- The level of external performance of an organization is a function of the degree of intensity of its internal *cohesion.*
- The variation in the degree of internal cohesion has a multiplier or leverage effect on the variation in the level of performance; thus, a doubling of the level of cohesion leads to an increase in performance of more than twice as much.

The strategic foundation theory can be summarized in four principles:

1. The *level of infection* of the TFW virus (taylorism-fayolism-weberism) is detrimental to the degree of cohesion of teams and the organization and tends to reduce the level of intensity of steering of activities.
2. the cohesion of teams and the organization is a key factor in the intensity and *quality of steering* and decision-making.
3. the level of steering intensity influences the degree of cohesion of the teams and the organization and tends to reduce the level of infection of the TFW virus.
4. the level of cohesion of the teams and the organization has an impact on its level of sustainable socio-economic performance.

Remember that sustainable socio-economic performance refers to economic performance (creation of financial value) that is compatible with the social performance of the company, i.e., the level of satisfaction of the needs in terms of quality of working life of all categories of personnel involved in the activity.

1.2.1.5 Integral quality of the organization. The three levels of integral quality are: the quality of products (goods or services) that benefit (external) customers, as well as the quality of operations and the quality of management, which produce beneficial effects on the internal actors of the company or organization, considered as "*internal customers*" (Figure 1.3).

The integral quality theory, a component of the Socio-Economic Theory, shows that the quality of management is an effective and efficient lever for ensuring the quality of the organization's operations and, by extension, the quality of its products. It is therefore relevant to act on the quality of management and operations in order to improve product quality,

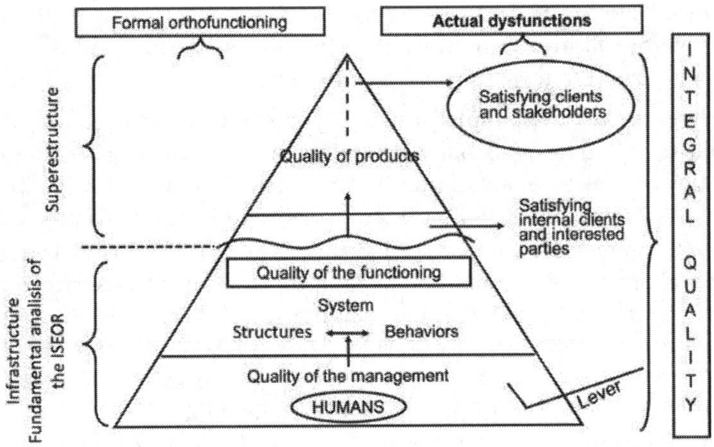

Figure 1.3 The three levels of integral quality of the company or organization (©ISEOR 2005).

instead of simply acting directly on product quality, as is often the case with quality approaches (certification, continuous improvement, etc.).

1.2.2 The Sales and Marketing Function

The concepts of the vital sales function and socio-economic marketing constitute the "all-sellers" theory in the organization.

1.2.2.1 The vital sales function. By focusing its analysis on internal dysfunctions and proposing solutions to reduce them, socio-economic management encourages better cooperation between the different functions of the company by demonstrating the strength of their *interdependence.* This is particularly the case for the production and sales functions, which are led to cooperate better for greater efficiency. Socio-economic management stimulates the different functions of the company, thanks to the interaction between production and sales departments performance.[2]

A well-filled order book allows manufacturing to reduce its dysfunctions and recycle its hidden costs. In the same way, an effort on the shop floor to reduce dysfunctions that have a commercial impact, by ensuring quality and delivery times, helps to stimulate the sales force. We thus move from a situation where the dysfunctions allowed the sales force and the shop floor to justify their own underperformance, to a new situation where the sound performance of the shop floor encouraged the sales department to increase its own. This makes it possible to go beyond the classic strategy-structure duality confined to the relationship between the marketing strategy and the sales department structure. According to the Socio-Economic Theory, structure and strategy issues must be addressed simultaneously.

Selling is a vital function. It is an intrinsic function of life. Let's rehabilitate this notion that has lost its meaning and has been misused by those who have connoted it in a negative way. As a play on words, we can say that it is a living function with a spelling mistake. Selling consists of creating *social links* within the organization, between the different people who collaborate and towards the outside of the organization. It also expresses the social and societal utility of what is produced.

A major element at the heart of sales is the notion of quality, the simplest definition of which is the ability of something to satisfy a need. When a good or a service is of proper quality, it facilitates its sale, and then the renewal of its sale through customer satisfaction. The same is true for the quality of service and reception in public, associative or voluntary services, based on listening to and respecting the client, who is called the user, according to tradition. Why not call him or her a client, the most beautiful term that can be given to someone who has a need that we propose to satisfy?

1.2.2.2 The "we are all salespeople" theory. The traditional organization of work has assigned the mission and responsibility of selling to certain people in the company. The principle laid down by the Socio-Economic Approach to Management, "*all salespeople*" in organizations, is a key message, whether in companies, public organizations or associations, in the market or non-market sectors. Provided that its ethical dimension is respected, selling is probably the noblest act of a human being. Selling is to provide a service to a person who has a legitimate need that we can satisfy through a social link. The profound definition of selling is to organize an exchange of resources, more or less balanced. It is also to provide the means to live in *dignity*, thanks to an income deserved by the work provided and the creation of value that one brings in the social and societal life.

Considering that everyone in the company can and should contribute to the sale is a powerful lever to develop *cooperation and internal cohesion*, in order to produce quality goods or services that satisfy customers or users. Where the TFW virus isolated salespeople, to the point of considering them as "separate" actors, socio-economic management introduces direct or indirect *sales acts* into the job of each person, from the telephone reception, through production, packaging, administrative services, logistics, up to the end of the process, i.e., the sale.

1.2.2.3 The role of marketing as a commercial laboratory. The usual territory of marketing is the external environment, the internal environment being positioned as the territory of human resource management and production activity management. Socio-Economic Strategy brings these two environments together, by proposing a marketing approach extended to the internal environment. It consists of listening to employees and volunteers in the same way as customers, in order to identify their needs. By treating staff members at all levels as *internal customers*, in an uncompromising and professional manner, the quality of the products, goods or services can be made sustainably better, more competitive and more profitable for *external customers.*

The TFW virus has very often isolated marketing from sales, the former considered as noble people who design products based on market research, the latter with a thankless job, at the service of the former, sometimes even scorned by them. Yet the needs expressed by potential consumers are often hidden and not very explicit. Market research does not make it possible to extract this information and these hidden needs. This is why it is necessary to develop techniques to detect and extract these needs, in order to build and formulate a response adapted to the real or potential market. Salespeople who are close to customers are better able to capture these needs. Better *cooperation* between salespeople and "marketers" makes it possible to detect innumerable unsatisfied needs among current or potential customers, provided that the channels for feeding back this information and processing it are organized. *Re-assembling* the territories of marketing and sales is very effective and efficient for sustainable sales action.

1.2.3 Socio-Economic Management Control

Socio-Economic Management Control is based on the theory of hidden costs and on the management of sustainable performance by means of the indicator *"Hourly Contribution to Value Added on Variable Costs" (HCVAVC).*

Its practice consists in developing acts of *self-quality control.* It should be remembered that the Socio-Economic Approach to Management calls for individual and collective awareness as a key factor in sustainable performance. This is fed by reflexes of satisfaction with work well done and a propensity for *productivity and quality* of products, goods and services.

1.2.3.1 Hidden versus visible cost–performance. Facts have a visible part and a hidden part, not observable or measured by the observer or witness. One of the main ways to increase sustainable performance is to make decisions according to a socio-economic rationality that is based on an *extended socio-economic calculation.* This more relevant calculation takes into account not only the usual visible indicators, but also new indicators to be set up to better detect hidden elements, not taken into account in the usual decisions. For example, the displayed and invoiced price of a product always hides the subsequent cost of after-sales, maintenance, repair or even destruction. *Socio-Economic rationality* allows us to say that buying at a higher initial price may be more rational than a seemingly cheaper price, whereas traditional economic theory claims that it is rational to buy the cheapest product at the time of purchase, even though it generates a higher full cost. *Integral cost* includes the initial face price and subsequent costs.

According to this principle, socio-economic theory has made it possible to enrich the model of investment choice, first tested in the Péchiney-Ugine-Kuhlmann group (Savall, 1979a).

1.2.3.2 The socio-economic balance (abbreviated as "economic balance"): a decision-support tool based on extended socio-economic rationality. A misinterpretation of the accounting model, symbolized by the "T-account" which clearly separates expenses and income, breaking the link between expenditure and income, has led organizations of a certain size to entrust the monitoring of expenses and income to different specialists. However, every action simultaneously involves expenses and revenues. This has led us (Savall, 1974, 1975a, 1979a; Savall and Zardet 1992) to experiment in a great many organizations with a tool for improving decision making, the socio-economic balance, abbreviated as the *economic balance.*

1.2.3.3 Hidden externalized costs. The notions of visible and hidden costs are related to a space of observation and action. Thus, actions initiated in one department have impacts on other departments of the company, and similarly, actions launched by a company have impacts on other organizations on a local, regional, national or international *territory.* Thus, the Socio-Economic Theory has from the outset identified the importance of the hidden costs of externalities, in time and space, with the identification of the ratio of external costs to internal costs (Savall, 1978b). The propensity for dysfunctions and their hidden costs to reappear is a factor of externalities overtime. A current dysfunction, not or poorly resolved, will produce a series of dysfunctions and hidden costs in subsequent periods. The consequences are not or poorly measured at the time the action is taken. Because of the two types of externalities in space and time, quantitative indicators alone are inadequate to correctly represent the issues at stake in a decision.

1.2.3.4 Managing sustainable economic performance using the Hourly Contribution to Value Added on Variable Costs (HCVAVC). The ratio of *indirectly productive time/directly productive time published* in 1978 has been refined and has become the ratio of productive investment time to directly productive time. This led to the concept of *Intangible Investment in Qualitative Human Potential Development* (IIQHPD). This refers to the endogenous transformation of the three components of human potential: human energy, *involvement behavior* and commitment to the company's or organization's activity, and the evolving *skills* of the actors. The IIQHPD is self-financing thanks to a recycling of hidden costs into added value creation, through *integral innovation* practices, evaluated every semester. The duration of the IIQHPD intangible investment allows to feed a *learning process* that produces a multiplier effect of performance resulting in a very high return on investment of 210% to 4014% (Savall, Zardet, 2008).

1.2.4 Socio-Economic Organization and Production Management

The TFW virus has neglected and obscured the importance of the organization of cooperation between people, teams, levels of responsibility, relations between excessively specialized workstations, between so-called operational staff and so-called functional or support function staff. In essence, the virus considered that organizing or structuring the *individual job* would be enough to ensure harmony in the processes. That if everyone performed their job correctly, the whole would *ipso facto* produce a good result. The virus ignored the conflictual dimension of human potential, underestimated the chronic power of desynchronization and that of personal or team strategies that do not spontaneously converge. In order to compensate for this widely observed lack of cooperation, the generic model of effective and efficient organization experimented by ISEOR in all kinds of companies and organizations is that of *synchronized (or orchestrated) decentralization.*

1.2.4.1 An effective "anti-TFW virus" practice is to organize synchronized decentralization. The Socio-Economic Approach to Management has become a *TFW antivirus*, compensating for the shortcomings caused by the taylorism-fayolism-weberism virus. The *symphony orchestra* offers a model of an effective and efficient productive team. Overtime, each musician, though individually competent and equipped with a score, improves his or her skills and behavior, producing sounds that are pleasing to the other musicians and to the audience, thanks to the *conductor's pedagogical action.* With its metaphor of the company as a theater play, socio-economic management conceives of an organization as an ensemble of musicians and conductors, officiating at all levels of the organizational chart.

The relevant division of labor according to the socio-economic approach is compatible with the indispensable cooperation that ensures the creation of value and sustainable performance. One of the most important roles of managers at different levels is therefore to organize cooperation and to facilitate it with the right personnel dosed multi-functionality. Cooperation appears to be the main variable sacrificed or neglected in the dominant theories (TFW virus) and the practices that follow from them.

1.2.5 Managing Human Potential

Since the TFW virus has promoted a materialistic and disembodied conception of the human being in professional activity, a function of repair and partial rebalancing has been organized in companies and organizations, successively called personnel management and then human resources management.

Some authors, abusing inappropriate metaphors, have claimed the highly questionable name of "human capital." From the outset (Savall, 1974, 1975a), socio-economic theory has criticized the use of the term "capital" because it evokes an alienable object, which can be bought and sold, inert like the most sophisticated or high-tech machine. Indeed, since the creation of value has been attributed to two factors, considered to be of the same nature, capital and labor, since the 19th century, all that remains is to assimilate labor to a transferable object, susceptible of acquisition, such as a machine or a material production good, which is a serious error.

However, the factor, unique in its kind, which makes it possible to create a product, good or service, to carry it out of good quality, to imagine improvements in this product or in the way of carrying it out, then to sell it, this factor is incorporeal and belongs to the person who is equipped with such capacities. Thus, any person endowed with such potential can do a little productive work, a lot or, on the contrary, abstain from it, *if this is his/her strategy and if his/her colleagues tolerate this strategy.*

The innumerable dysfunctions reported by people, in many companies and organizations, of all sizes, in all sectors, in all countries, profit-making or not, demonstrate that the abstention from providing this productive work of value, as one's personal potential would allow, is obvious, visible and observable in any company or organization. Our work has indeed shown that it is the quality of the management of people and activities that allows for the achievement of a sustainable socio-economic objective and ensures the survival-development of a company or organization, whatever its size. This has been observed in both private and public organizations.

We have therefore replaced the erroneous notion of human capital with that of human *potential*. This potential belongs to the person who holds it. Quality management is the method that enables this potential to be applied to a collective activity traditionally called *work*.

1.2.5.1 An unnecessary distinction: knowledge/ know-how (to do)/ know how to behave. Among the formulas that need to be reconsidered in relation to human potential are the expressions "social skills" and "knowledge." In all simplicity, socio-economic theory considers that the concept of *behavioral quality*, which is easily understood, covers what the expression "social skills" evokes.

As for the expression "knowledge," the problem is not semantic but functional. Indeed, knowledge is an ingredient of action, it is a necessary, but not sufficient, element to accomplish the action that brings performance and produces value. After more than a century of efforts in most countries to develop education, teaching and training, the essential problem of human, social and societal development is not so much to disseminate knowledge, because progress has been considerable, as to integrate it into effective socio-economic action. Thus, the crucial question is and remains the rate at which *knowledge is transformed into know-how.*

The expression "know-how" encompasses the notion of knowledge and gives it its full meaning. Know-how necessarily includes knowledge. But unfortunately, knowledge does not always lead to know-how, which is the *sine qua non* for the production of sustainable socio-economic value.

In the Socio-Economic Approach to Management, we will therefore speak, on the one hand, of *know-how* or competence, implicitly referring to knowledge, and, on the other hand, of behavior instead of "knowing how to behave."

1.2.5.2 Human potential management: a function integrated into all the organization's functions and shared with the human resources department. Human potential, carried by all the people active in the company or organization, is stimulated in all teams where humans are present, whether they are managers, owners or not, employees or volunteers. As soon as they produce value, in the activity of the company or organization, these people constitute the said *human potential*, an irreplaceable essential resource, whatever the extraordinary progress of the most advanced technologies.

The said *support function* of the personnel or human resources has correctly ensured the application of the legislation in favor of the personnel, the payroll and the recruitment. On the other hand, the sharing of the *human potential management function* with the other functions of the company or organization is more or less clear and more or less effective and efficient, depending on the company or organization.

The Socio-Economic Approach to Management ensures a better activation of the human potential. Our numerous experiences and applications have allowed us to identify and measure the waste, more or less important, of human potential that is not or poorly mobilized, both by a relative lack of involvement of people and by relative failures of management.

The numerous implementations of the Socio-Economic Approach to Management by ISEOR have allowed considerable progress in certain areas such as: the integration of new recruits, the development of staff loyalty, the structuring of professional development for all categories of personnel, as well as the dynamics and management of remuneration. The main tools, presented in Section 2.1.4 of this introductory chapter of this Treatise, are: the competency grid, the Periodically Negotiable Activity Contract and the Internal–External Strategic action Plan. They have also made it possible to demonstrate that the process of change (cf. 2.1.2), starting from a given situation in the company's operations and moving towards a new expected operation, through a deliberate strategic choice, constitutes a real *metamorphosis.* Its success requires a structured, planned and carefully programmed endogenous process as well as the anticipated allocation of part of the human, individual and collective energy. In this way, *the integral innovation* that allows the company to be in phase with the evolutions of its relevant environment could be built.

Such a deliberate and organized process is called *socio-economic intervention.*

2 SOCIO-ECONOMIC INTERVENTION TO CONCRETELY ORGANIZE THE ORGANIZATIONAL METAMORPHOSIS AND THE GROWTH OF SUSTAINABLE PERFORMANCE

Socio-economic intervention is an organized process of change management to simultaneously develop the social and economic performance of a company or organization that has deliberately decided to adopt such a strategy. This dynamic is generally driven by the support of intervener-researchers or certified professional consultants.

2.1 The Intervention Process in the Company or Organization

The short lifespan of the effects of an action or behavior explains the propensity for *cyclical degradation of the performance* of the company or organization.

2.1.1 The Rationale for External Intervention

Observation over the medium and long term shows that the *awareness* and *intention* of internal actors are *necessary* but *not sufficient* to drive change or metamorphosis, with a view to ensuring the survival-development of the company or organization.

The life of an organization is a permanent process that brings out the *resurgence* of dysfunctions and hidden costs, according to a natural periodic cycle analogous to that which affects the life of the human person. The course of human life can be likened to a process of activity that follows a *learning curve,* simultaneously individual and collective. This "switch" from the individual to the collective is a real transformation that implies successive mutual adjustments, according to iterations that constitute a *heuristic* process, of intelligent adaptive trial and error, source of improvement of socio-economic performance.

Why does a human being, naturally recalcitrant *a priori,* get involved in change, despite his/her natural resistance to change? Is it because they want to improve their working conditions? Is it due to a deep and recurring need to obtain satisfaction in a professional situation?

2.1.2 The Dynamics of Change: The Trihedron and the HORIVERT Architecture

Every energy system undergoes, over time, a degradation that physicists have called *entropy.* The company or organization, a dynamic system, is no exception to this rule. Organizational entropy is manifested by a loss of resources due to dysfunctions. A strategy aiming to improve its economic and social results must therefore reduce entropy by actions oriented

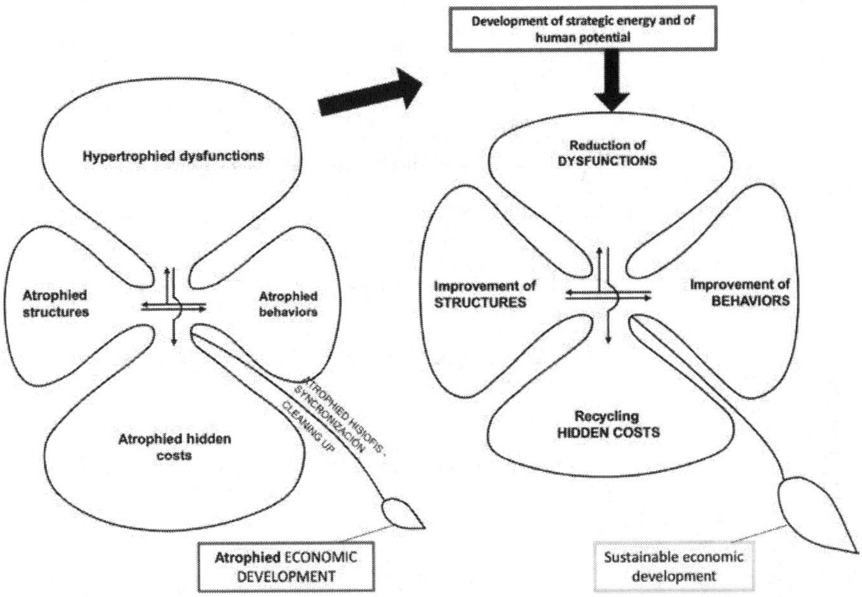

Figure 1.4 Strategic development through socio-economic intervention: From strategic weakness to strategic strength.

towards the *reduction of dysfunctions* and, consequently, the *recycling* of hidden costs into value added.

The first statement of the Socio-Economic Theory of organizations schematizes the phenomenon of entropy in the form of the first cloverleaf in Figure 1.4.

The Socio-Economic Theory of organizations[3] can be summarized as follows. An organization is a complex set of five types of structures (physical, technological, organizational, demographic and mental) that interact with five human *behavioral logics* (individual, activity group, categorical, affinity group and collective). This permanent and complex *interaction* creates pulses of activity that constitute the functioning of the company. The latter is composed of an ideal "*orthofunctioning*", degraded by dysfunctions. The regulation or adjustment of dysfunctions consumes resources that increase the cost of the company or organization's activities. These costs, which are neither measured nor taken into account in the decisions and actions, are called *hidden costs*.

Figure 1.5 of the triad is located between the two clovers. It explains the dynamics that transform the state of the productive system of the company or organization. The trihedron represents the dynamic learning process that makes the whole organization function and evolve over time.

2.1.2.1 The three driving forces of change dynamics. They are summarized in the trihedron diagram, each axis being successively a source of energy impetus for change.

The *improvement process axis* symbolizes the dynamics of change through the four successive stages (Figure 1.5), and the *management tools axis* symbolizes the contribution of management tools to the entire management team in the horizontal action of the socio-economic intervention. The *political and strategic decisions axis* expresses the fact that change cannot be achieved without a force of decision-making energy resulting from the interplay of the company's actors (managers, executives, staff). The will to deliberate change is essential, but it must go well beyond mere speeches of intent and be translated into concrete decisions

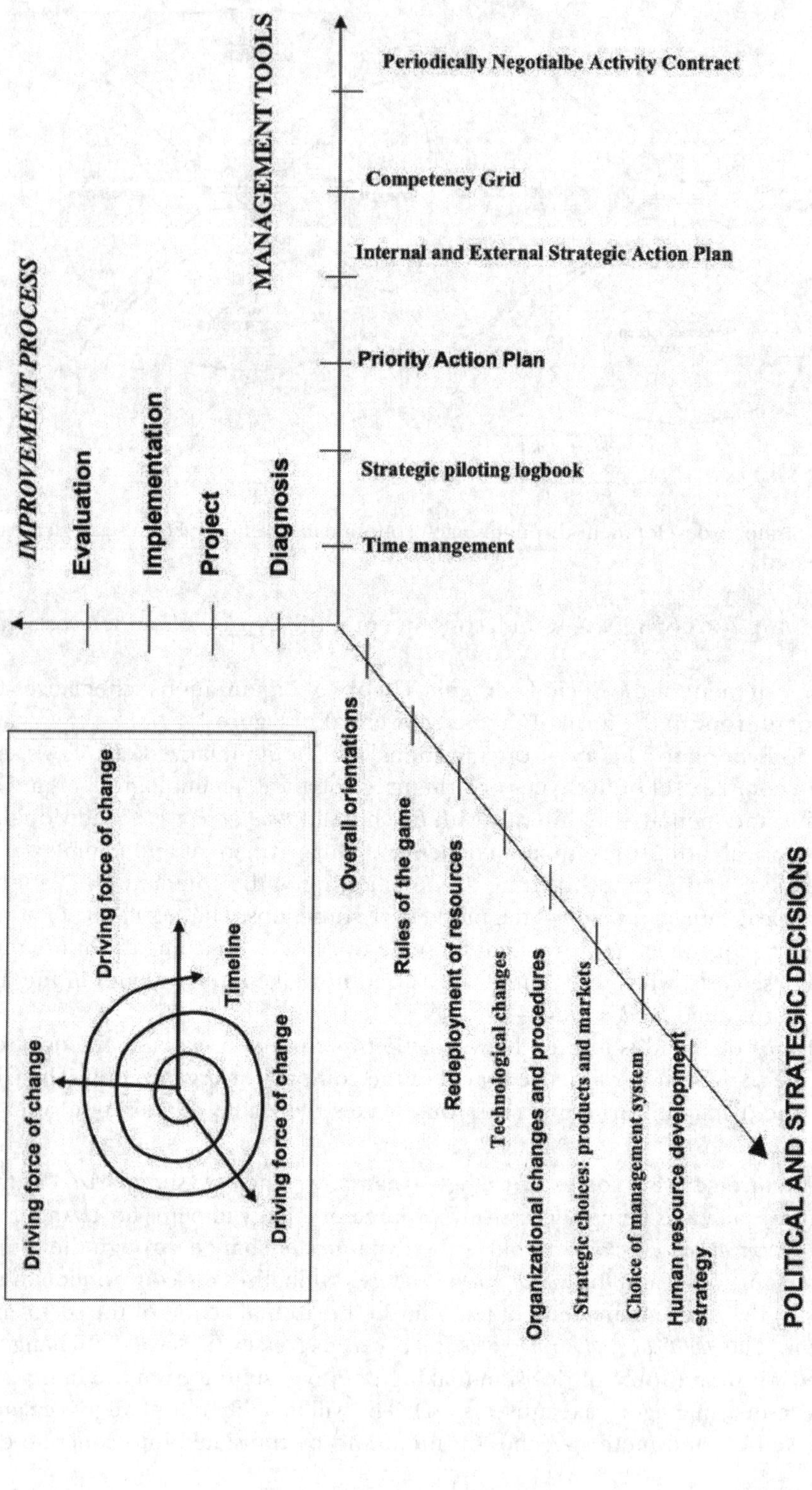

Figure 1.5 Articulation of the three driving forces of change.

to *transform* the company's various areas of activity. Thus, socio-economic management, in addition to introducing major innovative *strategic choices*, strengthens the *internal cohesion* of teams, the external coherence of the company's strategy and their fruitful interactions. Change can be likened to a *spiral of progress* that alternately follows the three axes: the diagnosis begins, the time management tool is implemented, strategic decisions are made, then their implementation becomes clearer... and so on over time.

The crucial importance of strategic *implementation* in relation to strategic choices is demonstrated by the many cases observed where a strategy remains an intention, a wish, a dream, as long as the rooting and concretization of these choices are not ensured by concrete actions. This means that, beyond the relatively visible "*superstructure*" of a company (its product portfolio, its clientele, its technologies, etc.), the relatively hidden "*infrastructure*" constituted by its internal management and operation (Figure 1.3) plays a decisive role, yet one that is neglected in most theories and professional practices.

2.1.2.2 The metamorphosis "theater play": the HORIVERT scenario (or method). Figure 1.6 HORIVERT (horizontal and vertical intervention) represents the organization of the actors' space and the roles they play in the "theater *play*" of metamorphosis.

The HORIVERT model has three components: a "static" model of the architecture of the actors who should be involved in the metamorphosis (Figure 1.6), a dynamic model of the impetus for change (Figure 1.5) and a model of the scheduling of actions called the *chronobiology of change* (Figure 1.7).

The change method developed by ISEOR is a synthesis between the advantages of the globality of change, envisaged by the *organizational development* approach, and those of the depth of change recommended by the *sociotechnical* approach (Savall, 1974, 1975a). Our method, called HORIVERT (Savall, 1974, 1975a, 1979a; Savall, Zardet, 1987; Savall, 2003ab), (Figure 1.6) consists of combining the management of change at the level of the company's management teams and top management in a *horizontal approach* throughout the company, with very concrete change actions carried out in several units of the company, which constitute the *vertical approach*. This produces a controlled propagation of the dynamic throughout the company. This method consists of synergizing the changes made at both the horizontal and vertical levels, through collective *emulation dynamics* and by making the changes proposed and made at the vertical level *consistent* at the horizontal level. This allows middle management to steer the change process, because the actions carried out at the horizontal level contribute to enriching its role, while facilitating certain transfers of responsibility to employees in the form of concerted delegation mechanisms that are put in place in the horizontal and vertical approaches. The HORIVERT method creates both economic performance and an increase in the *involvement and responsibility* of the actors, appreciated at all levels of the company or organization, which brings a surplus of social performance for the benefit of the personnel.

The HORIVERT architecture allows the integration of the top of the company and each of the teams in the management of change, by means of two devices that structure the functioning of the company or organization:

- Horizontal action consists in organizing *collaborative training clusters*, each cluster being composed of a line manager and his or her supervisors. The collaborative training on management tools is done in each cluster and allows to reduce the *natural resistance* to change.
- Vertical action in at *least two units* (departments, services, agencies, workshops) involves the management team of these units and their employees. In small companies (less than 30 people), vertical action mobilizes all the people simultaneously.

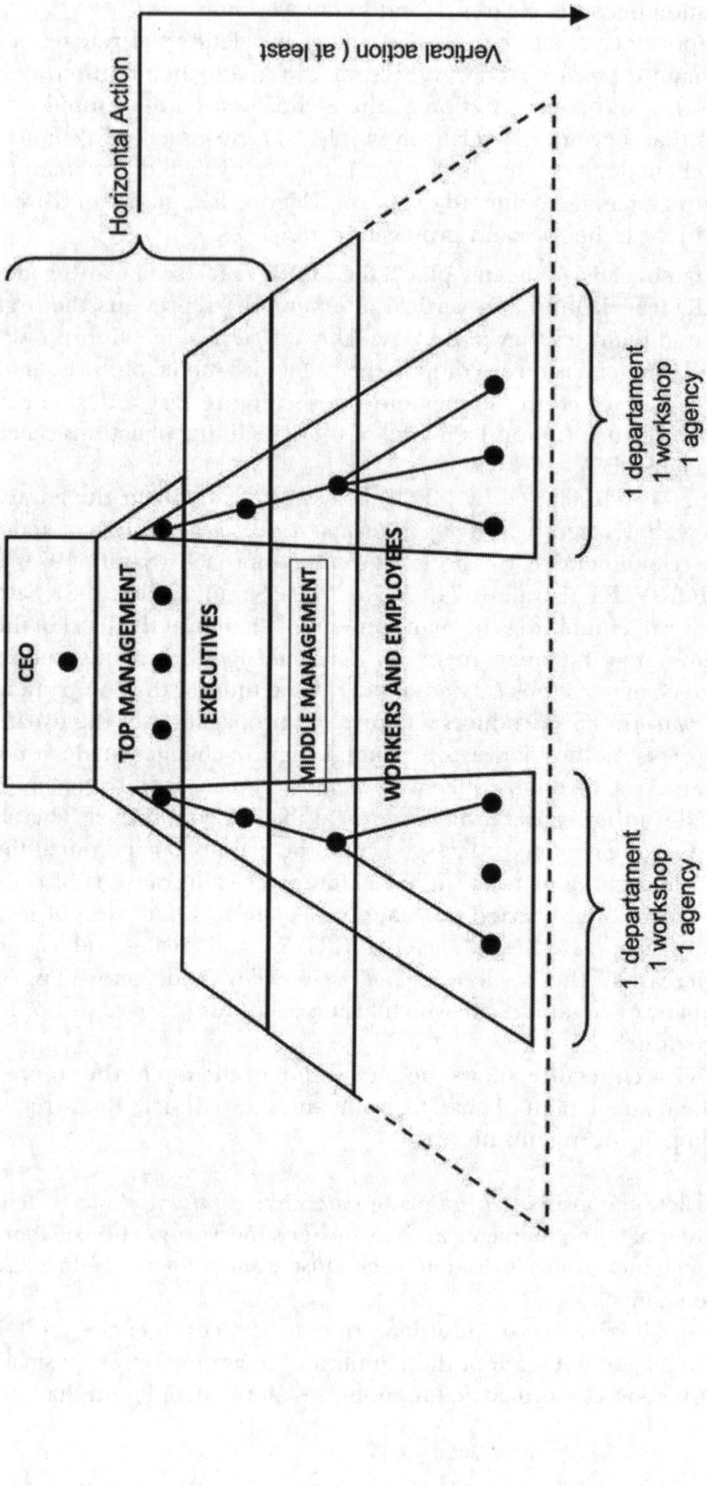

Figure 1.6 The HORIVERT architecture or scenario.

The HORIVERT scenario makes it possible, on the one hand, to ensure better integration of socio-economic intervention into the organization's strategy and, on the other hand, to resolve dysfunctions, both of a strategic nature and relating to current activity, thanks to the involvement of the actors (Savall 1974, 1975a, 1979a; Savall, Zardet, 1987; Boje, Rosile, 2003; Buono, 2001, 2003; Hayes, 2001). Figure 1.4 presents schematically the strategic development of the firm through socio-economic intervention. This intervention architecture (Figure 1.6) ensures that change is embedded in the firm from the top down to the grassroots level. It is also an ongoing architecture for learning and integration of people and activities over the ongoing life of the organization.

The HORIVERT model can be adapted to a wide variety of business cases. It can be applied to *large organizations*, such as a large pilot region of La Poste (Post Office) in France with 30,000 employees, the company Brioche Pasquier (4,000 employees), or in Belgium, FOREM (3,200 employees), as well as to *medium-sized companies*, such as Technord (350 employees), or *very small companies*, such as SCI Informatique or SLB Medical, which have 5 employees. In the case of very small companies, or *so-called "proximity" companies*, the approach is organized by grouping together 4 to 5 companies and has been named "HORIVERT multi-SMEs." It consists in organizing a horizontal inter-company action bringing together the managers of companies from various sectors, each accompanied by one or two executives or close collaborators. In addition, within each company, an in-depth vertical action is conducted.

This miniaturization of the HORIVERT model was conceived and applied by ISEOR for the first time in 1985, during an operation organized by the Chamber of Commerce and Industry of Lille – Roubaix – Tourcoing in about fifty SMEs, then in France since 1998 in 500 notary offices, in Mexico since 2001, and in Belgium since 2004, as well as in 250 proximity companies since 2016, in partnership with Actalians and then the OPCO-EP (Proximity Companies).

The Socio-Economic Intervention is announced and presented to the people of the company or organization by the management as a *strategic priority* mobilizing the entire company, without disrupting the current activity. The principle is that the improvement of the survival-development capacity, resulting from the intervention, cannot be done at the expense of the current performance. The numerous interventions carried out by ISEOR have shown that this is possible, thanks to the *substitution of calibrated time, necessary for the metamorphosis* action, for time wasted in the recurrent resolution of dysfunctions. The main condition for success is the *progressiveness* of the *change action* in the organization. Figure 1.7 schematically summarizes the *typical planning* of change actions that progressively recycle hidden costs, thanks to the progressive reduction of dysfunctions. This is brought about by the implementation of actions to improve socio-economic performance, through the *involvement of people*: management, supervisors, technicians and staff. ISEOR's scientific research program and successive pilot actions have made it possible to develop, over time, an effective and efficient protocol for *scheduling* change actions that take into account the particular *chronobiological rhythms* of each company or organization.

The successive editions of the book "*Mastering Hidden Costs*" (Savall, Zardet, 1st edition published in 1987) present the socio-economic intervention process in a comprehensive way. Its 7th edition, published in 2020, capitalizes on the lessons learned to date from the evolution of the socio-economic intervention method over the years.

2.1.2.3 From the search for a more efficient organizational mode to the discovery of the pre-eminence of people and activity management. The socio-economic intervention method underwent a paradigm shift around 1977. It was created in 1973, based on the *new forms of work organization* advocated by the Sociotechnical School, by adding the economic

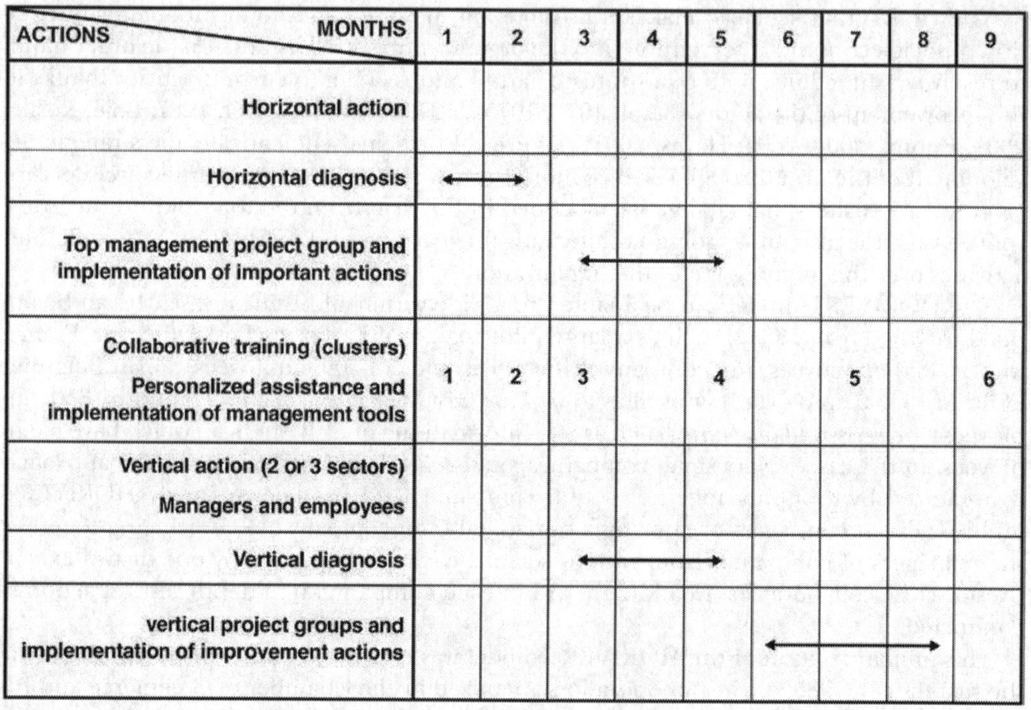

Figure 1.7 Schematic planning of the progressiveness of change actions, taking into account the chronobiologic rhythms of the company or organization.

dimension that was missing from this current of research, invested by psychosociologists from Northern Europe as well as sociologists (Jean-Daniel Reynaud, Philippe Bernoux, in France) and engineers (Davis in the United States).

Our initial research hypothesis was that it was possible to design and experiment with an *organizational model* that was simultaneously more stimulating for people (social performance) and more efficient and effective (economic performance). Our experiments in the early years showed us that this source of sustainable socio-economic performance was too static and that the said organization of work was important but not essential. All that remained was to pose a new hypothesis of a more dynamic nature, namely that the management of people and activities is the primary factor of sustainable socio-economic performance.

The hinge of this evolution was constituted by two major communications by Henri Savall. The first, at the symposium co-organized by François Perroux and Jean Piaget on the idea of regulation in the history of science (Savall, 1977a, 1978a). The second, encouraged by the Agence Nationale pour l'Amélioration des Conditions de Travail (ANACT), was presented at the IAE de Nice conference the following year (Savall, 1978b). The dynamic concept of steering has proven to be very operational, for 47 years, and more relevant to explain the origin of improvements in sustainable socio-economic performance.

The steering of activities consists of three main levers:

- stimulating human potential with stimulating information;
- synchronize people and actions;
- periodically cleaning up, the functioning of the company or organization.

This hypothesis has now been stabilized for 44 years: the paradigm of the quality and intensity of the management of people and activities has not been questioned, for the time being, during the thousands of experiments carried out: 2,150 companies and organizations, 72 sectors of activity, 48 countries and 110,000 people accompanied and observed in socio-economic interventions.

The intensity of the steering of people and activities in the organization is a key success factor for the organization's performance. The steering of proactive strategies is more effective and efficient when the company uses *decentralized vigilance indicators*, covering both its economic and social performance. This type of management requires not separating the three-time horizons, short, medium and long term, i.e., what concerns

- immediate management security: cash flow, monthly, quarterly and annual results
- multi-year development: future results of current actions and investments
- foresight: the future of business and product portfolios, markets and technologies, organization and human potential, in particular the recurring and growing need for new individual and collective skills and their updating.

The first lever, *stimulating* information, encourages actors to take effective action, which implies an expenditure of human energy, cooperative behavior and a contribution of skills.

The second lever, the *synchronization* (or orchestration) of activities and actors, refers to the development of real-time coordination practices of actors in activity processes. The lack of synchronization has two effects: a lack of *creativity* and a lack of implementation of *innovations* or operational improvements. Another effect is the tendency for priorities to get the output during the course of the activity, due to the *instability of behaviors* within organizations, subjected to unprecedented pressure from their competitive or normative environment and *contradictory requests*.

The third lever is the periodic *cleaning up* of dysfunctions. The organization is a living being that undergoes natural pollution throughout its life, as its organs (structures, procedures and behaviors) undergo inexorable degradation over time, due to the phenomenon of organizational entropy. This is why a *periodic up-dating of the dysfunctions* is necessary, taking into account their spontaneous resurgence. Thus, the *intangible production system* loses part of its efficiency and effectiveness if it is not periodically cleaned up (Figure 1.7 and 1.8).

2.1.3 A Participatory Process for Reducing Dysfunctions and Recycling Hidden Costs in Four Stages

The socio-economic method of *iterative* improvement includes the following steps:

2.1.3.1 The key role of the diagnosis, the mirror-effect and the expert opinion. The socio-economic diagnosis is focused on the identification of dysfunctions expressed by the active members of the company: leaders, managers, executives and staff, the principle being that improvements in the company's performance will be obtained by means of the resolution of poorly solved or unresolved problems that affect the quality of its operations. The idea is therefore to get the *witnesses of dysfunctions to speak*, as these are very rarely recorded in documents or indicators for the management of people and activities. Thus, the dysfunctional diagnosis is a combination of the familiar vision of the witnesses of the dysfunctions and the external, "new" or unaccustomed eye of the change process "accompanying" consultant or intervener-researcher. The results of the interviews are presented to all the people who have been interviewed, individually or in small groups, in order to produce a *shared image* of the problems to be solved, by means of the mirror-effect. The *mirror-effect* reduces the natural resistance to change because it appeals to everyone's consciousness by referring to individual and collective experiences. It produces a visible image of the dysfunctional life of the organization, which creates a *will for improvement* and new practices.

The history of the concept of socio-economic intervention shows that in the early years of our research, the diagnosis only involved processing the expression of the people concerned in order to produce the mirror-effect. Later, at the request of the companies and organizations, we added the *expert opinion* expressing the perception of the intervener-researchers or consultants, as a valuable complement.

After a decade of manual processing of the content of the interviews, ISEOR created and developed software to facilitate this processing. The design of the Socio-Economic Management Expert System (SEGESE) software took into account the phenomenon of *polysemy.* This means, in effect, that a word contains different meanings depending on the person interviewed and the circumstances. Symmetrically, the same generic problem can be expressed by very different words.[4] The software has thus made it possible to accumulate and structure an original nomenclature of more than *5,000 types of generic dysfunctions*. The diagnosis is therefore expressed in a mixed language combining the *generic ideas formulated by the interveners* from the software and the *specific ideas of the people who witnessed* the dysfunctions. The formulation of generic dysfunctions is done using an *inductive method* of content analysis, starting from the natural language of the people interviewed in their company and translating it into a generic language. This makes it possible to identify the same type of dysfunction, regardless of the differences in expression of the interviewees and the particularities of the company or organization.

The horizontal diagnosis aims to list the dysfunctions perceived by all the management and supervisory staff, in order to establish a general and transversal diagnosis of the main dysfunctions of the company. This will be completed by vertical diagnoses which will allow, in a second phase, to involve the base staff as well. Each member of the management and the supervisory staff is a member of a *collaborative training cluster* and is interviewed individually. The whole diagnosis, including the managers' expression, in the form of key ideas illustrated by the *witness sentences,* is presented to all the managers, gathered in the collaborative training clusters.

At least two sectors (departments, services, workshops or agencies) are then subjected to a more concrete vertical diagnosis. This consists of identifying dysfunctions and evaluating the resulting hidden costs. The set of *competency grids* (see 2.1.4 below) for the sector is used to deepen the analysis of the training-job match. Interviews focused on the dysfunctions of the sector are then conducted with each manager and supervisor in the sector. In addition, small group interviews, of 3 or 4 people, with the core staff make it possible to meet with 30 to 60% of the workforce, ensuring that the sample of people is varied in terms of profession, status, seniority, age, gender, etc. The vertical diagnosis is presented to the department's management, and then, in the presence of the management, to the core staff who were interviewed, in order to produce the mirror-effect that stimulates an appetite for change.

2.1.3.2 The participatory focus group to build solutions. A project process, set up to develop solutions and innovative practices, is equivalent to a double learning process, both individual and collective.

The *horizontal project* designates a set of improvement actions aimed at reducing the dysfunctions identified in the horizontal diagnosis and at stimulating the company's strategy. The diagnosis of dysfunctions and the *strategic project* are therefore the *two sources* that feed the search for improvement actions. The horizontal project is developed under the responsibility of the manager with the support of a focus group. The *project team* works alternately in *limited group, plenary group* and *work group.* It meets for a limited time, four times over a quarter, without affecting the usual level of activity. To structure the search for solutions, the key ideas of the *expert opinion* are grouped into 4 to 5 "*baskets* of dysfunctions", each basket corresponding to a *root cause* of dysfunctions is handled by a work group led by a member of the *plenary group.*

The *vertical project* is developed by a focus group, with the sector's line manager being the *project leader.* Work groups led by members of the plenary group make it possible to involve other people (managers, experts and rank-and-file staff) in the change process dynamics.

2.1.3.3 The implementation of improvement actions, a journey towards the expected performance and permanent evaluation as a compass to guide itself. A structured *implementation* of the improvement actions proposed by the different focus groups is decided by the Management, which allocates the necessary resources and sets up a system for evaluating the social, organizational and financial impacts of these actions. These actions will be self-financing by recycling hidden costs into value added, generated by the reduction of dysfunctions.

An in-depth *evaluation of the qualitative, quantitative and financial socio-economic* results is carried out 6 to 12 months after the start of the intervention. It allows us to identify the most *significant achievements* and to evaluate the gains in value added. In-depth interviews are conducted with management, supervisors and rank-and-file staff to identify actions and key results from the perspective of the different categories of actors involved. The *value-added gains* actually observed are compared with the cost of the action. This makes it possible to establish an economic balance that is no longer forecast but real, and to calculate *the return on investment* of the change action carried out by the company. This evaluation has an important impact. It allows the company to become aware of the improvements made and thus regenerates a *new cycle of energy for change* in order to compensate for the erosion, over time, of the effects of the improvement actions, as they have a propensity to decline.

2.1.4 The Implementation of Simple and Shared Management Tools Axis

The structured implementation of improvement actions is facilitated by the use of *six simple and stimulating management tools,* most of which are used by all staff.

The socio-economic management tools, implemented during a change process conducted with the involvement of the organization's stakeholders, allow for better control of operating costs, in particular by partially converting or *recycling* hidden costs into value added. These tools have also been applied to projects involving a variety of organizations, companies and institutions in a given territory, on issues that go beyond the perimeter of a single company, such as the guidance and integration of young people, illiteracy, and the organization of public-private partnerships in the health sector and in territorial animation (Bonnet, 1988; Savall, Zardet, 2005; Savall, Zardet, Noguera, 2004; Savall, Goter, Bondin, 2019). Concrete examples of these socio-economic management tools can be found in the many chapters of this Treatise, which illustrate a wide variety of cases.

2.1.4.1 Orchestrated individual and collective time management. The self-analysis grid and the concrete time management tools (TMT) allow the search for a more efficient structure of time use, by developing individual and collective programming of activity as well as concerted delegation.

2.1.4.2 Competency grid. The Competency Grid (CG) is a synoptic that allows the effective competencies available to a team and its organization to be visualized. It allows the development of an *integrated training plan,* particularly well adapted to each person and to the evolving needs of the team.

2.1.4.3 Strategic Piloting Logbook and stimulating indicators. The Strategic Piloting Logbook (SPL) brings together the qualimetric (qualitative, quantitative and financial) indicators used by each member of the management team to manage the people and activities in their area of responsibility. It allows for the measurement, evaluation and monitoring of sensitive parameters of operational and strategic activities, in order to *make decisions* on the management of these activities.

2.1.4.4 Internal–External Strategic Action Plan (IESAP) and Priority Action Plan (PAP). *The Internal–External Strategic Action Plan (IESAP)* clarifies the organization's strategy over the next three or four years with respect to its stakeholders, i.e., its *external targets* (customers, suppliers, partners, institutions, etc.) and its *internal targets* (leaders and managers to employees and workers). It is updated every year to take into account changes in the relevant environment.

The Priority Action Plan (PAP) is the agreed inventory of actions to be carried out in a six-month period to achieve the priority objectives, after arbitration on priorities and feasibility tests.

2.1.4.5 Periodically Negotiable Activity Contract (PNAC)

The Periodically Negotiable Activity Contract (PNAC) formalizes the priority *objectives* and the means made available to each person in the organization, through a personalized *twice-yearly* dialogue with the direct supervisor. A *variable compensation* bonus is attached, linked to the achievement of a combination of collective, team and individual objectives and self-financed by the periodic recycling of hidden costs into value added.

2.1.5 The Political and Strategic Decisions Axis

In order to be effective, the implementation of these management tools requires the compliance of certain rules of knowledge that have emerged over the course of 47 years of ISEOR's research and intervention:

- the conduct of a process must sustainably *involve* the different categories of actors (personnel or partners) in the construction and implementation of their *management tools.* At the top of the company, it is essential that those in charge define the strategic orientations, the rules of the game for the company's operation and that they validate the *action plans* defined at the managerial level, as well as those that concern several sectors of the company transversally. In each sector of the company, the method uses the *mirror-effect technique.* This allows everyone to become aware of the high cost of dysfunctions and then to design and implement solutions for improvement. This *mirror-effect technique* is also used in experiments on *territories* and issues other than business management. The mirror-effect is very stimulating for action, because *it makes the actors aware* of the problem and facilitates their *appropriation* of the improvement actions;
- the company needs an *external energy input* to identify and recycle its hidden costs and performances, not only because an external eye helps it to better identify such self-financing reserves, but also because it is necessary *to apply specific and structured methods of change management and implementation* of socio-economic innovations;

It should be emphasized that socio-economic intervention is generally accompanied by the implementation of the mission of internal consultants. This not only facilitates the appropriation of the method and tools by the company, but also contributes to the sustainability of the improvement process. The *internal interveners* play the role of socio-economic management consultants in the company, for a limited period of time (about 15% of their working hours), while retaining their usual functions and activities.

The *two conditions for success* that are beyond the control of the external consultant because they depend exclusively on the company's actors can be summarized as follows. It is necessary:

- that the company has a *pilot* (President, CEO, General Manager, Director) with the strategic *will to pilot him/herself* its organization, because this *piloting cannot be delegated*;
- that a certain number of actors in the company have perceived a sort of "*strategic threat*" in the external environment, which encourages them to accept to change their professional practices.

These are the prerequisites for the success of a socio-economic intervention, drawn from the lessons learned by our research team. The other conditions for success emerge during the process of change and are gradually integrated, in a *dynamic of orchestrated organizational learning*, to play a symphony of sustainable global performance.

2.2 Intervention-Research Methodology and the Respective Roles of the Researchers and the Actors in the Company

The Socio-Economic Theory contributes to the methodology of research and its epistemological foundations. Thus, the concept of intervention-research is not the same as that of action research. Indeed, intervention research is based on the recognition of the *impossible neutrality* of the researcher and his/her work of scientific intention, because it has a deliberate societal purpose.

Two movements of scientific progress are activated: *close observation* of observable facts on the one hand and epistemological consolidation on the other, *epistemology* being the analysis of the validity of concepts and theories.

2.2.1 Characteristics of Intervention-Research in Companies: Rigorous and Dynamic Observation of the Object Studied

Intervention-research is characterized by the commitment of researchers to accompany the company in a deliberate process of transformation, as in medical science, and to evaluate the effects (Savall, Zardet, Bonnet, Cappelletti, 2019).

The ISEOR researcher is involved in an organizational project, without abandoning his or her academic identity, ethics and research project. He/she is immersed in the organization, without any desire for neutrality or so-called objectivity (Savall, 1974, 1975a, 1979a; Savall, Zardet, 1987; Moisdon, 1984). He/she interacts with a wide variety of actors, alternating his/her "geopolitical" positions (Savall, Zardet, 1996, 2004). The actors of the enterprise are *ordinary scholars* according to Girin's (1981) wise expression. In cognitive interactivity with researchers, actors implement scientific and technical knowledge, consciously or by reflex. They play different roles: co-producers of knowledge, contributors and providers of information, co-evaluators of research and experimenters of knowledge as end users. Observation shows that research is not the monopoly of professional researchers.

We develop cumulative research that allows us to build a *continuum between fundamental and applied research*, to move from "contemplative" research of phenomena to transformative research (Arendt, 1994), where experimentation is a recognized mode of validation, in the manner of the life and natural sciences. We practice replication, which is the application of the same research protocol over many years by many researchers (Kwesiga, Pattie, 2006). In medicine, for example, it is practiced systematically through very tight control over the quality of research, consisting of observing a common methodological protocol, applied by all researchers across the countries of the world who participate in research recognized by institutions and peers.

2.2.2 *The Role of the Intervener-Researcher in Close Proximity to the Company's Actors*

ISEOR's intervener-researchers ensure an intermittent but regular presence within the organization, equipped with an explicit research strategy involving the co-construction of innovative knowledge with the actor-experimenters. The teamwork of the intervener-researchers facilitates learning and the development of their skills. Pioneering companies are engaging in intervention-research programs that are clearly different from the usual missions of consulting firms. One condition for bringing together practitioners and researchers is to identify together an original managerial problematic, both specific (contingent) and generic, in order to define objectives and a research methodology relevant to both parties (Savall, Zardet, 1996, 2004; Plane, 2000, Buono, Savall, Cappelletti, 2018).

Let us point out here that the communication of concepts and theories, in order to better integrate them into action, uses *metaphors* of deliberate though careful pedagogical intent.

2.2.3 *Proximity to Medical, Clinical, and Fundamental Research*

The experimental approach that has become established in medicine consists of *observing* the initial situation, identifying the protocol and the prescribed "solutions," applying the treatment to patients, before *evaluating* the effects and thus validating the hypotheses through *experimentation* (Savall, Fière, 2007, 2014). From the outset, in 1973, our objective was, in the same spirit, to validate, according to the principle of transformative research, the results of transformations that reveal certain profound properties of the object studied, as well as their impacts on the company or organization.

Indeed, like the human being, the company or *organization is a living being.* The proximity of methods between medical research and intervention-research can be observed on the following points: rigorous observation with explicit research protocols, the desire to better diagnose the patient before adopting a treatment that will allow him or her to cure or mitigate the effects of his or her illness, the continuum between applied and fundamental research, the organization of *research in teams,* and finally the principles of generic contingency, contradictory intersubjectivity and cognitive interactivity.

2.2.4 *Epistemological Consolidation of the Scientific Value of Concepts, Theories, and Methods: Three Pillars of "Generic Constructivism" Proposed by the Socio-Economic Theory*

The three fundamental epistemological principles proposed by *the Socio-Economic Theory* are:

1. *cognitive interactivity,* by which concrete knowledge is elaborated and co-constructed, between researchers and between researchers and practitioners;
2. *contradictory intersubjectivity,* a substitute for the impossible neutrality of research, whereby subjectivities and differences between actors and between researchers are recognized, made explicit and used to construct relevant local generic knowledge.
3. *generic contingency,* recognizing the specific character of each case, as well as the existence of generic elements in each. Our concept of "generic constructivism" makes explicit the lineage of a constructivist epistemology inspired by Piaget (1975, 1988), but applying to the acquisition of collectively shared knowledge and seeking repli-

cable generic knowledge. Cumulative intervention-research allows for the consolidation of generic results through successive iterations of validation.

In a joint research program between management researchers at ISEOR and medical researchers, our concepts above were applied to the case of medical research (Savall, Fière 2010).[5] Here is the synthesis:

Cognitive interactivity means that by making the patient talk, the hospital doctor, practitioner-researcher releases important information to make the diagnosis. If we are not successful, we do not obtain the information necessary to identify the pathology and then to evaluate the effects of the treatment. Information about the detection of certain symptoms can only be obtained with the expression and collaboration of the patient.

The principle of *contradictory intersubjectivity* expresses the fact that it is essential to obtain information from different points of view of actor-witnesses, situated in the field of the object studied. Thus, the patient feels certain things, while other people around him observe other symptoms. It is by gathering this information that we can establish a diagnosis of the pathology and the state of health of the patient. At the treatment stage of the disease, the same phenomenon is observed: the patient must take his/her medication and observe its effects. Without the narrative of the patient and his/her entourage, scientific knowledge cannot be built, because it is very dependent on what the patient agrees to do: does he take his/her medication or not? In medical research protocols, the number of refusals to take medication, or the number of times it was not taken, is carefully noted in order to interpret the relevant information, allowing the description and explanation of the evolution of the pathology and the evaluation of the effectiveness of the treatment.

Generic contingency admits that each case is specific and singular, while seeking a core of knowledge that is not specific, which will be found in other cases.[6] In management sciences, a battle is waged between those who postulate that everything is unique and that it is therefore not useful to look for the 'universal' knowledge, stigmatizing standardization which crushes the finesse of analysis that would be possible through in-depth observation of the unique case. In the opposite camp, the complexity of the object studied is mutilated by simplistic models and algorithms. According to the principle of generic contingency, the cases of patients all have their individuality, but a hard core of what is common to them is sought. This type of study is the basis of therapeutic trials, which are validated by a statistical study, on a population of 100 case-patients, for example.

2.2.5 *Scientific Consultancy, Positioned Between Professional Advice and Intervention-Research*

What is the difference for the company between a contract concluded with a consultant and an intervener-researcher (Savall, 1989)? Consultants are commonly considered as service providers who must "strongly adapt" to their clients. *In contrast,* one of the challenges of an intervener-researcher team is to transform the traditional client/supplier relationship into a balanced, mutually respectful partnership. The team of researchers then becomes a real partner and transparency increases between the two parties involved. The company sometimes even solicits the opinion and advice of the intervener-researchers, based on their scientific expertise, before making decisions in the areas concerned by the intervention-research in progress.

What's the difference for the intervener-researchers? Intervention-Research, also called *scientific consultancy,* is socially useful and explicitly committed research, in line with the idea of the citizen university and *citizen science.* One of the evaluation criteria is the scientific evaluation of satisfaction, by observing how companies and organizations succeed in improving their practices and their socio-economic performance, by applying new knowledge. Methodological rigor, the requirement of specifications negotiated at the outset and regularly evaluated, and the periodic evaluation of the evolution of practices and performance are major criteria for intervention-research and scientific consultancy, in order to ensure the internal and external validity of research results.

2.3 The Evolution of the Socio-Economic Theory Since 1973

Our first fruitful hypothesis to enable us to construct the theory of socio-economic management was to consider that the *management sciences are experimental in nature,* contrary to the generally accepted idea that the humanities and social sciences are of a different nature from the other sciences. We believe that such a difference is a mere postulate and has never been demonstrated.

Our numerous experiments in a wide variety of contexts have allowed us:

- to *corroborate or invalidate* certain hypotheses formulated at the beginning of our research work
- to discover results that were relatively *surprising* compared to our initial intuitions.

This allowed us to identify two categories of surprises related to both obstacles and factors that facilitate change. The longitudinal nature of this research, which lasted several decades, has allowed us to consolidate the validation of our hypotheses.

2.3.1 The Most Spectacular Surprises

They mainly concerned the very *high level of hidden costs* that we calculated, together with thousands of actors in the 2,150 companies and organizations in which our intervention-researches took place.

- The hidden costs of dysfunctions are in the range of 10 to 95% of the turnover of companies or the total budget of organizations, private or public. In the countries of the euro zone, this corresponds to a *loss of financial resources of €20,000 to €70,000 per person per year.*

  Similarly, the level of recycling of hidden costs into recovery of value added allowing the company or organization to self-finance, up to 35 to 55% of the hidden costs calculated during the initial diagnosis.
- Another surprise was the wide variety of generic dysfunctions identified in dialogue with numerous actors and recorded in the expert system software that we created at ISEOR
- 5,021 types of generic dysfunctions were identified and constitute the unique knowledge base created by ISEOR, based on intervention-researches that took place in 72 sectors of activity and 48 countries.
- The level of resistance to change of all actors, without exception, in companies and organizations, including those who wanted and decided on the change strategy, expected to be useful for the survival-development of their company or organization.

2.3.2 The Company or Organization is an Open System, of a Socio-Technical (Emery & Trist, 1960) and Socio-Economic Nature (Savall, 1973, 1974)

Our experiments have shown, from the outset, the relevance and power of the global or systemic approach to the company or organization and its socio-economic performance. We were able to observe the dissemination of activity flows throughout the company, outside the beaten track of the official organization represented by the organizational chart. Similarly, the strong dynamics of *contagion* and propagation of *organizational pathologies*, from one person to another, between two teams or between two levels of responsibility. As early as 1976, we were able to trace the chains of propagation of dysfunction (Savall, 1977a, 1978a, 1979a, 1979b; Savall, Zardet, 1987).

We have also observed two important vectors of the dynamics of change in practices: emulation between the actors, as well as the *act* which proves to be more effective than the word. Both of these factors explain the importance of the example set by those who are most convinced of the value of metamorphosis, in the dissemination of new practices that lead to improvements.

2.3.3 The Pre-Eminence of Human Behavior Over Structures

Without underestimating the importance of structures, the experiments have shown their relative, theoretical and virtual character. They appear as influential, but not determining, *moderating variables* in the process of producing performance.

- The strength of individualistic behavior: the intensity of the lack of reflexes and know-how of teamwork has appeared as an almost universal phenomenon, an important cause of many dysfunctions. The educational system, in teaching and even in the family, is probably a major cause of this.
- The phenomenon of the lack of managerial courage, a sort of rupture between the idea and the intention on the one hand and the act of managing people on the other, consists of a person, whether a manager or not, not taking the risk of displeasing other people in acts of management.

2.3.4 Discovery of the Five Natural Characteristics of Humans That Shed Light on the Phenomenon of Organizational Metamorphosis

The close and long-term observation of professional situations and change actions in a great many companies, of about 110,000 people, over the last 47 years, has made it possible to formulate a micro-theory, derived from socio-economic theory, which makes it possible to understand, on the one hand, the fundamental cause of the very many dysfunctions observed and revealed by the members of the organizations diagnosed, and, on the other hand, the factors that need to be mobilized in order to make a success of the process of change in the company or the organization. Section (1.1.2.4) above presents and develops these five characteristics: all persons are *intelligent, comedian, strategist, disobedient, and amnesiac*.

2.3.5 Generalized Concept of Learning

Our experiments have shown that learning is not an exceptional act that takes place in a particular period of skill acquisition by an inexperienced young person, to prepare for his or her professional life, or by an experienced adult to develop or change his or her profession. The phenomenon of learning can be found in the concrete daily life of organizations, and the learning curve is presented as a key concept in socio-economic theory and management (see §1.1.2.1). Carrying out a non-routine job requires a period of adaptation and the recall of relatively forgotten knowledge. Leading a team towards a new activity implies the acquisition of new technical and orchestration knowledge. Managing an important company project requires the memorization and implementation of know-how, which is not a reflex action and which requires re-learning and measuring its effectiveness and efficiency.

This means that learning is found everywhere in the activities of a company or organization and that quality management of people as well as its effectiveness implies a particular *pedagogical patience*, of reminding of the working methods to facilitate the memorization of the good reflexes by the collaborators, at any level of responsibility that one is, in the company or organization.

When this learning time is not properly ensured, dysfunctions and hidden costs of a high level follow. The return on investment of this learning time has been shown to be very high: between 210 and 4,014%. One hour invested in learning avoids between two and forty hours lost in dysfunction regulation (Savall, Zardet, 2008).

Our experiments have shown that the vast majority of people in professional situations are capable of "taking the permanent elevator": which leads from the abstract to the concrete and vice versa from the concrete to the abstract.

Interactive pedagogy regularly takes this very formative elevator. It is at the heart of an effective change management method, because it allows most people to get involved and be effective in the organizational metamorphosis actions.

2.3.6 Demonstration of the Almost Universal Ability of Humans to Perform Qualimetric Measurements in Their Work Environment

Many authors and practitioners have stated that some things cannot be measured, that they *cannot be quantified.* This is to deny that history shows us that *scientific progress* has consisted in identifying and describing the significant phenomena of the universe and then, progressively with the help of appropriate instruments, in assigning numerical values, albeit imperfect, to these phenomena. Regarding the dysfunctions and hidden costs in companies and organizations, our experiments have shown that every person records, consciously and often unconsciously, information about his or her professional environment. Nearly 3,000 socio-economic diagnoses carried out with the involvement of 110,000 people have shown that it is possible, by means of interviews with witnesses of dysfunctions (directors, managers, employees), to calculate the economic impact, known as hidden costs, with the *same approximation* as the usual compulsory accounting kept by companies. It should be remembered that *it would be impossible to calculate hidden costs without the help of these witnesses of the dysfunctions.*

Our long-term research on the phenomena of *contagion through dysfunctions* demonstrates the transversal character of dysfunctions. They cross all the partitions invented by man, whether they are hierarchical, functional or project-based in organizational design.

As a corollary, it is important to incriminate the archaic representations of the company or organization, in the fields of teaching, professional training and consulting in management and organization of the company, stubbornly segmented into relatively compartmentalized functions. Indeed, these practices do not take into account the observable functioning of companies and organizations which is systemic in nature, as well as its process of generating sustainable socio-economic performance.

As a provisional conclusion, at this stage of the reasoning, our initial hypothesis that the *residual factor of the production function* (Savall, Zardet, 2011a, 2013) could be illuminated by the concept of hidden costs-performance, has been validated thanks to the measurement, unprecedented, of hidden costs in 2,150 companies and organizations.[7] The hidden cost–performance variable is now the missing link between the macro-economic approach of the production function and the evaluation of hidden costs-performance identified in firms and organizations. Malinvaud's team had found a residual of about 50% of the economic value of production, unexplained by the two traditional factors of capital and labor (Carré, Dubois, Malinvaud, 1972). At the level of the firm, our work has made it possible to find a value of hidden costs varying between 10 and 95% of sales.

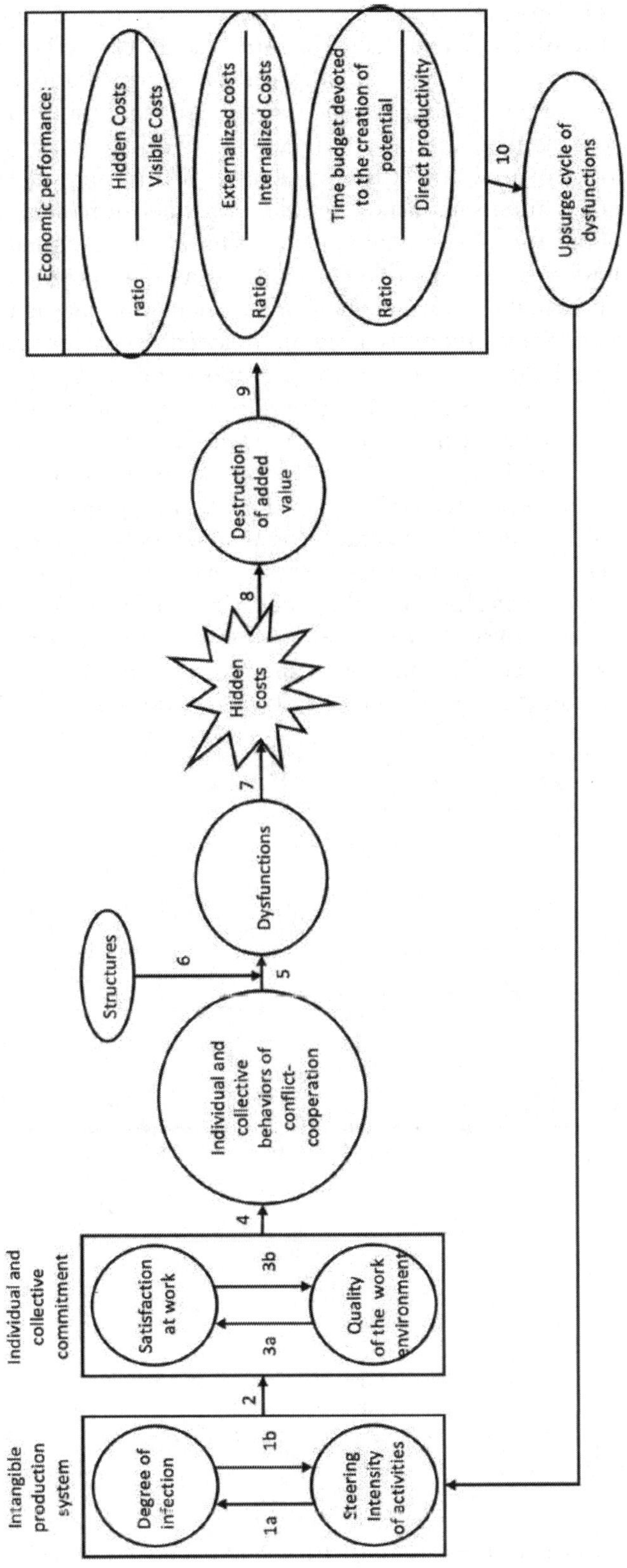

Figure 1.8 Current modeling of the socio-economic theory of hidden costs-performance (Savall, Zardet, 2011a, 2011b, 2013, 2014b)

The multi-level model proposed by socio-economic theory is therefore based on an *isomorphism* hypothesis, from the societal level to the individual level, via the organization and the work team. The current version of our model articulates organizational and individual performance: how does the performance of the individual in an organization and inserted in a work team influence the performance of the firm? It reveals an implicit but fundamental underlying dimension of the model: the variables of a corporate social responsibility (CSR) development policy and its impact on organizational performance.

The construction of the Socio-Economic Theory has followed a cumulative research process, allowing the knowledge gained to be consolidated and advanced according to successive statements. This, together with systematic experimentation, has made it possible to reinforce the robustness of this theory, as it has approached new problems and new fields of investigation, whether it be companies or organizations, or local, regional or national territories, considered as sets of entangled organizations subject to complex phenomena. Schematically, this path of scientific intention centered on the study and *qualimetric modeling* of change processes (A, B, C, D, E... in Figure 1.9) allows, over the years, the creation of new research know-how, incorporated and used in the following processes. Socio-economic intervention is practical, operational and can be applied by both research teams and consulting professionals. This interaction between researchers, management practitioners and consultants is evidence of a conception of the University's societal role and responsibility based on their cooperation and synergy, sources of innovation (Savall, Zardet, 1995, 2001). Like the life and natural sciences, the humanities and social sciences lend themselves well to this scientific path based on the experimentation of concepts and theories (ISEOR, 2003).

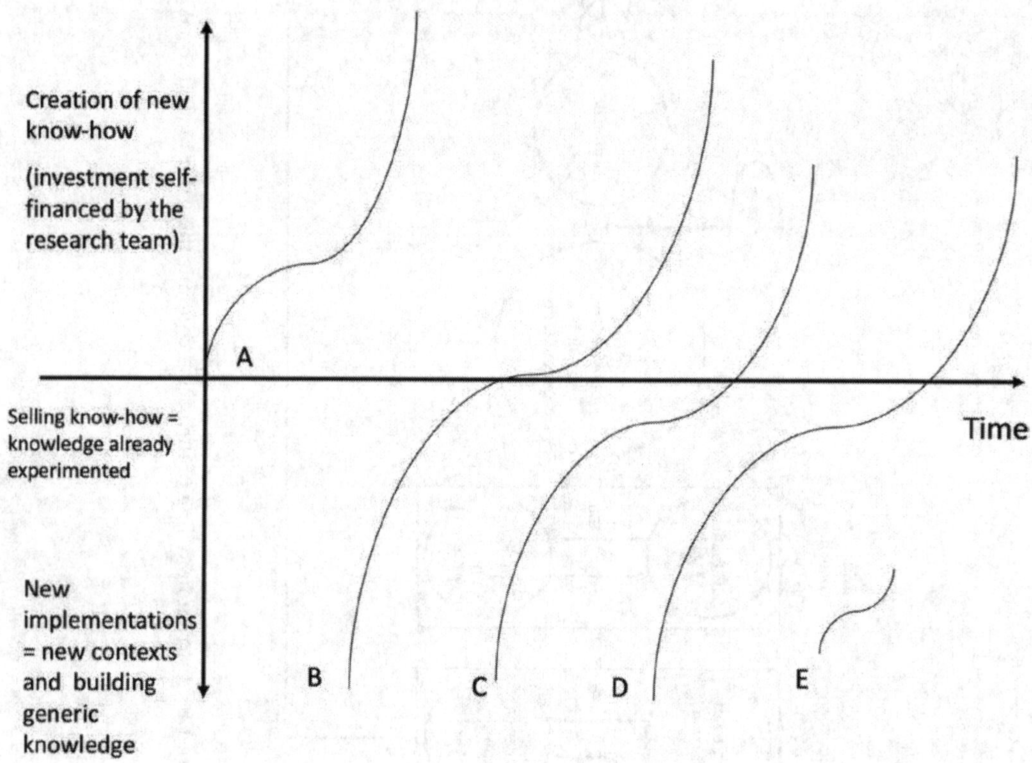

Figure 1.9 The process of creating new knowledge from intervention-researches.

3 PROSPECTS FOR A POSSIBLE SOCIO-ECONOMIC STEERING OF SHARED PROSPERITY

Our multidisciplinary training in economics, management sciences, political sciences, literature and accounting, forged during our studies in higher education, has enabled us to build cognitive reflexes on a transdisciplinary basis. Our self-training, within the framework of our research in these fields, has provided us with a valuable complement from the sociology of work and organizations, applied psycho-sociology and ergonomics. Our view of the knowledge of each of these disciplines has been broadened, with a spirit of openness that has never left us (see summary biographies at the end of the book).

Fascinated by the phenomena that inhabit organizations, whether productive or not, profit-making or not, with material or spiritual heritage, our look has never been confined within the conventional boundaries that separate one organization from another in a given territory, and that separate the different levels of territory from one another.

This transdisciplinary substrate encouraged us to adopt the principle of isomorphism or homothety between the *different levels* of analysis: the individual, the group or the team, the company or the organization, the territories: local/regional/national. We will therefore not enter into the debate, which in our view is sterile, on the difference in approach that should be adopted according to the level of analysis at which one is situated. Too strict a division constitutes an obstacle to the progression of knowledge. What seemed interesting to us in order to understand the complex universe, especially the economic and social one, is to study the *links* that exist between the different elements that make it up. The knowledge that we are looking for is found in the "elevator" that links the individual, his or her team, the company, the local territory and then the regional and national territory.

3.1 Some Lessons to be Learned From ISEOR's Experiments

In the special issue of the journal "Revue Française de Gestion" devoted to the theme of research valorization, we summarized the main results that have an impact on managerial practices in companies and organizations (Savall, Zardet, Bonnet, Cappelletti, 2019). Our intervention-researches carried out for 47 years, in 48 countries, in 2,150 companies and organizations, with the involvement of 110,000 people, have constituted our vast research laboratory. Here are the results of our research in a nutshell.

3.1.1 Extending the Scope of the Hidden Cost–Performance Concept

Hidden costs constitute an intangible source of *self-financing capacity* for the socio-economic development of a company or organization. They represent a potential of *socio-economic productivity*, which can be mobilized without degrading the conditions of professional and personal life. Hidden costs provide an approximate measure of the informal *economic power* of individuals and teams within an organization. It is a power that is often *involuntary*, of *destruction* of economic value, of value added, despite the action of the formal organized powers of a company or organization.

At the level of a local, regional, national or international territory, hidden costs can be identified and measured, with the same approximations as national economy indicators such as GDP, in the form of *hidden macro-costs*. Thus, we have published an estimate of the hidden cost of absenteeism in France to the tune of *108 billion euros in 2020* [study conducted for the Sapiens Institute (Savall, Cappelletti, in newspaper "Aujourd'hui en France," November 2019)].

3.1.2 Performance Paradigm Shift: Contractualization or Subordination?

Our theory of the five natural characteristics of the human being has been abundantly validated by close scientific observation of the behaviors of a very large number of actors in professional situations and in processes of change taking place in a wide variety of contexts: 48 countries, 72 sectors of activity, 2,150 companies and organizations of private, public or associative status. Our experiments have made it possible to *contradict the simplistic models* of behavior underlying many theories, both in the field of economics and management. The representations provided by these established theories, which are the basis of teaching and professional training, accommodate the reductive model of the subordination of employees to decision-makers at all levels in the organization. Thus, managers are supposed to follow the directives of the general manager, senior managers are supposed to follow the directives of the managers, middle managers and supervisors are supposed to follow the directives of the managers and then, in turn, technicians, blue-collar workers, and rank-and-file employees follow the orders given by the supervisors. This theoretical *hierarchical scheme* is contradicted by the abundance of multiple and innumerable dysfunctions that we have observed in organizations and that have been revealed by all these categories of people.

Subordination is a legal presupposition, a principle that is consistent in the exceptional situations where the law intervenes to resolve conflicts in an organization. This *legal fiction* has its raison d'être in resolving relatively serious disputes in courts of law or in situations of regulated conciliation. This principle, according to which the organization of hierarchical relations allows a group of people, a team, an establishment, a company or a group of companies to function, is reassuring but *unrealistic.* The somewhat rigorous *observation* of *behaviors* in professional situations, within organizations, invites us to *look for another principle* to explain by which psycho-sociological and technical mechanisms, a company or organization reaches its objectives, obtains a financial result in general positive, in spite of the strength of the five natural characteristics of the human.

Our hypothesis, largely validated by numerous experiments, close and rigorous observation of the actors in action, as well as the evaluation of the socio-economic results of the activities, is that there exists a hybrid *contractualization system,* partly formalized but above all informal and effective. Thus, the production of a good or a service, its provision to a client or a user, constitutes a system of innumerable *micro-negotiations* between the people who produce or sell and distribute, by means of processes that constitute a chain of acts, in the sense of the *value chain.* The concatenation of these acts implies numerous permanent negotiations on the ground, in the team, the workshop, the office. In so-called productive organizations, the thread of these negotiations is the production or distribution process of goods and services.

Dysfunctions appear as deficiencies, failures, non-quality of these micro-negotiations that *have not reached their goal,* i.e., orthofunctioning. The *TFW virus* is the cause of *53%* of the dysfunctions observed. Indeed, the three organizational principles it defends: *hyper-specialization,* the *design/realization dichotomy,* and the *depersonalization* of processes and the concrete organization of work constitute obstacles to the development and success of micro-negotiations, which, according to the Socio-Economic Theory, are the main factor in performance.

Actions to improve sustainable socio-economic performance are oriented towards *stimulating* these micro-negotiations, which constitute a real "breathing space" for the company or living organization. The hidden costs measure the destruction of economic value due to these "negotiation-breathing" accidents.

Thus, the good practices of respecting the quantities ordered in a delivery to a customer, producing the required level of quality, respecting a deadline, reaching the level of productivity required by the company, will be well served if all the people involved in the processes concerned *mutually adjust* their productive behavior and mobilize their skills to do well. In all these cases, the system of micro-negotiations generated by the *cooperation required* by the inescapable division of labor will have functioned correctly. This is the statement of *our contractual approach to performance.*

3.1.3 Unprecedented Value Added of Intangible Investments

For two centuries, *investment* has become the engine of prosperity and economic progress. Industrial and material investment dominated until the last few decades. The *calculation of profitability and return on investment* has been mainly applied to material and technological investment. The models of investment choice mainly emphasize the calculation of forecasted profitability of material elements. Our work has shown that *intangible investment in the qualitative development of human potential (IIQDHP)* has a very high rate of return and that it constitutes a very interesting adjunct to material investment since it also makes it possible to increase the return on investment of the couple [material investment + intangible investment].

Any theory tends to become, over time, a more or less dogmatic ideology and ends up being deviated from its substance and its original purpose. Thus, the production function $Y = f(K * T)$ could initially be interpreted as representing the complementarity of capital and labour factors (Carré, Dubois, Malinvaud, 1972). However, another use based on a different interpretation eventually prevailed in the history of this theory. It is the *substitution* of the capital factor for the labor factor that has won the historical battle. Thus, capital is no longer really the tool that increases human productivity, because the machine has acquired the reputation of having intrinsic productivity thanks to a simplistic mathematical formula manipulated by the users. Certainly, the machine has advantages in the eyes of some: less disobedient than humans, more docile if maintained, but it is not very creative, whatever the promises of artificial intelligence. Moreover, humans feed the market with their varied and evolving demand, thanks to their decision-making and purchasing power, while the machine is inert and... "doesn't go to the market to buy"!

3.2 Macro-Economic Foundations of the Theory of Human Potential as the Only Active Factor of Value Creation

Our eight years of research on macroeconomic theory and the history of economic thought, between 1965 and 1973, have had a profound impact on our scientific vision of economic activity, especially under the influence of the great Spanish economist Bernácer. This physicist, a visionary economist, proposed as early as 1922 a theory, of great topicality, a century later, on the explanation of crises, chronic unemployment, related to the phenomenon of hoarding of dormant savings and speculative investments that dry up the irrigation, through money and purchasing power, of the whole economic activity (Bernácer, 1922, 1945; Robertson, 1940; Savall, 1973, 1975b, 2012, 2018; Gephart, 2018ab).

Equipped with the importance of the *time factor*, so present in Bernácer's theory, we began the construction of the socio-economic theory in 1973 (Savall 1974, 1977a, 1981). This allowed us to identify the ephemeral nature of the effects of structures and behaviors, the *chronic resurgence* of dysfunction and *value destruction* in the form of hidden costs, and the obsolescence of action models, management techniques and economic policies.

Bernácer's contributions to our work on economics and management were complemented by those of the great French economist François Perroux. François Perroux's (1975) dynamic approach to economic theory, provided us in particular with *the concept of "active unit* capable of shaping its environment through its energy" as well as the dialectical concept of *conflict-cooperation* that characterizes economic and social relations (Perroux, 1979; Savall, 2013).

3.2.1 Critique of Some Key Concepts in Macroeconomics

3.2.1.1 The two factors, capital and labor, of value creation in the so-called production function. The *Socio-Economic Theory,* the conceptual framework of the socio-economic *management* method, contributes to the understanding of the mechanisms of economic *prosperity,* crisis and chronic underemployment, beyond the sole perimeter of the firm. It is based on the *pre-eminence of human potential* over capital in the process of creating economic value.

The Socio-Economic Theory (Savall, 1974, 1975a; Delors, 1975; Perroux, 1979; Ansoff, 1981; Savall, Zardet, 1987; Savall, Zardet, Bonnet, 2000; Boje, Rosile, 2003; Péron, Péron, 2003; Buono, Savall, 2007, 2015; Sorensen, Yaeger, 2012; Conbere, Heorhiadi, 2018) considers that the only *active factor* in the creation of value is the Human Potential. The history of economic thought has highlighted the three main factors of economic value creation: capital, labor and nature. However, these three factors are not of the same kind. Nature is a given exogenous to humans. Capital is an accumulation of economic value, mainly created by humans. Work represents the human activity that transforms nature and uses capital as a tool for producing economic value. Some economic theories have privileged the value of work, considering that any incorporation of work in a good or a service creates value. In reality, it is the *matching* of a good or a service with a demand based on the need of a consumer that *ultimately* attributes its value to this good or service. In fact, stocks, never sold or distributed to consumers, lose their economic value.

3.2.1.2 Financial capitalism versus entrepreneurial capitalism. Bernácer proceeds to a non-Marxist critique of financial capitalism, based on a radical critique of the rent and the speculation, a kind of economic predation that leads him to condemn the interest of capital but to rehabilitate entrepreneurial profit.

In the continuity of Bernácer's work, who was also the director of studies at the Bank of Spain, we consider that investment or disinvestment must take into account the *integral—or global—performance* of an organization and make a *qualimetric* evaluation of it in order to make decisions for sustainable development. However, accounting and financial systems, in their dominant conception, maintain the ephemerality of performance. They do not encourage maintaining or developing performance over medium and long periods (more than one year). *Entrepreneurial capitalism,* creator of enterprises, products and jobs, shrinks, becomes discouraged, lacks financing, as financing is *diverted to the strings of* relatively sterile *speculative bubbles,* generated by the overabundant influx of errant capital that hypertrophies the speculative spheres and mechanisms (Bernácer, 1922; Savall, 1973, 1975b, 2012, 2018). On the contrary, the lack of capital willing to invest in a real and sustainable way in *productive circuits,* caused by the excessive attractiveness of *speculative* markets, condemns companies to underdevelopment or mutilation, due to the lack of financing for truly productive activities.

3.2.2 Should We Choose Between a Macroeconomic Approach and a Microeconomic or Management Approach? Both are Necessary and so are Mutually Linked to Understand Sustainable Value Creation

Having appreciated what the macro-economic approach brings, which is very useful for piloting the economic and social prosperity of territories, and convinced of what *proximity* allows, within an organization, within a space and a perimeter more concentrated than a territory, our research in economics and management has shown that the two approaches are indispensable and complementary, as each feeds the other. The example of the calculation of GDP, a macro-economic indicator rooted in the accounting indicators of companies, offers a good illustration.

In our opinion, the macro-economic approach has not been equipped with suitable instruments to constitute a reliable observatory of the economic activity of the territories. After our doctorate in economics, we were convinced by the limits of remote observation, indeed one can see other planets thanks to sophisticated instruments, or even one can observe mountains from a distance, but not microbes. The observation of viruses requires proximity and special instruments. By analogy, it is within organizations, at a short distance from people and their activities that we have been able to observe for almost half a century the numerous dysfunctions and the destruction of value that they cause in the form of hidden costs.

It was not a good idea to separate economic sciences and management sciences at the scientific level. The scientific fertilization of economic and management theories requires a reciprocal openness that the movement of matching, then distancing, then matching again and so on, will allow for a better observation of the relevant phenomena of these two *sui generis* inseparable levels: the activity on a territory and the management of the organizations that compose it.

In short, at the end of our research in macroeconomics, in 1973, this level of analysis appeared to us to be unsuitable for the effective management of economic and social prosperity. In the animation of economic activity in the territories, the primacy of the firm as a crucible for the creation of economic and social value appears.

The last chapter of this treatise will present the concept of *Socially Responsible Capitalism* as a coherent framework for socio-economic management, as well as the notion of societal responsibility of the individual, the family, the organization, and the local, regional and national territory. Illustrating the principle of isomorphism, the HCVAVC indicator (hourly contribution to value added on variable cost), calculated at the scale of a company, will be assimilated to a "nano-GDP" at the scale of a nation. It could be used as an indicator to measure the evolution of social responsibility at these different levels.

CONCLUSION

Our scientific research program has focused on socio-economic theory and the management methods that have been derived from it for over half a century. Its objective was to demonstrate that an economic regime and a system of management of organizations taking into account *human potential* could ensure sustainable economic and social prosperity, by being at least as competitive as the regimes and methods that have historically succeeded one another and been established in society.

This research has produced concomitantly a *theory of management* that has been extensively tested in a variety of sectoral and national contexts, a *theory of knowledge* with scientific intent based on a *theory of integrated epistemology*, and a *theory of interactive pedagogy* as a lever for change, organizational transformation and sustainable prosperity.

This Treatise on Socio-Economic Theory and Management brings together 113 chapters written by our partners and witnesses to this vast international research program: professional user practitioners and academics: teachers and researchers. The book presents these main theoretical contributions as well as pragmatic contributions rooted in these experienced theories.

The main conceptual keys are *the visible and the hidden*, the holistic approach of the enterprise or organization as well as sustainable performance, completed by dialectical conceptual pairs: conflict-cooperation, social-economic, dysfunction-orthofunction, static-dynamic.

At the time of the COVID–19, when the exacerbation of health, social, political and economic crises enhances awareness of the need to renew our practices in the economic and social world, by intensifying innovation, the Socio-Economic Theory and the management method that results from it offer perspectives that are both innovative and pragmatic. They remind us, in a kind of human and social ecology approach, that the *human being is part of nature* and deserves as much interest nowadays as the respect of the physical and climatic environment. Questioning models, theories, principles, methods and other artifacts and then reconstructing them is probably a salutary and feasible action. From then on, the notion of economy will cease to appear as a burdensome constraint and will regain its source *altruistic* dimension, i.e., the creation of value to be shared with other people, of which it has been unfortunately deprived.

NOTES

1. See also Section 1.2.3.3 "Hidden Outsourced Costs"
2. See Chapter 22 Pascal Pasquier & Amandine Savall.
3. See General references annex at the end of this Treatise
4. See Chapter 3, Harbi, Savall, Zardet, & Ziani
5. See chapter 32, Thiébaut & Fière
6. The association of the two dialectical terms *contingency* and *generic* translates the idea that the notion of contingency recognizes specificity and that this is compatible with the search for generalization of knowledge that is the very definition of science.
7. See below Section 3.2.1, "Critique of some key concepts in macroeconomics"

Note: The general references to socio-economic management theory (SEAM) reported in the body of the text of the chapters (such as Savall, Zardet, . . .) appear in the appendix at the end of this Treatise and not in the specific references of each chapter.

PART II

THE ORGANIZATION OF THE ISEOR RESEARCH CENTER, PIVOT OF AN INTERNATIONAL NETWORK (CAPITALIZATION, VALIDATION, AND DIFFUSION OF SCIENTIFIC AND PRACTICAL KNOWLEDGE IN MANAGEMENT)

This page intentionally left blank.

CHAPTER 2

JUNIOR INTERVENER-RESEARCHERS AT THE ISEOR RESEARCH CENTER

Discovery and Integration Process

Pierrick Govart and Suzon Roche

ABSTRACT

This chapter presents a four-handed testimony from two researchers newly integrated by the ISEOR research center after respectively 20 months and 6 months of internship. They present the story of their first months of integration, their surprises and the specificities of the working methods of the research center. In particular, they describe how they learned to set an example, how they sought to strike a balance between autonomy and cooperation, and how they analyzed the induction process and its impact.

INTRODUCTION: WHY CHOOSING TO WORK AT THE ISEOR RESEARCH CENTER

The first author is an intervener-researcher who always had the project of becoming a management consultant. She has followed the entire graduate program in socio-economic approach to management since the end of her bachelor degree. She was convinced by the method taught by the ISEOR's intervener-researchers as they used to devote two to three days per week with client companies to put into practice the methods and tools of the socio-economic approach to management. She began to practice on her own and in focus groups and she could observe their positive impacts. Then, she joined the ISEOR research center for an internship at the beginning of her first year of the master's program.

SEAM Treatise, pages 47–51

The second intervener-researcher spent a dozen years as deputy managing director in a small company. During his first year of master program, he conducted a socio-economic intervention and he also been convinced by the impacts and relevance of the methods and tools of the socio-economic approach to management. These achievements convinced him to join ISEOR to conduct interventions on a larger scale, which he did during his second year of the graduate program.

1 AT A SCHOOL OF EXAMPLARITY: PRACTICE FIRST PRIOR TO ADVISING

1.1 Being Immersed in Methodological Humility

What struck us first upon our start at the ISEOR research center was the high level of productivity enabled by a meticulous orchestration of work methods and communication, coordination and cooperation mechanisms. The first day gave the feeling of discovering a new dimension of space-time. We also had to quickly learn a new language, the discovery of a lexicon considered as the first buoy of the junior intervener-researcher. It is useful to remind ourselves of this learning period when meeting face to face with actors from client companies and organizations, as they also learn some of this language. We have also relearned how to use a calendar, a tool that we thought we had mastered until now.

1.2 Learning to Steer (ourselves)

As junior intervener-researchers, we are required to steer ourselves at the kick-off of our own integration process. We had to anticipate and prepare the stages of our integration, training needs, and the content and level of our activity. This guidance, coupled with the management tools presented in the third part of this chapter, allowed us to quickly take up responsibility. We never felt we were spectators of our induction, but rather the primary actors.

1.3 Preparation and Capitalization

Prevention is better than cure as preventing dysfunctions is often much less time-consuming than regulating them. Each intervener-researcher must therefore learn a key practice of the profession: getting prepared. In order for a "play" not to turn into an improvisation session, a comedian has to prepare his/her script. Having prepared the script enables each comedian to harmoniously find his/her position and role in the play.

The counterpart of the preparation is capitalization. It is implemented after each training session through writing a summary note. Once assembled, all the notes constitute an integrated training manual that is built up on an ongoing manner. Capitalization also takes place after an intervention operation. It is beneficial to both the client who keeps track of outstanding achievements and to the intervener-researchers who may replicate best practices identified with other clients.

1.4 Action Taking

During our previous professional experience, the tool that had most convinced the CEO during the year-long intervention was the decision sheet (Savall & Zardet, 1987, 1995). This management tool fosters transition from decision to action. At the ISEOR center, decision sheets are filled in at each and every meeting. It enhances the commitment of the actors to implement decisions, and whenever needed the negotiation of the necessary means, in particular in terms of time budget.

2 STRIKING A BALANCE BETWEEN AUTONOMY AND COOPERATION

2.1 Team Organization: Welcome to the Matrix Organizational System

The ISEOR research center has chosen a matrix organization, which may seem surprising for a structure of about thirty employees. Each intervener-researcher, even when a newest recruit, is a member of a team led by a "vertical" team leader who ensures that the workload of the members of his or her team is feasible and help them manage their workplan. Team leaders also have to listen to the intervener-researchers' requests for training and for vacations.

Each team member is also involved in several project teams, led by an activity manager for each intervention-research "site." These teams are set up for the completion of a service or a mission, and are disbanded at the end of the mission, after a few months or a few years.

Finally, on the day of his or her arrival, each junior intervener-researcher is assigned a mentor, who is neither his or her vertical team leader, nor his or her work site activity manager. Mentor's role is to welcome the junior, to train him/her on the functioning and procedures of the ISEOR center as well as the methodological habits required for his/her integration.

Such an organization requires absolute rigor due to the multiplicity of actors. But this rigor has the advantage of encouraging us to get prepared to any meeting and to make it efficient. Preparation can be less formal when dealing with a single contact person and not asking too many questions.

2.2 Diversity of Activities

One of the main interests of the profession of intervener-researcher at the ISEOR center is the variety of activities that it offers: intervention-research for different clients, collaborative training, publications, international development activities of the socio-economic approach to management, teaching, etc. As newcomers, junior intervener-researchers also benefit from a wide array of activities, even when beginning as interns and they are quickly involved into one or more intervention research "work sites." In our case, we started to pilot interventions on our own in very small businesses within four months after the beginning of our internship contract. Intervener-researchers also cooperate in publications. Such teamwork allows to step back from our work and often to discover the history of the company, its key actors or the evolution of the socio-economic theory since its creation almost half a century ago.

2.3 Diversity of Actors and Importance of Teamwork

Our most important finding over the two years of the university graduate program in socio-economic management at iaelyon school of management, was the experience of the effectiveness of organized teamwork. These two years had been a learning process of the symphonic discipline practiced at the ISEOR center.

In general, teamwork is dedicated to high value-added activities. The more people are around the table, the more value we believe must be created. But at ISEOR, we also use teamwork as a lever for action taking and we are used to teaming up when we don't feel like performing a specific activity such as writing a paper. Indeed, motivation is much greater when not being isolated.

At the ISEOR center, the practice of interaction is an ingrained methodological reflex. These interactions take place within structured mechanisms, without being a pretext for reducing informal communication. At the ISEOR center *warm communication* is advocated as it is beneficial to enhance the quality of communication and master dysfunctions as opposed to our previous experience, sending dozens of emails per week to our colleagues, even while they were close and had time available for a high-quality exchange.

3 INVESTING IN THE POTENTIAL OF JUNIOR RESEARCHERS

3.1 Sustainable Integration

As candidates, we very quickly got the feeling that the research center aims at loyalty. Conducting three to five job interviews for an internship contract in a structure with about thirty employees is far from commonplace. The tone of the interview was quite pragmatic. It was not a question of showing off one's best side by hiding the dust under the carpet. The emphasis is on the difficulties that we might encounter, particularly in adapting to work methods.

From the very start, the vertical team leader gave us the feeling that we were being listened to. At each stage, exhaustive notes were systematically taken. This listening behavior didn't not stop with the note-taking. Everything that was said was dealt with, even in the long term, even when we ourselves had forgotten what was said as the integration process was structured while flexible. For example, it was common for the new employee to update either the training manual or the scheduling of an itemized operation chart. This is a document that specifies the steps, people and times for each step. The milestones of the integration process were monitored with the sponsor, the vertical team leader and the top management to structure the integration and strengthen ownership to the company.

The ultimate proof of the willingness to invest in the potential of new researchers is the signing of a periodically negotiable activity contract (PNAC). PNAC is a management tool aimed at formalizing the priority objectives and the resources made available to each person in the company. The achievement of the PNAC objectives results in a bonus (Savall & Zardet, 1987). It is constructed, negotiated and signed with the vertical team manager, in cooperation with the activity managers. It is also an initiation to negotiation.

3.2 Meaning and Coherence

What probably most confirmed our motivation to continue working at the ISEOR center after our internship was, on the one hand, the meaning given to the work and, on the other hand, the *coherence* between words and actions. Indeed, ISEOR center is a company where managers are not only explaining *how to do* things, but take the time to explain the *why* and give real meaning to the work. This commitment to explaining the basis, the reason, the rationale behind a gesture, a method, a tool, a product or a concept is a considerable motivating factor.

And not only does ISEOR explain why things should be done in a certain way in companies, but we are used to practicing what "we preach." The high level of consistency between words and deeds is therefore also an important motivating factor.

3.3 Heuristics and Interactive Pedagogy

There is no knowledge without doing since skills are acquired through practice. Thus, at the ISEOR center, training requires *doing*. This is why we immediately put the methods and tools into practice, and why we were quickly involved in the field in front of clients. This approach was accompanied by the right to make mistakes and the duty to be rigorous. As new employees, we felt a real sense of benevolence, not complacency. Thus, at the beginning of our recruitment, we were surprised by the impression that the company had more confidence in us than we had in ourselves.

3.4 Ongoing Integrated Training

At the ISEOR center, training activities are integrated. It is carried out in specific sessions, but it is also everywhere, at all times, embedded in the background of all the activities. For example, a backing operation with two intervener-researchers would lead to a mutual contradictory evaluation. The control and the "OK for print", i.e., regarding a diagnosis before the presentation of the mirror-effect in a company, are also conducive to the transmission of pedagogical messages by the management to the intervener-researchers. The advanced seminars represent two full days per semester and they are also privileged opportunities for integrated training.

CONCLUSION

One can be convinced that the integration of newcomers to ISEOR is an effective process, when one considers that the first researcher who initiated this chapter was the sponsor of the other co-author approximately one year after her own recruitment, and that the second researcher was himself the sponsor of a new trainee researcher only three months after his own recruitment.

CHAPTER 3

A TAMED DIGITALIZATION PROCESS TO SUPPORT THE DEVELOPMENT OF THE SOCIO-ECONOMIC APPROACH TO MANAGEMENT

Nouria Harbi, Henri Savall, Véronique Zardet, and Ridha Ziani

ABSTRACT

SEGESE software is a major IT application designed at ISEOR since 1987 to support the socio-economic diagnoses operations. The design method of this application and the key role of the users in the initial development and in the ongoing enrichment of the knowledge base for 35 years are key and original characteristics. This tool illustrates the principle of a "tamed" digitalization, the adaptations of roles and working methods of computer experts and user-experts in socio-economic management.

The evolution of computer science has been continuous since the 1950s, both in terms of hardware and methodology. This science has moved from the large "mainframe" systems to the personal computer, thanks to the miniaturization of electronic components, which has allowed to reduce the size of the hardware and increase its performance and power. Design and development methods began to take into account the needs of users, integrating them later in the process of technological change. Indeed, it was necessary to wait for the implementation of project management methods and to become aware that the involvement of IT users is essential, not only to avoid psychosociological problems linked to resistance to change, but also to involve them in all stages of the projects, the role of users being essential in the needs analysis, testing, validation and acceptance phases.

SEAM Treatise, pages 53–61

This chapter presents our 35 years of project management experience developing computer applications at ISEOR (Zardet, Harbi, 2007). We have designed and developed a business application SEGESE (expert system in socio-economic management) with several variants, as well as several other management applications: socio-economic management control, contact management, etc. This chapter emphasizes the role of the end-user, who is not limited to acceptance, but enriches the knowledge base and makes the applications evolve during their practice.

1 PRESENTATION OF THE SEGESE SOFTWARE

1.1 Functional Description

SEGESE is a WEB application, developed since 1986 by the ISEOR research center in cooperation with the INSA de Lyon computer science team directed by Professor Jacques Kouloumdjian (Zardet, Harbi, 2007). It has been developed to model the knowledge acquired on the functioning of companies. It is structured in the form of a tree of themes, sub-themes, sub-sub-themes and key ideas related to the dysfunctions of companies.

In 2021, the database is made up of approximately 5,600 key ideas, divided into 6 themes, 48 sub-themes and 270 sub-sub-themes. This *generic* tree structure was built by capitalizing on more than 2,000 cases of companies and organizations and accumulating knowledge as SEGESE was used, by carrying out horizontal, vertical and integral socio-economic diagnoses (Savall & Zardet, 1987). The user's role is to isolate extracts previously selected from his exhaustive note-taking of the interviews—the "*field-note quotes*" expressed by the actors—and then to classify them in the themes/sub-themes/sub-sub-themes/key ideas tree. He/she then proceeds to classify the sentences, considered as contextual knowledge, in the *generic* knowledge base of the software. This approach allows him to build the *mirror-effect* (Figure 3.1), which allows the actors who have expressed themselves to validate the user's interpretation of their expressions.

This interactive method allows the *specific* and contextual ideas of the actors to be compared with the *generic* ideas chosen by the user, who knows the context of the company. The analysis of the actors' expressions confronts the user with a difficulty inherent to qualitative information, that of *imprecision, or even semantic instability* (Krief and Zardet, 2013). Indeed, in the same company, the same word can have different meanings depending on the people who use it, or even depending on the times at which the same person expresses himself/herself. An automatic content analysis that cannot integrate the specificities of the context would inevitably give erroneous results. SEGESE allows the user to create new key ideas to address specific issues. Simple quantitative treatments are possible, to "express the meaning of qualitative materials and increase their cognitive value added" (Savall and Zardet, 2004): frequencies of expression of dysfunctions by theme, sub-theme, sub-sub-theme and key idea or by population of actors.

However, since these were semi-structured interviews within the framework of a socio-economic diagnosis, a lexical analysis that would be limited to quantitative descriptors would be inappropriate. Indeed, the phenomena of "obsessed fixed ideas" and "taboos" (Savall & Zardet, 1996, 2004) during dysfunction interviews are such that the frequency of expression of a dysfunction cannot be equated with its real importance within the organization. Moreover, our research, in close interaction with the field, has taught us that, in order to appropriate the results produced by a third party, the actors, whether researchers or not, need a traceability that allows them to appreciate what interpretation was made of their discourse

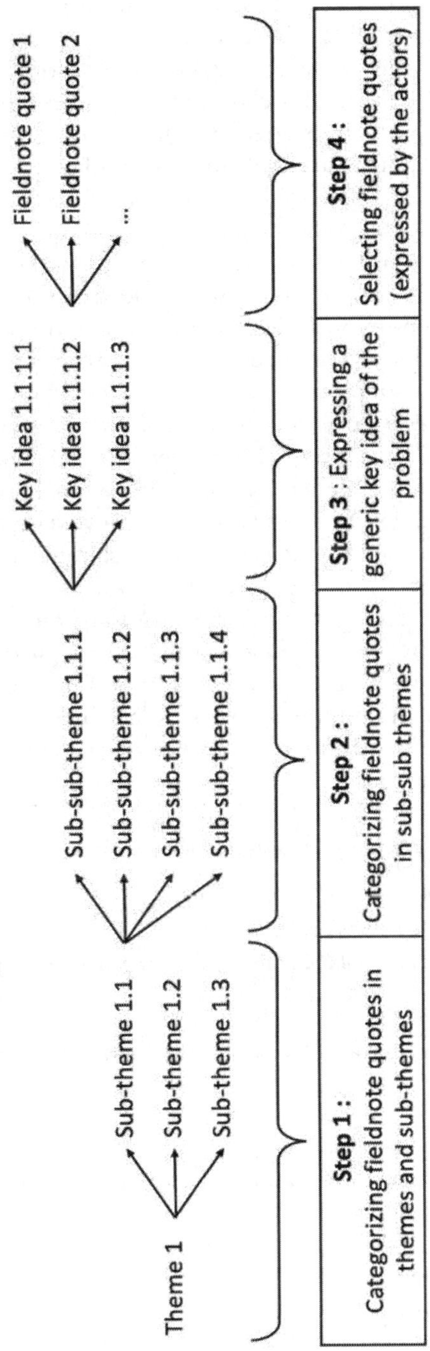

Figure 3.1 Tree structure and stages in the construction of the mirror-effect.

and by what "mechanisms" this third party led to the results presented. From this point of view, no other data analysis software provides, to our knowledge, sufficient traceability between the "raw" materials and the results of the analysis.

It is in this spirit that the SEGESE software was designed with the primary goal of restoring a "mirror-effect" image (Figure 3.2) to the actors.

It helps the users to organize their materials, structure their notes, carry out their processes and analyze the situation, but it is above all built to be presented to the interviewees of the field. The interface between the key idea and the witness sentence allows the latter to check, thanks to the traceability, the quality of the reformulation made by the user, from the original words or expressions. This constitutes a form of quality control by the actor-practitioners (Savall and Zardet, 2004). The re-ordering of discourse by SEGESE generates, in practice, a very good interaction. On the one hand, because the *mirror-effect* highlights the ideas shared by the majority as well as the "minority" ideas; on the other hand, because the key ideas, especially when they express dysfunctions, are better accepted by the actors when they are associated with witness sentences emanating from themselves and...which they cannot therefore reject. The interest and objective of the diagnosis are twofold. On the one hand, it establishes a very precise inventory of the dysfunctions perceived and expressed by the actors. On the other hand, it is essential to involve the stakeholders in the diagnosis phase, before mobilizing them in the change phase, which often generates a certain reluctance on the part of the stakeholders. The fact that the improvement actions stem from the dysfunctions identified and expressed by the stakeholders significantly reduces their resistance during the implementation of these actions.

In addition, the results produced by the SEGESE software encourage the interaction sought between intervener-researchers and field workers, through the very structuring of the presentation of the results. SEGESE thus appears to be a tool for producing a medium that encourages "interactive communication" between different actors. The software is easy to use as it has been designed through the principles of classification of the manual

Working Conditions (*theme*)

- **Equipment and Supplies (*sub theme*)**

  Difficulties obtaining supplies (*key idea of dysfunction*)

  "We are going to open a job center, but invitation cards have not been delivered yet." (field note quote)

  Lack of computer equipment

  "There is a real lack of computer equipment at the headquarter as well as in the regional sites."

- **Working Hours (*sub theme*)**

  Working hours are not adapted (sometimes)

  "Working hours are detrimental to productivity (e.g., some employees are allowed to start at 7:30 a.m. while clients only show up at 10:00 a.m."

  "There is a tradition of starting at 7:30 a.m. while there is no client until at least 8:30 a.m. As a result, there is a one-hour idle as compared with those have other work schedule.

  "At the supervisory and management levels, leeway granted to employees hinders employees' workload planning."

Figure 3.2 Example of "mirror-effect" results obtained using SEGESE software.

approach that was used by the ISEOR researchers before its creation. It is, therefore, very close to manual cutting.

1.2 Technical Description of SEGESE

SEGESE is an application developed within the framework of a research project initiated in 1985 in collaboration between two partners: INSA Lyon and its computer science research team directed by Professor Jacques Kouloumdjian, and ISEOR, a management research center directed by Professor Henri SAVALL. The objective of the project was to apply artificial intelligence techniques to the field of human resources management, based on the study of different types of knowledge representation and expert system development tools.

A first prototype was created in 1986 within the framework of a management research master program internship with the Prolog language, in order to study the feasibility of the project and define the specifications of the tool. This model was consolidated by a prototype, within the framework of a doctoral thesis in computer science (Harbi, 1990), developed with the mixed chain inference engine GURU. The prototype was tested and validated by ISEOR researchers in 1987, by carrying out 16 diagnoses for the food company Belin, which allowed the application to be consolidated. Several full-scale test applications followed with Giat Industries in 1990 (40 diagnoses), La Poste in 1990 (15 diagnoses), Lenôtre in 1992 (10 diagnoses), etc. Since then, SEGESE has been used to develop all of ISEOR's socio-economic diagnoses. It is marketed and made available to companies and franchised consulting firms in socio-economic management and to master's and doctoral students.

Since the 1990s, SEGESE has undergone several changes in response to changing needs and technological advances (Ziani, 1991). Currently it is a rich web application with a 'multilayer' architecture, developed under Microsoft Blazor, which uses a web service (WCF) for business processing and the provision of data stored in a database. The application is now accessible on the Internet from a web browser, under certain access conditions.

The new intuitive user interface and the business processes of the web service are the result of a close collaboration between the ISEOR management, its researchers and the IT team. Concerned about the strong involvement of the different actors in the continuous updates of this application, we opted for agile methods in the conduct of this type of project. The technologies used in the development of SEGESE are mainly Microsoft technologies such as C#, Blazor and SQL server, except for the design of the output reports, where SAP Crystal Reports was the chosen tool.

Starting with the SEGESE Professional version, different variants have been developed according to the new needs of users: a version for SMEs (Small and Medium Size Enterprises) with the same structure of themes, sub-themes, and sub-sub-themes, but with a base of key ideas limited to about 500, and versions for targeted diagnoses on: strategic intelligence, business and marketing practices, human resources management, socio-economic evaluation, and the self-evaluation of an academic publication. In addition, the in-depth socio-economic diagnosis and the SME socio-economic diagnosis versions have been translated into several languages: English, Spanish, Portuguese, Dutch, including a base of key-ideas of dysfunctions, translated as ISEOR's intervention-research activities become more international.

2 USERS AS PROACTIVE ACTORS IN THE DIGITAL TRANSFORMATION

2.1 Contribution to the Functional Evolution of an Application

The SEGESE tool was built with the participation of users from the beginning in 1985. The project management methods used facilitated their active participation. The construction of the knowledge base of the first version of the SEGESE Expert System required dozens of long work sessions between the team of computer scientists and the team of socio-economic management experts at ISEOR, whose objective was to extract the know-how of the specialists using cognitivist techniques. The successive updates were carried out according to agile methods, with strong interaction with the users and the continuous integration of evolution and adaptation requests. This is how the participation and involvement of the user in the development and updates of the tool have favored its integration into human know-how, in terms of "tamed" digitalization.

2.2 Contribution to the Construction and Enrichment of the Socio-Economic Knowledge base

By using SEGESE, the internal users of the company or the ISEOR intervener-researchers has made a strong contribution to the progressive and incremental construction of the knowledge base.

2.2.1 At the Level of Generic Dysfunctions Called Key Ideas

Initially, SEGESE included about a hundred key-Ideas. This version allowed 16 diagnoses to be made in 1987. The database of key-ideas has been completed as socio-economic diagnoses have been carried out in different companies in different sectors (Figure 3.3). Currently, it contains 5,600 key-ideas, divided into six dysfunctional themes (Figure 3.4), which were developed through more than 3,000 diagnoses.

The creation of generic dysfunctions (key ideas) was most intense during the first diagnoses with SEGESE. Once the sectors of activity and company sizes diversified, the number of key ideas created decreased (Figure 3.3).

2.2.2 In Terms of the Structure of the Classification

The growing number of key ideas during the 1990s (Figure 3.3) required an improvement in the structure of the classification and its refinement, by adding a third level, that

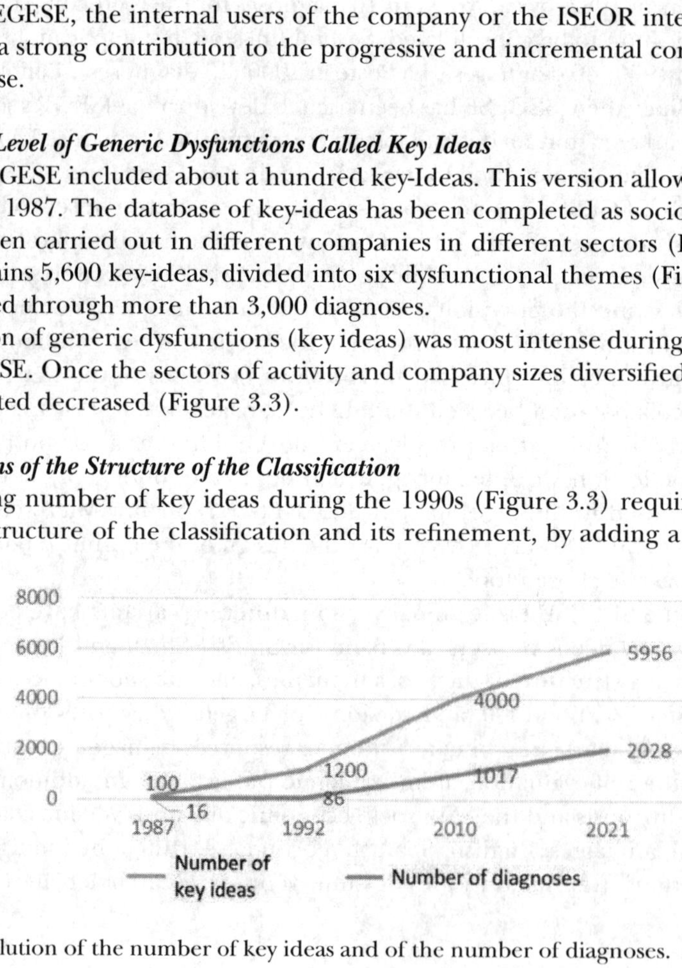

Figure 3.3 Evolution of the number of key ideas and of the number of diagnoses.

	THEMES	Number of fieldnote quotes resorting to each theme	Number of key ideas per theme	Fieldnote quote/Key ideas ratio
1	Working Conditions	15,797	843	18,74
2	Work Organization	16,825	1,079	15,59
3	Time Management	8,741	567	15,42
4	Integrated Training	4,652	433	10,74
5	Communication-Coordination-Cooperation	15,066	1,057	14,25
6	Implementation of the strategy	20,034	1,623	12,51
	Overall amount	**81,115**	**5,602**	**14,48**

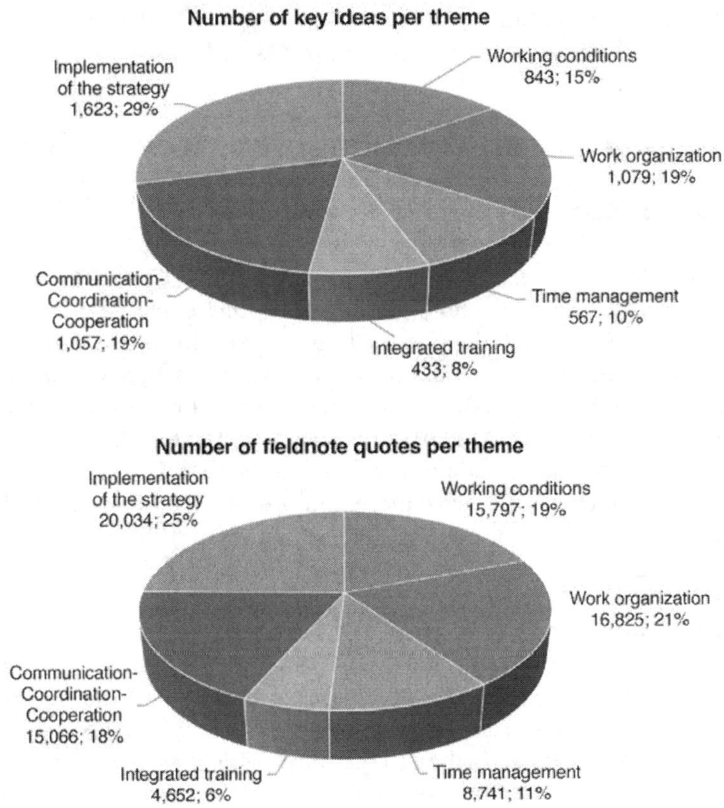

Figure 3.4 Distribution of key ideas and fieldnote quotes by themes of dysfunctions.

of the sub-sub-theme (the nomenclature now has 270 sub-sub-themes), to facilitate the imputation of the fieldnote quotes. Indeed, the introduction of sub-subthemes reduces the distance between the key ideas and the fieldnote quotes, which increases the intensity of the mirror effect and facilitates its appropriation by the actors of the company. This improvement not only facilitates the work of users in finding the best assignment of a fieldnote quote to a key idea, but also the evolution of the socio-economic diagnosis method.

The distribution of key ideas by theme is not an indicator of the "objective" importance of dysfunctions, as it reflects the perceptions of the actors, which don't reflect performance. The most "weighty" themes are also those that have a more limited improvement in the project phase following the diagnosis. Integrated training (8%), time management (10%) and working conditions (12%) are the most dynamic themes in the phase of defining improvement actions, even though the expressions are weaker than the other three.

2.2.3 In Terms of Socio-Economic Research and Innovation

The "SEGESE G" module (G for Generator) was designed to generate specific classications. It allows the creation of a complete tree structure of themes, sub-themes, sub-sub-themes and key ideas. The key ideas are created by the user in an incremental way as the diagnoses are carried out. This module makes it possible to generate variants of SEGESE to carry out diagnoses in new domains for the needs of research in socio-economic management. For example, an inter-company diagnosis on the problems of intergenerational management in companies made it possible to create a SEGESE G classification on this theme or others such as tetranormalization, or the foresight approach of jobs. To date, approximately 70 diagnoses have benefited from this version of SEGESE G.

3 LESSONS LEARNED FROM THE USE OF TECHNOLGICAL TOOLS

3.1 Analysis of Company Data to Advance Research

The set of data on company dysfunctions accumulated over the last 35 years in the SEGESE software now allows for documented and precise analyses. For example, doctoral theses prepared at ISEOR include cross-cutting analyses through datamining methods on a wide variety of themes, such as cooperation (Khenniche, 2010). Sectoral analyses (Savall and Zardet, 2015) or comparative analyses between countries, or specific by company size (Savall et al., 2010) have been conducted. More generally, a large number of queries have been made to extract and analyze the data from the diagnoses drawn up with SEGESE, in order to identify new dysfunctions that have increased over time. The results of these analyses are published in books, academic articles and doctoral theses.

3.2 Digitalization for Socio-Economic Analysis

This part focuses on the SEGESE software package. However, various other applications essential to the scientific and management activities of the ISEOR research center have been designed and are used today according to the same principles. For example, socio-economic management control tools, such as the activity sheet, were designed by ISEOR's research staff and then developed in digital form before being made available to companies. This tool allows for forward planning of activities and major strategic projects, self-analysis of activities by person and by team, and management control by activity (Savall and Zardet, 2008; Ennajem C., 2010).

CONCLUSION

Our intervention-research practice, as well as the analysis of dysfunctions identified in companies, show the existence of frequent and often serious dysfunctions due to the lack of mastery of digital tools: lack of skills, unsuitable tools, etc. Thus, in the face of the prevailing technological fascination, in France as in other countries, the results of 3,000 diagnoses encourage caution and investment in user's skills. Digitization and digitalization are tools that can improve a company's productivity, provided that there is a major investment in human potential as well as in skills development and collective rules of the game. Far from the substitution of capital/labor production factors, where technology is supposed to replace man, it is a complementarity of human potential and technology that seems by far the most human and most efficient way. At a time when some people advocate working from home, it is urgent to succeed in a fruitful combination between the use of technologies that support remote work and "collaborative human connectivity", which designates the current scientific program of the ISEOR (Savall, 2015).

REFERENCES

Harbi N. (1990). *Expert system in enterprise diagnosis.* PhD thesis in Computer Science and Applied Automation, under the supervision of Jacques Kouloumdjian. INSA Lyon.

Krief, N., Zardet, V. (2013). Qualitative data analysis and intervention-research. *Revue Recherches en sciences de gestion, 2,* 211–237.

Savall, H., Zardet, V. (2015). *A barrier to modernization of public services: the TFW (Taylorism-Fayolism-Weberism) virus. Case study.* Colloque AIRMAP. Lyon

Savall, H., Zardet, V. Datry, F. (2010). *Metamorphosis and sustainable development of SMEs. Comparative results France, Mexico and Belgium.* IFSAM Congress – Paris

Savall, H., Zardet, V., & Harbi, N. (2004). *Analyse spectrale de diagnostics socio-économiques: Traitement qualimétrique de données qualitatives, Colloque AOM-RMD-ISEOR, Lyon.* IAE Lyon.

Savall, H., Zardet, V., & Harbi, N. (2015). *Capitalization of 40 years of scientific knowledge in a research center: From SEGESE software to structuring researchers' and practitioners' knowledge for content analysis. A tool for collective learning.* Colloque AOM-RMD-ISEOR, Lyon.

Zardet, V., Harbi, N. (2007). SEAMES® A professional Knowledge Management Software Program. In A, Buono & H. Savall (Eds.), *Socio-Economic Intervention in Organizations.* Charlotte: Information Age Publishing.

Ziani, R. (1991). *On the implementation of P-RAM algorithms on feasible SIMD computers.* Doctoral dissertation. Computer Science Department, University of Warwick, Coventry, United Kingdom.

This page intentionally left blank.

CHAPTER 4

EXECUTIVE EDUCATION SEMINARS

A Scientific and Pedagogical System Complementary to Intervention-Research

Véronique Zardet and Karile Morel

ABSTRACT

Since 1987, inter-company executive seminars have been created at the ISEOR research center. Many executives, managers and employees of the companies where intervention-research projects take place have signed up to these seminars. A variety of seminars have been developed overtime. They are specialized by theme, audience or foreign language. These seminars create scientific and pedagogical impacts by consolidating a core of generic knowledge, alongside the specific knowledge of each intervention-research. They also enhance learning and changes in managerial and professional practices thanks to the diversity of the participants.

Twelve years after its foundation in 1975, ISEOR created inter-company professional training seminars. Their content is entirely focused on the Socio-Economic Approach to Management (SEAM) and they draw on the results of intervention-research projects carried out in all kinds of companies and organizations. These seminars have proved to complement intervention-research, both scientifically and pedagogically.

From a scientific point of view, they constitute a fundamental element of intervention-research that enables differentiation. Indeed, management consulting firms that carry out missions in companies don't offer this type of mixing and matching mechanism. This differentiation comes from the fact that companies, which start an intervention-research, will meet other companies which have been implementing socio-economic management for a year, two years, ten years, twenty years, etc. Thus, beginners, junior, senior and experienced managers meet up and their interactions result in remarkable impacts. The seminars have

SEAM Treatise, pages 63–72

been designed as a complementary system to the intra-company intervention-research processes. Like any executive education seminar, they aim at developing skills for both managers and internal consultants, but they also produce very fruitful exchanges between participants from companies of very different sizes, industries, regions, and even countries.

1 THE INTER-COMPANY EXECUTIVE EDUCATION SEMINARS AS A COMPLEMENTARY INTRA-COMPANY INTERVENTION-RESEARCH PROCESS

Over the past 34 years, various training courses have been created. Today, there are about ten of them, whose objective, content and pedagogical methods have been developed and adapted according to the evolution of intra-company intervention-research schemes. It is necessary to differentiate the fundamental seminars and the more in-depth courses.

1.1 Fundamental Seminars

They consist of two seminars whose content offer an overview of the major core and *core knowledge* regarding the major aspects of the socio-economic approach to management.

- The *Achieving change process* seminar. It provides an overview of the functioning and performance of a company or organization, the origin of dysfunctions and hidden costs, as well as the socio-economic methods of change management, in order to transform dysfunctions and hidden costs into value added in order to get sustainable enhancement of the socio-economic performance.
- The *Leading Teams seminar: interactive pedagogy*. Its pedagogy and content are focused on the learning of interactive and inductive pedagogic methods, to help participants transform their pedagogical and managerial leadership practices. It is intended for managers, internal trainers, internal or external consultants. Its content applies to the transmission of all kinds of knowledge, not only to the field of the socio-economic approach to management.

Both seminars are very innovative and question the usual principles of organization and management of the company, as well as the management of teams by front-line managers, middle managers and executives. The two courses complement each other and enable the understanding, application and achievement of sustainable improvement in socio-economic performance.

1.2 Advanced Courses

The in-depth courses develop a subset, a component or a dimension of the socio-economic approach to management. Their creation meets the needs identified during intervention-research projects in companies. They elaborate on targeted operational skills, such as the *evaluation of hidden costs-performance*, the elaboration of an *economic balance* of an *intangible investment project*, the implementation of *innovative commercial action plans*, etc. For pedagogical reasons, these courses are preceded by the fundamental seminar. The implementation of the concepts and tools developed in these in-depth seminars is a key pedagogical principle.

Between the different sessions (two or three depending on seminars, see Table 4.1), each participant has to implement concrete applications based on the content of the previous sequence in order to benefit from the feedbacks of the facilitators and from the other comments of participants when presenting them in interactive sessions.

All presenters are ISEOR intervener-researchers. They don't replace their ISEOR colleagues who intervene in a given company. Another characteristic to mention is that the superiors of the participants are asked to prepare with their superior a *statement of work* before each session in order to formalize the trainee's objectives, tools and actions. This process surreptitiously moves from a training seminar paradigm where participant attend the session to consume content, knowledge and relationships, to a logic where they co-produce new practices, while developing his/her own skills. The socio-economic executive training seminars become a tool for the development of the company's social and economic performance, as a complement to intra-company intervention-research on the one hand, and on the other hand an important contribution to the professional development of the employees.

Table 4.1 presents the range of in-depth training courses, all of which have a specificity:

- psychosociological dimension: *Managing behavior in a professional life*
- marketing & sales dimension: *Selling in a turbulent environment*
- economic dimension and management control: *Self-financing the company: The hidden resources*
- the role and action of the internal consultants: *Improving skills of internal interveners and strenghtening the socio-economic management practices*
- internal and external strategic issues specific to company managers applying socio-economic management: *The Number One* seminar
- the role and contribution of the non-managerial staff in socio-economic management: *involving all people in the company performance improvement.*

TABLE 4.1 The Executive Education Seminars Organized by the ISEOR Research Center (http://www.iseor-formations.com)

Title of the seminar	Duration	Main objectives
Fundamental seminars		
Achieving change processes	9.5 days 4 sessions at 4 to 6 weeks intervals	Implementing and accompanying change processes and enhancing profitability, efficiency, quality, competitiveness and sustainable social performance.
Leading Teams seminar: interactive pedagogy	4 days 2 sessions separated by 2 months.	This seminar is targeted at top managers, project managers, trainers and consultants. The objective is not to convey specific knowledge nor prescribing through words, but to develop action taking and how to make things happen.
Advanced courses		
Managing behaviors in professional life	3 days Two 2-day sessions separated by a month.	Management of behaviors by superiors, internal or external consultants in complex situations either in a context of a change process or in companies processed through socio-economic management.
Self-financing: the hidden resources	6 days Three 2-day sessions separated by 4 to 6 weeks.	Drawing on the hidden costs and performance methodology and on socio-economic management control to enhance the steering processes of activity profitability and sustainable economic performance.

(continued)

TABLE 4.1 The Executive Education Seminars Organized by the ISEOR Research Center (continued)

Title of the seminar	Duration	Main objectives
Selling in a turbulent business environment: "selling = human relations"	6 days Three tow-day sessions, separated by 4 to 6 weeks.	Seminar aimed at directors, sales and marketing managers as well as production managers. Objective is to trigger a surge in sales performance through leading and managing sales teams and enhancing cooperation of all company actors re: Sales and innovation: all sales-people.
Improving skills of internal consultants and strenghtening the socio-economic management practices	3 days Two 1.5 day sessions, separated by 2 months.	Seminar only aimed at top managers and internal consultants already trained in socio-economic management. The objective is to better lead change in their company and designing a support strategy by internal consultants.
Involving all people in the company performance improvement.	Three 1.5 sessions separated by one month.	Seminar only aimed at employees, workers and technicians who are not managers. Objective is to high-light the active participation of employees in the improvement of both the economic performance and the working conditions.
Number 1 seminar	A one-day seminar, twice a year.	Seminar aime at CEOs who are implementing the socio-economic approach to management. Main themes: company transition, cohesion of top managmeent teams, strategic bedrock, organizational choices, strategic decisions of new activities, growth and organizational structuring.
Seminars in foreign languages		
Socio-Economic Approach to Management: techniques & tools (in English)	2 four-day sessions separated by 4 to 6 months	Copy of the seminar "Achieving change processes" (see above)
SEAM Enhancement (in English)	A two-day session in June and in October each year.	Seminar aimed at furthering skills of those who have already attended the *Socio-economic approach to management: techniques & tools* seminar. Program is customized according to participants' needs.
Gestión socioeconómica de las empresas y organizaciones (in Spanish)	2 four-day sessions separated by 4 to 6 months	Copy of the seminar "Achieving change processes" (see above)
Perfeccionamiento en la gestión socioeconómica (in Spanish)	A two-day session in June and in October each year.	Seminar aimed at furthering skills of those who have already attended the *Gestión socioeconómica de las empresas y organizaciones* seminar. Program is customized according to participants' needs.

1.3 Foreign Language Courses

Since the 1990s, ISEOR has intensified its international development strategy. It has decided to offer the basic course Succeeding in Business in English and Spanish. The objective is twofold: on the one hand, to reach a non-French-speaking public, and on the other hand, to combine the course with the annual colloquiums organized by ISEOR each year in June and fall. Then, following the request of participants in the Making Change Happen course in English and Spanish, an "Advanced Socio-Economic Management" course was designed, the content of which is tailored to the participants' expectations, collected a few weeks before the course. This advanced course is also linked to the annual colloquia organized by ISEOR in June and fall.

2 CONTRIBUTION OF DIVERSITY TO THE MISSION OF THE RESEARCH CENTER

A retrospective analysis of the participants in the professional training courses that have developed over the past 34 years reveals a great diversity based on five main criteria (§ 2.3). This diversity is a source of scientific and pedagogical contributions to the activity of the research center.

2.1 The Scientific Contribution of Diversity in Seminars

Each company where ISEOR deploys an intervention-research project to implement and develop socio-economic management has specific objectives, a specific strategic situation and a specific economic and financial situation. Its activity is specific, as are its size and legal status. This set of specificities is taken into account in the negotiation of the intervention-research program, its objectives, its modalities, its schedule and its budget.

However, participants from these different companies are gathered in the same room in an executive education seminar, to consolidate their operational skills, intended to support the deployment of socio-economic management and its tools, each in their own company. As different as these people and their company context are, each inter-company seminar constitutes a scientific validation operation for the knowledge produced by the intervention-research project. Indeed, the specific and local knowledge, developed within a company, is validated in a generic way by other actors from other companies, because the actors discover, next to their specific local knowledge, generic knowledge valid whatever the context. The inter-company seminar adds a layer of validation of the relevance of this management method with different people. The variety of actors and companies in the same room increases the scientific quality of the results, just like a vaccine whose effectiveness does not depend only on the person who receives it.

The seminars also have a team-building impact on the ISEOR's research staff. Indeed, the leaders of seminars (who are also intra-company researchers) make "indirect" contributions to their colleagues who work within each company, by training and accompanying the participants in the seminar, from each cmpany. This develops team spirit and takes us away, once again, from the solitary management consultant at his/her client's. It also contributes to harmonizing the knowledge and skills of the various ISEOR researchers.

The oral evaluation at the end of each course, made by the participants ("What did you learn from this seminar?"), constitutes feedback that we use to guide the evolution of our knowledge and our methods. In fact, each of the seminars, just like socio-economic management, is systemic in nature. It produces, beyond its specific contributions, more diffuse effects on the integration of concepts, the link between social and economic, visible and hidden, individual and collective which transform the vision of the different participants. Participants in the courses also become aware of the existence of a robust scientific method and its value. This has a knock-on effect on their behavior and professional practices in their own companies. Indeed, the positive effects of the inter-company training course are reported by them in their company, and integrated more or less consciously into their work practices. This contributes, moreover, to modify their image of research in general, and in some cases even encourages them to implement socio-economic management and the executive education programs dedicated to it known in their environment.

2.2 The Pedagogical Function in the Research Process

If we admit that pedagogy is a modality to convince the patient to take care of himself/herself, the pedagogical challenge of the inter-company seminar is to explain the underlying principles of the socio-economic approach to management, so that the participants understand better and apply in depth and with less resistance in their respective companies, innovative scientific knowledge.

The "biological" diversity of the seminar is not an obstacle to pedagogy, on the contrary it is a stimulant. Indeed, what is treated in these is an advantageous complement of the accompaniment made by the ISEOR speakers in intra-company. First of all, each participant becomes aware that what he or she experiences in his or her company is also experienced by others in their own company, and that it is therefore not a very specific intervention, but rather a reasoned adaptation of a scientific research program.

Moreover, the distance from the daily workplace, in a different environment, produces psychological, physiological, ergonomic and sociological effects. It favors concentration on the participant, with less temptation to return to their daily tasks than if the seminar took place in the company site. It limits the distraction from everyday demands. This avoids the "confined" atmosphere with a close, routine and familiar human and social environment, and favors the discovery of new people, new companies, in an unfamiliar environment. We also note that additional training takes place "in the lobbys," in the form of exchanges between participants about their personal experience of socio-economic management (difficulties encountered and overcome, concrete positive impacts, etc.), which contributes to developing the idea of belonging to an innovative "network" of management practices. These seminars give rise to relationships between people and between companies, which sometimes continue. Sometimes, people from the same company working in different departments or locations discover each other by coming to the same seminar 200 or 500 km away from company site! Sometimes, people from two companies initiate exchanges, visits, experience sharing, and sometimes even business relationships. Their common "DNA," the socio-economic management, constitutes a factor of confidence between companies. For example, the Mexican avocado producer Aguacates Sanchez Hass has become a supplier to the fruit and vegetable trader Soly Import in Lyon, which in turn supplies the Savoie Poultry company, all three of which apply socio-economic management without having known each other before.

2.3 Criteria and Assessment of Diversity

To describe and qualify the diversity of the participants in the various seminars, six criteria have been selected among others:

- Concerning the company: its *size*, its *industry*, its *country* and the *stage of progress* in the implementation of socio-economic management;
- Concerning the participants: his or her *level of responsibility and job* within the company.

These five diversity criteria have allowed for a scientific analysis, which shows that diversity can be observed within each seminar on the one hand, and within all seminars on the other.

Zooming in on the last ten years, 920 persons have participated in a seminar (see Figure 4.2). Since the fundamental seminars are the basis for participating in the others, it is no surprise that they represent 46% of the total participants in the French track, ahead of

Sales processes in a turbulent environment and *Self-financing* the company (14% each), *Improving skills of internal consultants* (11%), *Managing behavior* (9%) and *Involving all people* (6%).

a. All company *sizes* are represented, including very large companies (over 5,000 employees) and very small companies, which are traditionally said not to invest in training for their employees. SMEs and mid-sized companies are dominant and host two-thirds of the participants in the seminars in French.
b. The breakdown by sector of activity shows that the business sector is dominant compared to the non-profit sector (21% of participants), and that trade and services account for two-thirds of participants. (Figure 4.1).
c. Regarding the countries of origin, the participants of the French-speaking seminars come mainly from France (77%), Belgium (13%), Switzerland (6%) and Lebanon (4%), knowing that 90% of the trainees come from companies that are in the process of implementing socio-economic management, in France, Belgium, Switzerland, Lebanon etc. The remaining 10% are management consultants, managers or company executives who come to discover the principles of socio-economic management, with the prospect of implementing it in their companies.
d. As for the deployment stage of Socio-Economic Management in the company; some participants have not yet started and come as "scouts." Then, during the first few months of starting a socio-economic intervention, the CEO and top management team sign up to socio-economic seminars, along with the internal consultants who accompany the intervention-research. Then, the main managers participate in the seminar. Finally, during the consolidation period after an initial period of intervention, the participants who have attended the *Achieving the change process* pursue with more in-depth seminar, as they are complementary to the internal support action, which is simultaneously led by a team of ISEOR intervener-researchers in the company. Then, as new managers are recruited in these companies, they first participate in the basic courses, to understand the meaning and scope of the socio-economic approach to management that their company has already adopted.

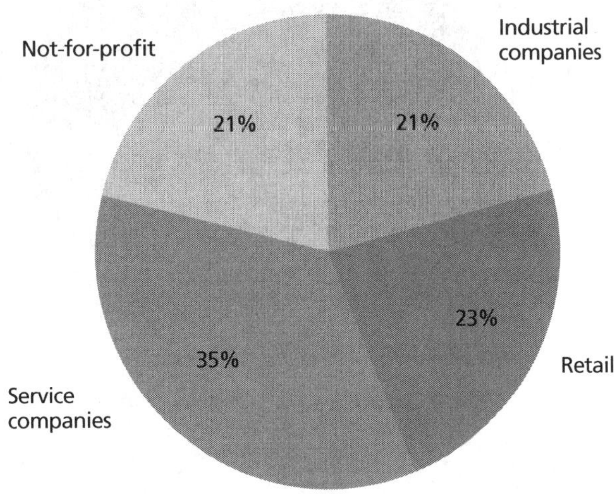

Figure 4.1 Distribution of seminar participants by industry sector (including all seminars).

e. The seminars taught in foreign languages, English and Spanish, have so far welcomed 158 participants, whose origin by country is as presented in the table. The largest percentages of the first four countries, Mexico, Lebanon, the United States of America and Spain, correspond to the development of both academic and professional partnerships that the ISEOR research center has built since the beginning of its internationalization strategy.

Countries of origin: 17 countries	Percentage of participants: total 100%	Countries of origin: 10 pays	Percentage of participants: total 100%
Mexico	35%	Saudi Arabia	1%
Lebanon	27%	India	1%
United States	18%	Argentina	1%
Spain	6%	Belgium	1%
Netherlands	2%	Qatar	1%
United Arab Emirates	2%	Canada	1%
China	2%	Kuweït	1%
France	1%	Columbia	1%

f. Finally, "internal" diversity is confirmed in each seminar and each family of seminars, as well as in all seminars, all families combined. In the same seminar, a company director, a manager in charge of a department, an executive or supervisor, an assistant, an accountant, a sales representative, etc., from different companies or from the same company, may participate side by side. We can thus understand that the interactivity between the participants is a powerful lever to allow each one to better understand what is at stake in their own company, in terms of dysfunctions, conflicts, innovative projects or sustainable performance.

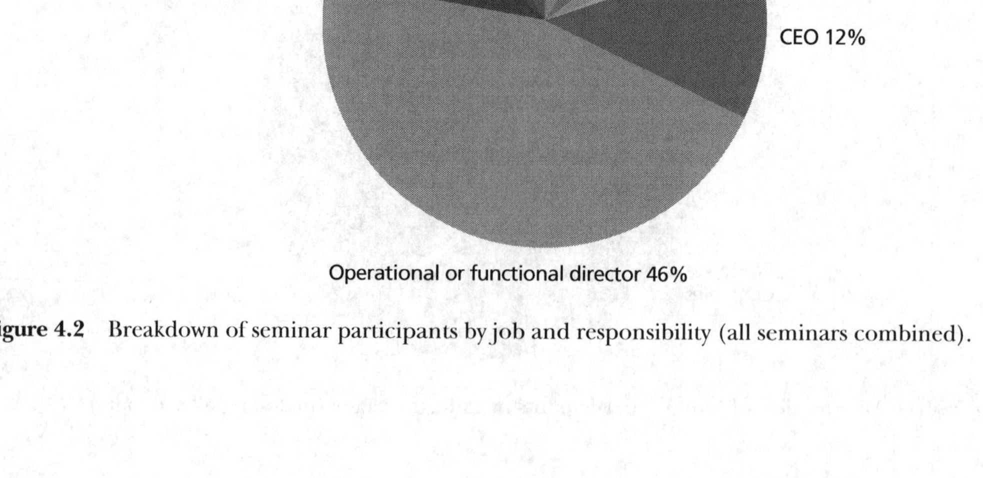

Figure 4.2 Breakdown of seminar participants by job and responsibility (all seminars combined).

CONCLUSION

The professional seminars organized and taught at the ISEOR research center are characterized by their "biological" diversity of the participating companies and individuals. It and thus constitute a system for building the demonstration that the socio-economic theory and the socio-economic approach to management illustrate the generic contingency prnciple: all participants are different but they share an experience that allow them to understand each other. Each actor, each company and each sector, each country is unique and specific, and yet the socio-economic theory and the socio-economic approach to management are applicable regardless of country, sector or size. In this respect, the research carried out at ISEOR has a "fundamental" character.

CHAPTER 5

CONSOLIDATING INTERVENTION-RESEARCH THROUGH COMMUNICATION AND DISSEMINATION MECHANISMS

Annual Conferences and the Journal *Recherches en Sciences de Gestion–Management Sciences–Ciencias de Gestión*

Véronique Zardet and Michelle Bonnard

ABSTRACT

To consolidate its intervention-research activities, the ISEOR research center has deployed three complementary mechanisms, largely self-financed, to produce and disseminate innovative knowledge in management: an annual conference with a professional focus that allows for the co-evaluation of research results and is extended by the publication of conference proceedings, and an annual international academic conference that aims for openness and multi-linguistic exchanges, and finally, a trilingual academic journal, *Recherches en Sciences de Gestion–Management Sciences–Ciencias de Gestión*, that advocates diversity, tolerance, and scientific rigor, and that has been developed since 1978 with a high level of ethics.

The ISEOR research center has created, in addition to its intervention-research activities in companies and organizations, several complementary mechanisms to consolidate its vocation to produce and disseminate innovative knowledge in management.

SEAM Treatise, pages 73–80

The main complementary mechanisms are: inter-company executive education—which is the subject of a dedicated chapter—the organization of annual conferences as well as the editing and management of an academic journal in management sciences, called *Recherches en Sciences de Gestion-Management Sciences-Ciencias de Gestión* Recherches. This chapter explains the rationale and characteristics of each of these mechanisms, which are self-financed or co-financed by the ISEOR research center: an annual professional conference, an annual academic conference and an academic journal.

1 THE HYBRID ANNUAL CONFERENCE WITH A PROFESSIONAL FOCUS

Organized every fall since 1989, this conference is intended to be a hybrid system between professionals and academics, between these two worlds that are often opposed, or at best unaware of each other, of business and higher education, of the public and private sectors. Its targets are students, managers, executives, consultants and teacher-researchers. Its ambition is to disseminate the results of experiments in the socio-economic approach to management in different contexts, countries, and types of companies, by their managers, by combining them with a theme that is renewed each year. This topical theme makes it possible to differentiate the conferences from one year to the next, and to invite consultants and managers who are particularly involved in this theme. Thus, in the last few years, the themes chosen were Challenges and opportunities of telework (2020), Tetranormalization: profusion of standards and business development (2019), How to work together? Challenges of intergeneration (2018), Tamed digitalization: at the service of the human being and sustainable performance (2017), Business innovation: all sellers in organizations (2016), Companies, value(s) and prosperity: Socially responsible capitalism (2015), etc.

1.1 Organization of the Conference

This conference is organized in partnership with Jean Moulin University and iaelyon business school. It takes place on the university's premises, a sort of symbol of a bridge between higher education and the business world. It is also an integral part of the education of iaelyon students, who learn the principles of socio-economic approach to management in class, and then have the opportunity to exchange with managers who have been experimenting with socio-economic management in their own companies, sometimes for years or even decades. This conference is an extension of their training, which is based on the principle of alternation. Since 1985, ISEOR's teacher-researchers have created bachelor's and master's degree programs within the university based on the knowledge created by experiments of the socio-economic approach to management. This department within iaelyon, called the University School of Innovative Management (EUGINOV), which was created in 1995 by Henri Savall, is based on the pedagogy of alternating teaching at the university with internships -or professionalization contracts- in companies, and on the mixing of students and professionals returning to school in the same classrooms (Voyant et al., 2018; Delattre, 2021).

In order to allow the dissemination of the results of the experiments outside of France, the professional conference is organized in three languages (French, English, Spanish) and thus constitutes an international opening for EUGINOV students. Presentations are given in the native language of each speaker, and translated simultaneously into the other two languages.

This professional conference also constitutes a mechanism for the co-evaluation of research: indeed, the leaders present the results of the implementation of the socio-economic approach to management in their company or organization, in the form of an oral presentation, often accompanied by visual support (PowerPoint type). No prior submission is necessary, as the program is designed based on requests to managers, consultants and teacher-researchers. The content of the exchanges during the two days is recorded and then transcribed by the ISEOR team. The transcripts are then sent to their authors and validated by them, and a book of proceedings is published by a professional publisher. This collection of works, which has been in existence for more than 20 years, includes numerous testimonials written by company directors who have applied socio-economic management, which constitute as many track records of the evaluation of the research. This process of producing proceedings allows professionals to publish elements of research evaluation, most of whom are not used to or interested in writing written texts. Doctoral students supervised by ISEOR and DBA students in research centered programs co-organized by ISEOR are also invited to present the progress of their intervention-researches in companies at this professional conference, alone or in co-intervention with the head of the organization where they are working.

1.2 Attendance at the Various Professional Conferences

On average, about 220 participants attend the annual professional conference. The audience is international. Over the last 16 years, 29 countries have been represented: Europe 8, Asia 7, Africa 6, North America 3, South America 4 and Oceania 1.

The proportion of academic participants, including 50 to 100 students from the EUGINOV center, is approximately 53%. These participants are divided into speakers (29%) and mere participants (71%). The high proportion of mere participants corresponds to students for whom the conference is a complement to their training. This is corroborated by the language distribution of the mere participants: 90% French-speaking, 7% English-speaking and 3% Spanish-speaking. Among the English-speaking mere participants, there has been a group of about ten MBA students from the University of San Scholastica (Duluth, Minnesota) for the past five years, supervised by their professors Alla Hcorhiadi and John Conbere, who come to consolidate their training in socio-economic approach to management.

Over the past 16 years, the presenters have been composed of 80% French speakers, 8% English speakers and 12% Spanish speakers.

2 A HYBRID CONFERENCE MAINLY AIMED AT ACADEMIA

2.1 Academic Partnerships

Since 1998, the ISEOR research team has been organizing an international academic conference lasting two to three days, in partnership with the Université Jean Moulin, which hosts the venue, along with iaelyon school of management, as well as international partners.

- On the one hand the Academy of Management of the United States. Four divisions have been involved in the 22 years since this partnership was established: Research Methodologies (RMD), Organizational Development and Change (OCD), Management Consulting (MCD) and Social Issues in Management (SIM);

- On the other hand, the International Institute of Costs for conferences more focused on analysis and management control. The International Institute of Costs brings together about fifteen Latin language associations specialized in auditing, management and management control in Europe (France, Spain), and especially in Latin America. The originality of this institute is to federate teachers-researchers and professionals in the field of cost analysis and management. It organizes an international congress every two years in one of the member countries. On three occasions, the congress has been organized in Lyon in partnership with ISEOR and the American Accounting Association (AAA). Brazil is a member country of the International Cost Institute.

Since 2020, a new partner is associated with the following international event: The International Society for Organization Development and Change (ISODC), an Anglo-Saxon association of academics and professional consultants in the field of organizational change

2.2 Challenges and Objectives of the Academic Conference

This conference represents an opening for the dissemination of research work to different types of work and approaches to management research. It also allows to position the results of research in socio-economic approach to management in relation to other research streams.

Its openness is represented by the different research methodologies mobilized by their authors: qualitative, quantitative or hybrid, as well as the angles of approach of the research work (intra-organizational, inter-organizational, sectoral) or the fields: strategic management, change management, human resources management, management analysis, management information systems etc.

Only a few papers were presented by ISEOR researchers, teacher-researchers or doctoral students. The majority of French and foreign speakers present work from other approaches.

Like the professional conference, the academic conference is a place to promote and defend tri-lingual practices (French, Spanish, English). Thus, all the panels are organized in simultaneous translation, completed by workshops by language, that is to say in general 5 panels and about twenty workshops during the 2 days. One of the major challenges is to promote a real recognition of the contributions of Latin American research, by having North Americans and Latin Americans come to France, each one speaking in his or her own language to present his or her research work.

This conference has a very broad international appeal, since over a period of 16 years, 52 different countries have been represented, including 18 in Europe, 10 in Asia, 9 in Africa, 7 in North America and 8 in South America.

2.3 Participants to the Academic Conference

Based on the academic conferences organized from 2004 to 2020, about 200 people participate each year in the congress, of which ⅔ are actual speakers and ⅓ are non-speakers. The international character of the congress is reflected in the very high proportion of foreign speakers: 56%, including 20% English speakers, 30% Spanish speakers and 6% Portuguese speakers. The Portuguese-speaking public participates in particular in the conference organized in partnership with the International Institute of Costs, of which Portugal and Brazil are active members. The non-lecturer participants are French-speaking for 61% of them, in particular doctoral students, Master's students and professors-researchers, English-speaking for 19%, Spanish-speaking for 19% and Lusophone for 1%. This confirms a recurring observation in academic conferences around the world: travel by French or foreign colleagues is most often associated with paper presentations, with universities only funding travel if a paper has been accepted at a conference. Otherwise, travel is based on self-financing by the teacher-researcher or doctoral student, which is not very common in the academic world.

The international recognition of ISEOR in the academic world owes much to the recurrent organization of this international academic conference. This recognition was reinforced a few years ago in 2018 during a major survey conducted by the National Foundation for Business Management Education (FNEGE) on the world's most influential professors in management. Henri Savall, founding president of ISEOR and professor emeritus at IAE Lyon, Université Jean Moulin was the first French ranked (Kalika et al., 2016).

In the organization of this international conference, ISEOR brings to the University efforts, means as well as logistic and scientific organization. 2,427 academics from 52 countries who did not know Lyon, nor Jean Moulin University. As a result it has enhanced the contribution and reputation of the university, without significant financial cost on its part. Indeed, the main financial means are provided by ISEOR, by distributing newsletters several times a year, by ensuring contact several times a year with several tens of thousands of recipients of this newsletter, but also by building and publicizing an innovative management theory through various means of distribution, without any major subsidy from the French public authorities. Depending on the year, research grants are obtained for this congress from the university, the Rhône-Alpes region or the Ministry of Research, amounting between 1,000 and 5,000 € in very good years. This international conference is obviously, like the vast majority of academic conferences, a loss-making event, whose main function is to disseminate and connect the network of teacher-researchers among themselves, as well as with the business world and organizations.

3 THE ACADEMIC JOURNAL *RECHERCHES EN SCIENCES DE GESTION–MANAGEMENT SCIENCES–CIENCIAS DE GESTIÓN*

The academic journal *Recherches en Sciences de Gestion-Management Sciences-Ciencias de Gestión* (hereafter RSDG) was founded in 1978 as a series within the journal Économies et Sociétés, then directed by François Perroux. The journal RSDG was designed to develop management sciences, when there were only two in France. In 2001, it became an autonomous journal under the name Sciences de Gestion. It was one of the few journals in the discipline of management sciences to be recognized by the CNRS in the 1980s and 2000s. It was forced to change its name in 2004 following the usurpation of its name by a journal in management sciences and became the journal *Recherches en Sciences de Gestion*. The academic world being not exempt from turpitude, the legal steps did not allow the journal Sciences de Gestion to keep its name. In 2004, in connection with the development of international academic and professional conferences, it expanded and its name took on its full form *Recherches en Sciences de Gestion–Management Sciences–Ciencias de Gestión*, creating an English-language series and a Spanish-language one, each of which publishes one issue per year of original articles in English and Spanish respectively. Since 2018, the journal has been published in electronic format.

Since its creation, RSDG has been scientifically edited, managed and financed by the ISEOR research center, which devotes about 1/3 of a full-time equivalent to it, in addition to external expenses such as anti-plagiarism software, printing costs, etc. It was founded by

Henri Savall, who ensures the scientific direction in collaboration with Laurent Cappelletti, full professor at CNAM and program director at ISEOR for the English-language collection, and Véronique Zardet for the Spanish-language collection.

3.1 The Editorial Line of the Journal

Like the academic conference, the RSDG journal is characterized by an open editorial line: thematic, methodological and epistemological openings. It advocates diversity, tolerance and scientific rigor, and appreciates transversal themes such as trust, value or social responsibility. It is a generalist academic journal in management sciences, with a special focus on epistemological and methodological articles, for which there are few French-language publications. Today, it is positioned among the top academic journals, ranked at the 3rd level by the National Foundation for Business Management Education (FNEGE) since the early 2010s. This ranking has had a strong impact on the number of article submissions received and articles published each year. For the reviewing of the articles, three independent scientific committees have been designed, composed of French (about 100 members), English (40 members) and Spanish (40 members) speaking professors-researchers. The international academic network of ISEOR has allowed the progressive construction of these scientific committees, representative of a wide variety of methodological choices, paradigms, research themes and French and foreign academic institutions.

3.2 Published Articles

How to make research results known to the greatest number of people, with an ethic of "not serving oneself"? In its 43 years of existence, RSDG has published less than 10% of articles on ISEOR's research. It has achieved its goal of contributing to the management science research community, particularly in France, in exchange for reducing a certain academic hostility towards ISEOR.

A statistical study of 20 years of publication (2001–2020) shows 727 articles published, an average of 7 per year, with a clear acceleration in recent years to 50 articles per year, since the switch to electronic format. The internationalization of the journal can be observed through two complementary indicators: on the one hand, the number of original articles published in French (75%), English (13%) and Spanish (12%); on the other hand, the number of authors' countries of origin: French articles come from authors from 27 different countries, 10 of which are in Europe; English articles come from 20 different countries, 9 of which are in Europe, 4 in Asia, and 4 in North America; finally, Spanish articles come from 9 different countries, 2 in Europe, 6 in South America, and 1 in North America.

The distribution of articles by field (Figure 5.1) calls for several comments. The large number of articles in strategic management (20 to 25% of the total number of articles) is probably explained by the lack of French-language journals in strategic management, given the number of authors working in this field. 7 to 10% of articles are published in methodology and epistemology, given that there is no dedicated French-language journal in that field. Moreover, despite the existence of specialized journals in human resources management, finance, marketing and sales management, or management control, the journal very regularly welcomes articles from these fields. This proves that, in addition to specialized journals, there is room for generalist journals of rank 3. The RSDG journal, which is less standardized

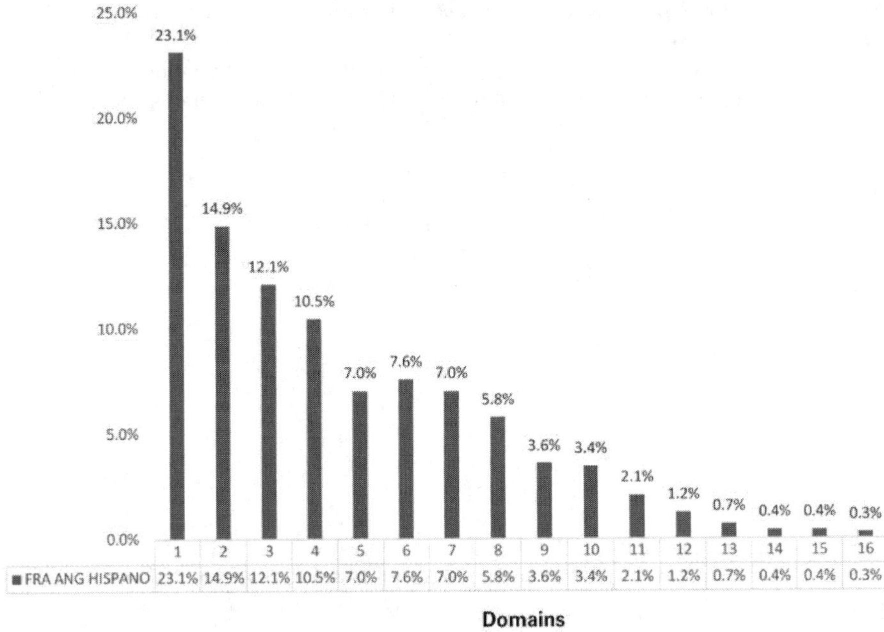

Figure 5.1 Distribution of articles published by field in the RSDG journal from 2001 to 2020, all languages combined. *Key:* (1) Strategic Management; (2) Human Resource Management; (3) Social responsibility; (4) Financial theories and financial management; (5) Accounting and management control; (7) Epistemology and research methods; (8) Organization behavior; (9) public service management; (10) Overall approach to company performance; (11) Information systems; (12) International management; (13) laws and tax management; (14) Organization theory; (15) Quantitative management research methodology; (16) Industrial systems.

than the specialized journals in the above fields, probably allows for the acceptance of articles that are more heterodox in their content or in their structuring.

CONCLUSION

The professional and academic conferences are multidisciplinary, as is the journal RSDG. The whole system illustrates a conception of citizen science, which does not only belong to academics, but to all the actors of society, contributing to democracy through their research results. The systemic dimension inherent to socio-economic theory is extended in this system: the conferences, the RSDG journal and the organization of the ISEOR are all systemic in nature, the links between these components producing human and scientific synergies. The conferences are also intended to disseminate the scientific knowledge developed by the ISEOR research center to the academic community and to all professional practitioners of the socio-economic approach to management, starting with managerial leaders.

REFERENCES

Delattre, M. (2021). Teacher-researchers and social responsibility: The "Socio-Economic Management" group in conjunction with ISEOR at iaelyon. *Management & Social Sciences.*

Kalika, M., Liarte, S., Moscarola, J. (2016). *Impact of management schools on France.* Study conducted for the FNEGE. Paris: FNEGE.

Voyant, O., Krief, N., Goter, F., & Dupouy, J. (2018). Strengthening the complementarity between explicit training and Implicit Education for Social Responsibility. *Management & Social Sciences.*

CHAPTER 6

THE SOCIO-ECONOMIC APPROACH TO MANAGEMENT (SEAM)

A Fruitful Theory and Method—Contributions to the Collective Work and Specificities of Doctoral Theses

Alexis Roche

ABSTRACT

This chapter presents the contribution of the doctoral theses prepared in the ISEOR international research center over the past 46 years. It highlights the contributions of theses and intervention-research for a citizen science, at the service of practitioners and not only of researchers. It shows the variety of companies and organizations in which the intervention-research have been carried out, as well as the diversity of the issues addressed according to the systemic approach of the research center. Finally, it presents a wide variety of themes of interest to companies and organizations.

The conception of ISEOR's research is that of its societal utility, since all research must include a contribution to society, or at least strive to have one: to help resolve conflicts and treat dysfunctions, transforming hidden costs into value added. In doing so, this work, like medical research, must be scientifically robust and constantly innovative to cope with the changing and evolving environment. One such practice of innovative and in-depth field research is the work of a doctoral thesis in management science. This chapter is based on an analysis of theses defended using socio-economic theory. The goal of a doctoral thesis is to structure the analysis of a problematic that will be investigated in depth over several years. The dissertation is a way of learning methodological skills, of developing theoretical and

SEAM Treatise, pages 81–89

practical bases for research, and of publishing methods for communicating results. The doctoral dissertation, as conceived at ISEOR, is thus an exercise in communicating knowledge for the purpose of collective learning, which aims to serve practitioners in companies and organizations and to change the conception of doctoral research.

1 INNOVATIVE AND APPLIED RESEARCH IN A WIDE RANGE OF ORGANIZATIONS AND CONTEXTS

The specificities of the management science thesis compared to other publications, such as the writing of scientific papers or articles, are characterized by the duration of the investigation, 3 years, on the research theme. This work is based both on a theoretical positioning in relation to the literature, the currents of thought and the existing theoretical frameworks, as well as on a consistent methodological positioning, for the robustness of the knowledge accumulated during the research. This results in a work of about 300 pages: the doctoral thesis in management sciences, which validates a diploma of "bachelor + 8 years" level. This is a mandatory step for anyone wishing to apply as a professor-researcher in France and abroad, in a higher education institution. However, one third of the PhDs who have defended their thesis at ISEOR, thanks to their skills acquired within companies and organizations, embark on a career as a company director, manager, consultant, or project manager.

Unlike other research centers that directly propose thesis topics to their doctoral students or orient them towards a theme in their field of specialty, ISEOR allows doctoral students a great deal of freedom in the choice of themes and the content of the thesis. The "unique" requirement is innovation, particularly managerial innovation, around an overall systemic research project, which covers the entire perimeter of the company or organization and may include several management sub-disciplines: strategy, finance/management control, human resources, marketing/commercial management, and information systems management. The socio-economic methodology and theory created and developed by ISEOR are like the roots at the origin of the trunk of a tree, which serves as the basis for subsequent developments. Thus, the cumulative themes of investigation of the different researchers constitute branches that strengthen the trunk. The idea is to allow creativity, leaving a large degree of freedom to the researcher, while relying on a common scientific methodology that can be reproduced. The goal is to confirm hypotheses, at the heart of socio-economic theory, on a wide variety of research themes, "scientific observation fields," sectors of activity, countries, or company sizes. Such a "field" corresponds to a company or organization in which the researcher intervenes over time. He observes work situations, takes notes, analyzes documents and intervenes by "experimenting" with the company's actors, implementing tools and methods aimed at better understanding his research topic and improving company practices. The branches that develop, through this research, enrich the theoretical and methodological model with observable practical results for practitioners. The objective is to obtain knowledge applicable to other organizations.

2 PERMANENT TEAMWORK AND THE CONFRONTATION OF IDEAS AS A SOURCE OF SCIENTIFIC RESEARCH

ISEOR is a research team that has developed since its creation in 1975. The researchers work as a team on the same fields of scientific observation. They can also work in different fields but compare their results, their work and their hypotheses with the other researchers in the team. Thus, one of the specificities of the research center, in addition to teamwork on the "scientific observation field," has been the establishment of a monthly research seminar, since the beginning of ISEOR in 1975, to compare the points of view of the researchers, doctoral students and PhDs of ISEOR, and those of the invited professor-researchers, members of other research centers. This makes it possible to be enriched by the criticisms and views of others. This confrontation also takes place in a more traditional way with the rest of the scientific community, during academic conferences regularly organized by French and international scientific associations.

In addition to the monthly research seminars, each doctoral student has a research director, whom he or she meets very regularly on a one-to-one basis, to direct his or her research and to finalize a quality thesis. Complementarity is organized between the individual supervision by the thesis director and the collective exchanges that take place during the monthly doctoral seminars. Many doctoral theses in management in France exceed the three years allotted by the regulations of the Ministry of Higher Education and Research. Thanks to the method and regular confrontation with the team, most of the theses supervised at ISEOR are defended within three years, despite a very strong involvement in the field of scientific observation, which consumes a lot of time. Moreover, in addition to professor-researchers, the thesis jury systematically includes a company or organization manager, as a witness to the intervention-research process that led to the development of the thesis,

The ISEOR research center claims a conception of responsible and citizen science, generating useful and practical knowledge, at the service of the real performance of organizations. It is about helping companies to function better. The goal is to invent "vaccines" based on scientific knowledge, in the form of professional practices, tools, and instructions for use, with long-term effectiveness for companies and organizations. Doctoral theses are part of the innovation "production machine" associated with team-based "intervention-research." As mentioned above, doctoral students are required to have a strong involvement and interaction with the field, the field of observation of the research, and to rigorously validate the results obtained.

ISEOR has developed specific intervention-research methods, known as qualimetric intervention-research (Savall & Zardet, 1996, 2004). They are qualimetric because they "measure" qualitative, quantitative, and financial elements, including hidden costs (Savall & Zardet, 1987). Data collection in intervention-research consists of observation methods, interviews, and document collection. This intervention-research methodology is based on strong interaction with the actors in the field over time with the aim of creating new knowledge. It aims to transform work situations through the direct intervention of the researcher, to observe and measure the effects. Indeed, it is by means of a transformation of the object studied that we could reveal certain properties that we cannot detect by placing ourselves outside of this object. (See introductory chapter, Savall & Zardet, section 2.2).

3 A CUMULATIVE AND ARBORESCENT THEORY THAT FINDS ITS SOURCE IN THE OBSERVABLE REALITY OF ORGANIZATIONS

This "field" is described as a scientific observation field because it is the place where rules of knowledge are discovered thanks to the formulation of hypotheses and their confrontation with the observed "reality," followed, if necessary, by the formulation of new hypotheses. The researcher looks for evidence in the form of facts that can be observed by the actors in the organization or by other researchers, such as words, gestures, environmental elements, and figures. The basis of the method is the close observation of phenomena and listening to the actors in the situations studied (leaders, managers, employees). The whole socio-economic theory was thus created and progressively formalized from observations and listening, ensuring an important theoretical robustness. This robustness of the roots and trunk is consolidated by successive observations over time, within the same organization, as well as by other people, new doctoral students, of the same phenomena, in numerous organizations, in various sectors, in 25 countries. The core of socio-economic theory is based on the most durable hypotheses. Indeed, every hypothesis has a long-life span, from a few days to a few years, or even a few centuries. This successive and long-term research, which forms the basis of a robust cumulative approach, makes it possible to confirm certain cause-and-effect links and the impacts of good management practices. The challenge is to find on the one hand, specific knowledge elements—considering and respecting the diversity of organizations and their context—and, on the other hand, generic knowledge. The latter generally have a longer period of validity and apply to different organizational contexts.

We speak of hypotheses, on the one hand because of the lifespan of a rule of knowledge, but also because the doctoral student, like any human being, has the freedom to make mistakes and progresses by heuristic trial and error, i.e., learning by trial and error. His hypotheses are confirmed by a succession of elements of evidence that confirm or deny them. For example, the doctoral student may make an initial observation: "a manager speaks up and his teams seem to be remotivated." The researcher then seeks to formulate hypotheses: "Thanks to this or that, the leader's words are effective and motivate people." He integrates other variables such as time: "What can reduce motivation in the short term but increase it in the medium to long term? The back and forth on his field or scientific observation grounds then allows the researchers to verify whether these hypotheses are validated, under what conditions, and whether they need to be refined or new ones formulated.

4 A RESEARCH CENTER THAT BUILDS A BRIDGE BETWEEN ACADEMICS AND MANAGEMENT PRACTITIONERS

The ISEOR research center is original in its longevity, 46 years in 2021, in its methods, in its systemic openness to the different branches of management sciences, and in the robustness of its knowledge production mode, due to the confrontation with scientific observation fields and other researchers. The aim of his scientific approach, to really help companies with a social and societal utility, permeates all his methodology and irrigates his theory. A theory is robust when it links the universe of words with the universe of observable facts in the field (see the introductory chapter, Savall & Zardet).

Table 6.1 presents an analysis of the themes and key concepts explored by the 213 theses prepared at ISEOR. The list of defended theses is presented at the end of this treatise.

TABLE 6.1 Analysis of the Themes and Key Concepts of the PhD and DBA Dissertations Prepared Within ISEOR

Themes	Key-concepts	Countries	Thesis number
Evolution of living conditions in and outside of work	Evolution of working conditions and information technology	United States	3
	Increasing digitalization of companies	Tunisia	20
	Integration of new technologies	France	11
	Changing expectations and lifestyles of "young people"	France	7

(continued)

TABLE 6.1 Analysis of the Themes and Key Concepts of the PhD and DBA Dissertations Prepared Within ISEOR (continued)

Themes	Key-concepts	Countries	Thesis number
Evolution of living conditions in and outside of work (cont.)	Analysis of work and non-work life	Mexico	14
	Analysis of dysfunctional stress and performance	Switzerland France	109
	Evolution of managers and the status of supervisors	France	6
	Need for recognition and positive evolution	France Belgium	130
	Need for personal enrichment. Fun at work, Internal-external friendliness, proximity of management, positive image, consideration of professional and personal projects	France Belgium	111
Absenteeism management	Absenteeism at work	France	8
Systemic approach and qualimetric measurement	Multi-dimensional socio-economic management model. Qualimetric approach (qualitative, quantiatative, financial)	United States France	92
Management of Human Potential	Creative capacity of teams of workers	France	16
	Involvement of individuals in strategic processes	Tunisia	45
	Link between trust and performance	Mexico	96
	Management of intangible investments	France	64
	Social regulation of structures and behaviors	France	41
	Loyalty and attractiveness of young entrants	France	111
	Management of non-viloent deviant behavior	France Belgium	110
Innovation management and corporate strategy	Innovation process	France Mexico	30; 83
	Ambidextrous innovation dynamics	France	145
	Proactive strategy	France Mexico	76; 98; 19
	Differentiation strategy	France	146
	Spin-off strategy	Tunisia	132
Marketing management	Internal–external marketing management	France	34
Sustainable performance	Evaluation of the sustainable performance	United States	89
	Day to day management (domination-submission model) and sustainable management (negotiation and reciprocal recognition-respect of actors)	France	133
	Sustainability of management methods	France	135
Management of interfaces between actors	Role of front-line managers and interfaces management	France	81
	Managing interfaces between actors	France	125
Integral quality	Integration of the quality dimension	France	54
	Socio-economic apporach to management and articulation with total quality management and organizational control	Brazil Tunisia	58; 127

(continued)

TABLE 6.1 Analysis of the Themes and Key Concepts of the PhD and DBA Dissertations Prepared Within ISEOR (continued)

Themes	Key-concepts	Countries	Thesis number
Integral quality (cont.)	Contribution of the socio-economic approach to management to lean management and to Kaizen for its efficiency	China	191
Link between quality-of-care and organizational quality	Adequacy of ISO 9001 and quality of care	France Belgium Switzerland Lebanon	66; 71; 93
	Strategy of public health and social organizations	France Belgium Columbia Lebanon	63; 65; 91
	Reconciliation of socio-economic and care objectives	France	60
	Caregiver and client mimicry	France	23
Management of family businesses	Family businesses and international development. Endogenous factor of sustainable development.	France Belgium United States	139
Internationalization	Internationalization	France	10
Strategic vigilance	Strategic vigilance	France	49; 67
Corporate Social responsibility	Social responsibility of enterprises	France	97
	Overall steering and measurement too for CSR	France Belgium Switzerland	117; 140
Scientific methodology	Computer science and methodology to help process scientific data	France	25
	Articulation of intervention-research and engineering research	France	105
Relations between researchers and practitioners	Dynamic cooperation between researchers and practitioners	France	88
	Know-how transfer between consulting firms and companies	France	38
Articulation of different hierarchical levels	Synchronized decentralization	France	29
Territory management and articulation between macro-meso-micro levels	Innovative job creation strategies	France	59
	Efficiency of public policies. Reconciling internal and external environments.	France Mexico Lebanon	61; 106; 131
	Acting on the local institutional environment for better information management	Central and Eastern Europe	82
	Steering inter-organizational cooperation on territorial strategies	France	116
	Territorial governance and public–private territorial strategy	France	143

(continued)

TABLE 6.1 Analysis of the Themes and Key Concepts of the PhD and DBA Dissertations Prepared Within ISEOR (continued)

Themes	Key-concepts	Countries	Thesis number
Territory management and articulation between macro-meso-micro levels (cont.)	Innovative networks. Mesoeconomics. Inter-organizational cooperation	Mexico Senegal	102 ;118; 136
	Developing the cooperation of non-governmental organizations	Lebanon	203
Inter-company management	Cooperation of stakeholders in multi-comany management	France	144
Entrepreneurship	Structuring of company and post-creation companies	France	32
	Entrepreneurial skills	France	114
	Entrepreneurship and overall performance	France	163
Information systems	Stimulating information systems to generate action	France Mexico	18; 69
	Clean-up practices	France	48; 110
	Links between hidden costs and information systems	France	47
Management control	Integrated management control	France	68
	Decentralized management control	France Belgium	121
Management of working time	Behavior of managers and managers' time management	France Germany	62
	Strategic management of working time	France	75
Illiteracy	Remedying illiteracy situations	France	78
Change management	Steering performance and change management	France Portugal Ghana Togo Mexico Liban Benin Morocco	12; 15; 85; 86; 126; 161; 192
	Measuring the level of resistance to change	France Brésil	128; 180
	Transformation of mental and cognitive maps	France	105
Budgetary management	Efficiency of budgetary management and socio-economic approach to management	France	107
Human Resource system	Effectiveness of sanctions–rewards systems	France Belgium	90
	Effictiveness of recognition systems	France	133
	Compensation system	France	39
Management of cultural organizations	Cultural organizations	France	124; 181

(continued)

TABLE 6.1 Analysis of the Themes and Key Concepts of the PhD and DBA Dissertations Prepared Within ISEOR (continued)

Themes	Key-concepts	Countries	Thesis number
Intercultural management	Local cultural advantages and modern insurance systems. Traditional solidarity.	Algeria	129
	Common language and intercultural skills. Intra and inter cultural differences	Angola Thailand France China Vietnam	52; 113
Sales management in not-for-profit organizations	Sales function in medico-social institutions	France Belgium	164
Union management	In-depth study of union dynamics	France	4
Working conditions and violence	Treatment of violence in high schools. Links between organizational dysfunction and violence	France	94
Professionnalization of sports clubs	Professionnalization of sports clubs	France	104
Role of the leaders	Impact of leadership management on performance	Turkey	112
	Management team and strategic bedrock	France	204
Public–private specificities	Profit and non-profit organizations Public–private comparison	France	9
Cultural organizations	Management of arts organizations	France	101
Integration of norms and standards	Tetranormalization et banking risks	France	178
	Norms and standards and socio-economic approach to management	France	141; 162
	Reasoned integration of norms and standards	France	205
Skills, training and employment	Training/job matching	France	5
	Concerted delegation	Burundi	70
	Integrated training	Burundi Morocco Tunisia	40; 73; 108
	Organizational learning	Mexico Lebanon	95; 133
	The knowledge-creating organization	Mexico	99
	Employability development	Tunisie	122
	Transformation from a job logic to a skills' logic	France	80
	Articulation of individual and collective skills	France	179
	Steering the transmission of skills and know-how by front-line managers	France Belgium	137

Note: The thesis numbers correspond to the list in the Appendix at the end of the Treatise.

REFERENCES

Buono, A., Savall, H., & Cappelletti, L. (2018). *Intervention-research in companies and organizations. From conception to publication.* Information Age Publishing.

Roche, A. (2013). Reconnaissance et performance: Proposition du concept de reconnaissance activatrice et d'un modèle intégrateur. *Thèse de doctorat en sciences de gestion,* Université Jean Moulin Lyon 3. [Recognition and performance: Proposal of a concept of active recognition and of an integrative model. PhD Disertation. University of Lyon 3].

Savall, H., (1977). *Manuel de formation doctorale: Construction de la thèse.* Document ronéoté. 47 p. [Training manual for doctoral students: WP. Lyon, France: ISEOR].

Savall, H., & Zardet, V. (1995). La dimension cognitive de la recherche-intervention: La production de connaissances par interactivité cognitive [The cognitive dimension of intervention-research: The production of knowledge through cognitive interactivity]. *Revue Internationale de Systémique, 10*(1–2), 157–189.

Savall, H., & Zardet V. (2004). *Recherche en sciences de gestion, approche qualimétrique, Observer l'objet complexe.* Economica. English translation in 2011 [The qualimetrics approach: Observing the complex object]. Information Age Publishing.

This page intentionally left blank.

CHAPTER 7

THE "HENRI SAVALL–ISEOR FOUNDATION"

Michel Grivel and René Charmasson

ABSTRACT

Organizations are discovering that their performance can't be exclusively financial and short-termist. The time to reconcile economic, social, societal and environmental requirements is coming. Capitalism has to be more human to succeed. Some business leaders recognizing the relevance of ISEOR's research works have decided with its leaders to create the Henri Savall-ISEOR Foundation to reward virtuous practices of overall performance management and bring their contribution by inviting managers who wish to go further, thanks to the results of Socio-Economic research and its field methods proven for half a century.

FOREWORD

Evolution of the "Reason for Being" of Companies and Organizations

Since 2019, with the French PACTE law, companies and organizations are invited to redefine their *reason for being*, whereas until now only profitability, maximization of profits with, as a good priority, the remuneration of shareholders were recognized as criteria of success. Leaders and managers who went beyond these criteria of success did so because they had the intuition and the conviction that, in order to succeed in the long term, *capitalism* had to be *humanistic* as well, whereas this quality of the global economy, desired by the majority of citizens throughout the world, was neither identified nor measured.

The reason for being, as understood by the legislator, is to go beyond the economic performance that is always essential to ensure survival and development. It is the company's

SEAM Treatise, pages 91–98

mission, its usefulness, its consideration of social issues, its contribution to society and to the environment in which it is embedded; the immediate environment such as the city, the region or the country; the distant or wider environment with commitments and practices of non-aggression of the planet gradually becoming practices of safeguarding and improving it in its biodiversity and through its climate.

Let's add that these new management practices of companies are progressively the object of labelling registered on the K Bis of companies, or by the certification B Corp[1] recognized at the international level. In other words, the reason for being, enriched with social, societal and environmental criteria, will be displayed as quality in the eyes of third parties. It becomes an example, which will progressively encourage the greatest number of companies to join this virtuous process.

ISEOR's Research Work

Since 1973, the *Research Institute of Socio-Economic Approach to Management* (ISEOR) has been working on the development of a scientific approach that will allow companies to change their view of the notion of performance and to act accordingly (Savall 1974–1975–1979–1981). The first research works focused on the *enrichment of human work* within organizations by demonstrating that poor conditions of life at work created numerous harmful *dysfunctions* that reduced the profitability of the whole. The status of the employee is profoundly modified. His or her role is evolving from that of an executor to that of a contributor to performance. The employees of the company and the organization become a living asset, a source of performance. This work has demonstrated, before its time, the relevance and necessity of the social approach now advocated by Corporate Social Responsibility (CSR). We know that the dissemination of the results of this research has already contributed significantly to this awareness (Savall, Zardet, 1987, 2008; Savall, Zardet & Bonnet, 2000, 2008).

By developing and deepening its research work, by intervening within companies and organizations to test and develop tools for measuring non-performance, such as the analysis and calculation of *hidden costs*, ISEOR researchers have, through their *intervention-researches* in companies and organizations, demonstrated to directors and managers that all social, societal and now environmental performances can improve the financial performance and profitability of structures. This happy consequence is fundamental, because it reinforces this essential notion of *humanist capitalism*. The economic world needs finance and investors as long as the latter choose not to be aggressive and to contribute to the sustainability of multi-performance. This is not only desirable, it is possible.

Furthermore, the Socio-Economic Approach of ISEOR has highlighted the double identity of the employee who is also a citizen, responsible in his city, his region, his country and today the world which has become a village. By considering the company or organization as a *system open* to its environment, ISEOR researchers have developed other tools for societal and environmental performance. From this point of view, the international deployment of the Institute's research in Europe, the Middle East and the entire American continent has enabled it to design and/or adapt its overall performance research methods by taking into-account the endemic variables present in these organizations, within their city, their region and their country.

1 WHY CREATE THE HENRI SAVALL–ISEOR FOUNDATION?

At a time when the practices of reconciling economic, social, societal and environmental performance are progressively on the agenda of our organizations, it is important to highlight and value the socio-economic achievements as we have outlined in the foreword. These achievements often originate in the humanistic values held by leaders, managers and teams of employees. They can be inspired by readings, conferences, university courses, some of which are directly derived from ISEOR's socio-economic research, but they can also find their source in education, civic life or another crucible. In all cases, they are born of the conviction that the sustainable presence of these values for all economic agents is becoming a requirement. If capitalism fundamentally allows for entrepreneurial freedom, its characteristic of being humanistic must be disseminated worldwide because it becomes vital.

The reason for being of the Foundation, created by informed leaders and by the founders of ISEOR, is therefore to put the spotlight on the remarkable socio-economic achievements that have led to the virtuous conciliation between the performances mentioned above. This conciliation is virtuous because the performances enrich each other and contribute to the prosperity of the whole. If these positive results are obtained by actors who are not necessarily familiar with ISEOR's research, they are no less remarkable. The founders of the Foundation, who are familiar with the work of ISEOR, also intend to recognize these practices, which are implicitly socio-economic in nature, as expressions of the values that they hold dear and that have been tirelessly developed and enriched by the research laboratory and its founder Henri Savall.

Its purpose will therefore be to:

- To highlight the remarkable socio-economic achievements, although not formalized by the ISEOR intervention-research method, in order to stimulate and encourage similar practices;
- To intensify the dissemination of socio-economic thought and knowledge that demonstrates that the relevance of management centered on the simultaneous development of human potential and the enterprise proves to be sustainable, effective, efficient and competitive.

2 THE FOUNDATION UNDER THE AEGIS OF THE FONDATION DE FRANCE

In December 2019, the founders of the Henri Savall-ISEOR Foundation, composed of busi ness leaders, accountants and research leaders of the constituent entities of ISEOR, have chosen to commit themselves for five years and to create their foundation under the aegis of the Fondation de France.

Creating a foundation under the aegis of the Fondation de France makes it possible to free oneself from the procedures for management and recognition as a public utility, since they are carried out by the Fondation de France as soon as it has given its approval to house the candidate foundation. This accreditation allows the founders and managers to devote themselves entirely to the vocation of their newly created foundation, which is recognized as a structure of general interest by the Public Authorities through the Fondation de France.

More precisely, the Foundation is a flow Foundation which does not invest its assets from donations. It commits the funds provided by the founders and may receive regular donations from donors to support its projects. The initial commitment is made by the founders.

It is a minimum of 200,000 euros brought within a maximum period of 5 years. In France, donations made by the founders as well as by the donors benefit from the tax advantages reserved for donations.

3 THE FOUNDATION'S MISSION

To complete the terms of Chapter 1, the Foundation, created in December 2019, aims to *promote and disseminate good management practices that take into-account the general interest and the common good in an uncertain world undergoing profound change.* It is part of a non-partisan mission to promote socially and ecologically responsible humanist capitalism, concerned with overall performance in the short, medium and long term.

Its mission is to highlight exemplary practices in reconciling economic, social, societal and environmental performance. This highlighting is based on socio-economic research of organizations as an engineering for the development of overall sustainable performance. This research, conducted by Henri Savall and the ISEOR Research Center for more than forty-seven years, has proven itself from a scientific point of view. However, they are still insufficiently disseminated and too often ignored by the general public.

This research has made it possible to introduce practices that allow the conversion of hidden costs linked to company dysfunctions into value creation for all economic actors. It challenges financial approaches, mainly focused on the objectives, often only financial, of managers and/or shareholders, which deteriorate the sustainable economic, social and environmental value of any organization concerned.

This research is intervention-research based on observations proving that financial management alone is based on a very incomplete approach to the factors of economic performance, focusing on capital flows, technological investments and labor costs. This reductionist approach is today in total contradiction with the new social and environmental responsibilities (CSR). It neglects the fundamental active factor of value creation that is Human Potential, composed of energies, competencies, and individual and collective behaviors. Finally, it distorts the essential role that financial investments could have in scientific, industrial, cultural or service projects that are innovative, useful and sustainable, which our world sorely needs today.

4 THE FOUNDATION INTENDS TO RECOGNIZE THE ACTORS WHO ACT FOR A RESPONSIBLE AND MULTI-PERFORMING MANAGEMENT

The Foundation wishes to distinguish *once a year*, through awards, actors who explicitly or implicitly implement responsible management, of a socio-economic type at levels such as: private or public companies and organizations, inter-company or territorial actions, public policies of a socio-economic type, actions in favor of international standards and norms making economic objectives compatible with social, societal and environmental objectives.

These prizes may concern actors, individuals or legal entities, who are responsible for achievements such as evaluations of company practices that implicitly respect socio-economic management, pioneering work by chartered accountants and company financial directors, qualimetric evaluations of the performance of inter-company cooperation actions, qualimetric evaluations of the search for overall performance at the territorial level, actions to make international standards and norms compatible and innovative academic or pedagogical work at all levels of education. The winners can therefore belong to the following categories:

- Managers or members of a company or organization other than a single person, French or foreign,
- Chartered Professional Accountants and/or interns preparing their diploma,
- Local and/or territorial authorities,
- Researchers or professor-researchers in university research teams and/or laboratories, French or foreign.

The Foundation's managers have defined these categories for the following reasons:

- Actors acting within companies and organizations are the bearers of practices that reconcile economic, social, societal and environmental performance,
- Actors acting within accounting firms and memorialists leading their clients, through their consulting approach and their actions, to go beyond the sole objectives of economic profitability and/or tax optimization and to seek the complementary reconciliation of social, societal and environmental performance,
- Actors from local and/or regional authorities who are the bearers of practices that reconcile economic, social, societal and environmental performance,
- Actors in university or laboratory research centers who contribute to the evolution of practices that seek to reconcile performances.

The prizes awarded by the Foundation are distinctions supplemented by endowments of up to €10,000 per prize. There are a maximum of four prizes per year, i.e., one prize per category, plus a special prize awarded by the jury. The awards are presented during annual ceremonies highlighting and promoting the prizewinners through articles in the print or digital media. A golden book of the Foundation will be published and will allow to remember the distinctions over the years.

However, certain categories of potential winners such as companies, profit-making organizations, accounting firms or memorialists are not fiscally eligible for the Foundation's financial endowments linked to the awards. In this case, the endowments will be paid to non-profit and general interest organizations, research centers chosen by the award winners and with the possible support of the Foundation. The choice of the recipients of the endowment linked to the prize is a complementary testimony to the social, societal or environmental commitment of the prizewinners. This testimony are presented during the award ceremony and relayed in press articles, interviews and the guest book.

5 EXAMPLE OF A COMPANY IMPLICITLY PRACTICING THE SOCIO-ECONOMIC APPROACH TO MANAGEMENT

5.1 An Evolution With a Strong Research, Innovation, and Anticipation Component

Ciril Company, now Ciril Group, was created in July 1978 with its founders as shareholders. Since its creation, its financial structure has been family-owned. It is still family-owned after the transmission to the second generation.

The company's first vocation was the edition of software, often specific to the new ranges of mini and micro-computer equipment of the 1970s and 80s, which allowed small and medium-sized companies to equip themselves. During its first years of existence, Ciril produced software for nearly 200 SMEs and SMIs in the fields of management and industrial production.

At the dawn of the 1980s, Ciril's managers shifted their focus from specific software development to the production of sector-specific software packages, i.e., standard software with evolving functionalities and quality, aimed at a specific profession, market or sector: first of all, software packages for local and regional authorities, then for the private hospital and clinic sector were produced. Today, 40 years later, the publishing of software packages for local authorities is still a core business, giving the group a leading role in France and in the French overseas departments and territories.

Following a strategic analysis of the evolution of the healthcare market and in view of the heavy investments to come, this activity was sold in 1997 to allow Ciril's R&D teams to concentrate on the buoyant local authority market and thus gain in excellence. To facilitate this strategic refocusing, Ciril's managers decided in 1998 to immediately expand their field of activity by integrating two other companies through external growth, thus enabling them to address an installed base of 350 customers. Everything became possible.

Since its creation, the company's managers have inscribed research and innovation in their DNA, allowing engineers to have the best development tools and to master the rapid evolution of computer systems, both in terms of hardware and software. The R&D teams have not hesitated to rework existing software already on the market several times in order to design new versions with greater value added in terms of the technological tools used and the functionalities.

It is this appetite for research that led the managers to take an interest in the field of geomatics (computerized geographic and cartographic systems), starting in 1993. The research activity, has integrated a team of researchers, working in close connection with specialized laboratories, French and foreign. This work led to the creation of the subsidiary Business Geografic in 2001.

During the 20 years of its existence, the subsidiary has developed by continuing to rely on the strengths of research and innovation. Its regular organic growth, completed by external growth, has allowed it to become a key actor in its market and to be a core activity of the current Ciril Group.

With the same concern, the company's managers asked themselves how to overcome the technological disruption caused by the Internet, high-speed networks and the emerging technologies of Cloud Computing. It was clear that users would gradually become accustomed to using their applications remotely, no longer wanting to be in charge of operating their own computer systems, and constantly demanding advanced information processing technologies that could be used with high levels of security. This vision and anticipation led to the creation of the SynAApS Cloud Computing activity, which meets the requirements of the other two software activities while creating its own customer base based on the strategy of high quality/security of data processing and storage. This new activity has obtained the appropriate international certifications and approvals enabling it to operate effectively in its market segment.

5.2 This Evolution Would not Have Been Possible Without the Reconciliation of Performance

To say that the company's managers were unaware of the emerging work of socio-economic research would be inaccurate. In 1978, Ciril's founder was largely inspired by the early work of ISEOR on the enrichment of human work, the strong need to take into-account the human capital of any company, with the corollary of reducing dysfunctions and the additional costs of regulation and return to normalcy. Without going so far as to practice the method of precise quantification of hidden costs and then that of procedures for reporting dysfunctions, with a view to reducing them, Ciril's management team has set in stone the following management principles:

- The company's primary asset is its employees, their skills and excellence, their ability to work together, and their understanding, sharing and commitment to the company's strategy,
- Each employee working in a team has the right to a space of responsibility that allows him/her to express his/her talent. This is possible with the organization of a bottom-up and top-down information system that allows them to position themselves well and to contribute well.

5.3 Social Performance Enriches Overall Performance. More Than That, it Feeds it!

Like any company, Ciril GROUP is a system that is open to its environment, both near and far. Its employees are also citizens, living in the city, and it would be absurd and dangerous to ignore this when they are within the company. It is fundamental that the management of the company take into-account this essential societal component, starting with the critical analysis of its vocation. Thus, to this day, Ciril GROUP managers attach great importance to the following principles or criteria:

- The principle (or criterion) of utility: Is the company's vocation, through the products it designs and sells and through the services it provides, useful to society and citizens? In other words, would society be poorer if these products and services did not exist? The relentless pursuit of usefulness is not only a societal requirement, it also leads the company's teams to excellence.
- The principle of non-aggression of the environment: How to tolerate that the exercise of a profession is destructive of the environment? All the components of the company are concerned. Of course, this is true for the Cloud Computing activity, which must evolve towards a "zero carbon" operation. But it is also true for the means of transportation used by employees, for energy savings, for waste management, with the corollary of eliminating non-recyclable waste.

Societal and environmental performance complements economic and social performance and contributes more and more strongly to the sustainable development of the company and the society in which it operates. This is the basis of the CSR approach, which today inspires company managers without them being explicitly aware of the Socio-Economic Management approach of ISEOR.

If the Foundation had existed, Ciril GROUP could have applied for the Foundation's annual prize. As this foundation does not exist, it chose to be one of the founders. Once the award had been obtained, Ciril GROUP would have dedicated its endowment to the association "Ma Chance Moi Aussi," created in 2015 by a retired industrialist. The association Ma Chance Moi Aussi supports the most vulnerable children from families with educational difficulties. Children who, like all children in the world, have potential within them. In collaboration with the families and the school, the accompaniment allows them to grow up serenely and to build a future. The meaning of the action is to work towards equal opportunities, to find a sustainable social cohesion, and to share a feeling of belonging to the Republic. By going beyond distinction and choosing this, Ciril GROUP's managers express their commitment to social, societal and civic responsibility.

CONCLUSION

Thus, the Henri-Savall ISEOR Foundation, by highlighting the actors practicing a management based on overall performance objectives, contributes to finding socio-economic solutions that will allow our society to respond to the numerous economic, social, societal and environmental challenges that will shape the world of tomorrow. By going to meet these virtuous actors, the founders hope that they will find in ISEOR's research results the methods and approaches that will allow them to progress further and continue to play a major role in our current societies marked by numerous turbulences.

NOTE

1. The B Corp or B Corporation or B Lab certification is a certification granted to for-profit, commercial companies that meet societal and environmental, governance and public accountability requirements. The name is an abbreviation of "Benefit Corporation," meaning a company that is known to have a beneficial impact on the world while being profitable. This certification is awarded by B Lab, a non-profit organization based in the United States, Europe, South America, Canada, Australia and New Zealand.

BIBLIOGRAPHY

1979: Henri Savall—*Reconstructing the company. Socio-economic analysis of working conditions.* Preface by François Perroux. Paris: DUNOD, 275 pages.

1980: Michel Grivel—*The impact of the management style of company directors and executives on the nature of working conditions in a computerized administrative environment*—Thesis, 3rd cycle, Lyon II and Lyon III Universities, 300 pages

1989: Henri Savall—*Enriching human work—Economic evaluation.* Preface by Jacques DELORS -Editions DUNOD 275 pages

1992: Henri Savall and Véronique Zardet—*Le nouveau contrôle de gestion. Hidden cost-performance method.* Editions Eyrolles. 399 pages

2015: Henri Savall, Michel Péron, Véronique Zardet, Marc Bonnet—*Le capitalisme socialement responsable existe.* Editions EMS – Management et Société

CHAPTER 8

SCHOOL OF THOUGHT IN THE HUMANITIES AND SOCIAL SCIENCES AND MORE SPECIFICALLY IN ECONOMICS AND MANAGEMENT

Application to the ISEOR Research Center

Roland Pérez

ABSTRACT

This contribution tries to answer the following questions: what is a school of thought in the humanities and social sciences in general and in the field of economics and management more particularly? How are they constructed? How do they develop? What do they become? Using this analysis grid, how can we situate ISEOR as a school of thought in the socio-economic field? We recall the conditions of its creation, its development over several decades, its activities and products, its institutional recognition

As this book is intended to become a reference publication—a "treatise" in a chosen field, "Socio-Economic Approach to Management" (SEAM), it is legitimate to ask whether this field and the collective that supports it constitute entities that are sufficiently assertive to distinguish themselves from other scientific, institutional or praxeological initiatives that can be observed in neighboring or comparable fields. More precisely, the question that this contribution wishes to answer is the following: was/is ISEOR the basis of a School of thought in the field of economics and management?

To try to answer this question, we will proceed in stages, starting with a definition of the very notion of School of Thought (ST), an operational definition nourished by a more general reflection

SEAM Treatise, pages 99–106

on the "movement of science" in general and more particularly in the field of human and social sciences (HSS), of which the disciplines of economics and management (EMS) are part.

1 ON THE "SCIENCE MOVEMENT"

These general aspects having been the subject of previous publications (Godelier & Pérez, 2015; Pérez, 2016), we will simply recall them briefly:

1.1 Scientific Practices and Paradigms

a. Exploitation vs. exploration: This distinction goes back to J.G. March (1988, 2008) and concerns all activities, via the stability of the framework of analysis or exercise of these activities. Exploration results in innovations; these may vary according to their purpose (process innovation vs. product innovation) and according to their scope (incremental vs. breakthrough innovation).
b. Scientific activity is paradoxical in that, although the aim of research is to produce new knowledge that will allow for major innovations, the practices implemented to achieve this are most often based on the strict use of protocols, to which are sometimes added some incremental innovations in the methods used, but without calling into question the initial conceptual framework. The whole constituted by this framework and the research practices and protocols that it authorizes constitutes a paradigm, as defined by T. S. Kuhn (1972). The attachment to the dominant paradigm at a given time expresses a majority current of ideas (commonly called "mainstream"), and thus a more or less supervised orthodoxy.
c. Sustainable heterodoxy and paradigm dynamics: We have proposed the concept of "*sustainable heterodoxy*" to express "a heterodox positioning in relation to the dominant paradigm and which resists, not only the test of time, but the various tests of validation in use in the scientific community considered..., founding in turn a new paradigm" (Pérez, 2016). Thus, in the history of science, a dynamic of paradigms is observed

1.2 On the Specificity of Human and Social Sciences and the Ambiguity of Economic and Management Sciences

1.2.1 The Human and Social Sciences Participate in the General Movement of Science Mentioned above, Notably in This Dynamic of Paradigms That Have Marked Its History

However, they present specificities that distinguish them from neighboring scientific fields and that complicate the paradigmatic dynamics. For the most part, these specificities are due to the relationship between the researcher and the research field; a relationship particularly emphasized by C. Levi-Strauss. This osmosis between the researcher and his/her field of research potentially presents numerous consequences which can constitute as many biases affecting the research carried out:

- behavior of the researcher "immersed" (*embedded*), or even participating in the activities studied (intervention-research);

- reactions (individual or collective) of the people in the environment studied (Hawthorne or Western Electric effect);
- the so-called "performativity" or "self-fulfilling prophecies" effect (Merton R.K., 1949; MacKenzie D.A., 2006) expressing the contribution of the discourse on a given item to the construction of this item;
- interactions between product and process: this aspect is less known, but nevertheless very sensitive in Human and Social Sciences: "the processes appear as *by-products*, or *induced products*, sometimes as important, if not more so, than the main product" (Pérez, 2017).

It is understandable that these scientific specificities, themselves very diverse from one HSS discipline to another, do not facilitate the stability of commonly accepted paradigms in a given social space, and *a fortiori* their international acceptance. It is therefore difficult to speak of a universal science, ignoring socio-cultural contextualizations (including linguistic ones), which are an essential component of Human and Social Sciences.

1.2.2 Heterodox Postures That Are Easy to Take but not Very Sustainable (Pérez, 2016)

The specificities of Human and Social Sciences, recalled above, favor the emergence of heterodox positions, based on a dissatisfaction linked to an overly orthodox reference to the dominant paradigm and using, to replace it *at a minimum*, new concepts and new schemes of analysis. As *words are not worth much*, the Human and Social Sciences have seen a flowering of heterodox, not to say heterogeneous, positions, more than in other scientific sectors. The risk, however, is to reduce these innovations to a few semantic elements, or even to a simple posture, sometimes to an imposture. This situation has been detrimental to the HSS, which could be considered, by many scientists in other fields, as soft sciences, or even pseudo-sciences.

1.2.3 On the Ambiguity of Research in Economics and Management

This domain of Human and Social Sciences has tried to escape the relative lack of consideration that sometimes affects the HSS by positioning itself in each of the segments that make it up (Pérez, 2004, 2016).

1.2.4 Economics and Hard Science Mimicry

This positioning is well known and does not date from yesterday. For a very long time, economists have dreamed of giving their discipline a status comparable to that of the physical sciences. Some of them may believe in it—especially researchers who came to economic research after studying the so-called "*exact* sciences." The result has been a formalization that calls for excessive mathematization, which is in fact quite conventional, since it is based on hypotheses that are often limited (rationality of actors, constraints on resources, utility functions, etc.). The creation of a *Bank of Sweden Prize in memory of A. Nobel*—commonly called the "*Nobel Prize in Economics*"—has reinforced this attempt by Economic Science to escape the status of soft science that used to be associated with Human and Social Sciences. Despite a few exceptions, this ersatz Nobel has accentuated the hold of the *mainstream* and the so-called neo-classical paradigm in this sector of knowledge.

1.2.5 Management Sciences as "Engineering Sciences" of Organizations

Management sciences were born as knowledge of *action based* on practices implemented in companies by managers who themselves came, for the most part, from the world of engineers. For a long time, a workshop/company was managed like a bridge was built, i.e., in a rational approach of flow and process optimization, without any particular consideration for the people composing the unit. In relation to this classical positioning, considering the Management Sciences as an appendix of the engineering sciences, the criticisms came from the world of the Human and Social Sciences itself, considering that the actors of the concerned organizations were too much ignored/neglected and proposing new tracks taking into-account these actors and their psycho-social characteristics. We have been able to speak of the "*clash of paradigms in management sciences*" (Pérez, 2004).

2 ON THE DYNAMICS OF SCHOOL OF THOUGHT

Since a school of thought brings together a certain number of people united by a common "Reason for Being," the existence of any school of thought is based on two complementary components: one of an ontological type concerns this "raison d'être" characterizing the grouping studied and allowing us to speak of a "school"; the other is of an eventual and organizational nature concerning the modalities of creation, evolution and the future of this specific entity

In the scientific field considered here, the reasons for being are to be linked to the "movement of science" mentioned above, in particular to that of the paradigm to which any school of thought in this field refers—explicitly or implicitly.

As far as the eventual and organizational dimensions of these schools are concerned, it seems possible/necessary, as for any finalized human organization, to distinguish several phases in their life itinerary:

- Their emergence and their respective contexts
- The main stages of their development
- Their future for those that are no longer relevant

2.1 Emergence of Schools of Thought

A school of thought is not born *ex nihilo,* whatever its founders or their disciples may say; there is always a "before" and hence the need to explain the context that allowed/favored the emergence of the considered school of thought. In the scientific domain in particular, this "before" necessarily exists, as the founder(s) of a School of Thought must necessarily refer to a state of knowledge, if only to show/demonstrate in what way the analyses presented propose a new paradigm likely to compete with, or even replace, the current paradigm(s). The history of any School of Thought, especially in the scientific field, thus calls for a prior presentation of the "landscape"—in historical, sociological, and geopolitical terms—in which the people concerned are situated and act.

For one cannot ignore the actors themselves and their personal trajectories. One cannot speak of a School of Thought without referring to at least one person who played a major role in its emergence, or even to an initial group whose conditions of constitution and internal organization should be explained further upstream...

Thus, the understanding of the emergence of a School of Thought calls for the crossing of the approaches of the two conceptions of historiography, conceptions that themselves constitute Schools of historical science: that of event-based history focusing on acts and persons, and that of the so-called "Annals" (Braudel 1960), which is part of a broader framework, allowing for the explanation of the context.

2.2 The Development of Schools of Thought

Since each school of thought constitutes a singular history, it would be futile to reduce each of them to a uniform development model. However, it is possible to propose some indicators that appear significant in the evolution of any school of thought, as in any social entity constituted around a finalized project, its "raison d'être" as mentioned above.

Number and evolution of members: this apparently simple quantitative indicator must be relativized according to the School of Thought considered; here the members are known and listed, there they are users whose importance can only be summarily evaluated. Nevertheless, with a constant definition, the evolution of such an indicator is significant.

Localization and territorial expansion: This geopolitical dimension completes the previous criterion. Most Schools of Thought have emerged in a specific place and many of them keep this place in their name (e.g., "Frankfurt School" in political philosophy). However, they are led to spread, here and there, according to the activities of their members, to become internationalized, which allows them to take place in other institutional and socio-cultural contexts, notably linguistic.

Activities and products: all Schools of thoughts are led to develop activities in relation to the desired goal. In the scientific sector, this translates into work that gives rise to publications in various media, books, articles, audio-visual documents, digital site and into transmission activities, either via the above-mentioned media or directly, courses, seminars, conferences, etc.

Organization: The very term "School" carries the idea of this transmission of work emanating from the School of Thought and of the coherence of the activities of its participants in relation to the founding principles of the said School of Thought. This implies an organization which, according to the School of Thought considered, can be more or less rigid, ranging from a strict, even sectarian regime—of the "Grand Master" and disciples type—to an open and tolerant mode of functioning.

Tensions and conflicts: these cannot be ignored; any new School of Thought generates, during its development, tensions and conflicts, even if it does not wish to create them *a priori*. These difficulties can arise both externally and internally: in the first case, hostile reactions can emanate from other Schools who are worried or even irritated by the emergence of a new School of Thought whose development could harm them. Internally, tensions may arise between founding members or with uncooperative followers; this may degenerate into open conflict, or even lead to a split in the School of Thought; history shows many examples of this, especially in the philosophical, political and religious domains.

Recognition: this indicator reflects, contrary to the previous ones, the approval of the society concerned by a School of Thought of its work and activities. In the scientific field, this recognition can take various forms, ranging from the editorial success of a particular publication emanating from a School of Thought to a prestigious distinction awarded to one of its leaders, highlighting the recipient's School of Thought.

2.3 The Future of the Schools of Thought

Like any human construction, a School of Thought cannot be immortal, even if such a wish may be that of its promoters or lauders; just as there was a "before," there will be an "after"... If their duration of existence is extremely variable, being able to be expressed in terms of centuries for philosophical or religious Schools of Thought, it is much more restricted in the field studied here, that of scientific Schools of Thought, notably in Human and Social Sciences and more particularly in Economic and Management Sciences.

A key moment in their development is the succession of the founder or the initial group. Following the example of the business world, where the law of the "third generation" is observed, few School of Thoughts in the scientific sector studied can report a lifespan spanning three successive leaderships, that is, in most cases, only a few decades.

After a School of Thought has faded away or broken up, the members who made it up usually join the new Schools that have taken over and of which they were sometimes the initiators; thus participating in this movement of science that is observed throughout human history.

3 ISEOR AS A SCHOOL OF THOUGHT

The preceding considerations make it possible to approach an argumented answer to the question posed, by placing it in a more general reflection on the evolution of knowledge and the dynamics of the Schools of Thought that express it. After a few introductory observations, the specific case of the ISEOR will be presented

3.1 How to Study a School of Thought in Human and Social Sciences?

The question may appear simple, even simplistic, to an outside observer: it is a question of "research on research"; consequently, researchers in Human and Social Sciences seem to fall into the easy way out, or even to be navel-gazing, by taking themselves as the object of study. Behind this cliché, a real dilemma arises: should a Human and Social Sciences researcher studying a Human and Social Science School of Thought belonging to the School of Thought he/she is studying or not? Each situation has opposite advantages and disadvantages.

Being outside the School of Thought has several advantages in terms of objectification and comparison with other Schools of Thought, but entails losses of information, especially those that cannot be collected via published documents or collected testimonies.

On the other hand, belonging to the studied School of Thought and being, consequently, in a position of "involved" or "participating" research, presents obvious advantages, notably in terms of observation time, information collection and interpretation of "weak signals." On the other hand, this position can present various methodological and even ethical risks. We are indeed in the situation described by the theorem of Lévi-Strauss, but in an even more marked way. Precautions should therefore be taken to accompany such research procedures.

Whenever possible, we recommend that these studies of Schools of Thought in Human and Social Sciences be carried out by a tandem of researchers—one internal, but slightly distanced, notably in terms of dependency relationships with those in charge of the School of Thought concerned; the other close, but nevertheless external. In any case, it is recommended that the authors of the study—*a fortiori* if there is only one—specify their position in relation to the object of study. This is not yet the practice in Human and Social Sciences, but it seems to us desirable, even necessary.

3.2 Application to ISEOR

It seems possible to apply the framework of analysis and the approach previously outlined to the experience of the creation of the ISEOR Research Center in 1975 and its development since then.

To get to the heart of the matter, we can put forward the following elements, beginning by specifying our position on the methodological and ethical level with respect to our object of study. We have known the ISEOR since its creation and have followed its activities and those of its principal members from time to time. Our attitude is globally empathetic towards this School of Thought, its members and its activities, while being totally independent of it in professional or personal terms.

a. **Context of creation:** ISEOR was created in Lyon, in 1975, by Henri Savall, with a small group of researchers (including Alain-Charles Martinet). The initiative was based on several correlated principles:
   - *Theoretically*: the new institute focused on the analysis of dysfunctions within finalized human organizations (the theory of "hidden costs-performance") and on the ways and means to remedy them, the "Socio-Economic Approach to Management" (SEAM); Henri Savall is situated in a double intellectual filiation; that of Germán Bernácer and that of François Perroux.
   - On the *methodological* level: the research conducted at ISEOR is of the "embedded" type, using Piaget-like clinical methods.
   - At the *institutional* level: the institute plays a dual role: on the one hand, as a professional partner (consulting and training) with the entities studied; on the other hand, as a research and teaching center with respect to the higher education institutions to which its members belong. This ambivalent situation accentuated the heterodoxy of the creation initiative.

b. **Development:** this has taken place over several decades and can be assessed by several indicators: the number of members has grown from a small group in 1975 to more than a hundred researchers in 2020; the area of influence, starting in Lyon, has expanded, via associated members to several cities in France (Montpellier, Paris, Strasbourg, etc.) and internationally (French-, English-, and Spanish-speaking countries).

   However, the organization remains centralized in Écully around the founder and his close relations, with relays in the associated teams and collectives where the influence of ISEOR is preponderant (ADERSE, Association of the Friends of François Perroux, etc.).

   Tensions and conflicts have not been lacking in this institution, as in all finalized human organizations: internally with the departure of researchers and externally with various institutions: university (Lyon 2), CNRS (section 37), ISMEA, etc.

c. The **activities and products** attest to this development: the fundamental activity of analysis and consulting in companies has concerned more than 2,000 organizations; it is coupled with a training activity, both in companies and at the university, completed by a training through research concerning the supervision of more than 200 doctoral theses. This intense activity is also expressed by the organization of about a hundred national or international conferences and is reflected in scientific publications including several dozen books and several hundred articles and communications.

d. **Finally**, this extraordinary activity has been the subject of institutional recognition: in France, for example, with the Rossi Prize awarded by the Academy of Moral and Political Sciences (Institut de France) jointly to Henri Savall & Véronique Zardet, or internationally, with agreements with the *Academy of Management* (AOM-USA), the International Cost Institute (IIC-Europe and Latin America) and the International Labor Office (ILO).

On the basis of the elements available to date, the main indicators of which have been recalled above, we can consider that, although the initiative taken in 1975 to create the ISEOR was heterodox in nature, it has proved to be sustainable and has given rise to a School of Thought in the field of Economic and Management Sciences applied to finalized human organizations. The present SEAM treatise illustrates, if need be, this observation.

What is the future of this School of Thought in socio-economic management? It is obviously too early to answer this question. This School of Thought and the institution that generated it—ISEOR—will have, like any comparable collective adventure, to ensure generational succession beyond the tutelary person of its founder. This succession has already begun, but it will have to become clearer in the coming years, allowing its members to make their own contributions to the inexorable movement of the history of science within human societies.

REFERENCES

Akerlof, G. A., & Shiller. R. J. (2009). *Animal Spirits: How human psychology drives the Economy and what it matters for Global Capitalism.* Princeton U. Pr.

Berry, M. (1983). *Une technologie invisible—L'impact des instruments de gestion sur l'évolution des systèmes humains.* W.P. CRG -École Polytechnique, Paris.

Braudel, F. (1960). *La démographie et les dimensions des sciences de l'homme.* Annales. Économies, Sociétés, Civilisations, 1960, p. 493.

Brondizio, E. S., & Pérez, R. (2017). L'École de Bloomington. In Cornu M., Orsi F., Rochfeld J. (Eds), *Dictionnaire des biens communs.* Paris, P.U.F., p 474–477

Caillé, A. (2005). *Dé-penser l'économique.* La Découverte-MAUSS, Paris.

David, A., Hatchuel, A., & Laufer, R. (2000). *Les nouvelles fondations des sciences de gestion.* Vuibert, Paris.

Godelier, E., & Pérez, R. (2015). Sur l'hétérodoxie soutenable en sciences sociales: Regards croisés sur les itinéraires de James March et Elinor Ostrom. *Revue de l'Organisation Responsable,* 7(2), 11–23.

Kuhn, T. S. (1972). *La structure des révolutions scientifiques.* Flammarion, Paris.

Latour, B. (1996). Avons-nous besoin de paradigmes ? One has wrongly accused Thomas Kuhn of a sociologism that he rejected. *La Recherche, 290,* p. 84.

Lévi-Strauss, C. (1950). Introduction à l'œuvre de Marcel Mauss. In M. Mauss (Ed.), *Sociologie et anthropologie.* PUF, Paris.

Mackenzie, D. A. (2006). *An engine, not a camera—How financial models shape markets.* MIT Press, Cambridge (MA).

March, J. C. (1988). *Decisions in organizations.* Oxford, Basil Blakwell

March, J. C. (2008). *Explorations decisions in organizations.* Stanford University Press.

Merton, R. K. (1949). *Social theory and social structure.* Plon, 1953.

Pérez, R. (2017). L'articulation marchand-non marchand—Cadre général d'analyse et application à la nouvelle économie numérique. *Entreprise & Société, 1,* 51–96.

Pérez, R. (2016). De François Perroux à Elinor Ostrom: la nécessité de postures hétérodoxes en sciences économiques et de gestion. In Blardone G. et Savall (Eds.) *Compétitivité et activité économique* (14° J. Fr. Perroux), Lyon, ISEOR éd., p. 169–176.

Pérez, R. (2004). Le choc des paradigmes en sciences de gestion. In Garel G. et Godelier E. (Eds.), *Enseigner le management.* Hermès, Paris, p. 120–130.

Segrestin, B., & Hatchuel, A. (2012). *Refonder l'entreprise.* Paris, Seuil.

Sen, A. (1999). *Development as Freefom,* (French translation: Knopf A. (2000), A New Economic Model, Paris, Ed. Odile Jacob.

Teulier, R., & Lorino, P. (Eds.). (2005). *Entre connaissance et organisation : l'activité collective,* La Découverte, Paris.

PART III

STIMULATING THE DEVELOPMENT OF SMEs, VERY SMALL- AND MEDIUM-SIZED ENTERPRISES (BUSINESS CREATION, FAMILY BUSINESS, CULTURAL . . .)

This page intentionally left blank.

CHAPTER 9

THE RESTAURANT THAT DIDN'T EXIST YET

Barbara Filippazzo

ABSTRACT

This chapter explains in which way and with which method the socio-economic management and the ISEOR team accompanied me in order to realize my project of creation of company: "the restaurant which did not exist." Indeed, we co-constructed with the ISEOR team a tailor-made intervention program to reduce as much as possible the dysfunctions and to recycle hidden costs in a preventive approach by using the method of scenarios.

When I had the desire to implement my business creation project "The restaurant that didn't exist" I immediately asked myself how the ISEOR team could accompany me. Indeed, it seemed obvious to me that I would use the socio-economic method to structure, organize, steer, and manage my team, but I had not yet imagined how the socio-economic intervention process could also be applied to the design of a business before its activity starts.

1 HOW BUILD A TEAM TO CREATE MY COMPANY ?

In 2014, my professional dream was to create an Italian-inspired "*bistronomic*" restaurant. It was a complete business creation: from the customized construction of the building to the restaurant offering. Indeed, our historical family business owned a vacant lot in an industrial zone, ready to be built to accommodate this restaurant project. It was therefore necessary to surround with the right people to build it in good conditions. Several questions related to the creation of this new company then arose: Where to start? Who should I surround myself with? How to go about it? What method should I use?

SEAM Treatise, pages 109–119

Very quickly, I saw two concurrent projects taking shape: the real estate project headed by my elder brother and the restaurant project for which I was the captain. Indeed, it was important to differentiate the management of the real estate project from that of the operation, in order to avoid a possible confusion between a "lessor" type partner and an associate. Thus, the objective of steering the governance and management bodies was quickly replaced by the objective of organizing the steering of these two projects in parallel.

According to experts in the hospitality industry, the economic viability of a business is traditionally conditioned by three criteria: "location, location, location." The quality of the location of my future restaurant was guaranteed by the ownership of this land: in the heart of a dynamic and fast-growing industrial zone, at the strategic crossroads of the Lyon metropolitan area's food wholesale market and the major agri-food and logistics head offices, next to the main freeway junctions and the southern ring road of the city. However, my key objective was to ensure the economic viability of this restaurant project by means of a strong identity, without relying solely on the quality of its location, in particular by developing an adapted offer of products and services.

In view of the stakes of this large-scale project (we will see later the size of the restaurant and the investment), I chose to be accompanied by the ISEOR team in order to move from dream to reality, that is to say to build a strategic project and to prevent, upstream of the opening, the dysfunctions and hidden costs customary in a business creation. ISEOR's support consisted in helping me build a coherent and innovative offer, write the premises of the dream and "put the ideas down" by structuring them in a strategic macro-planning (Filippazzo, 2016, 2018).

This chapter thus shows how I mobilized the socio-economic approach to management to anticipate dysfunctions, based on my personal experience. This general problem quickly turned into a multitude of concrete problems to be solved, both internally and externally, in terms of products-market, human resources, organization, economic and social aspects; for example: how to maintain the construction deadlines of the building in order to plan the recruitments and the start of the activity? How to clarify the positioning and the ambiguous role of my brother to gain in efficiency and productivity? How to take into consideration the recurrent staff turnover in the restaurant sector while avoiding the traditional overstaffing at the opening of a restaurant? How can innovative management of the future team, in a sector where practices are often "archaic," allow for the development of employee loyalty through empowering tools and practices? How to ensure that the restaurant's offer provides a competitive edge, or how to build an adapted offer of products and services to differentiate itself in the catchment area (Savall A., & François, 2015)? How can I build economic and budgetary projections over three years, without any history and given my perfectible financial skills?

2 IMPLEMENTATION OF THE SOCIO-ECONOMIC APPROACH TO MANAGEMENT TO BUSINESS CREATION?

2.1 Presentation of the Restaurant Creation Project

In 2014, when I started to concretize this business creation project, I was then 27 years old. Holder of a master's degree in hospitality management from the Paul Bocuse Institute. I had previously followed a university course at the IAE of Lyon in team management and quality, within the Euginov department, an internal school of the IAE specialized in socio-economic management. I had the chance to do my master's apprenticeship, then four years in a position of operations manager of the franchisee network in a group of restaurants in

Lyon practicing the socio-economic management for over 15 years. This professional experience allowed me to acquire real management skills. Thanks to the integrated training within this restaurant group, I put into practice the socio-economic theory (Savall, 1974–1975; 1979; Savall and Zardet, 1987, 1995) discovered during my university studies.

Of Sicilian origin, my project consisted in creating a "*bistronomic*" restaurant of Italian inspiration. The objective was to combine tradition and modernity, thanks to a warm place and an innovative cooking, which takes again old typical Italian receipts by bringing them a key of contemporary cooking, containing fresh and raw products which we would transform on the spot.

This is how we propose a menu that changes every week in order to respect the seasonality of the products and to keep our customers loyal, while constantly creating new associations of flavors and textures. We make fresh homemade pasta every day that we offer on the menu but also for take-away. An undeniable advantage, after clarifying our respective roles, was my brother's role as a family investor, allowing me the flexibility to build a custom-made building, where we now welcome 120 customers inside, and 100 customers on our shaded terrace, surrounded by green spaces. The restaurant is of easy access by car with over 75 parking spaces. Our primary business is traditional catering, complemented by a seminar room that can accommodate up to 40 people.

The Cavatello restaurant team is currently composed of 10 people: four in the kitchen and four in the dining room, including myself, as well as two apprentices (one in the kitchen and one in the dining room). I have decided to implement a policy of measured versatility, both within each team, dining room and kitchen, and between the two teams. For example, in the kitchen, all the employees change jobs every month and a half, so that they regularly practice all the jobs; in the dining room, it's even more frequent, everyone changes jobs almost every day, when all the staff is sufficiently trained. In addition to this multi-skilling, each person is also responsible for a cross-functional mission such as operation management, stock management, training, card creation, etc. A team of two employees oversees each of these missions and meets regularly with management for validation. This organization allows us to build loyalty and value among our employees, and to stimulate them so that each one is a driving force at his or her level to improve socio-economic performance.

2.2 ISEOR's Accompaniment Process

We have co-constructed with the ISEOR team an intervention program for the creation of this company. Indeed, since September 2014, we have been supported, through a combination of inter-company training and personalized support internal to the company. The inter-company trainings provided by ISEOR are very useful because they allow participants (myself, managers, and even some employees) to exchange with participants from various professions, companies and sectors. The value added of this device is important, because the problems which are approached there and the improvement of the targeted competences (management control, a market study, management of the human potential, sales...) concerns any manager or leader.

In order to transform our desire into reality, during the first meeting with the ISEOR team, we mainly expressed our expectations and needs. The "objectives of the intervention-research" (Buono, Savall, & Cappelletti, 2017) were then worded as follows:

"*To ensure the financial set-up and economic viability of the activity*": it was key to help me acquire the technical and sales skills to best steer the different partners of the creation project (lawyer, banker, chartered accountant...), and thus accompany me to build a solid, realistic and ambitious provisional budget;

"To steer the different governance and management bodies to ensure the projected opening date" (planned for about 18 months after the start of the intervention-research), by organizing structured relations between governance and management, by ensuring the integration of the different partners and external service providers, as well as by defining the recruitment policy and an adapted socio-economic management system;

"*Work out a short, medium and long term strategic project"* by identifying the values and the main political axes to be inculcated in the future teams, by formalizing the strategic project thanks to socio-economic tools such as the Internal and External Strategic Planning, the Priority Action Plan AP, the competency grids and the scheduling sheets by operation (FOO). It was also a question of setting up a competitive watch and an in-depth market study to root the commercial policy in the territory. (Savall and Zardet, 1995, 2005)

These objectives were then translated into dedicated support systems:

- A steering group to manage governance-management relations and ensure the smooth running of the intervention-research;
- Personalized assistance focused on the economic viability of the forecasted budget;
- An "offer and concept" focus group to consolidate the services and identity of the restaurant and to carry out a market analysis;
- A "human resources" focus group to deal with the recruitment of the team, the management policy of the organization and the socio-economic tools for steering, for which I asked some people from my professional circle to conduct "expert interviews," particularly on the issue of recruitment.

Each of these devices was regularly activated over the 18 months of the intervention-research process (Table 9.1). The rhythm of the intervention was coordinated and paced according to the progress of the creation project. The interveners, in close collaboration

TABLE 9.1 Planning of the Intervention-Research

	Mois																		
Méthodes	**1**	**2**	**3**	**4**	**5**	**6**	**7**	**8**	**9**	**10**	**11**	**12**	**13**	**14**	**15**	**16**	**17**	**18**	**19**
Personalized assistance IESAP Forecasted budget and economic sustainability	1	2	3	4	5		6		7			8		9		10		11	12
Project group Concept, business proposal and internal layout		1	2			3			4			5							
Project group Recruitment, management, and organization								1		2			3	4	5	6	7		

with me, designed this planning according to the milestones of the creation process (building permit application, trips to Italy, etc.) and the forecasted opening date of the restaurant.

As this was my first business creation project, I also contacted the Chamber of Commerce and Industry (CCI) to know more about their support system. Nevertheless, the systems they offered seemed incomplete in view of my socio-economic approach to business creation. Indeed, the Chambers of Commerce mainly train managers in the orthofunctioning of the company, whereas the socio-economic method allowed me to move to a foresight and "preventive" vision of the dysfunctions: to anticipate them, to measure them and to analyze them, without being "naive" or utopian, and by practicing the method of the scenarios. But, thanks to its network and access to their company database, the Chamber of Commerce allowed me to carry out a competitive watch. I also took part in several events that it organized in our catchment area, to give me visibility and thus promote my project, even before it was born!

2.3 Significant Achievements of the Coaching Process

Thanks to this accompaniment, I managed to structure my ideas and thus move forward on different priority axes. In fact, this process allowed me to question all the themes, including those that I thought I had mastered. Indeed, a business creation implies regular and multidisciplinary adaptations and improvements. Table 9.2 shows the various themes (column 1) that we worked on during 18 months, as well as the tools developed and used (column 2) and their impacts in terms of qualimetric results (column 3).

Figure 9.1 and Table 9.3 present the Internal and External Strategic Planning developed as well as the details of the service offer, developed according to the methodology proposed by ISEOR (Savall & Zardet, 1995, 2005).

Table 9.4 presents another significant achievement: the integration and training schedule for the restaurant team. The two managers were hired three weeks before the restaurant was scheduled to open, and the rest of the team was hired two weeks before. The detailed integration and training program for the first two weeks is presented below.

TABLE 9.2 Themes, Tools, and Impacts Targeted During the Intervention-Research

Themes	Tools/Details/Processes	Impacts/Qualimetric Results
Time management	• Macro-planning (see above) • Internal and External Strategic Planning (see below) • Detailed planning of operations • Interviews with experts and choice of advices.	• Steering/Knowing the goal • Improved time management • Providing the team with a strategy and the guiding thread of targeted objectives
Offer: products and objectives	• Product lines mapping (see below) • Looking for brand name/Graphic designer/graphiste/Trademark registration/History of the company	• Survey of the catchment area • "Individual" axis: Offer of "tavola calda" • Creating an identity of the place
Economic sustainability	• Qualimetric budgeting (see below) • Economic balances for the recruitment. Training/Induction	• Less than 5% budget difference between forecasted and actual budget • Calculated decision-making process
Human Resources	• Integration and induction planning (see below) • Competency grids (see below)	• Recruitment of the team 8 to 15 days before kick-off • Formalizing to enhance awaareness and to harmonize processes.

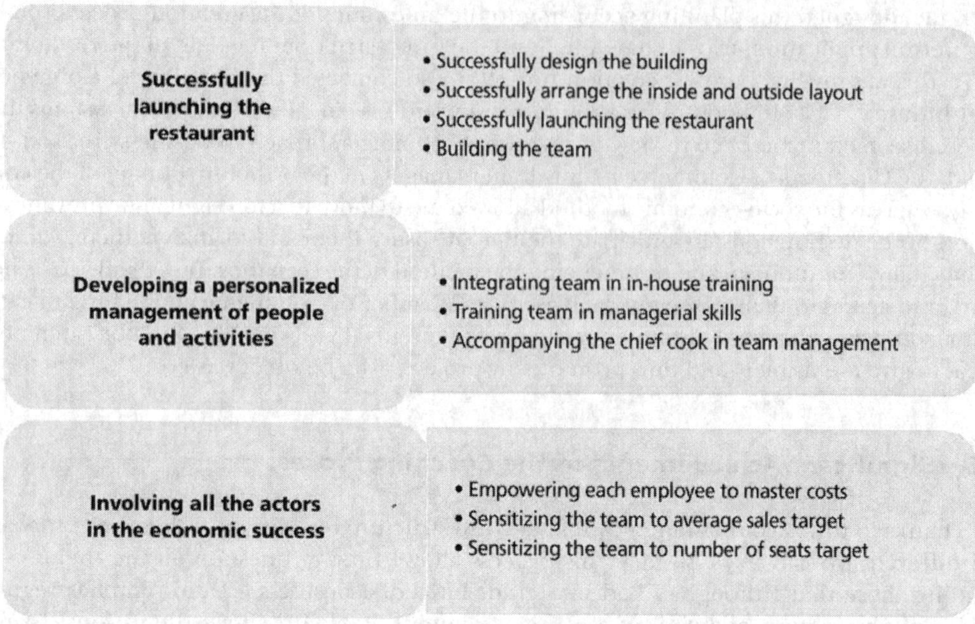

Figure 9.1 The first Internal-External Strategic Action Plan (IESAP) of the start-up company

Table 9.5 represents the team's "target" competency grid, as the aim was to project the evolution of each person after six months of operation.

3 WHAT LESSONS FOR FUTURE ENTREPRENEURS ?

What I retain today, four years after opening my restaurant Cavatello in November 2016, is to have succeeded in imagining the orthofunctioning in my business creation project, while considering several scenarios according to the hazards. Indeed, this "preventive" coaching allowed me to move from the dream to a realistic project by writing down the main lines, daring to "lay them out" and formalize them using tools that allowed them to be structured.

In this way, I advanced, step by step, while training myself. I learned that I had to master my time management, that I had to promote the concept when it did not physically exist, which allowed me to dare to think about several hypotheses. Such a process is key in a business creation project because it allows the concrete projection of the entrepreneur. This projection is facilitated by the "scenarios" method, where the entrepreneur studies a multitude of working hypotheses, instead of limiting himself/herself to a single scenario that leaves no room for the unexpected. This method implies the regular updating of all the scenarios, notably by exchanges between all the actors of the project and the formalization step by step of the retained options. These actors were the architect, the chartered accountant, the lawyer and the various service providers such as the kitchen designer, the furniture manufacturer, etc. ISEOR's support through the use of the socio-economic approach to management method enabled me to reduce the dysfunctions and to recycle hidden costs that I wanted to avoid, by means of developing my skills in time management, communication-coordination-cooperation and concerted delegation.

TABLE 9.3 Identification of the Service Offer

Product Lines	Product/Service	Market	Technology	Human Potential	Volume/Capacity/Duration
Lounge	Variety of drinks with and without alcohol	Truck drivers/workers/ handlers/employees/ executives	Counter	**Bartender:** *Special skills:* welcoming + assistance to clients	About 30 clients 10 minute average attendance time + cosy place for 15 clients
Tavola Calda	Fast food, warm and cold food displayed or take-away	Truck drivers/workers/ handlers/employees	Tavola Clada private space/ eaten standing and kitchen	**Bartender + Part-time waiter:** *Specific skills:* welcoming + assistance to clients	About 30 clients
Restaurant	Culinary delights and daily specials	Employees/executives/ groups/workers	Restaurant and kitchen space	**Restaurant room team:** *Specific skills:* welcoming + speed	110 seats + 124 terrace restaurants
Seminars	Room+ breaks + lunches	Companies	Dedicated space at the first floor: 49.7 square meter + kitchen party room at the ground floor: 42.8 square meter + kitchen	**Staff to be recruited:** *Specific skills:* sales	45 participants

TABLE 9.4 Team Integration and Training Schedule

Week #42				Week #43			
Day	**Themes**	**Duration**	**Persons involved**	**Day**	**Themes**	**Duration**	**Persons involved**
1st day: Monday, October 17	*Integration:* concepts, corporate values, management principles	3 hours	All team	6th day: Monday, October, 24	*Communication–Coordination–Cooperation:* Individual meetings, including personalized assistance on calendar and log-book	1 hour per client	All team
	Welcoming training: telephone reception, taking care of clients and claims	3 hours	All team		*Customized workshops:* Sorting out, Cleaning up, Sorting out, Setting up the tables (TBD).	4–5 hours	All team
2nd day: Tuesday, October 18	*Management tools:* calendar, time management, PAP, PNAC, resolution sheet	3 hours	All team	7th day: Tuesday, October, 25	*Preparing the kitchen* for tomorrow's samples, completing clean-up and sorting out the kitchen and receiving produces	All day	Kitchen team
	Active selling training: Explanation of the menu and products, What is selling? Simulation	3 hours	All team		*Preparing the room:* Explanation of the winelist, completing sorting out room and lounge and the reserve, receiving products	All day	Room team
3rd day: Wednesday, October 19	*Opening and closing training:* company facilities, room, and kitchen	3 hours	All team	8th day: Wednesday, October, 26	*Tasting dishes of the menu:* Setting up kitchen, samples for taste at 12:30 p.m. before sorting out	3 hours	All team
	Training on cashing: cashing and paying out, using the cash drawer, checking cash drawer balance, simulation	3 hours	Room team		*Report on tasting:* explanation of the produces and of winelist	3 hours	All team
4th day: Thursday, October 20	*Inventory management training:* Taking stock, ordering, inventory taking	3 hours	All team	9th day: Thursday, October, 27	*Setting up the launch:* room, kitchen, place, cloakroom. Debriefing.	Starting at 11:00 a.m.	All team
	Food sanitation: HACCP norms and standards, organization of the kitchen, intervention of outside companies	3 hours	Kitchen team		Debrief of the evening, Short team meeting, Areas of improvement, Feed-back.	1 hour	All team
5th day: Friday, October 21	*Tidying up and displaying rooms:* Dining room, kitchen, seminar rooms, offices, terrace	4 hours	All team	10th day: Friday, October, 28	Overall setting up before opening	TBD	All team
				Opening of the restaurant is fixed on Monday, November 7th, 2016, after an 11th integration and training of all team			

TABLE 9.5 "Expected" Competency Grid After 6 Months of Activity

Competences to reach after a six-month period	Skills Grid																												
	Within the organization at the beginning of the period																												Observations
Operations	Operations:																									Specific know-how			
	Day-to-day management																			Development management									
	Management				Common Core					Service						Kitchen													
Actors	Steering acitivity-time management	Steering and reporting on time management	Participating in the PAP process	Participating in the PNAC process	Opening and closing the restaurant	Participating in the service to clients	Participating to cooking	Presenting and promoting the menu	Welcoming (clients, internal clients, leads, suppliers)	Bartender	Waiter at TAVOLA CALDA	Managing bar inventories	Managing receipts	Producing in the restaurant	Managing restaurant and respecting procedures	Production in the kitchen	Managing kitchen inventories	Maintaining the workstation for cold food	Maintaining workstation for hot food	Participating in rules and procedures improvement	Steering the activities of seminars					Foreign languages			
CEO	■	■	■	■	■	■	■	■	■	■	■	■	■	■	■	◪	◪	◪	◪	■	■					■			
Chef Cook	■	■	■	■	■	◪	■	■	■	□	◪	□	□	□	□	■	■	■	■	■	□								
Senior Cook	■	■	■	■	□	□	■	■	■	—	—	—	—	□	—	■	◪	■	■	■	—								
Apprentice Cook	■	■	■	■	□	—	◪	■	■	—	—	—	—	—	—	◪	□	■	◪	■	□								
EPR	■	■	■	■	□	■	□	■	■	—	◪	—	—	◪	□	◪	□	■	◪	■	□								
Butler	■	■	■	■	■	■	□	■	■	■	■	■	■	■	■	□	□	□	□	■	■								
Senior Bartender	■	■	■	■	■	■	□	■	■	■	■	■	■	■	■	□	□	□	□	■	■								
Senior Waiter	■	■	■	■	□	■	—	■	■	◪	◪	□	◪	◪	◪	—	—	—	—	■	■								

CONCLUSION

A business creation project requires both a training effort for the entrepreneur and a work of anticipation and preparation of the project as such. A business start-up raises a lot of questions, and what we retain as a key factor of success is to accept to project oneself and that the scenarios can evolve. This "flexibility of work" was materialized by "back and forth" (articulations) and regular updates of all the socio-economic tools (Figure 9.2). This allowed us to imagine and design our project, even though it was initially unclear, despite our strong determination to see it through.

This socio-economic support allowed us to avoid many dysfunctions, with the support of a budget. Some of them remained, despite all our efforts to avoid them: staff turnover, although lower than elsewhere- and the difficulties to start some of the activities (seminar and "tavola calda" activity).

Nevertheless, overcoming the difficulties of these first four years of activity has allowed us to develop new skills, such as concerted delegation, strategic patience and economic steering. Our improvement and development projects are no less important. Indeed, we are working every day towards greater organizational and managerial maturity, through greater autonomy and discipline in the use of socio-economic tools. The stakes remain unchanged, especially in the context of the global crisis since 2020: to gain in productivity and professional development of each employee. The opening of a second entity should allow us to start an exciting entrepreneurial adventure again, with the contribution of a socio-economic team.

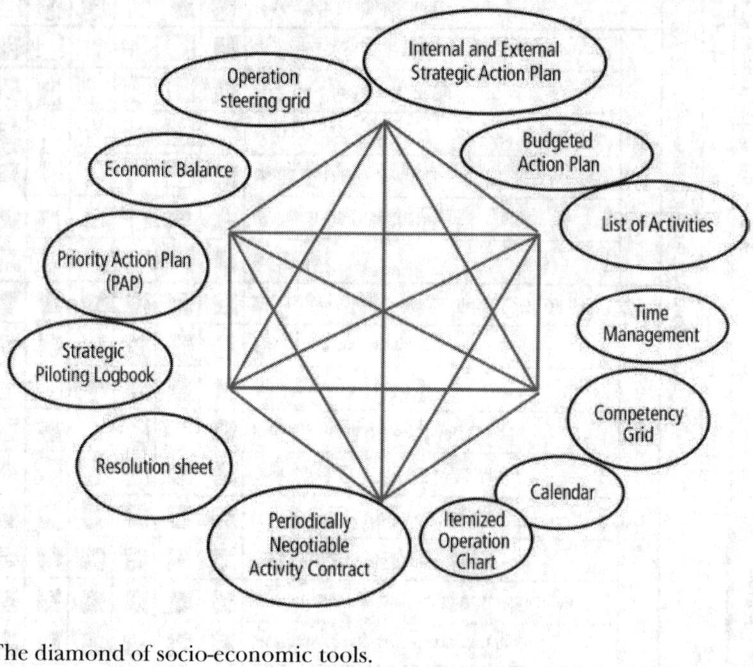

Figure 9.2 The diamond of socio-economic tools.

REFERENCES

Filippazzo, B. (2016). *"The restaurant that didn't exist...."* Presentation at the ISEOR Fall Colloquium, Lyon.

Filippazzo, B.(2018). *Developing work reflexes in a rigorous manner by considering intergenerational.* Presentation at the ISEOR Fall Colloquium, Lyon.

Savall, A., & François, P. (2015). *Conception d'une stratégie de différenciation: Contribution de la recherche-intervention socio-économique.* Presentation at the colloquium co-organized by ISEOR and the Academy of Management.

CHAPTER 10

THE CREATION OF SUSTAINABLE ENTERPRISES

Contributions of the Socio-Economic Approach to Management (SEAM)

Christophe Combaudon and Helga Fouré-Joopen

ABSTRACT

The improvement of interactions between the structures and behaviors of actors during the start-up phase of an enterprise is an important factor to take into account in terms of consolidating its survival and development. This contribution analyzes the results and impacts of a process of setting up a socio-economic approach on the performance of a company in the creation phase based on 12 scientific observation fields.

Our objective is to study the improvement of the sustainability of post-creation enterprises, in relation to the integral quality of management, because few works have exposed its importance until now. After the presentation of the problematic, we explain the field and the object of our research, and then approach the contributions and limits of the academic contributions as well as the concepts of the Socio-Economic Approach to Management (SEAM) applied to the object of our research. The applied research methodology section leads us to the application cases and the outcomes of the intervention-researches, which are commented on in the last section.

SEAM Treatise, pages 121–128

1 POST-CREATED COMPANIES

Beyond the ease of creating a business, its sustainability remains an important challenge: indeed, 50% of the businesses created disappear before reaching their sixth year of existence (INSEE, 2017) . This high mortality generally occurs in the "pivotal years" of the business, between 2 and 5 years, when the probability of failure increases by 50% compared to the first years and represents double the rate of the later years.

The explanatory factors commonly put forward are either internal, such as the size of the company, its age and financial factors, or external, such as economic periods or the sector of activity. Nevertheless, we observe that despite these explanations, the high failure rate remains constant.

Many authors such as Crutzen and Van Caillié, (2009), Khelil et al. (2012), Smida and Khelil, (2020) have tried to give an answer to the question of the sustainability of start-ups. Fayolle (2012), Verstraete T. et al. (2012) and Osterwalder (2002) have made numerous contributions, demonstrating that the improvement of the structure of a startup based on its "business model," is an important factor of sustainability (Combaudon, 2015). Other research, such as that of Bruyat (1993), exposes the importance of the profile and behaviors of the entrepreneur for the success of the creation of his company. More recently, through the principle of effectuation, Saravhasty (2011) insists on the behaviors necessary for the success of the entrepreneur. Some works (Degeorge and Messeghem, 2016; Torrès, 1997) have focused on the importance of the integral quality of management in the context of business creation. But approaching business creation only from a structuralist or behaviorist perspective has many limitations.

By integrating the research mentioned above, we ask the question: How can we improve the durability of these companies in the creation phase? The study of the links between the structures and the management appears to us as a key factor of improvement of the sustainability of the companies in phase of creation.

1.1 Scope and Purpose of Our Research

Experiments were carried out on 20 post-creation companies, having been in existence for 3 years. These were single-site structures belonging to various sectors of activity, with a workforce of between 1 and 10 people. This research was longitudinal and transformative, with an analysis of materials covering a period of 24 months. The scope of the research object was focused on the link between global management and the sustainability of the company in its creation phase.

1.2 SEAM Concepts Applied to the Research Object

The Socio-Economic Approach to Management involves a strategic analysis based on three elements (Savall & Zardet, 1987, 1995):

1. The internal potential of the company as a strategic vector;
2. Internal resources as the driving force of the company;
3. Strategic implementation as a potential multiplier.

The Socio-Economic Theory proposes a management model that closely integrates the social dimension of the enterprise and its economic performance (Savall and Zardet, 1987).

It includes overall management methods and tools based on human potential, which is considered to be the only active factor in the creation of value added in organizations. Technical and financial capital is itself an "inert" factor or tool (Savall et al. 2015).

Savall (1975) developed a fundamental hypothesis: the level of economic performance of an organization depends primarily on the quality of the interaction between human structures and behaviors within the organization. A rigorous and rapidly effective change management method allows for the implementation of concepts, with operational methods and tools such as the qualitative, quantitative and financial diagnosis (evaluation of hidden costs), the competency grid to evaluate individual and collective skills the time self-analysis grid to analyze one's activity, the priority action plan to decide which actions to implement, focus groups to improve negotiation, communication and cooperation between actors, economic scales to make more reasoned decisions, piloting logbooks to monitor the progress and effects of actions...

We applied the methodology of socio-economic research-intervention (Savall and Zardet, 1987) by integrating an important requirement in terms of observation of field materials and the implementation of the intervention model. Applied to post-creation companies, our research-intervention takes into consideration the development of human potential as the main factor of efficiency in the short and long term, as a guarantor of its survival and sustainability (Fouré-Joopen and Combaudon, 2017).

2 RESULTS FORM THE CASES OF POST-CREATED COMPANIES

We present the 20 fields on which we tested the hypothesis that the joint improvement of structures and behaviors improves the survival and development of post-created companies.

The diversity of the fields observed was very interesting to contrast the contexts of activities. Through the observation of different sectors of activity, we confirmed that the vital principles of survival-development of the young enterprise are not the concern of a specific sector of activity. Thus, the search for improvement in structure-behavior was generalizable and could be a source of generic contingency (Savall and Zardet, 1996, 2004). It should be remembered that generic contingency corresponds to the identification of invariants in organizations, which thus constitute a base of knowledge common to all organizations, identified in conjunction with the specificities of each case and each situation (contingency).

We processed the materials according to a qualimetric approach (Savall and Zardet 2004), which makes it possible to simultaneously elaborate qualitative knowledge (expressed with key words from interviews with the actors of the organizations) and quantitative knowledge (expressed with key numbers and mathematical treatments using quantitative and financial data).

The qualimetric approach allows us to restore all the richness of the field materials:

- The qualitative form improves and makes knowledge more clearly explicit,
- The quantitative form allows us to better measure the meaning of the remarks by reducing the subjectivity and facilitating the comparison of the elements studied,
- The financial form is a monetary translation of the field observations.

At the beginning of our research-interventions, these companies had been operating for an average of 3 years and had been accompanied for 24 months. All of the fieldwork is summarized in Table 10.1.

TABLE 10.1 Presentation of the 20 Cases of Enterprises in the Post-Creation Phase

Field	Kind of industry	Number of employees	Revenue of the company at the beginning of the intervention-research	Duration of the intervention-research
1	Trade in organic and natural products	6	€ 1,106,000	24 months
2	Short distance transport	6	€ 954,000	24 months
3	Management Consulting	2	€ 89,000	24 months
4	Home automation	3	€ 800,000	24 months
5	Industrial Automation	10	€ 1,757,000	24 months
6	Online games	8	€ 753,000	24 months
7	Thermoformed confort soles	2	€ 44,300	24 months
8	Development of artificial intelligence software	6	€ 897,000	24 months
9	Installation of solar panels	2	€ 446,000	24 months
10	Car washing, cleaning and renovation	10	€ 172,000	24 months
11	Children's amusement park	3	€ 178,000	24 months
12	Bakery	6	€ 125,200	24 months
13	Trade in organic and natural products	5	€ 1,501,000	24 months
14	Manufacture of food supplements	1	€ 83,000	24 months
15	Secretarial services for companies	3	€ 144,000	24 months
16	Communication agency	3	€ 126,000	24 months
17	Indoor soccer room	4	€ 243,000	24 months
18	Dietary advice	1	€ 56,000	24 months
19	Sales of artisanal ice cream	3	€ 370,000	24 months
20	Hosiery	6	€ 1,435,000	24 months

2.1 Main Outcomes

According to Savall and Zardet (1995), social performance can be considered improved when the organization registers positive results on the six main themes of working conditions, work organization, communication-coordination-cooperation, time management, integrated training and strategic implementation. In the course of our work, we carried out qualimetric diagnoses enabling us to measure the dysfunctions at the start of the research-intervention.

In these post-created companies, we observed a certain number of dysfunctions that we classified in the different themes linked to the social performance defined beforehand (Figure 10.1); the most frequent dysfunctions were related to

- time management: lack of planning, difficulties in managing priorities, managing deadlines, etc.
- strategic implementation: difficulties in making the strategy clear, in sharing the strategy, etc.
- work organization: problems in the distribution of tasks, missions, functions, lack of procedures, difficulties during staff absences, etc.

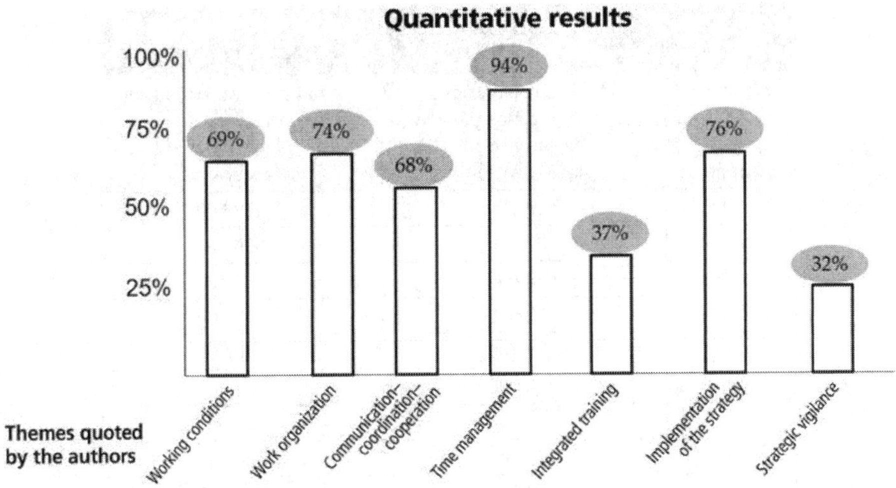

Figure 10.1 Frequency of the main dysfunctional ideas in all 20 small companies.

We also found that there was less sensitivity on the part of the actors to certain themes such as work organization, communication-coordination-cooperation, and even more so to integrated training and strategic vigilance. Yet, these themes were of major importance for the organizations studied in the post-creation phase (Combaudon, 2015).

As part of the diagnosis, we also measured the financial impact of these dysfunctions. As a reminder, the definition of hidden costs given by Savall and Zardet is as follows: "*Hidden costs are costs that are not identified in the information systems that a company has, such as budget, profit and loss account, general accounting, cost accounting, and dashboard. By symmetry, visible costs refer to all the cost items that appear in these same information systems*" (1987).

Any dysfunction that occurs in the company and that is regulated generates a cost that is detrimental to the survival-development of these post-creation companies. The average amount of hidden costs in the observed post-creation firms was € 25,900/person/year (Table 10.2).

After the implementation of the socio-economic innovation process on all of our sites, we observed notable qualimetric evolutions. In particular, these include increased vigilance on the part of these companies in the post-creation period, allowing them to adapt better (Fouré-Joopen, 2014); an improvement in individual and collective skills that allows for an increase in the level of professionalism; an improvement in communication with a better transfer of information; a better organization of work allowing for better regulation of absenteeism; and better time management allowing for the recovery of hours to develop the activity, sales turnover and profitability.

At the end of the process, we noted a positive evolution on the six themes, as expressed by the actors consulted (Figure 10.2).

Table 10.3 shows a significant drop in hidden costs 24 months after the start of the intervention, which led to a significant improvement in self-financing and therefore in the survival and development of the enterprises in the post-creation phase.

All the post-created companies, even those that had financial difficulties at the beginning of the intervention, have passed the 5-year mark, at least partly due to changes in structure and behavior that have generated self-financing through the significant conversion of hidden costs into value added.

TABLE 10.2 Amounts of Hidden Costs at the Beginning of the Intervention

Companies	Hidden costs per person and per year at the beginning of the intervention	Overall amount of hidden costs at company level at the beginning of the intervention
1	€18,700	€ 112,500
2	€ 59,400	€ 356,300
3	€13,600	€ 27,100
4	€ 52,800	€ 158,400
5	€ 12,100	€ 120,700
6	€ 6,000	€ 47,900
7	€ 11,000	€ 22,000
8	€ 25,800	€ 154,600
9	€ 12,000	€ 24,000
10	€ 5,500	€5,500
11	€ 17,200	€ 51,500
12	€ 11,000	€ 67,500
13	€ 16,300	€ 81,300
14	€ 20,400	€ 20,400
15	€ 37,000	€ 1,111,000
16	€ 22,500	€ 67,700
17	€ 39,100	€ 156,300
18	€ 67,300	€ 67,300
19	€ 42,600	€ 127,700
20	€ 287,000	€ 172, 300

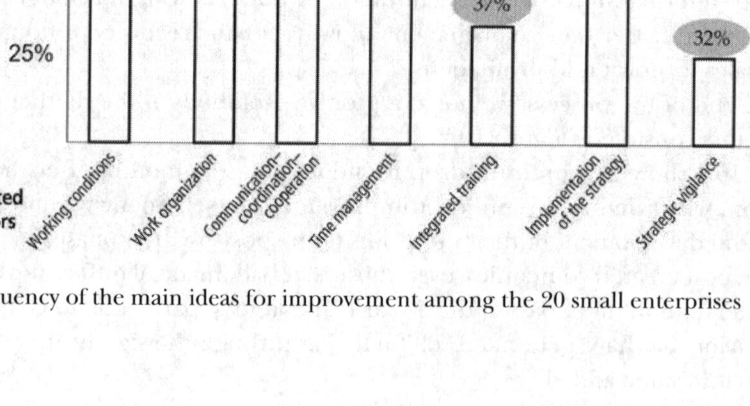

Figure 10.2 Frequency of the main ideas for improvement among the 20 small enterprises

TABLE 10.3 Conversion of Hidden Costs Into Value Added

Kind of industry	Amount of hidden costs at the beginning of the intervention	Amount of hidden costs converted into value added	Percentage of reduction as compared with the beginning of the intervention
Trade in organic and natural products	€ 112,500	€ 63,000	56%
Short distance transport	€ 356,300	€ 100,000	28%
Management Consulting	€ 27,000	€ 17,000	62%
Home automation	€ 158,400	€ 76,000	47%
Industrial Automation	€ 120,700	€ 63,000	52%
Online games	€ 47,900	€ 24,000	50%
Thermoformed confort soles	€ 22,000	€ 8,000	36%
Development of artificial intelligence software	€ 154,600	€ 68,000	44%
Installation of solar panels	€ 24,000	€ 12,000	50%
Car washing, cleaning and renovation	€ 5,500	€ 30,000	545%
Children's amusement park	€ 51,500	€ 26,000	50%
Bakery	€ 65,700	€ 22,000	33%
Trade in organic and natural products	€ 81,300	€ 37,000	45%
Manufacture of food supplements	€ 20,400	€ 16,000	78%
Secretarial services for companies	€ 1,111,000	€ 59,000	5%
Communication agency	€ 67,700	€ 19,000	28%
Indoor soccer room	€ 156,300	€ 77,000	49%
Dietary advice	€ 67,300	€ 30,000	45%
Sales of artisanal ice cream	€ 127,700	€ 41,000	32%
Hosiery	€ 172,300	€ 74,000	43%

CONCLUSION

The improvement of the interactions between the structures and the behaviors of the actors of a company in post-creation is an important factor to be taken into-account to consolidate its survival and its sustainability. The human potential is an essential energetic factor to create a competitive advantage.

The academic interest of our work is to open new fields and research objects in the field of entrepreneurship that also interest students. Students are often deprived of managerial tools and post-creation reflections, because the dominant models in entrepreneurship education are focused on the ante-creation phase, via the construction of the "business model" and the "business plan."

The interest for practitioners, creators or coaches, is also obvious, because the vast majority of them are not very aware of the overall management of the small enterprises.

Based on twenty or so cases, these results have a certain limit. It is obviously necessary to continue by integrating other small enterprises in the post-creation phase, other fields of investigation such as foreign companies in the post-creation phase, and other forms of activity in the post-creation phase such as self-employed companies.

REFERENCES

Bredart, X., Levratto, N. (2018). Business failure, default and bankruptcy: better understanding them to overcome them. *Revue internationale P.M.E., 31*(3–4), 29–34.

Bruyat, C. (1993). *Business creation: epistemological contributions and modeling.* Gestion et management. Doctoral thesis in management sciences. Université Pierre Mendès-France–Grenoble II.

Crutzen, N., Van Caillie, D. (2009). Towards a taxonomy of entry profiles in a failure process: a focus on micro and small firms in difficulty. *P.M.E International Review, 22*(1), 103–128.

Combaudon, C. (2015). *The joint improvement of structures and behaviors, a factor of survival-development of enterprises in the creation phase: cases of intervention-researches conducted in 12 enterprises.* Doctoral thesis in management sciences. University of Lyon

Degeorge, J.-M., Messeghem, K. (2016). Poursuite d'opportunité entrepreneuriale et modes de management, *Finance Contrôle Stratégie,* 19–2.

Fayolle A., Degeorge J.-M. (2012). *Dynamique entrepreneuriale Le comportement de l'entrepreneur,* Brussels, De Boeck. 288 p.

Fouré-Joopen, H. (2014). La dynamique coopérative inter-organisationnelle dans les réseaux innovants: le facteur confiance dans le cas de deux clusters français, Thèse de doctorat en sciences de gestion. University of Lyon

Fouré-Joopen, H., Combaudon, C. (2017). *The measurement of human capital: A survival factor for the VSE in a failure situation.* 15th Congress of the International Cost Institute & 4th Transatlantic Congress of Accounting, Auditing, Management Control and Cost Management in partnership with ISEOR, Magellan, IAE Lyon, Univ. Jean Moulin & the American Accounting Association. June

Khelil, N., Smida, A. and Zouaoui M. (2012). Contribution to the understanding of new venture failure: qualitative exploration of the multiple dimensions of the phenomenon. *Entrepreneurship Review 11*(1), 39–72.

Osterwalder A., Pigneur, Y. (2002). *Business Models and their Elements.* International Workshop on Business Models. Lausanne, Switzerland.

Sarasvathy S.D, Germain O. (2011). Effectuation, a pragmatic and pragmatist approach to entrepreneurship, *Revue de l'Entrepreneuriat, 3*(10), 67–72.

Smida, A., Khelil, N. (2020). Rethinking the entrepreneurial failure of emerging small firms. *Revue Internationale PME, 23*(2), 65–106.

Torrès, O. (1997). For a contingent approach to the specificity of the SME. *Revue internationale P.M.E., 10*(2), 9–43.

Verstraete T., Krémer, F., Jouison-Laffitte, E. (2012). The business model: a theory for practices. *Entreprendre & Innover. 1*(13), 7–26.

CHAPTER 11

INTERNAL STUCTURING AND EXTERNAL DEVELOPMENT

The Challenges of the Second Generation of a Family

François Filippazzo

ABSTRACT

The transition between two generations of SME owner-managers is always a very sensitive stage in the life of family businesses, between continuities and ruptures. This chapter shows how this transition was managed with the support of the socio-economic method of change management. The new generation of managers invented the second generation-organization in the service of a strategy of diversification of its products.

For more than four decades, a family business in Lyon has thrived, driven by its founder. This company was born in the early 1970s and operates in the fruit and vegetable wholesale sector (inter-company trade). As an intermediary, it is in a somewhat fragile position, as suppliers and customers increasingly seek to work directly together (Pardo & Paché, 2015; Bousquet, 2018).

At the turn of the 2005–2010 period, the second generation of manager-owner took over from the founder. The current leader became aware that the organization of the company was no longer adapted to continue the development of the activities. The idea of transforming the internal organization of the company was gradually born, in parallel with the important structural investments that the company had to face. The central question was how to accompany and succeed in the change.

SEAM Treatise, pages 129–136

In 2015, the incoming owner-manager turned to ISEOR to lead the change process. The accompaniment of this internal, then external, change began in November 2015 and continues to the present day.

This chapter discusses the levers that have favored the metamorphosis of this company. The first part shows the importance of investing in internal structuring to grasp external opportunities. The case study and the course of the intervention are then presented, before drawing the main lessons in the third part.

1 CHANGES IN A FAMILY BUSINESS AS THE FIRST AND SECOND GENERATIONS PASS THE BATON

At the beginning of the 2000s, we noticed important and profound changes in the business and strategic positioning of our company, within the production-import-ripening-final customer chain. The market became much less favorable, in particular because of new strategies of certain customers, such as those of the large-scale distribution which seek to circumvent the intermediaries to organize themselves their supplies of fruits and vegetables. In addition to this external strategic diagnosis, we had to clean up a somewhat old image of the company and relaunch an investment policy, the last significant investments dating back to 1995.

In parallel to these external challenges, we were measuring the time to invest in the company's new strategic projects, such as the relocation of the company's three main sites to the heart of the new food hub in the Lyon region. This strategic choice, made between 2006 and 2009, allowed us to meet the ever-increasing demands of our customers with larger, more modern sites, new ripening and storage facilities, and new equipment. As far as the teams were concerned, it also appeared necessary to involve key employees to become actors in this strategy in a different way. From then on, the management structure inherited from my father was no longer adapted: a "patriarchal" manager and employees who all reported directly to him, with no real organizational chart. Many SMEs live with this type of organization. However, as soon as the founder leaves, they become fragile, due to insufficient internal structuring.

Our case illustrates several contributions of management research. First, family businesses and the specificities of their management and governance are the subject of growing interest (Cappelletti & Savall, 2014), particularly because of their important role in the national economic fabric. Second, our company's experience testifies to the existence of intangible capital embodied by individuals, but very little formalized (Savall A., 2014). Talking about intangible investment in the development of human potential then constitutes a small revolution for managers like us.

If the previous observation is simple on paper, in reality it is difficult to change an organization that has worked well for over 30 years. Of course, the leader is not the only one who orchestrates the activities in the company. It is a matter of discovering the "hidden managers" who will work with him or her to manage the company's teams and performance. This construction of a new organization comes up against work habits and legitimate fears linked to this transformation. Stimulating such an internal change implies accepting to engage in a process of trial and error. It is necessary to experiment along the way, i.e., to understand that the solution does not exist and that it has to be built within the company.

We are certainly concerned with the emergence of new skills in the company. But we also made a clear diagnosis of the structure of its activities, which were characterized by an excessive dependence on a flagship product: bananas. The major strategic challenge was to diversify products and sources of supply. This challenge required financial investments, which were self-financed given the company's very solid economic and financial situation. On the other hand, it also required mobilizing the skills, time and energy of people to travel and meet new producers, then learn to import and mature new products, to develop the company's offer.

2 INVENTION OF A NEW ORGANIZATION TO SERVE AN AMBITIOUS STRATEGY

In November 2015, the company took the leap into a new adventure consisting of inventing and implementing a new organizational structure. To achieve this goal, a team of three ISEOR practitioners accompanied us in this transformation, the first major stage of which lasted nearly a year (Savall, 1974–75; 1979; Savall and Zardet, 1987).

This support for change consisted first of all in carrying out a diagnosis to identify the dysfunctions and evaluate our untapped productivity potential. Interviews with all the people in the company allowed them to express themselves freely on the quality of the operation. Many dysfunctions came to light. This is not an easy exercise for a manager, whose ego and certainties can be somewhat shaken (late deliveries, duplicate tasks, searching for carts, etc.). From an economic point of view, we have discovered a source of € 38,000 of hidden costs per year and per person. In a financially strong company, this hidden cost pool was a real surprise. This snapshot of dysfunctions revealed management problems. It was a totally new experience in our professional life, but it was essential to pursue the desired metamorphosis.

The focus group that followed this diagnosis phase allowed everyone in the company to get involved in the search for solutions. The main focus of the work was to build teams and to propose to some people in the company to become managers. The figure below shows the evolution of our work organization between 2016 and today (see Figure 11.1): we have moved from a centralized organization around a manager, the leader, to a decentralized and more flexible organization.

The years 2017 and 2018 allowed for the cultivation of this new organization by ensuring that the skills of new managers were developed through regular training and coaching. Managerial skills were particularly developed to better pilot skills in teams and the development of versatility in people. It is clear that one does not become a manager overnight, simply because of a hierarchical position. This evolution has not yet been completed and is still ongoing. One of the major managerial innovations implemented was the installation of a socio-economic management tool called the Periodically Negotiable Activity Contract (PNAC).[1] This tool corresponds very well to the idea of proximity management that we wanted to put in place within the company: to give managers the levers to act with a certain autonomy with their employees and to bring to life a spirit of negotiation to involve everyone in the new strategic projects.

In parallel with this work of internal structuring of our company, we have relaunched a policy of investment necessary to remain competitive. The two significant examples of tangible investments made are the creation of new cold rooms for the storage and ripening of fruit and the acquisition of new machines to package new ranges of fruit (avocados).

With material investments in machinery complemented by intangible investments in organizational development, we had the necessary tools to activate the second generation of the company's product-market strategy. This second generation in the strategy is mainly focused on product-market diversification. We launched an important work to decrease our dependence on our main product (Filippazzo, F., 2017). Our choice of diversification was avocado for three reasons: it is a high value-added product (high average selling price and

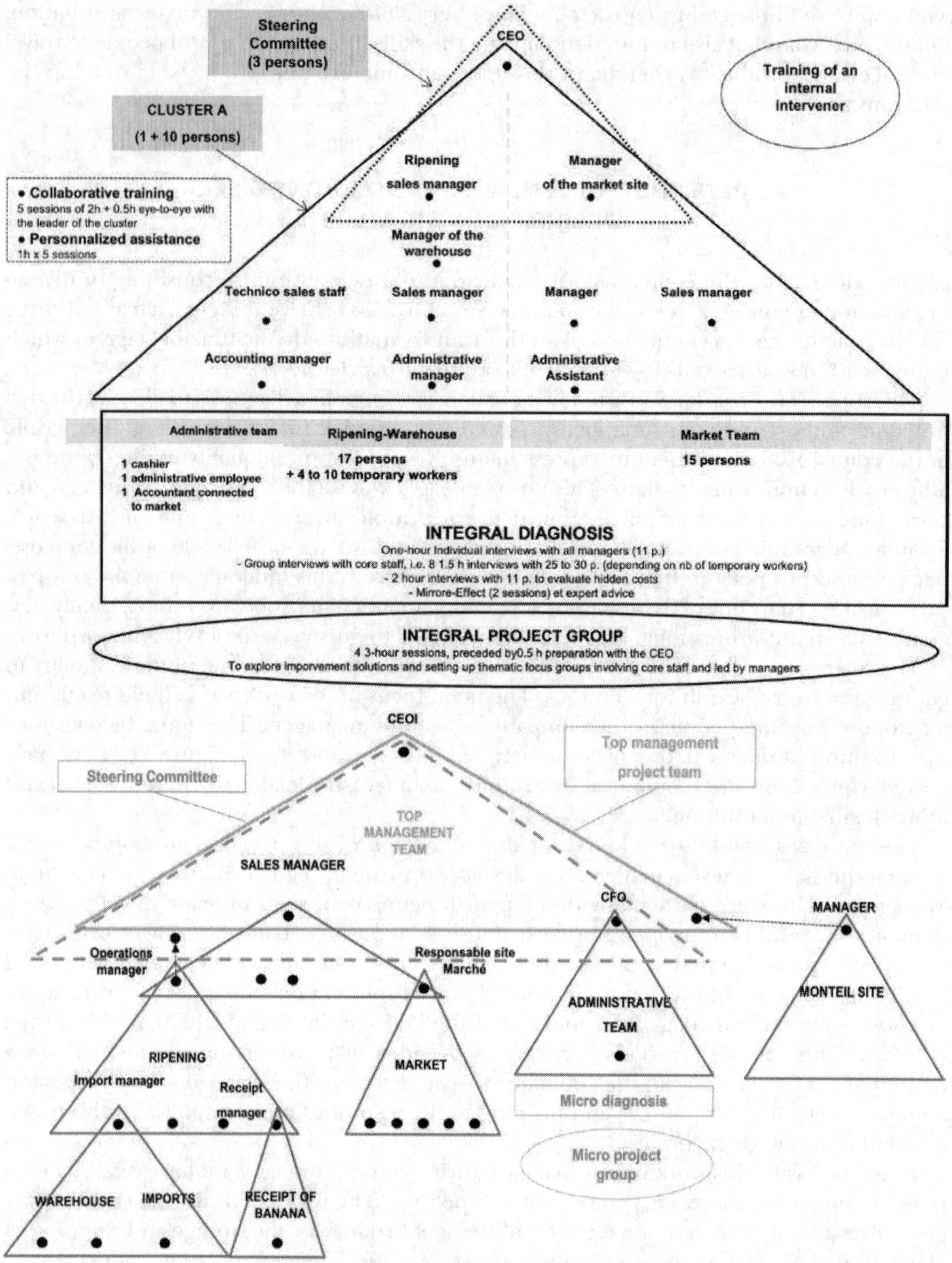

Figure 11.1 Evolution of the Work Organization Between 2016 and 2020.

strong increase in demand worldwide), which requires, like banana, know-how in ripening and knowledge of producing countries in Central America and Africa. In three years, we have succeeded in this diversification challenge: avocados have become the company's second most important product in terms of sales turnover. Because of our position as an importer, we have also developed a range of citrus fruits from South Africa (lemons, oranges, pomelos) in order to pursue this diversification strategy.

This strategic development would not have been possible without the efforts made to grow the human potential of the company. For example, the introduction of avocado in our product range has allowed us to expand the team of ripeners and increase our ripening skills, which adds value to the product between the producer and the final customer. Another example was the creation of new activities in the warehouse. These are no longer just handling tasks, but new packaging and quality control activities that have emerged and are enriching people's work.

Figure 11.2 illustrates the trajectory of important changes in the life of our company over the past four years. We started internally to achieve our ambitious external strategy (Savall and Zardet, 1995).

For a long time, we were reluctant to use external support. Organizational and strategic consulting is not considered easily accessible to SMEs. For the CEO, many questions arise: which method to choose? What is the right investment to make? How to evaluate the return on investment? In addition to these questions, the CEO is also uncomfortable with a new role: change management. He/she is the first person whose professional practices are called into question. After this experience, we measured all the benefits brought by the involvement of our employees in this project. This allowed us to overcome the difficulty of thinking that it was not possible to communicate with the teams on fundamental subjects.

3 ASSESSING THE IMPACT OF THE CHANGE ON THE COMPANY'S PERFORMANCE

The presentation of the company's results can be done from two angles: the significant achievements observed and the evolution of our Hourly Value-Added Contribution on Variable Costs (HCVAVC).

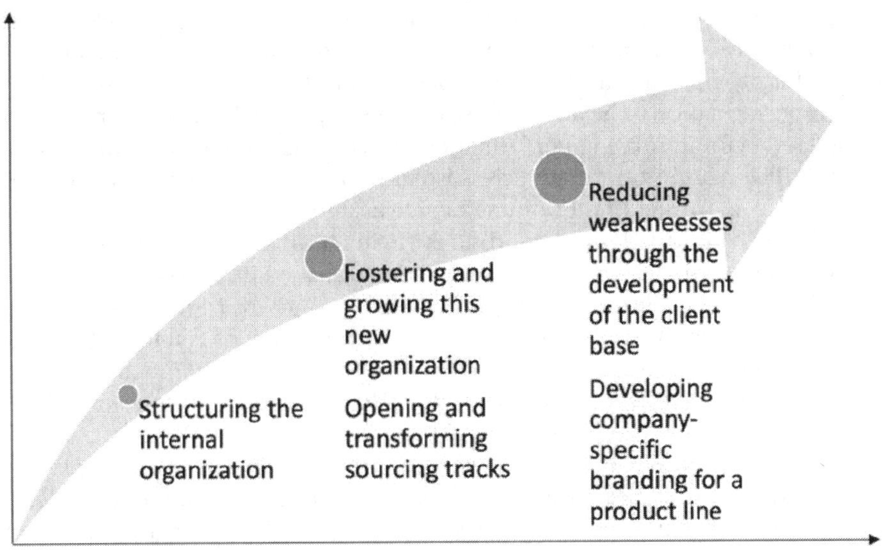

Figure 11.2 The company's organizational learning curve.

- **Implementation of organizational bedrock and of the human potential**
    - **11 new managers and their team developed in 20 months**
    - **Set up of PNACs in 10 months**
- **Self-financement** of the qualitative development of human potential
    - At the ripening and at the warehouse: **a 9% productivity increase** + investing in the training of employees
    - **At the market:** improved mastering of the costs
    - Mastering overall working time in a context of sharp increase of activities (banana)
- **Development of the ambition and of the strategic potential**
    - Diversification of products and suppliers
    - **Stronger belief** in strategic choices thanks to robust organizational and managerial bedrock
    - **Conversion of hidden costs into added value**
- **Strenghtening of strategic consernsusat top management level**
    - **Strategic bedrock**

Figure 11.3 Summary of the main milestones achieved between 2016 and 2020.

Figure 11.3 summarizes the major achievements observed. From our position as manager, it is the management of human potential that has brought real value added to our company. Three major levers of this management seem to me to be particularly decisive. The first is the improvement of communication-coordination-cooperation. We have gone from a very embryonic situation to a real resource for carrying out the company's projects. This has given meaning to the strategy and to everyone's work, because it is a new way of teaching within the company. The second lever is the installation of a "laboratory" organization. We used this method of experimentation to build the managerial structure, and then we kept it as a reference framework for product innovation. In other words, management has led us to develop a new form of courage to try things we would not have done before. Finally, the third lever is the PNAC, which has stimulated interactions between managers and employees and operators, to instill an effective dynamic on productivity and work atmosphere. This tool has helped us to develop concerted team autonomy, an indispensable ingredient in such a turbulent strategic environment.

On the quantitative and financial front, we also noted significant improvements that are reflected in the progress of an overall performance indicator: the HCVAVC. We quickly adopted this performance indicator proposed by ISEOR, which puts into perspective two fundamental levers for improving performance in a company: the contribution margin and hours worked. The margin on variable costs isolates the fixed costs from the analysis, those that do not evolve according to the volume of activity and that are nevertheless necessary to carry out our activity in the desired conditions (material investments, infrastructures, salaries, etc.). In other words, we analyze the value added created in the company, which allows us to finance our strategy and generate profits. The second lever for improving economic performance is hours worked. We seek to improve productivity by reducing the number of hours worked, which are currently diverted by the regulation of dysfunctions, by redirecting them to projects that create value added. The HCVAVC thus illustrates the value added generated per hour worked (Filippazzo, F., 2018).

As we can see in Figure 11.4, the evolution of this indicator has been progressive. This curve can be explained by the investment in human potential that we have made. Indeed, new management staff have joined the company, which initially increased the number of hours worked. They have contributed to the development of strategic projects which have stimulated the increase of the margin on variable costs in a second phase.

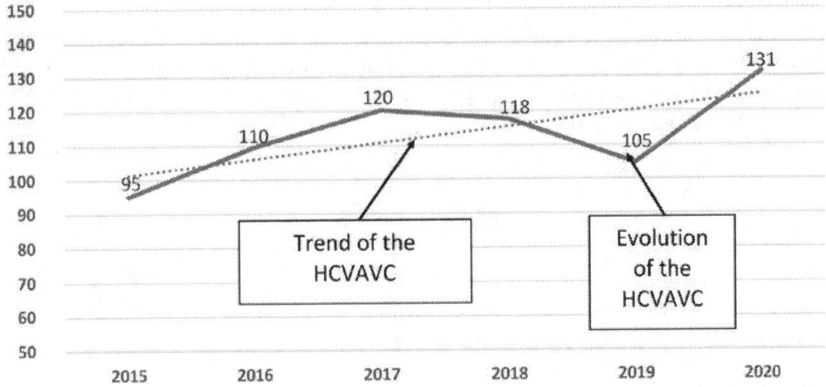

Figure 11.4 Evolution of the HCVAVC between 2015 and 2020.

While this indicator may seem complex at first glance, it provides a very concrete approach to managing the overall performance of a company. The increasing evolution of this indicator, beyond its absolute value, is a real indicator of the financial health of the company and its capacity to move forward. In our company, the HCVAVC went from € 95 in 2015 to € 131 in 2020, a 38% increase. The expected hours of all staff and temporary workers in the company increased by 35.1%, while the Variable Cost Margin increased by 86.7%.

CONCLUSION

Without ISEOR's coaching approach, the transformations we have made in the company's operations and life would not have been possible at this speed and with this magnitude. We have learned at least two *lessons* from this experience. The first is that learning about the company's business know-how must necessarily be accompanied by learning about management. Thus, we have understood that the methods for involving people are inseparable from the capacity of these same people to innovate in their job. The second major lesson concerns the primary source of value creation in our companies: this value is created every day, every hour worked by each person in the company, and it is made up of countless "small actions" that are implemented.

The reflection of these lessons is measured thanks to the HCVAVC, which integrates the two levers of strategic steering of the company, namely hours and value added on variable costs. From the point of view of the external dimension of the strategy, it is necessary to work on this value added on variable costs in order to constitute it, i.e., to innovate in products and markets. In its more internal dimension, the challenge is to make better use of human time and to control expense ratios. It is the meaning of management to stimulate the commitment of people who create value added. Finally, we have integrated the idea that the organization of our company is also a field of innovation within which we must try out experiments.

NOTE

1. The Periodically Negotiable Activity Contract (PNAC) is a management tool based on the following principle: every six months, managers negotiate with each member of their team a small basket of target-mean pairs to be achieved in the next six months. At the end of the six months,

an in-depth evaluation of the achievement of the objectives is carried out and a quality-productivity bonus is awarded to the individuals according to the results obtained. This tool develops managers' negotiation skills, permanent cooperation with all employees and provides a lever for synchronized decentralization of the implementation of the company's strategic projects (Savall, 1979; Savall and Zardet, 1987)

REFERENCES

Bousquet, C. (2018). *The articulation of individual and collective competencies to the company's strategy.* Doctoral thesis in management sicences. University of Lyon.

Cappelletti, L., & Savall, A. (2014). *Control practices of foreign subsidiaries of a family group: Results of an intervention-research.* AFC Congress.

Filippazzo, F. (2018). Assessing the return on investment in human potential in a dynamic SME. In H. Savall & V. Zardet (Coord.). *La digitalisation apprivoisée: au service de l'humain et de la performance durable.* EMS.

Filippazzo, F. (2017). Business innovation at the service of business strategy. In H. Savall & V. Zardet (Coord.). *Business innovation: All sellers in organizations.* EMS.

Pardo, C., & Paché, G. (2015). *Wholesale trade, business-to-business trade: The challenges of intermediation.* EMS.

Savall, A. (2014). *The endogenous factors of sustainable performance of the internationalization of the family business: longitudinal case of intervention-research.* Doctoral thesis in management sciences. Conservatoire national des arts et métiers – CNAM.

CHAPTER 12

LEARNING TO BE A LEADER

Julien Vinay, Muriel Legendre, Laura Bondin, and Olivier Voyant

ABSTRACT

What is a leader? A human being? Unquestionably. This chapter is the story of a man who embodies this idea. The transmission of a family business is the setting; the father, the son and the employees are the main characters.

The literature on learning to be a leader is scarce.

Sometimes it is the account of a theorist, probably too far from the realities to avoid conceptual caricatures. At other times, it contains the account of an "out-of-the-box" practitioner, far removed from the concerns of the leaders who make up the French, not to say European, or even international socio-economic fabric. For example, the authorized biographies of Steve Jobs (Isaacson, 2011) or the unauthorized biography of Bernard Arnault (Routier, 2003) cannot be considered as testimonies of learning about being a leader.

In this chapter, there are no baobabs or oaks. We have chosen to write the story of a company that resembles a bonsai tree. Its size is small enough to pretend to be human, large enough to require a managerial structure.

The authors, with eight hands, have chosen to use the "I" to embody the words of the leader, the "we" for those of the participants. This rare voice on the learning path of "being a leader" – part one – and of socio-economic management – part two – as well as the distanced testimony of the speakers – part three – aim to answer the following question: "How do you learn to be a leader?

SEAM Treatise, pages 137–143

1 LEARNING PROCESS TO BECOME A LEADER

Many leaders are satisfied with reading a few books, attend conferences, and participate in networks. I chose to be accompanied by intervener-researchers. I made this "crazy" decision on my own, without really knowing what door it would open.

1.1 Never Without my Father

My name is Julien Vinay. I am 47 years old, with 2 children. I run the family business "Vinay Matériel," which specializes in the trade of equipment for the building and industry. We currently employ 42 people and have an annual sales turnover of €12.6 million. This company was created in 1993 by my father. He was a tireless worker, devoted "body and soul" to the company. He dedicated his life to it.

At the time of the company's creation, many young construction managers were leaving their companies to become self-employed. My father used to say to them, "You just have to take the equipment and then pay me." He had a confidence and a benevolence pushed to the extreme of service, without necessarily being in profitability. He was more into service than into selling. Beyond a commercial relationship, his customers appreciated his values. Products became almost secondary: we were selling relationships more than products.

I took over the company in 2008.

Those who have had a similar experience know this rule: the father leaves... but he is never far away! For years, he came. First, because he didn't trust me, then because he was attached to the company. The last few years, he was there more to keep busy and stay in the mood. He knew he was no longer needed. Unlike in the beginning, he was not "annoying," if I may say so. He no longer went behind my back to make a contrary decision. He was trying to help.

When he felt I was ready, he stepped aside. He did try to leave the company for a month or two... but he came back. It was his life and the employees liked him. He was a father figure, and there was a mutual benevolence towards this company memory, in the good sense of the word. He was touched by the loyalty of the employees. Despite the change in management, the story continued.

My father, Guy Vinay, left on August 19, 2020. He died of a mountain accident. Only his death could make him leave this company. We have received many testimonies from customers and employees. He left just after the construction of the new store, just before the computerized inventory management. He knew we were on the right track.

1.2 Without my Father, Who am I?

My father left appeased by the direction I was taking. If he had been able to prepare for it, he would have said to himself, "I can leave because my son is ready. He was attached to what he had created, he was attached but there was a lot of generosity on his part. He didn't talk much; he talked more to those around him than to me. I know that he was proud to have built a company and to see his son continue the adventure.

Compared to him, I don't want to do everything. I want to leave room for the employees. The "35-tooth rake" structure was unbearable. I therefore chose to structure a team, to give responsibility, to delegate and to define a few rules, in particular concerning stock management. In addition, I wanted to free myself from the permanent pressure and to take a step back and distance myself from the events. To achieve this, I gradually freed myself from some of the operational aspects to work on a strategic vision.

Have I become a leader? I don't know when you can say that you are a leader. Without "passing the buck" to stakeholders, I think I started wearing the "suit" during the 2014 diagnosis. It was the first major project I wore. It was MY project. My father never said "no" to me, he could never have said "no" to a process that could help me. During our first interview with the workers, he said he didn't like the notion of "Chief." Their answer, "the leader is a conductor," suited him and reassured him. I also put the "suit" on when I set up middle management; it will be (more) complete when the greatest number, that is to say all of them, from accounting to reception, have understood where I want to go.

Rather than answering the question "who am I?," I prefer to imagine the answers of my relatives. My father would say, "He's too nice. I kept his kindness by being more directive. My mother would say "It's not easy... he follows in his father's footsteps: he knows how to surround himself with the right people and keep them." I can hear my sister saying, "I don't know how he does it! It was not in my character to become a manager and the dimension taken by the company is beyond her. Finally, my wife. If she doesn't tell me, she trusts what I do. She is not really worried about the fact that I will succeed in making the company sustainable. What she is most concerned about is that I'm going down. She's counting on me to continue to step back, to preserve myself.

2 SOCIO-ECONOMIC MANAGEMENT LEARNING PATH

On February 3, 2014, I made the decision to be accompanied by intervener-researchers specialized in Socio-Economic Approach to Management, and then to participate in the course "Succeeding change," organized by ISEOR . In retrospect, I think that this decision marked, in a way, my "birth" as a manager: it allowed me to make an intangible investment, without which the Human being cannot develop; it "forced" me to leave the company to train: sometimes, you have to know how to accept to extract yourself (for a while) from the company in order to better take care of it.

After 7 years of coaching, I believe I have understood the following "golden rules."

2.1 Respecting One's Commitments

Since my encounter with the "Socio-Economic Approach to Management," I have bought a new plot of land, built a new building. Despite the difficulties, I have not given up. In the past, some people criticized me for not following through. This time, I asserted my choices. I became persistent. I became persistent, but it was not natural. From this rule, I retain the following principles:

- An idea has no value; only its implementation can reveal it;
- The leader must show managerial courage (to say, to do) and understand that deciding is not imposing but negotiating and selling;
- Making resolutions and implementing them maintains trust, which is naturally fragile and ephemeral.

At present, some employees are losing their sense of responsibility. I think that my desire for rigor was imposed without (sufficient) trust. Socio-economic management must become a daily practice. We have to get to the "heart" of the method. For me, this is the moment when everyone can trust each other. All employees must receive the trust of their manager and the boss of the company. To ensure that everyone (re)adopts the right methodological approach, I have decided to measure, in a decentralized way, the rate of implementation of our commitments. I hope that the latter will signify an increase in mutual trust.

2.2 Structuring the Company in a Heuristic Way

In 2014, we conducted a diagnosis. My fear was to be criticized, but it turned out to be more complex in reality: I became aware of the lack of a management system. In 2021, we will repeat this diagnosis experience. My fear is that the managers will be criticized; at the time of the focus group, I hope to discover the unimaginable strength of everyone's action.

The transition from one date to the other was accompanied by the following "discoveries":

- Participative management contains two "golden" principles: benevolence is not complacency; participative is learning to say "no";
- Modern management aims to increase the influence of the first circle and not to "lock up" 100% of the employees in the first circle: when the number of employees increases or in the case of multi-sites, the company is in danger.

As far as structuring is concerned, it will have been heuristic, designed by trial and error, by trial and error. It is not enough to decree a new organization for it to work. It is necessary to design an initial team, to test it over several months, or even several years, before considering involving 100% of the employees. For this work, focus groups and concerted delegations are structuring methodological elements.

In 2018, with the support of stakeholders, I prepared the announcement of my new organization. To outline (generic?) win-win arguments, the following points were identified:

- In a changing world, we must learn to change regularly,
- I need you... but where you can make the most of yourself,
- As a leader, my role is to define the why and the what, not the how.

2.3 Renewing Your Strategic Ambition

In my first meeting with the intervener-researchers, I presented the idea of acquiring a piece of land and constructing a building. They urged me to be reasonably cautious: how do you build on an organization made of (shifting) sand? I decided to listen to them. Thus, MY first project was not material but intangible: I chose a container (Socio-Economic Approach to Management) to create content (land and building): soil expertise, development of the current premises, return on investment, nostalgia, family and sectoral conformity, renting part of the premises, development of the parking lot and stocks, creation of a refectory, meeting rooms, offices, an archive room, toilets and showers... the subjects and questions were numerous. Currently, the old building (1,500 m^2 on a 3,800 m^2 plot) is reserved for rental and storage. After buying a 6,000 m^2 plot of land, for which it was necessary to remove asbestos from a building and destroy it, I had a 3,800 m^2 building built with 70 parking spaces: 35 for the staff, 35 for the customers.

In 2020, I wondered about the opportunity to acquire a new site. After my exchange with the speakers, I retain the following principles:

- You have to learn how to pilot nearby sites before piloting distant sites;
- Is the opportunity compatible with a socio-economic strategy?
- Is the manager's idea, the short time, compatible with the implementation, the long time?

In case of incompatibility, decisions are contaminated by the TFW virus.

From a conceptual point of view, I remember that the years 2014 to 2017 will have been those of the implementation of "old" strategic ideas. From 2017 onwards, the strategy took the form of proactive and forward-looking writing.

2.3 Upgrading our Practice of Steering and of Economic Performance

Learning socio-economic management involves Hourly Contribution to Value Added on Variable Costs (HVAVC) , hidden costs and economic balances. In the company, the HVAVC indicator has made it possible to integrate two "golden rules":

- Sales cannot be equated with the value added created;
- There is no point in piloting the euros if you don't pilot the expected hours.

During the 2014 diagnosis, hidden costs, which were under-estimated, were valued at €1 million, i.e., 10% of sales turnover and 35% of value added. Faced with such figures, I became aware that the "customer" likely to bring in the highest value added is the company itself. To complete this awareness, I used, in particular for the building project, the "economic balance" as a decision-making tool.

All of these elements were brought together, between 2015 and 2016, in a document entitled "management control policy."

3 DISTANCED TESTIMONY OF THE INTERVENER-RESEARCHERS

The executive's account refers indiscriminately to "intervener-researchers" This term includes an ISEOR franchisee consultant and ISEOR interveners who accompanied her behind the scenes, or even on stage when the executive visited the Institute's premises.

In order to provide a distanced testimony, we have chosen to present a visible side of the action, called "technical," and then another hidden side, called "political."

3.1 Technical Intervention System

During the project's launch phase, the father and son participated in a mechanism called the "steering group," a form of antechamber intended to give birth to a (new) leader. Within this forum, organized at ISEOR, three recurring themes were discussed: strategic content, who to involve and the concordance of times.

As early as 2014, the leader understood that we were not going to take "the keys to the company," but that we would work to ensure that he took them. To achieve this, we developed a thermostatic word, allowing us to put him in a comfortable temperature: when he was hot, we had to cool him down; when he was cold, we had to warm him up.

For 7 years, we encouraged him to produce multiplied hours (to do and not to do in the place of the collaborators) and to reinforce the capacity of all to act.

As for the transmission between father and son, we benefited from their benevolence, even their kindness. In a rather classical way, we understood that it was neither desirable nor conceivable to replace a "father" by a "son," but a "father" by a team taken in charge by the "son." Gradually, hyper-centralization gave way to synchronized decentralization.

When asked "*What is your favorite management tool?,*" the manager's answer was quick: *Internal and External Strategic Planning*! Strategic tools have enabled us to move from an oral culture, which was that of the "father," to a written culture, allowing the "son" to display his role-text and that of his team for the years to come. The leader is no longer only what he says, he is what he writes and wishes to achieve as a team. We could consider that learning to be a leader is inseparable from learning to be strategic.

3.2 Political Dimension of the Intervention

On January 14, 2019, the leader arrived at the ISEOR premises in the context of a tax audit. We introduced the session with the question, "What could we do that would be useful for you?" The leader's answer was: (a) Continue the change, despite adversity, past mistakes (?) . . . by changing the rules of the game; (b) Save (keep) the company. At the end of the session, the visible threat of the tax audit had become a hidden opportunity to: (a) Insure the company against the risks of non-compliance with regulations and bring it in line with its values; (b) Accelerate the computerized implementation of inventory management; (c) Renew relationships with current customers and intensify prospecting; (d) Expand our product lines; (e) (Re)think the Internal and External Strategic Planning, especially in its proactive and forward-looking function.

On September 14, 2020, despite the circumstances, the leader honored his commitment to come to the ISEOR premises. We had just learned, a few days earlier, of the death of his father, Guy Vinay. This session was introduced by a question from the leader: "I want to define a 20-year strategy... what do I want to do? After him... after me? We ended with another question: "What are Julien Vinay's 10 favorite words? Future strategies could contain, explicitly or implicitly, the following words: Love, Nature, Child, Sport, Share, Cultivate (self), Evolve, Build, Dream and Laugh.

CONCLUSION

This chapter has chosen to give voice to ordinary men and women in the service of an "out of the ordinary" experience. The learning path of a leader is not a "long quiet river." However, with humanity, perseverance and methodological support, we can witness the birth of a leader. Let us entrust him with the last words of this chapter: "To conclude, I want to tell you that the mission entrusted to me by my parents is one that I have no choice but to carry out. It is my duty."

REFERENCES

Isaacson, W. (2011). *Steve Jobs.* Éditions JC Lattès.

Routier, A. (2003). *L'ange exterminateur—La vraie vie de Bernard Arnault.* Albin Michel.

This page intentionally left blank.

CHAPTER 13

SURVIVAL-DEVELOPMENT OF VERY SMALL ENTERPRISES (VSE)

Support for VSE Managers

Gérard Desmaison and Thomas Rouveure

ABSTRACT

In France, Small Business Companies (SBC) represent 96% of companies but 50% disappear before their sixth year, mainly because of a lack of strategic anticipation. This chapter highlights the decisive character of the structure/behavior relationship at several phases of the entrepreneurial process. The strategic skills of the entrepreneur are a key dimension to increase the survival and development of the company. The entrepreneur's beliefs about each area of the Entrepreneur's Activity Nomenclature (EAN) change his behavior and, ultimately, the structure of the company. The HCVAVC is a synthetic indicator for measuring overall and sustainable performance of SBC.

Very Small Enterprises (VSEs) or microenterprises represent an important part of the French economic fabric: 96% of the number of businesses, nearly 20% of jobs (Insee 2018). Yet their mortality is high, 88% of businesses in liquidation are businesses with less than 5 employees and 50% of microenterprises created disappear before their 6th year.

The post-creation phase is critical, presenting three perspectives: failure, stagnation and development (Figure 13.1). The root cause of entrepreneurs in difficulty is the lack of strategic anticipation in a period marked by a large domination of immediate results activities. The origin is both external (new products, market evolution, ...) and internal (structuring of the offer, organization, motivation of the manager...).

In view of the high risk of precariousness of this entrepreneurial path, we question the support mechanisms for VSE managers towards sustainable performance. We first assess

SEAM Treatise, pages 145–152

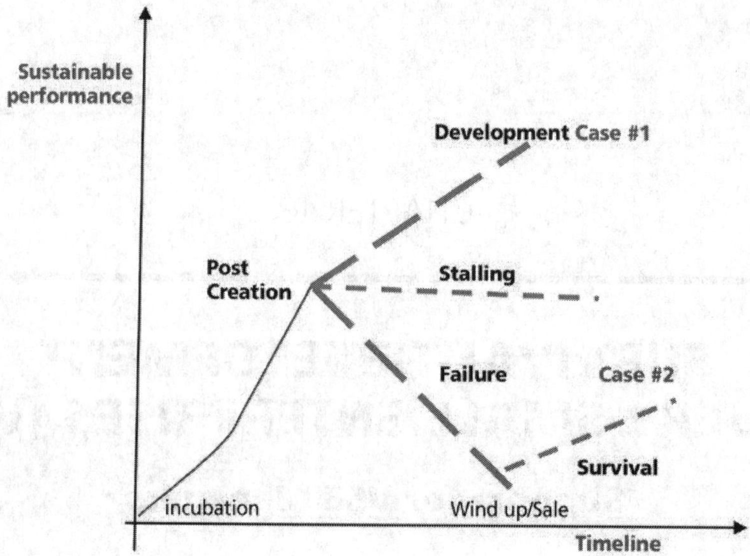

Figure 13.1 Evolution of VSEs in the post-creation period.

the support needs of VSE managers, then present two empirical studies illustrating support based on the concepts and tools of socio-economic management (MASE).

1 THE CONDITIONS FOR THE SURVIVAL AND DEVELOPMENT OF VSEs

To meet the need for versatility, the manager must broaden his or her horizons and develop a structured strategic vision: he or she is the guarantor of the VSE's overall and sustainable performance. The risk of isolation of the manager is a fragility that must be remedied (Lechat, Torres, 2016). Three conditions seem essential to ensure the sustainable development of the MSE.

1.1 Feeling Good in Mind and Body

The interest in the entrepreneur's behavior leads us to social psychology with attitudes as an anchor. Attitudes are defined as "the degree of evaluation, more or less favorable, that an individual develops about a behavior" (Grazzini, Boissin, 2013). Attitudes thus make it possible to analyze the entrepreneur's behavior.

"If I feel good in my body and my head, my company is doing well." The satisfaction of the basic needs of the VSE manager and the development of his human potential (Savall, 1974; Savall, Zardet 2005) are factors in the success of his company. This allows him to adapt to his environment, to create goods and services, to detect new needs and to innovate.

1.2 Developing a Comprehensive and Synthetic Vision in the Short, Medium, and Long Term

The work of Savall and Zardet (2008) proposes a structuring of the activities of individuals in the company using the nomenclature of activities, which "lists all the activities carried out by all the actors and allows for the monthly allocation of time spent." Rouveure (2018) proposed a nomenclature specific to the VSE: the Nomenclature of Entrepreneurial Activities (NAE). Composed of 6 domains and 24 themes of activities, it allows the manager to have a systemic vision of all the activities under his responsibility.

The literature recognizes the intuitive nature of executive decision-making (Julien & Marchesnay, 1988; Man et al. 2008), which is explained by the multiplicity of strategic, administrative and operational decisions that the executive must make. The leader must therefore devote time to developing a strategic vision for his company, allowing him to step back and make more informed decisions. This vision must be linked to two elements: the overall and sustainable performance of the company and the NAE (Nomenclature of Entrepreneurial Activities) in order to develop a systemic vision of the company.

1.3 Use an Integrating Management Indicator

The Hourly Contribution to Value Added on Variable Costs (HCVAV) is an indicator of the survival-development capacity of a company (Savall and Zardet, 1987). It is a strategic warning indicator, an average value, the result of multiple actions and interactions within the firm and its relations with its environment.

We now present two cases of application of support for entrepreneurs in the post-creation phase.

2 CASE STUDIES OF STRATEGIC SUPPORT FOR SMALL BUSINESSES

2.1 Epistemological Positioning and Research Methodology

Our study is positioned on a pragmatic constructivist paradigm (Avenier and Gavard-Perret, 2012). The external validity of this paradigm involves cumulative research that addresses the principle of "generic contingency" (Savall and Zardet, 1996, 2004). We adopt a methodology of "qualimetric intervention-research," an interactive method between the researcher and his or her field that aims at transformation (Plane, 2000). This methodology allows us to combine qualitative, quantitative and financial data from several sources of information: analysis of interviews, documents and direct observation.

We show, through the two cases, how socio-economic management allows for a comprehensive and systemic support of managers and their company:

- As a preventive measure in the post-creation phase (Development);
- In a curative way in the phase of difficulties leading to bankruptcy (Survival).

2.2 Development: Post-Creation Period

This study focuses on dysfunctions and Hidden Cost-Performance (HPC) based on an inter-organizational intervention-research conducted with 16 VSEs (0 to 4 employees) in the post-creation phase (2 to 4 years after the official creation of the company).

It revealed 157 dysfunctional phrases divided into 29 sub-themes. Table 13.1 shows the distribution by family of dysfunctions (Savall and Zardet, 1987).

The "Strategic Implementation" (MOS) family is the major source of dysfunction with more than 58% and concerns the entire sample. Table 13.2 details the main dysfunctions.

TABLE 13.1 Study 1—Frequency of Fieldnote Quotes

Categories	WC[a]	WO	CCC	TM	IT	SI
Frequency	3.2%	20.4%	1.3%	12.7%	4.4%	58.0%

[a] Description of acronyms: Working conditions (WC), Work organization (WO), communication-coordination-cooperation (CCC), Time management (TM), Integrated training (IT), Strategic implementation (SI).

TABLE 13.2 Dysfunctions of the Post-Birth Microenterprise (Rouveure, 2017)

Strategic implementation	601—Strategic directions	Lack of diversification
		No readjustment of the strategy
		Lack of a communication strategy
	604—Tools for strategic implementation	Error in cost assessment
	607—Personnel management	Poor employee management
		Difficulties in recruitment
	608 Management methods	Lack of a written strategy for the company

Inconsistency between strategy and behavior was noted by 6 entrepreneurs, i.e., 37.5% of the sample. To illustrate, when questioning a manager about his three priority development and improvement issues, a contradiction emerges: "And the third objective: to continue to perpetuate the activity and to engage in other activities in order to have an emergency margin. The entrepreneur presents a wish to perpetuate his activity and even to diversify, whereas he expressed a refusal to develop during the same interview: "I could not perhaps double but increase the activity by 50%. [...] I don't really want to expand. This cognitive bias is explained by variables that act on the manager's attitudes (Ajzen, 1987):

1. Behavioral beliefs: the "degree of appreciation of the activity" is the most representative characteristic, 75% of the sample is influenced by a high degree of appreciation. Conversely, 68.75% of the sample does not engage in activities that are not valued.
2. Normative beliefs: the proximity environment represents a major source of influence for the entire sample in the realization of certain actions and decisions.
3. Controlling beliefs: 100% of the group of entrepreneurs mobilizes skills from their previous experience and education for the benefit of their company. For 87.5% of the group, the absence of competence in a domain leads to an absence of action in this domain in the company.

The economic analysis then highlights a difficult economic situation for these companies: the HCVAVC is between 4€ and 50€, with an average of 18€. The economic impacts linked to the regulation of the dysfunctions amount to more than 245 000€, that is to say an average of more than 15 000€ of annual value added destroyed per company.

The lack of structuring in the strategy implementation process generates hidden performance costs that are not negligible for the survival-development of these companies: 8.75% of the average sales turnover and 19% of average production costs. The most representative component is the "non-creation of potential" which represents 42% and concerns 62.5% of the sample. There is a hidden performance within these companies that clearly allows them to reduce their risk of failure.

2.3 Survival: Period of Serious Difficulties

Failure is part of the life of the VSE and its manager. Serious difficulties lead to failure, which may even result in the liquidation of the company. Failure is a generator of learning and necessary for innovation (Cusin J., 2008). We analyze how a VSE manager can bounce back from an entrepreneurial failure through personal and operational support, which we call rebound engineering.

Our fieldwork, the non-profit association 60000 Rebonds, accompanies entrepreneurs who have gone into receivership after a series of financial difficulties. The objective of the support is to help them rebound towards a new salary or business project.

The materials come from our voluntary action within this association for 5 years, as creator of the antenna, sponsor and trainer of the accompanying persons of the Region Auvergne Rhône Alpes. This allowed us, through successive tests, to develop the engineering of the rebound. We have accompanied 5 entrepreneurs until the rebound and interviewed about twenty entrepreneurs after liquidation, before their support by the association.

In addition, we conducted a survey of 168 entrepreneurs accompanied by 60000 Rebonds who had rebounded. We thus consolidated the results of our experiment.

2.3.1 Reactivation of the Entrepreneur's Human Potential?

After a failure, the entrepreneur loses his or her bearings, resulting in a drop in the satisfaction of his or her fundamental needs (Physiological, Psychological, Sociological, Economic (PPSE): his or her Human Potential is atrophied. A collective and individual support (a coach and an operational sponsor) allows to reactivate it.

2.3.2 Rebound Engineering

Rebound engineering refers to the design of a set of techniques, processes, methods and tools that allow a failed entrepreneur to return to a situation that is acceptable to him or her. These tools, derived from Socio-Economic Management (MASE), have been adapted to the specific needs of the struggling entrepreneur (Desmaison, 2017). Easily assimilated and pragmatic, they provide a structured framework that can frame the changes in strategy necessary for a small structure (Savall and Zardet, 1995).

The 5 entrepreneurs of VSEs that we personally accompanied had a shorter rebound period than the national average: less than a year compared to 18 months. These tools are partially used by other volunteer coaches.

Used for entrepreneurs in liquidation, these tools can be used during periods of business difficulties and whenever the strategy is questioned (survival position).

2.3.3 The 2019 Impact Survey of Entrepreneurs Having Rebound (EAR)

Two findings from this survey of 168 VSE managers who have bounced back from liquidation illustrate the effectiveness of support for managers in difficulty:

- The feeling of the accompanied managers;

  On a scale of 1 to 5, the entrepreneur has, for the most part, recovered the satisfaction of his or her fundamental needs (in red, the feeling before, in blue, the feeling after support).

  They made the most progress on a personal level (reactivation of their human potential) and on a professional level (engineering the rebound).
- Accompaniment as a rebound gas pedal;

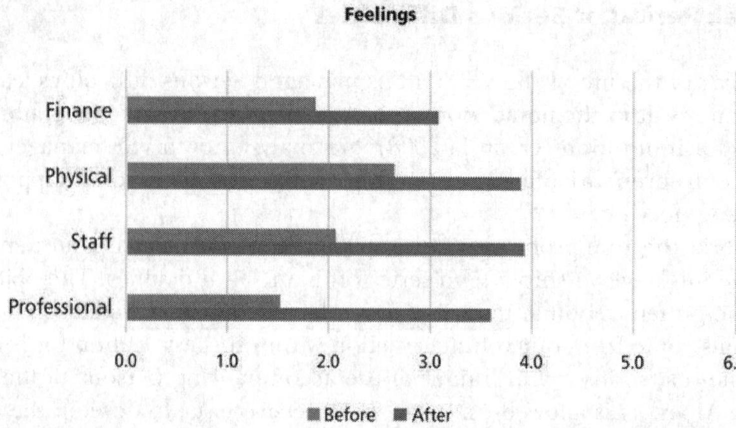

Figure 13.2 Feelings of the manager before and after coaching.

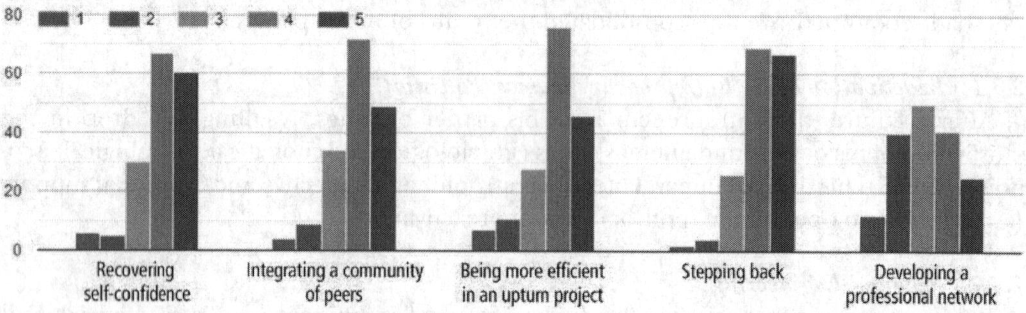

Figure 13.3 Benefits of coaching VSEs.

> We asked them how the association's volunteer support had contributed to improving different aspects of the rebound, according to a scale ranging from very little (1) to totally (5).

These results were attested to by numerous test sentences. The time saved by the coaching was estimated by those involved to be between 1 and 2 years. In periods of difficulty and survival, collective and individual, personal and operational support accelerates the revitalization of the VSE manager's human potential and provides management engineering in the event of a crisis.

3 DISCUSSION: THE CONDITIONS FOR THE DEVELOPMENT AND SURVIVAL OF VSES

The lack of effective time dedicated to strategy is a risk for the company's performance: a VSE manager tends to invest in actions with immediate results rather than actions to create potential, which makes his company vulnerable.

Strategic implementation requires specific support and more specifically raises the need for strategic skills on the part of the entrepreneur, to improve the management of his company and develop a balance of all the activities necessary for the proper development of his company: the NAE.

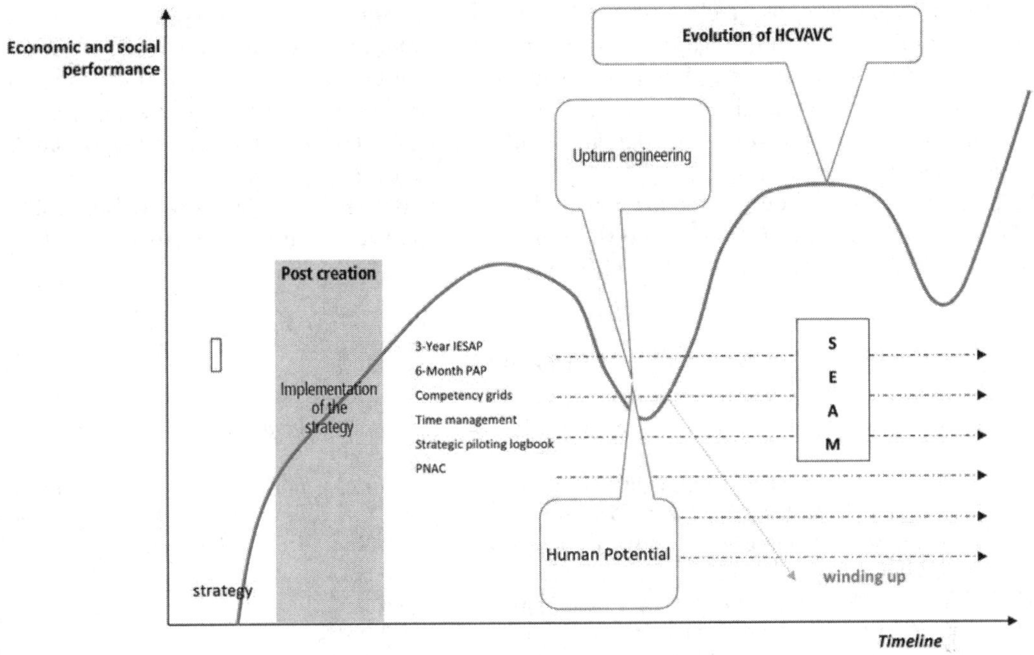

Figure 13.4 Development-survival of VSEs.

A systemic vision of the company, based on the NAB, leads to an overall and sustainable performance integrating the temporal dimension. The CHVACV is a simple and synthetic indicator for measuring sustainability. Strategic skills are a key dimension to increase the sustainability of the entrepreneur's job.

In each period of difficulty, the entrepreneur must bounce back for his company to survive. His rebound goes through a mourning curve (Kubler-Ross, 1969). For the entrepreneur, it is characterized by a descending curve (negative and counter-productive attitude, turned towards the past and refusal), then an ascending phase (productive attitude, turned towards the future and positive; Figure 13.4). Its accompaniment allows it to move from a state of pathogenesis to a state of "salutogenesis" (Augustin, Desmaison, 2019).

CONCLUSION

This study presents the determining character of the structure/behavior relationship at several phases of an entrepreneurial process: survival, development and failure. This relationship is just as important in the strategy of the MSE as in the individual strategy of the entrepreneur. The VSE manager must develop a systemic vision of his company, integrating all the activities under his responsibility, and relying on an overall and sustainable performance of the company. The results show the relevance of the qualimetric intervention-research methodology, facilitating the development of this systemic vision.

The theory of planned behavior (Ajzen, 1991) allows for an in-depth analysis of the beliefs of managers, which are the sources of influence of their behavior. The entrepreneur's beliefs on each domain of the NAE modify his behavior and, ultimately, the structure of the firm. The structure-behavior relationship appears to be decisive.

We have highlighted the close link between the manager and his company, between the physical and moral health of the manager and the implementation of the strategy. Not all VSEs have the financial strength to afford support. It could be facilitated by pooling costs, in particular through collective training of managers. Associations, union leaders and public actors also have a decisive role to play in facilitating survival-development actions for small businesses.

Small business entrepreneurs are particularly affected by the post-sanitary crisis of 2020. The results of this research may help them in rethinking their strategy, to ensure an overall and sustainable performance of their business.

REFERENCES

Ajzen, I. (1991). The theory of planned behavior. *Organizational Behavior and Human Decision Processes, 50,* 179–211.

Avenier M. J., & Gavard-Perret, M. L. (2012), Inscrire son projet de recherche dans un cadre épistémologique. In M.-L. Gavard-Perret, D. Gotteland, C. Haon, & A. Joliber (Eds.), *Methodologie de la recherche en sciences de gestion. Réussir son mémoire ou sa thèse* (2nd ed., pp. 11–62. Pearson Education France.

Cusin J. (2008), *Faut-il échouer pour réussir,* Ed. Paillot.

Desmaison G., (2017), *L'ingénierie du Rebond.* Congrès ADERSE, Bordeaux.

Desmaison G., Augustin B-M., (2019). *Entreprendre, échouer, rebondir. De la pathogenèse à la salutogénèse des entrepreneurs post-liquidation.* Colloque IDE, Lille.

Grazzini, F., Boissin, J.-P. (2013). Analysis of the mental models developed by French managers in the acquisition or takeover of SMEs. *M@n@gement, 16*(1), 49–87.

Julien, P.-A., & Marchesnay, M. (1988). *La Petite entreprise: Principes d'économie et de gestion.* Ed. G. Vermette.

Kubler-Ross, E. (1975). *Les derniers instants de la vie* (on death and dying, 1969), trans. Cosette Jubert, Labor et Fides.

Lechat T., Torres O. (2016). Les risques psychosociaux du dirigeant de PME: Typologies échelle de mesure des stressurs professionnels. *Revue Internationale PME, 29*(3–4), 135–159.

Man, T. W. Y., Lau, T., & Snape, E. (2008). Entrepreneurial competencies and the performance of small and medium enterprises: An investigation through a framework of competitiveness. *Journal of Small Business & Entrepreneurship, 21*(3), 257–276.

Nash, L., & Stevenson, H. (2004b). Success that lasts. *Harvard Business Review, 82*(2), 102–109.

Plane, J-M. (2000). *Méthode de recherche-intervention en management.* L'Harmattan.

Rouveure T. (2017). *Vers une performance globale et durable de la micro-entreprise—L'impact des compétences de l'entrepreneur.* PhD thesis in Management Sciences, Université Jean Moulin Lyon 3.

Rouveure T. (2018). Compétences et pouvoir d'agir du dirigeant de micro-entreprise. *Entreprendre et innover, 2*(37), 105–118.

CHAPTER 14

ORGANIZATIONAL DECODING IN THE 21st CENTURY

María Elizabeth Canllo de Montoto and Juan Matías Montoto Canllo

ABSTRACT

The objective of this chapter is to demonstrate the depth of our language when we relate to each other in the workplace and thus be able to determine the dysfunctions that are generated by lack of understanding or concealment of certain data and information on a daily basis.

The study was based on a family company with 130 employees in Argentina, which is dedicated to the distribution of mass consumption products. The socio-economic approach to management was applied in this company.

Through sterring meetings, a proximity to the managers of the different areas was implemented and it was possible to identify some meanings of the internal language. This then helped to work on the actual strategic path.

In today's world, management is much more complex than it was 100 years ago, when the first management theories began. Human relations are also evolving at an extraordinary and sometimes frightening speed. Therefore, today we must focus even more on the small details in order to better understand the people who make up the work teams, to manage them in a way that can evolve their human relations and thus the performance of organizations.

Within human relations we have identified different types of language codes within the framework of an organization. As defined by Avellaneda,

> A code? It is what allows us to identify and understand an information or message. What is decoding? It is to see the information that comes to us through diseases, symptoms, personal and organizational conflicts, which is showing us a way to understand and dissolve them. (Avellaneda, 2017)

SEAM Treatise, pages 153–161

In this chapter we want to transmit experiences decoding the language of a company and the results obtained from the better understanding of its actors.

1 RATIONALE AND OBJECTIVES OF DECODING THE LANGUAGE OF ORGANIZATIONS

What motivated us to carry out this research was the following problem: Is it possible to decode the internal language of the organization to better understand the internal functioning and help to make better decisions?

- How to increase productivity in an unstable environment?
- Is it possible to better understand people in order to motivate them?
- What are the right ways to stabilize the economics of the business?
- What methodologies can be used to reduce resistance to change?
- How can we avoid project implementation failures?
- Is it possible to better manage hidden and visible costs?

Through the support of sciences such as anthropology, psychology and psychopedagogy, during the process of implementing socio-economic tools, we try to improve the understanding of the hidden language of people within the company in order to improve and adjust actions and strategies, trying to enhance productivity by placing each actor in its best role and position.

When decoding we must discover the hidden language of all the people in the organization, since the non-externalization of some emotional states often causes labor relations to trigger moods of dissatisfaction that lead to great demotivation. If this situation is not discovered or unveiled, it generates a vicious circle in most of the people who are part of the organization. When we decode we can decipher codes that are deep and unconscious, we can discover the conflicts that are observed in companies, particularly with the same similarity as in the family that composes it in the case of family businesses.

We have found that the hidden language in an organization also has a hierarchy, there is a language between managers, another between line personnel and so on down the hierarchical ladder. Each of these languages is indecipherable to subordinate personnel or to management.

> The theory of the fragmented human beings, and in particular the isolation of the producer status, causes a kind of schizophrenia in the individual and generates a spontaneous state of conflict within organizations, as a result of an imbalance between conflict and cooperation. The conflict situation is not an anomaly; on the contrary, it is the most spontaneous, most frequent observable situation. On the other hand, it is up to the company or organization to know the existing combination between conflict and cooperation, to take responsibility and to take corrective measures to restore an effective and efficient combination to achieve an adequate level of performance. (Savall, Zardet, 2005)

Human behaviors are so varied that there is an infinity of combinations to analyze them. Taking as a paradigm of socio-economic theory that people are actors, comedians, strategists, intelligent and disobedient (Savall and Zardet, 2005), we discover that there are different reactions depending on the situation. Thus, a person may show some of these characteristics in his or her relationship with the environment. This is how we enter into the complexity of the diversity that exists in the world of internal relationships in the organization.

Savall and Zardet (2005) characterize human behaviors as follows:

> the instability of behavior, the spontaneous organizational disobedience also comes from a great permeability and continuity between life at work and life outside work, which function as two communicating vessels. Disturbances in one sphere spill over into the other, as do successes and beauties.

One of the hypotheses of H. Savall (1974, 1979) is: Human intervention is necessary to limit the spontaneous (natural?) erosion of the quality of actors' behaviors, over time.

Adapting the global strategy of an organization to each of the people who interact on a day-to-day basis among the teams is a challenge. It is not easy, as each speaks a different language, with all the vicissitudes that this entails. The question is: how does a manager or team leader act to align everyone towards a goal, if within each language an idea cannot always be described in the same way?

> Production reveals itself in the face of what it sees as exorbitant demands or unjustified reproaches. We have mentioned the lack of common language and communication. It is commonly a "dialogue of the deaf" that turns their backs on the two parties who have lost sight of the fact that they are working towards the same goal. (Savall, Zardet, 2005)

Certain patterns of observed behaviors derive from long-standing experience transfer from generation to generation. Not only within a business family, but also within each actor involved in management. For, within organizational psychology, we find that

> in the family/business we create everything that in our shared unconscious has meant life for our clan: not happiness, not achievements, not joy, but life. Our unconscious is interested in our survival and if it has recorded that certain facts, even negative ones, helped our business family to survive throughout generations—whatever the environment it has had to suffer and experience—all those who make up that clan will continue to repeat those patterns without realizing that this uncritical repetition is the cause of the problems that afflict them. (Avellaneda, 2017)

2 CASE OF A MEDIUM SIZE FAMILY BUSINESS

The company, where the socioeconomic management was implemented, is one of the logistics sector, of distribution of mass consumption products, with exclusivity of products produced by a multinational. Its portfolio includes beers, soft drinks, water, isotonic drinks, energy drinks and wines. This company has 2 owners, 3 managers, and 9 middle managers, who are part of the management, and 117 operating personnel. These 131 people are both direct and indirect, covering a geographic area of the 3 most important cities in the province of Santiago del Estero, Argentina. It uses 17 short-distance trucks and 4 long-distance trucks for its operations.

2.1 Context

The company's context is quite complex as it is influenced by several fronts that condition its autonomy and independence. For example, most of the strategic commercial decisions come directly from the national management, as well as the internal management methods and methodologies. As a result, they are not always adapted to the characteristics of each region and culture.

One of the global objectives of this mega beer producer is the drastic reduction of costs, he has an obsession to cut visible costs, and in most cases to outsource them to the distribution network. Thus, production planning policies, local commercial policies, decision-making policies centralized in Buenos Aires, are implicitly affected by this global objective of cutting visible costs. This has a great impact on the local management of each distributor, for example, stock outs, non-personalized commercial discounts by geographical area, high personnel turnover in different areas, centralized negotiations with unions, among others.

One of the outstanding variables is the high inflation that has plagued the country for several years and the changing and contradictory tax regulations. Argentina has inflation rates averaging between 25% and 40% per year, which complicates any attempt at medium and long-term planning in economic and financial matters, contribution margins, investments or new product development.

2.2 Development of the Socio-Economic Intervention

In 2013, we disembarked with the socioeconomic methodology (Savall and Zardet, 1987), seeking to introduce changes in global processes and convert hidden costs into productivity. In the company's distribution center, 13 individual interviews were conducted with all managers and 15 group interviews with 50% of the core staff. Table 14.1 shows the main dysfunctions diagnosed, with their frequency of occurrence and the causes identified by the stakeholders.

Table 14.2 presents the summary of the company's hidden costs (converted into euros), which amount to 727,000 euros in total, and 5,500 euros per person per year.

In addition, management and supervisors were trained and implemented socio-economic management tools. A distinction must be made between managers and owners and/or managers. In these cases, most of the managers had a quick response to the use of these tools, without forgetting that they had to be "reminded a couple of times" for the tools to be implemented.

With the first tool, the self-analysis of time, the stakeholders were afraid to reveal their own mistakes and failures in their daily activities. This tool was the one that cost the most at the beginning because none of them liked to reveal their own weaknesses and dysfunctions. The methodological help provided by us as internal consultants also helped to identify ways of looking at time and decode their visions.

With respect to the priority action plans and strategy planning, the managers have difficulties to project themselves in time, with respect to future action plans and improvement policies, in the assumption of not having the consultant's support in this tool, they would have been empty tools without synchronization or strategic support. There was a human resources training crisis, the managers were at the crossroads of what to write, what to plan and how to project themselves. However, the beginning of forward planning had many benefits for the organization as it allowed it to evolve.

The competency grids opened the minds of managers and senior management to see the gaps and areas where training was lacking and where there were no human resources within the organization to specifically fill those positions. This tool was easier to implement and to act upon. The only complication was deciding which training plans to start with.

The strategic piloting logbook took more time to implement, follow up and consultant support. The stakeholders had some delays in developing the qualitative, quantitative and financial indicators. Although they already had informal indicators in their heads that allowed them to make daily decisions, the transfer and formalization of the pilot indicators took longer. Like

TABLE 14.1 Summary List of Dysfunctions Identified in the Distribution Center

Elementary dysfunctions	Approximate frequency	Reasons given for the dysfunctions
Fines for truck shelters	Daily	Many tickets at night due to lack of visibility
Postponed Process of ballots	Daily	Reduction of rejection rate
Shortage of products from the plant	Ongoing	Plant ignores its responsibility
Truck drivers waste time to return and settle load	Daily	Only one checker and one SDL checking
Unscheduled phone calls	Daily	Regulation of dysfunctions
High maintenance cost of old vehicles	Monthly	Old vehicles
Logistic staff's absenteeism	Weekly	Sick leave, union's representation, Absence permit, shift switch, drunken state
Change process of goods	Weekly	Low quality, (flat, low content) or expired
Performance of non-required tasks	Daily	Customers who don't have the money when receiving the order
Overtime of sellers	Daily	Events that distract from the route (lunch, etc.)
Absenteeism of sellers	Yearly	Variety of reasons
Axum cell phone app not entirely used	Daily	Orders not available in the system. Hindrance to place the order when no access to inventory. Hybrid order are loaded here
Rejection of orders	Daily	Variety of reasons
Breaking of buns during delivery	Daily	Bottles that go loose without cases in the truck
Working hours without added value	Weekly	Lack of assistant
Reduced pension conditions for low temperature	Yearly	Union pressure
Out of stock	Yearly	CMQ stock break in beer
Sell out later than planned	Weekly	Progress problems
Shifts in function	Daily	Lack of administrative staff in each location
Loading disruptions	Weekly	High temperature on site
Lack of products	Ongoing	Due to the plant and not recognized
Lack of own trucks	Daily	Lack of maintenance. Old vehicles

time management, this indicator highlighted errors and dysfunctions in the areas. For this reason, people showed resistance in the creation of some of them. The fundamental message was that we were not looking for those to blame for the dysfunctions, but rather to prevent them, and that none of the actors is solely and directly responsible for them.

Finally, the periodically negotiable activity contract has been implemented several times since its first version. In the first two, there was no success because there was no follow-up by the managers, and at the time of evaluating and closing the contract, they were completed as just another obligation, without obtaining changes and improvements in management. In the last implementation closed at the end of 2019, we had the best results in management, execution and compliance by them.

We observed that the resistance to change camouflaged certain internal corruptions among the personnel, such as, for example, the crossing of commercial actions between different distribution channels without authorization, lending of returnable containers without receipts, theft of merchandise, among others. This delayed certain change processes.

TABLE 14.2 Evaluation of the Distribution Center's Hidden Costs

<table>
<tr><th rowspan="2">Indicators</th><th colspan="5">Component</th><th rowspan="2">Overall Amount</th><th rowspan="2">Risks</th></tr>
<tr><th>Overtime</th><th>Excess Salary</th><th>Over-consumption</th><th>Non production</th><th>Non creation of potential</th></tr>
<tr><td>Absenteeism</td><td>€ 500</td><td></td><td>€ 35,000</td><td>€ 12,500</td><td>€ 4,000</td><td>€ 52,000</td><td></td></tr>
<tr><td>Work accidents</td><td></td><td></td><td>€ 17,020</td><td></td><td></td><td>€ 17,020</td><td></td></tr>
<tr><td>Staff turnover</td><td>€ 320</td><td></td><td></td><td></td><td></td><td>€ 320</td><td></td></tr>
<tr><td>Non quality</td><td></td><td></td><td>€ 40,500</td><td></td><td></td><td>€ 40,500</td><td></td></tr>
<tr><td>Productivity gaps</td><td>€ 185,021</td><td></td><td>€ 255,000</td><td>€ 75,000</td><td>€ 97,694</td><td>€ 617,130</td><td></td></tr>
<tr><td>Overall Amount</td><td>€ 185,821</td><td>4.415 €</td><td>€ 347,520</td><td>€ 87,500</td><td>€ 101,694</td><td>€ 726,280</td><td></td></tr>
<tr><td>Economic concepts</td><td colspan="3">€ 537,806</td><td colspan="2">€ 189,194</td><td></td><td></td></tr>
<tr><td>Accounting concepts</td><td colspan="3">Overcharges</td><td colspan="2">Non production</td><td></td><td></td></tr>
</table>

Overall amount of hidden costs	Number of employees	Hidden costs per person per year
€ 727,000	131	€ 3,500

2.3 Social and Economic Impacts

Some outstanding changes were the reduction of time in making transcendental decisions, long-term strategic planning and clarity of management.

Despite all these difficulties, as can be seen in Figures 14.1 and 14.2, after one year from the beginning of the implementation of socioeconomic management, there was a large increase in productivity. In the following years, the country's economic, inflationary and financial situation started to become turbulent, with successive devaluations, so that the productivity index went down, went up, but remained at levels higher than those of the origin prior to the implementation. We assume that if the macro-economic conditions had been maintained, the productivity trend would have been increasing.

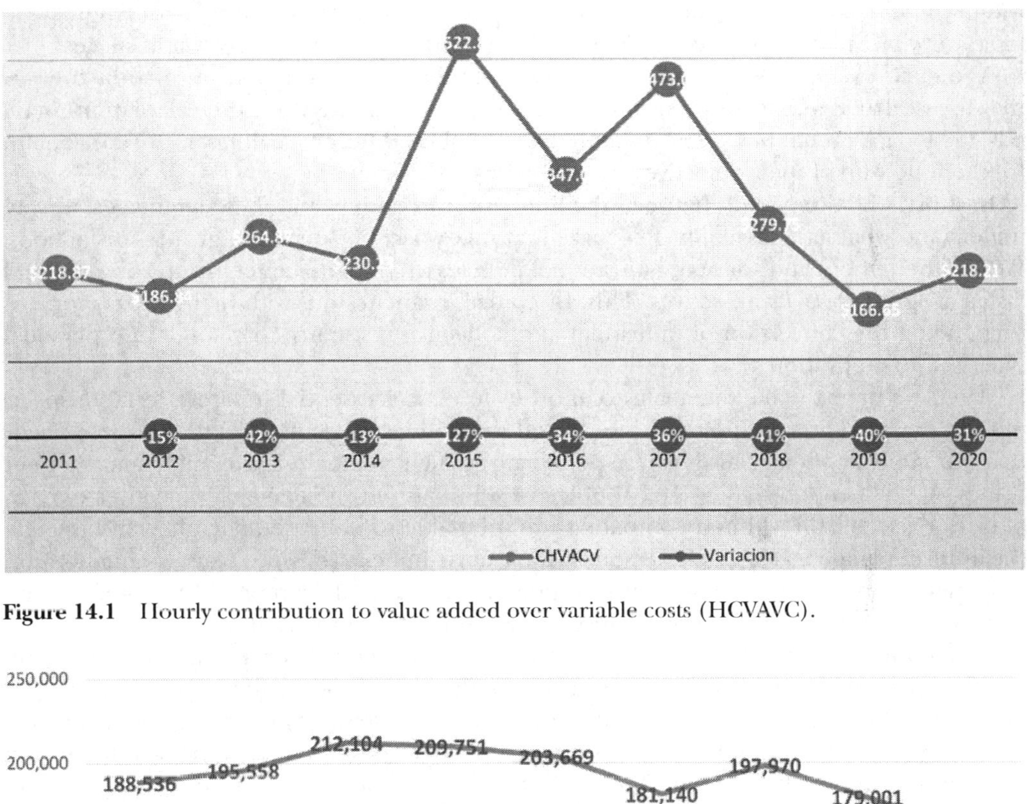

Figure 14.1 Hourly contribution to value added over variable costs (HCVAVC).

Figure 14.2 Sales volume in hectoliters.

As can be seen in this last graph, despite the fact that in 2015 when nominal sales volumes began to fall, it is observed that the company's productivity has a great leap, due to the investment in internal development and focus not only on the market and consumers but also on internal customers, and each of the collaborators and employees.

3 LEARNING AND KNOWLEDGE CREATION OUTCOMES

When we are negotiating objectives, ways of working and after several attempts we reach an agreement between bosses and subordinates, we learned that an affirmation from the subordinate does not always mean a Yes. Even though feelings of satisfaction are generated from having reached an agreement, we know that details and small print that were not addressed within the discussion are hidden. As long as we cannot bring these minutiae of language to light, we will continue to have hidden brakes on productivity and management success.

As a clear example, when managers present indicators, we often have to audit the way they are "calculated," as they may consciously or unconsciously alter the calculation methods due to lack of suitability. The effect is that they show different realities, more convenient for the follow-up of their objectives.

In short, when one reads between the lines and can understand these languages, we can understand what are the major objectives that mix work, personal and group satisfactions. We can then orient and adapt organizational policies to generate better group cohesion and faster progress towards objectives. This, of course, branches out with many effects, one of them being the conversion of individual and collective resistance to change into personal synergy and motivation.

When we want to take our team to another level, it is essential to know certain aspects of their personal life and not only job-related capabilities. We must find the possible needs that can motivate them. This is where personalized management or proximity management comes in, adapted not only to global objectives, but also to the personal objectives of each person. Each person within a company should be able to interpret, decipher and decode the different languages of each person in their environment (boss, colleague, collaborator, customer, supplier, etc.). We are thus defining a concept of becoming "therapists" (Savall and Zardet, 2004) that will be very important in and for the organization.

It is about trying to articulate people's strategies with the collective strategy of the team or the company (Savall, 1979), even if it means that people agree to give up part of their personal strategy if it is not compatible with that of the company or the team. Ignoring a person's extra-professional life, establishing a watertight partition, as recommended by the classical School of Management (Taylorism, Fayolism, Weberism) is a source of errors, tensions, interruptions and erroneous behaviors in the field of professional life (Savall, Zardet, 2005). The periodically negotiable activity contract makes operational the rapprochement of the company's strategy and those of the individual actors.

On the other hand, we need a certain pedagogy: because the technicality of the strategic plan very often needs a "translation" so that the messages disseminated are clear, so that they allow the actors of the company to relate them to their daily reality and so that the concrete actions that will emerge from them for the stakeholders, are precisely determined to be understood and put into practice (Savall, Zardet, 2005).

All stakeholders have powers, micro-powers, arguably multifaceted, some of which are visible and explicit, while others are hidden (Savall, Zardet, 2005). We had to review several priority processes and activities as they did not have the expected results, due to the informal powers of the actors.

During the decoding process and the evolution of organizational relationships, we benefited from the rigor of weekly meetings to align all members of a team towards a common goal, despite the fact that everyone has their own language or interpretation of the subject. It is also important to have a skepticism of indicator calculations, because if an indicator is well explained and motivates the responsible person, it means that it is on the right track.

CONCLUSION

The proximity of the management with the managers and of the managers with their teams allowed us to better understand our languages, behaviors and ways of working, to be more assertive in the face of all the turbulent changes of the context and to motivate. This generated confidence in each one of them, so that the strength and energy put by each one of them increased and spread to the rest of their colleagues. Sometimes we do not realize the mistakes we make and we allow the routine to blur the look to see the realities that happen around us. This generates an excessive vice that sometimes turns into chaos, when the outcome of a situation turns into uncontrollable situations. The whole process of application of rules, laws, knowledge, experiences is faded with the passing of time, if this management nurtured by emotions, projects, ideas and HR intentions is not sustained. It is very important and virtuous to be aware of our true role and to highlight our virtues as well as our mistakes, in order to leave indelible traces that mark paths of true transcendence.

REFERENCE

Avellaneda, N. (2017). *Decodificar una empresa es posible.* Editorial Palabrava, S.d.

This page intentionally left blank.

CHAPTER 15

EARNING MORE BY WORKING BETTER IS FEASIBLE

Laurent Paysac, Bertrand Paysac, and Mélissa Sanchez

ABSTRACT

According to the Marxist theory, the search for profit leads to capitalist exploitation and class struggle. Socio-economic theory shows on the contrary that the search for economic performance is inseparable from social performance. In this chapter, we present the case of a Lyon-based SME, SLB Médical, which designs and markets medical devices and articles for overpackaging medical products. ISEOR has been supporting this SME since 2016 in improving working life conditions and cleaning up its internal operations. Its outstanding achievements illustrate that it is indeed possible to earn more by working better.

According to neo-classical theory, man is a "homo œconomicus", his only motivation being to allocate factors of production, namely technical capital and human labor, with a view to maximizing his profits (Piotet & Sainsaulieu, 1994). This search for profitability by the capitalist entrepreneur is analyzed in Marxist theory as a form of exploitation of human labor (Marx, 1945). The maximization of profits then becomes incompatible with the satisfaction of employees, since it inevitably leads to class struggle between the proletariat and the entrepreneurs. In other words, economic performance prevails over social performance.

In contrast to classical liberal and Marxist theories, the fundamental assumption of socio-economic theory is that there is no need to oppose economic performance to social performance since they influence each other (Savall, 1974, 1979; Savall & Zardet, 1987, 1992). Other authors agree with this idea: Pfeffer (1995), Preston and O'bannon (1997) and Quairel (2006). Indeed, what neo-classical and Marxist authors fail to identify is that the firm's overall performance is only partially explained by the factors of labor and capital (Carré, Dubois, & Malinvaud, 1972). In reality, this performance is atrophied by dysfunctions

SEAM Treatise, pages 163–169

that impact both employee satisfaction and the company's economic performance. These dysfunctions generate hidden costs and performances (Savall, 1974) which only need to be recycled into value added, using a process based on the development of human potential. This is characterized by skills, behaviors and individual and collective energy (Savall, Zardet & Bonnet, 2014). The notion of "potential" is preferred to that of human capital, as these resources are inalienable and partially identified and revealed (Savall, 1974, 1979; Savall & Zardet, 1987; Cappelletti, 2010, 2012).

Where Marxist authors explain that economic performance goes hand in hand with class struggle, socio-economic theory argues that the search for socio-economic performance relies on bringing actors together to awaken their human potential (Savall, Péron, & Zardet, 2014; Savall et al., 2015). This chapter sheds light, based on this theory, on the answer to the following problem: how to create more economic value added without deteriorating social performance?

The case of an SME accompanied since 2016 shows that it is possible to simultaneously improve economic performance and social performance, thanks to operational improvements. This company designs and markets medical devices and overpackaging items for medical products. Its customers are public or private hospitals (doctors, pharmacists, nurses, etc.), service providers or associations such as home hospitalization structures. It enjoys a good economic performance, with strong average annual growth of 18% between 2012 and 2015. However, at that time, it was experiencing a very high staff turnover, strongly disrupting its commercial activity.

We present the company, its situation in 2015 and the socio-economic management support. A second section exposes the methods of continuous cleaning up of the organization, to prevent the appearance of hidden costs-performances. Finally, the socio-economic results in Section 3 prove that it is possible to earn more by working better.

1 SLB MEDICAL COMPANY: ITS SECTOR AND ITS CHALLENGES

Founded in 2001, SLB Medical co. markets articles and medical devices for the preparation and administration of injectable solutions, particularly in the treatment of chemotherapy, as well as protection and transport solutions adapted to these devices (infusion bags, syringes, vials). It is important to distinguish between the terms "Medical Devices" and "Medical Products." The former is a legal term, governed by European Regulation 745, which regulates the marketing of medical devices. This regulation essentially impacts the manufacturer of the medical device, since it must hold the "CE mark." Thus, according to this standard, SLB Medical co. acts as a distributor of medical devices, manufactured by a subcontractor holding the CE mark. The ANSM (French equivalent to FDA) is also vigilant and randomly audits the various actors in the sector, particularly in the monitoring of the medical device.

In 2015, the leader explained, "I am sitting on a gold mine, but I can't find people who want to dig with me." Indeed, in 2015 staff turnover was 183% and instability was 283% . To deal with this internal problem, frustrating and drastically slowing down the company's development, SLB Medical sought out ISEOR in 2015.

The accompaniment was intense for the first six months, starting with an integral diagnosis of dysfunctions and evaluation of hidden costs-performance (Savall & Zardet, 1987). This socio-economic diagnosis revealed €628,000 in hidden costs-performance in 2015, including almost € 80,000 related to staff turnover, due to regulations in terms of recruitment, training, integration and management of departures. At the same time, a business development potential of €490,000 was untapped. Faced with this situation, the manager decided to innovate, not in terms of products, but in his management practices.

In 2016, he decided to implement the tools and methods of the socio-economic approach to management (Savall, 1974; Savall and Zardet, 1987). The competency grid highlighted the need to develop the versatility of people and to enrich their work. An integrated training plan was put in place. The manager also developed the Internal and External Strategic Action Plan (IESAP) to formalize the long-term strategy (Savall and Zardet, 1995). The latter is specified every six months, thanks to the six-monthly Priority Action Plan (PAP).

All team members were involved in the operational implementation through focus group sessions. To encourage this recycling of hidden costs and performance into value added, a periodically negotiable activity contract (PNAC) was set up. It includes collective, semi-collective and individual objectives and is negotiated between each manager and his or her employee (Savall, 1979). The efforts made and measured to achieve the objectives are the basis for an additional half-yearly remuneration for each employee.

Beyond the change in management and organizational tools, this intervention stimulated a change in the mental structures of the company's actors. Indeed, under the impetus of the leader, the employees, previously "full-time healers", became the guarantors of the ortho-functioning, through a collective awareness.

2 CONTINUOUS CLEANING UP OF THE ORGANIZATION TO PREVENT DYSFUNCTIONS

We present the means implemented to raise awareness and make the actors responsible for preventing dysfunctions, by showing the virtues of this system through a concrete example.

2.1 Raising Awareness of Dysfunction Prevention

The presentation of the socio-economic diagnosis and the hidden costs-performances to the company's actors (80,000 € per year and per person in 2015) caused a shock, a stimulating mirror effect to show the need to "groom" the company's functioning. Cleaning up can be defined as the periodic maintenance of tangible and intangible objects that deteriorate over time (Bernadet, 1997; Ocler, 1999). The philosophy that has gradually taken hold through this search for continuous improvement can be summarized by the expression: "Work better to earn more."

The prevention of dysfunctions within SLB MEDICAL Co. consists first of all in showing how dysfunctions impact both social and economic performance. Indeed, dysfunction regulations are a source of frustration for employees, as these tasks are uninteresting. From an economic point of view, dysfunctions have significant knock-on effects. A delivery error requires a new delivery and collection, which in turn can lead to further dysfunctions. The time spent on an order is then multiplied by two, for the same sales turnover. This overtime could have been allocated to any other operation generating additional value for the company. The prevention of "non-products" (Savall and Zardet, 1987, 1992) is also part of this awareness-raising process, such as invoices not collected due to errors.

In addition, the manager attaches great importance to playing down errors, which represent opportunities to learn and improve.

2.2 Taking Responsibility for the Prevention of Dysfunctions

Several means of prevention have been put in place to prevent the appearance of hidden costs-performance.

Firstly, self-checking stages mark out each operation, whether physical or digital. The aim is to make the person carrying out an operation responsible for the quality of his or her own production, without relying solely on an external control, even if another employee can carry out a contradictory control. In the case of invoices checked before dispatch, self-checking and control have made it possible to reduce payment delays considerably. At the same time, a non-conformity is valued economically thanks to the hidden cost-performance evaluation method. This process has also made it possible to show the co-responsibility of each employee in the creation of economic value added for the company.

Everyone is involved in the process of cleaning up the way things work. For example, a steering tool or indicator deemed "dormant" is eliminated after cooperation. From this point of view, the implementation of socio-economic management tools has made it possible to considerably lighten the management of the ISO 9001 quality standard, as they meet a large number of the standard's criteria, without the need for additional indicators. These tools are also appreciated by the external auditor and facilitate certification (Sanchez M., 2020).

The prevention of dysfunctions is now a custom in the company, particularly in weekly team meetings. There is also a system dedicated to this task: the semi-annual mini-diagnosis. Each employee takes it in turns to express his or her views on perceived dysfunctions.

Improvement actions are then defined collectively, some of which may be incorporated into the next priority action plan. All the actors are thus involved in the implementation and evaluation of actions, which is an opportunity to increase their autonomy and skills. Finally, efforts to prevent dysfunctions are recognized as strategic objectives in the CAPN of each actor. The increase in performance generated is thus redistributed in the form of additional compensation to employees (see Table 15.1).

2.3 "Prevention is Better Than Cure": The Case of Order Management

Let's take the case of logistics and order dispatch. From the time an order is received until it is shipped, several preventive tasks exist at key stages of the process. For example, the picker highlights the important elements on the order, before the computer entry, to limit errors during the order preparation phase (which concentrates 90% of errors) and to facilitate the control afterwards. In the spring of 2020 (first containment due to covid–19), SLB Medical experienced a 23% increase in the number of orders to be shipped to hospitals. To prevent nonconformance regulation times from increasing, the warehouse worker proposed to increase the number of preventive checks, which represents an additional investment of 30 minutes per day. Between 2015 and 2020, the percentage of nonconformities on orders dropped from 1.21% to 0.59%.

3 "DOING MORE BY WORKING BETTER," AS EVIDENCED BY FIGURES

How and why has the company's socio-economic performance improved? To measure this evolution, we use the criterion of the Hourly Contribution to Value Added on Variable Costs (HC-VAVC; Savall and Zardet, 1987, 1992). Figure 15.1 shows its evolution between 2015 and 2019.

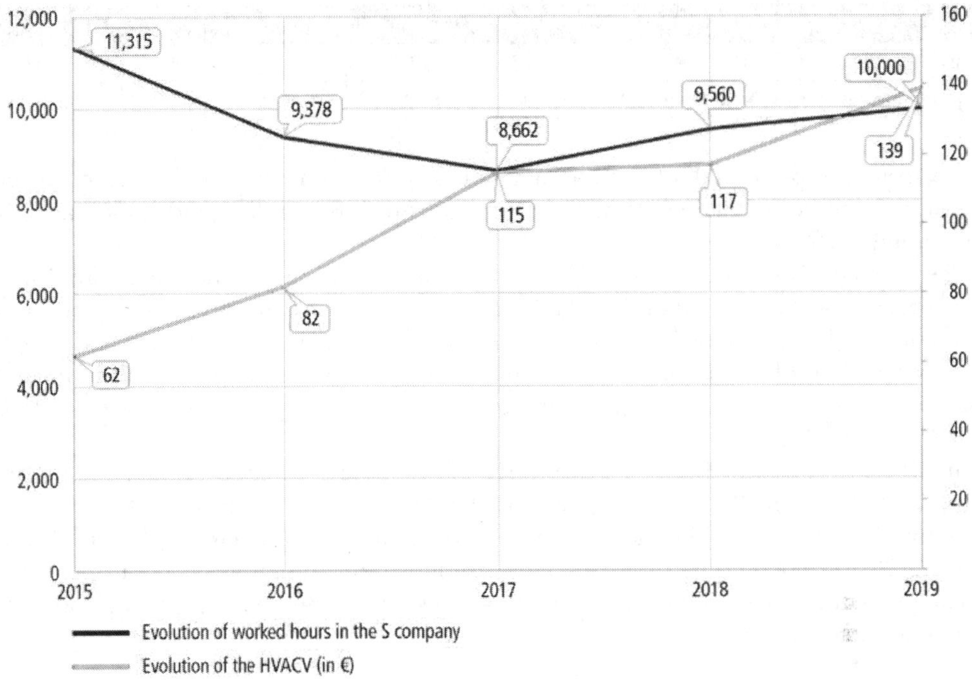

Figure 15.1 Evolution of hours worked and CHVACV between 2015 and 2019.

The improvement actions implemented have freed up hours worked that were previously dedicated to regulating dysfunctions. This time has been reallocated to higher value-added tasks, to dysfunction prevention or to strategic development actions. This virtuous circle is illustrated in the evolution of revenues, variable costs and hours worked.

Revenues have increased by 67% between 2015 and 2019 and net income has tripled over the same period. This can be explained by a commercial development that is now supported by several actors. Cooperation sessions of the leader with his team stimulated a market analysis and the strategic decision to develop a higher margin product line. New products were also developed under the company's brand. These additional resources were then used to finance a larger inventory of goods.

This increase in activity has led to economies of scale on merchandise purchases and a reduction in variable costs. With its new commercial clout with its carriers, the company also successfully negotiated a reduction in transport costs on purchases from 3.3% of sales in 2019 to 3.07% in 2020. It has managed to negotiate a maintenance of transport costs on sales (3.95% of the sales turnover in 2020, against 3.73% in 2019), whereas the tendency was an increase of 10% of these parallel costs. The sending of dematerialized invoices has reduced the cost of sending monthly invoices from 125 € to 10 €.

The number of hours worked and paid decreased by 12% between 2015 and 2019. Following two voluntary departures in 2016, the work organization was rethought in light of the competency grid. The manager has chosen to decompartmentalize the professions by developing cross-functionality and versatility among employees. Thus, the position of Quality Manager, held by the manager's son since September 2017, has been enriched with internal and operational management missions entrusted by the manager. The latter can now focus more on a strategic axis of external growth. The year 2020 was marked by the Covid–19 crisis: exceptionally, the company had to internalize the ESAT's packaging activity.

TABLE 15.1 CAPN Bonuses Paid by Year

Year	2016	2017	2018	2019	2020
Overall amount of the PNAC bonuses	€ 9,981	€ 9,040	€ 9,903	€ 12, 514	€ 18,000

This operation represented 3,143 additional hours worked compared with the forecast activity load (11,164 hours). The CHVACV thus amounts to 108 € in 2020 and could have been maintained at 139 €.

The manager is committed to redistributing part of the value added generated by the collective, semi-collective and individual efforts that make these results possible. Table 15.1 shows an overall increase of 80% in the amount of bonuses paid between 2016 and 2020. In order to build employee loyalty, the percentage of bonus paid is correlated to seniority: it represents 10% of gross semi-annual salary for the first three years, then progressively 12.5% and 15% thereafter.

In 2019, SLB Medical Co. had a workforce of 6 people compared to 7 people in 2015. Between 2015 and 2019, it is striking to note that the value added on variable costs has almost doubled (92.48%) while the number of hours required has decreased by 10% (11,315 hours in 2015/10,000 hours in 2019). This case illustrates the importance of hours spent managing dysfunctions, which lead to employee dissatisfaction and atrophy the company's economic performance.

CONCLUSION

The class struggle between the capitalist entrepreneur and the exploited employees is a recurring historical issue. Socio-economic theory refutes the opposition between economic and social performance. We are therefore interested in the following question: how to create more economic value added without deteriorating social performance? The case of SLB Médical speaks for itself. It implemented management tools and systems in 2015 and offers significant feedback on the prevention of dysfunctions.

In 2015, the manager regretted that he was "the only one to implement the product offer and to manage dysfunctions." The solitude of the manager has been transformed into a real team effort. Thus, the improvement of working conditions and operations has simultaneously stimulated the company's social performance (work enrichment, CAPN bonuses) and economic performance (increase in HCVAVC). Earning more by working better is therefore possible.

The energy and involvement of the manager are determining factors in setting up such a virtuous circle. This company shows great prospects for development. (Paysac, 2019).

REFERENCES

Bernadet, A. C. (1997). *Contribution of the practices of cleaning up to the improvement of the quality of the operation of the organizations.* University of Lyon: thesis of doctorate in management sciences.

Bourdieu, P. (2000). *Les structures sociales de l'Economie.* Editions du Seuil.

Cappelletti, L. (2010). Towards a socio-economic model of human capital measurement? *Revue Française de Gestion, 8,* 139–152.

Cappelletti, L. (2012). *Le contrôle de gestion de l'immatériel: une nouvelle approche du capital humain.* Dunod.

Carré, J. J., Dubois, P., & Malinvaud, E. (1972). *La croissance française: un essai d'analyse économique causale de l'après-guerre.* Editions du Seuil.

Friedman, M. (1970). A Friedman doctrine: The social responsibility of business is to increase its profits. *The New York Times Magazine, 13*, 32–33.

Marx, K. (1945). *Le capital.* Les Belles Éditions.

Ocler, R. (1999). De la nécessité de rendre les démarches qualité plus proactives, ISEOR. *Journée Tutorale Qualité* organized by GREFIGE/IAE, (p. 13). Nancy.

Paysac, L. (2019). Team stability: a daily challenge in an unstable environment. In H. Savall, & V. Zardet, *How to work together? Challenges of intergeneration.* EMS.

Pfeffer, J. (1995). Producing sustainable competitive advantage through the effective management of people. *Academy of Management Perspectives, 9*(1), 55–69.

Piotet, F., & Sainsaulieu, R. (1994). *Méthodes pour une sociologie de l'entreprise.* Les Presses de Sciences Po.

Preston, L. E., & O'Bannon, D. P. (1997). The corporate social-financial performance relationship: A typology and analysis. *Business & Society, 36*(4), 419–429.

Quairel, F. (2006). Is CSR transferable to the SME? Does the "responsible purchasing" policy of large industrial groups constitute a lever for the diffusion of CSR? *Oeconomia Humana, 4*(11), 19–23.

Sanchez, M. (2020). *The reasoned integration of multiple exogenous and endogenous norms to maintain the socio-economic performance of the firm.* University of Lyon: PhD thesis in management sciences.

This page intentionally left blank.

CHAPTER 16

HOW TO PROFESSIONALIZE MANAGERIAL PRACTICES IN FAMILY BUSINESSES

Éric Pernoud, Gilles Pernoud, and Françoise Goter

ABSTRACT

In this chapter we explore how the socio-economic management model allows family firms (FFs) to professionalize their managerial practices and increase their performance. Based on a intervention-research initiated in 2017, we highlight the managerial specificities of these firms, their main dysfunctions as well as the proven improvement actions. This chapter also makes explicit the characteristics of the methods and tools of socio-economic management that play a decisive role in resolving the difficulties encountered by family businesses

Family businesses (FBEs) represent the vast majority of businesses in the world, and in France about 83% of businesses (Radu-Lefebvre et al. 2020). Many of them complain about their difficulties in managing their operations and staff (Meier, 2018). This situation does not prevent them from growing. Leaders and their families are making progress in their managerial practices, but on narrow topics: digitalization, ERP, premises. The intervention-researches conducted by the ISEOR team in family businesses show a fairly degraded functioning in the teams, with a high staff turnover rate, numerous burn-outs and strong economic "bleedings"

This chapter shows how the professionalization of managerial practices in family businesses, with the help of the Socio-Economic Theory, allows for socio-economic performance. The first part of this chapter presents a state of the art of the main dysfunctions that jeopardize the sustainability of family businesses, as well as a selection of the concepts of the Socio-Economic Theory (SET; Savall, 1974, 1979; Savall and Zardet, 1987) that would make it possible to address these difficulties. The second part details the devices and methods

SEAM Treatise, pages 171–176

www.infoagepub.com

of the socio-economic theory implemented in the framework of an intervention-research conducted within the Savoie Volailles company. The third part presents the results of the intervention-research obtained.

1 MAIN OBSTACLES TO THE DEVELOPMENT OF FAMILY BUSINESSES

The in-depth study of family owned companies reveals three specific characteristics: (a) Managers are tired of managing their "core business" activities as well as their staff. They consider management to be more and more restrictive, particularly because of the proliferation of standards, the increasing complexity of personnel management regulations and the difficulty of implementing intergenerational management; (b) The new generations are adopting a less "patriarchal" management style, but are still imbued with "paternalistic" and poorly structured managerial practices; (c) The lack of professionalism in the managerial practices of the family members. Their socio-economic management indicators are classic, even rudimentary, and some employees take advantage of any confusions between family members to steer decisions in their favor or not to progress. Many decisions are based on emotions rather than on professional criteria.

How to professionalize the management of a family business? How to negotiate with each employee, especially family members, their place in the company and their professional future?

According to the socio-economic theory, efficiency requires ongoing negotiation between the actors (Savall, 1979). When the manager negotiates the commitment of his/her employees and contracts it, in different forms, this allows him/her to better know the level of skills, behaviors and working conditions of employees, and therefore to better integrate them into his/her decisions and actions. The tools of the socio-economic approach to management, in particular the Priority Action Plan (PAP) and the Periodically Negotiable Activity Contract (PNAC), facilitate this integration.

The first works in France on family businesses date from 1984 (Hirigoyen). More recent research shows the challenges linked to the durability of these enterprises, as 80 to 85% disappear before the third generation (Carlock and Ward, 2001). When the ability to innovate is blocked, the survival-development of family businesses is endangered (Ben Mahmoud et al., 2010). "The strategy for the future does not have to be established in continuity with the history of the family business. Nevertheless, it must necessarily take into-account the history, otherwise implementation difficulties could appear" (Savall A., 2014). The professionalization of the managerial practices of the family businesses is desirable: "proximity management and conviviality within the family business generate difficulties in managing the emotional behaviors of managers," and subsequently socio-economic difficulties (Savall A., 2014). Finally, power sharing, while preserving family harmony, is also a major challenge (Paré-Julien, 2016).

While their key success factors are certainly multiple, the results converge towards the difficulty for EFs to sustain their capacity for innovation, to overcome emotional difficulties and to agree on a business development strategy.

2 THE CHALLENGE: TO GET OUT FROM A PATERNALISTIC MANAGEMENT STYLE THAT CREATES BLEEDINGS

Savoie Volailles Co. is a family business created in 1976 and located in the French Auvergne-Rhône-Alpes region. It markets fresh and regional products in fruit and vegetables, butchery, delicatessen, cheese and groceries. It has five stores (10 to 18 employees each), two logistics warehouses, a central office and a head office, as well as a presence on about ten markets. The family owns orchards. The commercial policy is based on the proximity and quality of the products, from the soil. The company has about 120 employees and up to 160 in summer with seasonal workers. The two sons, CEO and MD, took over the management of the company created by their parents in 1976. They each had three children and 4 of them (2 from each brother) work in the company, as well as their respective wives.

In 2016, the sales turnover decreased in some stores and 2017 started badly on the economic front. In addition, the managers are experiencing difficulties in laying the foundations for a management that will ensure the transmission of the company between the 2nd and 3rd generations. The socio-economic diagnoses and the training sessions revealed several dysfunctions. The managers themselves regulate numerous dysfunctions on a daily basis. The staff turnover rate is high in some stores (60%), as well as in the butchery activity (132%). The other six family members (children and wives) would like to take on responsibilities, but are held back by the managers' centralizing "patriarchal" management. Family members alternate between phases of conflict and cooperation and sometimes lack objectivity when assessing (positively or negatively) the work of others. The lack of reliable indicators and family cohesion means that large-scale economic projects, such as renovating the warehouse and opening new stores, are often discussed but never implemented.

The managers and their family wished to implement socio-economic management, with the support of ISEOR, to improve cohesion within the family, both on the future of the company and on the future of everyone (family members and non-family members) in the company (Pernoud E et al. 2020). They also wanted to move away from a paternalistic management style and towards more professionalism. Of the 10 stores dreamed of by management, only 5 were opened in 2016, as family members felt that they were already having difficulty taking proper charge of the existing stores. The management of the stores is likened to "grocery store" management, with no clear strategy. Competition gradually developed and some employees did not correspond to the image desired by the family.

3 PROGRESSIVE PROFESSIONALIZATION OF MANAGERIAL PRACTICES

The socio-economic intervention in this family business started in July 2017. The first year allowed the implementation of the HORIVERT process (Savall and Zardet, 1987). In the following years, the accompaniment focused on the transformation of new business areas and the deepening of tools. Today, the intervention is still ongoing because the managers still want to improve the quality of their management.

Managerial practices have gradually become more professional. The first resolutions taken by the members of the family were to learn to prepare politically and technically the exchanges and work sessions, and to manage the activities and the teams more rigorously. The setting up of collaborative training clusters (teams of managers per activity) has also enabled the beginning of a structuring with perimeters to be piloted: management, commerce, logistics and markets. A pilot has been defined at the head of each of these areas. Indicators and communication–coordination–cooperation [3C] circuits have been set up to identify dysfunctions and improve the quality of decisions taken. The research-intervention device, in particular the steering group and the collaborative-training clusters, served as a springboard for family members to train, test their new managerial practices and refine their 3C devices.

At the end of 2017, a diagnosis and focus group (Savall and Zardet, 1987) with the management and the supervisory staff led to a new distribution of missions and roles, the construction of an organizational chart, a training path and mission sheets for the main jobs. "Vertical" diagnoses and focus groups were then conducted in three key sectors in 2018: a store, the Butchery activity and Logistics. Employees in these three sectors were interviewed about the company's dysfunctions and hidden costs. The implementation of management tools and a problem-solving method helped to reduce many dysfunctions and allowed a strong increase in skills and responsibilities.

The economic management of the stores used to be centralized with the managers and the purchasing manager. Today, weekly sales management by product family is carried out by the department managers, in cooperation with the store manager and the sales manager, according to a principle of synchronized decentralization (Savall and Zardet, 1987, 1995). Monthly accounting statements and inventories are used to better manage margins and orders. Seminars have been set up to prepare for sales highlights (sales actions, new products). A butcher/store manager pairing has been created, whereas previously the butcher's department was a "separate" department. The Logistics team has achieved productivity gains, in particular following the complete overhaul of the organization between the reception of goods and the preparation of orders. The development of economic balances on investment projects has had a positive impact on intra-family relations between shareholders. This tool has helped to objectify strategic intentions and reduce value judgments.

In January 2018, the biannual priority action plans (PAPs) were implemented in each team to promote the strategic breaking down of the company's Internal and External Strategic Action Plan (IESAP) (Savall and Zardet, 1995). The elaboration of the PAPs allowed the extension of the work launched after the diagnoses and to bring the teams together on common objectives. The fact that all actors are solicited on strategic projects, whether they are family members or not, decreases the feeling of privilege and increases team cohesion. Since early 2019, the company has implemented periodically negotiable activity contracts (PNACs) with employees. Two half-yearly interviews between an employee and his or her manager lead to the formalization of collective, semi-collective and individual progress objectives for the employee, evaluated after 6 months, and paid as a bonus. The PAPs and PNACs allow family members to better build and share the company's internal and external strategic objectives with non-members. People can project themselves more easily and understand the relevance of the proposed objectives.

In the past, family dinners served as a management committee and discussions mixed personal, patrimonial and managerial topics. The creation of a Management Committee in January 2019, composed exclusively of family members, and the introduction of "rules of the game" have also improved family cohesion. Precise criteria for evaluating employees and probationary periods have been defined. Now, everyone is more aware of the criteria for evaluating the quality of the work provided. Practices for managing activities and people have gradually become more effective, even if today not all areas and personnel are fully managed. The members of the family have found the courage to clean up certain situations, by putting an end to the "privileges" that certain employees and managers had granted themselves, who were taking advantage of the lack of management methods to work "comfortably" (workload, schedules, etc.). After three years of socio-economic management, the decline in stores sales turnover of the 4 stores, opened before 2016, has been stopped (Table 16.1).

The company's overall headcount has increased only slightly, through a combination of reduced hours, thanks to productivity gains, and recruitment linked to new strategic projects. Staff turnover and absenteeism have decreased significantly in two of the three sectors diagnosed (see Table 16.2).

Of the 1,150,000 Euros of hidden costs assessed in the E. Store and 882,000 euros in the Butchery activity, 76% have been recycled into value added. Ambitious projects have been

TABLE 16.1 Evolution of Economic Performance From 2015 to 2019

	Store of the family business focused on fresh food					%
Year	2015	2016	2017	2018	2019	2019/2017
Revenue	€18,573,496	€19,148,521	€20,797,468	€21,598,776	€22,788,776	+8.74%
Comparison with 4 other stores	€18,573,496	€18,824,562	€17,912,149	€17,890,689	€18,351,439	+2.40%
Revenue of the store opened in 2016		€323,959	€2,885,319	€3,708,087	€4,437,337	+35.00%
Variable costs	€12,261,808	€13,335,787	€13,877,574	€14,957,164	€15,200,000	+8.7%
Hours worked	Not evaluated	149,766 h	175,256 h	177,070 h	178,068 h	+1.58%
Hourly Contribution on Value Added on Variable Costs		€38.8	€39.48	€37.51	€42.61	+7.35%

TABLE 16.2 Trends in Absenteeism and Staff Turnover in the Three Sectors Diagnosed

	Store E.		Butcher		Logistic department	
	2017	**2019**	**2017**	**2019**	**2017**	**2019**
Absenteeism rate	8.43%	1.66%	11.87%	7.20%	5.33%	9.01%
Staff turnover rate	60%	19%	132%	36%	7%	48%

taken up or launched (new warehouse, meat cutting workshop, new ERP) and the opening of new stores is under discussion.

In July 2020, the family members set up an Internal School, one of socio-economic theory's key concepts. The Internal School is an "off-site" school whose objective is to ensure that the integrated training of employees runs smoothly. It provides trainers and trainees with interactive teaching methods and tools (Savall and Zardet, 2021). They realized that it is particularly difficult in family businesses to pass on know-how specific to family members, such as the choice and presentation of products, to non-members.

4 MAIN LESSONS LEARNED ABOUT MANAGEMENT IN FAMILY BUSINESSES

The management of family businesses is sensitive because it is largely based on affinity. Family members tend to trust their employees "blindly," as long as the latter have shown some results at the beginning and give the impression of behaving "loyally." There is little or no monitoring via indicators. The professional practices seem relevant on the surface, but hide situations that are socially and economically degraded for the company.

Paternalistic and directive management does not prevent the company from developing, but rather restricts its development. In a family business, some family members have difficulty finding their place: the tools and methods of socio-economic management make it possible to find out what each person is capable of doing and to define tailor-made activities and jobs. The use of IESP/PAP/PNAC tools limits the under- or over-interpretation of family members' strategies among themselves. It also shows that a strategy of one family member can be compatible or even complementary to those of the other family members.

The professionalization of the managerial practices of family members increases the degree of cohesion between them. The socio-economic theory allows them to share a common language and working methods, not just a common history. They also manage to understand each other better and to negotiate their "heritage" and their professional future. Moreover, the fact that the same tools are used by all increases transparency and gradually reassures non-members who fear favoritism. The "shared requirement" (Savall and Zardet, 1987) makes it possible to make each employee accountable.

Once they have achieved the desired growth, RUs tend to focus on immediate results, which are more visibly related to the company's core business. The satisfaction of immediate results also allows family members to better accept the demands of managing teams and activities. The balance between immediate results and potential creation actions, specific to THEOSE, allows a return to sustainable economic development. The measurement of intangible investment in the quality of human potential (IIDQPH) (Savall and Zardet, 2008) also explicitly shows the profitability of potential creation when it is managed. The company has learned to move from disorganized agility to structured agility, while better driving economic performance (Worley, A. Savall, Zardet, Bonnet, 2015). Finally, the transmission of skills from family members to non-members is not spontaneous; it should be structured, particularly with the help of pedagogical methods.

CONCLUSION

Taking into-account the specificities of family businesses does not mean developing a specific management for these businesses. This chapter shows that a general theory of the firm such as the socio-economic theory allows family firms to develop while respecting their specificities. Finally, the socio-economic theory helps family members to be more professional in their management practices.

REFERENCES

Ben Mahmoud Jouini S., Bloch A. and Mignon S. (2010). Capacités d'innovation des entreprises familiales pérennes. Proposition d'un cadre théorique et méthodologique. *Revue française de gestion,* vol. 200, no. 1

Carlock R., & Ward J. (2001). *Strategic planning for the family business. Parallel planning to unify the family and business.* Palgrave.

Hirigoyen G. (2014). *Family businesses: Challenges and performance.* Economica.

Meier O. (2018). Family business: succession and governance. *Le journal de l'économie.*

Paré-Julien D. (2016). Change of course for family businesses: Room for multigenerational management. *Gestion, 41*(3).

Pernoud E., Pernoud G., & Pernoud E. (2020). Socio-economic management, large-scale distribution and family businesses. In Savall & Zardet (Eds.), *Tétranormalisation: Profusion of norms and development of enterprises* (pp. 247–253). Editions EMS.

Radu-Lefebvre M., Barrédy C., & Fayolle A. (2020). Les nouveaux défis de la succession dans les familles entrepreneuriales. *Entreprendre & Innover, 44*(1).

Savall A. (2014). *The endogenous factors of sustainable performance of family business internationalization: A longitudinal case of intervention-research.* PhD thesis in management and management, CNAM.

CHAPTER 17

FROM A SMALL TRADITIONAL COMPANY TO AN INTERNATIONAL GROUP

Structuring the Growth of the Aganova Group

María Ángeles Rastrollo Horrillo, Marisa Rastrollo Horrillo, and Agustín Ramírez García

ABSTRACT

This research shows how the socio-economic model developed by ISEOR has contributed to overcome the internal barriers that made it difficult for a Spanish business group to take advantage of national and international markets. The findings reveal how organizational deficiencies are accentuated when penetrating international markets, due to the added difficulties of physical, psychological and cultural distance. And this occurs even in companies that have important competitive advantages, such as international patents. These results enrich the literature on firm growth and have important practical managerial implications.

While there is an extensive literature that analyzes the factors that favor small business growth, it is insufficient to explain how to overcome the obstacles that entrepreneurs face in structuring sustainable and profitable business growth. Research on barriers to small business growth has basically focused on three areas (Gherhes, Williams, Vorley & Vasconcelos, 2016; Fuller-Love, 2006): (a) the characteristics of the owner-entrepreneur that influence their ability to stimulate and manage the growth of their ventures, such as their previous education and experience or their entrepreneurial orientation; (b) the impact of size on the creation of business capabilities ; (c) the characteristics of the environment, arguing

SEAM Treatise, pages 177–183

how regulation and government support favor large firms and limit the competitive ability of small firms (Kurato, Hornsby & Naffziger, 1999) .

This literature concludes that the two fundamental weaknesses for the growth of small firms are: the high dependence on the entrepreneur's capabilities and the scarcity of financial and human resources, the difficulty to belong to networks, and the low capacity for innovation or market orientation (Liberman-Yaconi, Hooper, & Hutchings, 2009) due to their size (Gheres et al., 2016). Thus, it is argued that in small firms decision-making is centralized in the owner-entrepreneur, who is often involved in the execution of many decisions and spends a lot of time on day-to-day activities, to the detriment of strategic ones (Liberman-Yaconi et al., 2010). This use of time makes it difficult to plan and organize activities, and simple and informal organizational structures are common, with no definition of responsibilities or processes. Resource limitations would explain the lack of relevant information to improve decision making, and the difficulties in attracting and retaining qualified personnel.

The same line of thinking guides the literature on international ventures, identifying financial, technological and human resources (mainly the entrepreneur's knowledge and experience in international markets) and the networks developed by the entrepreneur as the main drivers of international ventures (Cavusgil & Knight, 2015). Moreover, the focus is on the interaction with environmental forces, explaining the influence of physical and cultural distance from foreign markets (Sui & Baum, 2014)), but without delving into the interior of firms starting to internationalize (Rastrollo-Horrillo & Martín-Armario, 2019). Existing research does not explain how small firms resolve the conflicts they face in satisfying culturally and geographically distant markets.

This research presents the findings of a socio-economic intervention (Savall & Zardet, 1987, 2008) conducted in the Aganova group, formed by two small firms, one of them an international start-up. It shows evidence of how the socio-economic model of the ISEOR (Savall, 1974, 1979, 2003) has contributed to identify and overcome the internal barriers that hindered the exploitation of national and international market opportunities.

1 THE AGANOVA GROUP: INTERNATIONAL START-UP FRUIT OF A STRATEGY OF GROWTH THROUGH RELATED DIVERSIFICATION

The essence of this business group cannot be understood without mentioning the figure of its founder. He is an entrepreneurial person who, although he did not have a university education, has a proven experience in the sector, derived from working for more than 15 years for a water supply company. This led him to set up on his own, creating in 2007 a first regional company dedicated to leak detection using traditional systems (Fugaqua) and at the same time collaborating with a leading European company in detection systems with the aim of financing the acquisition of the necessary technology.

The collaboration with the latter led to the idea of creating a different device for leak detection in large pipelines. To develop this idea, in 2012, he decided to create a new company, Aganova, initially formed by two people, the entrepreneur and an R&D manager. With the support of a research department of the University of Malaga, and after 3 years of research, he managed to patent the system in 2015, called Nautilus, after which he began the challenge of commercialization and the search for partners, to exploit the patent in a short time. That same year he got his first international sale and the entry of a venture capital investor, who not only provided the financial funds, but as his entrepreneur points out "*also knowledge to structure the financial part and for the definition of the business models of both companies.*" In order to reduce visible costs, the growth of Aganova's activity is carried out by taking advantage of Fugaqua's technical and administrative structure, sharing personnel and some equipment: "*Fugaqua generates cash-flow and allows Aganova to invest in R&D and penetrate international markets.*"

At the beginning of 2019, the owner begins the negotiation of the socio-economic intervention, because he felt that the project was in danger, due to numerous internal organizational failures. At that time, the two companies were both owner-managed and both in the process of growth. Fugaqua was expanding in the national market and had a staff of 33 people. Aganova, with 15 employees, had patented Nautilus in more than 50 countries on 5 continents, and was promoting growth through a wide network of international distributors. However, the sales figure was much lower than expected and they had difficulties to implement the strategic internationalization plan.

2 MAIN RESULTS OF THE SOCIO-ECONOMIC INTERVENTION

The intervention started in July 2019, with the aim of giving solidity to the Aganova Group, organizing the companies, in order to take advantage of market opportunities and ensure a profitable growth.

The socio-economic diagnosis (Savall & Zardet, 1987) helped to identify the organizational dysfunctions and root causes that affected the performance of this group of companies and the exploitation of their national and international market opportunities (see summary in Table 17.1). These dysfunctions revealed a lack of internal orientation of the management team, which distorted the focus of the company's attention, more centered on solving the numerous problems of quality failures or low productivity, instead of dedicating time to the piloting of activities and teams, to internal planning and coordination or to actively seeking new opportunities. While the entrepreneur exhibited proactive behaviors, the centralized management style prevented proactivity throughout the organization.

The economic profitability of international markets was not clear, and during the provision of services in several countries—Taiwan, Mexico, Colombia and Chile—there had been quality failures that jeopardized the investment made in these markets.

TABLE 17.1 Summary of the Qualitative Diagnosis of the Aganova Group

Main dysfunctions
Unsatisfactory working conditions: lack of space, schedules, bad working environment.
Difficulties to define the organizational structure (work and authority flow).
Lack of piloting of activities and workloads
Weaknesses in communication-coordination-concertation between staff and with external partners
Weaknesses in commercial activity
Weaknesses in the quality of customer service delivery.
Weaknesses in the development of the group's strategy: insufficient dynamism and lack of dedication of management to its implementation.
Shortcomings in people management: personnel selection and recruitment processes, competency piloting, uninspiring recognition and reward systems.
Lack of effectiveness of the management style, more dedicated to the urgent than to the important.
Weaknesses in the system of indicators for economic and strategic decision-making.

TABLE 17.2 Summary of Hidden Costs of the Aganova Group

Indicators	Overall amount
Absenteism	€ 60,900
Work accidents	N.E.
Staff turnover	€ 242,700
Non quality	€ 1,633,900
Productivity gaps	€ 386,400
Overall amount	€ 2,323,900
Hidden costs per person	€ 45,000

The dysfunctions had a high impact on the lack of quality, staff turnover and lack of direct staff productivity, generating hidden costs per person per year of €45,000 (Table 17.2). This quantification of hidden costs was key to making them aware of the need to work as a team and to take decisions that they had been postponing.

As a result of the training and cooperation meetings with the 10 managers and middle managers and the development of three project groups, actions for change were designed and implemented, which are summarized below, grouped into the following four areas:

1. *Development of a comprehensive group strategy*, with group corporate objectives set by management, and a breakdown of priority actions for each of the companies and their departments. Using the Priority Action Plan, all middle management and part of the staff participated in the formalization of the strategy, making it possible to innovate in the priority actions that each department would carry out during the semester to achieve the strategic objectives.
2. *Definition of a synchronized organizational structure.* The organizational chart of the group and of each company was redefined, clearly separating the structures and personnel assigned to each, and specifying the responsibilities of each department and each job position. Many important functions, such as accounts receivable management or purchasing, were not assigned. A corporate "Financial and Control Management" department was created, as well as an Administration department in each company; the area of activity of each company was delimited and a group strategic committee was created to promote common policies, taking advantage of the synergies between them. During the ten months of the intervention, many resources were devoted to defining processes at group and company level and to digital transformation. In addition, a system of meetings was put in place to develop real-time communication-coordination practices between departments, which were effectively maintained during the months of confinement, thanks to videoconferencing platforms.
3. *Economic piloting.* The group had a system of immediate key performance indicators drawn up monthly from accounting (sales, profits, cash flow, etc.). But they had no business or social performance indicators in terms of dysfunctions and hidden costs. Therefore, new indicators were created, such as leakage not identified on the first visit, or the amount of sales not invoiced due to errors in the provision of the service.
4. *Development of management skills.* The intervention provided the energy and tools to develop the managerial skills of the entrepreneur himself and of many of the managers. Within a few months, he appointed directors in each company, and he remained exclusively as CEO of the group.

Coordination meetings, the use of the PAP to share strategy and the adoption of time management tools (concerted delegation span, task scheduling) and competency grid management tools contributed to the effective exercise of leadership.

The results of the intervention were assessed as very positive by the company's management and staff. The change in the work dynamics, the closer leadership and the reduction of dysfunctions improved the work environment and the generation of value added. In the case of Aganova, the hourly contribution to value added over variable cost had doubled by the end of 2020. In the words of the entrepreneur and CEO of the group "After COVID–19 the company Aganova has hatched, something we expected 4 years ago, and in Fugaqua we have achieved a clear leadership in the Spanish market, we have improved the economic-financial results, the margins, and we have a team 100% focused on managing the business."

The entrepreneur also valued positively the effect of the socio-economic model on the cohesion of the group, stating "Some of the team had doubts at the beginning of the intervention, and in fact not all of them have evolved in the same way. But now the staff is very aligned, eager to grow, many conflicts have been resolved and conflicts between them have been resolved. Now everyone in the group speaks the same language, even though they are two companies with two very different business models."

3 LEARNING

The entrepreneur of the company had the characteristics proposed in the literature on growth and had the support of a wide network of partners who had helped him to enter international markets, generate technological innovations and access financial resources. But this had not been enough to ensure the success of its growth strategy. The research carried out shows the importance of socio-economic intervention in identifying and overcoming the internal conflicts that were hindering the growth of this business group. Specifically, two important lessons can be drawn to guide the growth strategies of small companies, one more general, and the other explicitly focused on the internationalization strategy.

The first lesson is that having internal information on dysfunctions and hidden costs is of vital importance for adopting more participative management and anticipating the organizational conflicts that arise during growth. Entrepreneurs often take it for granted that they have information about their company and maintain effective communication flows with their staff. On the contrary, we suggest that this is not necessarily the case, that this information must be developed consciously and methodically. Internal information about dysfunctions and hidden costs gives the opportunity to think about their root causes and act on them, thus fleeing the fatalism of apparent causes such as lack of time or financial resources. As the entrepreneur states "The model helps a lot to become aware of the problems to be solved, because they end up being normalized, believing that it is normal to lose so many opportunities and so much money."

The entrepreneur wanted to take advantage of the synergies between the two business structures to reduce visible costs, and this was generating much higher hidden costs. For example, in the international company the volume of hidden costs in 2019 was equivalent to 137% of sales, and in Fugaqua to 67%. In addition, the role of the entrepreneur must move from a centralized management style to one that promotes the active participation of staff in identifying internal and external opportunities and in implementing negotiated solutions. To do so, he needs socio-economic management tools to help him run a more decentralized and synchronized organization.

The second lesson alludes to the danger of embarking on a rapid internationalization strategy without strengthening the internal organization. The contribution of the socio-economic model to the effectiveness of the internationalization strategy is made explicit in three aspects. Firstly, the measurement of economic results, differentiating the immediate results from the investment in creating potential, makes it possible to become aware of the economic impact of quality failures resulting from the pressure of international markets. The higher visible costs of supplying foreign markets are well known, but the impact on the hidden costs generated by failed international projects is not so well known. For example, in the first major international tender obtained, they started the project without the necessary planning or clarification of the roles of the partners. This implied the dedication of several company directors of more than 20% of their working time for 6 months to solve the problems remotely, and the technical director had to spend 9 weeks at the destination to carry out the technical work, due to the deficiencies of the contracted personnel. The socio-economic intervention began one month after the start of this project and could be reversed in time. Secondly, the impact of previous failed pilot projects in other countries was higher, as the credibility with the client, with other potential clients in that market and with distributors was lost. Now it is more difficult to return to those markets, the distribution partner is more active, and a new plan has to be designed in those markets. Thirdly, they now have a clearer profile when it comes to choosing the most suitable distribution partner, as they not only facilitate sales but also service provision.

CONCLUSION

Using socio-economic intervention, this research provides evidence of the process of developing the internal cohesion of a company facing growth challenges, showing the impact of adopting an internal orientation in improving its external strategy (Savall & Zardet, 1995). Organizational deficiencies are accentuated when growth is in international markets, due to the added difficulties of physical, psychological and cultural distance. And this occurs even in companies that have important resources and competitive advantages, such as patents or financial and commercial partners. These results enrich the literature on firm growth.

With regard to practical implications, this study suggests that small growing firms should consciously develop their internal organization before embarking on growth strategies so as not to jeopardize the sustainability of the firm. Conclusions are also drawn for public policy on entrepreneurship, on the type of support services for the organizational development of ventures that should be promoted: those aimed at generating information on dysfunctions and hidden costs, promoting a synchronized organization and a participative management style based on negotiation with the staff.

REFERENCES

Cavusgil, S.T., & Knight, G .(2015). The born global firm: An entrepreneurial and capabilities perspective on early and rapid internationalization. *Journal of International Business Studies, 46*, 3–16.

Fuller-Love, N. (2006). Management development in small firms. *International Journal of Management Reviews, 8*(3), 175–190.

Gherhes, C., Williams, N., Vorley, T., & Vasconcelos, A. C. (2016). Distinguishing micro-businesses from SMEs: A systematic review of growth constraints. *Journal of Small Business and Enterprise Development, 23*(4), 939–963.

Kuratko, D. F., Hornsby, J. S., & Naffziger, D. W. (1999). The adverse impact of public policy on micro-enterprises: an exploratory study of owners' perceptions. *Journal of Developmental Entrepreneurship, 4*(1), 81–92.

Liberman-Yaconi, L., Hooper, T., & Hutchings, K. (2010). Toward a model of understanding strategic decision-making in micro-firms: Exploring the Australian information technology sector. *Journal of Small Business Management*, *48*(1), 70–95.

Rastrollo-Horrillo, M.-A., & Martín-Armario, J. (2019). Organisational barriers to nascent born-global growth: Learning from the inside. *Journal of International Entrepreneurship, 17*, 454–473.

Sui, S., & Baum, M. (2014) Internationalization strategy, firm resources and the survival of SMEs in the export market. *Journal of International Business Studies 45*(7), 821–841.

This page intentionally left blank.

CHAPTER 18

SEAM IN CROSS-CULTURAL CONTEXT

Omaya Kuran, Dolly Bassil, and Lara Khabbaz

ABSTRACT

The mosaic contextual profile of the MENA countries requires the adoption of innovative consulting approaches to reach the desirable change results. The three authors of this chapter being SEAM interveners in 3 different sectors: Public Sector, Private Higher Education, and SME-Performing Arts, in addition to their over 20 years compiled experience in working in different professional settings within the MENA region discuss the region cultural dimensions, the consulting tools and the intercultural communication skills adopted as part of organizational development and change (ODC) initiatives.

Through their proven effectiveness, SEAM adopted tools, methods and concepts play a substantial role in making it the innovative approach of choice to overcome cross-cultural challenges that might be hindering ODC.

Providing efficient and effective Management Consulting services in the Middle East and North Africa (MENA) region imposes numerous challenges to face and address in view of the mosaic contextual profile of the different MENA countries. Particularities relate mainly to Socio-Cultural background, Confessional background, Education System, Political affiliations among others. Addressing the noted challenges requires the adoption of innovative consulting approaches to reach the desirable change results.

In this chapter, the Socio-Economic Approach to Management (SEAM) (Savall, 1974, 1975, 1979, 1981, 2003; Savall & Zardet, 1987, 1996, 2004, 2011; Savall, Péron, Zardet & Bonnet, 2018) will be presented as an innovative management consulting model, allowing effectively intervening and inducing change in MENA professional and service providers' entities.

The three authors of this chapter being SEAM interveners in three different sectors (Public Sector, Private Higher Education, and SME-Performing Arts) in addition to their over 20 years compiled experience in working in different professional settings within the MENA

SEAM Treatise, pages 185–190

region discuss the region cultural dimensions, the consulting tools, and the intercultural communication skills.

SEAM relevance and effectiveness in dealing with different cultural particularities and challenges besides its agility and accommodation with different cultural perspectives and specificities will help interveners to apply it in different sectors across different cultures.

SEAM is based on soft as much as it is based on hard skills and resources; it cares for the growth and profitability of the company and equally cares for employees' well-being. SEAM intervener approaches the organization with the assumption that they are all inflicted by common dysfunctions. SEAM capitalizes on transformational relations and works on institutionalizing positive changes in the organization. Hence, SEAM involves all actors in steering change. Through their proven effectiveness, SEAM adopted tools, methods and concepts play a substantial role in making it the approach of choice to overcome cross-cultural challenges.

1 THE CASE OF A PRIVATE HIGHER EDUCATION INSTITUTION (KURAN, 2017)

Organizations are made up of diverse individuals who gather to solve problems and achieve common goals. Organizations do not exist independently of the individuals that constitute them. They integrate a diversity of people to construct a joint entity. The culturally diverse matter lies in every single sort of organization. Organizational members may be from different nationalities, different cultural backgrounds, different opinions, and speak different languages. In spite of these differences, they ought to interact and work together. Moreover, organizational change is closely related to individuals change. In many cases, an intervention is required in order to help individuals to develop new knowledge, skills, attitudes and behaviors. Such interventions can be holistic, highly structured and very focused on the achievement of closely specified outcomes, or they can be designed to help organizational members learn how to learn and encourage them to actively involve themselves in a self-directed process of professional development. Nowadays, organizations are often developing their businesses and building international strategies. Therefore, cross-cultural issues need to be overcome in order to deal with implementation of change.

Management is a combination of art and science. It is science since it applies universally accepted principles. It is art since it has to be appreciated through practical knowledge and experience. It also requires innovation and soft skills. It is essential that managers combine knowledge and information from different sources and use it wisely. Management education has a crucial role in today's world of disruption. Management has to be explained with real-time scenarios, in order for practitioners to solve current and complex problems rather than examples in how to tackle historical business problems. Therefore, a brand new perspective on management education is required especially for diverse business settings.

In an attempt to provide the required management education, a partnership between Faculty of Business and Management, University of Balamand and the Socio-Economic Institute of Firms and Organizations–ISEOR (Institut de socio-économie des entreprises et des organizations) Research Center affiliated to the University Jean Moulin of Lyon III developed a program that provides business executives and practitioners with advanced set of competencies and research skills, allowing them to produce context-specific and impactful solutions to business challenges. This goal is accomplished by equipping participants with unique and field-tested research methodology in Socio-Economic Management and coupled with Qualimetrics integrating qualitative, quantitative and financial metrics. The Socio Economic Approach to Management (SEAM) is an intervention process that aims to transform enterprises and allow them to survive and prosper in a new competitive and varied world of business.

The DBA program develops manager's ability to cope with cross-cultural environments and perform well in a new cultural setting. SEAM proved to be applicable in different cultural perspectives and specificities, since it takes into account the cross-cultural factors when carrying out intervention research within organizations. SEAM has been used in a wide range of different settings. SEAM researchers intervene in many organizations that vary in terms of scale, context and focus. Hence, they have considerable evidence pointing to its successful application regardless of the cultural diversity. SEAM consultants consider that dysfunctions and hidden costs are present in any organizational setting. The dysfunctions could be rooted in working conditions, work organization, communication-coordination-cooperation, time management, integrated training, and/or strategic implementation issues (Savall et al, 2008). The hidden cost is any cost that is not explicitly stated on the company information systems, such as absenteeism, work-related injuries and diseases, staff turnover, productivity gaps and quality related problems (Savall and Zardet, 2008). Therefore, they propose a systemic approach to diagnose dysfunctions and root causes, measure hidden costs and provide the process and tools to reduce them. SEAM participatory nature generates long term positive changes in the organization. For change to be positive and long-lasting, all actors (although diverse) are involved in steering the change.

SEAM is based on emotions as much as it is based on processes. Since it cares for improving performance and profitability of the organization and equally cares for the well-being of all members. SEAM is a higher level approach to participative management that is shown through evidence to reveal great results for the adopting organizations. SEAM interventions in a variety of organizations in different parts of the world, resulted in improving human interactions through building common language for all actors. Hence, SEAM is relevant in a universal context and contributes to organizations in order to incorporate all the diverse members to build a cooperative and common entity. Therefore, the DBA program attracts doctorate from different nationalities, different cultural backgrounds and practicing in different industries.

2 THE CASE OF A PUBLIC ENTITY IN LEBANON (BASSIL, 2018)

Public sector organizations are requested to be more responsive to the needs and demands of the communities they serve. Thus, they are under the urge of being restructured with a purpose to provide better, quicker and additional services to their clients. Furthermore, in view of the accelerating pace of change at the society level, citizens require from their governments, besides quality, quantity, and speed in service provision, new solutions and approaches to respond appropriately to their changing demands (Daglio, Gerson, and Kitchen, 2015). Such an enhancement in governments will allow re-establishing confidence in the public sector.

In view of these prevailing challenges and demands, the public sector in Lebanon is interested of being an object of a restructure with the aim to introduce new principles and common grounds in Public Management in Lebanon. This will lead to high performance organizations, developed enough to respond to the national challenges and citizens demands (OMSAR, 2011).

PEP, a public organization responsible to guide and supervise all forensic work in Lebanon, with emphasis on forensic medicine, suffers from poor management in general and strategic management in particular. The bureaucratic, hierarchical, and non-participatory approach of public management limits PEP work effectiveness and performance. Furthermore, the prevailing culture and leadership style within PEP impose limitations in encouraging organizational development and change (ODC) initiatives and instigating the creation and adoption of innovative ideas by civil servants. In particular, as a public entity, PEP has limited autonomy and flexibility in decision making which is based on rules and regulations and driven by procedures. This is due to the fact that management is done by career public servants whereas control is done by politicians. It operates under a limited budget with almost absent strategic and tactical planning, accountability measures, as well as internal and external communication-coordination-cooperation.

SEAM, a vital ODC method, was adopted to induce a change process to improve PEP strategic management and to upgrade its performance to respond to the needs and demands of citizens it serves. SEAM approach builds on evidence and tested theories collected through previous interventions in the public and private sectors and in different places of the world. Accordingly, SEAM is considered to be a rigorous and reliable approach, agile, and relevant for adoption and effective use in different types of organizations including public entities. The approach adopted by SEAM is in line with the current dynamic work of the OECD on Public Sector Innovation and its different investigated and tested elements (OECD, 2014). Through SEAM intervention in PEP, the interaction of different components associated with the organizational design, structure, processes, culture, and technology was investigated to reveal how these interactions support or inhibit initiatives leading to innovation in the public-sector based on a strategic thinking. A capacity building structure for PEP innovation was then developed based on the identified and assessed organizational elements. Furthermore, SEAM allowed to manage risks, complexity, uncertainty, and unpredictability prevalent within the PEP through its experimental, non-traditional organizational development and change approach.

SEAM innovative practices are designed differently than the traditional "command and control" management models. The adopted practices in PEP intervention included: (a) engaging all actors in the process of change and related decision-making processes. Parties affected by the change were also consulted; (b) directing and engineering the change and related processes towards achieving predefined strategic and operational outcomes that would ultimately lead to the improvement of the PEP services with a social impact; and (c) operating within the different layers of PEP and even through other organizations as well as sectors through emphasizing collaboration, cooperation, and coordination as modes of interaction among all parties. Since public organizations do not possess all the means to induce all desirable changes, SEAM helped to modify the role of PEP from a solitary actor, to a collaborator, coordinator, and knowledge agent. This was essential to contribute to increasing the capacities of PEP to create partnerships with other public sectors as well as with private and not for profit sectors and even with citizens themselves. Such partnerships are currently considered to be the new models allowing to increase the effectiveness and efficiency of public organizations through emphasizing "inter-dependencies and citizen-centricity."

Based on the above notions, SEAM is considered to be an innovative ODC approach, that is substantial to increase the effectiveness of the strategic management of any public-sector entity, which would ultimately positively impact its performance and ultimately its governance.

3 THE CASE OF A PERFORMING ARTS BUSINESS (KHABBAZ, 2018)

Following October 17 Revolution in Lebanon and the COVID19 pandemic that caused a severe economic crisis and currency devaluation, "fresh dollars" became highly required for every business to survive. Therefore, almost all Lebanese businesses are trying to export their products or to operate abroad to get fresh dollars. Performing arts businesses have a big opportunity despite all challenges to expand to the regional countries like the United Arab Emirates, Saudi Arabia, Kuwait, Qatar, etc. where investors are ready to finance performing arts' productions. This is due to governments of these countries that are encouraging this sector and considering it as an integral part of their educational and cultural advancement. Henceforth, opera houses and theaters were built, festivals and concerts were recently launched and they are all ready to receive talents and work of arts from the Arab region and abroad.

Lebanon has been the source of creativity and art in the Arab region due to its cultural diversity and heritage, freedom of speech and openness, and mostly due to the existence of an artistic identity that was established centuries ago. This is one of the main characteristics that differentiate Lebanon from other Arab countries and gives an edge for Lebanese artistic productions over other productions from the region.

In this manuscript, the case of Chateau Trianon Theater (Lebanon) will be tackled. A SEAM intervention was conducted in this theater in 2016–2018 and had remarkable results on the business overall performance. This intervention tackled artistic performances of this theater and the improvement of their tangent services; with an outlook to performing in local festivals outside the Chateau Trianon premises. To be able to sustain and grow the business, the managing directors decided to perform in the aforementioned countries outside Lebanon for several reasons. These reasons can be the same language, the common social topics, the need for talents in these countries, the high demand for artistic performances, and the availability of resources for production and hosting. The internal intervener who conducted the first intervention will be handling the second with the same team (artists, technicians and some of the administrators). The objective of the second SEAM intervention would be: "to be ready to adapt to the new normal, the new audience, and the new work place." This objective will be reached with the help of SEAM methods and tools that helped to overcome Lebanese internal cultural diversity (among other transformative changes) that made a significant evolution in the first intervention. In the second intervention, SEAM will help overcome the cross cultural diversity across the Arab region.

The shared governance and vision alignment are already established and will be further fostered in the second intervention using the integral diagnosis, mirror effect, and projected hidden costs that could be prevented. Re-ensuring orchestration between the three categories of actors is key to success in the new environment. Tools like Competency Grid (CG) and Time Management (TM) will be reapplied and carefully the new normal and new environment will be considered.

In addition, agility and flexibility improvement is needed and will be boosted through the use of a SMARTER IESAP, PAP and PNAC under different futures to cope with the multiple uncertainties and occurring disruptions. The full engagement of the internal stakeholders fostered by SEAM concepts, methods and tools will help warranting a similar engagement of the external stakeholders. If the actors are prepared and well equipped, they will be ready to overcome all challenges outside. SEAM will help the company build an anticipated scenario for performing in the Arab region with less dysfunctions. SEAM is the approach of choice for Performing Arts businesses not only across disciplines but also across cultures!

CONCLUSION

The three cases demonstrated that SEAM is effective in the MENA region. This chapter argues for the suitability of SEAM in different industries (higher education, public sector and performing arts) regardless of backgrounds, languages, social settings, and values. The chapter emphasizes the specific features of SEAM to prove that it is universal and that it familiarizes with diverse cultural perspectives. SEAM factors for change processes are holistic and participatory. The Socio- economic approach highlights transparency, justifications for the change and alignment of actions. Results showed that concern for human potential were success factors when leading change. The identified SEAM success factors also include conveying a complete communication across the organization and adapting change approach to all cultures.

REFERENCES

Bassil, D. (2018). *Developing Public Organizations through an Innovative Change Approach: An Intervention in Lebanon.* DBA dissertation. University Jean Moulin, Lyon 3, France & University of Balamand.

Daglio, M., Gerson D., Kitchen H. (2015). *Building Organizational Capacity for Public Sector Innovation.* Background Paper prepared for the OECD Conference "Innovating the Public Sector: from Ideas to Impact" Paris, 12–13 November 2014.

Khabbaz, L. (2018). *The SEAM Contribution to the Management of Theatrical Performances: The Case of Château Trianon – Lebanon.* DBA dissertation. University Jean Moulin, Lyon 3, France & University of Balamand.

Kuran, O. (2017). *SEAM Contribution to meet the internal and external challenges in a private Lebanese university.* DBA dissertation. University Jean Moulin, Lyon 3, France & University of Balamand.

OMSAR. (January 2011). *Strategy for the Reform and Development of Public Administration in Lebanon.* Office of the Minister of State For Administrative Reform (OMSAR) – Republic of Lebanon.

CHAPTER 19

FROM THE ARTIST-DIRECTOR TO THE DIRECTOR-ARTIST

The Case of Very Small Performing Art Organizations in France

Isabelle Horvath and Caroline Adoumbou

ABSTRACT

In a context of budgetary constraints, artistic organizations must resolve the equation between economic performance and creation. But they often come up against an image conflict between art and business. From an intervention-research, we show in this chapter how an artist-manager of a Very Small Performing Arts Organization (VSPO) can develop managerial skills in order to perpetuate his activity and deploy his artistic project. This experiment highlights the improvements in the management of the organization and the need for intra-organizational learning to build a dialectical relationship between art and management.

The economics of the performing arts (theater, dance, music, opera...) characterized by Baumol and Bowen's law (1966) highlights the inevitability of increasing costs in this so-called "archaic" sector. Contrary to the "progressive" sector, i.e., industrial and commercial, the improvement of productivity is weak. Indeed, a musical work meets criteria such as its duration or the number of musicians, which cannot be reduced while the costs of structure, staging and salaries increase. Moreover, since the economic goal is not profitability, the public authorities and donors must cover the costs. However, the budget of the State and local authorities for culture oscillates between decline and stagnation. In France, the number of small performing arts organizations with less than 10 employees has been increasing steadily for the past 10 years. It is around 60,000 in 2018 (Ministry of Culture). Since 2015,

SEAM Treatise, pages 191–198

the worsening economic crisis in the field of culture has led artists to multiply employers and eventually create their own structure. As for patronage, despite the tax benefits, it rarely exceeds 5 to 10% of a cultural institution's budget in France (Tobelem, 2019). Theater managements look for material solutions such as lightening the programming to compensate for the lack of resources.

But this cost-based approach is limiting. It does not take into-account the possible improvements in the organization's overall performance through the development of internal resources, based on the management of a renewed inter-actor collaborative process (Datry, 2006). This steering requires the implementation of a managerial approach that theater directors, especially those of very small performing arts organizations, are not trained to use.

How can managers reveal and develop these managerial skills? To address this issue, we report on an intervention-research conducted in the creation and cultural mediation ensemble *Brins de Voix.*

1 NECESSITY OF THE MANAGEMENT OF VERY SMALL PERFORMING ARTS ORGANIZATIONS

1.1 Artists and Managerial Skills

The artists of the very small performing arts organizations are "project workers" (Heusch et al., 2011, p. 17), at the head of organizations with few or no employees. They manage teams with variable geometry depending on the programming. The activity is characterized by a predominance of creative work, while the artist-leaders must jointly assume organizational and administrative tasks. The difficulty lies in the association of a process of steering the activity with the creative process. However, "it proves impossible to separate the work from its material or organizational conditions of elaboration" (Benghozi, 1995, p.85). The artist-managers hold managerial competences such as coordination, planning or strategy, unexploited because of a conflict of image between the art and the company (Bérubé, 2019) or the art and the management (Chiapello, 1998). To overcome it, the profession and its practices need to be rethought and reconstructed (Horvath, 2011) through a process of organizational learning that professionals call for (La Scène, 2016).

1.2 Challenges of a New Profession

Our intervention-research (Adoumbou, 2019) has highlighted the fact that in very small performing arts organizations, there is little to no strategic management of resources. These resources are used on an ad hoc basis to allow for the realization of a project. The desire of the actors in the cultural sector is such when it comes to creation and their "passion" job, that they are sometimes totally caught up in the artistic dimension alone, excluding any anticipation of the use of resources. They are not aware that their activity pushes them to change their posture and their profession. They therefore need to move from an "all-artistic" approach to one that takes into-account organizational and financial aspects, which will enable them to perpetuate their organization and therefore their artistic project.

According to Gessler (2008), a qualification is acquired at a given moment and can be attested by a diploma. A competence, on the other hand, is the result of a process of continuous improvement and progression. This distinction between qualification and competence is particularly relevant to the managers of very small performing arts organizations.

For some of them, it is more a question of highlighting skills than acquiring them. Indeed, certain aspects of the artist's job (simultaneous management of several employers, use of a rehearsal and performance schedule, etc.) call for management skills, but these are rarely identified as such.

2 THEORETICAL AND METHDOLOGICAL FRAMEWORK

2.1 The Socio-Economic Theory in the Light of the Actor-Strategist Theory

Socio-economic theory (Savall, 1974–1975, 1979; Savall, Zardet, 1987, 1995) is based on the resources of the organization (Penrose, 1959): Products, Markets, Technology, Organization and Human Potential. These five strategic data constitute the structuring elements on which an organization, whatever its sector or size, reflects in order to develop a strategy. The company's internal environment is essential because it constitutes the strategic foundation (Savall and Zardet, 1995, 2004), a factor that multiplies social and economic performance. This strategic foundation is built through the cohesion of the actors, who act as a lever to improve business processes, in particular the capacity for organizational innovation, by mobilizing their internal resources to find solutions to dysfunctions that reduce the organization's performance.

Each actor can be considered as a strategist with his or her own, more or less clear and conscious objectives (Crozier and Friedberg, 1977). The organization is then defined as a social construct that can only exist and develop if it takes into account the strategies of its members and if it ensures them a certain autonomy. It is a space of cooperation and interdependence between actors who each have their own, sometimes contradictory, interests. It is therefore a universe of conflicts of interest, a set of structured games. The actors' strategies can be of two kinds: offensive, when they want to seize opportunities, and defensive, when they want to escape the constraints imposed by the organization.

The link between these two theories is as follows: according to the socio-economic theory, the performance of an organization depends largely on the level of involvement of its actors, while the theory of Crozier and Friedberg identifies that this level of involvement is a function of the degree of convergence of the actors' interests with those of the organization. The idea according to which steering and management promote the alignment of the organization's objectives with those of the actors is fruitful for the management of very small performing arts organizations.

In order to obtain a higher level of involvement from the very small performing arts organizations managers, an intervention-research type methodology was chosen to accompany the actors in the process of transforming their practices.

2.2 Interest in Implementing Socio-Economic Management in the Field of Performing Arts

Intervention-research conducted according to the socio-economic intervention method (Savall and Zardet, 1987, 1996, 2004) enables organizations to develop resources by acting on their dysfunctions rather than by committing additional financial investments. Indeed, the quantified evaluation of hidden costs, the economic consequence of identified dysfunctions, allows actors to envisage a better allocation of resources. Since artists are known for inventing solutions within constrained frameworks, it was interesting to conduct an intervention-research of this type. Moreover, this methodology allowed for a high level of involvement of the actors, which contributed to the improvement of the collaborative process.

Since our approach had a dual objective of changing practices and changing the conflict between art and management, we conducted a series of "management" interviews, in addition to the socio-economic intervention, in order to assess the level of assumption of the managerial function in the organization as well as the posture of the actors vis-à-vis management (Adoumbou, 2019).

3 RESULTS OF THE EXPERIMENT

3.1 Presentation of the *Brins de Voix* Company

3.1.1 Structure and Design of the Research

The intervention-research took place in the very small structure *Brins de Voix,* whose purpose is cultural mediation and the creation of lyrical performances. A socio-economic diagnosis was carried out on the basis of 20 semi-structured interviews with nine categories of actors (Table 19.1). They aimed at collecting the dysfunctions perceived and experienced by the people. The diagnosis gave rise to a mirror-effect, an oral presentation of the key ideas of dysfunction illustrated by the expressions of the actors. The analysis by the researcher gave rise to an "expert opinion." This was followed by a project phase, aimed at developing innovative solutions and actions to reduce dysfunctions, according to a participative process involving managers, leaders and employees. The provision of management tools to the managers facilitated the concrete implementation of the solutions. Table 19.1 presents the profile of Brins de Voix and its objectives at the start of the research.

3.1.2 Difficulties and Challenges for Brins de Voix

At the beginning of the intervention, *Brins de Voix* faced several difficulties and challenges: the administrative structure was non-existent, the activity was not profitable and the resources were poorly used, which endangered its sustainability. Many projects were abandoned before completion due to a lack of efficient management. The managers, both with backgrounds in the arts and social sciences, had three objectives: (a) to improve the level of management of the organization and to develop the artistic project; (b) to ensure the sustainability of the activity but also to identify and formalize the existing competencies of the actors; (c) to set up an organizational learning process.

3.2 Stages of the Transformation

3.2.1 Identification of Managerial Competencies

We listed eight competencies: managing competencies, steering resources, motivating employees, making communication fluid, developing the organization's strategy, guaranteeing quality, planning work, and ensuring the distribution of work, based on the definition of management proposed by Thévenet (2018). These competencies served as a reference for the "management" interviews, which aimed to identify the tasks that fall under management and their perceived level of assumption of responsibility in the organization.

The managers identified four key competencies: ensuring communication within the organization; developing strategy; planning work; and distributing work (Table 19.2). The other

TABLE 19.1 Structure and Design of the Research	
Date of establishment	2010
Creator's profile	Graduate in lyrical song/PhD in Managment/MS in politics and communication
Personnel administration	Internal single desk for occasional shows
Number of directors	2
Legal form	Not-for-profit
2015 revenue	€ 18,000
Number of permanent employees (while not on the payroll)	1.5 full time equivalent
Temporary jobs and internal contacts	Musicians, dissemination managers, stage directors, wardrobe masters, actors, technicians, graphist designers, board members, volunteers
Activities and products	Shows creation and sale/cultural outreach/educational activities
Objectives of the organization by engaging in the process	Diagnosis of the functioning of *Brins de Voix*/Creation of new activities/Activities restructuring/Dévelopment of existing organization/enhancement of value for money/design of strategic objectives
Number of qualitative interviews of dysfunctions	10 (Musicians, administrative staff, directors)
Number of qualitative interviews	4
Number of interviews with managers	6
Nombre of project groups	3
Nombre of personalized assistance	10
Status of the researcher	Intervener-researcher/Co-director of *Brins de Voix*

TABLE 19.2 Level of Ownership of Managerial Functions

List of activities assigned to managers	Percentage of activity identification by the directors who were interviewed
Steering resources	8.0%
Managing resources	8.0%
Leading employees	8.0%
Enabling the quality of communication among employees	87.5%
Designing strategic objectives	62.5%
Ensuring the quality of services	8.0%
Planing and scheduling operations	37.5%
Dividing up operations among employees	37.5%

four (managing skills, managing resources, motivating staff and ensuring quality) do not appear at all in the managers' speeches, which allows us to suggest that they are not identified. Yet the dysfunctions expressed underline the need for them: "At certain times, I would have liked to have had someone firmer in front of me, perhaps to manage human behaviors that generate bad energy, wasted time and a bad work atmosphere." (Professional Musician)

3.2.2 A Tool for Managing Skills

Beyond the identification of these key competencies, we were interested in their level of management by analyzing the witness sentences of the "management" interviews and by

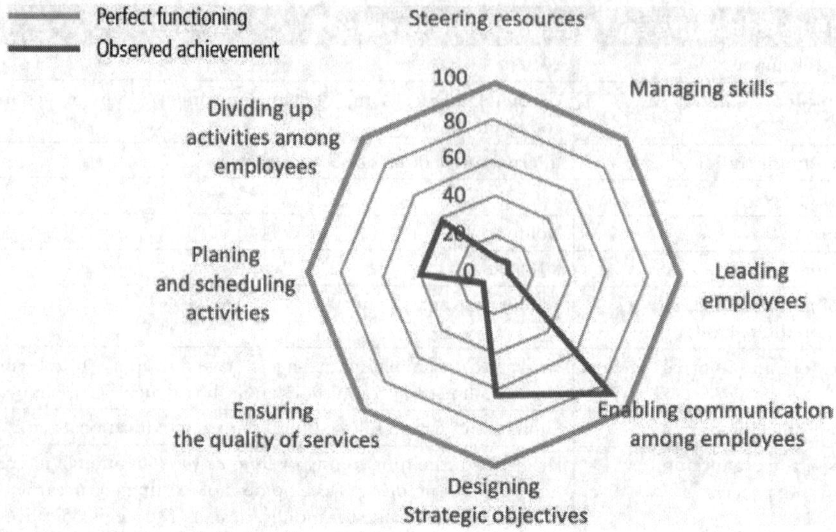

Figure 19.1 Managerial skills wheel.

observing the dysfunctions reported in the socio-economic diagnosis. It emerges that certain activities appear in the speeches, but not in the dysfunctions: we hypothesize that they are only partially taken care of. Conversely, some activities appear in the dysfunctions, but not in the discourse: we can then make the same hypothesis. Finally, some activities do not appear in either the discourse or the dysfunctions and allow us to hypothesize that they are not supported at all. Table 19.2 summarizes the level of support established for each function, based on the management interviews.

In association with this table, we propose to the managers an inventory of their skills in the form of a wheel representing the different functions (Figure 19.1). Coupled with a questionnaire on dysfunctions and on management, this wheel makes it easy to discern which skills need to be developed and which need to be consolidated.

3.3 Observed Improvements

The development and installation of managerial competencies had positive impacts on the socio-economic performance of the organization. Evaluation interviews took place at the end of the intervention, which highlighted interrelated improvements:

3.3.1 In Terms of Economic Performance

- Lower expenses and charges with a recycling in hidden costs: €5,000 recovered out of the €7,500 identified.
- Establishment of partnerships and exchanges, search for in-kind donations: donations have increased by 127% in one year.
- Increased revenues: sales increased by 233% in one year.
- Implementation of a strategy for the development and sustainability of the activity: the number of unprofitable shows has decreased by 20%, leaving room for small forms that can almost always be financed through self-production.

3.3.2 In Terms of Social Performance

- Reduction of the stress and mental load of the actors.
- Increased team cohesion.
- Increase in the level of involvement of employees.
- Improvement of the internal and external image of Brins de voix.
- Activation of human potential.

Other points remain unresolved, such as the management of premises. Indeed, the multi-site work alone generates numerous dysfunctions in terms of loss of time or equipment.

CONCLUSION

The problematic concerned the capacity of the TPOSV to develop managerial skills in order to improve the overall performance of the organization in a context of rationalization of resources, perpetuation of the activity and deployment of the artistic project. The experimentation in the Brins de Voix ensemble has shown that intervention-research is a process of introspection and learning (Argyris, Schön, 2002) that allows one to question and better understand one's practices. Instrumentation stimulates transformative action. It has highlighted two essential contributions: the first is methodological. A new tool for managing skills was born from the complementarity of the dysfunctional diagnosis with the "management" interviews, thus completing the range of socio-economic tools. The second is that the dialogue between economic and social performance (Savall, Zardet, 1987, 2020) and inter-actor cooperation (Crozier, Friedberg, 1977) contribute to the reconciliation between art and management, which is necessary for the sustainable structuring of artistic and cultural organizations.

REFERENCES

Adoumbou, C. (2019). *L'installation d'une fonction managériale dans les Très Petites Organisations de Spectacle Vivant: cas de deux recherches-interventions.* PhD thesis, Université Jean Moulin Lyon 3.

Argyris, C., & Schön, D. A. (2002). *Organizational learning. Théorie, méthode, pratique* (M. Aussanaire & P. Garcia-Malgares, trans., 1996). De Boeck Université, Paris.

Baumol, W. J., & Bowen, W. G. (1966). *Performing arts—The economic dilemma.* The Twenthieth Century Fund, New York.

Benghozi, P. J. (1995). Les sentiers de la gloire: savoir gérer pour savoir créer. In *Des savoirs en action. Contributions de la recherche en gestion.* L'Harmattan, Paris, pp. 51–87.

Bérubé, J. (2019). L'entrepreneuriat en commun comme force collective pour les artistes professionnels. *Revue française de gestion, 2*(279). 151–164.

Chiapello, E. (1998). Artists versus managers. Le management culturel face à la critique artiste, Métailié, Paris.

Crozier, M., & Friedberg, E. (1977). *The actor and the system.* Editions du Seuil, Essais, Paris.

Datry, F. (2006). *Les performances des projets de conception et de fabrication de décors lyriques. Cas d'expérimentation dans un opéra national.* Doctoral dissertation in management science. University of Lyon.

Gessler, M. (2008). A competence portfolio for professionals in the creative industries. *Creativity and Innovation Management, 22*(3), 280–294.

Heusch (de) S., Dujardin, A., & Rajabaly, H. (2011). *L'artiste entrepreneur, un travailleur au projet, L'artiste, un entrepreneur?* Université de Lièges, Bruxelles.

Horvath, I. (2011). *Développement d'outils de management et actes de langage dans les entreprises de spectacle vivant.* PhD thesis, Université Jean Moulin, Lyon 3.

Horvath, I. (2013). Une approche prospective du métier de directeur d'entreprise de spectacle vivant, *Management & Avenir, 5*(63), 98–114.

La Scène. (2016). Stanislas, Nordey. *Redevenir des pionniers, 82*, 14–17.

Ministère de la Culture. (2018). *Morphology and economy of the cultural field, cultural practices and uses.* www.culture.gouv

Penrose, E. (1959). *The theory of the growth of the firm.* Wiley.

Thévenet, M. (2018). Les 100 mots du management, Que sais-je? n° 4004, PUF.

Tobelem, J. M. (2019). Quel avenir pour le mécénat culturel?, Cahiers français, Financer la culture, *La Documentation Française,* pp. 44–54.

CHAPTER 20

DEVELOPMENT OF MANAGERIAL SKILLS AND SUSTAINABLE PERFORMANCE OF SMALL BUSINESSES IN THE LIBERAL PROFESSIONS

Renaud Petit and Véronique Zardet

ABSTRACT

The results of socio-economic management implementations, conducted in 200 small companies in the liberal professions, illustrate the main consequences of managerial deficiencies. The qualimetric data obtained made it possible to determine the generic and contingency elements of the four major sectors of regulated liberal activity accompanied: medical, paramedical, legal and real estate professions. But the most remarkable result of this intervention-research is to highlight the capacity as well as the speed of these companies to recycle their important hidden cost-performance deposits.

The regulated liberal professions represent an original sector of activity, employing 250,000 full-time equivalent employees for 110,000 companies in France and yet largely unknown? If we refer to the French and English-speaking management publications, or to the scant number of reports distinguishing regulated liberal activities from other liberal activities. Whatever their sector of activity, these very small organizations have a common problem: regulated liberal professionals (doctors and paramedics, legal professionals such as lawyers, bailiffs, agents…, and architectural professionals such as architects, surveyors, town planners…) did not receive any training in management or in management during their studies, even

SEAM Treatise, pages 199–209

though they were very long. They thus find themselves "business managers" facing multiple challenges. This chapter summarizes five years of intervention-research conducted since 2016 in 200 regulated liberal structures, within the framework of an institutional partnership with the OPCA ACTALIANS, which in 2020 became the OPCO focused on local businesses (OPCO EP). The major deficiencies in managerial skills are first analyzed. Then the partnership between ISEOR and the OPCO EP is presented, in its objectives and the intervention-research methods deployed. The main dysfunctions and hidden costs are then exposed, before showing the significant actions implemented by these structures and their impact on the economic performance of the company.

1 A MAJOR MANAGEMENT DEFICIENCY IN THE MICRO-ENTERPRISES OF THE REGULATED LIBERAL PROFESSIONS

Why are the companies of the regulated liberal professions of little interest to the management literature? These professionals, who are very well trained in their profession, all suffer from a lack of training in the management of their business. How many of them imagined during their studies that one day they would be at the head of a company, with a team of collaborators and associates, confronted with production, sales and promotion activities, financial management and investment choices, or strategic choices of partnership, internal or external growth, etc.?

The profession of manager is neither identified nor valued in comparison to the profession and technical expertise. The working methods that these liberal professionals have acquired during their studies are essentially individual, which then creates numerous difficulties due to the lack of common and shared working methods. Moreover, most of these professionals form partnerships, but observation shows significant gaps in communication-coordination-conciliation and cohesion between partners. The same observation extends to the relations between liberal professionals and their collaborators.

The regulated liberal professions are today affected by the crisis, with a consequence for some of them a decrease of the sales turnover, of the incomes and a threat on the jobs within the agencies, firms and very small enterprises. But these companies, whether they are economically successful or on the contrary in serious economic difficulty, have very few plans and suffer from a lack of strategic project.

From the point of view of managerial practices, the status and ethical stance of the liberal professional are in tension with the exercise of an activity in a team, moreover in a managerial role. This tension is characterized by difficulties in negotiating changes in practices with their partners, in order to define new common practices. Moreover, they have great difficulty expressing themselves on their own professional difficulties and even more on those of their colleagues.

In addition to this, we can add to this a behavior often observed—but nevertheless not in all professions—on the part of these liberal professionals of elitist. This type of behavior singularly affects the relationship between liberal professionals and their collaborators in several ways. First of all, there is a form of ostentatious deference on the part of employees towards their line manager, which can limit their appreciation of constructive criticism. In addition, such elitist behaviors have an impact on their conception of people management and their view of the ability of others to improve their practices and performance. For example, some doctors refused to allow the results of hidden costs to be presented to their colleagues (secretary and nurses), arguing that they would not understand. Or later, in the research phase of improvement actions, others felt that staff had better things to do than to be involved in focus groups, in which their contribution would be insignificant. The socio-economic change management process is thus intended to modify the mental representations of both parties.

2 OBJECTIVE AND CONTENT OF THE PARTNERSHIP BETWEEN ISEOR AND OPCO EP

ISEOR's interventions with the regulated liberal professions began in 1998, at the initiative of the notarial profession (Cappelletti, 2010). For more than ten years, a support process was conducted with 500 notary offices, located in 11 different regions of France, urban, semi-urban or rural, with between 1 and 70 employees, with three major objectives: (a) to improve the quality of operations, management and service to clients; (b) to meet the new competitive challenges and the increased demands of clients; (c) to support them in the implementation of the ISO 9000 quality standards.

This innovative approach to liberal practice was spotted by the profession of architects, which in 2009 contacted ISEOR to experiment in the Rhône Alpes region with support for some twenty agencies to improve economic and social performance, in a context of very low profitability in the sector, which was hit hard by the real estate bubble.

The success of this pilot action led to the implementation of a national support plan for the development of skills initiated by the OPCO ACTALIANS, with which ISEOR concluded a multi-year partnership in 2015, whose general objectives for the benefit of companies of liberal professionals were:

- Develop the quality of the internal organization of microstructures and services to their clients.
- Increase their economic performance and competitiveness in a context of strong competition.
- Strengthen social dialogue and internal cohesion to develop the involvement of human potential.
- To make microstructures from the same or different sectors of activity cooperate, through a collaborative training group bringing together several microstructures.

For the OPCO, the major stakes are:

- To support innovative actions in the direction of VSEs/SMEs, for which the OPCO EP is invited to act as a priority.
- To respond to the new missions expected of OPCOs in terms of supporting VSEs/SMEs in terms of skills management
- Helping companies affected by the crisis through an action that is both "preventive and curative."
- Promote its ability to be close to the local area, by implementing a territorial action and seeking ad hoc partnerships (Professional Unions of Regional Orders for the relay of territorial information).

From 2016 to 2020, 200 support initiatives have been conducted in 176 different companies in the four main regulated liberal professions: medical (35%), paramedical (1%), legal (9%) and real estate (55%).

The intervention method has been miniaturized and adapted to micro-enterprises (Savall, 2003; Cappelletti et al, 2009; Cappelletti, 2010) and has been deployed according to the following operating procedure, for structures with up to 24 employees: support is provided over a maximum of 10 months, at the rate of half a day per month; five collective training sessions are organized, for the manager(s) accompanied by his/her close collaborators (e.g., partners), within the framework of a training session for the manager(s): associates), within the framework of collective inter-structure collaborative training sessions; finally, 5 sessions within each microstructure allow the personalized accompaniment in situ (2 sessions of socio-economic diagnosis and 3 sessions of innovation focus group). For SMEs with more than 25 employees, the work scheme is entirely intra-company. The accompaniment ends with the joint elaboration with the managers of each micro-structure of the qualitative, quantitative and financial results of metamorphosis identified by the actors themselves.

3 IMMEDIATE RESULTS ON INTANGIBLE INVESTMENTS: PARTICULARLY OF MICRO-ENTERPRISES IN THE LIBERAL PROFESSIONS

3.1 Main Dysfunctions Identified

The dysfunctions are identified from interviews conducted with all the actors: managers, partners, employees. They give rise to a mirror-effect presented to all. A cross-sectorial reading of these 200 diagnoses allows us to summarize the main black points as follows. The interior layout is not always designed with a view to the functionality of storage spaces, the reception of the public or the comfort of employees. The equipment is not always in line with the needs of the professionals either. Essentially computer-related, the main difficulties relate to the lack of network performance, poor data security or the approximate mastery of professional software. The lack of work rules and procedures illustrates the glaring absence of common work methods, as if the professionals thought that physical proximity was a guarantee of collective work based on the "natural" sharing of information. No doubt the perceived pressure of daily life prevents the mobilization of time resources dedicated to the transfer of know-how. This can also be explained by communication-coordination-cooperation mechanisms that are either deficient or non-existent. Here again, physical proximity means that regular meetings, held in good conditions, to discuss operational activities or internal functioning, are not perceived as necessary. The immediacy and physical proximity of these meetings encourage abundant but disorganized and disturbing exchanges of information. The urgency of the situation is one of the feelings most often expressed by professionals, a consequence of the lack of anticipation and measurement of the time required for activities. The absence of indicators for managing time resources makes it difficult to plan and schedule activities, which ultimately reduces the quality of the work performed, including customer service. Finally, the lack of a clear division of powers and responsibilities is common, especially when the company has several managers. When formalization and strategic coherence are absent, they disrupt decision-making and implementation. Operations are sometimes "siloed", as if the managers were living together without any concern for overall managerial coherence, due to a lack of time for communication-coordination-cooperation other than "between two doors."

3.2 Significant Hidden Costs and Performance Recycled

The 176 microenterprises studied have an average workforce, including managers, of 7 people. The overall average of the Hourly Contribution to Value Added on Variable Costs (HCVAVC) is 43 euros (high standard deviation: between 10 € and 125 €) for an average amount of hidden costs per person and per year, calculated at the beginning of the process, of € 31, 000 . Hidden costs thus represent on average 55% of the sales turnover or revenue, with very strong heterogeneity of the companies' situations (see Table 20.1).

TABLE 20.1 Spread-Sheets on the Evolution of Performance Indicators for Each Sector

Order numbers	Sector	Staff	HCVAVC	Hidden costs/ person/year	Evolution of HCVAVC	Conversion rate	Variation of VAVC
	(Average)	6	€ 35	€ 27,551	14%	38%	
1	Architectural trade	12	€ 25	€ 21,100	20%	42%	€ –22,105
2	Architectural trade		€ 34	€ 17,300	3%	47%	€ –87,563
3	Architectural trade		€ 36	€ 20,100	11%	47%	€ 27,060
4	Architectural trade		€ 10	€ 15,400	10%	35%	€ 5,320
5	Architectural trade	5	€ 12	€ 19,400	0%	57%	€ 0
6	Architectural trade	6	€ 50	€ 70,000	–8%	21%	€ 31,686
7	Architectural trade		€ 50	€ 24,500	–22%		€ –544,330
8	Architectural trade		€ 39	€ 24,300	3%	58%	€ –6,828
9	Architectural trade		€ 57	€ 21,400	18%	56%	€ 91,950
10	Architectural trade		€ 22	€ 32,100	186%	59%	€ 271,313
11	Architectural trade		€ 24	€36,600	25%	58%	€ 58,854
12	Architectural trade	6	€ 32	€ 31,800		19%	€ 0
13	Architectural trade	5	€ 61	€ 34,900		25%	€ 0
14	Architectural trade	11	€ 39	€ 77,700			€ 0
15	Architectural trade	4	€ 80	€ 105,000		42%	€ 0
16	Architectural trade	5	€ 68	€ 27,300	–38%	36%	€ –2,964
17	Architectural trade	6	€ 33	€ 29,400	21%		€ 11,988
18	Architectural trade		€ 48	€ 38,000	–6%	60%	€ –66,834
19	Architectural trade	9	€ 39	€ 33,200	3%	31%	€ –115,170
20	Architectural trade	6	€17	€ 26,500		56%	€ 0
21	Architectural trade	3	€ 27	€ 30,300	7%	31%	€ –39,963
22	Architectural trade	5	€ 34	€ 35,100			€ 0
23	Architectural trade	3	€ 26	€ 28,300	8%	35%	€ 15,322
24	Architectural trade	8	€41	€ 33,100	61%	32%	€ 137,371
25	Architectural trade	5	€ 39	€ 25,100		30%	€ 0
26	Architectural trade	7	€ 65	€ 20,200		30%	€ 0
27	Architectural trade	3	€ 21	€ 30,200	5%	63%	€ –5,771
28	Architectural trade	6	€ 42	€ 51,400	–19%	97%	€ –39,722
29	Architectural trade	5	€ 22	€ 21,700	0%	67%	€ 37,994
30	Architectural trade	3	€ 15	€ 43,700	47%		€ 49,295
31	Architectural trade	4	€ 28	€ 26,900	0%	30%	€ 0
32	Architectural trade	5	€ 18	€ 46,000	6%		€ 7,285
33	Architectural trade	2	€ 39	€ 15,700		57%	€ 0
34	Architectural trade	9	€ 26	€ 58,600	19%	53%	€ –103,930

(continued)

TABLE 20.1 Spread-Sheets on the Evolution of Performance Indicators for Each Sector (continued)

Order numbers	Sector	Staff	HCVAVC	Hidden costs/ person/year	Evolution of HCVAVC	Conversion rate	Variation of VAVC
35	Architectural trade	6	€ 22	€ 24,100	186%	32%	€ 271,313
36	Architectural trade	6	€ 30	€ 29,300	–23%	46%	€ 12,104
37	Architectural trade	3	€ 22	€ 54,000	–9%	38%	€ –10,944
38	Architectural trade		€ 35	€ 101,100			€ 0
39	Architectural trade	13	€ 40	€ 24,700	15%	32%	€ 220,932
40	Architectural trade	6	€ 22	€ 49,500	9%	63%	€ 48,242
41	Architectural trade	7	€ 24	€ 24,600	–4%	48%	€ 9,831
42	Architectural trade	5	€ 39	€ 25,700		11%	€ 0
43	Architectural trade	10	€ 19	€ 37 300	47%	29%	€ 107,616
44	Architectural trade	14	€ 41	€ 17,580	–10%	3%	€ –48,271
45	Architectural trade	5	€ 51	€ 29,400	4%	37%	€ –842,405
46	Architectural trade	6	€ 56	€ 21,200	0%	61%	€ 65,520
47	Architectural trade	5	€ 52	€ 20,000	13%	46%	€ 72,549
48	Architectural trade	6	€ 31	€ 29,100	5%	7%	€ 7,177
49	Architectural trade	5	€ 37	€ 32,800	18%	40%	€ 122,691
50	Architectural trade	7					€ 0
51	Architectural trade	2	€ 52	€ 22,700	1%	32%	€ –2,499
52	Architectural trade	2	€ 10	€ 24,500	20%	39%	€ 5,260
53	Architectural trade	3	€ 17	€ 26,500	–12%	71%	€ –4,200
54	Architectural trade	6	€ 38	€ 31,900		28%	€ 0
55	Architectural trade	6	€ 41	€ 20,160	–2%	54%	€ 41,288
56	Architectural trade	3	€ 37	€ 21,000		38%	€ 0
57	Architectural trade	4	€ 32	€ 19,500	47%	43%	€ 124,556
58	Architectural trade	6	€ 52	€ 46,000	2%	15%	€ 9,710
59	Architectural trade	23	€ 60	€ 29,200	–5%	26%	€ 311,943
60	Architectural trade	5	€ 33	€ 34,000	–6%	21%	€ 22,928
61	Architectural trade	9	€ 58	€ 26,700	22%	50%	€ 155,298
62	Architectural trade	9	€ 29	€ 17,700	24%	40%	€ 221,299
63	Architectural trade	8	€ 34	€ 24,900	65%	45%	€ 310,860
64	Architectural trade	2	€ 36	€ 25,500	0%	20%	€ 20,160
65	Architectural trade	4	€ 28	€ 27,800	57%	27%	€ 199,320
66	Architectural trade	13	€ 63	€ 39,100	–24%	16%	€ –310,359
67	Architectural trade	5	€ 26	€ 61,000	45%	57%	€ 93,352
68	Architectural trade	6	€ 28	€ 47,500	–14%	53%	€ 26,564
69	Architectural trade	8	€ 39	€ 27,900	–1%	40%	€ –13,397
70	Architectural trade	7	€ 65	€ 69,500	–8%	12%	€ –269,490
71	Architectural trade	3	€ 28	€ 27,600	4%	34%	€ –6,136
72	Architectural trade	3	€ 36	€ 31,500	0%	46%	€ 13,014
73	Architectural trade	12	€ 38	€ 28,200	5%	13%	€ –31,792

(continued)

TABLE 20.1 Spread-Sheets on the Evolution of Performance Indicators for Each Sector (continued)

Order numbers	Sector	Staff	HCVAVC	Hidden costs/ person/year	Evolution of HCVAVC	Conversion rate	Variation of VAVC
74	Architectural trade	6	€ 24	€ 23,600	8%	17%	€ 20,876
75	Architectural trade	3	€ 23	€ 28,200	17%	10%	€ 26,608
76	Architectural trade	3	€ 35	€ 40,500	9%	39%	€ 119,490
77	Architectural trade	7	€ 44	€ 44,600	5%	22%	€ 205,764
78	Architectural trade	5	€ 27	€ 23,000	–4%	20%	€ 33,021
79	Architectural trade	6	€ 36	€ 23,900	4%	59%	€ 49,732
80	Architectural trade		€ 35	€ 21,800		35%	€ 0
81	Architectural trade	3	€ 65	€ 27,000		25%	€ 0
82	Architectural trade	8	€ 33	€ 134,800			€ 0
83	Architectural trade						€ 0
84	Architectural trade	7	€ 24	€ 23,600	8%	17%	€ 0
85	Architectural trade	7	€ 23	€ 28,200	17%	19%	€ 0
86	Architectural trade	6					€ 0
87	Architectural trade	4	€ 44	€ 44,600	5%	22%	€ 0
88	Architectural trade	7	€ 27	€ 23,000	33%	20%	€ 95,463
89	Architectural trade	5	€ 28	€ 29,700			€ 0
90	Architectural trade	5	€ 23	€ 21,100			€ 0
91	Architectural trade	6	€ 40	€ 21,600			€ 0
92	Architectural trade	6	€ 16	€ 11,500			€ 0
93	Architectural trade	14	€ 43	€ 27,900	2%	81%	€ 304,819
94	Architectural trade	6,3	€ 29	€ 35,700	–14%	23%	€ –27,268
95	Architectural trade	5	€ 21	€ 44,100	33%	36%	€ 69,230
96	Architectural trade	28	€ 38	€ 47,500	–5%	59%	€ 662,012
97	Architectural trade	6	€ 18	€ 18,400	0%	45%	€ –3,600
98	Architectural trade	4	€ 35	€ 27,600	–14%	18%	€ 5,750
99	Architectural trade	3	€ 37	€ 21,600	–5%	39%	€ –41,500
100	Architectural trade	18	€ 31	€ 25,600	20%	50%	€ 182,896
101	Architectural trade	1		€ 23,700			€ 0
102	Architectural trade	9	€ 34	€ 50,900	6%	20%	€ 20,048
103	Architectural trade	2	€ 30	€ 8,800	10%	27%	€ 2,640
104	Architectural trade	7	€ 36	€ 26,800	–6%	19%	€ 16,984
105	Architectural trade	3	€ 34	€ 52,900	26%	36%	€ 35,550
106	Architectural trade	5	€ 14	€ 51,500	129%	67%	€ 136,736
107	Architectural trade	5	€ 34	€ 36,800			€ 0
	Average	7	€ 42	€ 29,380	4%	30%	
1	Profession of law		€ 42	€ 18,000	0%		
2	Profession of law		€ 33	€ 17,500	0%		
3	Profession of law	10	€ 33	€ 54,600	24%	38%	€ 65,365

(continued)

TABLE 20.1 Spread-Sheets on the Evolution of Performance Indicators for Each Sector (continued)

Order numbers	Sector	Staff	HCVAVC	Hidden costs/ person/year	Evolution of HCVAVC	Conversion rate	Variation of VAVC
4	Profession of law	9	€ 35	€ 35,100	–3%	10%	€ –10,975
5	Profession of law	2		€ 29,400			
6	Profession of law	2	€ 57	€ 44,900		26%	
7	Profession of law	12	€ 63				
8	Profession of law	4					
9	Profession of law	2	€33	€ 27,400	9%	45%	€ –32,550
10	Profession of law	4	€ 67	€ 38,000			
11	Profession of law						
12	Profession of law	17	€ 49	€ 30,800	–2%	19%	€ –48,870
13	Profession of law	4	€ 26	€ 59,500	38%	23%	€ 80,724
14	Profession of law						
15	Profession of law	6	29 €	€ 3,080	–31%	48%	€ –94,986
	Average	9	61	€ 41,094	5%	40%	
1	Medical professions	5	€ 40	€ 42,100		30%	€ 0
2	Medical professions	4	€ 104	€ 43,200	–15%	79%	€ 2,760
3	Medical professions	5	€ 38	€ 24,400	18%	65%	€ 73,365
4	Medical professions	12	€ 57	€ 17,300			€ 0
5	Medical professions	9	€ 71	€ 35,400	–7%	38%	€ 155,137
6	Medical professions	9	€ 57	€ 13,100	25%	33%	€ 278,012
7	Medical professions	15	€ 55	€ 22,700	–4%	28%	€ 0
8	Medical professions	10	€ 62	€ 28,700	–3%	45%	–€ 30,176
9	Medical professions	13	€ 51	€ 25,800	–12%	44%	€ 187,920
10	Medical professions						€ 0
11	Medical professions						€ 0
12	Medical professions						€ 0
13	Medical professions						€ 0
14	Medical professions	8	€ 93	€ 46,280			€ 0
15	Medical professions		€ 79	€ 51,600	16%	17%	€ 324,219
16	Medical professions		€ 74	€ 30,400	23%	17%	€ 184,871
17	Medical professions		€ 125	€ 49,400	1%	19%	€ 391,288
18	Medical professions		€ 98	€ 48,700	3%	13%	€ 62,925
19	Medical professions		€ 76	€ 42,600	0%	29%	–€ 102,600
20	Medical professions	2	€ 56	€ 37,600	18%	34%	€ 29,258
21	Medical professions	2	€ 39	€ 28,000		26%	€ 0
22	Medical professions	12	€ 44	€ 34,000	2%	46%	€ 21,393
23	Medical professions	2	€ 40	€ 38,200			€ 0
24	Medical professions	2	€ 63	€ 75,000			€ 0
25	Medical professions	2	€ 39	€ 60,840			€ 0

(continued)

TABLE 20.1 Spread-Sheets on the Evolution of Performance Indicators for Each Sector (continued)

Order numbers	Sector	Staff	HCVAVC	Hidden costs/ person/year	Evolution of HCVAVC	Conversion rate	Variation of VAVC
26	Medical professions	13	€ 46	€ 23,700			€ 0
27	Medical professions	4	€ 55	€ 43,700	31%	94%	€ 43,749
28	Medical professions	7	€ 34	€ 18,200		22%	€ 0
29	Medical professions	6	€ 68	€ 21,600	1%	36%	€ 9,398
30	Medical professions	7	€ 67	€ 51,500	–24%	35%	–€ 159,955
31	Medical professions	7	€ 33	€ 30,700	6%	67%	€ 38,676
32	Medical professions	12	€ 31	€ 28,200	6%	57%	€ 49,816
33	Medical professions	5	€ 56	€ 89,200	18%	65%	–€ 4,320
34	Medical professions	8	€ 70	€ 32,600		10%	€ 0
35	Medical professions	2	€ 39	€ 64,800	49%	64%	€ 77,838
36	Medical professions	16	€ 24	€ 26,700			€ 0
37	Medical professions	23	€ 70	€ 34,100			€ 0
38	Medical professions	28	€ 70	€ 31,800			€ 0
39	Medical professions	19	€ 70	€ 42,700			€ 0
40	Medical professions	7	€ 41	€ 54,260			€ 0
41	Medical professions	2	€ 44	€ 41,260	23%	59%	€ 16,008
42	Medical professions	3	€ 60	€ 87,000	–13%	30%	–€ 34,140
43	Medical professions	4	€ 34	€ 20,900	21%	47%	€ 2,892
44	Medical professions	2					€ 0
45	Medical professions	6	€ 112	€ 90,500	–25%	21%	€ 183,316
46	Medical professions	23	€ 40	€ 27,700	13%	37%	€ 168,450
47	Medical professions	5	€ 78	€ 82,200	–14%	42%	€ 39,182
48	Medical professions	11	€ 47	€ 25,000			€ 0
49	Medical professions	3	€ 78	€ 76,700			€ 0
50	Medical professions	8	€ 111	€ 76,500	–25%	31%	–€ 319,220
51	Medical professions						€ 0
52	Medical professions	23					€ 0

At the end of the change process, after 10 to 12 months, the average rate of conversion of hidden costs into value added is around 38%. The companies are therefore in a development dynamic, confirmed by the increase in sales turnover of nearly 20%. This is proof that part of the time resources, initially dedicated to the regulation of dysfunctions, have been reallocated to commercial and production actions. It is also likely that the increase in sales turnover has also contributed to the creation of new manpower needs and recruitment. Indeed, the expected hours have increased by 5%, which means that the workforce has increased, taking into account the slight decrease in the weekly working hours of the managers.

Significant differences in HCVAVC are noted across the business sectors. The average HCVAVC in real estate is €35, while the average CHVACV in the medical and legal professions is €61 and €42 respectively. But it is the amount of hidden costs per person per year that varies the most, with medical occupations showing an amount of over €41,000, while real estate is €27,500. Finally, although the conversion rates are roughly the same (between

30% and 40%), the evolution of the real estate HCVAVC is much more remarkable (14%) than that of the other sectors (4% for law and 5% for medical). Medical or law activities are more profitable, but the margin for developing the productivity of real estate companies is very important as soon as managerial innovation actions are implemented (Delattre, Zardet & Petit, 2015).

3.3 The Different Actions Implemented

Among the main outstanding achievements observed at the end of the change process, the implementation of internal procedures to improve work represents 20% of the actions. The need to build and share work rules is one of the priorities of this type of company. For more than 15%, the organization of more frequent and regular internal meetings proves to be a privileged lever to respond to the difficulties of communication-coordination-cooperation. The construction and use of activity management tools (11%), particularly on a financial level, was also observed, as well as more precise planning (9%) aimed at better anticipating unforeseen events and avoiding that work in a hurry remains their "trademark." The arrangement of the premises to improve their functionality (8%), combined with an investment in IT tools (computer, printer, software), illustrate the need to implement actions to improve the work infrastructure. Finally, the numerous improvements relating to training (6%), skills management (5%) and recruitment (7%) show the central place of human potential in the development of companies in the liberal professions.

4 HOW THE PLURALITY OF ACTIVITY STRENGHTENS EXCHANGES ON MANAGERIAL PRACTICES

The need for liberal professionals to develop their managerial skills is obvious. The results of the interventions highlight the convergence of dysfunctions and significant achievements. The construction of multidisciplinary groups, generating an effective sharing of difficulties and good managerial practices, has overcome the ideology of believing that "my company is special." This is all the more true as the diagnoses carried out have shown a "universality" of dysfunctions whatever the sector. The qualitative, quantitative and financial results obtained were rapid and significant, perhaps more remarkable than in larger companies. Employees and collaborators recognize that the time taken by the manager to "take care of them through action" is extremely profitable. The agility of this type of company, visible in their ability to decide and implement quickly all together, is an undeniable asset for their development and longevity.

Some points of vigilance remain. A directive accompaniment is necessary for the passage to action. Implementing actions is not easy and, faced with the weight of daily life, the sustainability of good practices is not guaranteed beyond the support, without external energy. In the case of companies with a more complex governance, with several partners, if issues such as remuneration levels, the allotment of time budgets that don't create revenue, sales volumes, etc. are not clearly addressed, the risks of blockage, or even painful separation, will continue to loom large. Finally, the lack of anticipation of the succession of a business remains one of the main causes of mortality of small businesses.

We have also observed specificities specific to certain sectors. Thus, the strong influence of the level of diploma and the status in the relations generates a significant relational distance between the managers of companies in the legal professions and their team (lawyers, notaries, bailiffs...). Many of the companies we have assisted have sought to take greater account of their human potential. On the contrary, the real estate professions have the particularity of not attaching enough importance to common working methods, due to the lack of organized communication-coordination-cooperation and to the overall economic productivity, which is the source of the companies' sustainability. We were also surprised to note the reticence in the act of selling, as well as the lack of courage in customer relations, both in terms of managing deadlines and managing billing and collection. As for the medical and paramedical environment, the problems of management and governance turn out to be a real headache as soon as the number of associates increases, especially since the remuneration of professionals in this sector is much higher than in other sectors. In addition, the difference in remuneration between managers and employees is such that the presentation of the HCVAVC to the teams was a tense moment for them because the subject is often taboo.

CONCLUSION

This assessment of four years of intervention-research gives us the opportunity to draw up a panorama of the microenterprises in the liberal professions, which are little known to social science researchers, pass under the radar of national indicators, and are also neglected by the consulting profession, given their limited size and sometimes their financial capacity. Support for the evolution of managerial tools and practices is an opportunity to activate the development of internal human resources in a conscious and coherent manner, without resorting to the opinion of the accountant, who is too often unaware of the dynamics of economic performance.

It was also an opportunity to develop the skills of the ISEOR's intervener-researchers, who are called upon to support decision-making on all sorts of topics: legal, accounting, data analysis, human resources, technical, commercial... It also carries a societal responsibility, insofar as the speaker-researcher supports managers who are often solitary in their decision-making, even though they assume strong economic and employment responsibilities. Finally, the microenterprise in the liberal profession is a business like any other, perhaps a victim of size discrimination on the part of other economic actors. Ironically, small businesses, as a whole, represent nearly 25% of salaried employment in France.

REFERENCES

Cappelletti, L. (2010). Le management de la relation client des professions: un nouveau sujet d'investigation pour le contrôle de gestion. *Management et Avenir, 1*, 339–363.

Cappelletti, L., et al. (2009). L'implantation d'un système de contrôle de gestion au sein d'entreprises libérales: cas des offices de notaires. *Comptabilité-Contrôle-Audit, 15*(1), 79–103.

Delattre, M. ; Petit, R., Zardet, V. (2015). Ar(t)chitectes et management: histoires d'introduction d'outils de management chez les architectes. *Revue Gérer et comprendre, 2*, 4–15.

INSEE (2013). *Les professions libérales réglementées.*

CHAPTER 21

MANAGEMENT AND TRAINING OF FRENCH NOTARIES

Results of 20 Years of Transformation of a Profession

Xavier Daudé and Laurent Cappelletti

ABSTRACT

For more than 20 years, ISEOR has conducted transformative intervention-researches with the notarial profession, its offices, its departmental chambers, its regional councils and its Superior Council. The main transformations observed in the management of notarial professionals, in their training and in the functioning of the offices are described in this chapter, as well as the perspectives they generate and the progress that remains to be made.

Since 1998, ISEOR has conducted intervention-researches in management and quality, on the one hand with French notaries in 600 notary offices and on the other hand with the training department of the National council of Notaries and the National Education Center of the Notarial Profession (Savall, Zardet, Cappelletti 1998–2020; Daudé, 2009, 2012). These observations, conducted over a period of 20 years, provide exceptional scientific material, combining macro and micro data on the management and training of a profession. This chapter outlines the results obtained.

SEAM Treatise, pages 211–216

1 THE ORIGINAL STATUS OF THE NOTARY: A PUBLIC OFFICER WHO RUNS A BUSINESS

In France, there are approximately 6,800 notaries' offices, employing 60,000 salaried employees and managed by more than 15,000 notaries, a little more than half of whom practice as partners. A notary's office is, on average, composed of 8 employees and managed by a single notary or several associated notaries. In 2020, the offices received about 20 million clients and achieved a total revenue of 8 billion euros. Approximately 80% of this revenue consists of legal activities related to family law (inheritance, marriage, divorce) and real estate law (purchase, sale of a property). For these activities, notaries benefit from a state monopoly and must respect a regulated tariff. But they are in competition with each other, since their clients retain the choice of their notary. Approximately 20% of this revenue consists of non-monopoly activities with free pricing, mainly in business law, asset management and real estate negotiations. In this market, notaries compete with each other, as well as with other professionals such as lawyers and accountants (Daudé, 2009; CSN, 2020).

The notary is a member of regulatory structures that control and animate the profession, ensuring compliance with the rules. They are appointed by decree of the Ministry of Justice and registered in a Chamber grouping together the notaries of the same geographical department. Each Chamber is part of a Regional Council attached to a Court of Appeal. The action of these bodies is part of a policy determined and conducted by national council of the profession (CSN). The latter has an institutional role in defining the policy and a unique regulation for the profession. Notaries are thus organized as regulated liberal enterprises: they are company directors and public officers (Daudé, 2009; CSN, 2020).

2 METHODOLOGY FOR SCIENTIFIC OBSERVATION OF THE NOTARIAL PROFESSION

In order to improve the quality of the management and operation of offices, the notaries of France, at the instigation of the CSN, its training department and departmental chambers, have called upon teams of researchers from ISEOR. These teams first intervened between 1998 and 2004 in 350 notaries' offices (Rymeyko, 2002; Cappelletti et al., 2009) to carry out intervention-researches consisting of implementing the socio-economic approach to management (Savall, 1974, 1975, 1979; Savall, Zardet, 1987, 2008). Then, between 2005 and 2020, they intervened in 250 notary offices to implement management according to the ISO 9001 quality standard (Cappelletti, Noguera, Plane, 2012). The two management models, socio-economic and ISO 9001 quality, have thus been implemented in a total of 600 offices since 1998, involving about 6000 notaries and collaborators, using the same miniaturized intervention-researches method adapted to very small firms called multi SMEs-HORIVERT HORIVERT processes (Savall, 2003; Buono, Savall, Cappelletti, 2007). The intervention-researches carried out in parallel over the period with the training department of the national council and the national institute of notarial training on the organisation of notaries' training made it possible to analyze the data collected in the 600 offices and to exploit them in a more collective way.

The multi-SMEs HORIVERT method follows the principles of the HORIVERT intervention-research method (Savall, Zardet, 1987) but presents miniaturized devices adapted to very small firms and liberal firms (Cappelletti, 2007; Buono, Savall, Cappelletti 2018a, 2018b). The method is composed of three axes: a change axis made up of intra-company devices for diagnosis, focus groups, implementation of improvement solutions and their evaluation; a tool axis made up of inter-company devices for training in six fundamental management tools: time management, strategic piloting indicators, tables of skills, internal and external strategic action plan, priority action plan and periodically negotiable activity contract; finally, a political axis for synchronizing the whole. In one region, the offices were gathered in groups of four to five offices. Each office in each group was involved in an intra-company scheme (work within its office) and an inter-company scheme. The intervention was coordinated in each region by a steering group composed of elected notaries from the region.

3 OUTLINE OF THE RESULTS OF 20 YEARS OF TRANSFORMATION

The results of the intervention-researches make it possible to outline the progress made by French notaries in terms of management, administration and training, the weaknesses that remain to be overcome and the opportunities that need to be seized.

3.1 The Paradox of the Notarial Profession: Although it Has a Monopoly, it Must be Agile

Fluctuations in the real estate market, the constant evolution of family law laws and the harmonization of European regulations that periodically threaten the loss of the monopoly, are sources of strategic constraints for notaries. They require the continuous improvement of the management of notarial offices in order to motivate employees, create more added value, finance the development of new services and meet the increasing demands of clients. Like other professions, notaries are also faced with increasing competition and the demands of their clients. Inter-institutional competition is sometimes fierce between notaries in the monopoly sector, despite the discipline organized by the profession. Inter-professional competition can also be real with lawyers, chartered accountants and real estate agencies on activities in the free sector, such as business law and real estate negotiation. The notary must also deal with the increased demands of his employees, who are asking for greater involvement and a share in the results. The notary must in some way transform himself into a leader and offer his staff training, career plans and profit sharing to stimulate their commitment to work (Cappelletti, 2007; Cappelletti, Khouatra, 2009; Cappelletti, Noguera, Plane, 2012).

Notary offices have made considerable progress in 20 years to gain agility. First of all, in the digital field, with the dematerialization of acts allowed since 2008. Since 2018, the electronic authentic act can be signed remotely, via a videoconference. This digital strength has enabled notary's offices to resist better than other professions in terms of work organization, in the face of the constraints imposed by the Covid crisis. Secondly, in terms of demographics, the notary's office has opened up and regenerated considerably in 20 years, since the number of practicing notaries, both salaried and associated, has risen from approximately 8,000 in 1998 to more than 15,000 today, thanks to the political will of the profession as well as the Macron law of 2015 opening up access to the profession of notary. In addition, the notary profession has become more feminine, since women now represent 53% of notaries and 70% of employees. The evolution of the organization of the training of notaries and their employees has contributed to this regeneration. It was completed in 2018 with the creation of the national institute of notarial education, the notarial profession's leading school, which now brings together all training for notarial professionals at regional sites.

3.2 The Creation of the National Institute of Notarial Education/ INFN: Strengthening the Cohesion of the Professions

The national education center was born of the provisions of the decree of July 19, 2018, which came into force on October 1, 2018, a text that operated the merger of the former notarial training establishments, i.e., 11 Notary Professional Training Centers- and the 15 Notary Professional Institutes.

3.2.1 An Old Professional Training System Placed Under the Supervision of the Ministry of Justice

The teaching of notarial principles and practice is closely linked to the notarial schools, which were born of the spirit of the law of 25 Ventôse year XI (16 March 1803). Prior to this fundamental law, the regulations and corporate traditions only envisaged apprenticeship as a method of training, the "working time" as it was known. If the principle had been established, it is due to the initiative of the profession itself that these notary schools were created. The first one was founded in Bordeaux in 1830 by the Chamber of Discipline, an initiative that was progressively taken up in most of the departments and an ordinance of 4 January 1843 entrusted the Chamber of Discipline with the task of ensuring the theoretical and practical instruction of candidate notaries.

The law of August 12, 1902 and a decree of August 3, 1905 recognized the notary schools, which were under the sole responsibility of the Minister of Justice, organized their operation, the terms of the professional training period and made official the diploma of first notary clerk issued by these establishments. Despite numerous requests from the profession, notably at the National Congresses of Notaries, the introduction of university diplomas into the training course came only belatedly. The guidelines of decree n°73–609 of 5 July 1973 relating to the professional training of notaries and the conditions of access to the functions of notary, the founding text, are as follows:

- a distinction between the initial training of notaries and that of their associates,
- the creation of new establishments around this distinction,
- the notarial education centers (CFPN), in charge of the training of future notaries,
- the notarial schools, in charge of the training of collaborators, providing a uniform education in all schools,
- a high level university education for access to the functions of notary with the higher diploma of notary, the characteristics of which are defined by the decree of 5 July 1973,
- the requirement for all notaries to hold at least a law degree (four years of higher education),
- a correspondence course for clerks entrusted to a dedicated institution,
- a national coordination and control structure: the national education center (CNEPN).

The notarial profession nevertheless retained a purely professional course of study, modified in 1989. This organization underwent numerous changes, on the one hand in the educational field with the creation, in 2008, of the bachelor in the field of notary public and a diploma for notarial professions that replaced the diploma of first notary clerk, and on the other hand structurally with the creation of the INFN on October 1, 2018, by the effect of decree n° 2018–659 of July 25, 2018.

3.2.2 The Reasons That Led the Profession to Create a National Education Institution

The National Institute of Notarial Education INFN is a public utility institution under the supervision of the Keeper of the Seals, is a structure that today includes 75 administrative employees, a thousand teachers and 3,900 students spread over 15 teaching sites in France. The INFN is presided over by an Advocate General at the supreme court (Cour de Cassation), surrounded by a Board of Directors of 10 members composed of notaries, employees of notary offices and academics. The establishment is structured around a headquarters in Paris. The profession's desire to create a national structure is based on several observations:

- in the age of social networks, a training system divided into 26 establishments was no longer visible to students, teachers and partners of the profession;
- in spite of the control exercised by the profession, pedagogical disparities were noted between the training establishments for the same training courses;
- regional institutions sometimes struggled to organize a strong and audible communication on the training courses and the opportunities in the profession.
- small regional institutions sometimes lacked attractiveness to students.

The creation of a national notarial training establishment thus aimed to create a more legible and visible identity for students and a stronger sense of belonging to the same profession, to ensure pedagogical unity in all teaching sites, to have a new "strike power" in terms of communication, to develop continuing education for notaries and their collaborators, to organize scientific work, colloquia and conferences and to ensure their dissemination, to allow for international influence and finally to reduce operating costs.

3.3 The Contribution of Innovative Managerial Practices in the Offices and Avenues for Progress

In terms of the quality of the management and administration of the offices, significant improvements have been observed within the offices. The annual revenue of notaries' offices, which in total has tripled in 20 years, while the number of notarial professionals, notaries and collaborators, has only increased by 20% during the same period, is an illustration of this, even if a fraction of the tripling is due to the increase in property prices.

In detail, in about 75% of the 350 offices in the socio-economic management implementation sample, the intervention had positive economic impacts both on the immediate result and on the deferred result: the creation of potential (Cappelletti, Khouatra, 2009). However, in about 25% of the offices, the improvement in management quality, although existing, was less significant. The analysis shows that in these cases, the lack of involvement of the notary in charge of the office hindered the implementation of management tools and the creativity of the focus groups, which led to a certain disappointment among the employees.

At the end of the intervention, the increase in the economic performance of the offices was evaluated economically in each office by measuring the recovery of hidden costs. On average, the positive effects reduced the loss of value added by 37%, resulting in gains of about €40,000 per office, or about a 10% increase in their margin on variable costs. The intervention-researches thus made it possible to discover in most of the offices the capacity to conduct agile strategies in the face of a competitive environment and endogenous economic resources (Savall, Zardet, 1987, 1995, Savall, Péron, Zardet, Bonnet, 2015).

The observations made during the intervention-researches in ISO 9001 quality management within the sample of 250 notary offices, have made it possible to identify the contributions and limits of a standardization approach to human resources management for the profession. On the one hand, each of the offices, according to its needs, has formalized its quality plan and its underlying themes, a real guideline for the improvements to be made to its concrete organization (Cappelletti, Noguera, Plane, 2012). On the other hand, persistent limitations have been observed with regard to the effects of a standardization approach within notaries' offices, which represent areas of progress for the future. For example, the ISO quality approach does not address the issue of salary levels and in particular the variability of salaries according to the efforts of each individual. Moreover, the tools and mechanisms provided for in an ISO 9001 quality approach require the sustained involvement of notary managers to ensure their durability. However, this involvement is not always forthcoming, probably because the notary's initial training did not make him sufficiently aware of the importance of management, training and quality.

CONCLUSION

Beyond their contribution to the improvement of the quality of management and training of notaries' offices, the 20 years of transformative observation of the ISEOR within the notarial profession represents a formidable "phenomenology of a profession" whose exploitation of the knowledge produced is far from complete.

REFERENCES

Cappelletti, L. (2007). Intervening in Small Professional Enterprises: Enhancing Management Quality in French Notary Publics Offices. In A. F. Buono, & H. Savall, (Eds.), *Socio-economic intervention in organizations* (pp. 331–354). Information Age Publishing.

Cappelletti, L. (2012). *Management control of the intangible. A new approach to human capital.* Dunod.

Cappelletti, L., & Dufour, N. (2020). *Innovative management of standards.* Géréso Editions.

Cappelletti, L., & Khouatra, D. (2009). L'implantation d'un système de contrôle de gestion au sein d'entreprises libérales : cas des offices de notaires. *Comptabilité-Contrôle-Audit, 15*(1), 79–104.

Cappelletti, L., Noguera, F., & Plane, J. M. (2012). The standardization of human resource management. The case of the regulated liberal professions. *Revue de Gestion des Ressources Humaines, 85*, 3–17.

Conseil Supérieur du Notariat. (2020). www.notaires.fr

Daudé, X. (2009). Training and development in the notarial profession. In *Management des professions libérales réglementées.* Paris, Economica, Collection management socio-économique.

Daudé, X. (2012). *The metamorphosis of a regulated liberal profession and its capacity for innovation—The French notary's office.* Mémoire pour le diplôme supérieur de notariat, December, CFPN Paris.

Rymeyko, K. (2002). *Strategic stakes of the regulated liberal professions, changes in management practices and impacts on performance. Cas des offices de notaires.* Doctoral thesis in management sciences. University of Lyon.

PART IV

SUPPORTING THE DEVELOPMENT OF MID-SIZED AND LARGE COMPANIES

This page intentionally left blank.

CHAPTER 22

NEARLY 40 YEARS OF SOCIO-ECONOMIC APPROACH TO MANAGEMENT

Lessons Learned Regarding the Notion of Dynamic Equilibrium

Pascal Pasquier and Amandine Savall

ABSTRACT

This chapter presents the results of nearly 40 years of application of the socio-economic approach to management in the Brioche Pasquier company, from the point of view of a key managerial concept: "balance," which is both a compass and a deliberate policy for running the company and managing the 3,440 people who work there. The concept of balance is detailed in various forms: external strategy, internal organization and structure, people management, human resources...

This chapter presents the results of nearly 40 years of application of the socio-economic approach to management in a French company operating in the agri-food sector. Brioche Pasquier has been applying the principles and tools of Socio-Economic Management since 1984, when the managers of the time met with Henri Savall and his team from ISEOR. This chapter presents the results from the perspective of a key managerial concept: "balance," which is both a compass and a deliberate policy, dear to the current manager for commanding/leading/governing his company of 3,400 people.

SEAM Treatise, pages 219–228

1 FIGHTING THE "TFW" ORGANIZATIONAL AND MANAGERIAL VIRUS: THE CONCEPT OF DYNAMIC BALANCE

The concept of the "TFW virus" (Taylorism, Fayolism, Weberism) developed by ISEOR denounces archaic managerial practices that promote, on the one hand, the hyper-specialization of skills, professions, products, and sectors, and on the other hand, the separation of design and execution, and finally the depersonalization of management. This universal virus has been observed in all the companies that ISEOR has accompanied, regardless of their size, sector or geographic location. This virus, introduced in all educational curricula, favors the proliferation of inefficiency, ineffectiveness and therefore hidden costs. The three principles promoted by Taylor (1911), Fayol (1016) and Weber (1947)—hyper-specialization, separation of design and implementation, and depersonalization—run counter to a balanced managerial system that admits paradoxes and resolves them through reasoned practices, aiming to re-establish a symphony between the individuals and teams called upon to work together to create performance. This managerial system is contained in the socio-economic approach to management.

Unfortunately, the external social and economic environment is pushing companies towards "anti-socio-economic management," jeopardizing the notion of balance, particularly in the case of Brioche Pasquier. Indeed, its external environment is characterized by: the hyper-specialization of skills and professions, the increasing regulation via an unlimited proliferation of standards and rules of all kinds, the "Food Bashing"—acute societal criticism of industrial food, said to be "unhealthy"—in an increasingly global and digital framework that is changing consumer behavior. Thus, these issues require managerial adaptations, with ambivalent consequences, on the one hand positive (e.g., safety and traceability, accessibility, modernization and innovation) and on the other negative (complexity, individualization, corporatism and hyper-specialization).

It is in this turbulent context that Brioche Pasquier's manager claims a balanced policy, strategy and management, as Jean Grenier (1969), a French writer and philosopher, proclaimed: "it is as noble to strive for balance as for perfection; for it is perfection to keep the balance."

2 IMPLEMENTATION OF THE SOCIO-ECONOMIC APPROACH TO MANAGEMENT AT BRIOCHE PASQUIER

2.1 Presentation of the Company and its Context

2.1.1 Brief History

"From a family bakery to a company with 3,400 employees."

The story begins in 1936, in a small town in Maine et Loire, where Gabriel Pasquier's family bakery built its regional reputation with brioche. In 1974, 5 sons took over the family business and created Brioche Pasquier. Why Pasquier ? Why Brioche? Very quickly, when the company was created, the choice of the surname "Pasquier" as the company name came naturally: to immediately give a reference point to future consumers: "I know who makes the brioche I buy." And the word "brioche" specified what the family business historically made: the nature of its products. The 5 brothers decided to go and offer their famous brioche, protected by a bag, in supermarkets. The idea was revolutionary for the time and met with great success. The following decades saw the appearance of new products, quickly adopted by the general public, such as the "Pitch" in 1986 or the "Pain au lait," the brand's best-seller. The

TABLE 22.1 Key Events in the History of the Family Group

1974	Creation of the company
1977	Opening of the first site in the West of France (Brioche)
1984	Start of the partnership with ISEOR
1986	Opening of the second site in région Rhône Alpes Region (Brioche)
1992	Diversification with a new range of pastry products
1993	1st merger-acquisition in the Pastry product line in France
1998	Starting to export
1999	Building of a Brioche production site in the North of France
2001	1st merger-acquisition in Italy (Brioche) Launch of the 3rd range of Rusk products with a Spanish company
2004	Construction of the 2nd Spanish site
2007	Acquisition of bread production companies Creation of the "International" activity: anchoring and putting down local roots
2012–2013	Acquisition in the United States
2014–2016	Construction of a site in the United Kingdom
2017–2019	Acquisition of a minority stake in a distribution company in South Korea

company developed by establishing itself everywhere with, to date, 14 industrial and commercial sites in France and 4 sites and commercial subsidiaries abroad. Today, it offers a wide range of pastry and biscuit products (Pasquier, 2009, 2017, 2019). It is the fresh product (the brioche is a product that is eaten fresh) that led the company to decentralize, organize and structure this decentralization.

2.1.2 Products and Markets

The flagship product, the brioche, has guided the decentralization strategy. Brioche Pasquier has developed the notion of proximity, as the brioche must be fresh to satisfy its consumers. This desire has been translated into major choices. From the outset, the company kept the same brioche-making process as the one used in the family bakery, regardless of the industrial tools subsequently used. The company has chosen to work directly with mass distribution in order to avoid multiple intermediaries. Finally, if the company were to develop, it would not only remain in its village but would be established close to its customers and consumers.

In 40 years, the family group has become the undisputed leader of the Viennese pastry industry in France. It is also a major player in frozen and fresh pastries, as well as in rusk products.

2.2 Course of the Intervention Since 1984 and Significant Achievements

2.2.1 Choice of the Socio-Economic Approach to Management

In the 1980s, the company's strong growth led it to seek out and implement management and management methods that corresponded to the values and fundamentals held by the Pasquier brothers (Pasquier, 2016). Socio-Economic Approach to Management (SEAM) immediately appealed to them: the Pasquiers' educational principles were in line with those of SEAM; a state of mind that corresponded to what the managers wanted. The advantage of the SEAM, beyond the theoretical principles, lay in a methodology that proposed concrete tools to apply these managerial principles that were important to the managers. (Savall, 1974–1975, 1979; Savall and Zardet, 1987, 1995).

The trihedron represents a complete management system, where each of the three axes is important:

- Axis 1: problem-solving process (diagnosis/project/implementation/evaluation);
- Axis 2: management tools and machinery: the socio-economic management system is based on the instrumentation (tools, bodies) of managers for the collective and individual steering of teams with strategic vision tools:
  - at 3 years: since 2010, the implementation of the "Business Plan" tool for each site, activity and the group with the People/Products/Markets/Technologies;
  - at 1 year: the development plan and the budget;
  - at 6 months: Pasquier Improvement Contracts (PICs) and half-yearly seminars on the sites;
  - at 1 month: the monthly recommendation;
- Axis 3: political and strategic decisions.

The family-owned group is a company with a decentralized system for the executive, and concentrated for a strategic vision, in order to tend towards more accountability and proximity. Its management system is based on an organizational and managerial structure with the shortest possible hierarchy: first the Site, the cornerstone of this management system, then the Activity and the Group, with its support functions that synchronize and orchestrate (Figure 22.1).

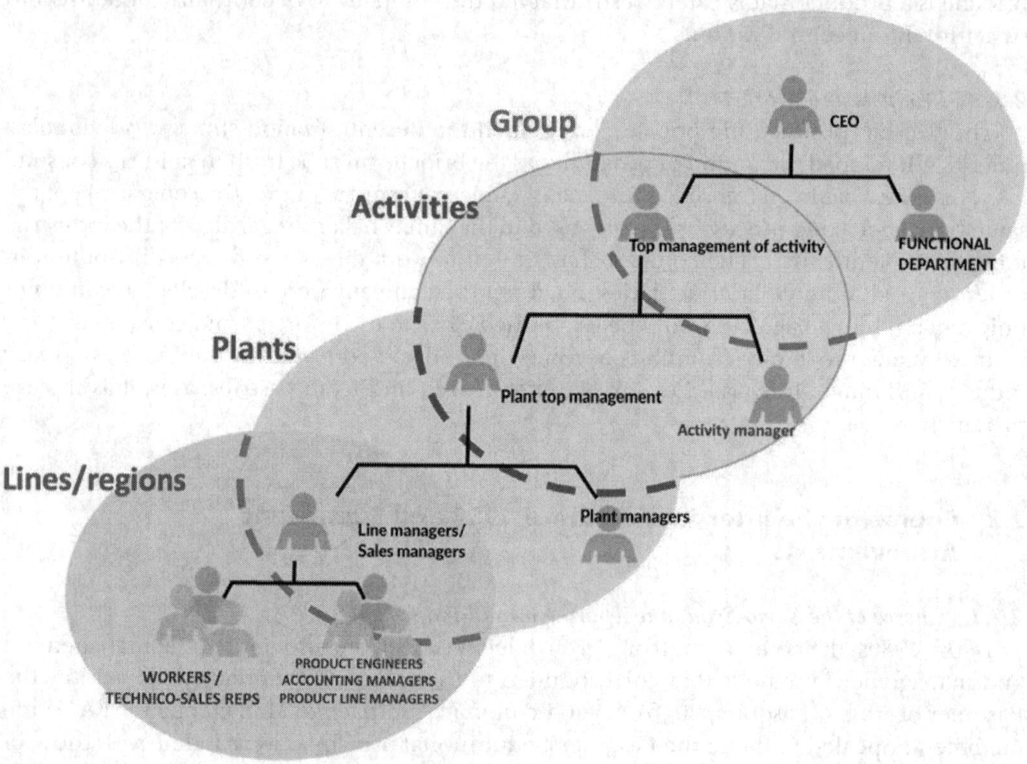

Figure 22.1 The four structural levels of the company.

Other bodies have been set up, such as product lines, business lines and focus groups. These are groups of skills that are tasked with creating innovation or carrying out projects and ensuring their implementation within the company.

2.2.2 Full-Scale Sites, on a Human Scale: A Strategic Choice

"*The site is the life of the company*": One of the fundamentals of the company is that the site is the cornerstone of this management system.

"*To produce is to sell, to sell is to produce.*" This translates into a process of synchronized decentralization (Figure 22.1): each site is managed and directed by a pair of general managers: industrial and commercial, living in the same office, to facilitate permanent exchanges between industrialists and commercials with a view to making the best decisions, including the constraints of each. The site is a human-sized entity (less than 300 people) which allows for a short hierarchy (assistant > manager > management). It is clearly identified and structured into measurable entities.

In order to implement its political and strategic decisions, its challenges and its priority projects, the company set up in 1986 a tool called the "CAP." This half-yearly "contract" makes it possible to bring the management system to life through clear and defined "orders" to all employees.

An illustration called the "CAP cartoon" was created to facilitate its presentation and understanding by all employees (see Figure 22.2).

The company is like a boat at sea, piloted by a crew to reach its objective. Before the expedition, this crew has already defined its objective and its strategy to reach its goal. During the voyage, they are confronted with an environment that is constantly changing. It must therefore adapt in the short or medium to long term. He must show agility and flexibility by adjusting his objectives and strategic axes if necessary to reach his destination.

The socio-economic organization of work implies, beyond the expression "all in the same boat," an overall approach to the work carried out, versatility (the "hands on" concept), accountability through the assignment of tasks to each individual (each team being responsible for the entire manufacturing process up to the packaging of the product), with the objective of satisfying internal and external customers.

Figure 22.2 CAP comic strip.

TABLE 22.2 A Dramatic Evolution of Human Productivity Indicators: 1986 to 2019

Years	Revenue in million Euros	Employees (Full time equivalent)
1986	27	350
2019	703	3,440
Growth in 33 years	× 25	× 9

2.3 The Various Desirable and Achieved Balances, Elements of Performance

Balance is a complex, multi-faceted and intrinsically dynamic concept. Balance is by essence precarious, unstable and variable from one moment to the next. The current economic and societal context, as a consequence of the health crisis linked to covid–19, proves once again that balance is necessary to ensure and preserve the sustainability of the company.

2.3.1 Balance in the External Strategy

2.3.1.1 Diversification of activities and business lines. The strategy of diversification into several activities that the company has pursued for several decades has made it possible to better spread the risks between activities and consequently to cushion the effects of the economic crisis. It shows that the notion of balance is necessary to preserve the company's sustainability, and to avoid weakening it by being present in only one field. Ensuring sustainable economic results requires maintaining a balance in the areas of activity: the economic performance of a group cannot be based on a single activity.

2.3.1.2 Different distribution channels. The company must constantly adapt to the changing behavior of all consumers, with the sole objective of satisfying them by making the product accessible wherever and however it is consumed. This is why the company is present in the traditional distribution channels (supermarkets, "drive-through" and stores, and out-of-home consumption), in online commerce and in other new channels.

2.3.1.3 Trade in France and abroad. In this era of globalization, the French buy products from all over the world... And the reverse is true. To ensure its sustainability, the company has turned to the international market in order to seize new business opportunities, new markets and win new consumers (Savall A., 2014; Worley et al., 2015). The company has chosen to manufacture its products in most of the countries where it has developed, by having a French team working on site, capable of transmitting the company's management system and know-how to teams of local personnel. The latter bring to the French teams everything that the company does not know in the country: the culture, the legislation and regulations, the consumer habits, the knowledge of suppliers, customers and distribution networks and channels... (Savall A., 2014).

2.3.2 Balances in the Internal Strategy

2.3.2.1 Organizational structures. The key word for maintaining the balance between the functional and operational staff is the notion of counter-power to avoid the feudality of the operational staff and the technical drift of the functional staff. As for the balance between sales and industrial staff, it can be summed up by the phrase "*to produce is to sell, to sell is to produce*," which must be the final objective for every employee in the company: to work to satisfy the consumer. We produce buns to sell them, and it is by selling that we feed the production lines. The two jobs are therefore closely linked.

2.3.2.2 Vision and action. Vision is used to project the company, to establish a roadmap that provides a clear overview of the strategic axes and helps us reach our objectives. Action allows us to keep a sense of reality, thanks to our proximity to our teams and our clients. It feeds the medium and long terms vision on a daily basis. It often leads to remaining agile and flexible.

2.3.2.3 Demographic structures: Age pyramid, male/female distribution. The balance sought is to have different generations working together with contrasting expectations. Trust and the ability to question oneself are the key words. For the older generation: trust them for their ability to pass on the management system and their know-how; and for the younger generation: learn to listen to them and hear their proposals for modernization.

As for the balance between men and women, which is necessary for the proper management of the company, many women hold management and executive positions, including in the plants.

2.3.2.4 External recruitment and internal mobility. They all arrive with their own experience and a fresh eye. They come, each in their own way, to question the working methods and make them evolve to improve the company's performance.

2.3.2.5 Individual responsibility and teamwork. The CAP cartoon illustrates the importance of teamwork. In order to achieve the desired success, it is necessary to assign, formalize and pilot the individual and priority actions of each of the actors.

2.3.2.6 Decentralization and orchestration. The choice of a decentralized system on the sites gives power to each entity, while ensuring harmony, especially in the face of external influences. This necessarily implies an orchestration function (by the Site, Activity and Group levels), which can only be exercised if the orchestrating team has complementary skills. In fact, it is necessary to first designate a subject and assign it to people (musicians) so that they deal with it according to their skill levels, or to plan a training process and, simultaneously, assign a conductor to the Site, Activity or Group level.

2.3.2.7 The manager, a necessary conductor. Bringing together expert and competent actors in extremely specialized fields requires orchestration. In the company, it is the managers who play the role of orchestra conductor, which is essential for the synchronization of players and activities (see Figure 22.3).

2.3.2.8 Area of competence and overall approach. The first is necessary for a manager to be legitimate, recognized and respected, but the second is essential to feed comprehensive thinking and make better decisions. Managers in difficulty are often those who do not have a clearly identified area of competence such as finance, quality, human resources, production, sales, etc. The area of competence is a prerequisite for orchestration. It establishes legitimacy, allows one to remain current (by cultivating one's field of expertise) and to question. This is how it has its role to play in the evolution of the company. Moreover, this area helps the manager to get through difficult periods and thus to give himself the means to bounce back better.

2.3.3 Balancing Performance

2.3.3.1 Social performance and economic performance. Economic performance only exists if the company's employees clearly know their place and function in order to contribute to economic performance, hence the importance of structuring and organizing the company in order to identify and clarify the place of each person.

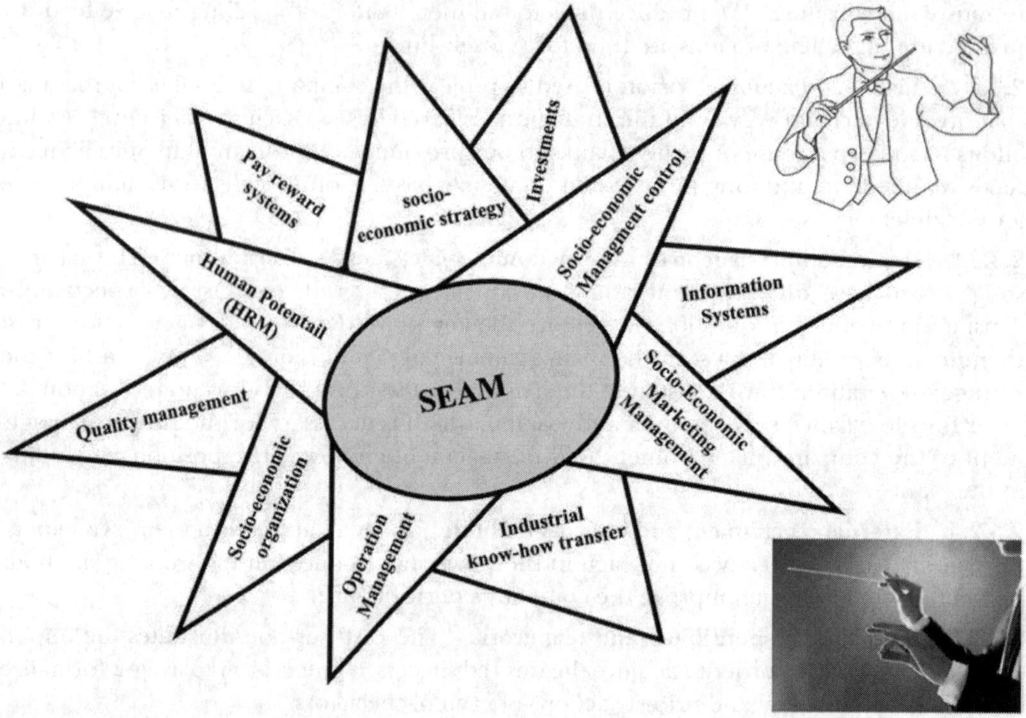

Figure 22.3 Socio-economic management star ©ISEOR 2013

2.3.3.2 Short term and medium and long terms projection. Short-termism is essential in a society where immediacy is omnipresent through the media. But it is only viable and can only exist if there is a medium and long terms vision in the background.

3 WHAT LESSONS CAN BE LEARNED ABOUT "BALANCE"?

These four decades of permanent search for balance in the management of the company have enabled us to draw a number of lessons for those who wish to practice this "notion of balance." Indeed, in order not to "put all one's eggs in one basket," the concept of balance is a daily guide for the leader or the socio-economic manager in his or her strategic, managerial or organizational decisions. It is a concept that can be applied in all circumstances: decentralization, internationalization, diversification, growth, etc.

First of all, it is a matter of analyzing, reflecting and deciding on any decision by systematically associating a *balanced reflection between social and economic aspects.* Whatever the nature of the decisions to be taken, the social and economic characteristics are indeed inseparable. Any decision should be taken not only according to its socio-economic impacts but also, and above all, according to the way it is implemented, particularly in terms of human organizational structures: cooperation circuits, assignment of roles, working tools and devices.

Secondly, *taking into-account a "client"* is essential. Indeed, the notion of balance is more easily applicable when the leader, the manager or, more broadly, the employee, conceives his decisions and actions for a "receiver" or "client." This client can be external, in the usual sense, or internal, in the sense of an internal stakeholder of the company who has needs to be satisfied. Indeed, the decisions to be taken and implemented must be understood in terms of the needs they must satisfy. Actions cannot be self-centered on the decision-makers themselves.

Finally, the complexity of managing a company consists in *managing paradoxes.* The idea of balancing decisions is not, paradoxically, to make choices between seemingly opposite options, but to reconcile all the variables, expectations and constraints. The search for balance requires the leader or manager to be less dogmatic and less rigid. His role is to avoid *"binarism" and the excessive imbalances* of his very turbulent strategic environment. The latter is "pressing" in the sense that it exerts technical pressures (finance, industrial engineering, technology, etc.) on the company and its decision-makers in all directions, which can easily cause them to drift away from this notion of balance. To balance his decisions and avoid extremist drifts, the manager must take care of his *proximity* to the teams and the quality of his tools. A manager must *stimulate the five senses* that nature has given him, in order to be close to his environment. This stimulation involves observation, active listening, touch, and even taste and smell, especially in the food industry. These managerial actions are promoted within the company by a strong policy: "*getting hands-on*" and "*working with*" the teams. The manager regularly visits the field to check whether the theoretical decisions he makes correspond to the reality on the ground. This proximity allows him to adjust his/her vision of the environment before decisions are made, or afterwards, to verify the quality of implementation and the need for any adjustments. All the more so since, in a terribly fast and changing environment, the obsolescence of decisions is accelerating. The complexity and velocity of this strategic business environment leads to another type of paradox to be managed: the need to act quickly and without delay, a sign of organizational agility and performance-creating reactivity, or, on the other hand, strategic patience and slow, serene hindsight to adjust the vision of the environment and avoid making hasty decisions that could destroy performance.

Thus, managers also strive to put in place measurement elements, more commonly called indicators, on all the subjects he/she pilots. Regular measurements, varied in nature and form (qualitative, quantitative, etc.), allow for a better quality of management and evaluation of the decisions made, and thus avoid imbalances or drift. For example, a site manager who needs to ensure the balance between operational and functional staff can monitor a very simple indicator: the presence and number of representatives of each category of employee in the product "Product series" (strategic product development groups).

CONCLUSION

The notion of balance, as we describe it, is more qualitative than quantitative. For example, each site management of the company is composed of a balanced binomial, with an industrial director and a commercial director at the head of the site. This pairing is nevertheless hierarchical, with a number 1 and a number 2. So balancing industry and commerce, in this example, does not mean respecting a strict "50–50," but simply a sufficiently important presence.

As explained earlier, the balance between "socio" and "economic" is crucial. This balanced system can be illustrated by a double scale where the first part represents human structures, organization, training and creation of human potential, while the second refers to the economic objectives established in five-year business plans, one-year development plans or six-month team improvement contracts. These two scales are not placed next to each other against the wall, but against each other: they balance each other (Figure 22.4).

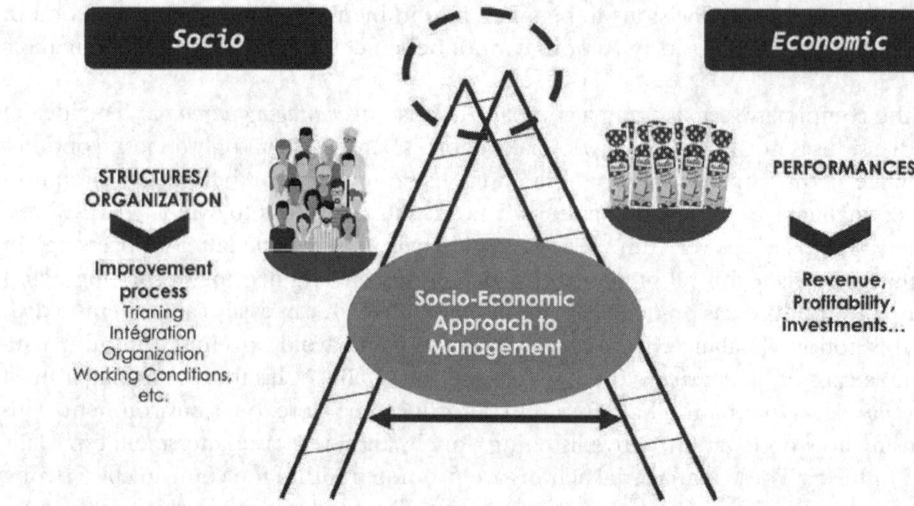

Figure 22.4 The double scale of socio-economic management.

REFERENCES

Grenier J. (1969). *Nouveau lexique.* Fata Morgana.

Pasquier, P. (2009). Two emblematic cases of sustainable economic development of companies. In H. Savall & V. Zardet (Eds.), *Management socio-économique: Une approche innovante.* Economica.

Pasquier, P. (2016). The fundamentals of the Brioche Pasquier company. In H. Savall & V. Zardet (Eds.), *Companies, value(s) and prosperity: socially responsible capitalism.* EMS.

Pasquier, P. (2017). *Business innovation: All salespeople at Brioche Pasquier.*

Pasquier, P. (2019). All sellers in the company and the role of the manager. In H. Savall & V. Zardet (Eds.), *How to work together? Challenges of intergeneration.* EMS.

Savall, A. (2014). *Endogenous factors of sustainable performance of family business internationalization—Longitudinal case of intervention-research.* Doctoral dissertation in management. Conservatoire National des Arts et Métiers, Paris.

Savall, H., & Zardet V. (Eds.). *Innovation commerciale: Tous vendeurs dans les organisations.* EMS.

Worley, C., Zardet, V., Bonnet, M., & Savall, A. (2015). *Becoming agile.* Jossey Bass.

CHAPTER 23

PROFESSIONALIZATION OF A FAMILY BUSINESS THROUGH HUMAN SUPPORT IN ORDER TO SUSTAIN VALUE CREATION

Victor Frontera and Victor Caumeil

ABSTRACT

The family business model is not only very particular, but also singular from one company to another. This paper aims to demonstrate that it is possible to maintain a family model in a fast-growing company, by professionalizing it. By relying on all the internal potential that will be put to use, by clarifying the role and prerogatives of management and finally by harmonizing practices and vision through a common language, the family business can be an extremely successful model both socially and economically.

Family businesses are numerous and their internal functioning is quite singular. We analyze how a company of this type manages to professionalize itself in order to continue creating value, relying on its know-how and its collaborators. We start by discussing the implementation of change, and then detail the proximity management as a way to professionalize this family business.

1 CRISIS OF BELONGING: CHANGE, A QUESTIONING

If it seems obvious that humans develop a particular relationship to change, this relationship must be analyzed by introducing the relationship of change to time. Time is an

SEAM Treatise, pages 229–234

incompressible universal unit that companies feel they lack. A change must take into-account the different aspects of time: rhythm, volume, calendar as well as the human difficulties it brings, called resistance.

When a company initiates a change, the first reflex of the people working there is often to continue working as before, while adding a new way of doing things. This inexorably creates a tension on the workload; quickly, two profiles of actors distinguish themselves:

- The one who wants to get by and accepts to change his practices and those of his colleagues. He/she therefore integrates the new methodology into his/her job. He will end up gradually reducing the amount of time spent on the change.
- The one who struggles or cannot integrate it and who does double the work, trying to apply two methodologies in order to keep control over the elements of his/her work. It will be necessary to help him/her to develop a greater confidence so that he/she appropriates a single new way of functioning.

It is necessary, for a company initiating a change process, to understand the time that it will represent. Regardless of the methodology used, the time invested will always be considered important, even though it is necessary for a sustainable integration of the change. The first year is often considered the most "indigestible," as new practices and methodologies are explained and gradually replace the old ones. This constant and important flow of new information can create a shock of belonging. The actors receive so much information and question so many practices that they end up questioning the coherence of all the elements at their disposal. It is following this questioning and thanks to this shock that everyone succeeds in going beyond the simple technical aspect of the change, in order to adhere to the meaning and make it their own. Thus, change always has an ambivalent impact on individuals. It creates discomfort and dissatisfaction, which are ultimately necessary feelings to access the benefits of a change, over time.

It is possible to complete the notion of time by the time taken by a manager, considered as "the one who knows," to accept the learning process of delegation. Considered as such, the manager confronted with the change has a direct impact on his or her employees. Indeed, the time it takes for the manager to learn to delegate is also time for the employees to "do nothing," as long as the manager himself does not spread the change. The case studied next is a demonstration of this.

In May 2014, the management of the trading company studied here, taken over by the son of the leader, reached a crossroads in its history. After 30 years, the historical leader had the choice to sell his group, or to expand his business from three to six stores, from 80 to 150 employees, but giving the reins to his son. After family cooperation, the decision was made to continue the business by taking the immediate external growth option. The only condition set by the young manager was to have full decision-making responsibility for the group.

The immediate problem was to identify the new human structural needs. It was necessary to move from a decision-making system concentrated on two or three people to a system divided into specialists, by professionalizing the company's entire strategic, managerial and operational system. Internal relations had to be structured, and people had to be hired for positions that did not exist at the time (HRM, Purchasing Department, Operational Manager, etc.). All these actions were aimed at ensuring the financial and human sustainability of the new group.

In human terms, the questions raised were: How to identify, keep and develop good employees? How can we remunerate the work of each person at its fair value, without making value judgments? Or how to instill strategy in each employee in order to guarantee the quality of reception and service in our sales outlets?

Finally, the historical manager had to psychologically accept the takeover by his son, in order to allow him to better engage with the teams already present and to integrate new employees.

It was then that the decision was made to implement, little by little, the principles of socio-economic management, with the support of ISEOR. The company first needed to learn how to objectively define the competencies for existing positions and those to be created, in order, for example, to give meaning to the internal promotions necessary for the proper functioning of the company.

This is how a first horizontal action of the management team and the direction was set up to identify the dysfunctions and to look for innovative solutions. Vertical actions then followed for two specific areas, following the same principle as the horizontal action. Training clusters were held in parallel to train managers (Savall 1974–1975, 1979; Savall and Zardet, 1987).

2 THE TRANSITION FROM A FAMILY MODEL TO A GROUP: PROXIMITY MANAGEMENT, A POSSIBLE RESPONSE

The abandonment of the so-called family management was for a time an option considered by the current manager, because it is generally perceived as amateurism. After several attempts at radical restructuring, it was considered that family management is in fact a way of managing the company which allows to give it meaning and to position itself as close as possible to each individual. The group could then keep family management at the heart of its strategy. However, it was necessary to organize the transition from a primary family management, where the manager is physically and intellectually omnipresent, to a professional family mode which allows the representation of the manager without requiring his physical presence. The group therefore initiated several actions, including new decision-making and communication channels so that the ideas transmitted and disseminated by each executive are heard as those of the "boss." The notion of synchronized decentralization (Savall, Zardet, 1987, 1995) was at the heart of this project.

The first step was to set up a management committee, with the delegation of some of the manager's functions to professionals recruited (internally or externally) to carry out specific functions such as those of HRM or operational manager. We had to increase the level of requirements as we went along to enable each person to understand his or her role and assume it without interfering with that of others: I no longer do everything by halves, but only my job, and very well.

The second task consisted in tackling the dogmas according to which a manager must decide on everything, that a loss of physical proximity leads to a cooling of human relations and that the representation of decision-making bodies by members of the management committee is a loss of power for the manager. The company director explained that the delegation of business lines, which until now had been held by him alone, to the members of his management committee allowed for a better "vertical-transversality" (Savall, Zardet, 1995, 2005) of the company's strategy. A good delegation of authority and a good understanding between the manager and his or her management committee make it possible to transmit the expectations as accurately as possible to all employees. The objective is general confidence: "the voice heard is the boss's."

After taking charge of the overall strategy and realizing that it was necessary to develop understanding and cohesion within the management committee, the next step was to revisit the management methods as a whole. The leader repositioned all the roles of the managers. With the growth of the group, autonomy without any control had taken over and created a lot of turbulence. Each person had taken the initiative to develop his or her own commercial management methods, which were not coordinated to compensate for the loss of managerial proximity that we mentioned earlier.

The need to speak the same language with all the employees appeared immediately after the restructuring of the management team. In order to better understand each other, a harmonized and homogeneous management of each person's performance was initiated, new work tools were created and each person was asked to practice a less face-to-face management, but more rigorous in respecting the new methods and practices. A great need for translation appeared, to better understand each other, because here again the system had moved from a primary mode, where oral communication was the major form of transmission, to a more rigorous system of formalization, written and monitored. One of the essential tools was the integration of the socio-economic management method (Savall, Zardet, 1987, 2005) designed by ISEOR, which greatly helped in the implementation of these tools and provided the energy that the company needed for such a project.

Nothing would have been possible if the management committee had not given meaning to all levels of the hierarchy. The last step was to change the way employees were appointed with their role and function, in order to instill the desired managerial philosophy in the operational bodies. Indeed, the majority of companies in the retail sector are made up of salespeople, so the objective was to make everyone understand that they were *not just salespeople* as designated by the collective agreement, but *sports advisors*! This made it possible to start a discussion on the interest in work and on the most vital function of the company, essential to its functioning. Little by little, everyone took responsibility for their own area, sometimes even to the detriment of the supervisor, who was in a permanent "function creep" (Savall, Zardet 1987). The change in mentality was sometimes difficult for managers at all levels to master. Managers with previously suppressed managerial functions thought they were losing power, while some advisors with no decision-making function granted themselves rights by exceeding their functions. Vigilance and rigor in the clarification of the expectations of each person has made it possible to begin the revalorization of roles through dialogue and the exemplarity of the entire decision-making chain.

You can't remember everything! The choice of writing rather than talking was a real challenge, especially since the retail business can quickly lead to being overwhelmed, which has the effect of distancing managers from part of their strategic role. This formalism allows for "forgetting" by making everyone realize that "writing things down" brings with it a collective responsibility to remember. The manager can move on, with peace of mind about the basic work to be done.

The professionalization of the language and the harmonization of practices have created an organization based on the self-checking of positions. From now on, a person wishing to evolve has a real knowledge of the expectations of the position to be filled. The company's human resources department is no longer validating a potential internal evolution based on value judgement alone. The company is able to understand a reasoned growth, individuals are more and more able to determine their own competencies, which helps to be more relevant in the choice of new managers.

In summary, the change has been total. All decision-making bodies have been modified, and everyone has changed the way they address each other. The change has given meaning and value to everyone in the company, regardless of their position. The pre-existing managerial models have been replaced by a common managerial model, inspired by socio-economic management, providing a common language (Savall, Zardet, 2011). Everyone now uses the same tools, which allows the sharing and fluidity of information transfers within the group.

The dynamic of collective value creation has been achieved above all through the involvement and empowerment of employees. This has been possible because the company's governance has succeeded in establishing a clear line in terms of management and operations. The socio-economic approach to management has served as the backbone of the organization to build its own managerial method. It is not a question of imposing a methodology, but of involving each decision-making sphere of the company in the construction of tomorrow's operation. Where each company had built its own management system, the definition and dissemination of a common company management method was a decisive factor in creating value.

The main challenge was to create humanization in the company, while keeping in mind that the company is composed of profit centers. To do this, sharing and listening to employees has taken on a more important and professional role. It was determined in which framework the listening is done: With whom? With whom? When? How long? To tell each other what... This is a real break with the old habits of an oral culture where people had the feeling that they were talking to each other, without anything coming out. In this new framework, rules continue to emerge, but they are explained and linked to the profit center. The actors are made aware of the economic aspects of the company, while remaining in discussion and negotiation (Savall, Zardet 2011). Each employee is made responsible for the functioning and treatment of dysfunctions, while understanding the social and economic impacts.

The creation of value depends above all on the involvement of employees in this process. Nevertheless, it cannot be decreed. Indeed, we have already discussed the interest of employees in their work, which is a determining factor. By restoring meaning and responsibility, employees understand that they are the main actors in value creation. It is not just a matter of responding to a position or a job description, but to the challenges of the business. Also, by giving meaning to the activities, everyone understands that they are part of a value creation chain. When everyone understands their role and the interest of their missions, a dynamic is created, areas of responsibility become areas of innovation and performance improves both economically and socially.

If the first argument that often comes up when it comes to attracting talent is the salary or related benefits, it is now a question of the meaning of work. The principle is to consider that if an employee, new or not, knows the direction of the company and the meaning it wishes to give to its actions, he is all the more reassured and stimulated. All this is structuring for a newcomer who then understands better that he can count on the others, because they too are part of a collective company dynamic, carrying meaning. Successfully positioning them in a common project while giving them meaning is an interesting key.

Finally, the creation of value has gone through a stage of collective awareness of untapped sources of socio-economic performance (Savall, Zardet, 1987, 1992). It is not simply a matter of asking each person what dysfunctions they feel or perceive, but of highlighting the collective responsibility in the way they are identified and dealt with. After having listened to everyone in individual or group interviews, they were asked to quantify the impacts of the dysfunctions, called hidden costs. From then on, new possibilities for decision-making were offered to the observed perimeter. All actors are able to detect these sources and implement concerted solutions to address them. A monitoring and steering system will be put in place to ensure that dysfunctions do not reappear or that they are brought under control.

Through this collective awareness and professionalization in the identification and treatment of dysfunctions, the company has gently succeeded in creating an improvement dynamic that is growing as individuals become more involved.After two years of work, the company's goals are on track, as sales turnover has improved from 68% in 2019 to 61% in

2020. The company has gained one point of customer satisfaction in one year (measured thanks to an innovative system), knowing that 1 point of increase in satisfaction is equivalent on average to 3 points of revenue gained.

CONCLUSION

Two issues seem important for the future of this company.

Firstly, it is necessary to succeed in getting people to accept the change. As the perception of the speed of change is different from one individual to another, everyone wonders about this speed. The tempo that management wishes to give to change can also be a re-thinking of its strategy. If a skill is determined by a deadline, a level of quality, a degree of autonomy and a budget, then the speed of change is a collective skill of the company. It must therefore master this, without abandoning anyone. Experience has shown that a change process must be maintained until a milestone is reached, where the change takes hold and grows exponentially.

Secondly, proximity management must be created and maintained. Taking care of employees cannot be decreed, it must be accompanied, by training the actors, while accepting the victories and failures. Integrating this issue into a strong political and strategic vision allows us to keep the right direction, otherwise, at the first obstacle, everything that has been put in place falls apart and the efforts made are in vain.

CHAPTER 24

INDEPENDENT LEADERSHIP AND SHARED GOVERNANCE

Jean-Claude Pénicaud-Tesson, Mireille Tesson-Pénicaud, and Yann Goudy

ABSTRACT

The managerial transformation of a company in the retail sector, in a movement of independent leaders, resulting from co-optation and linked together by professional sponsorship, is a complex and exciting process. It obliges the volunteer leaders to make a lasting commitment, in particular, to new management practices and to a change in the way the hierarchy works. The virtues of this transformation (a less solitary experience of management, an increase in the "competence – autonomy" of the different levels of the hierarchy and a measured and relevant acceleration of decision-making) are quite quickly perceptible and sustainably consolidate the company.

As managers of an independent company under the E. Leclerc banner, we experience the passion of entrepreneurship and the loneliness of the company manager on a daily basis. The E. Leclerc movement presents structural specificities that orchestrate these two dimensions of a manager's life. The experience of a new management approach, in our opinion, in the retail sector, has transformed our own perception of our role and our posture, and has had an impact on all our companies.

1 THE STRUCTURAL AND ORGANIZATIONAL ORIGINALITY OF THE E.LECLERC INITIATIVE

For more than 50 years, the E.Leclerc movement of independents has integrated men and women from all walks of life and all backgrounds. It gives them free use of the E.Leclerc

SEAM Treatise, pages 235–241

brand and the opportunity to access the full and complete governance of a store whose economic and technical viability has been validated.

1.1 Requirements Expected of a Member

Historically, only three main requirements are the counterpart of this integration into the E.Leclerc movement:

1. Respect of a low-price policy on the site concerned, evaluated via a periodically measured indicator (called OPUS)
2. Implementation of a profit-sharing and a participation of the employees in the results of the company (25% of the results distributed annually)
3. Active participation in the life of the movement by contributing to the work of regional, national and, in recent years, international workgroups.

In addition to these historical requirements, there is now a commitment to participate in training, to sponsor future company managers (future members of the brand) and a strong commitment to "increased compliance" with all regulatory constraints, in terms of the overall quality of the companies, particularly in terms of hygiene and health safety.

1.2 From the First Steps of a Young Manager to Managerial Emancipation

The first steps:

As E.Leclerc members, we are "co-opted" and supported throughout our journey in the movement, by a group of 4 to 5 "sponsors," E.Leclerc members themselves. This support is both human, by helping us to assimilate the culture and values of the movement, and commercial, by providing integrated and continuous training in our specific businesses and economic, by guaranteeing our initial loans. It contributes to securing the manager's first steps in the company, but also to cultivate specifically, with the manager, a sharp vision of his local independence (in the management of his site on his territory) in the service of the collective performance of the company at the national level, by consolidating the individual performances of each store. It is this permanent balance between local independence and capacity for action, on the one hand, and interdependence accepted at regional and national levels, on the other, that characterizes the company and obviously contributes to its atypical performance compared to its competitive environment.

The sharing of experiences is activated and maintained throughout the year at the regular rhythm of professional, technical and human exchanges, which punctuate the missions assumed, either at the regional level (regional purchasing centers), or at the national level (national structures: Galec, Scamark, Siplec and others).

On average, each member spends two days a week at the national level and one day at the regional level. It can be noted that although this time is not paid, it is a source of learning and that this absence from our companies frees up the space necessary for new entrepreneurs to emerge. The member thus has the mandate of the company (or of the region to which he/she belongs), and therefore the full responsibility of committing the company or its regional central office, to carry out, on behalf of the community, missions either to negotiate commercial agreements on a category of products, or to carry out business development projects (new markets, digitalization of the offer, etc.), or to ensure the management of national support functions (marketing, information technology, logistics, communication, publishing, etc.). Our organization has three original characteristics:

- The mandate entrusted to a member chosen for a specific area, on behalf of the community of members: his legitimacy comes from this mandate to be a representative of the company, credible and respected by his interlocutors (suppliers, service providers, third parties, etc.). At the same time, by committing the entire company through his decisions, the member, thus mandated, is obliged to continuously "self-check" his actions, in the service of the collective cause and under the indirect but permanent control of all his peers. In fact, since every decision taken at the national or regional level is intended to have an effect on the site of each store, all members potentially become the "customers who benefit or fall victim" to the decision of their peer. This informal but ultimately permanent de facto control is highly effective and has proven its relevance for several decades.
- A successful local initiative in an E. Leclerc store is always a source of innovation for the company and often the reason for a deployment that is easier to organize and more easily accepted by the managers of other stores in the company. As a remarkable example, the E.Leclerc "drive" was first tested and experimented on a local site before being approved by the company and proposed for deployment throughout the territory... But the decision is never imposed, it always remains at the initiative of the members on their site.
- The impetus and the accepted pooling of resources at regional and national levels is the permanent and lasting counterpart of the real independence of the manager on his site. The power of action that results from the pooling of resources (e.g., commercial negotiation, homogeneity of pricing policy, convergence towards good business practices, communication) ensures the movement's lasting cohesion, particularly in situations of crisis or tension in our competitive environment.

Thus, successful disruptive innovation is most often bottom-up (from local to national). Conversely, internal regulations, standards, communication and pooling are essentially top-down, from national to local.

It is in this context that the management of our stores is organized around an incessant back-and-forth between local initiatives, regional or national recommendations and/or prescriptions, sharing of experiences between colleagues, continuous adaptation to the avalanche of evolving standards (commercial, social and societal, financial and accounting, environmental and sanitary), external competitive stimuli and internal pressures from employees and time.

We can see here, without a doubt, a great proximity to the concept of synchronized decentralization (Savall and Zardet, 1995), which articulates the entrepreneurial initiative of the members and the national or regional synchronization of certain activities and policies relating in particular to purchasing, communication, information system tools and business software.

Through the diversified missions, repeated sharing and experiences at the three levels of involvement in the movement, the E.Leclerc member has the perception of acquiring an entrepreneurial "thickness," reinforced by the periodic reassurance offered by the positive, often agreed and politically correct evaluations of his sponsors and peers. In fact, just like a successful career in the administration, the experience acquired over the course of the missions in the company ends up making the member reach, "unwillingly" and with the benefit of age, the status of "baron" of the movement. This status often reflects more than a real increase in entrepreneurial skills, an insidious gentrification in the practice of the leader's power, lulled by the protection of the power of the brand. Since performance is often good, it is difficult for the manager to question himself or herself. The lack of ambition is a threat and the level of expectations declines proportionally.

This is where the loneliness of the entrepreneur is experienced, despite the environment of the sponsorship, the colleagues and the company. It is here that the fundamental question of the practice of the leader's power arises. It is here that the mutation towards a new approach may begin.

1.3 Towards Managerial Emancipation

In the retailer, the power to manage the company is often embodied by the member-manager, or the couple of member-managers, and it can easily and comfortably become very solitary, by adopting a classic scheme of a pyramidal organization with 5, 6 or even 7 hierarchical levels, in strict and zealous application of the statutory provisions of the collective agreement for the activity of large-scale retailing (cf. Figure 1).

To get out of this pre-written and ultra-majoritarian scheme in our sector can only be the result of the meeting between a chance and a conviction:

- The chance is that of being in a movement of real independent entrepreneurs where risk-taking, initiatives and local experimentation are always possible and even encouraged, as long as they respect the fundamentals of the movement in terms of its social and societal utility, both internally and externally
- The conviction is that of the independent manager who, becoming aware of the opportunity offered by this independence, decides to exploit it to rethink the comfortable organization of his company.

2 OUR EXPERIENCE OF THE SOCIO-ECONOMIC APPROACH TO MANAGEMENT

The conditions of the "crime" having been met, the act of this managerial emancipation only depends on the choice of the weapon of the crime: a project, a target, a method and actors.

- A "shifted" project: dare to manage and steer your company differently, reverse the order of things, no longer think of the result as an end in itself but as a result of the actions that precede it and that indirectly contribute to its achievement.
- A "simple" target: the "real" satisfaction of the customer as a common objective shared by all the actors of the company. The slogan is to make every daily action of every actor in the company an act that contributes, directly or indirectly, to the continuous improvement of the quality of the customer experience.
- A method: an authentically rethought management approach based on a new balance between economic and social performance (Savall et al., 2015)
- A commitment: to create the conditions for each employee of the company to be able to take responsibility and gain autonomy within the scope of their mission. (Pénicaud-Tesson, 2020; Goudy, 2020)
- Actors: all the company's employees.

Such a rethink is necessarily the result of a chaotic path between the multitude of so-called "breakthrough" managerial approaches that have been experimented with and relayed by an abundant literature. As is often the case, it is by sharing with another company director, in whom we have confidence, and who has tested a differentiating practice for himself and in his company, that we can find the reference framework on which to rely. In this case, it is the socio-economic management approach deployed by an industrial group in the food industry for more than 30 years in partnership with ISEOR (Savall, 1975; Savall and Zardet, 1987), which finally convinced us to initiate a process of change in managerial approach.

The setting in motion and the metamorphosis can only be implemented by the "top" of the company. It is the leader who must drive and illustrate the dynamics, the breakthrough, the change in practice to make the commitment to a new human management practice in the company credible and visible in the eyes of the entire team. Words are nothing if actions do not follow.

2.1 Transforming the Role of the Solitary Leader

Launching a disruptive innovation also generates loneliness for the leader, especially in a movement such as ours, where you have to prove yourself in order to convince others, often within a very short timeframe.

To illustrate this point and by way of example, one of the founding acts of change in our two companies was to rethink the practice of solo decision making by the manager. This ambition is very symbolic in companies where the leader is often perceived as holding "absolute" power, difficult to challenge, and deriving its legitimacy from its endorsement by its peers, who are themselves considered to be the historical referents of the movement.

In fact, the historical practice of decision-making in an independent supermarket can be summarized as follows (see figure 1): the manager, known as n°1, relies very classically, in a proven hierarchical scheme, on a director, known as n°2, who passes on in a direct or indirect line to the heads of departments (n°3) and/or departments (n°4) the instructions, instructions and arbitrations taken from the manager, who in fine pass them on to their employees. This "rake" organization is finally well accepted by both the second manager, who is satisfied to be the centralizing point of power in the eyes of his or her n–1s, and by the n–1s, for whom the existence of a single referent, who is not very intrusive because he or she is not very available, is quickly perceived as a comfort, resulting in a low risk of being really challenged

To complete the description of the initial organization, we should add the existence, in parallel to the relationship between the No. 1 and No. 2, of a regular activity between the No. 1 manager and his colleagues responsible for the main support functions (Finance, Human Resources, IT and Marketing, Quality and Customer Relations). The managers of the support functions operate in a direct and bilateral relationship with the manager and, in fact, occupy a position of No. 2 bis, No. 2 ter, etc., within their scope of responsibility. For the manager, this "juxtaposed pairing" also cultivates for each member of the pair (manager and head of a support department) the perception of a privileged direct relationship, often perceived as rewarding, with the manager. In the end, this organization is experienced as relatively comfortable by all the actors,p but ends up establishing a routine that does not motivate them, where ambition and the questioning of practices only exist very occasionally.

Based on this observation, after a horizontal dysfunctional diagnosis based on interviews with No. 2, No. 3 and No. 4 and group work with the same managers, the manager discussed with his front-line contacts, all the No. 2s, and decided to set up a collaborative space between the actors involved at the first hierarchical level, called without originality "management committee" or by shortening "Codir." This ex nihilo creation was accompanied by a profound upheaval of the historical organization chart, but also by new collective practices of communication-coordination-cooperation and, above all, of decision-making.

In one of the two cases of companies that we manage, the management committee is made up of the manager and the manageress (members), the historical director, the financial director, the human resources director and the food sales director. This composition has the particularity of echoing a new organization, in which the historical director of the site has seen the scope of the managers who were previously attached to him drastically reduced to be distributed among the other members of the codir, disregarding the standards of the profession and relying on the perceived competences of the other members of the Codir (Figure 24.1, Après). The objective sought and achieved was to distribute, including numerically, the company's managers so that each member of the Codir could, humanly and materially, ensure a real management of proximity to each manager who was attached to him. Thus, the historical director has gone from having more than thirty managers in the old organization to only five in the new one. At the same time, each member of the codir is now identified in the company as a "management referent," whose role is explicitly described to his or her teams as that of a facilitator-trainer-accompanist and no longer as a hierarchical superior.

The steering committee meets on average every 15 days on an agenda proposed by the manager and added to by the members according to current events. The floor is taken in rotation, and each member is asked to contribute to the final decision. A set of rules has been established to determine which issues are ultimately decided by the CEO after discussion in the Executive Committee, and which are collectively decided and assumed by the Executive Committee, following a debate. This new system has considerably modified the governance of the company and the conditions of communication-coordination-cooperation but also of cooperation.

In both companies, the cards have been reshuffled, and the managerial load of the store manager has been reduced and better distributed between the manager and the members of his management team.

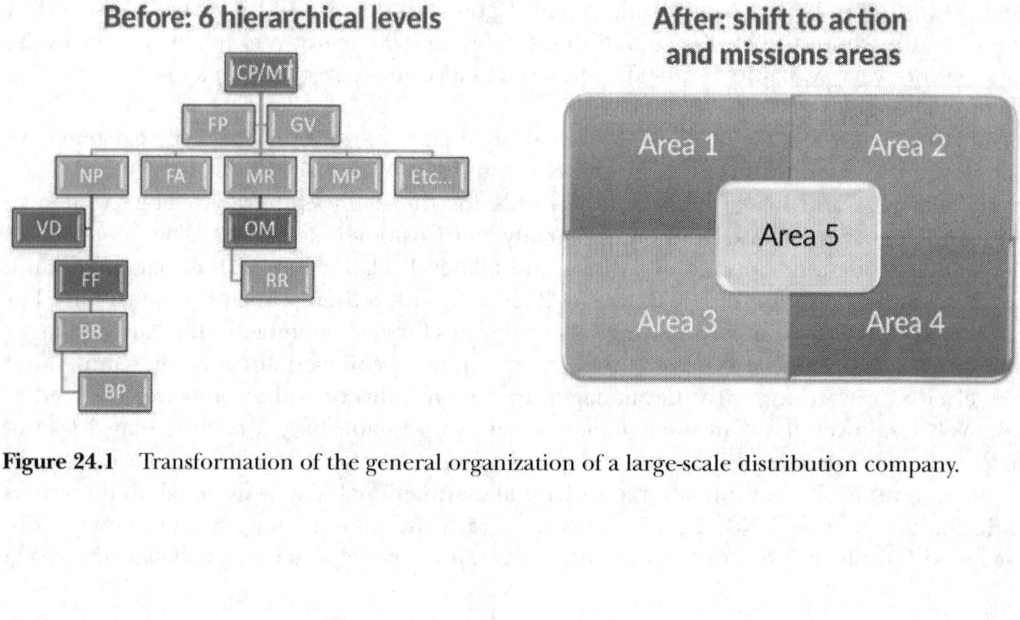

Figure 24.1 Transformation of the general organization of a large-scale distribution company.

2.2 Impact on the Role and Responsibility of the Members of the Management Team

This new mode of cooperation and decision-making allows, over the months:

- A real rebalancing of the perimeters of responsibilities between the members of the management team,
- A coordinated strategic de-multiplication,
- A better alignment on the language and the distribution of information to employees,
- A real acceleration of the communication and implementation of the decisions taken to the concerned actors of the company,
- Increased sharing of skills between members of the management team in their respective specialties,
- A significant increase in the capacity to explore and/or deepen specific or cross-functional projects, through a better distribution of workloads and adapted planning,
- A new, measured transparency of the most sensitive information.

CONCLUSION

This new organization has made it possible to significantly accelerate the implementation of the strategy, but also to improve feedback from employees. This virtuous circle of accelerated exchanges between managers and employees visibly contributes to the increase in skills and initiative of the company's actors. Innovation is of course subject to a real learning curve, which requires vigilance on the part of the manager with regard to his team, in order to organize a real sincere listening and patience with his employees.

The organization of the decision-making process allows the manager to concretely share the management of the company without losing control of it, but more operationally to foster a rise in cohesion and cooperation of his front line. Obviously, this reduces the loneliness of the manager.

REFERENCES

Goudy, Y. (2020). "Metanoia": Transforming the mind of each person to build the company of tomorrow. In H. Savall & V. Zardet (Eds.), *Tétranormalisation: profusion des normes et développement des entreprises* (pp. 240–246). Éditions EMS.

Pénicaud-Tesson, J. C. (2020). Management socio-économique et grande distribution. In H. Savall & V. Zardet (Eds.), *Tétranormalisation: Profusion des normes et développement des entreprises* (p. 233). Éditions EMS.

This page intentionally left blank.

CHAPTER 25

MASTERING GROWTH WHILE SUSTAINING BOTH PROFITABILITY AND HUMAN POTENTIAL

The Successful Challenge of an Agro-Industrial SME in Mexico

Isaac Sanchez, Arturo Guerrero Lizardi, and Véronique Zardet

ABSTRACT

Since 2005, Sánchez Aguacate Hass has relentlessly pursued a growth strategy based on the diversification of its products and markets, and the development of its human potential. The principles and tools of socio-economic management served as tutors to structure this growth, organize the concerted delegation, establish operational and strategic management indicators.

When you are an SME in the local, at best national, market, company growth is perceived as a double-edged sword: of course, it is often associated with increased power of the company in its market and increased profits; but on the contrary, to grow is to risk losing control of the company, and to venture into new and unknown markets. In Mexico, many companies that have internationalized beyond the United States have experienced severe economic difficulties, particularly due to customer defaults. The literature on growth and internationalization does not place much emphasis on the development of human potential (Rastrollo-Horrillo & Martín-Armario, 2019). It focuses on business strategies, distribution networks or creation of subsidiaries. Moreover, socio-economic interventions have shown that strong and poorly controlled growth is often accompanied by sudden increases in hidden costs. Of course, sales are growing very rapidly, but at the cost of lower profitability and value added. However,

SEAM Treatise, pages 243–249

in a situation of high strategic ambition, management team cohesion and concerted delegation between management, managers and staff are the key to internal and external success (Savall and Zardet, 2014).

In 2005, Sanchez Aguacate Hass was marketing its products in the Mexican market. Its leaders had the opportunity to participate in a performance development program led by COMPITE, a business support organization attached to the Mexican Federal Ministry of Economy. This program involved 5 companies and 5 consultants and was led by Drs. Savall and Zardet. It consisted of training, in an inter-company group, of the manager and one or two of his collaborators, an internal consultant and an external consultant for each of the 5 companies. Four one-week training-concertation sessions were distributed over the course of a year, between which a socio-economic intervention was carried out simultaneously in each company by the external consultant, the internal consultant, under the guidance of the manager and his close collaborators (Savall, 1974, 1979; Savall and Zardet, 1987). Sanchez Aguacate Hass was represented by its leader Isaac Sanchez and the external consultant Arturo Guerrero Lizardi. The Socio-Economic Approach to Management served as a springboard for its growth and development.

This chapter summarizes the stages in the implementation of socioeconomic management, traces the growth of the company since 2004 and the structuring that has accompanied it. It then analyzes the main keys to this controlled and profitable growth, emphasizing the continuous development of the company's human potential.

1 COMPANY METAMORPHOSIS

1.1 Brief Presentation of Sánchez Aguacates Hass

The company was founded in 1983 by Don Jesús Sánchez, father of Isaac and Israel Sánchez Mateo, in the state of Michoacán, Mexico. It is a region where the educational level of the population is low, both for personnel and managers. The family business has been involved in four main activities since its inception: growing, packing, transporting, and selling avocados.

In 2005, it had 54 people and no particular vision for growth. Activities were organized on a day-to-day basis, and for several hours a day, some of the employees were idle. There was little synchronization and absolutely no anticipation of activities. The structuring of the company was nonexistent: there was no organization chart, there were no really defined functions, there was only the owner, a buyer, a seller, an administrator and a couple of managers (Sanchez, 2007, 2014). Decisions were made in the morning, without any particular formalization, according to the issues that the leaders had in mind.

1.2 Implementation of the Socio-Economic Approach to Management

Between 2005 and 2020, there are 3 specific stages: the first in 2004 and 2005, during this training-accompaniment of approximately one year, with the support of an external consultant and the intervention and direct support of ISEOR consultants. A second stage, from 2007 to 2013, where the company was mainly supported by the external consultant. Then, since 2014, it has approached ISEOR for additional support from the external consultant, with direct support from him, remotely and in person twice a year. A team of ten internal consultants was formed, which gradually built up, then trained all the company's managers, conducted socio-economic diagnosis in each company entity and helped build improvement projects to reduce dysfunctions (Savall and Zardet, 1987). In 2018, the company organized a 2-day internal colloquium, where many executives, supervisors and internal consultants presented their outstanding achievements, in front of about fifty people.

1.3 Company Growth: Key Figures

1.3.1 Production Growth

Since its inception, Aguacates Sanchez has grown avocados in about ten orchards, totaling 165 ha, some located near the company's offices and others at a significant distance (up to 200 km), requiring truck transportation by personnel. This production has increased considerably in 15 years: from 465 tons per year, production has increased 5-fold, with 2,530 tons in the 2019–2020 cycle. The company has acquired new orchards, which today are not fully exploited for production. This is an investment, given the time needed to prepare the land for the crops.

The business expanded in 2012 into blueberry cultivation. It operated orchards that now represent 25 ha and produce 350 tons per year. Blueberry production generates a commercial margin of 42 million pesos, compared to 90 million pesos for avocados, with half the volume. This illustrates the much higher margin of the blueberry business.

Productivity has increased significantly thanks to the development of internal know-how and the hiring of expert employees trained in cultivation. For example, in 2004, 165 ha of avocado orchards produced 465 t, compared to 2530 in 2020. In 2016, blueberry crops produced 12 t per ha, compared to 14 in 2020 (+ 16%) (Sanchez and Guerrero, 2014, 2018; Zardet et al., 2015).

1.3.2 Growth in Packaging and Transportation Activities

The Packaging Business Unit is responsible for packaging part of the company's own production, another part that is sold to specialized export companies, as well as a significant portion of avocados purchased from local producers. The products are then transported by truck to national or international points of sale. In 2004 the company had 2 trucks, in 2020 it has 13, which provided 2,200 trips. The packaging activity represents about 19,000 t in 2020, 68% is destined for the domestic market, 32% for the international market.

1.3.3 Growth and Diversification of Sales

On a base of 100 in 2004, Empaque's sales volume (in tons) multiplied by 2.36, i.e., an average of +15% per year. This growth is the combination of organic growth in the avocado product line, diversification into blueberries, domestic expansion of its market and a deliberate export strategy. Thus, exports to Canada, the United States, Europe, Japan... and some recent countries now account for ⅓ of packinghouse turnover and generate margins well above the domestic market.

The company has developed its own sales outlets: the 6 branches now account for 23% of the company's turnover. In the last 2 years, it has created two new business units, in the face of persistent difficulties with its suppliers: a packaging box factory and a gas station. These activities, which were initially aimed at vertical integration (supply of fruit packing crates and fuel for trucks), have very rapidly developed their external sales: together, they now represent 17% of the company's turnover and 21% of profits.

TABLE 25.1 Some Key Business Growth Indicators 2004–2020

	2004	2010	2013	2020	Increase rate
Cultivated orchard areas (ha)	100	NC	105	310	× 3.10
Production in tons/ha	100	NC	NC	545	× 5.45
Sales in pesos (whole group)	100	NC	NC	441	× 4.41
Net profit (whole group)	100	249	339	1,255	× 12
Headcount (entire group)	100	655	1,047	2,621	× 26

The overall sales volume of the Sanchez group grew strongly: on a base of 100 in 2004, its turnover increased 12-fold, i.e., an average annual growth rate of 10%.

1.3.4 Growth in Headcount

From 57 people in 2004, the company grew to 680 people in 2020: 430 employees and 250 permanent, stable but intermittent indirect employees who harvest fruit in orchards and are employed by external service providers.

Table 25.1 summarizes the main key magnitudes of this fifteen-year trajectory. It can be seen that the increase in production is mainly due to the increase in productivity per hectare and human productivity. The growth in turnover and net income are significant. The group's overall rate of return has doubled from 5% of sales to 11%. In addition to the newly created activities, the business units that existed in 2004 have also significantly improved their overall economic productivity.

2 PROGRESSIVE STRUCTURING OF THE COMPANY

Starting from a very unstructured company of 50 people, the managers gradually structured the group to organize the activities in the form of 6 semi-autonomous business units, taking on a whole series of operational decisions themselves: orchards, packing, transport, (commercial) branches, box production and gas station.

In addition to the administrative services at the head office, each is headed by a manager, a member of the company's steering group, and has its own management team. A concerted delegation was organized between the group's management and the unit managers, then between each manager and his managers, resulting in a concerted delegation to administrative, commercial and production personnel (Savall and Zardet, 1987). This structuring has been accompanied by the development of professionalism in all areas of the company.

However, this did not prevent difficulties in financing growth. In fact, sometimes extreme ambition almost turned into uncontrolled growth. Growth financing for the purchase of new orchards, the box manufacturing unit and the gas station was done from operating profit flows, sometimes from personal family flows. This has resulted in weak financial liquidity. This investment/fundraising activity was limited to family members and was not shared with the steering group. In 2019, a strategic monitoring diagnostic followed by a project involved all members of this group. From now on, investment decisions and their impacts on cash flow are shared in the steering group, anticipated and better planned.

3 DEVELOPMENT OF HUMAN POTENTIAL AS THE CORNERSTONE OF PROFITABLE MASTERED GROWTH

Since 2004, the company has based its socio-economic development on a stubborn and regular search for dysfunctions and hidden costs, in order to implement socio-economic innovation actions that ensure growth and increase profitability (Guerrero, 2016, 2017), while innovating in terms of technology, products, markets, etc.

3.1 An Integrated and Sustained Training Policy at all Levels

Company owners and unit managers question each other very regularly, to develop their own competencies and get help in organizing the delegation of their multiple operational activities. In fact, the reflex is widespread not to want to delegate or teach, and the training action is a perpetual challenge. Because everyone would like others to think and act exactly as they do, with difficulty in accepting that everyone has their own way of thinking and learning. This is how the company decided to set up an internal school 2 years ago, a real permanent mechanism for identifying training needs, implementing integrated training actions often taken over by the managers themselves – also to develop the skills, autonomy and empowerment of employees. Integrated training has been the lever for growth: the company's general management has been learning to delegate its responsibilities to unit managers, building a management team, to dedicate itself every 6 months to priority strategic projects. This is how the steering group gradually freed up time to organize and structure growth and improved productivity. Gradually and steadily, a nursery of future managers has been built, identifying the key people to be trained, who will be responsible for entrusting them one day with the role of manager.

3.2 Development of Professionalism and Team Well-Being

In 2004, the company suffered from high turnover, low human productivity and a lack of dynamism and employee involvement. Very regular socio-economic diagnoses in the various entities of the company, carried out by the external consultant accompanied by internal consultants, resulted in focus groups, involving management and part of the staff. All these internal dynamics have resulted in important improvements for the personnel:

a. more pleasant physical working conditions: for example, investment in air-conditioned trucks for transporting personnel to the orchards.
b. the generalization of social security for all employees, while only 15% benefited from it in 2004
c. training programs in reading, writing and computer use for staff, with a room specially built for that purpose
d. training actions to develop competencies, increase versatility and people's interest in the job
e. periodic meetings led by local managers in the different units.
f. installation of periodically negotiable activity contracts (Savall, 1979) for all managers and employees, a system of half-yearly collective, semi-collective and indi-

vidual objectives accompanied by a salary supplement representing up to 14% of the basic salary

g. regular promotion of employees to supervisory positions, then to middle management and then to senior management. For example, the manager of the cashier's unit was an assistant accountant only a few years ago.
h. The role of managers has evolved strongly towards a more educational role, listening, setting objectives, preparing and directing priority action plans, implementing actions to reduce dysfunctions. The evolution of their role has been supported by regular training in the practices and tools of socio-economic management.

3.3 Contribution of the Socio-Economic Management Tools

Since 2005, the company has mobilized tools such as the internal external strategic action plan (IESAP) and the semi-annual priority action plans, to outline its growth path and choose actions to succeed in this progression (Savall and Zardet, 1995). On a semi-annual basis, the different units and the group evaluate the rate of compliance with the actions carried out. The priority action plan is the most effective tool in the company to develop and multiply IESAP's strategic axes (Sanchez, 2018).

Individual and collective time management tools have been installed, with the use of agendas for all managers, scheduling sheets by operation, semi-annual activity sheets to identify the allocation of priority time resources of managers. The meetings of the steering group and of the management teams of each unit are real mechanisms for negotiation and decision-making, which are evaluated from one meeting to the next. Concerted delegation fans have been created to help managers who have particular difficulties in delegating to their employees. Synchronization of the six units created in 2012 is now handled by the steering group, which meets every two weeks. Over the past two years, the hourly contribution to the value added on variable costs of each entity and of the group is evaluated monthly by the steering group and leads to decisions to maintain or even improve overall economic performance. Finally, this regular intangible investment for more than 15 years can be seen through the significant contribution of a team of ten internal consultants and one external consultant, whose respective roles are adjusted each year.

CONCLUSION

Sanchez Aguacate Hass has achieved, thanks to an intangible investment renewed every year for 15 years, a socio-economic development strategy that constantly seeks to combine: growth in volume and diversification; domestic market and internationalization; action on hidden and visible costs; productivity and quality. The main levers it regularly mobilizes are the activation of its human potential, to develop technical and managerial skills, to generate new, more responsible and autonomous behaviors, and to organize the delegation of commands to its employees, to take them out of current management operations and to organize strategic actions, to regularly devote time to strategic reflection and to make better informed and more concerted decisions.

REFERENCES

Guerrero Lizardi, A. (2016). L'implantation du management socio-économique dans une entreprise agricole mexicaine en forte croissance. In H. Savall & V. Zardet (Eds.), *Entreprises, valeur(s) et prospérité : le capitalisme socialement responsable.* EMS.

Guerrero Lizardi, A. (2017). Réduction des dysfonctionnements grâce à l'implantation de la gestion socio-économique. In H. Savall & V. Zardet (Eds.), *Innovation commerciale: Tous vendeurs dans les organisations.* EMS.

Rastrollo-Horrillo, M.-A., & Martín-Armario, J. (2019). Organizational barriers to nascent global growth born: Learning from within. *Journal of International Entrepreneurship, 17,* 454–473.

Sanchez, I. (2007). Implantation du management socio-économique et des contrats d'activité périodiquement négociables dans une PME mexicaine. In H. Savall & V. Zardet (Eds.), *L'hôpital élargi.* Economica.

Sanchez, I., & Guerrero Lizardi, A. (2014). Présentation de l'entreprise Frutas Finas Hnos et de la mise en place de la démarche socio-économique. In H. Savall & V. Zardet (Eds.), *La conduite du changement dans les entreprises et organisations.* Economica.

Sanchez, I. (2018). Les réalisations marquantes de l'entreprise avec la gestion socio-économique et le projet de consultants internes. In H. Savall & V. Zardet (Eds.), *La digitalisation apprivoisée: au service de l'humain et de la performance durable.* EMS.

Zardet, V., & Rasolofoarisoa, A. (2015). The challenge of a Mexican SME: Mastering growth and preparing the business transmission. In A. Buono, & H. Savall (Eds.) *The socio-economic approach to management revisited.* Information Age Publishing.

This page intentionally left blank.

CHAPTER 26

HOW TO SUCCEED A POST-DOWNSIZING LARGE-SCALE ECONOMIC RECOVERY

Françoise Goter

ABSTRACT

In the face of economic crises, the use of the Employment Protection Plan (EPS) is frequent but not very conclusive, both on the social and economic levels. Through the study of an intervention-research conducted within a middle size company, this chapter shows that the external environment alone does not explain the economic difficulties of companies and that a large part of the socio-economic performance is internal. This case study also shows how a proactive strategy, focused on hidden costs-performance, constitutes the "foundation" of a deep and sustainable restructuring, and allows for a large-scale economic recovery.

The habits of companies in economic difficulty are not changing much and the recent economic crises show that they are limited to the reduction of their visible costs. The cause invoked by companies to justify their economic situation is marked by fatalism, blaming the market for all its ills (Guyonvarc'h, 2017). Recourse to Employment Protection Plans appears to be the most relevant and efficient solution, with its share of downsizing and relocation. However, numerous studies have analyzed the consequences of such plans and their impact on the recovery of the company. Various perverse effects have been identified (Appelbaum, et al., 1987; Cascio, 1993, Kets De Vries and Balazs, 1997, Mishra, et al., 1998, Mone, 1994; Savall and Zardet, 1994; Mckinley, et al., 1995; Beaujolin and Schmidt, 2012). Among other things, restructurings related to employment protection plans are the source of many hidden costs that are detrimental to the socio-economic performance of companies (Savall, Zardet, 1987, 2015).

SEAM Treatise, pages 251–258

Based on the case of an SME in the French textile industry, this chapter shows how a company in serious economic difficulty can sustainably recover and avoid the deleterious effects of restructuring. The first part presents a state of the art of the main dysfunctions linked to Employment Protection Plans as well as a selection of concepts from the Socio-Economic Theory (THEOSE) (Savall, 1974–1975, 1979; Savall and Zardet, 1987) that explain these difficulties. The second part presents a intervention-research conducted within a SME in great economic difficulty. The third part details the devices and methods of the socio-economic theory implemented in the framework of the intervention-research and presents the results obtained. The fourth part analyzes the mechanisms of what could be a sustainable socio-economic recovery.

1 NEED TO MOVE AWAY FROM RESTRUCTURING FOCUSES ON VISIBLE COST-CUTTING

The literature studies two types of restructuring, "crisis restructuring" that results from economic difficulties and "competitiveness restructuring" motivated by the strategic policies of globalized groups (Beaujolin and Schmidt, 2012). Although their issues are different, their strategies are based on the same principles: reducing visible costs. The strategy according to which economic performance is achieved by reducing costs is almost a "convention" supported by financial ratios and their logic (Bernier-Khedache, 2019). In this logic, restructuring is particularly popular tool for corporate governance. Although restructuring had returned to the "backstage" (Foulon, 2020), each economic crisis brings them back. From an economic point of view, such plans, which are aimed at reducing visible costs, seem to be a sham, with an economic success that masks significant hidden costs. From a social point of view, the consequences are terrible for those who leave the company and those who stay. Working conditions are not very favorable (Guyonvarc'h, 2017) and some develop the so-called "survivor" behavior. Most restructurings result in long and laborious economic recoveries, or even do not allow the company to recover (Goter, Noguera, 2015). Recent studies on restructuring navigate between the theory of the back-and-forth, which claims that we should let nature take its course, and so-called social and solidarity theories, which invite us to frame practices through price correction and universal allocation (Cracco and Ghymers, 2020). Doesn't this research take us back to past socio-economic systems that have shown little effectiveness?

The socio-economic theory (Savall, 1974–1975, 1979; Savall and Zardet, 1987) studies the dangers of reasoning focused exclusively on cost reduction and demonstrates the effectiveness of steering visible and hidden cost-performance. This research, based on the socio-economic performance of companies and on the theory of human potential, seems to imply that company restructuring and traditional job saving plans are counterproductive. The HORIVERT method (Savall and Zardet, 1987), which allows the fundamental principles of SEAM theory to be applied at all levels of the company, seems to constitute a decisive element for a consistent and sustainable economic recovery. The concept of Socially Responsible Capitalism (Savall et al., 2016) would then be an alternative to restructuring as it is currently practiced. In this framework, if the reduction of visible costs is no longer the central element, what are the constituent variables of a vigorous and sustainable economic recovery? This chapter seeks to better understand the mechanisms of the recovery of a company in great economic difficulty and to identify the variables of action that will allow a real and sustainable socio-economic recovery to be achieved.

2 ECONOMIC DIFFICULTIES LINKED TO AN ACCUMULATION OF UNSUITABLE MANAGERIAL PRACTICES

The case selected for this chapter is a French family business founded in 1951 that designs, manufactures and sells sun protection fabrics. Its clientele is mainly professional (B to B) and composed of sun blind fitters. In 2005, the three managers, children of the company's founder, decided to sell the company to a large international group, world leader in sun protection with factories in the United States and France, and a distribution subsidiary in Australia. In 2007, the Group bought one of its biggest historical competitors (150 people), located a few kilometers away from the company and having several technologies, including an identical one. These two entities found themselves in great economic difficulty following the global crisis of 2008, and linked to a notorious overcapacity that followed, as well as to the growing obsolescence of a production tool on a technology that was not "core business." The buoyant niche market gradually turned into a commodity market. The arrival of a large number of competitors has led to a significant drop in prices. In 2 years, the sales turnover of the two entities fell by 60% for one of them and by more than 30% for the second. A first downsizing plan was carried out at Christmas 2008. The company went from 300 people to about 230. Several factors made the situation difficult: (a) cumulative losses over the last three financial years; (b) almost total financial dependence on the Group; (c) several major legal disputes with risks of several million euros; (d) few fundamentals in terms of working methods.

In 2009, the company recruited a new salaried CEO and asked him to turn the company around. The two entities, which had been competitors for over 30 years, had to learn to work together. After analyzing the possible synergies, the Group decided to centralize all existing support services in the unit that was first acquired. At the time of the launch of the Socio-Economic Intervention in April 2010, the company's cumulative financial losses amounted to 19 million euros. The administrative and financial, commercial and human resources directors of the time, as well as the historical shareholders, left the company. The two factories were aging due to the lack of innovation and the poor renewal of the production tool (premises and technologies). Despite the painful restructuring (66 people out of more than 300), the staff did not take the measure of the seriousness of the company's situation. Six to eight months after taking office, the manager realized that he would not be able to turn the company around on his own and wanted to initiate a socio-economic intervention. The manager knew about the socio-economic approach to management through a previous company in which he had had responsibilities about ten years before.

At the beginning of the socio-economic intervention, a horizontal diagnosis carried out with the management and the supervisory staff, followed by a focus group on the same perimeter, allows to do away with an elitist and unsuitable managerial practice. The report shows a lack of anticipation and vigorous decision-making in a severely deteriorated economic context, an abundance of resolutions that are difficult to program due to a lack of collective arbitration of priorities, planning and organization of activities. The company suffered from a lack of unity of command and a lack of authority. The absence of communication-coordination-cooperation (3C) mechanisms, as well as a significant compartmentalization at all levels, was noted. Everyone works without being concerned about the quality of the final product. Vertical diagnoses and focus groups were carried out in the four departments of the company. 80 interviews were conducted with management, employees and staff representatives. The dysfunctions and hidden costs identified were numerous. They highlight economic "haemorrhages" (Table 26.1) which would not have been detected via visible costs and show the inefficiency of a downbsizing carried out in the emergency of a reaction to a crisis situation,

TABLE 26.1 Summary of Hidden Costs Calculated by Sector and by Year in 2010

Diagnosed departments	Amount of hidden costs per person and per year	Number of employees in 2009 (Fulltime Equivalent)	Overall amount of hidden costs
Sales, Marketing, and R&D	€ 44,600	29.1	€ 1,300,400
Support services	€ 88,800	25.36	€ 2,251,900
Plant A	€ 35,900	112.4	€ 4,043,700
Plant B	€ 32,400	49.3	€ 1,602,100
Total	**€42,500**	**216.16**	**€ 9,198,100**

very costly and not backed up by rigorous socio-economic managerial practices (Goter, 2011). Between 2010 and 2011, the last two managing sons decided to retire.

3 MECHANISMS FOR A SUSTAINABLE SOCIO-ECONOMIC RECOVERY

Following the presentation of the diagnosis results, a "task force" operation was launched: the objective was to recycle as many hidden costs as possible into value added, euro by euro. Economic balances are carried out in the majority of departments, for any investment request made by a manager. More than 30 variable bonuses have been eliminated. K€ 900 of paid leave and modulation arrears have been cleared in the accounts. A bonus for employees has been introduced, through the use of the periodically negotiable activity contract (PNAC). Previously, only management staff benefited from a bonus system. Major investments in the modernization of the industrial tool (core business) and a significant improvement in working conditions have been made.

Despite multiple socio-economic innovation actions (Table 26.2), the damage caused by several years of economic crisis necessitates coupling the improvement of managerial practices with a 2nd downsizing. Between 2012 and 2013, the company went into receivership, refocused its strategy and adjusted its workforce from 220 to 144 people. One of the two factories in the process of becoming obsolete was closed, but the commercial potential was preserved thanks to the implementation of external solutions while keeping the know-how. This 2nd restructuring has been managed with the help of tools such as competency grids (CG) in order to avoid the departure of key skills. The indicators produced following the implementation of the socio-economic log-book (SELB)tool have progressively brought to light cases of serious professional disloyalty. The implementation of the Internal and External Strategic Action Plan (IESAP), the PAPs and the PNACs has been ritualized through a semi-annual strategic seminar. A new production work organization based on the principles of the Socio-Economic Organization was implemented in 2013. It provided for an Integrated Manufacturing Manager, Coordination Committees to decompartmentalize teams vertically and horizontally, and the deployment of local management.

In 2016, a social laboratory was set up in response to the outcry from staff when qualifications were introduced as a result of the regulatory obligation to comply with the revision of collective agreements, in this case the textile one. This system deepens the strategy of synchronized decentralization of skills management initiated by the new CEO. The GC tool has been repositioned at the heart of management and integrated training sheets have been produced in all sectors where process improvement was required. In 2017, a socio-economic assessment of the improvement actions carried out from 2010 to 2016 was deployed

TABLE 26.2 Main Results for the Period 2010–2014

Improvement in the quality of the products	• Reduction in customer claims. • Increase in foreign sales and better budget achievement. • Reduction from 80% to 30% of non-conforming products • Improved operational quality
Improvement of the quality of functioning	• Reduced average response time for customer complaints to 37 days • Improved management quality • Improved productivity without having to hire or replace some departures • Implementation of technical support in customers, a product manager • Reduced waste and recycling of some packaging • Positive response to the request for authorization to operate a 3rd production line • Modification of the main plant to physically integrate a manufacturing stage that was, for historical reasons, located outside the plant, in another very small building, and thus to have complete control over the quality of the product • Progress in the collective risk taking related to industrial and commercial forecasts • Renovation of the quality assessment and implementation of Quality Committees
Improvement of the quality of management	• Better procurement negotiations, creation of less costly chemical formula, and implementation of supplier quality assurance. • Improved quality of PAPs and PNACs, better distribution of key project management, increase in the rate of achievement of actions, development of cohesion around the Management Priority • Better quality of steering thanks to the PAP, Competency Grids and log-books • Establishment of a proximity management in one of the workshops • Mitigation of the effect of a "historical barony" in a production workshop

to re-energize the teams. Training sessions were conducted to strengthen managers' skills. Managerial relays have been set up in the main workshop to improve proximity management. In January 2018, a product manager function was again introduced. It is not fully functional, but it allows for the detection of major dysfunctions in the customer request management process and to take into-account changes in the various legislations impacting the business. The company has had difficulty avoiding reporting-type systems and focusing on management indicators. Nevertheless, relevant local management indicators and a simple and rapid method of interpreting the indicators provided were developed. Short-interval activities allowing coordination up to three times a day in the workshops, which operate on a 24/7 basis, have been set up. A new and particularly innovative role, that of Director of Human Potential Development (DDPH), was created in 2019.

The qualimetric approach (Savall, Zardet, 2004) of the evolution of the company's performance (Figure 26.1—Discontinuation of unprofitable activities, increase in productive potential, outsourcing of high-potential activities) shows a very clear economic recovery between 2008 and 2014, which intensifies between 2015 and 2020, allowing the company to be the European leader on its market. The combination of a graphical representation of the company's economic performance with the key achievements shows that the results obtained are not the result of chance and that they are linked to the relevance of the decisions made and the effectiveness of the efforts made by all. The economic gains achieved were mostly redistributed in salaries and used to finance investments.

The company's Hourly Contribution on Value Added on Variable Costs (HCVAVC) has increased from €38.92 in 2009 to €61.87 in 2019, an increase of 59% in 10 years. Over the same period, the 13% decrease in the number of full-time equivalent employees (FTE) masks a very marked increase since 2014. So much so that the company is on track to return to its 2009 FTE level.

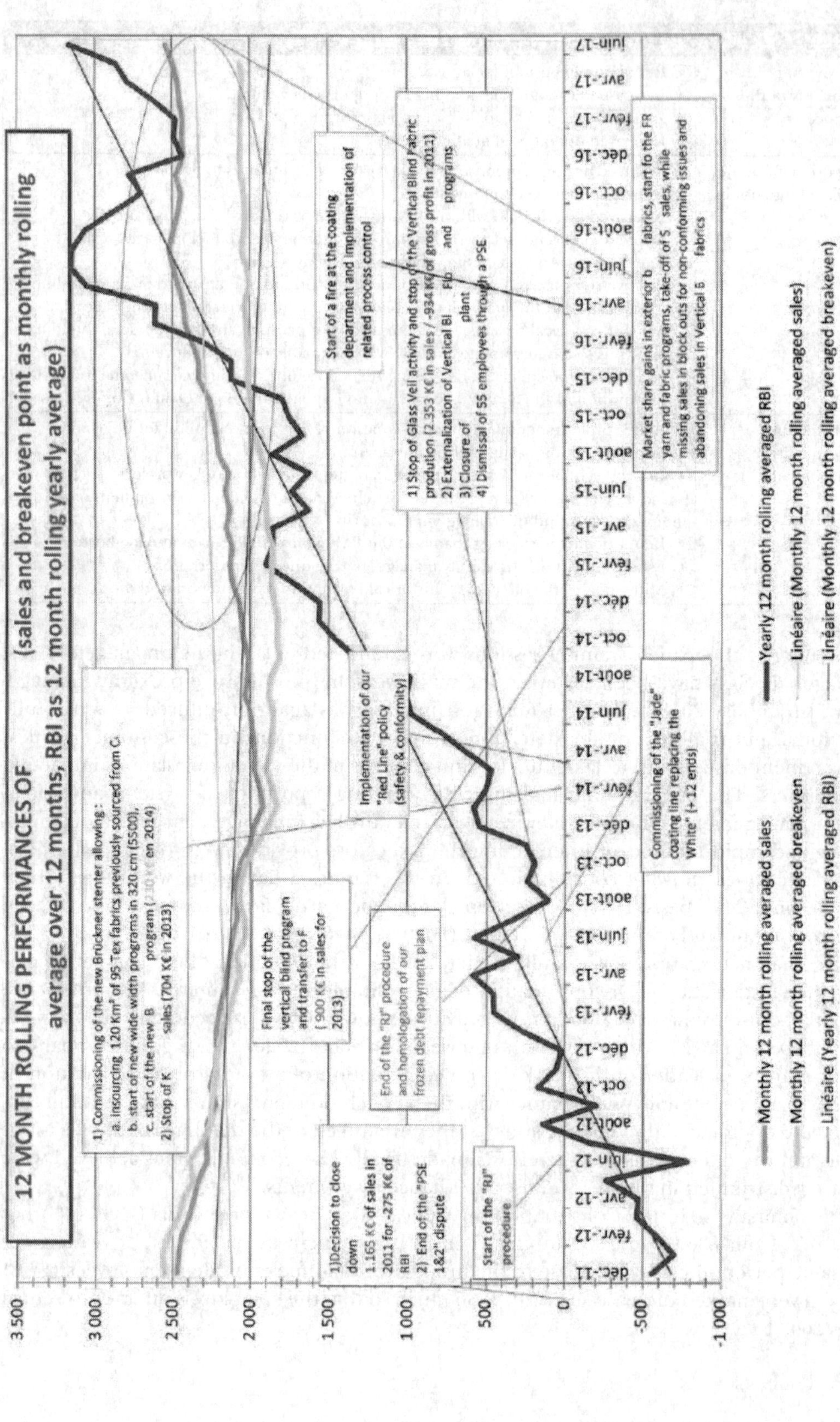

Figure 26.1 Company performance over 12 months.

Hourly contribution to value added on variable costs from 2010 to 2019 and percentage change

2009	2010	2011	2012	2013	2014	2015	2016	2017	2018	2019
38.92	34.53	38.85	41.83	47.14	53.68	55.39	55.73	60.02	61.36	61.87
—	–11%	13%	8%	13%	14%	3%	1%	8%	2%	1%

Number of equivalent full-time employees and percentage change

2009	2010	2011	2012	2013	2014	2015	2016	2017	2018	2019
216.4	215.1	221.3	198.4	142.6	148.2	158.4	163.2	166.59	177.07	188.71
—	–1%	3%	–10%	–28%	4%	7%	3%	2%	6%	7%

The return on intangible investment in qualitative human potential development (IIQH-PD, Savall and Zardet, 2014) for this company was calculated. Over the period 2010–2017, the overall rate of return on such an intangible investment is 65% and the company recovered the intangible investments made in 1.5 years.

4 MAIN LESSONS ON THE ECONOMIC RECOVERY OF COMPANIES

The socio-economic results of the studied company show a deep and sustainable growth. The two downsizings generated radically opposite effects. The first one, based mainly on usual criteria, did not allow the company to improve its results in depth. The second one, based on the tools and methods of the socio-economic approach to management, led to a whole series of improvements in managerial practices, operations and product quality. Unlike the first downsizing, the working conditions and working atmosphere following the second one are appreciated by all the teams.

It is not a particular strategic decision that allows the economic success of the company. It is the accumulation of a multitude of internal socio-economic innovation actions in various sectors and on a diverse scale that generates sustainable performance. The company has moved from a passive external strategy to a proactive internal-external strategy with the mobilization of its human potential throughout the socio-economic intervention, the leader has shown great courage and tenacity to fight against resistance to change and reductive economic reasoning. On several occasions, he put the company in "battle order", notably when it was sued for counterfeiting and during the health crisis. The tools and concepts of the Socio-Economic Approach to Management Model (SEAM) allow for an "elevator" between the different strata of the company, each actor better understanding the company's strategy and its contribution.

CONCLUSION

Restructuring action plans are considerably more effective when legal criteria are combined with rigorous socio-economic management practices. If the leader and the teams take the measure of the problem and the ideas are transformed into decisions and then into actions, the concepts of hidden costs-performance and shared requirements presented in the socio-economic theory allow a company to recover economically. The simultaneous implementation of the tools and concepts from the socio-economic approach to management avoids the perverse effects of restructuring. Finally, the case studied leads us to propose a new strategic practice for companies in great economic difficulty that would not lead to a restructuring of the company but rather to its reconstruction.

REFERENCES

Beaujolin-Bellet, R., & Schmidt G. (2012). *Les Restructurations d'entreprises.* La Découverte.

Bernier-Khedache, S. (2019). Le pilotage des effectifs: Une lecture conventionnaliste de la coordination entre fonctions contrôle de gestion et RH. *Revue française de gestion,* 31–49.

Buono, A. F. (2003). SEAM-less post-merger integration strategies: A cause for concern. *Journal of Organizational Change Management, 16*(1), 90–98.

Cracco, E., & Ghymers, C. (2020). Towards a sustainable economy through solidarity and responsibility: The opportunity presented by the 2020 crisis. *Management 2000, 6*(6), 183–211.

Foulon, S. (2020). The virus, gas pedal of restructuring. *Alternatives Économiques, 12*(12), 6–6.

Goter, F., & Noguera, F. (2015). Economic recovery: From company restructuring to company reconstruction. In A. F. Buono & H. Savall (Eds.), *The socio-economic approach to management revisited: The evolving nature of SEAM in the 21st century* (pp. 133–153). Information Age Publishing.

Goter, F. (2011). Le redressement vigoureux d'une entreprise en crise de transition. In H. Savall & V. Zardet (Eds.), *Réussir en temps de crise: Stratégies proactives des entreprises.* Economica.

Guyonvarc'h, M. (2017). Performants... et licenciés. Enquête sur la banalisation des licenciements, Rennes, Presses universitaires de Rennes, coll. "Le sens social."

CHAPTER 27

AN ORIGINAL AND EVALUATED EXPERIMENT TO STIMULATE THE SUSTAINABLE DEVELOPMENT OF SOCIO-ECONOMIC PRODUCTIVITY

Philippe Lacroix, Frantz Datry, and Rodolphe Bachaud

ABSTRACT

This chapter presents a concrete application of socio-economic intervention within the Belux subsidiary of the Manpower Group, whose objective is to improve the socio-economic productivity of teams by means of a methodology called "5 stars." This testimonial, co-written with the head of Manpower Group Belux, explains the construction of this method to improve the company's profitability and the involvement of its people.

The ISEOR Institute has been working with the Belgian subsidiary of the American group Manpower, a leader in the human resources services sector, for over ten years. This long-standing collaboration has allowed the construction of ambitious and original projects. This chapter describes the lessons learned from one of them, conducted from 2016 to 2020. What is it about? It is about building an original management methodology, which aims to sustainably increase the socio-economic productivity of teams, and which is based on two working hypotheses. The first recognizes the very high elasticity of human productivity and its high volatility. The second proposes to mobilize human potential as the main and sustainable lever for improving this productivity (Savall and Zardet).

Socio-economic productivity is defined here in terms of its two inseparable components, namely economic productivity per se and improvements in the quality of work life.

SEAM Treatise, pages 259–266

First, we describe the circumstances in which the group found itself and the problems it encountered, in order to develop an appropriate method for acting on socio-economic productivity through managers.

1 HOW TO EFFECTIVELY STIMULATE HUMAN POTENTIAL TO SUSTAINABLY INCREASE PRODUCTIVITY

1.1 Background

Manpower Group Belux is a national subsidiary of the large American group Manpower Group in the temporary employment and human resources solutions market for companies. This group, which is listed on the New York Stock Exchange, is established in 80 countries. The Belgian subsidiary achieves a sales turnover of approximately 330 million euros from a portfolio of more than 4,000 clients. It employs nearly 500 permanent staff, more than 37,000 temporary employees and 800 contractors. Contractors are a category of staff on permanent contracts with Manpower Group Belux and whose entire activity is carried out at client companies, in the context of specialized, high value-added, medium and long-term assignments. The services and products sold by Manpower Group Belux are numerous and grouped under three commercial brands. These are Manpower Enterprise for recruitment and placement services for temporary staff, Experis for the recruitment of permanent staff and contractors in the IT field for training services and Manpower Talent Solutions for human resources consultancy services (MSP-RPO-Coaching).

1.2 Improving Profitability and Developing the Involvement of People

The strategy of Manpower Group Belux is characterized by three main axes: (a) the strategic ambition for the period 2019–2023 is defined by three criteria: an operating profit of more than 6%, a staff engagement rate of more than 70% ("people survey") and a regaining of market share; (b) technological innovation and the digital transformation of work processes. A major investment is underway to transform the customer interface and improve the management of large volumes of data; (c) improving human productivity, operational "discipline" and quality of life at work.

While it is true that productivity is one of the key indicators measured each month by Manpower Group Belux and the group, the latter does not provide the solution for improving productivity levels when they are insufficient. It is therefore up to the Belgian subsidiary to find its own methods for continuously improving productivity.

1.3 Search for Hidden Costs is the First Step in Converting Them Into Value Added

As early as 2012, Manpower Group Belux had experienced the high elasticity of human productivity by discovering its hidden cost pool. Several very in-depth diagnosis made it possible to evaluate more than €16 million in hidden costs, or about €49,000 per year and per person. A first step had been to implement various actions developed in participatory focus groups, the effects of which had allowed a significant conversion of these hidden costs into value added (Lacroix, 2014). Figure 27.1 illustrates the increase in value added produced per hour of work from €62 in 2012 to €72 in 2013. (Datry & Savall, 2015; Datry et al., 2015).

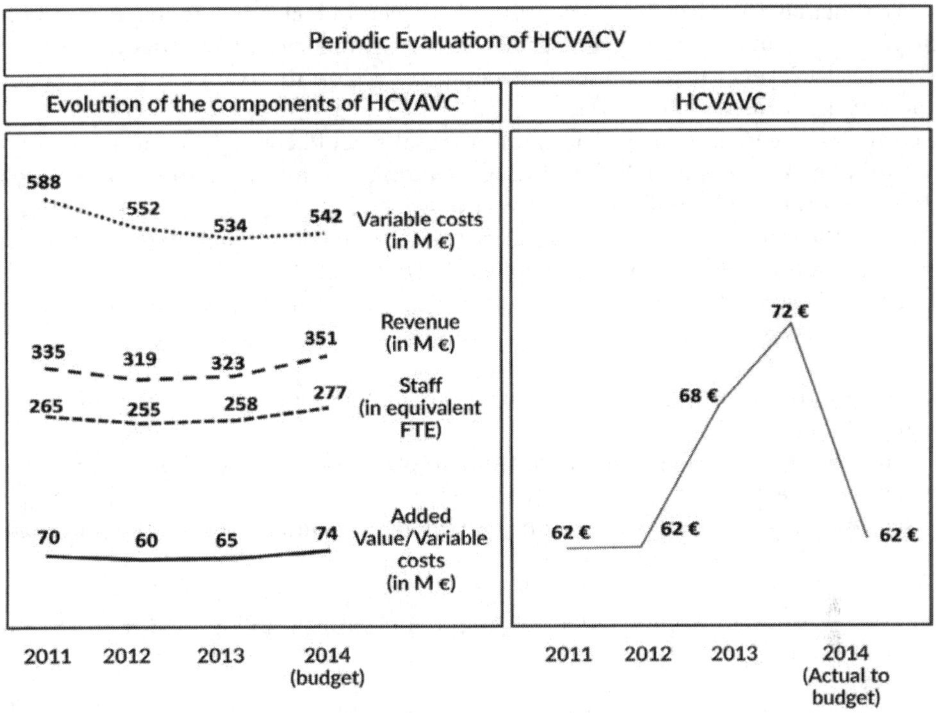

Figure 27.1 Periodic evaluation of the Hourly Contribution to Value Added on Variable Costs: Overall productivity indicator.

However, from the first months of 2014, we diagnosed the limits of some major structural adjustments. Indeed, despite very significant improvements in the functioning of Manpower Group Belux and a real gain in productivity, the latter was stagnating or even falling back with the hardening of the economic context. Competitors seemed to be doing better. Hidden cost sources, which were a source of productivity, were no longer being exploited and the technological changes envisaged in the strategy were likely to deteriorate without profound changes in working methods.

1.4 Getting to the Roots of Human Productivity

We have designed a methodology to activate and validate the hypothesis that sustainable productivity is played out in the control of the hours of activity of the people at Manpower Group Belux. Consequently, the role of management is the major lever for stimulating this productivity. The volume of working hours and their efficiency depend on the quality of team leadership provided by their manager. It is a question of getting to the roots of human productivity, i.e., of taking care of each employee and of all the hours worked by the company.

2 EXPERIMENTING WITH AN ORIGINAL AND EVALUATED METHOD: THE "5 STAR" OPERATION

Our fundamental hypothesis is that the reserves of productivity are considerable. However, the search for productivity does not have a good reputation. Managers are suspected, sometimes with good reason, of seeking productivity at the expense of quality of life at work.

The experimentation carried out responds to a threefold challenge: to achieve sustainable development of human productivity, without deteriorating social performance, at the local level where the levers for truly effective action to develop the company's socio-economic productivity are located (Zardet, Datry, Savall, 2017).

According to a certain managerial tradition, results would come primarily from decisions taken by the top of the hierarchy, according to a top-down logic. On the contrary, we have experimented with an original method that also stimulates a "vertical upward thrust" of results from the smallest organizational units, based on the development and strengthening of the orchestration role of proximity managers (Lacroix, 2020).

Called the "5 star" method, it is a device based on managerial proximity. The system consists of the following stages:

- a diagnosis session to identify the team's dysfunctions and evaluate the corresponding hidden costs
- a mirroring session with the whole team, to present the results of the diagnosis and define some priority improvement themes;
- six sessions to stimulate the team by seeking improvements in work organization practices and business know-how.

These six sessions are conducted according to a rigorous working method based on the following agenda

- Expression of significant achievements and difficulties encountered since the last session: the first step of a session is always to get everyone in the team to talk. The first step in a session is always to have everyone talk. The idea is to give everyone the opportunity to write freely about the positive achievements they have seen since the last session, as well as any difficulties or questions they have. This expression constitutes the living and concrete material of the session. In addition, it warms up the spirits—in the sense of a sports warm-up—so that everyone is present and involved in the meeting;
- Evaluation of previous resolutions: reviewing the resolutions taken during the previous session constitutes a mirror-effect, which has the objective of constantly evaluating the rate of implementation of the micro-actions to be done with clients and internally. This constant evaluation stimulates the team's motricity;
- Hourly contribution to the team's Value Added on Variable Costs: each month, a few synoptic economic indicator curves are projected and commented on in real time by the manager with his team. These indicators are put in front of everyone's eyes at the same time as the expression of significant achievements. Indeed, the challenge is to become aware together, as a team, of the causal relationships between the actions taken and their impact on the team's economic results. The objective is to never dissociate the measurement of economic performance in figures through indicators and the real actions carried out by the people with the customers. This logic is based on the concept of qualimetry (Savall and Zardet, 2004);
- Define the team's priorities for the coming month: each session is a powerful stimulus for developing proactive behavior by the entire team;
- Make resolutions in real time: resolutions are commitments negotiated by each team member with his or her manager. They are mini-contracts, the formalization of which encourages the actors to take action. In addition, this resolution sheet serves as a reminder;

- Schedule actions in real time: scheduling consists of entering the date and duration required to carry out the activities in the agenda. This programming is in fact an initiation to individual and collective time management. It is also a test of the realism of the priorities defined during the session: the objective is not only to make decisions and define priorities, but also to ensure that the corresponding actions can be effectively implemented by the team members.

The different points on the agenda of a team work session constitute reference points for structuring the meeting, without being a rigid framework that would risk drying up the creativity and spontaneity sought in this work methodology.

The 5-Star system provides a practical methodology for leading teams, but it also contributes to transforming the role of managers in the company. They themselves become the bearers of a methodology that they will disseminate within the company to their counterparts. In other words, all managers are gradually becoming a network of facilitators who can support any manager and any team in the company in making improvements, helping to drive change and more generally in bringing new energy to the team dynamic. This role of facilitator is nourished by local and specific experiences. The accumulation of these specific experiences allows the discovery of generic rules of knowledge of management intervention.

This methodology therefore conceals a transfer of intervention engineering in proximity. This transfer of engineering in team leadership is a major lever for the sustainable development of human productivity within the company.

This experiment was carried out on about forty units composed of teams of 4 to 12 people. These units are sales agencies and so-called "support" teams.

3 MANAGING PRODUCTIVITY: THE KEY ROLE OF MANAGERS AND COLLECTIVE LEARNING

After four years of experimenting with this new methodology, we can see its impact on the performance of the teams where it has been implemented. From a strictly economic point of view, the results appear to be robust and sustainable, as the temporary employment agencies have all been making an operating profit for three years now. This shows that they are highly resistant to a socio-economic context marked by increasingly frequent crisis cycles.

The "5 star" operation highlights the central role played by managers in achieving sustainable productivity gains. Indeed, productivity is particularly volatile. Its variations are due to many factors. The intensity of management control is one of the essential factors highlighted in the work of Savall and Zardet (2008), and confirmed here by our field experience.

This intensity of management is defined by three components:

- Stimulation: this is a contribution of energy from managers to their teams aimed at maintaining and developing their involvement and skills. This contribution of energy is achieved through the pedagogy of the managers with their employees: animation of integrated training to improve skills and advice in the execution of tasks;
- the synchronization of activities and people in time and space: the temporal dimension is particularly important here, as the time management of actors in companies is not given enough attention. The planning and programming practices of activities are particularly atrophied with regard to the speed of change;

Expert advice of the L. branch

PIVOTAL IDEAS OF THE MIRROR-EFFECT

- Fragmentation between company departments working in the same facilities
- Deteriorated accommodation, detrimental to working conditions
- Difficult cooperation between ops and consultants
- Overconsumption of time budget for some "retail" clients, exceeding time allotment
- Delayed production of service due to rigid allocation of clients and temporary workers
- Poor management of priorities: the pressure of clients disturbs the weekly work plan, resulting in permanent tight flow
- Piling up administrative processes (clients, time management)

UNSTATED IDEAS

- Incoherent opening hours in the case of a proximity service to clients
- Consultants seem to ignore the margin percentage, even though the 2016 budget objectives are high
- Need to strenghten Ops managerial skills through personalized accompaniment of his/her SOM and/or another Ops
- Lack of local initiatives to organize and sustain cooperation across departments
- Insufficient autonomy of consultants to choose priority activities, which impact pedagogy and teamwork

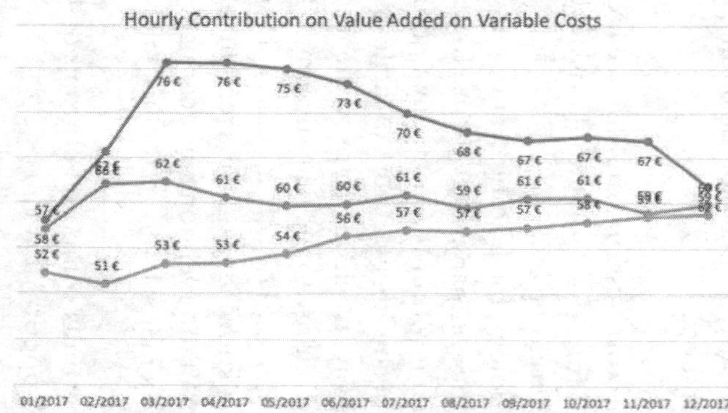

L. Branch

Qualitative results (Organization, management, sales)

- Improved cooperation between Ops and the 3 consultants (more frequent and efficient 3Cs)
- Dividing up hideous tasks among team members (administrative tasks, participation of Ops during over-activity periods)
- Opening hours of the branch 4.5 days per week (speeding up investment management for non-qualified patterns and emergencies)
- Efficient cross cooperation with HORECA local team (welcoming, sourcing applicants for Cora, etc.)
- Daily meeting at 4:00 pm during over-activity periods to prioritize and break tie
- New work organization for Cora (after a 24-hour time to reflection: rotating tandem every other week (each 16 hours per week on Cora while the other one is focused on its JO)
- Ongoing Cora client "education" (heads of departments)
- Lower rate of small clients outside Cora thanks to preventive actions regarding late customers (–2 hours/week)
- One consultant under recruitment
- Foreseen professional evolution of 2 consultants: one appointed Ops on V. and another becoming consultant on P.

Economic results of the branch: above 2015 and beyond budget requirements

- Increase of HCVAVC in January (€ 58 average in 2015) up to €73 in February and € 96 in March
- FTE increase: 58 in January, 73 in February and 100 in March

Evaluation of hidden costs in 2015—Branch L.

1) The hidden costs of job orders account for the other overtimes and non productions of the Ops and consultants and they don't use those time budgets to take care of clients requests. These hidden costs are notsummed up in the € 446,970 amount to avoid overlaping.
2) The breakdown of this hidden cost into the non-production and non creation of potential (50%/50%) considers the conversion of hidden costs into value added.
3) NAD: National Administrative Department

Margin rate	17.9%			HCVAVC		€ 46		
Elementary Dysfunctions	Calculation detail	ECONOMIC IMPACTS						
		Excess salaries	Overtime	Over-consump-tions	Non production	Non creation of potential	Risks	Overall amount
Overall amount		–	€ 265,019	–	€ 33,360	€ 19,950	–	€ 308,320
Equivalent FTEs	4.3	i.e.,	€ 71,700	per person per year				

Hidden costs/Added value on variable cost Ratio = €308,320/€499,206 = 61%

Figure 27.2 Example of a qualimetric evaluation of the socio-economic performance of a sales office.

- the cleaning up: of the organization of work, which has become obsolete with time and changes in the internal-external environment, but also of team leadership practices which tend to lose effectiveness and efficiency.

The control of working hours is becoming a central issue in order to move from the "dream" of converting hidden costs to their effective conversion into value added.

On the strength of this successful experiment, Manpower B&L is now developing a new management policy, the main lines of which are

- steering productivity at its "root": considering that the level of productivity is a function of the efficiency of each hour of work produced by any person in the company;
- Create a consensus within the management team around this issue and develop collective learning from successful experiments;
- develop effective and efficient operational management control practices: forward planning of hours allocated to activities (internal and external products-customers), time scheduling reflex and self-monitoring of time management by each person;
- strengthen the link between managers and management controllers: in particular by drawing up economic balances to measure the impact of the conversion of hidden costs on the creation of value added, i.e., the development of sales and intangible investments in the creation of potential.

Local managers become experts in qualimetry, constantly building links between organizational or commercial actions and the variations in performance measured by the Hourly Contribution to Value Added on Variable Costs.

The generic idea that emerges from this 5-star operation is that generic practices/manipulatives, to be used very frequently, based on experience and observation, are a lever to produce effects on performance. The question of time and recurrence of changes is an important determinant in these results.

Proximity implies that managers, instead of demanding a productivity that would be "natural", get closer to the field to observe very concrete dysfunctions, listen to people, and thus adopt an unusual posture. Indeed, instead of arbitrating and deciding, etc. It is first of all a question of listening and dialoguing, to make participative solutions emerge, which decreases the resistance to change of the employees but also of the managers themselves. Resistance to change on the part of managers is generally expressed by the desire to reuse "solutions" that have already worked, rather than adapting to the situation they are facing; however, the solutions they have already tried and which have given good results, included both the specific and the generic. They need to be helped to extract the generic and then integrate the new specific, which will provide a response based on experience and adapted to the new circumstances.

CONCLUSION

Socio-economic productivity and the involvement of people are directly and permanently compatible. It is the involvement of each person, at all levels, that makes productivity vary. It is essential to find it in all managers, who will then be able to instill it in each individual of their team through management actions. To do this, the manager invests small doses of time, but very frequently, in proximity with his team. It is in this spirit that the 5-Star intervention system was built, which serves both in the short and medium term to find solutions, to recycle hidden costs and thus to improve socio-economic productivity. In the longer term, this system encourages managers to learn an intervention-animation method that can be reused on a daily basis in their managerial practices.

REFERENCES

Datry, F., & Savall, A. (2015). Global-local (GLOCAL) creation of value-added. In A. Buono, & H. Savall (Eds.), *The socio-economic approach to management revisited.* Information Age Publishing.

Datry, F., Savall, A., & Lacroix, P. (2015). Seeking economic resources: SEAM intervention-research case in a Belgian subsidiary of a NYSE listed American group. In Conbere & H. Savall (Eds.), *Decoding the socio-economic approach to management.* Information Age Publishing.

Lacroix, P. (2020). Tensions between upward stimulation and top-down norm production at Manpower Belgium & Luxembourg. In H. Savall & V. Zardet (Eds.), *Tetranormalisation: profusion des normes et développement des entreprises.* EMS.

Lacroix, P. (2014). Socio-economic management in a Belgian company. In H. Savall & V. Zardet (Eds.), *La conduite du changement dans les entreprises et organisations.* Economica.

Savall, H., & Zardet, V. (2014). *Change management in companies and organizations.* Economica.

Zardet, V., Datry, F., & Savall, A. (2017). *Front line management, productivity and development of sales: Implementing SEAM in a publicly traded company.* SEAM Conference Duluth.

CHAPTER 28

LEARNING FROM THE IMPLEMENTATION OF THE SOCIO-ECONOMIC APPROACH TO MANAGEMENT AT LA POSTE

Joseph Gauchard

ABSTRACT

The economic and political evolution led to the evolution of La Poste and its structures in 1990. This led to a reform of the personnel management to take into account the constraints of the environment. The Institute of Socio-Economic Management was chosen to accompany this evolution under the conditions described below.

Joining this project of a treatise on socio-economic management to relate the experience of La Poste is for me to recall what I have implemented and the analyses I have drawn from it (Gauchard, 2016). La Poste, a company from which I am retired, wanted to see its statutory evolution accompanied by a managerial evolution. We will examine, in a synthetic way, the Why, the How and then conclude on the lessons, which arise from this experimentation towards 30,000 agents of the Post Office.

1 BIRTH OF A NEW LARGE PUBLIC COMPANY

The Post Office has always had a hybrid system, due to the reality of its public service missions and competitive activities. This resulted in the existence of a subsidiary budget that operated in the context of public finance until 1990. On that date, the law transformed the

SEAM Treatise, pages 267–272

Post Office from an administration to a company in the form of an "Autonomous Public Law Operator," for three main reasons

a. Users wanted to be recognized as customers.
b. The company, by escaping the context of public finance and the annuality of the budget, was able to project itself into the future and take responsibility for the management of its payroll.
c. Finally, the staff aspired to more creativity.

To this can be added the economic context that led to this evolution, characterized by: increasingly fierce competition, negative productivity and European deadlines that required rapid and continuous adaptation. It should be pointed out that the annexed budget did take care of the needs of the ordinary public service of the Post Office, but not sufficiently those related to its industrial and commercial needs.

After the successful launch of the slogan "Move with the Post Office," the Post Office could move itself. However, this was easier said than done in a company of 300,000 people, heir to a centralized, vertical, hierarchical and Napoleonic organization.

Let's quote some revealing words from the vocabulary of the time:

- Central Administration,
- External services,
- Heads of section,
- Brigade,
- Corps and ranks.

This shows a very administrative, not to say military, character!

Once the reform of the statutes was voted in 1990, it was necessary to tackle the reform of the structures to rebalance the functions towards the operational. In practice, the main structural changes were: the abolition of the 25 regional departments, the creation of 8 delegations by decentralization of the headquarters and the creation of a sub-departmental level, responsible for coordinating economic and employment areas.

This is how the Western Delegation came into being, and I will now present the evolution of its management.

2 IMPLEMENTATION OF THE SOCIO-ECONOMIC APPROACH TO MANAGEMENT AT THE WESTERN

I was personally in charge of the social relations department for the 30,000 postal workers in the West. A series of retreats for managers revealed a strong lack of training in management and economic culture.

All functions were "downgraded":

- Managers were doing supervisory activities,
- The supervisors were executing,
- The personnel functioned according to the Taylorian mode.

The cultural heritage, linked to the administrative aspects of the function, gave pride of place to costs, to the detriment of values and resources. Managers were responsible for their teams, but often by applying the rules at the expense of efficiency. At the same time, a large public debate in 1989 allowed us to find out what the staff thought of their company and its evolution.

Clearly, it was all very average. But a situation is never good or bad, it is what we do with it that makes it good or bad. Based on this, Jean Pichon, the Managing Director at the time, to whom I pay tribute, decided to launch a socio-economic intervention, which he wanted to be overall, rapid and validated by a steering committee. The objective was to obtain more professionalism among managers and to prepare for future changes (Pichon & Gauchard, 1993).

A contractual intervention-research approach was thus concluded with ISEOR. The first step was a training and cooperation program provided by ISEOR for the managers of the pilot sites in Brittany. Then, in the following years, it was extended to the 12 Western Departments through the intermediary of internal consultants previously trained and accompanied by ISEOR. Socio-economic management (Savall, 1975, 1979; Savall and Zardet, 1987) was thus established in the Grand Ouest delegation of La Poste, as a pilot delegation, in cooperation with the French Human Resources Department. At the same time, the diagnosis of the company was launched by ISEOR, with multiple interviews targeting all its levels. Dysfunctions and hidden costs appeared. This socio-economic basis allowed to highlight the internal causes leading to the search for managerial and organizational innovations.

This project was named DETI WEST:

- D for Development,
- E for Efficiency,
- F for Training,
- I for Involvement.

It was a strong strategic and human resources project, which gave me the opportunity to go around the Delegation, crisscrossing and plowing the land of the West, to sow the culture of socio-economic management, as the pilot of the team of internal consultants, which gradually grew to 12 people in a few years (Perret & Gauchard, 1992; Gauchard, 2009)

The certain result of this evolution was the appropriation of a different culture leading to the empowerment of managers through a number of actions:

- The definition of areas of responsibility,
- The provision of new management tools,
- The allocation of project portfolios,
- The transformation of speeches into actions,
- The availability of benchmarks and measurements,
- The contractualization of actions.

At the beginning of 1993 the project was implemented.

I then took responsibility for the Côte de Lumière Group located in Les Sables d'Olonne, along the Vendée coast and managing more than 600 people. I carried out a socio-economic diagnosis and set up the socio-economic management. Very good results have enabled me to regularly consolidate my gross operating surplus and my contribution margin to the company's results. The average increase of 6.8% in revenue over a full year has enabled me to maintain employment in my sector of activity from 1994 to 2000.

It now remains to draw lessons from this implementation.

3 LESSONS OF THE SOCIO-ECONOMIC APPRAOACH TO MANAGEMENT

The less you know what you are going to become, the more you have to say what you want to become."

Such was the climate of a company that wanted to evolve. The aim was to modernize the public service with a view to economic balance and social performance:

- by changing the vision: it was necessary to move from a closed administrative culture to an open economy through competition, because users/customers were becoming volatile.
- by managing time better: mastering time translates into the ability to manage human activity socially, economically or politically (Daniel 2009).

Personally, I have favored three tools for action.

3.1 The Resolution Sheet

It is a simple and efficient way to know who does what and when. Moreover, it allows the person in charge to assert his or her vision, by transcribing what has been agreed or decided. It is also a way to demonstrate one's ability to synthesize, to set an example and to have authority. It is a tool for the short or medium term.

3.2 The Priority Action Plan

If you don't have any objectives, there is no risk of achieving them. The PAP gives a clear vision of the objectives, understood by everyone. It also proves that each manager knows the daily life of the employees in his team. It is a powerful time management tool, an antidote to the age of impatience that prevails today. It is a tool for the medium and long term, integrating the political dimension of the company. When well designed, it gives meaning to work.

3.3 The Competency Grid

This support allows training to be adjusted to the common needs of the personnel and the company. With hindsight, it seems simple. However, as in all large organizations, there were rigidities, silos and layers of paperwork divided into archipelagos, sometimes complemented by conservatism.

My personal experience led me to consider that the major difficulty in a stratified company with multiple branches was the concerted coordination of the whole. It was necessary to weave links, bridges, mediations, all with the codes of social relations that I was in charge of at the beginning.

Moving from a vertical to a more horizontal management style is not so easy. The implementation of Priority Action Plans with multiplier sheets is one of the means (Savall and Zardet, 1995). It is a question of articulating the collective game as well as possible with respect for the individual, like a jazz band, where each musician has his or her share of initiatives in the common game. Rigidity, just like the excess of norms, has never allowed creative autonomy.

Time management becomes another tool, when the agenda becomes a decision-making tool and when the layers coordinate the times and moments of the steering meetings. It was a great achievement for ISEOR, as master of clocks, to succeed in planning these meetings according to an agreed rhythm. This allowed, for example, one of my colleagues to prepare his agenda in December for the entire following year. And it worked!

The fact remains that, in any reform, differences of interest can take precedence over the general interest, which is not or poorly formulated in managerial terms. Faced with this, socio-economic management knows how to give collective meaning to the steering, avoiding the withdrawal into oneself, so easy now in one's virtual bubble. The implementation of managerial innovations allowed a profound redefinition of the way in which the individual thought about his relationship with the group, but also how he understood his work. To illustrate this, I remember the visit I made to one of my managers who asked me to analyze the realization of his PAP. I agreed. His self-commentary on his strengths and weaknesses showed me the concordance of our times and actions. Good work. I also remember using a resolution sheet for every union hearing report, with implementation in accordance and reciprocity. Finally, I also remember the department of Ille et Vilaine and its Director who, in addition, launched and multiplied the CAPN (Daniel, 2009). Called progress contracts, this was a first in a public service in France.

Human beings are always concerned with giving meaning to what they do: there is no well-being without doing well. This means changing the organization for the benefit of everyone. Giving meaning to share leads to new behaviors. However, the will to do well, based on agreed and achieved criteria, must be recognized. This favors the achievement of employees and their successful integration into the company. The fairness of the manager has, by mirror-effect, the loyalty of the employee. The inequity of the manager can lead to burn out, engaging human responsibility. I think that from what I have learned from ISEOR and what I have done with it, this question of meaning has all its value in socio-economic management.

CONCLUSION

Managerial management is not an exact science that can be duplicated in the mathematical sense; it is above all a human science. This is what makes it so important and great. Its reliability is the result of field experiments, observations made, quantified and measured, comparisons made, and references obtained. These are the only bases that allow research and managerial implementation to progress. With ISEOR and socio-economic management, far from fashions, the company has gone from ready-to-wear to tailor-made and hand-sewn in this field. A know-how that needs to be made known.

To have applied it in Côte de Lumière, I can tell you that I did not risk to confuse the foam with the sea.

REFERENCES

Daniel, L. (2009). Implementation of socio-economic tools at La Poste. In H. Savall & V. Zardet (Eds.), *Management socio-économique: une approche innovante.* Economica.

Gauchard, J. (2016). Historical partnership with ISEOR. In H. Savall & V. Zardet (Eds.), *Companies, value(s) and prosperity: socially responsible capitalism.* EMS.

Gauchard, J. (2009). The experience of the approach within a large public company. In H. Savall & V. Zardet (Eds.), *Management socio-économique: une approche innovante.* Economica.

Pichon, J., & Gauchard, J. (1993). Extension strategy of socio-economic management in a region. In H. Savall (Ed.) *Évolution de l'expert-comptable : le conseil en management.* Economica.

Perret, A., & Gauchard, J. (1992). La Poste: une entreprise publique. Les enjeux et le nouveau management. In H. Savall (Ed.) *Qualité du conseil et mutation du service public.* EconomicaJoseph Gauchard.

CHAPTER 29

DEVELOPING ORGANIZATION AGILITY

Thomas G. Cummings, Christopher G. Worley, and Rickie Moore

ABSTRACT

In rapidly changing environments, organization agility can be a source of survival and also competitive advantage. In this chapter, we demonstrate how two methods developed in the USA and in Europe—Self Design and SEAM, helped organizations to continually develop and reinforce their agile performance either by keeping pace with changing conditions or by identifying and reducing organizational dysfunctions and the ensuing hidden costs. Using two mini case studies, we illustrate how the two methods were applied and outline the results that were obtained and sustained.

Organization agility is a crucial dynamic capability in rapidly changing environments (Teece, Peteraf, and Leih, 2016). It is defined as the ability to make timely, effective, and sustained organizational changes when and where they provide a performance advantage (Worley, Williams, and Lawler, 2014). Although knowledge of how organization design features enable agility capabilities has increased, knowing how to implement them in organizations is still in its infancy. We draw on two methods for organization improvement and change to explore how organizations can change themselves into agile performers: Self Design (SD) and the Socio Economic Approach to Management (SEAM; Savall, 1974, 1975, 1981; Savall and Zardet, 1987, 2018).

1 SELF DESIGN

SD helps organizations continually create and revise organization designs to keep pace with changing conditions (Mohrman & Cummings, 1989), which is essential for agile

SEAM Treatise, pages 273–278

performance. It involves multiple stakeholders and is typically led by a design team of key cross-functional or cross-level managers, employees, and staff. The team gains preliminary knowledge to carry out SD through readings, lecturettes, and cases examples about organization design and change management. SD starts with *clarifying strategy* to assess the organization's strategic objectives to assure they are aligned with emerging competitive conditions. Then, *valuing* defines the principles or values that will guide how the organization should be designed to achieve strategic objectives. They serve as criteria for *diagnosing* the organization's current design and performance capabilities and *designing* requisite changes. Proposed changes seek to align design features with each other to support agile capabilities. They guide organizational behavior in a strategic direction in line with the organization's strategic objectives and values. At this stage, the proposed design specifies the minimal critical features that need to be implemented while affording the organization's functional and operational units considerable freedom to tailor the design to their local conditions. Finally, *action learning* is used to implement the design. Organization members learn how to make requisite changes and enact new behaviors through an iterative cycle of learning by doing. They initiate changes, assess progress, and make necessary adjustments. This learning cycle continues as members learn how to implement and improve the design and alter it to fit changing conditions. Thus, SD provides organizations with the dynamic capability to continually assess and change themselves when and where it provides a performance advantage.

2 SELF DESIGN AND THE AGILITY JOURNEY AT CAMBIA HEALTH SOLUTIONS

In the face of dramatic changes in the US health care system, Cambia Health Solutions, a diversified nonprofit healthcare company, reorganized into two main divisions. Regency Health (RH) managed the firm's branded health insurance plan and Direct Health Solutions (DHS) administered its diverse operations in health care information technology and software development, retail health care, pharmacy benefit management, health care access, and freestanding wellness solutions. Cambia's senior leaders were concerned with the firm's ability to implement the new structure as well as its impact on the organization's strong people-focused mission and culture. They turned to SD to address these issues. It was led by a design team composed of representatives from the two divisions and relevant corporate staff. Members gained preliminary expertise in SD through readings and workshops; however, much of their learning occurred on-the-job with guidance from an external consultant.

SD began with serious consideration of Cambia's corporate mission called The Cause: "To serve as a catalyst in transforming health care, creating a person-focused and economically sustainable system." The design team and senior leadership staunchly reaffirmed their commitment to it. Similarly, analysis of the firm's strategic objectives and competitive environment confirmed the relevance of the objectives to evolving conditions in the health care industry. Next, the design team clarified the values underlying Cambia's corporate culture. It revealed deep and abiding care for employee and customer needs and steadfast attention to creating innovative and economical products and services. These values served as criteria to guide the team's design efforts.

The design team conducted an extensive diagnosis of the firm's existing organization design and agility capabilities. It included depth interviews with select Cambia managers and a survey measuring the firm's agility capabilities administered to all RH and DHS directors. The diagnostic results showed broad support for Cambia's mission and high satisfaction with working for a not-for-profit corporation that fostered a people-focused culture. However, employees struggled with what The Cause meant to their day-to-day work behaviors. How did "being a catalyst for transforming health care" translate into guidelines for treating customers? Members also voiced concern that existing practices and support systems did not align with the recent corporate restructuring. For example, it was unclear how individual, division, and corporate goals were determined; responses to strategic opportunities were slow and haphazard; and essential information and communication moved unevenly through the new structure. The information systems department scored particularly low on the survey, reflecting a poorly executed revision of the firm's information and control systems. Finally, and perhaps most importantly, the diagnosis showed widespread concern that Cambia lacked the dynamic capabilities needed to implement the new organization structure and to create "transformative innovations in health care" as called for in The Cause.

Based on the diagnosis, the design team concluded that Cambia's most pressing need for organization redesign was to build agile capabilities for continuously prioritizing and implementing mission-driven initiatives. Thus, criteria for redesign included prudent risk taking and innovation, accountability for decisions, coordination of customer-service tasks, and continuous change management. Based on these guides, the design team proposed relevant structural and process changes for Cambia. These included clearer more efficient and flexible work processes; coordination of key interdependencies across functions within RH and DHS and between the two divisions; closely integrated processes for strategic planning, goal setting, and resource allocation; decentralized decision making and accountabilities; and, performance management and reward systems contingent on achieving strategic objectives at individual, subunit, and corporate levels.

Finally, the design team orchestrated the implementation of the proposed changes at Cambia. It also coordinated the redesign program with other organizational changes occurring at the time, including realignment of the senior leadership team, modifications in leadership development programs, and reorganization of select business functions. The design team created several taskforces comprised of relevant management, employees, and staff to refine the proposed structures and processes and to facilitate their implementation. The taskforces included members with knowledge and experience of the respective design features. For example, the group charged with refining the redesign of the performance management system included human resource specialists. The taskforces were also responsible for helping to implement the changes. Members received special training in facilitating action learning, particularly helping organization members implement changes, evaluate their effects, and make necessary adjustments. Naturally, taskforce members gained much of this expertise in situ, helping organization members learn how to change Cambia by doing it.

During two years of action learning, Cambia's redesigned structures and processes were implemented producing significant improvements in agility capabilities and goal achievement. In contrast to the earlier results from the diagnostic survey, later surveys showed significant increases in Cambia's agility capabilities. In contrast to the diagnosis when almost all the agility capabilities scored below average, all were significantly above it at the two-year mark. Cambia continued to apply SD to its growth and development. For instance, in line with the mission of being a catalyst in transforming health care, collaboration between the RH and DHS divisions produced a breakthrough in digital health-care called *Journi*, an innovation to serve customers' personal health-care needs economically.

3 SOCIO-ECONOMIC APPROACH TO MANAGEMENT

The Socio-Economic Approach to Management (SEAM) addresses both the people and economic sides of organization performance (Savall, 1974; Savall, Zardet & Bonnet, 2000, 2008;

Worley, Zardet, Bonnet, Savall A., 2015). In addition, though its structure and approach, it helps organizations develop the analytical and change know-how to develop agile capabilities. Experimented worldwide in over 47 countries, the SEAM method has demonstrated its potential to enhance the economic performance of firms and organizations (Moore, 2005, Moore & Desmaison, 2015). SEAM involves a series of organization change activities including diagnosis, project and focus group planning, implementation, and evaluation. *Diagnosis* identifies and analyzes the dysfunctions in an organization, their resulting hidden costs, and the factors underlying them. SEAM's diagnostic focus on dysfunctions and "hidden costs" is unique. It uncovers the organizational policies, structures, and processes that can cause and reinforce innumerable dysfunctions in coordination and control, working conditions, goal achievement, and the like. These dysfunctions can be costly to productivity and efficiency, yet they are "hidden" in the sense that they are not captured by typical accounting or other management control systems. *Project and focus group planning* uses insights from the diagnosis to design management tools and organizational practices to reduce hidden costs or to convert them into visible performance improvements. *Implementation* involves translating the proposed designs into action levers for changing the organization. Depending on the magnitude of the redesigns, the proposed changes can address multiple features and processes of the organization and its subunits. Finally, *evaluation* involves assessing the effects of the changes on the organization's performance. Like diagnosis, it includes socio-economic appraisal of whether the changes reduced organizational dysfunctions and their hidden costs. This evaluation may signal the need for further diagnostic and change activities. As a result of the experimentation of SEAM over the last four decades, the results have led to extensive knowledge creation about management sciences and management interventions in organizations (Moore & Peron, 2010). Overall, by adopting a qualimetric approach, a balanced quantitative, qualitative and financial perspective, SEAM's change activities help organizations develop both the people and economic sides of agility capabilities.

4 THE SOCIO-ECONOMIC APPROACH TO MANAGEMENT AND BRIOCHE PASQUIER'S AGILITY EVOLUTION

Brioche Pasquier, the renowned French bakery, drew on SEAM to transform strategically from a domestic to a global competitor with strong agility capabilities (Worley, Zardet, Bonnet, Savall, A., 2015). The Brioche Pasquier Group (BPG), a family-owned enterprise, produces and distributes bakery products in Europe and the US. It works closely with local customers, sources ingredients nearby, and uses no artificial colors or flavoring in line with its core mission of producing quality fresh products. Because BPG's sources and customers are local, it takes pride in its small ecological footprint. The firm's growth and success with brioche products led the owners to consider carefully whether continued expansion and diversification might result in a bloated bureaucracy contrary to their family culture and values. They turned to SEAM for help in addressing this concern.

SEAM started with diagnosis of the dysfunctions and hidden costs of BPG's current organization structures and processes. It revealed inefficient and inflexible production processes, slow and erratic communication and coordination, and challenges translating strategic objectives into action. Based on the diagnosis, project and focus group planning proposed changes to address these dysfunctions and hidden costs. Plans included improvements in production processes, work designs, and sales and distribution methods. Proposed changes to BPG's strategic planning process included a rolling three-year plan that would be developed at corporate headquarters and updated annually. Implementation of the proposed changes was guided by an action plan that integrated the changes and tied them to specific action levers including the training and development needed to enact the new work behaviors. Finally, the evaluation phase of SEAM examined the effects of the changes on BPG's socio-economic outcomes and the hidden costs of its previous dysfunctions.

After the first year of implementation, BPG's changes showed significant improvements in socio-economic performance. Redesign of manufacturing processes increased the flexibility of product mixes, stabilized production schedules and working hours, and enhanced trust in management. These improvements translated hidden costs into value-added activity of about $19,000 per employee per year. Overall, the SEAM program reduced BPG's absenteeism from 4.5% to 1.5% and staff turnover from 90% to 11%. Product quality also improved, resulting in an 7.9% increase in profitability, which occurred despite the additional time, effort, and costs associated with implementing the organization changes.

As BPG expanded in Europe and eventually to the US, SEAM tools and methods continued to enhance its agile capabilities. They increased BPG's speed of adaptation and innovation. For example, quicker and more frequent attention to customer needs enabled faster and more innovative product changes compared to competitors. SEAM tools helped boost the production and sale of BPG's own product brands relative to its manufacture of supermarket brands. Supermarket brands decreased from 20% to 10% of total production while output of "Brioche Pasquier" products increased significantly. BPG's total revenues rose 18% despite its market share of supermarket branded products falling by 34%. SEAM methods enabled BPG to pay close attention to opportunistic changes in consumer markets and make timely responses. In the southern region of France, for instance, close scrutiny of demographic changes resulted in a whole new market for children's brioche products.

CONCLUSION

SD and SEAM were created independently from each other by scholars from the US and Europe, respectively. Naturally, they share certain similarities and differences. They both rely on diagnosis and learning. They help organizations learn how to continually assess themselves so they can change and improve accordingly. Both SD and SEAM adhere to a common set of humanistic and democratic values. They are not dedicated simply to helping organizations manage change and its economic outcomes. Rather, they have an abiding commitment to helping organizations create structures, processes, and practices that enable members to engage participatively in meaningful work that has positive human, economic, and more recently, sustainable consequences. SD and SEAM differ somewhat. SD is more emergent and learn-by-doing while SEAM is more structured and prescriptive. Thus, SD is likely to be a more uncertain and harder to manage change process than SEAM. In the end, neither SD nor SEAM was explicitly conceived to help organizations create agile capabilities. Yet, their values, change processes, and tools serve this purpose as Cambia and BPG would verify.

REFERENCES

Mohrman, S., & Cummings, T. (1989). *Self-designing organizations: Learning how to create high performance.* Addison-Wesley.

Moore, R. (2005). *Evaluation de la performance économique durable des entreprises: méthodes et pratiques américaines et européennes.*

Moore, R., & Péron, M. (2007). *Change and organizational performance: The importance of incorporating quantitative and qualitative assessment, in socio-economic intervention in organizations.* Research in Management Consulting Series.

Moore, R., & Péron, M. (2010). On the axiology and actionability of knowledge creation about organizations in management science research. *Turning to practice with action research* (pp. 179–194). Peter Lang.

Moore, R., & Desmaison, G. (2015). *In search of sustainable firm performance: The socio-economic approach to management interventions, the socio-economic approach to management revisited: The evolving nature of SEAM in the 21st century.* Information Age Publishing.

Savall, H. (1974). L'enrichissement du travail humain dans les entreprises et les organisations, Doctoral dissertation, Paris-Dauphine University, Published in 1975: *Enrichir le travail humain, l'évaluation économique.* Paris: Dunod. Translated in English in 1981: *Work and People: an economic evaluation of job enrichment.* Oxford University Press.

Savall, H., Zardet, V., & Bonnet, M. (2000, 2008). *Releasing the untapped potential of enterprises through socio-economic management.* Geneva: International Labor Office, and Ecully, France: ISEOR.

Savall, H., Zardet, V., Bonnet, M., & Moore, R. (2001). *A system-wide integrated methodology for intervening in organizations: The ISEOR approach.* Current trends in management consulting: 105–125.

Teece, D., Peteraf, M., & Leih, S. (2016). Dynamic capabilities and organizational agility. *California Management Review, 58*(4), 13–35.

Worley, C., Williams, T., & Lawler, E. (2014). *The agility factor.* Jossey-Bass.

Worley, C., Zardet, V., Bonnet, M., Savall, A., (2015). *Becoming agile.* Jossey-Bass.

CHAPTER 30

CONTEXTUALIZING SEAM IN THE BROAD MILIEU OF CONSULTING METHODOLOGIES

Eric J. Sanders and Tonya L. Henderson

ABSTRACT

There is a broad milieu of consulting methodologies available to the well-trained scholar-practitioner. General categories include expert (topic-specific technical guidance), doctor-patient (a variant of expert stressing the client's symptoms and perspective), and process consulting (helping an organization develop fundamental capabilities to sustain and expand near-term improvements). The Academy of Management's Management Consulting Division embraces all responsible, theory-supported consulting methodologies, and as past chairs of the Division, the authors explore the contribution of Socio-Economic Management (SEAM) to the field, with special attention to its action research implications.

1 CONTEXTUALIZING SEAM IN THE BROAD MILIEU OF CONSULTING METHODOLOGIES

SEAM originated in Lyon, France in 1974 and has since evolved from a small, niche methodology to one affecting over 2,000 organizations in 47 countries. Its influential predecessors include storytelling, complexity, and action research. A key innovation of SEAM is its combination of quantitative, qualitative, and financial research, known as qualimetrics. Cost accounting only accepts visible, measurable expenses and revenue to document the health of firms. Savall (1974) found this approach woefully inadequate to explain what really happens in firms and economies. By expanding the analysis to include measures of hidden costs

SEAM Treatise, pages 279–285

(including absenteeism, decreased productivity, misallocation of labor), and by adding human potential to the production function, he developed a broad-based model of how firms should work, which has proven very effective over the past 45 years.

SEAM is a detailed, rigorous approach to consulting. It is scientifically based and complexity-informed, using extensive qualitative and quantitative data to help organizations engage in participative problem-solving that affects the bottom line. SEAM has taken root on multiple continents and is well represented within the Academy, where it has gained respect in context with the full spectrum of consulting approaches. A common cohort of consulting is Action Research (AR), first described by Kurt Lewin (1951), which refers to a broad class of methods, each involving cycles of discovery, action/intervention, and reflection which may involve the application of expert and/or process consulting activities. Action research meets consulting where a consulting intervention creates new knowledge as part of an iterative process.

Consulting approaches can be grouped into three main categories: *Expert, Doctor-patient, and Process* (Schein, 1969). In expert consulting, an outside expert arrives at an organization to deliver a specific service, with a set of tools tailored to the task at hand. They unpack their bag of "best practices" and go through a proscribed process designed to bring about a specific effect that management is looking for. In doctor-patient models, the consultant brings process expertise and seeks to diagnose a presenting problem based on organizational symptoms (or confirm the client's self-diagnosis) and recommends a get-well plan or prescription of sorts. Finally, in process consulting, the consultant leverages the expertise of a client organization's members, facilitating interventions designed to elicit problem-solving and impart the consultant's skills into the organization. Figure 30.1 provides a simplified perspective using a Venn diagram, with our representation of the consultant's and clients' roles depicted as the large and small arrows respectively. A key factor to consider is that over the course of an engagement, the consultant may shift among these approaches, depending on the situation, as indicated by the joining arrows between the approaches.

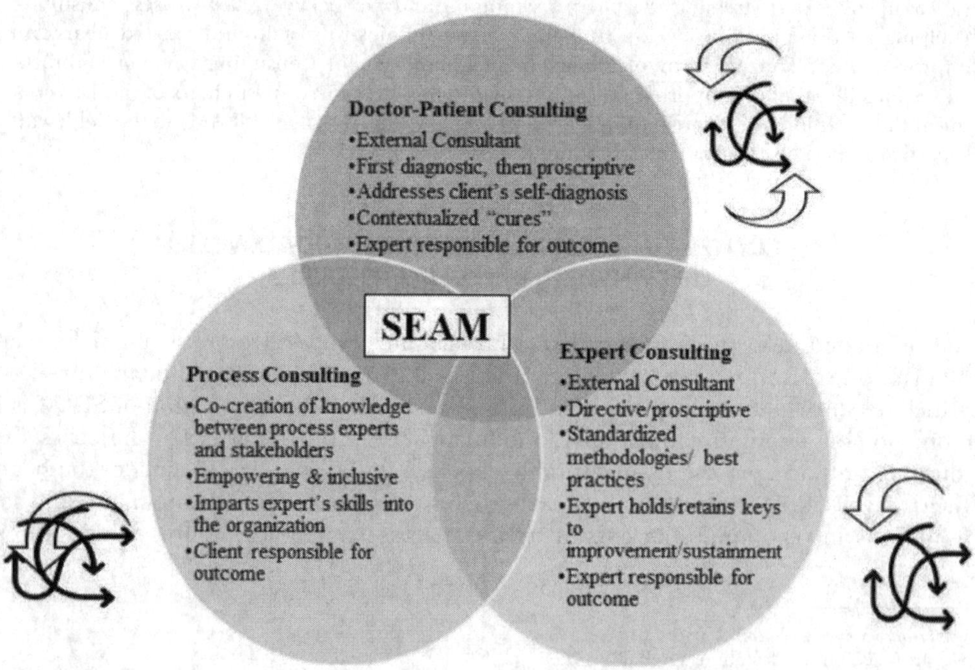

Figure 30.1 Consultant-client organization interaction by approach.

In this chapter we consider how SEAM fits within the broader context of these general frameworks, starting with that of the Expert Consultant. We give special attention to the pragmatic way that SEAM as a methodology accommodates the nuances of various approaches to address the complex nature of organizational life, emphasizing process consulting, but applying expert consulting and doctor-patient consulting styles as appropriate.

2 EXPERT CONSULTATION

Expert consultation began with the work of Frederick Taylor, Max Weber, and Henri Fayol. Taylor's work on scientific management supported vast improvements in efficiency, particularly in the manufacturing sector. Though widely maligned for the dehumanizing effects of its insistence upon one best way to do every job, ignoring the knowledge of low-level factory workers, Taylorism is sometimes credited with improvements in safety and pay (Weisbord, 2012). Fayol similarly developed a theory of management in which five core functions (Planning, Organizing, Commanding, Co-ordinating, and Controlling) were assigned exclusively to managers. He emphasized specialization of tasks, hierarchy, clearly delineated lines of authority. Similarly, Weber's work to standardize office procedures and his emphasis on formal power structures created the underpinnings of modern civil service. These three theorists had the collective effect of establishing a multi-generational trend toward designing command and control organizational structures through quantitative analysis that continues to resonate with today's large consulting firms and their clients.

While these concepts (and the consultants who helped implement them) did much to improve efficiency and fuel the economic engines of industrializing nations in the late 19th and 20th centuries, their combined effect over time was the denigration of the front-line worker to nothing more than a cog in the production machine (Weiner, 1967). Taylorism offered the would-be tyrant-manager with rationale for wholesale rejection of his workers' knowledge and perspective. Fayol, in turn, distorted the role of management in ways that dehumanized workers. Finally, Weber's love of hierarchies led to the creation of lumbering bureaucratic machines that are ill-suited to adaptation as market conditions shift. In each case, the critical component of working-level knowledge and innovation is undermined. The top-down nature of these ideas has led to decades of widespread abuse, known collectively as the "TFW virus" (Savall & Zardet, 2006).

Deming (1986) built upon these concepts to create Total Quality Management, with the decidedly more empowering twist of enabling workers to have a voice. His belief was that even the best workers cannot produce quality work when they are hindered by poorly designed processes. He stressed continuous process improvement supported by statistical process control, hoping to avoid knee-jerk reactions and misplaced blame for errors. The approach was rejected in the U.S., where command and control hierarchies ruled, but soon took hold in Japan, where decisions by consensus were more culturally accepted. That work kicked off the global quality revolution, leading to a variety of approaches, including:

- Six Sigma developed at Motorola (Harry, 1988) to reduce the error rate in manufacturing,
- Lean developed at Toyota (Ohno, 1998) to eliminate waste through empowering people,
- Capability Maturity Model (Chrissis, et al., 2011) for an integrated approach to process improvement and process synchronization across the enterprise.

These expert-based approaches benefit workers by improving their ability to produce products to specification, but do little to encourage innovation. In each case, the consultant advises the organization of the best way to do something, improving efficiency by enforcing structure and best practices or through quality-driven process improvements. This way of thinking is grounded in the mechanistic view of the firm, wherein each worker is a specialized cog in a well-oiled machine; they must each turn at a proscribed speed and angle to produce repeatable results. Although these approaches yield necessary improvements that enable industrialization and its economic benefits, they promote an overly simplified, diminished view of human contribution, except for the exalted perspective of a managerial elite.

3 DOCTOR-PATIENT METHODOLOGIES

The 1960s saw a movement from this mechanistic, hierarchical view, toward an increasingly humanistic one that was more attuned to biology and complexity-inspired views of the organization. Here the consultant's role is not "to tell you the right way to do your job," or walk you through a check-list of best practices, but rather to look at the organization's symptoms and suggest curative measures. This "organization as organism" approach yielded a variety of methods whose frameworks vary in their levels of formality.

Organization Development (OD) and various forms of humanistic management consulting fit in this category. Perhaps the best-recognized is the survey/feedback methodology developed by Rensis Likert (1961) and his colleagues to gather data from employees (and other stakeholders) in a reliable, quantitative way to diagnose problems and prescribe solutions. There are many forms of surveys and consulting firms that use them, all focusing on particular issues of concern, including employee satisfaction and employee engagement, customer satisfaction, organizational culture, organizational climate, leadership development, and various operational issues. Some enhance the data with a few qualitative questions, focus groups or interviews to provide anecdotal power to the numbers, and then recommend changes based on the data.

Another important form of doctor-patient consulting is the increasingly popular use of training and development and executive coaching to solve organizational problems. Methods include product, sales, and operational training, as well as executive coaching and leadership development. Advances include strengths-based development (Clifton & Anderson, 2002), and the focus on building emotional intelligence in addition to (or even instead of) deep product or process knowledge (Goleman, 1995). The results of these approaches are rarely measured in terms of business results, which makes them seem less valuable to the client. Thus they are the first "expense" to be cut when economic times are bad, even though in truth they could be a critical investment in human and organizational potential.

A common characteristic of doctor-patient methodologies is that the focus remains on the consultant providing expertise and tools unavailable to the client organization. They diagnose a problem that may or may not have been previously known to the client. Then they prescribe a solution, which may or may not work. In either case, the client owns the problem, but the consultant owns the solution, and bears the responsibility for both success and failure.

4 PROCESS CONSULTING METHODOLOGIES

Process consulting promotes sustained improvement and innate problem-solving capacity by leaving skills and knowledge behind. Here, the consultant does not presume to know the best solution, but instead asks questions and facilitates exchanges among workers, leaders, and other stakeholders in order to support organic problem-solving, teaching participants in the process.

Schein (1969) developed the concept of process consultation and his work on organizational culture and leadership (Schein & Schein, 2016, 5th edition) is perhaps the best-known work showing the value of this method to collaboratively diagnose and solve organizational problems with the client, so the client owns and embraces both the problem and its solution.

Process consulting methods offer frameworks for information-sharing and participative problem-solving. Emery and Purser's (1996) Search Conference is a structured, inclusive approach to problem solving and commitment to be enacted in a few days' time. Barry Johnson's (1992) Polarity Management uses the interplay among competing perspectives to elicit understanding. Appreciative Inquiry (AI) spawns cooperation among disagreeing parties through a positive connection with life, perceiving *what works* as mysterious and harnessing reverence as a generative force (Zandee & Cooperrider, 2008). In each case, process consultants set the stage for technical information to flow within the organization and be applied to the problem at hand.

Similarly, storytelling interventions engage a broad range of stakeholders without privileging any single perspective. Storytelling as organizational interventions began in the 1920s in the Hawthorne studies by Elton Mayo (1933) and his team from Harvard at Western Electric. Specific methods vary, but all leverage team members' perceptions, experiences, observations, rumors, emotions, and antenarratives. Consultants cross the barriers imposed by formal power structures to address the realities of productivity and the human spirit. The idea is that organizational life involves complex adaptive systems behaviors, with reality unfolding and changing over time (Boje, 2014). Recent developments, such as dialogic OD over the past decade, are another important application of storytelling in organizations to achieve outcomes not possible through traditional diagnostic OD methods.

Complexity-derived process consulting uses a variety of interventions. Eoyang (1997) offers complexity-derived tools for organizational contexts. Owen's (1997) Open Space Technology uses workshop designs that leverage individual choice and self-forming groups to maximize engagement. Brown's (2010) world café encourages dialogue through small group engagement within a large-group intervention on a given topic. These models treat organizational life as an emergent phenomenon, using various frameworks to set the stage for organic dialogue and problem-solving. In each case, the complex adaptive nature of human systems is leveraged to encourage co-creation of new knowledge and constructive change, and they all take time to succeed—from weeks to years, depending on the client's goal.

4.1 Action Research

The creation of new knowledge through successive research cycles gives rise to the close relationship between process consulting and action research, wherein interventions and their outcomes are documented in an iterative give and take between theory and practice. Action Research involves a diagnosis or discovery phase, wherein initial data is collected, and the baseline conditions are established. This phase is typically followed by an action or intervention and ultimately the documentation of subsequent sensemaking and results. Interventions may be derived from any of the three main consulting approaches, and data collection may be qualitative, quantitative, or mixed. Success may be judged on a variety of factors, using qualitative, quantitative, or a mixed approach, using measures that matter to the client throughout the project to document its value.

CONCLUSION: SEAM'S PLACE IN THE SPECTRUM OF SCHOLAR-PRACTITIONER APPROACHES

SEAM distinguishes itself among consulting methodologies in many ways. Chief among them is its incorporation of the strengths of a variety of perspectives, including qualitative, quantitative, and financial data (qualimetrics). SEAM's careful incorporation of the stronger aspects of each approach allows for the socially appealing, *softer* aspects of doctor-patient and process consulting (i.e., promoting employee voice) to blend with the efficiencies and monetary gains that are often associated with expert consultation approaches. To consult using SEAM requires formal training in the method. One cannot execute a SEAM intervention without understanding company financials and how to quantify the monetary cost of organizational functions.

While SEAM is most often described as a process consulting method, the economic and quantitative aspects of the model require technical expertise to be brought in from outside of the organization, as in expert consulting. SEAM also includes doctor-patient style exchanges in the diagnosis of dysfunctions using the HORIVERT analysis process, and subsequent treatment using SEAM techniques, such as the Internal/External Strategic Action Plan, Competency Grid, Priority Action Plan (PAP), and Periodically Negotiable Activity Contract (PNAC). The balance of the SEAM process applies various tools within the process consultation family (Table 30.1). For example, we see the application of storytelling in the mirror effect portion of the intervention, where the client is presented with data gathered from the organization to see life in the organization as it truly is, so they can then go on to build a new reality as it should be.

While many approaches lend themselves to one-time interventions, SEAM requires a long-term commitment from the entire organization, from the top down and the bottom up. This time commitment is the result of the thorough nature of a SEAM intervention and the necessary commitment to seeing the changes through multiple cycles of action research.

Given this examination of a virtual pantheon of consulting methodologies, it is our humble opinion that SEAM is truly a bridging methodology that falls into the process consultation family at its core, while including aspects of both expert consulting and doctor-patient consulting approaches. Thus, it falls toward the center of our initial diagram (Figure 30.1), as a method that uses the best of all consulting worlds to help build a better world.

TABLE 30.1 SEAM as an Integrative Methodology

Approach	Alignment with SEAM aspects/elements
Expert consulting	• Financial evaluations • Quantitative evaluations • Economic justification for SEAM
Doctor-Patient consulting	• Horivert analysis • Diagnosis of dysfunctions • Treatment tools (Competency Grid, PAP, PNAC...)
Process consulting	• Mirror effect • Improvement Process • Policy Decisions • Treatment tools (Competency Grid, PAP, PNAC...) • Developing client ability to sustain change • Interviews, Focus groups, etc. • Imparting skills into the client system for sustainment of the change

REFERENCES

Boje, D. M. (2014). *Storytelling organizational practices: Managing in the quantum age.* Routledge.

Brown, J. (2010). *The world café: Shaping our futures through conversations that matter.* ReadHowYouWant .com.

Chrissis, M. B., Konrad, M., & Shrum, S. (2011). *CMMI for development: guidelines for process integration and product improvement.* Pearson Education.

Clifton, D. O. & Anderson, E. (2002). *StrengthsQuest: Discover and develop your strengths in academics, career, and beyond.* Gallup Organization.

Deming, W. E. (1986). *Out of the crisis.* Massachusetts Institute of Technology, Center for Advanced Engineering Study.

Emery, M., & Purser, R. E. (1996). *The search conference.* Jossey-Bass.

Eoyang, G. H. (1997). *Coping with chaos: Seven simple tools.* Lagumo.

Goleman, D. (1995). *Emotional intelligence.* Bantam.

Harry, M. J. (1988). *The Nature of six sigma quality.* Motorola University Press.

Johnson, B. (1992). *Polarity management: Identifying and managing unsolvable problems.* Human Resource Development.

Lewin, K. (1951). Field theory in social science: Selected theoretical papers. Harper & Brothers.

Likert, R. (1961). New patterns of management. McGraw-Hill.

Mayo, E. (1933). *The human problems of an industrial civilization.* Compass.

Ohno, T. (1998). *Toyota production system: Beyond large-scale production.* Productivity Press.

Owen, H. (1997). *Open space technology: A user's guide, 2nd edition.* Berrett-Koehler Publishers.

Savall, H. (1974). *Enrichir le travail humain dans les entreprises et les organisations.* Dunod.

Savall, H., & Zardet, V. (2006). Impacts on some mainstream concepts in management theories and practice. *Paper presented at the Academy of Management (ODC Division) & ISEOR Conference proceedings,* Lyon, France, pp. 267-302.

Schein, E. H. (1969). *Process consultation: its role in organization development.* Addison-Wesley.

Schein, E. H. & Schein, P. A. (2016). *Organizational culture and leadership, 5th edition,* Jossey-Bass.

Weiner, N. (1967). *The human use of human beings: Cybernetics and society.* Avon Books.

Weisbord, M. R. (2012). *Productive workplaces: Dignity, meaning, and community in the 21st century.* Jossey-Bass.

Zandee, D. P., & Cooperrider, D. L. (2008). Appreciable worlds, inspired inquiry. In P. Reason & H. Bradbury (Eds.), *The SAGE Handbook of Action Research Participative Inquiry and Practice* (2nd ed., pp. 190-196). SAGE Publications.

PART V

LIVENING PUBLIC AND PARA-PUBLIC SERVICE ORGANIZATIONS: HEALTH, EDUCATION, LOCAL AUTHORITIES, ETC.

CHAPTER 31

SOCIALLY RESPONSIBLE POLICIES DO EXIST

Pierre-Alain Raphan

ABSTRACT

It is by planting seeds that we can hope to admire the forest one day. In politics, thoughts, ideas and projects are the seeds that allow us to target the root causes of our problems, to free up energies, to understand the major transitions (ecological, technological, economic, managerial), to prepare the future and to be able to envisage a sustainable world.

This is the meaning of each of its actions in the service of sustainable development objectives. This daily political life demonstrates the complexity of a system built by humans, which could prevent them, in the long run, from assuming their responsibilities towards future generations. I hope that this experience will inspire others.

Insanity is to do the same thing over and over again and expect a different result.

—Albert Einstein

With these words, Albert Einstein surely defined our scientific deficiencies and our comfortable reflex to return to habits.With the exception of the last European elections, abstention rates in France have been constantly increasing since the end of the 1960s, regardless of the scale of the election (municipal, regional, legislative, presidential...) and regardless of the political party in place.

If neither the scale of the election, nor the parties, nor the personalities and political programs have been able to reverse this curve, it is because the problem comes from elsewhere and is much more intimate. It is a matter of our political practices which are no longer adapted to the century in which we live.

SEAM Treatise, pages 289–296

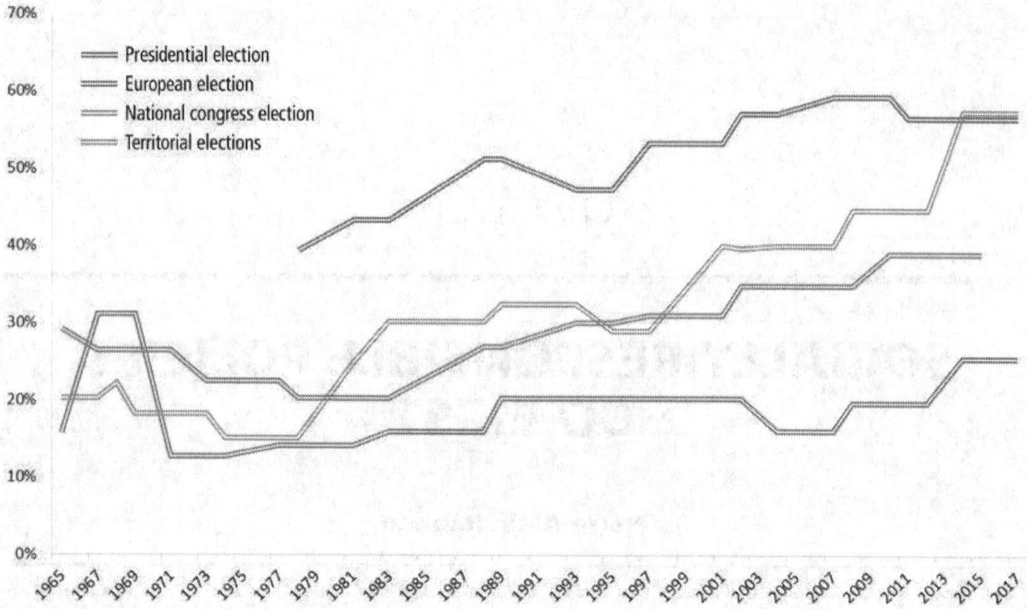

Figure 31.1 Abstentions in France.

In this alienating society, the political system must take a step back, take the time and the height to find the necessary distance and rhythm allowing it to pursue long-term actions. This system must recover the sense of the State, that is to say, to rethink its functions in time, to find subtle balances conditioned by values, to renounce isolating itself by replaying a domination. To have a sense of State is to trust in the intelligence and creativity of all. It means making our institutions agile, promoting innovation, whether technical, organizational or social.

The coronavirus crisis offers us this impetuous moment of introspection on our economic and democratic system, which have become their own enemies over time. Wouldn't it be an opportune moment, reasonable even, to rebuild our organizational modes around socially responsible practices?

1 AN ALARMING MANAGERIAL OBSERVATION

1.1 Focus on Human and Organizational Realities Linked to Poor Management

There are a few figures to know about employee engagement:[1]

- 88% of employees have no passion for their work.
- Employees who work in government have the lowest level of engagement.
- 86% of Human Resource managers think they are not on track with "leadership" development.
- 79% think they have a significant engagement problem.
- Only 6% think their performance management process is really worth the effort.
- 2/3 of employees feel overwhelmed.
- 50% of adults work more than 50 hours a week.

Unfortunately, current events know how to remind us how many signals we can no longer count that confirm these evocative figures. If we focus solely on public service, regular miscellaneous events remind us of their seriousness.

National Education:

- After the suicide of a school director in Pantin: What do we know about teachers'unrest?[2]
- Suicide of a teacher: another letter that accuses.[3]

Police:

- Suicides in the French police: the reasons of the illness.[4]
- Working hours, terrorist threat... the malaise of the police.[5]

Health system:

- Coronavirus: caregivers alarmed about their working conditions[6]
- "We are turning into robots": five caregivers testify to the deterioration of their working conditions in the public hospital.[7]

With each example, we see a process that highlights the absence of root cause analysis (Figure 31.2). This pattern is like trying to fill a leaky water bottle with more water, without realizing or wanting to realize that there are holes in the bottom of the bottle.So how can we force the political system to change its way of thinking?

2 EXISTING SOLUTIONS TO CONNECT TO THE POLITICAL WORLD

2.1 ISEOR's Findings and Solutions

Solutions exist, they have been tested and scientifically proven by the work of ISEOR under the orchestration of Henri Savall and Véronique Zardet (Savall, 1974, 1975, 1979, 1981;

Figure 31.2 Usual process of treatment of serious facts at the French governmental level.

Perroux, 1979; Savall & Zardet, 1987, 1992, 1995, 2004, 2005; Boje & Rosile, 2003; Buono, Savall, Cappelletti, 2018).

Called "Socio-Economic Approach to Management," they aim to propose a socially responsible capitalism and to engage in a practice based on listening, trust and the piloting of indicators related to hidden costs and performance (Savall, Péron, Zardet & Bonnet, 2015; Worley, Zardet, Bonnet & Savall, A., 2015). This requires us to review and rethink our relationship to work.

Professor Henri Savall's teams have identified a virus infecting the world: TFW.

The T refers to Taylor, whose doctrines advocated the hyper-specialization of individuals in an organization.

The F refers to Fayol, who saw as an absolute necessity the dichotomy between those who think the organization and those who execute it.

The W is Weber, drawing on a pragmatism that induces a strong depersonalization of tasks.

These three authors contributed to progress in their time, so it is the anachronistic application of their principles by our contemporaries that must be incriminated: taylorism, fayolism and weberism. Indeed, in the last century, everything has changed in our world, except these foundations that induce the norm. The TFW virus is widespread in all organizations, and it is not identified as a nuisance. It represents the common and widespread habit, the standard of management, without questioning its real effectiveness, let alone its humanity. This virus has created human and economic damage. If we focus on absenteeism alone, it costs society €108 billion per year,[8] including €32 billion for the private sector (study by the Sapiens Institute). Taking into-account these facts and the solutions to be brought requires a strong political will. This is why I had the idea to seize an opportunity.

2.2 The Story of a DBA Student, Trained at ISEOR, Who Became a Member of Parliament to Develop the Idea of the Socio-Economic Approach to Management

Following the meeting of Henri Savall, Véronique Zardet, Marc Bonnet and Laurent Cappelletti during my doctoral course (DBA) and my thesis on the subject of Artificial Intelligence and its impact on democracy[9] within the CORHIS laboratory of the Paul Valery University of Montpellier, I decided to train at ISEOR to deepen the scientific discoveries of their decades of work.

Because after these discoveries, I could not remain without doing anything at the risk of becoming an accomplice of non-assistance to society in danger. I therefore took the initiative to warn the public authorities by asking for an appointment with the President of the Republic François Hollande, the Prime Minister Manuel Valls, the Minister of Labor Myriam El Komri and the Minister of Economy Emmanuel Macron.

A few weeks after the letters were sent, only Emmanuel Macron had shown a strong interest in this vision by proposing an appointment with his advisor Philippe Martin. I remember a frank meeting about political realities, about our paradoxes and about the shared vision of the results of the ISEOR work.But as it stood, the rapid implementation of Henri Savall's recommendations did not seem obvious. This is why I joined the ranks of "La République en Marche" (LREM) in order to push this vision that I considered useful for the country. Since my election in 2017, I have undertaken various actions to integrate the importance of socio-economic management into political and economic practices.

3 SOCIO-ECONOMY POLICY ADVANCES

The challenge of turning Socio-Economic Management theories into a political object is a project in its own right. On these complex subjects, the difficulty is to be able to deconstruct deeply rooted thought patterns and intellectual schemas and, at the same time, to manage to give the impression to decision-makers that the idea comes from them.

Because the impact of the awareness and the scope of Socio-Economic Approach to Management theories comes down to accepting that each of us has been wrong from the beginning. However, in a French culture where mistakes are hardly accepted, a culture that is even more exacerbated in the political arena, any mistake ejects you, sometimes imperceptibly, from the system. It is like crossing a frozen lake without knowing if, at each step, the ice will crack under our feet putting an end, without warning and with the greatest intransigence, to our objective. This requires a long-term strategy, sensitive tactics, skill and unfailing patience.

The step that should not be missed was that of sensitization. Raising awareness, informing, annoying the system without irritating it and then acting were the key actions allowing each political opportunity to seize the subject as a potential response.

3.1 Fighting for the Inclusion of Management in the Law

3.1.1 Example of the "PACTE" Law

The first political opportunity was the construction of the law relating to the Action Plan for Growth and Transformation of Enterprises, known as the "PACTE" law (*Plan d'Action pour la Croissance et la Transformation des Entreprises*).

This was, for me, a very formative experience that revealed the political system within which we evolve. From the beginning, the will was to create workgroups by theme, in order to enrich the text proposed by the government. I proposed and took part in a group called "Passion at work," a title that made my colleagues smile because it seemed so naive in their culture. Only two colleagues, sensitive to this proposal, joined this workgroup.

Following this first phase, a Special Commission of the "PACTE" Law was created to steer the law through Parliament. I did not manage to join this commission for the simple reason that the majority group prioritized the members of the finance commission and the economic commission. As I am a member of the education committee, it did not seem relevant to the group to involve me in this reflection, ignoring the eight years I spent in a consulting firm, four years as director of a consulting firm and a doctoral course in management sciences.

Whatever, the priority was to get the idea across. So I approached the rapporteurs, the Minister of the Economy and his cabinet. None of them ever called me back. Appearing invisible to this system but aware of the stakes, I nevertheless tabled an amendment aimed at financing managerial innovation through the Banque Publique d'Investissement from the proceeds of the privatization of Aéroports de Paris and La Française des Jeux.

Bruno Le Maire had advocated that these proceeds would finance disruptive innovations. It was therefore sufficient to consider management as a disruptive innovation. During the presentation in the Chamber, I presented the findings of ISEOR and proposed this amendment. The rapporteur considers that the amendment is irrelevant because it is already satisfied, and she is against it. The Minister, Delphine Gény-Stéphann (Secretary of State to the Minister of the Economy and Finance), in the temporary absence of Bruno Lemaire, also considers that the amendment is irrelevant because it has already been met, and the government is therefore also against it. The rapporteur and the Minister therefore asked me to withdraw my amendment. Aware of the importance of the subject, I prefer not to withdraw this amendment and to re-argue it against the opinion of the rapporteur of the Commission and the Government. A debate in the hemicycle ensued and the amendment was finally voted in, both by members of the LREM majority and the opposition.

The rest speaks volumes about our managerial and democratic approach. Angered by the free vote of the deputies, the rapporteurs asked for an interruption of the session. The LREM deputies of the majority who voted for this amendment and myself were "given a dressing down" following the vote against the opinion of the Government. It was at this point that I took the time to recall that this subject had been submitted several times to the rapporteurs, the Minister, the Minister's parliamentary advisor, without response and that it was our duty to act on the root causes of malaise in our country especially when this subject had seduced the former Minister of Economy who became President of the Republic. In the continuation of the legislative process, the Senate will remove the provisions aiming at the privatization of ADP thus the associated provisions.

In the second reading of the text, I submit again the idea to the special commission. The rapporteur in charge of this article considers this measure to be "legislative blabla." The BPI was also against the idea, considering that it could already finance this type of action and fearing that there would be too many files to manage if "non-innovative" companies asked for this financing as a windfall effect. After several meetings, the Minister, visibly hostile, considered that the BPI's argument was not valid. At the second reading, the rapporteur and the minister gave a wise opinion, leaving the majority to take its responsibilities and include this provision in the "PACTE" law. And this is how the concept of management entered the French law:

> The fifth paragraph of Article 1 A of Ordinance No. 2005–722 of June 29, 2005 on the Public Investment Bank is completed by a sentence that reads: 'It contributes to the development of technological and managerial innovations.

3.2 Attempts to Discuss Pilot Projects

3.2.1 The Ministry of the Economy and Finance: A Key Actor

Beyond the strictly legislative aspect, we have undertaken various actions to promote this vision. The culture of socially responsible capitalism requires that we accept that another approach than our current practices is possible. To do this, we must ensure that decision-makers can accept the idea, test it and implement it. In this respect, we have had several awareness-raising actions.

The *Socially Responsible Capitalism* books were offered to Emmanuel Macron and Bruno Lemaire. We have also found terms close to Henri Savall's vision in these recent interviews, such as the article "Europe must be the continent of responsible capitalism." The book on the control of hidden costs and performance was given to Amélie de Montchalin. Awareness-raising brochures given to Olivier Dussopt and Alain Griset. Olivier Dussopt was the first to propose a series of meetings to study the idea of pilot projects within the civil service.

We are also studying the implementation of projects in two prefectures in the Paris region (the departments of Essonne and Seine-et-Marne), which have been attracted by the idea. As for the Parliament, during a day dedicated to control and evaluation, a space was dedicated to socio-economic management, allowing Henri Savall and Laurent Cappelletti to share their work with as many people as possible.

3.3 Intervention-Research Project in the National Education System

We are also working on launching a project within the French National Education System by proposing the creation of an R&D budget in the finance bill so that the EN can engage in action-research projects. The idea emerged from an initiative of a few parliamentarians from the Commission for Cultural Affairs and Education following the creation of a collective called "Teachers' Views." With the help of the company ChooseMyCompany,[10] we launched a qualimetric survey on a sample of 22,264 teachers, focusing on their quality of life at work. The result was clear.

- 13.5% have confidence in their hierarchy
- 9% would recommend a friend to become a teacher
- 7% feel supported in case of psychological difficulties
- 6% Appreciate the functioning of the French education system

The next step in the project is to engage teachers and their system in a dedicated action-research project.

3.3.1 A Special Place in French Research

Action research and the importance of the humanities and management sciences was one of the key points in the vision of French research during the study of the multi-year research bill, where I had the honor of being co-rapporteur in charge of investment and financing as well as the framing of the vision of research from 2021 to 2030, where the desire to direct more and more of the budget via the National Research Agency (ANR) on this type of project.

4 FOUR TRANSITIONS TO BE ACCOMPANIED

Overall, we are convinced that Socio-Economic Approach to Management is both a vision and a tool that would allow each organization to reduce its social damage while increasing its economic performance and/or its service efficiency.

Whether at the micro, meso or macro level, this practice aims to adapt to each situation. This could allow a country like ours to manage four transitions:

- ecological: based on the compass of sustainable development objectives
- technological: by betting on its ability to develop artificial intelligence, quantum technologies and sovereign tools
- economic: by adopting a new industrial vision of knowing and being able to produce locally, on demand and in a personalized manner. This will require the implementation of new business models, taking into-account the economy of attention and new technologies in the digitalization of organizations
- political, by establishing socio-economic management as a new system for listening to citizens

All this can only be achieved by developing the concept of sociation. Sociation is the competence of society as a whole, not only of its representatives or elites. Our system must ensure that everyone has a place in society and is aware of it.

The knowledge and mastery of new technologies could also allow us to put them at the disposal of our humanistic values as well as the requirements of individual and collective human intelligence. The idea would be to develop the concept of socially responsible artificial intelligence. For example, it is important to remember that France has committed itself, under the eyes of all the countries in the world, to a courageous and virtuous approach to setting sustainable development objectives. To do so, it has signed an agreement with 193 other United Nations member countries. This approach, based on 17 main objectives and 169 targets, is presented in three dimensions: economic, social and environmental.

What other field than digital technology and its many applications is better suited to meet this challenge? Approaches to digital technology are regularly based on a predominantly economic axis and focused on a narrow geographical vision.

By legislating on the directions that such tools can take and by basing our organizational approaches on Socio-Economic Management, we could loudly assert our humanistic values allowing us to go in the direction of the 17 development objectives and demonstrate that socially responsible policy exists.

NOTES

1. Office Vibes
2. http://www.cafepedagogique.net/lexpresso/Pages/2019/09/27092019Article637051680987824867.aspx
3. https://www.franceinter.fr/suicide-d-un-professeur-encore-une-lettre-qui-accuse
4. https://www.rfi.fr/fr/france/20190614-france-suicide-police-raisons-mal-etre
5. https://www.lemonde.fr/police-justice/article/2018/07/03/temps-de-travail-menace-terroriste-le-mal-etre-des-policiers-et-des-gendarmes_5325044_1653578.html
6. https://www.francetvinfo.fr/sante/maladie/coronavirus/solidarites/coronavirus_les_soignants_alarment_sur_leurs_conditions_de_travail_4148363.html
7. https://www.francetvinfo.fr/sante/maladie/coronavirus/temoignages_nous_nous_transformons_en_robots_cinq_soignants_temoignent_de_la_degradation_de_leurs_conditions_de_travail_a_l_hopital_public_4139829.html
8. https://www.institutsapiens.fr/le-cout-cache-de-labsenteisme-au-travail-108-milliards-e/
9. https://www.librinova.com/librairie/pierre-alain-raphan/intelligence-artificielle-democratie
10. https://choosemycompany.com/fr/avis-certifies/education-nationale/

REFERENCES

Cappelletti, L., & Savall, H. (2018). *Le coût caché de l'absentéisme au travail: 108 milliards €.* étude de l'Insitut Sapiens, France. https://www.institutsapiens.fr/le-coût-caché–2-l'absentéisme-au-travail–108-milliards-e–2/

Lemaire, B. (2019), L'Europe doit être un continent au capitalisme responsable, *Journal La Croix, 5* septembre.

Raphan Pierre-Alain (2020). *Intelligence artificielle et démocratie.* Librinova.

CHAPTER 32

THE SOCIO-ECONOMIC APPROACH TO MANAGEMENT AND HOSPITAL ORGANIZATIONS

Anne Thiébaut-Bertrand and Denis Fière

ABSTRACT

This chapter exposes the similarities between medical and socio-economic diagnosis approaches and between experimental research in medicine and intervention-research in management sciences. Two cases of socio-economic approaches illustrate the point, one conducted in the hematology department of the Lyon University Hospital and the other relating to the organization of blood transfusion. The similarity between these two methodologies is such that the socio-economic theory appears to be understandable to health care professionals. It should facilitate the identification and understanding of dysfunctions in hospital structures, to enable the definition of new practices in order to promote innovative strategic projects.

The hospital is on the move, even if this is not always visible from the outside. [For ten years [. . .] the public hospital has been undergoing major changes that have profoundly affected its missions and organization. The movement is largely driven by external upheavals, and the need to adapt is a major cause, perhaps a saving grace. The hospital is fortunate in that it is regularly subjected to exogenous shocks.

—Crémieux, 2007

These lines resonate strongly one year after the beginning of the health crisis generated by the pandemic due to a new Coronavirus. All health actors, public or private, liberal or hospital, have shown a remarkable adaptability that persists today. Organizations and practices have been turned upside down, some of them abruptly interrupting their activity, others

SEAM Treatise, pages 297–304

radically changing their department of assignment, with the sole objective of freeing up beds and human resources to take care of patients affected by the infection. De-programming, redeployments, "arming" conventional beds with critical care beds have become the daily routine for doctors, managers and administrative staff. The time will come to take stock, to value this work and this capacity to adapt.

However, the strong constraints of the public hospital were already well identified before the crisis and will reappear as soon as the health situation is under control. These internal and external forces require the adoption of strategic practices similar to those used by companies: define, implement, manage and evaluate a strategy specific to each institution, in order to improve its performance and guarantee its survival and development. Public hospitals must make strategic choices about their activities with a dual objective: to maintain the quality of their services and to control costs.

Numerous cases of socio-economic intervention-researches in different hospitals have enabled the methodologies of medical research and intervention-research to be compared with those of hospital researchers and practitioners.[1] This chapter explains how socio-economic theory applies to the public hospital, which implies that it is understandable by health care actors.

As hospital practitioners specializing in hematology (management of blood diseases) for several decades in two university hospital centers, and having participated in a socio-economic approach as part of our professional activity (Fière, 2000) and a doctoral thesis (Thiébaut, 2010), we outline the diagnosis approaches used in medicine and management sciences, as well as the research methodologies applied to improve knowledge. Illustrations are proposed from our experience.

1 PARALLELS BETWEEN MEDICAL AND SOCIO-ECONOMIC DIAGNOSIS APPROACHES

1.1 Medical Approach

The role of the physician is to respond to a patient's complaint, most often describing one or more symptoms. Hippocrates (45–370 B.C.) recommended that the physician examine the patient and question him or her within the framework of the "colloque singulier." The diagnosis process begins with an interrogation of the patient about his personal and family history, followed by the anamnesis and the description of the disorders that led him to consult. This is followed by a complete clinical examination with visual and auditory observation, palpation, auscultation and percussion. The doctor then has, in most cases, diagnosis hypotheses. The second phase aims at collecting arguments by performing complementary examinations (biological, imaging...), in order to validate or not the initial hypotheses by a set of arguments. Once the diagnosis has been made, the physician proposes a therapeutic strategy to the patient, which may include a combination of various means: surgery, radiotherapy, chemotherapy, psychotherapy, etc. The treatment is then prescribed and the patient is reconvened in consultation to evaluate the effectiveness and tolerance of the treatment. Thus, the diagnosis approach in medicine is organized around three axes: diagnosis tools, an approach to resolving the pathology or symptom, and an axis of decision making with patient involvement (Figure 32.1).

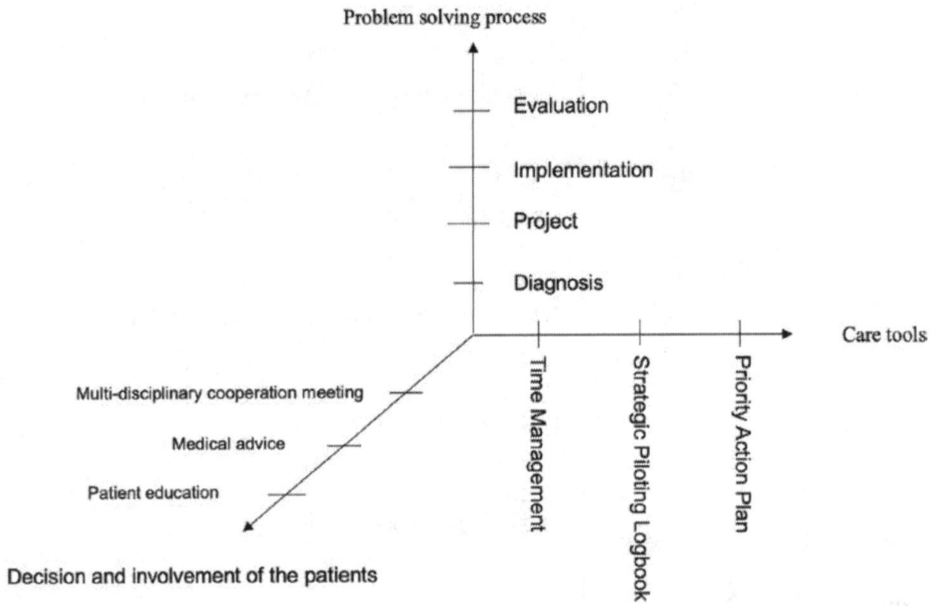

Figure 32.1 The diagnosis approach in medicine (adapted from Savall and Zardet).

1.2 The Socio-Economic Approach to Management

The socio-economic theory (Savall, 1974–75; Savall and Zardet, 1987, 2005) aims to identify the dysfunctions of organizations at the origin of hidden costs, which can be assimilated to organizational pathologies. It considers the company or organization as a complex whole comprising five types of structures interacting with five human behavioral logics. The permanent interactions between structures and behaviors cause more specifically deviations from orthofunctioning. These dysfunctions are classified into six families. The socio-economic theory, symbolized by a trihedron, involves methodological devices for change management, managerial tools for steering activities and people, as well as an axis of political and strategic decisions (Figure 32.2).

These two approaches have many similarities. The socio-economic approach to management consists of four phases: a diagnosis of the dysfunctions with an evaluation of the hidden costs based on interviews with numerous actors in the organization, then presentation of the diagnosis with a collective mirror effect. The triangulation of ODE data (interviews, documents, observation) allows access to reliable and robust data. The second phase is the proposal of innovative solutions by a focus group, followed by the implementation of improvement actions with different management tools (time management, competency grid, priority action plan etc.). Finally, the evaluation of the qualitative, quantitative and financial socio-economic results is organized one year later. Figures 32.1 and 32.2 illustrate the parallelism between the two approaches.

1.3 Points of Convergence and Specificities

Several elements of convergence appear between these two approaches: the research object is a living object. This is obvious in medicine. In management science, it is accepted

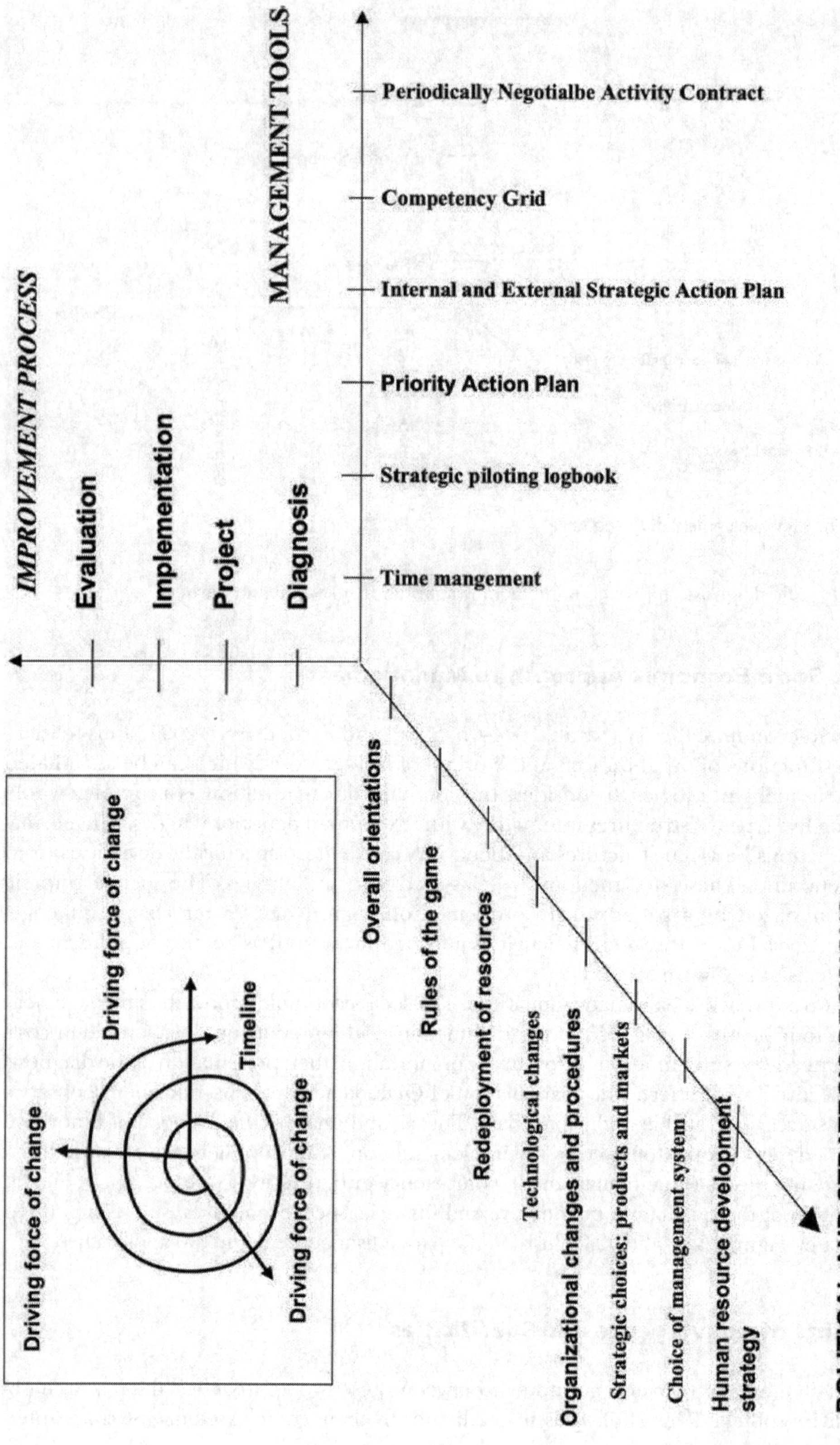

Figure 32.2 The trihedron of the socio-economic approach (© 1990).

that an organization is a system. F. Perroux (1975) proposed the concept of "active unit" to explain the survival and influence strategy of an economic agent in its environment. As for the human organism, it is made up of different interdependent organs (liver, heart, brain . . .) linked by hormonal, neurological or other connections. Vital connections, means of communication and coordination link these organs. In the same way, in an organization that has different organs or "departments" (human resources, production, finance, etc.), communication-coordination-cooperation tools are installed. C. Bernard (1947) reminds us, speaking of the human organism: "if it is necessary to break it down in order to understand it, the elements and parts that make it up only make sense when placed together." In medicine, pathologies are defined by a deviation from the normal, so-called physiological functioning of the organism. The request for intervention is formulated by a patient or an organization and thus follows a "suffering." Organizations, just like humans, suffer from pathologies, even if they are probably less aware of it.

Both diagnosis and therapeutic approaches are hypothetico-deductive and logico-inductive, based on a back-and-forth process. Medicine and management sciences are human-centered and borrow knowledge from related disciplines in the life, natural, human and social sciences. Finally, "performance" in health science consists of ensuring the well-being of the human body in all its complexity for as long as possible. The sustainable performance of an organization aims at maintaining its state of good health, its capacity for survival and development.

Nevertheless, humans have some specificities compared to organizations.

The life span of a human being is finite, which is not necessarily the case for an organization, even if it is subject to major changes. Furthermore, the approach to the subject is different: in medicine, the patient is a person and the doctor-patient relationship is part of the "singular dialogue" mentioned by Hippocrates. In management, the subject is a more or less large group of people, as any organization is composite, and human groups have their own complexities.

2 CLINICAL MEDICAL RESEARCH AND INTERVENTION-RESEARCH IN MANAGEMENT SCIENCES

2.1 Clinical Research in Medicine or Experimental Medicine

Claude Bernard is the founder of hypothetico-deductive experimental medicine, defined as research on human beings with a view to acquiring or extending knowledge that can be generalized: "The theory is the hypothesis verified after it has been subjected to the control of reasoning and criticism. A theory, in order to remain good, must always be modified with the progress of science and remain constantly subjected to the verification and criticism of new facts that appear" (Clarke, 1961). The importance of observation is thus re-established and C. Bernard opened the perspective of experimentation, advocating a transformative research in which the physician plays a true role of therapist. The role of clinical medical research is "to develop an objective approach to medical decision making that allows the integration of research results into the daily practice of the physician." (Matillon and Pellet, 1995).

Clinical research now follows a rigorous methodology "based on evidence," the "evidence-based medicine" of the Anglo-Saxons. Research projects are essentially therapeutic trials, aimed at verifying the efficacy and safety of a molecule in humans for a given pathology or symptom. Clinical trials are cohort studies, in which the physician-researcher manipulates the factor under study (the patient) and observes the effect (e.g., of a vaccine) on the previously defined endpoint (e.g., rate of protective antibodies against an infectious agent). The main advantage of the experimental study, compared to the observational study, is the *power of the causal inference* that it allows: the level of proof is higher. The researcher evaluates the efficacy and tolerance of the treatment administered in at least two groups of patients: group 1 receives the treatment to be evaluated and group 2 the reference treatment or a placebo. Thus, medical progress is made step by step, with each scientific advance allowing new hypotheses to be formulated, which are verified by a subsequent clinical trial, etc.

2.2 Management Intervention-Research

The transformative, qualimetric intervention-research designed by ISEOR (Savall and Zardet, 1996, 2004) also responds to methodological rigor. In his experimental investigations, the researcher is present in the field in order to establish lasting and frequent relationships with all categories of actors in the company. This is true longitudinal clinical research (Wacheux, 1996). The researcher seeks to access sources of information that are as reliable as possible, and to do this, physically approaches the spaces where the phenomena to be observed are taking place. His or her presence in the field makes it possible to validate pre-established hypotheses and to develop them. This is an empirical approach based on observation and experimentation in the field, where the researcher is involved in the action implemented. This intervention-research approach is resolutely "transformative," as opposed to so-called "contemplative" approaches (Avenier, 1989), and encourages the appropriation and use of knowledge by practitioners.

2.3 Convergences Between Clinical Medical Research and Management Intervention-Research (Savall and Fière, 2014)

In both cases, the research is empirical and the researcher is present in the field. The sequence of knowledge generation is as follows: Empirical observation → induction → logico-deductive hypothesis formulation → confrontation with reality through empirical observation, and so on. In both cases, knowledge is generated according to a heuristic process, allowing complex problems to be solved by intelligent trial and error (Savall and Zardet, 1996).

One of the points of divergence is probably the difficulty of comparing results on different groups in management science, because "samples" are difficult to construct "all things being equal."

The similarities outlined above help to explain why the socio-economic approach is easily understood by health actors. Thus, hospital management issues can be analyzed in the same way as any organization.

3 APPLICATIONS OF THE SOCIO-ECONOMIC APPROACH TO MANAGEMENT IN THE PUBLIC HOSPITAL SECTOR

We experimented with socio-economic management in the haematology department of a university hospital (CHU) where we were respectively head of department and doctor (Fière, 2000). This large department (a large SME) employed 150 people, 20 doctors and 130 nursing staff, hotel staff, etc., and had four units. The main improvements concerned (a) the working environment, equipment and logistics; (b) communication – coordination – cooperation within the department, in particular between doctors and nursing staff, which led to a drastic simplification of the system of meetings; (c) the role of management in consolidating behaviours, which are traditionally individualistic in the hospital environment; (d) the introduction of rules and tools for the organization of work, in order to harmonize hygiene practices, for example, and the rules for the care of transplant patients and donors

Moreover, a few years later, an important strategic reflection was conducted according to the same methodology. We analyzed the strategies for reconfiguring activities in public hospitals (Thiébaut, 2010). The mission of university hospitals is to provide care for all pathologies, but also to develop innovative diagnosis and therapeutic methods. Department heads are therefore led to make certain strategic choices for the development of activities, while ensuring that the quality of care is maintained or improved.

We studied transfusion support in patients with haematological malignancies. Transfusion of blood products is a controversial activity, but it concerns all types of patients and particularly those with hematological malignancies. These transfusions are indicated to compensate for insufficient bone marrow production due to the progression of the hematological disease itself or to the side effects of treatments. Transfusion support allows patients to maintain a certain quality of life, sometimes even as a condition for survival.

But blood product transfusions are expensive: 2.6 million euros per year on average for this hematology department. It is the primary cause of deficits in most departments, and a major cost item for hospitals with a hematology department. These blood products are exclusively delivered by the *Etablissement Français du Sang*, at prices fixed by the Ministry of Health.

This hematology department provides care and serves a large population. The activity is focused on the treatment of acute and chronic leukemia and related syndromes, and participates in the development of new therapeutic perspectives (e.g., allografts of hematopoietic stem cells with attenuated conditioning). The vast majority of treatments are carried out within the framework of therapeutic trial protocols.

Financial difficulties and the desire to develop innovative diagnosis and therapeutic techniques have led to a strategic project consisting of observing current organizational practices and then seeking solutions to improve the functioning of the department.

An in-depth analysis of the department's day hospital activity showed that transfusion activity is the most sustained there: 30% of the department's transfusions. The patients transfused in the day hospital either live near the university hospital's hematology department, or require a specific assessment and medical opinion within the department's competence, or come from outside, without the need for specific care. Indeed, regional hospital departments sometimes refuse, for financial reasons, to take charge of blood transfusions for patients from their region. In total, in this unit, 73% of the patients transfused fall into this 3rd case.

In six scientific observation sites, we conducted 30 interviews with nurses, doctors, managers, staff and patients, and identified major dysfunctions in time management, geographical organization, risk management and financial valuation. We then developed projects to improve this care and proposed tools to facilitate strategies for refocusing activities. This strategic project thus achieved its objectives both in terms of the quality of patient care and the financial impact. It has also shown that physicians have significant difficulties in introducing change into their practices, even though they practice the principle of the strategic project with their patients on a daily basis.

CONCLUSION

Diagnosis approaches in medicine and management sciences have many points in common. Similarly, clinical medical research and socio-economic intervention-research are both field intervention-researches. It is clear that the socio-economic approach can help hospital structures to analyze their dysfunctions and define new practices in order to conduct innovative projects. The similarity between the approaches and applied research in these two disciplines is an element that facilitates acceptance and understanding on the part of health actors.

NOTE

1. See the Appendix for a list of doctoral dissertations prepared at the ISEOR center and dealing with the sector of hospitals, in particular: Zardet, 1982; Thouverez, 1996; Krief, 1999; Bertezène, 2000; Leckie, 2001; Looky, 2005; Tabchoury, 2006; Thiébaut, 2010; Frachette, 2014; Le Lédan (to be defended)

REFERENCES

Avenier, M.J. (1989). Méthodes de terrain et recherche en management stratégique, Economies et Sociétés, Tome XXIII, n0 12, Série « Sciences de gestion «, n° 14, pp. 199–218.

Bernard, C. (1947). *Principes de médecine expérimentale.* Paris, PUF.

Clarke, R. (1961). *Claude Bernard et la médecine expérimentale.* Editions Seghers.

Crémieux, F. (2007). *L'hôpital en mouvement.* Esprit.

Fière, D. (2000). Le management socio-économique dans les hôpitaux: expérimentation dans un service d'hématologie des hospices civils de Lyon. In H. Savall (Ed.), *Le notariat nouveau.* Economica.

Matillon, Y., & Pellet, H. (1995). *La recherche clinique: de l'idée à la publication.* Directed by G. Landrivon and F Delahaye, Edition Masson

Perroux, F. (1975). *Active units and new mathematics. Revision of the theory of general economic equilibrium.* Dunod.

Savall, H., Fière, D. (2014). Comparative study of research methodologies in medicine and management. Case of socio-economic intervention-research of qualimetric order. *Journal of Medical Management and Economics, 32*(5–6), 354–370.

Thiébaut-Bertrand, A. (2010). *Contribution to the strategic analysis of activity reconfiguration to preserve and improve the quality of services/cost control in hospitals. Case of blood transfusion in French public hospitals.* PhD thesis in Management Sciences. Joseph Fourier University.

CHAPTER 33

COMPLEXITY, MAGICAL THINKING, AND SEAM

John Conbere, Alla Heorhiadi, and Dave Dobosenski[1]

ABSTRACT

Complex problems require a different mode of problem solving than simple problems. Magical thinking is a delusional management issue, and it is rooted in the TFW virus. Using a SEAM intervention in a rural medical center in the United States S, the authors describe how SEAM lessened magical thinking and prepared employees to manage complex problems.

This chapter introduces the concepts of complexity in organizational problem solving as well as magical thinking among managers within the context of a rural medical center in the United States. For five years, the medical center went through a SEAM intervention. These were the five years of organizational self-discoveries, growth, and change. The chapter makes the point that organizations that use SEAM have an advantage in dealing successfully with magical thinking and complex problems.

1 COMPLEX PROBLEMS

In the past few decades, thinking about problems that organizations try to solve has changed (Belrhiti, Giralt, & Marchal, 2018; Uhl-Bien, Marion, & McKelvey, 2007; Watkins et al., 2017). Previously the assumption was that any organizational problem could be solved by a linear logical approach. However, there are some problems that are different in scope from simpler problems. These problems are complex, and they cannot be solved through a step by step linear logic and top down management.

SEAM Treatise, pages 305–311

Complex problems involve too many unknowns and too many interrelated factors. The recognition of complexity came with the movement from the Industrial Era to the Knowledge Era, in which "knowledge is constantly increasing and being shared" (Weberg, 2012). Complex systems and organizations produce complex problems which are nuanced and require a nuanced approach as well as a new type of leadership. As Uhl-Bien, Marion, and McKelvey (2007) wrote,

> complexity leadership occurs in the face of adaptive challenges (typical of the Knowledge Era) rather than technical problems (more characteristic of the Industrial Age). As defined by Heifetz, (1994; Heifetz & Laurie, 2001), adaptive challenges are problems that require new learning, innovation, and new patterns of behavior. They are different from technical problems, which can be solved with knowledge and procedures already in hand (Parks, 2005). Adaptive challenges are not amenable to authoritative fiat or standard operating procedures, but rather require exploration, new discoveries, and adjustments. (p. 300)

We have found it helpful to expand the linear-complex model into a more nuanced scale, with an increasing order of complexity (Table 33.1).

When managers do not take the time to assess the type of problem with which they are dealing, they make fall into the trap of using a simple solution for a complicated problem when the problem is complex or wicked. When managers do use linear problem solving for a complex or wicked problem, the result is that the problem becomes worse (Nason, 2017). For example, the Covid–19 pandemic is an illustration of a very complex problem. Leaders who treated the pandemic as a simple problem (with solutions like "wait, this will be over soon" and "Covid–19 is no worse than the flu") made the virus spread wider. The outcome was a much higher rate of sickness and death than would have happened if the problem was recognized as complex and the different stakeholders, such as epidemiologists and health care providers were invited into the problem solving from the very beginning.

To manage a complex problem, leaders have to refrain from being the problem solvers. This is essential even if it is difficult for leaders who have learned that their role is fixing problems. Instead, leaders need to gather stakeholders in the problem, from all levels of the organization, to share their perspectives before any attempt is made to "solve the problem." The sharing is necessary because of the multi-faceted nature and emerging of complex problems. No leader can know enough to find the best way to manage the problem.

TABLE 33.1 The Spectrum of Problems

Problems	Simple	Complicated	Complex	Wicked
Logic	Linear	Linear	Non-linear	Non-linear
Description	Obvious cause & effect; Uses logic, routines, & established procedures	More detailed; Uses logic, routines & established procedures	Multidimensional; Multiple stakeholders; Dynamic, changing	Very complex; Constantly changing; Impossible to solve; Difficult to manage
Problem solving method	Top-down, hierarchical, managerial problem solving		Manage with explorative, collaborative dialogue among stakeholders	

2 MAGICAL THINKING, TFW VIRUS, AND COMPLEXITY

Trying to resolve complex problems like they are simple is magical thinking. We define magical thinking as a delusional, and often unconscious, belief that one can do the impossible (Conbere & Heorhiadi, 2018). In our experience, this type of thinking is common in the workplace. Some examples of magical thinking include: Adding more and more tasks to employees without removing any tasks and expecting that high quality of work will be maintained; promoting employees to supervisory positions without providing training on how to manage people and expecting these employees to succeed as supervisors; or leaders who do not put enough time and effort into steering the organization but expect the organization to meet its strategic goals. Magical thinking is harmful to employees and destructive of organizational productivity in long run.

The source of magical thinking in the workplace is the TFW virus, the predominate model of management in the western world.

> The TFW virus fosters the belief that employees really should be obedient to their bosses, and if they cannot measure up, then there is something wrong with them. The people, infected by TFW virus, accept the premise that doing the impossible can be done and thus should be done. At this point, the second side of the inner tension, which is "I cannot do all the work," is repressed and buried in the unconscious. It is easier for the person to bury the awareness that she cannot do the work, rather than admit that she cannot do it to numerous reasons—saving face, pleasing the boss, wanting praise or recognitions etc. (Conbere & Heorhiadi, 2016, p. 30)

The TFW virus is the metaphor to describe the mental model of modern management which evolved from the ideas of earlier management ideologists Taylor (1911), Fayol (1916) and Weber (1947), Savall (1974, 1981, 2006; Savall & Zardet, 1987, 2008;). See also "The TFW virus concept history" in Savall (2016).

Behind the metaphor are a series of assumptions. One assumption is that human beings in the workplace are rational and thus they must leave their emotional side at home. Another assumption is that employees should be obedient because, by selling their labor and time, they turned into human capital to be used for the good of the owners of the workplace. Leaders are assumed to be the elite—they know more, and they are superior—so their orders are always correct. As a result, an organization fosters the fractured workplace in which employees are depersonalized, heartless processes are common, and everyone is blind to the damage that the TFW virus has on organizational effectiveness and every person in the workplace.

The TFW mental model of management is based on the premise that linear thinking, i.e., rationality, can be used to solve workplace problems. For simple and complicated problems, the premise often works. As soon as a problem becomes complex or wicked, the premise no longer holds. Indeed, using linear thinking to solve a complex problem tends to make the problem worse (Conbere & Swenson, 2020). This fact is not new, but it has frequently been ignored—a demonstration of the blindness that comes with the TFW virus.

The modern workplace is getting more complex due to new technologies, globalization, economic and political changes, new norms and rules, etc. What once used to be a simple problem in an organization turns into a complex one without people being aware of it. For instance, once health care providers worked with insurance companies to be paid. The process was manageable. Now insurance companies may change their rules every year; the federal programs of Medicare and Medicaid impose additional restrictions; the Veterans Department imposes their own rules; electronic health records can be interpreted differently by providers; and coding issues can lead to problem that end up with non-payment. Many stakeholders and constantly changing rules make this a complex problem, at best, and perhaps a wicked problem.

Despite research that demonstrates that using linear thinking to solve complex problems tends to make the problems worse and not better, organizational leaders far too often ignore the research and persist in using linear approaches to complex problems.

3 THE EFFECT OF SEAM ON MAGICAL THINKING

One of the authors, Dave Dobosenski is the CEO of a rural healthcare center, and he is very familiar with both complexity and magical thinking in real life. He pioneered a SEAM intervention in a healthcare organization in the United States (Savall, Zardet, 1987, 2008, 2004, 2011). He became engaged in SEAM because he wanted to change organizational culture. As he was going through the interventions, he learned to recognize the complexity of problems and magical thinking of his employees. Here is an example.

The top leadership felt overwhelmed with work. Collectively all the top leaders decided not to respond to emails on weekends. However, on Monday mornings there were so many emails to go through that it was even more overwhelming. Then other problems started to arise, like missed information, delayed responses, or misunderstandings. The simple solution of stopping an email over the weekend did not address the complexity of the issue of being overwhelmed. The leaders had to consider contributing factors to the problem first, and think how to address these factors. (see Table 33.2).

As more department of the healthcare center went through the SEAM intervention, the CEO continuously asked employees to look at things through the lens of complexity. Here is an example. The surgical department in his medical center went through a SEAM intervention. The department started working on improvement projects—the Baskets. As it is seen from a Figure 33.1, all baskets were estimated as being simple. And this is how people approached problem solving, with fewer stakeholders and less time for thinking through the problem. The improvement work did not last long, and later more problems began to come up. The CEO encouraged the director of a surgical department to reassess the level of complexity of these baskets.

For example, a Basket on reducing charting and administrative work of physicians really turned out to be much more difficult than anyone expected. The local physicians and hospitals had to comply with national rules and demands. The electronic health record system was designed for a larger health care system and could be difficult to use. Providers did not have sufficient time during the day to complete the administrative work, so they might have to spend an hour or two at home on their records.

TABLE 33.2 The Problem of Overwhelming Email

Problem	Dimension of the problem: Contributing factors	What was needed to manage the problem
Being overwhelmed	• Fast organizational growth—new specialties, new services • Not enough delegation • Care-taking organizational culture (take care of everything!) • Changing government regulations, tetranormalization	• Establish priorities • Align resources and priorities • Change organizational culture

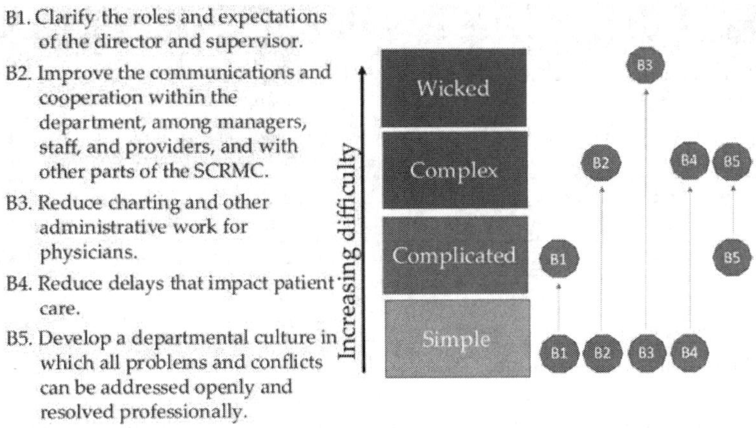

Figure 33.1 Spectrum of problems diagram at surgery department.

As people worked on the basket, they realized that what they thought were simple problems turned out to be a mix of complicated, complex, and wicked problems. They analyzed the situation and concluded that the problems were not simple, so they described them more accurately (Figure 33.1).

To manage complex problems, people need to be able to work together collaboratively. The SEAM process helped teams to improve their collaborative capacity. Below are some quotes from a qualitative assessment a year later.

> Initially there was a culture of skepticism, distrust and blame. Employees had learned that it was safest to stay silent and not "rock the boat." Involvement in the SEAM baskets in which members from all levels and departments was encouraged, and the focus was on collaborative problem solving, led to increased curiosity to learn and try new things. Consequently trust was rebuilt in leadership, and employees were more willing to take risks.
>
> Behavior changed followed changes in beliefs. Employees had been resistant to leadership and particularly to change efforts. The employee response was passivity, waiting out and attempt at change because they "knew" the change would not work anyway. SEAM created a venue for participation and engagement. Members from all levels of the organization learned that they could lead change projects and resolve differences through negotiation.

One of the primary practices of magical thinking is the belief that one can increase the amount one does without any loss of efficiency. Hospital employees cared deeply about their patients, and frequently took on more and more tasks without letting any tasks go.

> The new beliefs and behaviors reduced magical thinking. Rather than mindlessly accepting more and more tasks without adding resources such as training, time or more employees, employees began to negotiate for a workload that allowed them to succeed. Two SEAM tools facilitated the reduction of magical thinking. Managers used the SEAM time management tool and had to face their own inability to successfully do everything. Some who frequently had worked 70 to 80 hours per week came to see their many hours as hurtful to their efficiency, their health and their home life. Others saw that their model of overwork created a poor model for their employees.
>
> The priority action plan was the second SEAM tool that addressed time management. Managers in their magical thinking mode had taken on more tasks than they could do. By thinking

TABLE 33.3 Old and New Beliefs

Old beliefs	New beliefs
Nothing will change. This is the way we worked for ages.	We can change the way we work. It depends on us.
If I did something wrong, I will be blamed. Thus I am not going to say anything.	If something went wrong, I need to share this, so we all together can find a way to improve things
Communication is awful here. I do not know what is happening.	I am part of communication loops in the organization. My role is to make sure these loops work.
We are so busy. We do not have time to plan or meet.	We cannot afford not to meet and redesign things.

through the number of tasks they were attempting to do and the amount of time needed for each task led managers to drop some tasks, and to delegate or delay other tasks.

Dobosenski summarized the changes in beliefs that he saw as results of employees engaging in the SEAM intervention. The movement is from employees being fearful of using their potential, to feeling empowered to engage in the management of problems and change in a collaborative manner.

CONCLUSION

Many leaders do not understand complexity. Their use of linear thinking in the face of complexity can make the problem worse instead of solving the problem. What is needed is organizations in which employees at all levels feel empowered to enter safely into collaborative dialogue. The TFW virus has shaped the culture of many organizations into top-down management in which many employees are fearful of working in a truly collaborative manner.

Magical thinking, born of the TFW virus, is essentially delusion about one's capability. Steeped in the belief that one must be obedient to organizational authorities, one becomes blind to the consequences of one's actions. The possibility of collaborative efforts, necessary to managing complex problems, is undercut by the linear thinking that is typical of TFW virus thinking. The SEAM process, and particularly the participation in baskets, in which employees are empowered to work collaboratively, develops the collaborative capacity of organizations, and so helps create organizations that have the capability of managing complex problems.

NOTE

1. We are thankful to Dr. David Swenson from the College of St. Scholastica for his contributions about complexity.

REFERENCES

Belrhiti, Z., Giralt, A. N., & Marchal, B. (2018). *Complex leadership in healthcare: A scoping review.*

Conbere, J. P., & Heorhiadi, A. (2018). *The Socio-Economic Approach to Management: Steering Organizations into the Future.* Singapore: World Scientific Press.

Conbere, J. P., & Heorhiadi, A. (2016). Magical thinking as organizational dysfunction. *The Theory and Practice of Socio-Economic Management. 1*(1). 29–37.

Conbere, J. P., & Swenson, D. X. (2020). Hidden Costs, Unintended Consequences, and Complex Organizational Problems, and Why Leaders Often Ignore Them. *Organization Development Review, 54*(4), 21–27.

Fayol, H. (1916). Administration industrielle et générale [General and industrial administration]. Paris, France: Dunod.

Heifetz, R. A. (1994). *Leadership without easy answers.* Harvard University Press.

Heifetz, R. A., & Laurie D. L. (2001). The work of leadership. *Harvard Business Review, 79*(11) 131–141.

Nason, R. (2017). *It's not complicated: The art and science of complexity in business.* University of Toronto Press.

Parks, S. D. (2005). *Leadership can be taught: A bold approach for a complex world.* Harvard Business School Press.

Taylor, F.W. (1911). *The principles of scientific management.* New-York: Harper & Brothers.

Uhl-Bien, M, Marion, R., & McKelvey, B (2007). Complexity leadership theory: Shifting leadership from the industrial age to the knowledge era._*The leadership quarterly, 18,* 298–318. doi:10.1016/j.leaqua.2007.04.002

Watkins, D., Earnhardt, M., Pittenger, L., Roberts, R., & Rietsma, K. (2017). Thriving in complexity: A framework for leadership education. *Journal of Educational Leadership, 16*(4). 148–163. DOI: 1012806/V16/I4/T

Weber, M. (1947). *Theory of social and economic organization.* Translated by A. Henderson & T. Parsons. New-York: Free Press.

Weberg, D. (2012). Complexity Leadership: A Healthcare Imperative. *Nursing Forum, 47(4)*, 268–277.

This page intentionally left blank.

CHAPTER 34

IMPROVING MANAGERIAL SKILLS THROUGH THE IMPLEMENTATION OF THE SOCIO-ECONOMIC APPROACH TO MANAGEMENT

An Approach for the Survival and Development of the Hospital

Patrick Tabchoury, Donabelle Zakkour, and Rocks Mazraani

ABSTRACT

The services provided in Health Organizations need continuous improvement. Managers of the Healthcare Institutions have to be able to respond quickly to the increasing demands of the community they are serving. In other way, the leaders of health establishments must be trained and have the tools that allow them to monitor and to master the introduction of change and to help their organizations to overcome challenges especially in times of health or economic crises.

In this chapter, the aim is to present the socio-economic approach to management (SEAM) applied in three hospitals in the Middle East as well as the impact of this approach on the result and the development of managerial skills.

Every organization and company, whatever its size, is a place of learning. It is a place where theory and practice mix and where there is so much to learn, at all levels, without exception. Learning through policies and procedures, work processes, communication processes, hierarchical and transversal links and all the formal and informal collaborations.

The development of the competencies of the different actors in the company can never be the result of chance. It is the result of a process, directly or indirectly, explicitly or

SEAM Treatise, pages 313–319

implicitly, of a managerial skills development plan (Zakkour, 2013). It is the result of continuous, conscious, collaborative and concerted efforts by the company's internal actors at all levels. This requires a real commitment and therefore a process and methodology.

What about the hospital where each care unit, each department, is a small company in its own right? This small society, given the collaborative work in the process of accompanying and treating patients, where inter-individual relationships are charged with affect, is characterized by a quasi-familiar atmosphere. The seniority of the employees, when the turnover is low, accompanied by a training plan, favors a game of influence in this small company, which creates a power game between the members of this team considered as one family.

These games of influence, accepted and supported by the managers, medical or paramedical chiefs, have an effect, directly or indirectly, on both the economic and social levels. These influences, if the hospital does not apply an adequate competence management strategy, have a negative effect on the survival and development of the establishment. The impact on expenses is indirect, but it obviously influences the operating result through non-visible or hidden costs (Savall, 1974, 1975, 1980; Savall and Zardet, 1987). The competitiveness of hospitals implies an increase in the professionalism of the actors. In this respect, collective competence is a major competitive advantage.

If the hospital is distinguished by the level of quality of the medical and hotel services provided to patients, their families and visitors, the level of skills required is an essential asset for achieving objectives, in order to satisfy the growing demand of patient-clients. Competency development must therefore be considered an internal hospital policy and an integral part of its strategy, without forgetting that it is a necessary tool, which sometimes conditions the achievement of the decided strategy.

This chapter summarizes the contemporary challenges of the Lebanese hospital sector, the problematic, the methodology of the research and the impact of the improvement of skills on the development of the hospital.

1 THE CHALLENGES OF THE LEBANESE HEALTH SECTOR

The good health of individuals is a necessary condition for human development and the development of society. Good health is a right and a responsibility, conditioned by the security of the health system. The health crisis following COVID–19, with its repercussions in all developed, developing and underdeveloped countries of the world is a contemporary illustration in this challenge.

To fully integrate health into social and economic development, it is essential to invest in the health sector, based on a qualified, versatile, competent and efficient productive workforce. Dysfunctions have severe consequences and constitute threats. The current budgetary requirements of the health systems oblige to provide more and more services, more sophisticated and more diversified, with less resources, knowing that the persons in charge, directors, managers, doctors, heads of departments and other professionals are responsible for the quality of the services and acts provided in the hospital.

The financial constraints, the sometimes imposed pricing, the monopoly of certain suppliers, the delay in collecting certain debts, the challenge of developing technology, medicine and biomedical science represent a heavy burden. How can we cope with all this without continuous development of managerial skills?

However, the majority of healthcare executives are totally absorbed by the daily difficulties and find themselves drowned in crisis management. They spend their time managing day-to-day operations to the detriment of capacity building or management development (Savall and Zardet, 1987). Very few managers detect difficulties in time, appreciate their significance and take the necessary measures early enough. This is due to a lack of specific skills in hospital governance, especially at the strategic level, in management and development and in risk prevention, which is why a skills development approach is needed. The reform of managerial skills management applied to health care institutions allows the creation of a new framework for improving the hospital system, its internal management procedures and its steering tools. Such a reform implies an adapted systematic approach to skills management and an evaluation of the hidden costs-performance resulting from the lack of know-how and action skills.

2 PROBLEM STATEMENT

In the current context, and especially following the results and behavior of some Lebanese hospital managers during the COVID–19 health crisis, we note that most of them were mainly trained technically in their job, but little in crisis management and change management. The lack of managerial skills leads to many dysfunctions in the health system, which are not resolved or are dealt with too slowly in view of the increasing demands. Traditional basic management training is essential, but it is not enough. It must be reinforced, as one progresses in one's career, by continuous development of managerial skills in order to master the leadership and implementation of change. This managerial development is a necessity for the improvement of the organization's performance and a condition for the survival and development of hospitals.

Health organizations need methodological and practical assistance to implement a competency management approach in order to achieve the dual objective of improving performance and controlling costs (Tabchoury, 2006). The aim is to provide answers to the following questions:

- How can competency management be used to define the nature and modes of collaboration between the various professions in the hospital?
- How can competency management help the management team control personnel costs by improving the distribution of employees/work hours?
- How does competency management maximize the efficiency of resource use and minimize hidden costs?
- How does competency management positively influence social and career development?
- How can we improve qualitative, quantitative and financial results in the hospital by developing managerial skills and with which tools?
- How can competency management be used to deal with risks and unforeseen events, and to adapt the internal environment to respond effectively and rapidly to the new demands of the external environment?

In order to answer these questions, we start from the hypothesis that "the development of managerial skills focused on change management constitutes an essential investment to improve economic and social performance in a sustainable way. This investment in training can pay for itself in a very short period of time.

3 METHOD AND FIELD OF EXPERIMENTATION

The experimental work was carried out within the framework of the socio-economic theory created in 1973 by Henri Savall. The type of management proposed was created to speed-up the pace of transformation of companies and organizations in the new environment of globalization and exacerbated competition. H. Savall bases his theory on the key role of the human factor to act on the development or on the contrary contribute to the collapse of the company (Savall et al., 2015). All the actors within the company can play a major role in this change. They can use their powers, sometimes formal, sometimes informal, to slow down or on the contrary accelerate the pace of change.

The change methodology is based on a horizontal and vertical intervention within the company, which starts with a dysfunctional diagnosis based on individual and group interviews. The field of experimentation is made up of four health care institutions of different sizes, including three short and medium stay hospitals and one long stay hospital. These health facilities, located in the Middle East, provide both general and specialized care services. The experiment lasted eighteen months, during which time there was a back-and-forth movement between the field and the research laboratory. A total of 423 people were interviewed, individually or in groups, for the two types of diagnoses: horizontal and vertical diagnoses. The data was then processed to identify dysfunctions related to the lack of managerial skills and to evaluate the hidden costs generated by these dysfunctions.

Table 34.1 illustrates the evaluation of a vertical diagnosis in the maternity and pediatrics department of one of the hospitals, which represents approximately $854 per person per year.

Following the diagnoses, project groups were formed to develop and implement projects for socio-economic innovation and improvement of managerial skills. These projects aimed not only at the sustainable correction and prevention of dysfunctions, but also at ensuring a monitoring system to control and face potential future dysfunctions. Table 34.2 illustrates the composition of the Socio-Economic Improvement project group in the procurement department of one of the hospitals.

To ensure the implementation of the improvement projects, several socio-economic management tools were put in place. Training in the use of these tools was initiated in a group of managers, in order to enable the proper use and mastery of these tools by developing the skills of the people involved in the project.

The main socio-economic management tools used by the different actors are The Priority Action Plan (PAP), the Internal and External Strategic Action Plan (IESAP), the Time Management Grid (TMG), the Periodically Negotiable Activity Contract (PNAC), the Strategic lob-book (SLB), the Competency Grid (CG), the Behavioral Grid (BG), the Economic

TABLE 34.1 Vertical Diagnosis Maternity and Pediatrics in USD ($)

	Overwages	Overtime	Over-consump-tion	Non-production	Non-création of potential	Risks	Overall amounts
Absenteeism	1,800	N.E.	N.E.	N.E.	N.E.	N.E.	**€ 1,800**
Work accidents	N.E.	N.E.	N.E.	N.E.	N.E.	N.E.	**N.E.**
Staff turnover	N.E.	€ 93,800	N.E.	€ 29,800	N.E.	N.E.	**€ 123,600**
Quality defects	€ 21,700	€ 3,500	€1,100	€ 41,300	N.E.	N.E.	**€ 67,600**
Productivity gaps	€ 10,500	€ 10,300	N.E.	€147,300	N.E.	N.E.	**€ 168,100**
Overall amounts	**€ 34,000**	**€ 107,600**	**€ 1,100**	**€ 218,400**	N.E.	N.E.	**€ 361,100**

TABLE 34.2 Participants to the Socio-Economic Project of the Procurement Department

Project leader	Small group	Large group	Focus groups	Objectives
Procurement manager	• Director of the hospital • CFO • Procurement manager • Medical director	• Procurement manager • Nursing director • Care unit manager • Kitchen manager • Adminstrative director	Buyers Inventory managers	• Standardization of nomenclatures between all departments • Determination of common and department-specific items
			• Head nurses • Cook • Medical technicians • Maintenance technicians • Chief accountant	• Identification of : – Items needed to operate each department – Items to be stored – Consignment items – Minimum and maximum stocks – Annual consumption in quantity – Availability of materials from each supplier – Available suppliers for each article • Choice of suppliers

Balance (EB), the Resolution Sheet (RS), the Multipurpose Activity Sheet (MAS) and the Hourly Contribution to Value Added on Variable Costs (HCVAVC).

The audit of socio-economic tools is an essential phase in the development of the management skills of the various actors. It is an essential factor in assessing the level of compliance in the use of socio-economic tools. The two main tools audited in our field test were the priority action plans and the periodically negotiable activity contracts.

4 IMPACTS OF THE SOCIO-ECONOMIC PROJECT AND THE MANAGERIAL SKILLS DEVELOPMENT

After the implementation of the socio-economic project in these hospitals, interviews were conducted with the same people as those interviewed during the initial diagnosis. The main findings on the qualitative results can be summarized as follows

- An improvement in the quality of patient care and better application of accreditation standards and national and international norms.
- Improved human resources management: teamwork, working conditions, skills, autonomy, absenteeism, accidents in the workplace and working methods.
- Recycling of hidden costs resulting from failures into value added creation and minimization of the costs of services rendered.
- Progress in terms of technicality and medical equipment: imaging, dialysis, emergencies, laboratories, neonatal care, cardiac surgery, intensive care.

- Optimization of the use of physical space (sterilization, cafeteria, grouping of care units).
- Better recruitment and improved relations with physicians and improved attractiveness of new qualified physicians.
- Implementation of sustainable development actions: toxic waste, savings.
- Improved customer service quality: satisfaction, care, patient safety.

The improvement of social performance generated by the implementation of the socio-economic project and the development of skills is reflected in the improvement of working conditions and environment. The level of satisfaction of all categories of actors is more satisfactory following the improvement of managerial skills. The average satisfaction rates of patients, employees, patient visitors and doctors all exceed 90%, after the implementation of the project and following the same satisfaction questionnaires applied for each category of actors.

The turnover of each of the three hospitals increased. This allowed us to identify the impact of the implementation of the socio-economic project and consequently the improvement of managerial skills on the net income generated from various activities within the hospitals. We analyze this indicator by comparing it between the period prior to the socio-economic diagnosis and the two consecutive years during the implementation of the project. Figure 34.1 shows a comparison, for the three short and medium stay hospitals in our field, of the progression in relation to year 0: between +4% and +12%.

CONCLUSION

The development of managerial skills and the improvement of economic and social performance are major challenges for managers and caregivers. The development of skills through the introduction of socio-economic management created by Henri Savall and developed with his team at ISEOR allows hospitals to improve their economic and social performance. In our approach, after having applied socio-economic management, we then audited the socio-economic tools. This audit allowed us to deepen and deepen the use of these tools.

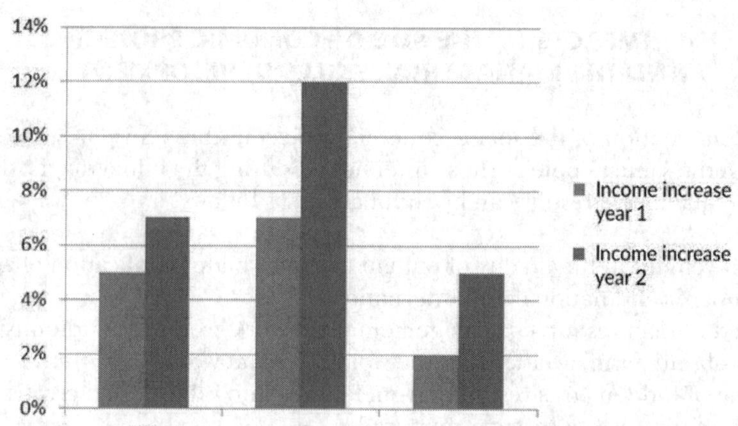

Figure 34.1 Evolution of revenues in the three hospitals.

Finally, an evaluation of the different basic indicators to reflect the results of the development of managerial skills through the implementation of socio-economic management showed the economic efficiency of this type of management. The evaluation of qualitative, quantitative and financial indicators showed the difference before and after the introduction of the socio-economic approach.

REFERENCES

Tabchoury, P. (2006). *La mise en œuvre du changement par l'introduction de la démarche socio-économique dans les hôpitaux privés au Liban.* Doctoral thesis in management sciences. University of Lyon.

Zakkour, D. (2013). *Development of managerial skills as a lever for economic and social performance: the case of nursing management in private hospitals in Lebanon.* PhD thesis in management sciences. University of Lyon.

This page intentionally left blank.

CHAPTER 35

INTERACTION BETWEEN REGULATION AND ORGANIZATION

The Case of the Hospital System

Frédéric Kletz and Jean-Claude Moisdon

ABSTRACT

The history of the implementation of activity-based pricing in the French hospital system reveals the difficulties encountered by the State in changing hospital organization, which is highly inertial given the complexity of this organization. Thus, the State has recently decided to test another intervention policy, by letting the actors in the field propose and experiment with changes in organization and financing. We can thus see a new form of articulation between regulation and organization taking shape. It is also a way of opening up the field of organization, no longer seen in the narrow sense of the hospital, but integrating the other health actors.

More than 15 years ago, the French government initiated a profound reform of hospital financing and broke with flat-rate financing; now, hospitals are financed according to their activity (Gervais 2015; Kletz, Moisdon 2015). The aim was to move away from the so-called "overall budget" reasoning, which was not very conducive to institutions' efforts to rationalize and innovate, and to encourage hospitals to review their organizational methods, by measuring their performance and identifying pockets of productivity and locations (clinical, medico-technical, or logistical and administrative services), which could give rise to new forms of organization or patient care.

SEAM Treatise, pages 321–326

1 ABP (ACTIVITY BASED PRICING), A LEAP FORWARD?

This system has had a considerable impact on the world of health care, by introducing a direct link between a hospital's activity, measured in terms of the number of patients[1] per category of pathology, and the financial allocation received from the Health Insurance. Hospital activity has indeed increased significantly, in terms of the overall number of admissions and hospital days (2 to 5% per year); on the other hand, there has been little change in organization, even though the pricing incentive was supposed to lead hospital actors to innovate in this area. Instead, it has caused hospitals to undergo a major shake-up and has made it difficult for staff to appropriate these changes, particularly in the face of the race to increase activity that it has induced.

This inability of hospitals to reform is classically linked to the characteristics of a professional organization, where the power of doctors is predominant and they are neither interested in nor favourable to seeing their practices influenced by management considerations. This diagnosis seems insufficient to us. Indeed, our intervention-researches in the hospital system have shown that many professionals have considered ABP to be an improvement over a particularly blind and unfair overall budgeting (Kletz , Moisdon, 2015). Some projects within institutions were initiated, but quickly ran out of steam.

To understand this situation it is useful to look at the hospital organization as a professional organization, but also as a production system. It may be considered inconsiderate to equate a patient and his or her suffering with a piece of metal passing from machine to machine, but as soon as one begins to analyze the functioning of the hospital, in relation to its performance (multiple: quality of care, safety, efficiency), one quickly arrives at this image: patient trajectories, passing through a certain number of points (consultation, service, imaging, laboratory, block, etc. In other words, a "patient pathway" is a process that can be used to manage the patient's health care needs, but which is not necessarily the same as the one that is used to manage the patient's health care needs. In other words, a "factory" where the operators are their own methods department, with no scheduling function. A tangle that is not very well controlled, which is held together by a significant "slack" and permanent mutual adjustment, where any attempt at reform, however modest (for example, changing the schedules of the manipulators in an imaging department), is often met with unexpected effects, coming from a world that is nevertheless close to colleagues and other clinical or hotel departments...

This organizational complexity has not escaped the attention of the central administration, which has been confronted for more than 50 years with particularly resistant institutions. This is why, fed with books and conferences from New Public Management and the work of American micro-economists, such as agency theory, it had, as a last resort, adopted the "black box" paradigm, giving up on entering this enigmatic world by giving it an incentive that was supposed to lead actors to reorganize themselves "in the right direction" (Lascoumes, Le Galès, 2005). This was to underestimate the fact that for these actors themselves, the box is also dark, perhaps a little less so, but dark all the same.

In other words, when the agent of agency theory is no longer an individual or a collection of undifferentiated individuals, such as consumers, but an organization, with its business rules, its history, its routines, the principal comes up against a "thing" that can certainly be transformed (having been made by humans, it can be modified by humans), but much more difficult than the principal dreams, and if it does change, it is often in an unexpected direction. Thus, although ABP has had effects that go in the expected direction, it has not led hospital actors to transform their internal modes of coordination and resource allocation. A "blind" development dynamic, taking advantage of various opportunities to increase the number of stays (and therefore revenues), without thinking about internal reorganization at the same time, has led to a fatal mechanism, known as price/volume regulation, which has resulted in a general drop in tariffs (affecting everyone, the deserving as well as the others) and growing tensions over workloads. This has produced a situation of social crisis, which has been regularly expressed for decades, but which has clearly become more pronounced since the introduction of the ABP, until it exploded recently with the irruption of the COVID 19.

ABP is certainly the most spectacular example of a problematic encounter between regulation and health organization, but there are others. Thus, since 2016, another incentive has been introduced, this time aimed at quality and safety of care, called IFAQ (Financial Incentive for Quality Improvement), a sort of rebalancing in relation to ABP, whose objective is efficiency. Similarly, although hospitals have improved their reporting and traceability procedures, they have not undertaken any profound changes in quality management.

2 EXIT FROM ABP: PATHWAYS AND EXPERIMENTS

For 15 years, ABP financing has remained in force, unanimously criticized on the grounds that it is adapted to certain types of pathologies (e.g., short surgical stays) and much less so to others (e.g., chronic diseases), for which the hospital stay is only an episode, most of the time brief in relation to the whole of the patient's course (Bourgueil, 2014). Indeed, the ABP, which finances only the hospital stay, does not encourage such coordination and, on the contrary, locks the hospital within its walls ... and in its superb relation to the rest of the health system (liberal medicine, medico-social etc.). The key words at the time were "pathways" and "coordination," which were used in all the speeches on the lack of incentives for efficiency (Savall, Zardet, 2005). Several commissions were successively set up to reform the ABP, but without much success, as the overall system gradually became very complex, to the point of creating a real "path dependency," in the sense of the economists. The ABP then remained the "least bad" of the systems, compared with the over-aged overall allocation or the old day price.

Faced with the flood of criticism, however, it was necessary to move forward. Two innovative shifts in the regulation policy occurred: experimentalism and the appeal to the field, accompanied by an undeniable concern for prudence and progressiveness, but also signs of a capacity for learning on the part of an administrative apparatus that its many critics deny it.

As early as 2013, care pathway management systems were experimented with, for example, for chronic renal failure or the elderly in loss of autonomy (PAERPA project). However, it is above all the 2018 Social Security Financing Act which, through its article 51, gives an unprecedented dimension to this experimentation strategy (Launois, 2020). A call for tenders for innovation has been issued to healthcare actors, based on apparently interesting foreign results, in order to set up adapted organizations, with funding from the health insurance system that departs from the usual rules. For example, several dozen hospitals, accompanied by the professionals in the towns concerned, are experimenting with the "bundled payment" model (episode of care), which consists, for certain surgical procedures, of remunerating not only the hospital stay but also the preparation and follow-up periods. The payment is an overall package that the participants in the experiment share. It is accompanied by an incentive aspect insofar as if health insurance expenditure proves to be lower than in the previous situation (for example thanks to a reduction in re-hospitalizations), the benefit is shared between the payer and the operators.

Similarly, the American model of Accountable Care Organization (IPEP), which consists of a group of health professionals and institutions taking charge of a segment of the population in an autonomous and coordinated manner, is currently implemented by some twenty groups in France (Lemaire et al, 2020).

These operations are innovative because of the step away from fee-for-service or stay-based pricing (T2ABP), but also because of the way they are constructed, which is the subject of genuine cooperation between the local initiators of the experiments and the administration. However, they remain organizational models driven by the central government and inspired by existing configurations.

The same article of the LFSS 2018/51 law also proposes that professionals in the field invent new organizations, likely to improve health care pathways and imagine adapted derogatory financing systems.

3 THE LOCAL INVENTION OF NEW CARE PRACTICES AND ORGANIZATIONS

This other call for proposals, aimed at initiatives prevented by the current operating rules, was very well received. A thousand projects have emerged, and after two successive selections (first by the ARS, then by a national committee), about 400 experiments should be deployed within five years. Currently, about one hundred have been authorized and have started. Their duration (4 to 5 years) should allow them to be observed and to set up in-depth evaluation procedures.

What are the characteristics of these projects that are emerging from the field? The vast majority of them target populations with specific health problems, such as chronic pathologies (cardiovascular, diabetes, cancer, etc.) or mental health problems, or fragile or at-risk populations (people suffering from obesity, the elderly, children in the child welfare system, etc.).

In addition to new methods of remuneration, which are a condition for the eligibility of projects under Article 51, several major types of innovation stand out, such as: (a) the integration of digital technologies into the care pathway or in prevention (tele-expertise, remote monitoring, training/education, etc.); (b) the creation of new work organizations that can result in the development of new professions (e.g., coordination or case manager) or new distribution of roles between professionals (e.g., prevention, detection or early screening entrusted to nurses, care assistants, home care workers, pharmacists, etc.) ...); (c) attempts to structure multi-professional and multi-disciplinary teams through the construction of partnerships; (d) the transfer of care activity locations : from the hospital to primary care, from accommodation to the home (*EHPAD hors les murs*), from specialized technical platforms to the home or pharmacies (*biology hors les murs*); (e) finally, the integration of new benefits or services in the basket of goods and services: support/accompaniment by psychologists, intervention of dieticians, occupational therapists, health promotion, development of adapted physical activity...

This is a wide range of innovations from the field, responding to three main objectives: to improve access to care, by “reinventing” the forms of construction of proximity: tele-expertise, moving mobile teams, changing the roles and functions of the health professions closest to the patients; to reduce the points of rupture in the care and health pathways, in particular between the hospital and the city; to respond to unsatisfied needs, by creating new services or benefits, especially in prevention (adapted physical activity, health promotion). These “innovations” are not always innovative, in the sense that they often take up an idea that has already been developed elsewhere (e.g., tele-expertise for wounds), but they are always innovative from an organizational or financing point of view, and often from both.

This last point ties in with the theme of this chapter, namely the concern for organization (Bloch, Hénaut, 2014): basically, everything happens as if the regulator takes note of the fact that an organization that is both singular and solidified by time will always remain opaque to him and will always send him unexpected feedback when he sends him a message that is intended to be an incentive. He then decides to delegate to those who work there, who in a way are lost like him, the task of elaborating their own organization, their coordination devices, their division of labor, their piloting, all things that are finally clear to all since it is the object of a collective design. It is easy to understand the considerable "reversal" that this state initiative implies. The tariff is no longer the starting point to which the organization as a whole should bend, but rather the end point of the reasoning; it is the tariff that must bend to the organization decided upon.

Obviously, the story has only just begun and we can sense the pitfalls that this adventure will encounter. Will the politician be able to hold such a distance (5 years!)? Will the pressure put on this or that project not pervert its meaning? For each project requires time to fully unfold and to allow its evaluation to fulfil its potential for collective learning. Another challenge appears: the need for an innovative evaluation of these projects. It is no longer just a question of judging clinical effectiveness, but also the soundness of the new processes invented, the consistency of cooperation, the reality of delegated activity, etc., all questions that the paradigm of the randomized controlled sample or its quantitative substitutes is incapable of addressing. But is this not the way forward? Indeed, the COVID crisis has demonstrated the dynamic inventiveness of the operational staff themselves in hospital organizations.

4 EVOLUTION OF THE HEALTHCARE SYSTEM

A new healthcare landscape is emerging, and a new place for the actors. Firstly, the public administration has changed its position by accepting to leave it to the actors in the field to propose new forms of collaboration and patient care configurations, rather than dictating decisions in a fatally blind manner in the face of a complex organization that escapes its control.

Secondly, a new place for healthcare operators themselves, who must learn to deal with the logic of others, to understand them better and to coordinate better in order to manage patient care.

Finally, a new role for actors who had previously been underground in the system, such as prevention or coordination actors: many of the Article 51 projects focus innovation on new forms of coordination between health actors, including the creation of new professional skills and the development of new systems. Approaches are also emerging that aim to deploy a holistic approach, integrating medical logic and the social characteristics of patients.

These developments, which involve an unprecedented transversality in patient care, with a pathway approach and coordinated, comprehensive treatment of patients, are a counterpoint to the current shortcomings of the healthcare system. They have an impact on the practices of professionals and on the organization and regulation of the healthcare system by the public authorities. In terms of public action, we are thus seeing the emergence of a new regime of government, no longer based on a posture of planning or regulation, but on the stimulation of collective exploration (Lenay, 2011, Cazin, 2017, Baly 2019).

We are seeing the grip of ABP gradually diminish. The same is true of management tools: always discussed and heckled when they are introduced, they can become part of the long term, deeply structuring the behavior of actors and irrigating the processes of choice and decision making, until the distance between them and the organization in which they were deployed becomes such that their replacement by other instruments is acceptable (Moisdon, 1997).

In the singular case of ABP, the Covid crisis undoubtedly accelerated these changes, by highlighting even more clearly the need to better monitor patients' journeys to and from the hospital. The challenge was not only to increase the capacity of the intensive care units, but also to help the actors to better coordinate with each other. Various forms of financing have become more attractive to the public authorities: financing based on the course of treatment, pricing based on the episode of care, and a population-based responsibility system based on the idea of clinical integration, instead of compartmentalized care by different health care actors.

NOTE

1. Homogeneous cohorts of patients.

REFERENCES

Baly, O. (2019). *The effects of intermediated flexible regulation: the case of the ambulatory shift in French health institutions.* Doctoral dissertation, Paris Sciences et Lettres.

Bloch, M.-A., & Hénaut, L. (2014). *Coordination et parcours. La dynamique du monde sanitaire, social et médico-social.* Dunod.

Bourgueil, Y. (2014): Les parcours, promesses d'efficience et d'équité? In *Parcours de santé, enjeux et perspectives.* Actualité et dossier en santé publique, n°88.

Cazin, L. (2017). *Regrouping for better governance? Le cas des hôpitaux publics français.* Doctoral dissertation, Paris Sciences et Lettres.

Gervais, A. (2015). T2A financing, hospital medical vision. *Journal of Medical Management and Economics, 33*(2), 117–122.

Kletz, F., & Moisdon, J. C. (2015). Metabolizing an economic incentive: expected and unexpected effects of new financing schemes in the hospital system. *Recherches en Sciences de Gestion, 1*, 185–205.

Launois, R. (2020). Article 51: evolution or revolution? From coordinated care networks to the payment of teams of health professionals: the same struggle. *Journal de gestion et d'économie médicale, 1*, 3–20.

Lemaire, N., Polton, D., & Tajahmady, A. (2020). Article 51: experimenting to innovate but also innovating in the way we experiment. *Les Tribunes de la sante, 1*, 35–42.

Lenay, O. (2001), *Régulation, planification et organisation du système hospitalier.* Doctoral thesis from the École des mines de Paris.

Moisdon, JC. (2005). 12. Comment apprend-on par les outils de gestion: Retour sur une doctrine d'usage. In P. Lorino (Ed.), *Entre connaissance et organisation: l'activité collective.* Paris: La Découverte

Moisdon, J.-C. (Ed.). (1997). *Du mode d'existence des outils de gestion.* Seli Arslan, Paris.

CHAPTER 36

THE SOCIO-ECONOMIC IMPROVEMENT PROJECT

A Source of Quality and Performance in Hospitals

Chantal Thouverez

ABSTRACT

Following an audit carried out in three departments of a hospital, the author identifies, in the first part, the dysfunctions and hidden costs affecting the patients, the health professionals themselves, but also the finances and the reputation of the establishment. The author then presents the socio-economic project and describes the improvement actions that were created during the first year to improve working conditions and services. Finally, the paper describes the socio-economic tools used. The competency grids and the priority action plan, for example, are high value-added tools in an environment that demands quality, efficiency, safety and serenity.

The content of this chapter has its roots in our work as an intervener-researcher in the hospital industry from 1990 to 1996, when we were preparing our thesis in Management Sciences (Thouverez, 1996). It therefore includes elements collected during this period but also during the following five years, when we were a consultant in the health sector. We will purposely take up our postulate or research thread for a better immersion in the past and to anchor our reflection in the present.

1 POSTULATE OR GUIDING THREAD OF OUR RESEARCH

The functioning and development of public hospitals are threatened by an understaffing of doctors and qualified care professionals, an absence of common strategic objectives and a

SEAM Treatise, pages 327–333

weakness in management. These institutions are also affected by internal communication problems, severe conflicts, strong compartmentalization between sectors, procedural shortcomings, and lack of training.

In addition, the type of structure that characterizes hospitals, both professional and matrix, does not facilitate the decision-making process or adherence to common objectives. All this affects the quality of services (medical, nursing, medico-technical, logistical and administrative) and affects performance. Indeed, many dysfunctions generate hidden costs that weigh on the hospital economy and on government health spending. Quality defects compromise the safety of users as well as the reputation of public establishments and encourage patients or their relatives to go to competing clinics and hospitals.

2 MAIN DYSFUNCTIONS IDENTIFIED

Our applied research took place in a hospital in the Rhône-Alpes region between 1992 and 1994, using the socio-economic intervention method (Savall, 1974, 1975; Savall, Zardet, 1987). Initially, three departments were subjected to a dysfunctional analysis. These were the operating room, a surgical unit and a medical unit. All three units had identical dysfunctions in the architectural structure, such as holes in the floors of the corridors, rooms and medical-technical areas. This caused nuisances such as noise when transporting equipment or meal trays, suffering for patients transported on stretchers, and sometimes sprains for the staff. In addition, no office had been provided for either the nursing manager or the head physician, which hindered them in the performance of their duties. The scattered storage areas for equipment, linen and supplies wasted the time of the different teams and delayed care.

2.1 Working Conditions

In the operating room, errors in the design of the premises resulted in unsuitable work spaces, such as the splitting up of three operating areas over a length of 80 meters. The absence of a clean and a dirty circuit, the off-center location of a sterilization unit for equipment and the common entrance for patients and professionals were also noted. These elements had negative effects on hygiene, on the one hand, and on the drudgery of the nurses' work, on the other.

In the surgical and medical wards, the small size of the rooms made it difficult to move beds around. In addition, old defects in the installation of windows prevented them from being opened in some rooms. Patients and caregivers complained about the lack of ventilation and heat in the summer. The blind pantries without ventilation did not allow for the evacuation of humidity. Finally, the absence of a washing and decontamination area forced staff to use the only bathtub, intended for patients, to clean soiled equipment.

In short, the building was dilapidated, sad, not very functional and generated non-quality, multiple incidents, waste of time, stress and tension. In addition, there were frequent equipment breakdowns and insufficient stocks of linen and supplies, which disrupted the work process.

2.2 Work Organization

There was also anarchy in the distribution of tasks, particularly in the scheduling of surgical procedures. Some doctors imposed, for example, three or four successive operations, without taking into-account the material and personal resources available and without referring to the nursing staff. In the early morning, surgeons were late by one and a half to two hours. These individual behaviors put patients, anesthetists and nurses on hold, and delayed the following operations. Professionals who could not eat because of the delay experienced hypoglycemia and fatigue. They were therefore not always concentrated and efficient. Finally, the systematic lengthening of the days generated overtime, anxiety and anger among nurses who were mothers and whose children were being cared for.

Other dysfunctions were often identified in cleaning and instrument preparation, due to a lack of procedures but also to insufficient skills, versatility, and motivation among the nurses. This resulted in errors in the assembly of surgical parts and in the packaging of boxes or bags. Untimely openings of sterilized boxes occurred in order to find the missing item, which reduced the stock of aseptic material, wasted time and exasperated the surgeons. In addition, the management of the blood supply was not rigorous, resulting in a lot of waste and hidden costs.

We cannot finish without mentioning the numerous internal conflicts of values, powers, territories, competences and people in this disorganized block, not to mention the quarrels with the staff of the surgery department due to the absence of drug prescriptions from the anesthetists before the patients leave the operating room.

In the surgical and medical wards, the lack of management, organization and evaluation of services by the nursing staff, as well as the lack of competence of the nurses, disrupted the progress and quality of care and compromised patient satisfaction. The professionals themselves expressed their fears and difficulties in providing technically complex care. Indeed, chemotherapy, the implantable chamber, thoracic drainage, endotracheal suctioning and emergency resuscitation procedures were not mastered by all the professionals and put patients at risk.

Therefore, with their consent and that of the managers, we created and used competency grids, designed according to the ISEOR model, in order to objectify personal competencies and those of the entire team. The reading of these grids clearly showed the strengths but also the weaknesses of the structure. The hidden costs of these three services were estimated at 3,029,740 francs per year, or 461,880 euros.

3 SOCIO-ECONOMIC PROJECT

The socio-economic improvement project is a process of dynamizing all the actors in order to modify structures and behaviors in order to improve quality, performance and also the atmosphere at work. Six general objectives were then defined: to reduce dysfunctions and recycle hidden costs, to improve working conditions, to reinforce the safety of services, to increase performance, and to improve communication-coordination-cooperation within the teams and between the different departments.

In the short term, we wanted to consolidate the functions of nursing managers by giving them an active role in the project phase. In the medium term, we wanted to diversify their skills by integrating a managerial dimension into their mission that had not yet been fully developed. Finally, we wanted to carry out a vast overall project to transform the functioning of the three services by integrating the director, doctors and managers of the surrounding sectors, such as radiology, pharmacy, dietetics, infection control and finance.

3.1 Project Construction Operating Method

The project was developed by a hierarchical workgroup and led by the sector manager. The latter assumes the role of project leader. The focus group is divided into two sub-groups: the small group and the plenary group.

The core group's mission is to keep abreast of the progress of the work of the core group and to ensure that the draft solutions are consistent with the objectives and strategic constraints of the hospital organization. The mission of the plenary group is to seek solutions for transformation within the department and to study the implications of these solutions on other sectors. The workgroups, composed of core staff, are tasked with considering specific themes and suggestions to complement the work of the plenary group.

3.2 Communication Strategies for Presenting the Project to the Teams

We communicated in advance with the management and the president of the Medical Commission of the institution in order to inform them of the points that we considered very urgent to correct and that were within their competence and legal responsibility. They considered our expert opinion relevant and shared our concerns. We obtained guarantees from them regarding the pre-anesthetic consultation and the blood bank, as well as the renovation of the operating room and the surgical unit. This support gave credence to the project and encouraged professionals to get involved in this phase of change. In general, the fact that strong decision-making actions are taken from the outset by management dispels some of the doubts in the teams about the feasibility of the project.

Given the discomfort observed among many employees when the results of the socio-economic diagnosis were presented, we wanted to start the project as soon as possible in order to avoid a form of discouragement or immobility among the staff. The enthusiasm of the researcher is, at this stage, essential to win over the participants. In this regard, we pointed out that during our half-day observation in the departments, we had noticed the presence of individual skills and abilities that deserved to be mobilized in the workgroups.

After presenting our objectives and the timetable, we clarified the values to be observed: respect for the Other, active listening, honesty, involvement, rigor and the search for the general interest. Furthermore, we used analogies to show that the project was an interesting, reconstructive and positive phase for those who would agree to participate in its elaboration and implementation. We indicated that we would be very present with the project leaders and available to them throughout the following semester, which gave the teams confidence in this introductory phase of the project.

3.3 Conducting the Project Sessions

The projects started one month after the feedback session on the results of the dysfunctions and hidden costs. Each project had a duration of six months. Every two weeks, we were on the hospital site for a whole day, to conduct individual interviews, answer the project leaders' questions, learn about their problems, look for solutions and prepare the next sessions. Although we had the project leaders in every small and plenary group meeting, the workgroups functioned autonomously, with the project leaders as the only referents.

3.4 Content of the Projects

The projects included twenty objectives and seventy-five actions for the operating room, and twelve objectives and thirty-five actions for the care units. They were developed according to the Priority Action Plan (PAP) model, created by ISEOR. It is a tool used in many departments, very structuring, stimulating and effective. The PAP is designed by the members of the plenary group and validated by the restricted group, which gives it a certain legitimacy and reliability. In line with the dysfunctions mentioned by the actors, it unites the professionals and encourages exchanges on specific themes leading to solutions or innovations. The PAP resembles an interview outline that also saves time in conducting meetings. It leaves a clear and synthetic trace of the objectives, the actions to be undertaken, the action carriers and the provisional calendar, thus facilitating the work of follow-up and control during the project and the final evaluation of the results.

In our case, changes were observed from the very first months because the PAP gives responsibility to the individuals who are "action carriers," while reinforcing their self-esteem. It strengthens team cohesion and is the most appreciated socio-economic tool among the health professionals to whom we proposed it between 1989 and 2000.

4 OUTCOMES OF OUR ACTION

We will mention here the main actions carried out following our expertise. In the operating room, the main improvements were as follows: complete renovation of four operating rooms and the corridor, extension of the sterilization rooms, creation of a space for filing files, creation of an SAS (explain the acronym) reserved for patients, installation of an office for the nurse, wall chart for planning operations, arrangement of cupboards and construction of a changing room, installation of a guard room.

In orthopedic surgery: renovation of the floors, creation of a pantry with a window and an office for the nursing staff and the head doctor, installation of a hydraulic bathtub and a decontamination room with installation of bins for soiled material and a machine for cleaning and disinfecting the basins.

In order to improve and modernize the equipment of the operating room, the following were acquired: anesthesia and surgical equipment: respirator, monitor, capnograph, laser optics, insufflator for laparoscopy, camera support, arthroscopic equipment, orthopedic table, decontamination bins, linen carts, equipment to improve patient comfort (heated blankets or armrests).

In medicine and surgery: anti-bedsore mattresses, thermal carts to keep meals at the right temperature, stocks of infusion supports.

The comfort of the rooms was also improved thanks to the acquisition of televisions, new window handles and ventilation strips, and toilet paper dispensers.

Improvements in the organization of the work of the operating room were as follows

- Appointment of a physician-coordinator
- Reinstatement of the nurse-manager as a team leader, notably through the planning of surgical interventions, supervision of work in the room and management of personnel; delegation of certain tasks from the nurse-manager to experienced professionals

- Creation of a procedure manual for instrument boxes, equipment decontamination techniques and the progress of each operation; definition of sterilization standards and daily controls
- Creation of hygiene and asepsis indicators in collaboration with the infection nurse; implementation of regular screening for nosocomial infections
- Creation of procedures for physicians

In surgery:

- Participation of the nurse manager in medical visits two days a week to free up nurses' time to work more with the nursing assistants at the bedside,
- Review of inventories, development of care protocols reviewed and validated by the chief of surgery,
- Consolidation to reduce the number of trips,
- Reduction of assembly line work and introduction of more personalized care, introduction of a daily post-operative medical visit.

In medicine:

- Strengthening of the planning and supervisory tasks of the nurse manager,
- Creation of a procedure manual covering the unit's nursing care, laboratory and radiological examinations, and creation of a dietary booklet to educate patients.

It should be noted that these different manuals were the result of group work between the medical nurse and the managers of the surrounding departments. They were given to each care unit of the hospital and were considered as very useful information tools by all the staff.

Finally, with the collaboration of the nursing managers, we introduced competency grids in the three departments, which gave very positive results regarding the mastery of care with high technological complexity.

It should be noted, in this regard, that we have often created competency grids in other places, with teams of nurses or midwives, in order to evaluate their initial level of mastery of care so that training actions can be proposed to them. Everywhere, skill acquisition has been noted as a source of quality, safety and harmony. It is, moreover, a tool that is well accepted by health professionals.

CONCLUSION

Before concluding this text, it is worth mentioning that the hidden costs of the three services have been reduced by 82% in one year. Internal communication has also improved considerably. We could also quote a phrase that was confided to us: "This Other that was unknown and foreign has become an interlocutor who no longer frightens us and with whom it is pleasant to cooperate." The reading of our applied research work over a period of ten years allows us to conclude that the socio-economic method has produced excellent results in the health sector, both in France and in Switzerland. At the end of our various mandates, it has also inspired professionals in hierarchical positions to commit themselves to quality and innovation. Some of them have trained in management engineering at ISEOR. This is a great proof of credibility and recognition.

We will now make a link between yesterday and today. In this year of the pandemic, in view of the management techniques used by hospital managers, on the orders of the government via the regional prefects and the heads of regional health agencies, we feel great sadness and compassion for these nurses and doctors who have been propelled into resuscitation departments at the bedside of people in respiratory distress and on artificial respirators, without having undergone the slightest technical training. Shouldn't we fear deaths linked to errors? Aren't the working conditions degraded by on-call and overtime injunctions likely to generate burn out, nervous breakdowns and suicides among health care personnel?

It is worrying that a certain number of these professionals are considering leaving the public service, after having been traumatized by this experience. Therefore, we consider that it is urgent to deeply restore the health system by allocating substantial financial means and by training more doctors and nurses. Management is another area that needs to be addressed. ISEOR's contribution, thanks to its ethics, its philosophical approach and the robustness of its tools, can certainly contribute to an improvement of the situation.

REFERENCES

Clément, J-M. (1994). *Essay on the hospital.* Boulogne-Billancourt: Berger-Levrault.

Mintzberg, H. (1991). *Le management. Voyage au center des organisations.* Paris: Les Editions d'organisation.

Nizard, G. (1994). *L'hôpital en turbulence. Les réponses managériales à la crise des établissements de santé.* Toulouse: Privat.

Thouverez, C. (1996). *Contribution of socio-economic management to the improvement of the quality of services and the functioning of hospital services.* Doctoral thesis in Management Sciences. University of Lyon 2.

This page intentionally left blank.

CHAPTER 37

RAMPING UP PUBLIC POLICIES

The Case of the General Labor Inspectorate in Angola

Kianvu Tamo

ABSTRACT

The cardinal virtue of public policy is the translation of the political authority's will into economic, social and environmental welfare of the national community. To this end, with regard to public management, especially in relation to working conditions in the civil construction sector, this empirical work, carried out in accordance with the theory and socio-economic analysis, proves that it is possible to accompany the achievement, by private and public companies, of overall performance. In fact, the detection of symptoms that hide high costs can open up avenues for an effective management of the General Labor Inspection.

This chapter presents an exploratory analysis of the functioning of the Angolan central administrative body of the Ministry of Public Administration, the General Labor Inspectorate (IGT), which covers the sectors of Construction, Industry, Petroleum, Geology and Mining, Transport, Energy, Health, Agriculture, Commerce and Services. This organization seems to lack effectiveness (Savall & Zardet, 1987) in view of the social, economic and environmental results recorded, particularly in civil construction companies. Indeed, in this sector of activity, which creates many jobs, many accidents are recorded.

We present in a first part, the inter-organizational action of the IGT and its difficulties of functioning and action. Then, in a second part, we explain the principles of the relevant socio-economic management to contribute to a better public management, in particular as regards accidents at work. Finally, a third part outlines the partial results of the exploratory research in progress with the IGT and the case of the Mota-Engil company.

SEAM Treatise, pages 335–341

1 INTER-ORGANIZATIONAL MANAGEMENT OF WORKING CONDITIONS

The General Labor Inspectorate in Angola has the general task of ensuring the application and compliance with the General Labor Law and the complementary legislation. The General Labor Directorate (GLD)is therefore responsible for inspecting working conditions at the national level, through its provincial directorates (see figure 1), which implies coordination mechanisms for compliance with the rules and regulations on safety and health at work, between numerous business units. However, their supervision is carried out exclusively by means of vertically transmitted information (Figure 1), which entails risks of interference not only within these units but also at the junction points (interfaces) between the different hierarchical levels. Thus, there is a lack of appropriate *communication-coordination-cooperation* mechanisms (Savall & Zardet, 1987), a vector for the exchange of operational information that is indispensable for strategic decision-making.

1.1 Informal Communication Based on Unreliable Information

The GLD periodically receives reports on occupational accidents from the country's companies. However, this information is not sufficiently precise, neither described (typification, classification) nor explained (correlation, causality) and therefore cannot become strategic information. Therefore, the regulation is limited to the application of fines punishing the units that transgress the norms and rules of safety and health at work.

Biased information: The operational information collected and compiled by the base units is biased because it does not respond to a standardized input protocol. As the sanctions that follow depend on the number of accidents reported to the control body, the tendency is for companies to underestimate the number of accidents in order to avoid increasing the fine.

Ineffective regulation: the information system does not allow for self-supply, i.e., exchanges of relevant technical information between actors. Thus, the IGT's regulatory action is limited to the application of fines to penalize offending companies.

1.2 Unsynchronized Coordination

The action of the General Labor Inspectorate (GLD) seems to have no impact on the economic, social and environmental results of the inspected companies in the civil construction sector.

A broken mechanistic bureaucracy: In a mechanistic bureaucracy (Mintzberg, 1990), the appropriate coordination mechanism is the standardization of processes, especially when the skills (technostructure) are lacking at almost all levels. From this point of view, the management structure of the GLD shows clear signs of vulnerability due to a lack of skills. It is this practical knowledge that makes it possible to control uncertainties (Friedberg, 1997).

Coordination without objectives: It is very difficult to coordinate the cross-cutting activities of several units when the actors do not know their objectives. They do so out of administrative routine, without associating the working conditions with the overall performance of the organization. This performance is a guarantee of the sustainability of development in the context of achieving the seventeen Sustainable Development Goals, including the eradication of poverty (Goal 1) and hunger (Goal 2) and the promotion of good health and well-being. It turns out that the quality of work in the organization (Tamo, 2001) is the lever for the conquest of the community's well-being (Perroux, 1991; Sen, 2000).

Lack of a shared language: the existence of a common tool is essential for cooperation between the stakeholders, in particular a plan that defines the objectives to be achieved in terms of working conditions.

A non-existent cooperation: The scope of action of the GLD is multidimensional and involves many actors from different administrative hierarchical levels (see Figure 37.1), macroscopic: the mesoscopic (local authorities) and microscopic.

An organized bureaucratic anarchy: Decision-making is the translation of cooperation. However, this administrative conglomerate, bringing together multiple bodies and services at different levels through an inspection procedure, cannot succeed in making rational decisions, i.e., solving identified problems. The organizational space relating to working conditions managed by the GLD appears as a certain organized anarchy, a "gabbage can" (March, 1991), mainly because of the lack of reliability of information, culture and sensitivity to the problem of work accidents.

2 THEORETICAL FOUNDATIONS FOR A SOCIO-ECONOMIC MANAGEMENT OF PUBLIC ACTION

At the basis of socio-economic theory, the functioning of an organization is the result of interactions between a set of structures and a set of behaviors that can have two outcomes: either *orthofunctioning*, the normal state, or *dysfunctions*, the pathological state. As Durkheim (1894, 2002) points out, the observation of social facts "confuses two orders of facts, very dissimilar in certain respects: those which are all that they should be and those which should be otherwise than they are, the normal phenomena and the pathological phenomena. We have seen that it is necessary to understand them equally in the definition with which all research must begin." Socio-economic theory has a panoply of concepts, models and methodological tools for understanding and explaining the dysfunctions observed in the production and delivery of services (Savall & Zardet, 1988, 1989). Table 37.1 compares the research processes in physiology and socio-economic management

2.1 Description of Operating Anomalies

The description makes it possible to typify operating anomalies, i.e., to distribute the observed phenomena in an orderly manner into categories, classify them and rank them. The socio-economic diagnosis method defines six themes (subdivided into sub-themes): working conditions, work organization, communication-coordination-cooperation, time management, integrated training, and strategic implementation.

Detection of functional anomalies: Through intuition, active observation and semi-structured interviews, the researcher identifies the symptoms that affect the object of study in

TABLE 37.1 Research Processes in Physiology and Socio-Economic Management

Symptoms	➡ Clinical Analysis ➡	Therapeutic actions
Classification Description (1)	Correlation Explination (2)	Prediction Prescription (3)
Dysfunctions	➡ Socio-economic analysis ➡	Innovative actions

comparison to the appropriate norms and classifies them. This leads to distinguishing what is functional from what is not, i.e., dysfunctional; in other words, the normal from the pathological (Canguilhem, 1943, 2010). According to Savall (1975, 1987), complexity comes from the fact that phenomena are not very visible, or even invisible, and must therefore be observed closely.

Characterization of dysfunctions: The attributes, i.e., the essential properties of each of the identified and characterized dysfunctions, are made explicit. This is followed by an assignment of indicators (absenteeism, accidents at work, staff turnover, quality defects and productivity gaps) that will allow their measurement.

2.2 Socio-Economic Etiology

As for explanation, the real object of science, it consists in explaining a fact (*explicadum*) and its effects and in analyzing (*explicans*) its antecedents in order to understand it; effects and antecedents having functional relations. Explanation is genetic, diachronic and synchronistic (Grawitz, 2001), deductive, probabilistic, functional or teleological (Nagel, 2006). The explanation in a socio-economic diagnosis is linked to the complex and permanent interaction between structures and human behaviors creating pulses of activity that constitute the functioning of the enterprise considered in interaction with its environment.

Causal analysis: The socio-economic method is both inductive and deductive: in socio-economic intervention-research, we extract from the stratified sedimentation of causes (invoked, deep, roots) observable and observed in the organization and in the environment. Indeed, it relates what Popper (1991) calls the three worlds, namely the knowledge base (science, epiteme), the inference engine (art, tekne) and the fact base (moral action, praxis) of policy demand (Tamo, 2006). Through causal analysis, organizational knowledge (Nonaka & Takeuchi, 2008) is created that is primarily relevant, i.e., emergent having the properties of multi-dimensionality, contextualization, globality, and complexity (Tamo, 2017).

Evaluation of hidden costs-performance: From the indicators of dysfunctions, we calculate the hidden costs traditionally ignored. These costs represent a potential source of organizational efficiency (Savall & Zardet, 1987).

2.3 Implementing the Strategy

The implementation of dysfunctional analysis and the evaluation of hidden costs leads to strategic implementation that aims at better overall performance. The compatibility of economic efficiency and human development, including economic, social, environmental and, ontologically, cultural and ethical, is not a zero-sum management (Savall, 1977). It is a synergetic "win–win" outcome for all stakeholders. Through this evolutionary and emergent process, strategic objectives are translated into innovative concrete actions.

Collaborative priority action planning: Defined and negotiated management objectives transformed into actions require communication, coordination and cooperation between actors and stakeholder groups. The instrument around which working relationships are built is the *periodically negotiable activity contract*. Its implementation presupposes the existence of a climate of trust between the partners. Thus, the coordination of activities not only calms exchanges between partners but also makes them more effective and efficient in the pursuit of negotiated objectives, thus countering the theory of transaction costs (Bensebaa, 2009). Indeed, "[the] principle of the 3Cs (communication, coordination, cooperation) aims to make internal communication more fluid and to prepare for the implementation of effective cooperation at the level of the company as a whole, while striving to avoid the formation of a refusal front thanks to more social dialogue. (Savall, Péron, Zardet and Bonnet, 2015).

3 GENERAL INSPECTION DIRECTORATE AND THE MANAGEMENT OF WORK-RELATED ACCIDENTS

The dynamics of organized action are based on the power exercised and the rules generated indispensable in a complex environment.

3.1 Scope of the Study

The GLD has its headquarters in Luanda, the Angolan capital, and carries out its action through local services spread throughout the national territory. Our research is exploratory and focuses only on work accidents, the data of which are entered by the companies and then transmitted and processed by the IGT. We also conducted semi-directive interviews on the same topic with officials of the IGT and the Mota-Engil company. The objective of the research was to understand and explain how the financial impact of work-related accidents in the Civil Construction sector was assessed, a field that covers various other objects of study, including occupational diseases, psychosocial risks, cultural differences, wage and behavioral discrimination, etc.

The main results obtained are:

- *Poor operating procedures*: In effect, site inspections are carried out in an unplanned manner, often based on denunciations from workers, social networks or the press. The published statistics of work accidents do not include all the information collected upstream via the manually filled forms. In other words, the mass of information captured is under-exploited. It would need to be digitized in loco (at the municipality level) in databases using more elaborate algorithmic tools.

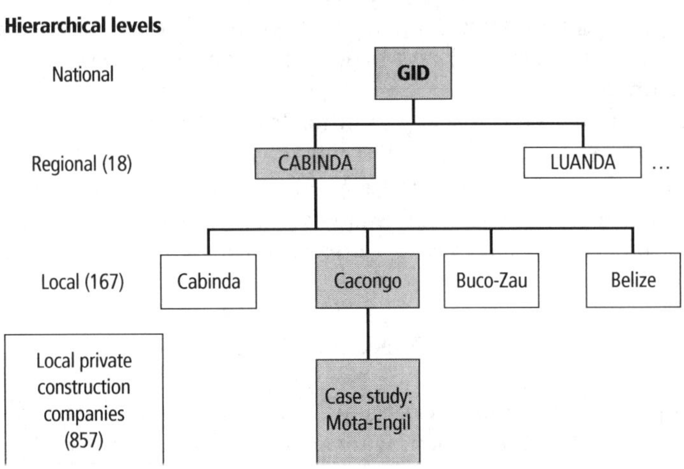

Figure 37.1 Organizational structure of the research field.

- *The costs of work accidents are underestimated*: In 2019, for all sectors, the estimated *direct costs* of work accidents are 419,879,496.80 kzs (about 1,050,000 Euros[1]) for 1,638 registered cases of work accidents,[2] accumulating 92,500 lost working days. This amount is multiplied by four by the IGT for *indirect costs*, i.e., approximately 4,200,000 Euros. The total estimated amount is therefore 5,250,000 Euros. This *total estimated amount is far below the real cost,* because the evaluation is very approximate. In fact, less than 20% of the accidents that have occurred are recorded (source: IGT interview). Regarding the qualification of accidents, the accident is said to be *light* when the work incapacity lasts less than 4 hours, *serious* if it lasts more than 8 hours and fatal when it is fatal. A finer gradation would allow a better identification of the severity of the disability. Direct costs are related to lost days, medical and hospital treatment, and funerals; as for indirect costs, the formula of applying a coefficient of 4, based on H. W. Heinrich's iceberg ratio dating from 1931, is completely arbitrary.

The application of the hidden cost-performance method would allow us to better identify the *hidden costs,* but also to partly convert them into *performances* that were previously ignored. Indirect costs are the costs of non-production, of regulation of dysfunctions by other colleagues and by the supervisor, of defects as well as administrative costs (investigation, report writing, recruitment, training…), material damage, post-traumatic stress without psychological follow-up of colleagues as well as other *human or intangible costs,* such as the effects on the quality of family and social life, irreversible psychosomatic impairment in case of death…

3.2 Study in the Mota-Engil Company

The branch of the Mota Engil company in Cabinda has an activity of assembly and disassembly, public buildings, operations and transport on site. It employs 569 workers, 88% male and 12% female, including nationals and expatriates. 83% of them are between 41 and 70 years old, which is indicative of the physiological vulnerability in a sector where the work is very hard. Moreover, from the point of view of school education, 58% have a primary level, 30% a secondary level and 12% a higher level. There is thus a *latent illiteracy.* A good part of the personnel finds it difficult to read, interpret and respect luminous and acoustic signals and safety instructions (pictograms), which are often poorly disseminated: obligation (helmets, headphones, boots, masks…) and prohibition (passage, fires…) and notices (toxic substances for example).

This exploratory study opens the way to other levels of research much more thorough, in particular descriptive, explanatory and prescriptive, going beyond the knowledge on its physiological effects. Indeed, a negotiated *intervention-research* in the activity units will show the interest to also evaluate the ignored financial costs concerning the affective and emotional effects of work accidents in a crisis context (Lebeau & Duguay, 2011).

CONCLUSION

This chapter proposes that the socio-economic approach to management lays the foundations for a *new public management* by opening up an interdisciplinary field of research. Indeed, the intelligibility of complex reality can be based on the cognitive interactivity and contradictory intersubjectivity of stakeholders. Thus, actions carried out within the framework of a socio-economic analysis can contribute to the improvement of the *overall and sustainable performance* of companies under the guidance of the General Labor Directorate.

The dynamization or *scientificization* (Habermas, 1968) of public action surpasses the ideal lineage of the Kantian hypothetical and categorical imperative, the Taylorian scientific organization of work, and the Weberian bureaucratic rationality: socio-economic management is a vaccine against the *TFW virus*[3] (Savall, Zardet, Bonnet, 2016).

NOTES

1. Exchange rate : 1 € = 400 Kz
2. 1,399 light cases, 214 serious ans 25 fatalities
3. Taylorism-Fayolism-Weberism virus

REFERENCES

Bensabaa, F. (2009). "Oliver Williamson. De l'économie des coûts de transaction au «williamsonisme»», in S. C. Petit and I. Huault (Eds.). *Les Grands Auteurs en Management* (2nd ed., pp. 353–372). Paris: Éditions EMS.

Canguilhem, G. (2010). *The normal and the pathological* (11th ed.). Paris: Quadrige/PUF.

Durkheim, E. (2002). *The rules of sociological method* (11th ed.). Paris: Quadrige/PUF.

Friedberg, E. (1997). *Le pouvoir et la règle. Dynamiques de l'action organisée,* Paris: Seuil.

Grawitz, M. (2001). *Methods of social science* (11th ed.). Paris: Dalloz.

Habermas, J. (1973). *Technique and science as "ideology."* Paris: Gallimard.

INE. (2018). *Objectivos de Desenvolvimento Sustentável. Relatório sobre os Indicadores de Linha de Base.* Agenda 2030. Luanda: Instituto Nacional de Estatística.

Lebeau, M., & Duguay, P. (2011). *The costs of occupational injuries. A literature review.* Montréal: IRSST.

March, J. G. (1991). *Decisions and organizations.* Paris: Les Éditions d'Organisation.

Mintzberg, H. (2010). *Estrutura e Dinâmica das Organizações.* 4ª Edição. Alfragide: Publicações Dom Quixote.

Nagel, E. (2006). *La estructura de la ciencia.* Barcelona: Ediciones Paidós Ibérica.

Perroux, F. (1991). *The economy of the twentieth century.* Grenoble: Presses Universitaires de Grenoble.

Pesqueux, Y. (2010). *Le Nouveau Management Public* (or New Public Management), https://hal.archives-ouvertes.fr/hal-00510878.

Popper, K. (1991). *Objective knowledge.* Paris: Flammarion.

Saussois, J.-M. (Ed.). (2016). *Les organisations. État des savoirs.* Auxerre: Éditions Sciences Humaines.

Sen, A. (2000). *A new economic model. Development, Justice, Freedom.* Paris: Éditions Odile Jacob.

Tamo, K. (2017). *A educação e a construção do conhecimento pertinente.* Luanda: Capatê Publicações.

Tamo, K. (2014). *Epistemologia da Gestão. O conhecimento do objecto complexo.* Prefácio de A. V. L. Ferreira. Posfácio de V. Zardet. Luanda: Capatê Publicações.

Tamo, K. (2006). *Elementos do Diagnóstico Socio-Económico do Sector Público.* Prefácio de H. Savall, 2ª edição. Luanda: Capatê Publicações.

Tateuchi, H., & Nonaka, I. (2008). *Gestão do conhecimento.* Porto Alegre: Bookman.

This page intentionally left blank.

CHAPTER 38

HOW TO INVOLVE EMPLOYEES TO WRITE THE HISTORY OF THE COMPANY

Norbert Deville and Olivier Voyant

ABSTRACT

A crisis is a useful pretext to activate the real, not to say unique, source of differentiation of the company, namely the Human Potential. Ten years ago, CETAF was confronted with an institutional, social and economic crisis. It made the choice of Human Potential. This chapter traces its journey and how the transformation allowed employees to write the company's history rather than undergo it.

The time has come to ask the question of the company's usefulness, to make a real introspection, more than necessary, in an economy of the unknown. This questioning is a lever for differentiation. To answer this question, wouldn't the real modernity be to look at the company from the inside rather than the outside? More often than not, we prefer to adopt the ostrich posture and look away from the outside. In order to break out of this conditioning, it is no longer appropriate to oppose, without any demagogy, the couple "Management + External" to that of "Personnel + Internal." Such a virtuous approach requires a perpetual upward and downward movement within the company, which should not be experienced as a constraint but as a process for creating economic and societal value.

In this context, sharing the history, the raison d'être and the ambition of the company with its employees means saying that the time for the conceptual reconstruction of the company is at hand. Thus, the employees must write and lead the future history of the company.

SEAM Treatise, pages 343–349

In order to share our approach to answering the question "how to involve employees in writing the history of the company," we will successively examine the theoretical contributions of authors and experts, the methodological contribution of socio-economic management, and the collective approach of CETAF.

1 THEORETICAL CONTRIBUTIONS OF AUTHORS AND EXPERTS

Since the publication of the PACTE law (*Plan d'Action pour la naissance et la Transformation des Entreprises*) in the French Official Journal on May 2nd 2019, public decision-makers have wanted to remove the obstacles to the growth of companies, thanks to a better consideration of social and environmental issues and a better sharing of the value created among employees. For Edgard Added,[1] the benevolence of the company enters a new era where its raison d'être is articulated around two (re)founding axes: the interest of the shareholder and that of the common good. According to the CEO of Publicis, the PACTE law could be an opportunity to seize in order to differentiate oneself in terms of business, employer brand or corporate social responsibility (CSR).

Regardless of social or economic interests, the time to rebuild the concept of the company seems to be, once again,[2] a hot topic. For a company concerned with the collective interest, what is its raison d'être? If history, the anchor of the company, can allow us to go on a quest for origin and memorial support, it seems necessary to sublimate it by asking ourselves about the paths of the future. The Observatory of meaning is the result of documentary work, qualitative interviews and a study conducted by the Wellcom agency (chaired by Thierry Welchoff) with the ViaVoire institute with a representative sample of 1004 people and published in September 2018. For the *Observatoire du Sens,* it is advisable to avoid taking a forbidden direction or a roundabout way, sources of disappointment. The quest for meaning must project the company towards the common meaning, namely a promise of meaning and sustainability. Placed at the center of everything, this promise could survive future turmoil and become the heart of future changes, instead of being the victim of them.

To achieve this, the incentive to action can be achieved through one of the tools available to managers and employees: "storytelling."

What is storytelling?

According to Mahy (2008), it is a way to create "desire, adhesion and commitment" through the use of "storytelling in the context of an innovation project." Companies must choose their stories and how to adapt them. In this respect, *storytelling* is an increasingly accepted way to achieve strategic and operational objectives in the service of their mission(s) of collective interest. Different narrative models are available to managers, but beyond the classifications, (Denning 2009) insists that "telling the right story" is the expression of a "core leadership competency, an ability that can help managers cope with (and achieve results in) the turbulent world" of the 21st century. Beyond competence, the authors insist on the need for a driven method. This is how the classic concept of storytelling is transformed into *Driving Telling,* a concept that has not yet been explored by the academic world.

To explain this concept, we have used a method that makes steering failures the root cause of all dysfunctions in companies. This is the socio-economic management method conceived by Professor Savall and developed with his team at ISEOR (Savall, 1974–75, 1979; Savall and Zardet, 1987).

2 METHODOLOGICAL CONTRIBUTION OR THE SOCIO-ECONOMIC APPROACH TO MANAGEMENT

The *Centre Technique d'Appui et de Formation des Centres d'Examens de Santé* (CETAF) was created on April 25, 1994 as a private non-profit association. This technostructure, which has been headquartered in Saint-Etienne[3] since 2003, has a role of supporting the Caisses Primaires d'Assurance Maladie (CPAM) with respect to their Health Examination Centers (CES). In this sense, CETAF is a public health actor, specializing in prevention engineering and health promotion. As such, it translates governmental public health strategies into concrete and operational actions including, in particular, the training of health professionals, the management of innovative prevention projects and public health research.[4]

If the period 2003–2006 was synonymous with strong growth for CETAF, the year 2007 heralded a sequence of visible threats, and therefore of hidden opportunities:

- The CNAM has stated its intention to halt the growth of CETAF in terms of objectives;
- A report by the *Cour des Comptes*, (Court of Auditors) on the period 2008–2009, destabilized the CES and CETAF;
- A general review of public policies resulted in a heavy and unavoidable budgetary constraint: –27% of credits between 2010 and 2013; a wave of retirements from strategic positions (including the Executive Director), four resignations and the economic dismissal of 7 people.

Faced with this situation, it was decided to call on an external service provider, in particular to capitalize on the know-how of retiring agents. Socio-economic management, proposed by ISEOR, was chosen for its ability to (re)place the Human being at the center of the company's concerns, in the service of socio-economic performance (Savall et al., 2015).

The story begins in May 2010 with a meta-objective, "To affirm CETAF as a proactive and efficient team for the Health Insurance," and a desire: to develop, simultaneously, actions of immediate result and creation of potential. In order to get out of a form of "ambient gloom," all employees were given the opportunity to express themselves on the social difficulties encountered and their economic impact. At the end of this sharing, four priority themes were discussed:

- Improving the animation of value-added activities,
- Reinforce the professionalization of management,
- Renovate the organization of teamwork,
- Mobilize all the actors through a proactive and contractualized strategy.

Thus, after listening, the search for and implementation of solutions made it possible to involve, in an incentive manner, all CETAF employees. The evaluation of the socio-economic results, carried out in 2013, resulted in a document of more than 170 pages, constructed jointly by the CETAF actors and the ISEOR stakeholders (Deville, 2013). Beyond the 150 sentences collected, which testify to an improvement in social performance,[5] the contribution of one hour of work to value added increased by more than 4% between 2009 and 2011. Without the mobilization of all, this value would have decreased by 15%. In addition, 62% of hidden costs have been reduced, which represents an amount of €29,000 per person per year. To obtain these results, the investment made, including the cost of the external service provider as well as the value of the time spent by employees, represents 3% of the overall volume of hidden costs. In other words, an investment representing 3% of the total amount of hidden costs allowed us to reduce the volume of hidden costs by 62%.

These results, which may seem spectacular, are in fact only anecdotal in view of the change dynamic that has been in place for more than 10 years at CETAF. The motto "Strengthening internally and opening up externally" has become a "breath" that guides the writing of history. This history is the result of a collective process whose main achievements are described below.

3 CETAF'S COLABORATIVE APPROACH

The involvement of CETAF employees in the history of their company is the result of a long learning process. It should be noted, as we will see in the following points, that this process must evolve permanently in order to achieve renewed socio-economic performance.

3.1 Breakfasts/Coffee Exchanges

Since 2005, management has organized quarterly breakfasts for all employees to share important information about the organization. In 2013, management was "forced" to note that, despite the use of several facilitation techniques, the top-down information was not generating much discussion.

It was decided to experiment with a new system: "discussion cafés," organized by employees. The above-mentioned information now follows a vertical pattern organized around the Pole Committee[6] and team meetings, via internal days if necessary (see point 3.3.). Between 2014 and 2019, 13 sessions were organized by employees, ranging from strategic intelligence to LinkedIn, via the shared medical file or quality of life at work. In the review conducted in 2019, this formula was favorably received by the majority of employees. The topics chosen meet expectations and the discussions are proving fruitful.

3.2 Internal Communication Media

Aware that the annual dissemination of the company's work program and activity report could not satisfy the demand for information from employees, CETAF created an in-house company newspaper "Trait d'Union" in 2014 and a regular publication on priority action themes "Infopap."

Between 2015 and 2019, 40 issues of Trait d'Union and 48 issues of Infopap have been published. Once again, the topics developed are popular and have evolved over time, making the information more readable and understandable. In 2020, Infopap was integrated into the internal magazine *Trait d'Union* to demonstrate the integration of socio-economic management tools into the life of CETAF.

3.3 Collaborative Training

It has become necessary to share knowledge with all CETAF employees in order to serve its strategy. This evolution of skills has been the subject of reflection in terms of training engineering. While it is necessary to call on service providers for some issues, others can be addressed by sharing knowledge among CETAF employees. The objective is to integrate a shared level of expertise within the company, which is essential to its proper functioning. For example, sessions have been organized on public health and socio-economic management. In order to obtain truly "integrated" training, these are preceded by a session of exchanges and sharing of practices, in order to meet the needs of employees.

3.4 Internal Days

This mechanism, which was set up at CETAF in 2012, is undoubtedly the most relevant for creating links within the company. Bringing together all the staff simultaneously, either "in the green" or in the company (alternating), these days allow employees to exchange outside the daily constraints related to their activities.

What is most interesting is the evolution of the organization that presides over them. Initially organized by management (agenda, program, logistics, etc.), they are now organized by a group of volunteer employees. The employees have a limited budget and are free to make proposals to management. The topics covered during these days are both varied and innovative. On a generic level, they deal with CETAF's values, policies and strategies.

For the past few years, complementary team-building activities have been offered in connection with the concepts discussed. The objective is to associate the concepts with their implementation. As an example, an activity was organized for the implementation of the SCAMPER method.[7]

3.5 Company Policies

The personalized assistance provided by the ISEOR staff revealed the need to develop company policies to promote the "channeled" creativity of the PASINTEX and PAP tools. Thus, three policies were developed within the framework of focus groups involving the management, the managers and a representative of ISEOR:

- A socio-economic management control policy (Deville, 2018),
- A human potential development policy (PDPH),
- A policy of communication, coordination and cooperation (3C)

The first policy, put at the service of a better management of CETAF, aims to: better manage human time; increase the economic sensitivity of employees; find strategic plans, systematically budgeted; strengthen the efficient management of activities and finally promote management dialogue.

The second policy (PDPH) defines the framework of the ideal aimed at promoting the well-being at work of its employees with the aim of improving sustainable socio-economic performance. Innovation, service, cooperation and trust are the values of CETAF, they must be supported on a daily basis by the PDPH, which now aims to: create and innovate; offer integrated, evolving and differentiated career paths; share the remuneration policy; develop the company's societal, environmental and economic responsibility and promote professional dialogue. (Deville, 2014)

The inseparable terms of the third policy are: communication, coordination and cooperation. This 3C policy, in conjunction with the PDPH and the CGSE, aims to "do things better together." It aims to create links and improve the collective, to give meaning, to support permanent change, to encourage dialogue, to make information understandable and appropriate, and to enhance the value of CETAF, its activities and its employees.

These three policies were the subject of an internal day of appropriation work. Sharing them has helped to remove uncertainties and to mobilize all employees in their implementation. It should also be noted that the formalization of these policies helps to write the future history of the company, especially since an annual monitoring system has been set up with one or two annual meetings of the Sectors' Committee to take stock of their implementation.

3.6 Seminar of the Poles Committee (COPOL)

The "COPOL seminar" is a recent creation, the first of which took place in September 2018. It responds to a need, expressed by both management and managers, to be able to sit down to create and share a common thought process in a place free from the turbulence and reflexes of daily life. The first seminar, prepared and held in the presence of a speaker from ISEOR, was the subject of intense preparation by the Director and the Deputy Director of CETAF, on the objectives of the seminar, its conduct (schedules, sequences, facilitation techniques, etc.), the role of the external speaker, and the evaluation of the seminar.

At the end of this first seminar, the participants considered that their expectations had been met, particularly with regard to the transparency of the exchanges and the richness of the contents: vision of CETAF today and tomorrow, argumentation of the strategic aims of PASINTEX, pre-solutions for the implementation of a budgeted PASINTEX, etc.

The second seminar took place in September 2020. It was prepared under the responsibility of the CETAF management with the involvement of managers, in particular for an update of the strategic intelligence matrices. In the future, it will be organized on an annual basis according to the alternation implemented for the internal days.

CONCLUSION

Regardless of the size, organization and sector of activity of a company, it is not easy to lead change, especially since for CETAF it was not a question of optimizing a particular process, but of restoring the association's sustainable performance.

It took about ten years to embed the change in CETAF's DNA and to ensure that it was present in the daily working lives of all employees. This necessary maturation, which avoided the wrong target, the application of costly and unsuitable solutions, and technocratic thought patterns, gave everyone the pride of working in THEIR company. The involvement of everyone in the described systems shows that the company's employees are able to write its history and its future and that they are able to make it known and recognized.

NOTES

1. Founding president of the circle of HR excellence, founder of the movement "the why project" and co-author of "the co-directors of the vintage" and the "HRD of the 3rd millennium." He organized the great forum of the raison d'être of the MEDEF in Paris, January 28, 2020.

2. As with every crisis, regardless of their form and the dramas they provoke, the health crisis that has been raging in the world since 2020 seems to be a "useful pretext" for the re-foundation of the company.
3. Cetaf employs 40 persons, including 9 researchers reporting to INSERM-Paris
4. www.cetaf.fr/ Website of the CETAF
5. For example, the following sentences illustrate an improvement in the work atmosphere: "There is a good work atmosphere within the Center"; "There is a decrease in conflicts between people", "There is a return of discipline, of a certain form of ethics," "The atmosphere has improved. You get to work with people you were not used to working with," etc.
6. Pole Committee is a team consisting of top and middle management.
7. The SCAMPER method is a creativity method to enrich an idea by going through the following filters: Subsitute, Combine, Adapt, Modify, Put to other uses, eliminate, Rearrange or Reverse.

REFERENCES

Denning, S. (2009, June–July) The art of storytelling. *Harvard Business Review.*

Deville, N. (2013). Socioeconomic performance of a Technical Support and Training Center for Health Examination Centers. In H. Savall & V. Zardet (Eds.), *Re-industrialization and multisectoral dynamization.* Paris: Economica.

Deville, N. (2014). How to be the partner of its institutional environment in the construction of its strategy? In H. Savall & V. Zardet (Eds.), *La conduite du changement dans les entreprises et organisations.* Paris: Economica.

Deville, N. (2018). How to better pilot and involve resources for socio-economic performance: socio-economic management control. In H. Savall & V. Zardet (Eds.), *La digitalisation apprivoisée : au service de l'humain et de la performance durable.* Caen: EMS.

Mahy, I. (2008) « Il était une fois… « or « la force du récit dans la conduite du changement «. *Communication et organisation, 33*(2008), 50–60.

This page intentionally left blank.

CHAPTER 39

NECESSARY COMMUNICATION–COORDINATION–COOPERATION TO FIGHT AGAINST THE BLOCKAGES OF LOCKED ORGANIZATIONS

Cases of Hospitals

Isabelle Barth and Marc Frachette

ABSTRACT

Hospitals have always been places of complicated interactions between physicians, nurses and management. Hospital organizations have reached a level of blockage and "lock-in" that is rarely reached, and that only a more "clinical" management approach combining a controlled level of communication–coordination–cooperation (3Cs) between its stakeholders can achieve. An in-depth diagnosis of the functioning of each structure, followed by a socio-economic project, a real "care plan" conducted with method, can help unlock the mechanisms of cooperation that are essential to hospital performance.

Despite the many calls for help from employees, despite the warnings of psychosocial risk experts, despite the figures for sick leave... Many organizations, companies or public bodies, large or small, are places that are felt by those who work there to be "locked"!

Some of these barriers are real and objective, others are experienced by the actors in their work life. Whatever the category, these barriers are very real obstacles to the performance of the organization, because they block all its fluidity. They are also the source of psychological suffering and self-censorship that are detrimental to the quality of life at work. They are the result of a technicist conception of management, with the development of procedures, rigid

SEAM Treatise, pages 351–357

hierarchies, specialization of tasks and services.They are also the result of a degraded management style that does not take into account human resources, based on power, dirigisme and often humiliation, even harassment.

In general, we have to wait for a crisis to erupt before governance comes out of its denial or blindness.This crisis can be internal, with classic symptoms: absenteeism or under-performance that are too obvious, strikes, legal proceedings, and a deteriorating image. It can be external with the inability to face a sudden change. A "blocked" organization is by definition incapable of adapting. A sudden increase in demand, or expected changes in the way the company operates, then bring the company to a standstill. Some leaders give up and the organization is doomed to "death." Others realize, either on their own or by force, that this is a crucial moment for awareness and the opportunity for a new beginning.

We have had the opportunity to work with many organizations that have experienced this awakening (Barth, 1994 ; Frachette, 2014). Hospitals and other health facilities are very representative of these locked-down organizations. It doesn't mean that hospitals are the only organizations to be locked.

We therefore propose to describe, through four cases of health organizations to show in what way they are locked, then the "unlocking" process through the installation of a management that we call "clinical" and which is based on dialogue and the "silo-breaking" of services.

Far from reporting on the whole process of socio-economic intervention, we point out the importance of communication-coordination-cooperation (3C) in restarting the flow of activity and energy in these four hospital structures.

1 EVERYTHING STARTS WITH THE DIAGNOSIS

One of the pillars of the socio-economic approach of the ISEOR is the diagnosis. We will briefly describe its characteristics (Savall, 1974, Savall & Zardet, 1987) and then illustrate it with the four pilot organizations.But before doing so, it is essential to give some background information on the evolution of French hospitals.

1.1 History of French Hospital Organizations

The French hospital system has a historical culture of organization and the search for health and social efficiency; this has been reflected since the time of the Hôtels-Dieu by a permanent desire for investigation and reform in parallel with the construction of the State (Imbert, 1982).

At the heart of this system, the doctors, who were responsible for medical activity, developed a power that had often experienced difficulty cohabiting with the managers (Mintzberg & Glouberman, 2002).

The modernization reform of 1958, by creating the University Hospitals, allowed the transformation of the hospital system by responding to the evolution of medical techniques; successive reforms organized the aspects of financing, the supply of care, the quality approach, and health cooperation (Pesqueux, 2002). All these fields have been supported by the executive, dealt with by the legislator and implemented by the health agencies. Over the decades, a large number of specialized bodies have appeared in all fields: financing, organization, quality, safety. These structures have developed in line with the growing complexity of the health system.

Caregivers found themselves confronted with the complexity of this governance without being invited to participate in its design or prepared to steer it; this new machinery, designed on the basis of real observations, effectively excluded the main stakeholders, who were deemed not to be sufficiently concerned by, or even opposed to, these new codes. As crises and budgetary constraints arose, health management came to a halt, giving way to top-down technical-economic approaches with a medical-economic vision centered on budgetary allocation. The doctrine of the hospital health system has become locked into a logic of executive, legislative, regulatory and technical decisions, instead of a management system integrating communication-coordination-cooperation mechanisms, sufficiently formalized and developed. This contextualization allows for a better understanding of the organizations in which we conducted the interventions presented here.

1.2 The Four Hospital Organizations: Presentations and Illustrations

We present here the results extracted from 4 intervention-researches over 10 years (2009–2019) which took place in health care institutions representing a total perimeter of more than 8,000 full-time equivalents (FTEs). 205 people were interviewed in medico-technical departments, clinical departments and management.

Case 1 is an acute care hospital with 2000 FTEs. The scope of the study was its internal use pharmacy (PUI); the objective was the reorganization of pharmaceutical activities. 27 people were interviewed (Frachette, 2014).

Case 2 is a private healthcare institution of collective interest (ESPIC) with an acute activity (MCO) of 1700 FTE. The scope was pharmacies spread over several sites and their management; the objective was to merge the pharmacies and harmonize activities. Thirty-two people were interviewed.

Case 3 is an MCO hospital (medicine, surgery and obstetrics) with 2,500 FTE. The scope of the study was a transversal process of care between clinical and medico-technical services; the objective was cooperation between the services concerned. 35 people were interviewed

Case 4 is an MCO hospital with 2000 FTEs within a group of 2000 beds. The scope of the study concerned two clinical medicine departments; the objective was the quality of functioning between clinical departments, pharmacy and management. 62 people were interviewed during the diagnosis phase, then 48 people during the evaluation phase.

1.3 The Socio-Economic Diagnosis

The initial negotiation phase of these accompaniments can be long, sometimes interrupted and then resumed, and in all cases needs to mature; thus, from the first contact, the intervener and the organization are in co-construction and begin to initiate this communication-coordination-cooperation process: communicate between the intervener and the institution, coordinate on the intervention protocol and agree on the objectives.

At the end of the information and cooperation stage, which allows for the definition of a customized intervention architecture, the socio-economic intervention always begins with a diagnosis of the organization's situation. This diagnosis phase, which is decisive for the transformation of the organization, is developed in chapter:[1]

This diagnosis, with its listening phase, gives the tone of this requirement. The socio-economic approach is the opposite of that used in response to calls for tender or calls for projects, which almost never involve cooperation: "we have had so many audits and we have never been listened to." At the end of the diagnosis phase, the design phase of the change project is held with the opening of an internal and external strategic action plan that links strategy to action. Only then will the implementation of these transformations allow for sustainable change management (6).

2 OBSERVING A LACK OF DIALOGUE

The socio-economic diagnosis is organized around six major themes: CDT (Working Conditions), WO (Work Organization), Time Management, Integrated Training, Strategic Implementation and the 3Cs for Communication-Coordination-Cooperation.

2.1 The CCCs: Definition and Issues

In socio-economic theory, the triptych Communication-Coordination-Cooperation plays a very important "streamlining" role in the organization. If we take up some elements of definition: Communication represents the exchange of information between actors, whatever the purpose; Coordination corresponds to information exchange mechanisms intended to achieve an objective; Cooperation allows actors to define a common objective. These three levers have shortcomings in the way organizations operate.

2.2 Locking in Due to the Failure of the 3Cs

In the observation sites we have used, many of the witness statements collected during the interviews concern the failure of the 3Cs within the teams or with management; these difficulties may have other organizational dysfunctions as their root causes. It is frequently the communication mechanisms that seem to be ineffective:

"There are no more joint meetings, meeting time is spent on schedules, top-down information"; "information from management is contradictory."

These difficulties indicate inefficient 3C systems: communication habits are not very agile and do not mobilize the teams.

It can also be the strategic approach that is poorly articulated with the needs: "the integration of newcomers is not planned, tutoring is not foreseen in advance" indicates 3C difficulties between human resources, managers and staff who welcome new recruits; "The internal tensions are due to a lack of clarity in decisions" illustrates the fact that decisions taken by management are neither agreed nor understood by managers and employees; "We are never fully staffed and on top of that there are job restrictions" indicates that beyond the job restrictions decided upon, the recruitment priority for jobs in tension is not sufficiently concerted.

The internal organization can also be questioned: "the functioning between managers and practitioners floats, it is not formalized"; "there is little delegation between practitioners and managers" illustrates the difficulties of 3C between different hierarchical lines, practitioners and caregivers.

Finally, problems of premises or equipment for working can accentuate the difficulties of cooperation: "the software does not work, the interfaces are inoperative and the maintenance times are long"; "it is difficult to connect, there are several codes and the software between the clinical and medico-technical services is not interfaced; as a result, we send faxes and make photocopies"; the consequence is the slowness of the 3C systems on patient files, which can thus delay treatment

3C's difficulties stem from the style and quality of management: constrained management, by injunction, with insufficient delegation, coupled with a lack of appetite for management among health professionals, leads to tensions that block hospital organizations.

Management is still anchored in a very subordinate paradigm (Moisdon & Tonneau, 1999) and has difficulty in evolving towards more agile negotiation and contractualization practices, involving the adoption of perfectly controlled and articulated communication, coordination and cooperation practices. When the 3C arrangements between decision-makers and field managers are fluid, the functioning of the organization and the mobilization of teams are quickly affected.

3 GET THE ORGANIZATION BACK ON TRACK

Once the diagnosis has been made, the next step is to set the organization in motion. The intervention process follows a well-established, multi-faceted protocol: setting up focus groups, training activities and developing tools to structure the future organization. We have chosen Internal and External Strategic Action Planning (IESAP). It is the tool that allows the redeployment of the strategy in a concerted, coordinated and communicated manner

3.1 IESAP: A Tool for a Shared Strategy

We present below the construction of an internal and external strategic action plan (anonymized and reconstituted from the different cases); this action plan integrates different themes related to the 3Cs; the strategic axes are directly derived from the elements of the diagnoses; the priorities correspond to the dysfunctions retained to lead the change. In a second phase, the actions are defined with the focus groups and validated by the management. In the right-hand column, we have indicated some elements of hidden costs that help prioritize actions; in fact, 30% of hidden costs can be reduced by actions that are well conducted over time, which allows us to remain focused on actions with greater social and economic value.

This IESAP identifies ways to improve the versatility of the actors and the 3C systems that will allow the good functioning of the activities. The management of the 3C systems, in particular via transversal actions between categories of managers, the steering of projects, and adapted management tools is a pillar to unlock the organization. The development of employees and their integration is a key intangible investment to anticipate blockages. Finally, institutional projects already underway are integrated into the action plan. These different axes require an effective 3C strategy to develop the management and performance of the organization concerned. The evaluation of the results after the implementation of the action plan allows us to gather feedback from the actors and to illustrate the mobilization of 3C actions.

3.2 Results of 3C's Actions

A socio-economic evaluation (Savall & Zardet, 1987) at the end of the change management approach was carried out in one of the hospitals; it illustrates the desire of decision-makers, whether they are practitioners, caregivers or their operational departments, to work in a more concerted manner and the fact that change management based on correctly implemented 3C measures rapidly produces effects. We call this approach "Clinical Management" (Frachette et al., 2019; Denis et al.2008).

Quick decisions were made concerning material resources: "the WIFI network is better than before" (decision to add terminals following a diagnosis that indicated problems with the connection to the patient file; before the diagnosis nothing had been done); "we had the support of the management for the purchase of carts" (without the meetings stimulated by the project the requests were not successful)

Internal functioning has improved: "between us it goes well, we are a united team despite the lack of recognition from the institution"; "the staff of the service are very available and adapt" (after one year of participative transformation), even if we still note a lack of 3C between management and the field. Some of the 3C mechanisms between managers and employees can still be improved: "there is still no communication on the projects from the managers."

The development of skills has improved following cooperation between the department concerned and human resources: "we have a good range of activities, it's changing" (development of versatility); "I finally got the training I needed" (internal departmental approach taken to management level).

The strategic approach is better understood and relayed: "the department is now recognized by the chiefs"; on the other hand, the functioning of decision-making bodies that are not well managed quickly leads to wasted time, misunderstood decisions, exhaustion and even low commitment: "the bodies always function badly."

Finally, we conducted an interview from a distance when we took up a new position (an interview during the period of containment of the Covid crisis); the manager interviewed indicated that the implementation of a socio-economic approach requires an important phase of cooperation, and that, if the middle managers accept the approach under the direct impetus of their head of department, the management finds it difficult to grasp the importance of setting up a participatory approach that does not quickly lead to solutions, despite the unease of a team in distress: "the cooperation does not go all the way down." The employees gradually understand the value of it, provided that the implementation of the solutions is discussed: "it is difficult to move from a posted plan to a concerted organization."

The condition for the success of such an approach is the adoption by the entire management line of a participative management style instead of a directive one: "cooperation requires an appetite, practice and a few tools; it relies on the manager, otherwise, in the end, it is the motivation that suffers.

Beyond the behaviors that are the basis of socio-economic management, what this department head remembers is the structuring provided by two tools: the competency grids that make it possible to map team practices and skills and to coordinate training plans; and also the articulation between the internal and external strategic action plan (IESAP) and its operational implementation in priority action plans (PAP), which stimulates all those responsible for actions and projects, right down to the operators concerned.

CONCLUSION

Many organizations are in a pathological state of operation. And the management only realizes this very late. Very often, it is the employees who sound the alarm.Paradoxically, hospitals are often acute cases of this. The suffering at work of the staff is real, the service to be rendered to the patients is degraded, the quality of care is in danger.

Socio-economic intervention, with its in-depth work on the diagnosis, based on the discourse of the actors, allows for the necessary awareness and builds the basis for the implementation of new strategic choices. We show from 4 cases that the failures in the dialogue, in all its forms (intra personnel, intra organizational, interdepartmental…) is one of the major causes of the blockages of the flows of the organization: flow of information, flow of people, flow of products … The organization is then like "locked," putting people in a situation of inefficiency, suffering, disengagement. The structured listening provided during the diagnosis, particularly during the interviews and the mirror-effect, frees up the word.

The project allows the redeployment of dialogues in confidence (10) with the theme of the 3C, and the PASINTEX is the tool for the development of a strategic implementation shared by all the actors. The unlocking is done, thanks to these 3 steps and these 3 tools from the socio-economic theory, allowing the organization to move towards the deployment of an overall performance, both economic and social. It is thus more agile and more capable of adapting to the changes imposed on it by its environment.

NOTE

1. See the presentation of the socio-economic diagnosis in the first chapter of this treatise.

REFERENCES

(1) Savall, H., & Zardet, V., (2003), Maîtriser les coûts et performances cachés. Paris, Economica, 4th edition, 2003.

(2) Imbert, J., (1982), Histoire des hôpitaux. Toulouse, Privat.

(3) Mintzberg, H., Glouberman S. (2002), Gérer les soins de santé et le traitement de la maladie, Gestion HEC Montréal, vol. 27, March 2002, 152 p.

(4) JORF. (1958), Ordonnance n°58–1873 du 30 décembre 1958, Journal Officiel de la République Française, p.1207v°, 31 décembre 1958

(5) Pesqueux, Y. (2002), Organisation: modèles et représentations, PUF, Paris, 2002

(6) David A. (2008), Logique, épistémologie et méthodologie en sciences de gestion : trois hypothèses revisitées, in Les nouvelles fondations en sciences de gestion, David A., Hatchuel A., Laufer R. (coordonné par), Vuibert-FNEGE, Paris, p.83–109

(7) Moisdon J-C., Tonneau D. (1999), La démarche gestionnaire à l'hôpital, tome I, Seli Arslan, Paris, March 1999, p.19

(8) Frachette M., Zardet V., Rieutord A., Barth I. (2019), La coopération entre services cliniques à l'hôpital et son impact sur la prise en charge thérapeutique, Journal de gestion et d'économie de la santé, vol. 37, N°3 2019

(9) Denis J-L., Contandriopoulos A-P., Pomey M-P. (2008), Editorial, Pratiques et Organisation des Soins, vol.39, n°3, July-September 2008, p.165–167 nécessaire CCC pour lutter contre les blocages d'organisations verrouillées

This page intentionally left blank.

CHAPTER 40

LISTENING AND MEDIATION AS A LEVER FOR TRANSFORMING A CONFLICTUAL STATE INTO A COOPERATIVE STATE

Laurent Bertrand and Renaud Petit

ABSTRACT

Listening and mediation are powerful levers of success for organizational change management. The transformation of the numerous individual conflicts and resistances, natural phenomena in organizations, into cooperation is the main managerial response to obtain collective performance. The remarkable qualitative, quantitative and financial results of the combined implementation of socio-economic management and the Non-Violent Communication approach, within an institution in the health and social sector, attest to this. The right mix of methodologist/mediator/therapist roles for managers is crucial for the sustainable and continuous success of cooperation in the workplace.

Implementing socio-economic management requires, in most cases, a strong involvement of the manager, as any change is synonymous with resistance. He is then led to combine a new method either with existing practices or to call upon additional specific approaches, often linked to the particularity of the organization's sector of activity. This is the case of the Aigues-Vertes Foundation, an institution for people with intellectual disabilities. Its activities and values aim to increase the social participation of people with disabilities, by reconciling their private life, their community life and their professional life in adapted places. The staff and accompanying professionals are trained to be good listeners, being confronted with complex and stressful situations, but they can nevertheless be impervious to management

SEAM Treatise, pages 359–365

issues, sometimes perceived as far from their primary concerns. The implementation of socio-economic approach to management (SEAM), coupled with Non-Violent Communication (NVC) practices, through their approach based on listening, has made it possible to deal with many conflicts and resistances. This chapter therefore focuses on the importance of listening and mediation as the main lever for a proximity manager in his action to change situations (rather individual) of conflict or resistance to a state of cooperation and cohesion (rather collective). First, the importance of listening in the SEAM change processes and in the NVC practices is analyzed. Then, a second part illustrates the implementation of the actions as well as the main results. Finally, the different points of convergence of the two approaches are presented, in order to bring out the managerial posture that enables the teams to build the meaning and responsibilities of their actions.

1 LISTENING: A LEVER FOR DETERMINING INDIVIDUAL AND COLLECTIVE NEEDS

The days of managing employees may be over (Collins, 2013) because if they have to be managed, then they don't belong. It is better to have meaning-driven collaborators who are able to make up their own minds what their company or team is about, decide how to contribute to it, and how to act to move forward. They must therefore be in tune with the meaning and identity of the company. When they are not, they are probably in conflict or at least in a position of resistance to any change.

In socio-economic theory, conflict is natural, i.e., the social group is inherently conflictual, so that trying to eradicate disagreements between actors in the organization is futile (Savall, 1974–75, 1979). The idea is rather to act in order to transform zones of conflict into zones of cooperation, because in their major part, social interactions are at the same time conflicts and "community of interests," the actors are as much adversaries as partners, since any exchange cannot be pure conflict or pure cooperation, since the actors cannot hide their egocentric interests (Perroux, 1973). It is not a matter of fleeing from conflict, or of fearing it, because it is not a priori good or bad, but rather of "knowing the nature of peace by understanding the true nature of conflict" (Follet, 1924), i.e., bringing out the meta goals in MASE or meta intentions in NVC.

Communicating is necessary for closeness, but not sufficient for cooperation. Sometimes, we communicate all the better when we have no intention of cooperating. It is the process of negotiation that allows us to move from communication to cooperation, the only proof that individuals are not in conflict, but in a mode of co-construction. Finally, the moment of rapprochement between two actors in conflict comes from the fact that a person progresses in his or her perception of himself or herself, a phenomenon of introspection, but he or she also progresses in his or her perception of the other.

In the NVC process, the human being is considered as a whole, composed of universal needs and feelings. To get closer and to know him better means to give him the opportunity to be fully in action. An empathic posture has the virtue of getting out of a two-dimensional work culture dominated by the simple dialectic Thinking/Acting. This mechanical aspect of organized systems influences relationships and contributes to the emergence of conflicts. Sometimes, in spite of a system that is supposedly well established and proven, differences in behavior appear to the detriment of the efficiency of the whole. Is there another parameter, outside of this system, that would connect people? NVC therefore seeks to take into-account the feelings of the actors in order to move from the binary Thinking/Acting approach to a three-dimensional approach: Connecting/Thinking/Acting (Miyashiro, 2013). Accessing the ability to understand the emotional characteristics of others allows for the identification of needs and the ability to name the feelings of the other which, in fine, allows for connecting. In concrete terms, we can better understand the relationships with all our colleagues, collaborators, partners, clients, suppliers, beneficiaries, public institutions..., all the stakeholders with whom we negotiate every day in our professional activity.

Listening is omnipresent in both SEAM and NVC practices. The socio-economic diagnosis is first of all a phase of listening to all the actors involved because "each individual, whatever his job, whatever his hierarchical level, is a witness to dysfunctions: he causes them, he suffers them, but he is also in a position to put forward suggestions, sometimes very concrete, to reduce these dysfunctions – this is the principle of the box of living ideas" (Savall & Zardet, 1987). The objective is to collect, through listening, information describing the lived phenomena and personal opinions of the interviewees. The combination of the individual information mentioned by each person, all of whom are observers of the facts, allows a general representation of the collective functioning. It is more a question of collecting raw expressions of dysfunctions than of looking for the causes, the interpretation of which is specific to the interviewee, but which is very useful in a project phase because it is a collective stage and "a consensus has already been established on the inventory of dysfunctions and their effects" (Savall & Zardet, 2004). This posture is close to an authentic or empathic listening proper to the NVC approach, without judging what is real or not, what may or may not seem important, but by carefully considering the nature of what is expressed, without arbitrary selection which would come from our own experience.

In addition, NVC mediation considers that the reformulation of the other person's needs is the tipping point towards the resolution of the conflict because he/she feels heard and understood, and therefore ready to cooperate being in confidence with the other. To a certain extent, the expert opinion has this same ambition, because this analysis aims at differentiating listening from believing. The facilitator must listen critically, in order to better express his or her position on the dysfunctions, their causes and their nature, beyond what the people have expressed. This may involve information that is "difficult for the actors to admit, but that the facilitator who has captured it expresses on their behalf (spokesperson and intermediation function)" (Savall & Zardet, 1987).

Whether in the context of socio-economic diagnosis interviews or in NVC practices, individual expression combined with the individual expressions of other actors in a given group results in an analysis, sometimes based on contradiction, devoid of judgment and therefore useful for negotiation and collective cohesion.

2 RESULTS OF THE COMBINATORIAL PROCESS OF TRANSFORMATION OF CONFLICT INTO COOPERATION

The combinatorial process presented illustrates the extent to which intangible investment is the pillar of the development of the Aigues-Vertes Foundation, with a total of more than 16,800 hours devoted to training and external accompaniment carried out in seven years (Table 40.1). All populations of actors are concerned, in systems that alternate individual meetings, group time, listening, mediation and co-construction.

The evolution of the combined investments in SEAM and CNV have given rise to numerous qualitative, quantitative and financial results. The first finding concerns cohesion, particularly that of the management team. Authentic listening and mutual trust have enabled the construction of a more successful Internal and External Strategic Action Plan (Savall and Zardet, 1995), but also teamwork, beyond the specificities of the business, which

TABLE 40.1 Overview of SEAM and NVC Assistance

Actions implemented	Categories concerned	Time budget
SEAM Product-Method (2015–2020)		
• Personalized assistance of the CEO • Top management team workshop • Personalized asssistance sessions and role of the internal interveners' manager • Accreditations of the top management team and of the internal interveners	Top management and middle managers (10 persons)	5,920 h
• it of the communication-coordination-cooperation systems and of the IESAP/PAPs • Diagnoses/ Project groups: – socio-profesional unit – Corporate service – Nursing care department – Socio-educational home team – Cohesion of the top management team • Socio-economic evaluation: – Socio-professional unit – Corporate service • Nursing care department	Top management, Middle management, Shopfloor (250 pers.)	
Non violent communication program (2013–2020)		
Basic training in Non Violent Communication	Top management, middle management and 52% of the staff (130 pers.)	3 days (21 h): 2,730 h
Accompaniment on mediating postures	Top management and middle management (27 pers.)	17 days (119 h): 3,213 h
Participating in mediating sessions	Top management, managers and staff (210 pers. and 700 attendance records)	A 118 average number of days each year from 2015 to 2020: 4,956 h
OVERALL AMOUNT of intangible investment		16,819 h

reassures the teams, who recognize the exemplary nature and coherence of managerial practices. This has facilitated the dissemination of SEAM practices and tools, to the extent that all the actors no longer express the unpleasant feeling of inequity of treatment from a managerial point of view.

The progress of cohesion can also be observed at the organizational level, with the merger of certain specialties and changes within each sector. For example, a historically "socio-educational" service is now part of the "socio-professional" sector. Internal transversality, which is often problematic in the health and medical-social sector (Zardet et al. 2011), seems to be increasingly accepted, and even desired, by the teams. We note here the capacity that professionals can have to link up, when a better knowledge of each other's work is brought about.

The overall evolution is just as visible at the level of communication-coordination-cooperation systems. For beyond the organizational chart, concrete and structured practices of interdisciplinary transversal exchanges have been put in place. The communication-coordination-cooperation mechanisms have been redesigned in terms of their content, frequency and composition. This is evidenced by the decrease in the average time spent in team meetings from 3 hours to 2.5 hours per week for professionals in the socio-educational sector and from 3 hours to 2 hours for those in the socio-professional sector. Meetings have become more effective, given the reduced time for managing conflicts and resistance, with more immediate resolutions. In addition, recourse to mediation has been greatly reduced, so that the time taken to resolve blockages is shorter, in the order of half a day, whereas previously it could take between 3 and 4 days.

The evolution of social indicators also illustrates the benefits of the combined process. Staff turnover has fallen very sharply from 23% in 2015 to around 8% in 2019, given the decrease in tensions and lack of collective cohesion. Workplace accidents have also decreased from 1.48% to 0.48% over the same period, while overall absenteeism remains stable, fluctuating between 6% and 7%.

The evolution of the treatment of hidden costs-performance is remarkable. First, it is possible to calculate them simultaneously, regularly and with the same effort in all sectors of the institution, including those that are considered less sensitive to financial data. Table 40.2 illustrates the data calculated and piloted by the teams themselves, accompanied by internal consultants. This is not data from diagnoses conducted by external researchers, but rather multi-faceted information from internal mini-diagnoses based on listening to dysfunctions, unmet needs, and a collective effort to calculate hidden costs and performance. These mini-diagnoses are the place where individual expressions are confronted, leading to the collective construction of qualitative, quantitative and financial objectives to be reached over a given period of time, so that everyone can help each other cooperate better. Beyond the hidden costs recovered by service, an overall objective of conversion of hidden costs into value added has been determined, so that each sector can know its percentage of contribution to the achievement of this overall objective. The point here is not so much to compare results, but rather to highlight that all sectors, and therefore all actors, are "stakeholders" in the evolution of the institution's socio-economic performance, whether they carry out a "core business" activity or a so-called "support" activity.

It is important not to forget the main beneficiaries of the collective cooperation: people with disabilities. All of this has contributed to the average decrease in their crises, as well as in the number of days of recourse to an external medicalized structure, from around 562 days of hospitalization in 2014 to 12 days in 2017. Finally, the volume of requests for complaint appointments with the General Management has also decreased, two appointments requested by families, were recorded in 2020.

TABLE 40.2 Treatment of 2019–2020 Hidden Costs for Each Department

Departments	Overall amount of hidden costs (2019)	Hidden costs recovered (End of April 2020)	Achievement percentage of collective objective in 2019	Remaining hidden costs to be recycled
Administration	SwF 126,400	SwF 66,500	887%	SwF 59,900
HRM	SwF 394,700	SwF 89,500	398%	SwF 287,700
Workshops	SwF 2,058,400	SwF 549,300	458%	SwF 1,390,000
	SwF 886,100	SwF 39,200	75%	SwF 843,200
Corporate service	SwF 247,900	SwF 84,000	373%	SwF 163,900
Nursing care	SwF 27,300	SwF 15,900	212%	SwF 9,700
Overall amount	SwF 3,740,800	SwF 844,400	400%	SwF 2,754,400

3 MANAGERIAL POSTURE TO BUILD MEANING AND RESPONSIBILITY FOR TEAM ACTIONS

The researcher could have an advantageous posture linked to his ignorance of the life history of the organization, of all the internal events perceived, positively or not, by the teams. He generally enjoys a special status, a certain aura, which he uses to manage the situations in which he is involved (Savall & Zardet, 2004). In this respect, the socio-economic diagnosis initiates trust at three levels (Savall & Zardet, 1987): the trust of the personnel towards the hierarchy, since it allows them to express themselves; the trust between the actors and the intervener, because the latter practices a very open listening without selection, nor judgement, a priori, and because he centers the interview on the dysfunctions and not on individuals; the trust between the intervener and the individuals, because he considers that all that is said is a sharing of moments of organizational life, that it deserves attention and allows him to help the intervener to organize change. In fact, it is a question of exchanging the roles of manipulator/manipulated, which is conducive to co-construction. The manager must listen to and observe his employees, if only to build a global trust in his system-team, similar to the one that an external researcher can weave. As we have observed, periodically organizing team mini-diagnoses is an appropriate way to stimulate permanent collective cooperation, based on empathetic listening to facts and not to interpretations.

Since conflict is part of organizational life, managerial avoidance is not a good strategy. The manager must be prepared to adopt the role of mediator/negotiator on a regular basis. Because by listening to the employees, the manager spots their concerns, their opinions, their reluctance, their moods or their stress, all of which are linked to their own individual needs. Nevertheless, he is asked to lead a team, so he will have to constantly mediate. This permanent mediation consists in preventing conflicts, rather than dedicating resources to deal with blocking situations between two or more parties, even though these resources are very precious.

Needs, whether they are professional or personal, when not satisfied, generate blocking situations. Sometimes these situations call for extreme behaviors that are totally inconsistent, incomprehensible or dissonant. The "therapeutic" dimension of the manager can be called upon in this case, because the facts can show that the blockage is individual and not systemic, or linked to the organizational functioning. The practice of NVC, in the case of the Aigues-Vertes Foundation, is useful for these situations, as long as the manager is "empowered" and trained to bring the individual to evoke his or her "life wounds" which are more personal in nature. It remains that these are situations of regulation and last resort reactions.

Finally, a good manager could thus be the one who, at times, seeks the more individual posture of the intervention-researcher by moving away from the manipulator/manipulated interactions, in order to make decisions according to the needs of the group and not by following his/her own emotions or intuitions. He/she will be more inclined to build methods and environments conducive to cooperation.

CONCLUSION

In socio-economic theory, the manager has three roles: methodologist, mediator and therapist (Savall et al., 2019), which require practices and devices conducive to listening, both individually and collectively, with the aim of provoking the most cooperation possible. The NVC approach, as implemented at the Aigues-Vertes Foundation, is not intended to promote psychological management, focused solely on the satisfaction of individual needs.

Some would say that the health and medical-social sector is better suited to this than other sectors. However, it is a question of placing human potential at the center of the organization, i.e., as the only lever for creating social and economic value added. The intangible investments made have indeed produced results. Among them, it is those of an economic nature that are the most remarkable, and this, in an environment where budgets for assistance to people with intellectual disabilities are decreasing. All means stimulating social performance are therefore good for developing economic performance.

REFERENCES

Collins, J. (2013). *Good to Great: Why some companies make the leap... and others don't.* Harper Business.

Follet, M.P. (1924). *Creative Experience.* Longmans, Green, New York.

Marshall, B. (2014). *Words are windows (or are they walls).* Éditions La Découverte.

Miyashiro, M. R. (2013). The challenges of empathy in the service of business – Beyond NVC. Éditions Jouvence.

Perroux, F. (1973). *Pouvoir et économie,* Dunod.

Zardet, V., Savall, H., Fière, D., & Petit, R. (2011). Managing interprofessional cooperation in the hospital. *Journal de Gestion & d'Économie Médicale,* Vol. 29, n°6–7.

CHAPTER 41

MODERNIZING THE ASSOCIATIVE MODEL IN THE MEDICO-SOCIAL SECTOR IN FRANCE

Frédéric Gloro and Denis Hamayon

ABSTRACT

The associative model in the medico-social sector is not outdated. It remains relevant for the development of social missions, particularly in the field of disability. However, it is necessary to recognize the existence of increasing difficulties in the management of these institutions, which constitute as many challenges for the modernization of their management. At least two areas could be the subject of a transformation of the associations: their governance and the implementation of a decentralized and synchronized management of their activities at the territorial level.

Many people think that the French status of the *association loi 1901* (non-profit associations) is no longer adapted for the good governance and efficient management of services for people with disabilities. The associative framework would have become obsolete to manage structures that often employ several hundreds of employees and accompany several hundreds of people with disabilities in their life course. Basically, we are witnessing a sort of "trial of amateurism" concerning the management of large institutions, whose operating budgets represent several tens of millions of euros. But in the face of this criticism, alternative solutions are rarely proposed. In this chapter, we would like to present another vision of things, based on our experience as directors of one of these associations, and to testify to the important changes achieved in several areas: the consolidation of the governance-management link, the transition from a highly centralized and pyramidal organization to a more decentralized and synchronized operation, the installation of a new management

SEAM Treatise, pages 367–372

model and effective managerial support for change. All these transformations have had very positive impacts in terms of the efficiency of the management of our association and the quality of our support to the people entrusted to us by their families.

1 THE ASSOCIATION MODEL IS ADAPTED TO THE FUTURE CHALLENGES OF THE MEDICO-SOCIAL SECTOR IF WE MODERNIZE GOVERNANCE AND MANAGEMENT

France has a fine heritage of medico-social associations created in the post-war period. This network originates from the mobilization of families, who invented structures that enabled their disabled children to be cared for throughout their lives. These private and supportive initiatives were a response to the inadequacy of public facilities directly managed by the State. Moreover, the State itself encouraged the development of these associations born from private initiatives, by progressively organizing their financing by public funds. It should be remembered that the financing of disability in France today represents approximately 30 billion euros per year contributed by the State, the Departments and the Social Security.

1.1 The Not-for Profit Association: A Model to be Developed

There is much to be done to change the structures of our professional organizations and improve the quality of support for people with disabilities. Our sector needs strategic renewal. Without claiming to draw up an exhaustive list, we can identify a few main challenges: repositioning all the organizations in the sector around a political project, transforming the supply of support services for people with disabilities and its financing, dealing with autistic disorders, and adapting support for people with disabilities as they age.

Among these challenges, those that affect the internal organization, governance and management of our associations appear essential. Of course, we want to defend this associative model, but not without recognizing its current limitations and the need to overcome them. One of the priorities is certainly to review our modes of governance. Our associations suffer from a lack of attractiveness to fill the functions of the governing bodies: Presidency, Bureau, Board of Directors. A generation of families and people involved in the social movement is currently disappearing and the succession is not well assured. Another facet of the challenge of modernizing our associative governance is its professionalization. Indeed, our institutions have become much more complex to manage than before. What criteria of complexity are we talking about? For example, the proliferation (Savall and Zardet, 2005) of financial, social and health standards, which is progressively transforming the costs of the core business of accompaniment to the benefit of regulatory funding (Gloro, 2020). We are therefore confronted with a real problem of training of our governance that needs to be managed.

The other essential facet of the transformations at work concerns the mobilization of all categories of actors in a meaningful associative project: members of governance, general and institutional management, supervisors, educational and health professionals, volunteers, families and residents. This is not a simple matter. From the outside, the functioning of our associations seems relatively uncomplicated. But in reality, we have to mobilize a wide variety of actors with different professional and personal interests and fields of action. Coordinating and synchronizing all these actors spread over dozens of establishments scattered over a territory is a matter of subtly adapted management.

1.2 An Example of a Not-for Profit Association: Adapei-Nouelles in the Côtes d'Armor, France

Adapei-Nouelles is celebrating its 60th anniversary in 2021. It is a parent association created in March 1961 to support mentally handicapped people. In a few figures, the association manages: 45 establishments and services, 1,350 employees, 82 million euros of budget and accompanies 2,600 people. The services of Adapei-Nouelles cover the whole territory of the Côtes-d'Armor department. Its activities and establishments are organized into three main areas: children, adults and so-called protected work.

In 2016, the not-for profit associations Adapei des Côtes-d›Armor and Les Nouelles merged to create a new organization. As is often the case with mergers, the general management changes and a new management team takes over the reins of the association. It was at this time that we built our new management model with the guidance of ISEOR (Savall, 1974–75; 1979; Savall and Zardet, 1989). In the following section, we describe the main lines of modernization of our organization and their impacts. We highlight one of the main keys to change that we have discovered and learned to manage better: the mix of directive and participative approaches to effective change.

2 THE MODERNIZATION OF THE ASSOCIATIVE MODEL REQUIRES PROFESIONALIZATION OF MANAGEMENT AND GOVERNANCE

2.1 A Steering and Governance System as a Pillar of Modernization

As we have already mentioned, there is a lot of criticism of the association model, on the grounds that it is less suited to the governance of large structures. In reality, many associations are poorly managed due to the lack of an overall orchestration system.

Our experience shows that the governance tool works as soon as a system of synchronized decentralization is put in place. This can be based on methods and tools such as those used in socio-economic management (Hamayon, 2015). The association's three-year strategic action plan is used to irrigate the strategic action plans of the establishments, which are in turn translated into local priority action plans at headquarters and in the various establishments and services (Savall and Zardet, 1995). The aim is to mobilize progressive circles to roll out the actions to the 1,350 employees, while giving them visibility on the overall strategic coherence of the association. In addition, the deployment of common socio-economic management tools across all the structures ensures a form of overall consistency for the association in the management of its various activities.

It is therefore a question of developing the overall management systems of associations. In our case, we have been involved for several years in a project dynamic. For the last 3 years, the dynamic has intensified thanks to the change in the general management of the organization. After five years of work, we have moved from the cyclical to the structural. We have noted that the level of commitment of the leader(s) is a key factor in the success of these transformations. In our association, we personally have a real desire to implement this type of policy. This is done in a process that is spread out over time, with successive phases of rejection and cohesion. It is a question of articulating multiple opposing forces, notably between the management and the local actors, by managing numerous establishments spread over the territory of the Department, with a relevant dose of synchronization between the Headquarters and the Directors.

2.2 The Indispensable Role of Local Managers, True Catalysts of the Associative Project

In the chain of actors and facilitators of the systems, we must not forget that local managers are the real catalysts of the deployment of the associative project. This hierarchical chain of actors and facilitators ensures the translation of the association's strategic project through its concrete implementation, particularly in the priority action plans.

Thus, we rely on the internal evolution of our employees and on the assumption of responsibility for problems at the right level. Support for the management of each facility is provided by its deputy director and department heads. They are the ones who are closest to the field, both in terms of day-to-day activities and in terms of the association's strategic changes, particularly in developing new forms of support for the people we serve.

When this change is underway, with everyone taking on more responsibility, issues of recognition and legitimacy arise. Many of these people are afraid of not being up to the task. A real individual and collective learning process is necessary, through the emergence of new practices of strategic steering and management tools. By distributing the burden of this steering, by decentralizing this steering while ensuring cooperation between all levels, we ensure a more rapid and effective strategic deployment (Datry et al., 2015). To do this, we rely on tools that structure the action: schedules, action plans, communication tools, proximity meetings, etc.

Previously, at the level of the Directors, we did not really have the skills to orchestrate the associative project. From now on, the aim is to increase the skills and responsibilities of these directors so that they are at the right level between the operational and the strategic, but also so that they play the role of transmission belts between the association's general management and the staff in the field, by relying on middle management.

Another issue is that of cohesion between the Directorates of the different establishments, as well as with the General Directorate (Savall and Zardet, 2014). The aim is to build an associative community at this level, and then to stabilize the new practices. In addition to human resistance, staff turnover but also crises, such as the Covid health crisis, regularly disrupt the level of cohesion achieved. Each new Director must also be involved in the general managerial and strategic culture of the company. For this, we deploy internal training in socio-economic management with the help of an "internal speakers' cell." This unit, made up of trained managers, is called upon to intervene throughout the association, to help all the managers of the other units but also to train new staff at all levels.

In addition, many difficulties remain with the synchronization with the Directors, the deployment of the strategy and its communication. We must therefore work constantly in close proximity with these direct collaborators, ensuring that the collaborators of the accompanied managers are directly involved.

2.3 The Effectiveness of Managerial Support for Change

At the beginning, we were in a very centralized and pyramidal organization with great difficulties in local synchronization. The challenge was also to get the administrators and families on board in order to consolidate the relationship between the new governance and the General Management. In this context, the request for interventions and managerial support for the change made sense, as an aid to steering a complex organization.

As the implementation progressed, socio-economic management proved to be a perfect counter-power to the classic hierarchical logic. This management system gives a place to all the categories of people present in an association: administrators, managers, directors, local staff, professionals, families, residents, volunteers, etc. Socio-economic management leads to a form of democracy on a daily basis. Everyone is aware of the organization's dysfunctions, but also of the ability to put oneself in project mode, to come up with solutions and implement them. Tools are used to support this deployment, with the internal and external strategic action plan (IESAP) serving as a common language and framework from top to bottom of the hierarchical pyramid. Furthermore, awareness of the evaluation of hidden costs and the return on investment by converting hidden costs into value added appears to be an important vector for change (Savall and Zardet, 1989).

The deployment of socio-economic management is accompanied by methodological, practical and pragmatic rigor. The tools and methods are a support in the daily management of activities, as well as in medium and long-term strategic management. Theoretical elements are mixed with practical interactions to do things on the ground.

The creation of a team of internal contributors is a school for them, but they also put themselves at the service of others to transmit new practices supported by tools and methods. Being an internal facilitator requires courage, as it means reaching out to other people, including those in a higher hierarchical position, to help them and pass on the methodological culture of socio-economic management.

This method is based on practice and action; it is by practicing that one discovers and clarifies the place and releases the potential of each person. This collective dynamic is a way of making a project together. Difficulties remain in the articulation of the steering between the General Management and certain areas of human resources or finance, which require strategic patience. We are thus in a participative management style, which is based on methods of team co-construction at all levels.

CONCLUSION

Change is a difficult practice, especially in a large organization in the non-profit sector, subject to many pressures. Far from calling into question the associative model, it is a question of consolidating and structuring it, in order to adapt it to the demands of the contemporary world. But since change is an eternal process, we must constantly make tradeoffs and reorganize our governance.

Through this chapter, we wanted to show how socio-economic management has been a way for us to review our governance, to structure the association but also to stimulate new energies. This has enabled us to better align and synchronize the different levels of the hierarchy with each other, as well as with the administrators, families, external institutions and users. This work should be pursued tirelessly, to take into account the new constraints that impact the association, as well as the renewal of our human resources. The exercise of a synchronized decentralization, in the sense of ISEOR, is a difficult art so that each one carries a part of the strategy in coherence with the overall associative project. We are thus pursuing our efforts in the animation and dissemination of a new associative model, which is consistent with our associative values and our mission of social utility.

REFERENCES

Datry, F., Fernandez, G., & Rateau, M. (2015). Cooperation for new services for disabled people, In A. Buono & H. Savall (Eds.), *The socio-economic approach to management revisited.* Information Age Publishing.

Gloro, F. (2020). Tetranormalization: Brake or lever for the development of medico-social organizations. In H. Savall & V. Zardet (Eds.), *Tetranormalisation: profusion des normes et développement des entreprises,* EMS.

Hamayon, D. (2015). Socio-economic management: At the heart of good governance and cooperation practices. In H. Savall & V. Zardet (Eds.), *Gouvernance et management: quelle coopération?* Economica.

CHAPTER 42

THE SOCIO-ECONOMIC DRIVE TO TRANSFORMATION FROM NON-GOVERNMENTAL ORGANIZATION INTO SOCIAL ENTERPRISE

Pierre El Haddad and Rana Barazi

ABSTRACT

Increasing societal needs and receding resources are driving NGOs to transform from funding dependency into social entrepreneurship. This comparative study undertaken within three different organizations demonstrated the effectiveness of SEAM to guide the transformations. The interventions protruded the need for inclusivity, strategic clarity, aligned competencies, and adequate management control, and guided the constituents into working symbiotically towards concerted objectives.

1 CIVIL SOCIETY IN SOCIAL AND ENTREPRENEURIAL BALANCE DILEMMA

Civil society occupies institutional voids created by incomplete markets or institutions (Ahlquist & Prakash, 2010; Markus, 2012). Literature cites three complementary foci of civil society starting with associational life as free and voluntary citizen action. The role and impact of civil society invites the interrogation over its values and goals thus introducing the teleological aspect for greater equity and justice (Edwards, 2014). Then as public sphere, civil society espouses "communicative action" and "discursive democracy" (Habermas, 1964,

SEAM Treatise, pages 373–380

2010). Non-Governmental Organizations (NGOs) may not share a common vision but commit to processes that allow participation and collective action (Edwards, 2014).

Traditionally, NGOs employ a charity model relying on public and private funding (Rashid, 2010). However, the expanding societal needs and depleting resources are subjecting NGOs to survival challenges. Most NGOs are transforming into social entrepreneurship that incorporates sustainability with social impact, hence shifting into less donor-dependency and more resource efficiency.

Increased pressures to improve effectiveness and greater competition over receding resources (Rashid, 2010) arose the need to develop their management functions and funding means (Kabdiyeva, 2013). NGOs, thus, need to develop corporate tactics and business models symbiotic with social entrepreneurship (Hénon et al., 2014; Peris-Ortiz et al., 2017). Pattern-breaking combinations of services and work organization tackled the dichotomy of business and profitability with the pursuit of social mission and value creation (Phillips et al., 2015; Luchsinger & Bagby, 1987). Connecting the social purpose with economic efficiency has therefore become the core transformation. Yet, NGOs find it difficult to identify themselves as social enterprises albeit progression toward revenue-generating ventures (Rashid, 2010). This transition entails profound organizational changes (Cummings & Worley, 2014; Worley et al., 2015).

2 SOCIO-ECONOMIC APPROACH TO MANAGEMENT—SEAM

The depth of change warrants applying SEAM that preconizes concerted steering and empowering employees to act as change agents in a collaborative drive (Datry et al., 2017; Voyant et al., 2016; Wright, 2011). In the same vein, the socio-economic theory holds that organizations sustain dysfunctions resulting from the interaction of structures with individual and collective behaviors (Savall, 1974, 1975, 1981; Savall & Zardet, 1987, 2008; Savall et al., 2015). The disclosure of hidden costs represents a shock treatment that tames defensive routine, primarily of executives, consequently initiating transformation (Bazigos & Burke, 1997; Conbere & Heorhiadi, 2015; Wright, 2011). The organizational metamorphosis requires collaborative reflection and action, bringing systemic and behavioral improvements concurrently. Such conversion evokes several pertinent theoretical concepts. The inclusivity in Organizational Development (Schein, 2010) relates to SEAM's human potential and hidden infrastructure. Active deliberation in civil society (Edwards, 2014) and reciprocity in the theory of cooperation (Axelrod & Hamilton, 1981) relate to contractualization. The duality of structure and agency in structuration theory (Giddens, 1984) echoes the structural behavioral interactions.

3 EPISTEMOLOGY AND MANAGEMENT DISCIPLINES

A social enterprise has competing social and financial objectives which need to be balanced, while avoiding mission drift remains challenging amidst that effort to generate revenues (Ramus et al., 2018). SEAM is adequate for such innovations being built on values that reconcile social and economic performance (Savall, 2003). SEAM interventions seek to understand and change human systems. Benefiting from a long-standing experience, it developed into a generic paradigm with proven robustness to apply to various settings. It is a pragmatic approach connecting theory and practice, and transferability and context, through abductive iterations and intersubjectivity (Morgan, 2007). SEAM is a post-positivist approach that seeks to verify theoretical inferences with quantified empirical observations.

Likewise, internal management control systems facilitate goal attainment and sustainable management in NGOs. It creates a performance measurement system for social enterprises through analyzing three reference fields: financial performance measured by realization of monetary objectives; social effectiveness measured by the impact on beneficiaries; and institutional legitimacy as compliance with mission statement (Bagnoli & Megali, 2011).

4 MULTISITE RESEARCH CONTEXT

Three interventions took place simultaneously within NGOs. Figure 42.1 illustrates the activity sector in which the participating organizations operate.

SPRING is a multi-disciplinary, multi-site organization of 600 employees, 43% of which have disabilities. They work in-house in labor-intensive tasks. SPRING offers primary, secondary, and tertiary services dealing with human rights and sustainable development. It has 12 regional sites in addition to headquarters where the intervention took place.

RESTORE is a rapidly growing tertiary service provider operating from a single office with 22 employees involved in landscape restoration and forestation. Initially a foreign funded project, RESTORE became an independent NGO competing with peers for resources.

SUPPORT is a tertiary service provider focused on home hospice care. It employs 17 people in its headquarters where the intervention took place, and one regional site. Services include home dispensed hospice care, and awareness and training.

5 FINDINGS

The findings are reported in two consecutive streams. First, diagnostic findings summarize the major dysfunctions as construed by actors, their explicative causes, and hidden costs to illustrate their impacts; second, prescribed solutions as devised by actors.

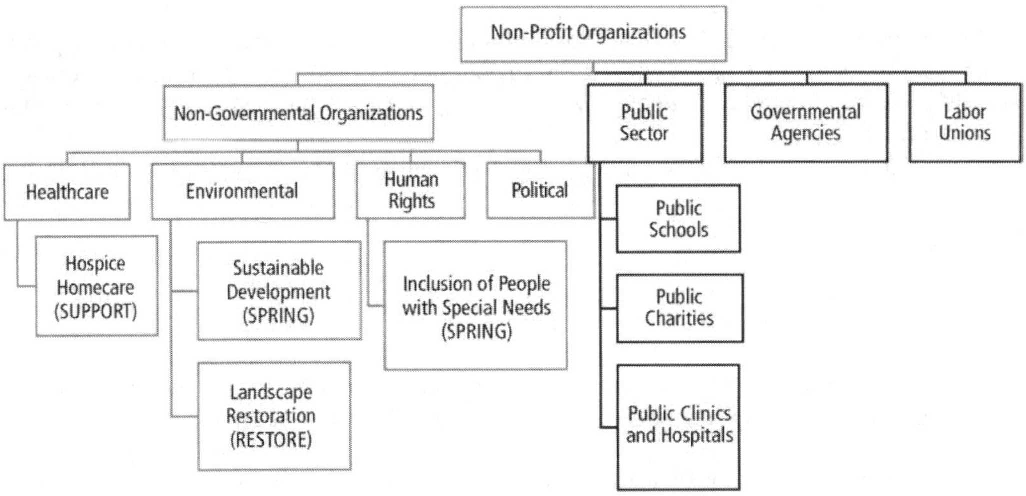

Figure 42.1 Activity sector.

5.1 Diagnostic Findings

SPRING was clustered along the inclusive HORIVERT process. The horizontal cluster included 11 executives; the vertical clusters were the human resources department (9 actors) and mobility program (4 actors). The analysis of dysfunctions yielded both convergences and bold divergences. The convergent perception is that the lack of a rallying strategy and controls cause loss of identity, demotivation and general lack of productivity. Illustrative quotes include:

> The long-term strategy of the organization is not well known, and certainly not the strategy of each department. This is actually our biggest problem, to know where we are going.
>
> The employees are demotivated because of the dissonance or the lack of coherence between management and the lower level.
>
> The lack of productivity is common throughout the organization. There are no clear objectives, no standards or indicators of performance.

However, divergent portrayals emerge. The first blames dysfunctions on loss of pride, a reduced humane drive, and the rift between old and new generations:

> Maintaining the human side is very precious but we need to be more business oriented, effective and efficient.
>
> The new recruits have a difficulty to take pride in their work, unlike the old volunteers that witnessed what our organization did for society and are more engaged in its mission.

The second party are economically sensitive, therefore protrude the importance and difficulty to steer towards more efficiency and financial stability:

> We are an NGO striving to be independent and sustainable, so our priority is to become independent financially. We help people, but we have to be financially viable.
>
> SPRING started as humanitarian and morphed into development, started as NGO and became a social enterprise. The weight of the foundational structure is making the transformation slow, slowly evolving. The celerity of evolution is not enough.

The disclosure of financial indicators and hidden costs fleshed out the extent of the problem. They revealed an HCVAVC of 6.75$/hour/per person. The mobility program averaged hidden costs of 140,000$ per person/year, totaling 560,000$ per year or 5% of the total organizational budget.

Concerning RESTORE, its small size and flat structure commended a holistic transversal diagnosis. The dysfunctions revealed concerns about the inadequacy of strategy to environment:

> If it happens that donors shift their attention from our focus, we will have a risk of cessation of activities, or at least a sizeable cut in our workforce.

Dysfunctions also revealed a changing perception about priorities and needed competencies that pertain to finding new sources of funding and the relevant set of skills:

> We are not anticipating competency needs for new expertise. This is essential in our scope of work because we are targeting new areas of activities.

One additional category addressed the need for vigilance and dynamic management controls:

> Strategy is not monitored nor reviewed frequently enough to brainstorm and take corrective measures. The rush and the load of work prevents reflective meetings from happening quarterly or maybe bi-monthly.

The cost of dysfunctions was a revelation for leaders previously comforted by growth figures and praise by their traditional donor. Hidden costs returned an astounding 880,000$ per year or roughly a third of total budget, despite an HCVAVC of 45$/hour/person. It is worth noting however that labor-intensive activities are outsourced.

However, despite having only 17 employees, SUPPORT was clustered. The horizontal cluster included the CEO and 5 unit managers while the vertical included the nursing unit with 4 nurses. The dysfunctions expressed by the managers at the horizontal level intersect with those expressed by the staff at the vertical level. They perceive a lack in strategic implementation, i.e., the definition, the choices, and the deployment of the business strategy:

> There is a strategy in the sense that we have vision, but nothing is written, and to what extent we can implement depends on the available funds.

The horizontal diagnosis showed dysfunctions mostly linked to work organization and subsequent issues in time management. These dysfunctions revealed dissatisfaction of the actors with the current functioning and management. They expressed issues related to shortages in staff competencies:

> It is not easy to attract workforce having the required experience and at the same time we don't have enough funds so this is a vicious circle.
>
> We need to empower the units for sustainability purposes.

In contrast, the vertical diagnosis revealed more practical field dysfunctions related to the provision of services including logistics and other operational issues. These were mostly linked to work conditions and reflect dissatisfaction of the actors with the current quality of management and service provision. The staff pointed out work conditions as causing extreme fatigue and stress, and incapability to achieve work/life balance. They also expressed a lack of motivation due to deficient clarity of strategic direction, which explains the high turnover rate.

> I am a nurse; I have no options for growth.
>
> It is clear that the monitoring and evaluation was not set from the beginning, we did not define a clear process.
>
> We are obliged to work outside the initial work hours, this affects my personal life.

To highlight the impact of the dysfunctions, the hidden cost was calculated based on a hypothetical value of 25$ for HCVAVC, which yielded 249,000$ annual impact, with an average of $14,500/person/year.

5.2 Innovative Solutions

Deliberations at SPRING revealed a classic example of a maturing organization. Its size and reputation and the ongoing intimate relation with the 'heroic' founders, shields constituencies from survival worries and explains the absence of any sense of urgency. Project teams, formed to design transformative solutions, grouped both social enthusiasts and the sustainability driven actors. Deliberations were frequently relayed to the founders by executives to ensure their endorsement and to ease them into their self-conceived objective to disenfranchise. The focus was to consummate the transformation towards a nimble and articulate social enterprise and the entrainment of actors using socio-economic tools. Three projects were prioritized: (a) Reviewing the strategy to emphasize entrepreneurship and efficiency while engaging the employees in the process, and a structural review to consolidate and simplify the business model. (b) Introducing a governance system and compensation scale that reward actors according to their performance. The governance system is being molded on the socio-economic tools, the Internal-external strategic action plan (IESAP), the priority action plan (PAP), and the periodically negotiable activity contract (PNAC) to align personal and organizational objective through continuous negotiation. (c) Developing actors' competencies to accommodate the shift towards entrepreneurship.

Behind RESTORE's dysfunctions stands a formative experience prone to compliance more than nimbleness required to survive competitive environments. The vulnerabilities originate from its previous sources of success. Founded as a project, it had a small and convivial team driven by a motivating cause, and paradoxically, stringent and massive procedures imposed by the donor. This is a classic example of growing organizations causing growing distances between functions, and veterans wary of additional layers separating them from the executives. From another perspective, stringent procedures are a source of assurance for good governance and compliance, but equally of inefficiencies that each organization must balance. The transformation of RESTORE was set to the pace of transversal teams encouraged by the director who appreciated the economic balance as brought by SEAM. This by itself was a considerable change in the organizational culture from the obedient compliance as source of success, to dynamic capabilities as prone by the socio-economic theory. One solution stipulated a shift from fund hunting towards revenue generating projects like natural reserve management and remunerated technical assistance. Another project related to improving strategic anticipation and competitiveness by reducing dependency on procedures and changing the balance towards nimbleness. This was tackled by developing a delegation span based on actor competencies and time management to decongest decision-making.

At SUPPORT, a new phase of the intervention started with remarkable enthusiasm and entrepreneurial spirit. As such, the transformation plans emphasized improving the overall productivity and efficiency, as well as a sway in the strategic orientation towards entrepreneurship.

On the strategy side, people were aware of the difficulty to sustain funding in a turbulent environment. Innovative sources of funding were sought. For that, revenue-making initiatives were undertaken in cooperation with volunteers and individual donors. Those included auctions for donated artwork or selling donated brand clothes. Management control, in terms of operations and people, focused on long-term targets and short-term results. It started by developing and applying quality planning and operation monitoring to ensure that the standard of performance is sustained. A monitoring and evaluation system was put in place for the internal and external performances.

The priority actions integrated the organizational strategy in the functions of each unit. Henceforth, the alignment brought a change in the focus of competencies needed, and the

TABLE 42.1 Synopsis of Change Projects in Three Lebanese NGOs Applying SEAM, Illustrating the Transformation Into Social Enterprise

Change projects	SPRING	RESTORE	SUPPORT
Strategy	• Shift from fund-hunting towards innovative revenue generating projects; promote entrepreneurial spirit; emphasize efficiency • Review structure, simplify into a more efficient business model		
Management control/governance	• overnance system and compensation scale for performance reward • Align personal and organizational objectives through continuous negotiation	• Improve strategic anticipation and competitiveness by reducing dependency on procedures, and change the balance towards nimbleness	• Improve management control by developing quality planning and operation monitoring • Develop M&E system for the internal and external performance
Competencies	• Develop actors' competencies to accommodate the shift towards empowerment and entrepreneurship in synchronized decentralization	• Develop a delegation span based on actor competencies and time management to decongest decision-making, and allow synchronized empowerment and individual responsibility	• Integrate organizational strategy with competencies needed. • Change of focus in the recruitment process and trainings needed

subsequent recruitment process and trainings scheme. Table 1 synopsizes the change projects in the 3 simultaneous NGOs, illustrating their transformation into social entrepreneurship.

6 DISCUSSION

SEAM was effective at protruding the challenges plaguing the NGOs and the contingent opportunities to drive to improve the quality of management. The interventions unleashed the spoke of actors. Voiced thoughts allowed them to identify ideas promoting creativity and designing them into action plans using integrated management tools. People were also able to deliberate initiatives using the financial indicator they have learned to use. The interventions also demonstrated that the transformation from NGO into social enterprise is not only essential to endure environmental shifts, but also feasible.

Comparatively, the interventions protruded the need for a clear strategy, aligned competencies, and adequate management control tools. The inclusive spirit underlying SEAM motivated the constituents to work in unison to transform their classic NGO model into social enterprise; from fund dependency towards revenue generating activities. This organizational growth is work in progress, as there is no end line for building the sustainable organization. However, the primary ingredient is the SEAM-mediated rallying of human energy towards concerted goals and decision-making.

REFERENCES

Bagnoli, L., & Megali, C. (2011). Measuring Performance in Social Enterprises. *Nonprofit and Voluntary Sector Quarterly, 40*(1), 149–165.

Barazi, R. (2020). *Application of SEAM as a project management methodology in non-governmental organizations: An intervention-research in Lebanon.* Doctoral dissertation, Université Jean Moulin Lyon III, France.

Bazigos, M. N., & Burke, W. W. (1997). Theory Orientations of Organization Development (OD) Practitioners. *Group & Organization Management, 22*(3), 384–408.

El Haddad, P. (2017). *Prescriptive management practice between theory and measurable outcomes: Improving performance of an international inspection and certification body.* Doctoral dissertation, Université Jean Moulin Lyon III, Lyon.

El Haddad, P. (2020). *Developing cooperation among NGOs: Exploratory research in Lebanon.* Doctoral dissertation, Université Jean Moulin Lyon III, Lyon. Retrieved from https://scd-resnum.univ-lyon3.fr/out/theses/2020_out_el_haddad_p.pdf

Phillips, W., Lee, H., Ghobadian, A., O'regan, N., & James, P. (2015). Social Innovation and Social Entrepreneurship: A Systematic Review. *Group & Organization Management, 40*(3), 428–461.

Ramus, T., La Cara, B., Vaccaro, A., & Brusoni, S. (2018). Social or commercial? Innovation strategies in social enterprises at times of turbulence. *Business Ethics Quarterly, 28*(4), 463–492.

Rashid, A. T. (2010). Canadian Journal of Development Studies/ Revue canadienne d'études du développement. Development through Social Entrepreneurship: Perspectives and Evidence from Bangladesh. *Canadian Journal of Development Studies, 30*(3–4), 441–455.

Wright, N. (2011). A journey towards organisation development. *Industrial and Commercial Training, 43*(7), 422–430.

CHAPTER 43

SEAM IN AMERICA

Cultural Compatibility for Teaching and Diffusion

Yue Cai Hillon, Debra Salsi, and Mark E. Hillon

ABSTRACT

The culture of an enterprise reflects beliefs about action. Values guide our actions and management tools are created to represent causal assumptions about how performance variables are connected. This cultural logic constrains how people act at work, but remains hidden because American management is so pervasive throughout the world. Alternatives are blocked. Authentically teaching SEAM forces the cultural self-reflection needed to unearth the barriers to adoption of innovative management. Our study draws on 13 years of data from American MBA students learning and doing SEAM in an intervention research course. Student reflections offered insight into the hidden cultural barriers to adoption of SEAM in America.

1 HIDDEN CULTURE

The culture of an enterprise reflects beliefs about how it should be managed, but this aspect of culture is largely invisible. American management has spread throughout the world and there are few outside vantage points for self-reflection on other options. Our experiences with innovative management education began in 2000 with the first SEAM (Savall, 1974, 1981; Savall & Zardet, 1987) course taught in America, David Boje's small business consulting course at New Mexico State University (Boje, Rosile, 2003). Training at ISEOR and interaction with SEAM intervention researchers around the world over a 20-year span has added to our knowledge and cultural insight. This study draws on 13 years of data from teaching

SEAM Treatise, pages 381–387

SEAM to American MBA students, all of whom had prior work experiences against which to compare this innovative alternative.

2 STUDENT REFLECTIONS ON SEAM

The one-semester MBA course format was the same throughout the 13-year period. Students read *Mastering Hidden Costs and Socio-Economic Performance* (Savall & Zardet, 2008) while conducting intervention research consisting of interviews, dysfunction diagnosis, mirror effect, and recommendation of project baskets for a local business client. Extensive class discussion supported the weekly learning-and-doing cycle. Clients covered a diverse range of industries and firm sizes ranged from 4 to 120 employees, all small enough to follow a hori-vert intervention design.

Between June 2010 and December 2013, a total of 109 MBA students in seven classes completed a post-project reflection on their learning experience. Table 43.1 summarizes results of asking if they perceived any relative advantages of SEAM and whether they intended to adopt any lessons learned on innovative management.

All students could see value in the approach, but despite our best efforts as educators, no more than 25% of students intended to apply some limited aspect of SEAM in their current jobs. Additionally, 5% expressed a desire to follow up for advanced training to become consultants if it was offered close to home. Another 5% stated that they had no intention to apply any aspect of SEAM because they already had a more preferred option. These findings were consistent with Rogers' (1995) diffusion of innovation model, especially the non-adopters who had weighed the relative advantages and said no to SEAM.

Students were learning, but we could only account for clear intentions from 35% of them. SEAM offers a practical applied science for improving management and organization, unlike anything taught in the standardized business school curriculum. Students experienced this process and benefitted from constant feedback as they learned to apply the approach in an actual enterprise. However, 65% of the students (a) Could see that the process was working as managers, employees, and owners progressed through the diagnosis of dysfunctions and mirror effect, (b) Understood the benefits of reducing hidden costs and releasing human potential, and (c) Had no better management options to suggest. Why did these students have no intention of applying even minimal lessons learned to improve their own personal circumstances at work? There were hidden barriers to adoption of SEAM in America that we needed to discover.

3 PERSONAL CULTURAL COMPATIBILITY WITH SEAM

Reflecting on our own experiences teaching international management seminars, we found that French students were brought up in a strikingly different educational system. Critical

TABLE 43.1 Decision to Adopt SEAM

Stated Intention	Percentage
Will apply some aspect of SEAM	25%
Would like advanced training	5%
Will not adopt SEAM	5%
No intention	65%

thinking was second nature and students had gained research skills to investigate and solve problems in their work. Business enterprises also operated differently, with much greater responsibility shown for developing human potential than in America. Discarding people was not in vogue. Management assumptions from American business schools had infiltrated slowly and more recently into France, and people knew that there were other alternatives.

With these ideas in mind, we changed our questions to students to ask about the cultural compatibility of SEAM for both the student and the client company. Between January 2015 and December 2019, a total of 104 MBA students in seven classes reflected on their learning experiences after the course. Table 43.2 summarizes themes of the second stage that revealed much more detail on the missing 65% with no expressed intentions. We will focus on this group because the *Compatible* and *Incompatible* groups showed similar patterns.

The *Maybe Yes* group expressed three themes characterized as favorable opinions without stating definite intentions. The *Maybe Yes – Personal* theme connected their nature or experiences with some aspect of SEAM. For instance:

> There's definitely a part of me that focuses on productivity and results rather than checking on myself or others to make sure they're happy with the way they're managed.
>
> I have an understanding for problems and there being an associated cost to everything that goes on in a business, whether we can quantify those things or not. I also appreciate being able to associate numbers to the things that are found and seem so subjective.

The *Maybe Yes – Tool* theme weighed the useful benefits of the process against difficulties in application, or commented favorably on the attributes of a specific tool. For example:

> I would interpret dysfunctions and their impacts differently than team members. This would occasionally make me question my understanding of this method, but I think that healthy discussions resulted from those differing interpretations.
>
> The ability to organize dysfunctions into various groups that have different effects on the business is key into structuring an action plan to reduce costs and improve the quality of product.

The *Maybe Yes – Pedagogy* theme offered comments on the learning experience itself and how the course was structured in a learn-and-do cycle. Students reflected that:

> Reading the textbook and witnessing the real-life application of SEAM methodology on a real business was a fantastic way to learn.

TABLE 43.2 Personal Compatibility With SEAM

Response	Theme Description	Percentage	Adopt?
Compatible	Perceived agreement with personal beliefs	6.73%	Yes 23.08%
	Some part of SEAM offers a useful tool	16.35%	
Maybe Yes	Personal—Agree with some aspect of SEAM	8.65%	No Intention 60.57%
	Tool—Usefulness may exceed challenges	14.42%	
	Pedagogy—Course design facilitated learning	8.65%	
Maybe No	Implied conflict with beliefs or inappropriate tool	12.50%	
Learning Challenges	Insufficient understanding of SEAM to reflect	16.35%	
Incompatible	Tools should be simple and produce quick results	9.62%	No 16.35%
	Conflict with beliefs not open to change	6.73%	

> I felt that I had all of these different tools and components but none of them fully made sense. The more we worked through it, and the more the project came together, the more sense it began to make. Completing the final project really helped to tie everything together.

Members of the *Learning Challenges* group had not been active engaged learners and therefore lacked sufficient understanding of socio-economic theory to reflect on whether or not they were compatible. The inability to reflect may have been part of a larger problem, as self-reflection is essential to learning. Passive learners also seemed unable to reflect deeply enough to access their own beliefs about management.

> I never felt like I fully grasped all the small details of the SEAM methodology.
>
> I cannot recall anything specific either way. [Compatible or Incompatible]
>
> I feel that it would definitely be beneficial to have had some exposure to these topics prior to this class.

This last group of students expressed no intention to adopt, reject, or even to continue weighing options. The standard MBA program requires prerequisite knowledge of all topics to be covered in the curriculum. Students expect not to learn anything new, just apply what they already know in a different context. "Incompatible" comments also strongly echoed these expectations against new learning, and added the belief that management tools should be simple to apply and quick to produce results. Efficacy in producing tangible and sustainable results did not enter into their reasoning, which also lacked a systemic perspective of the complex causal relations connecting dysfunctions throughout an enterprise. In effect, SEAM had violated their cultural expectations.

4 ENTERPRISE COMPATIBILITY WITH SEAM

Adoption of an innovation depends upon its complexity and compatibility as perceived by the culture into which it is being introduced (Rogers, 1995). Perceived complexity of SEAM appeared in the MBA student reflections as a justification for the choice not to learn. This was expressed in the *Learning Challenges* theme and also throughout the other themes as a reason to reject SEAM. Dissenting students believed that there were simpler ways to manage an enterprise. This generalization was not an isolated point. The majority of the reflections on the client's compatibility with SEAM were not comments about the culture of the enterprise, but rather mirrored the students' hidden beliefs about American management. Table 43.3 presents the enterprise compatibility themes.

Overall, the minority of reflections that directly related to cultural compatibility were much less insightful than the other themes. An *Incompatible Culture* was one in which management lacked genuine intent to improve company performance. Students reflected that management was not open to feedback, employees were not free to speak, nor were they respected or considered as essential value creators for the enterprise. Most incompatible clients were actively working against change. A *Compatible Culture* was essentially the opposite, with additional notes about the well-being and success of the company being tied to caring about employees and treating them like a family that was strong enough to talk openly about dysfunctions and ways to improve. The indirect reflections yielded less obvious insight.

Virtually all of the broader context themes voiced the assumption that management is a tool that serves a larger unacknowledged purpose within the rules and constraints of an economic system. This key idea was found in the indirect reflections expressing both compatibility and incompatibility. For instance, the *Appropriate Tool* theme expressed a rational logic of matching the general function of a tool with a problem: Most organizations have dysfunctions, SEAM is a tool to diagnose and correct dysfunctions, therefore, SEAM is an appropriate tool for most organizations. In several cases, this theme was also expressed as a stronger sentiment: The client needs SEAM. For clarity, this theme was about matching a tool to a need and made no judgment as to cultural compatibility of the enterprise culture with SEAM.

The *Tool Performance* theme expressed that a specific aspect of the tool's performance claims had been verified from the intervention research. For instance, the textbook claimed that employees would have knowledge of dysfunctions, they would share information if asked, the interview data would have consistent patterns, and the frequency of dysfunctions would reveal causal connections throughout the enterprise. When students experienced these words from the text coming to life in practice, they confirmed that the tool had performed as expected. This sense of internal consistency is the sort of compatibility that they expressed. Again, not a comment on enterprise cultural compatibility with SEAM.

The *Inappropriate Tool* theme was similar to the previous themes, but the student's own beliefs—not the textbook or the project experience—were the source of a claim to reject SEAM. There was a wide range of beliefs under this theme because they were constructed by and for the individual engaged in an act of self-delusion. However, the pattern was the same for all. A specific point from the project client or from the textbook was stated as the reason that SEAM was not applicable to the situation, then the specific was expanded to all cases. Most noticeably, each belief was easily disconfirmed. For instance, one comment dismissed intervention research in general by claiming that it had not revealed anything that the client did not already know. However, the diagnosis and reflections of many other students in the same cohort revealed that there was very little that managers did know. They had limited decision-making capacity for completing the priority action plan, they had not set clear task responsibilities and performance evaluations for employees, and they lacked time management competence. As one student noted, what managers did not know left everyone not "knowing what their tasks were and feeling like time was wasted, but also having a lot of work to do . . . in a very unorganized and dysfunctional way." Clients were also noted to have claimed they already knew about all of the problems mirrored back from the research, but students recognized this claim as a thin defense against accepting constructive feedback.

Other dissenters found that it was easy to take something from the textbook out of context to make a general rule. For instance, the text included some examples of manufacturing

TABLE 43.3 Client Cultural Compatibility with SEAM

Theme	Description	Percentage
Compatible Culture	Gave characteristics of managers and owners	10.58%
Appropriate Tool	Organizations have dysfunctions, SEAM addresses dysfunctions, therefore SEAM is the right tool	8.65%
Tool Performance	SEAM performed a function as designed	23.08%
Incompatible Culture	Gave characteristics of managers and owners	11.54%
Structure	Dysfunctions are unavoidably built into operations	5.77%
Inappropriate Tool	Belief that SEAM was wrong tool	13.46%
Size	Belief that SEAM does not work for small enterprise	11.54%
Learning Challenges	Insufficient understanding of SEAM to comment	15.38%

firms that had applied SEAM. These examples were then used to suggest that SEAM applicability was limited to manufacturing firms. SEAM would therefore not apply to their service industry project client. The reverse claim was also observed, that SEAM was not applicable to service firms.

The *Inappropriate Tool* theme also used the student's own specialized skill or bias as the basis for rejecting SEAM. For instance, claims were made that the client needed a solution that could not be provided by SEAM (e.g., marketing, leadership development, group therapy). As with all claims in this theme, the project data and other students in the class indicated more profound systemic dysfunctions destroying value. Finally, some commenters were opposed to the pedagogical method of using intervention research to learn SEAM and then elevated this bias to a general belief that research is an academic exercise of no benefit to business. Listening to employees and analyzing data is a waste of time because a true leader simply knows (i.e., tells) what problems need to be corrected.

Size was a sub-theme of the *Inappropriate Tool* theme because it was common to claim that SEAM was not appropriate for small enterprise. Some believed that the complexity of SEAM needed a large complex organization to discover networks of dysfunctions, or that only large firms could handle the additional workload and afford the high cost of consultants. Others chose an arbitrary size (e.g., 50 employees) as the minimum threshold for SEAM to be viable. Half of the respondents for this sub-theme noted surprise that SEAM had worked well for their small enterprise intervention research client, yet the belief was not abandoned.

Structure was one of the most revealing themes in the data because the comments exposed assumptions about management that had been designed into the enterprise structures. Decision-making always had a short-term time frame and a focus on quick results, thereby making short deadlines and a stressful work environment normal. High employee turnover was an essential part of the business model because it was assumed to lower costs. For intervention research, the constant stream of new hires was a challenge because they rarely stayed long enough to gain insight into dysfunctions. Although the client desired to improve and had the authority to make changes, their intentional focus on a short-term talent pool of employees was at odds with long-term value creation via human potential.

Beyond the short-term low-cost orientation, there were structural barriers built into the hierarchy. One client had a board of directors overseeing strategic decisions that was designed for structural inactivity, thereby making innovation in management difficult if not impossible. Even a favorable response to intervention research and a strong desire to follow through would be difficult to implement because of the structural bias to inactivity. In contrast to this clear but ineffective decision structure, a family business client had an unclear leadership structure. Decisions were being made, but employees and managers were unsure who was actually making the decisions. Another client was so regulated by their corporate office that they could not make changes to fit their local situation. For instance, all training was set by the corporate office and could not be altered. The overall result from the *Structure* theme was that dysfunctions were accepted as unavoidably locked into normal operations.

5 MANAGEMENT CULTURE

Desmaison and Vandenhove (2017) point to the difficulty of implementing innovative management practices that differ from current knowledge or accepted methods. They argue that management tools are artificial—someone created them to support a particular way of thinking about action. Values guide our actions, but American enterprise management does not share society's affinity for human rights and democracy (Hillon, 2005). This hidden culture defines management tools and performance variables, thereby constraining how people can act within an organization's logic.

We lost our humanity in the transition to modern machine civilization, forgot the need for imagination and critical thought, and found a wasteful purposeless materialism in its place (Mumford, 1934). Belief in a one-best-way to manage people at work became the only way. Maintaining order depends upon social and psychological detachment in the employment relationship so as to suppress awareness of an unfair arrangement that increases inequality (Hillon et al, 2016). The appeal of SEAM to some of our MBA students—hopeful working adults—echoes the need for social justice:

> Hearing the stories about how employees haven't had a raise in years despite growing profits. Collecting the perspectives of these disenfranchised employees and giving them a voice that might catch the attention of management was the most alluring part of the experience. Morally it feels wrong to me to grow rich on the labors and sacrifices of others.

Dignity must be restored to work. Capitalism can be socially responsible (Savall, Péron, Zardet, Bonnet, 2015, 2018). Teaching SEAM in America can help us restore what has been lost and what we have yet to achieve.

REFERENCES

Boje, D., Rosile, G. A. (2003). Comparison of socio-economic and other trans-organizational development methods. *Journal of organizational change management, 16*(1).

Desmaison, G., & Vandenhove, G. (2017). *From hidden costs to measurable performance: From heterodox practices to orthodox practices.* 15th Congrès IIC/ISEOR, June 2017, Lyon.

Hillon, M.E. (2005). *A comparative analysis of socio-ecological and socio-economic strategic change methodologies.* PhD Dissertation, NMSU & ISEOR/Jean Moulin (Lyon 3).

Hillon, Y.C., Kisiel, G., & Hillon, M.E. (2016). A Discursive Framework for Research in Management Consulting. *Recherches en Sciences de Gestion—Management Sciences—Ciencias de Gestión, 117,* 109–124.

Mumford, L. (1934). *Technics and Civilization.* Harcourt.

Rogers, E. M. (1995). *Diffusion of Innovations.* The Free Press.

This page intentionally left blank.

CHAPTER 44

LONG-TERM ORGANIZATIONAL CHANGE PROCESSES IN MEXICO

Martha M. Fernández Ruvalcaba and Graciela Carrillo González

ABSTRACT

The objective is to analyze the project of a group of professors-researchers of the UAM whose purpose was to adopt and adapt the ISEOR methodology to Mexican organizations, in order to explain the processes of long-term change in dynamic and highly institutionalized contexts. For this purpose, proposals of: E. Morin (Complex systems); H. Maturana (Organizations as human social systems); and Powell & DiMaggio (Organizational change from neoinstitutionalism). It is concluded that the evolution of the institutions generated a decoupling between the interests of the professors and the objectives of the project. Nevertheless, the application of socioeconomic theory and management is preserved in teaching and research.

The purpose of this chapter is to achieve a deep understanding of change processes with a long-range horizon, in dynamic environments and highly institutionalized organizational contexts. The question that guides our reflection is: what theoretical approaches help to understand and govern changes associated with the achievement of long-term project objectives in an organizational entity? To this end, the contributions of Edgar Morin, H. Maturana and Powell & DiMaggio are recovered. This analysis is anchored in the project of a group of professors of a Higher Education Institution in Mexico, which began in 1997 with a duration of ten years, whose objective was to form a research laboratory in organizational management and a doctoral program, taking as a reference the ISEOR and its alliances with the French University, adapting it to the characteristics and circumstances of a Mexican public university.

SEAM Treatise, pages 389–395

1 LONG-RANGE ORGANIZATIONAL CHANGE: A CONCEPTUAL FRAMEWORK

Understanding how organizations behave, in particular their long-range change processes, requires considering: the nature of the individuals that make them up, the social conditions and the continuous interdefinition of all their elements, through individual and collective action, in accordance with certain rules of coexistence. Different theories seek to contribute to this: E. Morín (1999) contributes elements from the notion of the complexity of systems; H. Maturana (2004) assumes the organization, from biology, as a system in which individuals interact both as biological beings and social agents; Powell & Di Maggio (1999) point out, from sociological institutionalism, the adoption of rules and regulations that simultaneously allow and constrain the behavior of social actors making community life predictable. From the contributions of these perspectives, gaps between planned change and resulting change are interpreted, in particular: the complexity of organizations, their identity as a social system and the processes of change.

1.1 Complexity in Organizations

In organizations, each individual plays several roles and has a multiplicity of identities that manifest his/her biological being and his/her cultural or social being in a physical environment (Morin, 1999). Under the logic of emergence, organizations are the result of the conjunction of relationships between individuals, which produce a system of qualities initially absent at the individual and overall level. Three principles characterize complex thinking (Llarandi,2018): the dialogic one, which associates in a dynamic context factors that at the same time complement and contradict each other; that of recursivity which breaks with the linear idea of cause-effect and recovers the sense of circularity, individuals generate society at the same time that society generates individuals; and the hologrammatic, which assumes that each element is a carrier of the whole, so that not only the part is in the whole but the whole is in the part, with each individual in a society, there is society as a whole with its culture and language present in the mind of the individual (Morin, 1999). Disorder is considered as an inherent aspect of the organization, given the sense of complexity (Morin, 1984), so that future states are unpredictable from certain causalities, since small changes come to produce unexpected states that affect individual and collective decisions.

1.2 Organizations as a Human Social System

In the consubstantial human being, his individual and social nature is defined as a system structurally determined and empathic with the system in which he performs (Maturama, 1985). However, "the behavior of a living being is only adequate if its structure and the structure of the environment in which it develops are congruent and if its structural changes occur in congruence with the structural changes of that environment, i.e., it adapts" (Maturana, 1985).

The Human Social System character of an organization is acquired from a network of interactions between individuals resulting from the coordination and cooperation between the members of a system that establishes an environment of coupling that guarantees its permanence. Organizations as social systems are characterized by being dialogic, incorporating in their interactions opposite qualities: the rational and the emotional, the individual and the collective, competition and collaboration, the social and the economic (Maturana, 2004), where the fundamental mechanism for communication is language.

1.3 Change Processes in Organizations

Given the interdefinition of the individual behavior of the members of an organization and of the social system, its characteristics change when the behavior of any of its members varies and/or when the rules of the game collectively generated are modified. The processes of change alter the stability of the social system, which interferes with its conservative character, constructed on the basis of social awareness or restrictions. The loss of members or the entry of new members with additional characteristics also leads to modifications, in two senses: the adaptation of the system and the success in the process of change or the destruction of the organization.

The new organizational institutionalism rejects the "rational actor" as a determinant in institutions and "concentrates on organizational structures and processes taking as a starting point the homogeneity of practices and agreements found" (Powell & Di Maggio, 1999). Organizational dynamics are not explained only by reference to individual actors but by their quality and their reproduction in structures that are self-sustaining, so that an individual chooses to adhere to certain institutions based on his or her expectations and previous experiences.

Meyer and Rowan (1991) point out the legitimacy of organizations as an element for survival, for which they create social and cultural systems beyond their productive function, where individuals who influence the trajectory of the organization are inserted. This legitimacy constitutes a mechanism that links the organization's behavior with belief systems and public opinion, so that change occurs in response to institutional pressure.

Institutions are rationalized and impersonal abstractions that define the normative obligations that actors take into account and that evolve slowly. Institutional change affects the status quo of organizations and in turn determines the system of beliefs and behaviors. Given the complexity of human organizations, the capacity to plan and govern change is reduced, as the strength of institutions traps creative individualism and social logic takes over.

1.4 The Conditions for a Long-Range Planned Process

Organizations adapt to institutional expectations. Consequently, organizational isomorphism, as a constraining process that forces a unit in a population to resemble other units with similar organizational characteristics (Hawley, 1968), consolidates population-level change in organizations (Hannan and Freeman, 1987). In this context, decision-makers learn to opt for appropriate paths and adjust their behavior to an appropriate standard confirmed by the actions of others through three mechanisms of change: (a) coercive isomorphism arising from formal and informal pressures present within the organizations on which they are dependent and by cultural expectations arising within society; (b) mimetic isomorphism arising from a force that encourages imitation of other successful organizations or standardized responses to uncertainty; and (c) normative isomorphism arising from professionalization to establish methods and control regulations for processes that contribute to legitimization.

Predicting or driving such change depends on several factors: the level of dependence of the organization on another organization; the level of centralization of resources by the organization; the level of uncertainty of the relationship between means and ends (Thompson, 1967). The more ambiguous the organization's goals, the greater the intention to follow a successful model (Meyer and Rowan, 1977). From this approach, the conditions for transformation are determined by various factors that affect not only adaptations but also isomorphisms.

2 THE LONG-RANGE PROCESS OF CHANGE

The change process we describe was generated with a group of 10 full-time professors-researchers in the area of research on strategy and management of organizations in one of the four academic units belonging to a public university in Mexico, the UAM Xochimilco (UAMX). The purpose of this process was to establish a research laboratory in the field of management that would adapt the experience of the Instituto de Socioeconomía de las Empresas y las Organizaciones (ISEOR) to Mexican circumstances.

2.1 Characteristics of the Organization—Period: 1998–2010

The Universidad Autónoma Metropolitana (UAM) has legal personality and its own assets. It is headed by a rector and is organized into divisions and departments. The divisions are established by areas of knowledge and the departments by specific disciplines. Each division is headed by a director and each department by a head. The governance of the university is vested in collegiate bodies: the Academic College, the Unit Academic Council and the Divisional Academic Councils. The Divisional Academic Council of Social Sciences and Humanities of the unit was responsible for approving the initiatives and resources associated with the project.

2.2 Background of the UAMX – ISEOR Project

In a timeline, the milestones that contributed to the shaping of the project were: the doctoral thesis "Interactions entre conditions de vie au travail et conditions de vie hors du travail. Applications à des cas d'innovation socio-économique" (Fernández, 1984); the professors who taught in the undergraduate program in administration, a field of knowledge considered highly professional;[1] their qualification through postgraduate programs; the establishment of international collaboration agreements between the Mexican National Council of Science and Technology and the National Foundation for Management Education of France; and the first international seminar of the master's degree in administration, a field of knowledge considered highly professional; the first international seminar of the master's degree in economics and management of technological change; the ECOS Norte Program, which supported during two periods (1998–2002; 2003–2007) the collaboration agreements between UAMX and ISEOR that led to the postgraduate training of 8 professors of the group and the realization of a congress in which the results of the collaboration were presented.

The initial objectives of the project were the development of research and the training of doctors in the field of administration, applying and adapting the consulting-research model developed by the ISEOR (Savall, 1974, 1979; Savall and Zardet, 1987) and, in a second stage, to offer a postgraduate program in socio-economic management of organizations as a strategy to give concrete form in the field of administration to the figure of the full-time professor-researcher, by adding consulting-research activities to his or her teaching functions.

2.3 Institutional Changes: Their Impact on the Consolidation of the Project

The core group of professors linked to the ISEOR project was constituted as a social system that, as the goals of teacher training were met, established deep interactions with specific objectives and a common language that boosted the consulting work during the first years and contributed to its legitimization. In 2000, an international conference was organized between UAM and ISEOR to close this cooperation program and to present some of the relevant results of the research-interventions obtained by the team of UAM professors (Fernández Ruvalcaba and Savall, 2004). Once the goal of training in theory and methodology was achieved and most of them obtained their doctoral degree in co-supervision (Martínez Vázquez, 2005; Peñalva Rosales, 2006; Ramírez Alcántara, 2006; González Pérez, 2006; Pomar Fernández, 2007; Brindis Almazán, 2007; Ibarra Cortés, 2008); that were the concentrating elements of the group's interests, the need for personal professional development arose in a broader context, offered by the institution of belonging, with greater external interactions, which evidenced the complexity of the system in the face of individual interests and decisions that had an impact on the collective.

On the other hand, the UAMX model's demand for multipurpose participation in university activities (teaching, research, management and discussion of current events) generated social pressure on professors that diverted them from the long-term project and from links with companies and organizations outside the university.[2] In addition, there were two institutional changes relevant to university activities: the emergence of the National System of Researchers (NSR), a national scheme that offers recognition and prestige to academics, based on the evaluation of scientific publications and training of graduate students; and UAM's own evaluation system, which considers teaching hours, number of published articles and participation in specialized events, which translates into monetary compensation that substantially increases the income of professors.

In the process of change, the focus of attention and action was centered on the dimensions that the actors believed they could regulate, according to their interpretations of the theoretical and methodological model of consultancy-intervention generated by the ISEOR. A postulate of such a model is that incorporating dimensions over which the actors do not have significant influence can lead to "paralysis by analysis": one can find reasons why a change project is unfeasible and act accordingly, self-fulfilling one's own prophecy. Such a postulate could be one of the factors that led to overestimating the effect of the reward systems imposed at the national level through the NSR and UAM itself, which privilege individual work and underestimate collective work, the pillar of any long-range organizational project.

3 THE UAMX-ISEOR PROJECT: A LONG-TERM CHANGE PROCESS

The professors involved in the UAMX-ISEOR project are individuals who play various roles within their organization, accentuating the dialogic character of the organization, since individualism, cooperation, solidarity and also competition prevail among them. The project, as a subsystem within their professional universe, demanded a series of behaviors and activities that were legitimized by the formally established agreements and conventions, but did not exclude them from other activities and links internal and external to UAM, giving rise to a complex environment, where many times the demands of their role as academics or researchers clashed with their role as university managers, consultants or with the requirements of the NSR.e ww

The elements of cooperation around the project were diluted and those of competition in the evaluation system increased. This was fundamental in the processes of change since the disparity between the interests of the professors and the objectives of the project generated a structural decoupling. In terms of the reformulation of socioeconomic theory (Savall & Zardet, 2005), the TFW virus infected not only at the level of the university, but at the level of the macro environment. A greater intensity of piloting activity would have been required to contain this effect. While it is true that the project objectives were not met in the terms initially sought (the creation of a research-intervention laboratory that would take advantage of and adapt the theoretical proposal and methodology of the ISEOR and the creation of a graduate program of studies along these lines), it did succeed in making the socio-economic theory and the socio-economic approach to management an explicit or implicit referent that is part of the mental structures of the professors who participated in the project. This far-reaching effect is manifested both in their teaching and in the research they carry out, and is regenerated and multiplied through the students in whose training they participate. The structure created from the project had to undergo a process of adaptation that has kept the group united, although the norms that define it today have been gradually modified under a logic of normative isomorphism that has forced them to adhere to and act according to the guidelines of the NSR and the UAM, since these are the ones that concentrate the resources on which they depend.

CONCLUSION

The structure created by the UAMX-ISEOR project is a complex system with all its properties, advantages and disadvantages, since it is immersed in a series of interactions internal to the project and UAM, as well as external to the university.

The conformation of this organization (UAMX-ISEOR), as a human social organization, concentrated the individual properties of its members, which added to the purposes of the project and its formalization, gave it a life of its own under a common dynamic and interests, legitimizing it around the project and later around institutional incentives. The evolution of the institutions (evaluation standards) at the national and university levels generated a process of decoupling between the individual interests of the professors and the objectives of the organization formed with the project, which diluted the links with ISEOR and reduced the activities planned for the long term. To date, the collective of professors remains, but the organization itself has been transformed, under the logic of an isomorphic organization, according to the new institutional framework of the country and the university to which they belong. However, it retains in its teaching and research activities the application of the socio-economic theory and the socio-economic approach to management.

NOTES

1. At that time, it was more important for teachers to have professional experience than master's degrees and doctorates.

2. In Mexico, the practice of linking companies with universities, particularly with public universities, does not predominate. There is an argument that points out the discordance of time to meet the needs of companies, among other elements.

REFERENCES

Brindis Almazán, L. (2007). *Estructuras de Organización para el Desarrollo Socioeconómico local: la comunidad artesanal.* Tesis de doctorado en cotutela en ciencias de gestión. Universidad de Lyon, UAMI.

Fernández Ruvalcaba, M. M. (1984). *Interactions entre conditions de vie au travail et conditions de vie hors du travail. Applications à des cas d'innovation socio-économique.* Tesis de doctorado en ciencias de gestión. Universidad de Lyon.

Fernández Ruvalcaba, M. M., & Savall, H. (2004). *El modelo de Gestión Socio-Económica en Organizaciones Mexicanas.* Ed UAM, ISEOR.

González Pérez, C.R. (2006). *L'organisation créatrice de connaissances. L'organisation synaptique.* Tesis de doctorado en cotutela en ciencias de gestión. Universidad de Lyon, UAM.

Hawley, A. (1968). Human ecology. In D. L. Sills (Ed.), *International encyclopedia of the social sciences* (pp. 328–337). Macmillan.

Hannan y Freeman, (1987) The ecology organizational founding: American Labor Unions, 1836–1985. *American Journal of Sociology, 92,* 910–943.

Ibarra Cortes, M. E. (2008). *Stratégie et gestion financières. Le cas de la municipalité de San Luis Potosi au Mexique.* Tesis de doctorado en cotutela en ciencias de gestión. Universidad de Lyon, UAM.

Martínez Vázquez, G. M. (2005*). La contribution du management socio-économique à l'aménagement des performances économiques et sociales. Cas d'expérimentation dans trois petites entreprises mexicaines* Tesis de doctorado en ciencias de gestión. Universidad de Lyon.

Maturana, H. (2004) Biología del fenómeno social en "*Desde la biología a la psicología.*" Coedición: Editorial Universitaria. Grupo Editorial Lumen. Argentina. 71–85.

Maturana, H. (1985) Entrevista Ecovisiones No. 6. *Talleres de Investigación en Desarrollo Humano,* España.

Maturana, H., & Varela (s/f). *La autopoiesis de Maturana y Varela: ¿Seres sociales o seres individuales?*

Meyer, J., & Rowan, B. (1991). Organizaciones Institucionalizadas: La estructura formal como mito y ceremonia. (Trad. Bruno Chaihuaque) en *American Journal of Sociology, 83*(2), 340–363.

Meyer, J., & Rowan, B. (1977) Institutionalized organizations: formal structure as myth and ceremony. *American Journal of Sociology, 83*(2), 340–363.

Morin, E. (1999). *Introducción al pensamiento complejo.* España: Gedisa Editorial.

Morin, E, (1984). *Ciencia con conciencia.* Anthropos, Barcelona.

Llarandi , C. (2018). Blog (https://profesionalesporelbiencom)

Peñalva Rosales, L. (2006). *Inducción al Aprendizaje organizacional en la Universidad Pública para el desarrollo de estrategias de vinculación con el sector productivo.* Tesis de doctorado en cotutela en ciencias de gestión. Universidad de Lyon, UAM.

Pomar Fernández, S. (2007). *La naturaleza híbrida de las organizaciones y el proceso de transferencia de modelos. El caso de las guarderías subrogadas en México.* Tesis de doctorado en cotutela en ciencias de gestión. Universidad de Lyon, UAM.

Powell, W., & Di Maggio, P. (1999). *El nuevo institucionalismo en el análisis organizacional.* FCE, México

Ramírez Alcántara, H. T. (2006). *Elementos estructurantes de la confianza y su relación con el desempeño en una universidad pública mexicana.* Tesis de doctorado en cotutela en ciencias de gestión. Universidad de Lyon, UAM.

Thompson, J. D. (1967). *Organizations in action.* McGraw Hill.

This page intentionally left blank.

CHAPTER 45

EVOLUTION OF BUSINESS SCHOOL'S BUSINESS MODEL

Gilles Guyot and Marc Bonnet

ABSTRACT

Business schools have developed since the second half of the 19th century and most of them have adopted the Wharton model, inspired by a scientist approach that neglects Human Potential. This model became widespread throughout the world under the pressure of accreditation systems, with the defect that the theories disseminated were not relevant. However, there is currently an evolution towards an innovative approach, as in the case of the qualimetrics intervention-research model implemented by ISEOR.

In the wake of the industrial revolutions of the 19th century, management and business education has gradually become increasingly important around the world (Hommel &al., 2014), and many schools have developed in Europe, the United States, and then in Asia. Today, there are more than 10,000 business schools in the world. Despite a great diversity of forms, the vast majority of them are based on a model that complements the fundamentals of the sub-disciplines of management (accounting, strategy, HRM, marketing, etc.) with a dose of social sciences (law, sociology, economics, etc.) and engineering sciences (computer science, production management and logistics). Today, they are faced with a rapidly changing environment (Gephart et al., 2019).

This chapter shows the drifts linked to an excess of scientism due to a need for academic recognition of a young discipline, and then the emergence of a new paradigm, which is ultimately not so far from the intentions of the founders (Guyot, 2012).

SEAM Treatise, pages 397–402

1 THE GENESIS AND DIFFUSION OF THE MANAGEMENT SCHOOL MODEL

Joseph Wharton is credited with the concept of *business schools* that differ from traditional business schools based solely on the transmission of good practices. In 1881, this Philadelphia ironmaster decided to create a school bearing his name within the College of Liberal Arts of the University of Pennsylvania. For this purpose, he created an endowment of $100,000 to train a new class of *businessmen* suitable for "those who were destined for efficient public service as well as for the struggle of business life. But he gave them a free choice of social science subjects, imposing only two "potato dishes": business law and accounting, and economics (money, taxation, industrial and service sectors). A teaching staff was recruited, mainly made up of doctors who had graduated from the University of Halle (Prussia) and who, from the 1890s, could be reinforced by the best of their doctoral students in order to cover the four years of the Baccalaureate.

The system was reinforced by the creation of the MBA, initiated by the *Harvard Business School* in 1908. Created by four academics, this original school, since it was a pure Graduate School, wanted to develop students' abilities in holistic judgment, decision-making and business management. In order to do so, in 1912, it developed its famous case method, which was derived from both the inductive reasoning method of its Dean, the historian Edwin Gay, and the "application" technique of the already famous *Harvard Law School*.

These teachings were very successful and by 1925 there were no less than 180 business schools. However, from the 1930s onwards, there was a certain confusion between the Bachelor's degree and the MBA, with professors tending to be more interested in consulting than in research. The renaissance came in the 1960s, following two Ford and Carnegie reports published in 1959, one by Gordon & Lowell and the other by Pearson. This was done within the framework of the *Carnegie Model*, whose principles had been established by Dean G.L. Bach, founder of the *Graduate School of Industrial Administration* (GSIA) at Carnegie Mellon University. Henry Mintzberg summarized these principles as follows (Mintzberg, 2004):

1. Research is paramount, teaching is second.
2. Research should be primarily descriptive, especially in understanding business and organizations.
3. Such research must be rooted in a set of underlying disciplines, including economics, psychology, and mathematics, which should be at the core of Master's courses and serve as the foundation for finance, marketing, accounting, etc.
4. The classroom is the place where students should be trained in analytical problem-solving skills such as operations research.
5. Special attention must be given to the doctorate to stimulate research and have graduates disseminate these ideas to other schools.

The new paradigm has been implemented by most American schools, and, later, spread around the world (Pettigrew et al. 2014). Far from the Principles cited by Mintzberg, the research is "descriptive above all" and, in most cases, the prescription is absent or not applicable in practice. If this research claims to be a "kind of physics," based on a Leibnitzerian epistemology (Churchman, 1971), it has, over time, drifted towards a scientistic approach, like economics. How can we explain such a sudden, mimetic break, contradicting all the traditions of academic freedom? There was strong pressure on the business schools from the foundations that commissioned the two reports, but it was also due to "the desire of the schools to improve the quality of their student recruitment and . . . the desire of graduate school professors to improve their status vis-à-vis professors in other academic disciplines. Clearly, business professors have always had an inferiority complex and felt an unquenchable thirst for respectability. This has led to a progressive alignment of management researchers with the cherished quantitative methods of economists. They thus forgot the reason why management sciences had been separated from other disciplines, because their role remains, above all, to train students for business life, to prepare them to be effective actors and efficient decision-makers (Barnard, 1938).

2 DISSEMINATION OF THE BUSINESS SCHOOL MODEL

The business school model quickly conquered the United States and, as early as 1916, the American Association of Collegiate Business Schools (AACSB) was founded, which was to play a decisive role in the success of this approach based on social science colleges (Hommel et al., 2014). the EFMD (European Foundation for Management Development), founded in 1971, decided in 1997 to create its own accreditation system called EQUIS. In ten years, EQUIS has accredited 183 schools and AACSB 874. This does not contradict the comparison of the number of member schools: 686 of which 363 are in Europe versus 1663 of which 632 are in the United States. The EFMD remains clearly regional while the AACSB has succeeded in globalizing by imposing a form of coercive mimicry (Di Maggio and Powell, 1983).

3 AN ERROR OF CHOICE OF RESEARCH METHODS ?

In the 1960s, management science research took an overly academic and positivist turn, which has only worsened by becoming more and more scientistic, contrary to Pearson's prophecy (Guyot, 2012). Hayek denounced it as early as 1974: "the 'scientistic' attitude is decidedly unscientific in the true sense of the word since it implies a mechanical and uncritical application of habits of thought to fields other than those for which they were formed. Some of the most serious errors of recent economic policies are the direct consequence of this 'scientistic' error." This is the reason why there is no epistemology of management research to date.

What is the true nature of management research? For some authors (Mintzberg, 2004) management is not "a science but simply an art and, above all, a skill. The art encourages creativity, and leads to 'ideas', to a 'vision'. Know-how, based on tangible experience, tries to make connections." Management science is an academic discipline that contains a set of sub-disciplines that can be studied or researched but cannot exist outside the whole. It is therefore not a silo of pure science but a strategic synthesis of action-oriented functions. Unlike the economy, management is a world full of individuals, with their own particularities, and each one plays its part in the whole. Managing well requires knowing how to get the best out of each individual while getting the best possible play from the team.

Because of the pressure from other disciplines, management actors have been assimilated to *'homo economicus'* driven only by their own interest. "Rejecting what we saw as the romanticism of analyzing business behavior in terms of choices, actions, and successes, we adopted a scientific approach seeking to discover laws and patterns and replaced all notions of human intentionality with a firm belief in causal determinism to explain all aspects of business performance. In fact, we have taught that business is reducible to a kind of physics" says Ghoshal (Ghoshal, 2005), before adding "I argue that academic research has had a very strong negative influence on the practice of management... More specifically, I suggest that, by propagating an ideology inspired by amoral theories, business schools have liberated their students from any sense of moral responsibility. Hirshman (Hirshman, 1970) had argued as early as 1970 that this "gloomy view has increasingly led management research to make excessive claims of truth based on biased and unrealistic analyses and cases." In sum, management research shouldn't consider humans as if they were commodities, but as human potential requiring an investment for its development and to create sustainable value (Savall, 1974, 1979; Savall & Zardet, 1987, 2004)

The conclusion that emerges from this analysis is that, today, we see companies complaining about the inability of academic research to solve their problems, while governments are increasingly concerned about the added value of social science research for society as a whole. It is time to return to the original goals of management by developing engaged scholarship methods, which are the only ones capable of studying complex social problems that most often exceed individual research capacities (Van de Ven, 2007)

4 NEED FOR A PARADIGM SHIFT

Even if we should not reject the considerable contributions of the different management disciplines developed sometimes in management schools or in management consulting firms or more often in the companies themselves. Of course, some authors consider that the research carried out in schools is relevant, but that it only lacks an appropriate translation for practitioners, who are judged incapable of understanding the codes of scientific approaches due to the fact that the community of teacher-researchers in management is locked up in their ivory tower. If there is some truth in the plea for the popularization of research for practitioners, through editorial supports such as The Conversation or Academy of Management Perspectives, the contributions of schools to the needs of practitioners are very insufficient, as shown for example in France by the FNEGE barometer. One reason given is that most management research is conducted in the paradigm of the complicated, not the complex. This need for a paradigm shift can be partly attributed to the profusion of variables to be taken into account in an interconnected world, where one cannot be satisfied with taking into account a few variables as in the case of statistical methods, even when one seeks to perfect the structural equations by adding moderating variables. In the wake of Dewey's work on abductive research, epistemologists recommend a paradigm shift from a mode of research mainly centred on deductive approaches to research that makes a better link between theory and scientific observation of complexity (Sarkey et al., 2004). This paradigm shift is considered particularly necessary in the field of management since it can be defined as a science of collective action that requires a practice-based approach in collaboration with actors (Lewin, 1951).

5 TRANSFORMING OR REINVENTING BUSINESS SCHOOLS?

The need for management research to be relevant to the challenges of complexity is becoming more and more pressing, particularly in order to meet the immense needs of public and private companies and organizations where actors suffer from strategic disarray in the face of the complexity of problems. Numerous authors invoke the need for management schools to better take into account their impacts on their stakeholders, not only at the level of companies, but also at the level of territories and society. This is the case, for example, with the AACSB accreditation standards, which give an increasingly important place to impacts. As an example, the Business School Impact System, (Kalika & Shenton, 2014) proposes an analysis grid to help business schools take into-account their impacts in a context of greater complexity than the sole evaluation of publications in academic journals. The question of the very legitimacy of business schools arises in the context of the crisis, in order to address the immense societal responsibility of management methods (Buono, 2016). Should we leave the role of producing actionable scientific knowledge in the field of management to corporate universities and consultants, or should we change the role of business schools?

6 EXPERIMENTS THAT BRING INNOVATION AND HOPE TO BUSINESS SCHOOLS

Harvard's model, which takes into-account the complexity of the case method and differs from the approaches of other business schools, has been inspiring in the context of the transformation of management schools. In particular, by drawing on case-based research methods, the Doctorate in Business Administration (DBA) programs that are now being initiated in most business schools around the world are strengthening the link between theory and practice in the field of management research. In the wake of clinical and action research methods, research-interventions in management research are beginning to be recognized by the academic community, particularly at the Academy of Management. Schools of management of the future are thus gradually being established outside the walls of universities and schools (Iseor, 2003) to meet the needs of society. For example, the CGS of the École des Mines de Paris (Moisdon, 1984) initiated collaborative research with companies to develop management engineering in a context of complexity. The qualimetric research-intervention approach developed at Iseor (Savall & Zardet, 2004) has many similarities with research in medicine (Savall & Fière, 2014), based on the model of university hospital centers, in close collaboration with medical faculties.

REFERENCES

Barnard, C. I. (1938). *The functions of the executive.* Harvard University Press.

Brammer, S., Branicki Linnenluecke, L., & Smith, T. (2019). Grand challenges in management research: Attributes, achievements, and advancement. *Australian Journal of Management, 44*(4), 517–533.

Buono, A. F. (2016). *Social responsibility of the business schools.* 2016 ADERSE conference. Lyon: ADERSE proceedings.

DiMaggio, P., & Powell, P. (1983). The Iron Cage revisited: Institutional Isomorphism and Collective rationality in Organizational Fields. *American Sociological Review, 48*(2), 147–160.

Churchman, C. W. (1971). *The design inquiring systems.* New York.

Gephart, R., Chet-Miller, C., & Svedberg Helgesson, K. (2019). *The Routledge companion to risk, crisis, and emergency management.* Routledge.

Ghoshal, S. (2005). Bad management theories are destroying good management practices. *Academy of Management Learning and Education, 4*(1), 75–91.

Guyot, G. (2012). *L'Internationale de l'Intelligence.* L'Harmattan.

Hayek, F. A. (1989). *The collected works of F. A. Hayek.* University of Chicago Press.

Hirchman, A. O. (1970). *Exit, voice, and loyalty: Response to decline in firms, organizations, and states.* Havard University Press.

Hommel, U., & Thomas, H. (2014). Research on business schools: themes, conjectures and future directions. In Pettigrew et al. *The institutional development of business schools* (pp. 6–35). Oxford.

ISEOR (2003). *The citizen university: Progress, modernization, exemplarity.* Economica.

Kalika, M., & Shenton, G. (2014). *BSIS values the economic and social impact of business schools on their territory.* Le Monde des Grandes Ecoles. December 2014

Lewin, K. (1951). *Field theory in social science.* Harper.

Mintzberg, H. (2004). *Managers, not MBAs.* Bennett-Koehler Publishers.

Moisdon, J. C. (1984). Recherche en gestion et intervention, *Revue Française de Gestion,* n°47–48, 1984.

Pettigrew, A., Cornuel, E., & Hommel, H. (2014). *The institutional development of business schools.* Oxford.

Pfeffer, J., & Fong, C. T. (2002). The end of business schools? Less success than meets the eye. *Academy of Management Learning and Education, 1*(1), 78–95.

Savall, H., & Zardet, V., (2004). *Research in management sciences: Qualimetric approach.* Observe the complex object, preface by David Boje (USA), ed. economica. English translation: The qualimetrics approach: observing the complex object, Information Abe Publishing.

Savall, H., & Fière, D. (2014). A comparative study of research methodologies in medicine and management: the case of qualimetric intervention research. *Journal of Medical Management and Economics, 32.*

Thom, R. (1990). *Apologie du logos.* Hachette.

Van de Ven, A. (2007). *Engaged scholarship.* Oxford University Press.

CHAPTER 46

CHANGES IN THE ENVIRONMENT OF UNIVERSITIES IMPACT IN THEIR STRATEGY

Towards a Paradigm Shift?

Claude Jameux

ABSTRACT

For the past twenty years, French universities have been facing three major changes in their environment: the globalization of higher education and research activities; public policy responses in terms of the autonomy of actors and the reorganization of the system; and a budgetary environment that has been constrained for a long time. This chapter argues that under the combined effects of these changes, a paradigm shift is taking place in favor of a strategic management approach. Universities must now respond to a strategic positioning constraint, develop their capacity for self-organization and revise the criterion of the sustainability of their projects.

Over the past twenty years, multiple transformations have impacted the actors and the system of French higher education and research. Put into perspective and linked, these transformations correspond to three major changes in their environment. Under their combined effects, a paradigm shift is taking place in the functioning of universities. It calls for a strategic management approach, understood as "a management style that emphasizes long-term development, proposes a vision of the future and refers to an institutional identity" (Tabatoni, 1996). This definition is appropriate for the temporal registration of the changes examined, which are part of the long term and at the same time outline the major trends for the future.

SEAM Treatise, pages 403–409

This chapter examines these changes and the paradigm shift they imply. It is essentially based on the experience acquired by its author at different levels of academic responsibility and should be considered as a step-by-step statement of a "thought in action" (Savall and Zardet, 1997) submitted for discussion.

1 UNIVERSITIES FACING THREE MAJOR CHANGES IN THEIR ENVIRONMENT

1.1 Globalization of Higher Education and the Knowledge-Based Society

1.1.1 Globalization: Beyond Rhetoric, Observable Effects

Globalization is often associated with the emergence of a knowledge market, where the boundaries between the academic and commercial spheres are diluted. Alongside labor and capital, science is seen as a production factor that explains the growth of nations and improves the economic well-being of societies. This is what some people call the advent of a knowledge-based society, with the possibilities offered by digital technology as a backdrop.

In this context, the globalization of higher education is generating competition between universities as well as with other public or private institutions, including foreign ones. As a result of the massification of student populations, the competitive forces are diversifying: the expectations of the user public are changing as a result of the digitization of activities, new educational service providers are appearing (e-commerce), and the number of substitutes for national diplomas is increasing.

Finally, in an open and competitive world, "being on the scientific map" is becoming essential for any university, hence the use of accreditation agencies that are supposed to guarantee the quality of higher education; hence also the quest for rankings, which has mobilized both the actors and the higher education system since the Shanghai shock (2003).

1.1.2 Knowledge-Based Society: The Essential Role of Universities in the Innovation Process

As an academic institution that combines education and research, the university is at the heart of the issue of innovation, understood in all its dimensions (scientific, technological, organizational and societal) and in all its forms (disruptive, process or usage-based). All the University's disciplinary sectors and all sectors of the economy are concerned. Thus, the richness and quality of interactions between higher education, research and socio-professional circles irrigate the creative capacities of actors in the innovation chain, the competitiveness of companies and, ultimately, the attractiveness of territories (Jameux, 2008).

Companies are approaching universities to feed their R&D activities with advances in research and to improve the quality of their human resources in innovative processes. For their part, universities are opening up to companies to develop research and development partnerships with high scientific, technological or societal stakes, and to strengthen the outlets for their training. Finally, the regions and their territories are helping to bring universities and companies together to build innovation ecosystems with a local or regional (business clusters, technopoles), national or international (competitiveness clusters) vocation.

1.2 Public Policy Responses: University Autonomy and Reorganization of the French Higher Education System

1.2.1 University Autonomy and Site Policy

The autonomy of French universities is the result of a long process of empowerment and was formalized by the law on the freedom and responsibilities of universities (2007). In addition to the institutional aspect of governance, which has evolved since then, this law reinforces the autonomy of management of institutions through access to extended responsibilities and competencies, particularly in budgetary, financial and human resources management matters. This autonomy is exercised within the framework of a site policy, aimed at coordinating training offers and research strategies in a given academic territory. The LRU law organized research and higher education clusters without disrupting the structural stability of institutions. The 2013 Higher Education Law law is more restrictive. Institutions must choose between three forms of grouping to ensure the territorial coordination of their activities: association around a lead institution, the university community of institutions or merger. With the December 2018 ordinance, another change is taking place with the possibility of creating experimental public establishments bringing together universities, schools and sometimes organizations within a single entity. Nine establishments were thus created in 2019.

1.2.2 Policy of Excellence: Investments in the Future

The policy of excellence is based on the program of investments for the future. The aim is to create multidisciplinary campuses that are visible and effective at the international level. To this end, the investments for the future concentrate a considerable amount of funding on the Initiatives of Excellence (Idex) and Science-Innovation-Territory-Economy Initiatives (I-site) projects. The Idex projects aim to create ten or so world-class universities with world-class scientific strength in a wide range of disciplines. The I-Sites aim to structure sites with a smaller scientific strike force but which demonstrate their ability to develop, with the support of local authorities, socio-economic partnerships in areas of excellence with a high innovation potential.

1.2.3 Excellence and/or Territorial Coordination: A Dual Movement to Spatialize the University System

Because of the volume of funding committed, the AIP is a powerful lever for recomposing the higher education system. For example, the funds paid out for Idex and I-Site at the end of the agreement and probationary periods amount to €217 million annually, while the increase in the subsidy for public service charges over the 2013–2016 period represents €272 million.

However, this restructuring based on excellence suffers from a lack of articulation with that based on territorial coordination. It is as if we were witnessing a two-pronged restructuring actions of the university system, resulting in a differentiated location of the system. Thus, at the end of 2018: one-third of the eighteen academic clusters do not have an Idex or I-site; three of the thirteen major regions do not have an Idex or I-site; outside of the Île-de-France region, four of these regions alone account for all of the Idexes (six) and nearly half of the I-sites (three out of seven).

1.3 A Constrained Budgetary Environment

Despite the rhetoric that emphasizes the benefits to be expected from university autonomy, the purse strings (excluding PIA and extra-budgetary funds) that feed them are tending to tighten. With a wage bill that represents on average 80% of operating expenses and that is mechanically increasing, the ring-fencing of public funding for universities actually means a decrease in their means (Cytermann, 2017). Universities are also faced with an increase in student enrollment and a need to upgrade their real estate.

In these circumstances, the search for complementary sources of funding (other than public) becomes crucial. Unfortunately, universities are having difficulty generating sufficient own resources of this type to sustainably complete the financing of their expenditures. This difficulty adds to the chronic underfunding of universities and further accentuates the fragility of their economic model.

2 STRATEGIC MANAGEMENT OF UNIVERSITIES: TOWARDS A PARADIGM SHIFT?

2.1 A Strategic Positioning Constraint

As a result of globalization, universities have progressively integrated a utilitarian component into their activities. Traditionally focused on their disinterested missions of producing research and disseminating disciplinary knowledge through training, all universities are now developing actions aimed at companies to promote innovation and student integration. Almost all of them claim to be territorially based. Some are building their scientific strategy on a European or global scale.

The essential point here is that we are moving from a paradigm of production/dissemination of disciplinary knowledge in a relatively protected and stable world to a paradigm of positioning these activities in the open and competitive world of knowledge, which is multi-scale, multi-actor, multidisciplinary and multi-resource. A first level of competence consists of positioning oneself in such an environment to ensure the coherence of the strategic project.

Whether one regrets it or not, it is illusory to think that universities are all in the same category. Because of the globalization of higher education activities and the restructuring of the French university landscape, strategic groups are emerging. Let us assume here, for lack of space, that a differentiation is established between:

- Universities that have developed a strategy of global coverage by grouping the major scientific sectors within a single omni-disciplinary entity;
- those that have chosen a strategy of differentiation based on interdisciplinary and cross-disciplinary themes with a high innovation potential;
- those that have opted for a strategy of specialization in a specific scientific segment of the knowledge market.

Three universities did not wait for the 2013 law to merge and have shown real proactivity: Strasbourg (Unistra) and Aix-Marseille (AMU) are two examples of the first category, while the University of Lorraine (UL) illustrates the second. In its Idex project, Unistra clearly states its strategic vision and identity: "Beyond borders, the University of Strasbourg, European by nature, international by vocation. For its part, AMU is just as clear in stating its strategic intention to be recognized as an "omni-disciplinary university of world-class standing. Finally, UL, which has an I-site, specifies its ambition to "become a leading European university" by emphasizing its "differentiation through (its) ability to respond to societal challenges by developing interdisciplinary approaches" and by stating its "multidisciplinary, entrepreneurial and innovative identity." Another example of a differentiation strategy is provided by the University of Savoie Mont Blanc, which intends to be recognized as a "research and professionalization university of the highest European rank, rising to the level of performance of its territory and differentiating itself by its ability to respond to the challenges of industrial, environmental and social transitions. Finally, the University of Avignon has long opted for a strategy of specialization in two areas of identity with strong national visibility: "agro-sciences" in connection with the presence of INRA on the site and "culture, heritage, digital society" in connection with the Avignon Festival.

These examples illustrate that a strategic project refers to a vision of the future and to an institutional identity. While all universities have now fully integrated the content and scope of an institutional project, they have probably not all become aware, or not in a uniform manner, of the fundamental questions that a true strategic project implies.

What category are we playing in? What type of university do we want to promote? What kind of university profile do we want to draw? What shared vision can we rely on? It is a considerable challenge for a university management team to formalize these questions and put them into words, otherwise any strategic project is a waste of time.

2.2 An Issue of Self-Organization

University autonomy has continued to fuel debate, pitting the advocates of institutional and managerial autonomy of institutions against the advocates of scientific and collegial autonomy of teacher-researchers (Leresche, 2009). These debates are not without interest, but let us admit that any organization, and the university is one, needs to be managed in the traditional sense of the term. The question is not to oppose these two types of autonomy, but to know how to reconcile the need for the former with the requirements of the latter.

The second aspect of the paradigm shift is associated with the extent of institutional autonomy granted. To overstate the case, one could say that universities are moving from a system centered on the application of directives, respect for norms and compliance with rules ("they receive instructions, they are supposed to apply them"), to a system that privileges their capacity for self-organization ("they have fewer instructions, it is up to them to self-determine according to their own projects"). Of course, autonomy is exercised within a legislative and regulatory framework, but the door is now open to experimentation. These experiments, which are not reserved for the EPEs alone, are all the more necessary since universities place their actions in systems of multi-actor competition/cooperation, where governance can only be shared between the public, private or mixed spheres.

However, the capacity of universities to self-organize is not self-evident. Indeed, how can we move from a governance that is historically and culturally organized around instructions, i.e., in relation to another person, to a governance that is organized around its own projects, while at the same time making its contribution to national policies? There is an identity shift to be made here, which consists of defining oneself in relation to oneself, in a self-referential posture. Some universities have succeeded in taking this step, others not yet. The case of Strasbourg is exemplary, since the three universities on the site did not wait for the incentive of "territorial coordination" to unite their destinies in 2009.

Another aspect of institutional autonomy is more organizational in the managerial sense of the term. Indeed, an analysis of the universities that have encountered difficulties in implementing the RCE, with deficit years, shows that beyond the simple technical problems of compliance with accounting standards, these institutions suffer from a management deficit at the level of the intermediate system. The increase in the power of central services that accompanies the introduction of the RCE creates problems of articulation between these services and with the training and/or research components (lack of horizontal and vertical cross-functional of services and of interoperability of their information systems). Moreover, many presidents rely on their director general of services and on central services, at the risk of cutting themselves off from the components and, through them, from teacher-researchers, who feel less and less involved as actors in the institution. The lack of dissemination of a strategic culture within the components, from the unit directors to the "driving forces" of the teams, accentuates this feeling of being sidelined.

It is a considerable challenge to (de)demonstrate the added value that the university as an institution brings to the components and their actors, in research as well as in training.

2.3 A Broader Criterion of Sustainability

For the dual reason of dependence on public funding and the unequal effectiveness of strategies for diversifying resources, the economic model of universities is fragile and does not allow them to exercise their autonomy to the fullest extent. This explains why the criterion of financial sustainability has rapidly become a criterion for evaluating the feasibility of each university's strategic project, particularly in terms of its educational offerings.

However, sustainability cannot be reduced to its financial dimension alone. Any strategic project should be examined from the perspective of three complementary questions: is it scientifically accessible, economically feasible and socially acceptable? An ambition that is not very credible in relation to the scientific potential of the research units, objectives that are disproportionate in relation to the resources that can be mobilized, or actions that are decided upon without any real prior appropriation by the institution's personnel, are all pitfalls for the sustainability of strategic projects. This type of questioning calls for a comprehensive analysis of sustainability, and not its reduction to the financial aspect alone.

One essential feature of the sustainability of a university's strategic project is its long-term nature, and therefore, ultimately, its acceptability to the driving forces of its social body, first and foremost among which are the teachers and/or researchers, who, as we have seen, rightly demand their scientific and collegial autonomy. Because a lack of acceptability always translates into a diminished sense of belonging to the institution, a balance must be sought between the contribution/adhesion to the university's strategic project and the sense of belonging to a discipline, seen as an emanation of the scientific community.

CONCLUSION

It is trite to say that a university is not comparable to a company, with a hierarchical line of command based on a Taylorian-Fordian (pyramidal) model of organization. It is less so to accept a dual system where a collegial model based on the academic freedom of teacher-researchers and the self-organization of disciplines coexists with an administrative model inspired by bureaucracy in the sense of Max Weber. By trying too hard to be inspired by the "New Public Management," the risk of a bureaucratic drift can destroy all the benefits expected from autonomy.

REFERENCES

Cytermann, J.-C. (2017). *La fragilité du modèle économique des universités, obstacle à l'autonomie.* colloque de l'Association des directeurs généraux des services, speech transcribed in News Tank, https://education.newstank.fr/fr/article/printable/96912.

Jameux, C. (2008). Société de la connaissance, université et territoire. *Recherches en sciences de gestion, 64,* 367–380.

Leresche, J.-Ph. (2009). Regards internationaux sur l'autonomie des universités et la territorialisation de l'enseignement supérieur. *Pouvoirs Locaux, 82,* 77–81.

Savall, H., & Zardet, V. (1997). Vers la "pensée en action" stratégique ou le non-dit dans le discours sur la stratégie—Proposition pour améliorer la qualité scientifique des recherches en stratégie. *Management International, 2*(1), 77–96.

Tabatoni P., (1996). Aspects de la gestion des politiques de la qualité dans les universités. In *Évaluation institutionnelle: stratégies de qualité, CRE-action* (Revue de l'Association des universités européennes), 107, p. 113–128.

This page intentionally left blank.

CHAPTER 47

KNOWING AND BEING ABLE TO BUILD ONE'S PATH IN AN INCREASINGLY COMPLEX AND UNCERTAIN WORLD

The Challenge of Knowing How to Become

Paul Rousset and Michel Grivel

ABSTRACT

In an increasingly complex and uncertain world, where most of tomorrow's jobs are still unknown, knowing and being able to build one's career path is becoming an essential skill, encompassing and exceeding professional skills and the triptych of knowledge/know-how/know-how to be. This skill, the ability to become, can be learned and trained through and for the experience processed and then integrated into new experiences.

Jostled by the accelerated evolution of technologies and globalization, professions are born, live by transforming themselves and die faster and faster. No one can claim to be doing the same job forever without changing or even disappearing. Even the reference to trades is disappearing in many sectors in favor of notions such as qualification, classification, skills, positions and jobs. As for career paths, they link more or less successful and capitalized experiences, are marked by the undergone and the intentional, by changes or the more or less constant, and mix more and more the personal and the professional and the different roles of life.

In this more complex, changing and uncertain environment, each person must know how to behave, invent, project, build and develop, make choices and act by transforming

SEAM Treatise, pages 411–418

what could be overwhelming into opportunities that they learn to seize. This requires a method of acquiring a particular skill in order to become the author of one's own personal and professional path. Beyond the "classic" skills, it is a kind of meta-skill, the knowledge of becoming that can only be built in relation to others, and concerns organizations as much as individuals. It becomes essential without replacing specific professional skills. It is added to knowledge, know-how and interpersonal skills, encompassing them and making them dynamic. It can be learned and trained in.

The challenge of knowing how to become has gradually become part of the concerns of the association *Trouver/Créer*, through its commitment to educational guidance, the promotion of this guidance to trainers and stakeholders from various backgrounds, and the development of multiple partnerships around learning, of which we present here some illustrations.

1 EMERGENCE AND DEVELOPMENT OF EDUCATIONAL GUIDANCE AND INTEGRATION

Geneviève Latreille (1980), a school and vocational guidance counselor who became a professor of social psychology at the Lumière Lyon 2 University, drew on her experiences, work and encounters to create a training center for school and vocational guidance counselors in 1967, with a multidisciplinary approach. She then convinced the Ministry to create in 1974 the university information and guidance units that would later become the SCUIO.[1] She then approached Denis Pelletier of Laval University in Quebec City, and his colleagues, the bearers of a new concept of guidance, the Activation of Vocational and Personal Development. Since then, the "educational guidance" movement has developed in Europe, which will profoundly change guidance practices. The individual is seen as the subject and not the object of his or her orientation, integration and personal and professional development. It is no longer a question of guidance but of training to know how to invent one's path throughout one's life.

Through this approach, experience appears as the foundation of all personal and collective construction, based on three principles:

- the importance of living and sharing experiences;
- the ability to reread and understand one's experiences individually and as a group, to process them in order to give them meaning;
- the ability to draw on them for future actions and projects.

Experiences are prepared, lived, processed and integrated by and for new experiences. This learning process allows individuals and groups to be more active in their personal and professional projects and actions.

Geneviève Latreille then linked her work with that of Carl Rogers, who focused on the person, and D. W. Winnicott to develop the concept of the "collectively found/created profession."

In 1986, a group of practitioners and researchers, including Robert Solazzi, from the CIO,[2] the ANPE[3] and several French universities, concerned with safeguarding and developing all these innovations, decided to found the association TROUVER/CREER, based at the Institute of Psychology of the university of Lyon 2[4] in memory of D. W. Winnicott and G. Latreille. In the '90s, it ensured the edition and the adaptation for colleges of educational manuals of the Quebecois choices. Robert Solazzi assumed the presidency, while linking the concepts elaborated by G. Latreille, D. Pelletier and D. W. Winnicott to the fundamental contributions of Edgar Morin and Jean-Louis Le Moigne, making "*complex thinking*"[5] the basis of an *Experiential and Paradoxical Approach to Guidance.*

Since then, the association has enriched its training, research and dissemination activities for those involved in guidance, integration, professional development and learning, developing in particular training courses that rely on the experience of participants, to make them live pedagogical sequences, process them with them to work on their meaning and scope, and thus better integrate them into their support practices.

Over the years, in collaboration with partners and professionals from various backgrounds, the members of the association, who are themselves reflective practitioners, have developed the method into an experiential, *paradoxical and cooperative approach* which has just been published (Defrenne et alii, 2021): *paradoxical* because paradox is a fertile reference point for living in a complex and uncertain world, relying on the opposites that coexist in a situation and learning to combine them through creative action; *experiential* because experience is a basis for acquiring the knowledge of becoming by placing past experiences, new experiences to be lived in the present and future experiences at the center of the accompaniment ; cooperative because cooperation is necessary to co-construct the support of individuals and groups, by encouraging cooperative interactions between individuals, with other professionals and the actors of a territory, around a common culture of guidance.

Today, the association is developing two main missions with professionals:

- it is an operator of training, pedagogical engineering, animation and coordination of collaborative research in various fields: secondary and higher education, vocational training and apprenticeship, employment, social and professional integration, management and human resources.
- It is a laboratory for exchanges, sharing ideas, conducting experiments and actions, enriching and deepening the approach, with capitalization and dissemination of the results of actions and research, particularly through training, conferences and publications.

2 AN EXAMPLE: THE CHOICE OF WORK-STUDY AND THEOREFORE OF EXPERIENCE AS A UNIQUE MODE OF TRAINING AT THE IUT LUMIÈRE LYON 2

Since 1992, TROUVER/CREER and ISEOR have had the opportunity to participate in the creation of the IUT LUMIÈRE, the only practice-oriented bachelor program in France that uses work-study programs as the exclusive mode of training, in order to help diversify the intake of high school graduates and reorient students who have failed. The objective is to train differently the public recruited differently, in response to identified needs, while activating them to build their personal and professional identity and to appropriate their knowledge to become.

Particular importance was given to the development, emergence and activation of qualities and skills that are not highly valued academically, but which are appreciated in a work situation. It was a question of establishing the student who becomes an apprentice as a subject, an actor and an author, and not just an object of his or her training, through an institutional project and various mechanisms. The latter put the accompaniment and processing of student experiences at the center of a cooperative process between teachers of various disciplines, between teachers and other educational personnel, between apprenticeship masters and academic tutors, and between companies and the institute of the university.

The fundamental elements of the project were as follows:

- *A specific recruitment* of students making them the main actors of the process: treatment of their grades in the same way whatever their baccalaureate; request to the candidate to state and analyze the contributions of his professional and associative experiences of all kinds and to explain the reasons for his choice of field and work-study program; association of employers to the auditions of choice of the promotion, but dissociating this collective choice from the choice of their apprentice, which is organized later during the schooling period.
- *The organization of a first year (under student status)* of preparation for a successful work-study program with : courses guaranteeing a professional level; personal and professional focus groups encouraging the individual and shared maturation of each student's project; tutored projects, in small groups or promotions, meeting the needs of companies or communities; very strict control of absences and lateness; support in discovering professions and finding companies; work with companies on their offer of missions, company recruitment forum; mutual trial internship with double tutorial supervision, all teachers being obligatory tutors; co-assessment with a booklet and internship report; processing of the latter with the possible (rare) search for another place for the contract.
- *A second year under a work-study contract* with : double tutoring and four periodic meetings, all of which give rise to a multidimensional (self-) evaluation; collective feedback from the work-study program that encourages the sharing of experiences, while preparing for the third year of the bachelor program by encouraging the apprentices to adopt a reflective posture on their presence in the company and to better measure what they could do or experience in an environment other than their own, necessarily restricted and focused on a particular context; writing and defending a dissertation that responds both to the concerns of the company and to the university requirements of documentation and hindsight; all of this is accompanied by the construction of practices and tools for monitoring the rise in professional competence of the apprentices (follow-up booklet, for example) in close collaboration with the ISEOR, its socio-economic method and its members invested in the project (Savall, 1974, 1979; Savall & Zardet, 1987).

Fundamentally maintained since then, this arrangement has proven its worth: contract breakage rates of less than 4%; two-year IUT success rates (73 to 94% depending on the DUT) well above national averages; second-year IUT success rates exceeding 95%; unemployment rates of around 4%; salaries rather higher than national averages... And above all : following an analysis conducted at the end of 2018 by the *Agence Emploi Formation* based on data published by the Ministry of National Education, Higher Education and Research, this IUT was recognized, for the second time, as the one with the highest "added value" for the success of its students in the 2-year Of the IUT, the "added value" corresponds to the difference between the "real" success rate and the "expected" success rate given the characteristics of the population.

3 AN EXPERIENTIAL AND COOPERATIVE APPROACH TO THE PARADOXES OF WORK-BASED LEARNING

Apprenticeship under work contract alternates teaching in the training center and work experience with the employer. These very different experiences are complementary and formative. This juxtaposition is, however, paradoxical because the training methods used are so different, not only according to the situations and work teams, but also according to the disciplines, the teachers and the strategies developed by the parties involved.

It is difficult to contextualize/decontextualize knowledge. Already in school, young people have been taught to dissociate their knowledge between disciplines rather than to link them, to experience different modes of learning and control, to consider school as separate from work and its issues. The major difficulty encountered by apprentices is therefore to manage to make the link, both at university between disciplines and between these and work situations. This is obviously difficult, especially since the young person has little experience and most courses continue to follow their academic logic.

While living through multiple transitions, the apprentice must therefore face this multipolar complexity and build his or her path by making links between everything he or she discovers and learns, between all the experiences he or she is given to live through, thereby instructing his or her future personal and professional choices. Obviously, this requires support that should be cooperative.

A collaborative research project developed with *Formasup Ain Rhône Loire*[6] from 2015 to 2019 has made it possible to make some progress in this area (Cimbaro et al., 2015). It was initiated following training courses for apprenticeship masters and tutors that Trouver/Créer had set up at the request of the apprenticeship administration. Based on the idea that it is not enough to be a good professional to be a good apprentice master, just as it is not enough to have a good command of one's discipline to be a good teacher and a fortiori a good academic tutor, these trainings develop an experiential approach that relies on the experience of the actors, makes them live experiences in training that are immediately processed to integrate them into action projects, putting the young learner at the center of the device.

Followed by a steering committee of which Michel Grivel (1980) was a member, the aim of this collaborative research was therefore to work, with the trainees, researchers and other learning actors, on the "field effect" of these training courses and the way in which they could be improved. This required monitoring of implementation, quantitative and qualitative field surveys with various actors (apprentices themselves, current and former apprentices, companies, apprenticeship masters, tutors, UFA managers, etc.), pedagogical-scientific cycles, and many other initiatives that gradually made us understand the need to professionalize all the actors and systems, and not only those in charge of tutoring apprentices.

A decisive contribution was that of Guy Le Boterf (2018), who co-hosted with *Trouver/Créer* a cycle on "Experience and Competence" that allowed participants to better master the distinction between "Having competences" and "Being competent." It was followed two years later by another cycle "Accompaniment and pedagogy of alternation" to share experiences and complementary contributions from Alain Dubois, Laurent Veillard (2017), Denis Amblard (2015) and Marine Pelé-Peycelon (2018).

The partnership shaping of programs, and even the co-elaboration of grids of competencies according to more or less identified needs and the job offers they target, are certainly unavoidable, but they only define capacities to be acquired or assumed to be acquired, and resources that can be mobilized; they are not enough to affirm that a professional, even a beginner, is competent. In order to build the appropriation of these skills, it is necessary to organize and sequence situational exercises ("one does not shoot flowers to make them grow"), and also to develop the reflective capacity of the apprentices, their self-assessment, through and for the professional experience.

A second phase of the collaborative research consisted in accompanying the apprenticeship units in their progress in this field, each in their own way, according to their strengths and weaknesses, and their motivations, all putting the professionalization of the apprentice at the heart of their practices: creation and co-engineering of "project" modules; definition of assignments in the company and construction of methods for their evaluation; work on the content and tools of tripartite follow-up meetings (apprenticeship masters, tutors, apprentices); facilitation of meetings of apprenticeship masters and tutors (sometimes with the apprentices); development of self-assessment grids of the increase in skills proven by analyzed acts; organization of return visits in both directions (after a stay in a work situation but also on return from time spent at the university); confrontation of the blocks of competence with actions in the field; work on the dissertation and its defence; apprenticeship cafés; organization of forums inviting professionals by the apprentices themselves; pedagogical conferences aimed at teachers, especially professionals, so that they use their own experience not to illustrate their courses but to better enable the apprentices to make sense of what they are experiencing, etc.

In doing so, the aim was and still is to find/create the paths to successful professionalization and to the construction by the young person himself of his knowledge of how to become, which will enable him to behave and make choices inside and outside the company, in a context where the skills needed for the future are more and more numerous and not yet known (Savall & Zardet, 2020).

It is already more than 30 years since Lucie Tanguy directed the collective writing of the famous "Unfindable training-employment relationship," this socially defined but scientifically undefined field of research. The aim was not to deny the existence of this relationship but to show how difficult it is to understand, how complex and changing it is, how it is mediated by a set of issues, realities and behaviors, both micro and macro socio-economic, individual and collective, public policies and specific actions with inescapable and increasingly accelerated changes in employability and career paths.

Under these conditions, training can no longer be simply teaching correctly defined knowledge that can then be applied, transmitting knowledge and know-how to students in the belief that they will instantly be able to mobilize what they have been taught but not necessarily learned. We must also make them professionals who know how to act competently and anticipate changes, learning to mobilize resources to better master complexity and uncertainty, and to make choices in this context, and thus to know how to become.

4 SECOND EXAMPLE: FROM THE WORKPLACE TO THE DISCOVERY OF PROFESSIONS, THE CONDITIONS FOR PRACTICING THEM AND THE CHALLENGES OF AN INDUSTRY

Obtaining a pre-bachelor (DUT) or a professional bachelor means that the graduate is capable of being effectively involved in a wide range of activities. However, preparing this diploma under a work-study contract, as is often encouraged for professional licenses, certainly opens the door to the professional world and the application in this world of the knowledge and know-how acquired in the training center, but also closes the door on a particular field of missions and a particular company, which inevitably cannot mobilize the apprentice's full potential. A double pitfall must therefore be avoided: the young person's rejection of lessons that he or she considers to be mostly useless, and his or her conviction that he or she will have difficulty doing anything other than what he or she has done in the company where he or she is/was an apprentice. However, knowing how to become requires exploring the field of possibilities, to understand that it is within reach.

During the creation of two work-study licenses in real estate, the *Institut du Droit Patrimonial et Immobilier* (Lyon3) asked *Trouver/Créer* to co-construct, with the managers of these licenses, an annual module initially entitled "Project." The aim was to help the apprentices to: get to know their partner professional environments better; build their personal and professional project; adopt a reflective attitude towards their learning experiences; prepare for their professional integration. The ambition was to allow the apprentices to build their capacity to know how to become, by making them progressively actors of their training by processing their apprenticeship experiences.

The pedagogical progression chosen was as follows:

- First semester: discovery of professions and organization of round tables by the students; processing of this experience from the point of view of professional and personal knowledge;
- Second semester: capitalization of the knowledge acquired during the first semester and construction of the personal and professional project; appropriation of the Skilvioo tool and elaboration of a skills CV.

The first semester was devoted to the cooperative discovery of: the diversity of professions and jobs, even positions, covered by the two licenses (real estate development and social housing management); the variety of conditions (material, human, managerial) of their exercise and the current evolutions of the practices and problems of the sector; this in relation to activities which were proposed to them, even imposed, such as the organization, at the end of the semester, of round tables Professions prepared and animated with the participation of professionals.

This pedagogical intention was a means of activating exchanges between apprentices on the work stations they occupied, the responsibilities entrusted to them, the activities of their companies, the trades and jobs for which they were preparing and the variety of their working conditions. He motivated them to interview their apprenticeship masters and/or company managers, as well as professional leaders, and to choose the themes and speakers they would prefer during the round tables.

They made this information their own and went from discovery to a certain knowledge of the trades and jobs in the sector and their professional environment, while acquiring other skills, such as: knowing how to organize themselves to meet and interview professionals; adopting a posture of observing and listening to other trades, other professional environments than their own; collaborating to organize an event, very material aspects to the animation of the round tables. In short, the apprentices have acquired a "different" knowledge of how to act than the one spontaneously thought of in their work situation, which is complementary to this one and indispensable to their future knowledge.

For the apprentices and those in charge of the training, the experience was very much appreciated from the first year; for the professionals invited to the round tables as well. They observed that the questions raised during the round tables resonated with those they were asking themselves. The system was therefore renewed.

There was one limitation, however: it had been planned to immediately ask the apprentices to identify the personal achievements of this experience, beyond a better knowledge of the trades and jobs for which their diploma prepared them. The apprentices found this exercise incongruous and had difficulty accepting it, especially since it was a semester-long evaluation test. Beyond the unavoidable and motivating emotion and the tension caused by the mode of evaluation implemented, the beginning of the second semester thus gave itself the time to process the experience, in all its collective, individual, personal and professional aspects. For the co-designers of the action, it was unthinkable not to take the time to process the experience, to give it meaning beyond, but also because of, the pleasure felt.

CONCLUSION

Such experiences, both individual and collective, need to be processed and integrated, just like the other experiences lived by the apprentices, in the training unit, in the company, elsewhere, so that they can invent their own professional and personal development, and so that they themselves can master the never-ending construction of their knowledge of how to act, mobilizing resources, and their knowledge of how to become.

This is a crucial issue for today's and tomorrow's world, which is more than ever changing and uncertain, complex and full of ruptures and opportunities, and which must be considered as challenges to be taken up for oneself, and in cooperation with other actors.

NOTES

1. SCUIO: Service Commun Universitaire d'Information et d'Orientation: Department of information and orientation
2. CIO: Centre d'information et d'Orientation: Center of information and orientation
3. ANPE: Agence Nationale pour l'Emploi/Pôle Emploi: National Employment Agency
4. https://www.trouver-creer.org
5. Complex thinking: The notion of complex thinking was coined by the French philosopher Edgar Morin and refers to the ability to interconnect different dimensions of reality. With the emergence of multidimensional, interactive events or objects with random components, one is obliged to develop a strategy of thinking that is not reductive or totalizing, but rather reflective. Morin calls this capacity *complex thinking.*
6. Formasup Ain Rhône Loire is a cross-industry and cross-university apprenticeship center. It is in charge of 3,500 apprentices and 130 work-study units.

REFERENCES

Amblard D. (2015). Le référentiel personnel de l'agir professionnel, un instrument de la professionnalisation de formateurs d'un dispositif de formation par alternance, thesis Lille1

Cimbaro Y., Vilcot T., et al., including Paul Rousset. (2015). *L'apprentissage responsable.* Afnor boutique.

Defrenne R., Faivre D., et al., including Paul Rousset (2021). *Trouver et créer un accompagnement de l'orientation tout au long de la vie.* Editions QUI PLUS EST.

Grivel, M. (1980). *L'impact du style de gestion des dirigeants et cadres d'entreprise sur la nature des conditions de la vie au travail en milieu administratif informatisé.* Thèse de doctorat de 3ème cycle, Universités Lyon II et Lyon III.

Latreille G. (1980). *La naissance des métiers en France 1950–1975, Etude psycho-sociale.* Presses Universitaires de Lyon.

Le Boterf, G. (2018). *Développer et mettre en œuvre la compétence.* Eyrolles, Paris.

Pelé-Peycelon, M. (2018). *Devenir Maître d'apprentissage: configurations et affordances pour construire sa pratique tutale en entreprise.* Thèse université Lyon 2.

Veillard, L. (2017). *La formation professionnelle initiale.* Presses Universitaires de Rennes.

Savall H., & Zardet, V. (2020). *Comment travailler ensemble? Défis de l'intergénération.* Éditions EMS.

CHAPTER 48

ENHANCING THE MANAGERIAL IMPACT OF MANAGEMENT RESEARCH TOWARDS DOCTORAL TRAINING IN MANAGEMENT ASSOCIATING ACADEMICS AND PRACTITIONERS

Michel Kalika, Jérôme Chabanne-Rive, and Marc Bonnet

ABSTRACT

As management research must increasingly make its managerial and societal impacts explicit, doctoral programs in management are now opening up to corporate practitioners and collaborative research. This chapter shows the example of two doctoral programs that contribute to this evolution: the DBA of the Business Science Institute, the EDEN program of EIASM and the hundreds of theses prepared at ISEOR.

Crises usually accelerate emerging developments. This rule was applied in business schools following the economic crisis of 1929, as their legitimacy was questioned from the point of view of their social responsibility (Bowen, 1953). The crises of 2008 and 2020 have accentuated the changes in the impact of management research. Among the signals identified, we note in particular the growing importance of impacts in the accreditation criteria of business schools by AACSB, AMBA and EFMD, the creation of the BSIS EFMD-FNEGE label dedicated to highlighting the impacts of business schools, as well as calls from the profession to increase the relevance of research and to provide effective responses to the transformation

SEAM Treatise, pages 419–425

of organizations in a world in crisis. This chapter demonstrates the importance of collaboration between faculty and practitioners to produce impactful research. After highlighting the need for collaborative research to achieve relevant impacts, we present two cases of doctoral programs incorporating this orientation, EIASM and BSI's DBA.

1 NEED FOR COLLABORATIVE RESEARCH BETWEEN ACADEMICS AND PRACTITIONERS TO ACHIEVE RELEVANT IMPACTS

For more than 70 years, management research has been focused on specialized areas of management, notably due to the dominance of positivist research approaches with a quantitative focus, advocated in the United States by the Ford and Carnegie Foundations. This research produced relevant results in a context marked by the relative predictability of the evolution of the business environment and the behavior of actors. However, the last few decades have been marked by an acceleration of interactions between management variables, due in particular to the digitalization of society and the globalization of the economy. This multiplication of interactions has progressively created a great complexity of situations, with an acceleration since the financial crisis of 2008 and the Covid crisis in 2020. Thus, sophisticated solutions validated through traditional research methods are no longer sufficient to help actors act in complexity (Bhaskar, 1975) and to achieve impacts (Gibbons et al., 1994). Complexity needs to be better taken into-account. Two main shortcomings are observed by the academic world itself (Bartunek et al., 2018):

- The hyperspecialization of management research into "silos": indeed, the complexity of situations is characterized by interactions between domains, which requires an overall and systemic approach;
- Observation of phenomena from outside companies or organizations, sometimes referred to as "ivory tower" research: the collection of reliable information on the complex situation is very limited or even distorted.

Obtaining relevant impacts in complex situations requires the use of innovative methods, such as action research or qualimetric intervention-research (Savall & Zardet, 2004; Buono, Savall & Cappelletti, 2018) to develop collective action engineering, a fundamental raison d'être of management sciences. Despite the strong mimicry observed in business schools over the last fifty years, changes have been observed, especially since Van de Ven's plea for engaged research (Van de Ven, 2007), due to the demands of management research stakeholders: accreditation bodies are asking for evidence of the impacts of management schools and their research, funders of management research and training are waiting for innovative solutions, even academic journals are being questioned about their impacts. The "evidence based view" research trend reinforces this trend (Pfeffer and Sutton, 2006).

We can thus observe the emergence of significant innovations in management research practices: collaborative research, such as action research and intervention-research, which lead to the creation of actionable knowledge in a complex context. They combine the rigor and quality of conceptualization of the academic world with the quality of observation of the complexity experienced by management practitioners in their professional lives. Thus, the model that ISEOR has been experimenting with for over 45 years has been judged very relevant by the leaders of the Academy of Management, with over 60 papers presented in ten years and the publication of a dozen books in the United States.

2 DEVELOPMENTS TOWARDS TRANS-DISCIPLINARITY IN DOCTORAL EDUCATION AND MANAGEMENT RESEARCH: THE EXEPRIENCE OF THE EDEN PROGRAM WITH EIASM

Doctoral education is central to scientific development. An important part of research activities is carried out within the framework of doctoral training and the management sciences sector is not left out. The doctoral experiences, the interactions and the accumulation of values that take place in this context have a formative character. Given the upstream nature of doctoral training programs, the content, postures and methodologies that are developed in these programs raise questions, particularly with regard to the hybridization of research practices involving management practitioners and academics.

To take a step back in the European context of doctoral education in management, it is interesting to observe the actions carried out over the last 50 years by the EIASM -European Institute for Advanced Studies in Management-. This was the beginning of the development of the academic community in management and the emergence of doctoral students in this field. However, the resources needed to support the development of competent doctoral students, scattered among the schools in Europe, represented a major problem. This was seen as an opportunity by the founders of EIASM to create a critical mass of experienced faculty in Europe to facilitate the growth and development of the scientific field of management.

EIASM was created in 1971 with the primary mission of being a key player in strengthening the role of doctoral studies in management in Europe. Since its foundation, EIASM has aimed at strengthening European management research, encouraging and facilitating the initiation and coordination of joint scientific research in management by leading European researchers, stimulating interaction between management academics in Europe, but also and above all, improving the development and quality of doctoral education in management in Europe.

The EIASM has conducted a reflection on the design and development of doctoral education in management—"Advanced Studies in Management." From the Institute's archives, the initial documents and discussions address many issues, including the challenges of doctoral education in management, the need to help doctoral students in management develop their research and pedagogical skills, the design of doctoral education in management, from the design and content of doctoral programs in management to the supervision of doctoral students, and the design and content of the doctoral dissertation in management. The debates on ideas and the evolving principles of design of doctoral studies in management have had a lasting impact on this scientific field in Europe. Between 1973 and 1988, EIASM organized and sponsored 31 European doctoral seminar programs, accompanying more than 800 doctoral students.

In 1988, EIASM launched a new initiative: the EDEN—EIASM Doctoral Education Network—and seminar series. Today, there are 7,000 graduate students involved in the program, with the support of 400 scientists. An average of 20 doctoral seminars are organized each year, for more than 350 students, representing 30 nationalities, with an average annual distribution of €50,000 to €80,000 in grants for 60 to 90 doctoral students.

The EDEN program has been organized around an integrated set of residential doctoral seminars that engage participants in systematic interaction, leading them to compare their approaches and cross-reference their research. It is a combination of intensive one-week seminars on advanced management research methodology and shorter seminars on the latest developments in their specific field of interest. This program involves doctoral students, their supervisors and their institutions, which allows for an alternation of locations and the creation of links with the main European management schools. These seminars thus have the potential to enable the sustainable creation of new networks of doctoral students, as well as the construction and strengthening of European academic communities of practice (Coughlan, 2018).

Thanks to its image and its competitive and organizational advantages (network core, autonomy, and flexibility), EIASM has proven to be very effective in three areas:

- The insertion of doctoral students into a highly stimulating system where European researchers can interact, within and between academic associations, sharing common concerns and goals;
- Helping doctoral students to position their own work in relation to European research in general: exposure to different research traditions and orientations; openness to global perspectives on the management environment; awareness of the challenges facing management science in Europe.
- The creation of a European network of very active trainers at the doctoral level.

EIASM also constitutes an ecosystem that favors openness to otherness in research approaches aimed at making an impact. It promotes the emergence and hybridization of research practices involving practitioner-managers and academics. To this end, three complementary means are mobilized:

- The organization of research workshops on themes corresponding to the challenges of companies and organizations in a rapidly changing European area.
- Trans-disciplinarity, as a leitmotiv of EIASM to ensure the development of a systemic vision, a necessary posture to deal with the complex problems of management in today's world. It allows us to compensate for the functioning of silos thanks to a very early awakening to the interests of trans-disciplinarity. The Institute promotes this approach by awarding an annual "Interdisciplinary Leader Award" for academic interdisciplinarity.
- The training of doctoral students in research methods that are not limited to the description or interpretation of management situations, but aim to make the link between theory and practice. For example, EDEN seminars have been organized on the theme of experimental research and action research.

3 EXAMPLE OF THE HYBRIDIZATION OF RESEARCH PRACTICES INVOLVING PRACTITIONER-MANAGERS AND ACADEMICS: THE DBA OF THE BUSINESS SCIENCE INSTITUTE

In order to maintain the legitimacy of management research in the long term with respect to stakeholders such as private and public organizations, as well as public funding authorities, it is necessary to design new forms of knowledge creation that generate impacts. It is important to distinguish several types of research impact. Beyond the academic impact of research, which is easily understood through quantitative metrics such as the "H index" or "impact factor" of publications, it is important to take into-account the managerial and societal impact of research. The managerial impact refers to the impact on the managerial practices of organizations, in terms of methods, tools, systems, processes or decisions. Societal impact assesses the contribution of research to societal and environmental changes.

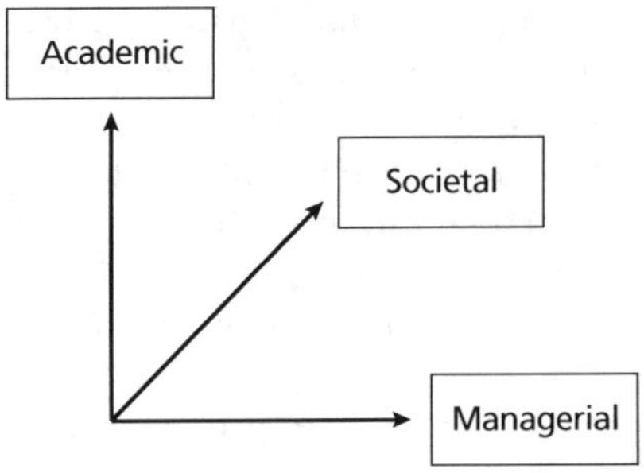

Figure 48.1 The three dimensions of research impact.

These three types of academic, managerial and societal impact concern different audiences (Figure 48.1).

- Academic impact concerns the academic community and regulates its functioning both internally, in terms of human resource management, and externally in terms of accreditation.
- The managerial impact concerns the leaders and managers within companies and organizations.
- The societal impact, understood at the global level, concerns citizens.

Although academic impact is easier to measure, the difficulty of measuring it should not lead us to give up.

But doesn't taking these different dimensions into account require different research methods? The "Doctorate in Business Administration" (DBA) is a pedagogical modality that involves experienced managers in a research process in which professors participate as advisors and coaches. The doctoral student manager contributes his or her research question based on his or her managerial experience and professional background. The professor brings his or her conceptual perspective, knowledge of the literature and mastery of methodologies. The motivations of doctoral students and professors are thus complementary:

- Doctoral students need to distance themselves from their problematic (Coghlan, 2007) in order to broaden their rationality and demonstrate reflexivity. This is all the more necessary since management situations are increasingly complex and there are no ready-made solutions (Buchanan, 1992). For example, the financial management of a large city requires taking into-account all the actors with contradictory requirements, while the financial approach only takes into-account a dimension limited to visible costs (Mottet, 2016). Moreover, the profession of managers does not consist of writing articles or theses, which requires coaching from professors experienced in the writing exercise.
- Since most management professors have been selected on the basis of academic criteria alone, unlike medical professors, they need better access to managerial and societal dimensions. Cooperating with practicing doctoral students, particularly in the case of DBAs, allows them to access quality data, taking into-account the multitude of interacting variables to obtain relevant impacts.

The processes of distancing and "distant familiarity" (Girin, 1981) must be carefully codified to foster positive interaction between practitioners and academics in the context of collaborative research. For example, in the case of the Business Science Institute's DBA doctoral program, whose quality processes have been formalized and validated by the achievement of international AMBA accreditation, procedures include several distancing devices:

- Regular, structured monthly meetings between each doctoral student manager and his or her supervisor,
- Regular presentations of work progress to professors and colleagues, notably during the international seminar in Wiltz (Luxembourg),
- Training seminars designed to take into-account the theoretical and methodological frameworks of management as a science of action.

This DBA, which is based on an international academic network organization, brings together the support team, more than 100 professors from different countries and nearly 200 doctoral student-managers (February, 2021) from 46 countries. The largest groups are from Germany, China, France and Ivory Coast. The pedagogy is face-to-face (Paris, Frankfurt, Shanghai, Abidjan, Bamako, Geneva, Bangkok, Douala, etc.) or remote, or most often mixed, and takes place in three languages (French, English, German). During the last week of September, all doctoral student-managers and their professors meet for an international seminar during which thesis follow-up, meetings, defenses and graduation take place. This networked organization, which has been based on the intensive use of information and communication technologies since its inception, combines flexibility and responsiveness, which is an asset for active managers scattered around the world. The fact that 80 managers have defended their DBA theses attests to the fact that a remote operation can be effective in the doctoral field.

The DBA is thus an artifact for building actionable knowledge (Beaulieu and Kalika, 2015) with impacts: in particular, it is advisable to position oneself in an attitude of scientific humility (Schein, 2013), avoiding both practitioner prejudice and professorial arrogance. Societal impacts are also achieved through the dissemination of results to the wider public, including a series of books published by EMS based on the DBA theses that have been defended.

CONCLUSION

Collaboration between practitioners and academics in the field of management research seems promising and seems to be accelerating, with the creation of dozens of new DBA and Executive PhD programs around the world each year. This is a sign of a transition towards a new model of management education.

REFERENCES

Bartunek, J. M., & McKenzie, J. (Eds). (2018). *Academic-Practitioner Relationships.* Sage.
Beaulieu, P., & Kalika, M. (2015). *Knowledge creation by managers.* EMS Publishing.
Beaulieu, P., & Kalika, M. (2017). *The DBA thesis project.* EMS Publishing.
Bhaskar, R. A. (1975). *A realist theory of science.* Leeds Books.
Bowen, H. R. (1953). *Social responsibilities of the businessman.* Harper & Row.
Buchanan, R. (1992). Wicked problems in design thinking. *Design issues,* 8(2), 5–21.
Coghlan, D. (2007). Insider action research doctorates: Generating actionable knowledge. *Higher Education, 54*(2), 293–306.

Coughlan P., Hargaden, V., Coghlan, D., Idris, A, &. Åhlström, P. (2018). The role of OM EDEN in building the EurOMA community, *International Journal of Operations & Production Management, 38*(8), 1664–1682.

Gibbons, M., Limoges, C., & Nowotny, H. (1994). *The new production of knowledge: the dynamics of science and research in contemporary societies.* Sage.

Girin, J. (1981), "*Quel paradigm pour la recherche en gestion?*" Economies and Societies, Volume XV, No. 10–11–12, Management Science Research Series, No. 2, pp. 1871–1889.

Kalika, M. (2017). *How to succeed in your DBA?* EMS.

Lejeune, C., Starkey, K., Kalika, M., & Tempest, S. (2019). The impact of business schools: Increasing the range of strategic choices. *Management international/International Management/Gestión Internacional, 23*(2), 88–98.

Mottet, V. (2016). *Construire une agglomeration transfrontalière: méthode pour surmonter les contradictions normatives.* EMS Publishing.

Pfeffer, J., & Sutton, R. I. (2006). *Evidence-based management.* Harvard Business Review, January, 62–75.

Schein, E. H. (2013). *Humble inquiry: The gentle art of asking instead of telling.* Berrett-Koehler Publishers.

Van de Ven, A. H. (2007). *Engaged Scholarship.* Oxford University Press.

This page intentionally left blank.

CHAPTER 49

SOCIO-ECONOMIC THEORY AT THE HEART OF STUDENT ENTREPRENEURSHIP SUPPORT

Sylvie Mira-Bonnardel and Isabelle Géniaux

ABSTRACT

Socio-economic theory constitutes a praxeology of entrepreneurial support, and more specifically of student entrepreneurship. Both a framework and a substrate for transformative coaching, socio-economic theory makes it possible to articulate the cognitive transformation of the student entrepreneur with the achievement of economic objectives. This chapter specifies the specificities of entrepreneurial cognition and the practices of coaching students in business creation projects, in order to explain how socio-economic theory offers an epistemological, methodological and operational framework for a renewal of these practices.

Since the first course in entrepreneurship was offered in 1947 by Harvard University, the field has exploded in university curricula, research projects, and the pathways for supporting students' entrepreneurial projects. Entrepreneurship is treated in four themes: the entrepreneur, entrepreneurial strategy, entrepreneurial finance and entrepreneurial coaching.

The coaching of entrepreneurs has become a real field of research (Chabaud, et al., 2010), treated from a methodological point of view (Verstraete, 2001), then with a transformative aim for the project and its bearer, with work on learning and cognitive transformation generating a modification of attitudes and behaviors, reducing inhibitions and consolidating the desire to undertake. The coaching is then less focused on skills and more attentive to the process and a better understanding of the entrepreneur and his cognitive patterns (Bakkali et al., 2010). Verstraete (2001) and Sarasvathy (2001) have shown on the one hand the specificity of the entrepreneur's cognitive processes and on the other hand

SEAM Treatise, pages 427–433

the influence of his cognitive prism on his entrepreneurial dynamics. This chapter deals specifically with the coaching of student entrepreneurs and shows how socio-economic theory constitutes both the framework and the substratum of a transformative coaching, combining cognitive transformation and the creation of meaning in economic achievement.

We first present the specificities of entrepreneurial cognition and the reasons why entrepreneurial coaching leads to its transformation. Then we specify the particularities of the coaching of student entrepreneurs and the importance of coupled processes of involvement/distancing. Finally, we show why the coaching of student entrepreneurs must be rooted in socio-economic theory.

1 SPECIFICITY OF THE COGNITIVE PROCESSES OF ENTREPRENEURS

Since the end of the 1990s, research on cognition has opened up the field of entrepreneurial cognition for a better understanding of the decision-making processes of entrepreneurs, notably with the work of Verstraete and Sarasvathy.

Verstraete (2001) describes the cognitive processes of the entrepreneur with three characteristics: strategic thinking, reflexivity and learning. Strategic thinking refers to the entrepreneur's vision, "the anticipation of a desired future." Reflexivity refers to the entrepreneur's ability to interpret and understand the events that surround him. Learning puts the entrepreneur back into his dynamic and concretizes his capacity to evolve between experience, knowledge, competence, motivation, and emotions.

For his part, Sarasvathy (2001) characterizes the cognitive process of entrepreneurs by distinguishing two cognitive logics: causal logic and effectual logic. The first is characterized by the anticipation of a desired future and the setting of objectives on the part of the entrepreneur; the effectual logic is based on the entrepreneur's ability to mobilize his resources and skills to deal with his current environment, even if this means modifying his objectives as he goes along. The causal and effectual logics converge on the importance of cognitive biases that limit the entrepreneur's own operational and strategic actions and his understanding of the environment. The entrepreneur's cognitive prism constrains his perception and considerably impacts his entrepreneurial dynamics and his understanding of data or analyses, de facto limiting their scope.

This is how a powerful cognitive filter constrains, reduces and rigidifies the entrepreneur's potential to act effectively, which is mainly determined by "the leader's ability to conceive and perceive the interconnection existing between the internal and external aspects of his organization and between the resources at his disposal and the activities he proposes" (Sammut, 2003, p.160).

A coaching program can therefore play a decisive role in the performance of the entrepreneur, either by boosting his or her growth in the post-creation/pre-development phase, or by consolidating his or her intentionality in the pre-creation phase, a situation that is generally characteristic of student projects in higher education institutions, whose educational mission is reflected in the entrepreneurial coaching of their students.

2 SUPPORT FOR STUDENT ENTREPRENEURS

Entrepreneurial support is by nature protean, complex and multi-skilled (Jacquemin et al., 2018). It is a co-constructed process engaged between a coachee and one or more coaches (Messeghem et al. 2013) mixing coaching, companionship, consultancy and mentoring.

Coaching takes the form of processes and contents, but also spaces, structures and networks. Processes and contents provide knowledge, methods and tools; spaces, structures and networks consolidate the legitimacy and recognition of the status of entrepreneur.

On the student public, Boissin et al (2007) have particularly well illustrated the issue of cognitive biases, by identifying students' beliefs about entrepreneurship. They showed the need to develop the capacities of student-entrepreneurs to transform their representations, which are too often anchored in a personal undervaluation.

In order to change the perceptions of the student-entrepreneur, support must be based on a detailed understanding of the student's career path and motivations, focused on the person rather than the project, and orchestrated within a mentoring rather than a teaching logic. The mentor fulfills a major function characterized by three dimensions: psychological, career and role model. The mentor does not provide technical skills per se; his or her objective is essentially to work on life skills and entrepreneurial dynamization, in a logic of vicarious learning.

It is necessary to articulate several methods in order to rethink students' entrepreneurial learning and to encourage their reflexivity: case studies, testimonies of entrepreneurs (who have succeeded or failed), researcher facilitation sessions, setting up of creation projects or even cases of application in the university course (Sammut, 2005). Indeed, it is important not to limit oneself to the interaction between a mentor and a protégé. The collective dynamic emerging from interactions with peers and relational networks offers an equally important learning crucible (Géraudel et al, 2012); in fact, it is a matter of effectively combining individual support and collective dynamics.

This individual/collective dialectic is precisely at the heart of the PEPITE schemes: "student clusters for innovation, transfer and entrepreneurship" set up in France by the Ministry of Higher Education and Research. The PEPITEs manage the "student-entrepreneur" status which allows students to access information, services, advice, incubation spaces, and even in some institutions to obtain educational credits for their entrepreneurial project. In association with public institutions of higher education, PEPITEs are mandated to offer support methods and reception areas offering services at very low cost, thus differentiating themselves from private incubators (Bories-Azeau et al, 2016).

The thirty or so PEPITEs that crisscross the French territory constitute entrepreneurial ecosystems, open to their socio-economic territory: on average per PEPITE, there are more than 60 active partners: academic partners, private and public funders, as well as numerous structures and associations working in the field of entrepreneurship without forgetting the socio-economic actors (companies and employers' organizations or movements; MESRI report, 2019).

The dynamization of support by the PEPITEs is reinforced by the Technology Transfer Acceleration Companies , created in 2010 by the Promising Investment Scheme (*Programme des Investissements d'Avenir*) . 856 million euros have been allocated to the creation of 14 Technology Transfer Acceleration Companies in France, created to develop the research of laboratories of educational institutions, all fields combined, through the creation of innovative companies.

This system supports student entrepreneurship because it is also students who activate the marketing of innovations by obtaining exclusive licenses on patents, often with funding for prototyping or sizing. These measures have strongly encouraged the development of field initiatives (Entrepreneuriales, Entrepreneur Days, etc.), innovative teaching methods (simulation games, virtual creation projects, entrepreneurial permits) and marked an important turning point in student culture by promoting the idea that "entrepreneurship can be learned.

From this impulse, many higher education institutions have integrated entrepreneurial support into their training offer. Higher education institutions often intervene before the start-up phase with the mission of instilling an entrepreneurial culture that allows the emergence of ideas and projects that can then be supported.

In our capacity as teacher-researchers in higher education institutions, respectively at the Ecole Centrale de Lyon and the University of Lyon 3, we have orchestrated business creation support programs, particularly with engineering students, drawing heavily on the contributions of socio-economic theory (Savall, 1974, 1989; Savall and Zardet, 1987, 1995). This theory provides the epistemological framework, the methodology and the operational tools for a transformative student entrepreneurial support.

3 CONTRIBUTION OF THE SOCIO-ECONOMIC THEORY TO THE COACHING OF STUDENT ENTREPRENEURS

The socio-economic theory presents a structural-behavioral conceptualization of the organization, the evaluation of the performance of an organization combines the economic and social dimensions, considering that behavioral variables of a psychological or physiological nature affect the organization. The energetic capacities of the individual interact with the structures in a reciprocal movement of adaptation/transformation (Savall & Zardet, 1987, 1995).

The epistemology of socio-economic theory is centered on intervention-research, whereby the researcher interacts with his or her field in a perennial, long-term relationship and a willingness to reciprocate through which the researcher learns as much from his or her field as he or she transforms it (Savall & Zardet, 1996, 2004; Buono, Savall, & Cappelletti, 2017). Intervention-research models are a particularly fruitful framework for accompanying student entrepreneurs, focusing on the enrichment and transformation of cognitive processes (Ben Mahmoud-Jouini et al., 2010). By building a long-term relationship of reciprocity between teacher-researchers and student-entrepreneurs, the coaching processes contribute to learning and reflexivity and are all the more transformative as they activate a reciprocal coaching model, with both the teacher-researcher and the student-entrepreneur in a learning and transformation situation.

From a methodological point of view, socio-economic theory allows us to root entrepreneurial thinking in a cognitive and reticular dynamic based on its three fundamental epistemological concepts: cognitive interactivity, contradictory intersubjectivity and generic contingency (Savall & Zardet, 1996, 2004).

Cognitive interactivity describes the process of developing knowledge and skills through successive iterations. Like the researcher, the student-entrepreneur will alternate phases of immersion in his or her project with phases of "distancing" necessary for the construction of a conceptual representation of the project. These phases are timed by the mentor, in this case the teacher-researcher, who punctuates the support with exercises that are not centered on the project, which facilitates distancing.

The *contradictory intersubjectivity* is a response to the impossible objectivity of the researcher and the student-entrepreneur and is implemented through the "mirror effect," a process that consists of submitting ideas and projects to different interlocutors, including other student-entrepreneurs and scientific, legal or financial experts. The mirror effect brings to entrepreneurial coaching the framework of cognitive transformation. Indeed, let's remember that the entrepreneur reasons according to specific cognitive processes, his entrepreneurial dynamics being controlled by his cognitive prisms. Implementing the mirror effect then offers a framework for cognitive transformation that leads the student-entrepreneur to become aware of his own biases in the discussion with his peers.

Generic contingency expresses the fact that, despite the specificity of each project, the multiplicity of analyses makes it possible to identify invariants and to set up patterns of action based on analogies. In this exercise, the mentor plays a very important role: the more projects he or she has developed or mentored, the more diverse entrepreneurial experiences he or she will be able to share, the more the student-entrepreneur will be able to draw from these entrepreneurial stories the invariants that will enable him or her to give meaning to his or her actions.

In terms of the operational tools proposed by socio-economic management (Savall and Zardet, 1987, 1995), the Internal and External Strategic Action Plan (IESAP) and the Priority Action Plan (PAP) structure the student-entrepreneur's actions. The IESAP allows the entrepreneur to project the desired image of his activity in the medium term in an effectual logic. The PAP provides the roadmap and aims to identify actions and their planning, the search for resources and skills, processes, and strategic decisions. These two interconnected tools provide the student entrepreneur with stimulation, as they transform objectives into actions, images into a vision and give meaning to his or her commitment.

With its roots in socio-economic theory, the coaching we provide to engineering students at Eole Centrale de Lyon articulates process and content, individual and collective, with a view to transforming and creating meaning (Figure 49.1).

Each of the phases of coaching constitutes a stage of individual transformation. The first stage is like a real maieutic where the student-entrepreneur builds, in the interaction with the teacher-researcher, the coach, the contours of his entrepreneurial project. The second stage is reassuring because the collection and analysis of quantitative and qualitative data and their translation into financial terms provides a feeling of mastery, especially for an engineer audience. During stage 3, the mirror effect offers, in the collective discussion with peers, a stimulation such as can be found in team sports, leading to collective learning and generally

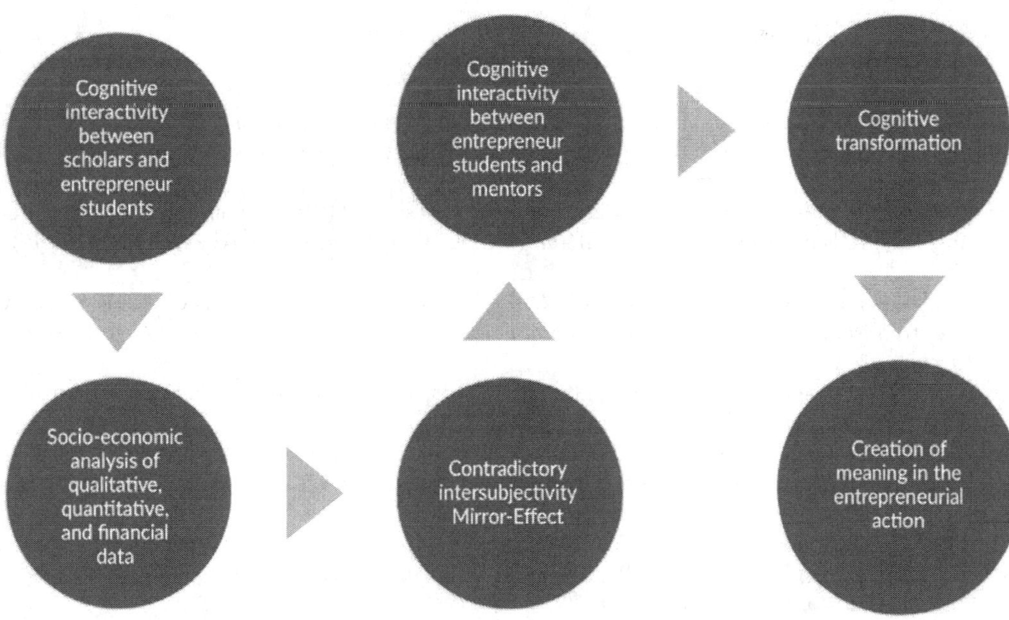

Figure 49.1 Coaching student entrepreneurs in a maieutic approach based on socio-economic theory.

inciting the student-entrepreneurs to totally rethink their project. The meeting with the mentor in step 4 allows for the identification and consolidation of the cognitive transformation in the logic of vicarious learning in step 5. The implementation of the PAP and PASINTEX tools during step 6 finally allows to give meaning to the reflection and to lead the action.

The temporal dimension must be taken into-account in the dynamics of the student-entrepreneur's support: the path we have built in 5 steps is necessary for the student-entrepreneur to emancipate himself from his cognitive biases.

CONCLUSION

Combining process and content, thought and action, individual and collective, socio-economic theory has allowed us to develop a program to support student-entrepreneurs with a transformative aim. Socio-economic theory has provided us with an epistemological, methodological and tactical framework for accompanying the student-entrepreneur in the realization of his or her entrepreneurial project and in the reduction of his or her cognitive biases. This cognitive openness constitutes the high point of the system implemented. On the one hand, it resonates with the educational mission of our institutions. On the other hand, the changes brought about are much more likely to guarantee the sustainability of the entrepreneurial dynamic than the operational work on the project.

Finally, our approach to accompanying student entrepreneurs is anchored in the paradigm of pragmatism, considering that action and interaction between researchers and the field allow us to understand and change the economic and social reality of the field and to generate scientific knowledge that is useful not only for the research field, but also for the advancement of management sciences, which has been materialized through several publications. If form precedes matter, socio-economic theory offers a particularly fruitful praxeology in the field of student entrepreneurship support.

REFERENCES

Bakkali, C., Messeghem, K., Sammut, S. Sylvie, (2010), Les structures d'accompagnement à la création d'entreprise à l'heure de la gestion des compétences, *Management & Avenir, 2010/9*(39), 149–162.

Ben Mahmoud Joiuini, S., Paris, T. Thomas, Bureau, S. Sylvain, (2010). La recherche-accompagnement: entre accompagnement et recherche-intervention. *Revue de l'Entrepreneuriat, 2010/2*(9), 56–75.

Boissin, J. P., Chollet, B., Emin, S. Sandrine, (2007). Les croyances des étudiants envers la création d'entreprise. Un état des lieux. *Revue française de gestion, 2007/11*(180), 25–43. DOI: 10.3166/rfg.180.25–43.

Bories-Azeau, I., Noguera, F., & Perroux, C., (2016). Accompagnement entrepreneurial: quelle maille territoriale d'intervention. *Gestion 2000, 33*(2–3), 161–180.

Chabaud, D., Messeghem, K., & Sammut, S. (2010). L'accompagnement entrepreneurial ou l'émergence d'un nouveau champ de recherche. *Gestion 2000, 27*(3), 15–24.

Geraudel, M., Jaouen, A., (2012). *Ecosystèmes d'affaires et PME.* Hermes Sciences Publications, Paris, 2012.

Jacquemin, A., Lesage, X., Verzat, C. (2018). Un écosystème tiraillé entre deux planètes. *Entreprendre & Innover, 2018/1*(36), 5–9.

Levy-Tadjine, T. (2008). *Intersubjectivity and singularities in entrepreneurship and management sciences.* Habilitation à Diriger des Recherches, Université de Bretagne occidentale.

Messeghem, K., Sammut, S., Chabaud, D., Carrier, C., & Thurik, R. (2013). Entrepreneurial coaching, an industry in search of performance levers? Management international/International Management. *Gestión Internacional, 17*(3), 65–71.

Mesri, Ministere de L'enseignement Superieur, de la Recherche et de L'innovation. (2019). *Evaluation of the PEPITE plan for student entrepreneurship. Recommendations for scaling up.* Report n°2018–108, January 2019.

Sammut, S. (2003). L'accompagnement de la jeune entreprise, *Revue française de gestion, 3*(144), 153–164.

Sammut, S. (2005). Entre former et accompagner, faut-il choisir? *L'Expansion Management Review, 116,* 50–53.

Saravsathy, S. (2001). Causation and effectuation: Toward a theoretical shift from economic inevitability to entrepreneurial contingency. *The Academy of Management Review, 26*(2), 243–263.

Verstraete, T., (2001), Entrepreneuriat: modélisation du phénomène. *Revue de l'Entrepreneuriat, 1*(1), 5–23.

This page intentionally left blank.

CHAPTER 50

THE ROLE OF MANAGEMENT SCHOOLS IN ACCOMPANYING THE TRANSFORMATION OF A PROFESSION AND SOCIETY

Marc Bonnet and Réda Gourine

ABSTRACT

The purpose of this chapter is to present the case of a school that shares with ISEOR an Aristotelian conception of science and teaching. This is the École des Hautes Études en Assurances in Algiers, with which ISEOR is linked, whose director prepared and defended his doctoral thesis in management within the framework of the ISEOR laboratory. This chapter also shows the importance of this type of school in contributing to the evolution of the professions and the prosperity of a country.

In antiquity, Aristotle partly differed from Plato's Academy and launched a form of school where knowledge is created dynamically by walking (Peripaten). The tradition of this was long lost in Europe, but it was perpetuated in the Arab world. This was the case with Averroes, who contributed in the 12th century to the development of scientific observation, for example in medicine. Similarly, Avicenna's accounts are about a philosophical and medical work advocating both philosophical quest and clinical experimentation" (Arkoun, 2010). Through the example of the EHEA school in Algeria, we propose to show that this type of Aristotelian-inspired school is necessary to accompany the evolution of society in a 21st century marked by rapid transformations in an increasingly complex world.

SEAM Treatise, pages 435–440

1 THE ROLE OF PROFESSIONAL SCHOOLS IN THE TRANSFORMATION OF PROFESSIONS

In the Middle Ages in Europe, vocational training was linked to an apprenticeship system based on the principle of imitatio, i.e., the reproduction of professional gestures and know-how. Guilds, and then companionship (Breton & Imbert, 2015), helped the professions to preserve and disseminate knowledge. Universities, on the other hand, remained more focused on speculative approaches, in the tradition of Plato's Academy created 2,500 years ago, then the University of Constantinople in the 5th century, followed by the University of Bologna in the 11th century after the collapse of the Byzantine Empire (Guyot, 2012). This tradition of division between theory and practice has continued to the present day in many parts of universities, with the exception of medicine, where an alternation between the university and the hospital world is organized. In the case of France, schools focused on technical professions were created at the end of the 18th century (Troger, 1989): École des Mines, École des Ponts et Chaussées, Conservatoire des Arts et Métiers, etc.). In Germany, the power of industry is based to a large extent on the quality of apprenticeship training, as well as on vocational universities such as the Fachorschule (Franz, 1994). In the field of management, the premises of commercial schools were initiated by the Hanseatic cities and Northern Italy in the 16th century, before the development of management schools in the 19th century and the structuring of business schools in the 20th century. Despite the existence of many internships, these management schools lack the link between theory and practice: they are based on a research model that is too academic, even scientistic, far from the principles of learning and "learning by doing" advocated by the epistemologist John Dewey, and often opposed to the active learning methods developed by Célestin Freinet (Freinet, 1956). Thus, companies and professions felt the need to create professional schools, such as the creation of the École Nationale d'Assurances in France in 1947.

However, the very rapid evolution of professions in the 21st century prompts us to reflect on an even closer interaction between the educational system and the professions. It is indeed necessary to foster the conditions for a harmonious transformation of the professions and to respond to the needs of society, by means of an ecosystem of innovation integrating theory and practice.

2 CONTEXT OF THE CREATION OF THE EHEA SCHOOL IN ALGIERS

The creation of a school of insurance professions has been a long term battle within the insurance sector in Algeria. The first initiatives date back to the 1990s, with the creation of an institute of finance, which had mainly developed training for the banking world. Towards the end of the 1970s, two Algerian-Tunisian schools were created: one in Tunis for banking and insurance, the other in Algiers for taxes and customs. Since then, these schools have trained most of the high-level executives in the insurance sector. Nevertheless, it did not offer enough places to meet the training needs of executives in the insurance sector in Algeria.

This is why the public authorities have encouraged the creation of the EHEA (School of Higher Education in Insurance) in 2012, in partnership with all the property and casualty insurance companies present on the Algerian territory. The capital has been progressively constituted by associating national and multinational insurance companies from the public and private sectors. The governance of the school is steered by a board of directors composed exclusively of CEOs of insurance companies who are involved in EHEA's projects and for whom the short-term financial result is not the only one of the school. The school's pedagogical committee is made up of senior executives from the sector, recognized as experts by their peers, as well as academics who assist the school in the development of degree programs.

The school currently offers 25 certification and degree programs and has trained 2,400 people since its creation. It has also set up committees for each branch and profession to develop and improve programs according to the needs of each profession: these committees take as their starting point the dysfunctions and shortcomings noted by professionals to develop the content of the programs, while giving them overall consistency. The school has also created a scientific committee and is becoming a space for dialogue between 140 professional and academic speakers to produce and disseminate knowledge in the field of risk management.

The school has established important links with major schools and universities in Algeria. For example, it dedicates a work space and documentation to doctoral students interested in insurance and facilitates access to experts in the sector and to certain courses. University professors are involved in the school well beyond their teaching duties, for example by actively participating in the school's various educational programs and development projects. In addition, each year EHEA organizes the sponsorship of some twenty students from leading schools for long-term training that leads directly to a job in the insurance field.

Specialized skills on targeted themes also require the use of an international network of partners on subjects such as big data, complementary or alternative finance (Islamic finance) or digitalization. Another challenge is to stimulate companies' proactive strategies, given the rapid changes in the insurance sector's environment. This requires the development of research programs in partnership between academics and practitioners, notably through doctoral programs. In this way, EHEA is progressively building an open ecosystem to enable it to achieve its ambitions.

3 THE ECONOMIC CONTEXT REQUIRES A TRANSFORMATION OF THE INSURANCE SECTOR

Algeria's development potential has many strengths (Connelly, et al., 2004): a young population, a highly qualified diaspora, numerous mining, agricultural and fishing resources, as well as a high rate of integration of local industrial production. There are opportunities to open up internationally, provided that agreements with the World Trade Organization, the European Union and the Arab Free Trade Area are implemented.

However, Algeria is undergoing a rapid change in its economy, all the more radical because the collapse of oil prices since 2014 requires a structural adjustment of the economy. In addition, the economic policy of state investment in industry and in structuring infrastructure (health, education, social housing) has proved disappointing. The Algerian economy can no longer be financed by the oil rent, nor by the real economy, where average hourly productivity has reached the low level of $6 per hour worked (CEIC, 2019)

This situation calls into question the possibility for the state to continue sustainably financing important social transfers such as pensions, social security and home ownership. The same applies to subsidies for everyday consumer goods, which also have perverse effects in terms of distorting competition. The social movements of recent years have also called into question the legitimacy of the political class and of institutions undermined by corruption.

In this context of change, the insurance sector has a growing role to play in covering the risks of the population such as those related to age (pensions), health and natural disasters. This is all the more necessary as risks are increasingly interacting, with cumulative effects: for example, a drop in income due to a loss of crops can also lead to health problems and risks for children's education. The unstoppable movement towards social and environmental responsibility also calls for numerous innovations in the area of coverage of new risks, including legal risks.

We must now improve customer relations by offering new products and avoiding the mimicry of large international insurance companies. Three examples can be given:

- *Parametric insurance*: unlike traditional insurance products where a claim triggers the compensation mechanism, citizens will increasingly need to be protected against life risks, such as the loss of purchasing power on essential products or food. Parametric insurance products can then be triggered according to price increase thresholds. Another example is protection against crop failure risks in a drought year. Refinancing of the risk could be provided both by insurance premiums and by a government-funded fund to replace existing subsidies.
- *Variable-cost insurance* provides an incentive for prevention: it consists of returning part of the premiums in exchange for risk prevention actions: this would contribute to the initiation of virtuous circles of individual and collective responsibility and risk reduction in all areas, including health.
- *Hybrid insurances* encouraging the renewal of local or family solidarity, drawing inspiration from the traditional forms of solidarity still practiced in Algeria such as the Twiza (Gourine, 2013).

Thus, new insurance products are to be developed in Algeria to protect citizens while making them more responsible. This calls for many innovations in insurance products to reinforce responsible behavior. These innovations in the insurance sector must avoid the risk of welfare behavior, where citizens would expect everything from a protective State: indeed, the State can no longer play this role alone, in a centralized manner, because of the decline in resources and the increase in the need for collective goods. Algeria must therefore reinvent a system that allows for the coverage of "human costs," according to the expression of François Perroux (1973), including a right to subsistence, the taking into-account of one's essential needs and the coverage of risks incurred in life. In such a system, insurance companies have a key role to play in advising and involving citizens.

4 INSURANCE COMPANIES NEED TO TRANSFORM TO ACCELERATE INNOVATION

To meet the challenges of the insurance sector in Algeria, insurance companies need to make progress and organizational learning in several areas:

- A very good knowledge of the market and its potential through a massive and quality data collection. This requires not only IT tools, but above all proximity to the citizen-customer. This implies transforming the sales professions to convince Algerians to become actors in risk management.
- The creation of innovative insurance products that respect both competitive standards, international social standards and those specific to Algeria.
- - The development of a digital transformation strategy to position itself in the blind spots of global giants of Big Data dominated by the United States and China. In this area, as in ERP, it is possible to find economies of scale by pooling certain resources between insurance companies.

- Governance and management steering systems for insurance companies that facilitate the transformation of the sector and synchronize development actions, at the interface between companies and the transformation of the role of the State.
- The control of the internal risks of the insurance companies through the mechanisms of incentive and control at the level of the customers (prevention and claims).
- The creation of capitalization products to invest in a territory where the financial market for the placement of assets is competing with informal investments considered more profitable.
- Controlling margins: current prices are often too low and it is necessary to improve actuarial and management control practices in order to perfect the pricing policy. This is all the more necessary as profitability is required to consolidate equity and finance prevention actions.
- The implementation of performance contracts for the commercial public sector within the framework of the State reform.
- The strengthening of operational compliance management, in order to improve reliability and transformation rates.

In order to carry out these transformations, insurance companies must implement change processes in an accelerated manner, choosing paths that are differentiated from one another and avoiding too much head-on competition. The EHEA school must accompany insurance companies in their transformation and innovation process. This requires the school to develop its role as a co-producer of knowledge and not just a transmitter of knowledge. The actors in the insurance sector must thus become "active units" in the sense of Perroux, through innovative management methods (Savall, 1974, 1979; Savall & Zardet, 1987).

5 EHEA AS A SCHOOL FOR THE DEVELOPMENT OF INNOVATION AND COLLECTIVE INTELLIGENCE

In order to respond to the sector's need for transformation and to bring added value to its ecosystem, EHEA follows the Aristotelian tradition (based, according to François Perroux, on an "alterocentric logos") (Perroux, 1964). Two characteristics can be highlighted: interdisciplinarity and implementation of a collective intelligence.

- Inter-disciplinarity: the school's strategy aims to break the isolation of strategy from the various disciplines of management sciences (Savall, 1974; Thietart, 1981), as well as from the disciplines of the humanities (Savall & Zardet, 2004; Boje, 2004). Indeed, managing an insurance company requires the integration of disciplines as different as actuarial science, management control, sociology and law.
- The implementation of a collective intelligence: EHEA can be a place for gathering and structuring the proposals of the various insurance actors to design and experiment with new insurance products. In this sense, the school gradually becomes a place of cognitive interactivity and "generic contingency" corresponding to the principles of intervention-research (Savall & Zardet, 2004). It can thus produce both a knowledge specific to each insurance company and a generic knowledge with impacts on all Algerian territories.

CONCLUSION

The EHEA strategy is an example of innovation in the field of education. It is a school whose production has a societal impact at several levels:

- For the insurance companies, a strong creation of potential allowing them to differentiate themselves from the international competition.
- For citizens, a contribution to the creation of innovative insurance products that meet their needs.
- For the State, the reduction of deficits, thanks to a greater responsibility of the citizens in the field of risk prevention.
- For the scientific community, the development of an innovative systemic approach in the field of risk management.

It is hoped that the example of EHEA will contribute to the renovation of the educational system, as was the case for other centers such as ISEOR in France.

REFERENCES

Arkoun, M. (2010). *The ethical and legal question in Islamic thought.* Vrin.

Berton, H., & Imbert, C. (2015). *Les Enfants de Salomon. Historical and ritual approaches to companionship and freemasonry.* Éditions Dervy.savall.

CEIC. (2019). *Algeria labor productivity growth.* CEIC publisher.

Connelly, M., Peyroulon, J. P., & Cunington, N. (2004). Algerian independence, a diplomatic revolution. *Revue Esprit, 10*(308), 142–156.

Franz, W., & Soskice, D. W. (1994). *The German apprenticeship system.* Diskussionspapier, No. 11, Universität Konstanz, Forschungsschwerpunkt Internationale Arbeitsmarktforschung, Konstanz.

Gurin, R. (2013). *Issues and socio-economic performance of innovative risk management actions building on a tradition of solidarity.* Doctoral dissertation in management sciences. CNAM Paris.

Guyot, G. (2012). *L'internationale de l'intelligence.* L'Harmattan.

Perroux, F.(1973). *Pouvoir et Économie.* Dunod.

Perroux, F. (1964). *L'Économie du XXe siècle.*

Thiétart, R.A. (1981) « la stratégie : aujourd'hui et demain «, *Revue Sciences de Gestion,* N°2.

Troger, V. (1989). History of technical education: between business and the state, the search for an identity. *History, Economy and Society, 8*(4), 593–611.

CHAPTER 51

CONTRIBUTION OF THE SOCIO-ECONOMIC APPROACH TO MANAGEMENT TO STEERING ACTION PLANS IN A CHANGING WORLD

Samia Khenniche and Sébastien Podevyn-Menant

ABSTRACT

Our society is faced with a profound change resulting from techno-scientific, economic and political transformations, which is particularly challenging for public action. At the same time, the multiplicity of its stakeholders and the increase in their demands reinforce the paradoxical nature of its performance. Socioeconomic approach to management, because it takes an overall approach to performance, understands short- and long-term results, and gives central importance to steering, contributes to the management of public action in times of change. By placing the principle of contradictory intersubjectivity at the heart of management, it makes it possible to overcome these paradoxes.

In recent years, the conduct of public organizations has been regularly questioned: in addition to the expected effectiveness of their actions, they have to face an injunction of efficiency and a growing pressure of accountability. In addition to this fundamental trend, there has been a more recent acceleration, reflected in a multiplicity of changes, which are greater in scope and depth than before. We are witnessing a mutation of our society.

The founding concepts and principles of socio-economic management (Savall, 1974, 1979; Savall and Zardet, 1987) are particularly useful for thinking about the evolution of public action, especially the risk of desynchronization between public institutions and the

SEAM Treatise, pages 441–447

population. This management approach provides a framework for understanding and action that makes it possible to embrace the different points of view of the actors involved and then to bring these views together.

1 PUBLIC ACTION, CHANGES AND TENSIONS IN GOVERNANCE

1.1 Ongoing Changes

The nature of the changes that have occurred since the 1990s is fundamentally different from those that occurred during the 20th century. It is no longer a question of crises in a system, which could predict a return to a previous situation, but of the transition from one system to another, of a "shift." This is expressed by the multitude of areas of change, their amplitude and the interaction that these different dimensions of the transformation have with each other. Three dimensions seem significant to us.

The first is a combination of technoscientific, organizational and economic revolutions (Giorgini, 2014). The technoscientific revolution corresponds to the impact of nanotechnologies, biotechnologies, computer science and cognitive sciences on human activity in all its forms. The organizational revolution, on the other hand, involves a shift from a vertical model to a more horizontal one in which it is possible to be both producer and consumer. Finally, the economic revolution is based on the advent of creative intensity versus productive efficiency.

The second dimension is the integration of environmental data into economic development models and, more specifically, the impact of human activities on global warming. This issue took on new importance with the creation in 1988 of the Intergovernmental Panel on Climate Change (IPCC), and their first report in 1990. Since then, reflection on the balance between the continued development of human activity and its sustainability has taken on an ever-increasing role in the public arena.

The third dimension lies in the evolution of relations between the actors of our democratic system. Distrust in elected officials and intermediary bodies is continually measured on the rise,[1] while election results show a persistent maintenance of abstention, questioning the reasons that lead to this situation: inefficiency, non-representativeness, loss of real power? At the same time, the advent of new information and communication technologies has provided citizens with information and communication tools that allow them to bypass traditional actors. This scissors logic—loss of confidence in traditional actors and the rise in capacity of even isolated citizens—raises the question of the durability of the current French democratic functioning.

The combined action of these three dimensions leads us to consider this period as a mutation of our society, amplifying the complexity of public action management.

1.2 Steering the Performance of Public Action

In addition to the current difficulties generated by the changes underway, there are questions that are consubstantial to the management of public action performance. Since all performance, whether in public or private organizations, is a "contingent social construct" (Chauvey, Naro, 2013), it requires the integration of the points of view of the various stakeholders. With regard to public organizations, these stakeholders are particularly numerous—users, citizens, taxpayers, inhabitants, territorial public institutions, State services, social actors, economic actors, agents, elected officials—and increasingly demanding of public organizations (Bartoli et al., 2011; Carassus et al., 2011; Cappelletti and Khenniche, 2017). This performance takes shape in a complex dynamic that brings together political projects, operational implementations, and concrete short- and long-term consequences on territories and populations (Khenniche and Henriot, 2021). While public organizations are now increasingly responsive to a population that wishes to have a say in the management of their activities, the multiplicity of interests with which public organizations are confronted requires them to make trade-offs (Brignall and Modell, 2000). Although these organizations are by nature part of a long-time frame, their concrete functioning reveals multiple time frames that can be explained by the different time horizons of political and administrative activities.

Moreover, performance management, understood as the ability to make relevant decisions in an uncertain and turbulent environment, is a particularly difficult exercise, especially when there are many decision-makers. Under the impetus of the new public management, public organizations, which have traditionally been governed by an administrative logic, are being driven by managerial practices with a view to strengthening the strategic steering capacities of the authorities that govern them. Numerous studies have reported on the failures induced by these practices. Emery and Giauque (2005) identify a series of paradoxes, such as the "managerialization" of policies, the multiplication of indicators on marginal elements, the promotion of managerial autonomy and political interference, and the call for integrated management by compartmentalizing bodies and levels. These paradoxes generate tensions in public governance (Mazouz, 2008), which are themselves sources of conflict.

On these two points, which are the taking into-account of the different points of view of the actors involved in public action and the complexity of steering public action, the contributions of socio-economic management are major. We have been able to measure these contributions in the context of an intervention-research conducted within a public authority.

2 SOCIO-ECONOMIC PERFORMANCE AND CONTRADICTORY INTERSUBJECTIVITY

2.1 Socio-Economic Performance, a Framework For Steering Public Performance

As we have seen, the performance of public action is complex to define and to manage. Socio-economic management is useful on both counts, for many reasons.

Because it approaches performance in its entirety by proposing a socio-economic performance, which does not dissociate the question of cost from that of value, with its concept of cost-performance (Savall and Zardet, 1987), socio-economic management makes the fundamental concept of cost-value actionable and makes it possible to approach the question of public action in all its complexity and richness.

Because this performance is understood in terms of the level and quality of so-called immediate results, but also in terms of the creation of potential, socio-economic management is concerned with the sustainability of performance and is in line with the concern for the long term inherent in any public action, as well as with the achievement of results in the shorter term, which is increasingly demanded by the public.

Because it defines management as the cornerstone of any search for performance, it revitalizes the capacity of organizations to lead their actions in times of change. As this steering is understood as collective, in particular through the principles of synchronized decentralization and contradictory intersubjectivity, socio-economic management considers multiple points of view as legitimate, places everyone at the heart of the organization's action and gives everyone a role as an actor; a saving posture to avoid being subjected to the changes underway.

2.2 Contradictory Intersubjectivity: A Principle of Action to Regulate Governance Tensions

Contradictory intersubjectivity "consists in confronting the relative and subjective points of view of each of the actors, by organizing and encouraging interactions between actors with points of view that are partly convergent and partly different, even contradictory" (Savall & Zardet, 2004, p.221). This focus, which everyone can use to apprehend an activity, allows us to observe a panorama that is more or less wide, a depth of field that is more or less great, and a wealth of details that are more or less important (Henriot, 2012).

This concept makes the disagreements at the source of conflicts intelligible. It allows us to understand situations of tension, particularly in public governance, not as a power struggle, but as the result of different and sometimes divergent visions, each of which is legitimate.

The point of view makes it possible to analyze the organization through the prism of the management situation (Girin, 1990), an activity that is constantly under construction and that is composed of actors who must accomplish "in a given time, a collective action leading to a result that is subject to an external judgment. "Who are the real participants? To what places and times is it limited? What result is expected? What authority exercises the judgment" (Girin, 1990, p. 144). Responses construct the meaning of a situation, which obviously applies to the management of public action.

In practice, different devices and tools make it possible to collect and consider the points of view of the actors. This is the case with qualitative interviews and the identification of hidden costs and performances in the socio-economic diagnosis. Socio-economic management tools, such as the internal and external strategic action plan, the priority action plan or the piloting logbook, developed by activating contradictory intersubjectivity and synchronized decentralization, make it possible to confront and then converge the different points of view.

3 SOCIO-ECONOMIC INTERVENTION WITHIN A LOCAL AUTHORITY

The community studied here is a commune of 50,000 inhabitants in the Paris region. Initially, the city wanted support in drawing up a roadmap for the implementation of a "performance approach." Our discussions aimed at defining the terms of our intervention with members of the administration—the operation manager, the general manager in charge of public performance issues, the Human Resource Manager—and the executive—the mayor, the deputy finance and HR officer, the chief of staff—allowed us to determine that the actors involved had a lot of trouble agreeing on the meaning of performance and that a much more in-depth action was needed.

3.1 The Shift From Specific Points of View...

Public performance was at the heart of the municipal project, and during the first 18 months of the mandate, everything was done as if this term was understood and accepted by everyone. The decision-makers considered it to be fundamental, and this was reflected in the creation of a dedicated deputy directorate general. In reality, this term had never been

Public management performance means coping with budget constraints. Our objective during this tenure is proximity: meeting inhabitants' requests, which also has to do with performance (Executive)	*An efficient public service has to meet citizens' expectations and contribute on time to concrete responses. The financial aspect doesn't raise the same issue.* (Executive)
The notion of performance can't be separated from innovation, risk taking and ambition (Top management)	*Performance requires to uphold activities resorting to common good* (Top management)

Figure 51.1 Expressions relating to the definition of public action performance (excerpt).

discussed, some thinking they understood it, others not daring to show their incomprehension. We therefore worked on a common definition of the performance of public action.

At the level of governance, interviews identified the representations of the performance of public action and revealed different, even divergent, definitions. The 14 interviews led to 14 different visions, sometimes revealing tensions in governance (see Figure 51.1). The expression of some reveals a vision of performance linked to the reduction of budgets, while others claim to exclude the financial question. Some associate performance with innovation, while others equate it with preservation of the existing. None of these views attempts to reconcile the different components of overall performance.

3.2 ... To a Co-Constructed Consensus

The diagnosis reports provided an opportunity to bring together the respondents from the executive and the administration, to present their different representations of performance and to compare their views. These exchanges were designed and conducted in such a way as to facilitate contradictory intersubjectivity and cognitive interactivity (Savall and Zardet, 1996; 2004). The clarification of the different points of view made it possible to identify misunderstandings, doubts and convictions, fears and aspirations, agreements and divergences, to deconstruct certain visions and to initiate the process of shared representation, in order to arrive at a common definition of the performance of public action in the city, as a common framework for the action taken by all (Figure 51.2).

This process was not without its difficulties. Indeed, co-construction requires verbalizing and clarifying implicit points of view. Then follows a necessary synchronization between the strategic ambition, the organizational choices and the modes of action. This coherence is complex; it is a matter of going beyond an agreement in discourse and reaching an operational consensus, in order to avoid the classic decoupling between discourse and action.

> "Ability to set a course and innovate to transform and surpass the community's current operations. The objective is to mobilize all the agents around efficient decisions, to offer a quality public service that meets the needs of the citizens, while respecting the budgetary constraints. It is also a question of translating into action the strong ambitions for the development and competitiveness of the territory, while preserving the general interest."

Figure 51.2 Definition of public action performance adopted.

This is indeed a new contribution of socio-economic management, which enables the transformation of management situations into action.

3.3 An overall and Controlled Performance

The operationalization of overall performance, defined by consensus between the executive and general management, has resulted in many concrete decisions. For example, at the level of elected representatives, mechanisms have been set up to share their points of view on the meaning—understood as meaning and direction—of city action. The elected representatives of the public policy clusters have introduced animation and coordination. The internal and external strategic action plan and the management chart (Savall & Zardet, 1987) have had a particularly marked structuring effect on performance management.

In previous terms of office, the overall coherence of the community's action was ensured by the trio of mayor, chief of staff, and director general of services, but each department worked without precisely articulating its action to that of the others, aiming for its own performance rather than overall performance. There was no formal framework to ensure the convergence of the various public action mechanisms. The internal and external strategic action plan made it possible to overcome this limitation.

Born of the common definition of overall performance, it was structured not by technical skills, but in three cross-cutting areas, referring to the different dimensions of performance (see Figure 51.2): "providing a sober and efficient public service," "building progress and success with the inhabitants," "strengthening the attractiveness and cohesion of the territory." It was then translated into priority action plans linked to management charts in each of the different departments.

New common performance measurement indicators were developed. Until then, the various departments had only quantitative or financial indicators for measuring resources. The points of view of the various actors were considered via results indicators, as perceived by the users, constituted in particular from surveys of the population.

CONCLUSION

These results demonstrate the relevance of the founding concepts of socio-economic theory in supporting the evolution of public action and overcoming the governance tensions inherent in it. The definition of a common approach to the performance of public action in a few months when the actors had been struggling with this issue for years, the co-construction of a shared political and strategic action plan instead of the multiplicity of compartmentalized action plans in place at the time, and the development of steering indicators that take into-account both the territory and the population, are all concrete achievements that attest to this.

NOTE

1. Reference: *Vagues fractures françaises, IPSOS, 2013–2020*

REFERENCES

Bartoli, A., Kéramidas, O., Larat, F., Mazouz, B. (2011), Vers un management public éthique et performant, *Revue française d'administration publique*, n°140, p.629–639.

Cappelletti L., Khenniche S. (2017), Développer la performance socialement responsable des collectivités territoriales : résultats émergents d'une recherche-intervention au sein d'une mairie, *Revue Politiques et Management public*, n°34/1.

Carassus, D., Favoreu, C., Gardey, D., Maurel, C. (2011), La caractérisation et la définition de la performance publique: une application aux collectivités locales, *Premier colloque AIRMAP*, Versailles-Saint Quentin

Chauvey, J.-N., Naro, G., (2013), Reporting et pilotage sociétaux : repenser la performance globale à l'aune des paradoxes de la RSE, *Comptabilité sans Frontières*. The French Connection, Canada, pp.cd-rom.

Emery, Y.; Giauque D. (2005). *Paradoxes de la gestion publique*, L'Harmattan

Giorgini, P. (2014) *La transition fulgurante : vers un bouleversement systémique du monde* ? Paris, Bayard

Girin, J. (1990), L'analyse empirique des situations de gestion, in Martinet A-C., *Epistémologies et Sciences de gestion*, Economica, p.141–182.

Henriot, J. (2012), Taking a decision in an ambiguous situation: the question of the gaze, *Revue Française de Gestion*, vol.38, n°225, p.129–146.

Khenniche, S., Henriot, J. (2021) Action publique : quête de performance et perte de sens, un éclairage par les tensions de gouvernance, *Revue Management international / International Management / Gestion Internacional*, vol. 25.

Mazouz, B. et al (2008), La gestion intégrée par résultats : concevoir et gérer autrement la performance dans l'administration publique, Québec, Presses de l'Université du Québec.

This page intentionally left blank.

CHAPTER 52

LOCAL AUTHORITIES AND MONITORING

Philippe Sauvannet and Marie-Christine Chalus-Sauvannet

ABSTRACT

The legislator, through three successive "acts" from 1982 to the present day, has profoundly modified the functioning of local authorities and drawn a new panorama of the organization of the French administration. Local communities have consequently become major players in economic, social and cultural life. Territorial monitoring was gradually put in place, with the aim of better adapting public services to the needs of citizens.

Decentralization has transformed the daily life of the French over the last three decades. Far from being a simple technique for organizing public services, it really corresponds, at least conceptually, to a concern for redistributing powers and bringing decisions closer to the places where they are applied (principle of proximity). As a result, local authorities have become major players in economic, social and cultural life.

There is less work on territorial intelligence than in the private sector (Bertacchini, 2010), but the predominant role played by local elected officials in view of the multiple transfers of competences should contribute to their development. Beyond the political will, how is this monitoring envisaged and in what framework does it fit? What about its implementation and the means allocated? Are local authorities ready to develop territorial monitoring systems?

Transformation of the institutional context, widening of the field of intervention and diversification of territorial professions are all changes that territorial authorities are facing. Before addressing territorial intelligence, it should be remembered that its management in local authorities is still little explored by researchers, particularly in management (Bousta-Jullien, 1999). Researchers who develop this theme most often approach it from the

SEAM Treatise, pages 449–454

perspective of performance control (Jaouhari et al., 2021). Local authorities are no longer a protected sector. The degree of demand from users is increasing, and companies do not hesitate to put them in competition before choosing their location. The political and even criminal responsibility of elected officials is now directly engaged by citizens, who no longer accept the verticality of a power for the duration of a mandate.

It makes sense to think about strategic intelligence for local authorities. Indeed, public management, which underlies the sustainability of a monitoring system, aims at producing results and increasing the potential of the community in the medium and long term, but it is also confronted with the challenges of the environment. Territorial intelligence is of interest to local authorities and public services because they need anticipatory information to make both operational and strategic decisions.

Thus, for the past four or five years, there has been a growing demand from local authorities to set up territorial monitoring systems, especially since the Local Social Action Center (LSAC) are required to do so. This chapter outlines the changes in the French territorial context and develops the challenges of territorial monitoring, before presenting the results of an exploratory research on territorial monitoring practices.

1 CHANGES IN THE FRENCH TERRITORIAL CONTEXT

The territory is now an actor that must ensure its development efficiently in a world that has become highly competitive, more and more exposed to new risks, but also to new opportunities. This is why the community of actors that constitutes the territory can no longer act in a dispersed manner and without an overall strategy. Like any strategic actor, a territorial community ("*territory*") must build and implement a real medium- and long-term strategy, translated into global and coherent action plans, based on a shared diagnosis, which cannot be a simple inventory of strengths and weaknesses (Savall and Zardet, 1995).

The increase in the mobility of goods and people has transformed the static vision of the territory and the urban context. The (territorial) borders inherited from the past are becoming blurred. Spaces are fragmenting, the citizen is becoming nomadic, virtual companies and the "local" are diluting in the light of the pervasiveness of European orientations, perceived or not but now the backdrop of policies that claim to belong to the local. (Bertacchini, 2001).

The phenomenon of peri-urbanization is growing, and cities are constantly expanding. If the means of transport impose both a new apprehension of the territory and new relationships, these do not disappear for all that. Information and communication technologies are transforming the world and changing our social practices as well as our relationship with space.

Today, local authorities must be careful not to break with their relationship with users, with whom they increasingly maintain an instantaneous customer/supplier relationship via social networks, where the services offered are discussed and evaluated.

1.1 Emergence of New Challenges

These developments require the identification of new challenges for the territory. Interactions between elected officials, the population and the administration are changing. A number of regions have programmed economic intelligence development actions: the first territorial program was launched in Essonne in 1995; the Basse-Normandie region has anchored its economic intelligence strategy in the long term since 1997. Other regions have carried out similar actions. These programs are mainly oriented towards raising awareness, training and supporting local SMEs. The latest decentralization laws have given the Region the responsibility for strategic development, particularly economic development.

The first assessment of territorial intelligence actions in France revealed: (a) a need to pool skills and information for economic and technological development; (b) a relative dispersion of actions: almost all regions have already launched economic intelligence experiments aimed at companies or groups of companies, but very few of them have initiated a truly integrated territorial intelligence approach, based on a steering and assessment "body"; (c) the need to better adapt economic intelligence tools to the context of the territory: the instruments for monitoring and making public information available are often installed without first having precisely defined their purposes, nor studied the methods for updating and processing content; (d) the desire of the regions to correctly monitor their major sectors of activity, to build loyalty and to anticipate possible threats and opportunities. Institutional actors or companies that yesterday adopted the status of active transmitters now find themselves in a fourfold position: transmitters, transformers, receivers and mediators.

Thus, territories find themselves in competition with each other and crises such as the heat wave of summer 2003, the clashes and violence in the suburbs, or more recently, the feeling of exclusion of certain social categories that exacerbates the differences between rural, urban and peri-urban worlds ("Yellow Vests") have highlighted their difficulties in anticipating and managing these events. This shows the need for territorial intelligence. How can it be understood and implemented?

2 IMPLEMENTING TERRITORIAL MONITORING

2.1 Prerequisites

Ideally, territorial intelligence requires the circulation of skills, vertically in dynamic back and forth, horizontally between functions and professions. It gives communities the operational means to anticipate:

- Developing, at all levels, tools and practices of anticipation;
- Integrating anticipatory information sensors;
- Redirecting priorities, meetings and discussions towards the future;
- Providing each manager with relevant indicators to ensure vigilance and control of results.

Managing change is first and foremost a question of political will and the ability to lead people towards a common project (Savall, 1974; 1979). It is the result of these collective and individual actions in the face of socio-economic constraints.

The creation of a territorial monitoring system requires the creation of a network of communication of information between the socio-economic actors;

- via a more important network of influence;
- by allowing the circulation of anticipatory information;
- by defending the interests of the territory through the surveillance of competing territories.

It is a question of transforming information into knowledge, knowledge into action (Polanco, 1999) and giving meaning to citizen and democratic representation. We have observed a growing desire on the part of local public leaders to implement mechanisms for capturing economic and social changes, in order to anticipate the evolution of the territory in order to act ahead of events, while encouraging the active support of inhabitants for the common territorial project.

Legal obligations now require local authorities to set up territorial monitoring systems. Thus, each year, then local social action centers must draw up an analysis of the social needs of their municipality, using tools for observing the needs of the population, in order to adapt the services provided to users. According to a local social action center manager, "a territorial watch seems to be a relevant tool, allowing the best adaptation of actions to the needs of the inhabitants." The local social action center director then proposes solutions to the elected officials to help them define their priority policy areas.

This territorial monitoring covers very diverse issues. For example, for a media library manager, it is a help "for the management of the team, the coordination of the animation policy," while the director of the museum considers that it would allow her to better prevent the risks of social movements and strikes of her staff.

Sometimes, setting up a specific watch is a first step: a watch system is implemented when a commune encounters serious socio-economic difficulties, for example (factories or labor companies about to close), or to get to know a population that has difficulty expressing its needs (e.g., new suburban populations).

2.2 Implementation Methods and Difficulties Encountered

The communities studied encounter many difficulties in organizing themselves with reliable and sustainable tools. Indeed, the existing observatories provide information that is too out of date, because changes are very rapid in reality and the information from national observatories is not always adapted to the community's context.

When implementing the territorial monitoring system, it is necessary to define the monitors, the strategic actors and the recipients. Since the development of territorial intelligence is most often internal to the local authority, an evaluation of internal skills is necessary... but it is rarely done. The selection of available local skills and information channels is an important step. It is a major transition in the attitude of local actors to encourage exchange and mobilization towards the territorial project.

In the territorial context, the delegation of authority that allows for the regulation of the system of interactions takes concrete form in the exchange between individual and collective actors: the local authority tries to identify, through a qualitative approach, the networks that exist on its territory. When this necessary monitoring action, which we describe as passive, has been carried out and has made it possible to identify and inventory the available skills, it is necessary to orchestrate them in order to bring the monitoring system to life (Chalus-Sauvannet, 2008). If the territories are all different in terms of their context, they are also different in terms of their internal skills and the ways in which they are identified. Our study has shown that local authorities under-exploit their internal skills. Better identifying their endogenous resources and potentialities in order to redeploy them and anchor the principle of vigilance are major areas for development.

2.3 Monitoring and Participatory Democracy: Contributions and Limits

The public administration regularly practices territorial cooperation: for the elaboration of a master plan or the realization of significant territorial projects, such as the development of territorial zones (master plans, territorial coherence schemes), or of neighborhoods or road projects. The consultation of the "natural" partners of these operations on the territory and their participation are common. Territorial cooperation, organized around representative groups with different points of view, is now tending to be extended to the whole population, including at the national level for the choice of major territorial development infrastructures (freeways, high-speed railways, nuclear infrastructures, etc.) with the National Commission for Public Debate.

Thus, participatory democracy is becoming more widespread and can prove to be a good support for territorial monitoring. However, its financial cost is often underestimated and the results are rarely measured. Moreover, uncontrolled use leads to a mass of information that is sometimes unusable, which clogs up the administrative services and generates dissatisfaction and frustration among users who have expressed themselves at the request of the community. This creates a misunderstanding that is fraught with risk. One of the most current examples is the Citizens' Climate Convention, whose 150 proposals are far from having been taken up *in concreto.* Finally, and above all, participatory democracy is not always synonymous with the representativeness of the population, as the same individuals often express themselves through multiple bodies and others never.

CONCLUSION

The institutional reforms have resulted in the development of national monitoring issues and more specific needs of communities. The difficulties encountered in setting up territorial monitoring systems have two facets: one is structural, essentially due to the interweaving of territorial structures: a commune may, in fact, be part of several Public Establishments of Inter-municipal Cooperation grouping together various communities, which obviously hinders the coherence and articulation of the watch; the other is related to the difficulties of changing the behaviors of agents, to position themselves in this changing environment and to understand the new roles assigned to them, in terms of proximity, capture and transmission of information.

REFERENCES

Bertacchini, Y. (2001). Du gisement des compétences locales et de leur transfert: quelles modalités? *Formes de l'engagement et espace public en Europe,* Metz, 5, 6 and 7 December 2001.

Bertacchini, Y. (2010). Intelligence territoriale: une lecture rétrospective. *Revue internationale d'intelligence économique, 2*(1), 65–97.

Bourdon J., (1996). *La fonction publique territoriale, Les collectivités locales en France,* Documentation française.

Bousta-Jullien Y. (1999). *Management public communal interactivité structurelle et cognitive, pertinence et action publique communale.* Doctoral thesis in management science, University of Lyon.

Chalus-Sauvannet MC (2005). *Décentralisation et collectivités territoriales*—Vers de nouvelles formes de management, Colloque Organization, development and change, in partnership with AOM and ISEOR, April.

Chalus-Sauvannet, M.-C. (2008). Veille territoriale—Enjeux et difficultés. In *Nouveaux regards sur le management public,* L'Harmattan, collection RECEMAP.

CNFPT. (2003). *Pratiques managériales,* Dossier sectoriel / rapport d'étape, 97 p.

Devès C. (2000). *Les collectivités locales face aux principes de la concurrence; les collectivités locales et le droit: les mutations actuelles.* Dalloz.

Jaouhari, L., Goumari, S., & Jaouhari, R. (2021). Management control tools and performance of local governments: A theoretical approach. *Revue Française d'Economie et de Gestion, 2*(4).

Lévy P., (1997), *Cyberculture.* Odile Jacob, Paris.

Polanco X., (1999). *Aux sources de la sociométrie.* Dossier n°2, Bibliométrie, sociométrie, infométrie, edited by J. M. Noyer, INIST-CNRS, Nancy.

CHAPTER 53

AN ORIGINAL EXPERIMENT IN EVALUATING THE IMPACTS OF NETWORKING THROUGH SOCIO-ECONOMIC ANALYSIS

Case of the Lyon Health and City Workshops

Pascal Brenot and Michaël Baska

ABSTRACT

Current methods of evaluating public systems underestimate the creation of value generated by these approaches, thereby jeopardizing the quality of the resulting public policies. The concept of socio-economic evaluation, derived from the socio-economic theory, provides methodological keys to better evaluate public systems. Using the case of the *Ateliers Santé Ville (ASV),* this chapter shows the hidden socio-economic performance of this scheme and describes the methodology used to achieve it. The results show that the ASV scheme, which is relevant from the point of view of public health, is economically viable.

The public policies of a local authority can take many different forms in order to respond to issues of general interest. They can take the form of the construction of public facilities or urban development operations. They can also take the form of procedures for issuing rights (building permits, authorizations for temporary occupation of the public domain, etc.) or services (social assistance, water distribution, etc.), as well as financial support (payment of grants). In this case, the evaluation of public policies seems rather easy, at least in terms of achievement and results, and even in terms of impact. Thus, it is easy to measure user satisfaction, or even the transformation of a given situation, and thus verify the achievement of

SEAM Treatise, pages 455–460

the objectives initially set for the local authority's public policies. They can also take the form of preventive actions: preventing the risk of accidents by improving roads to slow down the speed of vehicles, but also preventing the risk of delinquency, discrimination, or even risky behavior in terms of health. They may also aim to promote access to rights, particularly for people in precarious social situations. In this case, their evaluation appears more complex. How can we measure the effect of an educational drug prevention project on the target group? It is true that techniques for evaluating these public policies have existed for a long time, for example through monographs or cohort monitoring. But these techniques require a rigorous method of project management, which local authorities rarely have, due to lack of time and/or resources.

In the health and social field, for example, understood in the broadest sense of the term, the management and implementation of public policies mobilize many partners, primarily within the local authority, but also institutional partners (municipal social action centers, regional health agencies, hospitals, primary health insurance funds, mutual insurance structures, etc.) as well as a wide variety of professionals (health care professionals, social workers, specialized educators, prevention associations, support associations, access to rights, etc.). Their success in this area also depends on the participation of users and even local residents: this is the notion of health democracy. The management of public policy is based on the networking of these different professionals and local actors, which the legislator and the State services have been encouraging and promoting for the last twenty years. This is the case with the city health workshops, a networking approach initiated in urban neighborhoods with social weaknesses expressed in terms of relative monetary poverty, neighborhoods recognized as priorities for public action under the "city policy." The "urban policy" is a public policy of local development, based on an overall approach, aimed at neighborhoods considered socially fragile due to the concentration of a population with a significantly lower income level than the average of the urban agglomeration. These neighborhoods have a high proportion of job seekers, single-parent families and adults with little cultural capital. In terms of health, the population of these neighborhoods is also more fragile, with less easy access to rights and health care services. To implement the city policy, the State and local authorities sign city contracts that define a priority geography for intervention, specific objectives through the territorialization of public action, i.e., adapting it to the specific needs of priority neighborhoods, as well as project management engineering that allows for the democratic participation of residents.

Since 2001, the State has encouraged local authorities to implement a local development approach known as "health and city workshops" in order to propose territorialized actions to reduce social and territorial inequalities in access to healthcare and public health. This approach forms the basis of the health component of the Lyon city contract and the framework of the localized component of the Lyon local health contract, both of which were signed in 2015.

1 SOCIO-ECONOMIC ANALYSIS TO ENHANCE THE HIDDEN PERFORMANCE OF NETWORKING

A "city health workshop" (ASV) is an approach that makes it possible to implement partnership actions adapted to neighborhoods in difficulty. It is a cross-cutting approach, coordinating public action in the social, medico-social and health fields, with the participation of residents. Its objective is to reduce social and territorial inequalities in access to health rights, prevention and care. The ASV brings together associations, residents, health establishments, private health professionals, institutions and local authorities.

While health and care resources may still seem insufficient in relation to the needs of the population and political expectations, one may wonder about the appropriateness of mobilizing professionals and local actors to devote time, and therefore money, to working in a network for the benefit of a neighborhood and its population, rather than devoting this time to treating or at least accompanying the most vulnerable people. If, nearly 20 years after its launch, the ASV approach seems sufficiently relevant to be continued today, still mobilizing many health professionals and associative actors with very varied profiles, it is undoubtedly because they find it useful. But what about the public authority and the territory? What does the ASV approach bring to the community and the population? Is this networking relevant? How can we measure its added value? How can we evaluate the effects for professionals and local actors as well as for the community and the population?

These are some of the questions that arise when we talk about ASVs and, more generally, networking, which is very widespread in the field of public prevention policies. If we know how much the ASVs cost the local authority in terms of the payroll of the agents and employees involved, as well as in terms of subsidies and direct expenses, it is not inappropriate to try to evaluate the hidden performances as well, those that have not been measured until now. This is where the interest lies in using the socio-economic management methodology developed over 40 years ago by Henri Savall and ISEOR (Savall, 1974, 1979; Savall and Zardet, 1987), adapting it to evaluate and enhance, in the true sense of the term, the performance of the ASV network.

2 THE CASE OF THE LYON HEALTH AND CITY WORKSHOPS

Within the Lyon City Council, a local authority with more than 8,500 employees in more than 300 different professions, serving a densely populated area of more than 515,000 inhabitants, at the heart of a dynamic conurbation of 59 municipalities and nearly 1.4 million inhabitants, the Territorial Development Department (DDT) is responsible for developing, implementing and evaluating public policies that meet the challenges of social and territorial cohesion. Its mandate is to implement the prevention-health policy, with priority given to the most vulnerable people. Most of these people live in neighborhoods that are part of the priority geography of the city's policy and are covered by the city contract.

Through the process carried out with the invaluable assistance of ISEOR, the objective of the Lyon City Council and its DDT was to identify the performance of the ASVs. The intention was not to measure or evaluate the policy conducted in terms of public health, especially since it is very complex to evaluate precisely and objectively the real impacts of the local authority's action on the improvement of the inhabitants' health. We all know that if we stop smoking, if we eat and sleep better, if we play sports regularly, we are healthier. But it is very difficult to evaluate the effects of each of these health determinants, and equally difficult to differentiate between the responsibilities of the different actors (companies, local authorities, the population, individuals, health professionals, and even the rest of the world).

In undertaking the socio-economic evaluation of the ASVs, we set out to measure their performance, in particular the "hidden" performance that has not been measured until now. Such an evaluation of a network was new for Lyon City Council, and indeed few local authorities seem to have carried out such a study.

All the work carried out was the subject of a complete report including

- An expert opinion based on significant achievements and eight recommendations resulting from the interviews conducted.

- Principles of Socio-Economic Assessment.
- A qualitative analysis section followed by a quantitative analysis section.
- Management indicators and appendices to complete the report itself.

This underlines the importance of the work carried out.

3 ACHIEVEMENTS AND RESULTS

To carry out this approach, we set up a project team made up of the DDT employees most directly concerned because they are directly involved in the steering and coordination of the ASVs, i.e., a total of about ten people. These people received the necessary training to better understand and master the methodology of Socio-Economic Assessment (Savall and Zardet, 1987). In close cooperation with ISEOR, this project-team conducted some 80 individual and group interviews with about 60 people and 40 different structures, all of whom were directly and personally involved in the ASV. These interviews were carried out in two Lyon neighborhoods, included in the priority geography of the city contract, but with very different characteristics: the Guillotière and Duchère neighborhoods.

Located on a plateau to the west of Lyon in the 9th arrondissement, La Duchère is a social housing district dating from the 1960s, originally a symbol of social progress, initially built to provide comfortable and modern housing for the workers of the large factories then present in Lyon. But with the impoverishment of its inhabitants, life in this neighborhood has deteriorated greatly, as has its image. A major urban renewal operation was launched some fifteen years ago, with the demolition-reconstruction of more than 1,300 homes, with the aim of achieving a social mix, so as to reduce the proportion of social housing to less than 50% at the end of the operation, as opposed to nearly 100% at the outset, which generated profound changes in the population. In addition, and in order to meet the same objectives of social diversity and diversification of urban functions, numerous investments have been made in public facilities and spaces.

As for the Guillotière district, in the 3rd and 7th arrondissements, our second Socio-Economic Assessment test district has very different characteristics. It is a neighborhood in the old city center, very densely populated by people of various origins, where people from successive immigrations from southern Europe, North Africa and sub-Saharan Africa, the Middle East and East Asia live together, as well as students and people from higher socio-professional categories. A former very active river port of primary importance, located in the heart of the agglomeration, Guillotière has always fulfilled the historical function of a gateway to Lyon for newcomers, to find a job or a new life opportunity.

These two very different neighborhoods were chosen to better evaluate the impacts of the ASVs organized and conducted in each of them.

First, the work and interviews conducted with local professionals and actors made it possible to produce a qualitative analysis of the impact of the ASVs around five major themes

- The organization of work, in terms of better inter-knowledge of local professionals and actors; the development of cooperation, synergies and partnerships within the ASV and outside the ASV; the establishment of relationships between associative actors, institutions and health professionals in the neighborhood, thus creating a bond of trust; but also in terms of the production of coherent and complementary actions in line with the needs of the neighborhoods, actions made possible thanks to the ASV's methods of steering and animation.

- Communication, coordination and cooperation, in terms of facilitating links between neighborhood professionals, hospitals, city health professionals and voluntary associations; also in terms of cross-fertilization and effective meetings to strengthen expertise, make shared information more reliable and seek common solutions. The result is an increased readability of the DDT agents' involvement in the field, which is a factor of professional motivation.
- Time management, in terms of quality collective work; agreements between partners on work priorities; time saving in the mobilization of professional networks for the implementation of projects and the support or orientation of users.
- Integrated training, in terms of strengthening individual and collective skills thanks to the collective work carried out within the framework of the ASV; improving professional practices and implementing actions to avoid disruptions in the care pathways of the most vulnerable users.
- Project management, in terms of reinforcing the legitimacy of professionals from different professions and sectors to work on a shared strategy and joint actions; an innovative approach allowing better use of the territory's resources avoiding duplication and promoting economies of scale, stronger involvement of the inhabitants, greater proximity to the users, project engineering and tools that reinforce the adequacy of the action with the inhabitants' needs.

This qualitative approach was followed by a socio-economic evaluation of the resources optimized and the costs avoided thanks to the networking and prevention actions implemented in the districts concerned. It is based on the identification of two main categories of effects of the ASV, thanks to the exploitation of the exhaustive content of individual and collective interviews in the form of "verbatim":

- The "resource capture" effect for the district and its inhabitants: for example, material and financial resources and time spent by ASV members.
- The "avoided costs" effect for public action: for example, avoided health costs for beneficiaries and time saved for professionals and partners.

Thus, we were able to calculate that for the Duchère district, the effect of "resource capture for the territory" amounted to 427,400 euros, and the effect of "avoided costs for public action" to 498,200 euros, these effects being made possible by the mobilization of human resources representing 8 "full-time equivalents" (FTE), i.e., 7.5 FTE of professionals and 0.5 FTE of volunteers.

In the case of the Guillotière district, the effect of "capturing resources for the territory" was quantified at 60,700 euros and the effect of "avoided costs for public action" at 687,000 euros thanks to the mobilization of 8.75 FTEs (broken down into 8.25 FTEs of professionals and 0.5 FTE of volunteers).

4 MAIN LESSONS LEARNED FOR THE FUTURE

Combined with the multiplier effect of the mobilization of human resources of professionals and volunteers, the "resource capture" and "avoided costs" effects thus objectified make it possible to measure the value added of the networked work enabled by the ASVs, i.e., the calculation of the quantified volume of "hidden" performances (Savall and Zardet, 1987, 2008).

It is clear and objective that the performance of the ASVs is clearly superior to their costs, which also constitutes a steering tool for the allocation of public resources.

In qualitative terms, the outstanding achievements of the VSAs can be grouped around five key ideas:

- A better understanding and knowledge of the needs in terms of health, health care supply and access to rights,
- A strengthening of the capacities and skills of local professionals and actors to act on their own as well as in complementarity,
- A greater capacity to build and propose shared solutions,
- Optimization of resources,
- Increased information for professionals and residents.

Although it stimulates innovation and reinforces the efficiency of public action, the evaluation carried out with the assistance of ISEOR emphasizes that the ASV approach seems to be able to reinforce its strategic potential with greater integration into an overall local development project.

For the DDT, the socio-economic evaluation conducted on an experimental basis with the assistance of ISEOR has demonstrated its relevance in measuring the hidden performance of the network work that is at the heart of its teams' work.

In view of the renewal of the city contract in 2022, this experiment will undoubtedly deserve to be extended to all of our activities.

For Lyon City Council, which, like any large human organization providing public services, is faced with numerous societal, managerial and financial challenges, socio-economic management remains a field of innovation to be explored.

CONCLUSION

Through the case of the Ateliers Santé Ville, this chapter shows that the concept of hidden cost-performance used in socio-economic evaluation makes it possible to measure the hidden performance of public systems, which constitutes a significant advance for current evaluation practices in this sector. Moreover, this advance could help actors to better orient their public policy decisions.

REFERENCES

Savall, H., Goter, F., Bondin, L. (2019). Évaluation socio-économique des Ateliers Santé Ville, ISEOR Report, 333 p.

Savall, H., Goter, F. (2021). « Comment évaluer les impacts socio-économiques d'un dispositif public «, Article published in the ASAP Observatory.

Motard, C., & Tessier, S. (2016). Les démarches Ateliers santé ville: la promotion de la santé à l'œuvre dans les territoires. *Santé Publique, 6*(6), 729–733.

Savall, H., Cappelletti, L., & Raphan, P. A. (2020). *La méthode des coûts-performances cachés: outil stratégique et opérationnel d'évaluation des politiques publiques.* poster CNAM and ISEOR, Les rencontres de l'évaluation, Assemblée Nationale, 13 février 2020.

Zardet, V., & Goter, F. (2021). Les impacts socio-économiques du dispositif public des Ateliers Santé Ville? Article published in the ASAP Observatory.

CHAPTER 54

STRATEGIC PLANNING AND CHANGE MANAGEMENT IN PUBLIC ORGANIZATIONS

Integration of Socio-Economic Tools in Belgian Local Governments

Henri Talaszka and Xavier Pierre

ABSTRACT

Public organizations, in particular municipalities, need strategic planning and change management in a context of evolution of their strategic environment and a need to control public finances. Public managers need methods that allow them to set a course, identify efficiency gains and lead transformations while obtaining the support of their teams. Based on the case of 12 Belgian municipalities, this chapter shows how socio-economic tools (Internal and External Strategic plans, Priority Action Plans, Competency Grids, Time Management) meet the needs of managers.

Public organizations (POs), in particular municipalities and local goveernments, have strategic planning and change management needs in a context of evolution of their strategic environment and control of public finances. Public managers need methods that allow them to set a course, identify efficiency gains and lead transformations while obtaining the support of their teams. Based on the case of 12 Belgian municipalities, this chapter shows how socio-economic tools meet the needs of managers.

SEAM Treatise, pages 461–469

1 THEORETICAL FRAMEWORK

1.1 The Strategic Environment of Municipalities

Municipalities evolve in a dynamic and complex normative environment that is part of tetranormalization (Savall & Zardet, 1995): application of the General Data Protection Regulation, new phytosanitary norms or the new urban planning code. The phenomenon is aggravated by the diversity of the fields of action of a municipal administration: land use planning, security, culture or social affairs... For each of these, pressure for change is being exerted by higher administrative levels (States, Provinces), European and international conventions, but also by users-citizens-inhabitants. The latter are becoming more demanding and refuse to suffer from excessive bureaucracy and incomprehensible delays: they want to be heard, to obtain clear, rapid answers "with a smile." Residents want to be more involved in the choices that affect them. Digitalization – mobile applications for agents and users, integrated IT systems, dematerialization, etc. – is a technical and organizational challenge. – Digitalization – mobile applications for agents and users, integrated IT systems, dematerialization, etc. – is a technical and organizational challenge. Faced with these transformations in their environment, municipalities are adapting and have an interest in being proactive, which implies releasing resources to think, organize, equip and transform themselves.

1.2 Development of Public Performance

Since the 1990s, changes in public sector organizations have been made with fewer resources, without necessarily improving working conditions and services. The challenges of managing change are greater (Colerette, 2008). The communes are showing a desire to control the tax burden and debt. Containing taxes and cleaning up finances are common promises, along with ambitions to transform the territories and populations of the commune. The citizen expects actions and results, offering on this basis his confidence in the institutions. Effectiveness and efficiency sound like an injunction to maintain this trust.

Controlling expenditure while improving public action implies the search for sources of efficiency (Pierre, 2013): how to do better, with the same or even fewer resources, but above all how to work better together and methodically? The search for performance of POs is part of the New Public Management trend (Hoods, 1995), aiming at reducing dysfunctions through results-based management favoring empowerment of management teams, motivation of employees, autonomy of managers at all levels, all around the valorization of services provided to citizens (Mazouz et al., 2008; Cappelletti & Khenniche, 2017). Carassus et al. (2011) define public performance as "the ability of a public organization to control its human, financial and organizational resources, in order to produce a public service offer that is adapted, in quality and quantity, to the needs of its stakeholders and that generates sustainable effects for its territory. For municipalities, developing their performance consists of deploying strategic and operational decisions at the internal (organizational, human, financial) and external (public services, territory) levels (Pierre & Khenniche, 2016).

1.3 Dynamics of Adherence to Change

The internal dimension is often forgotten in strategic plans, to the detriment of cohesion, strategic strength and the ability to transform the external environment, like an *active unit* (Perroux, 1975; Savall & Zardet, 1995; Pierre, 2011). The development of public performance requires the adherence—to the strategy and to the changes that concern them—of management and operational teams. The main obstacles to change in the public sector are: *the size of the organizations, the multiplicity of actors, the broad missions, the limited financial resources, the numerous interest groups, the rigid legal framework, the collective agreements and the fixed informational and technological processes* (Jacob et al., 2008). Another difficulty is that of the dual elective and administrative hierarchy of the communes, which has a heavy impact on strategic clarity and the management of change when they do not collaborate effectively.

Change can only be driven by external pressure. Mobilizing people by listening to their expectations of transformation allows us to identify the gaps they perceive. These gaps are dysfunctions, pools of efficiency that can be measured financially in terms of hidden costs (Savall & Zardet, 1987). Public managers need methods that allow them to set a course, identify efficiency gains and carry out transformations while obtaining the support of their teams. These methods are often lacking and are generally incomplete.

2 METHODOLOGY AND SCIENTIFIC FIELDWORK

This intervention-research involved 12 municipalities in Wallonia-Picardy that responded to a project by the Province of Hainaut to offer training in socio-economic management tools (Savall & Zardet, 1987). The authors facilitated this training cycle in 2017–2018, with 99 participants (Directors general, directors, managers and project leaders). This cycle took the form of a series of collaborative training[1] and personalized assistance,[2] with project steering committees bringing together the Province and the Directors general of the communes. The system was based on strong interaction between actors and stakeholders, which made it possible to identify the needs of managers and to measure the adequacy of the socio-economic tools to meet them.

The situations of the municipalities and their sizes are contrasted: 7 have less than 10,000 inhabitants, 4 more than 10,000 inhabitants and one more than 50,000 inhabitants, which employs more than 1,000 agents, compared to about 100 in the small municipalities. In the latter, senior managers have already been trained in management and socio-economic tools, a strategic territorial action plan has already been established,[3] and projects to improve public performance have been identified and are being launched. This is far from the reality of other communes. The realities also differ financially, with some having significant revenues and others experiencing complicated financial situations (debt, loans, etc.). The relationship between elected officials and the administration is cordial in some communes, and at *loggerheads* in others, which has an impact on the serenity and efficiency of operations. The communal strategy is formalized in the larger cities,[4] whereas in the smaller ones, political priorities are poorly defined and the strategy is non-existent.[5] In terms of skills, the larger communes have problems of hyper-specialization and lack of cross-functionality, while the smaller ones suffer from a lack of skills, excessive versatility and a real difficulty in integrating technological and regulatory changes.

The problems of the municipalities therefore differ, as do their expectations with regard to socio-economic tools. Nevertheless, regardless of their size, the needs for strategic planning, efficiency and change management were recognized by the 99 managers of the municipalities.

3 RESULTS OF THE IMPLEMENTATION OF STRATEGIC PLANNING AND CHANGE MANAGEMENT TOOLS

3.1 Implementation of Socio-Economic Management Tools

The need for strategic planning and change management in communes, to develop performance and proactivity in a complex and changing environment, is significant. The tools developed by ISEOR are as much analysis tools as management tools: competency grid, self-analysis of time management, internal and external strategic action plan (IESAP), priority action plan (PAP), piloting logbook, periodically negotiable activity contract (PNAC).

These tools are not specific to the public sector; they have been widely tested and integrated in many public organizations In fact, 35% of the 2,000 intervention-researches conducted by ISEOR have been in the public sector. We focus on Internal and External Strategic Planning and Priority Action Plans—tools for strategic planning—and on the skills and time management grids: tools for analyzing available resources and sources of efficiency.

3.2 Internal and External Strategic Plan (IESAP) and Priority Action Plans (PAPs)

The IESAP and PAPs respond to stakeholders who want a clear, shared and stimulating strategy. In addition to the strategic orientations and objectives, they specify their breakdown into actions and projects, clarifying responsibilities and the implementation schedule for the duration of the mandate or the next six months, thus stimulating action. The IESAP is compatible with the regulatory expectations of a TSP and some municipalities have adopted it to formalize theirs and thus prioritize policy expectations and vision. Political vision is not the only key dimension of a commune's strategy. The Directors general express the importance of also integrating the commune's "core business" or "sovereign" functions into the strategic thinking, as well as the reality and coordination of available resources.

The integration of these strategic priorities requires an in-depth discussion between elected officials and the administration. Some Directors general hope to lock in policy decisions through a TSP, to avoid reversals or constant new demands. But strategic planning must remain flexible and the plan must be regularly reviewed, as a tool for dialogue that brings up disagreements and cognitive dissonance (Kenny, 2016). Another dangerous temptation is the multiplication of strategic priorities in an attempt to please the portfolio holders: education, security, cleanliness, land use, seniors, environment, etc. The inflation of expectations of results makes the IESAP unattainable, with a high risk of disillusionment (Colerette, 2008). To be realistic and to avoid running out of steam, it is advisable to plan major projects over the term of office: do not try to do everything at once, right from the start. This planning exercise makes it possible to integrate the legal-procedural-organizational obstacles. The exchange between elected officials and the administration is crucial.

Simple and synthetic, the IESAP is therefore a support for strategic dialogue between elected officials and the administration and encourages co-construction. Flexibility and the ability to (re)discuss the strategy are not friends of the elaboration of a TSP of several hundred pages. Formalizing 4 to 5 enlightening strategic axes is essential to mobilize and federate the agents. Their breakdown into objectives and actions clarifies the operationalization of the strategy. According to Colerette (2008), vague and not very operational instructions for change lead to "poor results." PAPs then help to organize the deployment of the strategy to the teams, stimulating the implementation of improvement actions and the coordination

TABLE 54.1 Priority Action Plan (Public Works Contracts Department)

Strategic Axes	Priority objectives	Priority actions
1 Better cooperation among departments to monitor public works administration and technicalities	1.1 Ensuring a better communication accross engineering and public works departments to prevent loss of time and mistakes. Enabling shared working methodsof public works to meet deadlines and get a quality of nprojects	1.1.1 Organizing a cross departmental meeting to give visibility to everyone's role and experience
		1.1.2 Clarifying constraints and procedural deadlines for each project, and create a spreasheet re. the projects kick-off (check-list) along with project timeline.
		1.1.3 Centralized archiving of project files
		1.1.4 Systematize a collegial analysis of offers by proceeding step by step
		1.1.5 Standardizing all road and building work procedures
		1.1.6 Centralizing paper and soft files data
		1.1.7 Creating contact databases for road and buliding works to be shared with public works contracts department

of available resources. The extract from the PAP (Table 54.1) produced by the head of a public procurement unit illustrates the search for public performance through the improvement of internal organization—in this case interdepartmental communication—and operationalization through concrete actions.

3.3 Competency Grids and Time Management

The organization's human resources are characterized by the time and skills available. Effectiveness implies having the necessary resources. Efficiency implies controlling their proper use and (re)allocating them to high value-added actions: those that serve the smooth running of the organization, the quality of public services and the implementation of strategic projects.

The competency grid (Savall and Zardet, 1987) responds to the need to clarify expected operations and available competencies. The analysis of the gaps between actual and expected stimulates decision-making about responsibilities and competencies. The reception of the competency grids by the participants was very positive: 90% of the participants completed it for their unit. The grid for the head of an urban planning department shows how the tool is filled in (Table 54.2).[6] The grid shows the vulnerable operations, because the competences are not yet effective (managing SOL procedures, following up on an infraction), or because there is a risk in the event of the absence or departure of a person (setting up a SAR, drawing up an urban plan). We also observe that some team members (AB, GH) are more versatile than others and we can analyze the risks of demotivation or even departure.

This tool sheds light on decision-making to better organize the activity: create duplicates at the counter, manage leaves, assign a new project. It targets the skills to be developed as a priority—thanks to the symbol of the circle—(AB-managing SOL procedures, GH-processing bonds), helping the manager to choose his or her "battles," his or her investment in time and energy. Indeed, it is advisable to avoid dispersion and to concentrate on a few priority actions during the next semester: putting such and such a person in pairs, having so-and-so train the rest of the team, pushing so-and-so to increase his practice. The development of

TABLE 54.2 Excerpt From the Competency Grid (municipality > 10,000 inhabitants) – ©ISEOR

Skills Grid—Urban Planning Department

Operations / Employees (N-1)	Urban planning department: Organization at the beginning of the period															
	Advising at the counter on building license	Advising on constraints	First research on urbanistic data for notaries	Processing and delivering notary requests	Analyzing and sorting out DIV 102 files	Ascribing official files numbers and delivering certificates	Preparing licenses for the city	License receipt	Analyzing a license request	Preparing a licensing file	Processing bonds	Land registery inquiry	Management land procedures	Monitoring violations	Setting up a SAR file	Working out town planning scheme
AB	■	■	■	◪	■	■	■	■	■	■	◪	■	(□)	◪	—	—
CD	◪	■	■	■	□	—	□	■	□	—	—	■	□	□	—	—
EF	◪	◪	□	—	—	—	◪	■	◪	◪	—	◪	□	□	(◪)	■
GH	◪	■	■	◪	■	■	◪	■	■	■	(◪)	■	□	◪	—	—

Key: ■ Full mastery of practice; ◪ Incidental practice or not fully mastered; □ Knowing principles without practice; — No theoretical training nor practice; ○ To be implemented

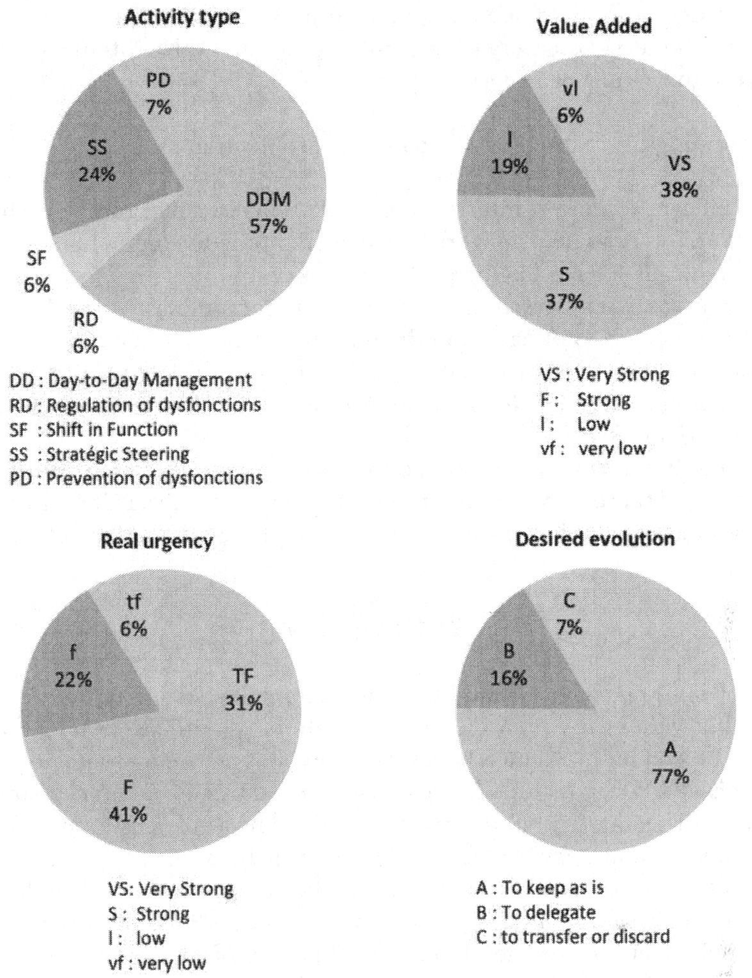

Figure 54.1 Results of time management analyses (based on 45 self-analysis grids representing 1,200 hours).

agents' skills is a lever of efficiency that translates into increased productivity and quality of service, and professional development for the individuals concerned.

With efficiency in mind, municipalities seek to control the time of their staff. The time self-analysis grid (Savall and Zardet, 1987) makes it possible to detect dysfunctions in time management (Savall & Zardet, 1987, 2020). The use of the tool requires a real effort: during a few days, the managers note all the actions they perform, measure them and characterize them. The participants showed an excellent degree of involvement in the exercise: 75% of the participants carried out their self-analysis, for an average of 4 days, and one person out of two formalized the main findings and actions envisaged to improve their time management. 45 self-analyses were collected, i.e., a total of 1200 hours analyzed, from which the following results are drawn (see Figure 54.1):

- Types of activities: Directors and managers spend on average less than 1/4 of their time on strategic steering actions, for a target of 50%.
- Value added: on average, 1 hour out of 4 is of low value added.

- Real urgency: more than one hour out of four is not mastered.
- Desirable evolution: on average 23% of the time can evolve within a few months, i.e., more than 1 day per week.

The main findings formalized by the managers are the following:

- The significant volume of interruptions (calls, emails, colleagues, etc.) hinders concentration, forces some managers to take work home to complete notes and analyses, or results in tasks not being performed or of lower quality.
- Many requests are expressed in an unclear manner and waste time. Disorganized requests from elected officials and the hierarchy are pointed out.
- Lack of delegation is recurrent, due to a lack of resources or investment in the training of their employees, with managers frequently saying to themselves: “it will be faster if I do it myself.”
- Time spent in meetings is considered excessive (often more than a third of managers’ time)—because they are not present in their unit to steer the activity and the strategy. Meetings are insufficiently structured, prepared and facilitated.

CONCLUSION

The analysis of skills management and time management sheds light on the sources of efficiency available within the communes. Observation of the process of integrating management tools in the communes shows the levers for exploiting them. Strategic planning tools help to formalize a strategy that has been co-constructed by elected officials and the administration, and to disseminate it to departments and teams, while ensuring their support for successful change. The strategy is a “cursor” for defining the value added in the municipality and making skills evolve, leading changes and reallocating resources. The development of strategy, internal cohesion and skills is a key to increasing public performance, improving the quality of public services and developing the character of an active unit of the commune, capable of transforming its territory according to its objectives.

REFERENCES

Cappelletti, L., & Khenniche, S. (2017), Coproduire la performance socialement responsable des collectivités territoriales: résultats émergents d’une recherche-intervention au sein d’une mairie. *Revue Politiques et Management Public.* 34/1–2 January-June /19–4.

Carassus D., Favoreu C., Gardey D., Maurel C. (2011), La caractérisation et la définition de la performance publique : une application aux collectivités locales, *Colloque AIRMAP.*

Colerette P. (2008), Pour une gestion du changement disciplinée dans l’administration publique, TÉLESCOPE, *Revue d’analyse comparée en administration publique,* ENAP, Vol. 14 n° 3, Fall.

Hood C. (1995), The “New Public Management” in the 1980s: Variations on a Theme, Accounting, Organizations and Society, Vol. 20, Issues 2–3, February-April, pp. 93–109.

Jacob R., A. Rondeau, F. Normandin (2008), La gestion du changement stratégique dans les organisations des secteurs public et parapublic : le point de vue des praticiens, TÉLESCOPE, *Revue d’analyse comparée en administration publique,* ENAP, Vol. 14 n° 3, Fall.

Mazouz B., Leclerc J. and Tardif M.J.-B. (2008), *La gestion intégrée par résultats : concevoir et gérer autrement la performance dans l’administration publique.* Presses de l’Université du Québec, Québec.

Perroux, F. (1975). Unités actives et mathématiques nouvelles. Dunod.

Pierre X. (2011), « *Pilotage institutionnel des coopérations interorganisationnelles – La mise en œuvre de stratégies territoriales* «, Éditions universitaires européennes, 416 p. Doctoral thesis in management sciences defended in 2010, CNAM. Paris.

Pierre X. (2013), "Solving the expenditure control equation while improving public action through a "magnifying glass" analysis of policy implementation in territories," *Transatlantic Congress of Accounting, Controlling, Auditing, Management Control and Cost Management, ISEOR & IIC, Lyon.*

Pierre X., Khenniche S, (2016), « Pilotage des coopérations avec les acteurs du territoire, levier de la performance publique?», *Colloque AIRMAP,* Poitiers.

This page intentionally left blank.

CHAPTER 55

STRATEGIC DEVELOPMENT AND IMPLEMENTATION

Managing Rythms and Relationships With Time—Case of a Congregation

François Du Penhoat and Maïté Rateau

ABSTRACT

In a multigenerational and multicultural religious organization, the relationship to time is not the same as in a company and is not the same for everyone. While everyone would like to see strategic projects move forward more or less quickly, the lack of a common methodology for building and implementing these projects makes it difficult to develop or even successfully accomplish the public interest mission. This chapter presents the results of a socio-economic intervention carried out within a religious congregation that enabled the emergence of a common strategic project for the community while managing the biological rhythms of each person.

This chapter studies the transformation that took place in a congregation that was accompanied by an ISEOR team in the evolution of its strategic project.

1 FROM INDIVIDUAL STRATEGIES TO A COLLECTIVE STRATEGY

In any organization, individuals live side by side and try to fulfill their mission, allowing them to implement their individual strategy. In the case of a congregation, these individuals are multiple, with different characteristics that the organization must take into-account.

SEAM Treatise, pages 471–478

1.1 Individuals and Strategies

The accompaniment of ISEOR was carried out with the house in Lyon, which is both a place where the missionaries of the congregation live and a place where social and religious missions are carried out. These missionaries come from Lyon and other provinces. Each one carries out his own missions that he wishes to carry out, provided of course that they correspond to the social and religious mission of the congregation. The average age of the members of the Province of Lyon is 76 years, that of the members of other provinces 37 years.

In the framework of the construction of a strategic project, it is difficult to unite all the individuals and their strategies. Indeed, with this age gap, missionaries have a different relationship to time (de Gaulejac, V. 2018; Monette, 1996), depending on their generation. On the one hand, there is a pre-retired generation, having completed many projects throughout their career and for whom there is no urgency to change and develop new projects and on the other hand, a younger generation eager to carry out projects and build the future. This relationship to time also differs because of the fact that many cultures coexist in the Lyon house (Lefebvre, 1997). The course of a day is thus different, with later or later starts and ends of the day, as well as a distinct intensity. This is true both on a daily basis and in the longer term. In addition, the congregation works in collaboration with external people, such as volunteers, some of whom are still active. Thus, in this particular context, the pace of progress of strategic projects, and in particular the strategic project of the house expected by each of the stakeholders, is very different.

The high turnover of staff constitutes another challenge for the construction of a common strategic project. Indeed, employees are sent on assignment for a fixed period, usually six years. For any organization, the arrival of new collaborators represents a significant challenge. In the case of the congregation, it is all the more important that this integration must ensure the rapid involvement of the newcomer in the strategic project which is not initially his own. Moreover, the house does not recruit according to its needs, it receives missionaries who are sent to it. The challenge for the organization is to adjust the integration process by adapting the organization's project to the new person.

A juxtaposition of scattered micro-projects has thus been put in place over the months and years, with each person building his or her own project. The resulting difficulty is not so much the result of this multitude of projects as the fact that they are not synchronized (Mintzberg & Romelaer, 1994). This makes it difficult to manage the overall strategic project in terms of time resources, financial resources, and even material resources. Indeed, resources are difficult to find and to manage. At the same time, state aid is decreasing in view of the economic context and the donors are aging people whose numbers are decreasing.

Thus, a different relationship to time, a high turnover of personnel with a necessary adaptation of the organization to the individuals, lack of synchronization of projects and decreasing financial resources are the major difficulties to co-construct a project. In addition, the organization and its members do not have a common methodology to build and implement projects. The organization feels the need to constantly readjust its project and to relearn how to work together. The problem raised in this context is: how can the community's strategic project emerge, while managing the biological rhythms of each member?

1.2 The Proposed Hypotheses

We present all of the hypotheses associated with the accompaniment of the congregation, responding to the stated problem, according to three categories (Savall & Zardet, 2004): descriptive, explanatory and prescriptive hypotheses (see Table 55.1).

TABLE 55.1 Body of Proposed Hypotheses

Descriptive hypothesis	Explicative hypothesis	Prescriptive hypothesis
The absence of a common strategic project favors the emergence of multiple individual strategic projects with no guaranteed consistency.	The non-mobilized actors, especially those of an association with its values, find projects to develop on their own, in line with their desires, their rhythms, the association's vocation, the image they have of it, and their respective environments.	The co-creation of a strategic project, integrating the different existing projects, allows to give meaning and coherence to all the projects, to involve the actors in the same strategic vision and to discard projects that would not make sense for the collective strategy of the organization.
Individual projects make it possible to manage a single speed: that of each project manager.	Different biological rhythms slow down the progress of collective projects and even immobilize/crystallize the actors. A long-term project without intermediate objectives makes it difficult to position the individual project	Negotiating a timetable for the progress of the strategic project makes it possible to involve people and give them visibility so that they can better understand how their individual project fits into the overall project in the shorter term.
The diversity of cultures in the same home is a pretext for not working together.	The different cultures of the people influence the way projects are managed without making them impossible.	Developing common working methods with all the players allows for the integration and better federating of the different stakeholders.
All resources (human, financial, material, etc.) are in sharp decline	The attractiveness of the religious function in France is decreasing and makes the search for human resources more difficult.	Making the common strategic project visible makes it possible to improve the attractiveness of the organization and to increase the resources to better accomplish the mission.

All of these hypotheses lead us to the root causes of the difficulties encountered in organizations, according to the socio-economic theory. We realize that it is these causes that limit the metamorphosis of the organization from an organization that has difficulty managing its strategic project to an organization that orchestrates and pilots its projects.

The root causes of the socio-economic theory are the steering defects, the synchronization defects, the lack of cleaning up and the defects of HISOFIS (Humanly Integrated and Stimulating Functional and Operational Information System; Savall & Zardet, 1987, 2020).

The HISOFIS concept questions the information circulating in organizations by analyzing its relevance and its contribution to organizational dynamics: is it understood and integrated by the actors and does it allow decisions to be made and therefore actions to be taken?

2 SOCIO-ECONOMIC MANAGEMENT AT THE SERVICE OF A CATHOLIC MISSIONARY CONGREGATION

We will first present the case study and then discuss the application of socio-economic management in the congregation.

2.1 Presentation of the Congregation

Founded in 1856 in Lyon by Melchior de Marion-Brésillac, this congregation is a community of Catholic missionaries from Europe, Africa and Asia. Its headquarters is currently

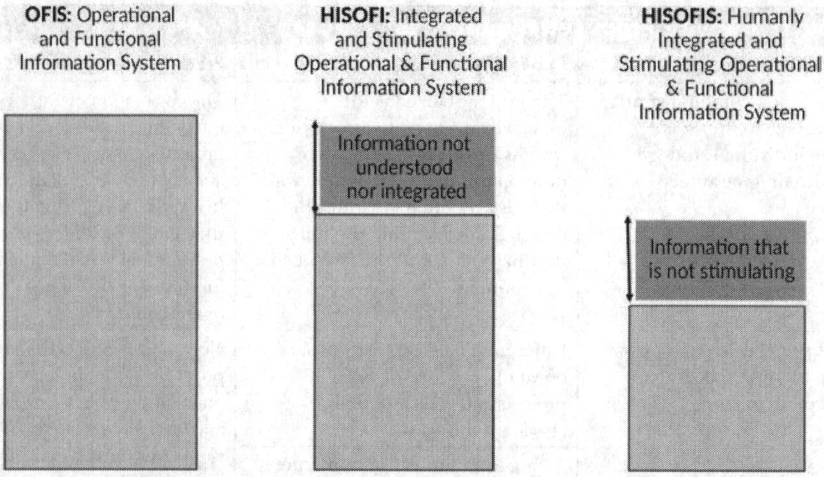

Figure 55.1 HISOFIS principle (Zardet, 1985, Savall & Zardet, 1987).

TABLE 55.2 Root Causes of Dysfunction (Savall & Zardet, 1987)

Root-cause of dysfunctions in organizations	Observed dysfunctions
Lack of synchronization	Lack of synchronization of micro-projects
Poor steering	Poor steering of the overall strategic project and lack of formalized strategy
Faults of HISIOFIS	Lack of communication on the strategic project. Seeking consensus and difficulty to take action
Lack of grooming	Routines adapted to a past situation, but no longer efficient at present

in Rome and it has 1012 members and associates, 15 of whom, priests and lay people from 25 different countries, reside at the house in Lyon. We are interested in building a project for the house in Lyon, a house of reference and identity for the congregation. It is both a house-place of life and a so-called international house, which fulfills its social, cultural and religious missions. In fact, it brings together the community of the members of the house, the Province, the employees and volunteers, the sisters, other members of associations as well as all other visitors and members who support the museum installed in its premises. It is thus a precious node of exchange, communication, outreach and crossbreeding. Its mission is to build bridges between different cultures and religions, not only with the entities of the congregation present in Africa, but also with African communities, the local Church, migrants, other cultures and other religions. The residents of the house in Lyon welcome many visitors, who come for formation or for renewal. Their objective is that everyone has a place in the house project, regardless of their rhythm.

2.2 Support to Develop a Strategic Project

The support provided by ISEOR is the result of a twofold request from the house in Lyon. The first came from the museum that the congregation owns. This museum, like most museums, was not profitable and was consuming more and more of the house's resources. Moreover, its position in relation to the house was not clear, because its contribution to the missions to be fulfilled by the congregation was questioned, and relations with the museum management were difficult. While the management wanted to develop the artistic influence of the museum, the Fathers wanted to improve the "quality of service" of the missions of the congregation. At the same time, the Council asked that the house define its project so that it would become an international house of reference at the heart of the congregation's mission, a place of welcome for the confreres and of privileged collaboration with associations and other religious or civil groups. According to the strategic project developed and proposed, it would obtain additional resources. During the summer of 2015, a project was developed according to the axes of the socio-economic management triad. Figure 55.2 summarizes the course of the accompaniment.

A diagnosis of the dysfunctions was carried out with 26 people in the house by an internal facilitator trained in the socio-economic intervention method by ISEOR (Savall, 1974, 1979; Savall & Zardet, 1987). He listed all the dysfunctions cited by the people, as well as the economic valuation of their impacts. Subsequently, a focus group was set up with working groups whose objective was to propose actions to reduce the dysfunctions and a strategic project.

At the same time, training in a number of management tools was provided to the members involved in the project, so that they could better manage their activities and the project in a methodical manner. These tools, detailed in Figure 55.2, allowed the development of a common language, the structuring of the reflection and actions to be carried out and the definition of some indicators to evaluate and adjust.

This process of accompaniment allowed the identification of numerous problems. The particularity of this diagnosis is that the theme of strategic implementation concentrated more than 30% of the expressions. Communication-coordination-cooperation, working conditions, time management and work organization were addressed in a balanced manner.

On the theme of strategic implementation, the actors raised the lack of updating of the strategy, its unsuitability to the environment, difficulties of coordination to elaborate the strategy and a lack of coherence between allocated means and fixed objectives. Regarding the management of rhythms, the impossibility of asking old people to change and the long delays for the implementation of new projects were highlighted. The need to change communication practices, strategy, and the internal functioning of the house (from welcoming

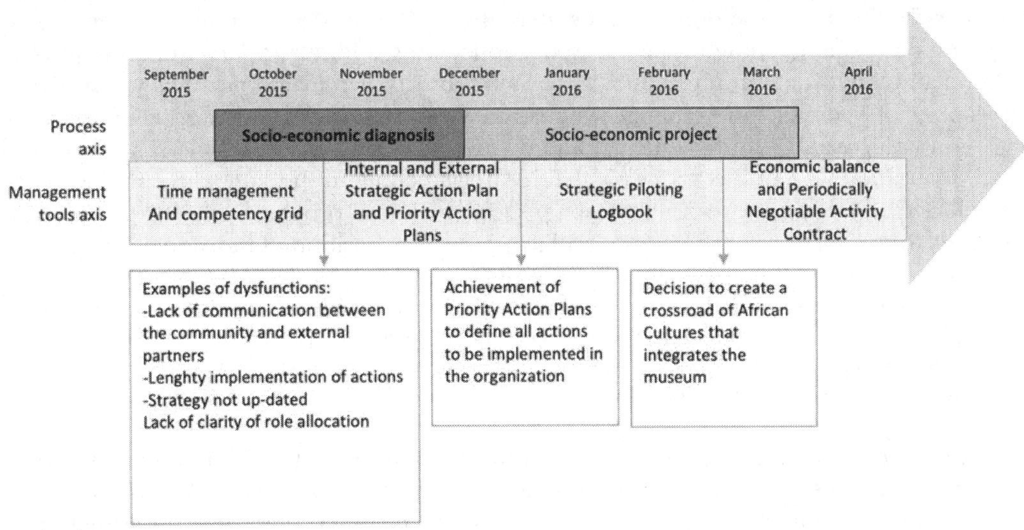

Figure 55.2 Summary of the socio-economic intervention.

new members to working with partners close to the congregation) was a strong point raised by a majority of the members of the congregation. The question that then arose was: how to make these changes happen?

The focus group was structured into eight workgroups with the following objectives:

- Internal objectives: to be a house of services (pole 1), to welcome (pole 2), to live together (pole 3), to manage finances (pole 10), to take care of health (pole 10) and to develop the house (pole 11).
- External objectives: Involve everyone, especially in annual events (pole 4), develop intercultural and interreligious activities (pole 5), define what is expected of the museum and its annexes (pole 6), develop pastoral care (poor, parishes, animation) (pole 7), and communicate (pole 8).

These divisions met for five months to propose solutions to certain dysfunctions and to build a common project for the transformation of the house.

2.3 A Unifying Strategic Project

As the sessions progressed and thanks to the iterative process of the focus group, the members developed an internal and external strategic action plan with three strategic axes:

- To make the house evolve as a node of exchange, communication and crossbreeding;
- To build something together that opens to the future and traces a missionary path;
- To have a missionary house in proximity to other actors.

One of the most important achievements of this accompaniment was the creation of a cultural center to regroup, pilot and synchronize all the projects responding to the missions of the house. This center makes it possible to fulfill the missions of the house by presenting the objects of African culture, without being a separate entity as was the museum. It was proposed that these objects be returned to the African populations. But they preferred that the fathers keep them because they are safer there than in some African countries. The center includes: permanent and temporary museum collections, a library, reserves of art objects, a cultural and linguistic training center, a media library, its own magazine and a website. It is also a place of listening and exchange which organizes conferences and inter-religious meetings, conferences and cultural activities and discovery classes.

Another advantage of this project is that it directs people in the same direction, with action plans that define the meaning of each person's action. It proposes a shared project that responds to the missions of the house, replacing the juxtaposition of individual projects.

> On the project itself, I would say that it has progressed well because we have brought together people of values and we have agreed on a project that is re-evaluated and reoriented every year, the strategic objectives are clear and the responsibilities defined; in this sense, there is enormous progress. (Provincial—Father François Du Penhoat)

The current challenges focus on the evaluation and adjustment of this new strategic project and the actions linked to it. The periodic evaluation of the project with a reorientation through the implementation of actions is necessary since the internal and external environment is evolving. This evaluation needs to be carried out in a structured way. A dynamic is already clearly felt in different aspects: work organization, work productivity and improvements in the financial situation. Our stated hypotheses are partially validated, but they fully contribute to show that the principles of socio-economic management are applicable in an organization where the management of rhythms is at the heart of the concerns and where the need to evolve has become inescapable.

3 DEVELOPMENT OF A STRATEGIC AMBITION BASED ON STRUCTURED AND PARTICIPATIVE WORKING METHODS

It is interesting to note that such a project could have ended and been limited to its implementation. However, it also developed the strategic ambition of the people and the organization. Thus, the internal and external environment stimulates change and evolution in an organization. However, it is difficult to bring about these changes without methodology. The triad of change is a strong element of socio-economic theory, which brings together the necessary ingredients to implement a strategic project and bring out this strategic ambition. Moreover, this strategic ambition seems to be nourished by a permanent action on the four root causes. Indeed, this makes it possible to limit the juxtaposition of micro-projects, to install new practices in a sustainable manner and to increase the speed of implementation of decisions, thus favoring the emergence of new actions.

Today, the creation of a crossroads, with multiple meetings and events organized, is an attractive project for missionaries. The willingness to evaluate and adapt expressed by the Provincial shows a new ambition to continue the outreach and fulfill many missions, without leaving aside existing projects. Moreover, in October 2020, a forum was created which is the counterpart of the cultural center, for the more religious aspects with three main concerns: to be a place of reflection and transmission of theological reflection on the Mission, especially in connection with certain universities and to help the missionaries of the congregation to analyze and revise their work and way of doing things.

CONCLUSION

Carrying out a socio-economic intervention in a congregation, a benevolent organization with its own specificities and similarities with other organizations, has shown that the principles of socio-economic management have made it possible to develop a strategic project that is shared, ambitious and managed. The three axes of intervention (structured continuous improvement process, management tools and political decisions) are the keys to address in depth the root causes of dysfunctions, which limit the rapid implementation of the strategic project and the creation of potential of each organization.

REFERENCES

De Gaulejac, V. (2018). T Plus on gagne du temps, moins on en a…Le rapport au temps dans la société paradoxante. Dans : Nicole Aubert éd., *@ la recherche du temps: Individus hyperconnectés, société accélérée : tensions et transformations* (pp. 39–51). Toulouse, France: Érès.

Lefevre, S. (1997). Rapports de générations. Une conjoncture socio-économique et culturelle, *Cahiers internationaux de sociologie*, CII : 183–198.

Mintzberg, H., & Romelaer, P. T. (1994). *Grandeur et décadence de la planification stratégique.* Dunod.

Monette, M. (1996). *Les nouveaux parcours entourant la retraite au Canada*: Résultats de l'enquête sociale générale. Ottawa: Statistique Canada.

PART VI

SOCIO-ECONOMIC STRATEGIES: ORGANIZATIONAL DEVELOPMENT, CORPORATE SOCIAL RESPONSIBILITY, "TETRANORMALIZATION," BUSINESS TRANSFERS, MERGERS AND ACQUISITIONS . . .

This page intentionally left blank.

CHAPTER 56

SEAM AS AN ORGANIZATION DEVELOPMENT INTERVENTION

Fifty Years of Common Ground

Peter F. Sorensen and Therese F. Yaeger

ABSTRACT

This chapter reviews SEAM within the context of Organization Development (OD) and Change. It compares the foundation and basic principles of SEAM with the origins and classic OD work of Beckhard and Blake, the two early contributors to whom the term Organization Development is attributed. We also address the parallels between recent developments in the field—Appreciative Inquiry, Agile concepts, and Strategic OD. The common ground of SEAM principles originated by Henri Savall in 1973 and 1974, almost 50 years ago, parallel concepts in Organization Development.

The term "organization development" was first coined by Richard Beckard and Robert Blake in the 1960s. In 1969, both authors presented their work as part of the original Addison-Wesley six pack of books in 1969. Four years later, Henri Savall (1974, 1981)) presented the foundation paper for the Socio-Economic Approach to Management. This paper discusses SEAM from the perspective of the field of Organization Development. The paper begins with a comparison of SEAM to these two early pioneering approaches to OD. The paper then presents comparisons with recent development in the field including Appreciative Inquiry, Agile, Strategic OD, and the ongoing contributions of the SEAM team.

SEAM Treatise, pages 481–485

1 SEAM: THE CLASSICS

SEAM clearly parallels the early concept of Organization Development (OD). For example, while the early OD contributors reacted to what they perceived as the major contributions to organization and management theory at that time, SEAM is even more explicit in citing the inadequacies of existing approaches to management and organization design. These inadequacies are described as a virus—the TFW virus, referring to the work of Fredrick Taylor, Henri Fayol and Max Weber, the early architects of management and organization theory in the 1930s and 1940s. The primary orientation of the early contributors to the field of OD is probably best illustrated by the Addison-Wesley OD six pack, a collection of six books by the six major OD contributors including Dick Beckhard and Robert Blake.

The parallels between SEAM and the values of Organization Development are made explicit in the quote "The socio-economic theory of organizations assumes that all employees, regardless of level in the hierarchy, are capable of innovation. As a result, the socio-economic theory of organizations prefers to pursue the optimization of human potential" (Worley, Zardet, Bonnet & Savall A., 2015, p. 30). The values and orientation which serve as the foundation of SEAM again parallel Douglas McGregor' s Theory Y while the TFW virus might be identified as another way of defining Theory X.

Another quote again illustrates the parallel between the values and orientation of SEAM and the values and orientation of OD, "Organizing in ways that tap human potential speeds up the process of converting dysfunctions resulting from the TFW virus into value-added work, of transforming low-value added activities into high-value added activity, and liberating socio-economic performance" (Worley, et al, 2015, p. 11). Other parallels between SEAM and the early contributors to OD include the concept of whole systems and organizational performance as presented in the work of Dick Beckhard. Here, Beckhard defines Organization Development as "an effort (1) planned, (2) organization wide, and (3) managed from the top, to (4) increase organization effectiveness and health through (5) planned interventions in the organization's processes, using behavioral science knowledge." (Beckhard, 1969).

Similarly, Robert Blake with Jane Mouton present in their contribution to the OD six pack, building a dynamic corporation through Grid development, a process which is similar to Beckhard in terms of a focus on the entire organization and a systematic process. For Blake and Mouton, the systematic process is the "Managerial Grid."

In brief, a number of parallels exist between SEAM and the early founders of the field. For example, an emphasis on planned change, system wide change, and similar to Blake and Mouton's Managerial Grid, the systematic change process is SEAM. One major distinction, however, may be the SEAM emphasis on the assessment of the economic cost of change and the focus on "hidden costs."

2 APPRECIATIVE INQUIRY

Although there are clearly a number of parallels between the major characteristics of SEAM and Organization Development, there are important contrasts when comparing SEAM with Appreciative Inquiry. The parallels between SEAM and OD are especially strong when one compares SEAM and organizational agility. But when comparing SEAM and Appreciative Inquiry there are again a number of similarities as well as differences. A comparison of these two approaches was recently presented in an article in the *Organization Development Journal* authored by members of the SEAM team and Benedictine PhD program. The following observations are based on that article (Sorensen, Yaeger, Savall, Zardet, Bonnet, Peron, 2010).

In terms of similarities, both approaches are associated with work at universities, SEAM with the University of Lyon 3, and Appreciative Inquiry at Case Western Reserve University. SEAM is associated with the work of Henri Savall and Appreciative Inquiry is associated with the work of David Cooperrider. The foundation work for SEAM was presented in 1973–74, while the first article on Appreciative Inquiry appeared in 1987. Both approaches have had significant international applications.

The major differences between SEAM and Appreciative Inquiry include differences in approach and process. SEAM focuses on a comprehensive and systematic approach to problem identification and problem solving as reflected in the concept of "hidden costs." In contrast, the major orientation of Appreciative Inquiry is to focus on opportunity and success as opposed to problem identification.

Drawing on the discussion in the summary of the comparison article cited above, two interesting observations emerge. SEAM, created by Savall in France, includes a number of citations from the U.S. management literature, while Appreciative Inquiry was developed in the U.S. but includes a number of references to the European tradition of social construction. Additionally, SEAM is characterized by the use of trained professionals while one of the most memorable and effective applications of Appreciative Inquiry was done not by trained professionals but by children.

3 AGILITY

In 2017, Worley along with Williams and Lawler, set forth a comprehensive statement on agile organizations in *The Agility Factor.* The Agility concept has become a popular concept in the field of Organization Development as evidenced by the recent 2019 OD Network conference highlighting the all-conference panel on Agility with Chris Worley as the keynote (as well as the recent Benedictine University Lecture Series celebrating the 25th anniversary of the Benedictine PhD Organization Development program).

The concept of the Agile Organization as defined by Worley and colleagues is characterized by "the ability to make timely, effective, and sustained change characterized by (1) a history of successful change that results in (2) profitability rates that are consistently (more than 80 percent of the time) higher than the average of their competitive group over time." And, "strategies, structure, and systems that can drive change and sustained performance. (Worley et al, 2015, pp. 16–17). This concept of agility is based on the Agility Pyramid with good management as the foundation followed by capabilities and agility. The agility routines include strategizing, perceiving, testing and implementing (p.18). In *Becoming Agile: How the SEAM Approach to Management Builds Adaptability,* the authors relate the story of the Brioche Pasquier Group, a French organization that applied the SEAM approach to developing and sustaining agility.

Here with the Brioche Pasquier we see further parallels in what has become one of the major approaches to Organization Development with the application of SEAM.

4 STRATEGIC CHANGE

In addition to Appreciative Inquiry and Agile, the field of Organization Development has increasingly moved to organizational strategy as an essential element of OD. Although both

Beckhard and Blake proposed system-wide change, their approaches tended not to deal explicitly with strategic change. The field has increasingly moved to Strategic Organization Development. In 1988, Jelinek and Litterer presented a paper at the National Academy of Management Conference, entitled "Why OD must become strategic," a paper which was later published in *Research in Organizational Change and Development.* This early paper was followed by Worley, Hitchin and Ross in 1996, *Integrated Strategic Change,* published by Addison-Wesley. This was followed by Yaeger and Sorensen, *Strategic Organization Development: Managing Change for Success.* This last reference includes an article by Head which reviews the historical role of Strategic OD.

Again, the parallels between SEAM and OD are clearly illustrated in the early development of SEAM. The following are abstracted from Henri Savall's original document presenting the bases for SEAM (Savall, as cited in Savall & Zardet, 2017, p. 295–296). This emphasis on strategic change continues through the years including Henri Savall and Veronique Zardet, 1987, 2017, *Strategic Engineering of the Reed; Reflections on socio-economic strategy and implementation).*

- A typology of change management strategies based on three criteria: the scope of the change (restricted to a local level or with a larger focus, on the whole company), the implementation procedure (top-down, bottom-up or hybrid: top-down-bottom-up-top down-bottom-up . . .), and the degree of involvement of internal actors (top and middle managers, supervisors, workers).
- The need to plan change
- The political will of the company
- Flexible and decentralized planning of the production circuits operations
- Dangers of not planning
- The need to economically assess change
- Analysis of the balance sheet in terms of value of the organizational change efforts

SUMMARY

This chapter has reviewed SEAM within the context of the field of Organization Development and as an approach to OD and Change. It has compared the foundation and basic principles of SEAM with the origins and classic OD work of Beckhard and Blake, two early contributors to whom the term Organization Development is attributed. This part of the paper draws primarily from their contributions to the Addison-Wesley six-pack. The paper then addressed the parallels between recent developments in the field – Appreciative Inquiry, Agile concepts, and Strategic OD. Here the paper drew primarily on several works dealing with Strategic OD, the recent work of Savall and Zardet, and earlier work by Yaeger and Sorensen et al, comparing Appreciative Inquiry and SEAM, and the recent publication, *Becoming Agile: How the SEAM approach to management builds adaptability.*

Although the development of the field of OD can be traced back to the early work of Beckhard and Blake in the 1950s and 1960s and SEAM with a shorter history, the 1970s clearly parallel the field of OD in a number of ways and can be considered an OD methodology within the field of OD. It is not only the historical parallels that are of interest, but the way in which SEAM and the field of OD have recently come together. The foundational concepts of SEAM and the OD classics are similar in that they both place emphasis on the total organization and organization effectiveness. The comparison with Appreciative Inquiry again draws striking parallels between OD and SEAM but also addresses one of the major differences, the clear emphasis on the ***economic*** measures and gains provided by SEAM and the costs of inadequate planning and change reflected in the concept of "hidden costs." With Agile, OD and SEAM truly come together with the collaborative work of one of the leading contributors to OD, Dr. Chris Worley, and the SEAM team of Zardet, Bonnet, and Amandine Savall.

But SEAM as an OD intervention does not end with the intervention itself but is characterized by important and ongoing contributions to the field of OD by the Socio-Economic Institute for Firms and Organizations and the University of Lyon, and the core faculty of Henri Savall, Veronique Zardet, Marc Bonnet, and Amandine Savall. These contributions include among others:

- Continuing contributions to the knowledge base of organizational change and improvement including work with Tony Buono and the book series, *Research in Management Consulting;*
- Expanding our knowledge of scholar-practitioner doctoral programs;
- Expanding our knowledge of global organization development through the international application of SEAM;
- The creation and hosting of the international Organization Development and management consulting PhD student conferences in Lyon and co-sponsored by the Academy of Management;
- Again, the contribution to the knowledge base of Organization Development and Management Consulting for their ongoing contribution in terms of panels and papers at the Academy of Management.

As evidenced here, the common ground of SEAM principles originated by Henri Savall in 1973 and 1974, almost 50 years ago, parallel concepts in Organization Development.

REFERENCES

Beckhard, R. (1969). *Organization development: Strategies and models.* Addison Wesley.

Blake, R. R., & Mouton, J. S. (1969). *Building a dynamic corporation through grid organization development.* Addison Wesley.

Jelinek, M., & Litterer, J. A. (1988). Why OD must become strategic. *Research in organizational change and development, 2*(1), 135–162.

Savall, H., & Zardet, V. (2017). *Strategic engineering of the reed: Reflections on socio-economic strategy and implementation.* Information Age Publishing. (1st ed. in French, 1995, Paris: Economica).

Sorensen, P., Yaeger, T., Savall, H., Zardet, V., Bonnet, M., Peron, M. (2010). "A Review of Two Major Global and International Approaches to Organizational Change: SEAM and Appreciative Inquiry," *O. D. Journal, 28*(4) 31–40.

Worley, C. G., Hitchin, Rossi, (1996). *Integrated Strategic Change,* Addison-Wesley

Worley, C. G., Williams, T. D., & Lawler III, E. E. (2014). *The agility factor: Building adaptable organizations for superior performance.* John Wiley & Sons.

Worley, C. G., Zardet, V., Bonnet, M., & Savall, A. (2015). *Becoming agile: How the SEAM approach to management builds adaptability.* John Wiley & Sons.

Yaeger, T., Sorensen, P. (2009). *Strategic organization development: Managing change for success.* Information Age Publishing.

This page intentionally left blank.

CHAPTER 57

A POWERFUL ORGANIZATION DEVELOPMENT RESOURCE THAT REMAINS OVERLOOKED

Joanne C. Preston

ABSTRACT

This chapter looks at the major alignments that SEAM and the values of ODJ have in common and the resource potential that this methodology has for change leaders. The topics covered are the importance of people's contribution to change, inclusion of the entire system, systems thinking, listening to all the stories about the organization, tying change to the bottom line, social responsibility, and hybrid consulting. All elements together make a powerful resource that has been overlooked in the change field. The goal is to make readers globally aware of the importance of this methodology and the usefulness that it has as a tool for change.

I have attended the Academy of Management for years and read numerous articles and books on a terrific technique called SEAM (Socio-Economic Approach to Management). To date, USA industries have little understanding even though this approach has been around for a long time (Savall, 1974, 1981; Savall & Zardet, 1987, 2008). In 2018, I was co-chair of a Dublin conference held for ISODC (International Society for Organization Development & Change). I was thinking about possible Key-note speakers that would appeal to both USA and European ODC (Organization Development & Change) people who would attend. I have known Henri Savall and, his daughter, Amandine, and thought that an introduction to SEAM might be terrific for the USA's attendees to hear. European companies know SEAM, it is not well-known in the USA.I thought it would be great for those practitioners attending the Dublin conference to learn about another resource that would help their practice. The participants loved it! They were amazed by SEAM'S comprehensiveness!

SEAM Treatise, pages 487–493

I am writing this chapter to educate people about this resource. SEAM is a little-known approach to management (Conbere & Heorhiadi, 2015) even though it has a solid track record as a change technique. My purpose in writing this chapter is to make SEAM a more widely known and used resource for ODC practitioners and change leaders globally!

1 PEOPLE ARE THE ORGANIZATION

In this chapter, I will reflect on why this resource matches the goals and values in ODC and why this will help implement change no matter what your role is in the organization. I will begin with an elementary idea that I have been actively trying to get academics and practitioners in our field to consider. This idea is that organizations are not living breathing entities on their own. My colleagues who worked with me in South Africa (RSA) during the change from apartheid to democracy quickly learned people are the organization (Preston, DuToit & Barber, 1996). Working with Mandela, we had to engage in interventions that changed the organization and began to change the people. It is the people who change the organization from the present state to the future state. The organization does not change itself!

We decided that the Beckhard & Harris change model (1987) needed a critical addition because of this experience. Their version made it clear that the organization would have a present state and a future state. This model encourages planned stages and steps that the organization takes called transition. The system comes closer to the future state with each implemented step. Our learning from RSA was that along with the carefully planned changes for the organization, the people have beliefs, thoughts, and behaviors (Old Reality) that made them successful in the present state. These values and behaviors generally must change in the future state (New Reality). We felt that along with each step or intervention planned for the transition that an equal intervention needs to happen with the people to help them made the needed changes for the new reality. If this did not happen, the people would not be prepared or able to behave successfully in the Future State. Therefore, we published Figure 57.1.

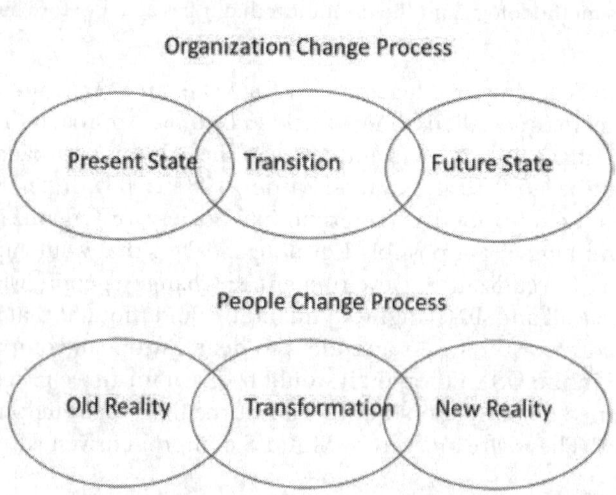

Figure 57.1 Organization change process (Preston, J.C., DuToit, L., & Barber, I. (1996). A potential model of transformational change applied to South Africa. In Woodman & Pasmore (Eds). *Research in Organizational Change and Development. 9*, JAI Press, p. 177)

Why is the concept of changing people relevant for SEAM as an OD resource? Well, SEAM is a tool that considers that the people make the changes to the organization. Process-wise, the SEAM models an action research approach of (1) an Intervention that is a whole systems approach, (2) Teaching Leaders about the SEAM approach, and (3) Coaching leaders through change (Conbere & Heorhiadi, 2015). As one can see, the focus here is on helping the people make the change by teaching and coaching until the completion of the process. Thus, this system of changing systems accounts from the beginning that people change the organization and build it into the steps for change.

2 CHANGES THE ENTIRE SYSTEM

What is most important is that the SEAM approach takes the client where they are at the present state and manages the change for the people step by step with encouraging help to succeed in the future state. All the people in the organization who receive this teaching and coaching are not just the top managers. In the SEAM theory, the core to making an organization better is developing the people (Conbere & Heorhiadi, 2015). When people grow, they are more engaged and more willing to provide their knowledge and ideas to make the organization stronger. The concept of human potential is integral to OD as well as SEAM.

3 EVERYONE TAUGHT SYSTEMS THINKING

As I have mentioned, SEAM is a system-wide approach to change in the organization, and this idea is central in OD thinking. SEAM also recognizes the OD concepts of systems thinking to help the organization learn (Senge, 1990). Here the individual asks how my behavior or a change in my area affects other parts of the organization. SEAM sees poor management as a potential dysfunction in the organization (Conbere & Heorhiadi, 2015). In this system approach, SEAM teaches managers to become better at managing people. Becoming a better manager and thinking about how my management and people influence the entire organization's success is a hallmark of systems thinking and solid OD practice. Managers and supervisors get little coaching on management tools, let alone interpersonal communication and conflict resolution in their lives. There is no guarantee that people have encountered this learning in their education. Consultants take for granted that they are familiar with the latest techniques in leading people. One of SEAMs goals is to train and sometimes retrain leaders on these fundamental skills to help people realize that what they do with their group does influence other groups and, ultimately, the organization's strategic running.

4 ALL THE STORIES HEARD

Because people are so valuable to the SEAM process, everyone describes the present organization to the consultants! As OD practitioners, we know and understand the value of collecting stories in a diagnosis to help get a quick snapshot of the organization now. One of the greatest advocates of story understanding is David Boje (Boje & Rosile, 2003). According to David Boje (2016) "Dialectic Storytelling" is integral to the SEAM process. What does dialectic storytelling mean? It is the ability to view stories from multiple perspectives and incorporate them into a reasonable representation of contradicting information. Dialectic, itself is seeing two opposing things as being true at once. For example, when two blind people touch an elephant, the one from the front says it is a sizeable thick snake; and one at the side says it is a large wall with a rough texture. Both these statements are contradictory but valid at the same time. Consultants that collect contradictory stories understand the richness of the present state of the system.

All the stories are helpful to aid in weaving the picture of the organization at that time. The more different the stories, the better the representation of "truth." In the SEAM method, positive and negative stories are collected not to evaluate the organization but to gather a deeper understanding. This process takes the first month with many practitioner consultants listening and gathering the stories from all organizational aspects (Boje, 2016). The "negative" stories are not deficits within SEAM but ways to discover positive untapped human potential trapped within the stories. The facilitator captures and analyzes how all perspectives paint a picture of what might be "truth." We know as change practitioners that there is no absolute "truth" but only a compilation of many people's understanding of the company at that time. These stories can reveal what SEAM states as costs or untapped human potential.

5 TYING TO THE BOTTOM LINE

These untapped human potentials or dysfunctions can cost the company huge amounts of money! SEAM closely uncovers, analyzes, and eliminates these costs to the bottom line that many OD interventions do not examine. What are these costs? These are the dysfunctions (Boje, 2016) that SEAM uncovers:

- *Working Conditions Themes*—lack performance evaluation, too much work, lack of reward, and no backup
- *Work Organization Themes*—lack of empowerment, top-down influence, and lack of networking of teams
- *3 Cs* (Communication, Coordination & Cooperation)—poor customer relations, and bad reputation, leaders at odds
- *Time Themes*—late delivery and wasted time on the wrong stuff.
- *Integrated Training Themes*—no formal training, lack of quality training, and lack of customer service training
- *Strategic Implementation*—no strategic plan and trial and error learning

These dysfunctions lead to what Savall calls Hidden Costs (Cappelletti, Voyant, Savall & Noguera, 2018). These costs are invisible to management because an income statement or balance sheet does not show them. Thus, the company's dysfunctions lead to unknown costs, for example, absenteeism, occupational injuries, staff turnover, lack of quality in production, productivity gaps, and many more (Boje, 2016). These expenses are driven by the deep-seated root causes such as excess salaries, over time, overconsumption, non-production, non-creation of potential, and risks. The root causes and hidden costs are imperceptible, and the dysfunctions of the organization show the invisible issues. It takes trained observers and analyzing all the stories by skilled professionals to discover these obscure problems. How much do these unknown issues cost an organization? There are over ~~1,300~~ 2,000 interventions carried out since 1973 (Conbere & Heorhiadi, 2015), and here (Table 57.1) an example of average hidden costs per industry.

As you can see by this table, these are expensive costs to organizations and, more importantly, affect any organization's bottom line. SEAM is the practice that can discover and

TABLE 57.1 Average Hidden Costs in 1991

Sector	Sector of Activity	Per Person per Year Costs
Industry	Electronics	$60,000
	Metallurgy	$23,400
	Glassworks	$46,400
	Household Appliances	$15,600
	Agro-food	$14,300
	Bank	$22,100
Services	Telecommunications Maintenance	$20,800
	Municipal Government	$10,400
	Major Distribution	$11,700

Source: Conbere, J., & Heorhiadi, A. (2015). Why the socio-economic approach to management remains a well-kept secret. *OD Practitioner,* p. 32.

eliminate these invisible costs to the bottom line—an advantage for any change leader who cares for financial improvement and human growth. The exposure and savings of these costs lead to the sustainability of the system.

6 SOCIALLY RESPONSIBLE CAPITALISM

SEAM is a socially responsible approach to improve companies socially and economically within the system. The idea of sustainable development is a long-term goal because SEAM emphasizes the people's development to build the organization. The changes in the structures and external influences drive these changes but are needed for the system's survival (Savall, 2017). Sustainable development coincides with and is integral to social responsibility. Management that supports sustainable development solves both short and long-term overall and holistic processes for both the employees and the organization. SEAM measures both profitability and the profitability of measuring investment into human potential. The integration of individuals, teams, and whole organization allows for the survival of the system. Thus, this approach builds an economic system that will last through building an intrinsic individual and collective responsibility for sustainability. SEAM (Savall, 2017) places human potential at the center to produce economic value and anthropological values. The individual's entrepreneurship, freedom to produce through democracy, respect for everyone's freedom, dignity, personal and collective development, and the taming of technology are the values that create sustainability. Developing the individuals to think sustainably, in turn, creates a sustainable organization.

7 HYBRID MODEL OF CONSULTING

From the previous section of economic hidden costs and sustainable development through human potential learning, this approach relies on a combination of expert, doctor, and process consulting skills for the facilitator (Schein, E, 1969, 1987). An expert consultant tells the people what to do and how to do it. A process consultant focuses on the client and the consultant's interaction to allow the client to develop the solution. The doctor's approach is to listen to the client's problems and diagnose the system's root cause. SEAM uses all three consulting techniques to produce high quality within the system. In addition to using these consulting tools, this approach weaves in action research as a methodology to understand the organization in the various stages as the change occurs (McSweeney, 2000). The use of these methodologies of ODC makes SEAM a hybrid model for creating change (Savall, A, Preston, Henderson, and Boje, in press). A combination of methodologies gives the consultant more information to assess the situation, modify it, and intervene effectively.

CONCLUSION

Throughout my many years as a global consultant, I have always been a generalist. I use the best technique for the system and the client at that time. I am not against having one methodology to sell to clients, but one method does not work in every instance. I read about and learn as many methods as I can so that when the time comes that I can apply a particular method or theory appropriately. SEAM is one of those techniques that shows versatility and is one of the only methods confronting the issue of financial issues in ODC. It is not a panacea for all systems. Even Henri Savall carefully chooses the organizations for SEAM (Conbere & Heorhiadi, 2015).

Because of all the concepts that I have explained in this chapter, I strongly advocate that more practitioners in ODC and change leaders become aware of the value of the SEAM methodology to an organization. SEAM is not self-explanatory, so change leaders need help, training, and supervision to use SEAM effectively. While in the present change leaders consistently overlook SEAM! I hope this book and specifically this chapter will make this approach more visible and more widely used in the future.

REFERENCES

Bechard, R., & Harris, R. T. (1987). *Organization transitions: Managing complex change* (2nd ed.). Addison Wesley.

Boje, D., & Rosile, G. A. (2003). Comparison of socio-economic and other transorganizational development methods. *Journal of Organizational Change Management, 16*(1), 10–20.

Boje, D. (2016). Storytelling dialectical method and the failure of Appreciative Inquiry as a scientific method of organization development and change. Paper given at the *International conference and doctoral consortium* June 9–10, Lyon, France.

Cappelletti, L., Voyant, O., Savall, H., & Noguera, F. (2018). 40 years of socio-economic approach to management (SEAM): What we know and where we go? Paper given at the *Academy of Management,* Chicago, IL.

Conbere, J., & Heorhiadi, A. (2015). Why the socio-economic approach to management remains a well-kept secret. *OD Practitioner,* 31–37.

McSweeny, B. (2000). 'Action research': Mission impossible? Commentary on "Towards the increased use of action research in accounting information systems" by Richard C. Baker. *Accounting Forum, 24*(4), 379–390.

Preston, J.C., DuToit, L., & Barber, I. (1996). A potential model of transformational change applied to South Africa. In Woodman & Pasmore (Eds). *Research in Organizational Change and Development. 9,* JAI Press, 175–200.

Savall, A., Preston, J., Henderson, T., & Boje, D. (in press 2021). How storytelling can make a difference in SEAM and other consulting approaches. in A. Savall (Ed). *Business Storytelling of Socioeconomics.* World Scientific Publishing Co Pte Ltd.

Savall, H. (2017). Macroeconomic roots and fundamentals of the socio-economic approach to management. *The Theory and Practice of Socio-Economic Management*, *2*(1), 1–27.

Schein, E. M. (1969). *Process consultation: Its role in organization development.* Addison Wesley Publishing Company.

Schein, E. M. (1987). *Process consultation*: Vol II. Addison Wesley Publishing Company.

Senge, R. M. (1990). *The fifth disciple.* Doubleday/Currency.

CHAPTER 58

ORGANIZATIONAL THEORY EARLY DEVELOPMENTS

Locating the Seeds of Socio-Economic Approach to Management (SEAM)

Richard Baker and Bruno Cohanier

ABSTRACT

Using an organization theory historic approach, the purpose of this chapter is to provide evidence that the seeds of the Socio-Economic Approach to Management (SEAM) were laid as early as the seminal work on motivation at the workplace of the Human Relations School in the 1920's. The main objective of this chapter is to show that SEAM contributes to tackle the reconciliation problem of the social and economic sides of business management which the Human Relations School failed to address properly and was subsequently criticized for.

The purpose of this chapter is to provide evidence that the seeds of the Socio-Economic Approach to Management (Savall, 974, 1981, 2003a, 2007; Buono & Savall, 2007; Savall & Zardet, 1987, 2008) which aims at improving an organization's socio-economic performance by reconciling the financial and social sides of management, were laid with the early works of the Human Relations School (HRS) in the 1930's with the significant difference that SEAM succeeded in addressing issues for which the HRS was unsuccessful.

Accordingly, we will first articulate the story of organization theories which emerged since the beginning of the 20th by providing the reader with a summary of Gruère's introduction and description of a matrix tool from a famous collective book entitled *Management, Aspects humains et organisationnels* (Aubert et al. 1991, 2010). We will then articulate the theoretical content of the different perspectives of this matrix from 1900 until 1960. This will lead to

SEAM Treatise, pages 495–501

finally demonstrate that the characteristics of SEAM which rely on the compatibility between social and economic performance were introduced by the transition from Classical School's "Directive Management" to the ideas initiated by the theoreticians of the HRS.

1 UNDERSTANDING OF THE EVOLUTION OF THEORIES OF ORGANIZATION

In an attempt to provide a global framework for the understanding of the evolution of theories of organization, Aubert et al. started to publish a study of the human and organizational aspects of management entitled *Management, Aspects humains et organisationnels* in 1991. In their 9th edition dated 2010, the authors have kept an interesting matrix largely inspired by the work of Stanford Professor Richard Scott published in 1981 under the title: *Organizations: rational, natural and open systems.* The purpose of this tool was to help practitioners and researchers who sought to clarify and improve the functioning of organizations by offering a meaningful story of the evolution of the various organizational models produced since the 1900's until the 1980's.

With reference to Scott's analysis, the structure of this matrix was to sort, and place theoretical developments produced successively or simultaneously by theoreticians/practitioners in an insightful manner on two axes explained in Figure 58.1.

These two axes translate "binary alternatives which, by successive sets, make it possible to locate modes of work organization and their theoretical currents attached" (Aubert et al. 2010, p. 15).

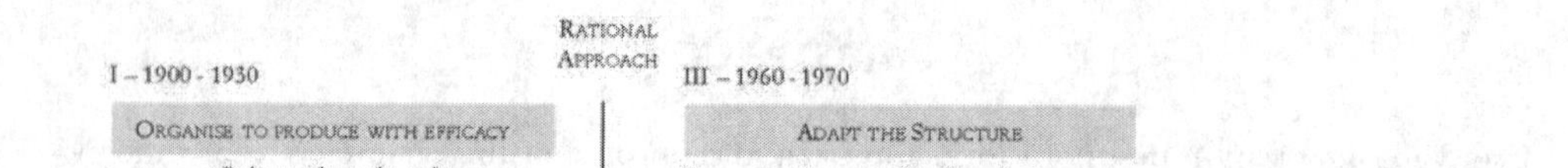

Figure 58.1 Organizational theories evolution matrix. *Source:* Revised and augmented from Aubert et al. (1991, 2010), *Management, Aspects humains et organisationnels,* P.U.F., p. 17

The matrix designed by Aubert et al. presents a vertical axis ranging from a rational to a social approach of how an organization is structured and operates: two exclusive yet interdependent dimensions of management. The rational approach edge of this axis is focused on technical and economic results through job rationalization. The dynamics of the social edge is concerned with the satisfaction and the motivation of the staff, with the search for a productive compromise. In other words, "while on the rational side the determination of objectives is obvious and the objectives arise from routine choices, on the social side, organization decisions are dictated by social arrangements, power relations, multiple influences, or norms" (Aubert et al., 2010, p. 16; Scott, 1981).

The horizontal axis is inspired by systems theory. At its left (i.e., before the '60s), a closed system describes autonomous and self-sufficient organizations. Leaders are mainly focused on the management of internal arrangements and their interrelations to maximize resource usage acting "as if the environment did not matter or at least not considering external variables as a priority" (Aubert et al. 2010, p. 16). At the right edge, the open system corresponds to the years after 1960. This perspective acknowledges that the internal dynamics of an organization is influenced by external elements (i.e., economic, cultural, social, technological, legal and political environment, etc...). This edge leaves behind the mechanical conception of the organization for an open and systemic one, which takes into account interdependencies. In other words, two-way interactions as well as the need to control as much as possible the environmental forces which shape the survival and development of organizations are vital (Aubert et al., 2010 p. 17; Scott, 1981).

2 ARTICULATING THE THEORETICAL CONTENT OF THE DIFFERENT PERSPECTIVES OF THE TOOL FROM 1900 UNTIL 1960

Using the storyline suggested by Scott (1981, 2003), the outcome of the Aubert et al. (2010) matrix representation displays two axes highlighting four areas. In coherence with the argument of this chapter, we will briefly describe the two first ones to chronologically provide a storyline unfolding organizational theories' development between 1900 and 1960.

2.1 Zone I: Closed System, Rational Approach

At the top left of the matrix starts a period which lasts approximately 30 years. Its most famous authors are Taylor, Fayol and Weber. They formalized the main ideas of the start of the industrial era centered on the North American industrial context. "Organize to produce with efficacy" is the title Aubert et al. (2010) have chosen to summarize the main aims and means of theories belonging to Zone I. According to the tenets of the Classic School, an organization is a "rational tool which serves clearly specified ends." Accordingly, authors suggest a "scientific" model of organization which allows companies to work in the best interests of stakeholders (e.g., Taylor's vertical division of labor putting "the right man at the right place" to perform tasks entrusted to managers and the ones devolved to performers who are told with great precision the "one best way" to perform their job). The organization is centralized and pyramidal, the production follows standardized procedures (Aubert et al., 2010, p. 18; Scott, 1981; Chandler, 1962, 1977).

Fayol sets out his military inspired "administrative principles" on which "any effective management of organizations should be based." Starting from the top of the hierarchy to reach the base, the management of men should be governed by authority and discipline and should follow "a directive process based on the division of labor, hierarchy and centralization." Any organization "will be better administered if there is a unit of command and a fair principle of staff compensation." According to Zone I theoreticians, this is a perfect fit because workers are supposed to be motivated by a rational system of salary based on a direct cause and effect link between the effort provided by the employee and the remuneration obtained which therefore is considered transparent and fair. In other words, leaders whose natural authority is essential, and executors who well understand their interest, both accept the rule of the game. No one in the organization can obviously disagree with this "one good scientific way of doing things." Hence, the rationality of the administrative principles must be imposed on all, if not self-imposed. Subsequently no more possible conflict can arise, and the efficiency of the organization can be maximized (Aubert et al., 2010, p. 19; Scott, 1981).

The third member of the tryptic, Weber, suggests the bureaucratic model of organization. It relies on explicit operating procedures which justify the concept of "authority" where rules are the common reference for all workers: "rule controls order." In other words: it is the control of a precise set of rules and techniques along with the consistency of authority and responsibilities which can solve management problems.

In this perfect and rational dreamworld where goals are known and tasks are circumscribed and repetitive, organizational change dynamics soon showed that scientific management downplayed the influence of informal phenomena and environmental forces. This, according to the matrix of Aubert et al. opened the way to the opposite organizational approach realizing with Herbert Simon that rationality was actually bounded.

2.2 Zone II: Closed System, Social Approach

Located at the bottom left of the matrix, Zone II covers the period between 1930 and 1960 still in the United States. This is a period marked by the economic crisis of 1929 which contributed to change some (Taylorian) men at work perspectives. Aubert et al. illustrate Taylorian era with the example of 1936's Charlie Chaplin's Modern Times showing a factory worker employed on an assembly line being force-fed by a faulty "feeding machine" where he screws nuts at an ever-increasing pace onto pieces of machinery, ultimately leading him to a nervous breakdown. This part of the movie reflects the consequences of rationalization which not only did not bear fruit, but caused unforeseen effects, such as absenteeism, turnover and braking. In reaction to these adverse effects, theoreticians of the HRS tried to give it a human face: some researchers started to undertake experiments in the workplace (e.g., Mayo at the Hawthorne plant on behalf of Western Electric). However, Zone II still belongs to the closed system part of the matrix because studies undertaken used "an average individual who was more like an average American" (Aubert et al., 2010, p. 20; Scott, 1981). This means that even if the tenants of the School have demonstrated the emergence of informal structures, the interpersonal power systems, the importance of status, communications, how informal structures influence formal systems, all being vital to understand the functioning of organizations, human behavior is considered quite predictable and if/when well-arranged should rationally and logically lead to organizational performance.

3 FROM "DIRECTIVE MANAGEMENT" TO HRS PROPOSITIONS: THE PREMISE OF THE SOCIO-ECONOMIC APPROACH TO MANAGEMENT'S SOCIAL AND ECONOMIC PERFORMANCE RECONCILIATION

Aubert et al. (2010, p. 20) stress the importance of contributions of the HRS theoreticians (e.g., McGregor, Maslow and Herzberg) who showed that men had complex motivations and did not react solely to materialism. Certain "intrinsic" motivations (e.g., participation in decisions and responsibilities, task enrichment, etc.) could lead to qualitative and quantitative performance which are superior to those obtained by the increase in controls and sanctions (i.e., the carrot and the stick). With Lewin and his colleagues underlining the importance of group dynamics (e.g., showing the advantage of the democratic style compared to other management styles), the notion of "group" became something more than the sum of its members leading the way to open systems conceptions of organizations of Zone III.

Despite its contributions, the HRS has been partially distrusted for different reasons articulated below (Aubert et al., 2010, p. 22). However, we argue that the transition from "Directive Management" (i.e., Zone I) to the HRS principles described above (i.e., Zone II), laid the early grounds for SEAM's objective to improve a company social and economic performance (Savall, 1974, 1981). These seeds were planted as early as the HRS started to formalize its work in the 1930's. We argue that the intervention research features of SEAM ensured its success on two main issues which the HRS was not able to tackle and was subsequently criticized for:

a. HRS theoreticians were not successful in their attempt to prove the existence of a clear relationship between leadership style and the conception of men at work on one side and worker productivity and organizational efficiency on the other;
b. The theories of HRS, like many of others identified in the matrix were built in reaction/ response/ aggregation to former theories. In that sense, HRS was able to contribute to some "humanization" of "professional-so-far-rational" circles but was criticized for going too far in its tendency to reduce organizational problems to individual psychological problems (i.e., "psychologism") overlooking the importance of formal organizational structures (Aubert et al., 2010, p. 21).

The SEAM intervention research approach actually tackles both critics listed above. Inspired by the seminal work of Germán Bernácer (1916, 1918, 1922), and evidenced by many articles and case studies arguing that social performance and management quality both strongly contribute to an organization's economic performance (Schuler & Jackson, 1987; Wright et al., 1994; Pfeffer, 2005 and Sanz-Valle et al., 1999), the fundamental proposition upon which it is based suggests the compatibility between social and economic performance (Savall, 1974; Savall & Zardet, 1987).

SEAM intervention research protocol is based on the Socio-Economic Theory which states that "the main factor of efficiency is the human development of the company. In any company, there are social, economic and financial losses due to dysfunctions linked to the interaction between company structures and human behavior. These dysfunctions are evidenced by anomalies, errors, disturbances and are expressed in the difference between the desired and the actual operations. They result in atrophy of the economic and social performance of each company and organization because the economic and social performance of an organization depends on the quality of the interaction of the structures of the organization and behavior of the men who act within this organization" (Savall, 1978; Savall & Zardet, 1989).

Departing from Lewin's (1947) unfreeze-change-freeze model, the process of intervention research alternates periods in the field with periods of withdrawal and analysis. The periods in the field lead to interpretations. Organizational practices are observed over time in order to follow their natural evolution and evaluate the effects of changes which are introduced (Savall, 1974, 1981; Savall & Zardet, 1987; Savall, Zardet, Bonnet, 2000; Buono, Savall, Cappelletti, 2018). In the second cycle of the intervention research there is a formulation of hypotheses, which are validated by a second immersion period. The alternation between periods leads to building reliable knowledge by sedimentation of facts (Miles & Huberman, 1984; Yin, 1989; Strauss & Corbin, 1990). By uncovering dysfunctions and their associated hidden costs, this type of intervention research both shows that worker's productivity is tied to leadership style (critic a. of the HRS) while not falling into the individual "psychologism" trap (critic b. of the HRS).

4 LIMITATIONS AND CONCLUSIONS:

The matrix shaped by Aubert et al. (2010) is useful to articulate the evolution of different succeeding or overlapping theories. It is of course not exhaustive nor exempt from shortcomings (e.g., it is mostly North American centric, and it does not foresee an exit after Zone IV). Yet, one of its advantages is that it shows that the evolution of these theories largely depends on the unfolding of historical moments. For this reason, we concur with Aubert et al. (2010, p. 26) that "to fully understand the theories, it is necessary to explore their genesis, to identify the axioms on which their logic is based, and to place them in their initial context. Science and ideology indeed maintain permanent relationships. Theorists seem to have often followed the dominant representations of their time and helped to formalize them. Each has worked to bring new light to evolving realities. It is as if the contributions of the researchers had enabled the widening of the field of vision of the practitioners. These have taken a step back by gradually integrating elements of reality that have been forgotten or overlooked. It is their view of the world that has been transformed and enriched according to the problems to be solved. Because they could no longer always explain or master events, they amended certain theoretical principles or abandoned them in favor of others deemed more relevant to support the change."

The HRS was highly criticized, among other things, for not being able to prove that its conception of men at work was clearly related to productivity and organizational efficiency. The SEAM intervention research protocol articulated above highlights this link by nature and facts. The theories of the HRS like many others were built over time as a binary response to former ones and as such were subsequently criticized for concentrating too much on individual psychology overlooking the importance of dimensions such as formal structures, the sociological and political components of organizations. This led to the ultimate criticism of the HRS which states that it considers the organizational system closed in on itself, according to open system and socio-technical approach (Emery & Trist, 1960). Once again, it is a criticism that SEAM easily overcomes because the nature of its intervention research protocol is to improve organizations by fostering the compatibility between social and economic performance.

The SEAM intervention research protocol is an effective and well accepted methodology for changing and improving organizations. It gathers the reconciliation characteristics promoted by tenants of the HRS which contributed to the advancement of theory and practice by departing from the Classical School paradigm. It has a cost in terms of both researcher and managerial effort which is largely out weighted by the contribution to knowledge and practice it delivers if one recognizes that organization science is a "crossroad work in progress" juxtaposing paradigms (Aubert et al., 2010, p. 14), each pertaining to a specific discipline where none has succeeded yet in gaining undisputed favor among the scientific and practitioner community.

REFERENCES

Aubert N., Gruère J.P., Jabes J., Laroche H., and Enlart S. (1991, 2010). *Management, aspects humains et organisationnels,* Paris, P.U.F.

Bernácer, G. (1916). *Sociedad y felicidad. Ensayo de mecánica social.*2ª edición 2015, Publicacions Universitat de Alacant.

Bernácer, G. (1918). Las monedas y las cuestiones sociales. *Revista Nacional de Economía:* 31.

Bernácer, G. (1922). La teoría de las disponibilidades, como interpretación de las crisis y del problema social. *Revista Nacional de Economía* (40), 47–72.

Buono, A., and Savall, H. (2007). *Socio-Economic Intervention in Organizations. The Intervener-Researcher and the Seam Approach to Organizational Analysis,* Charlotte, NC: Information Age Publishing.

Buono, A., Savall, H., & Cappelletti (ed.), (2018). *Intervention Research: from conceptualization to Publication.* Charlotte, NC: Information Age Publishing.

Miles, M. D., and Huberman, A. M. (1984). *Qualitative data analysis: A sourcebook of new methods.* Beverly Hills, CA: SAGE.

Pfeffer, J. (2005). Producing sustainable competitive advantage through the effective management of people. *Academy of Management Executive,* 19(4), 95–104 (reprinted from 1995, 9(1)).

Sanz-Valle, R., Sabatier-Sanchez, R., and Aragon-Sanchez, A. (1999). Human resource management and business strategy links: An empirical study. *The International Journal of Human Resource Management,* 10(4), 655–671.

Schuler, R.S., and Jackson, S. (1987). Linking Competitive Strategies with Human Resource Management Practices. *The Academy of Management Executive,* 1(3), 207–219.

Scott R.W. (1981, 2003). *Organizations: Rational, Natural and Open Systems.* Englewood Cliffs, N.J: Prentice Hall.

Strauss, A., and Corbin, J. M. (1990). *Basics of qualitative research: Grounded theory procedures and techniques.* Sage Publications, Inc.

Wright, P. M., Mac Mahan, G. C., and Mac Williams, A. (1994). Human resources and sustained competitive advantage: A resource-based perspective. *International Journal of Human Resource Management,* 5(2), 301–326.

Yin, R. K. (1989). *Case study research: Design and methods.* London: Sage Publications.

CHAPTER 59

NEGOTIATED COMMITMENT

A Key to Continous Improvement in the Chinese Companies That Have Adopted LEAN Management

Jean Ruffier and Ziyuan Tang

ABSTRACT

Ignorance of the defect of the socio-technical approach causes a general failure of Human Resources Management practices in Chinese companies. The submission paradigm is a real hindrance to increasing the performance of enterprises. Based on a case of socio-economic intervention-research carried out in a Chinese factory that has adopted LEAN, this chapter aims to highlight the relevance of the paradigm of negotiated commitment in the development of employee motivation in the search for continuous improvement and to confirm the motivational effect of the Periodically Negotiable Activity Contract.

Over the past forty years, the pace of introduction of modern managerial approaches has been steadily increasing in Chinese companies. However, our observation shows that Chinese companies that have adopted LEAN management have difficulty in continuously improving their performance. The purpose of this chapter is first to explain the causes of this difficulty, and then to position the concept of negotiated commitment, derived from socio-economic theory (Savall 1974, 1979; Savall and Zardet, 1987), as a managerial philosophy that enables companies to develop employee motivation in the search for continuous improvement. We take this opportunity to illustrate the motivational effect of the Periodically Negotiable Activity Contract by means of this case of socio-economic intervention-research carried out within a company practicing LEAN management in China.

SEAM Treatise, pages 503–508

1 KAIZEN, A BREAK OF TAYLORIZATION

LEAN is generally perceived by managers of industrial companies as one of the most relevant managerial approaches to increase the operational performance of the company. The principle of LEAN consists in continuously improving the economic performance of the organization (Womack and Jones, 1996). It is generally based on the implementation of KAIZEN (continuous improvement) (Liker and Hoseurs, 2008). The latter aims to make each employee aware of his or her responsibility, authority and freedom to make improvements at his or her level (Imai, 1986). According to our previous observations, the adoption of LEAN enables Chinese companies to achieve immediate growth in economic performance. However, sustainable growth in economic performance is difficult to maintain. KAIZEN is often at odds with the management methods usually used in China. From our experiences in these companies, we find that, on the one hand, employees rarely support improvements when they are top-down, and, on the other hand, the motivation of employees to make improvements at their level is very low.

Based on Shah and Ward (2003) who consider LEAN as an integrated socio-technical system, we believe that the performance growth of LEAN organizations is mainly due to two factors: (1) the instrumental concepts of LEAN; (2) HRM practices aimed at involving each employee, while respecting LEAN requirements. Indeed, contemporary developers of the socio-technical approach, initiated by Emery and Trist, emphasize the need to combine these HRM practices with the instrumental concepts of LEAN (Sawheny and Chason, 2005). The socio-technical stream has done a lot of work on identifying HRM practices that are conducive to LEAN adoption, productivity increase and incremental innovation. Unfortunately, this research hardly explains the link between the technical system and the social system, nor the conditions for motivating employees to become involved in the KAIZEN approach. Furthermore, the authors of these research studies are silent on the fact that the socio-technical approach does not in any way challenge the submission paradigm. This silence is a kind of godsend, particularly in China: it gives managers the illusion of modernizing and internationalizing their management, while allowing them to keep a directive mode of operation, considered archaic by most modern management thinkers. Taylorism has made it possible to integrate new categories of personnel into industrial production: once this integration has been achieved, it becomes a brake on the increase in the performance of companies, in that it blocks the true involvement of workers. Someone who wants to do something and knows how to do it will always be more efficient than someone who only moves according to the orders given to him. But accepting to rely on the autonomous will of employees implies abandoning a separation between conception and action, i.e., engaging in forms of Human Resource Management involving consultation and cooperation, which seems difficult in contemporary Chinese factories.

2 FROM THE PARADIGM OF SUBMISSION TO THE PARADIGM OF NEGOTIATED COMMITMENT

Companies aiming at LEAN while refusing KAIZEN do not exist only in China. Their management practices a form of schizophrenia, expecting a continuous improvement that would automatically follow from the adoption of HRM practices known to be "relevant" to motivate employees, while not granting them sufficient autonomy to make these practices work. In China, this tendency can go to the extreme of setting up a form of negotiation, while prohibiting any expression other than that of management (Ruffier 2015). It is therefore not surprising that management in these companies cannot rely on the active involvement of subordinates in the process.

The results of our successive works (Tang and Ruffier, 2019) show that Chinese employees are aware of the flaws of the submission paradigm: the adoption of LEAN causes an increase in work stress, a reduction in their autonomy, a depersonalization of tasks, a limitation of the skills used, etc. (Savall and Zardet, 2015). The impact of these defects on Chinese employees' motivation is considerable and employees become wary of any change. As a result, employees' resistance to submission is strong: they refuse to implement or support improvement actions imposed by company management, to report problems, to offer suggestions, to pass on their experience and know-how, believing that this might worsen their working conditions or job security (Tang, 2019). On the other hand, in the cases studied, the employee is able to consciously identify his needs and make demands on the level and duration of rewards. He is also able to modify his productivity when he perceives an imbalance between contribution and reward. The submission paradigm cannot guarantee a level of employee productivity (Tang, 2019).

In contrast to the submission paradigm, socio-economic theory proposes the negotiated commitment paradigm that leads to personalization in the work relationship (Savall, Péron, Zardet, & Bonnet, 2015). Negotiated commitment appears as a managerial philosophy adapted to the continuous improvement of the overall performance of companies. This managerial philosophy recognizes the existence of spontaneous organizational disobedience and argues that, through negotiation, it is possible to obtain from employees a genuine commitment to performance improvement. Commitments made by the company can be seen as the key factor in developing employee motivation to improve performance. The implementation of the negotiated commitment is based on the development of the Periodically Negotiable Performance Contract (PNPC), which helps to establish a negotiation between the employee and his or her direct supervisor, enabling them to reach an agreement on the improvement objectives, the means necessary to achieve the objectives, the rewards to be given to the employee, and the evaluation and control measures. As mentioned earlier, employees are demanding of the fairness of the reward/contribution ratio. The employee's perception of the fairness of this ratio is personal and subjective. Therefore, there is no management system that is relevant to everyone. The PNAC makes it possible to adapt the organization to the perception of each employee, by making choices that are relevant to both the employee and his or her manager. The sanction/reward system will work all the more effectively if it is seen by all as allowing both management and employees to act according to their perception of what is desirable.

3 CONTRIBUTION OF THE PERIODICALLY NEGOTIATED ACTIVITY CONTRACT TO EMPLOYEE MOTIVATION FOR CONTINUOUS IMPROVEMENT

Our latest intervention-research was conducted at an aeronautical company in northeast China (Tang, 2019), which specializes in machining and painting the body parts of civil aircraft. It has been practicing a Chinese version of LEAN for a number of years. But, as seems to be common in China, its HRM methods proved to be contradictory to the principles of KAIZEN. The implementation of a real KAIZEN is a real problem for the company. We therefore proposed to the management an intervention-research in three main steps: (1) diagnosis interviews; (2) development of PNAC; (3) evaluation interviews. The results of this study show an effective contribution of the PNAC to a stronger involvement of the employees in the continuous improvement process (see Table 59.1).

TABLE 59.1 Economic Consequences of the Evolution of Continuous Improvement

Dysfunctioning	Unsuitable mounting equipement to new parts manufacturing	Lack of appropriate procedures for to provide mounting equipments	Delayed identification of flawed parts manufacturing	Outdated work instructions	Unsuitable equipment layout standards for manufacturing	Overall amount
Amount of hidden costs in February: (Yuan/day)	141.75	42	614.25	28.65	56.70	883.35
Amount of hidden costs in August: (Yuan/day)	47.25	0	614.25	19.09	28.35	708.94
Improvement (Yuan/day)	94.50	42	0	9.65	28.35	174.41

We explain these results by the combination of a better perception of managerial action, a greater interest of the employees in the results, the feeling of a greater justice in the ratio of remuneration/contribution, and, especially, their greater autonomy.

3.1 Giving Meaning to the Organization

For management and managers, the development of the Periodically Negotiable Activity Contract (PNAC) implies a commitment not to punish a person at the origin of a dysfunction. This allows for greater transparency for employees and a more open and calm discussion of the causes of these dysfunctions. In China, it is customary to punish the perpetrator of a dysfunction regardless of the reasons he or she gives for the action. The contrary is often considered as a proof of weakness of the authority. It goes without saying that this pushes the authors of these dysfunctions to hide them, which does not facilitate their reduction. As a result, the choice not to punish, but to look together for ways to overcome dysfunctions, is perceived by Chinese employees as a considerable opening: suddenly the organization appears to be conceived more as a means of obtaining performance than as a means of crushing employees. For the workers, the Periodically Negotiable Activity Contract constitutes a credible commitment by the company. Employees are faced with a less risky and more predictable future, particularly in terms of pay and job stability. This is what we call giving meaning to the organization.

3.2 Increasing Expectations

Expectation refers to the employee's perception of the probability of achieving a given goal when he or she makes an effort to do so. The employee's expectation is based on personal characteristics (competence, ability, experience and self-confidence, etc.) and the perceived difficulty of achieving the goal. We believe that the development of the PNAC gives each employee the opportunity to negotiate with their manager and to set goals that employees will think are more relevant if they seem achievable. The PNAC makes it possible to set rewards that employees want, at the cost of efforts that seem within their reach. Employees are more likely to act if they expect a reward that is worth the effort. At the same time, the development of the PNAC helps managers to have a better vision of employees' future attitudes, as well as to better anticipate whether or not continuous improvement objectives will be achieved. In this respect, the development of the PNAC reduces the uncertainty of planning.

3.3 Increasing Organizational Justice

The development of the PNAC involves employees in the decision-making process. They can accept, modify or reject what their manager proposes. In interviews, Chinese employees recognize the relevance of this approach. They expect more distributive justice from it. The interviews also showed that the feeling that some people are overly rewarded is very demotivating: by making the reward system contractual and transparent, the feeling of arbitrary decisions is reduced. Management, on the other hand, achieves better collective control, while reducing the possibility of playing one off against the other.

3.4 Developing Autonomy at Work

The development of the PNAC contributes to establishing a participatory process that involves the employee in decisions on improvements and in the choice of evaluation and control indicators. On this point, the development of the PNAC is considered by Chinese employees as a practice which, on the one hand, increases their freedom of action in the management of their activity and, on the other hand, contributes to developing the feeling of being the initiator of their action. They feel responsible for their own behavior. They come out of submission, which implies that they only move to follow specific orders.

However, in the absence of a commitment from management on the possible renewal of their employment contracts, employees refuse to work on the dysfunction whose economic consequence is the most important (see Table 59.1). They are aware that their skills are limited to the tasks they have learned: an increase in the interchangeability of employees is therefore likely to worsen their job security. In our view, it is the lack of decision-making capacity on the part of local management that limits the effects of the PNAC, even though these effects are already substantial.

This difficulty does not seem specific to this company. In China, only the Communist Party has the right to form organizations to express the interests of any social group. The party's mission is to improve the situation of the employees, but the choice of means is the business of the party and not of the employees. Negotiating rewards with groups of employees is therefore a delicate matter. The autonomy given to employees here corresponds to a desirable emancipation of the latter, provided that it is limited to the narrow framework of punctual improvements, with an obvious economic interest for the enterprise.

CONCLUSION

Numerous studies conducted by both Chinese and foreign researchers have shown that Chinese workers are becoming more educated, more demanding, and less likely to adhere to the paradigm of submission. Our work here confirms that the submission paradigm is no longer appropriate for the current generation of Chinese workers. The failure of LEAN companies to challenge the Taylorian organization explains their inability to commit to continuous improvement. In China, many companies are reluctant to opt for HRM practices that break away from a vertical decision-making mode. To achieve this requires a profound change in the thinking of Chinese managers, but also of Chinese theorists. It must be admitted that the dictatorial mode practiced by the governmental authorities, down to the lowest levels of society, is not facilitating here. But on the contrary, our study proves that it is possible and interesting for Chinese companies to engage in negotiated approaches, as in this case with the setting up of a Periodically Negotiable Activity Contract.

This approach constitutes for the Chinese employees, but also for their management, a rupture of course, but this rupture is likely to reduce the conflict within the Chinese companies, because it allows the employees and their hierarchy to agree on common productive objectives, as well as on the means to reach these objectives. The productivity reserves that could be unlocked here are considerable. In the same way, the changes in attitude implied by the generalization of managerial philosophies, such as the one presented here, seem to us to be more in line with the search for innovation specific to high-tech companies that this country is trying to promote.

REFERENCES

Emery, F. E., & Trist, E. L. (1969), *Socio-technical Systems,* in Systems Thinking, F.E. Emery, Penguin Books Ltd, Harmondsworth.

Imai, M. (1986), Kaizen: *The Key To Japan Competitive Success,* China Machine Press, 1st edition 2012 Chinese version, p1–28, 1st edition 1986.

Liker, J. K., & Hoseus, M. (2009), Human resource development in Toyota culture, *International Journal of Human Resources Development and Management,* 10(1), p34–50.

Ruffier, J. (2015), *Strikes in China: actors, development, work, In Froissart, C. Labour, social struggles and the regulation of capitalism in contemporary China,* Presses universitaires du Septentrion, p87–97.

Shah, R., & Ward, P. T. (2003), Lean manufacturing: context, practice bundles, and performance, *Journal of Operations Management,* 21(2), p129–149.

Sawhney, R., & Chason, S. (2005), Human behavior based exploratory model for successful implementation of Lean enterprise. *Performance Improvement Quarterly, 18*(2), 76–96.

Tang, Z. Y. (2019), *Motivating Chinese employees to implement people-oriented KAIZEN: intervention-research in a Chinese LEAN management practitioner company,* PhD thesis, University of Lyon.

Tang, Z. Y., & Ruffier, J. (2019), What destroys Chinese workers' motivation to implement people-oriented Kaizen in Chinese Lean management practitioner factories, *Symposium organized by the Academy of Management, Management Consulting division, ISEOR, IAE Lyon and Université Jean Moulin,* Lyon, June.

Womack, J. P., & Jones, D. T. (1996). *Lean thinking: Banish waste and create wealth in your corporation.* Simon and Schuster.

CHAPTER 60

THE IMPACT OF SOCIO-ECONOMIC INTERVENTION ON THE DEVELOPMENT OF AMBITION AND STRATEGIC IMPLEMENTATION IN A MEDIUM SIZE AND IN A SMALL COMPANY

Jérémy Salmeron and Carole Bousquet

ABSTRACT

The objective of this chapter is to show the effect induced by the implementation of a socio-economic intervention on the ambition, on the design and on the strategic implementation as well as on the development of strategic competences of very small and small businesses. Based on two intervention-research case studies, the chapter highlights a methodology and systems that make it possible to reduce dysfunctions linked to strategy and improve the performance of these companies.

Strategy is a vast subject, both in the academic and practitioner worlds. The literature around this concept abounds, but conducting a concrete analysis and finding solutions remains a challenge for many practitioners who wish to develop the performance of their organization.

Moreover, the French entrepreneurial fabric is mostly composed of Very Small Enterprises (VSEs) and Small and Medium-sized Enterprises (SMEs). There are nearly 4 million of them in France, generating 43% of the value added created and employing the majority of the workforce, i.e., 6.3 million people. While research in the fields of entrepreneurship, strategic

SEAM Treatise, pages 509–516

management and human resources management highlights the innovative and agile nature of these companies, too few researchers are interested in the mechanisms of strategic thinking and even less in the effects of its implementation. This is the starting point of our research. We draw on two cases of longitudinal intervention-research conducted between 2015 and 2020 in the Rhône-Alpes-Auvergne region: one in a general surgery practice and the other in a fruit and vegetable ripening company, two contrasting sectors, seemingly not subject to the throes of disruptive innovations and little investigated in management science.

This chapter focuses on the impact of formalizing a strategy on the development of the social and economic performance of an SME, as well as on the contribution of socio-economic intervention-research to business strategy, like an (almost) invisible hand. Finally, the sequencing of the development of strategic ambition is illuminated via a socio-economic management tool: the Internal and External Strategic Action Plan (Savall & Zardet, 1987, 1995).

How to increase the strategic ambition and implementation of an SME?

In the course of various intervention-researches, we have regularly observed significant gaps between the strategy of companies and the internal resources mobilized to implement it effectively and efficiently. These mismatches between strategic objectives and the results obtained, on the one hand, and between results obtained and resources mobilized, on the other hand, have an impact on the company's performance (Bousquet, 2018). The work of socio-economic theory has identified three types of strategic dysfunction (Savall, 1974; 1979; Savall and Zardet, 1987, 1995):

- A strategy that is *over-dimensioned* in relation to available resources, particularly in terms of skills
- A strategy that is *undersized* in relation to available resources
- A mismatch between strategy and resources due to a lack of strategic formalization and steering

The central hypothesis is the following: the support and the action provoked by an intervention-research stimulate the different phases of the strategy (analysis, choice and implementation) and make it possible to improve both the strategic ambition and realism of the company.

This chapter shows how to increase the realism (without seeking the stratosphere) of strategy while being ambitious, ambition being defined as the ability to project into a new desired and performing state, in terms of matching objectives to resources.

In a turbulent environment such as the one we live in, the company director is at the heart of a dilemma leading him sometimes to movement, sometimes to immobility, alternating sequences of exploration of new resources and sequences of exploitation of his resources. While it seems obvious that strategy is a driving force for the company's development, all too often this development takes place in reaction and not in anticipation. This injunction of the environment mainly affects the company manager who finds himself having to oscillate between strategic announcement and operational brake. By going back and forth during the life of the company, he/she understands that it is better to remain cautious about the direction to give to his company. As a result, the nature of strategic actions and their scope change and a gap develops between the stated ambition and the observed reality. This gap between expected and actual functioning constitutes a dysfunction (Savall, 1979).

By combining Porter's definition (1980, 1985) and the work of Henri Savall and Véronique Zardet (Savall, 1974, 1979; Savall & Zardet, 1987, 1995), we agree to define strategy as the setting and combination of social and economic objectives to be achieved in order to generate a sustainable competitive advantage, by identifying and allocating the internal resources necessary to achieve these objectives.

We present the contributions of the socio-economic diagnosis to highlight and formalize the real problems encountered by the company concerning its strategy, its strategic ambition and its implementation. Then, we show how the support mechanisms of socio-economic intervention-research allow for the improvement of organizational practices in order to formalize a strategy, identify the necessary time resources and competencies, and deploy an effective and efficient implementation. Finally, we present some concrete tools that have accompanied the significant results obtained by the two companies.

1 DYSFUNCTIONS RELATED TO THE FORMALIZATION AND IMPLEMENTATION OF THE STRATEGY

The two intervention-researches conducted by the ISEOR team between 2015 and 2020 are as follows:

The fruit and vegetable ripening company S. is a family business located in the French Rhône-Alpes region, with 40 employees and two distinct adjoining sites: a wholesale market, for a retail clientele, and the ripening company, for a large and medium-sized supermarket clientele. The intervention-research (Savall and Zardet, 1987) started in October 2015, with an integral socio-economic diagnosis, followed by a focus group and in-depth coaching on strategic and managerial issues until the end of 2018. At the same time, management and supervisors were trained in socio-economic management and its tools. Management committee meetings and personalized assistance to the management have allowed to outline an internal-external strategic action plan from the first year, before leading to a strategy formalized in the form of a IESAP and multiplied in Priority Action Plans for the wholesale market and ripening sites.

The surgical practice P. is made up of 19 people: seven surgeons, an administrative manager, eight medical secretaries and four operating room nurses, spread over two sites for interventions and consultations. The surgeons operate in two different clinics, located about 100 kilometers apart. At the start of the intervention in 2018, the practice benefited from a miniaturization of the socio-economic approach to management: a full socio-economic diagnosis, a focus group and personalized accompaniment, with collaborative training actions for the management team pooled with other liberal professions structures (Savall, 2003).

During the socio-economic diagnosis, we collected the actors' expressions on the dysfunctions they observed and experienced in their daily work. We selected the dysfunctions relating to strategy from the nomenclature produced by one of the authors (Table 60.1). The table summarizes the problems identified, illustrated for the sample sentences expressed during the socio-economic diagnostic interviews.

In summary, in each organization, the strategy is not formalized and is, in fact, reactive. The decisions taken by managers are mostly made in reaction to a phenomenon (internal or external) in their environment. Concentrated in the head of the leader, the strategic actions decided upon take little account of internal and external clients-suppliers, whether it be the medical practice or the ripening plant. Vulnerable resources, especially strategic competencies, are perceived, but not followed by specific actions to remedy them. Similarly, strategic threats are identified but the strategy is not formalized, which considerably reduces decision-making in the short, medium or long term.

Both managers express difficulties in making strategic decisions. The fear of the "wrong choice" becomes paralyzing, increased by the isolation of the leader: as the strategy is not

TABLE 60.1 Main Strategic Roadblocks Mentioned by Organizations (according to Bousquet's classification, 2018)

Themes	Key Ideas	Ripening company	Surgery office
Choice of formalization of the company strategy	Lack of clearly defined strategy	"Strategy is not clear or defined for the ripening nor for the market and for the company at large" (Manager)	"I have information of the short term strategy, but I think that information is not sufficient for all"
	Deficiency in client-supplier cooperation	"I don't meet enough with wholesalers and semi-wholesalers. I would need a time budget for that" (Top management)	There is a relationship between the MD and the surgeon. In case we reject a patient three times in a row, he won't send us patients any more"
	Weaknesses on strategic competences	"In for or five years, we'll have to replace some managers. Therefore, we have to plan it in advance. You can't train them within one year for such positions." (Managers)	Not evaluated during the socio-economic diagnosis
	Strategic threats	"the problem is that society is changing. Relations with clients are difficult and our clients are different even though our working methods are the same" (Top management)	Not evaluated during the socio-economic diagnosis
	Difficulties to make strategic choices	"What sall we do in the future? Moving more to producing, like for the Italian grapes? Investing in producing?"	Not evaluated during the socio-economic diagnosis
	Lack of formalization of the strategy	"We shouldn't move to diversification. We have to master and strenghten our expertise"	Not evaluated during the socio-economic diagnosis
Strategic deployment and implementation	Lack of structured and implementation of the strategy	"There are far too many discussions and ideas, but we don't take action and implementation is too long" (Top management)	"There is no follow-up in the suggestions. We consider implementing something but it remains down the road"
	Lack or absence of communication–coordination–cooperation on the company strategy	"I'm experiencing difficulties to implement the strategy. There are many aspects I'm not aware of and they don't thing it would be helpful to let me know, while I would need it" (Manager)	"There is no strategic meeting. We only share information in the lobbies"
	Lack of economic sensitization of actors	"We are much more demanding with the employees of the ripening department. E.g., they have to fill in production forms" (Manager)	"Financial balance is not well understood by some colleagues"
	Lack of key socio-economic piloting indicator	"At the level of the team, our missions are not clearly defined. Such missions lack objectives and control, and management tools should be implemented" (Manager)	Not evaluated during the socio-economic diagnosis
	Difficulties regarding delegation and synchronized decentralization	"We follow and endure. We would like to be involved in the company strategy and it would help us better planning" (Manager)	Not evaluated during the socio-economic diagnosis
	Lack of evaluation of strategic implementation	Not evaluated during the socio-economic diagnosis	"There is no follow-up of ideas of projects. We'd rather implement a project but that's as far as it goes."

formalized, sharing it is more complex and the concerns or potential scenarios are not shared. This lack of communication slows down the top-down and bottom-up circulation of strategic information. Existing indicators are used more for reporting than for proactive management. However, there is no shortage of strategic ideas and desires, but they are rarely expressed and followed by real implementation: some projects are launched but do not come to fruition, generating demotivation and frustration throughout the company. Finally, the evaluation is not done: since the strategic implementation is itself considered dysfunctional, it is painful to evaluate unfinished projects.

These dysfunctions related to the strategy and its deployment also have significant economic impacts of about €708,000 (in 2016) or 42% of the total hidden costs of company S. and €252,000 (in 2017) for firm P or 35% of the total hidden costs.

2 CUSTOMIZED SUPPORT SYSTEMS TO IMPROVE STRATEGIC PRACTICES

The socio-economic approach to change management is broken down into three axes that are used concomitantly and progressively (Savall and Zardet, 1987): the process axis, systematically starting with a socio-economic diagnosis, followed by the project, implementation and evaluation; a tool axis, where management and supervisors are trained in common management tools: time management, competency grid, priority action plan and internal/external strategic action plan, strategic log-book and periodically negotiable activity contract. Finally, the last axis is that of political and strategic decisions, where the ISEOR's researchers accompany management in its changes to the rules of the game: resources, internal and external policies, products, markets, etc.

Management and supervisors are trained in the tools for developing and planning the company's strategy. Among them, the internal and external strategic action plan (IESAP) (see Tables 60.2 and 60.3) translates the company's socio-economic strategy, giving an image of the desired strategic situation over a 3 to 5 year period. It has two components: one based on the reduction of strategic obstacles (hidden costs) and the other on the necessary or desired development actions. The IESAP articulates actions targeting the internal environment of the company and its external environment. This strategic action plan is then broken down into priority action plans (PAP), the number of PAPs depending mainly on the size and structure of the organization, over the next six months. It is a tool for implementing strategic actions, which consists of multiplying strategic actions, ordering them and prioritizing them.

The formalization of these two tools is done through iterations and trial and error by management. Indeed, as we have said, the manager and his or her small team are often paralyzed by the fear of "bad" decisions. However, the socio-economic diagnosis and the launch of focus groups (process axis) are respectively a trigger and a catalyst for strategic actions: the improvement actions resulting from the focus group feed the strategic action plans and stimulate their formalization.

At this stage, it is important to emphasize the "placebo" effect of the researcher. On the one hand, this is due to the time allocated in the personalized assistance and other intervention mechanisms, time away from the operational level that allows the manager and the management team to seriously consider strategic and projective issues; on the other hand, although the researcher does not interfere in the substance of the decisions taken or desired, his distance and his questioning ("Is it realistic? To what extent? In what time frame? Is it enough?") reassure the managers when they make their choices.

3 THE IESAPS OF BOTH COMPANIES

The IESAPs were formalized and are presented in Tables 60.2 and 60.3. Although the form differs somewhat, the principle is identical. The strategic axes define the company's roadmap and are broken down into priority objectives, which represent the results desired by the manager. Then, each objective is broken down into concrete priority actions, which can both be included in the agendas and delegated to employees.

The benefits of formalizing IESAPs are multiple. First, the strategy is written down, so it can be discussed and communicated. Second, the exercise requires answering the following question: "What do we need to do (priority actions) to achieve the desired result (priority objectives)?" This question is crucial for implementation, as many projects fail for this reason. This first step therefore allows us to verify the feasibility of the actions envisaged.

In addition, in the face of the almost systematic isolation of the manager on strategic issues, IESAP makes it possible, by identifying the carriers or pilots, to make strategy "everyone's business." Any employee can become a pilot or a cooperator of a priority action, thus participating in the collective mobilization.

Finally, IESAP helps the company prioritize and plan its actions. The temporal distribution of priority actions allows the manager and his team to be realistic in terms of sustainability, taking into-account the operational requirements. Moreover, the segmentation by semester calls for an evaluation every six months of the realization of the actions and the achievement of the objectives, which considerably increases the probability of effective implementation.

CONCLUSION

At the beginning of any strategic formalization, there is an unwritten strategy (at least in the mind of the manager). The socio-economic intervention-research process makes it possible to formalize this strategy, particularly during personalized assistance and management committees with the researcher-intervenors, the manager and his or her close management team. The written and formalized strategy becomes easily communicable and can therefore be multiplied.

The previously observed lack of synchronized decentralization of the strategy is greatly reduced. It is therefore easier to orchestrate the multiplication of the strategy. Thus, the operational actors can more easily organize the feedback of operational information. Through a double effect of contradictory intersubjectivity and cognitive interactivity (Savall and Zardet, 1996, 2004), strategic scenarios are discussed, the strategy is re-evaluated, and strategic ambition gradually increases.

If, in VSEs and SMEs, the proximity of actors is an asset for organizational flexibility, it must also be the object of vigilance. For the agility induced by size cannot compensate for a lack of formalization that is a source of disorganization. Moreover, the size of VSEs/SMEs often leads to informal relationships that have a significant impact on organizational decisions. In order for management tools not to be perceived as cumbersome and rapidly "obsolete" (Le Boterf, 2001), it is necessary to combine structuring, organizational agility and the ability to adapt to change.

By delving into the heart of organizations, intervention-research makes it possible to define a "tailor-made" program, according to the company's needs. The identical methodological framework allows for adapted content, fed by the company's issues. The internal/external strategic action plan projects the organization into a medium-to-long-term future,

TABLE 60.2 IESAP in Company S (2017)

Strategic Axes	Strategic objectives	Actions	Persons ou services concerned	Provisional planing					
			L = Leader	2018		2019		2020	
	Expected outcomes / means	Actions	C = Contributor	S1	S2	S1	S2	S1	S2
Promoting our role of go-between through added value products and services for our suppliers and clients	Getting the F. certification	Leading to market F. implementation	L13-C4-C12	■					
		Leading implementation to meet L's requirements	L13-C3	■	■	■	■		
	Developing all employees' expertise on priducts: 100% of in house training	Training manuals on products	L13-C1		■				
		Tutorials on supply chain	L13-C5			■			
		Creation of an internal company school	P13-C8					■	
		Defining shared values and processes	P13-C2	■	■				
		Budgeted long-term communication strategy	P1		■				
	Recovering xT of volume with constant margin	Focused diagnosis and project	P4-C2	■	■				
Diversification to avoid being dependant on one product	Coherence between line products budget and actual to budget	Itemized operation chart for each campaign	P2-C4	■	■				
		Provisional planning of main campaigns	P2-C4	■	■				
	Mastering storage conditions, ripening and packaging	Mastering ripening process and launching of product A	P3-C6-C7	■					
		Improving products storage conditions	P1-C2-C3-C13	■					
		Sub-contracting (logistics, packaging)	P5	■					
Developing new opportunities for product B	Propsing a differentited product to our clients	Creation of a project group focused on product	P2-C3	■	■	■	■	■	■
	Enabling reliable partnerships	Sourcing suppliers	P2-C1	■	■	■	■		
	Getting new clients	Canvassing Client L	P2-C1	■	■				
		Exploring organic product selling opportunities	P2-C3			■	■	■	■
		Developing sales outside purchase centers	P3-C7	■	■	■	■		
Improving internal organization	Implementing a better business software	Developing the information system	P1-C13	■					
	Inventory and availability of data sources	Integrated training manual on key company functions	P13						
	Coverage of jobs	Competency grids for each service	P13-C2-C3-C4-C8-C9-C10	■					
		Training of managers	P1	■	■	■	■	■	■
		Succession planning	P11	■					
		Evolving organization (organization chart, provisonal management of jobs and competences	P1-C2-C11	■	■	■			
	Implementing shared procedures in all sites	Implementing the Ag process	P13-C8-C9	■					
		Sales validation process	P1-C2	■					
	Lowering work accidents	Planning gestures and postures training sessions	P1-C13	■					
		Tools to decrease Muslo-Skeleton diseases	P6-C2-C3	■	■				

TABLE 60.3 IESAP in Company P (2019)

Strategic Axes	Priority objectives	Priority actions	Leaders	2018		2019		2020	
				S1	S2	S1	S2	S1	S2
Increasing activity	Enhancing the office visibilty	Updating and developing the website	Dr1	X					
		Integrating robots'videos for pancreas, liver, chest, endocrinology	Dr1			X			
	Developing the activity of the office	Bariatric activity to be developped	Dr2		X	X	X		
		Liver activity	Dr3				X	X	X
		Attracting foreign customers	Dr4			X	X	X	
		Inquiring on adversiting and information rules regarding patients	Office manager		X				
		Creating an activity on another site	Dr5	X	X	X	X		
Improving productivity and well-being at work	Improving patients'database	Gatering databases	Office manager			X			
	Considering shared patients'database with the hospital	Access to patients' data from all offices	Dr1				X	X	
	Developing cooperation with partner offices	Radiologists	Dr3		X	X			
		Anesthesist	Dr3			X	X		
	Improving communication with operating room	Planning communication with stretcher bearers re. Equipement, etc.	Dr2	X					
	Periodic communication meetings	Creating an exchange system for the planning, operating room, overtimes, available slots, absenteesim, etc.	DR1	X	X				
	Improving exit of patients process	Creating an externalized secretary officeD	Office manager					X	X

while the priority action plan ensures regular implementation and evaluation, which provides the ability to reconcile short-term and long-term objectives, at the same time, in the same place (Salmeron, 2016). Finally, through its action, like an "invisible hand", intervention-research allows these companies to formalize their strategy, increase its ambition and ensure its realism.

REFERENCES

Bousquet, C. (2018). *The articulation of individual and collective competencies to the company's strategy: Intervention-research in an SME.* Doctoral dissertation in management sciences, Université Jean Moulin Lyon 3.

Le Boterf, G. (2000). *Construire les compétences individuelles et collectives.* Les Editions d'Organisation.

Porter, M. (1985). *Competitive advantage.* Free Press.

Salmeron, J.-C. (2016). *The socio-economic innovation process, an ambidextrous process?* Doctoral dissertation in management science, Université Jean Moulin Lyon 3.

CHAPTER 61

THE TECHNORD GROUP

An Industrial Adventure and Advanced Social Responsibility

Michel Foucart

ABSTRACT

The Technord industrial group has experienced an exceptional strategic and human trajectory, based on humanist values and the deployment of socio-economic management, which has accelerated the implementation of strategic vigilance practices that have fostered the development of new activities based on listening to customers and their expectations. This chapter also presents the singular trajectory of its historical leader, who decided to return to higher education in management at the age of 60, and organized the succession of the management with his son.

A quarter of a century ago in 1994, I met Henri Savall in Louvain-la-Neuve, Belgium. At that time, our company had grown to 70 people and had quadrupled its workforce in 10 years. I felt powerless to manage so many people, driven by the idea that private enterprise in the capitalist system should create dignified and sustainable jobs. I was off track... why did this concept of socio-economic management catch my attention?

1 THE INITIAL ATTRACTIVENESS FOR THE SOCIO-ECONOMIC APPROACH TO MANAGEMENT

The dominant discourse opposed finance and humanistic approach. I had searched, in vain, for possible accompaniments to bring the economic and the social closer together. It was

SEAM Treatise, pages 517–523

more an intuition than an established paradigm. Indeed, it was not in my foundations, as I have an engineering background.

My wife and I were obsessed with creating jobs and (re)giving men and women dignity through work. We also wanted to create a working community, like the sports, religious, tourist communities etc. . . . I found this definition in a dictionary: a community is a group of people who have a common heritage and share the *mission* and *purpose* of the company. It is a space of freedom where they can come to settle, to train, to take responsibilities, to break isolation, to create social links . . . In short, thanks to this community, it is a question of contributing to the happiness of the men and women who are there. It is a paternalistic vision of which I am not at all ashamed. Just as we wish for the happiness of our children, we wish for the happiness of the men and women in the company.

Moreover, with the current crisis, I note, in a very comforting way, that economic competition exists, but that the purpose of the fight is the durability of this work community. It is based on keeping a quality of relationships within the community based on our five values, which people have made their own: respect, trust, dialogue, common sense and high spirits.

Trust is fundamental. I never wanted to put a time clock on the workers' hours. Everyone has always declared their hours, under the supervision of the management. Because physical presence in the office under the eye of the manager is no guarantee of employee commitment and efficiency. The more trust you have, the more collaboration you get: it's a virtuous circle, as long as you display trust as a starting point. This is fueled, of course, by management tools . . . A priori, we trust this man or woman who comes to join this company community, who wants to do well and give the best of himself or herself.

Following a survey, during the covid period, among the staff, we had the idea to offer all our employees a telework kit. We gave them a comfortable chair and a large screen, connected to their laptop. We provided a desk for those who didn't have the physical comforts, so they could work in good conditions. I noticed recently on the telecommuting equipment order board that people only ordered what they needed. One would think that they would take advantage of this to order an extra chair . . . It was not the case, and this is encouraging! Of course, this equipment remains the property of the company, just like a toolbox.

In keeping with the logic of work communities, 12 years ago we were about to open up the shareholding to employees in order to share the ownership of this community, in addition to the profit sharing that has been going on since the beginning. My children, who are now running the company, will soon start this process again, with a different approach than mine. They will proceed in stages, but this employee shareholding approach seems to them to be very virtuous. I am amazed to observe the continuity of the management team, to keep the values and purpose of the Technord group alive, by leading exciting and inspiring projects.

A second very strong desire, from the very beginning of the company, was to create jobs, thus thwarting the prevailing idea that the only purpose of a company is to make a profit. We have demonstrated the opposite. In fact, today we are more than 400 employees, and our company supports 600 families on a daily basis, if we include our 200 loyal subcontractors.

2 SIGNIFICANT FACTS AND ACHIEVEMENTS OF THE COMPANY

2.1 Strategic Intelligence and Strategic Watches

We had an exceptional experience when we set up a group of strategic watchers with ISEOR about ten years ago. We had a medium voltage transformer station construction business, which had existed since the company's inception. But we didn't have a strategy, while there was a lot of existing know-how in the company, but it was completely diluted in other activities. The genius idea was to create a group of strategic guards for this line of business.

When we created this group of strategic guards for the Medium Voltage activity, we carried out a market study because we did not know our market well. We detected different development paths. From there, we built a IESAP (three-year internal-external strategic action plan) for the development of medium voltage. We defined our ambitions with budgets, actions consisting of identifying a new target of customers and new activities, as well as looking for correspondents among our suppliers. This involved identifying opportunities for collaboration with our strategic suppliers—the circuit breaker manufacturers—and with ORES, the electric power supplier in Belgium. This line of business has developed continuously since then. Before, we used to build transformer stations, which transformed 15 000 volts into 220 volts. Today we are in the European big league: we have received approval from ORES to build 150 000 volt substations, which we transform into 220 volts, before building domestic substations. This is a fabulous example.

Every year we revisit IESAP. The group of permanent guards, in which we have included young people, renews its strategic analyses. We have appointed a "boss" of the strategic watch group, who, on the basis of this experience, has transposed this system to other activities. One of the strengths of the group today is that it is forward-looking thanks to these strategic watchers. The strategy comes largely from the people on the ground, the employees. It is then a matter of putting it into practice.

The most recent activity, which started three years ago, concerns what is known as digitalization or "industry 4.0." The aim is to improve the efficiency of existing machinery to withstand competition from Asia. In the field of manufacturing, the aim is to increase the quality and productivity of the existing machine park. This is how the concept of Industry 4.0 was born. A spectacular example is that of accompanying the manufacture of champagne and controlling the fermentation curve of the grapes. At a certain point, oxygen is injected to stop the fermentation. Until now, this injection was done empirically. We have managed to write an equation that allows us to reliably anticipate the evolution of fermentation, depending on certain parameters. One of our young collaborators was trained in the fermentation phenomena of yeast, beer and wine. We focused on champagne because we are lucky enough to work with Moët et Chandon company. From now on, we anticipate the evolution of the fermentation, and we inject oxygen at the best moment of the fermentation to have the best quality of wine. This activity was launched from a strategic intelligence group focused on industrial IT.

There are currently 46 watchers in the company, some of whom participate in multiple groups. Our last seminar was fed by the results of the 6 strategic watch groups, each dedicated to a product line. For example, one of the groups is focused on data centers, thanks to the opportunity provided by our customer CHRISTAL Belgium. We now have an extraordinary market in full development.

2.2 The Articulation of Priority Action Plans and Periodically Negotiable Activity Contracts

In 1994, Technord began its collaboration with ISEOR, applying a method and tools for change management and continuous improvement. We started with a diagnosis of the company to measure hidden costs. At the time, we had 70 employees and the conclusions came as a violent shock, with 7 million Belgian francs per year in hidden costs for the entire company, or 100,000 Belgian francs per person per year! The enumeration of the dysfunctions represented a wall of lamentations which forced me to show a great humility, since it is never easy to see what is wrong, even if the identification of the problems offers a great source of progress.

After the diagnosis, the remedies! We have implemented the five tools developed by Professor Savall and his team. Tools that we are still using today! First of all, we set up IESAP, from which each hierarchical level and each department drew up its priority action plan. Then, each person was trained to improve their time management. The fourth tool was the competency grids in each team and finally the fifth was the strategic piloting logbook. This is a notebook that each person makes and in which he or she gathers his or her tools, documents and indicators for managing his or her teams, as well as the resolution sheets from each meeting and the meeting reports. This way, key documents are accessible to everyone.

One of the key tools is the periodically negotiable activity contract, negotiated between each manager and his or her staff to determine the progress objectives for the next six months, based on three axes. Firstly, the implementation of the PAP on a personal basis. Second, the reduction of dysfunctions generally observed in the previous six months. Thirdly, how to grow within the company and develop the well-being and development of people, particularly through training.

This articulation of the two tools of socio-economic management, the priority action plan (PAP) and the periodically negotiable activity contract (PNAC), is really spectacular and very concrete, as a tool for improving the synchronization of actions.

For example, at one point we had a cash flow problem. The common reflex is to turn to the accounting manager, asking him/her to delay payment to suppliers and to collect as soon as possible from customers. I refused to do this. We went through the entire cash generation process with the sales people, which is very rarely done. While we didn't systematically ask for a down payment at the time of the order, we started to include it in all the offers we made to our customers. Similarly, we have aligned the payment terms in our offers with the progress of our services. These are the two solutions that we have put in place, with indicators for evaluating these new practices.

We have also done a lot of work on the planning of key stages. Previously, when an order included, for example, a large transformer costing €200,000, the project manager, to be sure of having it on time, would order it immediately. And this transformer sometimes remained in stock for 8 months before being installed at our customer's site. The solution we came up with was to rigorously plan the order with our supplier, who also delivers it directly to the site. This allowed for significant recycling of hidden costs.

The people in the design office were given the task of drawing up monthly progress reports in order to propose monthly invoices, instead of waiting until the end of the work to invoice. Our accounting department sends an invoice to the client, with a copy to the engineer in charge of the site at the client's. Thus, in case of late payment, at the same time as the claim is sent to the customer, the project manager calls his customer contact to activate the payment. This has resulted in an increase in cash flow with the help of our sales staff.

We have included these new practices in the priority action plans (PAP), which are applied to the different departments of the company. This socio-economic management approach has accelerated the company's development, while contributing to the improvement of the social climate thanks to the communication-coordination-cooperation system. It has been well received by the staff and has allowed the development of participative management, sharing of responsibilities and motivation through empowerment. It is a way to make the staff grow so that they feel happy in the company.

Professor Savall and his team accompanied us for fourteen months to train us in the tools and their application. We have seen an overall improvement in the company and a better social climate within the company. The new generation of the company cannot imagine development without this method and its tools, which we continue to use today. Above all, they have taught us that the energy released by the reduction of dysfunctions can be reinvested in the overall improvement of the company. The result has been felt in terms of development, because we have been able to anticipate the evolution of technologies in our business and to identify the new needs of our customers, as we explained earlier.

2.3 The Periodically Negotiable Activity Contract (PNAC)

The magic, because it still remains magic today, is that a manager, four times a year, without waiting for a conflict, shows a minimum of consideration to his manager. This is a major act of recognition for employees.

The progress contract (PNAC) is a vital tool. It is also an opportunity to renegotiate between a person's personal life strategy and the strategy of the company community. It is important for the manager to take an interest in people's private lives, not to be intrusive, but because every element of a person's private life conditions his or her professional life: a birth, a divorce, the purchase of a house... This makes it possible to understand why an employee changes his or her behavior and strategy... The progress contract meeting makes it possible to discuss the strategies of both parties. The posture of systematic meeting allows to detect the important problems of the collaborators to try to solve them.

2.4 Preparing for My Master Degree for My 60th Birthday

As the company grew, I took great pride in being able to create jobs in the region. But the bigger the company gets, the more professional you need to be. This need for rigor and professionalism made me want to learn more about the basics of the method we were using.

In 2000, with the encouragement of Henri Savall, I decided to take the Master Program (*Diplôme d'Études Approfondies*) in management sciences at the Jean Moulin University in Lyon. Going back to university at 55 was a real challenge and a great experience. The courses were concentrated over a period of fifteen weeks, two days a week. Thus, on Thursday morning, I took the High Speed Train to Lille at 6 a.m. and I returned on Friday by the evening High Speed Train.

There were about thirty people in the class. Three quarters of them were young students, among whom were two female students, one the daughter of a Togolese minister and a young Asian, with whom I got along well. I was by far the oldest and this age difference was like a rejuvenating cure for me. I was enthusiastic and happy to meet competent university professors in subjects that were totally unknown to me, Professor Trouvé for the sociology of organizations, without forgetting the courses in management control or marketing, and of course, Henri Savall for socio-economic approach to management.

Thus, on Thursdays and Fridays at noon, I used to go and eat at the university restaurant... with my classmates.... I would sometimes do their socio-economic management homework and in return, they would give me the notes that I didn't take during the classes.... I really enjoyed this student life and rubbing shoulders with these teachers, wells of science and absolute humility.

This beautiful adventure of training for a diploma ended with a thesis and I didn't realize it at the beginning. I was rather reluctant, because what interested me was the training more than the degree. But I painstakingly began to write this famous thesis on the transmission of family businesses. It was one of the most difficult exercises for me, because I don't like to write and I had little time. But I managed to finish it and I defended my thesis at the Jean Moulin University. While waiting for my defense, I remember going back in time, experiencing the stress and the tense atmosphere of the examination hallways, just like in my early studies.

The graduation ceremony was held a few months later in the large auditorium. It was packed! On the podium, about fifteen professors dressed in their university gowns. When the names of the graduates of the Master Program in Socio-Economic Management were called out, and I heard mine, I walked down the steps—I was easy to spot with my grey hair—the whole amphitheater rose to applaud me . . . I was surprised, terribly moved and it was in tears that I received my diploma. I was surprised, terribly moved and it was in tears that I received my diploma. Recovering from my emotions, we all met at the cocktail party where everyone came to greet me and congratulate me. It was an unforgettable day.

2.5 The Successful Preparation of the Transmission of the Technord Company to My Son

I had a personal experience of taking over a family business that left its mark on me at the age of 35. Indeed, a TEI company that I managed for 10 years and which was very prosperous, fell victim to a division of the shareholders who wanted to sell this company. Fortunately, after three years of negotiations, I managed to buy back all the shares through the Technord holding company that I created for this takeover in 1988.

In 2000, at the age of 55, I created a family foundation under Dutch law, in order to make the financial landscape of Technord's ownership indivisible and thus guarantee the continuity of the governance. Initially, none of my four children wanted to work in the family business and I had therefore drawn up a project for a cooperative of employees who could ensure the Group's continuity, in partnership with the family shareholders. Unfortunately, this progressive and innovative project was refused by the Belgian tax authorities.

In 2000, my son Philippe decided to join me and after having occupied all the positions, from sales to purchasing logistics, the time came to organize his implementation as Technord's boss. I therefore set up a system of periodic meetings with Professor Henri Savall, who steered the sometimes difficult dialogue between the founder and his/her successor. Each work session was divided into three parts: first, Henri Savall and I, then my son alone, and then the father and son meeting to set up actions and resolutions. This method allowed us to build over time a Concerted Delegation Grid that served as a guide throughout Philippe's tenure as CEO in June 2010.

Today, I have become the "grandfather" of the Group, guardian of the values and mission. Technord is doing just as well, if not better, without me than with me. I am amazed at the deepening of humanistic values and the exemplary development of our group, which continues to practice the method and tools of socio-economic management.

CONCLUSION

For more than 25 years, the Technord Group has followed an exceptional growth path, while maintaining its founding values, supported by socio-economic management and its tools. We are proud to note that the company regularly receives awards for its job creation and social performance... the latest reward as we conclude this chapter at the beginning of 2021: it has just been recognized as one of the "best workplaces" for 2021, by being ranked in the Belgian top 10 of the Great Place to Work survey (which concerns well-being at work) organized each year independently by the Vlerick Business School (Belgium).

REFERENCES

Foucart, M. (2009). Two emblematic cases of sustainable economic development of companies. In H. Savall & V. Zardet (Ed.), *Management socio-économique: une approche innovante.* Economica.

Foucart, M. (2010). Industrial group in advanced technologies. Transmission of a family business in times of crisis. In H. Savall & V. Zardet (Ed.), *Management stratégique des professions réglementées.* Economica.

Foucart, M. (2015). The convergence of family and humanistic governance. In H. Savall & V. Zardet (Eds.), *Gouvernance et management: quelle coopération?* Economica.

Foucart, M. (2016). Finance at the service of business. In H. Savall & V. Zardet (Eds.), *Companies, value(s) and prosperity: socially responsible capitalism.* EMS.

Foucart, M. (2019). Reception, integration and professional development. In H. Savall & V. Zardet (Ed.), *How to work together? Challenges of intergeneration.* EMS.

Foucart, P. (2011). Independence and differentiation strategy. In H. Savall & V. Zardet (Ed.), *Réussir en temps de crise: stratégies proactives d'entreprises.* Economica.

Foucart, P. (2012). Transmission of firms practicing socio-economic management in Belgium. In H. Savall & V. Zardet (Ed.), *Les entreprises familiales: création, succession, gouvernance et management.* Economica Le groupe Technord: une aventure industrielle et une responsabilité sociale avancée.

This page intentionally left blank.

CHAPTER 62

CORPORATE CITIZENSHIP

A Common Good and the Search for Sustainable Performance

Christophe Fargier and Frantz Datry

ABSTRACT

Is the idea of corporate citizenship a simple slogan or, on the contrary, a strong principle that can guide the actions of the entrepreneur-manager? The experience of the Ninkasi group, a small business created in Lyon in 1997, shows that this concept exists, guides strategic choices and is embodied in the professional behavior of the company's managers and employees. We propose to give a meaning and a definition to this proposal of corporate citizenship.

After such a chaotic 2020, you may legitimately wonder how to build future plans for your company. It is in these moments of doubt that you rediscover the principles that have consistently guided your decisions for over 20 years. These principles can be summarized in a phrase that we need to define: corporate citizenship. It is a common good and a heritage. A common good, because we build for ourselves, as a manager-entrepreneur, and for others, whether they are employees-collaborators, associates, customers or partners. It is also a heritage made up of a wide variety of resources, among which the know-how held by the people in the company is certainly the most precious part for its future.

Seven years after its creation in 1997, the Ninkasi company, thanks to the will of its director, has integrated the principles and methods of the socio-economic theory of organizations to accompany its development. After so many years, a review of the key concepts that guide its strategic choices and the way they are implemented is proposed here.

SEAM Treatise, pages 525–530

1 PROPOSALS FOR DEFINING THE CORPORATE CITIZENSHIP

The company is a citizen because it is part of the long process of patient and persevering construction. How long does it take to build a successful organization, a recognized brand, stable quality products and trust within a distribution network? This is the fruit of patient work that is part of a deliberate strategy to build a real "work tool" that does not depend on the circumstances of the moment and the inevitable vagaries of the economy. Here we find an application of the concept of strategic patience (Savall and Zardet, 2020). The corporate citizen participates in the life of the city, of its territory and is concerned with producing positive externalities so that its development is in symbiosis with its environment. In this ecosystem logic, the company is nourished by its interactions with this environment: many strategic opportunities are born from encounters.

Secondly, this definition of the company involves refusing the mirage of maximizing short-term financial results, by deliberately distancing itself from the financial and excessively speculative capitalism that has invaded the entire planet in recent decades. This overly speculative capitalism, which strongly permeates the strategic choices made by many executives, is not the relevant framework for the socio-economic development of companies today and for tomorrow (Savall et al., 2015).

Does this mean that the corporate citizen is not interested in its economic and financial results? On the contrary, the economic responsibility of leaders, managers and teams is an indispensable condition for the survival-development of the company. The company is a citizen because it is constantly concerned with the competitiveness of its products and its profitability. Without short, medium and long term economic performance, the company is neither robust nor sustainable. Without sufficient and stable resources, it is not possible to build strategies based on the development of human potential, i.e., a future made of relative stability for people who wish to develop their professional project and their employability within the company. However, in an unstable environment, a clear framework and direction are necessary to mobilize the creativity and audacity of teams. The corporate citizen must create a structured internal-external environment that orchestrates a permanent process of trial and error, a source of controlled innovation. The challenge of using resources wisely for sustainable projects that integrate social, societal and environmental dimensions defines the framework of corporate citizenship responsibility.

In times of crisis, adhering to the principles described above may seem like a challenge. As we write these pages, the health crisis is affecting the entire planet and is obviously affecting Ninkasi's business. In this context, strong resilience is required to withstand the pressure on its director, managers and all teams. For a year now—first lock-down in March 2020—the cessation of the operation of part of the bar-restaurant activities has entailed a major financial risk for the survival of the group. Internal cohesion between management, managers and employees is one of the key elements of this resilience. This internal cohesion is a fragile "being." It is necessary to "over-communicate" internally to reassure and develop optimistic messages. This optimism is the fuel that allows us to gain support for a common project. This is not an idealistic vision of reality. On the contrary, this optimism is anchored in the constraints of the present. But it deliberately seeks an antidote to the ambient pessimism (Fargier, 2009).

The common thread of this resilience is undoubtedly the quality of the management of activities and people. Management performance is the real issue in the company. It is indeed management that constitutes the cement of internal cohesion. We must admit that managing has become a mission that is both essential and particularly difficult. Because managers are assigned the role of organizing and building what we call congruence.

In the course of our reflections, it appears to us that the key word for defining corporate citizenship may be that of congruence, in other words, the bringing together of various dimensions that are often perceived as incompatible. This concept of congruence can be observed at different levels:

- between the societal dimension of the company (citizenship) and economic—sustainable performance;
- between management practices—based on proximity and the role of managers in team development—and human values; and
- to match the quality of management, the quality of dialogue and the quality of professional behavior.

It is a matter of developing impact strategies that provide evidence that the company's socio-economic development model has positive externalities (Savall and Zardet, 1995, Savall et al. 2015). We can no longer be all talk or promise.

This congruence is the initial postulate of the socio-economic theory of organizations designed by Henri Savall and developed with the ISEOR team (Savall, 1974, 1979; Savall and Zardet, 1987). In other words, the separation of the social and economic dimensions is a conceptual sham. A sustainable socio-economic strategy is based on the necessary search for successive balances between social and economic performance (Savall and Zardet, 1995).

2 WHO IS THE NINKASI COMPANY?

Ninkasi is a Lyon-based company created in 1998 by its current founder-director. It has about 250 employees and is made up of a network of about 20 bar-restaurants, an independent brewery-distillery and a promotion and distribution activity for contemporary music. Several professions contribute to the identity and unity of a concept: producing and animating places of conviviality and sharing.

Ninkasi is the perfect alchemy between the production of quality beers, a restaurant offer in partnership with local actors and the organization of concerts and parties, all in warm and friendly places. In the end, we brew much more than beer, we create places to brew! Ninkasi, created in 1997 in Lyon, defends strong values of emergence, short circuits and the mixing of professions, audiences and styles. Ninkasi is a real "melting pot" of enthusiasts of all kinds: unconditional fans of bitter, acidic or barrel-aged beers, experts in indie rock, salsa or drum n' bass, serial devourers of double burgers, we are all here to share a good time together in our place!

Let's move forward a little in the definition of this corporate citizenship by developing a few complementary themes that characterize from our point of view the very notion of socio-economic strategy of organizations.

2.1 Some Illusions About Corporate Governance

The management tradition associates governance with capital and capital with decision-making power. However, close observation of how companies operate and the transition from decision-making to implementation shows that power is essentially in "doing" and not in "saying." We don't like to take inventory of the many product projects and business reorganization decisions that did not see the light of day or did not have the expected results.

Each time, one of the conclusions of these small and big failures is that we did not know how to organize the ownership of this decision by all the teams of the company. The experienced and lucid leader understands that his or her power is limited if the management and the teams are not involved. Power lies in "doing", i.e., in management and in the ability to invent and implement solutions. Human potential plays a key role in strategic activation (Savall and Zardet, 2015). It is up to managers to create this involvement, defined as the intrinsic motivation of employees. Trust, cooperation and motivation are not given, they are instead a permanent construction. Strategic ambition and results depend on our ability to mobilize people, i.e., their creativity, productivity and assumption of responsibility. Meaning and integrity must be given to activities and missions in order to enrich work and release human potential (Fargier, 2016).

2.2 A Company on a Human Scale

What if the successful company was human-sized? It seems obvious that size increases the difficulty of synchronizing activities and people in time and space. We consider that the so-called citizen company, or at least its units, should not exceed a certain size of around 300 people. Beyond that, it is probably unrealistic to think of acting effectively. As soon as the structure becomes too large and too complex, the costs of synchronization explode and greatly reduce the organization's performance. In the socio-economic model, this corresponds to a category of hidden costs now well identified and documented in a great deal of applied research (Savall and Zardet, 2016). It is necessary to structurally create the conditions for responsibility and autonomy for all categories of employees. Performance is achieved where professional actions are taken and decisions are made, in line with the company's commitments.

By giving autonomy to individuals and teams, we manage to implement an organization that makes the most of this autonomy, without it becoming a risk of losing control of projects, processes and resource allocation. This organization, which combines autonomy and direction, is called synchronized decentralization (Savall and Zardet, 1995; Fargier, 2007).

2.3 Entrepreneurship: Cultivating Experimentation to Structure the Company and Innovate

The company is a real laboratory. We cultivate all sorts of experiments in many areas: new products, new ways of organizing production, more efficient work methods and more lively interactions with customers. This conception of the company as a crucible for experimentation in all directions requires real know-how in terms of management. Indeed, it is a matter of encouraging local initiatives in teams, which are a source of creativity and innovation, and of synchronizing these initiatives correctly so that they lead to a concrete and measured result. The right to make mistakes and the duty to evaluate and learn from them are virtuous and effective practices. The management of change and the ability to adapt must become a pleasant way of breathing. This change is achieved by regularly reviewing processes, products and work organization. Being in motion means taking action and learning from the process.

A little soul-searching leads to the conclusion that the main driver of entrepreneurship is fun. The fun is in the doing together and the perception of the enrichment that comes from internal and external interactions. In the end, it's about having fun writing great entrepreneurial stories and getting teams on board with their implementation. In other words, dreams, intuitions or opportunities move from the stage of ideas to concrete realizations. The study of the market potential comes later. Later, the story goes that we were visionaries, when it was fun and curiosity that drove many of the company's strategic projects. For Ninkasi, there are many examples, such as the creation of a distillery to expand and diversify the range of spirits, sodas and syrups.

3 ECOSYSTEMS: BUILDING OTHER WAYS OF COOPERATING, CREATING SOCIO-ECONOMIC VALUES AND SHARING IT IN ITS EXTERNAL ENVIRONMENT

If the company must learn to experiment, it must also do so in and with its external environment. As transdisciplinary approaches are still quite limited, the way in which the firm weaves cooperative links with its environment is a future field of exploration. These links are complex and are organized at different scales: territory-firm-team-individual (Fargier, 2013; Savall et al. 2015). This fosters agility and makes it possible to mobilize resources and skills that the company alone does not possess.

The corporate citizen seeks to resonate with its relevant environment. Because of its limited size, it needs to build cooperations with multiple partners in its environment, as it does not integrate certain resources necessary for the development of its strategy. Here again, it is a know-how of internal-external synchronization that is at work to lead this type of development strategy. The success of the brewery and distillery in Tarare, just outside Lyon, illustrates how the company is anchored in its territory. This brewery has enabled the conversion of former textile industry buildings that historically occupied the Tarare valley for over 100 years. The de-industrialization of many French territories has left industrial wastelands that offer opportunities for today's companies, provided they know how to forge strong and balanced links with local players.

CONCLUSION

In order to avoid any misunderstanding, these remarks are not in any way an apology for the methods of organization and management of the company that claim to reverse the authority of management to the benefit of the employees. On the contrary, without synchronization, decentralization is ineffective and even dangerous. One could even say that unsynchronized decentralization leads to demagogic strategies. Thus, in this model of corporate citizenship, management's objective is to tirelessly build the conditions of compatibility between the necessary leadership on the part of management and the empowering autonomy of teams. This model of organizational development was forged by Henri Savall in the early 1970s. Since then, Savall and his team have been experimenting and developing more rewarding and efficient forms of work organization. Finally, Ninkasi is also a socially responsible company in that it develops a socio-economic strategy.

Know-how and trust are central values based on a more optimistic vision of the human being. It is the will to believe that it is possible to take a different path than the traditional forms of organization. "Friendship, love, trust and loyalty become reality because we believe in them. Of course, that belief can be betrayed, but it was better to be 'fooled by hope' than by fear" (Rutger Bregman, 2020).

The company believes that Man is good: "Putting openness to the world and to society at the heart of the purpose" (Olivier Frérot).

REFERENCES

Bregman, R. (2020). *Humanité. Une histoire optimiste.* Seuil.

Fargier, C. (2007). Approfondissement et consolidation du management socio-économique. In H. Savall & V. Zardet (Eds.), *L'hôpital et les réseaux de santé.* Economica.

Fargier, C. (2009). Implication personnelle du dirigeant et cohésion de l'équipe de direction. In H. Savall, V. Zardet, & M. Bonnet (Eds.), *Management socio-économique: une approche innovante.* Economica.

Fargier, C. (2013). La connexion de la stratégie de l'entreprise à celle du territoire, le pilotage d'un investissement important; une balance économique à la clé. In H. Savall, V. Zardet, & M. Bonnet (Eds.), *Réindustrialisation et dynamisation.* Economica.

Fargier, C. (2016). Réussite stratégique et management socio-économique. In H. Savall, V. Zardet, & M. Bonnet (Eds.), *Enterprises, valeur(s) et prospérité: Le Capitalisme Socialement Responsible.* EMS.

Frérot, O. (2019). *Vers une civilisation de la vie: entreprendre et coopérer.* Chronique Sociale.

CHAPTER 63

PRO-ACTIVELY REACTING TO THE TETRANORMALIZED BUSINESS ENVIRONMENT

Cases of a Lebanese Bank and a Small Family Insurance Brokerage Firm

Jocelyne B. Eid and George N. El-Rahbani

ABSTRACT

The notion of compliance and conformance with laws and regulations has gained the recognition in the market place to be not a simple back-office function but something that must be embedded into the fabric of the organization, in alignment with performance objectives, in a way that the organization as a whole can meet the obligations of various stakeholders: from the customers to suppliers, employees, investors regulators and others (Simons, 1994). The foundation of this work is based on two socio-economic intervention research projects undertaken in a Lebanese private Bank and a Small Family Insurance Brokerage Firm (SFIBF) aiming to enhance the management of complex norms and standards. The purpose of this work is to present the common mechanisms put in place via two socio-economic innovative projects. Within the context of this research projects, two interveners researchers one is internal (assuming an additional function as an Operational Risk Manager in the Bank) and the other is a consultant which are classmates share the common process and learning experience. This dual role enriched the outcomes of the intervention and the overall process as detailed in the different sections of the chapter.

This chapter presents two case studies involving the socio-economic approach to management (SEAM) management consulting method carried out in a private Lebanese Bank

SEAM Treatise, pages 531–536

and a Small Family Insurance Brokerage Firm. The research tension analyze the impact of management system of norms on organization performance and social responsibility. The chapter presents what has been carried out in common during both interventions, and illustrate the socio-economic tools applied at work as well as the main achievements in terms of social improvement and economic performance. The socio-economic innovative projects were evaluated through the current economic crisis in the Lebanese financial sector noting that both intervention results and reforms did help the Bank and the SFIBF to overcome the Lebanese complex situation, financial risks and stress.

1 CONTEXT AND BACKGROUND

From the start of its history, the Lebanese Republic has never experienced peace or political relief or economic stability. Currently, matters are not completely different, the country continues to be divided into several parties, political instability still reigns, and corruption is currently worse than ever.

Lebanon is currently facing overwhelming social and economic challenges as a result of decades' political corruption and war and their resulting impact on the government and the nation as a whole. To note that in this challenging situation, the economic activity in Lebanon is below potential, drastically affected by the unstable geopolitics and security situations. The major financial players in maintaining this stability in the country are insurance companies and Banks (Makdessi, R., & Mekdessi, S., 2014). The Lebanese financial sector is rather unique due to the fact that the financing of the government is mainly relying on commercial banks deposits growth. With a debt to GDP ratio of almost 155% a very large proportion of this government debt is held by domestic banks; therefore, the stability and the adequate management of these latter is a must (finance.gob.lb).

2 GENERAL OVERVIEW OF THE BANK AND SMALL FAMILY INSURANCE BROKERAGE FIRM

The research projects focus on the Lebanese Financial Sector. The first socio-economic project was conducted in a Bank operating principally in Lebanon offering a very well diversified range of products and services catered to Commercial, Retail and Private clients. The Bank employs 440 employees and has more than 50 years of banking tradition and a presence in the MENA region and European countries.

As for the second project, it took place in a SFIBF founded in 1999 as an insurance broking and risk management in the Lebanese market. Its employees help clients fully understand the range of risks they face especially in today's increasingly uncertain global business environment. Since 1999, clients have relied on the brokerage for trusted advice and to represent their interests in the marketplace. The Brokerage serves 30,279 clients who are enterprises of all sizes in every industry, and include individuals, multinational organizations, and government entities. The Brokerage deals with more than 12 Insurance companies, handling risk in more than 17 countries.

The business environment of both the Bank and SFIBF could be described as follows: serious political instability, highly competitive sector and stringent requirements of norms.

3 THE SOCIO-ECONOMIC INTERVENTION-RESEARCH AND PARTICIPATIVE PROJECTS

Both CEOs were looking for a consultancy method to assist them in restructuring the internal control departments responsible to maintain compliance. This methodology was needed to support their proactive vision of the incoming market and environment changes. The financial sector survival, stringent and complex norms in addition to work in silos and fragmented internal control system were mainly the trigger behind the restructuring idea.

As for the establishment of an agile internal control system to manage complex norms and maintain compliance notion of this chapter, the CEOs worries origin can be anchored to the country political instability that may cause business disruptions, the sanctions risk and an increasingly stringent regulatory environment. SEAM (Savall, 1974, 1975, 1981, 2003; Savall & Zardet, 1987, 2008, 2004, 2005; Savall, Zardet, & Bonnet, 2000, 2008; Savall, Péron, Zardet, & Bonnet, 2015, 2018) is probably the approach of choice to reform and improve the quality of the norms management in the Lebanese financial sector.

This paper will focus on the Tetranormalization effect on the financial sector and specifically its stemming hidden costs. Based on the observation during the intervention-research projects, the research hypothesis is that the socio-economic approach to management enable the creation of a unified system to manage complex norms, and generates simultaneously social and economic positive impacts: internal cohesion and efficiency-productivity.

3.1 The Findings

The topic of complex norms management in the financial sector has always been an interesting issue on how to really have efficient and effective control system?

Based on a 3-year longitudinal study (2017–2019), the researchers will share concrete common findings and results obtained in both organizations.

Negotiation with the intervener-researchers led to the interventions processes being designed according to the scientific organization development protocols. Following the socio-economic protocols the following was included: (1) a steering committee, whose members are the CEO and top-level management team; (2) collaborative training sessions and personalized assistance for all managers with a focus on the socio-economic tools, along with personalized assistance in customizing and implementing them; (3) socio-economic horizontal and vertical diagnosis and projects, involving the top and middle management and various departmental levels—these processes all include a participative inventory of dysfunctions and calculation of hidden costs, along with guidance to focus groups in preparing financial balances for socio-economic projects; and (4) integrated training of internal interveners to enable customization, embeddedness, and sustainability of the socio-economic projects.

In brief, the Bank and the SFIBF, like many other organizations believed they had very little weaknesses and that they were performing well. However, when the socio-economic diagnosis was performed and the results of the mirror effect were presented, the management realized the level of their weaknesses, the internal control inefficiency and the number of the dysfunctions they have.

Moreover, the calculation of hidden costs as opposed to the known costs recorded by the traditional accounting methods proved that what both organizations saw was merely the tip of the iceberg and that they had the bigger chunk lying in the dark. The result of the SEAM diagnosis revealed dysfunctions in six major areas that affected the mental state of the actors. The summary of the qualitative data analyzed indicated problems related to working conditions, work organization, communication–coordination–cooperation, time management, training, and strategic implementation. Furthermore, the work structure of the organizations affected the actors behaviors and the dysfunctions impacted the hidden costs which in turn affected the Bank and the SFIBF performance.

3.2 The Mirror Effect

The mirror effect caused a cultural shock and made actors more aware of the causes of the dysfunctions, as voiced by both steering committees:

- "We realized that policies and procedures are books on shelves no one use them or read them, they are obsolete and do not reflect new norms requirements." (SFIBF Manager)
- "We realized that one of our most critical dysfunctions is working in silos between in the most critical departments." (Bank CRO)
- "We discovered that the control board committees and top management team members were seemingly aligned, and they work in silos. We have no alignment between compliance and operations." (Bank CCO)
- "We cannot believe that we are asking our clients to sign all this forms." (SFIBF Officer)

The main root causes behind the disfunctions as voiced by the researchers- interveners are due to lack of steering, lack of synchronization and the lack of a unified Information system. The results of diagnosis, shocked the CEOs and the steering committees who took the decision to tackle dysfunctions by risk based approach. Focus groups were setup and piloted by the steering committee to address the dysfunctions revealed in the semi-structured interviews. The focused groups worked on minimizing dysfunctions, reducing associated hidden costs, improving department structures and improve actors' behaviors.

3.3 The Tetranormalization Observed Effects

The effects of Tetranormalization on both organizations is illustrated using a concrete example related to the implementation of the Data Protection Regulation promulgated by the European Parliament and the Council of the European Union. The implementation of this directive illustrate the existence of the four poles of Tetranormalization. The Tetranormalization four poles hidden cost calculation related to the data privacy law implementation (see Table 63.1).

TABLE 63.1 Tetranormalization Hidden Cost Calculation Example

	Bank	Brokerage Firm
Pole 1 Social Standards	$404,260	$32,000
Pole 2 Quality and environmental standards	$788,220	$19,000
Pole 3 Trade standards	$400,896	$98,000
Pole 4 Accounting & Financial Standards	$788,220	$43,000
Total	**$2,381,596**	**$192,000**

The evaluation of the hidden costs in both organizations as illustrated in table 1 shows that the most compelling empirical evidence was directly related to the accounting and financial standards in the Bank and trade standards in the SFIBC. These unaccounted hours in the implementation of norms and resulting from the Tetranormalization effects can be converted into added-value to improve the Bank and Brokerage firm performance and employees morals.

3.4 Achieved Results

In a high standardized sector and following the researchers' observation it seems essential to demonstrate the "normative agility" and transform the norms and standards projects into competitive advantage (Savall & Zardet,2013;Eid, J. B, 2020).

Therefore in the both cases, a structured organization chart was implemented and communicated at the end of December 2017 integrating the internal control functions aiming to ensure cohesion and teamwork to achieve common objectives. At the beginning of 2008, the Bank established a centralized norms and standards committee to manage proliferations of norms and calculate its hidden costs in addition to visible costs. Also in this regard, the Bank and the Small Insurance Brokerage firm developed internally a system to monitor and follow up on norms status. The code of conduct and the compliance and accountability plan were updated and developed.

Going back to the hidden cost, the interveners recalculated the hidden cost after 1 year of the intervention, the ending of a cycle, and proved quantitatively the recycling of 35% of these costs. Finally both organizations developed integrated training plans to be delivered to all employees to understand fully the norms requirements and support the compliance implementation.

4 MANAGERS AS DEVELOPERS OF HUMAN POTENTIAL AND TALENT

The CEOs and steering committees clearly stated that human potential is the lever of sustainable performance, as all the actors must support the socio-economic intervention projects in order to design and implement the Organizations' strategies in highly competitive market.

The Bank's vision had been defined by the following motto "Maintain leadership in the design and the launching of financial services while ensuring compliance with local and internal regulations." The Bank's mission is that of "Enabling our clients and our people to become leaders in an everchanging market." These values and missions resulted in the definition of managers' core responsibilities. In both organizations, all managers are in charge of implementing the strategy by serving the clients first and the management and development of talent by rigorously maintain a leadership management practice that guides all employees to success by integrating social and financial performance. As such the organizations and employees share responsibility of human potential development.

CONCLUSION

The improvement of the management control to better manage norms and standards led to a phase during which the Lebanese Bank and the SIBF made significant management changes evident mostly in developed managerial skills, reorganized work conditions, controlled implementation, the creation of transparency, and enhanced manager professionalism. The objective of the chapter is to test that the investment in human potential and the enhancement in management methods lead to socio-economic performance. The findings sustain the concept that, through the socio-economic management consultancy projects, actors learned that there were many hidden costs that lead to the disturbance of management, a factor which people were not conscious. These hidden causes led to additional financial expenses that were not presented in the information systems of the Bank and the Brokerage Firm. This study created awareness among all the actors with the intention of creating an image of the possible savings that could benefit the organization's development. Moreover, the findings illustrated that managers learned how to create a participative and democratic process that required the rectification of the symmetry of power, hence affecting knowledge creation. Both researchers believe that the common implemented system to manage norms is "A Message of Hope " for other their country, organizations and the world needed in this period.

REFERENCES

El Rahbani, G., & University of Balamand, Faculty of Business and Management. (2020). *Helping a Family Business Firm Become a Better Sr Provider for Greater Results Towards Stakeholders.*

Eis, J., & University of Balamand, Faculty of Business and Management. (2020). *The Intergation of Control Functions to Manage Complex Norms. The Case of a Lebanese Bank.*

Simons, R. (1994). How new top managers use control systems as levers of strategic renewal. *Strategic Management Journal, 15*, 169–189.

Makdessi, R., & Mekdessi, S. (2014). The Default Risk Management in Financial Institutions: Case of the Credit Risk in Lebanese MFIs. *Economics, 2*(2), 112–123. *Management Learning, 32* (1), 49–60.

Savall, H., & Zardet, V. (2004 ,2011). *Challenges and Dynamics of Tetranormalization.* 2005: 1st edition in French*: Tétranormalisation: défis et dynamiques.* Economica

Eid, J. B. (2020). The Integration of the Control Departments to Manage Complex Norms. The Case of a Lebanese Bank. In *Academy of Management Proceedings* (Vol. 2020, No. 1, p. 19381). Academy of Management.

CHAPTER 64

RIGOR AND RELEVANCE OF "RESPONSIBLE" STRATEGIC MANAGEMENT

Contributions of the Socio-Economic Theory

Alexandre Asselineau

ABSTRACT

Faced with current societal issues, integrating social and environmental considerations alongside the economic dimension has become as imperative as it is urgent. But some questions remain. First, considering social aspects is still often seen as a constraint on companies. Second, the operational execution of "responsible" strategies often deviates significantly from the initial intentions, due to the deficiency of strategic management in proposing methods that embrace the complexity of organizations. On the contrary, Socio-Economic Theory seems to provide a fruitful framework for creating the conditions for efficient, responsible, and humanistic management.

The inclusion of social and environmental dimensions in the "raison d'être" of companies, alongside economic performance, is a strong trend. It is gradually replacing a representation of the company as an isolated entity motivated by the sole quest for profit. However, this transformation is not without its difficulties, both in terms of theoretical considerations and of the transformations at work. The challenge is ambitious: to combine economic performance with social and societal requirements. This contribution focuses on the "responsible" strategic management of companies, i.e., the implementation of a strategy based on principles of social responsibility. Based on the assumption that the changes to be made require the use of a rigorous and structured methodology, we note that research in strategic

SEAM Treatise, pages 537–542

management is struggling to provide elements that can be used by practitioners. Socio-economic theory (SET) (Savall, 1974, 1979; Perroux 1979; Savall and Zardet, 1987) is a notable exception, providing a suitable methodological framework, based on a coherent concept of "socially responsible capitalism", which can accompany the transformation of organizations.

1 THE SOCIALLY RESPONSIBLE COMPANY

1.1 Rethinking the Role and Place of the Company

The famous article published by M. Friedman (1970) constitutes a severe indictment of the idea of corporate social responsibility. While the economist (Nobel Prize winner in 1976) admits that a manager may have a social responsibility in his private life, he must, as a representative of the interests of the owners of the company, "conduct business in accordance with their wishes, which are generally to make as much money as possible by complying with the legal and ethical rules of society. While the text lacks nuance, it is nonetheless interesting, particularly because it is fully in line with the dominant theoretical framework of neoclassical economics. The underlying idea that the firm is an entity independent of the "rest of the world," whose sole responsibility is to maximize its profit, is still influential today. Yet it is hardly tenable (Chanteau et al., 2017, p. 11): Contemporary societies expect, more than ever, a significant contribution from firms to the collective interest and strong social and environmental commitments, far from the excesses of a faceless and stateless financial capitalism.

Indeed, many companies are now integrating this need, albeit to varying degrees (De Jong and Van der Meer, 2017; Wang, Tong et al., 2016), allowing the concept of Corporate Social Responsibility (CSR) to flourish. It is recent, even if the integration of ethical approaches in organizations is not (Quairel and Capron, 2013), and not very stabilized, due to the polymorphous nature of the term "responsibility" and the numerous expectations associated with it (Ingham, 2011).

Defined as "the voluntary integration by companies of social and environmental concerns into their commercial activities and their relations with stakeholders" (European Commission, 2001), with the ISO 26000 standard, the idea of CSR now seems to be taking shape, even if a demarcation remains between the "convinced" who make it the core of their strategy and the more reticent. In France, the adoption of the PACTE Law (2019) allows companies to statutorily adopt a "raison d'être," i.e., a social or environmental mission, alongside the profit-making purpose of the activity. The evolution is significant, since it involves integrating the expectations of all of its stakeholders: not only is profit not the only objective, but it is even a "limiting factor" (Notat and Sénart, 2018, p. 16).

1.2 Economic, Social, and Societal Performance: Complementary or Opposed?

This conception considers that the company cannot prosper at the expense of the community, capturing most of the value created without considering the negative externalities generated (Porter and Kramer, 2011). But, far from neoclassical and Marxist theories that oppose profit and social and environmental issues, it advocates a model built on the complementarity between these dimensions, combining the assets of a capitalist system and extra-economic considerations: "shared value creation" (Porter and Kramer, 2011), or even a model of "socially responsible capitalism" for Savall, Péron et al. (2015).

But what are the consequences of a better integration of societal dimensions on the economic performance of the firm? The existence of a correlation between company competitiveness and the implementation of CSR approaches has not yet been fully demonstrated, even if, among others, a study conducted by France Stratégie evokes a significant positive impact (Notat and Sénard, 2018), with a higher performance gap (13% on average), in favor of companies practicing CSR. Nevertheless, it does seem that CSR has at least some observable direct and indirect positive benefits: corporate image and reputation, reduced consumption (water, energy) and social costs (Chanteau et al., 2017), and even strategic opportunities (Asselineau and Cromarias, 2011). De facto, some of the largest companies are fully committed to this path, becoming "companies with a mission" within the meaning of the Loi Pacte (Danone, Yves Rocher), or joining the B Corp Certification.

Thus, it seems possible to reconcile economic performance with social and societal issues. But... how do we do it?

2 HOW CAN STRATEGIC MANAGEMENT RESEARCH CONTRIBUTE TO THESE REFLECTIONS? A CRITICAL APPROACH

2.1 What Role for "Responsible" Strategic Management

"The issues for companies are no longer whether or not to engage in CSR, but rather how to manage CSR strategically and effectively (...). Despite shared enthusiasm, many companies find themselves facing significant challenges" (Wang, Tong et al., 2016, p. 535).

This issue of the articulation between the strategic project and the day-to-day operation of the organization falls within the scope of strategic management, which "deals with (a) major intentional and emergent initiatives (b) taken by managers on behalf of owners (c) involving the use of resources (d) to improve the performance (e) of firms (f) in their external environment" (Nag et al, 2007, p. 942).

Thus, "responsible" strategic management is about intentional and emergent initiatives built on a CSR architecture. It is particularly, but not exclusively, aimed at for-profit organizations, whose objectives are primarily oriented towards economic performance. Some organizations seem "genetically programmed" (Asselineau and Piré-Lechalard, 2009) to integrate the implementation of CSR (e.g., Biocoop, Malongo, MAIF, Pochéco, etc.). In many cases, however, the process proves to be complex: the expressed will struggles to find a real translation in the heart of the organization, actions remain peripheral, or generate internal tensions (Hengst et al., 2020; Crilly et al., 2016; Ashforth and Reingen, 2014).

Emphasis has long been placed on strategy formulation, with implementation assumed to flow naturally from it. This is wrong: it is established that strategy implementation requires at least as much effort as strategy design (Mintzberg et al., 2009). The "responsible" transformation of a company is indeed a formidable challenge (Hengst et al., 2020). Thus, the determination of a "raison d'être" can generate real complexity at the level of the company's internal managerial chain (Notat and Sénard, 2018). Similarly, the strategic vision, "a vibrant, idealized, verbal portrait of what the organization aspires to achieve one day" (Carton, Murphy, and Clark, 2015, p. 10) is in theory a first step for the inclusion of extra-economic dimensions in the organization's project, thus for the implementation of a "responsible" strategy. But if the literature offers some (rare) recommendations (Kantabutra and Avery, 2010), it is often very difficult to identify whether the vision proudly presented by the company is anything more than a simple communication vehicle.

2.2 Which Methods and Tools?

There are two reasons why it is difficult to identify methodologies for organizations wishing to implement responsible strategic management.

Firstly, the methods commonly used show a poor capacity to grasp the complexity of organizations and the actors that make them up. They are generally based on simplified conceptions of reality or easily measurable subdivisions (management of innovation, performance, information systems, etc.), to the detriment of an overall perspective. This is true of governance, governed by agency relationships (principal-agent), "contract nodes" or game theory models. Similarly, these approaches obey deliberate "top–down" logics (e.g., Balanced Scorecard), built on a dichotomy between reflection (decisions) and action (execution), whose efficiency can be criticized: In reality, like Adam Smith's pin factory, each employee contributes through his or her daily decisions, each of which impacts the organization. Hence the importance of looking at "emerging" strategies, except that they often amount to mere incantations: "If, with the new organizational methods, the emphasis is on employee motivation, commitment and accountability, no tool that could move these objectives from being wishful thinking to being unavoidable factors in the new organizational strategies has been put forward (...)" (Savall, Péron et al., 2015, p. 148).

Second, despite a high number of publications, strategic management research has little influence on the socio-economic world (Ployhart and Bartunek, 2019), even going so far as to question its very usefulness (Le Roy, 2017, p. 26). Some explain this by the methods used by researchers: external observation, unique and non-generalizable cases, etc. (Hengst et al., 2020).

On the contrary, this contribution is based on the idea that an economically successful and socially "responsible" company must be based on a coherent management structure that respects the structures and actors. This particularly ambitious project requires methodologies that are no less ambitious. It is therefore remarkable to note the response offered by socio-economic theory to meet these challenges.

3 WHAT ARE THE PROSPECTS FOR RIGOROUS AND RELEVANT RESEARCH IN STRATEGIC MANAGEMENT? CASE OF THE SOCIO-ECONOMIC THEORY

3.1 Moving Beyond the Dichotomy of Strategy Formulation and Implementation

The socio-economic theory provides a framework for reconciling the rigor of "scientific intent" with its usefulness for transforming organizations (Savall and Zardet, 1995, 2004). While there is still some debate about the compatibility of these two dimensions (rigor versus utility), TSE has made the decision from the outset: Management science is experimental in nature, and therefore must combine the knowledge of researchers and practitioners for the purpose of organizational transformation (Van de Ven and Johnson, 2006; Van de Ven, 2018). TSE assumes many similarities with medical sciences: the complex object studied (the company), is "alive, active and conscious" (Savall, 2018, p. 35), its observation cannot be carried out on the surface, but must involve many backs and forth between immersion (field) and distancing (laboratory). It is a matter of "caring for organizations to improve their health, discovering new pathologies or variants of existing pathologies, and validating the effectiveness of management tools, methods and practices with respect to the performance they expect" (id. p. 35). The methodology is tried and tested, based on three principles (cognitive interactivity, contradictory intersubjectivity, generic contingency), and proposes practical tools that organizations can use to align intentions and actions: In this way, the dichotomy between those who think about strategy (managers, researchers, consultants) and those who make it happen, the main difficulty of strategic management, can be overcome.

3.2 Towards an Efficient, Responsible, and Humanistic Management

Rethinking the way organizations operate to better balance economic performance and social considerations is a complex exercise, if we want to move beyond simple greenwashing. From this point of view, the socio-economic theory also seems to provide a relevant answer, thanks to an approach that combines a philosophical and macroscopic perspective of CSR and an operational perspective that provides a "toolkit" co-constructed with practitioners and scientifically proven. The theoretical foundations of the socio-economic theory promote the existence of a responsible social-liberal capitalism, incompatible with the "Taylorism-Fayolism-Weberism virus" (TFW) and laissez-faire financial capitalism, which "mutilate the creative dimension of human work" (Savall, Péron et al., 2015, p. 118). TFW relies on "human potential" as "the primary strategic lever for sustainable improvement of economic performance" (id., p. 121). It recognizes the complexity and interdependence of organizations and the actors within them, as well as the tensions arising from cooperation and competition, and places the individual at the heart of the entrepreneurial capacity of organizations, thanks to a series of coherent measures: strategic anticipation and vigilance, contractual negotiated commitment, synchronized decentralization, "3Cs," flexibility and training, competency grids, proximity dialogues, etc. These are all ways of (re)establishing the human potential of organizations. These are all ways of (re)activating individual and collective value creation capacities and limiting dysfunction.

CONCLUSION

At a time when the need to redefine the nature of the links between business and society has become glaringly obvious, we have emphasized the difficulties of implementing this new social contract in companies, after several decades of unbridled financialization of economies and "TFW" viruses. If CSR is now widespread in the discourse of public authorities, researchers and practitioners, there is often "a long way to go" in the reality of organizations. This may sometimes be due to a lack of willpower, but probably often it is due to a lack of appropriate methods. While most concepts from strategic management struggle to provide efficient solutions, we have highlighted the relevance and strengths of the socio-economic theory. This approach, based on the fundamental principles of "socially responsible capitalism" that places the individual at the heart of the organization's concerns, proposes a complete methodology, validated over more than forty years, by combining, in a rather unique way, scientific research and immersion within organizations. By asserting that a company's performance depends above all on the internal strength of its human potential, the socio-economic theory conveys a strongly positive message, reminding company managers that the most important thing is internal cohesion, and that they therefore have all the keys to success, provided they want them.

REFERENCES

Ashforth, B., & Reingen, P. (2014). Functions of Dysfunction: Managing the Dynamics of an Organizational Duality in a Natural Food Cooperative. *Administrative Science Quarterly*, 59(3), 474–516.
Asselineau, A., & Piré-Lechalard, P. (2009). «le développement durable, une voie de rupture stratégique?» *Revue Management & Avenir*, n°26, juin, p. 280–299
Asselineau, A., & Cromarias, A. (2011). «La RSE, un catalyseur d'innovations au service de la «vision» stratégique», *Revue Sciences de Gestion*, n°84, p. 29–48
Carton, A., Murphy, C., & Clark, J. (2015). A (blurry) vision of the future: how leader rhetoric about ultimate goals influences performance. *Academy of Management Journal*, 1015(1), 10–36.
Chanteau, J.-P., Martin-Chenut, K., & Capron, M. (dir.). (2017). *Entreprise et responsabilité sociale en questions, Savoirs et controverses*, Classiques Garnier.
Commission Européenne. (2001). «Promouvoir un cadre européen pour la responsabilité sociale des entreprises», *Livre vert*, version française, 35 p.
Crilly D., Hansen M., & Zollo, M. (2016). The grammar of decoupling: A cognitive-linguistic perspective on firms' sustainability claims and stakeholders' interpretation. *Academy of Management Journal, 59*(2), 705–729.
De Jong M., & van der Meer M. (2017). How Does It Fit? Exploring the Congruence Between Organizations and Their Corporate Social Responsibility (CSR) Activities. *Journal of Business Ethics*, 143, 71–83.
Friedman, M. (1970, September 13). The Social Responsibility of Business is to Increase its Profits. *The New York Times Magazine.*
Hengst, I.-A., Jarzabkowski, P., Hoegl, M., & Muethel, M. (2020). Toward a Process Theory of Making Sustainability Strategies Legitimate in Action. *Academy of Management Journal, 63*(1), 246–271.
Ingham, M. (2011). *Vers l'innovation responsable, pour une vraie responsabilité sociétale*, De Boeck.
Jullien, F. (1996). *Traité de l'efficacité*, Biblio Essais, Le Livre de Poche.
Kantabutra, S., & Avery, G. (2010). The Power of Vision: Statements that resonate. *Journal of Business Strategy, 31*(1), 37–45.
Le Roy, F. (2017). Le Management Stratégique en France: Facteurs de déclin et de renouveau. *Le Libellio d'Aegis, 13*(2), 21–29.
Mintzberg, H., Alhlstrand, B., & Lampel, J. (2009). *Safari en Pays Stratégie*, Trad. française, 2ème éd., Pearson.
Nag, R., Hambrick, D., & Chen, M.-J. (2007). What is strategic management, really? Inductive derivation of a consensus definition of the field. *Strategic Management Journal*, 28(9), 935–955.
Notat, N., & Senard, J.-D. (2018). «L'entreprise, objet d'intérêt collectif». *Rapport aux Ministres de la Transition Ecologique et Solidaire, de la Justice, de l'Economie et des Finances, du Travail*, mars.
Ployhart, R., & Bartunek, J. (2019). Editor's comments: There is nothing so theoretical as good practice—a call for phenomenal theory. *Academy of Management Review, 44*(3), 492–497.
Porter, M., & Kramer, M. (2011). Creating Shared Value, how to reinvent Capitalism—and unleash a wave of innovation and growth. *Harvard Business Review*, Jan.–Feb., 62–77.
Quairel, F., & Capron, M. (2013). "Le couplage" responsabilité sociale des entreprises et développement durable, mise en perspective, enjeux et limites. *Revue Française de Socio-Economie*, 11, 125–144.
Wang H., Tong L., Takeuchi R., & George G. (2016). "From the editors. Corporate Social Responsability: An overview and new research directions. *Academy of Management Journal, 59*(2), 534–544.

CHAPTER 65

IMPACT OF THE SOCIO-ECONOMIC MODEL

On Corporate Social Responsibility

Eva Conraud Koellner and Martha Ríos Manríquez

ABSTRACT

This chapter analyzes the impact of the ISEOR socioeconomic model on the corporate social responsibility developed by a company. It will address the intervention and delegation tools of the socioeconomic model as a particularly relevant strategy to involve employees in social responsibility actions. A case study of a self-diagnosis applied to the "human capital" of a primary sector company in Mexico, which has been implementing the socioeconomic management model for more than fifteen years, is presented to measure its perception of the achievements in corporate social responsibility.

This chapter analyzes the impact of the ISEOR's socio-economic model on a company's corporate social responsibility. The incentive and delegation tools of the socio-economic model will be addressed as a particularly relevant strategy to involve employees in social responsibility actions. A case study of a self-diagnosis applied to the "human capital" of a primary sector company in Mexico, which has been implementing the socioeconomic management model for more than fifteen years, is presented to measure its perception of the achievements in corporate social responsibility.

SEAM Treatise, pages 543–549

1 CONTEXTUALIZATON OF THE PROBLEM: CORPORATE SOCIAL RESPONSIBILITY IN ORGANIZATIONS

CSR currently represents one of the toughest challenges in the face of the demands of the various stakeholders of organizations, regardless of their size, sector or business activity. For many, CSR is nothing more than a means of avoiding fiscal commitments or a social marketing strategy, while for others it represents a milestone that is transforming companies to the point of turning them into agents of social change. There are many definitions to describe CSR (Dahlsrud, 2008). The Mexican Center for Philanthropy (CEMEFI) defines it as a "conscious and consistent commitment to fully comply with the purpose of the company, both internally and externally, considering the economic, social and environmental expectations of all its participants, showing respect for people, ethical values, the community and the environment, thus contributing to the construction of the common good" (Cajiga, n.d., p. 4). It implies assuming commitments in the economic, social and environmental areas, in a transversal manner in all the company's operations. This has been studied since the 50s from different perspectives, going from the vision of the entrepreneur to that of interest groups and three-dimensional models. In 2010, the reflection on social responsibility reached consensus with the publication of the ISO 26000 standard, which offers a diagnostic guide to measure social responsibility actions in seven areas: Governance, Human Rights, Labor Practices, Environment, Fair Operating Practices, Consumer Affairs, and Community Involvement and Development. The work of López, Ojeda, and Ríos (2017) highlights "human capital" as key to promoting social responsibility actions, by favoring employees' trust and sense of belonging, increasing their willingness to work through the granting of responsibilities and a willingness to share in the company's growth and profitability. This is reflected in productivity, efficiency, achievement of goals, quality of activities and therefore in a better financial performance and image of the company.

In the case of Mexico, interest in the concept of CSR arose as an echo of international trends reflected in the publication of norms, laws, guidelines and agreements, with the publication of ISO 26000 being a major reference point, but above all as a particular pressure derived from the international trade agreements signed in the 1990s and as a consequence of the global economic crisis, which led to a significant reduction in the profit rates of companies and thus a reduction in social welfare. In general, it is observed that in Mexico social actions are usually implemented in a welfare, paternalistic and charitable way, being still little established as a business management strategy. It is evident the fundamental role of the contribution of managers to act internally to shape the corporate image, establish the social role of the company and represent a behavioral reference for its employees. Vives (2014) finds that the main obstacles perceived by companies for the implementation of social responsibility actions are financial, explicit or implicit incentives in companies to not want to sacrifice profits and the relationship of remuneration with financial objectives. In the work of El Hila and Amaazoul (2013), they mention as an obstacle to CSR, the very tetranormalizations resulting from the proliferation of regulations and norms that seek to establish rules of healthy games but which in some way pose barriers to the competitiveness of companies, which, because they do not know how to integrate them into their processes, generate chronic hidden costs that reduce their performance and jeopardize their growth potential.

2 IMPLEMENTATION OF THE SOCIO-ECONOMIC APPROACH TO MANAGEMENT IN THE COMPANY

Since 1973, the ISEOR Research Center has focused on the development of strategies that jointly lead to the improvement of economic results and human and social performance of companies and organizations (Savall H., 1974, 1979; Savall & Zardet, 1987, 2009). To this end, a socio-economic management model was defined that integrates sustainable global management methods based on the human development of the company as the main factor of effectiveness in the short, medium and long term, with tools that stimulate the competencies of the members of the organization and optimize its resources to reduce dysfunctions and to recycle hidden costs (Péron & Bonnet, 2008). The effectiveness and efficiency of this model lies in its ability to articulate traditional management methods with a human and social vision of its functioning and its overall sustainable performance. In practical terms, the model observes the dysfunctions distributed in six key variables of the social performance of each company: working conditions, work organization, communication-coordination-cooperation, work management, integrated training and strategic implementation. Socio-economic theory considers the firm as a complex whole composed of five types of structures in interaction with five types of human behaviors (Savall & Zardet, 1987,1995). These permanent and complex interactions create the activity impulses that constitute the living functioning of the firm. However, it is possible to detect anomalies, disturbances, differences between the desired performance and the performance actually observed; these are the dysfunctions whose chronic nature generates hidden costs. The model is characterized by its focus on resistance to change, as a human characteristic. It allows a diagnosis to be made between the visible and the hidden in order to negotiate change.

Considering that the literature on aspects of social responsibility as a strategy for the competitiveness of organizations highlights the benefits of optimizing "human capital," production processes and interaction with stakeholders, the convergence between the socioeconomic management model and CSR will be analyzed through a case study.

3 CASE STUDY

The primary sector company has 680 employees and has been engaged since 1983 in the production, distribution, export and marketing of avocados and other farm products, located in the state of Michoacán, Mexico.

The socioeconomic importance of avocado production in the state of Michoacán derives from the benefits it brings to producers, marketers, industrialists, and consumers. It represents more than 70 thousand direct jobs and 300 thousand indirect jobs, accounting for 60% of Michoacán's agricultural GDP, 80% generated by small producers with less than five hectares (Cooperativas de Aguacate, 2017). However, the State of Michoacán, the world's largest avocado producer, is paying a very high cost for its cultivation, from both a social and environmental perspective (Nájar, 2016). In this regard, Martínez (2008) notes that, in the case of small and medium-sized companies, their lack of knowledge in management is one of the causes of their irrational use of natural resources, which leads to the externalization of costs, which end up being charged to their workers and/or society.

The company decided 15 years ago to adopt the socioeconomic management model (Savall et al., 2000), in response to the desire of its managers to break paradigms and continue growing in a sustainable manner. Based on the application of an in-depth diagnosis,[1] interactions were initiated between the directors, managers and collaborators, where, through a dialogue table, the ways of operating in the different areas of the company were shared.

Drawing a timeline, in 2004 (reference year for change) the need to implement a strategic change in areas such as: logistics, production, transportation, finance, traceability and administration was seen; from 2005 to 2012 some tools of the ISEOR model were applied, such as: an IESAP (Internal and External Strategic Action Plan), a PAP (Priority Action Plan), and CAPN (Periodically Negotiable Activity Contracts).

Taking as a reference 15 years of continuous implementation of this model and adoption of the tools by each of its collaborators, tangible results were reflected: the areas of logistics, production and traceability showed in the area of sales a gradual and constant increase of 8% annual average; this adds up to an economic benefit of 135% accumulated annually, which as a work team reverts a hidden cost to a gain and a dysfunction to continuous improvement, thus generating a profitable, reliable, efficient company, with adaptation to challenges.

In terms of CSR, there were also noticeable improvements such as 100% affiliation to Social Security, benefits stipulated by law: vacations, vacation bonus and Christmas bonus, a real salary registration with social security, not with the minimum, which meant the highest registered salary in the area. And from 2014 to date, profit sharing is provided. Likewise, workers are offered a safe, comfortable and dignified public transportation service, and temporary employees in the field are registered with the social security system. In terms of gender equity, equal pay is granted to men and women in the company for similar activities; the working hours of production personnel were modified to allow for a lunch break. Direct actions were incorporated for employees, such as paternal incapacity, economic retribution based on effort, and support and educational opportunities were established for personnel. The company also trained 13 managers in Socioeconomic Management at the ISEOR, France. As an additional benefit, staff are given the afternoon off on their birthdays, as well as workshops on reading, ceramics and self-improvement. Financial support was provided to an old people's home.

In terms of environmental protection, a photovoltaic cell plant was installed to generate electricity, and the company participates in weekly trash collection on roads and in town areas, as well as actively participating in the reforestation of some areas.

4 SELF DIAGNOSIS OF CSR IN THE COMPANY

As a complement to the implementation of the socioeconomic model tools, a self-diagnosis based on the Gonzalez questionnaire (Gonzalez Sanz, 2014) was applied in 2019 to the company's six business units. The questionnaire is divided into seven sections, one for each axis developed by ISO 26000: (1) Organizational Governance (OG), (2) Human Rights (HR), (3) Labor Practices (LP), (4) Environment (E), (5) Fair Operating Practices (FOP), (6) Consumer Affairs (CA), and (7) Community Involvement and Development (CID). Each of the sections sets out a series of indicators as statements regarding the actions and policies implemented by the company in the area of CSR. For each question there are three possible answers, indicating the one that best describes the performance of the company, from the perspective of those responsible for each department in cooperation with their subordinates. The same questionnaire was distributed to the six units of the company so that it could be answered collectively by senior management and area managers, in order to identify the perception and level of knowledge of employees in relation to the CSR actions implemented in the company.

TABLE 65.1 Results of the Self-Diagnosis[a]

Departments	GOB	HR	LP	EMP	FOP	CA	CIDP	Average
Management	0.54	0.64	1.22	1.25	1.15	0.52	0.44	**0.82**
Corporate services	0.25	0.18	0.63	0.10	0.08	0.16	0.08	**0.21**
Branch offices	1.04	0.82	1.41	0.65	0.92	1.12	0.76	**0.96**
Orchards	1.08	0.55	1.52	1.00	1.08	0.48	0.40	**0.87**
Packing	0.29	0.18	0.85	0.30	0.77	0.44	0.40	**0.46**
Trucking	1.42	1.55	1.52	0.45	1.69	0.76	1.20	**1.22**
Average	**0.77**	**0.65**	**1.19**	**0.62**	**0.94**	**0.58**	**0.54**	

Source: Own elaboration

[a] Organizational Governance (OG), Human Rights (HR), Labor Practices (LP), Environment (E), Fair Operating Practices (FOP), Consumer Affairs (CA) and Community Involvement and Development (CID).

Based on the interpretation suggested by Gonzalez's model, the following table (Table 65.1) allows us to compare the performance of each business unit in the different CSR indicators.

In order for these scores to be understood, the evaluation procedure is set out below, and then the result obtained by the company is commented on.

Up to 0.80: The company has great opportunities for improvement, since it does not yet have CSR-oriented management.

0.81 to 1.19: The company is already carrying out actions in the field of CSR, but good CSR practices need to be monitored.

1.20 to 1.69: The company has already assimilated the concepts of CSR and is clear about the commitments required for socially responsible management.

1.70 to 2: The company is well informed about emerging management issues and uses CSR to achieve its objectives, both economic and social.

As can be seen, the company had the highest score in Labor Practices, with a score of 1.19. This dimension includes as main indicators labor and labor relations to contribute to job creation, employment stability and decent work; to improve working conditions and social protection, including remuneration, working hours, vacations, hiring and firing practices, maternity protection and access to welfare services. Another indicator of coincidence with the socioeconomic model is social dialogue, which consists of facilitating agreements, negotiations and information exchange between employers and workers; as well as human development and training in the workplace, with the aim of improving people's quality of life, involving access to knowledge and information, and with political, economic and social opportunities, which expand people's freedom to decide their own destiny and live a valuable life.

The dimension that obtained the lowest average score was active participation in community development, with a score of 0.54. However, the results indicate a concentration of activities of this nature in a single department, which shows a clear concept of the commitments necessary for socially responsible management in terms of community involvement, through a closer and more productive relationship with the parties involved (government and society, community, internal public, customers and suppliers).

The dimension of consumer affairs follows with a score of 0.58, which makes it clear that the company is not taking advantage of its social responsibility actions as a social marketing strategy, which leaves great areas of opportunity for the company to position itself as a socially responsible supplier in the face of its competition.

The same occurs in the areas of environmental protection and human rights, where a clear interest of the company is identified in the responses, with the need to establish criteria for measuring and disseminating the progress achieved in terms of both human rights and environmental protection.

The governance score of less than 0.8 is the result of an implicit integration of aspects of social responsibility in the company's mission and values, and a lack of internal communication of the achievements made in this area, as well as the absence of a person responsible for monitoring CSR actions in the company at the time of the diagnosis. This dimension was in fact the one that was given priority once the self-diagnosis had been completed.

In terms of fair operating practices, the score was 0.94, which indicates concrete CSR actions, although a manual and code of ethics must be drawn up to reflect the practices carried out in official company documents.

Finally, it is worth noting the results by department, with Persea Trucking obtaining the highest score, which was the most recent department to be created by the company and where CSR issues were included in its design.

CONCLUSION

The diagnosis shows that the company has assimilated the concepts of CSR and is clear about the commitments required for socially responsible management. It clearly shows the impact of the actions undertaken through the tools of the socioeconomic model to achieve the goals set in terms of social responsibility, especially in its socioeconomic performance and attention to its personnel. The self-diagnosis applied to the company's personnel reveals the impact of the socioeconomic model on the perception of social responsibility, identifying labor practices as the variables most present, since the socioeconomic strategy is based precisely on the company's internal development. The principle of the socio-economic strategy is to provoke its progress starting from itself and not from its external environment, which will eventually benefit from this progress.

NOTE

1. Arturo Guerrero, external consultant, supported by internal consultants and remote assistance from ISEOR.

REFERENCES

Andia Valencia, W. (2015). La responsabilidad social: Análisis del enfoque de ISO 26000. *Industrial Data, 18*(2), 55–60. Obtenido de http://www.redalyc.org/articulo.oa?id=816/81643819008

APEAM. (Julio de 2014). *Importancia del aguacate en la actividad económica de México, 1996–2013.* Obtenido de mhaia: http://www.mhaia.org/wp-content/uploads/002_Misc_Files/Importancia_del_aguacate_en_la_actividad_economica_de_Mexico_2014-07-22.pdf

Argandoña, A., & Silva, R. (2011). *ISO 26000, una guía para la responsabilidad social de las organizaciones.* IESE Business School, Universidad de Navarra.

Barroso, F. (2008). La responsabilidad social empresarial. Un estudio en cuarenta empresas de la ciudad de Mérida, Yucatán. *Contaduría y Administración,* 226, 73–91.

Cajiga Calderón, J. F. (s.f.). *El concepto de responsabilidad social empresarial.* Centro Mexicano para la Filantropía.

Cooperativas de Aguacate. (2017, 2 de Julio). La exportación de aguacate genera dos mil 500 millones de dólares a México. *El Heraldo de México*

Cortés V., M. A., Muñoz Z., M. L., & Quintero G., M. L. (2014). Sistemas integrados de gestión y responsabilidad social empresarial en empresas agroindustriales de los departamentos de Cauca y Valle del Cauca, Colombia. *Informador Técnico, 78*(2), 140–147. https://doi.org/10.23850/22565035.97

Dahlsrud, A. (2008). How Corporate Social Responsability is defined: An analysis of 37 definitions. *Corporate Social Responsability and Environmental Management, 15,* 1–13. https://doi.org/10.1002/csr.132

El Hila, R., & Amaazoul, H. (2013). Impacts de la tetranormalisation sur les pratiques de RSE. *Recherches en Sciences de Gestion Management,* 96, 199–216. https://doi.org/10.3917/resg.096.0199

El Sol de México. (2017). Obtenido de El Tratado de Libre Comercio amenaza al aguacate y a la carne de res: https://www.elsoldemexico.com.mx/finanzas/el-tratado-de-libre-comercio-amenaza-al-aguacate-y-a-la-carne-de-res–241028.html1

Gonzalez Sanz, H. (2014). *Implantación de la Norma ISO26000 en las Pymes: Un estudio de caso.* Responsabilidad Social Empresarial. España: Universidad de Valladolid.

López Salazar, A., Ojeda Hidalgo, J., & Ríos Manríquez, M. (2017). La responsabilidad social empresarial desde la percepción del capital humano. Estudio de un caso. *Revista de Contabilidad, 20*(1), 36–46. https://doi.org/10.1016/j.rcsar.2016.01.001

Martínez, G. (2008). Gestión con responsabilidad social y los costos ocultos. *Revue Recherches en Sciences de Gestion,* 66, 113–133.

Martínez, R., Vera, M., & Vera, J. (2015). Responsabilidad Social Empresarial en las pequeñas empresas constructoras de Puebla, México. *Revista Global de Negocios, 3*(3), 31–41.

Mazzotti Pabello, G., & Solís Pérez, P. (2014). La ISO 26000:2010 y la paradoja de la responsabilidad social empresarial: Aproximaciones críticas. *Administración y Organizaciones, 17*(32), 99–117.

Nájar, A. (2016). Los daños ocultos que provoca el aguacate, el "oro verde" de México. *BBC Mundo.*

Ojeda Hidalgo, J., & Lira Silvino, G. (2014). Marco teórico de la responsabilidad social corporativa. En E. Conraud, *Responsabilidad Social en empresas multinacionales en el estado de Guanajuato* (pp. 21–52). México: Pearson.

Organización Internacional de Estandarización. (2010). *Guía de Responsabilidad Social.* Recuperado el 3 de Noviembre de 2020, de https://www.iso.org/obp/ui#iso:std:iso:26000:ed–1:v1:es

Organización Internacional de Estandarización. (2010). *Guía de Responsabilidad Social.* Recuperado el 3 de Noviembre de 2020, de https://www.iso.org/obp/ui#iso:std:iso:26000:ed–1:v1:es

Saldaña Rosas, A. J. (2010). Responsabilidad social empresarial: hacia una agenda de investigación en México. *Administración y Organizaciones, 12*(24), 75–89.

Vives, A. (2013). RSE:-¿Cuáles son los obstáculos para que las empresas sean responsables? *Diario Responsable.* Obtenido de https://diarioresponsable.com/opinion/16394-icuales-son-los-obstaculos-para-que-las-empresas-sean-responsables

Vives, A. (2014). Guías para la responsabilidad social en las pymes: Efectividad de herramientas de autoevaluación. *Revista Globalización, Competitividad y Gobernabilidad, 8*(2), 29–54.

This page intentionally left blank.

CHAPTER 66

TOWARDS A GENERAL MODEL OF HIDDEN COSTS INTEGRATING ECOLOGICAL ISSUES

Stéphane Trébucq and Jocelyn Husser

ABSTRACT

The purpose of this chapter is to associate the integration of ecology to the hidden cost model following the recent evolutions of the standards and the management tools. An integrated model of global performance is proposed and then associated with the hidden cost method. This model is essential for companies that must learn to integrate data related to their environmental impacts into their evaluation and management tools. The theory of hidden costs can thus be deployed in complex informational environments enriched with new social and environmental standards.

The business environment in the early 21st century has changed profoundly compared to the 1970s, when the hidden cost model was first developed. In 1987, the Brundland report popularized the notion of sustainable development, which is now omnipresent in the management sphere. Ecology has also become one of the major sources of concern for citizens, who are both producers and consumers (Savall, 1979). Freeman's (1984) proposal on the imperative need to satisfy stakeholders was widely accepted, before being introduced into many management and reporting standards. In the face of all the degradation that natural capital is undergoing, how can we revisit the concept of hidden costs-performance? These notions of cost and performance have themselves evolved, as we now speak of social and environmental costs and overall performance. This chapter discusses the integration of ecology into the hidden cost model, following the recent and important changes in the landscape of standards and management tools.[1] We then present an integrated model of

SEAM Treatise, pages 551–559

overall performance and illustrate the interest of broadening the concept of hidden costs to include ecological issues (2).

1 THE NEED TO EXTEND THE HIDDEN COSTS MODEL TO ENVIRONMENTAL ISSUES

The questions of responsibility and sustainability of business models have become unavoidable. The notion of "strong sustainability" also raises challenges in the face of management systems that are unable to inform managers about issues such as the rate of regeneration of renewable resources. The landscape of standards and management tools has thus been profoundly transformed since the first works devoted to the hidden cost model (Savall, 1974–1975, 1979a; Savall and Zardet, 1987). Ecological aspects now appear to be essential in the analysis of the cost-performance relationship.

1.1 New Standards Integrating Ecological Issues

Standards lead to the integration of societal aspirations, respectful of the environment. Ignoring them can jeopardize a company's legitimacy, make its products and services less attractive, increase the cost of access to financing, and degrade its employer brand, thereby reducing its attractiveness to future recruits. These are therefore hidden costs.

The first environmental grid on which there is a very broad international consensus is the GRI (Global Reporting Initiative) standard. It proposes a series of indicators according to several themes: consumption of materials, energy and water, effects of activities on biodiversity, greenhouse gas emissions, effluents and waste, and environmental assessment of suppliers. These indicators coincide with certain areas of action of the ISO 26000 standard (2010) on corporate social responsibility. In each of the standard's areas of action, a series of possible and conceivable actions is proposed, thus enabling an organizational audit of effective practices. The use of these normative sources thus makes it possible to advance in the characterization of the environmental performance of companies.

Since 2015, the more global issues of sustainable development have also been clarified within the framework of the United Nations. 17 Sustainable Development Goals (SDGs) have been issued, broken down into 169 targets to be achieved by 2030. The X30-037 standard clarifies the intersection between these SDGs and ecological aspects. Six SDGs are concerned by the environmental aspect: n°6 access to safe water and sanitation, n°7 sustainable and affordable energy, n°12 responsible consumption and production, n°13 fight against climate change, n°14 sustainable use of oceans and seas, n°15 ecosystems, forests, soils and biodiversity.

The SDG grid leads us to question the relationship between business and society and the creation of societal value by companies. It could then become relevant to differentiate between the hidden costs incurred by the company and those imposed on its external environment. On a financial level, responsible investors appreciate the environmental commitment of companies in the face of increasing regulatory requirements. This reduction in environmental risks normally also translates into a lower cost of capital (Dardour and Husser, 2016). The analysis of SDG 12 is a perfect illustration of the responsibility of companies to develop eco-designed products and services. It is concomitant with a circular economy logic (waste reduction, recycling, reuse). The delay of the company in these fields could considerably reduce the attractiveness of its products and services, and consequently lead to job losses.

Thus, hidden environmental costs can lead to hidden social costs. The reverse is also true, since dysfunctions in the social sphere can lead to ecological underperformance. Social and environmental aspects are therefore part of a system, with multiple interactions that must be integrated into an overall analysis of performance.

Moreover, the integrated reporting framework issued by the IIRC (2013, 2020) takes into consideration the various intangible capitals (Figure 66.1): the value creation process highlights a logic of incoming and outgoing capitals, subject to the impacts of the company's activity.

The IIRC approach identifies six fundamental capitals mobilized and affected by a company's activity, including natural capital. This approach invites us to revisit the model of hidden costs in order to integrate this new system of company management. According to the IIRC, natural capital corresponds to all resources and environmental processes, whether renewable or not, that provide goods or services (...). It includes air, water, land (soils), minerals and forests, biodiversity and ecosystem health.

To what extent are management systems actually capable of producing information about these different elements? In the framework of the hidden costs method created by ISEOR, the approach consists in particular of questioning the stakeholders (Savall & Zardet, 1987), with the risk that they will be much more prolix about social dysfunctions than environmental ones. In fact, the analysis of hidden environmental costs requires specific tools that allow for the precise analysis of physical flows.

1.2 New Tools for Integrating Environmental Issues

Several management tools allow for a very precise analysis of the environmental effects induced by the company's activities. In this context, we present the materiality map, followed by the new balanced scorecards and finally the life cycle assessment (LCA) methodology.

The materiality map visualizes the dialogue with stakeholders (see FD X30-031 standard). All CSR and sustainable development (SD) issues are included. They are assessed twice, with two interest scores, one from the stakeholders, the other from the company. The result is a matrix, in which the northeast quadrant contains the important topics shared by the company and its stakeholders, and the southwest quadrant the topics that are less important for all stakeholders. Two areas of disagreement appear in the two remaining quadrants. In the context of an analysis of hidden costs, the opinions expressed by internal and external stakeholders would help to better understand the differences of opinion.

The issues visualized in the materiality map should be related to the company's strategic objectives. Kaplan and Norton (1992, 2004) proposed to represent the strategy of companies in the form of a graphic tool. Initially composed of four axes (learning, internal processes, customers, financial), it was progressively amended in the face of the growing importance of CSR themes, into an "Integrated Scorecard," which integrates a fifth strategic axis, environmental. The study of cause and effect relationships between the different strategic objectives, and in particular the environmental axis, can help identify dysfunctions and therefore hidden costs.

Finally, the most reliable and scientific tool for assessing environmental impacts is LCA (life cycle assessment). The analysis is based on an inventory of the different physical flows (Figure 66.2), translated into environmental impact indicators. LCA provides clear information on the environmental impacts at the scale of a product or an organization. The indicators generated by the LCA can be used in a dashboard. Once the LCA calculations have been established and the method has been well integrated within the company, the analytical grid of hidden costs would allow a better understanding of the reasons why certain organizational

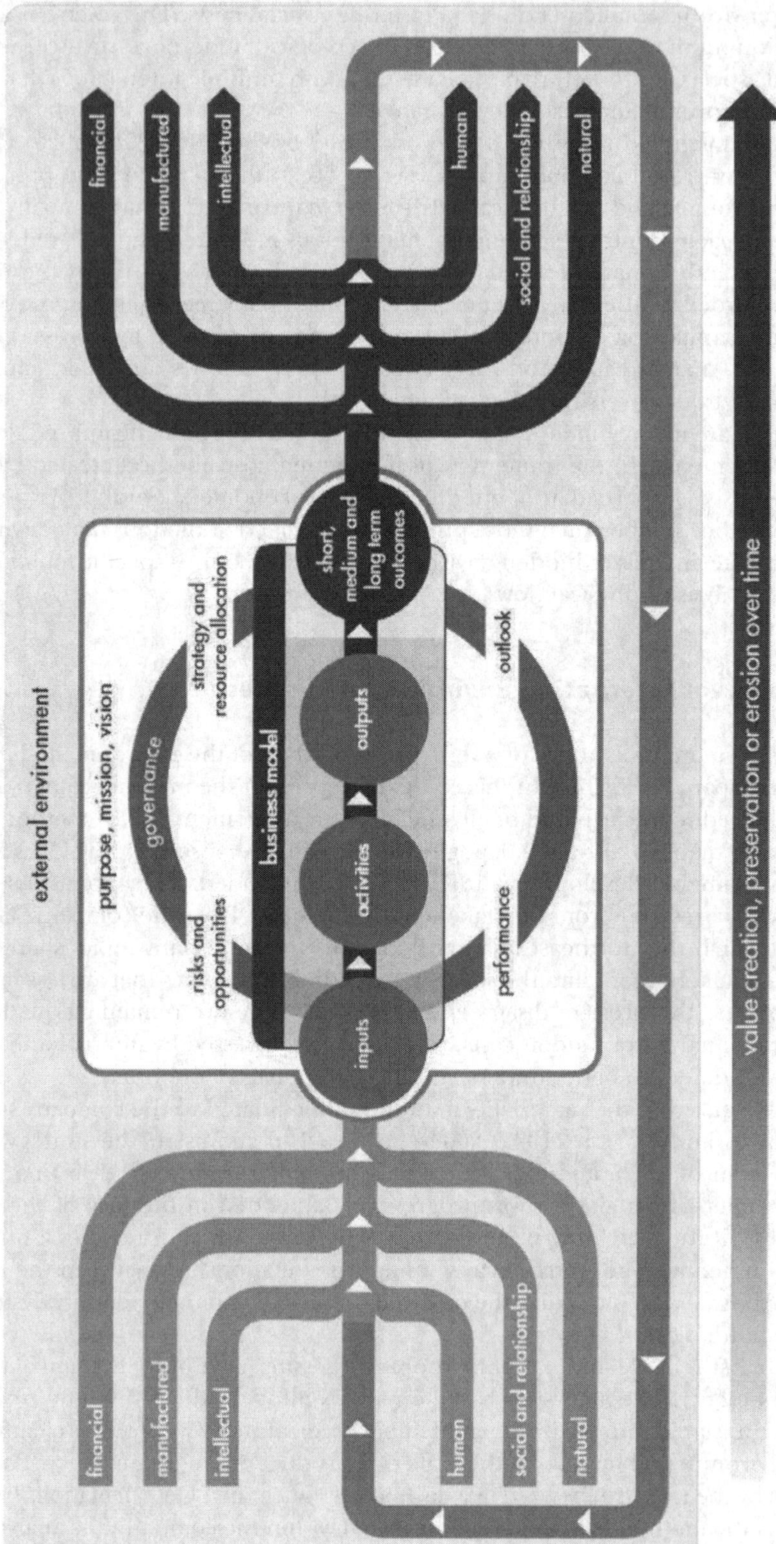

Figure 66.1 IIRC value creation diagram (International Integrated Reporting Council, 2020 version).

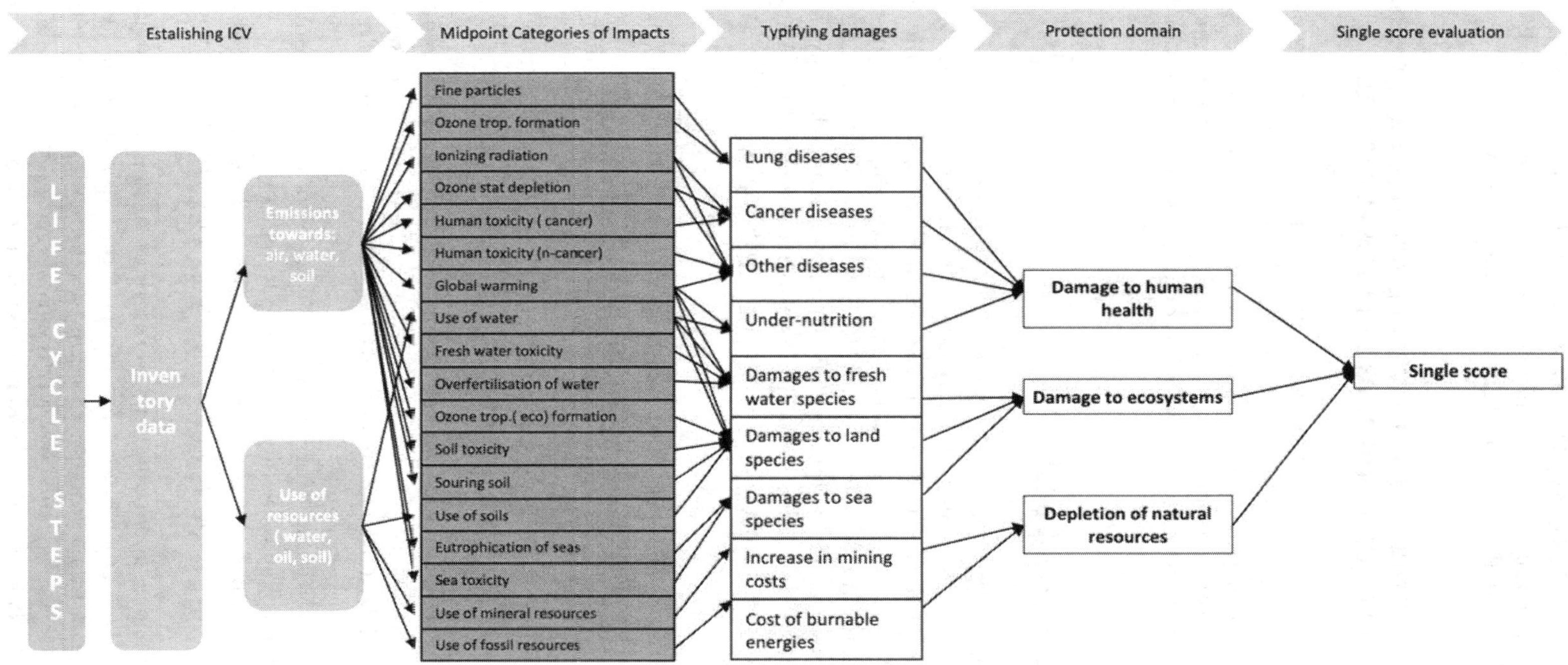

Figure 66.2 Calculation of the different impacts according to the environmental Life Cycle Assessment methodology (Jourdaine, 2020).

changes are not made. Three key blocking factors are likely to be communication, training and strategic implementation failures. Underestimating the associated risks or misunderstanding the lack of potential can lead to significant financial losses.

2 CONTRIBUTIONS OF THE OVERALL PERFORMANCE MODEL AND ILLUSTRATIONS BASED ON A FEW CASES

We discuss the possibility of taking hidden costs into account by using the concept of global performance. The latter has the advantage of integrating a series of diverse and recent issues, which no other management tool has yet managed to bring together and integrate. Without losing sight of the contribution of standards and tools to environmental management, we illustrate, using several cases, the inclusion of ecological aspects in the historical model of hidden costs.

2.1 Global Performance Model

The model shown in Figure 66.3 is the result of work undertaken by the CJD (*Centre des Jeunes Dirigeants*) and the insurance company Generali. The first is the EFQM model, corresponding to operational excellence (M1). The second corresponds to the consideration of stakeholders, with a view to creating value through partnership (M2). The third refers to the ISO 31000 standard on risk management (M3). The implementation of these three approaches requires, however, that a foundation be laid beforehand, clarifying the company's mission (S1), vision (S2), and values (S3). The governance system (S4) that has been put in place guarantees this. The company is invited to develop its vigilance and its transformation on four major transitions:

- The first is territorial (T1), encouraging the company to enter into a strategy of local cooperation in connection with the sustainability of its eco-system.
- The second is energetic (T2) and corresponds to the announced end of hydrocarbons.
- The third is digital (T3).
- Finally, the fourth integrates the circular economy (T4), in contrast to a linear logic leading to the depletion of resources.

All of these elements allow the company to innovate (L1), to differentiate (L2), to strengthen its brand equity (L3), to reduce its exposure to risks and to control the cost-quality-delay triptych (L4), and finally to optimize its sales and the seizure of new opportunities (L5).

The model makes it possible to bring together a series of often scattered and partial concerns. It makes it possible to be more aware of the risks incurred in the event that the company neglects certain transitions. It also suggests the complementarity of management approaches based on the concepts of continuous improvement, risk management and stakeholder management.

The global performance model can then be cross-referenced with the list of dysfunctions associated with the hidden cost model. A first cross-reference is made with the dysfunctions of "strategic implementation." Whether in terms of information systems (605) or strategic implementation tools (604), the company is encouraged to reflect on the issues of energy and circularity. It is also possible to identify the dysfunctions of "integrated training."

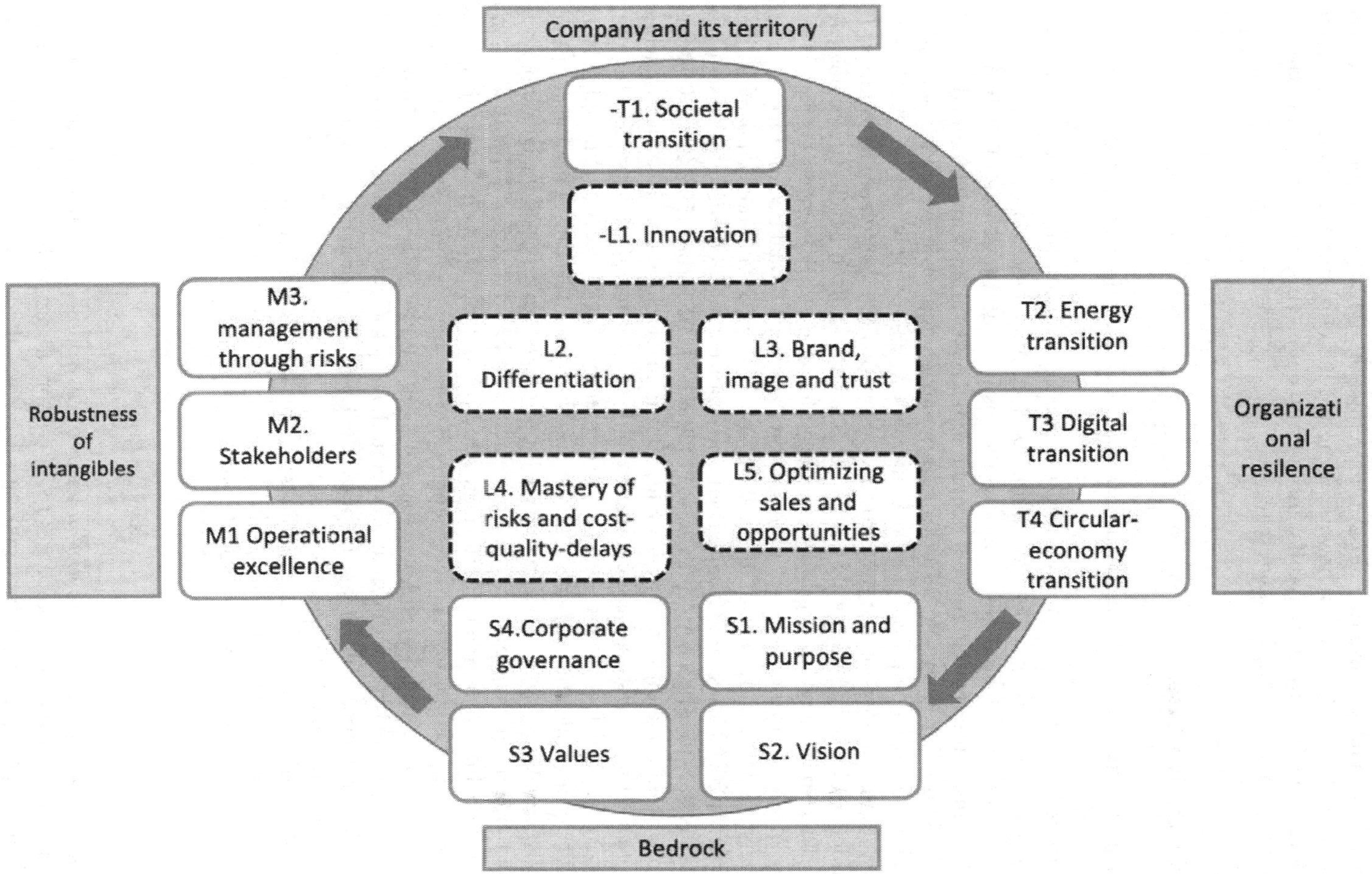

Figure 66.3 Global performance model (Trébucq, Pinault, & Kourda, 2020).

Indeed, the ability to make certain transitions (energy, circularity) depends on the use of training and certain specific skills (502, 503). The good environmental and ecological governance of the company also depends on the reduction of its dysfunctions related to communication (305). Within the framework of the hidden cost method, obvious interactions can be identified. We now turn to different cases that allow us to appreciate the nature and variety of these interactions in concrete terms.

2.2 Illustrative Cases

In order to illustrate our cases, we use the grid of dysfunctions used in the hidden costs method.

According to Aguirre (2020), if we take the case of wineries, they currently have only a limited capacity to embrace the entire global performance model. In general, their information systems are deficient (605), due to the insufficient knowledge of their managers (602). Training plans to integrate new environmental issues are not implemented (502, 503, 504, 607). This failure may also result from the management style, which is not conducive to exchanges between employees and managers (608, 309, 310). Jourdaine (2020), for his part, has shown the weakness of the information systems (605) available to wineries. They have difficulty identifying their stakeholders and lack the skills to develop an ecological approach. This type of dysfunction deserves to be added to the ISEOR grid.

In the ADAM company, the environmental approach began to take shape through a series of partnerships and the support of external experts. However, when the company wanted to have an AFAQ 26000 assessment, aligned with the requirements of the ISO 26000 standard, it became necessary to hire a person dedicated full-time to CSR issues (503, 207). This person organized the information system (605). The ability to involve all staff in a CSR approach, sensitive to environmental issues, was accompanied by a transformation of the management style, giving it a more participative and collaborative dimension (608). The availability of personnel to consider ecological issues requires a prior improvement in working conditions (104, 107). The implementation of an eco-design strategy for products also involved the creation of a new innovation-oriented department (201). The manager reduced a series of dysfunctions in order to improve the environmental performance of his company. The benefits of this approach are multiple. The commitment of the youngest staff has been reinforced. The company has increased its reputation and strengthened its bargaining power with customers. However, the company does not yet have an information system that is sufficiently advanced to continuously supply indicators comparable to those of an LCA. The skills available (503) can significantly reduce the extent of hidden environmental costs.

These illustrations confirm the usefulness of the ISEOR dysfunction grid, but also the possibility of its evolution on certain evaluation criteria, and finally the difficulty of a financial calculation of hidden environmental costs.

CONCLUSION

The implementation of a methodology in terms of environmental management such as Life Cycle Assessment now allows companies to be equipped with rigorous tools for evaluating the ecological consequences of their activities. However, the indicators resulting from such an approach do not allow for an appreciation of all the negative effects of poor environmental management. The latter has financial consequences on the company's performance.

Poor environmental performance has a negative impact on the company's brand image, reducing trust and the durability of relations with all stakeholders. From this point of view, the ISEOR dysfunction grid appears to be highly relevant in isolating a series of key variables for action. Strategy, training and communication are all levers for transformation. The integration of the themes of the global performance model could also be used to update this grid, as could the process of identifying and dialoguing with stakeholders. The theory of hidden costs and performance can now be deployed in information environments enriched with new standards and new management tools. However, a huge amount of analysis and accumulation of observations and materials is required if we want to reach a stage where artificial intelligence could be mobilized to assist decision-makers in their project of recycling hidden costs.

NOTE

1. See the academic conference series devoted since 2015 to "New Business Models." https://www.nbmconference.eu

REFERENCES

Aguirre, J. (2020). *Réflexion sur la préparation d'un plan stratégique pour les Vignobles K en utilisant une modélisation de la performance globale*, mémoire de master 2 Direction Financière Contrôle de Gestion et Audit Interne, IAE de Bordeaux.

CJD. (2004). *Le guide de la performance globale : 100 questions pour faire votre diagnostic et établir votre plan d'action.* Editions d'Organisation.

Dardour A, & Husser J. (2016). Does it pay to disclose CSR information? Evidence from French companies. *Management International*, 20, 94–108.

Freeman, R. E. (1984). *Strategic Management: A Stakeholder Approach*, Pitman Editions.

ISO 31000. (2018). *Management du risque: lignes directrices.* AFNOR.

Jourdaine, M. (2020). *Mise en place d'une comptabilité analytique environnementale mobilisant l'Analyse de Cycle de Vie (ACV) et l'Activity-Based-Costing (ABC): application au cas viti-vinicole*, Thèse de sciences de gestion, soutenue à l'Université de Bordeaux, 24 novembre.

Kaplan R. S., & Norton D. (1992). The Balanced Scorecard. Measures That Drive Performance. *Harvard Business Review, 70*(1), 71–79.

Kaplan R. S., & Norton, D. (2004). Measuring the Strategic Readiness of Intangible Assets. *Harvard Business Review*, 82(2), 52–63.

Trébucq, S., Pinault L.-R., & Kourda, H. (2020). Auditer la «performance globale: retour d'expérience d'un outil destiné aux PME françaises et proposition d'une nouvelle définition, 22ème Université de printemps de l'Audit Social «Audit social et RSE au travers du prisme de la chaîne globale de valeur», 28–29 mai, à paraître dans la revue *Management & Avenir.*

Trébucq, S. (2017). Mise en place d'une comptabilité carbone à l'échelle des produits: le cas d'une PME de la filière bois. *Recherches en Sciences de Gestion, 118*(1), 65–96.

X30-031. (2013). *Responsabilité sociétale—Gouvernance et responsabilité sociétale—SO 26000*, AFNOR.

X30-037. (2020). *Objectifs de Développement Durable de l'ONU, lien entre la Responsabilité Sociétale selon l'ISO 26000 et le Développement Durable*, AFNOR.

This page intentionally left blank.

CHAPTER 67

FROM THE TERRITORY AS A TERRITORY OF STANDARDS TO ISO STANDARDS WITHOUT TERRITORIES

Yvon Pesqueux and Benoît Pigé

ABSTRACT

Normative conflict is a tangle of norms that places people at odds with that they must live with in the society around them. The failure to take into-account the possible conflicting nature of standards is explained by the process of a-territorialization of international standards. The reference to "interested stakeholders" marks the shift from a status of a-territorial standard (ISOs were "industrial" standards) to that of political standards. This passage opens the question of multi-level governance art the level of territory by consensus with the more distant levels.

Modern society is experiencing the rise of multiple sources of standardization. While these sources can be grouped into a limited number of main streams (Savall and Zardet, 2005), standards nevertheless aim to cover all dimensions of human activity. The loss of the legal hierarchy, which ordered norms within a supposedly independent and omnipotent state, has opened she door to an increase in normative conflicts (Bessire et al., 2010). The consequence of normative inflation (Thibierge, 2014) leads organizations to paralysis (for those who can only endure norms) or to clientelism and lobbying (for those who seek to influence the normative process).

In this ineluctable chain of events, the way out seems to be that of the strongest. Nevertheless, the observation of organizations shows that: if organizations manage to influence the normative processes to obtain a respite from short-term pressures, they deprive themselves of the dynamic that contestation and the questioning of acquired situations bring. As a

SEAM Treatise, pages 561–566

result, they become fossilized and are overtaken by new competitors who are more attentive to the underlying social issues.

In the short term, the apparent stake is the control of the norm. In the medium and long term, the issue at stake is the coherence between the norms that govern the behavior of people within an organization. Normative conflict is not only a tangle of norms that make any action and decision impossible, it is also and more fundamentally a conflict that places people in a situation of contradiction with what they have to live with the society around them (Pigé, 2019). The schizophrenia that threatens organizations translates into an organizational disinterest that merely reflects the inability of human beings to reconcile the irreconcilable.

1 THE TERRITORY AS A TERRITORY OF STANDARDS AND NORMS

A territory is a geographical space that is imposed on the individual, but it is also a human and social construct (Pigé, 2018). This construct may seem "natural" as a consequence of a historical process (France, communes, regions, Europe, etc.) but it is always simultaneously the result of a human representation of some form of reality.

In this constructivist logic, a territory is distinguished from others by the norms that apply to it. These norms may be common or specific, but their unique combination makes the territory under consideration distinct from others (Pigé, 2015). For example, France shares many common norms with other European Union states, but it also has norms that are unique to it or that it shares with a limited number of countries. Similarly, the suburbs of large cities share French norms, but specific norms may also apply there that are not observed in city centers or in the countryside, but that can be observed in other countries, including on other continents. Negotiating the place of the norm in the organization thus requires taking territoriality into account (Cappelletti et al., 2015).

1.1 The Violence of A-Territorial Standards and Norms

A-territorial standards and norms are norms designed and enacted without specific reference to a territory. They are considered to reflect a globalized common good. This is the case for human rights and most standards issued by international organizations. For example, international accounting standards (IFRS) are supposed to provide the most accurate representation possible of the activity of the entities concerned. The ISO standards are supposed to offer the representation of a management system that is uniformly applicable throughout the world and regardless of the sector of activity.

This mode of representation is violent because it presupposes that the entity (or person) subject to the standards in question is in an environment that is itself implicitly considered as standardized. Thus, the systematic reference to market prices in the case of IFRS assumes that all the territories concerned by this standardization have markets that function in accordance with the implicit postulates of the accounting standards and therefore that market prices reflect a fair value. However, one only has to look at a number of countries that have adopted IFRS (e.g., many African states, but also China) to realize that the implicit framework of application does not exist or is not respected or does not correspond to local standards.

Normative violence emerges because there is an inherent normative power in the norm. To exist and to survive, the norm must impose itself. This is what constitutes its performativity, without which a norm "does not exist." This requirement for recognition and application, which is linked to the standard, refers to the game of standardizers. Because the standard generates power relationships, constitutes a market, and induces goodwill and rents, it becomes a tool for increasing the political and economic interests of the actors involved in its design and application (Savall and Zardet, 2005). The reference system then becomes a violent weapon against those who refuse to apply it, because this refusal challenges the underlying positions and interests, regardless of the legitimacy or otherwise of standardization.

1.2 Normative Conflict as the Cause of Normative Violence

Normative violence is not only due to normative power. It is only expressed if actors refuse to enter the normative game. Actors can refuse to enter the game because the norms they are asked to apply are in opposition to those that govern their daily lives. It is not necessarily a question of a desire to resist what comes from outside, but also of an impossibility of applying the requested norm, because it jeopardizes the equilibrium that governs the life of the community within a territory. For example, the financialization of transactions can brutally disrupt the exchanges in kind that take place within a community.

Implicit in the universal process of standardization is the assumption that all individuals are equal, but also that the common good can be defined at the individual level. The international norm gradually tends to be declined in concrete terms, assuming that each individual is in the same configuration and that there is a universal individual ideal (which could be the ideal of the anonymous individual of a society, the ant evoked by Henri Bergson, 1932).

Because each person is not only marked by the habits and customs of the community in which he or she is born, but also by his or her biological and psychic history, the normative perception differs from one person to another. These differences are accentuated when collective differences linked to belonging to societies that are both common and distinct are superimposed on these individual differences. Between the individual and humanity, the territories ensure the daily living together. This living-together must certainly evolve as society changes (including in its composition), but it presupposes that all norms be evaluated in terms of this living-together, which is necessarily embodied and territorialized.

The failure to take into account the possible conflictuality of norms is explained by the process of a-territorialization of international norms. As long as they remain at the level of principles and leave it to each territory to manage the concrete applications, normative conflict can be managed. For example, the principle of gender equality, which originates from the representations of Northern countries, can be considered a norm. This norm only becomes conflictual when it imposes concrete prescriptions on territories where these prescriptions emerge in contradiction to other pre-existing norms, which conceive this principle in another way. Thus, the norm of professional equality between men and women is based on the existence of collective institutions that take care of young or sick children. When local norms provide for a marked division of male and female roles in the family domain, conflicts may emerge between professional and family norms.

Recognizing the territorialization of norms means recognizing that a norm can, or must, only become concrete in relation to specific territories where governance modalities will govern the transformation of a principle into a technical prescription. Otherwise, the actors confronted with a standard that imposes itself on them have no other apparent solution than forced submission (ultimately generating violence), transgression or revolt.

2 ISO STANDARDS WITHOUT TERRITORY: FROM "STAKEHOLDERS" TO "INTERESTED PARTIES"

It is in the context of the growing importance of the reference to sustainable development, and more specifically to the energy transition, that it is important to underline today the reference to "interested parties," as is the case with the COPs (Conference of the Parties). This is the case of ISO standards and therefore of those of the "ISO package" (the certifiable ISOs of the "environment–social–economic" trilogy). With regard to the previous argument on the violence of a-territorial standards, the reference to "interested parties" marks the transition from their status as a-territorial technical standards (the ISOs were "industrial" standards) to that of political standards. This passage opens the question of a multi-level governance by consensus, without territory stricto sensu but allowing the territory level to build a consensus with the more distant levels.

The generality of ISO standards also indicates a more overall project of governance without reference to a territory, hence the expression used in this text of "standard without territory."

The three ISO standards that can be certified are

- the "Quality: ISO 9001 (version 2015)" standard, the mother of standards, as the other standards adopt the same concepts and structure, thus founding a broader conception of quality,
- the standard "Environmental management system" ISO 14001 (version 2015), and
- the "Occupational health and safety management systems" standard "ISO 45001" (version 2018"), putting an end to the "social-societal" tension and integrating the directives issued by the ILO.

These standards are a general reference, in the absence of national regulations which, when they exist, at least validate their contents by declining them for each field of activity, public or private. The other standards are certifiable on a voluntary basis, their legitimacy being a function of their successful use. This "quality–environment–social" trilogy aims to bring a little harmonization into the categories of tetranormalization.

Around the government negotiators, a COP brings together seven categories of "parties," in search of a common language and able to continue to participate in COPs and to apply their expectations independently of each other and even of the position of governments. For example, many U.S. municipalities continue to participate in the COPs and to implement their outcomes, despite the withdrawal of the U.S. government.

The "interested parties" are the following: scientists, notwithstanding the diversity of the fields concerned, NGOs (non-governmental organizations) despite their diversity, companies with regard to their commitments in terms of sustainable development, despite the diversity of their sector and size, trade unions despite the diversity of their nature and their rights in the various countries, local authorities with regard to the challenges of sustainable development at the meso and micro levels, associations for CSR and sustainable development, and representatives of minorities with regard to the respect of their rights.

The reference to "interested parties" makes it possible to step back from the violence of a-territorial standards, insofar as the renewed ISOs constitute the "first level" of multi-level governance by consensus. The ISO standards thus refer to the notion of "interested party" with regard to "common principles":

- a reference to continuous improvement as the foundation of a governance dynamic;
- a reference to significant thresholds built on the basis of defined objectives and monitoring indicators that are consistent in space and time, with reference to the principle of materiality and the challenge of comparability;
- the reference to the construction of a "management system" through the effect of composition between standards;
- the reference to the notion of "organization," thus the vocation of ISO standards to be applicable to both public and private entities; and
- the alignment of each standard with its contribution to the Sustainable Development Goals of the 2030 Agenda.

CONCLUSION: MULTI-LEVEL GOVERNANCE BY CONSENSUS

There can no longer be any standards without governance (de Rozario and Pesqueux, 2018), as standards constitute the substance that underpins the logic of their implementation with regard to "living together." So, between a territory as a territory of norms and ISO norms without territories, what kind of governance is involved?

The multi-level governance by consensus applies as well to the territories of standards as to the standards without territory in front of the question of sustainable development (which is also in some way that of "living together" sustainably). It has been proposed as a response to the limits of neo-Malthusian analyses of the "tragedy of the commons," which associate the depletion of natural resources with the absence of a rational social organization, and to institutional approaches that reduce environmental crises to problems of governance. The founding hypothesis of this governance is that the environment is a matter of multi-level regulation defined as the interlocking of the processes of developing norms and governance between the international, national, regional and local levels, which is why it is called "polycentric governance" (Marks, Hooghe, and Blank, 1996), since it makes it possible to take into account the articulation of the different scales of action involved in the regulation of natural resources Hooghe and Marks (2003) distinguish two types of multi-level governance by consensus, one limited to political or governmental responsibilities and competencies, and the other extended to several levels of competencies and to other territorial spheres, with regard to flexible fields of competence concerning all the modalities of "living together." It aims to make standards of disparate level and purpose compatible.

Multi-level governance by consensus is part of a logic of cooperation, compromise and joint elaboration of the rules of "living together" by articulating territorialized norms and norms without territory, in order to take into account the changes in scale that mark the territorialization of environmental policies, allowing the agents concerned to create a community of interest that makes cooperation and "living together" possible. "Polycentric governance" (Prenkert and Shackelford, 2014) has also been mentioned as a modality of "climate governance" composed of evolving coalitions with no clearly defined hierarchy, under the aegis of the United Nations, which plays a role as the generative component of a complex regime.

The OECD (2012) defines multi-level governance as

> the explicit or implicit sharing of decision-making power, responsibilities and competencies for policy development and implementation between different levels of government and territorial scales, that is: (i) between different ministries and/or government agencies at the central

> government level (horizontal coordination at the top level); (ii) between different levels of government at the local, regional, provincial/state, national, and supranational levels (vertical coordination); and (iii) between different actors at the subnational level (horizontal coordination at the bottom level.

Multi-level governance by consensus thus aims to articulate a territory of norms to norms without a territory, even if the criticism levelled at this type of governance (whether it is described as participatory or multi-level) is its potential for saturation, insofar as it gives rise to what can be described as "saturated governance", i.e., governance in which the management team consumes its resources in articulating with the "interested parties" both to meet their expectations and to be accountable to them, to the detriment of "doing." The question of how to challenge the anomie that is at stake with tetranormalization is therefore open.

In the face of the heterogeneity of normative sources put forward by the tetranormalization thesis, multilevel governance by consensus offers the beginning of a way out, not only because of the consensus that marks its substance, but also because of the project to integrate the different levels.

REFERENCES

Bergson, H. (1932). Les Deux sources de la morale et de la religion, PUF, 1959.

Bessire, D., Cappelletti, L., & Pigé, B. (Eds.). (2010). *Normes: Origines et Conséquences des Crises.* Economica.

Cappelletti, L., Pigé, B., & Zardet, V. (Eds.). (2015). *Dynamique normative, Arbitrating and negotiating the place of the norm in the organization.* EMS.

De Rozario, P., & Pesqueux, Y. (2018). *Theory of organizations.* Pearson.

Hardin, G. (1968). The tragedy of the commons. *Science,* 162, 1243–1248.

Hooghe, L., & Marks, G. (2003). Unraveling the central state, but how? Types of multi-level governance. *American Political Science Review, 97*(2), 233–243.

Marks, G., Hooghe, L., & Blank, K. (1996). European Integration from the 1980s: State Centric v. Multi-level Governance. *Journal of Common Market Studies, 9,* 356–371.

OECD. (2012). *Water Governance in OECD Countries: A Multi-level Approach, OECD Water Studies.* OECD Publishing. http://dx.doi.org/10.1787/9789264168244-fr

Pigé, B. (2015). La convergence internationale des normes comptables: Panoptique ou tour de Babel? *Recherches en Sciences de Gestion,* 106, 67–88.

Pigé, B. (2018). L'inscription du territoire et des institutions dans le temps long – Les enjeux pour la gouvernance des organisations. *Prospective et Stratégie, 9,* 63–75.

Pigé, B. (2019). Théorie et fondements théoriques de la Tétranormalisation. *Recherches en Sciences de Gestion,* 131, 215–240.

Prenkert, J., & Shackelford, S. (2014). Business, Human Rights and the Promise of Polycentricity. *Vanderbilt Journal of Transnational Law,* vol. 47, n° 451.

Thibierge C., et al. (2014). *Normative densification, discovering a process.* Mare & Martin.

CHAPTER 68

THE MANAGEMENT OF NORMATIVE INFLATION BY CONTROL AND MANAGEMENT FUNCTIONS

Case of the French Financial Sector

Nicolas Dufour and Imen Abdou

ABSTRACT

This chapter deals with the issue of the complex management of standards and regulations in the financial sector. Our objective is to illustrate the fact that standards can be anticipated, managed and negotiated. They require a clear positioning of the governance of financial institutions, but also a real and daily involvement of management and operational staff. The chapter addresses this issue through case studies in the French financial sector.

This chapter puts into perspective the way financial organizations anticipate and manage standards. The reinforced normativity is the result of the numerous crises and financial scandals of the XXI century. This sector perfectly illustrates the idea that standards are both the cause and the consequence of crises. On the one hand, standards, particularly prudential standards, are strengthened following crises, such as the subprime crisis or the sovereign debt crisis. On the other hand, these approaches, often based on complementary capital allocations, only deal with the consequences of crises and not with their causes (Bessire et al., 2010, Dufour, 2011, Yacoub, 2018). Faced with these challenges, the strengthening of standards is a major trend for the financial sector. We develop how this strong trend implies having to deal with potential contradictions in the management of standards, referring to the framework of tetranormalization (Savall & Zardet, 2005; Cappelletti, Pigé, Zardet, 2015).

SEAM Treatise, pages 567–573

These contradictions may be inherent to the standards themselves or may be the result of choices imposed by the application of multiple standards by a single financial institution.

1 DENSIFICATION OF STANDARDS AND NORMS IN THE FINANCIAL SECTOR

We highlight, through the managerial and academic literature, the challenge of strengthening standards in the different spheres of the economy, as a response to risk.

1.1 The Logic of Self-Control and the Risk Society

It is interesting to try to translate the impacts of this normative densification in the organization, based on the idea that the different bodies of norms respond to the paradigm of the Risk Society: the norm is a response to risk, consubstantial with our post-modern societies where we try to deal with risk through an attempt at standardization (Beck, 1986). The main axes of risk in post-modern society suggest the axes of normative densification: consumer protection, economic and financial risks, security and environmental risks.

1.1.1 Financial Security: A Cycle of Continuous Reinforcement

Let's take the example of an area that has been considerably strengthened in terms of regulation in Europe over the last ten years. Financial security regulations cover the risk areas of money laundering, fraud and corruption. As these risks are now perceived as major risks, the response of governmental and transnational authorities has resulted in a legislative and regulatory arsenal, which advocates a set of self-monitoring and whistle-blowing measures, particularly for private organizations. Let's take a look at the regulations implemented and the organizational measures expected to be applied. At the same time as these texts are becoming more and denser, contradictions appear when these regulatory developments are brought together with others.

1.1.2 Customer's Protection: Normative and Moral Hazards

For several years, it has been essential to take into account the context of normative hazard. The protection of customers and consumers is a very illustrative example. This field concerns several regulatory texts that have reinforced the control of commercial practices of financial institutions. These regulations are often the result of financial risks assumed by the subscribers of financial products and services, be it financial losses or non-actionable guarantees. Financial scandals and sanctions of institutions are all crises that provide examples of regulatory reinforcements perceived as necessary: RGPD regulations, MiFID II regulations on financial instruments, regulations on payment services, financial security law, directive on insurance distribution. These successive regulations impose a level of security and control in order to protect policyholders.

1.1.3 Prudential and Accounting Regulations: A Reactive Approach to Risk Management

It is essential to take into account the strengthening of financial and prudential regulations (solvency of financial institutions), including the risk of default by banking and insurance institutions. While these regulations are once again a response to risk, such measures have a limit. Indeed, prudential regulations deal primarily with the consequences of risks, through the allocation of capital, and to a lesser extent with the anticipation of the causes of risks.

1.2 Controlling the Densification of Standards and Norms: The Emergence of Multiple Supervisory Authorities

The densification and complexity of regulations imply taking into account a diversity of risks: prudential, financial security and customer protection. Indeed, the above-mentioned regulations relating to the three main categories of financial risks, i.e., financial security risks, protection against risks borne by clients and protection against financial crises, are each subject to controls. These different risks have seen the emergence of various control authorities, notably the ECB, the Banque de France, the AMF and the ACPR in the prudential field. In the area of customer protection, we can mention the DDPP, the ACPR and the CNIL. In the area of financial security (money laundering, fraud, corruption), we can mention the AFA, Tracfin, the DNLF, the BRDA or the ACPR. These are all entities that are supposed to intervene in the management and control of the proper application of standards, or in the production of doctrine and analyses of the way in which these standards should be applied...

2 CASE STUDIES OF NORMATIVE DENSIFICATION IN THE FINANCIAL SECTOR

These two cases illustrate the management problems inherent in normative densification. One example relates to the banking sector and the other to the insurance sector.

2.1 The Case of a Banking Institution

This first example taken from a doctoral research (Yacoub, 2018) focuses on normative contradictions and highlights the following dysfunctions:

2.1.1 Financial Ratio Conflicts

The NSFR (Net Stable Funding Ratio) and LCR (Liquidity Coverage Ratio) ratios pursue contradictory objectives, bringing into confrontation a short-term vision and a medium-long-term vision of liquidity management. The most surprising thing about these two ratios is that they are derived from the same standard. It should also be noted that these ratios are in contradiction with the transformation role of banks. Indeed, transforming liabilities by issuing assets, according to the historically established role of intermediation and transformation of banks, is partly called into question by this temporal management of liquidity. Indirectly, an increase in provisions will also reduce the financial results of institutions and thus limit their capacity to strengthen their capital.

2.1.2 Conflicts Between Accounting Standards

IFRS 9 and Basel III standards on the same subject of loan impairment are in competition. This competition between standards leads to redundant work, generates operational complexity and a lack of visibility in risk management. The most critical aspect of the loan impairment process is the staged approach, which categorizes an entity's exposures into three categories or stages, depending on whether there is a significant increase in credit risk.

2.1.3 Organizational Conflicts

Banks adopt the regulations without fully integrating them into the definition and construction of all their operational processes. Indeed, the standard penetrates all structures and spreads to all actors of the bank. Banking standards are becoming increasingly complex, even for banking professionals, who are confronted with a very large number of standards, as well as the links and interdependencies inherent in regulation. An internal process of integrating standards into the bank's organization is necessary in order to promote their effectiveness and sustainability.

2.2 The Case of a Life Insurance Company

In this chapter we study the normative response to financial risks, which induce multiple normative conflicts. Based on intervention-research conducted within a life insurance company, a subsidiary of a wealth bank (Dufour, 2020), we establish the following category of norm conflicts:

2.2.1 Conflicts Between Standards (LCB-FT, RGPD)

This first category of conflicts of norms illustrates the ontological opposition between, on the one hand, financial security regulations, which can be unfavorable to the insured and even result in intrusive controls and alerts, and, on the other hand, regulations on the protection of private data (RGPD), which concern the protection of personal data. This first type of conflict of norms is that of the oppositions inherent in the regulations themselves, which can be described as inter-norm conflict.

2.2.2 Conflicts of Interpretation (RGPD, Solvency II)

The second category of conflict is the very consequence of the interpretative nature of standards. The actors of an organization do not agree on the fact that the regulation applies or not, or they are opposed on the capacity or the way to apply it in the company. Opposition may even arise because of the threshold for the application of regulations.

2.2.3 Regulatory Conflicts

This category of conflict arises when regulatory authorities have a different assessment of how a standard should be applied. Organizations must then deal with different supervisory authorities to which they are accountable.

2.2.4 Conflicts in the Application of Standards

This category details what can be described as intrinsic to a single standard. In the application of standards, the problem of interpretation of texts implies that the organization subject to them should define the level of depth and the methods of application of the said standard. This issue of self-control of the standard has the consequence of generating conflicts between stakeholders of the organization, as to the level of compliance to be implemented. These conflicts may arise, for example, between business functions and functions in charge of compliance control.

3 MANAGERIAL PERSPECTIVES

This section makes reasoned proposals to help provide a framework for managing standards in organizations.

3.1 Managing the Integration of Standards and Norms

The policies, processes and controls necessary to enable an organization to manage the integration of standards must be deployed. These compliance policies require, among other things, the integration of processes for arbitrating on standards, but also for orchestrating the application of the standard within the entity.

3.2 The Compliance Budget and the Cost of Standards and Norms

Managing standards requires quantifying the impact of integrating them into the organization, given that increased regulation negatively affects the overall profitability of the banking sector. When integrating standards, the negative effects of increased standards should be anticipated: for example, customers should not have to pay for a financial institution to comply. It should not be possible to pass on the costs of regulation and compliance to customers (Dufour, 2018). Finally, managing standards involves a trade-off between the budget needed to be compliant and the risk of not implementing a standard and being sanctioned. This benefit-risk approach must be qualified for risks with an ethical/customer protection dimension or that meet an obligation of result.

3.3 The Risk Cost/Opportunity Trade-Off: Can Regulations Not Be Applied?

It seems important to us to address the principle that it is sometimes more detrimental to apply a standard in its entirety than to seek to adapt it to the sectoral and organizational context of a company. According to this principle, it is possible to make trade-offs on the application of regulations. This arbitration depends in particular on the probability of a standard being audited and the probability of sanctions in the event of an audit. Some standards are not subject to any control or sanction. The question of their application is above all ethical (the question of the goal sought) and refers more to the risk of reputation than to the risk of compliance. But this issue is dated: for many years, insurance companies wondered how to apply the regulations to prevent escheatment: faced with the absence of control and standards that were never sanctioned in the event of non-compliance, many insurers thus postponed their compliance projects. But in 2017, this deputy general manager we met explained to us: "Insurers' sanctions as of 2015 on this subject have thus reshuffled the cards and put the laws on the prevention of escheated contracts back on top of the pile. It took heavy fines to get projects in place and move the lines. Arbitration is allowed until the risk of sanctions becomes real. This raises an ethical question, however.

3.4 The "Stockholmization" of Control

Companies may "overtranspose" certain regulations under the effect of two types of pressure:

- pressure from their sectoral supervisory authority, which sees in the over-application of certain texts the fact that the company is ahead of other companies in the sector; and

- internal pressure from the organization, linked to the fact that showing over-application of the texts gives the impression that the risks are under control. However, this apparent ethics may nevertheless hide other underestimated or even unknown risks.

These observations are particularly noticeable in the financial sector. Some French financial institutions have departments of several hundred or even thousands of employees in charge of compliance, risk, internal control and audit. Let's also mention the excess of procedures and committees exposed by this compliance manager in 2017: "Our bank has 12 anti-money laundering procedures and 3 dedicated committees that meet every month. We are compliant but this represents a high cost for clients who pay for all these controls. In the end, we generate discontent because all these structures do not protect them any more but create management red tape."

How do you avoid redundancy or even "over-quality" in the integration of standards? A compliance director, in 2013, illustrated this as follows: "For the past 15 years, we have observed a trend towards the "stockholmization" of control: the banks multiply the controls and over-transpose the texts to please the supervisory authorities, who of course do not say that this is excessive. They are there to say when a rule is not respected, they are not there to give advice if it is applied in an inefficient or ineffective way. This is ultimately counterproductive because internal controllers lose their ability to alert as they manage risk in a bureaucratic or administrative manner."

3.5 Some Recommendations for the Management of Standards and Norms

The transdisciplinarity of the standard would make it possible to efficiently integrate the standard as a whole, in all the structures of the financial institution. Moreover, this transdisciplinarity allows for "cleaning up" linked to better management and elimination of redundancies. In order to avoid the above-mentioned drift, several areas of management of the standard seem relevant to us to develop:

- indicators dedicated to the management of the standard (quantity of standards applied, delay in the application of standards, rate of compliance per standard, customer dissatisfaction resulting from the application of standards, incidents with compliance impacts, are we saying better than the competition on compliance etc.) and
- A formalized budget dedicated to the management of standards: tools, human resources, dedicated governance.

It is essential to provide for arbitration mechanisms for the standard, such as a compliance committee. Indeed, efficient and effective management of the standard implies arbitrating the application of the standard itself, but also the best way to apply it (partially/totally/under what conditions). In addition, the creation of a structure for the management, optimization and coordination of the standard that brings together several experts in the banking sector would allow the transdisciplinarity of the standard within financial institutions, by having a synchronized management of the integration of the standard that goes beyond the disciplinary framework of the normative perimeter.

CONCLUSION

Like other recent research on the management of standards, continuing the search for a comprehensive managerial framework in the face of normative density is essential, even if it is only a partial response to the problem of the Risk Society (Cappelletti, Dufour, 2017, 2020).

The institutionalization of internal control or prudential standards is only one response, albeit a useful one, to the challenges of controlling major societal risks. Prudential risk and the various risks of the financial sector are very much framed by a set of risk control measures, which have become denser and even more piled up over the last 20 years. In the end, the spectrum of hyper-control returns with each crisis: trying to control, sometimes excessively, what often escapes us: the human factor, both in its behaviors that can create risk and in its reactions to a given risk.

REFERENCES

Abdou, I., (2018). *Les contradictions de la norme dans la maîtrise des risques bancaires: résultats d'une recherche-action conduite en position de praticien réflexif dans une banque régionale,* thèse de doctorat, CNAM LIRSA.

Bessire D., Cappelletti, L., & Pigé, B., (2010). *Normes, origines et conséquences des crises.* Economica.

Cappelletti, L., & Dufour N. (2017, October). La mise en œuvre de processus d'ingénierie normative comme réponse à la tétranormalisation. Cas du secteur des complémentaires santé. *Revue Management & Avenir,* n°95, 37–56.

Cappelletti, L., & Dufour N. (2020). «L'institutionnalisation des normes prudentielles. Résultats d'une recherche-intervention au sein d'une mutuelle intégrant Solvabilité II.» *Finance Contrôle Stratégie* [En ligne], 23–2.

Cappelletti, L., Pigé, B., & Zardet, V. (Eds.).(2015). *Dynamique normative. Arbitrer et négocier la place de la norme dans l'organisation.* EMS.

Dufour, N. (2011). «La financiarisation est-elle un vecteur majeur d'avènement d'une «société du risque» ?» *Management & Avenir, 8*(48), 258–271.

Dufour, N. (2014). *Le coût du risque, enjeu majeur pour l'entreprise.* GERESO.

Dufour, N., (2018, Juillet). Inflation réglementaire: Quand le risque de non-conformité devient un risque majeur. *Face au risque,* 544, 34–37.

Dufour, N., (2020). Gérer l'inflation normative. Le cas de la lutte contre le blanchiment dans une banque patrimoniale. *Annales des Mines – Gérer et Comprendre,* 139, 46–57.

Savall & Zardet. (2005). *Tétranormalisation; défis et dynamiques.* Economica.

CHAPTER 69

DIGITAL TRANSFORMATION

The Human-Digital Competitiveness (HDC)—Framework From Technological Determinism to a Socio-Economic Perspective

Emmanuel Monod

ABSTRACT

The high failure rate of digital transformation projects might be lowered by socio-economic approach to management. SEAM is not only holistic performance measurement system, but also an organizational transformation method encompassing workforce differentiation and business process innovation. However, SEAM shall develop digital dimensions such as development methods, technological infrastructure and enterprise architecture in consistence with the "Human-Digital Competitiveness" (HDC) framework. Combined with HDC framework, the SEAM stands as a customer-driven, people-driven performance management for improving the odds of digital transformation in companies.

Digital transformation is usually related by most of the consulting groups to the concept of business model innovation (McKinsey 2020; BCG, 2020). In parallel, the same consulting groups highlight that the failure of digital transformation projects remains exceptionally high reaching a failure rate 70% according to McKinsey (2018). Leading management consulting firms espouse the definition of digital transformation as "the use of technology to radically improve performance" (McKinsey, 2020, p. 3). This research claims that this discourse of the consulting groups focusing on business model innovation falls back to technological determinism (Markus & Robey, 1988). It neglects both human and organizational dimensions that contribute to the failure or success of digital transformation. Therefore, how

SEAM Treatise, pages 575–581

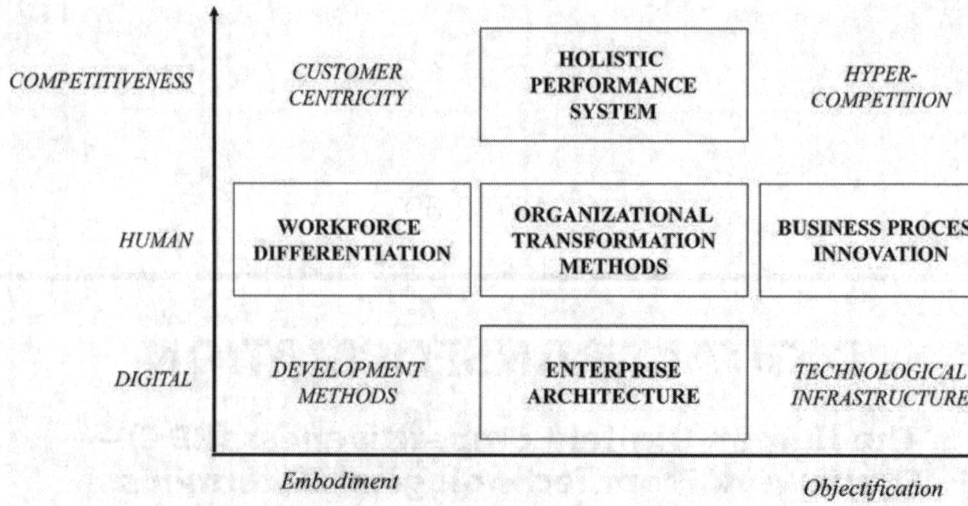

Figure 69.1 Digital transformation: The Human-Digital Competitiveness framework (HDC).

to combine the expectations of companies regarding economic performance with these social dimensions? This paper claims that socio-economic approach to management (SEAM) (Savall, 1974, 1975, 1979, 1981; Savall & Zardet, 1987, 2008) is a way to include these two dimensions. The relevance of SEAM for digital transformation is here described through the dimensions of the "Human-Digital Competitiveness" (HDC) framework, elaborated from a critique of the discourse of consulting groups on digital transformation, previously referred to as Human-Technology Performance framework (Monod, 2020; Figure 69.1).

This framework includes three dimensions: the competitiveness dimension, the human dimension and the digital dimension. Each of these dimensions might be differentiated along another axis related to their objectification or at the opposite to their embodiment following the Theory of Practice (Bourdieu, 1977, 2005). The research question is here "how can digital transformation implementation success improved through socio-economic management"? In order to respond to this question, each of the HDC framework dimensions is described hereinafter with a socio-economic perspective.

1 THE COMPETITIVENESS DIMENSION

The first dimension of the HDC framework, competitiveness, includes *hyper-competition, customer centricity* and *holistic performance management system.*

1.1 Hyper-Competition

Companies, and especially SMEs are now facing an environment characterized by hyper-competition, where competitive advantage is no longer be sustainable (Porter, 1979) but transient (Ilinitch, D'Aveni, & Lewin, 1996). Companies are forced to search for new ways of renewing their competitive advantage that can be no more protected under barriers to entry, but relies on links with customers, shareholders, research institutions, government but also employees. All these stakeholders were previously neglected in the five force models

(Porter 1979) relying on the assumption on a stable environment. Hyper-competition requires to include many additional performance measurements to the classical cost efficiency such as the speed of product innovation and process innovation. Economies of scale are no more relevant and require a conceptual shift is toward innovation (Volberda, 1996). The point is such innovation does not come from any of the "five forces" (Porter 1979), but rather from the employees, one of the main missing stakeholders of the "five forces" model. A socio-economic reading of hypercompetition highlights the importance of time management and communication-coordination-cooperation (3C) for the development of dynamic capabilities and transient competitive advantage. Moreover, the link with organizational innovation coming from workers is highlighted through socio-economic tools such as competency grid, periodically negotiated activity contracts and priority action plans (Savall & Zardet, 1995, 2018). Regarding the socio-economic approach of dysfunctions, time management is often related to the fact that managers and supervisors spend more time on routine tasks than on development activities. Such an analysis should stand as the premise of digital transformation, aimed to automate routine task in order to allow the frontline workers to focus on developmental and relational activities. Therefore, the socio-economic perspective on management allows to understand the social mechanisms that may contribute to the economic competitiveness through digital transformation. A second dimension of performance highlighted by the HDC model is customer centricity.

1.2 Customer Centricity

Performance measurement has been often criticized for focusing too much on accounting, neglecting customer perspective, internal process perspective, and innovation as well as learning perspective, as described in the balanced scorecard (Kaplan & Norton, 1996). Later, Kaplan and Norton (2004) stressed that people make processes work, generating satisfied customers, and subsequently financial results. The view that customers are not simply consumers, but rather contributors to value-adding is not new. However, digital technologies also enabled new ways of providing insights on how products are used through the data collected on platforms. Therefore, the perspective is shifting oward usage-based value enabled by digital technologies (Heinrichs et al., 2012). The contribution of the socio-economic approach to customer centricity is to connect this imperative to organizational dimensions (Savall & Zardet, 2017). For instance, working conditions dysfunctions may result from the silos between departments of a company, requiring employees to disturb their colleagues who need to serve current customers. Work organization dysfunction may be related to the lack of match between customer requirements and the current procedures of the company. Communication-coordination-cooperation throughout the company is an obvious requirement for an integrated customer centricity prior to any digitalization. Hyper-competition and customer centricity lead to a reconsideration of the holistic aspect of performance.

1.3 Holistic Performance Measurement System

Under the pressure of hyper-competition and customer centricity, such a holistic dimension of performance is now a requirement, but how to relate it to organization and technology? SEAM (Savall & Zardet, 1992) elaborates further relating dysfunctions to hidden costs through concrete disturbances or abnormal such as staff turnover, low-quality work, absenteeism, occupational injuries and disease and direct production gap. The direct production gap or direct productivity variance includes non-production or missed production. The second kind of hidden costs is the regulation of dysfunctions. They are grouped into two kinds of activities: human activities and product consumption. This classification of regulation is then applied to hidden cost calculation, which involves six components: overconsumptions, non-production production, non-creation of potential, risks, excess salary and time wasted. These six components are the financial consequences of dysfunctions (Savall & Zardet, 2008, pp. 28–29). In this respect, the performance measurement system developed by SEAM is much more comprehensive than the key performance indicators (KPI) or the balanced scorecard. They include in a management dashboard not only financial and economic indicators, but also social dimensions that may even be qualitative. However it requires for its implementation human dimensions described hereinafter.

2 THE HUMAN DIMENSION

The second dimension of digital transformation in the HDC framework, the human dimension includes the three components of the human dimension are *business process innovation, organizational transformation methods* and *workforce differentiation.*

2.1 Business Process Innovation

The least that can be said about business processes, is that the human dimension was either neglected as in the value chain (Porter, 1985), or considered as resistance to change in Business Process Reengineering (BPR), where IT was expected to replace middle managers (Hammer & Champy, 1993). However, a less visible trend, "Business Process Innovation" (BPI), suggested than, rather replacing people by IT, technologies might not only support workers but also be designed by the workers themselves (Davenport, 1993, 2008). Whereas a current trend in BPM focuses on process automation (Marr, 2019). BPI still stands in contrast highlighting the importance of support to human. SEAM includes numerous dimensions common with BPI such as work organization, communication–coordination–cooperation, but also of time management. However, BPI does not provide a comprehensive set of tools beyond process metrics, and definitely does not include social and qualitative performance indicators as especially such as management dashboard, competency grid, or periodically negotiated activity contracts that SEAM does include.

2.2 Organizational Transformation Methods

What kind of organizational transformation is relevant for digital transformation? Continuous improvement such as six sigma and lean management were challenged both by BPR and BPI, as described previously, and by agile methods described hereinafter. Behind these organizational transformation methods highly promoted by consulting groups, Organization Development (OD) grew out more discretely of the need for organizations to long-range problem-solving. OD also maintained ideals of humanistic integration of organizational processes with workers. The latest trends focus on the grounding in organizational science (Cummings & Worley, 2008). Whereas OD includes numerous common dimensions with SEAM such working conditions, work organization or communication–coordination–cooperation (3C), only SEAM allows to quantify potential benefits of change including economic, social and financial performance as well as both quantitative and qualitative performance measurements. Indeed, SEAM (Worley, Zardet, Bonnet, & Savall, A., 2015) through the identification of organizational dysfunctions and hidden cost provide a quantified objective to digitalization allowing to calculate its return on investment that no other organizational transformation does.

2.3 Workforce Differentiation

HR is a dimension of digital transformation highly neglected by most of the consulting groups, often limited to "digital talent management" (BCG 2020). Initially raised by the core competency framework (Hamel & Prahalad, 1990), an intense debate took place in the HR management discipline related to the strategic value of HR, such as workforce differentiation (Becker, Huselid, & Beatty, 2009) as opposed to the traditional view of HR (Lepak & Gowan, 2010). Instead of focusing on HR "functions" such as workforce planning or job definition, worldwide leaders have developed systems for managing and motivating their high-performance employees, ensuring that they take the strategically critical job positions. Workforce differentiation play a critical role in companies' digital transformation success. SEAM tools such of competency grid and periodically negotiated activity contracts relate workforce to strategy through internal-external strategic plan and priority action plans. Such a consistency between socio-economic management and workforce differentiation might also be articulated through the study of dysfunctions such as working conditions, work organization, communication–coordination–cooperation (3C) and integrated training. If digital transformation is undertaken is the perspective of helping the best employees to perform better rather than replacing them, digital workforce is a requirement prior to such transformation that might be enabled by the socio-economic perspective.

3 THE DIGITAL DIMENSION

Despite the spectacular developments related to performance measurement and human dimensions, SEAM may benefit from the HDC framework when it comes to digital dimensions that includes *technological infrastructure, systems development methods* and *enterprise architecture.*

3.1 Technological Infrastructure

A first research direction would be to apply the socio-economic approach to technological infrastructure. The difference between digital transformation and information technologies (IT) is that whereas the latter is related to the digitization of operations that has been conducted in companies since the late 1990s, through ERP or CRM systems, the second includes another level related to applications and external platforms. Without a technological infrastructure, however, such applications and platforms lack seamless operations. As a result, when they conduct digital transformation, they often focus customer experience without considering the importance of data. Companies must be able to provide seamless access to critical operational data for transaction execution and therefore need a robust and scalable operational, technological infrastructure (Ross, Weill, & Robertson, 2006). The link between technological infrastructure lies in the concept of automation of repetitive tasks that may be linked to hidden cost in SEAM.

3.2 Development Methods

Whereas most digital transformation literature developed by consulting groups refers to agile methods (BCG 2020), they do not describe the performance that results from the use of these methods independently from technology. Indeed, traditional information systems development methods usually create problems in software development such as the length of the development process, cost, and quality problems of the systems (Abrahamsson et al., 2003). By contrast, agile methods, such as eXtreme Programming are centered on people and interactions, fast response to changes, collaboration with the customer, and working software (Fowler & Highsmith, 2001). Therefore, a second research directions is here to describe the common points between agile methods and SEAM in order to improve the fit with digital transformation, a starting point being time management, but also working conditions and work organization.

3.3 Enterprise Architecture

The third research direction for SEAM to investigate in order to improve its suitability for digital transformation is enterprise architecture (EA). EA is an approach that allows to identify IT capabilities critical to enabling the firm's strategic objectives (Henderson & Venkatraman, 1993). Therefore, EA acts as a tool for aligning IT, business and digital transformation strategies. In short, EA can ensure that initiatives are global as opposed to fragmented and can leverage advantages gained through exploiting IT advantages. Rather than develop an exhaustive list of possible IT capabilities, a well-designed enterprise IT architecture highlights the IT capabilities that are most critical to a firm's strategic objectives and makes use of them (Ross, 2003). The socio-economic management tools may therefore benefit from the EA approach by including the IT strategic alignment into the management dashboard, and to include architectural considerations both in internal-external strategic plan and priority action plans.

CONCLUSION

This exploratory research highlighted the relevance of socio-economic approach to digital transformation as a way to include both economic expectations on performance and human dimensions without falling back into technological determinism. Whereas SEAM appears as a comprehensive performance measurement system bridging hyper-competition and customer centricity, such approach also includes human aspects of digital transformation such as workforce differentiation, organizational transformation or business process innovation. Research directions for SEAM in digital transformation include agile development methods, technological infrastructure and enterprise architecture (Savall & Zardet, 2019). Each dimension of digital transformation has been here described with SEAM through a framework previously used for analyzing the discourse of consulting groups on digital transformation, "Human-Digital Competitiveness" (HDC). So far, although social dimensions are acknowledged by consulting groups when it comes to resistance to change related to digital transformation, these dimensions are neglected both at the performance measurement level and that the digital level. Through the analysis of dysfunctions and hidden cost, SEAM stands as a theory that may allow companies to improve their success in digital transformation and achieve both economic, financial and social benefits

REFERENCES

Abrahamsson, P., Warsta, J., Siponen, M. T., & Ronkainen, J. (2003). New directions on agile methods: A comparative analysis. *ICSE '03: Proceedings of the 25th International Conference on Software Engineering* (pp. 244–254).

Becker, B. E., Huselid, M. A., & Beatty, R. W. (2009). *The differentiated workforce: Translating talent into strategic impact.* Harvard Business Press.

BCG. (2020). *The Evolving State of Digital Transformation.*

Bourdieu, P. (1977). *Outline of a theory of practice.* Cambridge University Press.

Cummings, T. G., & Worley, C. G. (2008). *Organization development and change* (9th ed). Cengage.

Davenport, T. H. (1993). *Process Innovation.* McGraw-Hill.

Hamel, G., & Prahalad, C. K. (1990). The core competence of the corporation. *Harvard Business Review, 68*(3), 79–91.

Hammer, M., & Champy, J. 1993. *Reengineering the Corporation: A Manifesto for Business Revolution.* Harper Collins.

Henderson, J. C., & Venkatraman, N. (1993). Strategic alignment: Leveraging information technology for transforming organizations. *IBM Systems Journal, 32*(1), 4–16.

Huselid, M. A., Becker, B. E., & Beatty, R. W. (2005). *The workforce scorecard: Managing human capital to execute strategy.* Harvard Business Press.

Ilinitch, A. Y., D'Aveni, R. A., & Lewin, A. Y. (1996). New organizational forms and strategies for managing hypercompetitive environments. *Organization Science, 7*(3), 211–220.

Kaplan, R. S., & Norton, D. P. (1996). Strategic learning & the balanced scorecard. *Strategy & Leadership, 24*(5), 18–24.

Kaplan, R. S., & Norton, D. P. (2004). The strategy map: Guide to aligning intangible assets. *Strategy & Leadership, 32*(5), 10–17.

Lepak, D., & Gowan, M. 2010. *Human resource management: Managing employees for competitive advantage.* New York: Pearson Prentice Hall.

Markus, M. L., & Robey, D. (1988). Information technology and organizational change: Causal structure in theory and research. *Management Science, 34*(5), 583–598.

Marr, B. 2019. *Artificial intelligence in practice: How 50 successful companies used AI and machine learning to solve problems.* John Wiley and Sons.

Matt, C., Hess, T., & Benlian, A. 2015. Digital Transformation Strategies. *Business & Information Systems Engineering, 57*(5), 339–343.

McKinsey. (2018). *A roadmap for a digital transformation.*

McKinsey. (2019). *Unlocking success in digital transformations.*

McKinsey. (2020). *Digital transformation: Improving the odds of success.*

Monod, E. (2020). Digital transformation: the Human-Technology Performance framework (HTC), *Transversus,* 19, 1–10.

Porter, M. E. (1979). The five competitive forces that shape strategy. *Harvard Business Review, 86*(1), 25–40.

Ross, J. W. (2003). *Creating a strategic IT architecture competency: Learning in stages* (MIT Sloan Working Paper No. 4314-03).

Ross, J. W., Weill, P., & Robertson, D. (2006). *Enterprise architecture as strategy: Creating a foundation for business execution.* Harvard Business Press.

Thomas, L. G. (1996). The two faces of competition: Dynamic resourcefulness and the hypercompetitive shift. *Organization Science, 7*(3), 221–242.

Volberda, H. W. (1996). Toward the flexible form: How to remain vital in hypercompetitive environments. *Organization Science, 7*(4), 359–374.

This page intentionally left blank.

CHAPTER 70

MANAGERIAL ENGINEERING AT THE SERVICE OF VISION-ROBOTICS

Amandine Savall, Hervé Henry, and Nylème Chettih

ABSTRACT

This chapter presents the case of a vision-robotics company that employs about 80 engineers. Engineers represent a very specific population to manage. It is therefore up to the company, which needs managerial skills to run its organization, to identify and train these young engineers in management. By intervening at the heart of this vision-robotics company, the ISEOR team of researchers was confronted with a high level of resistance to change in managerial and organizational practices. The local managers were more "flexible" and saw their resistance to change diminish as the intervention progressed.

This chapter presents the case of a vision-robotics company that employs about 80 engineers to develop highly innovative and technological robots. Engineers represent a very particular population to manage, due to their academic background and are characterized both by their engineering skills, their very sharp creativity combined with a lack of training in social sciences, such as management, management or communication. The company has asked ISEOR to help it face the difficulties of integrating the managerial dimension into the very well mastered know-how of robotics.

The first section will present the problems of a high-tech company confronted with the management of humans. The second section will present the Sileane company and its socio-economic intervention. The third section will analyze the lessons learned from this case.

SEAM Treatise, pages 583–589

1 THE CHALLENGE OF HIGH-TECH-HUMAN MANAGEMENT INTERACTION

New technologies are at the center of corporate debates and concerns, conveying the implicit idea that these new technologies, or "technical capital," can largely replace human labor. However, according to socio-economic theory (Savall, 1974; Savall & Zardet, 1987, 1995), human nature is characterized by five attributes: "intelligent, comedian, strategist, disobedient and amnesiac" (Savall & Zardet, 2016). Yet, these characteristics of human genius are both difficult to bring together in a technology while also proving to be limitations in the use of these technologies, which are new sources of hidden costs. This is why a material investment such as a new technology should always be accompanied by a large dose of intangible investment in training and support for humans using these new technologies (Savall, 1979; Savall and Zardet, 1992, 1995, 2008).

The project manager, "a new type of manager in a non-hierarchical universe" is represented as "the one-man band who succeeds in federating all the actors in his team, the one-off contributors recruited from within the company or from outside, in order to carry out the mission entrusted to him by the General Management and the clients" (Amghar, 2001; Boy, Dudek, & Kuschel, 2000; Raynal, 1996, 2000). Of course, companies have a great need for non-hierarchical project managers to carry out technological projects, but they also need hierarchical managers who take care of their employees, their skills, their behaviors and their contribution to economic performance.

According to Vannereau and Lemaître (2020), engineering students find it difficult to believe that this hierarchical need exists, and many of them are not convinced that managerial issues hold an important place in the engineering profession. They consider that an engineering student who does not develop an appetite for management during his or her higher education studies will never become a manager. However, in our opinion, even if engineering schools integrate some social and human sciences courses in the programs of engineering students, these are more introductory courses than the development of managerial skills for their future functions.

Moreover, there is a prevailing tendency for higher education courses and curricula to be hyper-specialized, leading many young people to value technical rather than managerial courses. It is therefore up to the company, which needs managerial skills to run its organization, to identify and train these young engineers in management.

At the beginning of the socio-economic intervention, one of the problems of this vision-robotics company was its "hyper-technicality" accentuated by a historical organization by trade. Indeed, the management had recently decided to move from an organization by trade to an organization by "Business Units" (BU). The aim of this new organization was to reduce the dysfunctions linked to the hyper-technicality of the teams, to revitalize the business and to improve the economic sensitivity of the engineers.

The profitability of such a company is essentially based on the control of two expense items: material purchases and hours worked. In the case of this company, purchases, which represent €4,500,000 in equipment purchases and €500,000 in subcontracting annually, have always been under control with a variation of +/– 3% compared to the budget. Nevertheless, the manager considered that the hours worked were too often beyond control, with the payroll representing €2,500,000 for 135,000 annual hours.

Another problem of this company was related to the difficulties of recruitment and training of employees. Newcomers were experiencing great difficulties in integrating. The same was true for the "army of trainees," representing 25,000 hours of annual activity, whose integration was not structured.

Finally, the company's growth had forced the management to reorganize and delegate management functions, increasing from about 5 to 25 managers. These new responsibilities required training: a real challenge when faced with a population of engineers whose belief in technical innovations is boundless, but who question and/or resist any non-technical change (human, organizational, managerial, behavioral, etc.).

2 INTRODUCTION OF THE SOCIO-ECONOMIC APPROACH TO MANAGEMENT IN THE SILEANE COMPANY TO CONSOLIDATE ITS STRONG GROWTH

Founded in 2002, the company builds machines based on robotics and vision, connecting cameras to robot arms to automate situations where machines, known as "blind," cannot function; for example, in random or unknown contexts such as handling fresh products or fragile and unstable materials. It carries out 20 to 25 projects per year, 15% of which are so-called "one shot" projects, carried out with a prototype machine. A project lasts from 9 months to 5 years, especially if it is a research and development project, with an invoiced budget ranging from €400,000 to €2,000,000. Between 2016 and 2019, the company has undergone a very strong growth in its workforce, going from 40 to 90 people and doubling its sales revenue, an increase of €7 million in 4 years. Its profitability is about 5% of sales in 2018, an *encouraging* but declining figure. The company, which offers innovative solutions, stands out and has grown thanks to strong creativity but has installed as a corollary a solid form of indiscipline in its teams, which are mostly engineers, aged 30 on average.

Figure 70.1 shows the organization chart of the management team and the number of employees per team.

The company is established on a market in permanent growth of 15% per year. Competitors are more or less numerous or even non-existent depending on the complexity of the projects. The company has opportunities for international development to enhance its differentiating factors.

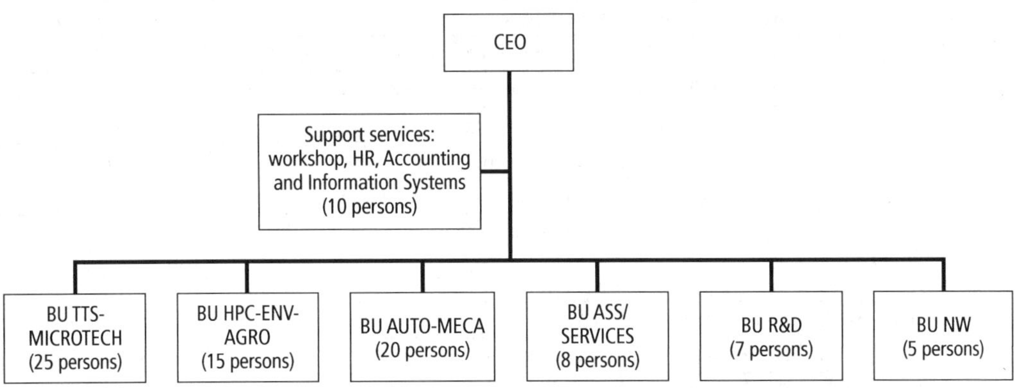

Figure 70.1 Organizational chart of a vision-robotics company.

2.1 Socio-Economic Intervention: Diagnosis of Dysfunctions and Hidden Costs

The intervention consisted in providing monthly personalized assistance to the manager for strategic management and to the administrative and financial manager for economic management. The first circle around the manager met every three months within a steering group of the intervention.

The intervention team implemented the HORIVERT methodology in 2018 and 2019: A horizontal action composed of a diagnosis-project with approximately 33 managers (individual interviews, mirror- effect, expert opinion of the speakers) and collaborative training sessions per BU completed by individual personalized assistance with the same managers. This support enabled the implementation of four socio-economic management tools: time management and concerted delegation, the competency grid and the integrated training plan, the priority action plan and finally, the piloting logbook using relevant and adapted indicators (Savall and Zardet, 1987). The vertical action involved two BUs: the vertical diagnosis consisted of conducting individual interviews with managers, group interviews with employees, and hidden cost interviews, followed by a mirror-effect and later an expert opinion. The internal contributors, under the supervision of ISEOR, contributed to these two diagnoses, which were followed by focus groups per BU, bringing together managers and employees to discuss dysfunctions and propose solutions.

Numerous dysfunctions were identified, grouped into seven themes and the associated hidden costs were evaluated (Table 70.1).

TABLE 70.1 Dysfunctions and Associated Hidden Costs

	Main dysfunctions identified during the diagnosis	Hidden costs = economic impacts of the dysfunctions
Piloting indicators, time management	Lack of piloting of workload and activities	€ 98,000
	Lack of synchronization regarding work organization	€ 43,000
	Lack of strategic piloting indicators ans system	€ 13,000
Commercial action plan and customer relationship	Fragility of the commercial action Unsuitable communication systems	€ 800,000
Training policy—integration and loyalty of the employees	Weak accoutabilily of the actors	€ 43,000
	Unsufficient guidance and support for the development of skills	€ 199,000
	Vulnerability of some operations due to lack of skills	—
	Difficulty in stabilizing the team/staff turnover	€ 394,000
Synchronized decentralization	Difficulties in implementing the new organization	€ 43,000
	Défaillances des dispositifs 3C et inefficacité managériale	
Purchasing and management of equipment	Lack of optimization of material resources	€ 70,000
Project management	Inefficiency of 3Cs flows on projects	€ 11,000
	Defects in the organization of projects	€ 957,000
Concerted delegation, enhancement of autonomy	Excessive shifts in function	€ 5,000
	Lack of clarity in the distribution of the roles and responsibilities	€ 5,000
Total amount of hidden costs		**€ 2,681,000**

The total amount of €2,681,000 of hidden costs identified corresponds to approximately 20% of the revenue and 400% of the annual result, or the equivalent of 58,300 working hours (more than one third of the working hours).

2.2 Significant Achievements of the Intervention Process

2.2.1 Development of Internal Cohesion and Managerial Practices

The analysis of the dysfunctions pushed the company to evolve its management practices and strengthen internal cohesion in accordance with the strategic foundation theory (Savall, Zardet, 1995). Thus, as of autumn 2018, the company set up regular collective and individual management and communication-coordination-cooperation mechanisms between the leader and his Steering committee (CODIR): for example, weekly activity reviews between each N and his N+1, weekly project meetings, bi-monthly Steering committee meetings, as well as sales meetings. These regular cooperation have been made more effective through the implementation of tools such as the resolution sheet.

In 2019, these practices were gradually extended to each BU. The machine project managers have become more powerful thanks to these local management rituals. The cohesion between the leader and his "number 2" has been strengthened. In April 2019, he was given responsibility for an additional BU. His formalization as the leader's right-hand man relieved the latter of part of his managerial burden. Since mid–2019, two hours every Friday are reserved for employees to work on improving the internal functioning of the company.

2.2.2 Developing Sensitivity and Practices for Economic Management

The economic awareness of the teams has notably concerned the commercial dynamics. From the beginning of 2019, the decentralization of the sales function was initiated in each BU, carried by all engineers, experts in their machine solutions. The implementation of this decision was accompanied by the creation of a piloting logbook, which brings together various economic indicators to serve the Steering committee. This period was marked by a drastic reduction in the number of interns: the company went from 15 interns (full-time equivalent) to "a few targeted profiles" in 2019. A few months later, the company strengthened the management of hours worked, via better use of the time reporting software per project. In July 2019, the management committee (COGES), where each machine project manager presents the profitability and progress of his or her machine project to the manager and his or her BU manager, was systematized monthly.

2.2.3 Strengthening of the Strategic Project and Symbiosis of Internal and External Environment Analyses

In 2019, the competency grid was implemented in the teams. At the same time, the leader and his first circle shared the strategic analysis of the company. A strategy was thus formalized in a PASINTEX and then in priority action plans. This is how the company has multiplied its analysis and its strategy at all levels and in each team. The company's strategic vision for the next 3 to 4 years can be summarized in four strategic axes: – to continue to develop market niches where unique machine projects require strong business expertise; – to develop the training offer and other services for current customers; – to cover the territory with a proximity network combining internal growth and partnerships; – to implement the "PACS" project based on the analysis of dysfunctions and the search for socio-economic solutions in order to improve internal processes and the functioning of the organization.

The clarification and formalization of this strategic project had an impact on the organization of the company: first, with the transformation of the "Automotive" BU into the "General Industry" BU, to respond to the third axis and to reorientate itself on projects of less than 500 000 €. The birth of this BU transformed a strategic threat into an opportunity and required a review of the organization of these new small-scale machine projects, since the historical organization was designed for projects over €500,000.

3 WHAT LESSONS CAN WE LEARN FROM THE EXPERIMENT?

3.1 Synchronized Decentralization

Decentralization makes it possible to give each hierarchical level and everyone more responsibility, and to give more autonomy to each person. Autonomy is a very important ingredient for engineers, who find it difficult to be "locked in." It also helps to retain them in a very volatile job market. However, synchronization is the essential complement to decentralization, because the performance of a company is created at the interfaces between people and services and requires that people be synchronized.

3.2 The Symphonic Discipline

The creative skills of engineers can sometimes fall into a form of indiscipline. The socio-economic management system does not aim to enforce discipline in the military and authoritarian sense, but to create a certain degree of symphony between all the players: engineers, salespeople, managers, executives… This symphony is necessary for performance. The objective is to avoid chaos, i.e., excessive indiscipline, not necessarily voluntary on the part of individuals, but independent and uncontrolled initiatives that destroy value instead of creating it.

3.3 The Development of Managerial Skills

The manager is the conductor who creates the symphony between people. However, the reign of technology and technique resides in the heads of all these engineering actors, who combine a weak economic sensitivity with a technical hypersensitivity. The manager must have at least a part of the technical skills of his team of engineers; this is facilitated when he is himself an engineer and puts his hand to the wheel in the projects that his team develops.

However, since engineers have not been trained (or have received very little) in management during their schooling, it is up to the company to create its own managers. According to Verza and Bachelet (2007), during this long training course, engineers could acquire organizational and managerial skills and the ability to manage the performance of their teams. First of all, it is necessary to set up a team training plan to develop a measured versatility. The next step is to set up a more inclusive work organization: from A to Z, hence the BU organization. This puts the external customer at the center of the team's concerns. Finally, the implementation of economic management practices, tools and indicators, particularly for hours of activity, makes it possible to better manage equipment purchases and the productivity of hours worked. The former is often relatively well controlled, while the latter is unfortunately too often considered the "preserve" of each individual, where "everyone does what they want with their time."

CONCLUSION

By intervening at the heart of this vision-robotics company, the ISEOR team of researchers was confronted with a high level of resistance to change in managerial and organizational practices on the part of all managers, and in particular the steering committee. Indeed, the first circle around the leader foments resistance because these management functions are often in "pain," caught between the leader and the teams of employees. More "flexible," the local managers saw their resistance to change diminish as the intervention progressed.

The second limitation lies in the difficulty of decentralizing the sales dynamic and the sustainability of this action over time. A highly technical product cannot be sold by a salesperson alone. The best people to sell them are the engineers who produce these machines, but they have difficulty devoting enough time to the commercial activity. The result is repeated cycles of full and then suddenly empty order books.

The third limitation is that it is less natural for an engineer to deal with people than with machines. Therefore, the sustainability of managerial efforts and the durability of the intensity of management are not guaranteed.

Finally, the emerging problem in this company is how to continue to do the same jobs and manufacture the same highly innovative and ingenious machines, while the expectations of employees in terms of personal comfort have intensified?

REFERENCES

Amghar, A. (2001). *Management de projet, du savoir-faire au savoir-faire.* Editions JCI.

Boy, J., Dudek, C., & Kuschel, S. (2000). *Management de projet.* De Boeck.

Fayolle, A. (1996). *Contribution à l'étude des comportements entrepreneuriaux des ingénieurs français.* Thèse de doctorat, Université Jean Moulin Lyon 3.

Henry, H. (2020). Siléane, l'innovation permanente en robotique, vision et intelligence artificielle: de l'indiscipline créatrice à la discipline symphonique. Dans *Tétranormalisation: profusion des normes et développement des entreprises.* Editions EMS Management & Société.

Raynal, S. (1996). *Le management par projet.* Editions d'organisation.

Raynal, S. (2000). *Le management par projet, approche stratégique du changement.* Editions d'organisation: Paris, France.

Siléane, « L'info du coolware », journal interne, septembre-octobre 2019

Vannereau, J., & Lemaître, D. (2020). La problématisation dans l'apprentissage du management en filière d'ingénieur. *Revue internationale de pédagogie de l'enseignement supérieur, 36(1).*

Verza, C., & Bachelet, R. (2007). Les ingénieurs deviennent-ils managers grâce aux projets? *LGIL papers LP/07/02.*

This page intentionally left blank.

CHAPTER 71

SEAM'S ROLE IN MERGER AND ACQUISITION INTEGRATION

Anthony F. Buono

ABSTRACT

Most merger and acquisition strategies continue to be dominated by financial analyses, legal considerations, and power plays by dominant groups as individuals jockey for position and influence. Rather than focusing on the inherent dysfunctions that can emerge in the combined organization due to the informal power held by organizational members—from low productivity, poor quality and reduced commitment, to voluntary turnover and related hidden costs and untapped potential—far too many companies seem to meander through post-combination integration. Drawing on an intervention in a U.S. hospital merger, the chapter illustrates how SEAM can facilitate the challenge of merger integration.

The overarching reason why firms enter into a merger or decide to acquire another company is the belief that the combination will allow the new entity to attain its strategic goals more quickly and less expensively than if the firm attempted to do it on its own (Haspeslagh & Jemison, 1991). The poor performance of combined firms, however, continues to raise questions about the efficacy of this strategy, as studies over the past several decades suggest that less than one-third of mergers and acquisitions actually achieve the operational, financial, and strategic objectives suggested in pre-combination feasibility studies (Coff, 2002; Elsass & Veiga, 1994; Koi-Akrofil, 2016; Lubatkin, 1983). Most merger and acquisition (M&A) strategies are still dominated by financial analyses, legal considerations, and power plays by dominant groups as individuals jockey for position and influence (Buono & Bowditch, 1989; Chatterjee & Brueller, 2015). Rather than focusing on the inherent dysfunctions that can emerge in the combined organization due to the informal power held by organizational members—from low productivity, poor quality, and reduced commitment, to voluntary

SEAM Treatise, pages 591–597

turnover and related hidden costs and untapped potential—far too many organizations seem to meander through the post-combination integration process.

1 THE SOCIOECONOMIC APPROACH TO MANAGEMENT IN MERGERS AND ACQUISITIONS

The SEAM approach to organizational analysis developed by ISEOR underscores that there is an inherent difference between what may be intended in a particular situation and the actual experience of key stakeholders—including employees, managers, customers, shareholders and suppliers (Savall, 1974, 1981; 1979; Savall et al., 1987, 2000, 2008,; Savall et al. 2001). The realization that organizational members readily draw on and exercise their informal power to accelerate or thwart the pace and direction of change raises a number of challenges for M&A-related integration efforts. Of course, the idea that the human side of mergers and acquisitions must be attended to is not a novel idea. A growing number of researchers and practitioners have been raising such concerns for the past thirty years. Yet, far too many organizations continue to treat the merger and acquisition process as an engineering exercise, as a series of rational decisions rather than a far more chaotic set of events (Ashkenas & Francis, 2000; Buono, 2005).

Most observers of the M&A process readily agree that the human dynamics that follow the combination of two firms are significant determinants of merger success or failure. Yet, this focus is often at the expense of the economic and political realities accompanying the change. The hybrid nature of the SEAM approach—the integration of social *and* economic factors—provides a unique and needed approach to post-M&A integration (Savall & Zardet, 1995).

As illustrated in Figure 71.1, such combinations have far-reaching and often dysfunctional effects on those involved (Buono, 2005). Based on over three decades of experience in studying and working with companies going through the merger and acquisition process, while initial reactions are frequently characterized by goodwill and a cooperative spirit, and senior management emphasizes the promise of the combined entity, the reality is often in stark contrast to such lofty promises. As suggested by the SEAM framework, under that seemingly positive surface, the experience of organizational members is often far removed from what is initially intended by senior management. In fact, a merger or acquisition can sufficiently transform the structures, cultures and employment prospects of one or both the organizations that they cause organizational members to feel stressed, angry, disoriented, frustrated, confused, and even frightened (Buono & Bowditch, 1989; Buono et al., 1985; Buono & Nurick, 1992). SEAM analysis can help managers focus on the nature of and resultant hidden costs due to these dysfunctions.

Most early M&A planning, however, emphasizes horizontal actions, focused on the upper echelons of the organization and basic changes in organizational structure. While such initiatives are important for the overall success of the combined entity, vertical actions – focused on key individuals and work units—tend to be guided by shortsighted decisions. Clearly, an integrated emphasis on both dimensions—the HORIVERT method suggested by SEAM analysis (Savall & Zardet, 1987, 2008)– would go a long way toward ameliorating many dysfunctions and hidden costs. A key dimension lies in the mirror-effect that is produced by feeding back detailed field notes, juxtaposing top-level executive quotes and perspectives, with those from middle managers and employees. HORIVERT facilitates the analysis of what might be thought of as the "hierarchy gap," when the perceptions and foci of senior-level management are often quite different from the attention and focus of middle managers, supervisors, and employees. While senior-level executives may have previously

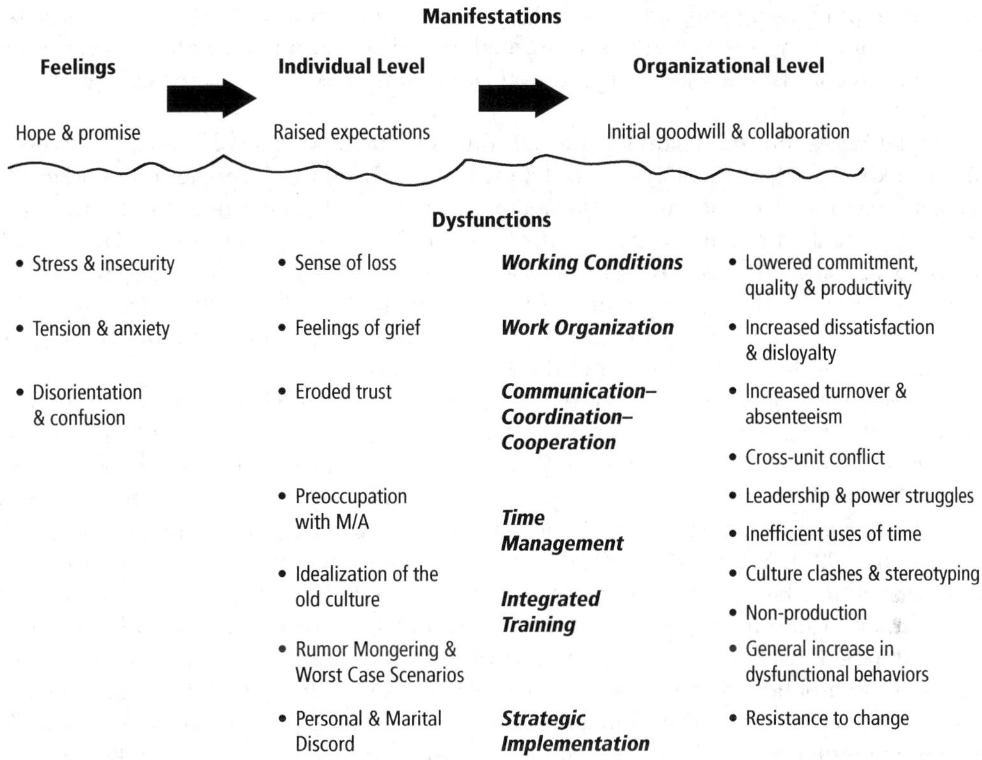

Figure 71.1 Illustrative human reactions, organizational dysfunctions and related SEAM Tools in Mergers and Acquisitions (Adapted from Buono, 2003).

worked through the stress and conflicts associated with such change, turning their attention to the next strategic moves, middle- and lower-level organizational members are still mired in the anxiety, confusion and anger that typically accompanies the initial stages of a merger or acquisition (Marks & Mirvis, 1992).

The decision to move forward with a M&A should be based on a full understanding of the human and operating challenges associated with integrating two organizations, going beyond the financial and legal issues that typically drive such decisions. The most essential elements in managing this type of operational integration emerge from an understanding of (1) the combination process itself, (2) its technical and human dimensions, (3) its cultural overtones, and (4) the reality that all real value creation occurs after the merger takes place.

SEAM and M&A integration: a case example

This chapter briefly examines the formation of a large regional medical center (RMC) in the United States during the early 2000s. The RMC was formed by a merger of two small- and medium-sized hospitals, combining the organizations into a single-site, state-of-the-art facility offering inpatient and outpatient services in one location. As a way of ensuring that quality healthcare would continue to be provided for the region, the boards of directors of the two hospitals determined that the institutions should merge. . The merger would combine the best of both hospitals, providing the resources necessary to bring currently unavailable services and physician specialists to the area, attempting to eliminate the need for travel outside of the area for the community's health care needs. Arguments for supporting hospital mergers in the past have focused on efficiency and lowered costs due to higher volume, such as savings in purchasing and operations. Along those same lines, some observers argue that the quality of care will improve thanks to medical collaboration and systematizing of best practice protocols. In theory, with greater efficiency hospitals can provide better care while lowering the cost of that care.

Hospital M&As, however, can be especially difficult due to a range of factors: (1) a disruption of medical staff; (2) leadership and trust issues; (3) cultural misalignment across the organizations; and (4) problems predicated by joint operating agreements under which the legacy organizations retain separate control over their assets and authorities. Despite lofty intentions and modest cost savings, hospital M&As are associated with a deterioration of quality care and the patient experience (Beaulieu, et al, 2020; Pearl, 2020; Schmitt, 2017). In SEAM parlance, in an effort to attain short-term cost savings administrators often ignore the long-term hidden costs inherent in the M&A process.

As firms attempt to capture the "softer" synergies related to their M&A plans, SEAM analysis becomes increasingly important. As reflected in Figure 71.2, managers face increased challenges as they move from financially-based, "hard synergies"—the visible costs and savings involved in the combination—to capture the "softer" synergies involving the transfer of core competencies and best practices and investing in their human resources (Coff, 2002; Eccles et al., 1998). Yet, as Marks (2003) underscores, even when companies look to the "softer" synergies (Figure 71.2) corporate staffers from acquiring organizations, armed with their charts of accounts, reporting cycles and planning approaches, tend to impose their systems on target firms and merger partners rather than engage in a true joint diagnosis and analysis of the situation. SEAM analysis forces recognition of the hidden costs, revealing the dysfunctions that underlie traditional accounting methods and financial assessments. The untapped potential and hidden costs in mergers and acquisitions continue to linger unless senior-level management intervenes to reduce (Figure 71.2).

In the RMC merger, the foundation of the integration strategy drew on the SEAM methodology, exploring the hidden costs that are inevitably associated with a combination strategy. Using mirror-effect analysis to surface issues and uncover areas of potential discontent

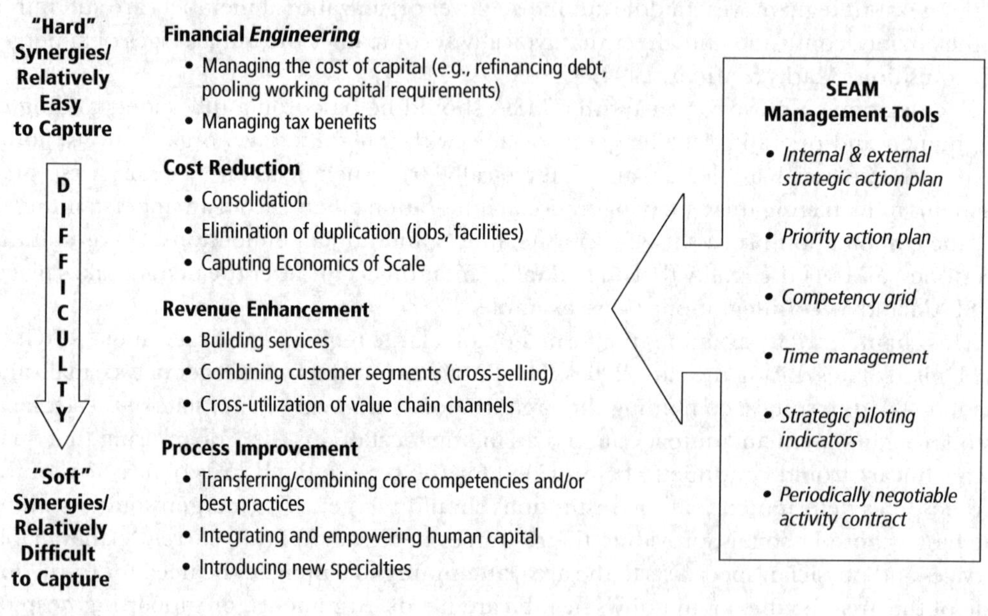

Figure 71.2 Illustrative merger synergies and related SEAM tools.

and untapped potential, RMC structured its pre-acquisition planning and post-acquisition integration efforts to maximize employee input and participation.

In preparation for the acquisition, an extensive intergroup mirroring exercise was conducted that focused on capturing the similarities and differences between the two hospitals. There were stark differences in the ways in which the staffs of the two hospitals viewed themselves and the "other." The senior management team focused on avoiding the emergence of a "winner–loser" mentality across the two staffs, working to raise awareness of the underlying dynamics and the need to establish a common language and understanding across the two hospitals.

The integration approach included:

- efforts to ensure that the staff of both hospitals were aware of the tasks and activities (and related costs of non-performance) that were critical for integration;
- regularly scheduled meeting focused on piloting the progress of post-merger integration initiatives (strategic piloting indicators);
- interviews (administrators, physicians) and focus groups (nurses, hospital staff) in order to analyze their perceptions (mirror effect reporting);
- priority action plans focused on integrating short-term objectives (e.g., completion of the new facility, transfer and care of existing patients) and longer-term goals (e.g., introduction of new specialties,...) while avoiding potential dysfunctions (e.g., "we" vs. "they" tensions); and
- HORIVERT process focused on integrating actions at the strategic and operational levels.

After three years of integration planning and construction of the new facility, the process successfully closed two hospital, combining them in one centrally located hospital. Over 230 patients were moved from the old hospitals to the new hospital in just eight hours. Reflecting on the success of the merger, RMC was honored with Healthgrades' (a leading resource that connects consumers, physicians and health systems) 2020 America's 250 Best Hospitals™ Award, a distinction that places the medical center in the top 5% of 4,500 hospitals assessed nationwide for its superior clinical performance. RMC was also noted for its overall clinical excellence across a broad spectrum of care.

3 LEARNINGS AND IMPLICATIONS

Most firms involved in the M&A process emphasize the importance of their people – yet in practice this approach seems more talk about their commitment to and the importance of "human capital" than their actual efforts. SEAM, in contrast, emphasizes human potential. Human beings cannot be considered as other resources, since organizational members are free to spend or withhold their energy according to the quality of the informal and formal contract they have with the company (see Savall, 1980). This is where SEAM analysis, with its focus on developing a set of practices that integrates the different disciplines—management, marketing, accounting, finance—into a coherent and interactive whole is clearly needed.

In the RMC merger, a key operational focus was supported by a concerted effort to: (a) retain and attract key talent; (b) involve organizational members from both hospitals in the planning and implementation process; (c) use focus groups to uncover key concerns and provide training and insight into merger-related dynamics; (d) support the combination with post-acquisition integration ceremonies and team-building activities; and (e) use post-acquisition training workshops focused on the lessons learned from the combination to enhance the core competencies of hospital administrators and staff. The SEAM process (diagnosis, project, implementation, assessment), cost analysis and mirror-effect reporting processes facilitated the integrated strategy. Hospital administrators realized that the nature of the desired synergies *required* truly collaborative and cooperative relationships across the two organizations. Rather than focusing solely on short-term reductions in costs and achieving the "hard" synergies in the merger, SEAM-based analyses provided a clearer indication of the strategies and tactics necessary to capture the longer-term, "softer" synergies inherent in true operational integration efforts.

CONCLUSION

Mergers and acquisitions by their very nature create significant upheaval in the lives of organizational members. The disruption caused by combination-related stress and anxiety, culture shocks and tensions, and job loss, relocation or realignment, obviously entails a number of dysfunctions and human costs that can trigger a series of negative reactions on the part of organizational members. A SEAM-based analysis during M&A planning helps to focus attention on these problems and the hidden dynamics and costs (Figure 71.1), uncovering potential dysfunctions. Managers who focus on them can begin to ameliorate these inherent dysfunctions festering under the surface, creating a stronger foundation for the new organization to achieve the critical operational synergies (Figure 71.2).

The good news is that a growing number of companies are beginning to focus on the post-M&A integration period much more systematically, appointing highly visible and well-respected integration managers to shepherd the two firms through what is often turbulent and unchartered territory as they attempt to function as a single entity (Ashkenas & Francis, 2000). Since these interorganizational strategies require a level of consultation and collaboration that goes well beyond typical patterns of management and organization (Buono, 1991), the time has come for managers (a) to understand the hidden costs involved in combining organizations, (b) to assess the gap between the experience of organizational members and the strategic plans of senior-level managers, and (c) to balance short- and longer-term dimensions of performance.

REFERENCES

Ashkenas, R. N., & Francis, S. C. (2000). Integration managers: Special leaders for special times. *Harvard Business Review, 78*(6), 108–116.

Beaulieu, N. D., Dafny, L. S., Landon, B. E., Dalton, J. B., Kuye, I., & McWilliams, J. M. (2020). Changes in Quality of Care after Hospital Mergers and Acquisitions. *New England Journal of Medicine, 382,* 51–59.

Buono, A. F. (1991). Managing strategic alliances: Organizational and human resource considerations. *Business & the Contemporary World, 3*(4), 92–101.

Buono, A. F. (2003). SEAM-less post-merger integration strategies: A cause for concern. *Journal of Organizational Change Management, 16*(1), 90–98.

Buono, A. F. (2005). Consulting to integrate mergers and acquisitions. In Greiner, L., & Poulfelt, F. (Eds.), *Handbook of management consulting: The contemporary consultant—Insights from world experts* (pp. 229–249). Southwestern/Thompson.

Buono, A. F., & Bowditch, J. L. (1989). *The human side of mergers and acquisitions: Managing collisions between people, cultures, and organizations.* Jossey-Bass.

Buono, A. F., Bowditch, J. L., & Lewis, J. W. (1985). When cultures collide: The anatomy of a merger. *Human Relations, 38*(5), 477–500.

Buono, A. F., & Nurick, A. J. (1992). Intervening in the middle: Coping strategies in mergers and acquisitions. *Human Resource Planning, 15*(2), 19–33.

Buono, A. F., & Savall, H. (2007). SEAM in the context of merger and acquisition integration. In A.F. Buono & H. Savall, *Socio-economic intervention in organizations: The intervener-researcher and the SEAM approach to organizational analysis* (pp. 385–399). Information Age Publishing.

Chatterjee, A., & Brueller, N. N. (2015). A new M&A methodology: Five lessons in anticipating post-merger resource interactions and challenges. *Strategy & Leadership, 43*(4), 26–37.

Coff, R. W. (2002). Human capital, shared expertise and the likelihood of impasse in corporate acquisitions. *Journal of Management, 28*(1), 115–137.

Eccles, R. G., Lanes, K. L., & Wilson, T. C. (1999). Are you paying too much for that acquisition? *Harvard Business Review, 77*(4), 136–146.

Elsass, P. M., & Veiga, J. F. (1994). Acculturation in acquired organizations: A force-field perspective. *Human Relations, 47*(4), 431–453.

Haspeslagh, P., & Jemison, D. (1991). *Managing acquisitions: Creating value through corporate renewal.* Free Press.

Koi-Akrofil, G. Y. (2016). Mergers and acquisitions failure rates and perspectives on why they fail. *International Journal of Innovation and Applied Studies, 17*(1), 150–158.

Lubatkin, M. (1983). Mergers and the performance of the acquiring firm. *Academy of Management Review, 8*(2), 218–225.

Marks, M. L. (2003). Making mergers and acquisitions work: A guide to consulting interventions. In A. F. Buono (Ed.), *Enhancing Inter-firm Networks and Interorganizational Strategies* (pp. 3–30). Information Age Publishing.

Marks, M. L., & Mirvis, P. H. (1992). Rebuilding after the merger: Dealing with 'survivor sickness.' *Organizational Dynamics, 21*(2), 18–32.

Pearl, R. (2020). 3 reasons hospital mergers fail. *Forbes,* January 28. https://www.forbes.com/sites/robertpearl/2020/01/28/3-reasons-hospital-mergers-fail/?sh=706a08d5790c

Schmitt, M. (2017). Do hospital mergers reduce costs? *Journal of Health Economics, 52* (March), 74–94.

This page intentionally left blank.

CHAPTER 72

CONSIDERATIONS ON THE SOCIO-ECONOMIC APPROACH TO MANAGEMENT IN THE CONTEXT OF A MERGER BETWEEN TWO COMPETITORS

Jean Caghassi

ABSTRACT

The industrial group GIFA has implemented socio-economic management since the year 2000. The main contributions were the creation of a strategic base common to two sites, the improvement of economic performances, the valorization of intangible activities and human potential, the implementation of an original management control system compared to the traditional accounting system. The contribution of socio-economic management was decisive in consolidating the merger of human and economic potential and ensuring the success of the merger of two sites with different cultures.

During a visit to Brioche Pasquier in 1999, with a group of visitors led by a foreman who surprised me by the extent of his understanding of the objectives and strategic stakes of his company, well beyond his technical skills, I was even more astonished to hear his manager, Louis-Marie Pasquier, recount the history of the success of his company, emphasizing how lucky they were to have met, some twenty years earlier, a consulting organization that had accompanied the development of their group ever since. If this cooperation had lasted for so long, I thought that this organization was worth contacting.

SEAM Treatise, pages 599–605

The company I was managing was then starting to think about its development and was faced with a problem of managing its growth. It took me a few months to succeed in meeting Professor Henri Savall and his team at ISEOR, and then to discover, quite quickly, the extent of the contribution that the socio-economic method could make to the development of the company, which a few years later became a coveted leader in its field.

1 HISTORY OF THE SOCIO-ECONOMIC APPROACH TO MANAGEMENT IN THE GIFA GROUP

1.1 The Company

The GIFA group is an industrial company, from the design to the realization and commercialization of emergency vehicles such as ambulances, with a strongly industrial culture resulting from its past belonging to a large automotive group. The bodywork market, which is extremely competitive, is occupied by companies of all sizes that have developed essentially from small-scale activities. In 1999, the company had an independent sales network and managed its positioning with respect to car manufacturers, partners interested in distributing their vehicles in specialized areas often neglected by their dealer networks.

In 1999, it had also taken control of its main competitor, a family-owned group of similar size but with a traditional culture, which was facing serious financial difficulties. This enabled it to strengthen its hold on the French market and to take an undisputed leadership position on the commercial level.

1.2 The Course of the Economic Intervention

1.2.1 A First Phase of Implementation of the Socio-Economic Management From 2000 to 2003

A horizontal and vertical diagnosis was carried out on the two sites, followed by projects and action plans carried out in 2001–2002, in parallel with the implementation of the steering tools proposed by the socio-economic management (Savall, 1974, 1979; Savall and Zardet, 1987). In 2003, a socio-economic evaluation was carried out to measure the improvement in economic and social performance (Caghassi, 2015, 2016). It also showed to what extent the commitment of the teams to the projects was a determining factor in their success, despite the operational difficulties, and allowed each site to benefit from the potential of the other, by promoting the recognition of their respective skills.

1.2.2 A Second Phase of Consolidation of Socio-Economic Principles and Management From 2003 Onwards

We had to consolidate our business management practices, establish the tools of socio-economic management, and share the strategy as closely as possible to the action level, by developing accountability. At the same time, at the commercial level, the company's capacity to react to more demanding markets had to be increased. The battery of performance indicators developed during the first phase finally made it possible to establish the link between economic and social performance at the level of each employee, based on objective, transparent and measurable criteria.

1.2.3 A Third Phase of Socio-Economic Management Control in 2004

In addition to the accounting management control system, the implementation of a socio-economic management control system (SMCS) has enabled us to differentiate our costs, to identify our sources of value added more precisely and in a transversal manner, by allocating material and intangible resources to each of the projects planned over 3 years. The approach was pragmatic, by accurately recording the hours spent by each person on their activities, based on a nomenclature of activities determined in cooperation with the actors (Savall and Zardet, 1992, 2008).

The managers had to change their way of working, by arranging slots in their agendas, by discovering that each of them had a personal interest in steering their activities in terms of time budgeting, and by monitoring the fulfilment of their commitments, without this being perceived as an intrusion into their operational autonomy. The CGSE has brought about real changes in the way people plan, delegate and manage their actions. It has made everyone aware of the importance of their intangible contribution to the development of activities. It has allowed us to value what no other accounting management system could do: objectively measure and quantify the company's human potential.

A direct consequence of this economic valuation, invisible in a traditional accounting plan, was to justify in an indisputable way, at the time of the sale of the company to the group that took control of it in 2010, an overvaluation of 26% compared to traditional valuation methods based on cash flow or analyses of material assets.

2 SOME MAJOR CONTRIBUTIONS OF THE SOCIO-ECONOMIC APPROACH TO MANAGEMENT

The socio-economic methodology has distinguished itself by its contribution in several areas.

2.1 Performance Improvements

The socio-economic method, through its approach of measuring hidden costs, is one of the few that allows for an economic valuation of elements that are usually considered intangible and rarely measurable, even though they are essential for improving the performance of activities. The socio-economic diagnoses evaluated hidden costs of 3,400,000 €, i.e., about 22,000 € per person per year, in an almost equal way on the two sites, whereas the CHVACV was fundamentally different between the two sites: 32 €/ h on A and 19 € on B.

This equivalence of hidden costs on the two sites was one of the founding elements of the cooperation that was built between the staff of the two sites. The focus groups, formed by bringing together the skills of the two sites, made it possible to determine the best alternatives for improving the performance of each site and, consequently, of the whole. Actions have been taken to organize a harmonious merger of the two sites:

- the creation of new functions, in particular an industrial department and a sales department
- a physical reorganization of the premises to facilitate exchanges
- the simplification of operational processes to delegate certain operations
- centralization of purchasing to promote economies of scale
- specialization of sites by product line
- the organization of subcontracting of certain manufacturing operations to more competent companies.

TABLE 72.1 Summary of the Socio-Economic Assessment (2003/2000)

	Total	Site A	Site B
Conversion of hidden costs into valeu added	1,870 K € Equivalent to 53%	670 K€	1,200 K€
Hourly Contribution to Value Added on Variable Costs	+ 20.0%	+11%	+ 25%
Revenue	+ 31.0%	+ 42%	+ 9%
Variable costs	+ 27.0%	+ 29%	+ 4%
Industrial productivity (in hours worked)	+ 8.6%	+ 8%	+ 16%

The economic impacts measured during the 2003 socio-economic evaluation (Savall and Krief, 2003) were edifying: a 53% recovery of hidden costs compared to 2000 and a 20% increase in the group's CHVACV (Table 72.1). This demonstrated that the actions implemented had had positive effects in all areas of commercial action, management and order fulfilment.

These performances should be compared with the amount of intangible investment of € 374,000 made by the company over 3 years to implement socio-economic management, which allowed for a conversion of hidden costs of € 1,870,000, i.e., an overall rate of return of 500% (€1,870K/€374K).

2.2 Strategic Engineering

The GIFA group's management team, with its many ideas for improving performance, often had difficulty translating them into action and getting the operational teams, which were not very involved in the decision-making process, to fully adhere to them.

The socio-economic management tools focused on strategy and strategic implementation proved to be particularly effective in ensuring the synchronized implementation of the management team's decisions with the operational teams, thanks to a process that allowed local management and field staff to feed into the strategic thinking process, through the direct involvement of each person in the search for solutions to dysfunctions.

This double top-down / bottom-up action was materialized with the triptych of strategic declination of the socio-economic method:

IESAP ➡ PAP ➡ PNAC

An internal/external strategic plan, IESAP, was drawn up by the management committee, establishing the major strategic orientations for the next 3 to 5 years in 4 strategic areas: products, markets, technologies, human potential and organization. It was then broken down into 3 priority action plans (PAP): the first for the coordination of the group's actions, the other two for each of the sites, with each site's PAP being validated by the general management. These were in turn translated into specific action plans for each of the services and departments, managed by their managers and prepared with the participation of their employees, while ensuring that they were consistent with the orientations of the master action plans.

The third stage of this process is the periodically negotiable activity contract (PNAC), a performance grid that integrates individual, semi-collective and collective objectives, established in accordance with the IESAP and the PAPs: they are the variation at the individual level and thus become the real "keystone" of the socio-economic management system, since they have a dual facet, both economic and social (Caghassi, 2015).

An economic facet, because the PNAC makes it possible, as soon as the objectives of everyone, from the manager to the operator or salesperson, are reached, to reward the achievement of these objectives on predetermined bases using objective indicators. In practice, the PNAC results in a salary supplement in the form of a half-yearly bonus as soon as the half-yearly objectives are partially or totally achieved. It thus makes it possible to distribute part of the additional economic performance obtained by achieving the objectives.

A social aspect, because by evaluating with each PNAC holder on a half-yearly basis the achievement of his objectives, the manager identifies with him the concrete means he needs to reach his objectives. As a result, the CAPN becomes a powerful tool for dialogue, listening and cooperation, considering the individuality of each person, rather than a tool for top-down control by the hierarchy, and even less so a tool for punishment.

The improvement actions implemented, and the socio-economic management tools have had a clear impact on improving the social climate, by structuring the link between economic performance and social performance, each of which has become indispensable to the other, and by ensuring that the strategic objectives defined and implemented at all levels are shared by all employees, regardless of their role and responsibility in the company.

2.3 A Common Language Between Two Companies With Different Cultures

Sites A and B, both active in the same sector of activity and with equivalent commercial positions in terms of market share, had very different operational characteristics, essentially resulting from their history. Site A, created in the 1960s by a large industrial company in the automotive sector, became independent in 1992, and was characterized by an industrial culture: an organization by function, an organizational chart with clear procedures, rules, a classic management system and controlled growth at the operational and financial level. Site B was a company created ex nihilo by a former salesman, which had very quickly taken on a significant dimension in the 1980s, with proven technical skills and producing quality products, but without succeeding in establishing a real operating structure that would have allowed it to control its growth; the diffuse and above all uncontrolled responsibilities generated significant energy losses and major financial losses, which led to its takeover by site A (Caghassi, 2015, 2016).

During the merger of the two companies, with such different cultures, formerly in head-on competition, it was necessary to manage, beyond the change in scale (the company went from a workforce of 40 to 170 people and from €10 million to €30 in sales), human relations between teams that did not know each other, distant from each other by 270 kms and, above all, very different work habits. In short, each site spoke its own language: industrial on the one hand, craft on the other, not always compatible in appearance, but it was essential to make each one recognizes, in mutual acceptance, the skills of the other.

We had to find ways to involve all the teams of the two sites in a process of change, by giving them the possibility of being actively involved, with coordinated initiatives. The socio-economic method provided us with the solution as soon as the evaluation of the hidden costs of the two sites was presented. All the teams felt concerned by the diagnoses, which showed not only internal dysfunctions at each site (skills, organization and management control systems) but also the interface between them. From a qualitative point of view, the human relations between the two sites, initially strained, were relativized by the evidence that each had to improve its own performance by converting its hidden costs into value, before thinking that it was up to the other to bow down to a supposed superiority. This had a considerable impact on the mindset of the teams working together, nipping in the bud any sense of vindication or grudge between sites. From then on, we no longer spoke industrial or artisanal language: the socio-economic culture and language became the common base on which the group would be anchored.

The credibility of the socio-economic approach was thus quickly assured by the power and particularity of the initial diagnosis, established from individual interviews conducted by the ISEOR staff in absolute anonymity, and then returned to all the teams in an unusual, transparent, and uncompromising form, highlighting the dysfunctions identified on each site to an unsuspected extent. The mirror-effect, which uses exactly the same phrases, expressions and reproaches expressed during the interviews, in which the people called upon recognize themselves (Savall and Zardet, 1987), enabled each team to become aware of its importance within the company and of the role it could play in it, as soon as what it had expressed was taken into consideration.

2.4 Valuing Intangible Assets and Human Potential

The Socio-economic management control is a real tool for controlling the human resources of an organization. Like what is regularly practiced in a production system (such as ERP) based on nomenclatures, time measurements and the use of organization methods, it is a tool that allows this notion to be extended to all direct and indirect activities carried out in the company. By establishing a detailed nomenclature of all the activities of a company in order to achieve its operational objectives in all areas, without being limited to the strictly material level, and by reconciling this general nomenclature with the nomenclature of each activity and the skills of each of the actors, it becomes possible to measure the adequacy of these skills to the workstations, but also the performance of each department and its employees (Savall and Zardet, 2008). In addition to measuring and improving performance in relation to the resources allocated, it becomes easy to forecast the resources needed to support the changes brought about by the strategic objectives, by anticipating the determination, allocation and implementation of resources.

The socio-economic management control thus becomes an essential management tool for feeding the competency grids of the various employees, determining training and new skills acquisition needs, restoring balance between departments, enriching organizational schemes by better distributing operational responsibilities, modifying job descriptions if necessary, programming career development in line with detected potential, and contributing in a transparent and objective manner to improving the performance of all activities.

What is major and particularly innovative is the ability of the socio-economic management control to give an economic value to all the elements of the organization, without limiting itself to materially measurable activities (purchases, raw materials, production time, etc.). This economic value, never reliably represented in traditional accounting schemes, fundamentally changes the perception of the importance of each activity and consequently the role of each employee in an organization. Because accounting values, without being contestable, are not sufficient indicators to value activities, and only partially measure the human potential of the company, the only real guarantor of its sustainability.

CONCLUSION

This chapter does not pretend to develop all the aspects of the successful implementation of socio-economic management. It is more modestly a testimony of its contribution to the successes recorded by a group, resulting from the merger of two historically competing companies, which succeeded in building the success of their merger on a common strategic base, enlarged and enriched by the diversity of their competences and their cultures.

As the manager behind this initiative, and despite the difficulties encountered in setting up the process, the managerial comfort I enjoyed at the end of the process was the best reward for the efforts made, while also underlining the satisfaction of the investors who have accompanied the company unfailingly for 18 years.

This comfort has also allowed us to prepare the transfer of the group, by choosing and building the best option to ensure the continuity of jobs and the recognition of the skills of the 200 or so employees who have contributed to the success of this industrial adventure.

REFERENCES

Caghassi, J. (2016). Rencontre d'un dirigeant avec l'ISEOR. In H. Savall & V. Zardet (Eds.), *Entreprises, valeur(s) et prospérité: le capitalisme socialement responsable.* EMS.

Caghassi, J. (2015). Le management socio-économique pour faciliter la relation gouvernance-management. In H. Savall & V. Zardet (Eds.), *Gouvernance et management: quelle coopération?* Economica.

Savall, H., & Krief, N. (2003). *Évaluation socio-économique dans un groupe de carrosserie industrielle.* Rapport de recherche ISEOR. Lyon

This page intentionally left blank.

CHAPTER 73

INTERNATIONAL COMMUNICATION IN AN INTERCULTURAL ENVIRONMENT—ILLUSTRATIONS

Jeannette Rencoret and Georges Peillon

ABSTRACT

Communication has proven to be a powerful lever for the Socio-Economic Approach to management of international companies. This chapter shows, thanks to three concrete examples, how the development and implementation of internal and external communication contribute both to the performance of the company and to the development of its reputation.

Desert of Al Sharja, Abu Dhabi. The wind sweeps the sand dunes, the heat overwhelms the tents. One of them hosts the press room with a place reserved for telecommunications, another dedicated to press briefings. A dozen foreign journalists are patiently waiting for the update on the joint maneuvers between France and the United Arab Emirates. Nothing happens. Then a bus arrives, pouring in about thirty people dressed in military fatigues. They are local journalists, gathered for the occasion by the Emirati press service.

On the shores of Lake Gruyère, the board of directors of this Swiss company with 200 employees met quietly to discuss the opportunity to enter the North American market. Already the market leader in high-voltage drivers in Asia and the Far East, the company is considering the risks involved.

On the terrace of the Kenzi hotel, some district officials and the management of the company building part of the Casablanca tramway are discussing the overall nuisance that has been polluting the lives of residents for nearly three years and are trying to find solutions, despite the expected gain from the new public transport.

SEAM Treatise, pages 607–612

These three cases illustrate, to varying degrees, an external communication strategy that has a direct impact on the performance and results of the objectives to be achieved. As a performance lever, a "good" communication strategy integrates, from the outset, parameters such as the messages to be disseminated, the communication targets to be reached, the budgets for the various tools to be implemented, and the methods of evaluating the communication. At the same time, an effective strategy evaluates the limits that must not be crossed, in terms of geography for example, or the possible risks and weaknesses that it must anticipate and formalize.

1 AN OVERALL STRATEGY TO FRAME THE EXTERNAL COMMUNICATION POLICY

In short, every organization should implement communication strategies that are understood over the medium term (2 to 3 years) to develop coherence and coordination of messages and actions. Indeed, it is thanks to an upstream conception, unfortunately often overlooked, that companies or organizations can develop dialogues with all their stakeholders: authorities, partners, subcontractors, customers, users, residents, elected officials, media, etc. These stakeholders shape their opinion, attitude, and behavior towards the company thanks to communication "gestures," and not only to simple marketing actions for example. It is therefore essential that this strategy presents a positive, credible image, consistent with the company's values (Wellhoff, 2010), its fundamental mission, which is its core business, and its long-term vision. On this last point, it is interesting to note that only the Swiss company has a real vision of its future. It can project itself to consolidate its position as leader in its hyper-specialized market and at the same time, it shares its activities with all its employees on a daily basis.

Moreover, it is important that the company has a general strategy, or global policy, which sets the major long-term orientations. Thus, the French company based in Morocco has a very paternalistic but also essentially commercial vision of its activity. Its presence in the country for some fifty years has enabled it to develop a high level of notoriety, despite name changes due to a succession of mergers and acquisitions. It is even often referred to in common parlance by its former name, given its involvement in daily Moroccan life. Its long-term strategy is essentially focused on the acquisition of new large public works contracts. In a way, it is living on an asset.

For the UAE Ministry of Defense, the situation is different. The political strategy is based on the Emirates' desired position in the Persian Gulf region. But there is also a desire to appear as a country that is strategically important to the Western powers. Thanks to the wealth provided by the dividends of the oil fields, it has a desire to position itself as a politically and economically reliable nation in a historically unstable sub-region. These notions are not necessarily made explicit to the population, but the gigantic financial resources guarantee a form of impunity in the strategic choices made.

2 EXTERNAL COMMUNICATION MEANS INTERNAL COMMUNICATION

Communicating externally with relevance and efficiency requires respecting a founding principle: it is advisable to address the internal side before communicating externally; if it is never good for employees to learn by way of the press or otherwise, a piece of news that concerns them directly, it is often catastrophic for the morale of the company to neglect the channels of dialogue and cooperation. This clearly means that internal communication and external communication are two inseparable wheels.

In addition to management actions, internal communication is used to unite employees, explain the company's Management, and take an interest in employees. Too often, internal newsletters are the showcase of the company's success (which is legitimate), while neglecting the fact that they are also the employees. The level of team involvement depends on the level of management investment in internal information and communication. Through the implementation of concrete and local actions, the level of involvement increases and leads to a significant improvement of the organization, thus reducing dysfunctions and hidden costs (Savall 1974, 1979; Savall and Zardet, 1987).

External communication is fundamental because it participates in building awareness (I trust), reputation (I know) and image (I like). This external communication must be adapted to specific targets, but also in line with the company's internal values. In fact, too great a discrepancy between, for example, a thundering and flashy advertising campaign and precarious working conditions for employees creates a gap in understanding and forms of mistrust that are detrimental to the company's dynamics.

Let's study the cases of three organizations with an international vocation, confronted with similar external communication issues, in different intercultural contexts. They must develop communication with stakeholders with divergent interests. But what is the place of the company's strategy? What level of foresight has been developed? Have these organizations qualified the intercultural environment in which they operate?

The Ministry of Defense of the United Arab Emirates (UAE) must promote its operational skills internationally, the Swiss company wants to conquer the North American market for electricity suppliers, and the French company must make hostile audiences accept long-term nuisances. The issue is not to compare their objectives, but to understand their modes of engagement and resolution of their respective constraints. When the bus of local journalists dressed as soldiers arrived on the tarmac in Al Sharja, the foreign correspondents opened their eyes in astonishment. How can journalists be so "submissive," under the orders of an official word assimilated to a kind of propaganda? The Emirati press service replied that it was always like that and that it avoided distortions in the information, the spreading of rumors and gave the certainty that the information would be taken up in all the media without exception.

Effective communication requires a company policy and strategy upstream, based on coordination and cooperation to obtain the participation and involvement of all staff. Because each employee contributes at his or her own level to the diffusion of the company's overall image.

The commitment of the employees to their organization is a major asset for successful external communication. At the Swiss manufacturer of high-voltage conductors, the 200 employees belong to a "family" of highly qualified professionals, whose qualification programs are constantly running, where talking circles are a reality in this human-sized company. On the other hand, only a very small part of the middle management of the Emirati staff seems to be informed and concerned by the technical, military, and diplomatic stakes of these Franco-Emirati maneuvers. In a quasi-feudal system of operation, and despite the high-level training of senior officers received at Sandhurst or West Point, only a very small part of the staff is informed, because the possession of information is assimilated to the control of power in a hyper-hierarchical system. Finally, in Casablanca, the 3,000 or so local workers who work on the project know nothing about the final project, and the French management motivates them solely on the legitimate aspects of public works safety and by offering more attractive salaries than local public works companies.

One may wonder about the links between [Communication-Coordination-Cooperation] and the quality of the external relationship with stakeholders. According to the major theories of communication and management, the more employees are informed of the company's actions and projects, the more they perform well and are invested in the organization. But why don't all organizations practice this? Often, time management appears to be an obstacle to sharing information internally, as if it were a "value" reserved for executives only (this is the case in the UAE). Secondly, company management often underestimates the level of investment of employees in the company project, whom they consider as producers and not as actors (this is the case for the metro construction company). Finally, internal communication is perceived as a cost for the company, forgetting that it is a real source of motivation (this is the Swiss case). As we can see, these dysfunctions linked to the place of internal communication led to managerial costs and image costs for the company. (Savall and Zardet, 1987; Desmaison, 1992).

In the context of international and intercultural relations maintained either for commercial or political purposes, it is fundamental that the various stakeholders, companies, governments, associations, NGOs, etc., understand that despite the different cultures and languages, it is important that they adapt to these cultural criteria. Communication messages must also be adapted. Thus, taking cultural parameters into account would have been particularly beneficial to the French company in Morocco, as well as to the Emirati ministry. But the company did not anticipate that local workers have different work rhythms and habits, just as the Emiratis did not anticipate the need for factual, accurate and immediate information from international correspondents.

Thus, communication is not only a simple channel of information. Another way of understanding intercultural models opens, offering a more complete vision of the quality of the relationship between communication, culture, project, and management.

3 COMMUNICATION BUILDS MEANING

Another corollary aspect is the integration of interculturality in the construction of meaning and communication. Indeed, the objective is to disseminate messages that are adapted to audiences and that conform to a human, social and economic reality. Thus, one of the major difficulties in Casablanca was to achieve proximity communication with residents who did not perceive the expected gain from a public transport system that would relieve congestion in an overcrowded city, but who focused on the nuisance caused by the giant works. The company had explained in all dimensions what this new tramway would bring in terms of quality of life but had failed to specify the nature of the work and the inconvenience of noise and air pollution. It focused on achieving the medium-term objective, without measuring the short-term social and economic impacts.

Societal responsibility, which represents the commitment of the company (said or unsaid, perceived or not) in the life of the city, its participation, and its contribution to a better life for the whole of the population is thus questioned. In all three cases, the company with the greatest social responsibility, the company building the metro in Morocco, failed in this respect, even though all the parameters were in place to obtain an optimal "image + notoriety + reputation." The first obstacle was that the project was not designed in relation to residents. During the first period of work, no local cooperation committee was set up, no space for dialogue was offered. The residents felt that the authorities were imposing nuisances on them: difficulty in leaving their buildings, increasing noise pollution day and night, inability to give a deadline.

The company then had to develop a wealth of communication skills to explain the nature of the work in an educational manner, to set up suitable working hours, to install sets of explanatory panels, and to broadcast precise deadlines in the media. The company's progressive consideration of the expectations of residents considerably slowed down the progress of the work. Almost two years of delay. But the multiplication of actors involved in the project also explains the differences in perception between the national and local authorities and the companies and their subcontractors.

Another important question is: are the communication messages issued compliant, relevant, and understandable? With the exception of the Swiss company, which wants to conquer the American market and is still reflecting on the relevance of its development, the other two companies have constructed their messages in a sometimes-haphazard manner. For the UAE, the essential message could be summed up as "we are extremely efficient because we have a lot of money," which is far from reassuring diplomatic and military partners and which left the few international journalists present perplexed... For the public works company in Casablanca, it is obvious that communication with residents was not anticipated. Is this an incomprehensible oversight for a public works company belonging to a global group, a form of contempt, or a lack of knowledge of the public and their ability to mobilize? Whatever the case, the costs incurred by stopping the work, carrying out local communication actions (posters, press, TV and radio campaigns) and setting up local cooperation committees were prohibitive. They had not been anticipated in the financial plan and, moreover, they led to a delay of almost two years in the completion of the work... Of course, the construction of messages is essential, but so is the anticipation of a communication strategy!

In turbulent market environments, it is important to anticipate and understand the cultural environments in which a company evolves. The case of the Swiss company is edifying. The company is led by an enlightened and intelligent manager with a very simple management style. The size of the company, barely 200 employees, is an asset and he often reminds us that it is the quality of the employees that makes the company rich. Located in the center of Switzerland, the company has conquered the Chinese market and all the markets of Southeast Asia. The quality of its products combined with a high level of technical expertise and unparalleled reliability has propelled the company to the top of the high-voltage conductor manufacturers. The desire to expand into the North American market was a logical next step since the main competitors were located there. But the board of directors first decided to send an exploratory mission to understand how American companies in its sector operate, their ways of thinking, their production rates, communications, etc., and not just the quality of their equipment. This humble approach paid off. For two months, two company executives, a technician and a manager walked around their competitors' facilities, talked to employees about their working conditions, and looked at the professional communications they produced. They drew up a detailed map of their competitors' ecosystems to get to know them better. The Swiss company thus integrated different cultural codes and thought processes to better adapt to its competitive market.

CONCLUSION

External communication in internationally oriented organizations is a key management tool. In the internal and external environment of the company, it is necessary to develop a coherent and integrated communication in agreement with the different partners to ensure a good performance of the investments. In addition, the professionalization of the communication function leads to the implementation of efficiency measurement tools.

Communication can be a powerful lever for growth, but also, in the case of non-communication, a powerful brake on the development of the company and its employees. The three cases illustrate this: the Swiss company, thanks to its efforts to anticipate and understand the American market, was able to adapt its offer in a hyper-competitive and high-tech environment. In the space of two years, it has maintained its position as world leader in its sector of activity. The UAE Ministry of Defense has not changed. The internal structures and the hierarchical culture have not evolved, and only colossal financial means have allowed the evolution of know-how. Finally, the French company in Casablanca, through an effort to question its operating methods, has succeeded in adapting, but with a colossal delay and prohibitive operating costs.

REFERENCES

Desmaison G. (1992). Les 3C management. Revue Brises, INIST, CNRS n°17.

Wellhoff, T. (2010). Les valeurs : donner du sens, guider la communication, construire la réputation. Editions Eyrolles.

PART VII

SOCIO-ECONOMIC MANAGEMENT OF HUMAN RESOURCES AND HUMAN POTENTIAL

CHAPTER 74

THE SOCIO-ECONOMIC APPROACH TO MANAGEMENT

A Metaphor From the Panarchy

Pedro Constantino Solís Pérez and Juan Castaingts Teillery

ABSTRACT

This chapter studies the ISEOR Socio-economic Model from the metaphor of panarchy and resilience to offer a new look at the cornerstone theory of ISEOR strategy, where the success of a firm's external strategy depends on the degree of internal cohesion. On the other hand, the individual and collective behavior of conflict and cooperation and their impacts on the internal cohesion of the firm are observed from another plane. The aim is to argue that the metaphor of panarchy and the postulates of the cornerstone of socioeconomic theory are consistent with each other for the study of current organizations.

The socioeconomic theory of organizations consists of a *bio-systemic* theoretical model of companies and organizations to carry out the analysis of their *management*, through an on-site intervention, which integrates economic and social variables with the purpose of improving the performance of the *interaction* between organizational *structures* and employee *behaviors* (Savall, 1974, 1979; 1980; Savall and Zardet, 1987; Savall, 2003, p. 33). The interaction between structures and behaviors manifests itself both as a *driving force* for the productive development of the organization and as a *promoting force* for dysfunctions, where the difference between the observed operational results and the operational results expected by the different actors involved is explained by their specific conflicting objectives.

The Institute of Socio-Economics of Enterprises and Organizations (ISEOR) was founded in 1973 by Henri Savall as a non-profit research association, whose epistemological basis is

SEAM Treatise, pages 615–621

carried out through a robust process of learning and conceptualization based on a series of experiments and interventions, where empirical evidence is collected from real cases of enterprises in the construction of scientific knowledge in *management.* The interaction between researchers and real cases of companies is considered as a principle of cognitive interaction, complemented with the principle of *contradictory intersubjectivity* that consists of a prolonged process of participation that allows comparisons through different points of view to enable the creation of knowledge (Savall and Zardet, 1996, 2004; Bonnet and Savall, 2014, p. 4).

Henri Savall and Veronique Zardet, main drivers of the socio-economic approach to management, publish in 2015 a work of reflection on the *new state of the art* of the socioeconomic theory of organizations and territories in the 21st century. *The Informal Production System* (IPS) is posed as a significant concept in individual and collective *conflict-cooperation* behavior that can cause dysfunctions in organizational structures, generating hidden costs that have a *value-added destruction effect,* thereby causing negative effects on the economic performance of the organization, to the extent that the level of individual and collective commitment affects the performance of the company, both to contribute to its improvement and to its devaluation (Savall and Zardet, 2015).

1 THE PANARCHY METAPHOR AND THE SOCIO-ECONOMIC THEORY

The metaphor, from the Greek *meta* (outside and beyond) and *pherein* (to transfer), consists of transferring concepts and models of thought from one field of knowledge, beyond its scope, to another field of knowledge with the purpose of pointing out similarities, approximations, conformities or analogies that contribute to improve knowledge and the cognitive value of what is studied.

The biological metaphor has been widely used in the field of business and organizations. The Darwinian evolution of species has been transferred in different ways to the understanding of organizations, assuming that they are living organisms, whose survival depends on adaptive variations to their environment, fighting for available resources against others, and relying on internal resources that allow enhancing strategic development options (Montoya L., Montoya I. and Valencia-Arias, 2016).

In fact, the socio-economic theory repeatedly uses images from biology and clinical medicine in the development of its conceptual constructs. In this sense, this theory is defined as a bio-systemic model[1] of firms, where dysfunctions are assumed as problems that prevent a correct biological, social and economic adaptation, diminishing and devaluing both their performance and the creation of value added. The biological approach manifests itself in images about the role that dysfunctions play in engendering hidden costs that affect sustainable economic performance:

> One could compare the company as a strategic vehicle that loses too much energy because of leaks or internal and external hemorrhages. The hemorrhages come from the numerous dysfunctions... that occur daily in all organizations and generate chronic overconsumption of technological, financial and human resources..." (Underlined by the authors, Savall H. and Zardet V., 2009, 2)

On the other hand, another central concept of socioeconomic theory refers to the metaphor of the TFW virus as the anachronistic survival of the principles of structuring, in the mechanistic design of enterprises, carried out by Frederick Taylor, Henri Fayol and Max Weber. The characteristics of this TFW virus are defined as follows:

> Most viruses are pathogenic. The degree of infection of the TFW virus in organizational models and in dominant managerial practices is referred to a deficiency of more or less important cooperation between participants in an activity—between individuals of a team or between the same sites of the organization, subsidiaries or departments... (Free translation, authors' underlining, Savall and Zardet, 2015, 33)

The characteristics of the TFW virus are related to the specialization and division of labor, with the separation between decision/conception and operation, as well as a depersonalization of work generated by rules, organizational charts, and standardized methods (Savall and Zardet, 2014). The socio-economic theory, on the other hand, emphasizes more on the increase of people's capabilities and skills, on a greater *organization* of the relationships between actors based on communication, negotiation and agreements from which pacts are established to renew *socially acceptable contracts.* In these contracts, results are established that increase performance and that are agreed under a pedagogical logic of quasi-democratic essence (Savall and Zardet, 2015, p. 32). A relevant aspect of hidden costs is related to the assumption that they are essentially the reflection of individual and collective insubordination of the actors, and as all insubordination is kept hidden.

Hidden costs also stem from complexities in the structures and activities of firms and organizations, their internal system and their relationship with the external environment, which may involve inefficiencies and dysfunctions of various kinds. Several concepts and constructs, described above, can be included in the socio-economic theory, closely related to the referential frameworks of complex adaptive systems, which will introduce problems linked to uncertainty, emergence and self-organization in entities (companies, associations or institutions), where the complexity lies in the fact that everything is intertwined, interwoven or entangled under a complexus: the parts are inseparable from the whole and the internal/external is interconnected. In addition, the complex relationships of this network often generate new elements and relationships not contained in its original structure, which are known as "emergences."

The central, structural *internal and external elements* linked to social processes and organizations are energy, information, self-organization/control, available instruments of reflection and knowledge about the environment and the organization, and operation of enterprises, organizations, adaptation and feedback/control. These elements form an adaptive and recurrent cycle, where the initial triggers are energy and information. They all interact with each other, with complex relationships involving recursion. For example, efficiency in the use of human, biological, physical and chemical energy depends on the quantity and quality of the internal and external information available, on the control and feedback systems implemented, on the reflective and strategic formulation capacity, and on the existing capacity for adaptation and self-organization. The deficient structuring of these internal relationships leads to inefficiencies and dysfunctions.

For the analysis of the processes of evolution of these structures, it is convenient to use the metaphor of panarchy developed by Holling (2001), which comes from the figure of the Greek god Pan, image of unpredictable change, and from the word hierarchy associated with the rigid and static. Assumed as an oxymoron, this new term represents structures that sustain experience, test its results and allow adaptive evolution. Thus, "panarchy is a representation of a hierarchy as a nested set of adaptive cycles. The functioning of these cycles and the communication between them determines the sustainability of a system" (Holling, 2001, p. 396).

For Holling (2001, p. 394), panarchy allows the understanding of the complexity of economic, social and ecological systems, through three properties that shape the adaptive cycle and future state of a system: (a) *the inherent potentiality or richness of the system* that determines

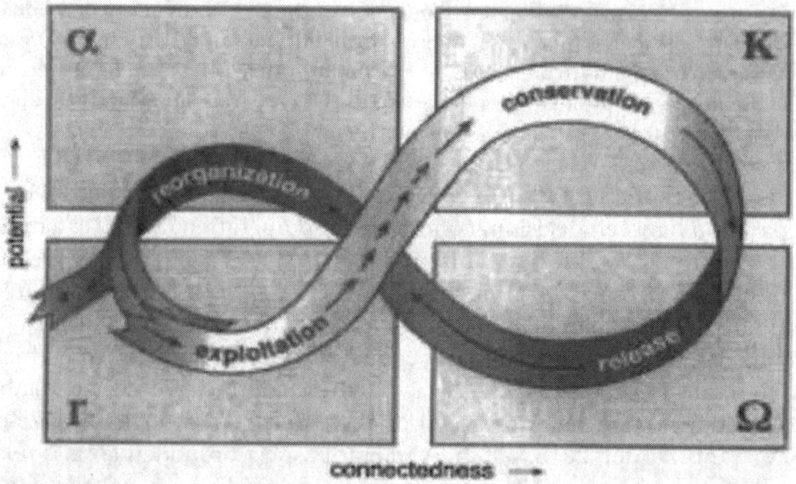

Figure 74.1 Representation of the four ecosystem phases and the flow of events between them. Taken from Holling (2001, p. 394).

the future range of possible options and the feasibility of change; (b) *the controllability or governability of a system* expressed by the degree of connectivity of the internal monitoring of variables and processes; and (c) *the adaptive capacity*, that is the resilience of the system, as a measure of its vulnerability to unpredictable and unexpected disturbances.

In the panarchy metaphor,[2] four phases of ecosystems are defined (see Figure 74.1) Phase 1. Exploitation as a time of growth where opportunities are taken advantage of; b) Phase 2. *Conservation* as a time of stability and rigidity; c) Phase 3. *Liberation* as a time of creative destruction, collapse and uncertainty; d) Phase 4. *Reorganization* as a time of great uncertainty, opportunity for innovation and restructuring (Pendall, Foster and Cowell; 2007, p. 8).

2 PHASES OF ADAPTIVE CYCLES AND CORNERSTONE POSTULATES

To transfer the panarchy metaphor to the socio-economic theory on the *strategy cornerstone*, we will use the theorems developed by Savall and Zardet (2016, p. 8–9) in this regard:

1. the success of the organization's external strategy is a function of the intensity of its internal strategy;
2. the level of the organization's external performance is a function of the degree of intensity of its internal cohesion; and
3. variation in the degree of cohesion has a multiplier effect (or leverage effect) on variation in the level of performance; thus, a doubling of the level of cohesion creates a more than doubling of performance.

In socioeconomic theory, the interaction between structures and behaviors is the driving force (energy/information) of social and economic performance growth, but over time rigidity and deterioration destroy the intensity of its internal strategy and the level of its external performance through hidden costs that collapse structures and behaviors. The ISEOR intervention methodology initiates in companies a process of self-organization, adaptation

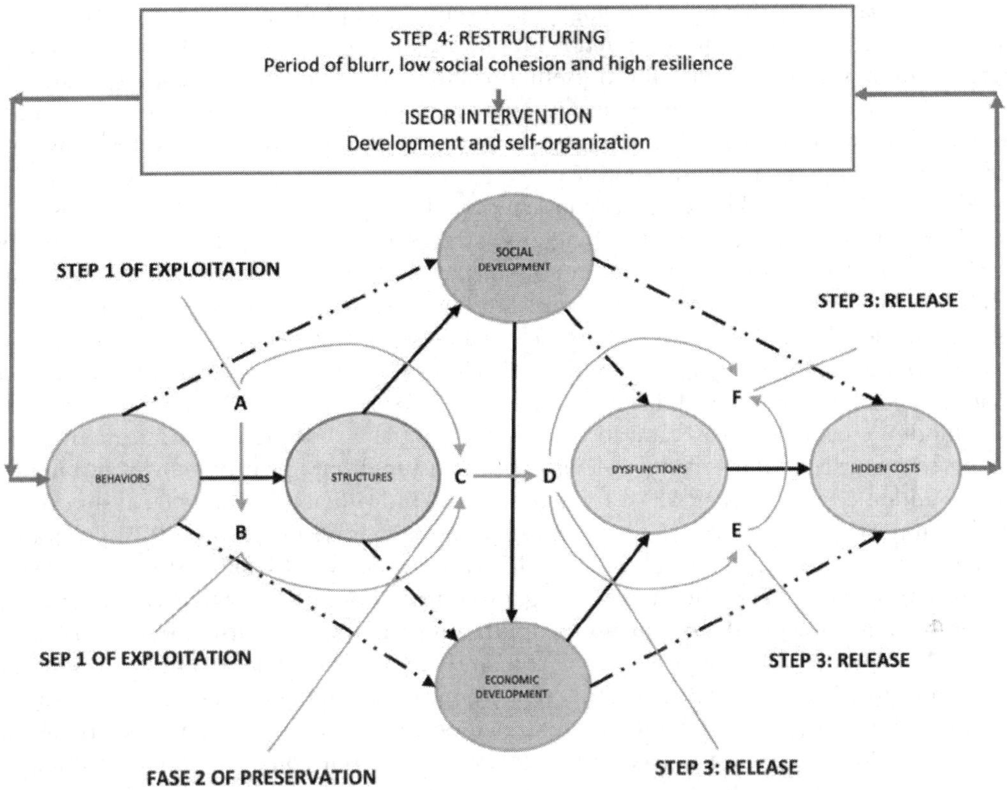

Figure 74.2 The panarchy metaphor and ISEOR's socio-economic theory. (Own elaboration)

and feedback to recover a driving force between structures and behaviors (see the process in Figure 74.2).

Within the ISEOR process, the phases and dimensions of the adaptive cycle of the panarchy metaphor are used to interpret the principles of the strategy cornerstone through complex adaptive systems.

Phase 1 Exploitation and Growth. This stage is characterized by a time of growth and exploitation of the *intensity* of the radiant energy transferred by its *internal strategy*, where at the beginning of this phase there is a low potential and low connectivity, which will grow according to the level of resilience capacity of people's *behaviors* to resist, absorb, adapt and recover in the restoration and renewal of their *basic functions and structures.* At the beginning, renewal and innovation activities seem chaotic and confusing, but in reality it is an evolution marked by progressive learning and increased participation at the individual, group and collective levels. The development of people's capabilities and skills is enhanced by increasing communicational connectivity. The emergence of a new order occurs through a progressive organicity of relationships between actors and the reconstruction of socially acceptable pacts and contracts. The gradual rise of social cohesion multiplies its effect on the increase of social and economic performance.

Phase 2: Conservation. This time of conservation refers to a period of stability and equilibrium based on a high potential for social cohesion, around a consensus perceived as belonging to a common project, which has a multiplier (or leverage) effect on performance and external performance. Internal connectivity is high, but now based on a greater structuring of the company in terms of technology, organization, administrative control and mental models. The connectivity and interactions of internal actors will be based on economic interests and on social and cultural representations that amalgamate social cohesion and also legitimize the exercise of power. There is a detriment of direct interactive communication among internal actors, so that the levels of individual, group and collective resilience are low. Structural rigidity increases significantly.

Phase 3: Liberation. This period is characterized by an entropic process of collapse, destruction and uncertainty. Structural rigidity is increasing, limiting the execution of the strategy and affecting the conditions and organization of work. The potential for social and economic performance decreases and tends to low levels. Connectivity is high in terms of structural and administrative controls, but nevertheless tends to decrease because communication, coordination and cooperation diminish along with social cohesion. Dysfunctions are manifestations of a loss of stability and a move away from harmony. Dysfunctions translate into hidden costs that release and lose energy, potentiality and internal strategic intensity of the company due to overruns, overtime, overconsumption, low productivity and higher risks. Hidden costs are essentially a reflection of the individual and collective insubordination of internal stakeholders. This insubordination is expressed in absenteeism, work accidents, personnel turnover and lack of quality and productivity (Savall and Zardet, 1987).

Phase 4: Reorganization. The time of reorganization manifests itself with great uncertainty, but at the same time it is the opportunity for innovation and restructuring. Internal connectivity is low, but the need for resilience is high and to that extent the potential is high. The need to restore basic structures and functions requires managing changes that recover energy, to enhance internal strategies and external performance. In this sense, information/communication processes are necessary to recover social cohesion and human potential to introduce social and technological innovations. The axes of socioeconomic intervention play a catalytic and driving role in reorganization and resilience through upgrading processes, management tools and political and strategic decisions.

CONCLUSION

The metaphor of panarchy and the four phases of ecosystems is consistent with socioeconomic theory and the postulates of the *strategy cornerstone.* In this sense, complex systems theory underpins the relevance of these postulates. The processes of self-regulation and entropy are cyclical, therefore, order/disorder relationships erode and collapse internal social cohesion as a central element of individual, group and collective resilience.

Finally, the network of complex interactions between interest groups usually leads to *various adaptation processes* that can be of three types: a) integrative, which provides stability; b) with alternative powers, which provides stability with alternative tensions; and c) negative with escalation to extremes, which provides conflict with self-destructive processes.

NOTES

1. biosystemic system implies homeostasis; this is the capacity to maintain a relative stability of the internal environment within adequate margins, despite internal and external fluctuations. All companies and organizations have homeostasis, which are processes of communication, regulation and control.
2. Note that there is an important relationship between homeostasis, strategy and panarchy.

REFERENCES

Castillo-Villanueva L. Y Velázquez-Torres D. (2015), Sistemas Complejos Adaptattivos, sistemas socio-ecológicos y resiliencia, Quivera, vol. 17, núm 2, julio-diciembre, pp. 11–32

Craig A, Angeler D., Garmestani A., Gunderson L. y Holling C.S. (2014). Panarchy : Theory and Application, Ecosystem, Núm 17, pp. 578–589.

Holling, C. S. (2001). Understanding the Complexity of Economic, Ecological, and Social Systems , *Ecosystems* 4, Núm 5, pp. 390–405.

Irusta, A. (2014). « *El concepto de gubernamentalidad. La economización de la política y el problema del Estado en Michel Foucault* », *Philosophia* 74/2, pp 39–59.}

Montoya L., Montoya I. y Valencia-Arias A. (2016) "*Metáforas biológicas aplicadas a las organizaciones II. Ensayos escogidos,*" Edición 1 Universidad Nacional de Colombia.

Raskin, P. (2008). World lines: a framework for exploring global patways, *Ecological Economics*, pp. 461–470.

This page intentionally left blank.

CHAPTER 75

CROSSED REFLECTIONS ON TRANSDISCIPLINARITY IN MARITIME EXPEDITIONS

Entrepreneurship and Crew Spirit

In memory of the dedication of a father to his son

Serge Péron

ABSTRACT

The complexity and the danger of the maritime expedition led very early to develop specific forms of association between partners. A contract between "merchant adventurers" and emigrants financed the voyage of the Mayflower. Trans-disciplinarity is a necessary dimension of these high seas, scientific, commercial, or political enterprises. Trust and solidarity are conditions of their efficiency. Despite technical progress, they remain and are embodied in the crew, both a living cohesive structure and a management tool. The French Navy has developed a discourse and practices around the crew spirit, in companionship with the entrepreneurial spirit.

When Henri Savall did us the honor of asking my mother and me to bring out in this work both the absence and the presence of my father, Michel Péron, he left me, to convince me, complete freedom of subject.

My father, perhaps to give me a hint, had dedicated to me "Transdisciplinarity: the foundation of Anglo-Saxon managerial thought" published under his direction and of which he had written the first chapter "Reflection on transdisciplinarity in managerial thought" by wishing me "Bon Voyage in transdisciplinarity, for a guy from the Navy." I was then finishing the first part of my professional life, spent as a commissioner in the French Navy. I

SEAM Treatise, pages 623–628

remembered having had, many years after the publication of this book, exchanges with him on this theme which was particularly dear to him, and which was strongly present in his work.

The following reflections echo his work and invite us to travel.

1 TRANS-DISCIPLINARITY AND "MARTIME EXPEDITION"

"Fools who entrust their person to the sea!" cries one of the characters in Erasmus' colloquies.[1] In his Institution of a Christian Prince, the same Erasmus compares the qualities required of a ruler to those of the captain of a ship: "one does not take to sea, to be the pilot of a ship, the one who is better than the others by birth, wealth or beauty, but the one who knows best how to hold a rudder, the one who is most vigilant and faithful."[2]

The conditions of navigation were not much safer than in the first third of the 16th century when the Mayflower landed on the shores of Cape Cod Bay. Sailing was and remains an adventure full of uncertainties and dangers. The complexity of the "maritime expedition" (a term used in maritime law to designate all persons who participate by their activities.in a transport operation by sea), marked by the risk specific to the enterprise for both persons and goods, by the resulting need for solidarity (obligation of assistance, "general average"[3]), has given rise to an autonomous law qualified as "maritime," combining, borrowing from and derogating from different legal disciplines. Specific insurance regimes, considering the prospects of gains and losses, have financed these adventures since Antiquity. For a long time, the "maritime expedition" found its financing in what was called "the big adventure loan": high interest rates compensated for the fact that in case of loss of the ship or the cargo, the sum lent was lost for the lender.

It was the creation of a shareholder company, combining colonists with English investors to operate a royal grant that financed the Mayflower's voyage, not a loan. The Pilgrim Fathers, acting as individual entrepreneurs, had, Michel Péron reminds us, "the financial support of the precursors of venture capitalists, the merchant-adventurers." He affirms the essential role of this maritime, commercial, and ultimately political adventure by underlining that "the company is the cornerstone of the American society since the signature of a contract between the pilgrims of the Mayflower, in 1620, even before their landing." Corporate America is America at all, a contractual community where social conscience is mixed with a sense of responsibility and individual rights. It is a micro-social structure coupled with a founding and cohesive institution.

Whatever the goals of ocean navigation—foundation of a colony, scientific research and exploration, commercial exchanges, surveillance and protection of ocean spaces, great nautical race, etc.—trans-disciplinarity is imposed. Trans-disciplinarity is one of the answers to the multiple challenges raised by the maritime enterprise. Interdisciplinarity or trans-disciplinarity? While interdisciplinarity sets up a dialogue and exchanges between disciplines to promote research on a global scientific issue such as climate change,[4] trans-disciplinarity works on complex objects that do not belong to one discipline, by linking them through different actions, thanks to collective rather than individual expertise, to the confrontation of points of view and to interactions. The overcoming of disciplines makes it possible "to ensure the synchronization of these various fields in an often-conflicting universe."

To free themselves from navigation from course to course, sailors were able to mobilize astronomical and mathematical knowledge, albeit incomplete, for the benefit of their missions, with audacity, capacity for anticipation, intuition and even a form of prescience. It was also necessary to design ships that were increasingly capable of navigating over long distances, capable of "holding the sea" in heavy weather and inspiring confidence in their crews: stability, in an environment where remaining motionless is almost impossible, is a vital issue, as recalled by the inglorious sinking of the Gustav Vasa in 1628, when it first left the port of Stockholm.

Historically, it is for the needs of maritime discovery expeditions that the greatest number of disciplines coexist on board ships: each of the two frigates with which Jean-François de Lapérouse set sail in 1785 for the Indian Ocean housed 110 officers, scientists, and sailors. "The officers and fourteen scientists, artists and technicians will have at their disposal an exhaustive scientific library, the best measuring and observation instruments. The most modern science and mechanics can offer the mission. In the "General State of the scientists, artists and sailors" embarked for the expedition one finds one or more surgeons, doctor, astronomer, geographer, cartographer, botanist, naturalist, meteorologist, physicist, clockmaker, painter, draughtsman, chaplains and an interpreter and a diplomat.

How not to recognize in this combination of scientific and artistic knowledge, joined to the scientific, technical, and nautical skills of the sailors, under the coordination and the authority of the expedition leader, an example of trans-disciplinarity in the exercise and the service of a mission? In 2005, an expedition of this type, conducted on a ship of the French Navy in Vanikoro,[5] mixing "in the same investigation archaeologists, scientists, amateur divers and state sailors," but also an ethnolinguist, an entomologist, painters, photographers, doctors... allowed to remove the doubt on the circumstances of the death of Lapérouse, in the wreck of his ship in June 1788.

The French Navy of the 21st century still has its scientists, from oceanographers to ballistic experts, its painters, and its chaplains. As the Ministry of the Armed Forces website states, "The official painters of the Navy constitute one of the oldest artistic corps, whose origins date back to the 17th century. The artists are painters as well as sculptors, illustrators, photographers or engravers." Of course, they participate in missions at sea, and are integrated for these missions into the crew, with officer rank. The Navy also maintains a close partnership with the Association of Marine Writers.

The environment in which the action takes place has obviously never ceased to fascinate throughout the centuries: complex, always in motion, subject to rapid changes, sometimes very violent. The movements are made with a relative slowness, at the rhythm of a life marked by the watches, the permanent watch, the waiting, and the isolation. In this confined universe, the success of the voyage (in the military navy, we speak of a campaign) is achieved through a great diversity of trades, sciences, knowledge, and techniques used for the needs of navigation, community life and the objectives of the expedition. And always, in difficult circumstances, the decision belongs to the commander.

2 TRANS-DISCIPLINARITY AND "CREW SPIRIT"

Even in the 21st century, in the age of satellite navigation systems, there is no expedition without a ship, and no ship without a crew, sometimes a small one, as is the case on modern commercial ships. Depending on the company, the flag of the ship, the number of sailors, the quality of training and the coexistence of different nationalities, the crew, as a cohesive structure, has reality.

The example of the French Navy is significant in this respect, as it is developing a reflection, a discourse, and practices inspired by the notion of crew and what it covers. This discourse is both strongly cohesive and inclusive. While dictionaries generally restrict the composition of the crew to personnel in charge of maneuvering and servicing a ship, apart from officers, the term used in the French Navy, recognized by the Academy, commonly refers to "all sailors, masters and officers embarked on a ship."[6]

Navy human resources managers regularly emphasize the importance of sharing the cultural identity of the institution during initial professional training, instilling its ethics and values, and teaching the duties and requirements of the profession. One of them, Admiral Sautter, wrote in 2004: "Whether we are talking about future officers or young recruits, we must develop and maintain solidarity and a crew spirit, i.e., a sense and taste for the work accomplished together.

Admiral Rolland,[7] who until summer 2020 was commander of the French surface fleet, composed of more than 100 ships, whose crews include between 10 and 2,000 men and women, emphasized during a conference that "facing the successes as well as the difficulties of a mission means strengthening collectively, it means progressing together toward a common goal." Achieving this objective "is not achieved by the mechanical application of processes or ISO standards… It is achieved by the commitment of each person in his or her function."

To maintain this individual and collective commitment in the long term, to be ready, in operations, to take the tactical advantage, to gain the upper hand over the adversary, the two most important levers are accountability and mutual trust. Admiral Rolland adds: "We need a common objective to align our energies and wills in the same direction. But the bow of the ship is not enough to give this direction, to give meaning to collective action. It is the commander's job to recall the mission, to federate and combine skills to carry out this mission successfully, despite the difficulties. Then, by progressing towards this common objective, each person gains confidence in the value of the group. An example of this confidence is the night watch commander on the bridge: often it is someone with only six or seven years of experience, whose training and qualifications are more important than rank, and whose responsibility during the watch is to steer[8] the ship, carry out orders and ensure the safety of the entire crew, some of whom are at rest. This is possible, says Admiral Rolland, "because this sailor has received solid training, has benefited from companionship, because he can count on a robust organization and, above all, because he is aware of the trust placed in him. Trust is at the heart of the crew spirit.

To command a warship crew is to be prepared to lead men and women into battle, and to prepare them for battle, which implies for all of them to accept the idea of death given and death received. In a recent book, Admiral Finaz, former director of the *École* de guerre and naval writer, differentiates between command and management, without opposing them. "To command a warship is not to lead it into battle all the time. It also means running a company, and therefore managing it. Managing also means undertaking, creating, innovating, "recombining to innovate again, taking risks if necessary, inventing the future (which is not only foreseeable, but it can also indeed be invented…), explaining it, sharing a vision (with the crews, the staffs or the collaborators), mobilizing the intelligence, experience and energy of the sailors, the teams, the personnel, arousing their performance and succeeding." And he adds: "to command is to use this performance for the mission."

Here we find some of the dominant traits, from the 17th century, of the Anglo-Saxon entrepreneurial spirit described by Michel Péron: "a certain ability to foresee the unforeseeable, to distinguish, as it was said at the time, between contingent and permanent causes, and to take risks by experimenting, to go beyond factual and numerical data in order to avoid being caught off guard, all of which are key points in entrepreneurial management in our time."

In combat or in business, writes Admiral Finaz, "the qualities necessary for this community alchemy of leadership are also themselves to be approached with a spirit of association", because to operate it needs teams, values, and collective commitments. Some of these associations "form for seafarers what our community calls the crew virtues. These are the pillars of our wisdom: autonomy and solidarity; function and responsibility; hierarchy and participation; exigency and benevolence; energy and culture; intelligence and courage; speech and time." The exercise of these virtues is both an individual and collective necessity. Commanders are the guarantors of this crew spirit, through their exemplary role and their own responsibilities. However, each person on board has a particular responsibility, and enjoys a degree of trust and recognized autonomy, which strengthens the solidarity and efficiency of the group, and contributes to its social cohesion, by providing both a sense of pride in belonging and the feeling of living an individual adventure.

Energy and culture? Intelligence and courage? Word and time? "Management is a pragmatic manipulation of energy on a daily basis. The sermons of the preachers of the American colonies . . . were intended to maintain a cohesion that had to be rebuilt every day. In a way, the same is true in the corporate field of the late 20th century. Free enterprise is not the result of a system but the fruit of experience. The spirit of the laboratory dominates. The key factor is then the pragmatic approach, which is based on a perpetual testing, on a constant faculty of adaptation.

The crew spirit and the entrepreneurial spirit, in addition to their transdisciplinary and sometimes intertwined roots, have very contemporary companion links. It is the same entrepreneurial spirit, noted Michel Péron in another book that presided over the founding of the American colonies and "the building of entrepreneurial societies by promoting pragmatism, self-confidence and creativity. These characteristics were favorable to the development of social life, cooperation, community activities, thanks to a positive relationship and communication. They meant autonomy and challenge, while resting on a strong concept of solidarity. This spirit is similar in many ways to crew spirit.

"Crew spirit and entrepreneurial spirit can sail together," writes Loïc Finaz—a beautiful marine expression that means for two ships to sail together, one able to support the other. A ship goes slowly on the high seas, but where it wants and when it wants. This reality of navigation in maritime spaces reminds us that the company is sometimes struck by evils which, in principle, the crew of the Navy will escape on board its ship. Excessive financialization, the attraction of short-term investments and immediate profit, the neglect of values and ethics in actions, despite their falsely reassuring presence in speeches, weaken the entrepreneurial spirit. The surveillance of maritime zones, sovereignty actions, all the training actions that contribute to keeping the crew ready for its missions, including combat, are part of the longtime frame of the high seas. The company, without having to set sail, knows how to remedy its problems and what benefits it can expect, but it does not always have the capacity, the will or the means to do so.

CONCLUSION

When a sailor puts down his or her sack for good, he or she often misses this crew spirit. And when he starts a second career in civilian administrations, the total absence of this crew spirit is striking. Fortunately, if science fiction keeps its promises, trans-disciplinarity and crew spirit still have a future ahead of them. Already, the vocabulary of space adventure, in reality as in the movies, draws from the lexical field of the navy—ships, gangways, cruisers, crews . . . and admirals. It is said that 180 days could be enough to reach Mars from Earth. It is as much as James Cook, during his second voyage, to reach the Antarctic polar circle from Plymouth, in January 1773. How many scientists and artists will the expedition be enriched with? My father could have smiled with me at these postmodern perspectives.

NOTES

1. *Colloques,* tome I, À l'enseigne du Pot Cassé, Paris, 1934.
2. Quoted by Charles Moulin, Érasme, Éditions à l'enfant poète, 1948.
3. General average is a specific rule of maritime law which allows to distribute among the owners of the ship and the cargo the losses and expenses resulting from the actions carried out by the master, in the common interest, constituting a voluntary sacrifice, in the presence of a real danger and with a useful result.
4. Approach taken in *Sciences et société : Répondre ensemble aux enjeux climatiques* ; Jean Jouzel & Julien Blanchet. *Avis du Conseil économique, social et environnemental,* October, 2017.
5. Archipelago of the Salmon Islands, in the Coral Sea.
6. 9th edition of the *Dictionnaire de l'Académie Française.*
7. Vice Admiral Jean-Philippe Rolland, Commander of the Naval Action Force (ALFAN), speaks at the Talk international lecture series, June 2018.
8. In the nautical sense of the term: "To steer with the rudder (which is the etymological meaning)," *Littré dictionary.*

REFERENCES

Péron, M., & Péron, M. (2003), Postmodernism and the socio-economic approach to organizations. *Journal of Organizational Change Management, 16*(1).

Savall, H., & Péron, M. (2015) Socially Responsible Capitalism. In *A.* Buono & H. Savall (Eds.), *The Socio-Economic Approach to Management revisited; the Evolving Nature of SEAM in the 21st Century.* IAP.

CHAPTER 76

GIVING MEANING TO WORK AND REDUCING PSYCHOSOCIAL RISKS

Nathalie Ombelets and Sandra Fattorutto

ABSTRACT

In companies with a social purpose, the emotional and mental load is high, which increases psychosocial risk, can affect the quality of life at work and even the health of workers, and deteriorates the company's socio-economic performance. In this context, the meaning that employees give to their work plays a fundamental role in containing psychosocial risk. The different tools of socio-economic management have specific effects on the meaning of work, in particular the tools of strategic multiplication and management self-control. The definition of the company's vision and the choice of its values also have an impact on meaning.

BY WAY OF INTRODUCTION: THE HISTORY OF STONEMASONS

In 1163, the king decided to carry out major works in Paris. He chose to go directly to the heart of Paris, to the island of the city. When he arrived, he saw three stonecutters very concentrated on their work. He addresses the first one:

"What are you doing, my good man?"

"Can't you see? I'm cutting a stone," the man replied gruffly."

The king then turns to the second stonemason:

"And you, can you tell me what you do?"

"I, my lord, work here to feed my family."

At this moment, the king observes the third stonemason who has remained behind in the exchange and is still concentrating on the work of the stone. The king walks up to him and asks:

"And you, what are you doing?"

Stopping to strike the stone, the stonemason stands up and looks proudly at the king:

"I, my lord, am building a cathedral!"

SEAM Treatise, pages 629–635

The objective of this chapter is to show the importance of meaning at work for the well-being of employees, especially at the psychosocial level and consequently its importance for the socio-economic performance of companies.

1 PSYCHOLOGICAL RISKS

1.1 Reducing Psychosocial Risks in Companies

In Belgium, the law of 4 August 1996 on the well-being of workers during the performance of their work formed the basis for a thorough reform of the legislation on health and safety at work. In the context of our work, we will retain this element: each employer must conduct a welfare policy based on general principles which are: avoid risks, eliminate them, or reduce them at source, prefer collective protection measures to individual ones, and ensure that employees are trained and informed. This policy must be integrated into the company's overall management.[1]

In 2014, the issue of psychosocial risks is clarified with a law and a royal decree:

- the Law of February 28, 2014, completes that of August 4, 1996, as to the prevention of psychosocial risks at work including, in particular, violence and moral or sexual harassment at work;
- the Royal Decree of April 10, 2014, on the prevention of psychosocial risks at work.

Psychosocial risks at work must now be considered in the company's prevention policy, like all other risks that may affect the health and safety of employees. Psychosocial risks at work are defined as "the probability that one or more workers will suffer psychological damage which may also be accompanied by physical damage as a result of exposure to components of the organization of work, the content of work, working conditions, conditions of working life and interpersonal relations at work, on which the employer has an impact, and which objectively entail a danger."[2]

The origin of these risks lies in the working conditions and the organization of work. The Belgian Knowledge Centre on Well-being at Work[3] talks about the "5 Ts":

- the organization of work: the organizational structure (horizontal-vertical), the way tasks are distributed, the work procedures, the management tools, the management style, the general policies conducted in the company.
- the content of the work: the employee's task as such: the complexity and the variation of the tasks, the emotional requirements (relationship with the public, contact with suffering, having to hide one's emotions...), the mental load, the physical load, and the clarity of the tasks.
- working conditions: the modalities of execution of the work relationship characterized by the types of contracts and schedules (night work, shift work, atypical schedules...), learning opportunities, career management and evaluation procedures.
- working conditions: the physical environment in which the work is carried out, i.e., the layout of the workplace, work equipment, noise, lighting, substances used and working positions.
- inter-personal relations at work: this includes internal relations (between workers, with the direct supervisor, the hierarchical line...), but also relations with third par-

ties, possibilities of contact, communication, and quality of relations (cooperation, integration).

1.2 The Analysis of Psychosocial Risks in a Social Enterprise: The Example of the Société Wallonne Du Crédit Social (SWCS)

The SWCS is a public organization in Wallonia. It offers an alternative solution to the banking sector that makes access to property and the renovation of housing possible in a sustainable development perspective. SWCS has about 105 employees.

A psychosocial risk assessment survey was conducted in 2017 by a specialized external organization. Beyond the risk assessment, its objective was to make recommendations to take adequate preventive measures. The survey focused on the 5Ts detailed above and improvements were proposed for each of the 5Ts. In a company with a social purpose, the theme "work content" is central; it includes the following aspects: emotional load, mental load, and the meaning of work.[4] When one works with a precarious public, the emotional load and the mental load can be particularly strong and constitute an important stress factor.

The emotional load is mainly related to the following elements:

- being aware that one's mistakes can have serious consequences for the beneficiaries;
- being confronted with people in difficult situations such as illness, death, loss of a job; and
- being exposed to risks of aggression.

The mental load is more the result of contextual elements such as administrative burdens, interruptions in work, the increasing complexity of work or the management of emergencies.

2 MEANING AT WORK

In the context of a high emotional and mental load, the survey concluded that the importance of meaning at work makes it possible to contain psychosocial risk. The dimensions analyzed by the survey for meaning at work were:

- My work is interesting.
- My work is useful.
- My work is compatible with my personal values.

Given the organization's mission, which is to enable access to home ownership for the underprivileged and to encourage the renovation of their homes, the results in terms of "meaning at work" are excellent. Most of the staff feel involved in the "fight against poverty," in the "support of the most disadvantaged," in the "social approach" in particular with regard to the way banks operate in granting loans.

Moreover, in recent years, most of the new employees recruited have come from the banking world. When asked about their motivation, they tell us that they are "looking for meaning" and are ready to make salary concessions to find it. The usefulness of each employee's work is based on the company's positioning: to be an alternative for those who do not have access to bank credit. This is a positioning in relation to the human element, which is essential in the eyes of the employees.

3 MEANINGFUL TOOLS

3.1 Socio-Economic Management Tools

A quality of life at work policy is mainly based on the quality of management: the respect of the balance between professional and private life, the quality of the organization of work and of communication-coordination-cooperation, in a preventive approach of psychosocial risks.

Since 2010, the SWCS has been progressively deploying the different tools of socio-economic management (Savall and Zardet, 1974–1975, 1987, 1995). This chapter insists on the specific effects of some of them on meaning at work.

3.1.1 The Involvement of All Levels of Personnel in Improvement Focus Groups

The ISEOR continuous improvement method allows us to place the human being at the heart of the company's performance and to establish a real dialogue between managers and staff on the dysfunctions that hinder the smooth running of a company, dysfunctions that are very often considered taboo (Ombelets, 2011).

Listening to the staff is considered very favorably: "It's good, our opinion is taken into account." The staff clearly receives the signal that the hierarchy considers the ideas of the actors in the field and recognizes the value added of human potential in the design of improvement projects. The involvement of staff in the diagnostic interviews and subsequent working groups is a sign of healthy collaboration.

Going further, when it comes to implementing certain actions resulting from the improvement project, the piloting of some of them by the staff allows them to feel empowered and invested with a mission. There is a double gain here: the valorization of the personnel through their involvement in the project and the improvement of the company's performance.

The 5T classification of psychosocial risks is intrinsically linked to the six families of dysfunctions in the socio-economic diagnosis (Savall, 1980; Savall and Zardet, 1987), which make it possible to carry out diagnostic interviews (Table 76.1).

TABLE 76.1 Interactions Between the "5Ts" and the Six Domains of Socio-Economic Diagnosis

	5 Themes				
SEAM	Working conditions	Work organization	Content of the work	Work life conditions	Interpersonnel relations
Working Conditions	X			X	X
Work Organization		X	X		
Communication-Coordination-Cooperation					X
Time Management		X			
Integrated Training	X		X	X	
Implementation of the strategy	X	X	X	X	X

3.1.2 A Tool for Involving Staff in Corporate Strategy Broken Down Into IESAP/PAP/PNAC

According to a publication by the French Ministry of Labour, Employment, Vocational Training and Social Dialogue, entitled "Work management and psychosocial risks" (Coutrot and Sandret, 2015), 30% of employees who have neither an individual appraisal interview nor quantified objectives are overexposed to psychosocial risk factors: high psychological and emotional demands, existence of ethical conflicts, insecurity, less social support. These employees also more often report poor physical and mental health.

This study shows a link between the absence of evaluation meetings and psychosocial risks. If the criteria are considered by the employee to be "precise and measurable," the individualized evaluation can be a space for debate on the work, which does not allow for the negotiation of the workload, but rather for the reinforcement of certain resources (autonomy, support, recognition, etc.), thus enabling the employee to cope.

The first tools implemented in the company are the IESAP, the PAP and the PNAC. The Internal and External Strategic Action Plan (IESAP) allows formalizing and structuring the internal and external global strategy. It is broken down into six-monthly Priority Action Plans (PAP) at the team level, and then into Periodically Negotiable Activity Contracts (PNAC) at the individual level, allowing for a complete irrigation of the strategy at all levels of the company (Savall and Zardet, 1995). The regular use of these tools within each department makes it possible to develop a common vision and language: each employee has the same level of understanding and knows the purpose of the projects he or she must carry out. This is the first step that any company can take to give meaning to work.

Here is an example of an objective from our IESAP "Develop our marketing function." This objective, which may seem broad and without any individual goal, translates into clear and measured personal objectives for the employee in the field, such as: "Make ourselves known to three new potential partners in order to develop our social support orientation offer." This approach also allows us to enhance the employee's value, who can see how he or she contributes to the company's overall strategy, and to reassure him or her: he or she knows where we are going in the short and medium term, within what timeframe and with what resources. The letter "N" in the PNAC, which stands for "Negotiable," takes on its full meaning in the context of the psychosocial risks mentioned above. The employee and his or her superior negotiate the objectives and the means necessary to ensure that the objectives are achieved serenely. This negotiation, which is fundamental to the success of the PNAC negotiated between a manager and his or her employee, is the social aspect of the tool which, coupled with rigorous time management, allows for the smooth running of routine management activities and management development.

3.1.3 The Involvement of Line Personnel in the Design of the Internal/External Strategy: Our Internal and External Strategic Action Plan/Priority Action Plan Development Method

The company develops and updates its IESP during an annual strategy seminar, which brings together the directors and team leaders. The team leaders are the link between the Executive Committee and the field staff and play a key role in "selling" the plan and making it operational.

As "salespeople" of the SWCS strategy to the field, their buy-in is essential. To use an ISEOR metaphor, they facilitate the transition from a gaseous state (ideas) to a solid state (actions taken and measured) to improve the company's overall performance. This is where the challenge lies: mobilizing human potential to act depends on the meaning we give to the actions to be taken.

3.1.4 Individual Accountability Through Self-Management Control

SWCS has recently implemented a costing of its activities, based on individual time self-measurement. This new practice is part of the broader framework of the implementation of a management control function (Savall and Zardet, 1992, 2008) within the company. The implementation of this time measurement, which coincided with the communication of the results of the psychosocial analysis, allows us to respond to certain pitfalls expressed by the personnel on the organization of work and more precisely on the distribution of working time and mental load.

The company seized this opportunity to allow staff members to value their working time, and thus conduct a constructive dialogue with their managers, in an objective and documented manner.

An essential and meaningful point in this new project was the method of creating the activity lists, based on which the staff measures their time daily. The nomenclatures are structured in management-security activities linked to the competency grid and the management-development activities from IESAP. This breakdown of activities linked to socio-economic management tools reinforces strategic coherence and gives meaning to field actions.

It is still too early to evaluate the improvements linked to this time measurement, but the testimonies of staff members show that this time measurement has already had several impacts:

- It leads to a better organization of work and, in some cases, makes it possible to question this organization to reduce the mental load.
- It encourages reflection on hidden costs.
- It provides new relevant global or local management indicators.

3.2 Other Meaningful Tools

In addition to determining its internal/external strategy, SWCS quickly wanted to define its vision and values as levers of performance. The functioning of the company is quite particular because it is a public organization that has historically worked with partners from the private sector, which constitute its "front-office." In this context, it is easy to understand that the vision and the values carried by the company and its partners can be totally different. However, the company decided to design its value system by involving both its staff and its partners: a real challenge!

For the company, it was also a question of clearly defining its positioning, to mobilize and motivate the employees to build this superb cathedral together. Quite naturally, SWCS opted for a method of building its values based on the HORIVERT model (Savall and Zardet, 1987): facilitation and construction sessions of a management/executive level cluster and interdepartmental groups organized over a short period of time. This dynamic of horizontal and vertical reflection resulted in better internal cohesion within the company, as well as with its partners, and increased employee mobilization. To make these values live within SWCS and with its partners, we have developed a program to promote these values. First, we personalized each value with a totem, an object that symbolizes it. Periodically, when a department has been particularly successful in achieving an objective, that department is honored by receiving one of the totems that illustrates the "performance." This program can be seen as a recognition mechanism that complements the periodically negotiable activity contract.

CONCLUSION

Whatever the size, the sector, the shareholding (private or public), the purpose (social or economic) of a company, it lives and grows thanks to its "stonemasons" who must be protected from psychosocial risks. The loss of the meaning of work affects both social and economic performance and we have illustrated the extent to which socio-economic management contributes to developing the meaning of work, to improving well-being but also performance and efficiency, through the following levers.

- Participative improvement processes (diagnosis of dysfunctions, calculation of hidden costs, search for improvement actions).
- The development of the managerial role and managerial courage and the central place reserved for employees who must be taken care of.
- The tools of socio-economic approach to management.
- The implementation of a socio-economic management control.
- Participatory processes aimed at defining the company's values and mission.

Socio-economic management provides a basic principle, the socio-economic balance, as well as a common language and structuring tools, which are invaluable for controlling psychosocial risks.

NOTES

1. Federal Public Service Employment, Labour and Social Dialogue. https://emploi.belgique.be/fr/themes/bien-être-au-travail
2. Act of February 28, 2014, supplementing the Act of August 4, 1996 on the well-being of workers during the performance of their work as regards the prevention of psychosocial risks at work including, in particular, violence and moral or sexual harassment at work.
3. https://www.beswic.be/fr/themes/risques-psychosociaux-rps
4. Also clarity of tasks, which will not be discussed here.

REFERENCES

Coutrot, T., & Sandret, N. (2015). Work management and psychosocial risks. *Dares Analyses*, 3, 1–10.

Ombelets N. (2011). The creation of value added in three critical phases of the life of an organization. In H. Savall & V. Zardet (Eds.), *Réussir en temps de crise. Stratégies proactives des entreprises* (pp. 139–144). Éditions Economica.

https://emploi.belgique.be/fr/themes/bien-être-au-travail

https://www.beswic.be/fr/themes/risques-psychosociaux-rps

This page intentionally left blank.

CHAPTER 77

HOW TO CONTRIBUTE TO THE DEVELOPMENT OF MANAGERIAL SKILLS IN SMEs

Sébastien Payre and Aline Scouarnec

ABSTRACT

The mastery of the managerial function, although essential in terms of survival-development of SMEs, is only rarely mentioned in the literature and in the professional world. We consider that it is necessary to go beyond the difficulties that are regularly encountered in the exercise of the manager's job, to implement a support approach that will support it. In this respect, the mobilization of the competency grid contributes to de-dramatizing situations, but also and above all to initiating a dialogue between members of the management and supervisory staff to make the professionalization of managers possible.

1 THE CONCEPT OF COMPETENCES FOR MANAGERS

1.1 Despite an Abundant Literature, the Manager Is Defined in a Superficial Way

Despite the existence of numerous scientific articles, books, blogs, etc., there is no shared definition of management and the managerial profession. One of the few authors to have proposed a definition is Mintzberg (1973), for whom the manager is "any person who has responsibility for a formal organization or one of its sub-units."

A review of the francophone literature (Payre and Scouarnec, 2015) allowed us to propose a synthesis of the missions and roles of managers in four main fields: managing activities and

SEAM Treatise, pages 637–644

production; leading teams and supervising people; contributing to strategy development; and contributing to organizational changes. We propose to use the definition we have proposed (Payre and Scouarnec, 2015): "[...] any person who performs a supervisory function, whatever his or her hierarchical, functional or divisional position (or lack thereof) as well as his or her status within the company; with one or more persons who may or may not themselves perform a supervisory function on a principal basis." Thus, the profession of manager and the function of supervision can be practiced outside the formal authority or rather the formal organization.

1.2 The Concept of Competence Is Also Difficult to Define

The concept of competence has been the subject of numerous studies, without a unanimous definition being given in a definitive manner. We are faced with a concept that covers, totally or partially, knowledge, know-how, behavior, interpersonal skills, the performance of a task and more recently soft skills.

The approach proposed by the socio-economic theory is original compared to previous works because it is based on the concept of human potential, considered as the only active factor of value creation (Savall and Zardet, 2005). We therefore move from an individual approach to a systemic approach to the functioning of organizations and Human Resources Management. Above all, the survival-development of organizations no longer depends solely on material or financial capital, but on the ability of management and supervisors to "mobilize" the potential of the organization's actors. This radically changes the prism or the angle of approach to competence because we do not seek to hide or renounce the development of competences, but on the contrary to develop them, with the help of a tool that is the competency grid. To our knowledge, socio-economic management is the only scientific approach that proposes a tool for the diagnosis and management of skills. Its originality also lies in the fact that it measures the quality or mastery of operations, and not just knowledge or know-how.

2 CONTRIBUTION OF THE COMPETENCY GRID FOR SME MANAGERS

2.1 Observing the Difficulty to Handle the Management Function

After more than 15 to 20 years of action-research and/or intervention practices, we have made a shared and edifying observation. Whatever the sector of activity or the legal form of the organization, the problems are persistent, whether in companies or non-profit organizations.

We have selected 5 cases of action-research and interventions in which we have participated since 2013 and which have one thing in common: the difficulty of holding a managerial posture, in the absence of HR support and definition of the managerial mandate. The common points between these organizations include:

- difficulties identified by management in terms of management practices and cohesion;
- a lack of satisfactory assumption of the supervisory function by all or some of the managers; and
- the search for common management practices and methods.

2.2 A Structured Approach and a Rigorous Methodology to Support Organizations and Managers

The five cases are made up of two socio-economic interventions and three cases of action-research (more than ten companies, establishments, or services) with a prospective aim, in order to propose an initial grid of managerial skills (see Table 77.1).

In the first two cases, the implementation of socio-economic management was carried out with methods adapted to the size of the SME. Thus, the second case saw the implementation of an action comprising a horizontal diagnosis and project, to which were added two vertical actions in different companies, whose managers were the same. In the first case, the socio-economic intervention was adapted to the small number of employees in the SME and built in a global way. Table 77.2 presents the main methodological devices used in these research-interventions.

For the following cases, we used the prospective study of professions (Boyer and Scouarnec, 2005) which constitutes a method of strategic management of people. This method makes it possible to develop a diagnosis through a study report, which focuses on the main internal and external changes facing companies and to propose, through scenarios, the main changes in terms of organization, human resources management and professions that may result from them.

For case 4, the initial prospective study was extended in the form of an action-research project, the objective of which was to support the merger of two medico-social foundations. The Table 77.2 presents the main methodological steps used in these action-research projects.

2.3 Straightening Out the Hierarchy and Developing Managerial Skills

One of the most notable contributions of the implementation of socio-economic management (Savall and Zardet, 1987) is the straightening of the hierarchical line, which translates

TABLE 77.1 Presentation of the Cases

	Case 1	Case 2	Case 3	Case 4	Case 5
Activities	SME manufacturing industrial parts	Family owned SME in the sector of transport and travel agencies	Branch of communication and advertisement	Medico-social foundation: religious sisters of a congregation	Mutual benefit organization
Sectors	Industry	Tourism	Advertising	Healthcare	Social-welfare
Workforce	Less than 30	Ranging from 10 to 60	Flexible	More than 1,000	Several hundred
Context of the intervention	Significant questioning of the production manager.	Managerial cohesion and leadership practices are not well developed.	Many technological changes and strong competition.	Merger of the two foundations that provided psychiatric care.	Increased competition and changing health needs.
Main issue raised by the manager	Difficulty for a technician to become a manager of his former colleagues	Difficulty in developing management skills and increasing internal cohesion.	Demand for rapid evolution of the management function within the companies of the sector.	Development of common management and managerial practices in the context of a merger project.	Contribute to change in the context of strategy development in a participatory manner.
Research method	Socio-economic intervention-research		Action-research focused on foresighting		

TABLE 77.2 Methodological Devices and/or Steps Used

Socio-economic intervention (Savall and Zardet, 1987)	**Job foresighting**
Steering committee Monitoring and steering the research process with Management.	**Contextual understanding** Identifying knowledge on the subject and elaborating the sample of supporting companies and expert actors.
Socio-economic diagnosis Identifying dysfunctions and evaluation of hidden costs	**Preformalization** Formalizing a first draft and identification of trends.
Collaborative training and personalized assistance Training in management tools and themes to promote their implementation.	**Designing scenarios** In-depth analysis of the subject with experts and practitioners to formalize foresighting scenarios.
Socio-economic innovation project group Find solutions to prevent and solve dysfunctions.	**Validation of scenarios** Final formalization of scenarios and trends identified in connection with one or more analysis models.

into the enrichment of managers' work and their greater autonomy. Managers and executives have found significant room for maneuver in their function, significantly improving their working conditions.

The second contribution of the implementation of socio-economic management is the noticeable improvement in communication-coordination-cooperation, within the hierarchical line including the Management. Internal cooperation frequently develops within the hierarchical line and with the staff and the management. Solidarity between managers is increasing. One of the reasons for the lasting acceptance of socio-economic management in these SMEs is the fact that it provides a common working method for all managers. This contributes to more action, to a clearer assumption of the managerial posture, and to more efficient energy expenditure than before within the hierarchical line. A change in mindset is reflected in a greater sense of perspective on the part of managers and executives. Hierarchical actions are conducted in a more collective and coordinated manner.

3 LEARNING OUTCOMES FOR THE PRACTITIONERS, INTERVENER-RESEARCHERS, AND STUDENTS

What lessons can be drawn from this research about the professionalization of managers and their preparation for taking on the role of supervisor? How to develop management skills in SMEs in particular?

3.1 The Lack of Mastery of the Manager's Profession Calls Into Question the Ability of Companies to Survive and Develop

Even if some organizations are aware of the importance of mastering the management function, few of them launch improvement initiatives in this area. However, they end up becoming vulnerable to this. Often, internal activity and cohesion are literally carried by the leader and a few managers.

The hidden costs (Savall, 1974, 1979; Savall and Zardet, 1987) assessed are very significant, as the two research-interventions reveal: between 25,000 and 70,000 euros per person per year. We can attempt to measure the direct economic impact of the lack of mastery of the management function by using hidden costs-performance (Payre, 2017). The direct economic impact of the lack of mastery of the managerial function represents about 50% of the costs identified in Table 77.3.

3.2 Rapid Improvements If Management Agrees To Invest in the Quality of Its Management

Contrary to what we sometimes hear in companies, the lack of mastery of the management function and the lack of development of skills in this area is not a question of the person, the profile or the background. It is much more a question of whether the company or organization really invests in the training and coaching of its managers.

The recourse to the "providential" man or woman coming from outside to replace the managers in place is not a relevant, acceptable and especially effective solution in the medium term. We agree with Noguera and Plane (2016), for whom legitimacy and leadership in teams are acquired through exemplarity and action. Socio-economic management contributes precisely to this. The development of managerial skills cannot be achieved solely through training seminars, coaching, etc. A structured and rigorous process is needed, which allows for a "360 degree" approach that addresses all dysfunctions without complacency, which is the case with socio-economic management.

3.3 Managerial Development Must Be Piloted and Give Rise to Exchanges Between Managers and Management

Leaders and members of management committees sometimes find it very difficult to identify the needs and support methods of managers to develop their managerial skills. Implementing a policy for the development and improvement of management practices based on a detailed diagnosis of the problems encountered by managers is a fruitful approach. Therefore, the use of the competency grid greatly facilitates decisions on training, work organization, evolution of the hierarchical mandate and managerial development. Upward and downward exchanges between managers and the management team help to identify

TABLE 77.3 Summary Table of Hidden Costs Related to the Lack of Mastery of Management in the Two Research-Intervention Cases

Generic Ideas From the Expert Advice	Hidden Costs and Performance
Managerial Role and Quality and Quality of Management Support	**€ 1,092,100 Soit 49.40% de l'ensemble**
Lack of organization and management of activities and excessive demands	**€ 183,900***
Weak cohesion within the management team and difficulties in exercising the hierarchical function	**€ 28,200***
Inadequate time management practices and management control	**€ 26,400***
Lack of management of behaviors and respect of the company rules of the game	**€ 101,200***
Lack of professional dialogue and cooperation within the company	**€ 540,900**
Insufficient mastery of the managerial mandate, of the hierarchical posture and lack of common working methods within the management.	**€ 211,500**

* Underestimated given the time available

and organize support needs (Savall and Zardet, 1995). In the appendix, we present the first version of a generic manager competency grid, developed from the five selected cases. We freely drew inspiration from the management and business management skills repository produced for the FNEGE (Scouarnec et al., 2019), to formalize the generic operations.

CONCLUSION

How can we begin to answer our question about the development of managerial skills in SMEs? The question is far from trivial, as the managerial function and the hierarchical posture are increasingly questioned. Many of them are facing challenges or questioning of their practices (Thévenet, 2012), know-how and skills in management. However, few publications emphasize that many line managers in SMEs come from the field and are much more technical experts than managers.

Becoming a manager is not only a matter of using management techniques but also of a deliberate policy of professionalization (Mispelblom Beyer, 1996) and managerial development. To exercise a managerial function requires specific, even new skills that need to be identified and developed in SMEs. The implementation of socio-economic management contributes, through the provision of a common methodology, to the managerial and HR development of SMEs. The use of the competency grid, of which we propose a generic model, makes it possible to identify the concrete difficulties of mastering the management function, not to sanction or blame people, but to accompany them.

APPENDIX 77.1 Skills Grid

Work organization at the start of the period																														
Activities	Operations																													
	Day-to-day management																		Development operations											
Actors	Managing activity and distributing the workload	Procurement management and ordering	Planing projects and activities	Processing and monthly checking payroll	Steering projects and budgets	Preparing Priority Action Plans	Measuring performance through indicators	Regular use of log-books	Evaluating skills and training needs	Checking the implementation of rules, norms, and procedures	Controlling use of human , financial, and equipment resources	Respecting and implementing decisions	Communicating with internal and external clients	Managing 3C systems (meetings)	Complying with 3Cs and decision systems	Communicating actions to subordinates and superiors	Team-building and leading team	Managing sales actions, point of sale, and reception	Ongoing vigilance	Contributing to strategic implementation	Anticipating recruitment needs	Improvement actions	Advising internal and external clients	Developing employees' skills	Use of digital tools					Observations

Key: ■ Mastery of current practices □ Knowledge of principles without practice ◪ Occasional or not entirely mastered practices — Neither theoretical nor practical knowledge ○ To be created

REFERENCES

Blake, R., & Mouton, J. (1964). *The Managerial Grid: The Key to Leadership Excellence.* Gulf Publishing.

Boyer, L. (2010, Janvier). Les managers de proximité jouent un rôle essentiel dans les entreprises. *Courrier Cadres,* pp. 82–85.

Drucker, P. (1952). *The Practice of Management.* Harper & Row.

Fayol, H. (1916). Administration industrielle et générale. *Bulletin de la Société de l'Industrie minérale,* Paris.

Mintzberg, H. (1984). *Le manager au quotidien,* 1ère édition 1973. Editions d'Organisation.

Mispelblom Beyer, F. (1996). Le management entre science politique et méthodologie d'encadrement, *Les Cahiers d'Evry,* n°4, Février, Evry.

Noguera, F., & Plane, J. M. (2016). "introduction." In F. Noguera & J. M. Plane (Eds.), *Le leadership: recherches et pratiques* (pp. 1–5). Vuibert.

Payre, S. (2017). Les PME françaises s'occupent-elles de leurs managers? Principaux dysfonctionnements managériaux et RH à l'origine des difficultés de prise en charge d'une fonction d'encadrement. *Revue de GRH,* 2017/2, n°104, 35–60.

Payre S., & Scouarnec A. (2015). Manager: Un métier en mutation ? Essai de lecture rétro-prospective pour dessiner les contours du métier de manager et les accompagnements RH nécessaires, *Revue de GRH,* n°97, juillet-août-septembre, pp. 3–16.

Scouarnec, A., Brillet, F., Payre, S., Tissioui, M., Joffre, C., & Keuleyan, R. (2018). Configurations Ressources Humaines: vers une grille de lecture prospective et innovante. *Communication au congrès de l'AGRH,* Lyon.

Taylor, F. W. (1911). *The Principles of Scientific Management.* Harper Brothers.

Thévenet, M. (2004). *Quand les petits chefs deviendront grands,* Editions d'Organisation.

Thévenet, M. (2012). *Managers en quête d'auteurs.* Manitoba/Les Belles Lettres.

White, R. (1963). Ego and Reality in psychoanalytic theory. *Psychological Issues, 3*(3), Monograph 11, 1–210.

CHAPTER 78

RECYCLING HIDDEN COSTS

Importance of the "Serial Learner"

Jean-Marie Peretti and Soufyane Frimousse

ABSTRACT

In the current context of accelerating transformations, organizations must become agile and set up a learning ecosystem to continuously develop new skills and make their employees talented. This requires that each employee becomes a "Serial Learner." A Serial Learner is someone who can learn and develop outside the box. The key is to create the conditions for everyone to learn. The question is no longer what to learn, but how to create a permanent learning dynamic. How can we ensure that each work situation becomes a learning situation and reduce hidden costs? There are many similarities between learning and integrated training developed by the ISEOR team under the leadership of Professor Savall.

The theory of hidden costs encourages organizations to look for solutions to deal with the dysfunctions that weaken them and slow down their performance. This theory was invented by Professor Henri Savall in 1974, at a time when the need for measurement in the social and human resources field was recognized to improve the overall performance of the organization and make it more accountable (Savall, 1974, 1979). This period was marked by the development of the first attempts at human resources accounting and the creation of the obligation, in 1977, for French companies to publish a social report. In this context, the contribution of the theory of hidden costs was fruitful. The central hypothesis of this theory is that the sustainable performance of a company depends on its social and economic performance. The identification of organizational dysfunctions is therefore of major interest.

The development and dissemination by Henri Savall and his team, within the ISEOR (Institut de Socio-Economie des Entreprises et des Organisations), of a method (Savall et

SEAM Treatise, pages 645–649

al., 2000) which is situated in socio-economic management control and is based on qualimetric research-intervention have had a considerable impact on the progress of organizational management. It is not surprising that its creator is cited among the twenty most influential authors in the world in economics and management, according to the manager survey conducted in 2016 by the FNEGE (National Foundation for Management Education in Enterprises).

The axes of socio-economic management control encompass a qualitative module focusing on working conditions, work organization, communication–coordination–cooperation, time management, integrated training, and strategic implementation (Savall and Zardet, 1987). An interview guide was developed to carry out socio-economic diagnoses in these areas, in order to identify dysfunctions in organizations and measure their hidden costs.

In the current context of accelerated transformation, organizations must become agile and implement a learning ecosystem to continuously develop new competencies for their employees and make them talented. The goal of inclusive talent management is to make people "all talented" (Peretti et al., 2008). This requires that every employee becomes a serial learner. Being a "Serial Learner" becomes an essential talent (Frimousse and Peretti, 2019). The Serial Learner is the one who has the ability to train and learn by thinking outside the box (Anglade, 2015). He is attentive to the changes that affect his job and anticipates the new skills to be developed. They become actors in the development of their employability. To continuously acquire relevant new skills, the serial learner relies on the 70–20–10 learning model (McCall, 1996).

According to Daniel Belet (2017), the interest of the learning organization lies in its ability to structure itself to ensure the professionalization of people in order to professionalize its activity. In a learning organization, all members learn from each other. The learning of some promotes the learning of others. Individuals and the group are invited to learn how to learn. Learning faster than the competition is the only way to remain competitive. "Learn or die." The key is to create the conditions for everyone to learn. The question is no longer what to learn, but how to create a permanent learning dynamic. How can we make every work situation a learning situation and reduce hidden costs?

1 LEARNING ERA: LEARN OR DIE

The 70/20/10 model is the result of research on the learning process and the acquisition of skills conducted by McCall, Eichinger and Lombardo of the Center for Creative Leadership (1996). This model divides the way we learn and train into three distinct areas: 70% of our learning is through our experiences and practices, 20% through our social interactions and 10% through a formal mechanism through traditional training channels. The interest of the model is to consider the environment as well as the appetite of employees for training. On-the-job training and action training are gradually inserting the idea of skills development into the fabric of daily work.

The 70/20/10 model makes organizations aware of the obsolescence of training methods that do not take the environment into account, as well as of employees' appetite for training and the need for a new approach to skills development: learning.

The term "learning" is defined by the place and role given to users in the management of processes and by the radically inverted—"learner-centered"—nature of learning. The notion of learning developed by Philippe Carré corresponds to the sustainable set of dispositions favorable to the action of learning, in all formal or informal situations, experientially or didactically, self-directed or not, intentionally or incidentally. Learning is based on the idea of lifelong learning by emphasizing the role of the "learning social subject" in the development of individual and collective competencies (Carré, 2018). Learning brings training and work closer together, to the point of merging them.

The question is no longer what to learn, but how to create a permanent learning dynamic (Cerdin and Peretti, 2019). How can we ensure that each work situation becomes a learning situation?

The organization must create the conditions for learning in order to encourage learning based on systemic interactions. The employee is considered as a potentially proactive subject who is responsible for his or her own learning rather than as an actor who reacts to the training intentions of others, as a "learner" rather than a "trainee." The motivation of learners, the proposal of self-training methods to identify the necessary data and the environment that puts employees in a learning situation are the pillars of learning. The notions of trust, empowerment, support for the professional development of employees, reflection on problems encountered in the workplace, the right to make mistakes, recognition and acknowledgement, taking the initiative, and autonomy are valued and developed by the learning organization. The organization is thus called upon to become "learning," "enabling," and not just "qualifying."

The qualifying organization develops individual and collective skills through traditional training activities (seminars, conferences, etc.). The learning organization differs from a qualification logic and relies on the formative dimension of work through experiential approaches and local resources (feedback, tutoring, coaching, etc.). People are trained in the various situations in which they find themselves, to find answers to their questions, their problems and their challenges. The trainer-tutor has a role of learning facilitator, in charge of accompanying projects in terms of content, method and relationship. The trainer-tutor moves from "face-to-face" to "side-by-side" with the learner.

2 TURNING THE ORGANIZATION INTO A LEARNING ECOSYSTEM

As part of their continuous professional development policy, companies are changing their training model in order to develop the learning abilities of each employee. They are adopting Serial Learning, which is based on the proactivity of learners and the sharing of the training function. The challenge is to transform employees in their daily relationship with their professional activity, with knowledge and with the continuous adjustment of their skills. Serial Learning contributes to reinforcing flexibility, adaptability, and innovation thanks to its impact on the entire training value chain: identification of needs, development of a skills enhancement program, implementation and finally evaluation of acquired skills.

Serial Learning implies the desire to learn, daily. Daily training becomes a watchword ("One learning a day"). Training is no longer planned; it is integrated into daily work. Turning employees into serial learners helps them to develop their skills and thus ensure sustainable employability. Learning becomes continuous, collaborative, and informal. Serial Learning impacts all three forms of learning: experiential learning, collaborative work, and formal training. It allows the organization to respond much more efficiently to the challenges of its environment and its markets.

Successful transformation requires the organization to constantly reinvent itself and all employees to continuously develop new skills. Serial Learning is based on a learning culture that focuses on increasing the number of learning opportunities. This mastery of the art of learning everywhere, all the time and from all possible sources of knowledge, and of continually adapting to one's environment, is based on the construction of a learning ecosystem.

To create a true learning ecosystem, the company systematically develops certain approaches. It develops skills sharing, experiential training, creates learning communities and sets up co-development workshops, uses MOOCs and "blended learning," optimizes tutoring, mentoring and coaching and ensures that the skills acquired are certified and put into practice. The way in which work is organized and interactions are encouraged is crucial to stimulate learning. The company instills "learning" transformations, communication and teamwork methods, managerial attitudes and techniques, pedagogical devices and learning resources. It promotes lifelong learning as a central visible value, in terms of evaluation of practices, recognition and valuing of skills. In this way, the company becomes a talent factory for Serial Learners, a guarantee of continuous improvement, operational excellence, sustainability, and recycling of hidden costs.

There are many similarities between learning and integrated training developed by the ISEOR team under the leadership of Professor Savall (Savall and Zardet, 1987). The precursors of socio-economic management propose a variety of socio-economic management tools, including the integrated training manual. This training method covers all professional training practices aimed at ensuring the adequacy of training for jobs by striving to reconcile the satisfaction of current and future employee development needs with the skills needs of their organization. The Integrated Training Manual (ITM) is a useful tool in the implementation of integrated training actions. Its purpose is to jointly improve the performance of the organization and the skills of its members (Savall and Zardet, 1987).

Integrated training is therefore based on detecting and exploiting potential and preparing for the new requirements of the environment. It is a question of adaptation. It is a question of building skills in line with the organization's strategy, while taking care to consider training as an investment with medium and long-term benefits. Hence the importance of matching training to jobs and employee expectations with the proposed organizational conditions and content. Indeed, unbalanced ratios cause dysfunctions within organizations, which generate hidden costs that contribute to inflate the cost of goods and/or services and consequently affect their competitiveness.

CONCLUSION

Nearly fifty years after its invention by Professor Savall, the socio-economic theory based on hidden costs is still relevant and encourages organizations to seek solutions to deal with the dysfunctions that weaken and slow down their performance. This is only possible if all employees keep up with the pace of change. They must continually develop new skills. This mastery of the art of learning everywhere, all the time and from all possible sources of knowledge, and of continually adapting to one's ecosystem, is called learning. From this point of view, serial learning makes each employee responsible for the development of his or her professional career and for increasing his or her skills.

REFERENCES

Anglade, A. (2015). Les serial Learners. *RH Info*, 31/08/2015.

Cappelletti, L., Voyant O., & Savall, H. (2018). Quarante ans après son invention: la méthode des coûts cachés. *ACCRA*, 2018/2 (N° 2), 71–91.

Carré, P. (2018). Apprenance: Sens, Contresens, Performance? In S. Frimousse & J. M. Peretti (Eds.), *L'apprenance au service de la performance.* EMS.

Cerdin, J. L., Peretti, J. M. (Eds.). (2019). *L'apprentissage et sa réussite.* ISTE.
Frimousse, S., & Peretti, J. M. (2018). Tous apprenants: Serial learner et rebel talent. In S. Frimousse & J. M. Peretti (Eds.), *L'apprenance au service de la performance.* EMS.
Frimousse, S., & Peretti, J. M. (2019). Serial learner, un talent à développer. *Mag RH,* N°5, mars.
McCall, M., Eichinger, R., & Lombardo, M. (1996). *The career architect development planner.* Lominger Limited.
Peretti, J. M. (Ed.). (2008). *Tous talentueux.* Eyrolles.
Véro, J., & Zimmermann, B. (2018). À la recherche de l'organisation capacitante: quelle part de liberté dans le travail salarié ? *Savoirs* 2018/2 (N° 47), 131–150.

CHAPTER 79

CONTRIBUTION OF THE SOCIO-ECONOMIC APPROACH TO MANAGEMENT (SEAM) TO THE RENEWAL OF THE TERRITORIAL HUMAN RESOURCE MANAGEMENT MODEL (HRM)

Anne Loubès and Florence Noguera

ABSTRACT

Although many experiments in territorial HRM were undertaken, about ten years ago, within various territories, through employer groups, regional mobility poles, provision agreements and territorialized networks of organizations, the results today seem mixed. After analyzing the causes of the difficulties in implementing territorial HRM, this contribution proposes ways to rethink territorial HRM, using the concept of socio-economic management.

The territory is nowadays considered as a real lever of action relevant to HRM issues, especially through the development of territorial networks of organizations. The territory is like a social construct, consisting of actors who interact around shared resources, which promotes links between public and private actors (Fort et al., 2016). The first work on the implementation of a territorial HRM was conducted in local productive systems (SPL) and competitiveness clusters. Set up by the French government to foster innovation in an economic sector, they were first studied from the perspective of inter-organizational collaborations and project management practices (Defélix et al., 2008) before being studied from an

SEAM Treatise, pages 651–656

HR perspective. In terms of public policy, in 2008 the State committed itself to developing collective and territorial approaches to HRM to implement professional or geographic mobility within employment areas. The national interprofessional agreement of November 14, 2008, devotes a specific article to the "territorial support dynamic." Territorial HRM appears to be a lever for development: the territory is perceived as a pool of skills by companies; it represents a fundamental issue in terms of the attractiveness of employees and company clients and is the main area of inter-organizational geographical mobility for employees (Noguera et al., 2015). Thus, the territory is a privileged space for collective action that offers new perspectives for developing collective projects and territorial HRM policies. In 2017, Uzan et al. outlined the emergence of a model of HRM extended to the territory and crossed by CSR for Arnaud et al. (2013), territorial HRM is a set of "organized human resource management practices (pooling of jobs, skills and training, mobility and territorialized PMJC) outside the traditional boundaries of the firm with the aim of strengthening the competitiveness of a geographically given territory." Although many experiments in territorial HRM were undertaken a decade ago in various territories, through employer groups, regional mobility poles, secondment agreements (Le Boulaire et al., 2010) and territorialized networks of organizations, the results today seem mixed (Coutetret et al., 2019). One of the reasons for this is the cognitive deficit in human resources management of the actors involved in the conduct of territorial HRM projects.

Territorial HRM, which consists in transposing a set of HRM practices, systems and methods used within companies to the level of a territory or an employment area, is difficult to implement. Indeed, territorial HRM is not a simple extension of corporate HRM (Saint-Germes et al., 2013), as the multiplicity and nature of the actors call for an adaptation of tools and devices (Loubès et al., 2012).

The complexity of territorial HRM comes from the fact that a "territory is singled out by the fact that the actors involved [...] are not linked to each other by hierarchical relationships, they are legally independent" (Zardet and Noguera, 2014, p. 6).

After analyzing the causes of the difficulties in implementing territorial HRM, we propose ways to rethink territorial HRM, mobilizing the concept of socio-economic management.

1 TERRITORIAL HRM: A DIFFICULT ANCHORING IN TERRITORIALZED ORGANIZATIONAL NETWORK

Different studies show the difficulties and limits of territorial HRM. In competitiveness clusters, Arnaud et al. (2013) show the difficulties of implementing an HRM policy, despite the tools and processes of shared HRM. Three factors complicate the development of a territorial HRM policy within the competitiveness cluster: "the reality of members who are not instantly mobilized, which hinders the dynamics of mutualization; the resistance to change that some actors express in the background regarding the idea of evolving collectively on the HR dimension; the heterogeneity of members' expectations" (Arnaud et al., 2013, p. 29). Regarding territorial human resource management, Mazzilli (2016) shows the difficulty of developing a common collaborative strategy: the deployment of a Territorial HRM encounters tensions related to collaborative work and the diversity of partners in the process. The work carried out in the competitiveness clusters (Calamel et al., 2011, p. 190) shows that "although collaborative and mutualized actions have been implemented in terms of training, employee mobility, and territorial forward-looking management of jobs and skills, the fundamentals of the HRM systems have not changed: the subordination link, methods of evaluation and remuneration... have remained unchanged." Based on a five-year longitudinal study of a technology park, Couteret et al. (2019) highlight a case of TMJC[1] failure. An idealized representation of technology, which they describe as technocentrism, and an overly pressing temporality are the two reasons for this failure. "CPs engaged far too quickly in practical considerations and, to justify themselves, conferred on the classic tools of Provisional Management of Jobs and Competences (PMJC) the power to solve all their problems" (Couteret et al., 2019, p. 46). Everaere and Glée (2014) found the same phenomena in other TMJC projects.

Regarding the evaluation of TMJC schemes, Bories-Azeau and Loubès (2013) confirm based on two case studies, the difficulty of developing adapted tools for evaluating territorialized partnership actions, as well as the limited consideration of the territorial level as an action space favorable to externalities.

The implementation of a territorial HRM project is difficult because it relies on the cooperation of many actors, spread out over the territory. Cooperation between them is generally not spontaneous, as it is affected by rivalries, relationships of autonomy and domination, and egocentric attitudes that drive their relations. There is a loss of resources and energy, and a lack of teamwork at the inter-organizational level, which hinders the achievement of expected performance.

2 POSSIBLE WAYS TO RETHINK THE TERRITORIAL HRM MODEL

Faced with these numerous difficulties, how can we rethink the territorial HRM model? The socio-economic management approach offers a relevant framework of analysis and action to think about new orientations aiming at enriching the territorial HRM model.

2.1 Contribution of the Socio-Economic Approach to Management to the Implementation of a Territorial HRM Project

The fields of application of the socio-economic approach to management are multiple: the organization or company, but also the territory conceived as a set of organizations, institutions, and companies. Socio-economic management is a management method that closely integrates the social, human, and economic dimensions (Savall and Zardet, 1987). The socio-economic management method is a facilitator for the implementation of a territorial HRM because it helps to build a Territorialized Network.

This method is organized around three axes (Savall and Zardet, 1987): the political and strategic decisions of the Territorial Networks concerned, the process of transformation and continuous improvement and the specific tools of socio-economic management. The first axis of political and strategic decisions provides the necessary energy impulse to the stakeholders of the Territorial HRM project to define their collaborative, shared and mutualized project. The second axis of the implementation process is a method of inter-organizational project management, composed of a succession of cycles of resolution of the problems encountered by the stakeholders. Thanks to shared inter-organizational diagnoses and project management expertise in the critical implementation phases of the territorial HRM project, the stakeholders can define a concerted, shared, and mutualized vision. The last axis concerns the management and HR tools to be implemented within the territorialized network of organizations. For example, these are tools to help with strategic implementation, which help clarify the Territorial Networks' strategy over the next three to five years regarding its external targets (customers, suppliers, competitors, institutions, public partners (e.g., public employment service) and internal targets (managers, employees, executives, etc.). It is updated each year by the stakeholders to consider the evolution of its internal-external environment. This contributes to the implementation of a shared governance within the Territorial Networks. Skills and job management tools can also be implemented, particularly in the regional mobility hubs. These PMJC tools enable the effective skills available in the partner companies to be visualized and their concrete organization. They also contribute to the elaboration of integrated training plans particularly adapted to each person and to the evolving needs of the network's companies. Finally, among the tools that can be implemented in the Territorial Networks, let's mention the shared socio-economic management dashboard, which includes qualitative, quantitative, and financial indicators used by each network manager to manage the people and activities in his or her area of responsibility. It allows for the measurement, evaluation, and monitoring of the implementation of actions and the sensitive parameters of the operational and strategic activities of the Territorial Networks.

2.2 New Directions for Rethinking the Territorial HRM Model

By integrating the perspectives offered by socio-economic management (Savall and Zardet, 1995), several research paths are possible and can be envisaged to rethink the model of Territorial HRM structured by territorial network projects of organizations open to mobility as well as digital transformation.

2.2.1 Structuring Through a Territorial Organization Network Project

First, a territorial HRM project requires the emergence of collective actions to regulate and manage the collaboration between companies. Bories-Azeau et al. (2007, p. 3) specify that it is necessary to have: "mechanisms of coordination and adaptation of activities between the agents of the territory and to take into account elements such as the densitý of the really existing social relations; the sufficiently long duration of these networked relations; an efficient circulation of information and a territorial proximitý (combination of geographical, organizational and institutional proximity)." Territorial HRM is like a network, in the sense that the network qualifies the nature of inter-organizational, cooperative, and non-hierarchical relationships. These collective actions can be organized through Territorialized Networks. These networks facilitate the management of the territorial and collective dimensions of projects between various stakeholders. Recent advances suggest strengthening actions in favor of collaboration and sustainable stakeholder engagement. To make stakeholders converge towards a common representation, it seems important to invest in inter-organizational shared diagnoses (Michaux and Defélix, 2019), to provide managerial expertise to project management (Couteret et al., 2019), or to constitute a collective actor whose commitment is meant to be sustainable by forming a duo of human and non-human "boundary-spanners"—project manager and digital platform—(Loufrani-Fedida and Saint-Germes, 2018).

2.2.2 The Territorial Mobility Hub at the Heart of Territorial HRM

A second possible way is to deploy, at the scale of a territory in support of the territorial Network a mobility space like those deployed on the internal market in large companies such as the SNCF or Crédit Agricole. The concept of a "mobility pole," which is associative, multi-partner and territorial, consists of pooling resources between companies and facilitating not only personal projects to create a business, but also transfers from one company to another in the same local employment area (Defélix et al., 2008). Mobility hubs can thus help support the external mobility of employees for an association or group of companies in an employment area (Babeau, Janand, & Noguera, 2017). Regional mobility hubs thus make it possible to optimize the management of professional mobility, by offering diversified career paths and developing an innovative approach to territorial mobility management. The regional mobility centers support member companies and employees undergoing professional transition. Located in an employment area, the mobility center pools resources in terms of job analysis and management. Organized on a territory, it encourages employee mobility by helping them build their professional project. As early as 2008, based on the theory of transitional labor markets in connection with flexicurity, Gazier emphasized the role of social partners, firms, and territories in the development of "protected mobilities" and cores of stability.

2.2.3 The Role of Digital in Territorial HRM

Behind the territorial dynamics, the question of digital is omnipresent, although it is too rarely addressed. While collaborative platforms of all kinds are flourishing, what about HR solutions for territorial areas? Loufrani-Fedida and Saint-Germes (2018) analyzed the case of Nice Sophia Antipolis and showed the key roles of the project manager and the digital platform named "eDRH." This platform, considered as an acceleration artifact, includes 15 services and 3 main modules. It subsequently integrates an inter-company mobility platform, which serves as a support for a sustainable commitment from a variety of actors. It gradually becomes a translation tool for the project and its coordination artifact.

This case study shows the importance of HRIS as a structuring element of territorial HRM dynamics. Thus, the question of aligning HRIS with territorial logics must be asked. On what basis should this alignment be organized? On the sustainable commitment of the PPs who will find operational tools and concrete answers? On the political or strategic positioning of a territory, of a Territorial Network of organizations?

In summary, the process of implementing socio-economic management contributes to renewing the territorial HRM model because it allows the involvement of all the stakeholders in the territorial HRM project. Each partner company and employee participate in the definition of actions and collaborative, shared and mutualized tools of the territorial HRM project. The quality of the management is clearly improved, the collaboration and the cohesion of the stakeholders are reinforced. This contributes to a shared governance within the Territorial Network, open to mobility and digital transformation.

NOTE

1. The TMJC (Territorial Management of Jobs and Competences) is the set of devices and practices made available to several companies on a territory or an employment area to improve HRM and to anticipate changes in terms of jobs and skills.

REFERENCES

Arnaud, N., Fauvy, S., & Et Nekka, H., (2013). La difficile institutionnalisation d'une GRH territoriale. Une étude de cas exploratoire. *Revue française de gestion, 2*(231), 15–33.

Babeau, M., Janand, A., & Et Noguera, F. (2017). Les Espaces Mobilité dans une grande entreprise publique: d'un modèle contingent à un modèle transférable au territoire ? *6ème colloque AIR-MAP,* Nice, juin.

Bories-Azeau, I., & Et Loubes, A. (2013). L'évaluation des dispositifs de GPEC à l'échelle territoriale: vers un renouvellement des pratiques? *Management & Avenir,* 1(59), 157–175.

Calamel, L., & Et Mazzilli, I. (2011). *GPEC territoriale: Quelle contribution à la sécurisation des parcours professionnels?* revue du CEREQ, Formation et emploi.

Couteret, P., Bornarel, F., & Virgili, S. (2019). L'échec de la mise en œuvre d'une GTEC: une étude longitudinale. *Gestion 2000,* 2019/4 Volume 36.

Coutetret, P., Bornarel, F., & Et Virgili, S. (2019). L'échec de la mise en œuvre d'une gestion territoriale des emplois et des compétences: une étude longitudinale. *Revue Gestion 2000,* volume 36.

Defélix, C., Culié, J.-D., Retour, D., & Et Valette, A. (2008). Travailler au sein d'un pôle de compétitivite: un défi pour la gestion des ressources humaines? In R. Beaujolin-Bellet, P. Louart, & M. Arlier (Eds.), *Le travail, un défi pour la.* Éditions de l'Anact.

Defelix, C., Colle R., & Et Rapiau, M. T. (2008). Prendre en compte le facteur humain au sein des pôles de compétitivité: la longue marche vers l'innovation sociale. *Management & Avenir,* vol. 20, no. 6, 2008.

Everaere, C., & Et Glee, C. (2014). Une GPEC territoriale? De l'outil de gestion à l'institutionnalisation d'une nouvelle forme de GRH. *Management & Avenir,* vol. 73, no. 7.

Fort F., Bories-Azeau, I., Noguera, F., & Peyroux, C. (2016). Accompagnement entrepreneurial : quelle maille territoriale d'intervention ? *revue Gestion 2000,* mars-avril/mai-juin.

Gazier, B. (2008). Flexicurité et marchés transactionnels du travail: esquisse d'une réflexion normative. *Travail et emploi,* 113, 117–128.

Le Boulaire, M., Degruel, M., Et Defelix, C., & Et Retour, D. (2010). Nouveaux territoires, nouvelle GRH? Quand la GRH se "territorialise." *Entreprise et Personnel,* N° 288.

Mazzili, I. (2013). Construire la GRH territoriale: une approche par les dispositifs de gestion et la théorie de l'acteur-réseau, Thèse de doctorat, université de Grenoble.

Mazzili, I. (2016). Dans les rouages de la GPEC territoriale: surmonter les tensions pour élaborer une stratégie collaborative. *@GRH,* 18(1).

Michaux, V., & Et Defelix, C. (2019). Conduire un diagnostic partagé en contexte inter-organisationnel: enseignements théoriques et pratiques. *Revue de Gestion des Ressources Humaines,* n°111, janvier-février-mars.

Noguera, F., Bories-Azeau, I., Fort, F., & Peyroux, C., (2015). Management des compétences territoriales et création de valeur. *Recherches en Sciences de Gestion-Management Sciences-Ciencias de Gestión,* 108, 25–44.

Pichault, F. (2002). La question de l'alignement stratégique dans le cadre des nouvelles formes organisationnelles. *Revue de Gestion des Ressources Humaines,* N° 46.

Saint-Germes, E., & Et Loufrani-Fedida, S. (2013). L'instrumentation de la GTEC au service de l'articulation entre compétences individuelles et employabilite: le cas de la plateforme eDRH06. *Congrès AGRH.* Paris, France.

Uzan O., Bonneveux, E., Bories-Azeau, I., Condomines, B., Delattre, M., Houessou, B., Hulin, A., Loubès, A., & Raulet-Croset, N. (2017). De la GRH instrumentale à la GRH partenariale: l'impact des stratégies territoriales, n°103, *Revue de GRH.*

Zardet, V., & Et Noguera, F. (2014). Quelle contribution du management au développement de la dynamique territoriale? Expérimentation d'outils de contractualisation sur trois territoires. *Revue Gestion et Management Public,* vol. 2, n°2.

CHAPTER 80

EXPLORATION OF CONVERGENCE AND NORMATIVE ARTICULATION IN THE FIELD OF PROFESSIONAL TRAINING

Arnaud Muret[1]

ABSTRACT

This chapter explores two possible and desirable avenues of evolution in the vocational training sector in France, through normative convergence and articulation of norms:

- The first is in a systemic plan apprehending a long time, which would make it possible to reconcile the life course of an employee.
- The second is in a more operational level based on an engineering recombination articulating "human capital" and economic capital.

The coherence of the life-course could be improved by converging the professions of skills operators (OPCO) and social protection groups (SPG) by imagining the creation of groups operating on the life-course (GLC).

Then it is a matter of designing a Region/OPCO experiment aimed at exploring the simultaneous unification of economic and "human capital".

This chapter explores two avenues of evolution in the vocational training sector, both through normative convergence and through the articulation of norms that evolve in spaces that do not, a priori, meet:

- The first is in a systemic plan apprehending a long time allowing to reconcile the life course of an employee.

SEAM Treatise, pages 657–663

- The second is at a more operational level, based on a recombination of engineering that articulates human and economic capital.

The first part proposes to renew the coherence of the life-course by converging the professions of skills operators (OPCO) and social protection groups (SPG) by imagining the creation of groups operating on the life-course (LG).

In the second part, it is a question of designing a Region/Opco experiment aimed at exploring the simultaneous unification of economic and "*human capital.*"

1 IMPROVING THE COHERENCE OF THE LIFE COURSE BY BRINGING TOGETHER THE OPCO AND SPG PROFESSIONS?

Parity management is mainly active in the social protection[2] and training sectors. Each of these sectors embodies a part of the social life of employees and individuals. Each of them is defined, constituted, and governed by a complex normative system that has sedimented over time. It therefore has hard layers. These systems may appear to be "mutually exclusive" and to create different worlds and actors who nevertheless intervene in the lives of individuals, and particularly employees. In the social protection sector, there are groups operating in the fields of health, dependency, savings, social action, and retirement, with joint governance. These are the Social Protection Groups.[3] In the field of professional training, they are skills operators (OPCO) whose governance is also based on equal representation.

Initially, the focus of the SPG was on supplementary pensions, then it became provident funds. With each reform, the financial volume of this focus has shifted towards life insurance, particularly in those sectors with a very large financial base. Today, in the SPG, the historical share of supplementary pensions only represents a "small" part of the total activity; nevertheless, it remains significant enough to be taken into consideration in the political decisions of the SPG. In the training sector, a shift in the barycentre of the origin of the activity's resources is also observed.

The funding bodies for vocational training were initially and mainly financed through training insurance fund mechanisms. Then, they were transformed into approved parity collecting bodies (OPCA) whose resources were supplemented by an equalization mechanism via a parity fund. With the 2018 law, these organizations became skills operators (OPCO) and their main resources[4] are allocated by a national public body, *France compétences*, managed in a quadripartite manner. The use and destination of these resources are strongly regulated by the public authorities.

Today, the joint governance of the SPG is at a crossroads, as is the case for the OPCOs. Indeed, if the governance of the SPG continues to develop in a purely insurance-based logic, and moreover by integrating risk management—for example, "Fire, Accidents and Miscellaneous Risks"[5]—this may raise questions about the legitimacy of their being players in the "general interest." Their roles could be strongly questioned, particularly by the market and by capitalist or mutualist companies that would also be able to fulfill them. Although the problems of the OPCOs are not quite the same, the question of the legitimacy of governance also arises in the long term. The growing share of resources allocated by the State to the OPCOs and the associated allocation rules mean that the degree of freedom in decisions and management given to the governance of the OPCOs is considerably reduced. This may raise questions about the value of such governance in the long term and about the fact that this activity could be integrated into *France Compétences*, a public operator.

At this crossroads, the governance of the SPG and the OPCOs, both of which are composed of social partners, could look for new areas of development by refocusing on their identities and by attempting to renew the coherence of the life course of employees and individuals. When we look back at the origins of the SPG and the professional training financing bodies, their genetic codes are notably those of the insurance mutualization logic and parity management. Why not bring them together? Indeed, there is a common normative genesis that has diverged about their missions. Why not start again from the genesis of these two worlds and make a normative convergence?

This approach would have the advantage of reinforcing the notion of "general interest" that parity management carries, its legitimacy and would position the structure more distinctly in relation to the actors (States, companies, mutual insurance companies, etc.) by bringing together parts of the social life of individuals in the same whole and thus also considering the individual.

In this way, both political and operational synergies would be numerous, and implementation would be relatively quick since it would mainly be a matter of engineering. In practice, this would consist of aggregating the OPCOs with the SPGs, creating Life Course Groups (LCG).

To do this, it would be necessary to change the ANI that created the SPG to broaden their scope of action so that the summit[6] associations of the SPG would include training concerns in their decisions. This would be the opportunity to create this new type of vehicle (GLC) resulting from the legal transformation of the SPG. This would be done in the same way as within the SPG, mutual insurance companies, provident institutions and private insurers exist and co-exist, there would be an OPCO with its own rules and governance.

Operational synergies would be strong. For example, links could be made between provident funds, savings, health, and training, by mobilizing training as a tool for prevention and dissemination of good practices. Also, an insurance product of the "training contingency" type could be designed, distributed to companies, and managed by the branches. Lastly, EIGs of IT resources could be extended, to provide companies and employees with extremely fine, penetrating and dense distribution networks throughout the country, as well as a rich, more complete, transparent, simple and readable service offer for everyone.

Such an approach, aimed at bringing together the OPCOs and the Social Protection Groups, would strengthen the role of the joint action as guarantor of the "general interest" of companies and their employees by taking care of retirement, provident, health, savings, and training. This approach would make it possible to bring together the hyper-fragmentation of the social life of an employee, of an individual, so that his or her life course (learning, producing, and benefiting) could find a renewed coherence by creating Groups operating on the Life Course.

In the previous part, a normative convergence was explored from a common genesis. In this second part, the articulations of norms evolving in spaces that a priori do not meet are investigated, having for the only common point a word, capital. Yet would it be possible to seek to unify economic capital and "human capital" simultaneously by responding to the needs expressed by companies and their employees, based mainly on the adequacy between human and financial engineering?

2 DESIGNING AN EXPERIMENT AIMED AT SIMULTANEOUSLY COMBINING ECONOMIC AND "HUMAN CAPITAL"

In a crisis, to avoid the economic collapse of the country and its social consequences, public authorities focus on injecting money into the economic circuit on the one hand to support and respond to the demand of companies and on the other hand in social protection systems that act as social shock absorbers.

The injection of money into the economic circuit by the public authorities aims to respond to demand, which is implemented by companies and associations. The public authorities, State, Region, Europe, etc. to support this response, will by various devices "economic aid" give or lend money to companies. However, these aids will be in relation to a need of investment of the company and the answer that the company brings to answer the demand. These investments are going to concern investments that can be mobilized and amortized. This aid consolidates the "economic capital of the company."

To date, there are many financing mechanisms based on banks, public or private funds that have been tested. However, this financial assistance to the needs expressed by the company will only provide a complete response when it is realized through the production of work. It seems that there is no company that can produce without human intervention. There is always at least one "man" who brings his skills and contributes to the production through his work.

Work is based on a skill, an acquired expertise, but this capital must constantly be adapted, developed, and transmitted. Today, there are Skills Operators (OPCO) whose function is to finance employee training so that employees acquire, consolidate, or develop skills. The need and choice of training for employees is based on the company's vision of the situation and its market. Based on this vision, the company encourages its employees to take this or that training. These training courses are, in turn, paid for by the skills operators if they are considered a priority by the branch in which the company operates, the level of funding being set by the branch. This system aims to support the financing of the company's "*human capital.*"

In the reorganization of the landscape of vocational training financing, the eleven OPCOs were created based on the grouping of professional branches, using criteria of coherence in terms of trades and skills, sectors, common challenges in terms of skills, training, mobility, local services, and the needs of companies. In this case, among these eleven OPCOs, there is the OPCO for local companies (OPCO EP), which groups together 54 branches, mainly craft trades excluding construction, private individuals, etc., representing 4 million employees and nearly 400,000 companies with fewer than 50 employees, including 384,000 with fewer than 11 employees, i.e., approximately 30% of companies with at least one employee in France.

The OPCO of local companies is built to finance apprenticeship, to help the branches to build professional certifications and to accompany SMEs to define their training needs. It provides a service, a response to a company sociology: where directors and human resources managers are almost non-existent. It is essentially the head of the company who wears and assumes all the hats within his company as director of operations, administration and finance and human resources. Although knowing the importance of human resources, the business manager is mainly focused on how to provide the service and make sure that there is money coming into the business. These business leaders must constantly realize the intersection of the "economic capital" and the "*human capital*" of their companies and they can rarely delegate these tasks.

Today, the financing of the company's "economic capital" and that of the "human capital" are done in distinct and parallel circuits. Circuits that only talk to each other marginally or very occasionally and have very different processing times for their files. In the health crisis that is having a strong impact and where one of the challenges is to overcome the economic crisis that it induces, it is important to question the opportunity to work on uniting the financing mechanisms of "economic capital" and "human capital" to contribute to the success of the economic and social recovery of the country.

The question is how, in this context of crisis, to facilitate the life of companies and allow them not to be torn by the tension induced by distinct financing circuits and timeframes, even though they have the same objective for the company manager.

The regional level seems to be the most relevant among the work areas that could lead to the unification of "economic capital" and "human capital" financing methods, with a view to ensuring proximity and considering territorial economic and labor issues. In this approach, the key player is naturally the "Regional Council."

Indeed, according to the law of March 2, 1982, then that of August 13, 2004, and finally January 27, 2014, economic development is the main field of intervention of the regions. Given the importance of this competence for the development of the local territory, the legislator has charged to coordinate the actions of the various local levels in a concern for consistency to avoid duplication and increase the effectiveness of local economic interventions. It has a coordinating and leading role in economic development. It has a tool at its disposal which is the territorial agreement of concerted exercise. This instrument has clarified the exercise of competences when they are shared between several levels of administration.

The Regional Council is also responsible for defining the system of aid to companies. These take the form of services, subsidies, interest subsidies, loans, and repayable advances, at zero interest or at more favorable conditions than the average bond rate. It also decides on the granting of these different categories of aid. Like other local authorities, the region can grant its guarantee or surety for a loan contracted by a private person, the risk borne by the authority being substantial since it will have to make up for any default by the company. The region has tools to act on the economic capital of companies.

In addition, since 1983, the region has been responsible for vocational training and apprenticeship, a responsibility that was confirmed by the law of August 13, 2004, on local freedoms and responsibilities, which made the region the lead agency, a role that is justified in view of the powers it has in the context of economic development. The purpose of the regional plan for the development of vocational training and guidance is to analyze the medium-term needs of the region in terms of employment, skills, and qualifications, as well as the programming of vocational training actions for young people and adults, considering the situation and the economic development objectives of the region. This document is drawn up by the region within the regional committee for employment, training, and vocational guidance based on guidance documents presented by the President of the Regional Council, the representative of the State in the region, the academic authorities, the employee trade unions and the professional employers' organizations.

Finally, the Regional Council is also an interlocutor of the European Union, for the implementation of European public policy. Indeed, the European Union relies on structural funds that allow the financing of development actions in the direction of less favored regions, and more particularly, actions to support economic development. The law of January 27, 2014 (MAPAM law) also strengthens the role of the regions in this area by providing for the management of certain European programs as a managing authority.

The Regional Council, strengthened by the competences given by the State in terms of territorial economic coordination, economic support, legitimacy to intervene in the field of vocational training and actor of European public policies, can play a key role in the unification of financing of economic capital and "human capital" of companies.

In this approach, an experiment would aim to reconcile the financing of the economic capital of the company and that of "human capital." It is based on the idea of coupling and, at the same time, the process of instruction of an economic aid file by a Regional Council or its instructing structure to that of a financing of training or a HR (human resources) service by an OPCO.

To do this, the proposal would be to associate, upstream of the instruction of economic aid files by a region, the possibility for the OPCO EP to intervene in financial and HR matters on the file.

There are several possible ways of doing this. Either,

1. it is considered that the scope of intervention of the OPCO is only on its branches and companies of the associated interprofessional, in this case the OPCO intervenes with its own means; or
2. the OPCO can intervene on a much wider field. In this approach, the Region, together with the State, could temporarily entrust a European Social Fund (ESF) or National Employment Fund (NEF) envelope to intervene on a wider scale based on its expertise, as part of its know-how in terms of investment in "human capital." In this case, the OPCO can also associate its own resources when the requesting companies are within its field of competence.

Operationally, as soon as a company applies for economic support to the Regional Council or its representative, the OPCO services are informed. The company's HR needs are then simultaneously examined whether they are expressed.

1. If the company has expressed a need for training, skills to carry out the implementation that the economic assistance would bring, then the OPCO responds to this request.
2. If the company has not expressed a need, the services of the Opco would accompany the company on a HR diagnosis and according to what emerges, the OPCO would offer HR and financial support.

This experimentation would ultimately be based on engineering work between normative systems with numerous rules. This would make it possible to cohabit and synchronize them for work on the different dimensions that make up the company.

CONCLUSION

In this chapter, two axes have been examined. In the first, a normative convergence has been explored from a common genesis, based on the individual, the employee, and his/her needs throughout his life. In the second, we looked at the articulation of norms evolving in spaces that are *a priori* different, based mainly on the adequacy between human and financial engineering, while seeking to reconcile the needs of companies and the individuals that make them up.

NOTES

1. Muret, A. (2003). *La qualité en recherche : la construction d'une norme française.* Thèse de doctorat en socio-économie de l'innovatIon. École Nationale de Mines de Paris.
2. Social protection covers: Health protection, the pension system, family policy, disability and dependency, savings, social protection for job seekers.
3. The joint committee of social protection groups are managed by a summit association, a concept created in an agreement on the governance of joint social protection groups on July 8,

2009, whose Board of Directors includes equal representation of employers and employees. The Board of Directors of the *Association sommitale* defines the political and strategic orientations of the group. The Summit Association is a decision-making body, not a management body. The groups therefore have a single management structure, pooling management resources to serve companies, employees, and retirees. The group includes at least one AGIRC pension institution, one ARRCO pension institution and one provident institution. But it may also include a mutual insurance company or an insurance company. Whatever the structure belonging to the group, it must be involved in compulsory supplementary retirement or collective or individual supplementary social protection. The groups manage not only the AGIRC-ARRCO supplementary pension, but also offer coverage against life risks such as work disability, supplementary health, retirement savings, death, and dependency coverage. They are aimed at companies for their employees within the framework of a group contract or at individuals within the framework of an individual contract.

4. These resources are supplemented, depending on the branch that joins the OPCO, by contractual resources and occasionally by voluntary payments from companies.
5. It is therefore a different family of insurance from that of personal insurance or life insurance. Indeed, P&C insurances cover damages and the protection of goods, while the life insurance protects people, it can be health, accident, death, or life insurances.
6. The concept of the "*summit association*" was created in an agreement on the governance of joint committee of social protection groups on July 8, 2009. The Board of Directors is composed of equal numbers of employer and employee representatives. The Board of Directors of the *Summit Association* defines the political and strategic orientations of the group. The Board is a decision-making body, not a management body.

This page intentionally left blank.

PART VIII

SOCIO-ECONOMIC MANAGEMENT CONTROL

This page intentionally left blank.

CHAPTER 81

OVERCOMING THE POVERTY OF CONVENTIONAL MANAGEMENT CONTROL PHILOSOPHY THROUGH SEAM

R. Murray Lindsay and Henri Savall

ABSTRACT

Management control in the Anglo-Saxon world has largely followed a cybernetic philosophy since the turn of the 20th century, with Robert Anthony's (1965) conceptual framework having had a profound influence. The dominance of this philosophy has made it difficult to conceive of control in an alternative way, hampering a wider audience from appreciating what SEAM has to offer. However, Anthony's (1988) comments regarding his framework's shortcomings, which have been largely overlooked, provide exceptional clarity in signposting the key issues underlying what Hofstede (1978) refers to as "the poverty of management control philosophy." They also serve as a lens for viewing SEAM in a new and compelling light.

Since the turn of the 20th century, management control (MC) in the Anglo-Saxon world has largely followed a cybernetic philosophy (Giglioni and Bedeian, 1974; Hofstede, 1978). The dominance of this philosophy has made it difficult to conceive of control in an alternative way. This hampers a wider audience from appreciating what a postmodern theory like SEAM has to offer because the fundamental discrepancies in assumptions regarding individuals, organizations and the very nature of control make the two philosophies, in a Kuhnian sense, "incommensurable."

Robert Anthony's (1965) conventionally based framework has had a profound influence on the accounting profession through its adoption in teaching circles as the "bible" on MC.

SEAM Treatise, pages 667–674

However, what has been largely overlooked are Anthony's (1988) comments regarding its shortcomings. They provide exceptional clarity in signposting the key issues underlying what Hofstede (1978) refers to as "the poverty of management control philosophy." They also help to overcome the above impasse by serving as a lens for viewing SEAM's contributions in a new and compelling light.

1 ANTHONY'S FRAMEWORK

Anthony (1988) defined MC as "the process by which managers influence other members of the organization to implement the organization's strategies" (p. 10). However, this process was viewed narrowly. Specifically, MC is divorced from the processes of strategic control (involving strategy formulation and revision) and task control. Instead, its focus is on reporting financial information involved with planning and execution centered on responsibility centers and their managers. Further, except for considerations of rewards and motivation, MC excludes personnel activities associated with management.

Anthony's cybernetics model is often taught through the analogy of controlling a building's temperature to a predetermined standard with the use of a thermostat. It begins with a planning process serving to coordinate units and establish performance standards. Actual performance is then compared with the budget/standard. This comparison influences behavior through two key principles. The first is "management by exception," whereby management attention is focused only on significant performance deviations from standard. The second involves the evaluation (and motivation) of managers through "responsibility accounting." These principles continue to be reflected in every introductory managerial accounting textbook today.

However, controlling an organization is vastly more complicated than controlling a building's temperature. In particular, the relative importance of personal needs (goals) driving behavior varies across individuals and changes over time. Moreover, participants act in a self-interested manner in pursuing their personal goals and these may not always be consistent with the organization's goals. This potential conflict led to framing a management control system's central purpose around encouraging goal congruence. As Anthony explains: "The system should be designed so that actions that it leads people to take in accordance with their perceived self-interest are actions that are also in the best interests of the organization" (p. 70).

2 ASSESSMENT

Anthony (1988) acknowledges the relevance of general systems theory (GST) for the study of MC. GST describes a system in terms of the energy flows occurring as a result of the interactions among the various elements within a system's internal and external environments. SEAM's elaboration of the nature of these interactions is useful for understanding GST and not inconsistent with Anthony's brief description (pp. 25–26). As portrayed in Figure 81.1, SEAM conceptualizes the internal environment as involving interactions between structures and behaviors occurring at the individual, group, department and organizational levels. Work structures include physical (e.g., working conditions), technological (e.g., level of automation), organizational (e.g., strategies, division of labor, organizational structure and decision rights, personnel systems, rules, policies, and performance measurement systems), demographic (e.g., age, training, education, knowledge, personality traits)

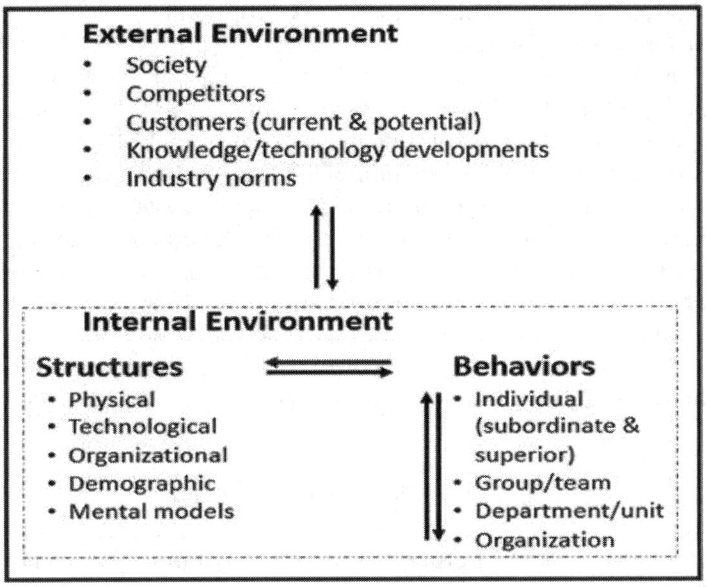

Figure 81.1 Energy flows reccurring within the overall system.

and mental structures (e.g., management style and attitude toward control, decision logics in use, professional ideologies, culture).

GST attempts to "optimize" the overall system rather than its component parts. However, a prerequisite is the ability to understand the dynamics of behavior (which underlies performance). As Figure 81.1 reveals, this is difficult because organizations are complex systems involving many different types of interactions. Moreover, standards of performance may not be known, and they derive from people, making them both involved in setting the standard and the means for attaining it (Hofstedt, 1978). Also, the use of simple cause and effect logic is problematic because in a complex system behavior has a context. Consequently, GST focuses on understanding interactions within the overall system instead of studying the parts in isolation. It is the nature of these interactions and people's needs that impact (energize) behaviors; consequently, they need to be understood.

Anthony (1988) recognizes that the cybernetic model, as described above, does not reflect these complexities. For example, in addition to recognizing Hofstede's (1978) significant criticisms of applying a cybernetic model to organizations (p. 58), he appreciates that the process of control is influenced by people's personal needs (p. 69), informal information (p. 36), the nature of the informal interactions among participants (p. 67), participants' cognitive filtering of information based on their mental models in use (p. 55), and the structure of the internal environment in which the control system is embedded (pp. 25–26). He also recognizes that behavior is motivated less by the formal control system and hierarchical directives than by the structure-behavior interactions occurring within the system (pp. 25–26, 37). A further weakness is that the actual meaning placed on the term "system" is very narrow, referring only to the planning, coordinating and control functions (p. 27). In particular, "coordination" is used only in the sense of enabling responsibility centers to follow the same set of operating assumptions.

Notwithstanding, Anthony writes that "probably the most serious weakness" of the model—one that impedes the achievement of its central purpose—is the lack of knowledge about how best to measure the degree to which actual performance was congruent with the organization's goals (p. 74). This arises as a result of treating the process of control as a "black box" because the dynamics of behavior cannot be observed (p. 37). Anthony therefore cautions that the financial focus of MCS "tells only part of the story" and can be "dangerously misleading" (pp. 21–22, 57). He thus recommends that superiors need to incorporate judgement when evaluating subordinate performance at higher management levels.

Despite these concerns, the determination of how best to motivate (rather than measure) goal congruence continues to dominate thinking about management control. This has led to focusing the research agenda on issues such as the appropriate performance measure(s) to use, how to set targets (imposed or participatively) and at what level of difficulty, and whether and when subjectivity should be introduced in performance evaluations. Increasingly, the dominance of agency theory, with its pessimistic assumptions regarding human behavior, has led to framing motivation largely in terms of providing financial incentives for meeting carefully chosen, objective performance targets (Ghoshal, 2005).

3 SEAM

SEAM overcomes these concerns in three key ways by combining social and economic considerations into a single framework (as represented in the first two words underlying the SEAM acronym). First, SEAM places fundamental importance to human potential (and its development and use) because people are the only *active* factor driving productivity, quality and innovation. Human potential reflects the innate capacity and desire for employees to create value (i.e., reflecting productive energy). It is comprised of individual and collective energy to act, competencies, and behavior (i.e., the way people interact with others and their work). Energy represents the capacity or tendency for intense activity. It consists of both a stock and a flow. As one exerts effort, the stock of energy needs to be replenished through stimulating communication and information. On the other hand, if a stock is not used, a reduction in motivation occurs, which underscores the emphasis SEAM places on empowering employees.

SEAM recognizes that employees are not always obedient or submissive. They possess informal powers where they can give or withhold their *energy* depending upon the nature of their interactions within the organization, as Anthony recognized. Consequently, for goal congruence to occur, people must no longer be viewed as another (inanimate) resource at the company's disposal, where the correct behavior can be bought or controlled into fitting the needs of the organization (i.e., McGregor's [1960] Theory X). Instead, SEAM teaches that management's essential task is to develop, use and unleash human potential in an organizationally cohesive manner by creating the appropriate *conditions* (i.e., internal environment) where employees perceive their personal goals are best achieved through efforts aimed at achieving organizational goals (i.e., McGregor's Theory Y).[1] This orientation underpins SEAM's focus on the quality and intensity of "management steering" for promoting human potential as the key requirement in realizing an organization's strategic ambition.[2]

Second, analogous to physical systems which follow the 2nd law of thermodynamics, SEAM's concept of management steering reflects the natural tendency for organizations to drift into dysfunction or incoherence (cp. Kaplan, 2006). Entropy results in energy losing its capacity to perform productive (value-added) work even though inputs remain the same. Within organizations, entropy manifests itself in such ways as when the wrong strategies are pursued (i.e., failing to adapt), organizational priorities and/or employees' roles in achieving them are unclear, activities are done badly, excessive bureaucracy and hierarchy exists, conflict occurs among organizational units and/or employees, and when employees lack motivation to perform to their full potential. Moreover, since energy cannot be created or destroyed in a closed system, but only transformed from useful to non-useful forms (the 1st law of thermodynamics), new sources of energy must be continually introduced into the system to permit the organization to survive and adapt.

SEAM's starting point is that entropy is natural once a state of equilibrium is reached due to ongoing structure-behavior interactions. These interactions are not only a driving force, essential to the value-added production, but also the cause of conflicts and disorder that produce dysfunctions resulting in a reduction of productive energy. They lead to "hidden costs" impairing both current and future performance that go unreported by conventional accounting systems, analogous to Miller and Vollman's (1985) "hidden factory" in the field of operations. The importance of unearthing dysfunctions is crucially important. As Argyris (1990) ruminates, if a manager believes it necessary to take action to prevent subordinates from shirking their responsibilities, why not explore what causes them to act in counter-productive ways instead? Otherwise, Argyris writes, the control system will simply perpetuate defensive routines that bypass and cover-up the fundamental problems. Organizational learning occurs only if the causes of dysfunctions are sought through engagement with the underlying problem.

Through studying the nature of dysfunctions as part of their interventions in organizations, ISEOR's research team has developed a typology of organizational dysfunctions. They are identified in a biannual process involving the collection of data and information through a unique approach (called the HORIVERT method) and methodology for measuring hidden costs (called Qualimetrics). To reflect the complexity of understanding organizational reality, this information is then submitted to another unique process (called the "mirror-effect") that permits reality to be socially constructed. This process leads to a shared and more "objective" view of the dysfunctions at work and assists in obtaining employee buy-in. Finally, a process has been created for prioritizing and eradicating dysfunctions through projects that are implemented using SEAM's management tools.

The upshot is that SEAM implements GST in the manner that Anthony ideally espouses. Specifically, Anthony (pp. 7, 26) writes that MC requires information about the flow of energy (as manifested in behavior) that explains the behavior occurring within the system. However, Anthony does not follow this prescription because he considers the dynamics of behavior to be a black box, incapable of being observed, let alone measured. In contrast, by providing a method for identifying and measuring dysfunctions as a regular organizational rhythm, SEAM identifies the non-productive energy flows and, in so doing, stimulates positive energy for their eradication. This is a major differentiator from conventional thinking based on seeking static equilibrium through implementing "best" practices. The fact that entropy is inevitable necessitates thinking in terms of dynamic equilibria. Specifically, each organization must periodically advance to a new (temporary) equilibrium and SEAM provides general tools and methods for this purpose.

The approach to performance measurement is the third way SEAM overcomes the limitations of Anthony's model. Anthony states that performance should be judged using two criteria: efficiency and effectiveness. He uses the analogy of an engine for the former, whereby the most efficient engine is the one producing the most energy per unit of fuel consumed. However, in practice, efficiency is often considered, at best, only in terms of how well a responsibility center controls costs relative to a standard, which fails to capture the output side. At worst, in uncertain environments, efficiency is ignored because the relationship between inputs and outputs cannot be established, resulting in results control only. SEAM overcomes these difficulties by measuring efficiency through the indicator, HCVAVC, which represents employees' actual average hourly value-added contribution. HCVAVC is measured as follows:

$$\text{HCVAVC} = \frac{\text{Sales} - \text{variable costs (= output of productive energy)}}{\text{Total number of paid hours during the year (= the key energy input)}}$$

The reporting of HCVAVC serves two important functions. First, in highlighting that employees are at the centre of value creation, it conveys the importance of developing and utilizing human potential. Second, HCVAVC motivates (stimulates) management in two important ways to continue with the process of identifying and eradicating dysfunctions in a virtuous cycle, much like reporting the "cost of quality" did in the early days of the quality movement. One way this occurs is through the calculation of the increase in value-added that is theoretically possible if all identified hidden costs were converted into value-added activity. (This value is obtained by multiplying HCVAVC by the number of labor hours estimated to be wasted, as determined in the diagnosis phase.) The other is through measuring the change in HCVAVC (i.e., productive energy) across periods. The amount of change reflects progress in transferring latent (unproductive) energy into productive (value-added) energy through the elimination of dysfunctions.

Turning to effectiveness, Anthony (1988, p. 35) assesses effectiveness in terms of the relationship between the outputs of a responsibility center and the strategic objectives of the organization as operationalized through the critical success factors underlying strategy implementation. As a financial measure, HCVAVC is incapable of fully reflecting strategic performance. Consequently, SEAM uses three management tools to overcome this limitation. Specifically, it establishes the organization's strategic priorities through the "priority action plan" (which are then linked to departmental objectives) and employees/teams are tasked with their accomplishment through each employee's "periodically negotiated activity contract." The "strategic indicators logbook" is then used to capture performance relative to these priorities and commitments.

4 CONCLUDING COMMENTS

The poverty of conventional management control stems, in the first instance, from the adoption of a cybernetic underpinning that does not reflect the complexity of organizations and the humans within them. Goals are a given and there is a natural inclination to view people merely as "things"—a means for their attainment, like any other resource—rather than more properly as both the goal and the means. This results in a simplistic and shallow view of the social-psychological processes governing human behavior and thus organizational performance (Hofstede, 1978). Given this view (along with the related assumption of *homo economicus*), it was only a small step to focus MC around the idea of *motivating* goal congruence—rather than viewing control systems in terms of attempting to achieve goal congruence. This occurred because of the framework's second major weakness: the inability to measure its central concept—the degree of goal congruence—because it was assumed to be a black box. And unless one was prepared to abandon any notion of control, the inevitable consequence was "command and control"—focused around rules, directives, rewards and punishments—that results in second order conditions whereby the presumed untrustworthiness of employees becomes self-fulfilling through the defensive reasoning it motivates (Argyris, 1990; Ferraro et al., 2005).

In contrast, SEAM adopts a living systems perspective and places fundamental emphasis on the concept of human potential and its utilization. As a result of the natural tendency for living systems (organizations) to drift into dysfunction or incoherence, SEAM is based on the view that peace and consensus must be socially (re)constructed through "management steering" for the purpose of (re)creating the conditions to foster harmony between individual and organizational goals. Further, SEAM incorporates a unique process for rigorously measuring its central concept—the utilization of human potential—that serves to identify impediments as well as to motivate its continual improvement. It does this in two ways. One is through the process of identifying dysfunctions and measuring their associated hidden costs as a proxy for the level of latent (non-productive) energy associated with entropy. The other is by measuring progress in converting latent energy into value-added activity by measuring changes in HCVAVC from period to period.

By abandoning a cybernetic framework for a more realistic view of the functioning of organizations along with the ability to measure progress involving the utilization of human potential, SEAM offers a much-needed redress to the poverty of management control thinking in a manner that overcomes many of Anthony's criticisms of his own model.

NOTES

1. Anthony (pp. 70–71) appreciates this point when he quotes, approvingly, the following passage by McGregor (1960): "the essential task of management is to arrange organizational conditions and methods of operations so that people can achieve their own goals best by directing their own efforts towards organizational objectives."
2. SEAM's concept of "management steering" ("pilotage") can be broken down into three levers: (i) producing stimulating information; (ii) synchronizing activities; and (iii) the need to periodically "clean-up" structures and behaviors causing dysfunctions because of the phenomenon of organizational entropy (discussed shortly). The activation of these levers is facilitated by six tools and a specific method for detecting and eradicating dysfunctions that inhibit human potential (see Savall, 2003, 1974, 1979; Savall & Zardet, 1987, 2008).

REFERENCES

Anthony, R. N. (1965). *Planning and control systems: A framework for Analysis.* Harvard Business School Publications.

Anthony, R. N. (1988). *The management control function.* The Harvard Business School Press.

Argyris, C. (1990). The dilemma of implementing controls: The case of managerial accounting. *Accounting, Organizations and Society, 15*(6), 503–511.

Ferraro, F., Pfeffer, J., & Sutton, R. I. (2005). Economics language and assumptions: How theories can become self-fulfilling. *Academy of Management Review, 30*(1), 8–24.

Giglioni, G. B., & Bedeian, A. G. (1974). A conspectus of management control theory: 1900–1972. *The Academy of Management Journal, 17*(2), 292–305.

Ghoshal, S. (2005). Bad management theories are destroying good management practices. *Academy of Management Learning and Education, 4*(1), 75–91.

Hofstede, G. (1978). The poverty of management control philosophy. *The Academy of Management Review, 3*(3), 450–461.

Kaplan, R. S. (2006). The competitive advantage of management accounting. *Journal of Management Accounting Research,* 127–135.

McGregor. D. (1960). *The human side of enterprise.* McGraw-Hill.

Miller, J. G., & Vollman, T. E. (1985). The hidden factory. *Harvard Business Review* (September–October), 142–150.

Savall, H., (2003). An updated presentation of the socio-economic management model. *Journal of Organizational Change Management, 16*(1), 33–48.

Savall, H., & Zardet, V. 2008. *Mastering hidden costs and socio-economic performances.* Information Age Publishing. (Initially published in French in 1987)

CHAPTER 82

MANAGEMENT CONTROL AS A PARADOXICAL SPECIALITY

Yves Dupuy, Gérald Naro, and Denis Travaillé

ABSTRACT

The contribution questions the edge of management specializations, and more particularly that of management control. The latter is in fact the result of a paradoxical convergence between multiple technical imperatives and a global organizational vision. This paradox could be extended to the whole of management and, consequently, invite a decompartmentalized conception of research, teaching, and practices in this field.

The question of the specialization of managerial actors touches on the foundations, structures and exercise of socio-organizational power. In a related way, it questions the very conception of the research and training sectors concerned. Yet this specialization is often presented as an obvious necessity because it is considered inseparable from competence. At worst, the compartmentalization, lack of coordination, and territorial conflicts to which it could lead can be reduced by an atypical specialist: "the" management controller. Supposedly capable of controlling "everything", and consequently of becoming a specialist in everything, the said controller would even evoke, at the very least, the strange figure of a sort of "a-specialist."

To give substance to this hypothesis, and its possible consequences, we propose to examine a few trajectories of reflection and training of teachers or practitioners who are "management control specialists." The history and observation of practices, training and research generally describe their *a priori* well-defined activity: that linked to the implementation of formalisms and calculations that are supposed to translate the sole economic-financial

SEAM Treatise, pages 675–681

rationality of organizations and allow them to master it. Implicitly, the "specialist" in management control is thus linked to the accounting and financial field.

However, the fundamental intention of control, as stated above, is much broader, as it also aims to ensure the structural coherence and human cohesion of the organizations being controlled. It therefore seems to call for extended questioning of the sharing and the very meaning of the totality of the representations, formal and informal, of the complexity of these organizations of their information system. In this way, and beyond, it calls into question organizational intelligence, and thus the essential springs of human resource management.

Three scientific currents are thus called upon, which must be brought into convergence and harmony within the framework of management control, its scientific definition, its teaching, and its implementation in the field of organizations. Academic works and approaches, as well as multiple practices, testify to the possibility and contributions of such a perspective and to the ways in which it can be achieved. A few significant cases will be mentioned here.

1 THE DESIGN OF A TRAINING COURSE AS A CONVERGENCE OF THREE "NON-SPECIALIZED" TRAJECTORIES

This principle of convergence is illustrated first by the design and then the adaptation of a master's degree organized around management control technologies. The success and durability of this training program have gone hand in hand with a constantly renewed scientific and pedagogical reflection, based on the above-mentioned axes: formal economic rationality, the adaptation of information systems, and an in-depth understanding of human resources.

1.1 From Rational Production Management to Control Through Hidden Costs

Costing was created for factories and by engineers. The "analytical management accounting" was then called "industrial accounting" (Rimailho, 1936). It was based on the figure of calculable costs, as an explicit and complete translation of the degree of rationality of organizational production processes: periodic product, service, and function costs. At the same time, operational research was mobilized, with tools such as average cost calculation, linear programming, or the PERT graph. The objective of linear programming was to calculate the productive combination that minimized a cost function. PERT was to define the solution that would minimize the time required to complete a project. In all these cases, the implicit assumption was that these costs or delays could be reduced—and therefore controlled—by formalized production or project management programs.

This was without considering the evolution of organizations and their environment, and therefore with costs increasingly linked to variations in indirect costs, and therefore, implicitly, to hidden costs. Therefore rational production management has had to evolve towards logistics, as a broader and more qualitative approach. From the point of view of management control, this resulted in the need for a socio-economic approach (Savall, 1974–1975, 1979; Savall and Zardet, 1987), to better couple the social dimension and the economic performance of the organization. The aim is to go beyond control by visible costs to flush out hidden costs, ignored by financial accounting, diluted in the totality of expenses or absent from product accounts, and consequently "invisible" to managers, particularly those responsible for production. Identifying and analyzing dysfunctions then allows for the implementation of improvement plans, thus reducing these hidden costs.

Management controllers must therefore both know and master the economic and numerical representations of the organization (Dupuy and Travaillé, 2013) and know how to place them in a critical perspective. This is all the truer since IT resources are pushing for a proliferation of data, without ensuring that their meaning is improved. This raises questions about information systems and their role in management control.

1.2 From Computerized Data Management to Control Through the Meaning of Representations

The figure of automatically controlled management, and thus controlled, has challenged and questioned control and management controllers since the early days of organizational information systems and operational research. The latter would make decision-making processes "structurable," even "programmable." Automated data processing systems would thus allow the "algorithmic" production of organizational choices, and correlatively their evaluation and control. Initially limited to a few repetitive operational processes, notably production management, as mentioned above, this "algorithmic" management will soon claim to extend to the entire organization. We are then talking about "integrated management systems," "expert systems," or even "inter-organizational" systems. Such systems tend to make management control unnecessary, except perhaps on a very overall financial level.

But the underlying assumptions of such management "models" are hardly resistant to the complexity and instability of organizational processes. The failures and limitations of management algorithms have multiplied. They give back to the management controller the status and power of a major player in the design of the organization's information system, and not only of its accounting and financial system. Nevertheless, the hypothesis of the complete digitization and automation of management and control has recently come back into force. Algorithms and expert systems are now being introduced under the mysterious oxymoron of "artificial intelligence." And above all, at the same time, organizations are taking control of their data. They are increasingly outsourcing the storage and compilation of their data to cloud service providers. From there, "deep-learning" is developing, presented as a soon-to-be unavoidable substitute for the learning of the organization's members, and therefore for their own intelligence and control.

In the end, the management controller would see himself dispossessed of the very heart of his mission to create cohesion, in that artificial intelligence would supplant anyone in the overall intelligence of the organization. Because it is also in the sociological spirit of time, this type of hypothesis fundamentally questions human resources management.

1.3 From HRM to Control Through Organizational Intelligence

For a long time, human resources, like financial or technical resources, had to be subject to management control to ensure their efficiency and effectiveness. As the denominator of a productivity/expense ratio in the income statement, human resources as a resource had to be managed with economy. Attempts to "activate" this resource, in terms of investment, and according to human resource accounting were proposed during the 1970s. They failed to overcome the problems of valuation and came up against fundamental accounting principles. In particular, the development of international accounting standards under IFRS and the overtaking of legal form by economic substance have accentuated the relegation of human resources to the status of expenses. However, the development of thinking on intangibles, by bringing back into fashion the notion of "human capital," a concept developed by neo-liberal economists (Becker, 1964), is pushing management control to consider this complex object differently.

If financial accounting is struggling to integrate "human capital" not as a cost, but as a value-creating investment, it is in management control that the most fruitful questions and advances are being raised. As early as the 1980s, the importance of actors in the value creation process was highlighted in what was considered to be the revival of management control, which was then accused of having lost its relevance. It was a question of moving from remote, centralizing and hierarchical management control, aimed at controlling from "above" the organization's responsibility centers and their responsible managers, to transversal and participatory management control, aimed at steering processes from the political and cognitive autonomy of the actors (Lorino, 1995): "from top–down control to bottom–up empowerment," was the title of a famous book published in the United States by one of the representatives of the "relevance lost" movement (Johnson, 1994).

Henri Savall and the ISEOR, by taking an early interest in the hidden costs and socio-economic dimension of performance, have long made it clear that performance control in organizations depends on the involvement and cooperation of the players. They then set out to develop a complete management system in which management control and HRM are no longer considered as two specialized managerial functions but must instead coordinate closely in the management of the cost-value relationship (Savall and Zardet, 2008), even if it means that they will disappear as disciplinary specializations in favor of an overall socio-economic approach. Long before the idea of interactive control was developed (Simons, 1995), ISEOR highlighted the importance of social interaction at the heart of organizations. One of the most stimulating elements of this approach is ultimately the idea of management control as organizational intelligence. Intersubjective cooperation, mutual adjustment, and the co-production of problem solving in action are major elements. They have a particular resonance at a time when organizations must manage the uncertainty and complexity generated by the health crisis.

Reflecting these principles, a convergence and cooperation of research and diversified disciplinary axes have made it possible to overcome, in the above-mentioned training, the tensions between technical and financial specialization and a global and generalist approach. The recruitment of students and, beyond that, the control processes that can be observed, confirm the relevance of such an approach.

2 THREE TYPICAL MANAGEMENT CONTROL PRACTICES ILLUSTRATING THE CONCEPT OF "A-SPECIALIZATION"

Current management control practices largely illustrate the principles of convergence and consistency mentioned above. Sharing, co-construction and debate are the key points, illustrated below by three representative examples.

2.1 The Accounting Foundations and the Accountants in Question

Within universities, training accountants are very often assigned ambitious control functions. For these "traditional" accountants, steeped in an administrative and normative culture, this means questioning their knowledge and practices, particularly in the areas of budgeting and cost evaluation, as if these categories were no longer self-evident.

For example, establishing an intelligible link between the budget and the resources actually available requires an often-counterintuitive effort to hybridize representations and their uses. This is typically the case for calculated expenses. Here, apparently simple, albeit fussy, administrative rules constantly collide with research programs or training courses and the thinking of their managers. What does it mean to "amortize over one year"? Why this or that total amortization period? How can one make people understand and accept such an immediate amputation of possible "expenses," that is, of the only *a priori* intelligible accounting category? The accountant who thinks he is summoning up the obvious here is bound to fail. Experience shows that, on the contrary, he must work closely and continuously with the managers concerned, even if they are themselves "specialists" in . . . management.

Similarly, the category of "costs" gives rise to many misunderstandings. What is the cost (cost of what, in other words)? Evaluated according to what spatial and temporal perimeter? For what reason? How do you respond, for example, to a training manager who is convinced that one "more" student costs "nothing"? How can we legitimize the comparison between the calculated cost of one course and another? Once again, the creation of meaning obviously depends on the sharing of data, the discussion of their elaboration and the co-construction of their interpretation. It is as if, in short, the accountant-controller had to "despecialize," while the non-accountant-controller had to make part of the way towards the accounting specialty. This is indeed a process of hybridization. Such a process seems to be at work, in similar forms, in many other organizations.

2.2 The Information System as a Support for Cooperative Control

Management control can therefore be understood as a mediator within the organization. By creating shared representations of performance and strategy, it becomes a producer of meaning and cooperation between the players. This is particularly important in a professional bureaucracy (Mintzberg, 1982), where an administrative and a professional sphere struggle to share common objectives. Between the representatives of management and the administrative hierarchy, who are the guarantors of economic and budgetary objectives, and the professionals, who are the guarantors of the norms of their profession, management control is faced with paradoxical problems. As Cyert and March (1963) wrote, organizations are made up of individuals with disparate goals, and this is perhaps where the art of management control lies, in that it makes it possible to articulate interests and representations based on differentiated logics.

A typical example is that of a university hospital where a manager from the Medical Information Department (DIM), in close collaboration with the management control department, facilitates exchanges between representatives of the administrative hierarchy and representatives of health professionals, in particular the doctors in charge of the units. The highly visual operating room dashboards are used to confront different points of view and interests with a view to cooperation in making strategic decisions for the hospital. The dashboards combine the properties of interpretative flexibility and the actors' confidence in the validity of the information they contain. They thus play the role of frontier objects (Star and Griesemer, 1989), allowing different worlds to dialogue and cooperate, for the benefit of collective intelligence. This process is very similar to the one observed at the University and to those developed by other organizations subject to sometimes different imperatives.

2.3 Management Control as a Vector of Organizational Intelligence

At the *Commissariat à l'Énergie Nucléaire et aux* **Énergies** *Alternatives* (CEA) in Marcoule, management controllers develop management methods that are typically based on organizational intelligence. In a professional world of researchers and engineers, with little interest in economic performance, they are responsible for implementing a management control system imposed both by the constraints of public management, in particular the implementation of the framework of the *Loi Organique relative aux Lois de Finance,* and by the injunctions of an increasingly competitive environment. Management control is therefore intended to produce meaning by creating, through interactivity, representations that can be shared by the group. It serves as a common thread in project meetings, during which site management, laboratory directors, engineers and functional managers interact around performance indicators and dashboards. This process, which is largely facilitated by business intelligence tools, gives rise to new ideas, responses to threats or opportunities, and emerging strategies. Management control plays a driving role here in that it stimulates and energizes organizational intelligence in the service of strategic thinking.

Thus, in the three cases mentioned, the accountant, the specialized professional, the researcher, the engineer, and other managers find themselves in search of a harmonious management system because it is as decompartmentalized as possible.

CONCLUSION: FOR A DECOMPARTMENTILIZATION OF TRAINING, RESEARCH AND PRACTICES

These few examples of approaches and practices illustrate the culmination of perspectives and concepts that have been traced for a long time within ISEOR. In auditing, as in other areas of management, it is a matter of decompartmentalizing, and therefore of "de-specializing"—of "a-specializing"—research, training, and practices. This requires, fundamentally, that we overcome the very prevalent confusion between specialization, professionalization, and competence.

Thus, it is ultimately the very concept of management as a scientific and pedagogical discipline that is called into question. To what quality of training can the extreme differentiation of so-called "professional" courses lead, if not to displays that mimic the definition of the most common commercial products? What can be said, in parallel, about the contribution of research that is so specialized that it almost never leaves a strictly compartmentalized academic cenacle? These fundamental socio-economic questions remain largely open.

REFERENCES

Bollecker, M., & Naro, G. (2014). *Le contrôle de gestion aujourd'hui: Débats, controverses et perspectives,* Vuibert.

Becker, G. S. (1964). *Human Capital, A Theoretical and Empirical Analysis.* Columbia University Press for the National Bureau of Economic Research.

Cyert, R., & March, J. G. (1963). *A Behavioral Theory of the Firm.* Prentice-Hall.

Dupuy, Y., & Travaillé, D. (2013). *Les bases de la comptabilité analytique de gestion,* 3ème édition, Economica.

Johnson, H. T. (1992). *Relevance regained. From Top-down control, to bottom-up empowerment.* The Free Press.

Lorino, P. (1990). *Comptes et récits de la performance,* Les éditions d'organisation, 1995.

Mintzberg, H. (1982). *Structure et dynamiques des organisations,* Editions d'Organisation, Paris.

Rimailho, E. (1936). *Organisation à la française.* Paris, Delmas, volume 3, 1936.

Simons, R. L. (1995). *Levers of control: how managers use innovative control systems to drive strategic renewal.* Harvard Business School Press.

Star, S. L., & Griesemer, J. R. (1989). Institutional ecology, "translations" and boundary objects: Amateurs and professionals in Berkeley's Museum of Vertebrate Zoology, 1907–1939. *Social Studies of Science*, 19, 387–420.

CHAPTER 83

THE SOCIO-ECONOMIC APPROACH TO MANAGEMENT AS A CONCEPTUAL FRAMEWORK FOR STRATEGIC COST MANAGEMENT

Miguel Juan Bacic

ABSTRACT

Strategic cost management (SCM) uses a set of tools to increase the value of products and reduce costs with the objective of improving the competitiveness of companies. However, it lacks a broader conceptual framework that discusses and understands organizational complexity and the interaction of human and technical structures that lead to dysfunctions and hidden costs. Socioeconomic management offers such a conceptual framework, which allows for a better interpretation of organizational reality and better results when applying SCM tools.

The question for many companies is how to maintain and/or increase their competitiveness in today's uncertain and turbulent times. To obtain good results and maintain a sustainable position in the market, the company must be permanently able to generate value for customers and obtain a revenue stream (as a function of the value generated) that is greater than the cost of producing that value.

Value is the degree of utility that the good or service has for customers. Utility arises from a set of factors that generate benefits for buyers; these may be elements that increase their performance or contribute to cost reduction. This utility-value must be validated by the market when it is transformed into exchange value.

It is the task of strategy to manage the value-generating elements, since, in principle, the greater the perceived value, the higher the price that can be charged (if the differentiating

SEAM Treatise, pages 683–689

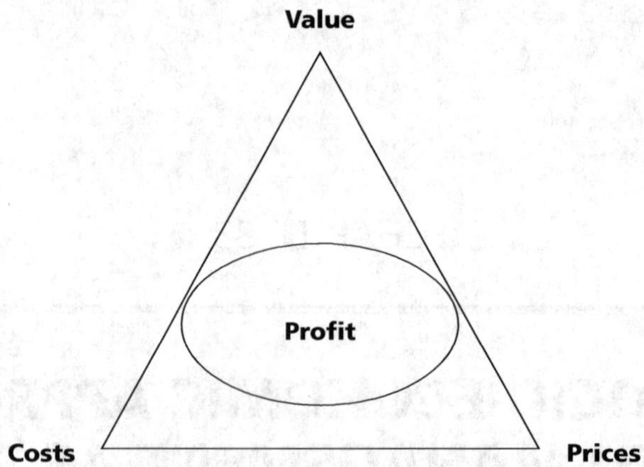

Figure 83.1 The three pillars of profit: costs, value, and price. *Source:* Maital, 1994

elements are safeguarded), and the greater the profitability. Since the production of a good or service incurs costs, which arise from a set of activities carried out, the strategy must also be sensitive to the cost elements and the activities carried out, which generate value and costs simultaneously. Balancing these three elements—value, prices and costs—is a basic function of the company, both in defining strategy and in day-to-day management. According to Maital (1994), these are the three pillars of profit, represented in Figure 83.1 as the angles of a triangle within which the company's profits are found.

The greater the distance between the angles of the triangle, the greater the profits. Cost management must be understood in this context: costs do not necessarily have to be reduced; they must be increased if they contribute to generating greater value and, therefore, higher prices and greater profitability. The task of cost management is to maximize the difference between Cost and Value. Strategic cost management (SCM) has an important role to play in this mission, helping with its concepts and tools to increase productivity and rationalize costs, with a view to maximizing the cost-value differential.

In this chapter we discuss tools and concepts related to strategic cost management, with the objective of understanding how to underpin competitiveness. We show that socioeconomic management and the study of hidden costs are the general conceptual framework from which to improve the results of the application of SCM tools.

1 CONCEPT OF THE STRATEGIC COST MANAGEMENT

It is possible to think of two major fields of interest for cost management, one concerned with the control and improvement of current costs, the other with supporting the construction of a favorable future situation in terms of costs. The first field is of a more operational nature, the interest consists in improving what exists. The second has a more direct connection with strategic actions and aims at supporting the construction of a favorable future position in terms of costs. Both should be understood as fields of cost management, since the improvement and construction of a competitive situation in terms of costs are of interest to the company.

According to Slavov,

> Cost management comprises the set of philosophies, attitudes and artifacts that seek a favorable situation in terms of costs, within a systemic perspective, based on improvement and value generation and on the development of an understanding of cost drivers, where the emphasis can be operational and strategic. (...) when the emphasis of management is strategic, several characteristics are considered, for example: greater long-term importance, commitment of top management, greater risk and greater breadth in the scope of decisions, among other characteristics. When the emphasis is operational, on the other hand, the importance is greater in the short term, in the activities of middle management, there are fewer risks and the scope of decisions is more limited. (Slavov, 2013, p. 152)

Strategic management accounting is "a formal information system that presents a strong external orientation—in addition to internal information both financial and non-financial—collecting information about customers, suppliers and competitors that allows companies to define, implement and modify their strategy" (Pinzón et al., 2006, p. 88). The SCM, based on strategic management accounting information, seeks the construction of a favorable situation in terms of costs, within a systemic perspective based on the improvement and generation of value for the customer, the control of costs within this perspective and the development of an understanding of the cost drivers (short and long term), always supporting the maintenance and increase of the company's competitiveness (Bacic, 2011, p. 141). The SCM must manage a set of demands that, at times, may seem contradictory, such as reducing costs without destroying internal competencies.

In a vision that views the company as a system that can be continuously improved, it can be stated that managing costs is synonymous with projecting, building, maintaining and improving the company's cost position, seeking to increase its competitiveness, in accordance with the company's strategy. It is necessary to act on the elements that cause costs, trying to reduce them and maximize the value generated for the customer. The adoption of a systemic perspective means that, in addition to the internal aspects, all the elements with which the company is related outside its internal field (suppliers, customers, community, environment, etc.) must be considered, either to strengthen them or not to affect them negatively.

Understanding SCM in this way, it can be seen that it plays an important role in the construction and improvement of the company's competitive situation and in the adequacy of the Value-Cost relationship. There is a set of concepts supported by tools that can be applied as can be seen in Podmoguilnye (2019) and Smolje (2016).

Necessary factors for cost management within this perspective are the long-term vision and the existence of a management policy, within the company, that encourages trust among people, that understands improvement actions as fundamental, that develops long-term relationships with suppliers and that supports innovative ideas. All these tools require a long-term systemic vision, relationships of trust between the parties, continuous improvement efforts and the ability to act on the variables that affect the interaction between people and structures within organizations. Paradoxically, they are orphans of a general conceptual framework that understands and studies the organizational complexity that arises from the interaction between people and structure. Socio-economic management applied to hidden costs and performance (ISEOR methodology) offers an adequate and broad conceptual framework for better application of SCM tools.

2 THE SOCIO-ECONOMIC APPROACH TO MANAGEMENT: CONCEPTUAL BASIS OF SCM

The socio-economic approach to management is based on the socio-economic theory of organizations (Savall, 1974, 1979; Savall and Zardet, 1987). This theory understands that organizations are complex and have physical structures and human behaviors that interact during their operation. The complexity of the interaction of the various elements necessarily leads to dysfunctions (Savall, 2007).

Dysfunctions generate hidden costs (Savall and Zardet, 2008, p. xxiii). Socio-economic management assumes as a hypothesis that there is always a difference between the situation that the various stakeholders (interested parties, or actors) of the organization expect and the present situation. There are six areas of dysfunctions that cause this gap: (1) working conditions; (2) work organization; (3) communication-coordination-cooperation; (4) time management; (5) integrated training; (6) strategic implementation (Savall, Zardet, & Bonnet, 2000, 2008, p. 16). These dysfunctions generate hidden costs and performance, which are not visible because there are no accounting accounts to record them, or if they exist, they do so partially and do not show these costs in an integrated manner, or the information does not lead to actions to recycle them into value added. Hidden costs "are those that are not identified, quantified or controlled in the company's traditional financial statements, such as general accounting, analytical accounting or budgetary control" (ibidem, p. 31). They are therefore difficult to quantify and control through traditional management tools (ibidem, p. 31). Hidden performance consists of the recycling of hidden costs into the creation of not yet estimated profit potential (ibidem, p. 32).

Hidden cost indicators can be physically observed and measured. They are: (1) absenteeism; (2) work accidents and occupational diseases; (3) staff turnover; (4) non-quality; and (5) lack of direct productivity. They derive from dysfunctions. It is possible to measure the economic consequences for the companies of the indicators observed by means of their valuation considering the components of the hidden costs which are: (1) Excess salaries; (2) overtime; (3) overconsumption; (4) non-production; (5) non-creation of potential; (6) risks (ibidem, pp. 30–34).

Figure 83.2 summarizes the relationship between dysfunctions and hidden costs.

Hidden cost and performance management is extremely broad and encompasses the set of tools to reduce the impact of dysfunctions. The tools and concepts that have their origin in the SCM literature and that we present in the next topic can (and should) be used within the context of socioeconomic management.

3 STRATEGIC MANAGEMENT CONTROL: TOOLS

We present below some of the tools most often mentioned in the literature dealing with SCM. It can be observed that all of them presuppose the achievement of results from the improvement of the interaction structures-people, allowing to lower costs and increase value.

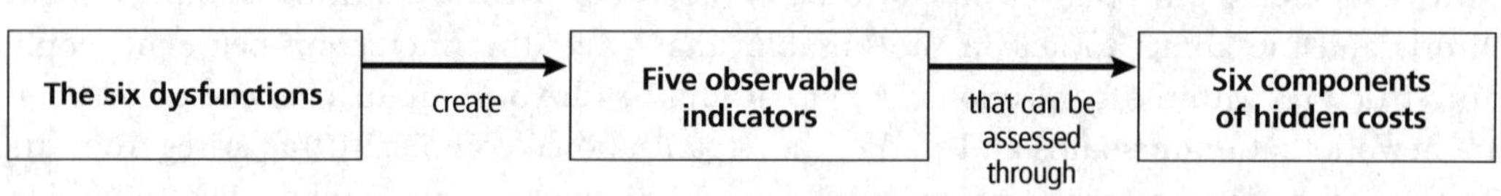

Figure 83.2 Conceptual framework of hidden costs and performance management. Source: own elaboration.

3.1 Kaizen Cost

Sakurai (1996) calls kaizen cost the Japanese practice of continuous improvement applied to costs. This management practice is based on the introduction of small daily improvements in products and processes. It also implies abandoning the view that standards are difficult to achieve and adopting the view that they can be surpassed through continuous improvement. The kaizen cost comprises visible cost reduction activities for each product and for each period, thus leading to an overcoming of standards (Sakurai, 1996, p. 52). It is considered that workers can participate in much of the work performed by specialists and it is imagined that the critical thinking of a group of people—who are in direct relationship with the process—can produce a continuous flow of incremental improvements, which lead to permanent cost reduction.

3.2 Quality Cost Control

The action on quality costs impacts the core of the company, trying to reduce waste and nonconformities. An important point to consider in the reduction of quality costs is that actions on the factors causing these costs are not direct (or mechanical). There is a reasonable complexity and, when the factors are complex, it is not possible to use ready-made formulas. Observation, study and reflection are required. The learning of the management team plays a fundamental role.

A factor that is part of the nature of any process and that generates quality costs is variability. Collaboration and employee training are indispensable elements in controlling variability. Market relationships with suppliers contribute to increase quality costs. The solution is the development of long-term relationships, in which price is not the only element to be considered and attributes such as delivery conformity with the specification, punctuality, and the ability to contribute to the improvement of our company are valued.

The control of quality costs requires perspective, it must be long term, being indispensable the learning and the development of relationships of trust between the parties (employees × management, company × suppliers). The most favorable environment for such a program is one in which TQM is practiced.

3.3 Target Costing

Target costing is the process by which the desired cost of a product is obtained. Such a process is prior to the introduction of the product in the market. The target cost (or allowable cost) arises from the difference between a certain selling price that the company considers consistent with its market strategy (target price) and the desired profit. The target cost is an ex-ante cost that must be obtained as a condition for the mass production stage to begin. Once the targets have been reached (which means careful planning of all pre--production aspects: specifications, components, suppliers, production process, etc.), the concrete conditions of mass production are studied and the standards are determined. The standard cost is set only after the desired target cost has been reached.

Obtaining the target cost starts at the product design stage. Given the allowable cost, a target cost team with representatives from the project and design (or engineering), marketing, purchasing and production departments, with the help of accounting (to provide information), studies how to reach the target before starting the production stage. Several techniques and methods are used, such as value engineering, design analysis, process variation reduction, negotiation with suppliers, etc. The process of obtaining target cost is iterative in nature (Sakurai, 1996).

3.4 Inter-Organizational Cost Management or Networking (Development of Relationships With Suppliers, Distributors and Other Agents)

The factors of the network system within which the company acts are intangible and refer to the nature and patterns of interaction established with a set of agents within and throughout a given industry (production chain, sector). Such a system is made up of a group of supplier companies and customers, articulated from a web of relationships, which may present different levels of cooperation, trust and coordination. The quality of the relationships established between suppliers, distribution channels and customers—and the capacity to articulate noble factors for the network—will define the system's competitive potential, its costs and its innovative capacity. This opens up the possibilities of cooperation between agents and of obtaining profits from the articulation of activities within the "value chain" of each company. Long-term relationships make it possible to develop trust and collaboration between the parties in a more profound way than in market or short-term relationships. The management of this form of cooperation also opens up the possibility of developing partnerships with companies outside the value chain that can generate possibilities of combined profits (Souza; Rocha, 2009).

CONCLUSION

The socio-economic approach to management offers an adequate conceptual framework for dealing with the complexity of organizations and the increasing uncertainty of the business environment. The tools of SCM make it possible to improve both the physical parameters related to the productivity of the resources with which the company operates and their quality, help in the creation of products of adequate (or greater) value for customers and improve the network of relationships within which the company is inserted. The result is, at the same time, better performance and lower costs.

The concepts and tools of SCM have the function of rationalizing costs, improving processes and products, contributing to the best possible adjustment of the Value/Cost ratio. Its application within the company induces changes in the productivity parameters of processes and inputs. It can also imply lower purchasing costs. Understanding the conceptual basis of socio-economic management when applying SCM tools allows for more robust results.

REFERENCES

Bacic, M. J. (2011). *Gestão de Custos. Uma abordagem sob o Enfoque do Processo Competitivo e da Estratégia.* Juruá Editora.

Maital, S. (1994). *Executive Economics.* The Free Press, MacMillan Inc. [Traducción al portugués: Economia para Executivos. Rio de Janeiro: Editora Campus, 1996].

Nakagawa, M. (1994). *ABC.* Custeio baseado em atividades. Atlas.

Pinzon, P. A., Elorza, M. L. V., & Vásquez, J. M. S. V. (2006). Aportaciones de la contabilidad de gestión a la calidad del diseño: especial referencia al contexto de las cadenas de suministros. *Revista Iberoamericana de Contabilidad de Gestión.* Vol. IV, num. 7. Enero–junio 2006.

Podmoguilnye, M. G. (2019). *Costos para una gestión estratégica y sustentable.* Thomson Reuters La Ley.

Sakurai, M. (1996). *Integrated Cost Management: a company wide prescription for higher profits and lower costs.* Productivity Press. [Traducción para el portugués: Gerenciamento Integrado de Custos. São Paulo: Editora Atlas, 1997].

Slavov, T. N. B. (2013). *Gestão Estratégica de Custos: Uma Contribuição Para a Construção de sua Estrutura Conceitual.* Tese Doutorado. FEAC, USP, Programa de Pós-Graduação em Ciências Contábeis. (Orientador Welington Rocha)

Smolje, A. (2016). *Reducción de costos. Ideas, técnicas y casos.* Buenos Aires. Thomson Reuters La Ley.

Souza, B. C., & Rocha, W. (2009). *Gestão de Custos Interorganizacionais.* Atlas.

This page intentionally left blank.

CHAPTER 84

ENTREPRENEURIAL RISK AS A HIDDEN COST

Daniel Farré and Susana T. Máspero

ABSTRACT

The influence of the Stakeholder Theory on Financial Accounting is notorious at the moment of not considering the Cost of Entrepreneurial Risk. The chapter analyzes the hypothesis of incorporating the sacrifice for such risk as an economic cost, except for considering it together with the value added within the hybrid concept of accounting profit, and expressing it in all the analytical processes of the socio-economic theory in order to optimize the sustainable surplus value. When made visible, it makes it possible to identify other strategies such as prevention, value chain management, association to the business, replacement of shareholder structures and reinvestment of surpluses, among others, improving the holistic management of Risk.

The economic-social framework represents a scenario of increased risk for entrepreneurs. Two decades after the use of the acronym (VUCA) in the business world, exacerbated by the effect of the COVID-19 pandemic, there is consensus that the social economic context is characterized by Volatility, Uncertainty, Complexity and Ambiguity, four elements that significantly increase the economic risk of entrepreneurs in for profit organizations. At the same time, repayment rates to Capital have declined globally. The combination of the two effects is detrimental to business sustainability. If we hide risk and do not manage it better, the current tendency of managers, who do not risk capital but are rewarded for results, will continue to choose increasingly adventurous alternatives to try to capture higher rate options, with less likelihood of long-term survival.

SEAM Treatise, pages 691–697

1 ENTREPRENEURIAL RISK AS A COST FOR MANAGERIAL ACCOUNTING

In the economic line of vision of the General Theory of Cost (Osorio and Cartier, 1992), every sacrifice necessary for the achievement of an objective is considered a Cost. The entrepreneur, by investing capital and assuming responsibility for a business, incurs a set of risks that, from the subjective point of view, imply the sacrifice of risking a potential loss (Farré, 2010), therefore, it is appropriate to appreciate it as a cost in any management process. In the same way, the Socioeconomic Theory (Savall, 1974, 1979) categorizes it as a Hidden Cost, which entails the danger of not taking it into account in the business decision-making process.

On the other hand, mainstream Financial Accounting, aligned with the Stockholders' Theory, does not allow considering it as a cost. By setting as its economic objective the maximization of "the" basic equation of the accounting profit, which arises from the difference between revenues and costs from a fiscal perspective, it cannot discern whether or not this amount covers the expectations of repayment of the owners' sacrifice. Paradoxically, having a positive profit does not in itself express economic convenience. If the amount does not cover such effort, it is neither "useful" for the entrepreneur nor "beneficial" for the economy as a whole. Seen in this way, the terms utility and profit lose their meaning, and the term costs remains incomplete in a Decision Making analysis because it does not reach all the stakeholders of the business under analysis.

This apparent polysemy of the term Costs is solved with a teleological vision, as Oscar Osorio (Osorio, 1986) already expressed: "We must accept that those sacrifices may be measured in different ways and valued differently, depending on the objective pursued."

Leaving out the sacrifice of the owners in the basic equation is useful for calculating the taxes to be paid to the State, but it is not useful for the holistic management of the Company with a vision of sustainability, which is the focus of this chapter.

2 THE SURPLUS VALUE AS AN INDUCTIVE GOAL OF DECISION MAKING

The constructivist-structuralist sociological theory (Bourdieu, 1979) defines Illusio (etymologically: "in" enter and "ludum" play) as the interest that social agents have in participating in a game of relationships and habitus as the subjective system of expectations and predispositions that influence their way of thinking, feeling and acting accordingly.

Taken to the socio-economic field, if we do not manage to generate Illusio (socio-economic Illusio) no type of value added will be generated, either because of the agents' ataraxia, or because of the lack of contribution of Accounting in revealing and disseminating the value-added relationships and associated sacrifices, impacting the habitus of the stakeholders necessary to carry out the business. Each stakeholder will be interested if he/she is aware that what will happen in the socioeconomic game will have meaning (value) and will exceed the sacrifice (cost) that his/her involvement will mean.

Agency theory (Charreaux, 1987) highlights the asymmetry of information and develops the imperfect information hypothesis, explaining the impact of information management on power. The transparent mapping of the strategy and the conceptualization and synthesis of the critical monetary and non-monetary elements of the business make it possible to reduce the asymmetry of the exposed information, a fundamental element of the Harvard cooperative negotiation model in order to activate the win-win game focused on the communion of interests.

The target-indicator to be used to guide the actions of companies cannot be the current financial accounting profit, which is clearly stockholder-oriented, since it does not meet these requirements. It must be replaced by an algorithm that broadens the scope in terms of the subjects considered and the time horizon. From our point of view, if we advocate for the inclusive sustainability of the socioeconomic ecosystem, we must act ex ante, in Decision Making, projecting long-term future information, considering the balance of all stakeholders, with the Confucianist vision of homus reciprocrans. Explaining historical information in moments of Accountability is usually late.

The business action to be undertaken will be beneficial if the value to be generated allows repaying the efforts (costs) of all the agents involved. If there is more than one alternative that meets or exceeds this condition, one of those that generate surpluses should be chosen according to the distribution and weighting criteria. Unlike the financial accounting profit, the guiding indicator will be the projected value added, for which the costs (which net the value generated) should be calculated considering the repayment request of each of the stakeholders based on their own perception of the effort to be made.

In line with the above, the shareholder is one more stakeholder. We propose to externalize their repayment requirement to the sacrifices associated with their investment, as a cost by calculating the periods exposed to risk of the invested capital monetized at a rate relative to the magnitude of the risk assumed. The difference between value and costs thus calculated ceases to represent the accounting profit and becomes an indicator of capital gain. Any positive (or neutral) surplus projected will be "useful" or "beneficial" for the stakeholders as a whole, as long as the distribution criterion that allows visualizing equilibrium in each of the business-participant relationships and generates the socio-economic Illusio of all is met.

The intensity of such Illusio will depend on the degree of balance projected, as stated by Farré, Sánchez, Zardet and Savall (2011, 2013) according to the planning horizon, the subjectivity of the participants and the uncertainty of the contex, namely:

> Type 1: unstable equilibrium, minimum indifference point or survival point: it is the lowest value for which the stakeholder is willing to participate;
>
> Type 2: of satisfaction, is the lowest value for which the stakeholder is satisfied to participate, which gives the business a higher probability of existence; and
>
> Type 3: loyalty or permanence, is the value for which the stakeholder exceeds his satisfaction to the point where he acquires a commitment that makes him loyal to the business and gives him, based on a greater distribution of value, a greater probability of existence in the future.

Plusvalue equal to zero in type 1 represents the frontier from which "it starts to be worthwhile" to carry out the action under analysis, although it expresses fragility for the long term. In their perception of type 1 repayment, many of the agents take into account that, by participating, they can convert their value potential into value, which would otherwise be lost over time. The first threshold may be conjuncturally low. The emergence of higher repayment alternatives puts their future commitment at risk.

3 ENTREPRENEURIAL RISK MANAGEMENT TO RECYCLE HIDDEN COSTS AND INCREASE HIDDEN RETURNS

The visibility of the economic impact of risk in for-profit companies will have two main effects:

1. When comparing decision alternatives, many of the high-risk, high rate-of-return alternatives, which in the traditional view are the winners, will no longer be prioritized over more sustainable alternatives that project a higher surplus value.

2. Managers will be able to analyze different alternatives to optimize costs by reducing risk. Just by reflecting on the behavior of the cost of risk in the last approach of the three typologies, a first applicability of this concept can be observed: If the owner proposes a strategy of distribution of surplus surplus value closer to the type 1 equilibrium in order to keep more repayment for himself, sustainability will be reduced and his cost of risk will be higher. Paradoxically, the overall surplus value will go down, and there will even be scenarios in which his own difference between value and cost will be lower.

Applying the synergistic approach of the Multidimensional Value Chain based on the collaborative strategy present in Drucker's Ethics of Interdependence (Confucian-based), it will be possible to identify actions that are usually hidden, among others:

- Replacing the conflict of interest negotiation approach of the monodimensional and confrontational homus economicus with the community of interest approach of homus reciprocans.
- To balance the power relations in the Multidimensional Value Chain by applying the long-term vision of the Socioeconomic Theory. From the analysis of the strengths of each of its links, ideas will emerge to mitigate the weaknesses of the company's positioning, carrying out integration actions with agents of common interests to gain greater bargaining power. But there will also be gains in the case of ceding degrees of power in the strengths, in exchange for greater loyalty of the agent with whom the company is negotiating, as in the case of supplier development or long-term agreements with future price stability.
- Replace uncertainty with certain costs of a lesser amount than the now visible cost of the risk assumed, identifying risks that can be prevented, planned, and/or mitigated.
- Share business risk with other stakeholders, involving them in the business, under different models:
  - Offering them, ex ante, participation in the surplus value to be generated, making it feasible to negotiate lower fixed prices, with a variable differential associated with the success of the business.
  - Changing the variable bonus model for managers, using the capital gain indicator as the basis for calculation, which net the cost of risk, instead of the profit or rate of return from the accounting equity view, which hides the dysfunctionality of extreme decision making in search of fictitious returns.
  - Condition costs to the contingency in businesses with uncertain contexts. For example, in agricultural businesses, include part of the premium for flood insurance.
- Optimize the shareholder mix: Since risk is an element with a high degree of subjectivity, shareholders do not measure it in the same way, nor do they give the same importance to sustainability over time. Even less do they ask for a similar rate of reward for the sacrifice. Classifying the different groups of shareholders by their degree of involvement with the company (owners, employees, speculative investors) and understanding their propensity or aversion to risk and investment horizon (long or short term) will allow finding the mix that optimizes the cost of business risk.
- Apply countercyclical prevention strategies: In periods of relevant surpluses, allocate a percentage of them to reinvestment in the business, without considering it as a shareholder contribution, since it has already been repaid with the amount requested ex ante. Such capital does not require additional future repayment because it does not represent an effort, therefore it does not generate future costs.

Not managing it will be worse. The "Laissez faire, laissez passer" effect will result in a higher cost for the owner, requesting a higher repayment for having to assume such risk.

4 CASE STUDIES OF COST OF RISK REPLACEMENT IN NOT-FOR-PROFIT COMPANIES

Not all companies have profit as their main objective, nor do they require repayment for the risk associated with the capital invested. Even in free market economies, there are hybrid value chains, with both for-profit and not-for-profit links. Is there a sacrifice for investment risk in these chains? In many cases, capital contributions are not made in explicit financial form. If there is an individual contribution from each member, it is perceived as a contribution to the viability of the objective for which the organization was established:

- In consumer cooperatives, members obtain goods or services at lower prices than in the traditional market.
- In worker cooperatives they obtain jobs that allow them to activate their value potential, which would be lost if they were unemployed.
- In credit unions they manage to disintermediate financial institutions by obtaining better rates, both for those who contribute their savings and for those who apply for loans.

In non-profit organizations there is a different philosophy of management, another concept of repayment, seen from the social or environmental improvement. The community is the main recipient of the investment. Sustainability management, i.e., the risk of not being able to meet the objectives of the different stakeholders, is more important than financial risk management. Even the State's contribution does not require explicit financial recovery, because the function and expected return is the generation and/or maintenance of sources of employment and their positive impact on the economy.

5 APPLICATION CASE: MOVEMENT OF "RECOVERED COMPANIES"

At the beginning of the 21st century, the "Recovered Factories" movement began in Argentina, later known as Companies Recovered by their Workers (ERT). Faced with the economic megacrisis, a group of owners of heavily indebted companies, with zero or negative profit projections and no market of investors willing to buy the company in progress, decided to initiate the closure of their factories by declaring them bankrupt. To avoid the loss of employment, the workers of these factories united, took over the plants to prevent their emptying and closing and maintained the economic activity by organizing themselves under the form of Worker Cooperatives.

After two decades of sustainability, in order to understand the reasons for the viability of productive processes that were unviable for the entrepreneur, we selected one of the iconic companies of the ERTs (Chilavert Artes gráficas) and interviewed Plácido Peñarrieta, one of its worker-founders who today is still part of the group that manages the cooperative.

From the beginning, they replaced the main objective of the company. They replaced the previous profit motive with the objective of generating employment, forming a Worker Cooperative. The employees assumed the role of management while maintaining their jobs, which they repaid with the income generated by sales. At no time was there any requirement of repayment for the entrepreneurial risk, typical of a for-profit company vision. At the beginning, because they had not contributed capital that they were risking, but unpaid work (months owed during the crisis). And then, when they started to generate genuine funds (surplus to costs due to salary withdrawals), they saved them (foreseeing to pay the amount due to the State) or reinvested in machinery improvement and updating. With the new vision of business management, reinvestment is not perceived as a sacrifice to be repaid, so it is not a cost.

Two decades of surplus value validate that the change of approach meant win-win relationships: customers obtain quality products at prices they consider fair, suppliers have economic activity, workers have jobs that allow them to convert their value potential into value, repaid with wages commensurate with their effort, the former owner improved his position with respect to the bankruptcy alternative, and the State fulfilled socioeconomic objectives that would have cost much more than the amount anticipated for the severance payment.

To close the interview, Peñarrieta, who still proudly considers himself a graphic worker, told us that years ago a professional questioned his management because he considered it was not "profitable," biased by his concepts of traditional accounting. From our perspective, the anecdote only reinforces our proposal to change the target indicator to favor the sustainability of organizations that generate value added under a more holistic win-win approach.

CONCLUSION

In order to fulfill the inclusive and sustainable vision enunciated, we chose to assume the Community of Interest (COI) accounting approach, based on the Stakeholder Theory with a homus reciprocans vision, as we understand it to be optimal to the interdependence negotiation approach that privileges to focus on the common points shared by all stakeholders (highlighting their mutual needs and obligations), instead of measuring conjunctural negotiation forces in the traditional method of conflict of interests contrary to Confucian ethics, which considers abusive the use of power in any kind of human relationship.

From this vantage point, we suggest that Decision Making should not be based on the basic historical equation of Financial Accounting but on the holistic projected value added (or surplus value) of all Stakeholders, netting value minus costs for each of them, without leaving any of the usual costs that are hidden for traditional Accounting.

In particular, it seems important to us to incorporate the cost of entrepreneurial risk in for-profit companies, instead of leaving it intermingled within the hybrid concept of utility of financial accounting, and to express it in all analytical processes of the socio-economic theory, to identify alternatives or lower risk scenarios in order to optimize the target surplus value.

When made visible, it allows a better study and conceptualization of its essence, and enables other risk management strategies with better holistic results. Management Accounting thus plays an active prescriptive role ex ante in Decision Making, in pursuit of the sustainability of profitable businesses rather than a passive explanatory role of the causes of failures.

In this line, the chosen case aims to create awareness of situations where the cost of entrepreneurial risk acted as a burden to the sustainability of a business that is maintained over time after two decades, by changing the approach and management objective.

REFERENCES

Bourdieu, P. (1972). *Esquisse d'une théorie de la pratique, précédée de trois études d'ethnologie kabyle.* Droz, Geneva.

Charreaux, G., & al. (1987). *De nouvelles théories pour gérer l'entreprise.* Economica.

Farré, D. (2001). "Support to the multidimensional approach to value creation." VII International Cost Congress. León, Spain.

Farré, D. (2009). *Linking Stakeholder Theory with management approaches and techniques: Multidimensional Value Chain and Multifocal Balanced Scorecard.* XI International Cost Congress. Trelew, Argentina.

Farré, D. (2010). *Reducing the economic cost of business risk.* Proceedings of the II Transatlantic Congress on Accounting, Control, Auditing and Cost Management. Lyon.

Farré, S., Zardet, & Savall. (2013). *Analysis of surplus value equilibrium in the face of different sustainability strategies.* III Transatlantic Congress on Accounting, Controlling, Auditing and Cost Management. Lyon.

Freeman, R. (1984). *Strategic management: A stakeholder approach* (Vol. 1). Pitman.

Menger, C. (1871). *Principles of Economy.* Von Mises Institute.

Osorio, O. (1993). Towards a general theory of costs in accounting. *Cost and Management Journal.*

Osorio, O., & Cartier, E. (1992). *General Cost Theory: A necessary framework.* In Accounting, Finance and Auditing in the Iberoamerican Integration Process Scientific Event, Havana City, Cuba.

Porter, M., & Kramer, M. (2011). Creating Shared Value. How to reinvent capitalism and generate a wave of innovation and growth. *Harvard Business Review.*

Savall, H., Zardet, V., & Farré, D. (2011). *The entrepreneurial risk management dimension in the economic balance of the socio-economic theory of hidden costs-performance.* IIC Congress, Punta del Este, Uruguay.

This page intentionally left blank.

CHAPTER 85

SOCIO-ECONOMIC MANAGEMENT CONTROL, A LEVER FOR CHANGING ORGANIZATIONAL STANDARDS

The Case of Operating Norms and Occupational Health

Thierry Nobre and Laurent Cappelletti

ABSTRACT

This chapter presents how the socio-economic approach (SEA) contributes to giving management control its dimension as a lever for change to improve the medium- and long-term performance of organizations. This analysis focuses more specifically on the theme of health. First, a synthesis of research-intervention shows how ESA implements change in a health organization based on the different stages of socio-economic intervention. Then, a second approach shows how ESA tools through standardization integrate the concern for occupational health to transform the organization.

Socio-economic management control has the peculiarity in the field of management control of offering "at the same time" tools and methods for measuring and controlling performance, as well as for change and problem solving (Savall, 1974; Lindsay et al., 2015; Lindsay et al., 2015). Distinguishing itself from classical management control systems, particularly by mobilizing the theory of hidden costs and performance and that of Tetranormalization (Savall, 1974, 1975; Savall, Zardet, 2005), socio-economic management control proves to be singularly useful in contributing to approaches to changing organizational norms, affecting, for example, operations or occupational health. To illustrate this, this chapter presents

SEAM Treatise, pages 699–705

the case study of a new organizational norm in a hospital (Nobre, 1999, 2006; Nobre et al., 2011), followed by two cases of adaptation to occupational health and organizational norms by companies and states (Cappelletti, 2021).

1 CASE OF A HOSPITAL IMPLEMENTING A NEW ORGANIZATIONAL STANDARD TOWARDS MORE DECENTRALIZATION

Change management in a hospital is generally considered a complex process in a complex organization (Nobre 2006). Among the causes identified for this situation, the sociological configuration and power relationships figure prominently in explaining the hospital's transformation difficulties. Socio-economic management control, through its intervention mechanisms and managerial engineering, makes a significant contribution and provides operational solutions for removing the traditional obstacles to change management in this specific context. We illustrate this observation with a case study conducted using a socio-economic intervention-research method in a medical imaging department of 60 people, within a hospital. With 400 beds and 1000 people, the hospital was expecting a change, even though the actor supposed to lead the change was very passive, even resistant to change. As part of the preparation of the establishment's project, each head of department had to propose a departmental project and define the strategic and change axes for his department. When the departmental projects were presented, the contribution of the head of the imaging department was totally insignificant and out of step with expectations. Moreover, the situation in this department was very dysfunctional, in a very tense environment. The problem was therefore the following: How to lead the change in a hospital context when the institutional pilot of the change does not want it?

The researcher was asked by the head of the institution who, given the stalemate, wanted an external intervention to initiate and stimulate the expected strategic change. The intervention-research took place over a period of 18 months with the four main stages of socio-economic management control: the realization of an organizational diagnosis, the creativity phase defining potential avenues, the decision phase and the implementation phase. The tools and methods used during this research made it possible to remove the obstacles specific to the relationships between actors traditionally identified in hospitals. In this case it was :

- the director of the institution requesting the change,
- the head of the department, the official and facial pilot of the project, who, given his position, should have been the project leader, but who in fact proved to be very passive
- the health executive, the actual pilot of the change,
- the other actors, mainly the other radiologists, who were in a wait-and-see situation.

The approach was based on a socio-economic approach, with an organisational diagnosis, identifying dysfunctions and hidden costs, and then methodological support in co-production with the various actors in the organization (Savall and Zardet, 1987).

The results of the mobilization of socio-economic management control in this case are mainly at three levels: objectification of the situation, achievement of the operational objective of carrying out a service project, with the definition of an action plan, and the evolution of the strategic management of the service, thanks to a smooth handover for the governance of the service. The main dysfunctions and hidden costs observed and the factors explaining the initial stalemate are presented in Table 85.1.

TABLE 85.1 The Main Dysfunctions Observed (amounts in thousands of euros for 43 people)

Table: Processes	Heures	Montants
Time of the schedules	433	20.6
Patients' prioritization rules	347	16.1
Protocols	900	112.1
Tel appointment booking	1,000	47.7
GAP relationships	52	2.5
Booking validation system		100.0
Jittery screens	225	13.7
	2,957	**312.7**
Table: Premises and equipment		
Booklets printing problems	900	69.2
Unopenable door of room 3 when there is a bed	58	3.5
Door overlooking elevator remaining open	41.67	2.3
	1,000	**75.0**
Table: relationships with other services		
Intervention delays	**125**	**33.1**
Table: unintuitive patient pathway		
Patient being lost. Need to look for the patient	52	6.3
Preventive checking of forms	43	2.6
Impacts on delayed check-ups		Not evaluated
Negative impact on brand image		Not evaluated
	95	**8.9**
Table: Cost of coordination with stretcher bearers		
Systematic regular calls	666.67	0.9
Calls for changes	2,133.33	101.8
	2,800	**102.7**
Overall amounts	**6,977**	**532.4**

The application of socio-economic management control has made it possible to achieve the initial objective of creating a service project, identifying the strategic axes that structure the evolution of the service, in coordination with the strategic axes of the institution. These axes are summarized below. They are the result of a system of workgroups involving all categories of actors in the department and units interfacing with the imaging department:

Patient pathway: Reorganization with architectural transformation of the administrative and medical reception areas, of the first-floor scanner results area, architectural reorganization of the ultrasound area, second floor reception area, reorganization of the MRI interpretation area, reorganization of waiting areas

Actions defined: Reorganization of diaries, 2nd floor scanner diary, MRI diary, ultrasound diary, imaging secretariat, telephone platform, online appointment booking, Block 12 problems, reorganization of patient care in the scanner and MRI, secure access to the 2nd floor department.

Departmental strategy: development of tele-radiology, adaptation of the imaging offer to internal demand, participation in work concerning the relevance of requests.

The awareness caused by the diagnosis and the mirror-effect presented to all the department's staff led to an awareness on the part of the head of department who agreed to hand over the leadership of the department. This transition led to two fundamental managerial changes: on the one hand, an internal transformation of the department that defined the internal steering procedures and formalized the delegation of operational responsibilities translated into effective managerial practices, and on the other hand, new relations between the department and the management of the institution that allowed for an effective strategic and operational link.

2 CONTRIBUTION OF THE SOCIO-ECONOMIC MANAGEMENT CONTROL TO ADAPT TO OCCUPATIONAL HEALTH STANDARDS

Studies on health and quality of life at work agree that the level of absenteeism in a company is a good indicator of this. They also confirm that at least two thirds of the causes of absence are due to defects in the quality of work life and personnel management (Savall and Cappelletti, 2021). In normal times, absenteeism at work is a well identified French disease whose cost to the nation varies between 80 and 120 billion euros per year, i.e., around 4 points of annual GDP lost. It represents an average cost or loss of value added of about 4,000 euros per active person per year, which is expressed mainly in terms of non-production and replacement wages. In times of health crisis such as that of COVID, given the additional psychosocial risks and deteriorated working conditions, absenteeism from work tends to worsen, further aggravating the costs that it generates in normal times. It is therefore necessary, in normal times as well as in times of crisis, to set up a health-oriented socio-economic management control in companies, based essentially on the qualitative, quantitative and financial control (Q.Q.Fi) of absenteeism. Such Q.Q.Fi, or qualimetric, management control is paradoxically still not widespread in companies, even though absenteeism is a major source of economic loss. It can take a miniaturized form in small companies and more developed in large. In concrete terms, it consists of periodically:

- identifying the dysfunctions caused by absenteeism at work.
- evaluating the costs and the loss of value added that they generate.
- identifying the root causes of absenteeism in order to identify those on which the company can act;
- inventing corrective and/or preventive actions to reduce compressible dysfunctions, i.e., those that have causes on which the company can act, while ensuring that the costs of the improvement actions are lower than the costs they aim to reduce;
- Evaluate the improvement actions implemented to continue or modify them.

Table 85.2 gives examples of dysfunctions related to absenteeism considered by the health-oriented management control of an IT service and engineering company (SSII) with around 30 employees.

Studies show that the dysfunctions caused by absenteeism and the costs they generate are reducible in a proportion varying from 35% to 55%, by appropriate corrective and/or preventive actions. By symmetry, this means that a part of these dysfunctions is incompressible, their causes being independent of the working conditions and management of the company. Nevertheless, on the one hand, the compressible and incompressible part of absenteeism can only be identified through a rigorous management control analysis. On the other hand, the compressible part of absenteeism generally represents such a potential

TABLE 85.2 Examples of Absenteeism Costs in an IT Services Company Measured During the COVID Crisis

Themes	Cost of Health-Related Dysfunctions
Work-related illness	There were 2 employee burn-outs linked to the deteriorated working conditions (and the anguish of the situation) which resulted in 300 hours of sick leave for the employees concerned. On the one hand, the salaries of the absent employees were fully covered by the company, i.e., additional salaries of 300 h × € 20 (hourly rate of the employees concerned) = € 6,000. On the other hand, the work of the depressed people in professional illness was left in suspense while waiting for their return, that is to say non productions of 300 h × € 46.3 (HCVAVC : Hourly Contribution to Value Added on Variable Costs) = € 13,890
Non quality	Errors in compliance with sanitary standards lead to risks of contamination and therefore risks of absenteeism. Not economically evaluated at this stage.
Low productivity and abseeteeism	The overtime of production of the missions linked to the sanitary constraints is estimated at 800 hours over the year, i.e., a hidden cost of 800 h × € 46.3 (HCVACV) = € 37,040. The tiredness of the personnel linked to the periods of over activity resulted in a total of 50 hours of absence. These were short-term absences not covered by the company in salary terms. The work of the absent persons is left pending, i.e., non production of 50 h × € 46.3 (HCVACV) = € 2,315.
Work-related illness	The lack of training of the heads of missions in the respect of the barrier gestures generates risks of contamination and administrative closing of the company. Not economically evaluated at this stage.
Non quality	A client who was not well received by the company in terms of health was contaminated by COVID. He cancelled a mission that had just started for a budget of € 50,000. This is a non production of 50,000 € × 80% (1 – margin rate) = € 40,000.

value added that it is economically and socially absurd to neglect it. Thus, in the case of the IT services company taken as an example, the total costs of absenteeism were evaluated at 99,000 euros, of which 40%, i.e., 39,000 euros, were converted into value added through improvement actions at a much lower cost of around 10,000 euros: an action to improve psychological working conditions consisted of more frequent monitoring of telecommuting and face-to-face employees to break their isolation and an in-depth and repeated action to learn health standards and barrier gestures (Savall, Cappelletti, 2018; Cappelletti, 2021).

3 SOCIO-ECONOMIC MANAGEMENT OF NORMS AND STANDARDS, A LEVER FOR CHANGE THAT CREATES SUSTAINABLE PERFORMANCE

Careful observation of the countries that seem to be the most resilient to the COVID crisis in terms of both health and economics, such as Japan, Korea, Taiwan or to some extent Germany during the first wave of the virus, shows the importance of collective competence in managing norms, "norms" being defined as the formal (laws, decrees, etc.) and informal (recommendations, advice, etc.) rules that guide human behavior to control risks. Indeed, the public authorities of these countries have acquired a competence in the governance of standards, in this case sanitary standards, and their companies a competence in the management of these standards that is superior to ours. In particular, these countries rigorously apply the OANE process—orchestrate/arbitrate/negotiate/ethics—identified as a root cause of quality according to the socio-economic theory of Tetranormalization (Savall, Zardet, 2005; Cappelletti, Dufour, 2020) and studies on the socio-economic management of standards (Bessire et al., 2010; Cappelletti et al., 2015).

For a government, it is a matter of creating adequate mechanisms for the orchestration and governance of a new norm when it involves its population, negotiating the conditions of its implementation with the stakeholders concerned, arbitrating the conflicts it may provoke and elaborating a set of positive and negative sanctions for its respect, clearly explained, in order to generate a real ethics of the norm in the population. This process is itself adapted within the companies in order to best respect the standard in question. In these countries, such collective competence is also exercised in other areas of norms than health, the financial, social and commercial areas (Cappelletti, Dufour, 2020). It is therefore no coincidence that companies in these countries—Germany, Japan, Korea, Taiwan, etc.—are often also champions of the health sector. It is therefore no coincidence that companies in these countries—Germany, Japan, Korea, Taiwan, etc.—are also often champions of product exports, which require remarkable agility in adapting to the specific standards of client countries. France needs guidance and learning in this area, both from its public authorities and its companies, as illustrated by the conflicts of standards that mark the COVID crisis: for example, the hesitations over recommendations governing the wearing of masks, the excessive rigidity of regulations governing hospital operations, the decrees distinguishing between essential and non-essential products, or the conflicts of standards that can handicap vaccination campaigns against COVID in France.

In both small and large organizations, difficulties have also been observed in assimilating health standards and enforcing them on employees and customers. For example, both Amazon warehouses and restaurants have had to suffer administrative closures for serious non-compliance with prescribed sanitary standards. Poor management of standards—whether sanitary, commercial, financial or social, which are the four areas of greatest normative intensity (Savall and Zardet, 2005)—entails visible and hidden costs. "Hidden" is understood to mean that they are not recorded or are poorly recorded in the accounts. This represents a considerable whole cost (visible cost + hidden cost) in terms of additional implementation time, sanctions for non-compliance (e.g., financial penalties) and operating losses when the risk targeted by the standard is realized (e.g., the risk of administrative closure). By symmetry, investment in an appropriate standards management process appears to be highly cost-effective, given the much higher costs of mismanagement that it avoids. Collective competence in standards management will serve companies and governments well beyond the COVID crisis as a powerful driver of health, social and economic performance. Basically, to rebound on a French debate, it is not a shock of simplification of standards that France would need, as the flow of standards cannot be stopped since the demand for risk control is growing everywhere, but a shock of governance of standards by public authorities, relayed by a shock of their management control in companies (Savall, Cappelletti, 2021; Cappelletti, 2021).

CONCLUSION

Through the cases of change in norms affecting the organization of work in the broadest sense by a hospital, a consulting firm and states, the chapter wished to illustrate the ability of socio-economic management control to contribute to change at microscopic as well as more macroscopic levels. The observations drawn from this application of socio-economic management control should also allow the identification of conceptual isomorphisms that are valid at the different levels of the organization: micro, meso and macro.

REFERENCES

Bessire, D., Cappelletti, L., Pigé, B. (Dir.) (2010). *Normes. Origines et conséquences des crises.* Economica.

Cappelletti, L. (2021). «La gestion des normes et le contrôle de gestion au service de la santé». *Revue Française de Comptabilité*, n°549, Janvier.

Cappelletti, L., Dufour, N. (2020). *La gestion innovante des normes.* Géréso Editions.

Cappelletti, L., Pigé, B., Zardet, V. (Dir.) (2015). *Dynamiques normatives.* E.M.S.

Lindsay, M., Cappelletti, L., Ennajem, C. (2015). "Understanding SEAM as an innovative plateform in management control for change and human potential development." *Academy of Management Annual Meeting*, Vancouver, August.

Lindsay, M., Savall, H., Zardet, V., Cappelletti, L. (2016). "The Socio-Economic Approach to Management (SEAM): Introducing a "Positive" Postmodern Approach to Managing Radically Decentralized Organizations based on Calculating Hidden Costs and Performance." *Management Accounting Section Midyear Meeting*, Dallas, January.

Nobre, T. (1999). «L'hôpital: le modèle de la bureaucratie professionnelle revisité». *XXe Congrès de l'AFC*, Bordeaux, mai.

Nobre, T. (2006). «Pour une lecture en hypertexte des organisations par la recherche action: le cas du changement à l'hôpital». *Finance Contrôle Stratégie*, 9(4), décembre.

Nobre, T., Merdinger-Rumpler, C. (2011). «Quelles étapes pour la conduite du changement à l'hôpital?». *Gestion 2000*, 3(11). mai.

Savall, H., Cappelletti, L. (2018). *Les coûts cachés de l'absentéisme au travail.* Étude pour l'Institut Sapiens, novembre.

Savall, H. Cappelletti, L. (2021). «La gestion des normes, facteur clé de succès économiques et sanitaires». *Les Échos*, 4 janvier.

This page intentionally left blank.

CHAPTER 86

HOURLY CONTRIBUTION TO VALUE-ADDED ON VARIABLE COSTS (HCVAVC) AS A CONCEPT AND TOOL TO MANAGE THE CREATION OF VALUE ADDED

Cécile Ennajem and Mohammed Ennajem

ABSTRACT

The HCVAVC makes it possible to measure the economic value generated by a unit of work time. In normal operation, when a solvent product (good or service) is generated, it generates an assessable value based on the hourly contribution to value-added over variable costs. The opposite reasoning leads to a non-contribution to the value added when a dysfunction appears and produces ipso facto a hidden cost.

The HCVAVC, coupled with the six areas of dysfunction, makes it possible to raise the awareness of the company's actors to the notion of wealth creation and to make the strategic and operational management of the creation of socio-economic value added tangible.

The literature on the traditional organization of work (Taylor, 1911; Fayol, 1916; Weber, 1924) aiming at increased productivity is numerous, but it rarely considers the components of the organization (individuals, groups, structures, environment). Other approaches, such as the sociotechnical approach (Emery and Trist, 1969), consider the organization as a system open to its environment, whose efficiency depends on the joint optimization of the technical organization of work and the social organization. His main contribution was to

SEAM Treatise, pages 707–713

show the existence of several efficient forms of organization, and that the quality of social life is improved by the satisfaction of the needs of the actors in their work environment.

The socio-economic theory was inspired by the socio-technical approach, adding the economic dimension (Savall, 1974–1975) and proposing the concept and tool of Hourly Contribution to Value on Variable Costs (HCVAVC) to analyze and develop the value added. The concepts of hidden costs and *conversion of hidden costs into value added* (Savall, 1974–1975, 1979; Savall and Zardet, 1987, 1992, 2008) are at the center of operational and strategic management control systems as well as of value added creation.

The concept of HCVAVC is an innovative tool for steering the creation of value added. This chapter is structured in three parts: a) Definition of the concepts and elements of calculation of the HCVAVC; b) Dynamics of the creation of value added and c) Strategic and operational piloting of the creation of socio-economic value added.

1 CONCEPT AND CALCULATION OF THE HCVAVC

In the socio-economic calculation method, the value-added on variable costs (VAVC) is always higher than the accounting[1] value-added, because it integrates fixed external costs; it represents the level of value creation necessary to cover structural costs. The VAVC therefore corresponds to the value-added created by the company on all its purchases, including purchases that are *not* considered directly incorporable into the activity.

By aiming to improve socio-economic productivity through the means of action available to the company to improve its VAVC, it differs from the dominant conventions for determining and steering accounting value-added. The HCVAVC in relation to the number of expected hours (HA) determines the socio-economic productivity indicator called HCVAVC, which constitutes an operational and strategic steering indicator for the actions of all the actors in the company.

The calculation of the HCVAVC is as follows:

Revenue – Adjusted variable costs (VC) / number of expected hours (EH).

The HCVAVC represents the average value of one hour of human activity within the company, whatever the job, functional or operational of the person. The number of expected annual hours (HA) corresponds to that of all the employees of the company or organization. Thus, a drop in demand, an increase in external purchase prices, or a drop in human productivity or product quality will result in a drop in HCVAVC. The variability of expenses depends on the rules of proportionality (level of activity) and on strategic options (organization of conferences, participation in trade fairs, etc.): we thus speak of *mechanical or strategic* variable expenses (Savall and Zardet, 2008). In public service organizations or associations, the HCVAVC is calculated by adding up all the fixed costs and, if applicable, the result (Ennajem C., 2011).

2 CREATION OF SOCIO-ECONOMIC VALUE ADDED

Socio-economic theory refutes the difference between internal and external productivity due to the porosity between the organization and its environment because the creation of socio-economic value added has no established boundaries. This value is questioned each time a performance gap is noted both internally and externally, in relations with partners, customers and suppliers. The absence of external impulses leads to a lack of internal action and vice versa.

To create value added, one of the first reflexes that crosses the mind of a company's management is to develop tools and means of production. This approach, which makes sense in principle, sometimes requires the acquisition of expensive material resources (material investments) and human resources (human potential), to ensure "perfect" control of production and a real capacity to adapt to changes in rhythm and organization. The creation of value is therefore not a self-generated process. On the contrary, it is the result of a set of actions on different levers (strategy, governance, production, human resources, customer relations, marketing, sales, new technologies), which allow to improve the economic and social performance of the organization, by striving to reconcile immediate results and creation of potential.

The human potential represents a lever and a primary active factor in the process of creating added-value through its *energy, competency* and *behavior* (Savall and Zardet, 2014, 2015). The creation of value added is activated by identifying dormant pools of hidden cost, then mobilizing them to organize a "re-creation of value" by activating and revaluing material and especially human resources, which have long been devalued but are so precious.

The creation of value added is also achieved through situations of inter-organizational cooperation, which allow to multiply and better organize this creation of value added over time (Ennajem M., 2020). As the result or outcome of a succession of organized actions, the creation of value added is also synonymous with "convention": the value created is always the result of a convention with organized variants, whose process is considered essential to ensure an equitable sharing of the value created between the stakeholders for a continuity of the relationship. This is the principle of fair margin therapy (Ennajem M., 2020). Finally, the creation of value added is also an "investment" that uses the economic to serve the social and vice versa, in a responsible approach to structure a societal and sustainable socio-economic model.

Let's take the case of a "dry cleaning" activity: considered in isolation within a shopping center, a traditional calculation of margin on variable costs and accounting analysis of profitability would have sealed the fate of this activity. In a socio-economic vision, the search for a strategic and operational unit, creating value added, of the whole [hyper market + shopping center stores] was privileged. Indeed, the shopping center needs the dry cleaner to attract customers. Since it is part of the same dynamic, the dry cleaner, thus considered as part of the same company (shopping center), gains by maintaining its activity.

3 STRATEGIC AND OPERATIONAL MANAGEMENT OF SOCIO-ECONOMIC VALUE-ADDED CREATION

In socio-economic theory, the term "piloting" has the strong sense of making decisions, like the airplane pilot who approaches the runway with his passengers and crew and chooses the appropriate method given the visibility and length of the runway! Piloting includes making decisions, implementing them, and evaluating them before continuing or modifying the actions (Savall and Zardet, 1987, 1995)

The HCVAVC concept-tool gives concrete substance to strategic and operational management, which consists of monitoring and analyzing the level of HCVAVC and its three components (turnover, variable costs, hours) each month, to continuously groom and act on the six families of dysfunctions (working conditions, work organization, communication-coordination-cooperation, time management, integrated training, and strategic implementation). The progression or regression of the HCVAVC provides information on the creation

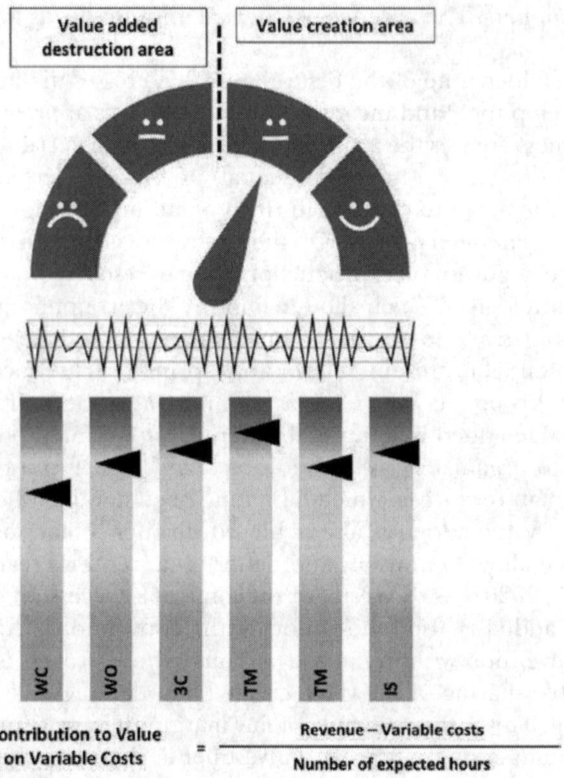

Figure 86.1 Socio-economic performance gauge. Figure created by authors and adapted from excerpts of images in the following site: "Manager attitude," Guillermou, 2017; https//images.app.goo.gl, https://www.f-legrand.f

or destruction of value. The objective is to chart a course with the organization's stakeholders so that they contribute positively to the creation of value added.

Socio-economic performance is thus conditioned by socio-economic innovation actions on these six variables (Figure 86.1). A mirage of increased socio-economic performance can arise, for example, from an increase in the HCVAVC following non-socio-economic actions, such as the abrupt cessation of training activities or the reduction of communication-coordination-cooperation times, which are apparently aimed at saving time, but which are likely to generate new dysfunctions. The mirage consists in believing in a positive result, which is temporary because it will unfortunately deteriorate in the following months or year.

The HCVAVC makes it possible to monitor overall economic performance by relying on three levers to increase its level:

- Increase sales by developing products and services and by better controlling the sales margin.
- Reduce or stabilize variable costs by reducing the cost of purchasing materials, equipment, and other items (without seeking the lowest costs at all costs, which are often synonymous with hidden costs due to the boomerang effect), by repatriating subcontracting or by reducing the quantities consumed, by producing less waste for example.
- Reduce the number of hours worked hours[2] and review their allocation: analyze the distribution of hours between dysfunctional hours, orthofunctional hours that create

immediate results and those that create potential. Action on the control of hours worked takes different concrete forms: reducing temporary contracts and the use of temporary staff, reducing overtime and additional hours, not replacing an employee who leaves in the same way, etc.

The value of human working time calculated with the HCVAVC is more relevant than the sole salary cost of human working time, traditionally used in management control. Indeed, it also includes the structural costs necessary for the staff to carry out its activity, as well as a share of the result. The HCVAVC (e.g., 30€) thus represents the average value of an hour of work and not its average cost. A person who works one hour produces a value added of 30€, which allows him to cover his salary costs, a share of the structural costs and to generate a share of the profit. If he loses one hour to regulate a dysfunction, it is as much value added lost.

Moreover, it is possible to calculate different values of HCVAVC. For example, if the company invests heavily in training its staff, the hours dedicated to creating potential will be greater, without the value added increasing. We can then recalculate a HCVAVC excluding these hours of potential creation, to check whether the HCVAVC excluding investment in training has improved. In this case, we suggest that certain principles of accounting[3] information be applied (principles of prudence, materiality, and good information) and that the practice of amortizing intangible investments be used to avoid erroneous interpretations. Indeed, the future of the company depends on a regular maintenance of hours of potential creation, a real-life insurance of the company.

In summary, the HCVAVC is a synthetic indicator for measuring the creation of value added, which allows the company to manage its real available resources. The interpretation of the evolution of the HCVAVC (growth, decline, stability) allows management and governance to prepare decisions. As an illustration, Table 86.1 presents some of our results on the evolution of the CHVAV in three companies from different sectors of activity (Ennajem M., 2020).

The three companies have conducted a socio-economic transformation project (diagnosis, improvement project, implementation, and evaluation), which has led to an increase in CHVAV, thanks to better management of human work time, with profound organizational changes, accompanied by material and especially intangible investments (new equipment, new plant, integrated training, new communication-coordination-cooperation system, etc.). These companies have improved their operating results (gains in productivity, efficiency, competitiveness, profitability) but also the creation of potential: development of skills and capitalization on the know-how of management and staff. The economic steering via the

TABLE 86.1 Creation of Socio-Economic Value Added in Three Companies

Case n°1	Case n°2	Case n°3
Industrial company of the construction and fitting out of emergency vehicles Case	Hybrid network of breweries-restaurants and musical events	IT consulting company
• Two sites (A & B) • Workforce: 183 people	• 11 sites • 157 employees	• 4 agencies • 57 employees
Sales : € 30.7 M	Sales : € 15 M	Sales : € 4.4 M
HCVAVC evolution (N to N + 2): + 25%	HCVAVC evolution (N to N + 4): + 14.7%	HCVAVC evolution (N to N + 3): + 5.9%
Conversion of hidden costs: 60%	76%	67%

(continued)

TABLE 86.1 Creation of Socio-Economic Value Added in Three Companies (cont.)

Case n°1	Case n°2	Case n°3
Organizational value added		
• Clarification of the roles and responsibilities of the actors at both sites. • Reorganization of product lines. • Unification of accounting. • Improvement of team synchronization and cohesion. • Professionalization of relations between teams. • Use of management charts and indicators. • Respect for internal and external commitments (production and delivery deadlines, etc.)	• Development of the role of the manager: teams of less than ten people • Delegation, autonomy, and empowerment of individuals. • Overhaul of accounting and control processes. • Professionalization of human resources management. • Matching staffing levels to workload. • Use of piloting logbooks, resolution sheets, planning-programming methods	• Sharing of skills between internal resources and external providers (for software development). • Encouragement of versatility and cross-functional cooperation. • Involvement and participation of technical experts in sales processes. • Structuring of communication systems. • Better management of trade-offs and priorities. • Activity management: scheduling sheets per operation, programming, piloting logbooks)
Social value added		
• Material investments: computers, air conditioning… • Integrated training: management of on-board electrical systems, forklift operator's license • Increase in skills and qualifications • Enrichment of tasks, concerted delegation. • Balance between permanent and temporary staff. • "Win/win" objective contracts. • Participation and profit-sharing	• Improvement of physical working conditions. • Integrated training actions to develop skills • Involvement of management in steering training with competency grids. • More attractive social and remuneration policies: profit-sharing, PNAC bonus	• Improvement of physical working conditions (headquarters and agencies) • Continuous improvement of skills through the formalization of integrated training manuals • Common integration program for all employees • Capitalization of know-how • Better distribution of tasks and workload • Attractive social and remuneration policies.
Economic and financial value added		
• Consolidation of the group's reputation. • Internalization of R&D. • Sales growth: alliance strategy, new partnership agreements… • Stop internal competition between the two sites to curb contract losses. • Reduction of quality defects in assembly, welding, finishing, parts quality, incomplete files • Reduction of absenteeism and work accidents (prevention and training) • Cost-value management of activities.	• Consolidation of the external image • Public–private partnerships • Opening of new stores • More listings in large and medium-sized stores • Major production investments: new factory, bottling tank, distillery. • Innovations in the product-services offer. • Reduction of unscheduled absences. • Cost-value management of activities	• Structuring of the offer in products/services • Better management of subcontractors (choice, quality, cost, deadlines). • Decentralized management control (combined management of hours, activities, and profitability of operations).

Source: Ennajem, 2020

HCVAVC shows that human resources play an active role in the creation of organizational, social, economic, and financial value added (Table 86.1).

The growth of the HCVAVC reflects an improvement in competitiveness and productivity and confirms that a part of the hidden costs has indeed been converted into visible performance.

CONCLUSION

The HCVAVC concept-tool helps to raise the company's awareness of wealth creation and to show each actor the way to positively participate in a process of improving the company's overall productivity. The reference to this concept is also useful to materialize the economic value of human time. Indeed, the measurement of this indicator and its coupling to the six areas of dysfunction helps to think about alternative choices to manage the working hours of the actors, and especially their decomposition to analyze their impacts on the creation of value added. The HCVAVC allows us to look at the what, but more at the how (Goethe's quote from his Faust): of course, the coordination mechanisms help to define the common "what," but also to formalize the "how," the steps and the concrete actions to be taken to reduce dysfunctions, which are a source of visible or hidden performance loss.

NOTES

1. Book value-added (calculated from the sales margin) = Sales margin + Production – External consumption (consumption during the year from third parties)
2. The Multipurpose Activity Sheets (MAS) system, which originated in socio-economic management control, makes it possible, based on the principle of self-declaration, to become aware of and quantify the time spent on each activity (to quantify the hourly volume of a project, to share and distribute time resources between two partners, etc.). (Savall and Zardet, 2008).
3. Ten fundamental principles govern accounting in France. They are defined by the French Commercial Code: going concern, independence of financial years (...), prudence, materiality, good information.

REFERENCES

Emery, F., Trist, E. (1969) *Socio-technical systems,* In *Emery Systems Thinking.* Penguin.

Ennajem, C. (2011). Évolution du rôle du contrôleur de gestion dans un contexte de contrôle de gestion décentralisé. Thèse de doctorat en Sciences de Gestion, Conservatoire National des Arts et Métiers, Paris.

Ennajem, M. (2020). *Le pilotage de la création et de la répartition de la valeur ajoutée dans les systèmes de coopération inter-organisationnelle.* Thèse de doctorat en Science de Gestion, Conservatoire national des Arts et Métiers, Paris.

Martory B. (2009). *Le contrôle de gestion sociale.* Vuibert.

CHAPTER 87

ANALYSIS OF THE SOCIO-ECONOMIC RISKS OF ORGANIZATIONS

A Current Vision

Francisco Javier Quesada Sánchez and Mª Ángela Jiménez Montañés

ABSTRACT

At present, organizations are linked to and subjected to a set of changes and threats that condition their socioeconomic behavior. This set of threats translates into business risks, which must be identified and assessed in order to mitigate the negative effects they can have on the economic and social performance of organizations. This chapter presents and analyzes the importance of the study of risks at present and their management, under the perspective of the COSO Model and the ISO 31000 Standard, considering the different classifications of risks that can and should be identified. Finally, we conclude with a brief description of the risks that should be identified in the audit activity, applying the Risk Model identified in the International Standard on Auditing ISA-ES 315.

At the present time, organizations are linked and subjected to a set of changes and threats that condition their socioeconomic behavior. This set of threats translates into business risks, which must be identified and assessed in order to mitigate the negative effects they can have on the economic and social performance of organizations.

This chapter presents and analyzes the importance of the study of risks at the present time and their management, under the perspective of the COSO Model and the ISO 13000 Standard, considering the different risk classifications that must be identified.

Finally, we conclude with a brief description of the risks that should be identified in the activity of auditing accounts, applying the Risk Model identified in the International Standard on Auditing ISA-ES 315.

SEAM Treatise, pages 715–720

1 BUSINESS RISK AND ITS CURRENT MANAGEMENT

The concept of risk is closely linked to uncertainty, which implies that all business activity assumes a risk. In the changing economic situation in which we find ourselves, entities have assumed the need for adequate risk management, in order to become "risk-smart companies", which must define three levels of responsibility in risk management: a) responsibility for risk governance, b) responsibility for the structure and management of risk and c) responsibility for risk ownership, including the measurement, identification and monitoring of the different types of business risks (Deloitte, 2010).

Within the risk analysis it is necessary to identify the degradation impact that the risk may affect an asset, which can be expressed as a percentage; it is the materiality of a threat and the probability of occurrence of an event, occurrence or event that may affect the organization's assets. The level of risk can be calculated by multiplying the impact by the probability and as a function of the event, probability and impact (Cormican, 2014). This valuation involves determining the cost derived from the value of the affected assets considering, in addition, the damage produced on the asset (personal injury, financial loss, service interruption, loss of image and reputation and decrease in performance). The level of risk will make it possible to establish the risk threshold, i.e., the maximum level of risk that the company is willing to bear. The study of costs linked to the level of risk is related to the theory of hidden costs, which are those that are neither identified, nor quantified, nor controlled in the company's traditional financial statements nor in budgetary control (Savall, 1974, 1979; Savall et Zardet, 1987; Savall, Zardet, Bonnet, 2000).

A relevant variable in the study of business risk is the cost of prevention or the cost of risk protection. This cost can be considered as the cost borne by companies in order to keep the level of risk below the risk threshold. In this way, the break-even point or equilibrium cost can be quantified at the cut-off point of the protection cost curve and the risks borne. Below this point, risks will be kept below the established threshold.

In order to keep risks below the risk threshold, it is necessary to carry out an adequate "Risk Management": Enterprise Risk Management, also known as ERM (Enterprise Risk Management) in the 21st century. It is an inherent and critical activity for any organization, although risk systems must be integrated with the strategy, decision making and culture of organizations (PwC, 2014).

Risk management and internal control are closely linked. The risk management framework most widely accepted by professionals is the COSO Model, which emerged in 1995, edited by the Committee of Sponsoring Organizations of the Treadway, made up of representatives of five private sector organizations in the United States. It was created with the mission of creating and providing knowledge on three major topics related to enterprise risk management, internal control and the fight against fraud. This first model has evolved over the years is now called COSO III or "COSO Enterprise Risk Management–Integrating with Strategy and Performance" (COSO, 2017). This report highlights the importance of enterprise risk management in strategic planning and its integration at all levels of the organization, as risk influences and aligns strategy and performance across all departments and functions and therefore improves the company's value chain.

On the other hand, it is relevant the management model proposed by the ISO 31000 Standard, published in 2019, a non-certifiable standard that provides methodology, principles and guidelines for business risk performance. It can be applied to any type of entity. It establishes that risk management incorporates all those coordinated actions to direct and control the risks to which organizations may be exposed. Management has to do, above all, with the quantification of risks, for which it is essential to define two elements within this process, which are consequence and probability.

This standard considers that the advantages of the application of risk management are: Improve the identification of opportunities and threats; Optimize business management; Increase confidence in stakeholders; Establish a basis for decision making; Improve controls and follow-up and monitoring methods; Optimize incident prevention and management; Minimize losses associated with business processes; Encourage organizational learning at all levels.

The COSO CSR framework notes that Corporate Governance, including sound oversight, is a prerequisite for effectively identifying, assessing and addressing the full spectrum of enterprise risks. Therefore, incorporating CSR-related risks into a company's governance structure and processes is critical to overcoming the challenges many companies face in managing these risks (COSO & Wbcsd, 2018).

2 TYPES OF ORGANIZATIONAL RISKS

Business risks can be classified from different points of view, and there is no single criterion. The classification of risks depends on the organizations' own characteristics (Rodriguez, Piñeiro, & De Llano, 2013). There are several organizations and professionals and academics who have established risk classification, although we consider that the following categories can be established:

2.1 According to Operations

Operational Risks: derived from the activity itself carried out by the company related to the operating cycle and which are reflected in the Income Statement.

Extra-operational Risks: derived from the possible risks assumed from the rest of the operations.

2.2 According to Business Activities (ISO, 2018)

Systematic Risk: Refers to those risks that are present in an economic system or in a market as a whole. Their consequences can affect the entire business network, as is the case, for example, with large-scale economic crises from which no company can escape. They can also be caused by accidents, wars or natural disasters.

Non-systematic risk: These are risks arising from the financial and administrative management of each company. In other words, in this case it is a specific company that fails and not the market or business scenario as a whole. They vary according to each type of activity and each case, as does the way in which they are managed.

2.3 According to their Nature (ISO, 2018)

Financial risks: they are all those related to movements, transactions and other elements that have an influence on business finances: investment, diversification, expansion, financing. They arise from fluctuations in financial variables that affect the organization's result.

They arise from the volatility of financial markets and the complexity of financial instruments. Within this type of risk, the following can be identified:

- Market risk related to fluctuations in the price conditions of the markets where the company operates. The comprises the influence of multiple external factors related to the behavior of sales prices, costs and availability of resources; the influence that certain general variables of a macroeconomic nature, such as interest rates or exchange rates, may exert on the company's financial and operating variables could also be considered (Rodriguez, Piñeiro, & De Llano, 2013).
- Credit risk derived from non-compliance with payment obligations binding the company's customers, suppliers or partners. Within this, default risk, migration risk, exposure risk and collateral risk can be differentiated.
- Liquidity risk: this type of risk refers to the uncertainty associated with the return on an investment in order to obtain the liquidity of the investment. It can be considered as the capacity of a company to sell its assets in cash immediately without incurring losses.

Economic risks: in general terms, economic risks include all those that affect the company's economic activity, both internal and external. Economic risks affect decisions related to the company's profits. This type of risk derives from actions linked to the company's internal policy, product and service distribution policy, the emergence of new competitors or changes in consumer trends. Operational risks can be included, which affect processes, people, systems and the company's value generation. Examples include internal fraud, external fraud, poor employment and occupational safety practices, inadequate practices with customers, products or business, damage to physical assets, failures in the execution of systems, cost reduction processes and talent management (Ernst & Young, 2011).

Strategic risks: they arise as a consequence of the fulfillment of the organization's strategic objectives. Among them, extreme margin reduction, changes in technology, brand erosion, aggressive competitor, failure of a new project, market stagnation can be highlighted (Slywotzky & Drzik, 2015).

Legal or compliance risks: they refer to compliance with certain legal and regulatory environment. They derive from factors such as convergence of regulations and global standards, complex business models, greater efficiencies caused by market deceleration, increased stakeholder expectations, increased criminalization of offenses. They are considered as the basis of the Ethics and Compliance Program and Work Plan of the organizations (Deloitte, 2015).

2.4 Corporate Social Responsibility Risks

These are the environmental, social and corporate governance risks, known as ESG risks, which influence the profitability, success and survival of organizations. The definitions of these are shown in Table 87.1 (COSO & Wbcsd, 2018).

3 BUSINESS RISKS FROM THE AUDIT PERSPECTIVE

The audit of the Financial Statements is the last phase of the accounting process, the purpose of which is the supervision of the same by an independent professional. It is considered as the accumulation and evaluation of evidence, based on a set of qualitative, quantitative and

TABLE 87.1 Definitions of Corporate Social Responsibility Risks

Types of risks	Components	Definition
Environmental risk	Climate change, natural resources, pollution and waste, and environmental opportunities	The effect that an entity's actions have on climate change in terms of greenhouse gas emissions, in addition to waste management and energy efficiency. Given the renewed efforts to combat global warming, aspects such as emissions cuts and decarbonization have become more relevant.
Social risk	Human capital, civil responsibility, stakeholder opposition and social opportunities	Human rights, labor standards in the supply chain, any exposure to illegal child labor and more routine issues such as, for example, respect for workplace health and safety standards. A social rating also arises when a company that is well integrated into its community has a "social license" to operate with consent.
Corporate governance risks	Governance and corporate behavior	A set of rules or principles that define rights, responsibilities and expectations among various stakeholders in the governance of corporations. A well-defined corporate governance system can be used to balance or align interests among stakeholders and can serve as a tool to support a company's long-term strategy.

Source: COSO & Wbcsd, 2018

analytical information that allows analyzing the correspondence between the information presented in the financial statements and the mandatory accounting principles and standards.

In the audit process, a selective analysis of the company's activity is carried out: organic, functional and economic-financial (Trigueros & (coord.), 2020, p. 11). It constitutes an element of protection of the legitimate interests of all its users: shareholders, investors, creditors, workers, analysts or the state and guarantees the transparency of the information derived to the stakeholders. It not only verifies the data provided by the accounting balances, but also issues an opinion, using generally accepted auditing techniques.

To facilitate the planning and execution of audit work, auditors use a Risk Model. This model should provide a link between the procedures performed and the opinion issued by the auditor. Audit Risk is the risk that the Auditor may issue a favorable opinion on significantly incorrect Financial Statements. This may occur in the event that the Financial Statements are materially incorrect and also the Auditor, during its examination, fails to detect errors.

The audit risk model is contained in ISA-ES 315 (Instituto de Contabilidad y Auditoria de Cuentas (ICAC)), which deals with the identification and assessment of the risks of material misstatement in the financial statements through knowledge of the entity, its environment and its internal control.

This standard is considered the basic pillar for the development of the audit activity. The auditor's objective is to identify and assess the risks of material misstatement due to fraud or error in the financial statements and in the assertions contained therein. The risks of material misstatement in the financial statements refer to risks that relate generally to the financial statements as a whole and potentially affect various assertions. They may arise from deficient internal control. Also, the auditor's knowledge of internal control may cause him to have reservations about the integrity of management and the reliability of records.

CONCLUSION

This final risk of the Statutory Auditor is a combination of several different risks:

1. *Inherent risk*: constituted by the possibility inherent in the activity of the entity that there are errors of importance in the accounting process, from which the Annual

Accounts are obtained. These are errors arising from the complexity of the operations, lack of expertise, inexperience or lack of attention of the personnel, etc.

2. *Internal control risk*: the possibility that these significant errors in the accounting were not detected by the entity's internal control systems.
3. *Analysis and substantive sampling risk:* consisting of the possibility that any material misstatement that exists and has not been brought to the attention of the internal control system would not be detected by the application of appropriate audit tests.
4. *Detection risk (ISA-ES 200, A.42 to A. 44):* depends on the auditor's work. It is related to the nature, timing and extent of the audit procedures. It is determined based on the audit procedures and their application by the auditor, depending on proper planning, staffing of the work team, application of professional skepticism and supervision of the audit work.

REFERENCES

Cormican, K. (2014). Integrated enterprise risk management: From process to best practice. *Modern Economy, 5*(4), 401–413. doi: http://dx.doi.org/10.4236/me.2014.54039

COSO. (June 2017). https://www.coso.org/Documents/2017-COSO-ERM-Integrating-with-Strategy-and-Performance-Executive-Summary.pdf. Retrieved October 17, 2020.

COSO, & Wbcsd. (2018). https://www.coso.org/Documents/COSO-WBCSD-Release-New-Draft-Guidance-Online-viewing.pdf. Retrieved September 23, 2020.

Deloitte.(2010). Retrieved September 2, 2020 from https://www2.deloitte.com/content/dam/Deloitte/co/Documents/risk/RiskIntelligence/Risk%20Management%20of%20the%20risk%20(2).pdf.

Deloitte (April29,2015).RetrievedNovember16,2020,fromhttps://www2.deloitte.com/content/dam/Deloitte/co/Documents/risk/PresentacionEvaluacion%20de%20RiesgosdeCumplimiento%20(April%2029_2015)Clients.pdf.

Ernst & Young.(2011). Retrieved November 16, 2020, from https://riskandopportunities.files.wordpress.com/2014/11/los_nuevos_riesgos_en_los_negocios.pdf

Instituto de Contabilidad y Auditoria de Cuentas (ICAC). (n.d.). Instituto de Contabilidad y Auditoria de Cuentas (ICAC). Retrieved November 27, 2020, from http://www.icac.meh.es/NIAS/NIA%20315%20p%20def.pdf

ISO. (2018). https://www.iso.org/obp/ui#iso:std:iso:14001:ed-3:v1:es. Retrieved November 23, 2020.

ISO. (2018). https://www.iso.org/obp/ui#iso:std:iso:31000:ed-2:v1:es. Retrieved October 26, 2020.

PwC. (2014). https://www.pwc.es/es/publicaciones/gestion-empresarial/assets/temas-candentes-gestion-riesgos-empresas-espanolas.pdf. Retrieved October 21, 2020

Rodriguez , M., Piñeiro, C., & De Llano, P. (2013). Risk Mapping: Identifying and Managing Risks. *Atlantic Review of Economics, 2*, 1–29. Retrieved September 15, 2020

Slywotzky, A., & Drzik, J. (May 2015). Countering the Biggest Risk of All. *Harvard Business Review, 83*(4), 78–88. Retrieved November 17, 2020, from https://www.researchgate.net/publication/7929215_Countering_the_biggest_risk_of_all

Trigueros, J. A., & (coord.), D. A. (2020). Audit. Includes the Draft of the new LAC Regulation. Madrid: Francis Lefebvre.

CHAPTER 88

COST CALCULATION, MANAGEMENT INDICATORS, "BUSINESS INTELLIGENCE" AND "BUSINESS ANALYTICS" FOR URBAN AND METROPOLITAN TRANSPORT SERVICES

Daniel Carrasco and Daniel Sánchez Toledano

ABSTRACT

Nowadays, companies and organizations have at their disposal a wide range of transversal technological possibilities, which constitute an opportunity to improve their management. Our study is oriented to the analysis of the information systems and the exploitation of the data of a public transport company, on the totality of the global dimensional matrix of the organization, for the definition of management indicators and scorecards, which allow the generation of adequate information to know the reality of the organization and to support the decision-making processes at different levels of responsibility.

In today's world, organizations are increasingly becoming complex realities in which the various institutional actors that make up the organization or its environment coexist in a system whose success depends on their ability to align different interests with a common objective.

Thus, issues related to the strategic definition of its business model, the development of its operations, the organization of its personnel, the management of its assets, the configuration

SEAM Treatise, pages 721–729

of its products and services, and its customer service, constitute the dimensional axes on which its management matrix is configured and which define its success or failure.

There are many issues to be addressed when dealing with the problems presented above: on the one hand, those linked to the orientation of innovation, R&D&I[1] and sustainability strategies and models, in their multiple aspects (environmental, financial and social, etc.); on the other hand, those relating to the implementation of these strategies in specific investment, quality, marketing and sales, logistics and supply chain, financial management, risk management and management control policies.

In addition, organizations are currently operating in a technological ecosystem that requires them to articulate policies to develop their activities through ICT tools (Information and Communication Technologies) and Artificial Intelligence, also taking into account their cybersecurity, as a critical element to operate safely and protect their external and internal agents.

Indeed, companies and organizations have a wide range of technological possibilities (machine learning, IoT, Big Data, Blockchain, Robotics, etc.) of a transversal nature, which pose a future radically different from that of past decades and which constitutes a real challenge for their managers and for the social researcher.

However, although much of the debate is focusing on the technological level, we cannot forget that people are at the center of the issue, since they are not only the ultimate raison d'être of the existence of any organization, but also the key element that, at all levels, determines its success or failure.

Therefore, we cannot forget key aspects such as change management and knowledge management or the codes of ethics and good governance, as well as transparency, as key elements of the Social Contract of the Entity with its internal agents and with the Community. Thus, the scenario described above contains a whole organizational universe that defines a wide field of interest for both the professional manager and the social researcher, as mentioned above.

It is within this framework of ideas that our study proposal finds support, focused on the overall analysis of the management dimensions, from the plane of research related to the disciplines linked to the analysis of information systems and the exploitation of data, in order to improve the knowledge of organizations.

For this purpose, we try to conceptualize and describe the main tools linked to this purpose.

From the calculation of costs, revenues and margins at all levels and for the entire overall dimensional matrix of the organization (cost of consumption, centers, agents, activities and processes, products, etc.) to the definition of management indicators and scorecards, through the development and implementation of "Business Intelligence" or Institutional Intelligence tools, as the first aspect of the phenomenon.

Indeed, the first aspect is to generate adequate information to know the reality of the organization and support the decision-making processes at different levels of responsibility (top management, middle management, operational management) and to comply with the obligations of accountability to society.

But there is a second aspect linked to this reality that starts from the first one. Once we have the information and the appropriate architecture of the databases that support it, it is necessary to analyze its content and exploit it to generate knowledge and improve the organizational dysfunctions and inefficiencies that are generated in organizations.

In this field, techniques linked to data mining, big data and predictive analytics that allow the detection and recycling of hidden costs into value added (Savall, 1974, 1979; Savall and Zardet, 1987; Savall, Zardet and Bonnet, 2000) are becoming increasingly important.

and the identification of business opportunities, as well as the subsequent organizational reengineering processes that enable the overcoming of dysfunctions, the enhancement of revenues and the exploitation of strengths and, consequently, the promotion of competitiveness, continuous improvement and business and organizational success.

Examples of improvements introduced by such tools include, among others, the implementation of fuel saving policies, vehicle preventive maintenance planning, determination of the optimal fleet renewal point, review of the vehicle acquisition policy based on the comparative analysis of makes and models, or review of human factor management to improve staff absenteeism.

1 PERSPECTIVES AND EVOLUTION OF MANAGEMENT TOOLS IN ICT ENVIRONMENTS IN THE FIELD OF PUBLIC TRANSPORT

In accordance with the approach outlined in the previous lines, it is necessary to approach the conceptualization and description of the theoretical tools described above and to propose a sectoral case study to illustrate an example of the application of the referential theoretical framework.

In this field, we have chosen the case of urban and metropolitan public transport and the public or private companies that operate as concessionaires of this service. Our choice is motivated by the fact that within this framework, there is a great potential for the application of the techniques described above, especially due to the growth and importance of the sector and the remarkable technological development it is experiencing: geolocation of vehicles, generation of intelligent transport networks, development of Smart-cities, development of multimodality, concern for sustainable mobility.... This circumstance, together with our experience in the implementation of analytical management systems in the sector, justifies its choice as a case study.

Within our theoretical framework and from the point of view of the disciplines linked to analytical and management accounting information systems, there has been a remarkable evolution from the first practices existing before and after the industrial revolution, oriented by a machine and Taylorist vision, to those defining management today.

In this context, the existential crisis experienced in the discipline due to the social and economic changes of the last decades of the 20th century and materialized at the dawn of our century by a technological, social and industrial revolution, places us in a radically different environment.

Aspects such as globalization, micro-segmentation of customers and markets, the generalization of uncertainty environments, the explosion and development of Information and Communication Technologies (ICT), the Internet of Things (IoT) and Industry 4.0, virtual reality or Artificial Intelligence (AI) have made it clear that it is necessary to develop new tools and a new language in the field of organizational management.

We are at a critical moment in the human relationship with business, which is manifested in enlightening data such as those formulated by the McKinsey consulting firm's report (Chinn, 2020), which predicts that, in the European Union alone, 59 million jobs (26% of the total) are at risk of disappearing, or the conclusions of the 2019 Davos Forum, which estimate that 65% of today's children will work in professions that do not yet exist today. These are predictions that are necessarily linked to a rethinking of educational systems and employee training processes in companies and, as discussed, their alignment with management systems.

From the point of view of our analysis, we are experiencing an evolution that we could summarize under four main headings:

- Formulation of models and calculation tools and accounting management and economic-financial management. The classical development of the discipline has allowed the formulation of various management tools: standards, inventory valuation, cost/volume/profit analysis, program budgets and zero-based budgets, performance measurement systems, incentive models, etc., which are widely used by managers of organizations and much discussed in the academic literature.
- Development of integrated information systems. As indicated above, ICT technological developments have enabled the integration of management systems, making possible the generalization of Enterprise Resource Planning (ERP) systems as key elements for achieving decisive advances in scientific and professionalized data-based management.
- Implementation of "Business Intelligence" (BI) tools. The aforementioned generalization of ERP's and ICT has allowed and forced the implementation of Discovery Data tools, which facilitate the exploitation of the growing volumes of information generated and its articulation on multiple dimensional axes oriented to decision making.
- Development and implementation of Business Analytics (BA) solutions and techniques. The next stage of the described process is the exploitation of information for scientific management based on data, through the generalization of the use of algorithms, data mining techniques, predictive analytics and big data.
- Development of Artificial Intelligence (AI) tools. The next stage is linked to the advance of autonomous systems that introduce rational thinking and acting capabilities, and these are techniques that are already being developed and applied to a greater or lesser extent in many fields of activity (medicine, engineering, economics, transportation, etc.).

In fact, and with respect to the scope of our case study, there are very advanced developments in different fields such as the design of intelligent transportation networks or the promotion of autonomous vehicles.

2 IMPLEMENTATION OF AN ANALYTICAL ACCOUNTING MODEL AND BUSINESS INTELLIGENCE TOOLS IN A PUBLIC TRANSPORT COMPANY

Nowadays, urban and metropolitan transport plays an essential role in the economic and social structuring of cities and population centers all over the world, acquiring a critical relevance the organization of models that make possible an adequate framework that guarantees the fluidity, economy, universality and sustainability of the displacements of its inhabitants, through an adequate combination of the different existing means of public and private transport.

For public authorities, it is essential to organize mechanisms for the provision of this service in any of its forms of management, taking into account the achievement of adequate levels of efficiency and sustainability, which are determined and conditioned by factors such as population density, orography, urban planning, spatial layout, etc. For this reason, transport operators' managers must develop tools to promote these objectives. Autonomous vehicles, geolocation, Smart-cities, sensorization, intelligent transport networks, alternative fuels, user support Apps (transfers, lines, timetables, etc.), cell phone payment, are examples of the many advances that are being applied to improve a service of a nuclear nature, for the maintenance of our economic and social model, and its sustainability in the face of challenges such as climate change.

We present below a case of implementation of an analytical accounting model and "Business Intelligence" for a public public transport company. Transportes Interurbanos de Tenerife S.A.U. (TITSA) is a public limited company of the Cabildo Insular de Tenerife, which throughout its 30 years of evolution and history, has become a benchmark in public passenger transport at national level. The main activity developed by TITSA is the provision of collective public transport services of passengers by bus on the island of Tenerife, which is part of the archipelago of the Canary Islands.

TITSA is the main public transport operator in Tenerife and manages the bus stations of La Laguna, La Orotava, Puerto de la Cruz, Buenavista del Norte, Guía de Isora, Adeje, Granadilla de Abona, Güímar, Candelaria, and the Santa Cruz interchange, as well as the garages and depots of La Orotava, La Laguna, Santa María del Mar, among others. It offers urban services in the capital of Tenerife, Santa Cruz, in La Laguna, Los Realejos and in Guía Isora, La Orotava, Los Realejos and Arona, as well as interurban, school and occasional transport services. TITSA buses provide service 365 days a year, 24 hours a day, with a network of approximately 3,700 stops distributed throughout the island territory, providing service with a network of 160 lines, more than 500 vehicles, more than 33 million passengers and more than 35 million kilometers traveled per year, with a staff of 1,724 professionals, of which 1,381 employees are drivers.

The company decided to undertake this project both to guarantee compliance with the law and its reporting obligations, and to modernize and improve its management in many ways: generating quality information for decision making, improving the basic information for setting prices and fares, increasing the company's transparency, favoring internal and external benchmarking, contributing to improve the financial sustainability of the service, etc.

To this end, the first step was an analysis and diagnosis of its information systems, defining the appropriate data integration strategy for the scope of the project, after which it was possible to define the analytical model, the set of selected scorecards and management

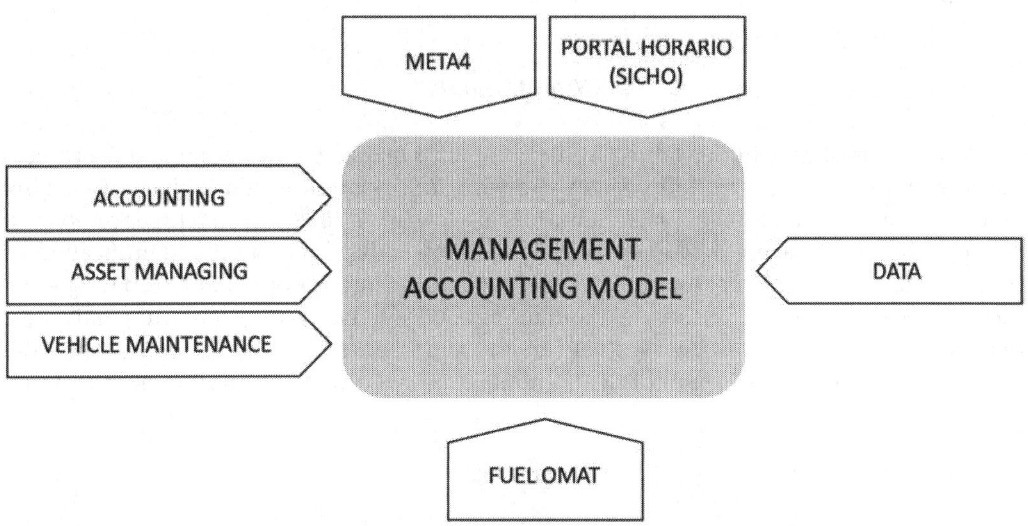

Figure 88.1 Integration of management systems. *Source:* Own elaboration.

indicators, and the implementation and integration of the computer system, with a project duration of 10 months.

The following groups of tools were used to build the structure of the dashboards that configured the BI tool:

- Dynamic tables for the numerical exploitation of the different dimensional variables defined in the model[2] (cost elements, centers, vehicles [make-model, fuel type, . . .], lines, service kilometers, passengers transported, workshop hours, driver hours, etc.; see example of cost table by type of line in Figure 88.2).
- Bar charts for the schematic exploitation of the different dimensional variables defined in the model (cost elements, centers, vehicles [make-model, fuel type, . . .], lines, service kilometers, passengers transported, workshop hours, driver hours, etc.; see Figure 88.2).
- Percentage distribution graphs of the different dimensional variables defined in the model (cost elements, centers, vehicles [make-model, fuel type, . . .], lines, service kilometers, passengers transported, workshop hours, driver hours, etc.; see Figure 88.2).
- Scatter plots of the different dimensional variables defined in the model (cost elements, centers, vehicles [make-model, fuel type, . . .], lines, service kilometers, passengers transported, workshop hours, driver hours, etc.; see Figure 88.3).
- Information exploitation graphs to identify the entities that exceed certain levels of dispersion in relation to the different dimensional variables defined in the model (cost elements, centers, vehicles [make-model, fuel type, . . .], lines, service kilometers, passengers transported, workshop hours, driver hours, etc.; see example of table of dispersion of costs/km by type of vehicle model—outliers—in Figure 88.4).
- Batteries of key performance indicators (KPIs) of the basic analytical axes of management (personnel costs, service lines, passengers transported, kilometers traveled, etc.; see example of table of KPIs of costs, revenues and margins per passenger and kilometer in Figure 88.5).

CONCLUSION

This is a successful case, highly valued by the company's management insofar as it is a project that has enabled the generation of highly valuable information to guide decision-making and improve the operator's management. It is also a critical first step for the development of predictive analytics, big data and data mining models that facilitate the identification of trends, anomalies, hidden costs, etc. and enable the continuous improvement of the public service in multiple facets: fuel savings, containment of pollutant and greenhouse emissions, improvement of traffic congestion, fleet renewal and maintenance policy through the determination of the optimal point of fleet renewal or preventive maintenance interventions.

NOTES

1. Research, Development, and Innovation.
2. Such tables and graphs provide for the dynamic and evolutionary presentation of data by periods to allow temporal comparisons of the information.

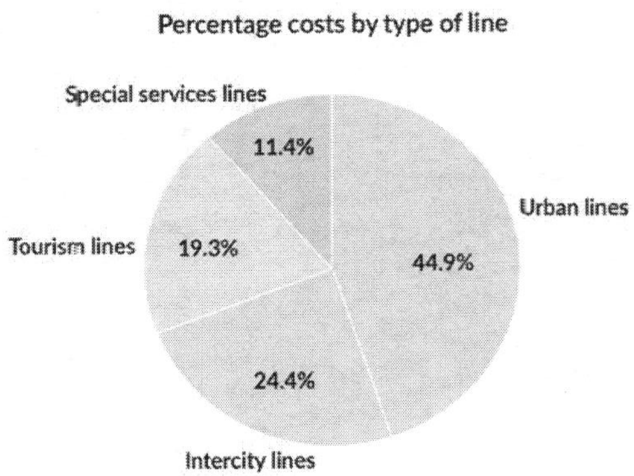

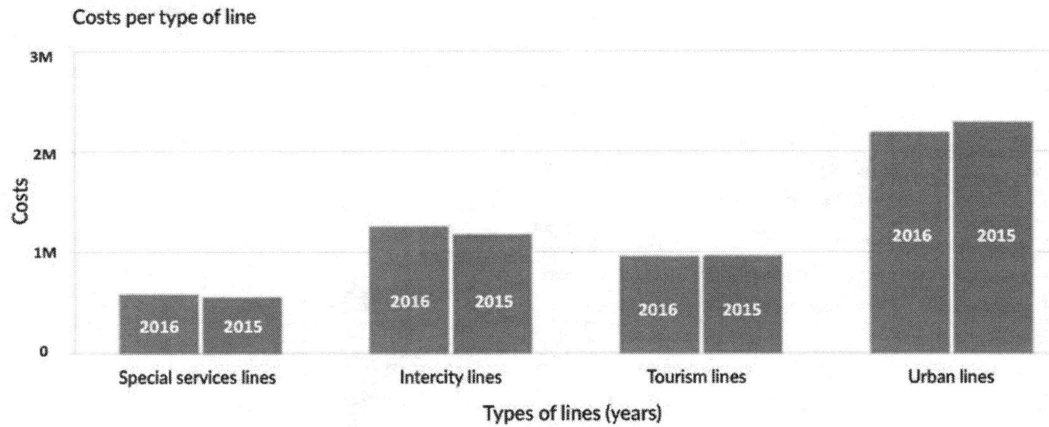

Types of lines	Cost	Number of travels	Cost/travel	Kilometers	Cost/km
Special service lines	€ 1,141670.35	872,416	€ 1.31	843,719	€ 1.35
Intercity lines	€2,439,999.75	1,901,319	€ 1.28	1,806,521	€ 1.35
Touristic lines	€1,023,736.29	1,495,905	€ 1.29	1,421,068	€ 1.35
Urban lines	€4,477,205.66	3,496,167	€ 1.28	3,293,931	€ 1.36

Figure 88.2 Cost scorecard by type of line. *Source:* Own preparation.

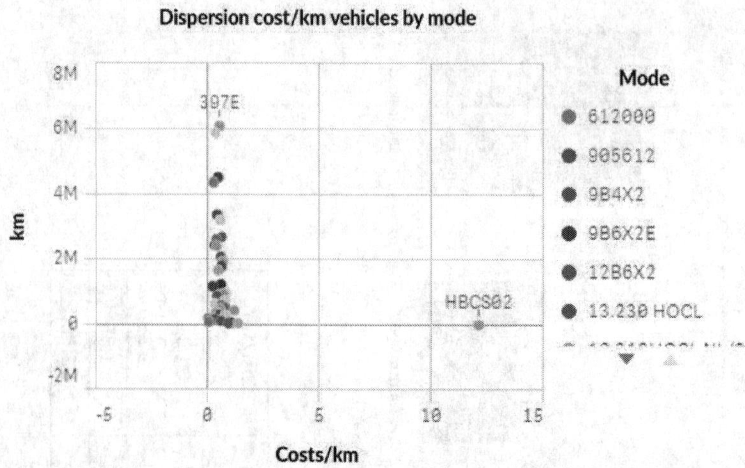

Figure 88.3 Scorecard of cost/km dispersion by vehicle model. *Source:* Own elaboration.

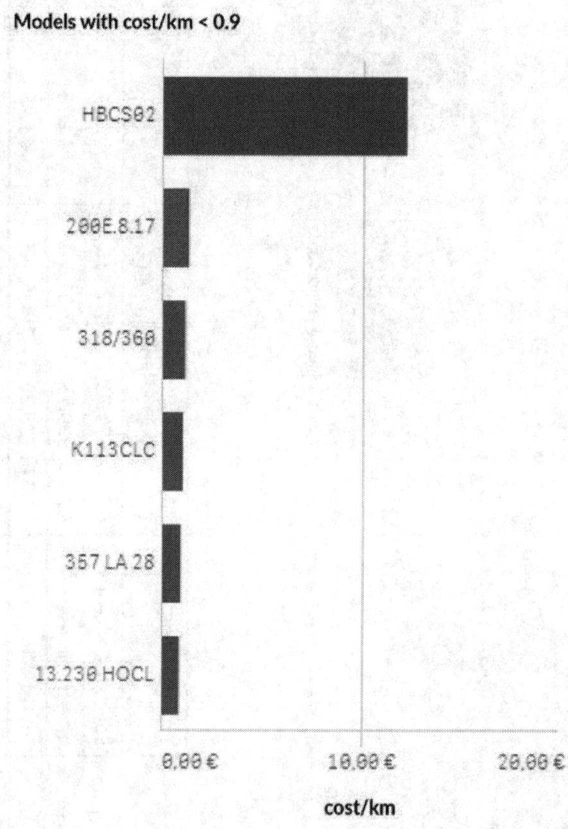

Figure 88.4 Scorecard of cost/km dispersion by vehicle model "outliers." *Source:* Own elaboration.

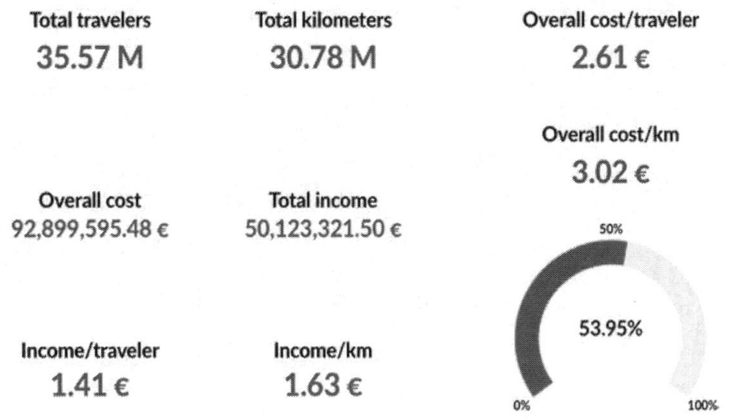

Figure 88.5 Table of KPIs for revenues, costs and margins per passenger and kilometer. *Source:* Own elaboration.

REFERENCES

Chinn, D. Klier, J., Stern, S. y Tesfu, S. (2020): *Safeguarding Europe's livelihoods: Mitigating the employment impact of COVID–19.* McKinsey.

Monteiro Chacón, M.J., Sánchez Toledano, D. y Oliveira Araujo, A (2014): La inteligencia Institucional y Cadena de Valor de la Información: El caso de la Universidad Federal de Rio Grande do Norte. Revista Evidenciaçao Contábil & Finanças, Vol.2, n°3. 88–103.

Sánchez Toledano, D., Carrasco Díaz, D. y Sánchez Toledano, J. (2014): Observatorio de Costes y Financiación del Transporte Urbano Colectivo: Un programa de investigación. *Investigaciones europeas de dirección y economía de la empresa,* Vol. 20, N° 1. 33–40.

Sánchez Toledano, D.; Flores Ureba, S. y Sánchez Toledano, J (2011): El cuadro de mando integral como herramienta de gestión al servicio público de transporte urbano colectivo. *XXV Congreso Anual AEDEM.* Valencia.

Sánchez Toledano, D.; Flores Ureba, S.; Carrasco Díaz, D., y Sánchez Toledano, J. (2011): *International Congress on Cost Control.* Barcelona.

This page intentionally left blank.

CHAPTER 89

THE CHARTERED ACCOUNTANT AND THE DECISION SUPPORT OF MANAGERS

André Rostan and Marc Rostan

ABSTRACT

Beyond his interventions in accounting matters in companies and organizations, the chartered accountant is frequently asked by the manager to assist him in certain decisions. He is also led, in view of his own observations, to propose improvements or corrections of anomalies, to improve an operation or limit a risk. He will be even more effective in his proposals if his approach is structured by a method and tools, while adapting to the personality of the manager, the final decision maker. But he will also have a key role to play in ensuring that a decision taken becomes a reality.

If the primary mission of the accountant in a company or organization is to assist, in one form or another, in the preparation of the annual accounts, he/she is called upon throughout his interventions to respond to the requests of the managers, to enlighten them on certain decisions they are considering taking.

But he is also led, on his own initiative, by analyzing the figures or from information of any kind that he/she may have knowledge of, to encourage the managers, as a preventive or curative measure, to modify their practices or to take certain decisions, to remedy an error, to limit a risk, to improve management or to take advantage of an opportunity.

Based on situations experienced during many years of professional practice in a medium-sized firm in a medium-sized city, we will clarify and classify the methods of intervention that we have used over the years to help managers in their decisions, by answering the questions: Who? What? How?

SEAM Treatise, pages 731–738

1 THE ORGANIZATIONS CONCERNED, THEIR MANAGERS AND THEIR RELATIONSHIPS WITH CONSULTANTS

1.1 The Organizations Concerned

The clientele of the firms intervening in the context defined above is composed of small and medium-sized businesses, liberal professions, craftsmen or structured craft enterprises, small shops, supermarkets, construction companies, professional associations, non-for profit organizations, etc. The size of these organizations ranges from one person working alone to several dozen or even several hundred people, in a variety of legal structures: sole proprietorship, one-man business, limited liability company, joint stock company, association, economic interest group, etc.

1.2 The Managers Concerned

In addition to the diversity of organizations, we are dealing with a diversity of managers. From the craftsman or the shopkeeper, most of the time not very familiar with accounting and legal matters, to the engineer, who is more easily sensitized to management, to the business lawyer, who knows perfectly well how to read the annual accounts, or the judge at the commercial court, who is particularly sensitive to the difficulties of companies.

1.3 The Relationship Between the Manager and the Accountant

The relationship is therefore not the same according to the manager's profession and knowledge of management. It also depends on the functioning of the individuals and the characters in presence. But it is up to the chartered accountant to find the right way to build a constructive and efficient relationship of trust, by adapting his approach according to the manager, notably according to the one who knows, the one who does not know or the one who thinks he knows.

2 THE ACCOUNTANT'S SKILLS

2.1 Basic Skills

The basic training of the chartered accountant and his experience lead him/her to give advice in accounting matters, but also to have rather solid notions in legal, fiscal, social matters as well as in finance and management: knowledge that is constantly updated and enriched by his experiences.

The field of competences is thus vast but cannot of course be perfectly mastered in its most specialized aspects. The chartered accountant is therefore regularly led to call upon specialists, as soon as he/she has identified a subject of which he/she has a good command of the contours, but not necessarily all the subtleties.

2.2 Complementary Skills

Some professional accountants can develop specific knowledge and experience in a given sector. For example: associations, transport, the public sector… Others are led, because of a parallel initial training or by taste, to develop competences in fields such as: legal, taxation, social, data processing, management of heritage...

As far as we are concerned, we would like to mention a training course in socio-economic analysis provided by ISEOR, which, beyond the direct assistance provided in the management of our firm, has enabled us to carry out some specific missions in this field and, in a general way, to better apprehend the consulting missions.

3 ORIGINS OF DECISION SUPPORT: TRIGGERS

In SMEs, the decisions to be taken in terms of accounting proper are limited and it is generally the professional who, due to the technical nature of the matter, is required to take the appropriate decisions for the presentation of the accounts

But for management decisions in the broad sense, the manager often needs an independent opinion: assistance is therefore, depending on the circumstances, either requested by the manager from the certified public accountant or proposed by the latter.

3.1 The Request Comes From the Manager

The occurrence of an important event, the lack of specific knowledge or the need to support a decision that has almost been taken requests in this area are varied and of varying importance. We can illustrate this with a few examples.

3.1.1 The Choice of the Legal Structure at the Time of the Creation

If the chartered accountant is solicited at the time of the creation, it is important for him/her to determine the future of a company that he/she does not know and whose managers he does not know well, to propose the mode of exercise which seems to him/her the most appropriate.

3.1.2 One of the Most Frequent Requests: The Choice of the Financing Method of an Investment

The choice of the investment itself is made by the manager who knows the needs of his business well. But once the choice of the investment is made, he often calls upon the chartered accountant to identify and choose the most appropriate method of financing for the situation: loan, leasing, long-term rental, use of all or part of the available cash flow...

3.1.3 Acquisition of Business Real Estate

The choice is generally between direct acquisition by the company or acquisition through a structure such as a real estate investment trust. The latter solution is generally preferred because of the flexibility and ease of transfer that it allows. But beware of preconceived ideas in this matter, it is not THE solution in all cases: it is important to clearly define the objectives sought, whether immediate or long term, and to consider the determining impact of taxation.

3.1.4 Transmission Missions

These missions are often time-consuming and require the presence of not only the chartered accountant, but also the lawyer and often the notary around the manager. Each transfer being it requires a "tailor-made" approach.

3.2 The Proposal is Initiated by the Firm

The examination of the accounting data, but also any information brought to the knowledge of the chartered accountant, whatever its nature, as well as any fact observed by him, can be the source of an intervention with the manager to enlighten him on a situation and to encourage him to take possible measures.

3.2.1 An Important Moment: The Meeting to Present the Annual Accounts

A meeting between the manager and the chartered accountant, sometimes sufficient but always necessary, it is the obligatory annual point of passage: a privileged moment to take stock of the situation and to draw the manager's attention. Let's illustrate with a few examples.

3.2.1.1 Anomaly in the overall financial situation detected during the examination of the accounts. Imbalance of the balance sheet due to a lack of financing for an investment, a company in difficulty, too much customer credit, etc.: measures must be taken, and if necessary, decisions to file for bankruptcy or to follow up must be made.

3.2.1.2 Anomaly detected in the accounts: late payment of VAT. Due to delays in payment by certain clients and the resulting cash flow difficulties, the accountant of a construction company with around 100 employees was not declaring all the cash received. The deferred payment of the VAT allowed to limit the bank overdraft. The firm drew the company manager's attention to the risk involved (tax adjustment, late payment interest, bad faith penalties of up to 80% of the amount of tax concerned, personal liability) and sent him a letter to encourage him to regularize the situation as soon as possible, which was done without delay.

The inconsistency being detectable by simply reading the annual accounts, the tax authorities, without surprise, launched an audit and notified the corresponding adjustment. But to show that he was aware of the situation, the manager communicated the letter from the firm to the auditor and, during a final exchange with his superior, the latter decided not to apply the maximum penalties: the beginning of regularization had been considered.

3.2.1.3 Anomaly observed in a retail business: drop in the commercial margin. At the end of a financial year, a drop in the commercial margin was noted, both in relation to that of the previous financial years and in relation to that of a second business of the same nature operated by the same manager: this made it possible to detect thefts committed by a salesgirl. This allowed the detection of thefts committed by a saleswoman and the initiation of procedures for complaints, reports, trials, convictions, etc.

3.2.1.4 Evolution of the company and legal structure not adapted to the current situation. As the company or the context evolves, it is necessary to regularly question the validity of the legal structure and to adapt it, if necessary, to ensure a better functioning, to limit the risks, to facilitate the transmission, keeping in mind that there is no perfect solution and that one often chooses between disadvantages.

3.2.2 Findings not Related to the Accounts

Let us cite a few examples.

3.2.2.1 Turning a constraint into an opportunity: example of the ISF (Wealth Tax). At the time the ISF was introduced, the drafting of the corresponding declarations made it possible to highlight the unbalanced structure of certain assets; this was the case, for example, of assets made up essentially of real estate, which could eventually be a source of problems when inheriting property, due to possible difficulties in selling part of it quickly and paying the duties in due time. This is followed by a suggestion to restructure the estate, if necessary, with the help of a specialist. It is important to remember that the current limitation of the wealth tax to real estate assets should not make us lose sight of the need for a regular overall review of the composition of certain assets, particularly with a view to succession or transmission.

3.2.2.2 Personal situation of the directors. The meeting to examine the annual accounts is also an opportunity to review with the directors their personal situation: matrimonial regime or civil partnership or marital life; donation or not between spouses ("donation to the last living person"); existence of a joint account or not; measures taken as a preventive measure in case of death, etc.

And to suggest for example to a married couple of about fifty years old, without children, to adopt the matrimonial regime of the community.

Or to suggest to a couple living together to ask themselves the question of marriage: "I am not saying that you should get married, but think about it, taking into account the long-term implications: assets, death, survivor's pension.Also consult your notary. And decide whether to get married or to stay in your current situation, but with full knowledge of the facts.

3.2.3 No Matter How Well-Founded the Observations Are, the Case is Not Always Won or Not Immediately

In a sole proprietorship, the manager takes more than he earns and puts his business at risk if he persists. More than once, the answer is: "That's how you make a living." And so they continue... as long as it is possible.

In a printing company, the turnover regularly decreases. It is obvious that measures must be taken. Suggestion to the manager: "You are a nice man with good contacts, perhaps you could do some canvassing. Immediate and unequivocal answer: he/she crosses his arms. Obviously, he/she doesn't feel like it, it bores him.

Whether it is a question of doing or not doing, it is the manager who ultimately decides. And once the unsuitable situation or the worrying evolution has been brought to his attention, he will behave in full knowledge of the facts: doing nothing thus becomes a choice, a decision on his part and, in fact, an action. It is up to him/her to assume the consequences. Even if he is frustrated, the chartered accountant will have fulfilled his duty of advice: one does not make people happy despite them, and one must accept this.

But, except for emergencies requiring an immediate insistent intervention, he must not resign himself, know how to persevere and regularly come back to the charge: if one does not always obtain immediate success, it is sometimes necessary to give time to time and, to the manager, the time necessary to integrate new ideas calling into question his vision or his practice. If one persists, the famous resistance to change can be overcome!

4 TOOLS AND METHODS

If you want to be efficient, keep track of the studies carried out, and later find the reasons why such and such a decision was taken, an adapted formalization is necessary. Keeping in mind that the study carried out at a given time for a given entity can be used again in the future for a similar case.

4.1 Initial Phase: Getting to Know Each Other—Interview and Note-Taking

4.1.1 The Interview—Hidden and Real Demand

Except in the case of a new contact, the intervention is greatly facilitated by the good knowledge that the chartered accountant already has of the entity concerned. This is a factor of success and time saving, if, regardless of how long the relationship has been in place, the sense of observation, a critical mind and reactivity are maintained: a permanent fresh eye.

Whether it is a request from the manager or a suggestion from the firm, an interview is essential. An interview means building trust, listening, observing, discussing, and taking notes. And if the request comes from the manager, it is important to clearly identify the objective he or she is seeking behind an apparent request, there is often a hidden, unformulated or poorly formulated request.

A typical case, for example, is a project to set up a company: what is the goal? A real association? A protection of the patrimony? A social status for employees? Is this request appropriate?

We also note the need, when dealing with non-specialists, to avoid professional jargon by using simple and understandable words. For example, to avoid confusion, it is better to talk about "input/output" rather than "debit/credit."

4.1.2 Note Taking

Memory is volatile and relying on it is risky: note-taking is therefore essential. However, taking notes too briefly can lead to the evaporation of important information or to not understanding the meaning of what you have written previously. It is therefore necessary to take notes that are as comprehensible as possible, to write complete sentences with subject, verb, and complement. Who hasn't had difficulty finding the exact meaning of notes taken some time ago, because there are only nouns juxtaposed and not a single verb?

But since, in order not to make the speakers lose their train of thought, there is not always the material time to write down everything exhaustively during the meeting, it is good to allow time to reread and complete the sentences without delay, so as not to lose the meaning of what was said. It is also a good idea to take time to reread and complete the sentences without delay, so as not to lose the meaning of what was said and to find, sometimes long afterwards, the reasons that led to a particular decision being taken rather than another, without forgetting to highlight the strong points that should lead to action.

4.2 Documenting Decisions: Minutes or Resolution Sheets

A detailed report may be necessary. But for practical actions to be implemented quickly, a resolution sheet is an excellent support: What actions are to be taken? Who is doing what? By when? In what form? Distributed to all participants at the end of the meeting, and tested on several occasions by us, it has proven its effectiveness. An operational model is proposed by ISEOR, within the framework of the concept of socio-economic management (Savall, 1974, 1979; Savall & Zardet, 1987).

4.3 The Specific Mission Letter if the Mission Requires a Particular Study

Validating a mission to be accomplished, as provided for by professional standards, this specific mission letter can complement or replace the resolution sheet, and materializes the request made, the objectives sought, the means to be implemented, by whom, the deadlines...

4.4 The Final Report—Validation of the Mission Accomplished

Experience has shown us that very few of our senior managers take notes. Therefore it is essential to quickly materialize the interviews and conclusions by means of an appropriate report which, serving as a common reference for the observations made as well as for the recommended actions, the decisions taken and the results obtained, allows them to be validated. And to highlight the mission carried out.

4.5 For Studies of a Certain Complexity, a Tool Proposed by ISEOR: The "OMSP" Grid

This "Objective-Products, Method-Products, Service-Products" grid is a very useful methodological tool for structuring any study to be carried out (Savall and Zardet, 2004). It allows for a coherent ordering of the approach followed, and constitutes a general, effective and reusable operational model for comparable interventions. Over time, the grids used constitute the memory of the firm's know-how.

For this purpose, one can consult the work cited in reference: "Evolution of the Certified Public Accountant: Management Consulting," which presents the very interesting results of a work group set up by the ISEOR and a small group of certified public accountants (called COMEC), and which functioned for about ten years to develop the consulting role of the certified public accountant in very small businesses and SMEs. Applications in companies, training and publications have been produced because of this collaboration (Zardet & al, 1992).

IN CONCLUSION: THE ACTIVE ROLE OF THE CHARTERED ACCOUNTANT

The chartered accountant must respond to the solicitations of a manager, bring him/her to get out of the daily routine, to take a step back, to become aware of a risk that he is running and that he is causing others (employees, family, partners) to run by allowing certain situations to continue. He/she must ensure that he is doing what is necessary by contacting him regularly.

His/her behavior is key: be observant, reactive, keep a critical mind, have the courage to see, say and do. He/her must accept that sometimes he will not obtain satisfaction, or not immediately, but he/her will have played his role as an advisor by alerting. He/her must also teach the manager not to hesitate to consult us before making any important decision that may fall within our competence, according to the adage that "prevention is better than cure," and to advise us without delay of any important event that requires our intervention.

In short, we must be available, physically, and intellectually, to listen, to exchange, to propose, to incite and to insist, and then to have the satisfaction of seeing that decisions taken in cooperation are followed by action. And to be gratified, sometimes, with a few thanks...

Let's never forget that helping to make decisions is good but acting to make them happen is better!

REFERENCES

Savall, H. (coord.) (1992) *Évolution de l'expert-comptable—Le Conseil en Management*—Paris: Economica.

Zardet, V., Rey, J.P., Joly, J.B., Debouvry, M.C., Rostan, A., & Culine, L.(1992). COMEC: COnseil en Management par l'Exeprt-Comptable in Savall, H. (coord.) *Evolution de l'expert-comptable—Le Conseil en Management.* Paris: Economica.

This page intentionally left blank.

PART IX

ECONOMICS AND MANAGEMENT: ARTICULATION AND CONTINUUM

This page intentionally left blank.

CHAPTER 90

TOWARDS A PARTICIPATIVE MANAGEMENT OF COMPANIES AND THE ECONOMY

Gilbert Blardone

ABSTRACT

The socio-economic theory is part of responsible and sustainable economic foundations inscribed in a socially responsible capitalism. Financial capitalism leads to crises whose origins were exposed as early as 1922 by the Spanish economist Bernácer. The ultraliberal ideology attributes to the market the capacity to regulate itself. A two-level strategy, the firm and the general economy, is needed to move from traditional management to participatory management by all actors involved. The author advocates the social and solidarity market economy, built from the enterprise and based on the substitution of a humanist ideology for ultraliberalism, in order to improve the living conditions of the population. Socio-economic theory shows that the existence of considerable reserves of productivity delays or prevents the creation of jobs.

Socio-economic theory is part of responsible and sustainable economic foundations inscribed in a socially responsible capitalism (Savall, Zardet, Bonnet & Péron, 2015). In order to understand this capitalism, it is necessary to look at other economic models and in particular at other forms of capitalism.

Jacques Attali (2013) argued for "an economy that brings together all entities producing goods or services, whether market or non-market, in a way that is economically viable and useful to both employees and customers, to their communities and to subsequent generations" because our economic model seems to be reaching its limits. Indeed, this model seems to feed crises that are linked and transboundary: financial and economic, social and environmental, political and philosophical but also organizational. Let us remember that

SEAM Treatise, pages 741–748

the positive economy socially adapts capitalism without modifying its aims and management methods. On the contrary, the social and solidarity-based market economy brings other goals and other management methods. This economic vision goes beyond capitalism and leads to another economic system. Thus the organization of the capitalist company is too often directed by the only short-term maximum profit required by the shareholders. This leads to a selection of managers chosen for this sole purpose. However, we observe that as soon as the situation deteriorates, for example a "less buoyant" market, their competences prove to be too narrow, insufficient or unsuited to deal quickly with situations that escape them. They are unable to develop alternative strategies involving all the actors concerned to respond rapidly to market changes. The notion of survival-development of the firm is then forgotten (Savall, 1975, 2012, 2018). The workers are then used as the only shock absorber and adjustment variable to the crisis, while a form of immobility gains the company (Leroy, 1990). Our economic model is capitalism, but it takes various forms over time; today, it is often solely financial and speculative.

1 FROM LIBERALISM TO ULTRALIBERALISM

This form of capitalism has led and continues to lead to a succession of crises, the origins of which were exposed as early as 1922 by Germán Bernácer, a great Spanish economist (Savall, 1973, 1975, published in U.S. in 2015). One of the most important crises of the 20th century was on December 23, 1973, when the price of a barrel of oil suddenly rose from $3 to $12. This was the first oil shock to cause a wave of panic in the West. It was the fear of running out of dollars to pay for oil imports, which was then the main energy source. All countries decided to increase their exports to earn dollars. Milton Friedman (1995), an American economist, then proposed to open the borders to competition free of all constraints. This is a major turning point where we have moved from liberalism, with its rules, to ultraliberalism and its refusal of rules. According to Friedman, the market is self-regulating, and any public intervention prevents a return to automatic equilibrium by the very fact that the market functions. The ultraliberal ideology has been generalized by the multinationals, which have made it their preferred doctrine.

> These multinational companies each have hundreds of subsidiaries. They have enormous financial means at their disposal, and escape all control. They exercise exorbitant political power. They alone benefit from the liberalization of trade on all levels. (Allais, 1999, p. 85)

However,

> the total liberalization of the movement of goods, services and capital on a world scale . . . is only possible, it is only advantageous, it is only desirable within the framework of economically and politically associated regional groupings, grouping together countries of comparable economic development, with each regional association reasonably protecting itself vis-à-vis the others. (Allais, 1999, p. 72)

This is what François Perroux called "mastering globalization" through "organized trade zones" (ZEOs), in partnership with each other. Maurice Allais explained, with regard to unbridled competition:

> Generalized globalization between countries characterized by very different wage levels and exchange rates can only lead, in the end, to unemployment, reduced growth, inequality, and mis-

ery of all kinds in the developed countries. It is neither inevitable, nor necessary, nor desirable. (Allais, 1999, p. 76)

We are then in an anarchic globalism.

2 A "CRISIS OF INTELLIGENCE" (MAURICE ALLAIS, 2001, 2005)?

Obviously, since 2007, Western leaders have not understood this. This is what made Maurice Allais say "the crisis today is above all a crisis of intelligence. It is ridiculous to remedy only the effects. It is the causes that must be addressed." And this struggle must be pursued according to a single principle that must transcend all others: "the economy must be at the service of Humans, not Humans at the service of the economy" (Allais, 1999, p. 93). Maurice Allais joins François Perroux (1961, 1996), an economist and Professor at the Collège de France, for whom the economy must be the economy of "all humans" (Barre, Blardone, Savall, 2005).

The English economist Keynes (1936) in his "General Theory of Employment, Interest and Money" in 1936 advocated, in order to get out of the 1929 crisis, an economic policy that would bring into play both the "consumption gas pedal" and the private or public "investment multiplier." Bernácer (1922, 1945, 1955), in a more radical way, explained that crises are congenital to the existence of speculative markets. "Markets are full of capital, attracting and capturing it. They fail in the productive sectors where real value is created, which dries up their financing, destroying employment and social welfare" (Savall, 1975, 2012, 2018, Savall, Zardet, 1987, 2005).

The problem is that capitalism is nowadays equated with the large groups that maximize profit and have been developing for 200 years. The criticism of capitalism refers to this negative image of rent, predation, and destruction of small businesses. There is another kind of capitalism, that of the entrepreneur who takes risks. We must restore the term capitalism in its essence and not in its hypertrophied use.

We must not try to adapt capitalism but to go beyond it by gradually changing the economic system. This means replacing the current management of companies by capital alone with a participative management of all the actors concerned. We must remember that maximum profit is no longer the main goal of management; it is a means to the service of investment. The new objective is therefore to cover the real needs of the populations, profit being only a means of action. Today, the domination of capital is asymmetric. It is sometimes an effective domination in the retention of value creation, which leads to economic abstentionism (Savall, Zardet, 2005), and sometimes an illusory domination with regard to the informal powers of all the actors, which can be translated into hidden costs and performances (Savall, 1974, 1981).

This critique of capitalism concerns, in particular, large companies listed on the stock market that are constantly seeking maximum profit. Small and medium-sized enterprises and craft enterprises are generally more motivated by their technical and commercial success or by their art than by the search for maximum profit. For them, profit often remains a necessary means to investment and innovation, not an end. This refers them to the entrepreneurs of the Solidarity and Social Market Economy.

Attacking the causes of repeated crises means attacking the very foundations of the system that is causing them today, financial capital and its ultraliberal ideology that inspires its economic, monetary and social policies. It is also an attack on those who produce it, with the increasingly dominant influence of the American multinationals and, following them, of multinationals throughout the world. It is an evolution towards a wild and unhealthy capitalism. Yet it seems forbidden to blame the globalization of trade as the cause of unemployment. Yet the doctrine of free trade, which removes all obstacles to the free movement of goods, services and capital, creates a globalist economy lacking any truly appropriate institutional framework. It is dominated by the law of the jungle, leading to countless miseries and job losses for millions of unemployed (Allais, 1999).

The ultraliberal ideology attributes to the market the capacity to self-regulate.

> This is to forget that the market economy is only an instrument and that it cannot be dissociated from its institutional and political context. There can be no efficient market economy if it does not take place in an appropriate institutional and political framework. A liberal society is not and cannot be an anarchic society (Allais, 1999, p. 86)

The economy today lacks a real system of regulation and develops within an anarchic framework (Allais, 1999). The crisis that Europe has been undergoing since 2007 in a completely open economy has already put it firmly on the road to underdevelopment. There is a slowdown in economic activity, as well as unemployment, poverty, precariousness, a sharp rise in inequality, company relocations, and the increasingly obvious domination of foreign investments, particularly Chinese, over the economies. The two criteria of underdevelopment: *internal disarticulation and domination—external dependence*, are already largely met (Perroux, 1961).

3 FOR A PARTICIPATIVE MANAGEMENT OF THE COMPANY AND THE ECONOMY: THE SOLIDARITY AND SOCIAL MARKET ECONOMY

A two-level strategy is needed to move from traditional enterprise management to participatory management by all the actors concerned: the enterprise level (microeconomic) and the level of the general economy (macroeconomic). This two-level work reflects the history of socio-economic theory and methods of transformation, which has constantly sought to move back and forth between these levels. From global economic analysis inspired by Germán Bernácer (Savall, 1973, 1975) and François Perroux (1979, Savall, 1979) to the deployment of a methodology of change within firms (Savall, 1974, 1979, Savall, Zardet, 1987) that itself feeds into socially responsible capitalism at the global level (Savall, Péron, Zardet & Bonnet, 2015).

Such a change in management system can only be achieved gradually from today's realities. The successive crises must constitute a gas pedal of these changes, because it maximizes the weaknesses and contradictions of financial capitalism. These weaknesses are clearly perceived by public opinion and make them aware of the need for change. The so-called solidarity and social market economy (SSE), already in place in many sectors, is the embryo of a possible future system based on the enterprise. It is neither a theory nor a prefabricated system, but a system whose elements exist and have proven their effectiveness. It responds to the problems posed by the crises and offers a way out, while at the same time being able to gradually replace the system in place. By addressing real needs, it has a wide scope of application.

The process of implementing a participative management of the company can be worked on from different axes, especially for capitalist companies in difficulty.

- A diagnosis on the real state of the company must be established on the exact situation of the threatened company. It is a question of knowing the precise reasons for its difficulties: profit judged insufficient by the shareholders or individual owners; unsuitability to competition; obsolescence of management, equipment or products and services offered as well as unused productivity reserves that prevent job creation. Measured in more than 2,000 firms by ISEOR, these reserves are between 20,000 and 70,000 euros per person per year (Savall & Zardet, 1987, 2008a, 2008b, 2014; Savall, Zardet & Bonnet, 2000, 2008). In all these cases, the innovations to be made to make the renovated firm viable again should be identified by the diagnosis.

- Public support facilitates the reconversion of a firm in difficulty. It varies according to the location of the enterprise, its "territoriality" and the state of public opinion.
- A new status: Cooperatives or mutuals in co-management. The management of the enterprise is then transferred to the actors (workers, capital providers, lenders, suppliers, customers). It becomes a cooperative or a mutual co-managed by the solidarity actors. It should thus mobilize all the stakeholders in the elaboration and implementation of a project of social and economic change.
- Administrative, accounting and technical support. The conversion of the enterprise into a cooperative being a complex legal, financial, economic and technical operation, the actors must be able to count on an external support in all the fields.
- Interprofessional and social relationships, Relationships can be established, on the one hand with other enterprises of the cooperative and capitalist sectors, on the other hand with universities, research centers, professional training institutions, information and communication institutions. It would be in the interest of the enterprises of the social and solidarity market economy to form networks among themselves that would allow them to support each other and to better face capitalist competition and the evolution of the economic situation. These horizontal links are essential for the social and solidarity market economy to be always at the forefront of research and innovation, attentive to the real new needs of the populations. The social and solidarity economy will thus contribute to creating a society in which all men and women will feel both responsible and valued. Social democracy will complement political democracy.

Men and women, instead of being used as an adjustment variable to the economic situation, can, through the social and solidarity market economy, once again become the purpose and the driving force of the economy and society.

4 THE SOCIAL/SOLIDARITY-BASED MARKET ECONOMY AND THE PARTICIPATORY MANAGEMENT OF THE ECONOMY (MACRO-ECONOMIC APPROACH)

The social and solidarity market economy is built from the enterprise, its basis is the enterprise. But the microeconomic context of the enterprise is strongly dependent on the general macroeconomic context that constitutes its environment. That is to say, the economic, monetary and social policies at the local, regional, national, European and global levels in which it operates. The future of the social and solidarity market economy is the revival of the activity and the morale of the actors.

The process of participatory management of the economy could be developed in six stages:

1. *Progressive generalization of the social and solidarity market economy* at the level of enterprises in five areas of action: local, regional, national, European, global. The companies of the social and solidarity market economy exist. Their number is growing steadily,

especially in France. But the participatory management method assumes, in order to last, an attitude of mind favourable to dialogue among the various actors, very different from that of confrontation, which is dominant today. Born at the local level from the companies, the social and solidarity market economy can thus extend its influence in wider spaces: region, nation, groups of nations in Europe and in the World.

2. *Substitution of a humanist ideology for ultraliberalism.* The "Washington Consensus" of 1989 has become the Charter of ultraliberalism adopted by all Western governments. However, the great contemporary economists François Perroux, Maurice Allais, but also Joseph Stiglitz (2003) and Paul Krugman (2012) have constantly reminded us that the economy must improve the living conditions of the population and not deteriorate them. They have tried to remind us of the rules of the game, of a dynamic market economy "at the service of man, not man at the service of the economy." Getting out of the crisis means first of all getting out of this "oversimplifying and destructive" ideology (Allais, 1999) and the austerity policies that it imposes on the population, while at the same time favoring speculation on the financial markets, which generates exorbitant gains for a small minority.
3. *Pre-financing* of economic activity through an active monetary policy. The process will take place over time and must therefore be accompanied by a dynamic monetary policy of pre-financing innovations so that indispensable financial means are made available without being under the domination of financial markets and their speculators. Socio-economic theory shows that the existence of considerable productivity reserves delays or prevents the creation of jobs. The dynamic would be in the satisfaction of "new" needs (Savall, 1974, 1979; Savall, Zardet, 2014). One of the priority objectives of the recovery of activity is the return to full employment, which implies a selection of investments according to this objective. In France, a 5% growth rate in GDP is equivalent to the creation of about 100 billion euros. One point of growth should provide about 100,000 jobs. We have three million unemployed. This is how long it would take, with a minimum growth of 5% per year, to find full employment, i.e., no more than 5% of unemployed.
4. *Community preference* adapted to this time in Europe. A new "Community preference," adapted to today's realities, for example through anti-dumping measures completed, if necessary, by ecological taxes aimed at the quality of imported products or social taxes encouraging producers to treat workers better, etc., would make the European Union a real "organized trade zone" (OTA).
5. *Democratization of the functioning of the European Union.* "The construction of Europe must be based on a confederation of sovereign states and the populations of the member countries must be closely associated with the construction of Europe" (Allais, 1999). "There can be no democracy if there is no sharing of forms of knowledge, information and if there is no living deliberation on everything that constitutes a common world" (Rosanvallon, 2013). The European Union does not have to change its institutions but to make them work more democratically because they are currently managed in an overly bureaucratic and technocratic manner. The evolution towards a social and solidarity-based market economy will facilitate a democratization of the Union, which will strengthen the support of the people.
6. *Controlled globalization through the construction of "organized trade zones."* The European Union would thus meet the three criteria of an OTA: it would be composed of countries economically and politically associated around common projects, with comparable levels of economic and social development, while respecting each other's cultures and interests (Perroux, 1961; Allais, 1999). The current power rela-

tions could be replaced by partnerships between countries and groups of countries on a global scale, respectful of the cultures and interests of each. Trade wars and currency wars would give way to international cooperation. On the other hand, the G20, a fragile and timid body for cooperation, could be the place for exchanges and proposals for the creation of exchange zones organized on a global scale, cooperating with each other.

The repeated crises show that the market does not regulate itself. To counteract its dysfunctions, all economic actors, especially the State and the States, must be able to play their role in an economy whose three engines, consumption, investment and exports, will function normally to satisfy the real needs and well-being of the populations. It is this ideology, both realistic and humanistic, that drives the social and solidarity market economy. It is one of the possible ways towards a new economic-political order that is socially responsible and human in dimension.

5 FOR A "COMMON WORLD"

This "common world" (Rosanvallon, 2013), based on solidarity, is within our reach, provided that we detoxify ourselves from the ultraliberal ideology that came out of the great fear of 1973. It is a matter of abandoning the old outdated and destructive recipes of economic, monetary and social policies based on austerity. We must put all our resources and all our potential to good use, through an economy "for Man and for all Men" (Perroux, 1961, 1996). Money is not a taboo but a force that must be put at the service of the economy. Work and creative imagination are the foundations of the wealth of nations and deserve to be the first beneficiaries. Companies, the basic cells of any economy, must be able to mobilize the creativity and dynamism of all the actors concerned, associated in a participative management in order to satisfy the real needs of the population. It is in this vision that the works of the socio-economic theory are inscribed. The company, the association, the commune, the region, the nation, Europe and the world are vast fields of action. Given the resistance capacity of financial capitalism, the current economic system, the emergence of a solidarity and social economy with participative management can only be a long-term adventure, the first stage of which is being played out, as of today, at the level of companies.

Utopia is the truth of tomorrow.

—Victor Hugo

REFERENCES

Allais, M. (2005). *L'Europe en crise, Que faire ? Réponses à quelques questions. Pour une autre Europe*, Paris, Ed. Clément Juglar.

Allais, M. (1999). *La mondialisation, la destruction des emplois et de la croissance*, Paris, Ed. Clément Juglar.

Allais, M. (2001). *La passion de la recherche. Autoportrait d'un autodidacte*, Paris, Ed. Clément Juglar.

Attali, J. (2013) «Manifeste pour l'économie positive», *Le Monde*.

Barre, R., Blardone, G., & Savall, H. (2005). *François PERROUX, le centenaire d'un grand économiste*, Ed. Economica.

Blardone, G. (2014). *La Crise 2007–2014: Chronologie, analyse et perspectives*, ISEOR Éditeur.

Blardone, G. (1990). *Le Fonds Monétaire international, l'ajustement structurel et les coûts de l'Homme,* Paris, Ed. de l'Épargne.

Blardone, G. (1995). *FMI, Endettement du Tiers Monde et ajustement structurel. Approche méthodologique et appliquée. Les cas de la Tanzanie et de Madagascar.* En collaboration avec Lothar CAVIEZEL. Berne, Ed. Peter Land.

Bernácer, G. (1922). La teoría de las disponibilidades como interpretación de las crisis y del problema social. *Revista nacional de economía.*

Bernácer, G. (1945). *La doctrina funcional del dinero.* Madrid: Consejo Superior de Investigaciones.

Bernácer, G. (1955). *Una economía libre, sin crisis y sin paro.* Madrid: Aguilar.

Friedman, M. (1995). *Essais d'économie positive,* Paris, Ed, LITEC.

Keynes, J. M. (1936). *Théorie Générale de l'emploi, de l'intérêt et de la monnaie,* Paris, Ed. Payot.

Krugman, P. (2012). *Sortez-nous de cette crise, maintenant* !, Paris, Ed. Flammarion.

Leroy, M. C. (1990). *Stratégies des collectivités locales. Tableau de bord.* Paris, Berger-Levrault.

Manifeste des économistes atterrés, Paris, éd. LLL. Les liens qui libèrent, 2010. 630 signataires, 68 p.

Perroux, F. (1961). «*De l'avarice des Nations à une économie du genre humain*» dans *L'économie du XXème siècle,* Ed. PUF ; 3ème ed., PUG, 1996.

Rosanvallon, P. (2013). «Comment vivifier la démocratie», Le Monde (Paris), pp.20–21.

Savall, H. (1975a). *G. Bernácer, L'hétérodoxie en science économique.* Dalloz, Collection des grands économistes.

Savall, H. (1975b). *Enrichir le travail humain : l'évaluation économique,* Dunod. traduit en anglais «Work and People, *an economic evaluation of job enrichment*...» Oxford University Press 1981 ; 2° edition Charlotte, États-Unis: IAP, 2010.

Savall, H. (1979). *Reconstruire l'entreprise. Analyse socio-économique des conditions de travail,* Préface de François Perroux. Dunod.

Savall, H., & Zardet, V. (1987). *Maîtriser les coûts-performances cachés,* Economica, 7° édition : 2020. Traduit en anglais *Mastering Hidden Costs and Socio-Economic Performance,* Charlotte: IAP, États-Unis, 2008 b.

Savall, H., Zardet, V., & Bonnet, M. (2000). *Releasing the Untapped Potential of Enterprises Through Socio-Economic Management,* Genève, ILO-BIT, 2° éd., 2008.

Savall, H., & Zardet, V. (2008a). Le concept de coût-valeur des activités. Contribution de la théorie socio-économique des organisations. *Revue Sciences de Gestion—Management Sciences—Ciencias de Gestión,* 64.

Savall, H. (2012). *Origine radicale des crises économiques : Germán Bernácer, précurseur visionnaire,* Charlotte, North Carolina, USA. Information Age Publishing. (IAP),.Traduit en anglais : *Radical origin of economic crisis : Germán Bernácer, a visionary precursor.* Palgrave Macmillan (2018).

Savall, H., & Zardet V. (2014). *Reconstruire l'entreprise. Fondements du management socio-économique,* Dunod.

Savall, H., Zardet, V., Bonnet, & Péron (2015), *Le capitalisme socialement responsable existe, Paris: EMS éditions.*

Sliglitz, J. (2003). *Quand le capitalisme perd la tête,* Paris, Fayard.

CHAPTER 91

FOR A EUROPE OF ORGANIZED EXCHANGE ZONES

A Socio-Economic Approach to Decentralization

Jean-Simon Tabournel

ABSTRACT

To fight against the disparities that weaken the European Union, it is necessary to transform it into an Organized Trade Area (OTA), in the words of François Perroux and Maurice Allais. An OTA brings together states with the same culture, with comparable levels of economic and social development, with a common project that they decide to implement in a concerted and flexible manner. The OTA project is imperative for a Union that wants to be a force of proposition in world regulation

"Penser l'Europe," the founding work of Edgar Morin (Morin, 1987; Morin & Naïr, 1997), constitutes an opening onto the complexity of the continent: Europe dissolves as soon as we want to think about it in a clear and distinct way, it splits up as soon as we want to recognize its unity (...). The notion of Europe must be conceived according to a multiple and full complexity (...)

> The difficulty of thinking Europe is first of all this difficulty of thinking the one in the multiple, the multiple in the one: the unitas multiplex. It is at the same time the difficulty to think the identity in the non-identity. Also, to conceive how the European unity lies in the disunion and the heterogeneity, we will have to resort to two principles of intelligibility suitable to elucidate the complex phenomena of this order: the dialogical principle and the principle of recursion.

SEAM Treatise, pages 749–757

a) The dialogical principle unites two antagonistic principles or notions, which apparently should repel each other, but which are inseparable and indispensable to understand the same reality. The problem is therefore to unite antagonistic notions to think the organizing, productive and creative processes in the complex world of human life and history. In this way, the dynamics of states are combined with those of federalism, the race to implement a large internal market with the opening to the open sea and Darwinist competition.

b) The principle of recursion goes beyond the notion of simple regulation and feedback. It opens onto self-production and self-organization: it is a generating loop in which the products become in turn creators of what produces them, in uninterrupted productive loops. These loops take the form of vortices, which are made of the meeting of antagonistic flows becoming complementary to constitute a self-organizing form and an active unity. Thus, from the 15th to the 19th century, the development of capitalism, cities, philosophical, scientific and technical knowledge are both products and producers of a self-generating loop that stimulates its internal developments and integrates them into a kind of maelstrom that will give rise to the great discoveries of the 20th and 21st centuries.

These two principles are at the heart of complex thinking, which negotiates with uncertainty and can imagine the organization. It is thinking that can link, contextualizing, globalizing, but at the same time recognizing the singular, the concrete. It is in this spirit that we have worked on the theme of the transformation of Europe into zones of organized exchange. The problematic is the following: The European Union appears as a compact mass but fragmented between Nations and States. Stuck on the small cape of Asia, not efficient enough in its self-organization, and, for this reason, too open to the winds and storms of the sea.

The question is then: in what way would the transformation of this complex unit into a zone of organized exchanges (OTA), then into an OTA of proximity, be able to give it a new lease of life, while allowing it to better adapt its institutions and to better embrace its time shaken by the "world's turmoil" (Gomart, 2019)?

We start from International Relations, geopolitics and geoeconomics, and gradually move towards mesoeconomics and the socio-economic approach. This reflection is articulated in five points.

1. The European Union: an indispensable mutation
2. The differentiated nature of the European Union
3. On which grounds do we want a new strategy?
4. From a zone of organized exchanges to zones of proximity and a better understanding of territories.
5. The considerable influence of the socio-economic approach and contractual regulation for the success of the new strategy: towards a policy of civilization.

1 EUROPEAN UNION IS ON THE TRESHOLD OF AN INDISPENSABLE MUTATION

In 2020, the European Union will have approximately 600 million inhabitants, thirty or so States and a wide variety of characteristics, both demographic and economic, with great differences in production, income, and types of consumption. This diversity is further accentuated by the idea that each state has of its place and role within the Union, in relation to its geopolitical position, its history and its conception of democracy.

These attitudes, while certainly legitimate, weigh on the overall dynamics of a Union whose governance is highly verticalized, through the Commission and the States, and would need to be more flexible to better adapt to the constant clashes of international competition. Firstly, because through crises, the Union is gradually becoming aware that in a world that is changing awfully fast, it can only continue to constitute an island of peace and (relative) prosperity if it leaves the shores of "soft power" and approaches the shores of "hard power" both for internal and external purposes. This means a different modality of growth and development and a different relationship to the world. It means a power policy.

Secondly, because it is currently achieving a mode of growth that is too weakened by international competition, as much as too focused on competition within the zone itself, and this situation must be corrected through a restructuring of productive capacities. From now on, it seems to us, it will be necessary to be more flexible, to identify and give impetus to identified territorial groupings, with their growth poles, their axes of innervation of the area, their subcontracting capacities, all realities that are indispensable to the new strategies that the new European Commission wishes to assume.

This strategy will involve the States: it is therefore necessary to conceive, in coherence with the European regional policy, a new cooperation between States, a cooperation of proximity, with the aim of bringing to a successful conclusion the projects in progress (such as the Mont Blanc tunnel, among others), but also to bring about new projects with the ambition of enhancing the value of the territories in this or that sector, across borders.[1] This is a concrete example of the coupling between States and Regions in a territorial development strategy.

2 SIGNIFICANT DIFFERENCES EXIST IN THE EUROPEAN UNION

What is the geo-economic position of the European Union in 2020 (Dumont & Verluise, 2015; Thourot, 2019)? It is characterized by a differentiation of GDP per capita and specificities in the types of capitalism in action.

2.1 A Differentiation of GDP Per Capita

GDP per capita in purchasing power standards (PPS) allows the comparison of GDP per capita of Member States and in relation to the EU average (24,900€, base 100 in 2012).

Four groups of states can thus be distinguished:

- The 8 countries with a GDP per capita index well below the EU average (47–70): Bulgaria, Romania, Croatia, Latvia, Hungary, Poland, Estonia, and Lithuania. All these states joined the EU after 2003.
- he 9 Member States with a GDP per capita index below or close to the EU average (71–99): Greece, Slovakia, Czech Republic, Slovenia, Malta, Cyprus, Spain, Portugal, Italy ;
- The 3 Member States with GDP per capita above the EU average (100–115): Finland, France, United Kingdom.
- The 8 states with an index above 115: Austria, Belgium, Denmark, Germany, Ireland, Netherlands, Sweden, and Luxembourg.

These data are eloquent testimony to a systematic policy of successive enlargements, which jeopardizes economic and social coherence, hence the need to "re-establish" a hard core of countries making up the euro zone. These statistical data, which testify to a structural situation, mark quantitative differences reflecting more fundamental differences, without seeing any determinism in them.

2.2 Specificities in the Types of Capitalism in Action

In the name of what do we want to enter the logic of a zone of organized exchange?

Let us distinguish, with C. Saint-Etienne (1993, 2010) and M. Albert (1991), two fundamental types of capitalism: Anglo-American and Rhenish.

Anglo-American capitalism designates the economic and financial system in which the creation of shareholder value takes precedence over the construction of economic value added, especially if the rates of return on dividends are fixed in advance and must be achieved. This is the pre-eminence of shareholders, especially majority shareholders, pension funds and other "activist" funds. It is a specific conception of the company whose objective is the rapid maximization of the share value for the shareholders, on the financial markets and with the rating agencies.

Rhenish capitalism, in the words of Mr. Albert, refers to the system in which there is a kind of balance between the economic and the social, where, in some cases, a kind of management "contest" between employers and employees' unions is reached, where the emphasis is rather put on the economic capacities, the social interest of the company and its raison d'être, both economic and societal. The social interest is defined as the superior interest of the company itself, considered as an autonomous economic and social actor, pursuing its own ends, distinct from the objectives of shareholders, employees, creditors, or suppliers, but corresponding to their common general interest of ensuring the continuity and prosperity of the company. It seems to me that European "values" incline more towards the philosophy of Rhenish capitalism than towards the Anglo-Saxon dynamic.

3 ON WHAT GROUNDS DO WE WANT A NEW STRATEGY?

Two points are decisive: to rebuild Europe as a structured interior space, strategically combining a policy of supply and a dynamic of demand; to decentralize the areas of production and marketing by bringing into play, both at the level of the States and at the level of the territorial frameworks, the principle of subsidiarity—thus by giving priority to projects and strategies of proximity and complementarity.

It is around the zones of organized exchanges of proximity that we propose a new internal architecture for the European Union. It is not, of course, a question of separating these zones, let alone setting them in opposition to each other: each one has its own specificities, as shown by the economic and social results. The idea is, on the contrary, to consolidate these areas from within, so that they become stronger through their production and their own market, so that they no longer depend on the large, anonymous, and bureaucratic European market. Linked in a different way to the contributions of the EU, these areas could thus strengthen themselves and, at the same time, cooperate better with neighboring or more distant areas, bringing into play the relations of specialization, industrial density and therefore the structure of their inter-area "external" trade.

Until now, the dynamics of EU construction have followed a vertical path through the States: subsidies come from Brussels to each State, and the distributions are vertical, from top to bottom. We propose to complete this dynamic in part: each area receiving what it needs and distributing it according to its strategic criteria, the whole would thus gradually reach a more integrated productive structure and better inscribed in its geo-economy. On a political level, this new orientation does not call into question state sovereignty, but it does require more cooperation, and therefore more spirit of negotiation. We are thus during a new dynamic of integration, pluralist, compatible with the policy of the Regions, but organized taking into account explicitly qualitative and not only quantitative criteria.

4 FROM AN AREA OF ORGANIZED EXCHANGES TO AREAS OF PROXIMITY AND A BETTER UNDERSTANDING OF THE TERRITORIES

We have answered the ethical question: "On what grounds do we want to rewrite European construction?." We must now address what is (or should be) a zone of organized exchange and why we want it to be decentralized.

It is a question of nations and groups of nations, while preserving their personality and the sense of their interests, cooperating for common objectives and projects. Each area, for its relevance and viability, should fulfill four conditions: a common culture, similar standards of living, comparable levels of development, and common objectives and projects, according to F. Perroux and M. Allais. Perroux and Allais (Perroux, 1964, 1969, 1976, 1981, 1982; Allais, 2005; D'Hombres et al., 2011; Association François Perroux, 2005, 2008, 2016).

The European Union is an example of an OTA. But it is imperfect. Indeed, it has not (yet) defined its geographical, or rather geopolitical, limits. It has yet to specify what really falls under the jurisdiction of the States and to clarify the status of the Commission: a proposing body, a decision-making body or a body for implementing the Union's policies? It must reinstate the Community preference (Article 44 of the Treaty of Rome), which implies that priority is given to the internal market over the external market, the latter being considered a mere complement to the former. This means that a significant proportion of the goods and services used must be produced in the zone, with imports providing the rest. Thus, for M. Allais, the abandonment in 1973 of the Community preference and the priority given to external dynamics (20% of GDP) over the domestic market (80% of GDP) resulted in a reduction in real gross domestic product per capita[2] of at least 30% and probably 50%. At the same time, domestic production has been under permanent pressure from wild and predatory competition, leading to relocation, unemployment, and austerity, thus undermining the Community's growth and development potential.

A real organized exchange zone would make it possible to revive a strategy of autonomous production, translating a voluntary policy of "structural preference"—precise and flexible—capable of expressing the requirements of a relative independence of the countries considered.

This preference of structure would be based on a "dynamic of industrialization," as Perroux (1969) writes:

> However useful the global policy may be, it is a selective policy that decides on the three structures by which the policy of independence is realized:
>
> - The structure of supply of novelty (research, information technology, atom, executives)
> - The structure of renewal of the economic apparatus (growth industries, new industries)
> - The structure of offensive export (export drive, specifically driving exports).

These three structures are obviously interacting; they support and consolidate each other; it is their organization and cohesion that make their strength and their power of intervention, as well as their dynamics of propagation.

Thus, behind the term of internal market, a real strategy of restructuring of social and economic potentials is placed and developed, which responds to a chosen and wanted strategy, capable of resisting and intervening intelligently on the external markets. What is a common culture, at the level of a union of peoples and states with about 600 million inhabitants? Apart from a few aspirations and abstract principles, a few "values," what do Anglo-Saxon, Latin, Germanic, Mediterranean and Balkan cultures have in common? Have we thought about the representation of the world that these peoples have? What is their image of the Other? Have we considered the weight of religions, their conception of the world, the respective weight of States, the structured autonomy of civil society?

For all these reasons, it seems to us indispensable, while keeping the framework of the European Union, which in a way constitutes our Common Good, to structure it in *small OTAs, or OTAs of proximity*, capable of making peoples cooperate with each other, with a more open mutual understanding, who know each other better, whatever their conflicts or differences may have been before, and whose proximity makes them more familiar. Let's put it another way: as long as the aim in Europe was to create a common market open to the winds of global competition, the economic and commercial dynamic prevailed. Now that, in 2021, a new commission is at work, with legitimate ambitions to "beef up" the European economy and consolidate the internal productive market; now that the global geopolitical and geostrategic situation is in full mutation; now that politics and socio-economics must join forces to meet international challenges, a decentralization of certain European productive structures must take place: more flexibility is needed, because more adaptability is required, with a view to greater resilience.

It is in this spirit that we propose to structure the European space into a few small EAZs with the following characteristics: a limited number of States, therefore an identified surface area, with its regions and growth poles, and its territorial network; a cultural neighborhood, truly shared values, a common horizon; a willingness to enter into real cooperation between partners capable of bringing mutual benefits. This schema does not mean that one local OTA is uninterested in the others—especially since they would continue to be part of the same "great European whole." It means that within the framework of proximity strategies, neighbouring countries, together with their neighboring regions, strengthen their cooperation and deepen their cultural links, in coherence with all the projects already launched, often a long time ago. The institutional interventions of the Commission would continue, but new projects could be born and developed, in coherence with the ERASMUS dynamic or others.

This project of a local Organized Trade Area Exchanges would make it possible to regain control of entire sections of territory that have been neglected in a perspective of unbridled globalized competition. It would be a matter of taking back control of a new approach to space and territory: taking advantage of the ecological and energetic transition to rebuild local agriculture, developing the biotopes of a new industrialization, in relation with the industrial policy stated by Commissioner Thierry Breton, strengthening the relations between the pilot companies of the zone and improving the subcontracting policy. These activities would be, and already are, part of a common space, the Union, and concern national spaces, unequally endowed with resources and differently polarized and innervated, where States, Regions, Länder, Departments or the equivalent work. Up to now, cooperation flows have favored large industrial projects, largely due to structures of sovereignty, and involving several States. Thus, Airbus, for example, involves cooperation between the United Kingdom, France, Germany and Spain, with two assembly sites outside the European Union; the European Intervention Initiative, in the military field, brings together France, Spain, Germany, Belgium, Denmark, Estonia, the Netherlands, Portugal and Finland. These major projects have given rise to numerous design offices, SMEs, SMIs and other public/private partnership structures.

5 THE CONSIDERABLE INFLUENCE OF THE SOCIO-ECONOMIC APPROACH AND CONTRACTUAL REGULATION ON THE SUCCESS OF THE NEW STRATEGY

A new "approach" to regional planning, based on the raison d'être of companies, the reclamation of interior space, ecological concerns, and the indispensable renovation of social policies, seems to us to be invigorating. It requires the development of existing business networks, to restructure them around the IT revolution, robotics and artificial intelligence. It also requires a revival of territorial diagnoses: at the level of economic action zones identified as living areas and employment areas, living zones and meeting zones, allowing to put in synergy economic project, employment objectives, cultures and socio-cultural traditions. This leads to a socio-economic type of diagnosis (Savall, 1974, 1979; Savall and Zardet, 1987).

The new OTA structure would be initiated by a systemic, multidisciplinary diagnosis, leading to a collective and concerted innovation project, followed by an evaluation of the actions and results in the social and economic fields. The aim is to promote meetings, cooperations and the creation of realistic prospective projects adapted to the characteristics of the territory concerned and to the policies implemented, through these layers of decentralization.

And it is at this stage of development that socio-economic management (Savall and Zardet, 1987, 2021) shows its full relevance: it is a matter of making the collective project more flexible and adaptable. This type of management creates partnerships, keeps the partners on their toes, in a dynamic of struggle-competition, with meetings, negotiations, cooperations and exchanges, through which contractual regulation takes on its deepest meaning, in the respect of the various parties to the collective project.

Here is what François Perroux wrote in 1978 about balance and regulation:

> An important point needs to be elucidated which refers to Jean Piaget's notion of structure, and which, at the moment when we approach the politics of economic regulation could suffer from ambiguity. Self-regulation, as we recall, is essential to Jean Piaget's notion of structure (...) In short, the only economic regulation that interests agents obliges observation and analysis sooner or later to go beyond the submission of man to things (inert goods moved in a homogeneous space perfectly foreign to man), into the ways of the progressive submission of things by agents, by actors, launched jointly in a struggle for liberation that loosens the constraints of nature and the eliminable constraints of society. The policy of contractual regulation is in perfect and necessary harmony with the whole theory of regulation and equilibration. (...)
>
> Regulation by contract is an aspect of social regulation. Its effectiveness is a function of the nature and content of the social organization that makes the parties capable of contracting, let us say of proceeding to a humanly significant exchange of intentions and wills on a legitimate object (...). The contract, the contractual way, considering the diversity of the situations of the individuals and the groups, is a specific mode of regulation, which completes, refines and softens the regulation by the social and political order.
>
> Contractual regulation can avoid sudden and violent changes, which always generate high economic and social losses. If it becomes a part of people's habits and permeates their minds, it should even reduce the virulence of conflicts and eliminate those which, rationally and practically, can be eliminated (...) Contractual regulation cannot therefore be considered apart from the diffusion of education and culture and the improvement of people's material lot. It relies on the social learning of individuals and groups that has the chance to develop in all the concrete situations of the activity. That is to say that the organization of the industries and the regions (and other territories, we add) can benefit a lot from the regulation by contracts, concluded from one subgroup to the other and between each of them and the public authorities. (...) Our

future depends on a renewed interpretation of the economy and the invention of new rules for the social game.

These writings of 1978, what have they not been read, honestly interpreted, meditated and implemented… But should we be surprised? Between the moment when healthy reflections open new horizons, new ways of thinking and acting, and the time of the first realizations, doesn't it take one or two generations? This is an inescapable reality that politicians must integrate into their strategies, in an uninterrupted game of interactions.

CONCLUSION

This is the challenge: should we continue to build the European Union from above, as a regulated free trade zone—or should we not build it differently, precisely insofar as it is not only an economic or commercial project, but increasingly a strategic design, on the political as well as the socio-economic, societal, cultural and military levels?

To accede without caution to Darwinist free trade and unequal competition is to dissolve the Union and build on sand. To reach a real status of organized trade area completed by OTAs of proximity, is to create a pole of solidity, coherent and integrated, but in a pluralist way, capable of putting in synergy the whole of its potentials in partnerships with poles and external States.

This would be a Europe "necessary to the world." It would be more than a political choice, it would be, in fact, "a policy of civilization."

NOTES

1. Thus, the renovation of the Oloron-Saragossa railroad, which would help to open Aragon and bring Aragon closer to New Aquitaine.
2. Out of inflation.

REFERENCES

Albert M. (1991). *Capitalisme contre capitalisme.* Editions du Seuil

Allais, M. (2005). *L'Europe en crise ? Que faire ? Réponses à quelques questions. Pour une autre Europe.* Editions Clément Juglar

Association des Amis de François Perroux (2005). *Le centenaire d'un grand économiste: François PERROUX.* Economica

Association des Amis de François Perroux (2008). *Comment vivre ensemble: conditions économiques de la démocratie.* ISEOR Editeur

Association des Amis de François Perroux (2016). *Compétitivité et activité économique. Quel avenir pour la France et l'Europe ?* ISEOR Editeur

Dumont G. F., Verluise P. (2015). *Géopolitique de l'Europe.*_PUF

Esposito, M. C., &Azuelos M. (coordonné par). (1997). *Mondialisation et domination économique – La dynamique anglo-saxonne.* Economica

Gomart, T. (2019). *L'affolement du monde.* Tallandier Essais

d'Hombres, E., Savall, H., & Gabellieri, E., (coordonné par). (2011). *Humanisme et travail chez François PERROUX.* Economica.

Morin, E. (1987). *Penser l'Europe.* Gallimard.

Morin E., & Naïr S. (1997). *Une politique de civilisation.* Arléa.

Perroux, F. (1964). *L'économie du XXè siècle*. PUF.
Perroux, F. (1969). *Indépendance de la nation*. Aubier-Montaigne.
Perroux, F. (1976). *Les Droits et les Devoirs Economiques des Etats dans le domaine financier et monétaire* in *Justice économique internationale*. Gallimard.
Perroux, F. (1978). Équilibre et Régulation. *Revue Economie Appliquée*. Archives de l'I.S.M.E.A tome XXXI – n°3–4 . Librairie Droz. Genève.
Perroux, F. (1981). *Pour une philosophie du nouveau développement*. Aubier. Presses de l'Unesco.
Perroux, F. (1982). *Dialogue des Monopoles et des Nations*. PUG.
Revue Sciences Humaines n°1 – 1990 et n°47 – 1995.
Saint-Étienne, C. (1993). *L'Europe contre le capitalisme*. Armand Colin.
Saint-Étienne, C. (2010). *Guerre et paix au XXIè siècle*. François Bourin éditeur.
Thourot, P. (2019). Ramses 2020: un monde sans boussole. *Paysans société* (6), 32–37.

This page intentionally left blank.

CHAPTER 92

THE SOCIO-ECONOMIC APPROACH TO MANAGEMENT

A Lever for Action in Organizations of the Southern Countries

Geneviève Causse and Pierre Hidalgo

ABSTRACT

In the 1980s, the reforms implemented by international donors in sub-Saharan countries generally consisted of transplanting management methods considered universal. The use of the socio-economic method, by considering the specificities of the context, made the reforms more appropriate and acceptable. After examining the problems posed by the reforms, the presentation of a few activities implemented in accordance with values very similar to those of ISEOR shows how socioeconomic management can be a lever for action for countries in the South.

By countries of the South, we mean those in sub-Saharan Africa in which we have had the opportunity and pleasure to work for decades.[1] It was during our fieldwork that we became aware of ISEOR's work and that cooperation existed in various forms. The scope of the ILO's work at that time was very broad. In 1972, the government of Niger called on the ILO to set up a project for the rehabilitation of Nigerien enterprises, financed by the United Nations Development Program (UNDP). This project, which was launched in 1973, was directed by Pierre Hidalgo from 1980.

At that time, we were in the period of structural adjustment programs (SAP), imposed by donors as a solution to underdevelopment. These programs consisted of privatizing most of the public enterprises and transplanting the management methods used in developed countries and generated many problems. The project manager, with the consent of the political

SEAM Treatise, pages 759–765

leaders, initiated large-scale projects related to the management of organizations and the training of executives and managers. After a few years of implementing innovative methods, the discovery of the socio-economic method (Savall, 1974, 1979; Savall and Zardet, 1987) confirmed the way we were proceeding, which logically led to cooperative actions.

After examining the problems that arose at the time and the need for innovative methods, we discuss the important dimensions of the method that are appropriate for the countries in the zone (§ 1). We then present some examples of activities implemented with values very close to those of ISEOR (§ 2).

1 NEED TO CHANGE THE MODEL AND THE SEARCH FOR SOLUTIONS

The conclusions of the diagnoses carried out on the management of organizations in the countries of the sub-Saharan zone,[2] as well as those of academic studies, were unanimous: the organizations are not performing well and the way they are managed is irrational. It was therefore necessary to devise solutions adapted to the context.

1.1 The Findings

These findings relate to the two areas of activity of the ILO's representation in the field: company management and the training of managers and executives.

1.1.1 Management of Enterprises

The titles of various articles at the time testify to the need for change: "Can an African company be restored by respecting the word of the ancestors? (Henry, 1988), "How to reconcile tradition and modernity in the African company" (Olomo, 1987). Management itself is questioned: "African management: myth or reality?" (Dia, 1991), or "Africa [is not] sick of management" (Bourgoin, 1984).

These observations of poor performance, as traditionally measured, mainly concern large public or private companies. Their causes are the difficult transfer of technology in the field of management (Causse, 1993) and the principle of universalism of management methods.

1.1.2 The Training of Managers and Executives

Until recent years, due to the lack of sufficient management science trainers, most African managers and executives were trained in a developed country and followed programs that inculcate "best practices," i.e., those of the countries where they are taught.

In developed countries, the ultimate training for the executive role is done on the job, in an organized setting, where the graduate student gains the necessary practical experience. "An African student graduating from even the best Western business school, and who is given important responsibilities upon his return, will not have the opportunity to acquire the necessary experience" (Causse, 1993, 22). Unable to acquire the necessary practical knowledge and unwilling (or unable) to admit his inadequacies, "there is a great risk that he will confine himself to his role as a leader, having the authority conferred on him, but without ever acquiring competence" (Ibid., 22).

1.2 The Search for Solutions That Consider Specificities

The essential characteristics of African culture make it possible to highlight the relevance of solutions that consider the principles of the socio-economic method and the tools recommended.

1.2.1 *Essential Characteristics of African Culture*[3]

An important characteristic with consequences in the field of management is "the place of elders": *"There is a natural hierarchy that is sometimes difficult to reconcile with the principles of organization, personnel management, and the establishment of control procedures"* (Causse, 1993, 24). It explains the military-type organizations, the significant hierarchical distances, sources of "irresponsibility." We are faced with the difficulty of decentralizing (d'Iribarne, 1990).

Then comes "collectivism," in the sociological sense of the term, where solidarity takes precedence over individualism, which can lead the individual into situations described as irrational. Thus, in the company, the distribution of wealth within the community of belonging may precede its production, or at least it is independent of it. Solidarity explains the mode of recruitment. Western" management methods based on individualism and competition, and therefore a source of conflict, are not relevant in this context.

Let's add the difficulty of separating private and professional life, a separation that is taken for granted in the Anglo-Saxon management style. The expressions used to characterize the African enterprise, whose boundaries are blurred, are significant from this point of view: "family enterprise" or even "village enterprise" (Zadi Kessy, 1998).

1.2.2 *Some Principles of the Socio-Economic Method Consistent With African Culture*

These cultural characteristics are echoed in the writings of the creators of the socio-economic method on the values that, in our opinion, form the basis of this method:

- "Personal gain at the expense of any community is not acceptable" (Savall et al., 2015, 149);
- "... there is no dichotomy between professional and personal life" (Ibid. 152);
- "The entrepreneur cannot be content with being a creator of economic wealth, for he or she must also be a creator of meaning (values) and a creator of social ties,..." (Ibid. 152);
- "We must, in fact, rethink the organization no longer as a closed world but as an open system with porous boundaries where professional and personal problems interact" (Ibid. 152);
- "Misunderstanding an employee's non-work life,..., is a source of errors, tensions, misinterpretations and misbehaviors in the field of work life" (Savall and Zardet, 2005, 168).

Some concepts often used fit well with the characteristics of the context, such as "interdependence," considered as a relational value requiring reciprocity (trust, honesty in business,...). Giving to stakeholders (family, village, ethnic group) is not without counterpart. Gifts are followed by counter-gifts of various forms (financial contribution, flexible jobs,...).

1.2.3 *Recommended Management Tools*

If we look at the small "community" African enterprise, in which the functions of decision and control are not separated, the principles mentioned above are fully applicable. These are the most numerous in Africa. On the other hand, public enterprises, as well as societal enterprises, are more subject to universal management methods.[4] In these enterprises, the methods and tools imported have deteriorated over time or have never been properly used. The use of an overall approach (of the Horivert type), involving management and operational staff, is likely to shift the very hierarchical mode of regulation towards new, more participative, and more motivating managerial practices. The examination of some experiences of activities carried out in the field in innovative projects, in accordance with the normative precepts of the International Labor Organization (ILO), to which the ILO belongs, highlights the common values that underlie the cooperative actions that have taken place between the ILO and ISEOR.

2 EXAMPLES OF PROJECTS IN LINE WITH THE SOCIO-ECONOMIC METHOD, SHARED VALUES AND COOPERATION ACTIONS

We have chosen three examples that highlight the shared values between the two organizations ILO and ISEOR.

2.1 Examination of Some Projects

We emphasize the innovative approaches adopted in each of these projects.

2.1.1 The Pedagogical Method Implemented in the National Management Development Centers

Expert reports about enterprises emphasized the need to train managers to accelerate the development of countries. The ineffectiveness of the actions recommended until then (traditional training seminars, expert missions) led the head of mission to create Management Development Centers.[5] The term *development* chosen is significant.

The training was aimed at a small group of people in a work situation, of equivalent hierarchical level, to allow group work. The participants committed themselves to sharing their experiences and to carrying out a project to improve the functioning of their department. The program was divided into four or five phases, each of which included a training and exchange workshop lasting a few days, followed by a return to the company for a few weeks, the final phase being the presentation by each participant of the proposed improvements and the methods of implementation.

Teamwork, learning autonomy, developing critical thinking and mutual enrichment were the valuable contributions of the method. Moreover, this type of training has a multiplier effect because during the periods in the company, the participant works on his project within his team. The results obtained were tangible for the individuals, for the companies and for the country.

2.1.2 The Approach to Developing Training Plans

A mission to develop training plans took place in 1986 at the request of a large public mining company located in the Aïr desert.[6] The term *training plans* is generally used to refer to the tables drawn up within the personnel department.

Based on the socio-economic principle that people only fully adhere to systems in which they have been involved, an innovative method was implemented. The proposed method consisted of a normative phase (job profile) followed by an observational phase (evaluation of possible gaps in relation to the norms). At the end of these two phases, the training plan was developed.

The particularity of the approach lies in the normative phase. The "specifications" for each position, including the work to be done, the way to do it, the way to behave and the way to represent the work relationships, were developed by consensus, using a participatory approach. The job profile for level N was drawn up by a committee made up of employees occupying a position at level N, level $N-1$ and level $N+1$.

The assessment phase was carried out by a development committee led by the employee's line manager, whose role was to determine the direction of the gap between the individual and the norm: if the gap was negative, a training plan was envisaged, and if it was positive, the individual's promotion could be considered. The method was therefore also a career management tool.

An important collateral benefit was that the participants of the committee, who had been led to reflect on certain required aspects of behavior, often improved their behavior, even before any training action.

2.1.3 Organizing Leadership Conferences

Conferences were organized for the general managers of companies and other organizations. In view of the difficulty of decentralizing and delegating, we decided that one of them would be on the subject: "What is a (well) organized company? There was a lot of discussion about the difficulty of delegating as well as about time management, information systems, employee motivation and shared values.

In the same vein, a conference aimed at the general managers of public companies, considered to be poorly managed by an overly lax management, was entitled: "Can we manage a public company as we manage a private company? It provoked debates likely to change behaviors.

These conferences were reported in the national newspaper,[7] which increased the impact and confirmed the participants' feeling of having a national mission.

2.2 Shared Values and Cooperative Actions

The principles and values that prevailed during the implementation of these projects are close to those that emerge from the socio-economic theory, which explains the common actions that we will report on.

2.2.1 Shared Values

The adoption of a *participatory approach,* present in all activities, echoes the literature on the socio-economic method, particularly the emphasis on proximity dialogues that "seek to better integrate the minority into the decision-making process in the framework of a 'collaborative and participatory democracy'" (Savall et al., 2015, 145).

In the area of training, the desire to go beyond *the stage of knowledge and to integrate knowhow, knowhow, and even knowhow* to be paramount. At the end of the training, the individual must be able to do his or her job but also be able to lead a group and participate in social cohesion in an "open system."

All the actions, even those dealing with a specific field, were considered according to *an overall, multidimensional approach.* The interaction phenomena between the stakeholders were taken into consideration, regardless of the activity and the level at which it took place. This approach is close to the "Horivert" process of the socio-economic method.

2.2.2 Cooperative Actions

These are in two areas: participation in thesis defenses of ISEOR doctoral students in which the authors of this article have been asked to be members of the jury, and major collaborative publications.

In 1996, G. N'Kanagu's thesis, *"Contribution of the integrated training method to the improvement of business performance in Central Africa: The case of Burundian businesses"* was undoubtedly one of the first intervention-research experiences in African businesses. The results were significant, as the author indicated at the time of the defense: "The company agreed to invest in us.

In 1998, K. Tamo's dissertation, *"Proposal of an interpretative model of human development likely to improve the performance of African organizations: application to the Angolan public administration,"* showed that the socio-economic method could be adapted to public organizations.

In 2000, H. Yamuremye's dissertation on the ambitious topic of *"The contribution of concerted delegation practices to improving the functioning of management teams"* showed that delegation practices are possible. We were surprised to find out, during an intervention in Burundi in 2008, that H. Yamuremye was responsible for a course in socio-economic management at the Université Lumière in Bujumbura.

In 2005, L. Looki's thesis, *"Proposing a socio-economic management approach to improve performance—The case of Togo and Ghana,"* had as its field of study a private clinic in Lomé, which one of the authors had the opportunity to visit two years after the defense. The process that was put in place continued.

As far as collaborative publications are concerned, let's mention first the book *"Le conseil en management. A guide for the profession,"* published by the ILO, under the direction of M. Kubr. The latest edition in 1998 presents the socio-economic method.

In 2000, the book "Unleashing the untapped potential of companies through socio-economic management," whose authors are H. Savall, V. Zardet and M. Bonnet, with the participation of P. Hidalgo (a member of the ISEOR Scientific Committee), was published jointly by the ILO and ISEOR. A new edition was published in 2008.

In 2009, a chapter of the book coordinated by ISEOR officials was written in collaboration: *"Contribution of socio-economic management to solve universal social problems." It is included in the part of the book dealing with the theme "Sustainable social responsibility of the company: contribution of socio-economic management."*

CONCLUSION

The approaches used in the implementation of the ILO's technical cooperation activities for the development of countries have been mostly innovative. The ILO's values have led to a participatory approach, respecting the individual and making economic and social performance compatible. These values, which are also those considered by the socio-economic method, have led to a rapprochement between the ILO and IESOR. Among the reference values, "proximity management," which is at the heart of the socio-economic method's approach, makes it capable of providing the solution for the countries of the South. It allows for the integration of specific behaviors of the context and thus for progress in the knowledge of "African management."

NOTES

1. Mostly Western African countries.
2. See the World Bank Report on the Observance of Standards and Codes.
3. We take into consideration those common cultural patterns of the region studied
4. In a public company, regardless of where it is located, rigorous management of public money does not allow any deviation from the rules of public accounting. In a company, or "controlled" company, the rules of good governance apply. Naturally, respecting universal rules does not prevent certain practices, such as the creation of social funds intended to deal with events relating to personnel.

5. *The Centre National de Perfectionnement à la Gestion de Niamey* (CNPG) was created in 1986 as part of a government program to rehabilitate businesses, under the supervision of the Chamber of Commerce, Agriculture, Industry and Handicrafts, with the support of the ILO-UNDP project. A similar center was created in 1990 in Conakry. These centers are still in operation.
6. Mission carried out by G. Causse and P. Stern (HRM Specialist) in the Sonichar company in Anou-Araren.
7. Cf. Le Sahel" of July 26–27 and 28, 1985 following the conference: "What is a (well) organized enterprise?"

REFERENCES

Bourgoin (1984). *«L'Afrique malade du management»,* Ed. Jean Picollet, 218 p.

Causse, G. (1993). Le transfert de technologie dans le domaine du management. Application aux pays en développement d'Afrique francophone, *Revue Intercultures* n° 22, juillet, p. 15–30.

Causse, G. & Hidalgo, P. (1986). *Conception de la formation et incidence sur les stratégies mises en œuvre au CNPG,* Note pour servir de préambule au dossier remis à la mission d'évaluation PNUD du projet CNPG, 6 p.

Dia, A. L. (1991). Le management africain : mythe ou réalité, *Revue Internationale PME,* vol. 4, n°, 29–48.

D'Iribarne, P. (1990). Face à l'impossible décentralisation des entreprises africaines, *Revue française de gestion,* n° 80, sept-oct., p. 28–39.

Henry, A. (1988). Peut-on redresser une entreprise africaine en respectant la parole des ancêtres ? *Annales des Mines,* Septembre, 86–94.

Kubr, M. (1978,1998). (sous la direction de), Une voix alternative: la méthode socio-économique, au chapitre « Amélioration de la productivité et des performances, in *Le conseil en management. Guide pour la profession,* p. 496–500 et annexe p. 783–799.

Looki, L. (2005). *Proposition d'une gestion de type socio-économique pour l'amélioration des performances. Cas du Togo et du Ghana.* Thèse de doctorat de sciences de gestion. Université de Lyon.

Maertens, E., Causse, G., Bonnet, M., & Hidalgo, P. (2009). Contribution du management socio-économique pour résoudre des problématiques sociales universelles, in *Management socio-économique : une approche innovante,* coordonné par H. Savall, V. Zardet et M. Bonnet, Ed. Economica, 167–188.

N'Kanagu, G. (1996). *Contribution de la méthode de formation intégrée à l'amélioration des performances des entreprises en Afrique centrale : Le cas des entreprises du Burundi.* Thèse de doctorat de sciences de gestion. Université de Lyon.

Olomo, P. R. (1987). Comment concilier tradition et modernité dans l'entreprise africaine, *Revue Française de Gestion* n°64, sept-oct., 91–94.

Tamo, T. (1998). *Proposition d'un modèle interprétatif du développement humain susceptible d'améliorer les performances des organisations africaines : application à l'administration publique angolaise.* Thèse de doctorat de sciences de gestion. Université de Lyon.

Yamuremye, H. (2001). *La contribution des pratiques de délégation concertée à l'amélioration du fonctionnement des équipes de direction.* Thèse de doctorat de sciences de gestion. Université de Lyon.

Zadi Kessy, M. (1998). *Culture africaine et gestion de l'entreprise moderne,* Ed. Ceda Abidjan, 245 p.

This page intentionally left blank.

CHAPTER 93

HIDDEN RISK

Socio-Economic Theory and Crises

Robert Gephart

ABSTRACT

Hidden risk involves potential threats to organizations that are neglected or tacitly accepted. These risks create hidden costs unaddressed in formal accounting reports and information systems. They undermine revenue, impede organizational performance, and engender crises. SEAM processes can recover some these costs. But when unaddressed, the costs can accumulate and evolve into crises. The current chapter addresses the nature of hidden risk, how it emerges in organizations, how hidden costs produce dysfunctions that make society more risk-prone, and how SEAM's six new management tools, along with Ethnostatistics, can help manage hidden risks and prevent organizational crises.

Hidden risk reflexively creates hidden costs in organizations that are seldom addressed in capitalist production. This chapter focuses on how hidden risks can be detected and managed using the Socio-Economic Theory of Management (SEAM: Savall, 1974, 1981; Savall & Zardet 1987; Savall, Zardet & Bonnet 2000; Buono & Savall, 2007). SEAM research established how hidden costs emerge as unintended side effects of wealth production (Beck, 1992). These costs include the "surplus expenditures and opportunity costs" excluded from the organization's accounting information system" (Buono & Savall, 2007, p. 425) that impede organizational performance. They can amount to 15% to 42% of business turnover or revenue. Although 35%–55% of hidden costs can be recovered by SEAM processes (Bonnet, Savall, H., Savall, A., & Zardet, 2018, p. 450), this value added is lost when hidden costs are not identified and managed, producing hidden risks. Hidden risks thus exist as invisible or unaddressed threats to organizations that can become crises.

SEAM Treatise, pages 767–772

SEAM focuses on harnessing hidden costs in organizations to enhance organizational performance. Hidden costs occur in individual organizations but reflect system wide problems threatening societies. These costs have created a new social paradigm – "the risk society" (Beck, 1992) "where the risks and hazards systematically produced" in modern economies need to be "prevented, dramatized... (and) limited" (p. 21). These risks harm economies and can engender economic actions that "exceed the limits of what is tolerable" (p. 21). It is important to prevent the acceptance of 'normal risks' that have become "a dominant force in history and society" (Beck, 1992, p. 22), and the harmful consequences that modern productive forces have hidden and ignored.

This chapter develops and elaborates the concept of hidden risk in organizations. It explains how to use the SEAM Approach to uncover hidden risks and hidden costs in contemporary organizations, and how SEAM tools can overcome dysfunctions that enhance organizational risks. The socio-economy is conceptualized as a risk economy, allowing hidden risks to be understood in socio-economic terms. The Taylor-Fayol-Weber (TFW) Virus metaphor of SEAM is use to highlight this key ideological risk to organizational functioning. The role the TFW virus plays in creating hidden risks and impacting organizational performance is described. The chapter then explains Qualimetrics (Savall & Zardet, 2004, 2011) and Ethnostatistics (Gephart, 1988; Gephart & Saylors, 2018), two methods that can be used to address hidden risks and costs. Qualimetrics integrates qualitative, quantitative and financial data to provide better descriptions and measures of hidden costs and hidden risks (Savall & Zardet, 1996, 2011; Gephart & Savall, 2018). Ethnostatistics (Gephart, 1988, 2006) explores how numbers and performance measures are produced, assessed and used rhetorically in documents and discourse.

The key chapter questions are (a) what is hidden risk and how does it emerge in contemporary organizations? (b) How do hidden risks produce costs related to organizational dysfunctions that occur in risk society organizations? and (c) How can one use Qualimetrics, Ethnostatistics and SEAM practices to manage hidden costs and hidden risks in organizations during crises?

1 THE SOCIO-ECONOMY AND NEVER-ENDING CRISES

Advanced capitalism creates a never-ending crisis cycle (Habermas, 1973; H. Savall, 1975, 2018). Crises are activated by sequential failures of (a) the economic system that cannot produce the number of "consumable values" sought by citizens (1973, p. 49), leading to (b) an administrative system failure to produce important rational decisions. This leads then to (c) failure of the socio-cultural system to produce "action motivating meanings" for works (1973, p. 49), resulting in (d) a legitimation crisis for the state when it fails to create general work motivations or produce positive responses to government actions.

Legitimation crises are further enhanced in the risk society. Early industrial society was one where "the logic of wealth production dominates and constrains the logic of risk production" (Beck, 1992, p. 12). But capitalism has shifted to one where the logic of risk production now dominates the logic of wealth production and there is need to remediate the critical risks of wealth production: the "irreversible threats to the life of plants, animals, and human beings" (Beck, 1992, p. 13). These threats risks can no longer be dismissed as unfortunate, silent, side-effects of production since they are globalized. Organizations in risk society now face the issue of how to prevent or minimize "the risks and hazards systematically produced as part of modernization" (Beck, 1992, p. 19).

Despite this, advanced capitalism retains a focus on maximizing explicit revenues and cutting explicit costs to achieve the goal of economic efficiency. Hidden risks and costs, and hidden potential and value, are ignored. SEAM provides an alternative to conventional management that uncovers the benefits, as well as the waste, unanticipated side effects, and damages that emerge from advanced capitalism. SEAM is oriented to enhancement of human and organizational potential rather than its destruction. Thus, management theory's emphasis on explicit costs and revenue excludes consideration of hidden costs and unexpected side-effects that underlie risk societies and that become sources of hidden risks that engender crises. An important feature of SEAM is its ability to assess hidden costs and assign precise cost estimates to accumulated risks in organizations, and to produce evidence-based knowledge for improved crises responses.

2 THE TFW VIRUS AND HIDDEN RISKS

Advanced capitalism employs an ideological mindset or logic that emphasizes cost cutting, with unfortunate implications. SEAM (Savall, 1974, 2007, 2016) has developed the "TFW Virus" metaphor, based on the work of three classical management theorists—Taylor, Fayol, and Weber—to highlight the core principles and problematic implications of advanced capitalism. These principles have become reified conceptions and distorted descriptions of management theories, transformed into rigid tools for management. The principal features of the virus are (a) use of hyper-specialization in organizational structures to be efficient; (b) separation of work design from work activity; and (c) depersonalized job design that assumes workers are naturally lazy and require management control (Gephart and Savall, 2018, p. 264; Hazelbaker, 2016, 2–16). The visible symptoms of the virus are (a) employees are assumed to have limited skills and to be replaceable, (b) silos differentiate people and areas of work, (c) dysfunctions are common due to problems with co-ordination, (d) employees are rigidly controlled by with fixed job descriptions and policies, and (e) employees are assumed to be unthinking beings who under-valued relative to management.

The foundational premise is that increasing profit requires ongoing cutting of explicit costs. Labor is assumed to be the most flexible factor of production (vs. land and capital) and the most controllable cost. Extensive cost cutting and labor force reductions become the best practices to improve organizational performance, defined solely in financial terms (Bonnet, et al., 2018). The TFW virus limits employees' quality of work life, restricts their range of work activities, hinders engaged activity, lowers performance, and can create dysfunctions and dissatisfaction (Bonnet, et al., 2018, p. 448).

SEAM argues that the financial and operating practices of organizations infected with the TFW Virus create significant hidden risks that create hidden costs that undermine profit, inflict unnecessary dysfunctions and costs on organizations, and limit the development of organizational or human potential. Human potential is essential in order to identify and manage hidden risks and costs (Bonnet, et al., 2018, p. 447). These hidden risks and costs cannot be covered by further cost-cutting but they "can be harnessed and hidden human potential can be released by identifying and overcoming dysfunctions" (p. 447).

Hidden risks are potential threats to organizations that are unnoticed, neglected or normalized. The key risk posed by the TFW Virus is its emphasis on developing structures that create dysfunctions and impede human potential. The sources of hidden risk include: everyday activities that create dysfunctional structures that impede work performance; unanticipated threats that are not addressed due to more pressing issues; recurrent problems or dysfunctions that have been normalized; and negative side effects of normal and useful value creation activities. Hidden risks thus require actions to address and control them and risk remediation can produce tangible, visible costs

Hidden costs destroy value-added (Savall, 2007, p. 7), or create opportunity cost due to failure to gain value added where it was available. Hidden costs have 6 components.

The first three components are costs the organization can avoid: excess salaries, overtime, and overconsumption. The next three costs are nonproduction, non-creation of potential, and costs stemming from risks the enterprise endures. These hidden costs are grounded in 6 areas of organizational dysfunction Savall, Zardet & Bonnet, 2008, p. 30–33): working conditions, work organization, communication-coordination-cooperation, time management, integrated training, and strategic implementation.

Classical accounting does not record hidden risks or measure hidden costs and cannot control these. There are however, risk-based indicators of hidden costs: absenteeism, occupational injuries and diseases, staff turnover, non-quality production, and productivity gaps (Savall, et al., 2008, p. 33). When incorporated into visible cost accounts, hidden costs negatively impact income in terms of the ledger but they are often unrecorded and thus become lost earnings (p. 31). Yet hidden costs are high in organizations (Savall, et al., 2008, p. 30) and impact immediate performance by limiting resources for production in the present, and limiting the creation of future potential due to scarce resources.

Hidden costs have another side: hidden performance. Hidden performance is a reduction in hidden costs, or, the creation of unmeasured gains. Hidden performance is not recorded because it is a prospective resource, not a current revenue source (Savall, et al., 2008, p. 31). SEAM "puts the enterprise on a development path where the reduction of hidden costs and the identification of hidden performance are critical" (Savall, et al., 2008, p. 31). This contrasts with conventional management approaches that capture information on only visible performance.

3 ELABORATING SEAM

SEAM (Buono & Savall, 2007) is a change intervention process to help enterprises become more effective by focusing on controlling hidden costs, enhancing hidden human potential, and overcoming dysfunctions. The initial step in the process is diagnosis of dysfunctions and evaluation of hidden costs (p. 8). Hidden risks generally constitute or operate as indicators of hidden costs but are not often explicitly examined in SEAM. One contribution of the chapter is to clarify how hidden risks can be linked to hidden costs.

Hidden risks are the starting point for understanding hidden cost production. This first intervention step requires the intervenor/consultant to meet and interview organizational members to obtain their descriptions of organizational dysfunctions, and estimate their frequencies and impacts. The second stage involves cooperation among organizational members who develop innovative organizational solutions to the dysfunctions (Savall, 2007, p. 8). Third, implementation and improvement actions are developed and taken. Finally, the change outcomes are evaluated using qualitative, quantitative, and financial performance information (p.8). The change process is a "metamorphosis" (p. 8) in the organization to engage employees in two actions: (a) a horizontal action where the executive team and middle management work together ascertain dysfunctions and implement solutions, and (b) a vertical action where two or more units involve their management team and line personnel in ascertaining dysfunctions and hidden costs. This process enhances the link between the company's strategy and the socio-economic intervention's goals (p. 9) and embeds the change in the organization from its top management team to its shop floor. The process promotes collective learning to ensure dysfunctions and solutions are addressed by the people, at all levels, who encounter these issues.

There are two methodological approaches to understanding the production of numbers—Ethnostatistics and Qualimetrics—used by SEAM to identify and harness explicit and hidden revenues, costs and opportunities related to hidden risks. Ethnostatistics is important to broadening the scope of qualitative descriptions of hidden and explicit revenues and costs in organizational performance. Ethnostatistics uses an interpretive perspective to understand the production and meaning of statistics (Gephart, 2006, p. 418) and financial measures used in crises (Gephart, 2014), including the rhetorical or persuasive uses of numbers. Each of the three levels of ethnostatistics contributes distinct insights into the performance of an organization. First level ethnostatistics explores construction of numbers in everyday settings, using in-depth ethnographic field research on the practices of people involved in creating and using numbers. This brings important variables, practices and processes to light and allows a better description of the contextuality and complexity of constructed realities that can enhance the evidence used in SEAM interventions. First level ethnostatistics helps to identify alternative practices, gaps, and issues that are missed by examination of performance in formal financial numbers produced for accounting records. Second level ethnostatistics puts statistics to work to test assumptions about statistical interpretations and explore alternative statistical tools that could yield differing results. This process uncovers limits to current practices and methods, and identifies alternative performance measures and statistics that are more meaningful. Third level ethnostatistics explores the rhetoric of statistics by analysis of the language of statistical texts. This shows how statistical claims are used to persuade people of certain truths or features in texts, and raises questions about the 'unbiased' validity of statistical interpretations and applications.

Qualimetrics is a SEAM based methodology that uses qualitative, statistical, and financial data to overcome limits of institutionalized measurement systems. Qualimetrics complements Ethnostatistics. It seeks to recover "hidden data" (Savall & Zardet, 2011, p. xxix) that are omitted from accounting reports. Hidden data including hidden costs are revealed by qualitative information and observations collected in interviews and documents. In SEAM, the researcher quests for what the actors do not say, the hidden quantitative information that exposes fundamental factors that explain organizational performance. The qualimetric approach uses "the logical and semantic continuum between ideas and numbers"—qualitative, statistical and financial data—to allow each component to contribute to the meanings of the other two components (p. xxx). The qualimetric process thus involves collection of qualitative data from actors that describe their setting, work practices, and outcomes. Next, actors work to determine the key dysfunctions and how frequently these occur—the statistical second. The third—financial—step is to estimate the hidden costs of dysfunctions identified in the first two steps. Then, actions to overcome dysfunctions can be developed based on accurate and validated evidence on the organization's functioning. This can be enriched by use of ethnostatistics in description and evaluation of counting practices. Ethnostatistics is thus important for understanding the broad context of performance measurement facing organizations, identifying intangible yet implicit phenomena that impact how organizations operate, and effectively analyzing hidden risks, hidden costs, and hidden performance of concern to SEAM.

4 SEAM IN PRACTICE: CRISES

Six "new" tools of management – Internal/External Strategic Action Plan, Priority Action Plan, Competency Grid, Time Management, Strategic Piloting Indicators, and Periodically

Negotiated Activity Contracts (Savall, Zardet & Bonnet, 2008)—provide important techniques to improve management practice. They create information to identify and manage hidden risks and costs and facilitate conversion of hidden costs into value-added (Savall, 2007:12). The tools also enhance the visibility of risks, threats and dysfunctions, and opportunities and can also enhance the effectiveness of crisis management planning and responses by practitioners.

The lessons to be learned here are that (a) SEAM practices could likely improve Governmental responses to the COVID crisis, (b) many organizations and leaders are reacting in traditional ways that result in practices that enhance the TFW virus and cripple organizational responses, and (c) hidden risks, costs and their transformation into hidden value is possible but difficult without recognition or use of the socio-economic approach to management.

REFERENCES

Beck, U. (1992). *Risk society: Towards a new modernity.* Sage Publications.

Gephart, R. (1988). *Ethnostatistics: Qualitative foundations for quantitative research.* Sage.

Gephart, R. (2004). Normal risk: Technology, sensemaking and environmental disasters. *Organization and Environment, 17*(1), 20–26.

Gephart, R. (2006). Ethnostatistics and organizational research methodologies: An introduction. *Organizational Research Methods, 9*(4), 417–431.

Gephart, R. (2014). Using prosperity to construct an economic crisis: Alberta's "Bitumen" Bubble. *Recherches en Sciences de Gestion, 105.*

Gephart, M., & Svedberg H. (2019). Introduction to risk, crisis and emergency management. In R. Gephart, C. Miller, & K. Svedberg Helgesson (Eds.), *The Routledge companion to risk, crisis and emergency management* (pp. 3–13). Routledge.

Gephart, R., & Savall, H. (2018). The TFW virus: Ideology and global risks. In D. Boje (Ed.), *The Emerald handbook of management and organization inquiry* (pp. 263–276). Emerald Publishing Limited.

Gephart, R. P., Jr., & Saylors, R. (2019). Ethnostatistics. In P. Atkinson, S. Delamont, A. Cernat, J. W. Sakshaug, & R. A. Williams (Eds.), *SAGE research methods foundations.* SAGE.

Habermas, J. (1973). *Legitimation crisis.* Beacon Press.

Buono, A., & Savall, H. (2007). *Socio-economic intervention in organizations: The intervener-researcher and the SEAM approach to organizational analysis.* Information Age Press.

Bonnet, M., Savall, H., Savall, A., & Zardet, V. (2019). The socio-economic approach to management: Preventing economic crises by harnessing costs and creating sustainable productivity. In R. Gephart, C. Miller, & K. Svedberg Helgesson (Eds.), *The Routledge companion to risk, crisis and emergency management* (pp. 447–463). Routledge.

Savall, H., & Zardet, V. (2019). Bernácer's topical theory of crisis and unemployment. In R. Gephart, C. Miller, & K. Svedberg Helgesson (Eds.), *The Routledge companion to risk, crisis and emergency management* (pp. 228–257). Routledge.

CHAPTER 94

HIDDEN COSTS STEMMING FROM SITUATIONS OF UNCERTAINTY

The Case of Cyberattacks

Philippe Laurier

ABSTRACT

The company is a social body concerned with its survival, even before aiming for profitability or growth. Its organization and its choices will be influenced by this imperative. Threats to this survival, such as the growing risk of computer attacks, are not easily measurable ex ante by decision-makers and create uncertainty that hinders the optimal allocation of resources, and thus cause hidden costs. Moreover, the mere possibility of such an attack, weighing on the processes and decision-making function of the company in a diffuse manner, lowers its performance and cohesion.

The company is a social body that is ultimately concerned with its survival (presence of stakes). This preoccupation makes it operate choices in front of various threats, or bets when this decisional process is affected by uncertainties: *uncertainties-bets-consequences.* Among the consequences of such a chain of events are hidden costs.

1 UNCERTAINTY GENERATING POSSIBLE HIDDEN COSTS

One of the situations leading to this type of choice concerns computer attacks by cryptovirus -with data encryption and then ransom demand- which have become commonplace against companies. This type of event, or its simple statistical possibility, raises questions prior to making choices:

SEAM Treatise, pages 773–779

- What is my risk, as a decision-maker, as a manager of the company under attack?
- What will be my gain—often comparable to avoided costs—according to the various possible choices?

Such a situation is illustrative of a relationship between "unforeseeable costs" and "hidden costs" (Savall, 1975, 1979; Savall and Zardet, 1987, 1992). The former are not considered predictable with sufficient certainty in the eyes of decision-makers; their probability and magnitude are difficult to estimate ex ante, even for insurers. The latter do not appear in the accounting and economic information system of firms and are the result of a suboptimal operation or organization (Savall, 1975, 1979; Savall and Zardet, 1987). This suboptimality is a consequence of a computer attack or, more to the point of our reflections, of the hypothesis of such an attack. The mere presence of this uncertainty leads to a decrease in efficiency in the company, affecting behaviors, relationships, and processes.

It is therefore necessary to distinguish between the hidden costs of a computer attack and those of the possibility of an attack; our reflection focuses on the second point. Indeed, if computer attacks generate damages ranging from the most obvious (a non-production in case of blocking of the company or an attack on its brand image) to the most discreet (such as under productivity or non-quality), the possibility of an attack, and then—if the attack has occurred—the possibility of a solution by a ransom, also cause visible or diffuse inconveniences. Three periods are discernible regarding these hidden costs resulting from uncertainties, with specific nuisances:

- Before any attack, when the proper functioning of the company is disrupted by the hypothesis of the occurrence of such an event.
- During the event, if it occurs, when the capacity of reflection is handicapped by it and monopolized by the search for a way out, which in turn takes the form of a gamble.
- A posteriori, when the trauma suffered and the hypothesis of a repetition of the event sometimes give rise to less effective behavior.

2 COMPANIES ARE DEADLY BODIES

Cryptoviruses are intended to paralyze the victim. When key functions are permanently blocked, the hacking becomes potentially lethal (maximum stake[1]) for the affected company. Death can be considered in three ways:

- As an organization likely to suffer a lethal attack from an economic point of view, by forced cessation of its operations, with bankruptcy filing;
- Or to undergo a destructive attack from a human point of view, when the shock of the crisis weakens psychologically the individuals, reduces their lucidity and their capacity to react. The human factor is currently underestimated in the evaluation of the damage caused by computer attacks; there are weaknesses which, by a boomerang effect, will lead to other costs for the company.
- Moving from an individual level to a collective level and to an attack that destroys its cohesion, the company appears as a living organism if it remains coordinated and united in the face of a threat, and as long as it manages to overcome or transcend its

internal oppositions, from the manager to the shareholder or the employee. In fact, all the members of this company -decision-makers or spectators—are not identically involved in these choices and by these choices; their personal risks -patrimonial, professional, reputational—are of different magnitude and nature. In this respect, the company is not a homogeneous and coherent body, but an entity torn by opposing interests revealed and exacerbated by an IT crisis or by its perspective. Thus, the gain and the risk differ for the various members of the company, which influences their postures and their choices. The moral dimension is also appreciated in a divergent way by these protagonists, faced with the dilemma of whether to pay a ransom.

3 WEIGHT AND COST OF UNCERTAINTY

The company faced with a computer threat is not forced to make a single choice, but a series of successive choices, which occur mainly at two stages of the attack:

3.1 Uncertainty About the Event

The first choice occurs upstream, when the company is faced with an initial uncertainty: will it be attacked, and if so, how much damage will be done? Should it invest in a security system whose effectiveness it is unable to predict, because the uncertainty weighs not only on the possible attack, but also on the random performance of the shield.

It does not know whether it will be under-investing defensively (allowing an attack to take place), over-investing (corresponding to an economic waste of scarce resources, notably its cash flow and available time), or investing inappropriately to prevent attacks. Ambiguity is expressed in three forms, resulting from too much, not enough or inadequacy.

3.2 Uncertainty About the Outcome

The second period of choice occurs later when the company under attack is offered a ransom by the hacker, in exchange for the promise of a decryption key. There is a certainty of the event—happened and in progress—and a first approximation of the amount of the damage; however, the hazardous nature of the good provision of a key amount to making a bet, or a refusal to bet when the victim refuses the payment.

These bets are taken under conditions of imperfect information (on the probability of occurrence of an event, and on the extent of its consequences) and incomplete lucidity (anxiety disturbs the decision-maker, who differs from the *homo economicus* of the theory). The initial difficulty in measuring the gains and risks for choices is reinforced by the psychological tension during the crisis. Bets are taken in a partisan, hostile and changing environment: the hacker is an actor in the game, after having been its generator. His choices interfere with those of the company.

This two-stage uncertainty generates attitudes that oscillate between abstentionism -when doubt leads to refusing to make a choice, such as investing in random security and then paying an equally random ransom- and, as an absolute survival reflex, accepting any investment or ransom (Savall, Péron, Zardet, Bonnet, 2015).

4 THE HIDDEN COSTS OF UNCERTAINTY

Three types of disturbances can be discerned, in addition to the harm of an attack per se and the price of the initial security investment:

4.1 A Decrease in Productive Performance

The company worried about a possible attack is forced to modify its behavior and organization to ensure its security. Such modifications generate costs, some of which are hidden, since companies often find themselves less efficient in the management of their day-to-day operations,[2] and less rapid in the processing of their business and in their exchanges with the outside world. This first type of ed performance is sometimes quantifiable, such as for losses measurable in time (overtime in the hidden cost-performance model of Savall and Zardet, 1987).

There are also effects expressed in money, such as purchased safety tools that duplicate previous equipment. Our field study highlighted that a significant part of the improvements in the security of information systems obtained by an investment could have been obtained by tools at a more moderate price; many managers, subjected to an anxiety-provoking argument from security vendors, overpay for the promised results, driven by the reassuring hope of an equivalence between expensive pricing and strong protection.

4.2 A Decrease in Decision-Making Performance

This is the result of uncertainty, which mobilizes minds and provokes a wait-and-see attitude, immobility and even apathy, as well as sterile overactivity and contradictory decisions.

Testimonies collected from managers who have been victims of hacking are astonishing because of the repeated thanks that are addressed to such and such an external person who has been present during the crisis, and who has brought a calmer and more dispassionate view of the accident. These thanks are related to the costs avoided by such a presence: the latter often mitigated the decline in decision-making performance that the company was about to suffer in the chaos.

A common observation during such attacks is indeed the difficulty of SME managers to make decisions that would normally have appeared simple to them. If it is true that the complexity of a crisis makes it difficult to manage, in fact, even the most ordinary actions and decisions suddenly seem complex to managers; it is first their capacity for analysis that is reduced.

The decrease in decision-making performance experienced by the company can be divided into two categories: on the one hand, a disruption affects the decisions to be made as a result of the IT crisis, and which would not have existed without it; on the other hand, a disruption affects decisions that would have been made even without the crisis, such as validating a hiring, negotiating a commercial agreement, or prosaically organizing one's agenda and leading a meeting.

The crisis management assistance units that are brought in to support a manager during an attack answer questions that are often high-level on the technological side, but low-level on the managerial side, to the point where the main contribution on this last aspect lies in listening and giving advice of simple common sense: a manager then expects to be helped to gather his ideas, to resume a normal rhythm of reflection, and to know how to prioritize daily priorities again, in addition to those of the event. Otherwise, there is a cost consisting in the fact that a process internal to the company but not directly affected by the hacking takes a disproportionate amount of time, or that the decision is less relevant, less adapted to the expectations of a customer or a supplier than it would otherwise have been. This last notion is difficult to measure to the point that insurers have made it a practice to include in their cyber insurance system assistance provided on the spot by a telephone assistance unit. In doing so, they reduce both the "unpredictable costs" (we don't know what a hack will cost, but we know that it will cost less with good assistance) and the "hidden costs" (again, we don't know what the lower performance of the decision-making system will cost, but we estimate that it will cost less with assistance)

4.3 Decreased Commercial and Relational Performance

A frequent subsequent distrust is observed among victims, who prefer to take fewer risks through fewer contacts. A representative case is that of an art gallery owner, victim of a takeover of her email by an unknown person who stole and modified her password. This email was one of her commercial vectors, because clients contact her through this medium. The hacker used the address book of this account to send mails asking for financial assistance to the recipients. The trauma of the attack was enough for this manager to refuse to open certain e-mails from an unknown sender for years. A mental reflex designed to protect herself from a booby-trapped attachment that could steal her password again, but which results in a loss of business opportunities.

Note the increasing nature of the damage: the losses are nil on the first day since any new contact would have taken time to turn into a possible purchase. They increase thereafter. This character is also accumulative, since a new satisfied prospect would have contributed to the word-of-mouth that drains other contacts. A first reputational deficit came from the counter-advertising done to the clients of this gallery at the time of the attack, since they were solicited unpleasantly, some of them having paid, driven by their generosity. The second one gives its full value to the term deficit, with a decrease of notoriety consecutive to this aversion to open mails and to exchange.

The first of these two losses would be qualified as an intangible cost but not strictly speaking hidden. The second, which results from a discrete change in behavior, a self-censorship, is reflected in a drop in commercial and relational performance. The measurement of this hidden cost will consist either in evaluating the number of lost contacts—initial impact—or the number of lost customers—final impact. Another approach would be to quantify the efforts to be made by the gallery to compensate for this loss, for example by phoning the senders of letters—if they are identifiable—to check their seriousness, or by multiplying the number of openings intended to re-establish contacts with its visitor base outside the Internet.

Despite its extreme character, this case highlights a type of cost present on a smaller scale among many victims or witnesses of attacks. To this should be added the damage suffered by third parties, for example an artist looking for a gallery owner to exhibit. This "collateral damage" leaves the perimeter of a company to embrace that of a community.

5 THE UNEQUAL DISTRIBUTION OF THE COSTS OF UNCERTAINTY

5.1 Distribution Within the Company

Paying a ransom, i.e., paying a swindler, is an ethical transgression that is often judged differently by each person, according to moral and materialistic criteria (the scruples of paying lead to impacts of different magnitudes from one member of the company to another). The resulting differences of opinion sometimes contribute to the breakdown of *affectio societatis*.

In one case, an SME was subjected to a cryptovirus for two weeks; this length of time weakens the cash flow, as most disbursements continue to be made due to direct debits, while the data needed to bring in funds by initiating invoicing becomes unusable. As the blockade continued, dissension grew among the shareholders over a possible ransom payment, which was supposed to liberate them, but where the prospect that the bankruptcy of the company would or would not lead to their personal bankruptcy was apparent. Such behavior is reminiscent of Nicolas Bernoulli's "St. Petersburg paradox" (1713), where a gambler's decision will be influenced by the size of the potential gain or loss, not in absolute terms, but in proportion to the gambler's wealth. This discussion of costs, from the most obvious to the most hidden, cannot ignore the implications for the career or wealth of the person who bears them.

Added to this is the fact that the final payer is sometimes different from the decision-maker, the author of the choices. This is particularly true of hidden costs, whose degree of detectability and readability also differs from one actor to another. Thus, in the presence of uncertainty – in the face of information that is imperfect in quantity and quality, and of a conjectural nature – the inequality is not confined to access to the right information for the various actors, since a second asymmetry concerns the capacity or otherwise of each actor to act on the costs, while a third concerns the unequal distribution of the harm recorded by each. The bias between actors is threefold: of information on costs; of possible action on these costs; of damage caused by these costs, distinctly on each.

These items are intertwined: the choices adopted by the decision-maker within a company reshape the situation, and therefore the costs and the uncertainty attached to them; his action will modify the information and the damage.

The potentially lethal nature of a computer attack reinforces the sensitivity of this uncertainty-betting-consequence chain because the break-up of the attacked company, which until now has been the bearer of the costs, would disperse part of them unequally among its various stakeholders.

5.2 Distribution With Actors Outside the Company

The costs, which give rise to internal disagreements as to their distribution, are at the same time the object of debatable distribution keys with other protagonists, external this time. The IT threat generates uncertainties, the weight of which is borne unequally, since the targeted companies assume the bulk of the costs, while their IT (and IT security) service providers conversely draw on it as a source of revenue, without sharing either the risks or the doubts with their related costs; such precariousness becomes, on the contrary, a source of gain for them.

CONCLUSION

The threats of computer attacks appear as a condensation of uncertainties, to a high degree since they play with the existence of the company, while being concentrated on sometimes very short intervals of time. This concretization of possibly extreme and immediate stakes gives to these facts the appearance of a textbook case, allowing to observe in vivo the disruptions undergone by the companies put in a position to bet for their survival. The context of maximum uncertainty pushes to their paroxysm many hidden costs usually present on a smaller scale in the daily life of companies. These situations thus constitute revelations, microscopes that enlarge for our eyes dysfunctions that were until now too small to be easily observed.

NOTES

1. We will see that the stakes can go beyond the disappearance of the company if the attack causes external losses in addition to internal ones.
2. The feeling of insecurity is often a bridle -as is a safety regulation- that adds checks, prohibitions, restrictions, complexity

REFERENCES

Allais, M. (1953). Le comportement de l'homme rationnel devant le risque : critique des postulats et axiomes de l'école Américaine, *Econometrica, 21*(4), 503–546.

Bernoulli, N. (1713). *Specimen theoriae novae de mensura sortis.*

Laurier, Ph. (2020). *Les cyberattaques et leurs préjudices dans les entreprises. Les rançons lors d'attaques informatiques.* Publication Institut de Recherche Technologique IRT-SystemX, France.

This page intentionally left blank.

CHAPTER 95

SUCCESSFUL SDG TRANSFORMATION THROUGH SOCIO-ECONOMIC CO-CREATION

Raymond Saner and Lichia Yiu

ABSTRACT

The 2030 Agenda represents unprecedented opportunities for doing well *and* doing good. To leverage this historical momentum and succeed in overcoming the Covid–19 pandemic, communities, businesses and governments together need to identify innovative ideas, products, services and processes for new wealth creation in a sustainable and inclusive manner. According to WBCSD, 12 trillion US$ of value creation and employment could be realized. The three dimensions are conceived as forming an interdependent whole, requiring policies that are intersectorial, multi-stakeholder, inclusive, participatory and transparent. This chapter proposes ways to implement such a holistic sustainable and partnership-based development strategy.

Two critical international agreements must be achieved in the next decades to ensure that the world remains sustainable and not be ravaged by pandemics, extreme weather patterns, famine, displacement and armed conflicts. They are the 2030 Agenda for Sustainable Development (inter alias SDGs) and the Paris Agreement on Climate Change. Both agreements demand a systemic "reset" and comprehensive transformation.

This transformation has to be far reaching and encompassing all aspects of human life from social interactions, economic activities, and political orientations to mankind approach to the planetary ecosystems. Underpinning this transformation is the recognition of the necessity to re-balance economic growth, social equity and environmental viability to achieve longer term wellbeing and quality of life.

SEAM Treatise, pages 781–787

This chapter aims to propose a conceptual framework to transform the complex relationships between governments, businesses and civil societies from adversaries to partners in order to achieve the SDGs. This journey of reaching sustainability needs to be infused with a commitment to socio-economic co-creation at its core.

1 CONTEXT

The consequences of Covid–19 pandemic – 1.8 million deaths, 80 million of infected people and hundred millions of job losses – continue to devastate the global system. However, the major economic and social disruptions have also created a generational opportunity to fix the broken wheels of the current system and to build forward a more equitable and sustainable world. As stated by the UN Secretary General Guitterez in his July 2020 Nelson Mandela Lecture,

> The response to the pandemic, and to the widespread discontent that preceded it, must be based on a New Social Contract and a New Global Deal that create equal opportunities for all and respect the rights and freedoms of all. The New Social Contract, between Governments, people, civil society, business and more, must integrate employment, sustainable development and social protection, based on equal rights and opportunities for all.[1]

A new Social Contract and a New Global Deal could only be achieved if countries and their business and other stakeholders join forces and agree to a socio-economic approach in co-creating a new deal of collaboration. Such a new global social contract is encapsulated in the 2030 Agenda and its 17 Goals. Successful implementation and achievement of its 169 targets would deliver the new social contract for "the world that we want" (UNDG, 2013).

A conceptual framework to facilitate cross-sector partnerships and to forge a new Global Deal through the application of socio-economic co-creation (Savall, 2017) and following the guiding principles of Organization and Social Change and Development (OSCD) model proposed by Saner & Yiu (2012) will be presented below.

2 2030 AGENDA TRANSFORMATION AND SECTORAL ACTORS

Applying an OSCD perspective, three sectors need to be considered from a holistic and interactive change perspective. The quality of interactions among them and their respective institutional capabilities can determine to a large extent the success of SDG implementation. They are:

1. An effective, efficient and inclusive government able and willing to cooperate with civil society and the private sector,
2. A business sector that participates in contributing to sustainable development by aligning its production processes with the SDGs and engaging with local communities.
3. A civil society which engages in co-creation of sustainable solution together with the governments and businesses and monitors the progress.

A key task of the OSCD approach is to build transitional management and organizational mechanisms to facilitate a cross sector participatory process based on the use of co-creative design tools for the implementation of the SDGs. Through contextualized SDGs that reflect local socio-economic needs, local ownership could be strengthened. Deeper information exchanges within these sectors and acknowledgement of the diversity of perspectives can then be created allowing for alternative and novel solutions to emerge.

The ensuing discussion clarifies the respective roles and potential contributions of the three sectors and highlights the organizational and cultural changes that entail.

2.1 Government's Role and Contribution to the SDGs

The 2030 Agenda has been proposed as an "indivisible whole" due to strong interdependencies of the social, economic, and environmental dimensions which exist between and within the goals. Some of these goals and targets are mutually supportive, others are constraining or reducing (Nilsson et al, 2017). The interlinkages and interdependencies amongst the 17 SDGs (David LeBlanc, 2015) make it more difficult to find the right policy mix and coherence needed without Cross-sector contributions.

Hence, moving the SDGs forward at national or subnational levels will be a balancing act between policy trade-offs and multiplier effects while bundling goals together where possible. It needs to amplify the positive outcome of some goals and curtail the negative impact of others. An effective change process will require dedicated resources, strong institutional capacities, base-line data and timely feedback and policy coherence. An organizational change program will be called for to identify the strategic pathways of implementing smartly the 17 goals in the 10-year remaining duration of the 2030 Agenda. Three anchoring elements highlights the government's contribution to this change process are:

2.1.1 Resource Allocation

Resource constraint is often one of the main barriers leading to failed change. Prioritization is a must at all administrative level, i.e., nation, province, city or municipality. This strategic planning depends on whether the SDGs can be financed by regular budget, whether sufficient number of competent experts are part of the change process and whether the strategy is coherent. Equally important is a government's ability to consult and negotiate with key stakeholders, e.g., citizens, business, academics, and NGOs to generate a broadly agreed priority list of development actions. Inclusive engagement of stakeholders and open dialogues are necessary to avoid policy bias, fragmentation and exclusion of key stakeholders and vulnerable groups. Platforms to facilitate such engagements need to be identified, built, and maintained as part of the capacity building program.

2.1.2 Governance and Information

Besides budgetary discipline, the government is expected to safeguard the SDG principles of transparency, accountability, inclusiveness, equity and partnership so that a fair and just society functions. This governance function can only be achieved through open communication and information sharing with stakeholders and citizenry. Achieving good governance often represents another cultural orientation with new norms, rules and skillsets.

2.1.3 Policy Coherence

To accelerate SDG progress and effective use of available resources, local governments should engage in cross-sector policy coordination and at the same time forge government to stakeholder policy consultations. (Saner & You, 2017). Policy coordination and consultation (inter alia PCC) requires know-how and ability to design and operate governmental policy mechanisms (Saner, 2009a, 2009b). Without institutionalizing PCC practices, government officials will continue to work in vertical silos at the expense of coordinated horizontal or networked interfaces needed to achieve greater policy impact and desired outcome.

Establishing transparent and standardized operational procedures, fostering complementary culture and norms, and building cross sector teams are the priority tasks of the OSCD intervention to realize the socio-economic co-creation of values and achieve policy coherence.

2.2 Business Role and Contribution to the SDGs

The SDGs represent unprecedented opportunities for "doing well by doing well" (Benjamin Franklin). Improving a company's positive impact on the SDG while at the same time attempting to reduce its potential negative impact requires strategic vision and committed managers who act as boundary spanners between internal processes of an enterprise and the external threats and opportunities. Business adoption of SDGs resonates with a socio-economic approach to management (SEAM) developed by Henri Savall (1974, 1975, 1981) and colleagues of ISEOR (Savall, Zardet, 1987, 2008; Savall, Zardet, Bonnet, 2000; Savall, Péron, Zardet, Bonnet, 2015). SEAM focuses on both people and financial results and offers a philosophical and managerial change theory to enterprise development. It incorporate financial accounting, social values, care and partnership with employees.

Businesses are key partners driving the needed transformation, especially of the SDG 7, 8, 9 and 12, which suggest a change from fossil to renewable energy sources (SDG 7), economic growth and decent working conditions (SDG 8), infrastructure, industrialization and innovation (SDG 9) and sustainable consumption and production (SDG 12). Opportunities presented in these sectors, according to the World Business Council for Sustainable Development, represent an estimated 12 trillion of value creation and related employment. Adopting SEAM will steer business toward contributions in reducing multidimensional poverties that inhibited the development of full human potential for the majority of the world population (SDG 1). This alternative vision and approach to business management will be more organic and responsive to the needs of the community than simply "doing no harm" through the compliance with responsible business codes such as the OECD Responsible Business Guidelines.

To ensure sustainable and mutually beneficial cooperation with other actors, the role of Business Diplomats (Yiu & Saner, 2018) is needed to bridge the sector divide and to generate a multitude of constructive interactions with other parties. Cross-sector interactions offer opportunities for innovative products and services and contributing to the attainment of the SDGs. Meanwhile, this role also supports the realization of corporate citizenship in a community.

2.3 Civil Society and Co-Creation of SDG Implementation

The United Nations Conference on Trade and Development (UNCTAD) estimates that the financing gap for achieving the SDGs in developing countries will be US$ 2.5–3 trillion per year (UNCTAD World Investment Report, 2014). Channeling available finance towards the SDGs is constrained by a range of challenges. Limited fiscal space and institutional capacity to formulate a pipeline of bankable SDG investment projects and weak financial systems plagued with waste and corruption constitute major barriers in closing the financing gaps. Civil society could play an active role in identifying grass root needs, creating SDG projects and monitoring their actual implementation through meaningful engagements. More importantly, credible CSOs reinforce public trust when domestic resources (tangible and intangible) are mobilized. It is also an indispensable part of good governance by constituting a civil society monitoring network to track how SDG funding is being used. Grass root feedback to the Voluntary National Report of the country help identify actual progress of SDG implementation.

Social Contract as a means to ensure full engagement of society's major stakeholders should be part of the National SDG implementation plan and stipulate conditions for a grand partnership in the country. It could forestall the well-studied collective action problem or social dilemma, a situation in which all individuals would be better off cooperating but fail to do so because of conflicting interests between individuals that discourage joint action (Ostrom, 1971, 1965). Collective rule-arrangements that realign individual incentives, or rules that specify permissible actions is the proposed way out of this common trap (Ostrom 2012; p. 80).

While governments and businesses alike are at the tipping point for behavioral change, civil society organizations need to rise to the challenge and ensure conducts of all parties are aligned to the principles of the 2030 Agenda and results streamlined to the SDGs. Accountability and concrete representations of the NGOs will constitute the good governance of this sector.

Proposition 1: *An integrated approach to social, economic and environmental development and cross-sector collaboration as the base for building better futures*

Building a sustainable environment, society and economy (the three dimensions of the 2030 Agenda) has been strengthened thanks to the additional pressure resulted from the signing of the Paris Agreement on climate change. Paris Agreement requires the signatory governments to be transparent on what their respective countries do to halt climate change through nationally determined contributions (NDCs). In addition, the related protest movement of the youth make it difficult for governments and society to ignore the alarming signs of accelerating climate change and pending disasters.

Convergence of social and economic dimension of sustainability are less developed than the one on environmental sustainability. However, the investment and business communities are moving increasingly more towards a socially aware and inclusive approach to investment and business conducts. New instruments have been created such as Social Impact Investment and investment products based on ESG criteria (Environment, Social and Governance). But social factors of investment still lag behind. More needs to be done through regulatory measures. Voluntary measures alone do not generate sustained good business behavior.

Didier Reynders, EU commissioner of Justice on due diligence (2020), mentioned that a large survey of CEOs of major European companies received over 600 responses. Out of which more than half from individual businesses and from a large sample of Member States. The results showed that voluntary action to address human rights violations, corporate climate and environmental harm, although incentivized though reporting requirement, has not brought about the necessary behavioral change. The study found that only one in three businesses in the EU are currently undertaking due diligence which takes into account all human rights and environmental impacts. 87% of CEOs surveyed complained about shareholder pressure to generate short-term profit and claimed that longer-time horizons would improve performance and innovation.

Regarding corporate governance EU has three main objectives: (a) to foster longer time horizons in corporate decision-making; (b) to incentivize sustainable business models; (c) to increase corporate accountability for human and environmental harm. Such regulatory efforts need to be complimented by civic actions and oversight.

SMEs, less visible than large corporations, on an aggregated level have higher environmental footprint and need to contribute equally to a sustainable future. Literature estimates that SMEs contribute 60–70% of industrial pollution in Europe (OECD, 2018). Engagements of the local community in support of the regulatory mechanisms are therefore inevitable especially when it comes to the business practices of the SMEs. Building Forward Better without the partnerships and collaboration of the civil society and local community would remain elusive.

Proposition 2: *Collective socio-economic action as the basis of partnership stipulated in SDG 17*

The neo-liberal economic model of the Washington Consensus produced the financial crisis of 2008 and revealed its lack of sustainability when faced with a pandemic crisis. Alternative economic futures are needed to get out of the dead-end of the current mainstream thinking.

Alternative conceptions of the economy as has been offered by scholars and pioneers on socio-economic approaches to sustainable economic and social development like Henri Savall (Socio-economic approach to management, 2017), Beat Bürgenmeier (Environmental economics, 2019), Peter Utting (Social and Solidarity Economy, 2014) and others need to be revisited.

New modules, laws and practices are needed to make our economy sustainable, equitable and committed to preserving public goods. Through Cross-sector partnerships, involvement of research and academic communities, will amplify the learning capacities of the societies and institutions in this pursuit of new social contract. More cooperatives, social enterprises, solidarity-based self-help initiatives are needed[2] to create a non-zero sum arrangement.

Nicolas Schmit, the EU commissioner in charge of jobs and social rights, has recently stated that "Social fairness is essential for economic prosperity for all."

For sustainable development to work, all stakeholders need to be part of the multilevel partnerships in co-creating solutions to enable achievement of the 17 SDGs. Business, Civil society and governments need to find alternative narratives and tools in making these partnerships effective and deliver the kind of results that accelerate the transition to a more sustainable and inclusive future.

Proposition 3: *NGOs as Intermediaries and Transitional Mechanisms for SDG Transformation*

Sustainable development is a bottom up approach where one person has one voice in contributing to the creation of a collective future. This common future cannot be dictated by experts or by the elite who often lack social empathy and have shown little ownership in reducing the plight of poor people and in contributing to the creation of a socio-economic and sustainable future. CSOs rooted in local communities are well placed in playing the link-pin function to harness locally available social capital and other immaterial assets and to mainstream marginalised voices into the larger narrative of SDGs.

Common futures without safeguarding individual dignity and wellbeing for all would miss the mark. NGOs are challenged to be part of the intermediary mechanisms and platforms that steer the SDG progress forward.

3 FINAL REMARK

The OSCD technology mentioned above needs to be anchored in the globally networked intelligence system in order to be able to simultaneous intervene at different system levels and at a much larger scale than is the case with traditional Organisation Development approaches.

NOTES

1. UN Secretary-General's Nelson Mandela Lecture: "Tackling the Inequality Pandemic: A New Social Contract for a New Era, New York, 18th July 2020
2. For more information on the various alternative forms of organising the economy see website of the UNTFSSE- https://www.cfainstitute.org/en/about/press-releases/2018/new-reports-by-cfa-institute-and-the-pri-find-that-risk

REFERENCES:

Burgenmeier, B. (2019). *l'économie au pluriel.* Edition Mardaga, Brussels, Belgium.

Kingombe, Ch., & Saner, R. (2018). *Public–private partnerships and foreign direct investment as determinants of SDG achievement.* OECD PCSD Partner Platform, Paris Created on Jan 30, 2019

Remarks of Commissioner Nicolas Schmit at the informal EPSCO dinner organized by the Finnish Presidency on a "Strategic vision for social and employment policies in the future EU," 9 December 2019, https://ec.europa.eu/commission/commissioners/2019–2024/schmit/announcements/remarks-commissioner-nicolas-schmit-informal-epsco-dinner-organised-finnish-presidency-strategic_en

Saner, R., & Yiu, L. (2012). *Known unknowns of mainstream ODC: Need to move beyond current "borders."* Academy of Management ODC Newsletter, summer 2012.

Saner, R., Saner-Yiu, L., Golub, N., & Sidibe, D. (2017). Implementing the SDGs by subnational governments: Urgent need to strengthen administrative capacities. *Public Administration and Policy, 20*(2), 23–40.

Saner, R., & Yiu, L. (2017). No policy coherence? No poverty reduction. *Strategic Review: The Indonesian Journal of Leadership, Policy and World Affairs,* 7(2), 12–16.

Savall, Henri, (2017). Macroeconomic roots and fundamentals of the socio-economic approach to management. *Theory and Practice of Socio-Economic Management,* 2(1).

Speech by Commissioner Reynders in RBC Webinar on Due Diligence in RBC webinar on due diligence, April 2020, https://responsiblebusinessconduct.eu/wp/2020/04/30/speech-by-commissioner-reynders-in-rbc-webinar-on-due-diligence/

Utting, P. (2014). Raising the visibility of social and solidarity economy in the United Nations system. Chapter taken from *The Reader 2014: Social and Solidarity Economy—Towards Inclusive and Sustainable Development.* (ITC and ILO).

UN Development Group. (2013). *A million voices: The world we want. A sustainable future with dignity for all.* UNDG Millennium Development Goals Task Force. https://unsdg.un.org/sites/default/files/The-World-we-Want.pdf

Yiu, L., & Saner, R. (2017). Business diplomacy in implementing the Global 2030 Development Agenda: Core competencies needed at the corporate and managerial level. In H. Ruel, *International Business Diplomacy: How can multinational corporations deal with global challenges?* Advanced Series in Management, Volume 18, 31_56, Emerald Publishing LTD.

This page intentionally left blank.

CHAPTER 96

SAVING COMPANIES, ENTREPRENEURS, AND JOBS

Robert-Louis Meynet

ABSTRACT

The amicable and judicial treatment of companies in difficulty is in France a field that is little known in the world of socio-economic analysis. However, there is a time when the search for hidden costs is prioritized, first by a social restructuring that is always urgent, inevitable and indispensable (article L 631–17 of the Commercial Code), and then by an enrichment of the tasks of the employees who remain to lead to very important gains in productivity (+ 30% on average).

The Judicial Administrators are in France the Agents charged by court decision, to administer the property of others (Article L.811.1 of the Commercial Code) or to exercise functions of assistance or supervision in the management of such property. This chapter deals with the company in financial difficulty, which seeks the help of the Commercial Court or the Court of First Instance, which appoints a Judicial Administrator, a professional in business law and figures, to assist the management in its attempt to restructure amicably or judicially in order to ensure its survival. The company has most often made operating losses for several years, which has led to cash flow difficulties to the point of causing a cash flow impasse, legally referred to as "cessation of payments." In the presence of a state of cessation of payments, the manager of a French company is obliged to place himself under the protection of the Commercial Court or the Court of First Instance, which then appoints a Judicial Administrator.

SEAM Treatise, pages 789–794

1 ROLE OF THE JUDICIAL ADMINISTRATOR IN RELATION TO AILING COMPANIES

Following the two oil shocks of 1973 and 1979 and since 1985, the French legislator has entered into a quasi-permanent reform of companies in difficulty for both economic and legal reasons. The economic reasons are related to an increasingly globalized economy and the emergence of countries with low labor costs, which have disrupted or even destroyed entire parts of the Western economies. The result has been the failure of Western companies, without any link to the failures of the managers themselves. Indeed, the defensive competition for the preservation of commercial margins has led to a sustained increase in corporate failures. The presumption of fault on the part of the director has thus gradually disappeared from criminal business law.

1.1 Legal Proceedings

Since January 1, 1986, the French legislator has allowed failing businesses to draw up a safeguard or recovery plan, after the opening of a safeguard or recovery judgment, under much faster and easier conditions than the previous texts.[1]

It has provided them with professionals appointed by the Courts, to assist companies in difficulty, alongside the usual advisors, lawyers, and accountants. The Judicial Administrators, with economic, financial, and legal training, oversee assisting the manager of the company in difficulty, in order to draw up a draft recovery plan to be validated by the Court. Their mission is to preserve the maximum number of jobs compatible with the profitability and durability of the company. They intervene alongside the *Judicial Representatives*, who are responsible for checking the company's debts and then liquidating it, if the recovery plan or the company's sale plan does not allow all the debts to be paid. Their mission is structured in three "observation" periods, of a maximum of 6 months; and they must regularly report to the Court on the evolution of the accounting results of the sick company.

If, on the legal level, the Judicial Administrator must act in accordance with the provisions of the free VI of the Commercial Code, he is left free to his imagination on the management level. His mission leads him to take steps with the management of the company, but also with the representatives of the employees, the customers, the suppliers, the co-contractors and in a general way with any person or company likely to help the recovery of the company, by transforming the accounting losses into operating balance, then into profits.

Because the deterioration of the cash flow is such that the salaries of the month preceding the Court's judgment could not be paid to the employees, the French legislator calls upon an organization, the AGS (Assurance de Garantie des Salaires), which pays the salaries in place of the employer, knowing that it is an advance to be reimbursed as soon as possible. The company then finds a calmed social situation, favourable to dialogue and management actions which consist, in most cases, in reducing the costs on which it is possible to act, before imagining in a second time the development of the turnover.

Time is limited: the mission of the Judicial Administrator is carried out in an extremely short time span of only a few weeks, during which the company has enough cash to pay all the expenses with its own cash flow. A company that manages to balance its operations in less than 6 months has a very high probability of being saved, while a company that remains in deficit will have to be sold, with impact on jobs.

During this period, the components of our action are in all respects similar to the missions carried out by ISEOR and Professor Savall's teams (Savall, 1974–75, 1979; Savall and

Zardet, 1987), except that our time frame to act is much shorter. The Judicial Administrator needs the manager and his knowledge of the company to identify very quickly all the areas of improvement, but he can act alone if necessary. He needs the employees' representatives and often the employees themselves, so that they adhere to new decision-making, manufacturing or communication processes, but he can also impose them, if their implementation meets too many obstacles. Safeguard and receivership procedures therefore leave very little time to search for hidden costs and to implement restructuring measures.

It is precisely this very short period that constitutes a major obstacle in the chances of a company's recovery and in the search for hidden costs. This haste is linked to a judgement that has been rendered, published in the press, opposable to all, which publicly determines the remaining life of the company. The economic consequences can quickly turn out to be disastrous regarding suppliers, customers and, more generally, the co-contractors of the sick company.

1.2 Prevention Procedures

New policies for the prevention of business difficulties have appeared in recent years at the initiative of the Commercial Courts, with the active participation of the Judicial Administrators. Their objective is to intervene much *earlier* in the process of proven difficulties or the status of payment transfers. They are called *Ad'hoc Mandate* and conciliation and have the great advantage of remaining confidential, while giving the President of the Court who has opened these procedures the power to suspend the payability of a debt for up to two years (in the absence of an amicable agreement), with respect to one or more creditors under private law, except for public debts. The President of the Court can even authorize the *Ad 'hoc Mandate* or the Conciliator to advertise—anonymously or not—to sell the company. Legally, the "ad 'hoc Mandate" procedure is discreetly prolonged from 4 months to 4 months, without any time limit, to end up with a conciliation which can last 5 months. Economically, it does not allow for the freezing of all liabilities as of right, as in Safeguard and Judicial Reorganization, but in practice, it is noted that the company pays very few liabilities during this restructuring phase, private and public creditors[2] being particularly understanding. As for the banks, they participate without fail in all the necessary meetings until an agreement is reached, which often consists of freezing the medium- and long-term bank debts and continuing the short term loans. The deadlines granted by the banks are in fact very important moratoria for the company, which is then limited, during the prevention procedures, to paying salaries and essential suppliers.

These preventive procedures are very popular and are unanimously preferred by the managers of companies in difficulty. They also give more time to restructure the company and to look for hidden costs. Nevertheless, these amicable and confidential procedures can only be successful if, each month, the forecast and actual data reflecting the main parameters of the company's activity are presented. Knowing the turnover, the result and the EBITDA in a very short time is therefore essential to carry out discussions with the company's creditors, in particular the banks or the public creditors. Therefore the lack of experience of an external accounting firm that does not prioritize the use of management control tools or the absence of an internal accounting department within the company are major dysfunctions that must be identified very quickly by the conciliator.

2 THE MANDATORY COHABITATION OF A MANAGEMENT AND A JUDICIAL ADMINSTRATOR IN SEARCH OF HIDDEN COSTS

The capacities and possibilities of managers to adapt very quickly to a profound restructuring and consequently to a questioning of their economic model vary from one manager to another, from one company to another, from one region to another. Employees, too, are in favor of a rapid change in the existing model. It is in this context that we have been practicing our professional activity of Judicial Administrator, exclusive of any other, for more than 40 years and counting to date more than 12,000 judicial missions.

Over this very long period, we have observed that, on average, it is possible to maintain the existing turnover, by reducing various costs and in particular that of the wage bill, by approximately 30% in SMEs with less than 100 employees. The reduction of jobs must of course be accompanied by other costs, for economic as well as psychological reasons, in the same proportions. In this situation of very serious crisis of the company, the techniques of recovery implemented by the Judicial Administrator consist in taking as a basic data the existing turnover and in reducing the expenses to reach as soon as possible an operating balance, then a profitable management.

2.1 The Example of a Group of Companies in the Women's Underwear Industry

This group of companies suffered a cyber-attack at the end of 2019 causing damage estimated at more than 10 million euros, in addition to accounting losses made in 2018 and 2019 for a cumulative amount of several million euros, for a consolidated turnover that dropped from 60 to 50 million euros.

At the suggestion of and with the active participation of the court-appointed administrators, the management has undertaken, since the opening of the receivership, a very high-quality restructuring effort in a very short time. The Management, the employees' elected representatives and the employees themselves have all become aware of the need to rethink the economic model that had prevailed in the group created 40 years ago.

This group of companies has 1,000 employees, nearly 70% of whom are abroad, in the women's lingerie sector. Within 4 months, a cost-cutting plan to combat hidden costs has reached an annual amount of more than 6 million euros in France, without reducing the turnover potential. Personnel costs account for one third of the annual gain from these cost savings. The other two thirds are the result of geographic reorganizations (elimination of sites), strategic repositioning with simplified product ranges, cost sharing in purchasing and sales, and reduced recourse to subcontracting, not to mention actions on logistics flows (quality control, folding, scoring, labeling) and simplified legal structures. Participation in trade shows has been rationalized and digital sales developed to offset the decline in sales in stores. The simplification and reorganization of certain processes not only saved costs, but also improved the economic performance of the company's players, first and foremost those among the remaining employees who accepted new, more versatile positions.

This first step, carried out in all directions during this 4-month period, sometimes in a brutal and violent way, was a necessity to re-establish a self-financing capacity at least balanced within the time limits granted by the collective procedures. The process has been successfully completed and will continue with a new stage of research into the hidden costs resulting from these new processes and this new organization, to continue to improve productivity.

It has allowed us to stabilize our cash flow and the Court and the Public Prosecutor's Office are no longer worried about an increase in the company's liabilities. It is now possible to envisage a positive exit from the receivership, either by the group with its own human and financial resources, or with the arrival of a third party in the group's share capital. The Judicial Administrator must now prepare a draft plan, in which the profitability obtained from now on must be put in relation with the payment proposals made to the creditors, over a maximum period of 10 years.

2.2 The Example of a Bookbinding Company

Bookbinding is an ancillary and complementary activity to printing. It consists of binding and shaping already printed leaflets and magazines. This sector of activity is suffering from a reduction in volumes due to an accelerated shift from advertising to digital technology and relocation to countries with low labor costs. The French market is concentrated on five players. Company B has been in business for over 70 years with 85 employees. We intervened following a drop in its volume of activity within the framework of a conciliation procedure, which failed because of a business model that has become structurally loss-making since the beginning of 2015: turnover has fallen by 13% in 5 years and expenses, particularly salaries, which represent more than 66% of turnover in 2019, have remained stable in absolute terms in recent years.

The liabilities declared on the day of the Safeguard and admitted for an amount of 700,000 euros were an encouraging parameter to undertake a large-scale social and organizational restructuring. Nevertheless, the manager, grandson of the creator, wished to sell most of the share capital he held in the company in the weeks following the opening of the safeguard by the Court. An experienced professional, employed by a printing company, then became the majority shareholder. His arrival allowed to immediately improve the company's turnover by 300,000 euros per year, by adding a binding activity using unused premises (1,400m^2).

Our first investigations led us to recommend a large-scale action in view of the number of employees, most of whom were hired before 1990. The turnaround of this company had to solve the problem of maintaining the turnover, with a reduction of about 25 jobs, to maintain the other jobs in the long term and make them much more versatile.

Several months were necessary for the new manager, assisted by the Judicial Administrator, to reassure the customers who had to remain confident in the company's chances of recovery. Restructuring practitioners know how delicate these operations are from a technical, psychological, and also industrial point of view because they require investments in new and more automated, even robotized equipment, which must be financed.

After 16 months of effort, the 25 jobs have been eliminated and the Salary Guarantee Insurance has exceptionally intervened to finance the cost of the redundancies, which will have to be reimbursed in 24 months. In this complicated legal and economic context, turnover was maintained overall with a loss of around 10%, largely compensated by a sharp reduction in the cost of purchasing goods and in particular raw materials, external charges (reception costs, travel, customer gifts), a reduction in subcontracting and a major agreement on the annualization of working hours. This restructuring period absorbed the cash available on the day the Safeguard was opened, but the customers agreed to shorten their payment terms, which made it possible to maintain a positive cash flow.

In the end, the company submitted a draft Safeguard Plan to its creditors, with a projected positive self-financing capacity of nearly 200,000 euros per year, to pay off liabilities of around 700,000 euros over 10 years, after integrating self-financed annual investments of between 50 and 100,000 euros. These forecasts are deliberately pessimistic and include a forecast turnover reduced by 10% to 4.6 million euros.

The Court has recently adopted the safeguard plan, which signs the return of the company to the real economy, where it will have to be able to pay both its new expenses and its old debts contained in the safeguard plan. It must therefore continue to seek productivity gains to ensure its survival, and even its development, in a context where commercial margins are still falling.

CONCLUSION

The globalization of trade no longer spares any sector of the economy, and results in lower sales prices and cheaper labor. In this context, trade margins are inevitably shrinking and companies have the greatest interest in seeking gains in overall economic productivity (Savall and Zardet, 1987) in order to survive and even prosper.

Every year, France experiences a little more than 50,000 business failures, which can no longer ensure the normal payment of their operating expenses and loans. It is in this context, in connection with these economic difficulties, that the Judicial Administrator intervenes by court order, to deal with the difficulties within the framework of prevention procedures, which are characterized by their confidentiality.

If the dysfunctions of the company are very important, the judicial treatment can effectively help a company to return to profit and to pay its debts. Nevertheless, whether the treatment of difficulties is amicable or judicial, companies need long-term support to identify their hidden costs, then convert them into productivity gains (Savall and Zardet, 1987). This is now the path to be prioritized as soon as clients no longer tolerate unjustified price increases in a situation of strong competition. On this precise point, the expertise acquired over several decades by ISEOR and Professor Henri Savall's teams in the research and conversion of hidden costs is a precious support to reach this objective of sustainable competitiveness.

NOTES

1. In particular, the law of July 13, 1967
2. For public creditors, the Commission of the Heads of Fiscal and Social Services very often grants payment terms of 18 to 24 months and sometimes even 36 months.

CHAPTER 97

CONTRACTUAL EFFICIENCY: SOCIO-ECONOMIC APPROACH TO MANAGEMENT VERSUS AGENCY THEORY

The Case of an IT Services Company in Morocco

Tariq Zidi

ABSTRACT

The contractual approach of the firm presents the firm as a node of contracts between its stakeholders. The divergence of interests between the parties generates tensions and conflicts and pushes each party to the contract to adopt various strategies to preserve its interests. To resolve this dilemma, socio-economic theory has shown that replacing subordination in the relationship between the stakeholders of the firm by the establishment of a contractual relationship based on recognition, negotiation and discussion makes it possible to minimize the risks inherent in the agency relationship and thus to generate a greater commitment of the agents to the objectives of the organization.

The *contractual approach of the firm* presents the company as a contractual system between different individuals and parties. The contract, by nature, is intended to ensure a certain balance between the expectations of its various stakeholders. However, one of the major characteristics of the contract is its incompleteness. Because of this incompleteness, one of the parties (the agent) may seek to gain maximum benefit from the situation to the detriment of the interests of the other party (the principal), who is harmed. The contractual approach to the firm was developed to overcome the limitations of the neoclassical approach, by trying

SEAM Treatise, pages 795–801

to define the most efficient organizational form, where the contractual relationship between the principal and the agent is balanced.

The Socio-Economic Approach to Management offers a vision of the firm and of management based on transparency and the search for collaborative efficiency in the relationships within the organization. Considering the teachings of contract theory, specifically agency theory, does socio-economic management allow for organizational and contractual efficiency within the firm?

This question can be broken down into several points:

- Does socio-economic management include a conceptualization of the contract?
- To what extent does socio-economic management provide practical answers to the problems related to the incompleteness of the contract raised by agency theory?
- Can socio-economic management help to overcome the divergence between the interests of the principal and the interests of the agent?

1 SOCIO-ECONOMIC APPROACH TO MANAGEMENT VERSUS AGENCY THEORY

"We define an agency relationship as a contract by which one or more persons (the principal) engage another person (the agent) to perform some tasks on his behalf that involves a delegation of some decision-making power to the agent," these are the words used by Jensen and Meckling in 1976 to define the agency relationship. The theory of agency proposes to explain this relationship and its implications in terms of divergent interests and motivations between the principal and the agent, which divergence is a source of costs for the principal.

In the context of a firm, agency theory explains the tension that exists between the principal (shareholders, employers) of the firm and the agents (manager, employees), due to the divergence of their interests. The former has an interest in the latter behaving in such a way as to increase the shareholder value of the firm. The agents, on the other hand, have an interest in increasing their income and consequently in focusing on the size of the firm, for example. This contradiction between the interests of each party generates tensions and conflicts. Agency theory is based on two main assumptions. The first assumption is that, in a relationship, individuals seek to attract the maximum amount of profit and interest. The second assumption is based on the idea that the contract is by nature incomplete and that individuals seek to take advantage of this incompleteness. This is what the authors of the theory refer to as information asymmetry, since managers enjoy a privileged position about access to information on the management of the firm, which is not the case for shareholders or owners who are exposed to moral hazard, adverse selection and managerial opportunism.

To counteract this disadvantage, the principal tends to use agency theory to provide controls and incentives to encourage the agent to act to achieve specific goals that are in the principal's interest. "The principal can limit divergent interests by providing an appropriate incentive system for the agent as well as monitoring means to limit aberrant behavior by people." (Jensen and Meckling, 1976). Monitoring and incentives come at a cost to the firm, called agency costs. To mitigate them, an ex-ante contract has the role of balancing the relationship between the principal and the agent.

However, the implementation of such mechanisms is costly for all parties, since the principal and the agent bear *monitoring and obligation costs* respectively. The principal seeks to protect himself/herself from the agent's opportunism by engaging a set of monitoring and incentive mechanisms, while the agent is obliged to show good faith and commitment to the principal's interests.

The Socio-Economic Approach to Management, with its hidden cost-performance approach (Savall, 1974, 1979; Savall and Zardet, 1987, 1995; Savall et al., 2015), provides innovative solutions to this dilemma that characterizes agency relationships. Indeed, agency theory states, as we have just seen, that on the one hand, the principal seeking to increase its shareholder value incurs additional costs and expenses; on the other hand, the agent seeking to increase the size of the firm, to secure and maximize its revenues, resorts to hidden strategies to achieve its goal. These two objectives clash and create tensions between the principal and his agent.

Socio-economic theory proposes a different reading of the relationship, where the principle of subordination gives way to a dynamic relationship based on negotiation and recognition of the actor as an autonomous entity with a specific identity, objectives and expectations (Savall and Zardet, 2005a). Experimental work evaluated from socio-economic theory has shown that a contractualization relationship based on recognition, negotiation and discussion allows for a greater commitment of the actors (agents) to the objectives of the organization as a whole. This creates more value added, to the satisfaction of all stakeholders, thanks to the ability of this approach and its management tools to reduce the risks inherent in the agency relationship, notably information asymmetry, moral hazard, and agent opportunism. Negotiation allows for a personalization of the relationship and thus a shift from a hidden strategy to a *visible and negotiated strategy* (Savall & Zardet 2005a), and thus paves the way for greater commitment on the part of the agent.

By improving the quality of the interaction between the structures of the organization and the behaviors of the actors, the managers release financial resources that allow them to increase the size of the company and its shareholder value at the same time. "The economic and social performance of an organization depends on the quality of the interaction between the structures of the organization and the behaviors of the men who act within this organization" (Savall, 1978).

The central assumption of socio-economic management is that "the level of economic performance of an organization depends on the quality of the interaction between the structures of the organization and the human behaviors, which act within this organization" (Savall, 1977). The quality of this interaction defines the degree of organizational efficiency and effectiveness of the firm. However, this interaction is inherently complex and difficult to control. As a result, it is a source of dysfunction at the origin of social, economic, and financial losses. These dysfunctions reflect the gaps between the desired functioning of the organization (orthofunctioning) and its actual functioning. By focusing on the analysis and then the action on the dysfunctions, socio-economic management makes it possible to improve the *organizational efficiency* of the company and consequently its socio-economic value for the benefit of all its stakeholders.

2 CONTEXT OF THE COMPANY STUDIED

The company evolves in the Moroccan economic context, where SMEs are mostly very small structures, the studies conducted on the subject showing that failures affect more particularly this category of companies. Indeed, over the period from 2009 to 2015, the bankruptcy rate of SMEs in Morocco was 16% (El Manzani, 2018). In 2017, according to the study conducted by Inforisk, a total of 8, 088 SMEs[1] went bankrupt. This is more than double the number of SMEs affected by bankruptcy in France, where according to the Bank of France,

4,000 cases of bankruptcy were recorded in 2017 (El Manzani, 2018). The sectors most affected by bankruptcy in 2017 were trade and repair, which accounted for 34% of the 8088 failing SMEs, followed by real estate, with a rate of 22% and construction with 16% of all failing SMEs.

El Manzani et al (2018), in their exploratory study on the factors of entrepreneurial failure of Moroccan SMEs have highlighted three categories of factors: the external environment; the specificities of SMEs and the entrepreneur.

The SME studied belongs to the new information and communication technologies sector. Before implementing socio-economic management, the company, like all Moroccan SMEs, encountered management, organizational and financial management difficulties. As a company manager, to alleviate the company's difficulties and improve its performance, I approached the academic and research world, ISEOR, and thanks to this, we were able to carry out a process of change within the company by implementing socio-economic management.

3 IMPLEMENTATION OF THE SOCIO-ECONOMIC APPROACH TO MANAGEMENT IN THE COMPANY

We started this project in 2011 with the conviction to make our organization a socially responsible and sustainable company. Before the implementation of Socio-Economic Management, the staff turnover rate was very high, it represented more than 30%, for a turnover of about 300,000 euros per year.

With the help of the tools proposed by socio-economic management (Savall and Zardet, 1987), we built an internal and external strategic action plan, which gave us a very clear vision of the company and provided meaning for all the employees. This approach also allowed us to listen to all stakeholders, both economically and socially/environmentally (Zidi, 2019, 2020).

Through the socio-economic intervention, we identified the dysfunctions of the company to move towards greater social responsibility. We followed different steps to build a global and sustainable performance: realization of a diagnosis with the listening of the stakeholders and the collaborators, collection of data and documents, observation. This diagnosis enabled us to identify major dysfunctions in six areas: working conditions, work organization, communication-coordination-cooperation, time management, integrated training, and strategic implementation. We then organized a dialogue within the management and with the employees.

We estimated a hidden cost of 69,000 euros (690,000 dirhams), which is high for a Moroccan SME of 12 people. Once the diagnosis was completed, we defined a socio-economic innovation project, with the objective of improving overall performance, via the implementation of socio-economic management of Corporate Social Responsibility (CSR), to improve working conditions and professional life.

4 OUTSTANDING ACHIEVEMENTS

Following the diagnosis, we organized the management of human resources to place the human and social aspect at the center of the company's organizational structure and strategic decisions. Thus, the company adopted an HR policy based on training and a participatory decision-making policy. It has also revised its remuneration and motivation policy and improved the working conditions and environment. We have also introduced a transparent management system for employees and all stakeholders. This allowed us to set up the competency grids, the internal and external strategic action plan (IESP), the priority action plan (PAP), the periodically negotiable activity contract (PNAC) and a company Strategic Piloting Logbook (Savall and Zardet 1987).

At the end of the first evaluation, we obtained satisfactory results. Indeed, the collective indicators showed that the delivery times to customers and the social indicators had begun to improve. Working conditions and the social climate have also improved, and we have observed a better efficiency of the commercial action. Governance and organizational reforms have been put in place thanks to a clear vision of the company. Indeed, our strategy is formalized in the short, medium, and long term.

Through the diagnosis and implementation of socio-economic management, we have put in place practices of corporate social responsibility, while moving towards overall performance. As far as standards are concerned, socio-economic management allows us to detect hidden costs, to recycle them and to invest in standards that are not mandatory, but which serve CSR.

We have also noted progress in strategic decision-making, as the company has gained in cost reduction and in the release of its potential. We have also improved our image, thanks to CSR and improvements in social performance. Social performance has translated in several ways: better motivation at work and involvement of employees, development of skills, improvement of indicators with a decrease in the staff turnover rate to 4%, compared to an industry average of 15–20% (Figure 97.1).

In terms of staff evolution, the company has grown from 12 people at the time of the project launch to 50 people in 2017 to reach a staff of 80 at the end of 2020 with a projection of 120 employees at the end of 2023.

From an economic point of view, we have observed an increase in sales revenue (Figure 97.2), a greater control of hidden costs which have become visible to the company, a diversification of activities, a repositioning of the company on more profitable segments but also a capitalization of knowledge.

Then we went beyond that, we created a corporate foundation that acts on the societal and environmental aspects, with a reduction in our energy bill. We have also developed new projects, as we are now helping agricultural producers to become self-sufficient. Moreover,

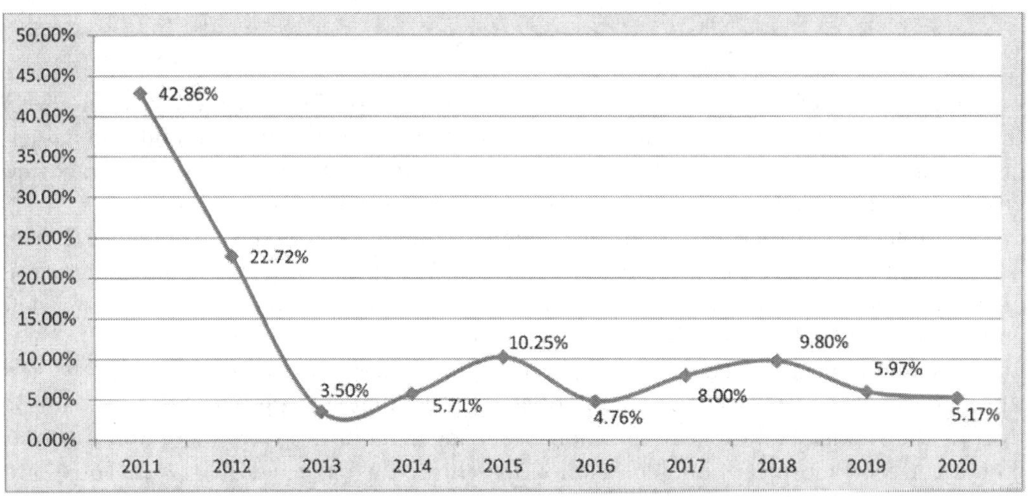

Figure 97.1 Evolution of the staff turnover rate between 2011 and 2020.

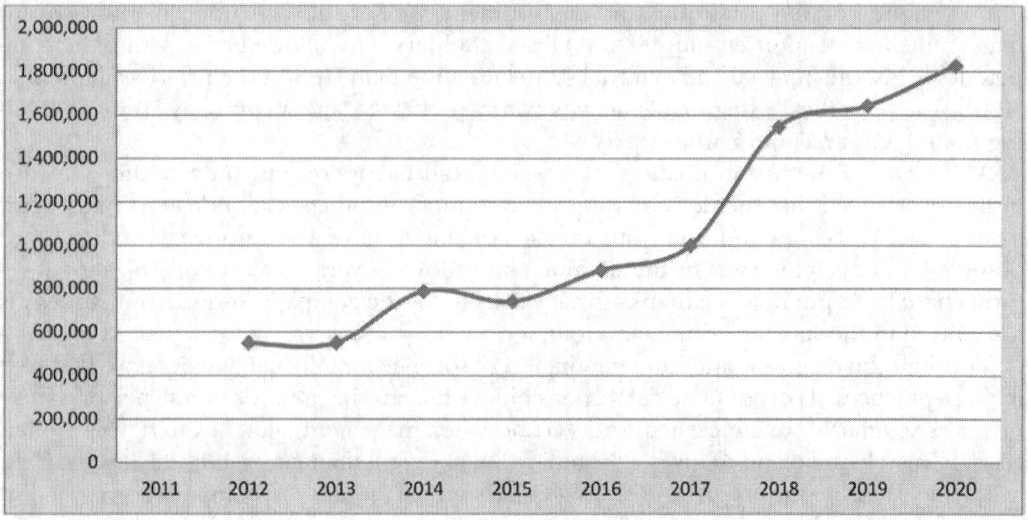

Figure 97.2 Evolution of the company's sales revenue between 2012 and 2020.

as a computer software development company, we recruit young people, university graduates who have completed five years of higher education, to help them enter the world of work. We initially had 12 employees and we have grown to 80 people in 8 years (from 2011 to 2019). Thanks to the recycling of hidden costs, we have set up an *internal school* where we train our employees so that they can be operational to manage projects. In the field of education, we are helping parents to become more autonomous, so that they can allow their children to go to school.

We have developed steering tools and proposed participative management, through the establishment of deliberative commissions on new projects. This is possible thanks to an *agile steering* and the creation of our foundation, composed of 12 employees, which acts in the environmental and societal fields.

CONCLUSION

The implementation of the socio-economic management of CSR has allowed a change in the organization, on the organizational, economic, social, environmental, and societal levels. All this progress has allowed the company to be active in recruitment, to attract new customers but also to have a brand image in Marrakech and in Morocco.

We conducted the socio-economic management implementation project under a double label: that of a manager and company director and that of a researcher in management sciences. This position is not without difficulties and ambiguity for both the company's staff and us. In such a situation, it is not always easy to find the right balance between the two postures to best meet the requirements of each. The posture of researcher requires keeping the necessary distance from the research object as a guarantee of rigor and scientific objectivity of the results. However, the position of manager requires involvement and rigorous monitoring of the project's implementation to achieve the expected objectives. To resolve this dilemma, throughout our project and research process, we alternated between the field and the theory.

NOTE

1. In a statement to the Moroccan magazine "Tel quel," the president of the Moroccan Confederation of Small and Medium Enterprises (a trade union which claims more than 8,000 members) estimates this figure at more than 10,000 bankruptcies. He explains this discrepancy between reality and the published figures by the fact that "Entrepreneurs are ashamed to admit their failure, or do not declare themselves in order to continue to practice in the informal," issue of 02 FEBRUARY 2018.

REFERENCES

El Manzani N. et al. (2018). Les facteurs de l'échec entrepreneurial des PME marocaines : une étude exploratoire, *Marché et organisations* 3 (n° 33), p. 105–144. DOI 10.3917/maorg.033.0105.

Michael C. Jensen, William H. Meckling, (1976). Theory of the firm: Managerial behavior, agency costs and ownership structure, *Journal of Financial Economics, 3*(4), 305–360.

Zidi, T. (2019). *Le management socio-économique de la RSE et la performance globale de l'entreprise: cas d'une PME de services marocaine.* Thèse de doctorat de sciences de gestion. Université de Lyon

Zidi, T. (2020). Le management socio-économique de la responsabilité sociétale de l'entreprise et la performance globale: cas d'une PME au Maroc. in Savall et Zardet (Ed.). *Tétranormalisation : profusion des normes et développement des territoires.* Éditions EMS. 337–340.

CHAPTER 98

THE GLOBAL HERITAGE VALUE CHAIN

Technological and Social Innovation

Claudia Rocío González Pérez and Pedro Constantino Solís Pérez

ABSTRACT

The management of cultural heritage is analyzed from the interactive networks of the global heritage value chain, using the scope defined by the relationships between stakeholders in the tetranormalization at global, regional and territorial levels. The processes of technological innovation, public management and social innovation are referred to from the concept of territory as the space where socio-economic activities are carried out, as a meta-organization, to manage the actors involved in cultural heritage projects. The case of cultural heritage management in Tepeyahualco (Puebla) is presented.

Cultural heritage is a human construction from which a community recognizes itself, through its belonging to an individual and social history that it inherits, values, protects and recreates through an institutional and technological framework. The Territory-Community relationship is at the origin of the stories, narratives and traditions of human groups. Cultural heritage evolves over time, and is therefore reinvented and modified as a process, being reconstructed by the communities themselves or through the mediation of public administrations. The following is a case of cultural heritage valuation, integrating concepts of socioeconomic analysis with the levels of analysis of the global value chain of cultural heritage and the innovations required by the community at the local/territorial level.

SEAM Treatise, pages 803–809

1 THE GLOBAL HERITAGE VALUE CHAIN: INTERACTIVE NETWORK OF ACTORS

Interactions between the global and the local move through different scales and complex networks linking a wide range of actors. The global is constituted by macro-structures that support configurations of practices, conventions and institutions that define the government and governance of commercial, financial, business and agent circuits (states, civil organizations, producers or consumers). These macro-structures are mediated by differentiated power relations within global production chains and by the socio-cultural links that crisscross nations or states. Global networks are inserted or embedded in diverse and dispersed geographic spaces that are global, regional or local territorial in nature.

The planetary nature of networks leads to a growing interdependence and joint evolution of human and ecological systems. For Paul Raskin (2006), human systems are shaped by behaviors (political, economic and social institutions) and ideas (values, knowledge, ideology, spirituality, arts and culture). On the other hand, the environment includes the ecosystems, mineral, hydrological, climatic, physical, biological and chemical processes of the biosphere. This global unity of human and ecological systems is presented in a nested structure of sub-global regions and local territorial systems with their own characteristics, establishing interactions between the different scales (see Figure 98.1).

The economic, social and political development of a community is linked to its cultural heritage; therefore, this heritage participates in the global, regional and global interactions mentioned above. The evolutionary nature of the institutional framework at the global level is also governed by entropic processes that deteriorate and destroy it. In this case, the "world order" is constituted by political, economic, social and technological institutions where "new emerging realities" become global risks (dysfunctions) that alter and deteriorate their institutional performance, requiring adaptations or transformations that allow them to reorganize a "new world order" based on their resilience capacities.

The disruptive processes that occur between global, regional and local interactions are analyzed under the approach of tetra-normalization (Savall and Zardet, 2005), which aims to identify the problems that transform the established global rules on social and economic issues due to the entropy of sustainable overall performance. A tetra-normalized environment is characterized by a strong and excessive density of rules and standards in four core

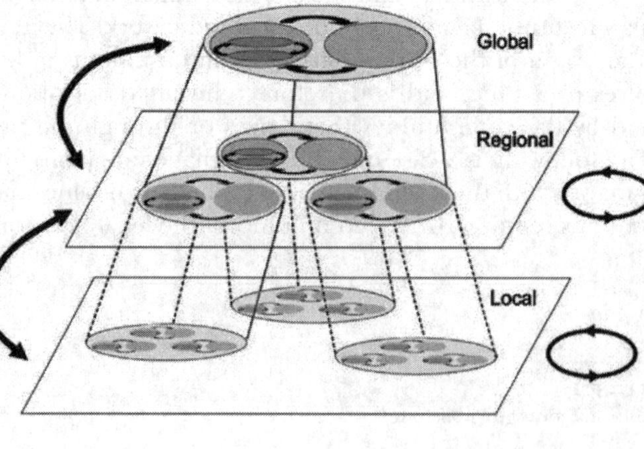

Figure 98.1 Interactions between and across different scales. *Source:* Raskin (2006, 4).

areas: (a) accounting and financial; (b) commercial; (c) quality, safety and environment; and (d) social (Petit et al., 2015).

> The perimeter of tetranormalization includes all those factors that touch, affect, alter, disturb and disrupt the rules of the economic and social game, due to competitive dynamics, strategic ambitions, hegemonic and economic forces, crises, and the reactions of stakeholders, both companies and public and private organizations, as well as local, regional, national and supranational public and private institutions. (Savall & Zardet, 2005, p. 25)

Heritage includes the unity of human and ecological systems. Therefore, it links at the same time the aspects of nature and culture, encompassing geography and natural territories, but embedded and impossible to dissociate from symbols and meanings. Moreover, Cultural Heritage is located in an economic, social and political institutional framework dense with rules, norms, certifications and laws. The identity importance of Cultural Heritage makes it an integral part of modern life and an irreplaceable basis for current and future development.

Cultural Heritage is located in the interactions of local, national, regional and global levels where the tetranormalized environment is reflected in the proliferation of norms, standards, rules, laws, certifications, accreditations from the flourishing of institutions and public and private organizations that seek to promote creativity, innovation, protection and assurance of activities and behaviors, but that have densified and dispersed energy in dysfunctional and entropic processes.

In the case of the safeguarding, restoration and enhancement of Heritage, it is even more evident how different normative elements and standards at different levels, Global-Regional-Local, affect and pull the decisions of public administrations. Cultural Heritage both by its local nature and its international competition is increasingly difficult to manage.

However, the capacity for resilience and self-organization is found in each individual community as a source of diversity, as an evolutionary driving force for the enhancement of Cultural Heritage.

2 TERRITORIAL MANAGEMENT AND CULTURAL HERITAGE VALUE CREATION

The Cultural Heritage value chain is linked to Cultural Tourism and the Sustainable Development Plans of the United Nations Development Group (UNDG) to promote collaborative work at the global level aimed at safeguarding, protecting and developing cultural heritage.

The analysis of global value chains begins with the dimensions at the global level (top-down) with an input-output structure between producers and consumers, with a geographical scope of countries and territories and with an economic governance structure made up of companies and international organizations that exercise asymmetric power and develop explicit coordination of the network (Gereffi and Fernandez, 2016). At the other extreme, the dimensions at the local/territorial level (bottom-up) involve the technological upgrading of processes and functions to achieve certifications and compliance with norms and standards, the involvement of local industry actors to carry out technological upgrading, and a local territorial governance, where a collaboration of institutional actors is carried out.

Cultural heritage is created and reconstructed at the local/territorial level by the communities involved or through the mediation of public administrations that promote development programs. Three main activities are involved in the recreation of cultural heritage:

production, management and socialization. The creation of the added value of Cultural Heritage takes place in a space of local/territorial social governance of an inter-organizational and inter-institutional nature, where several actors participate. They require management tools to elaborate a collaborative strategic plan with the actors involved.

At the local-territorial level, municipal or district governments do not have the competencies and capacities to realize the convergence of the cultural heritage value chain with the related activities of tourism, environmental protection and the creation of local productive chains that can help improve the quality of life of the community: increasing their income, improving their health, enhancing their education and favoring their artistic enlightenment.

The socioeconomic management approach to organizations refers to a method of intervention in which a group of intervener-researcher become involved in an organization to analyze dysfunctions and hidden costs, and then propose actions to improve its social and economic performance (Savall, 1974–75; 1979; Savall and Zardet, 1987). However, a socio-economic intervention process can be applied in spaces of inter-organizational cooperation, to take charge of the relationships between the actors involved and the piloting of a plan that reinforces an effective and efficient cooperation of the strategy implemented in a territory. (Pierre, 2010; Girard, 2015)

> The concept of territorial management is associated with the idea that there is a need to manage the actors involved in projects taking place in a territory, such as public policies. The territory then becomes a "meta-organization." (Pierre et al., 2015, p. 341)

Cultural heritage plays an important role in the process of building an identity and a significance specific to each community, whose specificity and particularity are manifested in the multiple exceptionalities of the human relationship with its ecosystem, as a result of a history that has evolved over time and will surely evolve in the future. However, community social governance must fit into the institutional framework constructed in regional and global value chains, where global economic governance is the result of the asymmetric power of global companies and institutions, where technological innovation and its transfer through standards, certifications, rules and tetra-normalized procedures are established and defined at the global level, and which communities must incorporate and transfer to the local/territorial level.

3 FROM TECHNOLGICAL INNOVATION TO SOCIAL INNOVATION

In the global value chain, technological innovation plays a central role in the development of economic governance, since dominant firms establish international competition based on their capacity to classify, select, adopt and exploit the technologies necessary to maintain current and future survival (MacCarthy, 2003). The ability to impose conditions on entry into the value chain translates into demands for standards, quality levels and control of certifications. These demands represent the need for a more efficient transformation of inputs into products, reorganizing the production system or introducing superior technology.

Social innovation, on the other hand, has arisen in response to the acceleration of global crises, growing inequality and the deterioration of ecosystems (global warming, social discrimination against ethnic minorities or women, globally spreading diseases such as the covid19 pandemic). The concurrence of several negative entropic processes results in the institutional and organizational framework at the global level increasing its tendency towards disorder and the tetranormalization of the components of the global system.

Social innovation refers to the need for local communities, territorially located, to establish links between people, groups, organizations and institutions to facilitate cooperation, communication and a more cohesive governance around development strategies.

> Also, we forge a territory and a community, which generates its own opportunities and makes the most of its talent and competencies. But Social Innovation does not stop at this ambitious goal of improving and generating added value in relationships to promote innovations. Its ultimate goal is to apply this relational model to respond to the future challenges we face as a society. In short, what we are aiming for is a new governance that promotes the generation of new social capital as a basis for Social Innovation. (Domanski et al., 2016, p. 26)

4 CULTURAL HERITAGE MANAGEMENT IN TEPEYAHUALCO, PUEBLA

Tepeyahualco is a municipal capital in the State of Puebla, Mexico. The municipality has promoted the creation of a development plan to alleviate a strong emigration of its inhabitants who have no job prospects. The work is peasant, agricultural and livestock farming, and the human system of the territory interacts strongly with the ecological system, from the very meaning of Tepeyahualco, which in the language of the native peoples symbolizes "in the roundness of the hills." The interaction between the rural condition and the native landscape nature is characterized by tangible and intangible patrimonial values such as the archaeological zone of Cantona, the Railway Station, the Alchichica Lagoon, the San Carlos Fort in Perote, as well as famous patron saint festivities and remarkable natural landscapes.

The idea is to reuse the building of the Municipal Presidency, located at the foot of the hills and in front of the town's church, for an urban revitalization project, to improve mobility and habitability. Community participation in projects that imply a process of economic and symbolic valorization is analyzed.

The revitalization of the public space of the town of Tepeyahualco as well as the proposal for the reuse of some buildings of heritage value, are at the beginning of the first work link of the interpretative chain of heritage, which seeks a) the valuation of heritage; b) the development of restoration, rescue, rehabilitation and reuse projects and c) the integration of the result to a cultural market. In this last link, the enhancement of heritage aims to connect heritage with the territory in order to later achieve a cultural tourism proposal.

Including the participation of institutions, associations, agencies and interested organizations, has the purpose of sharing knowledge and experience in different aspects of the project. Cultural management is a tool for the development of sustainable projects, where symbolic and material value are combined in a physical object. This conjunction is of interest to the public, but also to professionals in restoration, conservation and reuse. This is an effort to create projects that are developed by and for the community through the following points:

Technological innovation. The process of valorization of cultural heritage begins with the complexities of the tetranormalized processes, since regulations, certifications and technical requirements that originate in international, national, state and local spheres intervene, which need to be attended to and fulfilled. These aspects have to do with the care, protection, architectural design and assurance of heritage, which are aspects linked to specialized technical innovations (upgrading). The appropriation of technological innovation becomes a process of participation and collective learning among the actors involved.

Management, Planning and Budgeting. A cultural management project at the local/territorial level implies the participation of the inhabitants of Tepeyahualco, involved in the design of the interpretation plan, as well as the owners of haciendas and points of potential tourist attraction, together with a professional body of researchers, academics, analysts and government representatives, with the purpose of gathering all the necessary information from the village as well as from its inhabitants, in order to expose the needs of the parties involved and with this, propose solutions. This can be achieved with an Internal and External Strategic Action Plan (PAEINTEX) (Savall and Zardet, 1995), which reflects the interests and negotiation between community, business, organizational and institutional actors, and their coordination in territorial governance, as well as the necessary budget for its implementation and periodic evaluation of the results achieved. A Strategic Management Plan was integrated with two tools: a Community Participation Plan and an Interpretation Plan, specified in three projects (revitalization, reuse and management), in such a way as to concretize an integral approach to the conservation of the urban and architectural environment.

Social Innovation. An intervention to valorize cultural heritage includes technological innovation, management and planning at the local/territorial level, but above all the possibility of an effective realization that is only achieved through the process of social innovation to the extent that the actors involved modify and recreate the modes of integration and cooperation among them (governance), realizing a social organization of innovation, where as in the case of Tepeyahualco, it has specific, unique and particular aspects of its identity as a human and ecological system.

CONCLUSION

The study of different cases of Latin American rural territories has shown the diversity and heterogeneity of the subcontinent; there is no single way to incorporate cultural heritage into sustainable development. What can be said is that communities come out stronger with strategies and projects to revalue and re-signify their cultural heritage in the face of external modernity, establishing more social mechanisms and discursive forms, inducing social innovation as opposed to mere utilitarian technological innovation.

A Global Heritage Value Chain necessarily requires the revision of the first and original link, which is the territory where customs, landscapes, real estate and values are found. Heritage is a local element that can become a link in the global chain. The need to situate the analysis of cultural heritage in territorial value chains and its capacity for articulation in global value chains implies recognition of the economic dimension of heritage, of its forms of linkage from the local to the global, and the necessary articulation between economic governance and social governance.

REFERENCES

Domanski, D, Monge N., Quitiaquez G. y Rocha D (2016) "*Innovación Socialen Latinoamerica*," Fundación para la Innovación Social y Uniminuto, Bogota.

Gereffi G. y Fernandez-Stark K. (2016) *Global Value Chains Analysis: A Primer, Duke Center on Globalization, Governance and Competitiveness,* Duke University, Second Edition.

Girard, S. (2015). *Contribution à l'analyse des pratiques de coopération inter-organisationnelle territorialisée—Le cas de l'Insertion par l'Activité Économique.* Tesis de doctorado en ciencias de gestión. Universidad de Lyon.

Petit R., Delattre M. y Ruat T. (2015) *Adaptation of HORIVERT to Architects,* en *The Socio-Economic Approach to Management Revisited. The Evolving Nature of SEAM in the 21st Century,* Ed. Information Age Publishing, Charlotte, NC.

Pierre, X. (2010). *Pilotage institutionnel des coopérations interorganisationnelles dans la mise en œuvre de stratégies territoriales—cas d'acteurs de l'efficacité énergétique et du développement durable* – Tesis de doctorado en ciencias de gestión. Universidad de Lyon.

Pierre X., Beck E., Broggio C., (2015). Transorganizational Intervention and Meso-Socio-Economic Approach to Territorial Management: The Case of a Network of Environmental NGOs. en *The Socio-Economic Approach to Management Revisited. The Evolving Nature of SEAM in the 21st Century,* Ed. Information Age Publishing, Charlotte, NC.

Raskin, P. (2006). *World Lines. Pathways, Pivots, and the Global Future,* Boston: Tellus Institute.

CHAPTER 99

THE IMPORTANCE OF THE ROLE OF INTERMEDIARIES IN THE CREATION AND MAINTENANCE OF COLLABORATIVE NETWORKS

Laura P. Peñalva Rosales and Silvia Pomar Fernández

ABSTRACT

The research is approached from a descriptive and explanatory perspective of the role of intermediary organizations as generators of trust and governance, facilitators of communication and readers of reality; hence their relevance for the conformation of organizational networks. For this purpose, a documentary analysis is carried out. The importance of these organizations is exemplified with the presentation of the case of the Instituto Nacional del Emprendedor (INADEM), an organization created by the Mexican federal government that supports entrepreneurship and micro, small and medium-sized enterprises that have the potential for growth.

The interconnectedness of the world economy makes markets and production in different countries increasingly dependent on each other. Thus, new forms of social organization are emerging that are capable of building their own agendas for discussion, generating internal communication mechanisms and generating solutions to specific problems, which in the end can influence government agendas. The emergence of these new forms of organization builds local governance despite global ungovernability.

Intermediate organizations belong to the group of these new actors, which do not supplant the functions of the State or the market, but rather try to generate a bridge between them, acting as functional renovators of the system.

SEAM Treatise, pages 811–816

This chapter attempts to determine the importance of the role of intermediaries in the solution of organizational and business problems. From the documentary analysis of various sources on the role of intermediary organizations. Then, the case of INADEM is briefly presented. The objective is to exemplify the relevant elements for the work of intermediaries and to argue that their presence is more important than they are recognized, due to the role they play in the creation and maintenance of collaboration and knowledge networks in the inter-organizational framework.

1 CONTRIBUTION OF INTERMEDIARIES

The concept of intermediary covers different types of actors, situations, contexts and subject matter of mediation. "Intermediaries are defined by their position between two culturally split spaces, and by their performance of a mediating function between the two (positional or functional definition)" (Moguillansky, 2007). The difference between origin, professional occupation, position, beliefs, values, purposes, culture, knowledge; that occurs between individuals who want to establish a relationship, generates discrepancies. Intermediaries perform mediation actions.

In general, an intermediary is a "reciprocal translator," catalyzes and moderates the dynamics of intergroup relations, promotes the balance of power between actors; provides "popular pedagogies" Mike Featherstone (1991: 74). The inescapable conditions for the common project to prosper are: to get all the actors involved to participate in a committed manner and work side by side; to generate an adequate organization of the work; to have tools for the management and evaluation of progress; and to let the actors make their own decisions within their own sphere of concern. This, in turn, could give rise to an innovative project where harmony between the social and the economic is achieved (Savall and Zardet, 1987, 1995). In the present era, with electronic commerce via the Internet, new ways of establishing contact and communication between companies and customers, of promoting the product or service, forms of payment, exchange of information; in short, new business models and new market coordination mechanisms are emerging. Commercial intermediaries are not disappearing, but rather reconfiguring their role. Direct communication between suppliers and consumers causes an overload of information that makes them require intermediaries to help them collect, collate, interpret and disseminate information (Peterson et al., 1997; Del Águila Obra et al. 2000) in a more synthetic and organized way, allowing both parties to make better decisions. However, the role of generators of trust, communication and mediation to solve problems does not change, and generates virtuous circles of inter-organizational action.

The collaboration of a third party, who intervenes in a mediation process, is necessary to jointly reach an agreement in a negotiation process; but also, as Savall and Zardet (1995) refer, it provides other types of support: helping to create a dynamic for driving change through participant observation and also supporting the interactive co-production of knowledge. In particular, it helps to create "From a postmodern perspective a dynamic collective memory is in dialectical relationship with local knowledge created through intervention-research" (Boje, 2002: 52).

On the other hand, the existence of multiple forms of power makes it indispensable to negotiate with each individual in order to obtain his cooperation in the plan to change social relations or to reduce the dysfunctions in which he participates and a change of attitude towards the project. The information and knowledge available to the organization constitute an important input that modifies its innovative capacity.[1] In this sense, the creation of information networks is decisive. The heterogeneous nature of the inter-organizational fabric contributes, via these networks, to reduce uncertainty and strengthen the capabilities of companies, making learning processes horizontal (Casalet 1999).

One way of generating inter-organizational networks is through intermediate organizations that promote linkages, information exchange and mutual learning, thereby building local governance, even though the organizations may be in a situation of global ungovernability. Intermediate organizations generate linking devices that facilitate the transmission and transfer of knowledge, they are creators of sociability, allowing organizations to communicate, organize and act together to raise their demands, meet their needs and generate the development of collective strategies (Chavez, Sourrouille, 2016); (Zayas Barreras et al. 2017). To understand how at the level of organizations the construction of a new governance is possible, we first define the intermediate organization to which we refer and its nature.

Intermediate organizations are those in which the mix of reflexive goals—which are oriented inward to the organization itself—and transitive—which arise from instances outside the organization and originate an intentional impact of the organization on its environment—is such that the organization finds a balance between the needs of the environment and its own. While it is true that economic authority guides the performance of these organizations, political authority strongly influences their goals and processes. It is precisely because of this sui generis mix that such organizations manage to become organizational intermediaries and, at the same time, generators of social capital whose main support is trust.

This figure of intermediate organization is the one that supports excluded or disconnected actors to: gather the means and competences, access the necessary investments and infrastructures to share projects.

2 ROLE OF INTERMEDIARY ORGANIZATIONS

How does an intermediary come into being? The reasons can be varied:

1. When the parties who want to enter into a relationship do not know how to do it, do not trust each other and then look for someone to guide them in the establishment of dialogue, negotiation and agreements, and trust him to act critically but impartially on the subject of agreement.
2. When, in a commercial relationship, the supplier does not have all the elements or conditions necessary to bring the product or service directly to the consumer, and it is costly or impractical for the consumer to reach the supply directly; in this case, the intermediary covers that part of the supply chain to generate a value chain.

The role of intermediary organizations is to act as generators of trust and communication. It allows the creation of links that generate virtuous circles of inter-organizational action. During this process, one cannot avoid confronting the diversity of action logics and improvement orientations of the different actors. However, this confrontation makes it possible to create modes of collective legitimization and to generate transactional spaces for learning and negotiation.intermediate organizations manage to stimulate synapses within the social fabric by generating linking devices that facilitate the transmission and transfer of knowledge. They allow organizations to communicate, organize and act jointly.

The fundamental pillars in the nature of these organizations are: (a) their coordination mechanism, (b) their purpose or aims and (c) their way of building legitimacy (Bozeman, 1987). Monitoring the state of quality of trust between organizations makes it possible to periodically correct the "cursor's" position, which will require tools and practices for reviewing and evaluating the rules of the game.

The coordination mechanisms used by intermediate organizations are constituted on the basis of:

1. Affective trust, founded on the mutual personal knowledge of the actors (Mangematin 2002);
2. Legal-rational trust, based on the bet that the established interaction will obey general rules and normative devices, which guide action and exchange.
3. Trust through commitment to professional values, which is nourished on a daily basis by the solidarity that serves as a normative device to ensure the transformation of a promise into concrete service practices.

Confidence that an organization is capable of interrelating with another is built by analyzing its professional discourse and practices, its technical or managerial competencies, its behavior as an institution and its previous relations with other institutions. Some of these organizational forms, called intermediary organizations, emerge from the State itself with the purpose of fulfilling those functions that are part of its duty but that it is not able to cover adequately, mainly due to a lack of knowledge of each of the micro social environments in which its decisions are installed and of the particular effects caused by them; these are the decentralized organizations that act as intermediary organizations.

Intermediaries have different ways of financing themselves, according to their context and subject of mediation. Commercial intermediaries provide a service for which they charge, by means of a surcharge, the receiver of the good they transfer or a commission to the producer from whom they place the good. Financial intermediaries charge a commission to the financial fund they place. Government intermediaries have an annually allocated budget. They can also be financed by civil organizations, foundations, international organizations, or similar, when they work in communities to which a benefit is to be provided.

3 THE CASE OF THE NATIONAL ENTREPRENEUR INSTITUTE (INADEM)

INADEM was created to support the development of MSMEs. It operated from 2014 to 2019, with the purpose of boosting productivity and including informal companies to economic formality. It made available to entrepreneurs "programs and tools to give them the possibility to access credit; innovation; productive scaling; market entry; access to relevant information, and technological incorporation" (INADEM, 2018: pp.48).

INADEM used to publish calls for proposals aimed at entrepreneurs and businessmen. During its lifetime, it granted 723,466 million pesos (€29,172), supported more than 92,000 entrepreneurs and 575,486 companies (INAI, 2019).

INADEM performed an important function for the country's economy, through various support programs it tried to benefit small entrepreneurs who did not have the financial resources to start a business, develop it or make technological improvements. As an example, the company BATIAL,[2] formed by three Mexican entrepreneurs graduated from the National Autonomous University of Mexico with a degree in petroleum engineering and dedicated to the maintenance of cisterns, performing inspection and cleaning of water tanks using submersible robots.

In 2016, the entrepreneurs learned of the existence of INADEM and decided to apply for three calls offered by the institution. The first consisted of training to be able to form a company, the second in support for the development of technology, and the third in support for entrepreneurs with computer equipment. At the beginning of 2018, BATIAL began to operate formally with its first robot design. After several prototypes that they were perfecting, they managed to win ninth place, out of 1066 projects, in the 11th Santander Award for Entrepreneurial Innovation.

In April 2019, the Chamber of Deputies voted a ruling to eliminate INADEM, proposing to manage support to MSMEs and entrepreneurs from the Ministry of Economy, with the argument of improving and increasing economic support so that all entrepreneurs can access support in a transparent manner, so that such support does not arrive through intermediaries, and to have an administration that spends less and is more efficient.

In view of these purposes, we find several contradictions with the disappearance of some intermediate organizations, such as INADEM.

- We are seeing the disappearance of intermediate organizations that are in charge of a function of coordinating actions: monitoring the state of quality of trust, installing evaluation tools and practices, raising awareness about the inconsistency of projects or decisions; and listening critically and lucidly.
- Most MSMEs are not companies that are in the growth and development phase, so they need specific and intensive support, in terms of technical assistance and training that really contribute to their development, which is missing.
- The training promoted so far does not pay attention to entrepreneurship and innovation, which should be promoted to generate more jobs.
- The strategies that will enable the company to continue interacting cooperatively and commercially with different agents in the context are not yet explicit. Integration into value chains is in question.
- Innovation and entrepreneurship are limited, especially the technology-based entrepreneurship needed to develop a National Innovation System.

CONCLUSION

The lack of professionalism and the abundance of poorly corrected dysfunctions are factors in the loss of trust among the different actors. These dysfunctions are seen as the sign of a certain "dysfunction" of human behavior, as a lack of managerial and technical skills. The existence of intermediate organizations is very important to support entrepreneurial actions or to give the possibility of growth and problem solving, through the organizational networks they generate and the necessary tools, to those companies that have managed to show such a possibility.

The disappearance of intermediate organizations should consider the social role they play, since, being closer to the social actors at the micro level, they are creators of inter-organizational communication and promoters of collaboration and knowledge networks, as well as interlocutors with the State. This has allowed them to generate new capacities, knowledge and learning that has opened up the possibility of change.

NOTES

1. The organization's ability to transform and create from the sum and correct use of its individual skills and collective knowledge.
2. These data were obtained from interviews carried out by UAM students advised by Professor Pomar.

REFERENCES

Boje, D., & Rosile, G.A. (2002). "Comparison of socio-economic and other transorganizational development methods" En *Journal of Organizational Change Management.* Volume 16 Number 1 2003: Socio-economic approach to management.

Bozeman, B. (1987). *Todas las Organizaciones son Públicas. Tendiendo un puente entre las Teorías Corporativas Privadas y Públicas.* Colegio Nacional de Ciencias Políticas y Administración Pública y Fondo de Cultura Económica. México.

Casalet, M. (1999). Redes de innovación en la construcción del mercado en México. / ISBN: 9687637250 / Nacional Financiera y Flacso / (Biblioteca de la micro, pequeña y mediana empresa; 11) / México

Chávez, M.; Sourrouille, M. (2016) Redes sociales y territorialidad bolichera de sirios y libaneses en el sudeste de Río Negro, Argentina (1900–1950) *Anuario de Historia Regional y de las Fronteras,* ISSN: 0122–2066, vol. 21, núm. 1, 2016/ Universidad Industrial de Santander / Bucaramanga, Colombia.

INADEM. (2018). *INADEM.* Recuperado el agosto de 2020, de Informes Anuales 2014–2018: httpas:// www.inadem.gob.mx/fondo-nacional-emprendedor.

Jiménez Quintero, J.A.; Del Águila Obra, A.R. y Antonio Padilla Meléndez, A (2000). Implicaciones estratégicas del comercio electrónico basado en Internet: modelos de negocio y nuevos intermediarios /pags. 63 a 78 / *ICE TRIBUNA DE ECONOMIA* / enero-febrero 2000 número 783.

Mangematin, V. et Thuredoz, C. (2002). *Des mondes de confiance. Un concept a l'épreuve de la réalité sociale.* CNRS Editions.

Moguillansky, M. (2007). La figura del intermediario cultural para pensar los procesos de integración regional. *IV Jornadas de Jóvenes Investigadores.* Instituto de Investigaciones Gino Germani, Facultad de Ciencias Sociales, Universidad de Buenos Aires, Buenos Aires.

Zayas Barreras, I.; Zayas Barreras, R.A.; Heiras Palazuelos, M.J. (2017). Clúster agrícola como factor de desarrollo en las empresas del municipio de Angostura, Sinaloa En *Revista Mexicana de Agronegocios,* ISSN: 1405–9282. vol. 40, enero-junio, 2017, pp. 525–539 Sociedad Mexicana de Administración Agropecuaria A.C. / Torreón, México.

CHAPTER 100

IS TODAY'S MANAGEMENT SCIENCE UP TO THE TASK?

Guy Devillebichot

ABSTRACT

For half a century, "scientific and technical knowledge" has been of a rare abundance. However, humanity has come to jeopardize its real conditions of survival!

Do economic and management thoughts have something to do with this fiasco? Or with such a serious absence of general policy? How can we discern tracks of renewed relevance, to be elaborated in common?

In memory of three of my Masters from beyond France:
G.L.S. SHAKLE (RU)
Albert TEVOEDJRE (Benin)
Shigeo SHINGO (Japan)

Such a question requires a lot of humility.[1] It questions each member of a community of researchers. And, beyond that, each one is, even more than yesterday, aware of it, if not instructed. We cannot pretend to answer it in a few pages, nor even to reach a tangible or perceptible "useful result."

I appeal to the free and critical spirit necessary to any scientific approach; to the theoretical and practical distance that is always indispensable; and finally, to the curiosity and intuition of which each person is capable; to his or her effort (and joy) to *produce usefulness* for all and for everyone. Here, to begin with, is a not very original mental experiment.

A "physicist" at the foot of an apple tree from which a fruit is going to fall. *Law of nature?*[2] of the fall of bodies[3] (2) (3) (4). A force that makes the apple fall.[4] But since the apple is

SEAM Treatise, pages 817–823

placed on the branch, we must admit that a "force" must have put it there. What force? The answer is biological and not physical.

Conclusion of stage (would say François Perroux [1903–1987]): the curiosity is better satisfied by the couple of "sciences" *physics and biology*, than by only one of them. And it is not a question of a superficial curiosity which would be of "metaphysical or theological" order, in contradiction with the ways of seeing of Auguste Comte and Claude Bernard.

From time immemorial, humanity has known painful conditions of existence for its members, all mortal. Despite everything, we have survived our common ancestors. On the scale of the long history, the *traces* of the *tangible* human heritage[5] exist and are the object of constantly enriched updates.[6] It is the same of the immaterial heritage whose "reconstitution," even more difficult, follows ways undoubtedly more complex. In short, we would like to know more about the ordinary life of all these people who are our distant ancestors.

Let's bet that the *intangible* "achievement" of humans outweighs their material achievement. Although these ancient "traces" are perhaps difficult to know, the risk being to underestimate the material exploit.

For reasons linked to the survival on which everything depends, the two "feats" are mutually linked in an inescapable way. Scientific and technical knowledge is intangible, even if it does not constitute by far the whole of knowledge.

In dead memory, it no longer exists. And, alive, everything depends on the use that one makes of it, relevant, *humanly*.

1 RELATIONSHIP

In short, two "dynamics" are present (let's think of them as globalized or regionalized, as we wish). Those of "material realities" R 1: Dyn (RM), and those of "ideas and knowledge" R 2. With, of course, a mutual relationship that can be written $R\,1 \leftrightarrow R\,2$

Rl corresponds to the "facts" let's say "physical" and/or "biological," R 2 to the "ideas" by nature, "intangible" (facts of human and social order):[7] (7)

Now: "short film" on the essential "variable": population (P). We are interested in its quantitative evolution. The more we go back in time (until the "African big-bang"), the less we know about it. Here are some "data" since the year 1800:[8] (8)

1800: 1 billion
1930: 2 billion (after WW1)
1960: 3 billion (after WW2)
2000: 6 billion
2020: 7.8 billion

The fundamental meta relation $P \leftrightarrow Y$ calls for a separate analysis (Y being production).

Hervé Le Bras distinguishes between three demographics: "statistical," "qualitative" and "mathematical."[9] And we can no longer hide various things under the carpet…

Quantitatively, $Y = f(K, L)$, K being "capital" (material) and L "Labor." Depending on the field, one can observe "complementarity," or on the contrary, possible factorial "substitution."

But K is not a "primary factor." It is a "production detour" (since Böhm-Bawerk). The 2 "primary" factors are Nature and Labor, hence: $Y = f(N, L)$ [10]

Finally, it would be better to write $Y = f(E, N, L)$, E designating energy, or better: $Y = f(En, Ew)$.[11] (11) At this point, "physical science" is pushed to its limits, with the fundamental notions of entropy (and of neguentropies?).

2 EMERGENCE OF URGENCIES AND PRIORITIES

After the sentence of decomposed reflection, back to the essential: the metarelation P ↔ Y. It did not wipe us off the planet. Even if the theorem of Malthus (1766–1834) has been able to exert its deadly influence here and there.[12]

For other major risks, linked for example to epidemics and war (chemical and nuclear weapons of mass destruction since the middle of the 20th century), the globalized dimension of reflection becomes inevitable. If the risks of world war have not appeared since 1945, it is because individuals (known or unknown) have succeeded in "producing" peace. But in addition to the proliferation of military means of destruction, new risks of general collapse have appeared[13] (climate change, damage to biodiversity, etc.). New paradigms are needed to initiate a necessary change of direction as soon as possible.

The scenario of aggressive "competition," which has become obsolete, would be succeeded by a new era, that of cooperation (inevitable!): all knives would be put in the checkroom, and violent, hateful, and domineering practices (whether voluntary or not) would be put to bed for good.

Is it conceivable that "management science" refuses to deal with the problem of priorities and urgencies, as well as the challenge, first at the global level? For what good is it if we supposedly 'optimize' (in detail!), if globally we do not know how to manage the risks that can quickly make our planet uninhabitable for us? First, to become aware of the realities as they are, as far as we can foresee their evolutions, those for which we are totally "responsible."[14]

To confront challenges of this kind, let us repeat, the time is no longer for generalized confrontation between companies, between nations, between leaders eager for "empires," sitting on "States" or multinational groups. People expect something else: a generalized spirit of cooperation and mutual aid. It is enough to list the "problems"/challenges in order of gravity and urgency.

What is the use of all kinds of productions and the products they generate, if not for the better life and happiness of human beings? If not, what else? To tell the truth, there is nothing gigantic about the ingredients of happiness. At the individual level, there are 4 ingredients:

a. a satisfactory state of health
b. a sufficient income to be free from want
c. good relationships with others
d. success in work (and more generally in activities)

This is a seemingly simple and clear breakdown. Let's be grateful that companies and organizations of all sizes are working on it with drive and socio-economic-environmental efficiency. But it is still necessary to deepen these 4 dimensions and their interrelations. As an example, for c) Quality of working life (QWL) is a good objective as long as we do not forget the QWL of those who are not "at work"!

The question of "full employment" (and good employment) is of course central, nothing being worse than being unemployed. Fourastié (1907–1990), who had spent his life thinking about the long term (LT), launched the idea of 40,000 hours (of "work" over a lifetime). This "prospective" vision, specified before 1970, remains of great interest today. It is still necessary that this idea of 40,000 hours be really understood in all its richness and complexity. One thing is certain: the positive effects of the reduction of working hours are multiple. Everyone can reflect on this freely, whether they are employees, volunteers, or ordinary citizens.

3 ABOUT THE CONCEPT OF PRODUCT

The increase in "productivity" calculated correctly is the basic rule of all management, but it does not mean that the quality of the "product" should be neglected in all respects. It does not mean *ipso facto* increasing the quantity to be produced. It simply means lowering the cost per unit produced. In addition, it is necessary to integrate all the hidden costs, both internal in the sense of ISEOR and external in the sense of Pigou 1920 (to be defined progressively with care and integrated into the ad-hoc accounts).

The concept of product itself needs to be clarified. A product is that which does not exist unless one decides to produce it (and it is a wave and not only a corpuscle!). Its meaning is much wider than we usually think.[15] Peace, freedom, private but also public liberties (essential to maintain private liberties),[16] rights (even of the most affluent), and duties (even of the most deprived) are products. They do not begin and end with the enterprise, a productive market organization, whose function is to produce goods and services and not to "make cash," contrary to what is often taught is of course part of the common "goods" but it is not identified with the Common Good. One of the fundamental common goods is the development of the ability to communicate between the citizens of the world (of the 5 continents), and not only between the "great leaders."

The question of language is essential. It is possible that "true communication" between two average citizens "of the little people" is richer than between great leaders stuck in their games and strategies of power and roles of "representation." The construction of a common language requires translations that are not betrayals! It is a long-term work: work for linguists whose "production" also has a meaning. It is not undoubtedly linked to the "supremacy" of any single language. It refers to the fundamental differences between cultures for thousands of years. Thus, Western culture is not the same as Chinese culture, or Indian culture, or the culture of various countries with a Muslim tradition (even if the latter is much more recent). And then? Are we (and who?) willing to have one "civilization" crush all those that exist? And by what right, please?

On the contrary, let's recognize the diversity of cultures (and of "values"), it is obviously a source of wealth! If the fundamental principle of non-violence prevails, even if it is penalized. The great "wise men" of humanity must do some productive work, integrating the contributions of those of the past. Is it so complicated to put them in relation of mutual communication? To manage such a program, a mobilization of all intelligences is required. Specialists in the "hard" sciences, of course, but also in the human and social sciences, which are generally less expensive. Their work should be transparent to the small peoples and put under the appreciation of "wise men" from all over the world (such as the Club of Rome, or Budapest), of institutions already created, dormant, and which have become a terrain of confrontation instead of cooperation and mutual aid.

4 PROGRESS

The production function Y = f (K, L) will still have some virtues, from the world space to that of the smallest "enterprise." Behind the K/L cleavage lies the question of product sharing: Capital on one side, Humans on the other. The blurring is total, and the confrontation is in the making. How can we avoid the question of the right of ownership and use of K and L? L can be, as we know, classified among the privately (or publicly) appropriated K goods. Moreover, in the Investment that generates K, there is of course the Intellectual Investment. Thus,

L is the bearer of K. Who is the owner of it or of its use? As for the question of the "sharing" of Y, then the "K-me" and the "L-me" confront each other, I first, and then the others.[17]

In parallel to a real progress of a "science of the improvement of activities," for which our "management science" is only an incomplete premise, a work of historians is to be developed in a resolute way. History, as a scientific discipline, is like management science. They belong to two different poles: one turned towards the past that cannot be changed, the other oriented towards the future whose course can be influenced. "Better knowledge" on one side, "better action" on the other. As we know, history as a science faces many difficulties such as access to certain "archives."

For example? The fact that we are today facing a possible generalized collapse is a sign that humans, with their way of "managing" . . . have taken it like a foot.[18]

Is the great RESET advocated by Klaus Schwab (born in 1938) among others desirable? Associated with a notion of Industrial Revolution that is not sufficiently elaborated, does it correspond to needs? Doesn't it favor above all the concentration of power, the scenario of conflicts between rival powers, the attack on the most fundamental freedoms (public and private)? The so-called "surveillance capitalism" certainly has its uses: tracking down terrorism, drug trafficking, organized tax fraud of all kinds.

In my humble opinion, we need to do it differently. Computerized" relations between historians from all over the world should be organized . . . a better knowledge of the past will result. At the same time, great adventures on a global scale can be launched. Starting with the cleaning of the oceans and the space which has become a zone of no right.

BY WAY OF CONCLUSION

- The Preface of François Perroux to the Pléiade Edition of Marx, 1968
- A questioning on collective intelligence, a social construct
- A key? One man = one voice.

NOTES

1. To answer it, but also by asking it.
2. Galileo Galilei (1564–1642), the founder of physics, had investigated this question before 1600. He was taken to task by the Holy Office. Imprisoned from 1633 he died in 1642, without having left his jail. In Cathar country, we know the damage of intolerance.
3. Aristotle was mistaken when he tried to state this law.
4. Newton (1643–1727) was credited with the discovery. For him, the Anglican schism was a good thing. Although he did add to the work of the Polish Copernicus. Newton, far from Florence and Rome, was not worried. He was even buried in Westminster Abbey. His law was UNIVERSAL.
5. In the French language the term "*Patrimoine*" has been imposed, but "*Matrimoine*" could have been just as appropriate. A study of language practices in this respect would not be useless.
6. Because of the new scientific and technical skills, archaeologists and anthropologists work much better than in the past. Let's think about remote sensing and DNA decoding (see Evelyne Heyer "l'Odyssée des gênes" Flammarion 2020).
7. The individual "brain" can be considered as a "black box." What could be the case for a collective brain?
8. Let us not forget Victor Hugo's famous line: "this century was two years old. . . ."
9. Even reduced to "renewed sets," demography is valuable. See W. Petty (1623–1687), successive contributions by Lotka (1880–1949), Volterra/Brelot (1931), and Fanny Delebecque.

10. This is not so much the physiocracy of Quesnay (1694–1774), but the "pono-physiocratic" doctrine (ponos: work in Greek) of Effertz (1656–1921).
11. See, for example, Gaël Giraud (born in 1970), J.M. Jancovici (born in 1962), and before them Georgescu Roegen (1906–1994) and the vast current of proponents of SYSTEM DYNAMICS (Simon, Boulding, Forrester, the Meadows couple: Club of Rome (1972), Brundtland report (1987), work of the IPCC, etc…) On the French side again, J.L. Le Moigne and his female teams, Edgard Morin, and, among others, Jacques Lesourne (1928–2020) cf. his 1976 book written with fervor.
12. It consists in the elimination of those who have not been invited "to the banquet of nature," P knowing the forced decline to adjust to an insufficient or badly distributed Y.
13. The foreseen existence of this "collapse" is still contested by "optimists" whose unconsciousness can be feared, or by "pessimists" who add to it. It is fundamental to see clearly (exact and soft sciences all mobilized). Concerning the sanitary crisis: see Edgar Morin: *Changeons de voie: les leçons du coronavirus* Denoël – 2020: obligatory reading!
14. Refer to AFD website, *10 ans pour réagir* (17.12.2020)», Dominique Bourg
15. See the work of Elinor Ostrom (1933–2012), from which it emerges, as one might expect, that not all useful products take the private market form, far from it. The study of the latter has been more specifically developed by good economists. One sometimes wonders whether they have really understood Adam Smith himself; and money and its creation, delicate and serious matters in any society, have been the subject of much debate.
16. See Jacques Mourgeon: *Les libertés publiques* – Collection Que Sais-je – Édition 2005 augmentée.
17. The differences in wealth and income have become quite indecent in many countries. One finds there occasionally "classic deviated capitalism" or "Chinese-style, African-style, Indian-style or even Middle Eastern-style" for short.
18. For the last 3 centuries, the price signal has played a fundamental theoretical and practical role (with a summary accounting). No living species on Earth seems to have been satisfied with such a poor information system of evaluation and communication. This was undoubtedly a decisive advantage for mere survival. It is time to transform the "imperfect" into the "present" to have a "future."

REFERENCES

Ducroux, A. M. (2002). Les nouveaux utopistes du développement durable. *Autrement.*

Fondation GoodPlanet et Arthus-Bertrand Y. (2021), Cap 2030, une décennie pour changer le monde

Brandt W. (1985), La course aux armements et la famine dans le monde 1988

Tévoédjrè A., Tinbergen J., Câmara H. (1978), *La pauvreté richesse des peuples,* Editions Economie et Humanisme/Editions Ouvrières.

Fondateur Association Mondiale de Prospective Sociale

Sen A. (1999), l'Economie est une Science morale.

Cohen, D. (2015). *Le monde est clos et le désir infini.* Albin Michel.

Coriat B. (2020), La pandémie, l'anthropocène et le bien commun.

Larrouturou P. (2020), 7 solutions pour éviter l'effondrement.

Chapoutot J. (2020), Libres d'obéir. Le management ; du nazisme à aujourd'hui.

Billeter J.F. (XXXX) Leçons sur Tchouang-Tseu » -Denys Lombard

Culture indienne : Michel Hulin – Vandana Shiva – Isabelle Filliozat

Culture musulmane : Eva de Vitray-Meyerovitch « Anthologie du Soufisme »

Fromm E. (1976), Avoir ou Être

Témoignages personnels :

- 1965: Premier Congrès mondial Econométrie – Mise en garde Ragnar Frisch
- 1977 AISE Tokyo: Danse «mondialisée» de K. Boulding

- 1978: Colloque de Nice (Jacques Lebraty): Henri Savall présente la méthodologie nouvelle des coûts cachés de l'ISEOR, axe de recherches particulièrement prometteur !
- 1989: Colloque de Toulouse avec Shigeo Shingo créateur du SPT

Notion d'intelligence individuelle et ses 4 dimensions (cognitive, corporelle, émotionnelle, algorithmique)
Intelligence collective: références nombreuses et inégales

PART X

EPISTEMOLOGY AND RESEARCH METHODOLOGY

This page intentionally left blank.

CHAPTER 101

THE SOCIO-ECONOMIC APPROACH TO MANAGEMENT (SEAM) USES ENSEMBLE STORYTELLING, ABDUCTION-INDUCTION-DEDUCTION, AND SELF-CORRECTING METHODS FOR HIGHLY RIGOROUS, EFFECTIVE, AND ETHICAL ORGANIZATIONAL INTERVENTIONS

Grace Ann Rosile and David M. Boje

ABSTRACT

We contend that the Socio-Economic Approach to Management (SEAM) is so extraordinarily effective in improving organizational performance in large part due to its collaborative strategies coupled with highly rigorous organizational research methods. We view SEAM's collaborative methods through our own lens of Ensemble Storytelling. Using this lens, we find evidence of five forms of Ensemble Storytelling relevant to SEAM.

SEAM employs some of the best practices of organizational research in their interventions, including collaborative processes. In this way, they frame what we call 'Ensemble Storytelling' (Rosile et al., 2021) within an inquiry approach that meets highly rigorous standards of qualitative research. In this chapter, we will demonstrate how SEAM practices (Savall, 1974,

SEAM Treatise, pages 827–836

1981) are highly compatible with Ensemble Storytelling, and how SEAM interventions incorporate long-accepted and laudable organizational research methods. We offer these two perspectives on storytelling and research methods to provide deeper insights into how and why SEAM has enjoyed such noteworthy success over multiple decades.

In Part I, we explain Ensemble Storytelling. We address five aspects of Ensemble Storytelling, and explain how SEAM is complimentary to these forms of conversational storytelling interviewing (Boje & Rosile, 2020). In Part II we consider ways in which SEAM (Savall & Zardet, 2008: 206) and storytelling use the 'Abduction, Induction, and Deduction' (AID) successive spiraling phases of the research process championed by Charles Saunders Peirce (1958, Volume 8, section 385; Volume 2: 266, 515, 624).

These AID spiral phases are theorized by Peirce (1958) as a "self-correcting" research methodology. Popper (1963: 318), by contrast, wanted to avoid the fallacy of induction, by (1) the trial and error of the scientific method and (2) using falsification instead of just verification of one's theories and what Peirce called abduction. For Peirce the AID successive approach is a continual process of arriving closer and closer to the truth, if one keeps sampling. The final part of this chapter offers a summary and conclusions, where we will explain how SEAM arrives 'closer to the truth' (Larsen, Boje, & Bruun, 2021) using Ensemble Storytelling with AID and self-correcting AID in conversational storytelling and change management processes.

Please note that SEAM intervenor/researchers may not use the same terms relating to 'conversational storytelling' as we use here (although SEAM does incorporate explicit discussion of Peirce's AID model). SEAM gathers verbatim conversation as part of its diagnosis and used in Mirror Effect meetings. It keeps interventions on track with a scientific method, which interanimates qualitative, quantitative, and financial information. Thus, regardless of terminology, we find the SEAM practices embody 'true storytelling' and Ensemble Storytelling principles (Larsen, Boje, & Bruun, 2021).

Further, we believe that this compatibility of SEAM concepts with Ensemble Storytelling and with widely acknowledged theories of organizational research methods deepens

Figure 101.1 The abduction-induction-deduction spiral.

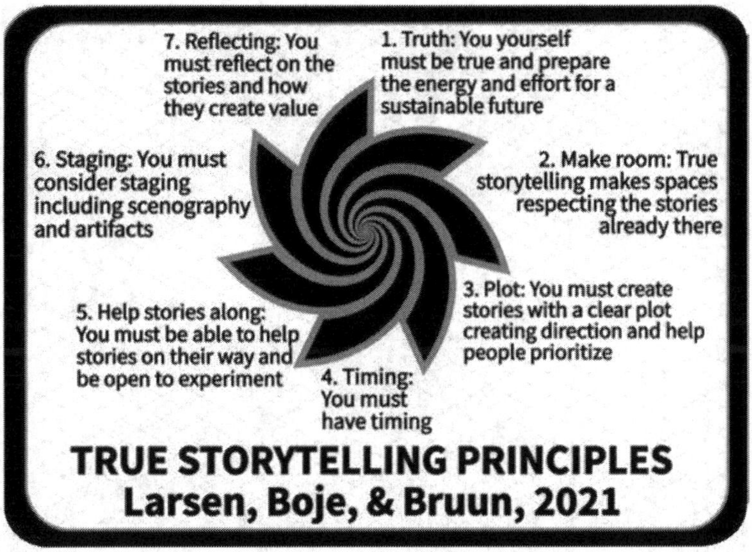

Figure 101.2 True storytelling principles (Larsen, Boje & Bruun, 2021).

our understanding of SEAM. The evidence of SEAM's success and effectiveness has been well-documented for over 20 years. However, SEAM successes encompass more than mere profits (Savall & Zardet, 2008), as SEAM methods also foster corporate social responsibility (Savall a al., 2015, 2018). SEAM researchers received a national award in France for their contributions to understanding and measuring corporate social responsibility (Zavall et al., 2018, p. xxxv). This present essay seeks to add to our understanding of why and how SEAM works with what we term "Ensemble" collaborative processes within a context of AID self-correcting research methods.

1 FIVE FORMS OF ENSEMBLE STORYTELLING

Ensemble Storytelling refers to collaborative ways that storytelling can involve multiple voices in co-creating ("together-telling") stories. For us, storytelling is broadly defined as more than a clear, linear, beginning-middle-end narrative with a plot (Boje, 2001; TwoTrees, 1997, 2000). We take a broader view to include multiple streams of narratives that exist before, and from which current elements of "the" story eventually emerge. Of course, "the" story is also subject to change as it evolves and is placed in different contexts with different audiences over time.

As some story elements emerge in living story webs, others become submerged or overlooked. For these reasons, we study "living story" (Boje, 2001; TwoTrees, 1997, 2000) in all its dynamic networking, retrospective- as well as prospective-sensemaking, and told as well as 'untold stories' (Hitchin, 2015) aspects of storytelling. We stress the relationship of this broadly defined view of storytelling to SEAM.

The "Ensemble" part of Ensemble Storytelling has its roots in the performing arts, where instead of one star, an entire set of performers share equally in the role of "star" (Rosile et al., 2018; and Rosile et al., 2021). Rosile et al. (2021) studied their concept of Ensemble Leadership (Rosile et al., 2018) through their participant-observation research with the Coalition of Immokalee Workers (CIW), whose motto is "We are all leaders." That research

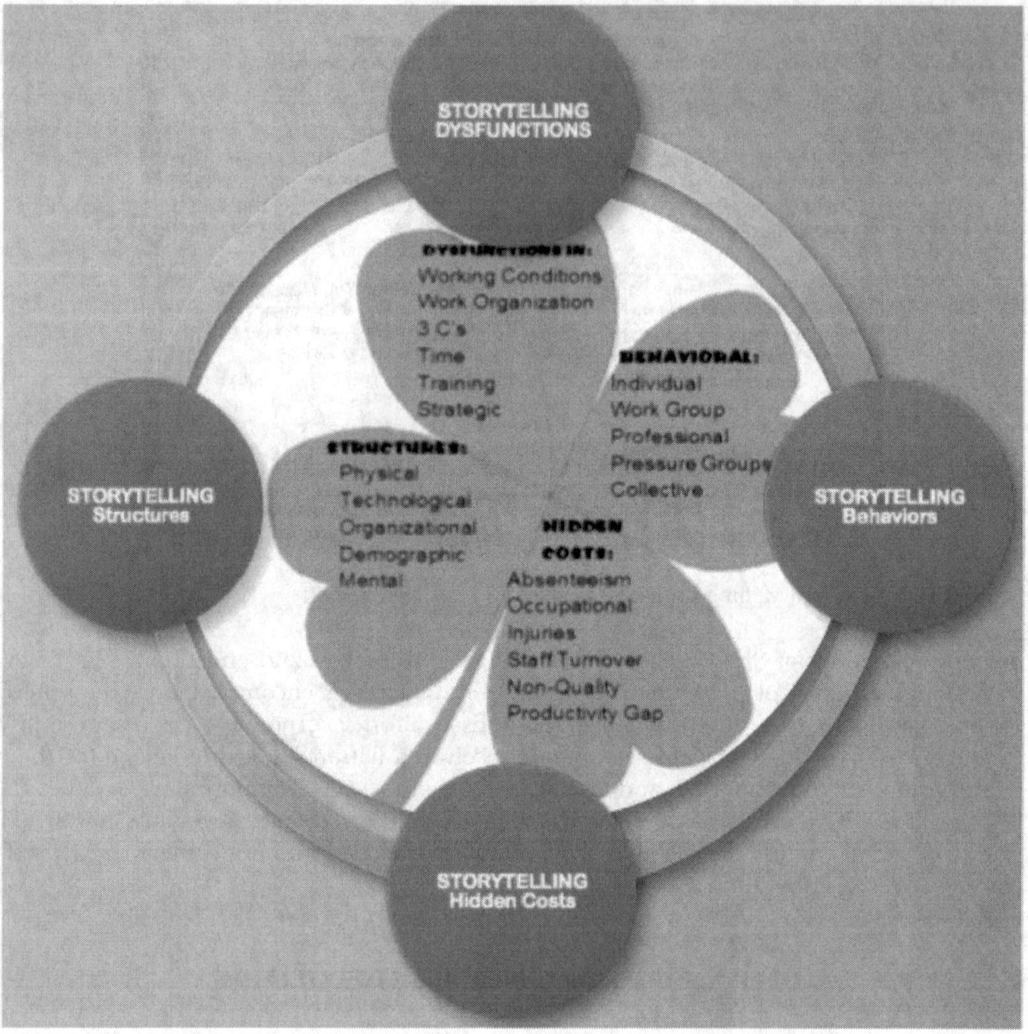

Figure 101.3 How storytelling can be part of the SEAM 4-leaf clover diagnosis.

revealed 7 Ensemble Storytelling processes by which the CIW enacted their motto in their de facto Ensemble Leadership organizing style.

We will use the five (5) aspects of Ensemble storytelling identified by Rosile (2016) and Rosile et al., (2021). The first three (3) are all aspects of "Together-Telling" and are 1) Ensemble Story Elicitation, 2) Ensemble Story Role-sharing, and 3) Ensemble Authorship. The fourth category is Collaborative Mediums including things like Theatrical Performances. The fifth and final aspect of Ensemble Storytelling is Ensemble Socio-Materiality and Political Economy. We turn now to the first of our 5 "together-telling" processes, Ensemble Story Elicitation.

Ensemble Storytelling Elicitation is key to understanding all Ensemble processes, as it emphasizes the role of listening. Good storytelling research elicits the stories of others, and replaces interrogation with elicitation. Once a story is elicited, the story researcher attentively listens. In this previous sentence, we might equally well substitute the words "SEAM intervenor/researcher" for "story researcher." SEAM intervenor/researchers are trained to take verbatim hand-written notes. This process shifts more of the narrative power to the interviewee and away from the interviewer.

This is in contrast to the interviewer who tapes the interviewee's comments, while holding for themselves the power of the "record/off" switch, and while choosing how closely attention needs to be paid to the interviewee. Instead, the process of hand-written notes can be much more personal and respectful, and so very different in tenor from methods using printed questionnaires and even semi-structured interviews. The respect and deference conveyed by taking notes by hand puts the interviewee and the interviewer into a much more equal power relationship. This more egalitarian relationship lends itself to what we call "conversational" storytelling (Boje and Rosile, 2020) as opposed to the more hierarchical connotations of the interviewer-interviewee relationship.

Our second Ensemble Storytelling together-telling process is Ensemble Story Role-sharing. This refers to sharing the roles of story-teller and story listener. The SEAM consultants are not solely process consultants who never make recommendations. Instead, SEAM intervenor-researchers are both process consultants and expert consultants. Once they have completed their interviews, the SEAM practitioners promise to offer at least three (3) recommendations. This makes sense, based on their many years of experience using SEAM in so many companies. Further, this again balances the power between story-teller and story-listener as the two trade roles at different points in the process. We consider this switching of roles to be role-sharing. We believe this sharing to be another aspect of a power-sharing "conversational" type of storytelling (Boje & Rosile, 2020).

Ensemble Authorship is our third form of Ensemble Storytelling. In the mirror process, SEAM intervenor-researchers present direct quotes and themes emerging from the interviews, and they invite feedback. Participants may disagree with what is presented, but what is more usual is that people recognize that stories of the problems consist of their own exact verbatim quotes. Recognizing this, it becomes easier to come to common understandings of problems and to collaborate to design the "experiments" that can address these problems.

Ensemble Storytelling Collaborative Mediums and Theatrical Performances constitute our fourth type of Ensemble Storytelling. SEAM has strong underpinnings in theatrics. However, they do not engage in elaborate collaborative art and theatre processes to train and educate their membership like the Coalition of Immokalee Workers (CIW) (Rosile et al., 2021). Instead, SEAM uses the direct verbatim quotes of the organization's members to provide the "script" for their special version of organizational feedback. This organizational feedback, generically known as the "organizational mirror," becomes the "mirror reality theatre" in SEAM. Extensive use of verbatim quotes yields a process we characterize as the collaborative together-telling of Ensemble Authorship.

Our fifth and final aspect of Ensemble Storytelling is Ensemble SocioMateriality and Political Economy. This feature is easily visible in the profit-sharing plans required to be a part of every organizational project "experiment." Such profit sharing could not be token amounts but rather had to be at least a significant (10% portion) of the salary of each employee engaged in that project experiment.

2 ABDUCTION, INDUCTION, AND DEDUCTION AND SELF-CORRECTING METHOD

Pierce's (1931–1935) classic approach to research as abduction, induction, and deduction (AID) in a self-correcting cycle is especially well suited to the dynamic ongoing processes of organizational changing and developing. We see several ways in which SEAM incorporates this AID process.

First, SEAM considers abduction by avoiding a too-early diagnosis of problems. Instead, SEAM begins with a very open-ended and indirect questioning of a broad range of organizational members both laterally and horizontally (called the "hori-vert" process). One example of this abductive process is described in Rosile (2008). In this article, a case example of an actual use of the SEAM process is offered as an exemplary model, and is the basis for an exercise on practicing open-ended interviews for needs assessment. The case example is based on an actual consultation where SEAM researcher-intervenors were asked to design an equipment-maintenance training program. However, the intervenors did not assume that the organization's diagnosis of this training issue was to be accepted as the root of the organization's problems. After a thorough SEAM analysis, the true root causes of the problems turned out not to be training-related. The true root causes subsequently were revealed and addressed by the SEAM consultants (Rosile 2008). By using non-directive open interviewing at the pre-diagnosis stage, the SEAM method thus incorporates abductive reasoning (including intuitive hunches) of a broad cross-section of organizational members.

Abductive, inductive, and deductive processes may occur at any time and in any sequence throughout the SEAM intervention, however, each has a particular phase in which it is most explicitly considered. Thus while abductive reasoning occurs continuously through the SEAM process, it is most emphasized during the mirroring phase. Mirroring allows the organizational members and the researcher-intervenors together to reflect collectively on the meanings of the comments. Those comments constitute the "metascript" (Boje & Rosile, 2003) of verbatim field notes gathered during the extensive initial interviews.

After the mirroring effect meeting, organization members and the intervenors together plan their project actions using SEAM's DPIE tool (DPIE stands for Diagnosis, Project planning, Implementation, and Evaluation). In teaching consulting at the university, we use a succession of three small projects to form a DPIE spiral (Boje, 2011, 2017a, 2019; Saylors & Boje, 2014; Hillon & Boje, 2019).

These plans are not called "solutions" as with many organization development and problem solving approaches. Instead, SEAM calls these action plans "project experiments." It is at this phase that the organization tests its deductions. We view conversation storytelling induction inquiry as contributive to SEAM. We look at the ways organizations mired in

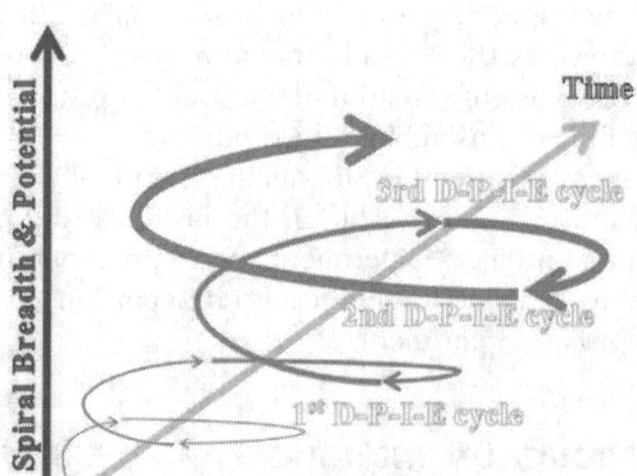

Figure 101.4 How we use DPIE in successive spiral for teaching student consultants.

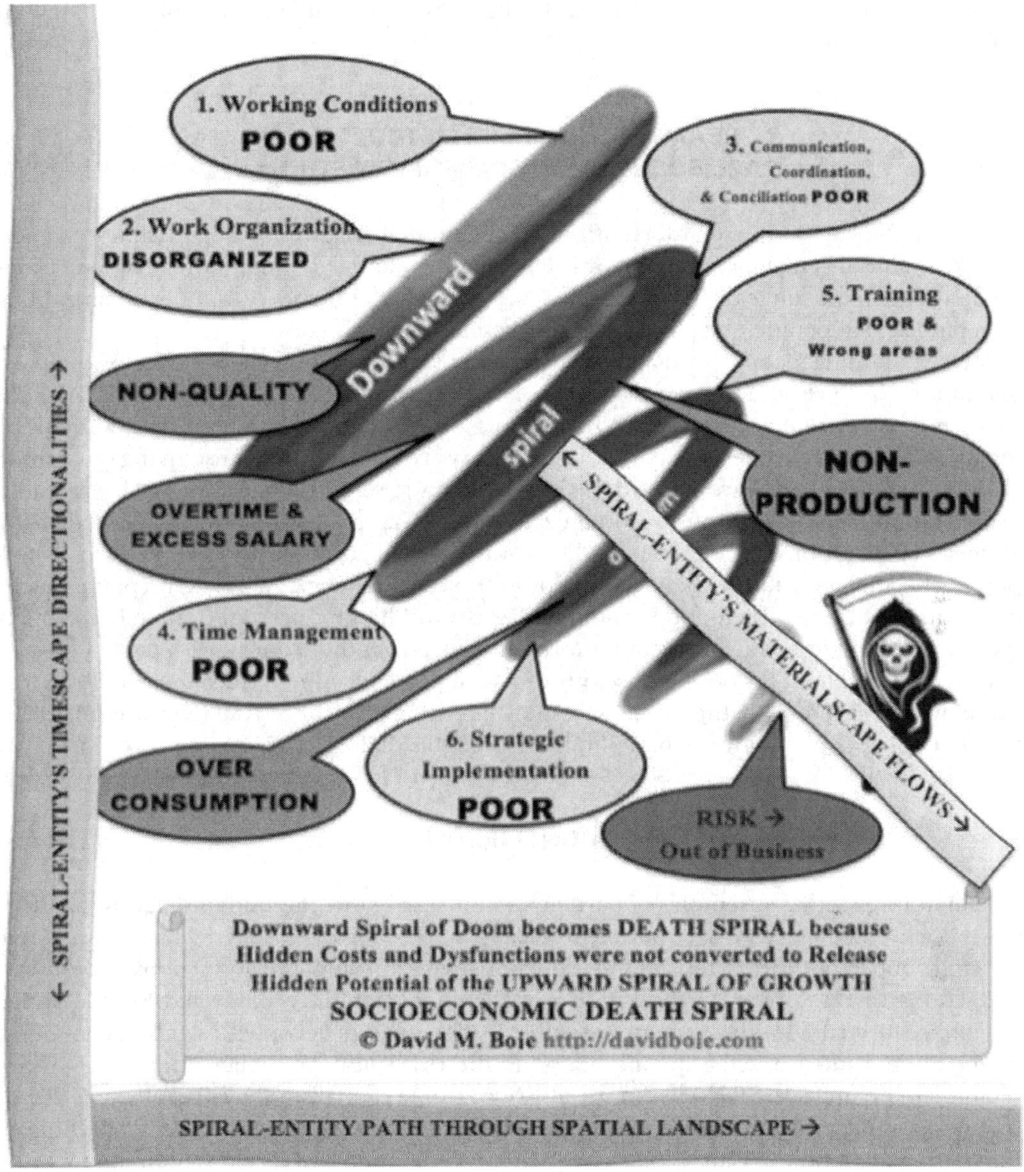

Figure 101.5 Often the potential of upward sprial comes from transfoming the downward spiral of doom.

dysfunctions, structural and behavioral recurring patterns, and hidden costs, yield downward spirals of performance and well-being.

The organization may deduce that certain process improvements have been correlated with improved efficiency in the past. This deduction might then be formulated as an inductive test, with more of a controlled "project experiment," to document specific actions leading to measured improvements in efficiency and effectiveness. If the "project experiment" shows improvement in organizational performance, then the savings or profits are shared with those who designed and implemented the experiment through previously-agreed-upon calculations. As mentioned above, this profit-sharing is an example of Ensemble Storytelling Political Economics.

3 SEAM AND ENSEMBLE STORYTELLING ARE FOCUSED ON SCIENTIFIC METHOD

We refer to SEAM's approach to scientific method, in how Diagnosis using qualitative, quantitative, financial (Qualimetric), Mirror Effect meetings, and DPIE along with ongoing training in tools clients can learn to use for themselves, builds resilience, and puts organizations on a path to democratic, socially responsible capitalism.

We are training people to diagnose the ensemble storytelling networking of their organization. *In Ensemble Leadership there are multiple kinds of networks, all entangled, hopefully, in a good, just, true, and beautiful way.* It is a move far beyond open systems double loops of feedback (retrospective-sensemaking) and feedforward (prospective-sensemking) to a third loop of 'intelligent adaptive networking,' by attuning ensemble storytelling with ensemble leadership. It has the kind of interorganization networking alliances, that CIW made with 17 mega corporations (from McDonald's to Wal-Mart) to adopt ethical 'worker-driven corporate social responsibility' behaviors (Rosile, Boje, & Sanchez, 2021). Our point is self-correcting not by just single loop (command & control hierarchies), of double loop (open systems adapting to extract more and more resources from the planet), with triple loop, we enter an ensemble network of 'conscious capitalism by convening ethical ensembles.'[1] It is therefore consistent with the 'socially responsible capitalism of SEAM (Savall et al, 2015, 2018). Triple Loop ensemble storytelling is thoroughly dialogical.

CONCLUSION

In sum, it takes actual ensembles of participation in a scientific method of diagnosis, abductive-inductive-deductive work to be able to create double loop open system change, and then do triple loop experiments, tests of the inductions, work through the abductions, modify the deductions, then assure the organization is in alignment with the ecology. As SEAM includes ensemble storytelling with a base of ensemble leadership this becomes a symbiotic mode of intervention, rooted in scientific methods and the IAD spiral. We believe the future of ensemble storytelling and SEAM lies in socially responsible capitalism (Savall et al. 2015, 2018) that has, as well, an ecological business modeling foundation (Spare & Boje, 2020; Boje & Jorgensen, 2020; Boje & Rana, 2020). Single loop capitalism, and its extraction model without consciousness, can give way to not just double loop open systems, but to an ecological and socially responsible capitalism.

NOTE

1. For more on our approach to Single, Double, and Triple Loop ODC, in relation to SEAM https://truestorytelling.blog/storytelling-organizations-are-perfectly-designed-to-get-the-results-they-are-getting-to-change-the-results-change-the-storytelling-system/ accessed Apr 14 2021

REFERENCES

Boje, D. (1995). Stories of the storytelling organization: A postmodern analysis of Disney as "Tamara-Land." *Academy of Management journal, 38*(4), 997–1035.

Boje, D. (2001). *Narrative methods for organizational & communication research.* Thousand Oaks, CA: Sage.

Boje, D. (2011). *The cycle and the spiral-antenarrative: a quantum-ontology-system manifesto.* NMSU Working Paper, accessed Apr 14, 2021 at https://business.nmsu.edu/~dboje/qm/fractal_rhythms_in_spiral_development.html

Boje, D. (2017a). Risky deleuzian double spiral-antenarratives and sensemaking of academic capitalism. *Routledge companion to risk, crisis and emergency management. Online prepublication PDF.*

Boje, D. (2017b). "Ensemble Leadership and Worker-Driven Social Responsibility Defeat Globalized Modern-Day Slavery" Keynote talk at Global Management Conference, Lille, France, 6–8 June 2017.

Boje, D. (2019). "The Future of the "Spiral Paradigm" in Climate Action." In *The Emerald Handbook of Management and Organization Inquiry.* Emerald Publishing Limited.

Boje, D., & Hillon, Y. C. (2017). The fifth epoch: Socio-economic approach to sustainable capitalism. *Markets, Globalization & Development Review* (MGDR), 2(1), Article [http://digitalcommons.uri.edu/mgdr/vol2/iss1/2].

Boje, D., & Jorgensen, K. M. (2020). A 'storytelling science' approach making the eco-business modeling turn. Journal of Business Modeling, Vol. 8, No. 4, pp. 8–25.

Boje, D., & Rana, M. B. (2020). Defining a Sustainably-Driven Business Modeling Strategy with a 'Storytelling Science' Approach. Chapter to appear in Markovic, S., Sancha, C. and Lindgreen, A. (Eds.), *Handbook of Sustainability-driven Business Strategies in Practice,* Northampton, MA: Edward Elgar.

Boje, D., Rosile, G.A., Herder, R., & Sanchez, M. (2018). "The Coalition of Immokalee Workers uses Egalitarian Rhizomatics to Overcome Enslavement in Corporate Supply Chains." *Business & Society.*

Boje, D., & Rosile, G. A. (2020). *How to Use Conversational Storytelling Interviews for your Dissertation.* Cheltenham, UK, and Northampton, MA, USA: Edward Elgar Publishing.

Czarniawska, B. (2004). *Narratives in Social Science Research.* London: Sage.

Gabriel, Y. (2000). *Storytelling in Organisations.* Oxford: Oxford University Press.

Hillon, Y. C., & Boje, D. M. (2019). Socioeconomic Triple-Spiral-Helix Response to Socially Irresponsible Capitalism. In *The Emerald Handbook of Management and Organization Inquiry.* Emerald Publishing Limited.

Hitchin, L. (2015). Method and story fragments. In M. Izak, L. Hitchin, and D. Anderson (eds.), *Untold Stories in Organizations.* London: Routledge, 213–238.

Larsen, J., Bruun L., and Boje D. (2021). *True Storytelling: Seven Principles for an Ethical and Sustainable Change-Management Strategy.* London: Routledge.

Peirce, C. S. (1931–1937). *Collected Papers of Charles Sanders Peirce,* Vol. I to VI, edited by Charles Hartshorne & Paul Weiss, 1931–1935, Cambridge, MA: Harvard University Press.

Peirce, C. S. 1958. *Collected Papers of Charles Sanders Peirce.* Volumes VII-VIII, edited by Arthur W. Burks, 1958. Cambridge, MA: Harvard University Press.

Popper, K. R. (1935/1959/1992/2000). *The Logic of Scientific Discovery.* Logik der Forschung first published 1935 by Verlag von Julius Springer, Vienna, Austria. First English translation by Hutchinson and co., then 1992 by London: Routledge, and again by Routledge Classics 2000. Accessed 6 March 2019 at http://strangebeautiful.com/other-texts/popper-logic-scientific-discovery.pdf and from http://www.math.chalmers.se/~ulfp/Review/logicscdis.pdf.

Rosile, G. A. (2007). Cheating: Making it a teachable moment. *Journal of Management Education, 31*(5), 582–613.

Rosile, G. A. (2008). "Avoiding Biased Questions for Training Needs Assessments." In Garguilo, T. L., Pangarkar, A. M., Kirkwood, T. *The Trainers Portable Mentor.* Pfeiffer/Wiley: San Francisco, CA, pp. 13–19.

Rosile, G.A. (2016). "Tribal Wisdom Contributions to the Socio-Economic Approach to Management" at joint *conference of the Academy of Management Organization Development and Change Division* and the Institute for Socio Economic Organization Research Conference in Lyon, France, June 9–10.

Rosile, G. A., Boje, D., & Claw, C. M. (2018). Ensemble leadership theory: Collectivist, relational, and heterarchical roots from indigenous contexts. *Leadership, 14*(3), 307–328.

Rosile, G. A., Boje, D., Herder, R. A., & Sanchez, M. (2021). The Coalition of Immokalee Workers uses ensemble storytelling processes to overcome enslavement in corporate supply chains. *Business & Society, 60* (2), 376–414.

Saylors, R., & Boje, D. (2014). Antenarrative spiral approach to SEAM.. In *Facilitating the SocioEconomic Approach to Management: Results of the First SEAM Conference in North America* (March). IAP.

Spare, M.; Boje, D. (2020). Utilizing Participative Action Research With Storytelling Interventions to Create Sustainability in Danish Farming. To appear *in Organizational Development Journal.*

Twotrees, K. (1997). Presentation at the Organizational Behavior Teaching conference, *meeting at Case Western Reserve,* Ohio.

Twotrees, Kaylynn. (2000). Seven Directions practice: A Practice for the Crossroads, *The Fourth R* (Vol. 92, August, Sept, October) published by CRENet (Conflict Resolution in Education Network).

CHAPTER 102

THE SOCIO-ECONOMIC THEORY OF FIRMS AND ORGANIZATIONS

Heterodoxy in Management Science

Laurent Cappelletti

ABSTRACT

The socio-economic theory of firms and organizations presents important fractures with the dominant theories in management sciences, which structure its orthodoxy. These fractures, which are explained and discussed in the chapter, are particularly noteworthy in terms of epistemology, methodology and the societal utility of science. They thus form the basis of a singular heterodoxy in management science, a powerful lever for disruptive knowledge.

Orthodoxy refers to the set of doctrines and theories held by the dominant fraction of a community. Six managerial theories emerge from our observations as being the ones most used by the management science community for work that is predominantly hypothetico-deductive and descriptive, the criterion being the neutrality of the researcher. These are the agency theories of Michael Jensen and William Meckling, the transaction costs of Oliver Williamson, the neo-institutionalist theories of Paul DiMaggio and Walter Powell, the value chain of Michael Porter, the organizational configurations of Henry Mintzberg and the resources of Gary Hamel and C.K. Prahalad. In light of this outline of the orthodoxy in management science, the socio-economic theory of firms and organizations (Savall, 1974, 1977, 1979; Savall and Zardet, 1987, 2020; Savall, Zardet and Bonnet, 2000, 2008; Savall, Zardet, Bonnet and Cappelletti, 2019), referred to as Socio-Economic Theory in this text, appears to be a *heterodoxy* and therefore marks fractures with the orthodoxy, particularly at the levels of *epistemology, methodology and societal utility*.

SEAM Treatise, pages 837–843

1 FIRST FRACTURE: THE SOCIO-ECONOMIC THEORY ASSUMES NON-NEUTRALITY AND NON-OBJECTIVITY OF THE SCIENTIST

At the epistemological level, the Socio-Economic Theory (SST) is heterodox by systematizing the explicitness of the implicitly normative conceptualizations that guide it (Perroux, 1975, 1979), thus transcending the debates on epistemological positioning (constructivist versus positivist), which are often futile as regards the quality of reflection on knowledge. Its epistemological foundations are based on the transformative observation of the object of study, the authenticity of the data and the *qualimetric approach*, thus breaking with the orthodox paradigms of *neutrality* and objectivity.

1.1 Transformative Observation as a Source of Robustness of Primary Data

For the socio-economic theory, the paradox of research data is that it is never given. The management researcher must collect it in a scientific observation field through "in vivo" *transformative observations* (Savall, 2001). It is in fact in the field of scientific observation – companies, organizations, territories, etc. – that the real world unfolds. – It is in the field of scientific observation – companies, organizations, territories, etc. – that reality is revealed, and that knowledge is revealed on the condition that this field is transformed. For the socio-economic theory, the field is "off the ground." It is the domain of fiction, that is to say "the opposite" of reality. Admitting that the management sciences propose to study the practices of actors in relation to the performance of organizations, the socio-economic theory considers that the concept of practice covers all three observable objects: written documents, oral expression and actions. Given the impossible *objectivity* of the researcher since he is a subject, this conventional representation, if not "objective," allows for the construction of a platform of knowledge of scientific intent, usable in each space of actors and for a certain time (Buono, Savall, Cappelletti, 2018). Therefore, by making the interaction between the observing subject and the object studied a foundation of its epistemology, SST deepens the question of the impossible *neutrality* of the researcher, who fully assumes his non-neutrality and its consequences on the limits of scientificity of his research. This does not mean that socio-economic theory advocates a monopoly of transformative observation in management sciences, since for it there is no single scientific method for making rigorous observations, which would be "the" method, but a plurality that respects the complexity to be studied. Nevertheless, it favors transformative observation to collect primary research data and thus illuminate knowledge from this perspective (Buono, Savall, Cappelletti, 2018).

1.2 Authenticity of Data as a Primary Epistemological Criterion

For the socio-economic theory, the central epistemological criterion is therefore no longer that of orthodoxy, objectivity and/or neutrality of the researcher, but authenticity. That of the researcher first, which he or she achieves by becoming aware of the influences of his or her choices and values and by revealing his or her theories, opinions, and research position (Buono, Savall, Cappelletti, 2018). That of the data that he or she then collects by making explicit in a comprehensive way what he or she observes. In doing so, the receiver of the research can appreciate the work of the researcher. Following on from this founding criterion, the socio-economic theory mobilizes complementary epistemological principles which are falsifiability and heuristics to which it adds *qualimetry* (Cappelletti, Faron, Fière, Savall, 2020). Because of the principle of *falsifiability*, knowledge acquires this status if it remains open to criticism on its value, otherwise it is a dogma or a belief. Thus, a piece of knowledge of today can return to the status of a mere hypothesis tomorrow, or even be abandoned completely. These changes of foot, if they are based on rigorous methods of observation, are an integral part of the scientific process. They are part of the heuristic method, rational trial and error, a learning process that characterizes the creation of robust knowledge. The principle of qualimetry consists in combining qualitative data with quantitative data in order to create knowledge (Savall, Zardet, 1996, 2004).

1.3 Qualimetry to Approach the Complex Object in Management

For the economist, the firm is a simple point in the macro and meso-economic space (Perroux, 1975, 1979). However, if we approach this simple point with a rigorous and precise method of observation, we realize that it is in fact already a complex universe. This universe is populated by individuals, groups and entities that maintain innumerable interactions between them. The organization is therefore not a homogeneous category; it is characterized by a great diversity of human, intangible and material elements that the orthodox models of management, both simplistic and sophisticated, do not correctly translate (Savall, Zardet, Cappelletti, 2021). The significant elements of the economic activity of an organization or a territory cannot be perfectly or completely measured by numbers or simply quantitative indicators. On the other hand, these elements can be identified and almost measured by keywords, key ideas, and various signs, in the form of so-called qualitative indicators. The *qualimetric approach* (Savall, 1974, 1979; Savall, Zardet, 1987, 1992, 1996, 2004, 2011) makes it possible to associate and combine these two categories of indicators. It provides a less distorted, less mutilated, less erroneous and less biased representation of economic activity, observed at the level of a company or a territory. From a methodological point of view, the *qualimetric approach* assumes that the analyst gets closer to the place of observation of the object or situation studied, that he/she triangulates the data he/she processes. These are obtained by observing the phenomena, exploiting existing documents and targeted interviews of human actors witnessing the phenomena to be studied, both individually and in groups, to maximize the information that allows for the elaboration of a conceptual and theoretical construction (Savall, Zardet, Cappelletti, 2021).

2 SECOND FRACTURE: THE METHODOLOGICAL APPROACH OF THE SOCIO-ECONOMIC THEORY BRINGS TOGETHER EPISTEMOLOGY AND MANAGEMENT

The heterodoxy of the socio-economic theory *methodology* for creating knowledge in the management sciences is revealed by its very name, *qualimetric intervention-research*, which places *basic research* and *applied research* on the same continuum, without separating them (Savall, 1977, 2003). Intervention-research is part of the evidence-based management paradigm, which brings together field approaches aimed at theorizing professional practices. It is resolutely heterodox by integrating "at the same time" *epistemological devices* to guarantee the scientific quality of the observations as well as *managerial devices*, to produce knowledge useful to companies and organizations, which is not well tolerated by orthodoxy (Cappelletti, Voyant, Savall, 2018).

2.1 The Reference Paradigm of Qualimetric Intervention-Research: Evidence-Based Management

The knowledge proposed from "in vivo" methodologies is subject to recurrent criticism from the orthodoxy. Some of these criticisms are of a scientific nature and concern their validity, while others are of a political nature and concern their alleged dependence on the field and the conflicts of interest that this would engender. The separation between theory and practice in management, which is refuted by heterodoxy but advocated by orthodoxy, refers to *evidence-based management* (EBM), which advocates the development of theoretical knowledge based on rigorous observation of facts, useful for managerial decisions (Pfeffer, Sutton, 2006). In connection with EBM, it is useful to mention in the discussion the concept of *"engaged scholarship"* forged by Van de Ven and Johnson (2006), which is like the socio-economic theory. It is based on two principles: "co-production of knowledge" between researchers and practitioners and "adversarial arbitration," i.e., the validation of observations through non-indulgent and mutually respectful discussions between researchers and practitioners.

2.2 The Three Integrated Epistemological Devices of Qualimetric Intervention-Research

Qualimetric intervention-research integrates three singular epistemological devices (Buono, Savall, Cappelletti 2018). *Cognitive interactivity* refers to the fact that the construction of collective knowledge results from a process of interaction between two or more actors. Each being the bearer of a snippet of knowledge contributes, through successive iterations, to build a knowledge shared by the actors of a team or an organization. This justifies the need for a partnership between the researcher and the scientific field of observation. *Generic contingency* refers to the fact that any situation is contingent but that an in-depth analysis reveals a generic component that can be found in other situations, just as the same atom can be found in different molecules. *Contradictory intersubjectivity* refers to the interactive process that allows two or more actors, starting from different subjective points of view, to construct, by means of iterations over time, an acceptable common representation. The general heterodox concept of *generic constructivism* encompasses these three principles. It allows, by successive replications of research-interventions carried out in always specific situations, to derive generic knowledge that can be transposed to other situations. How do we know that a knowledge is generic and not only local or specific? If users use it and validate it, we will say that it has a certain value. Knowledge is a convention until there is an innovation recognized by both communities, those of researchers and practitioners (Savall, Zardet, Cappelletti, 2019).

2.3 The Three Integrated Management Devices of Qualimetric Intervention-Research

Since epistemological devices are indigestible for organizations, *qualimetric intervention-research* integrates them into management tools that they can tolerate well. For this reason, the methodology integrates three managerial devices linked together to create a spiral of progressive improvements: a *political device* to engage the management of the territory's organization, an *instrumental device* composed of management tools, and a *processual device* to stimulate the collective resolution of problems.

The *political device* aims to stimulate the political and strategic decisions of the company's management concerning the negotiation of its objectives with the actors. For this purpose, a steering group meets periodically, involving the researcher and representatives of the management of the organization studied. The decisions of the management team give meaning to the use of the tools and a framework for the actions implemented to solve the problems. The *processual device* provides a problem-solving dynamic. It is composed of four steps: socio-economic diagnosis, project group, implementation of improvement solutions, and qualimetric evaluation. The diagnosis focuses on the dysfunctions that disturb the actors of an organization. It is composed of three main modules: qualitative, financial and presentation of results aimed at producing a "mirror effect" with the people interviewed. Once validated, the diagnosis serves as a work platform for the socio-economic project group. Its role is to invent solutions to reduce the identified dysfunctions and convert their hidden costs into visible performance. Once implemented, the solutions are evaluated to measure the performance generated. Finally, the tools of the *instrumental device* are used by all the managers of the observed company. There are six of them to instrument the six areas considered crucial to socio-economic performance: time management, the competency grid, the strategic piloting logbook, the internal-external strategic action plan, the priority action plan, the periodically negotiable activity contract, (Savall, Zardet, 1977, 1987, 2020).

3 THIRD FRACTURE: THE USEFULNESS OF THE SOCIO-ECONOMIC THEORY IS EMBODIED IN A CITIZEN CONCEPTION OF SCIENCE

The socio-economic theory refutes the orthodox presupposition that the practical *usefulness* of a research work, demonstrated through documented prescriptions or management tools, would be proof of non-scientific nature. On this question, the heterodoxy of the socio-economic theory consists in proposing, by means of its methodology, *contingent knowledge* useful to the organizations observed to solve their management problems. Then the reiteration of the same methodology on other scientific observation fields allows to identify *generic knowledge* whose usefulness is shared by many companies and organizations. Finally, the dissemination of knowledge to scientific, professional, and general public receptors gives socio-economic theory a societal utility in a *citizen science* perspective. For the socio-economic theory, unlike orthodoxy, the dissemination of research results to citizens is part of the scientific validation process. If not, the field is left open to conspiracy theories, *fake news* and other managerial fictions (Pfeffer, Sutton, 2006) that the citizen impregnates the organization or the territory where he / she works.

3.1 The Production of a Vaccine Against the Variants of the T.F.W. Virus

The *contingent utility* of the socio-economic theory consists first in co-creating with the companies and organizations observed their own vaccine against the variant of the "T.F.W. virus" that affects them. The socio-economic theory demonstrates that the most common management methods are infected by the "T.F.W. virus," i.e., the anachronistic use of the models of Frederick Taylor, Henri Fayol and Max Weber, which are based on a conception of the organization of work from another age, depersonalized, excessively specialized and centered on uniform procedures (Savall, 1974, 1975). Abundant *qualimetric intervention-researches* have identified that managerial dysfunctions are particularly rooted in six areas that constitute the factors of quality of life at work: working conditions, work organization, the communication-coordination-concertation triptych, time management, integrated training and strategic implementation. It is on these six levers that the socio-economic theory proposes to act through *proximity management* to improve the quality of life at work and the efficiency and effectiveness of the organization (Savall, Zardet, Cappelletti, 2021).

3.2 The Measurement of Hidden Costs and Their Sustainable Conversion Into Value Added

The *contingent utility* of the socio-economic theory also consists in systematically measuring the hidden costs of the companies and organizations observed and then converting them partially into sustainable performance. At the origin of the socio-economic theory, Henri Savall concluded that the macroeconomic approach was not able to account for the value creation process (Savall, 1974, 1975). He drew two conclusions from this. First, that an essential variable was missing from the traditional formula Y = f (K * L), where the value of production Y is a function of the quantity of capital and the quantity of labour. Second, that measurement tools such as national accounting, based on company accounts, do not allow for the detection and measurement of this unknown variable. This is how he created the methodology of qualimetric research-intervention, allowing a rigorous scientific demonstration and taking the form of a management method, to better study the phenomena and to better measure the creation of value within organizations. It was also necessary to qualify the residue corresponding to unmeasured variables. This is how he proposed the concept of hidden costs-performance (Savall, 1974, 1975, 1979; Perroux, 1979; Savall and Zardet, 1987; Boje, Rosile, 2003).

3.3 The Contingent Knowledge Versus Generic Knowledge Continuum

The *generic utility* of the socio-economic theory is not static but dynamic. The accumulation of convergent *contingent knowledge* generates *generic knowledge* that feeds the SST. On the other hand, suspensions in this accumulation, or even refutations by contradictory observations, erode the generic order of a knowledge. The socio-economic theory thus moves away from the orthodox conception according to which if research is a dynamic, the knowledge it produces would be a stock. For the socio-economic theory, knowledge and research are flows. Since 1974, replicable knowledge has been produced by the socio-economic theory through experiments in more than 2,150 companies, in 72 sectors of activity and in 48 countries (Savall, Zardet, Bonnet, Cappelletti, 2019).

HETERODOX CONCLUSION OF THE SOCIO-ECONOMIC THEORY

The three major fractures of the socio-economic theory with the orthodoxy in management sciences lead to the view that science is not a process reserved to produce generic knowledge. It is a process that is useful to society, i.e., that helps it to solve problems to make shared progress. This criterion of usefulness in management sciences imposes a proximity to the field, unless one considers that to be scientific, one must detach oneself from practice and from the observation of reality, whereas this leads, on the contrary, to leaving concrete science for abstract fiction. This is perhaps the most transgressive aspect of heterodoxy in the socio-economic theory, or its most gaping fracture line with orthodoxy, which consists in considering that a science that does not demonstrate its usefulness, either fundamental or applied, is no longer a science, in management as in other disciplines (economics, sociology, medicine, etc.).

REFERENCES

Boje, D. M., & Rosile, G-A. (2003). Comparison of socio-economic and other trans-organizational development methods. *Journal of Organizational Change Management, 16(1),* 10–20.

Buono, A., Savall, H., & Cappelletti, L. (Eds.) (2018). *Intervention-Research: from Conceptualization to Publication,* Charlotte, NC: IAP. Traduit en français : *La recherche-intervention dans les entreprises et les organisations,* NC: IAP*, 2018.*

Cappelletti, L., Voyant, O., & Savall, H. (2018). 40 ans après son invention : la méthode des coûts cachés. *Audit Comptabilité Contrôle : Recherches Appliquées,* 2(2) : 71–91.

Cappelletti, L., Faron, O., Fière, D., & Savall, H. (2020). Le Covid19 et l'essence de la science. *Le Monde,* 6 juillet.

Perroux, F. (1975). *Unités actives et mathématiques nouvelles.* Révision de l'équilibre général Paris : Dunod.

Savall, H., Zardet, V., & Cappelletti, L. (2021). Le capitalisme peut et doit être socialement responsable sur le terrain. In Y. Levant (Ed.), *Histoire, management et Société. Mélange en l'honneur du professeur Henri Zimnovitch,* préface André Comte-Sponville. E.M.S.

Savall, H., Zardet, V., Bonnet, M., & Cappelletti, L. (2019). Valorisation de la recherche par l'expérimentation en entreprise. Cas du modèle de management socio-économique. *Revue Française de Gestion,* 7(284), 149–169.

Van de Ven, A., Johnson, P. (2006). Knowledge for Theory and Practice. *Academy of Management Review, 1*(4), 802–821.

This page intentionally left blank.

CHAPTER 103

AN ARISTOTELIAN ARCHEOLOGY

CSR and the Socio-Management Paradigm[1]

Jean-Jacques Rosé

ABSTRACT

The singular strength of socio-management is to resolve the contradictions inherent to CSR and its implementation. The path follows the work of A. Smith, often misunderstood because the complementarity of the Wealth of Nations and Moral Sentiments expresses the same necessity. This complementarity is illustrated by two presidents of the Society for Business Ethics who adopt a similar Aristotelian response, borrowed by D. Bonnet, for whom socio-management, by going from hidden costs to hidden meaning, reveals the deep Aristotelian basis of socio-management.

Socio-management, innovative theory and practice, built in the wake of G. Bernácer (Savall, 1973, 2012[2]) and F.: *heterodox,* because it *transcends* the dominant ideologies (Savall, 1978,p.140). Exceptional structurally effective articulation of the *economic* and the *social* in a fruitful encounter with the current of the American *Corporate Social Responsibility,*[3] especially within the ADERSE.[4] Prospective programs that despair and unleash skepticism and vituperations of negative minds.[5] However, *socially responsible capitalism does exist* (Savall et al. 2015): with its strong roots and its international extension, it is a major actor in the effective implementation of a Social Responsibility organically integrated into management. The movement of this chapter is dialectical: the exploration of the aporias of CSR leads us to a rereading of Adam Smith, to shed light on a necessary Aristotelian archaeology that founds the *paradigm of socio-management.*

SEAM Treatise, pages 845–851

1 CORPORATE SOCIAL RESPONSIBILITY (CSR) AND MANAGEMENT: POLYSEMY AND APORIA

The circulation of CSR on the web measures the diversity of definitions (37 between 1980 and 2003), their sources and their frequency of use (Dahlsrud 2008). For G. Enderle (1996), this broad spectrum designates a field characterized by the *vigor of conflicts* resulting from the idea that corporate actions can and should exist under non-economic obligations: *CSR begins where the law ends* (Davis K., 1960). This conceptual framework is a set of theories, whose value is measured by the effectiveness of their use by actors. But at the same time, their unexpected adoption by political authorities[6] generates a proliferation of national and international incentives, norms, and regulations (Lépineux et al, 2016; Rosé 2011, 2019), aptly named by ISEOR as *tetranormalization* (Savall, Zardet, 2005): how the law, or its shadow, obscures rather than underpins or nurtures corporate responsibility. The outcome of this process is a mutation: *the beyond the law* is absorbed by the law. CSR is no longer the responsibility of companies, but ultimately the power of judges who sanction in the courtroom. Its judicialization is its negation (Soulez-Larrivière 2013; Rosé, 2019).

2 NOELIBERALISM AND CSR: A MISREADING OF ADAM SMITH

Complexity and contradictions tend to obscure the obvious, such as the guilty absurdity of philosophers for whom economic activity would be amoral by nature:

> "Morality is disinterested, it is even by this that it is recognized. The businessman who is honest only to keep his customers," Kant explained, "even if he acts in accordance with morality in everything, he is not acting morally for that reason. [...] The word management is now available, even in French, to say these things; why take the word ethics, which in this register can only bring illusions and confusions?"[7]

Alluding to those merchants, *butcher, baker, and brewer* (Smith 1991:82) whose trading, based on their *interest* rather than their *benevolence*, is used in a scholarly-looking rhetoric under the authority of Kant, to erase two centuries of contradictory interpretations: Das *Adam Smith Problem,* which traces the construction of economic thought from the moral chairholder's approach (*Theory of Moral Sentiments,* Smith, 1st edition:1759), in conjunction with his Investigations into the *Nature and Causes of the Wealth of Nations* (Smith, 1st edition 1776). His Scottish compatriot Gavin Kennedy (2005) bases the understanding of the work on the biography of the author, his first religious vocation and his formation by the masters of the Scottish Enlightenment: Shaftesbury, Burnet, Hutcheson, and Bentham (Jaffro, 2000). A pleiad of masters who inspired two fellow students: the young David Hume and Adam Smith, forced to think about what was happening to their culture and morality, confronted with the industrial revolution. Smith's place in the genesis of economic science obscures his influence in the history of philosophy, even though he never defines the invisible hand of the market independently of morality: "But Smith, as well as being an economist, was an ethicist who did not see the market as incompatible with morality" (Duska, 2000).

The contemporary exegesis is unanimous[8] as the *international conference* for the second centenary of the publication of the *Nature and Causes of the Wealth of Nations* verbally expressed it:

The identification of the Nature and Causes of the Wealth of Nations with the founding text of economic liberalism, as commonly perceived, appeared to be an absurdity that was not even addressed by the participants.[9]

3 THE CURRENCY OF ARISTOTELICIAN HUBRIS

Atlanta, August 2005, *Society for Business Ethics*, President Denis Moberg opens the opening session of the annual conference:

> Commercial affairs appear much too down-to-earth for such a lofty idea. The drudgery, competition, and time pressure so common in modern work life encourage foolishness not wisdom. Yet, as Aristotle reminds us, wisdom has two faces-one concerned with understanding the profound truths of life and the other with the practical judgments that all of us must make every day. And it is this practical side of wisdom that is so relevant to contemporary business. In fact, most modern companies accord special esteem to leaders by virtue of their practical-wisdom-related talents of "experience" and "good judgment." (Moberg, 2006)

Anaheim California, August 2008, *Society for Business Ethics*, President Richard P. Nielsen opens the annual conference:

> One of the oldest and best definitions of business ethics can be inferred from Aristotle. In Aristotle's Nicomachean Ethics Book I, is concerned with "the object of life" and the "ends of activities." Aristotle explains that "The end of economic [.] Science is [to create] wealth." In the Nicomachean Ethics, Aristotle also considers the idea of praxis within many different spheres of life as action that developmentally changes the actor and the external world. Putting these two ideas of economic/business activity and praxis together, Aristotle can be interpreted as suggesting that the purpose of business activity/praxis is to create wealth in a way that makes the manager a better person and the world a better place. Involuntary poverty is usually a bad thing. Poverty, like war, often brings out the worst in people. From an Aristotelian perspective, it is possible to simultaneously create wealth, be ethical, and be happy. (Nielsen 2008)

This crowd of American families evicted from their homes by the subprime crisis: the presidential address is entirely devoted to an analysis of the causes of this tragedy, the main one being the massive speculation of financial capitalism. The diagnosis and the response are based on the Aristotelian concept of hubris:

> In the Nichomachean Ethics, Aristotle also considers the idea of praxis within many different spheres of life as action that developmentally changes the actor and the external world. Putting these two ideas of economic/business activity and praxis together, Aristotle can be interpreted as suggesting that the purpose of business activity/praxis is to create wealth in a way that makes the manager a better person and the world a better place. (Nielsen, 2010: 299)

4 DANIEL BONNET: AN ARISTOTELIAN CONTRIBUTION TO "SOCIO-MANAGEMENT"

How to resolve these agonistic polarities (Fabiani, 2007) that generate hubris with tragic consequences? On the operational ground of ISEOR's interventions, the *Institut Psychanalyse et Management* (IPM) builds a multidisciplinary approach to "demystify the management of social risks at work" (Savall, Zardet, Bonnet, 2015). Bold ambition:

> Enantiology: enantios = opposite and ose = metamorphosis, which also gives the neologism "enantiosemia"—originates from the term "enantiodromia" designating the interplay of opposites in Heraclitus' philosophy. (Bonnet, 2019:221)

Density of these definitions that consonant with: "The symbol in the Greek sense of the word 'an enigma', but Heraclitus says it: 'the master whose oracle is at Delphi does not speak, does not conceal, he means' [10] [.]The enigma does not block the intelligence, but provokes it." (Ricoeur, 1965: 27)

To understand and master the aporias of management through a "process of transformation [.] in the interface of the cognitive and affective fields" (Bonnet, 2019:218–220), by means of methods based on a mixture of Freud's analytical approach and Aristotelian concepts, enriched by a historical journey of the *symbol* (Bonnet, Ibid.221–223). In this journey, the symbol connects words and *states of the soul*,[11] to reveal what is hidden, the primitive basis of socio-management, extended to a chain of interrelations of the fields: economic—*social—Psychological—Psychoanalytical—Ethical—Philosophical*, expressed in a Hellenic vocabulary, evoking the founding fathers of Western philosophy: Heraclitus and Parmenides guide us to *Aristotle's logical square* to articulate the logic of the major concepts of socio-management (Bonnet, 2020) by reference to Savall and Zardet (2004:432, 2005:499[12]). The *hidden costs* (economic field) refer to the *hidden instances* (psychoanalytical field). An extreme epistemic tension, in accordance with the *replacement of the external reality by the psychic reality* (Ricœur, 1965: 429), to the extent of the theoretical and operational stake[13] of the strategies of company:

> Savall's work (designating in the text the epistemology of ISEOR), like Plato's (The Republic), must "be rolled around" to discover its hidden meaning. One finds the place of the fathers, Perroux, Piaget, Morin, Gaston Granger... and a few others. The doxa sees only the shadows of the cave. Just like the characters trapped in the cave, it does not occur to them to look for the hidden meaning, or for what is hidden, to detach themselves and go and see behind. They only look at the shadows like images on a screen (what shows and is shown, but also what hides and is hidden). They do not realize that they are being manipulated by puppeteers. [Savall, like Socrates, asks questions about what is established, the habits that are assimilated to knowledge and reality. (Bonnet, 2010)

The cave is the whole world in which the industrial civilization, for Arendt (1961), rests on the transformation of the fossilized solar energy, stored in force of work *substituted to the human work* (slavery): or multiplier of the human work (increase of the productivity of the worker's work). This Human Labor to which Henri Savall devotes his permanent effort to *enrich* it from a diagnosis that remains spectacularly premonitory and relevant, four decades later, in the era of our societies in the process of galloping digitalization:

> The logical outcome of the evolution of our technicist civilization is the supremacy of technology, the mental, even intellectual enslavement of man to technology and the machine, whatever his level in the hierarchy of the organization and, often whatever his intellectual and mental capacities. (Savall, 1975–1989:26)

In the framework of the IPM, this profound *analysis* (in the *Freudian* sense) of a pragmatic rather than irenic socio-management, leads to its *Aristotelian* approach:

In Book VI, on the intellectual virtues Aristotle returns to the close connection of reflection, ethics and action, dismissing the validity of mere theoretical reflection: 'On the other hand, theoretical reflection which has no relation to action, and which is not creative has as its happy and unhappy consequence truth and error. Such is the object of all pure reflection while what characterizes at the same time the faculty of action and the faculty of reflection of the soul has for object a truth agreeing with the right tendency. (Aristotle 1965: 153; Bonnet D., ibid.)

For Savall and Zardet, the Aristotelian rigor of socio-management makes it possible to dislodge *hidden costs,* to defy prohibitions, whether they are economic, social, or academic. Against all obstacles and traps: *a combat sport,* as for sociology, according to P. Bourdieu (2001).

NOTES

1. "Paradigm: set of beliefs, values, techniques and model solutions, shared by a group of scientists" (Savall H., 1978: 139). In accordance with Goldschmidt V., 1947.
2. "This book was published in the United States… in French, tracing the macro-economic foundations of the socio-economic approach to management," Dedication of the author.
3. CSR in the following text or RSE, Corporate Social Responsibility: depending on the context
4. Association for the Development of Teaching and Research on Corporate Social Responsibility. https://www.aderse.org/
5. An emblematic exemple: Postel N., Sobel R. (Dir.), 2013.
6. A profusion of European Union texts, from the "Green Paper – Promoting a European Framework for Corporate Social Responsibility" in 2001 to the European Consensus on Development of 16 June 2017. In France, since the Grenelle de l'environnement, a succession of texts (laws, decrees, orders): article 1833 of the amended Civil Code; article 1835 of the Civil Code (integration of the raison d'être in the articles of association in application of the PACTE law of 22 May 2019.
7. Comte-Sponville, 1992: First publication in the Express of a text which is very dear to its author, available in three new versions referenced in the bibliography.
8. Dellemotte J. 2002,2005 – Diatkine D.2019 – Biziou M., Gauthier C., Pradeau J. F., French translators of *Theory of Moral Sentiments* (Smith, 1999)
9. Conference held at Nagoya University on April 12–15, 1990 (Mizuka H., Sugiyama C., 1993). Similarly, Biziou M., Gauthier C., Pradeau J. F., French translators of *Theory of Moral Sentiments* (Smith, 1999).
10. Diels-Kranz, Die Fragmente der Vorsokratiker, T. I, Héraclite, B.93. One will underline the proximity of the reading of D. Bonnet with the analyses of J. Vuillemin (1983) and J. Ellul
11. *Peri Hermênias* I,16 a, cité par Aubenque (1977:107) et Ricoeur (1965 :30–33)
12. Quoted by Bonnet, *ibid.* :4
13. One will underline the proximity of the reading of D. Bonnet with the analyses of J. Vuillemin (1983) and J. Ellul

REFERENCES

Arendt, H. (1961, 1983). *Condition de l'homme moderne,* traduction de G. Fradier, Préface de P. Ricœur, Paris: Calmann-Lévy

Aristote. (1936). *Organon: II. De l'interprétation,* Traduction et notes: J. Tricot, Paris: Vrin. Aristote, 1947, *De l'Ame,* traduction et notes J. Tricot, Paris: Vrin.

Aristote. (1965). *Ethique de Nicomaque,* traduction, préface et notes J. Voilquin, Paris: GF Flammarion.

Aubenque, P. (1977). *Le problème de l'être chez Aristote,* Paris :PUF

Bonnet, D. (2010). *Platon, Aristote et l'épistémologie de l'ISEOR Note de travail collaboratif.*

Bonnet, D. (2019). *Mettre en œuvre un processus de transformation au sein des organisations. Cinq tableaux pour caractériser une approche* énantiologie.

Bonnet, D. (2020). Dessiller les structures doxiques du langage et des discours dans les pratiques managériales. *Colloque International sur le Développement organisationnel et la Conduite du Changement,* ISEOR/Academy of Management (AOM).

Bonnet, D., & Garcia, M. (2012). Compatibilité de l'éthique de conviction et de l'éthique de responsabilité: l'hétérodoxie du management socio-économique, *4ème Colloque et Séminaire Doctoral International sur le Développement Organisationnel et la conduite du Changement,* ISEOR/Academy of Management (AOM).

Bourdieu, C. P. (2001). *La sociologie est un sport de combat,* Film documentaire: C-P Productions et VF Films.

Comte-Sponville. (1992). *Le capitalisme est-il moral*? Paris : l'expansion, N° 42

Comte-Sponville. (1994). Le capitalisme est-il moral ? *in Valeurs et vérités,* Paris : PUF

Comte-Sponville. (2004, 2009). *Le capitalisme est-il moral ? Sur quelques ridicules et tyrannies de notre temps,* Paris: Albin Michel.

Comte-Sponville. (2012). *Le capitalisme est-il moral? A l'épreuve de la crise,* Paris: Albin Michel.

Dahlsrud, A. (2008). How Corporate Social Responsibility is defined: Ananalysis of 37 definitions, *Corporate Social Responsibility and Environmental Management,* n° 15, pp. 1–13.

Duska, R. (2000). Business Ethics: Oxymoron or Good Business, *Business Ethics Quarterly,* Volume 10, Issue 1, p. 111–129.

Dellemotte, J. (2002). *Individu et coexistence sociale chez Thomas Hobbes et Adam Smith : une enquête sur le mythe fondateur de la science économique,* sous la Dir. d'André Hervier. Thèse de doctorat Économie Paris.

Dellemotte, J. (2005). *Das* A. Smith *Problem—Rappel et perspectives,* Texte de travail

Diatkine, D. (2019). *Adam Smith—La découverte du capitalisme et de ses limites,* Paris: Seuil.

Enderle, G. (1999). An Introduction to International Business Ethics, in Enderle G., Ed., *International Business Ethics – Challenges and Approaches,* University of Notre Dame Press

Goldschmidt, V. (1947). *Le paradigme dans la dialectique platonicienne,* Paris : PUF.

Fabiani, J. L. (2007). Disputes, polémiques et controverses dans les mondes intellectuels – Vers une sociologie historique des formes de débat agonistique, *Mil neuf cent. Revue d'histoire intellectuelle,* (n° 25), pages45 à 60

Jaffro, L.(2000). (Dir.). *Le sens moral – Une histoire de la philosophie morale de Locke à Kant,* Paris: PUF

Kennedy, K.(2005). *Adam Smith's Lost Legacy,* Great Britain: Palgrave Macmillan.

Lépineux, F., Rosé, J.J., Bonanni, C., & Hudson, S. (2016). *La RSE – Théorie et pratiques,* 2eme éd., Paris: Dunod.

Mizuka, H., Sugiyama, C. (1993). *Adam Smith—International Perspectives,* London: Macmillan.

Moberg, D. J. (2006). Practical Wisdom and Business Ethics, Presidential Address to the Society for Business Ethics – Atlanta, *Business Ethics Quarterly,* Vol.17, n°3, 2007, pp. 535–561.

Nielsen, R. P. (2008). *High-Leverage Finance Capitalism, the Economic Crisis, Structurally Related Ethics Issues, and Potential Reforms,* Society for Business Ethics Presidential Adress.

Postel, N., & Sobel, R. (Dir.). (2013). *Dictionnaire critique de la RSE, RIODD,* Villeneuve d' Asq: Presses Universitaires du Septemptrion.

Ricœur, P. (1965). *De l'interprétation—essai sur Freud,* Paris: Seuil.

Rosé, J. J. (2011). L'intérêt général au risque de la RSE- Une approche multiculturelle limitée pour une CSR discursive, in Trébulle F.G., Uzan O., *Responsabilité Sociale des Entreprises – regards croisés Droit et Gestion,* Paris : Economica.

Rosé, J. J. (2019). Devoir de vigilance : accomplissement dialectique de la RSE, in Schiller S., *Le Devoir de vigilance,* Centre de Recherche Droit Dauphine, Paris: Lexis Nexis.

Smith, A. (1991). *Recherches sur la nature et les causes de la richesse des nations,* traduction d'An *Inquiry into the Nature and Causes of the Wealth of Nation,* (1re éd. 1776) Traduit par Germain Garnier, revu par Adolphe Blanqui, Introduction et index par Daniel Diatkine, Tome 1 et 2, Paris: Flammarion.

Smith, A. (1999). *Théorie des Sentiments Moraux,* traduction de *The Theory of Moral Sentiments,* (1re éd. 1759) traduit par Biziou M., Gautier C., Pradeau J.F., Paris: PUF.

Soulez-Larrivière, D. (2013). Le marché de la vertu, in Garapon A. et Servan-Schreiber P., *Deals de justice. Le marché américain de l'obéissance mondialisée,* Paris, PUF.

Vuillemin, J. (1983). Le Chapitre IX du *De Interpreteratione* d'Aristote – *vers une réhabilitation de l'opinion comme connaissance probable des choses contingentes,* Philosophiques 10(1), 15–52. https://www.erudit.org/fr/revues/philoso/1983-v10-n1-philoso1300/203211ar

CHAPTER 104

THREE ELEMENTS FOR POSITIONING INTERVENTION-RESEARCH IN THE EPISTEMOLOGICAL DEBATE OF PLATO AND ARISTOTLE

Manuel Garcia and Emmanuel Beck

ABSTRACT

The reading of Plato and Aristotle still shows today epistemological convergences which question us. Plato develops an analytical approach and rigorous reasoning, while Aristotle invests in a global and systemic approach of an object in evolution thanks to its potential: "the being." The socio-economic theory applies a similar approach to organizations. Significant epistemological improvements have been made, on the one hand, to clarify the abductive process of analysis of the evolving organization, and, on the other, to make explicit the relations between contingency factors and invariants in a form of generic constructivism.

The scientific methods described by Plato and Aristotle never fail to reveal disturbing reflections of modernity. We have extracted three of them because of their proximity to the work of ISEOR: 1) Scientific truth imposes, according to Aristotle and Plato, an objective of social utility, positioning research in a perspective of progress for society; 2) The scientific method adapted to the confrontation with the Quantum for Aristotle, and to the treatment of ideas for Plato; 3) The insertion of the researcher in society. These three themes evoke two epistemological principles of socio-economic theory: cognitive interactivity and contradictory intersubjectivity (Savall, Zardet 1995b, 1996). These principles are present in the dialogues that Plato and Aristotle construct in a device of exchange that accompany, repair, correct and prepare at the same time. We can also position the analysis proposed by Aristotle who

SEAM Treatise, pages 853–858

questions the object and its movements in space and in time (Meta. H6, 1045 b), to deduce a potential. Plato moves away from this when he dialogues and observes before producing deductive and mathematical reasoning, which he will abandon for a more hypothetical, and less deterministic form (Phaedo 249 bc, Theaetetus 154 c).

This chapter attempts to compare their respective positions with the epistemology of the socio-economic theory (Savall 1974, and Savall & Zardet, 2004).

1 WHAT KNOWLEDGE? WHAT METHODS?

The distinction between science and technique seems clear enough for Plato. It is less so for Aristotle, who often uses the term "sciences" in the plural, to qualify different areas of intellectual and material production, scientific and technical, in a conception quite close to the socio-economic theory.

1.1 Scientific Knowledge

Both authors distinguish techniques from science because they do not make one wise or learned, mainly because of the process of learning by imitation (Epin. 975d). However, Plato is interested in them through observation, explicitation (Phil. 57a:59c), (Schul 1953) and confirmation of principles. Aristotle, however, sees it as an evolutionary and progressive process towards quality and learning (The Great Morality, L1, Ch. III, §5). In both cases, techniques reveal areas of porosity and interactivity with science on the utility of acting for the common good (Van der Eijk 2012).

Aristotle seeks to identify common characteristics of the sciences by proposing the study of "being" (Meta. 1003 a, 1003 b 19–35). "Being" is described by measurable characteristics, and it is observed through its power of actions, in a given temporality, it is "being in power." The scientist identifies it by his senses, by formulating non-demonstrable axioms and considered as universal, as well as with the help of precise characteristics and definitions. It seems to him impossible to separate the impressions coming from the senses from the information produced by reasonings, and calculations, because for him there is only one human reality (Meta. H,6, 1045b). His reflection leads him to consider that the contact with reality is not the simple verification of a reasoning, the knowledge is consubstantial of the being (De la gén. Cor. I, 2, 316).

This reunification of ideas, acts and facts in the globality of reality, contrasts with the analytical separations proposed by Plato who proceeds to a refinement from deductions and reasonings (Theaetetus 145a, Banquet 208a). The researcher's observations and interrogations are a priori legitimate (Meno 98c, d, 99a). In his case, movement, actions and time are analyzed separately, on the axis of renewal (Parmenides 129 e, 138 c, Banquet 207 d and s). The access to knowledge starts on perceptions followed by dialogues, summoning representations and beliefs, then by reasoning by deductions and analogical inferences (Banquet 207d, Parm.163 e). This leads the scientist to abstract himself in more and more elaborated reflections, with the aim of reaching the idea of all ideas, or the first cause. The return takes place by a descending dialectic, which verifies the deductions by their causal relations, without intermediate reference in the reality. This movement separates two worlds in the progression towards the higher level of knowledge, and in their flow towards the lower level. The fragility of the validation mechanism is circumvented by invoking a mystical environment (Rep. VI, 511 e), a form of superior knowledge consecutive to the immortality of the soul : reminiscence. The soul being familiar with all knowledge, it is possible to rediscover everything (Meno 81d). This allows him to bypass the absence of explanation for induction and intuition. He thus reinforces the place of deductive and analytical methods, by proceeding in a static way from similarities, which he considers as the indisputable trace of universal knowledge (Couder &, Séchan 1949).

1.2 Some Points for Reflection

Even if, many convergences exist between the two philosophers, their understanding of the universal and of the scientific object question us. For Aristotle, the universal is impossible to reach by thought (Meta. 982 a, b, 984 a), but it remains identifiable in the repetitions of results (Sec. Anal. 88a). Plato also seeks these regularities from a simplification of reality supported by a mystical interposition. However, a convergence appears in the approach, by adding to perception reasoned and rigorous explanations, in which mathematics can be integrated as well as hypotheses (Rep. VI 510 c, d, e, 511 a). The acceptance of a non-mystical human induction, based on intuition and metaphysical experience for Aristotle (Meta. 982a and b) remains however an important difference between the two philosophers.

Aristotle considers that the object exists by its movement and its power. This is the basic element for a universal science. It is not without recalling the concept of "active units" (Perroux 1975), which has a fundamental place in the socio-economic theory (Savall 1974, 1979). This universal science is quite comfortable with the presence of specialized sciences (Meta. 982b), provided that the invariants remain. Aristotle considers that the universal science is differentiated because of its absence of claim to direct by itself the action, it is neither manufacturing (Meta. 982 a, b), nor practical (Eth. Nic. VI, 7, 1141 a), it remains in a theoretical form. Plato, by being interested in the idea, seems to transform the scientific approach into an approach of the scientist as a scientific being. Science becomes a methodological exercise separating the object from its environment, even if utility and ethics are absent. Aristotle assumes the complexity of a systemic and contingent analysis of the being in its environment. The successive invariant and contingent results forge the experience of the observer, through the memory of facts, processes and reasonings (Meta. 980b, 981 a, 1017 a, b, 1019 a, 1020 a,e, Savall & Zardet 2004, 361, Piaget 1970). It is a deep interrogation of interactions, movements and transformations, the roles of memory and experience in an evolutionary framework, which resembles the Structures-Behaviors links in organizations (Savall & Zardet 1987, 1989 151–162).

2 THE GENERIC CONSTICTIVISM OF THE SOCIO-ECONOMIC THEORY AND ARTISTOTLE

For Aristotle inductions come from reasonings, dialogues, syllogisms (Prem. Anal. LI,4, 25b), hypotheses (Sec. Anal., LI,2, 71 b20, Mesquita 2015) associated with an experience. In the socio-economic theory, a looping system clarifies the role of induction, in a structuring back-and-forth between theoretical reflection and the results of induction (Savall, Zardet 1995b, 29–32). The constructivist dialogue between these two poles is developed from a body of hypotheses, which allows deductions and inductions to be inscribed in an abductive reasoning, as Aristotle envisaged it (Eth. Nic. VI, 1140a).

2.1 Invariants and Dysfunctions

The socio-economic theory has brought out three epistemological principles, two already mentioned: cognitive interactivity and contradictory intersubjectivity, and a third, generic contingency (Savall & Zardet 2004), which characterizes the identification of invariants. The first two suggest the establishment of a dialogue between the actors and the researchers, inserting the knowledge and the controlled actions in a process of validation of the descriptive, explanatory and prescriptive hypotheses, demonstrating the causal relations. The intervention-research constitutes a constructivist approach in the progressive acquisition of knowledge from observations and actions ordered in time (Piaget, 1970). The presence of the researcher does not alter the scientific objective, although it does cause modifications in the distribution of energies, provided that the researcher and the actors are capable of formalizing and anticipating the evolutionary movement. This is how the socio-economic theory forms an original epistemological bridge, by validating the place of induction in the research process, which considerably hindered Aristotle and Plato, obliging them to invoke a mystical form for the one, and an ethical one for the other. Observation and the clarification of phenomena make the organization a scientific object whose structures and actors' behaviors are analyzed, and whose dynamics of evolution and transformation over time are identified. The evidence thus leads to an interest in dysfunctions, accidents for Aristotle (Meta. 1014 a, Van Aubel 1963, Tessier 2015). Indeed, the movements and the potential of the being, being limited by dysfunctions, whose regulations consume factors of production, the search for an imagined and desired orthofunctioning, the good and the beautiful for Aristotle and Plato, takes from then on an ethical positioning. More than Plato, Aristotle insisted on the indispensable qualitative progression of competences through learning, for ethical reasons (Aristotle, The Gr. Mor., L.1, Ch.3, §5). This is the case in intervention-research for actors and researchers, as the whole of this work configures the intersection between contingent technique, and generic science, in a constructivist form. Aristotle's and Plato's boundary between technique and science evolves from a zone of porosity or interactions, to a domain of mutual enrichment.

2.2 Research and Ethics

In the Nicomachean Ethics, Aristotle separates the world into those who know and those who seek to know. "Happiness is the activity consistent with perfect virtue, for life is more pleasant for those who know and for those who still seek to know" (Ethics, X, VII). Plato defines the seeker as a lover of truth (Tim. 46d), he differentiates himself from the ignorant (Banq. 202 a, 204 a), he enriches knowledge, he has an important place in society (Rep. VI, 484–513), for good is largely the result of knowledge (Rep. VI, 508–514), and the essence of knowledge is beneficial to the individual philosopher and to society (Theet. 166 a –168 c).

By overcoming the separation imposed by Aristotle and Plato between technique and theory, the generic constructivism of the socio-economic theory, places the researcher in a position where his or her scientific experience and knowledge, both technical and practical, serve as a platform for induction and for his or her deductions. The researcher relies on the actions performed, the movements observed, the evaluation of their effects and the identification of causes. In this way, he perceives the sensitivity of the organization and accumulates information about the processes. Through the dysfunctions, he detects a part of the unused potential, which he must put into action. This is an important proximity to Aristotle, who advocates the creation of knowledge when he speaks of continuous improvement for the good. One can see in this a requirement for the researcher to introspect, a form of scientific and ethical reflexivity (Meta. 982 a, b, 983 a). The socio-economic theory joins Aristotle in his approach and in his requirements as a discipline in movement, according to which the insufficiency of experience corrupts the scientific capacities to search for universals.

Ethics appears rather little in Plato, whereas it transcends in Aristotle who addresses men of good will (Verbeke 1963, The Great Moral, Ethics to Eudemus, the Nicomachean Ethics). Today, ethics is often part of social responsibility, which, in order to exist in management, must go beyond the principles of action strictly limited to financial interests and agency theory. Ethics, in the organization, cannot be limited to the administration of a difference in conception between individual affairs and collective interests, it also questions research methods. One can distinguish two scales of control in organizations: one teleological linking acts and consequences, the other deontological setting the rules of behavior. This control then influences the form of relations within the organization, between organizations, and between organizations and the city. Thus, Aristotle's legacy opens the path taken by the Socio-Economic Theory (SET) towards promising forms of inter-organizational management, in a competition-cooperation form (Garcia, Delattre 2018, 2019). The socio-economic theory can thus move towards inter-organizational concerns that remain inscribed in a permanent search for the improvement of individual and collective competences of the actors, and for a perfection of the structures, avoiding the risk of imported or exported dysfunctions consecutive to a deficit of regulation of social and economic performances.

The absence of slackness, the quest for truth, goodness and beauty, constitutes an ethical ambition present in Plato and Aristotle. The place of the researcher would depend, according to them, on his commitment, which is generally analyzed in ethics of conviction and ethics of responsibility. For Plato, the commitment is total in the intelligible world, that of ideas, which is for him the place of scientific activity (Rep. VI, 507). For his part, Aristotle is involved in a scientific research accompanied by an ethical questioning driven by the relation to reality (Eth. Nic. VI, 7 1141 a). The ethics of conviction (Eth. Nic. 1140 b) must be, for example, controlled by principles of objectification of hypotheses. The ethics of responsibility is, on the other hand, backed by a device of putting into action, based on human qualities. Indeed, Aristotle addresses thoughtful men, having made the practice of virtues a conscious habit (Eth. à Nic. 1143 a). In fact, the honesty, and intelligence of the researcher are indispensable, and he must act in the perspective of the good. The contribution of the researcher and his place in the City are thus configured in the method, as well as in the epistemology and ethics, which induce particular human qualities.

CONCLUSION

There are many convergences between the reflections of Aristotle, Plato, and the socio-economic theory. The comparison is rich in lessons, because it lets us glimpse tracks of work structuring the relations between sciences and techniques, and especially between the analytical and static vision of Plato, integrated and dynamic of Aristotle. On these same points, divergences persist. The universal knowledge is for these two authors a demonstrable theoretical construction. It is separated from techniques by the wisdom it gives to scholars and the universal knowledge it allows to discover. However, Aristotle's analysis of the being and Plato's dialectical system start from the real, consequently from a form of utility, and return to it at the end of the reasoning. Aristotle differentiates himself by proposing the analysis of an object in its movements and transformations, he thus also questions time, in its successions and its simultaneities. The analysis may seem *a priori* more complex, but it is nevertheless much more useful. There are in this choice the premises of a true constructivist innovation because it places the search for invariants in an intellectual mechanism of successive deductions and inductions, as is specified by the socio-economic theory, which clarifies this intuition, in the intervention-research. The contingent, far from being a limit, becomes a complement fertilizing the universal.

REFERENCES

Couderc P., Séchan L., Platon et les sciences mathématiques, In: *Revue des Études Grecques,* tome 62, fascicule 291–293, Juillet-décembre 1949, pp. 450–459.

Garcia M., Delattre M., (2018), Réduire les conséquences des externalités et des dysfonctionnements par la gouvernance inter-organisationnelle territorialisée, *Communication pour le colloque ADERSE, Paris mai 2018.*

Garcia M., Delattre M., (2019), Réduire les externalités et les dysfonctionnements dus au déterminisme social : le cas de la relation du handicap à la professionnalisation, *Communication pour le colloque ISEOR-AOM, Lyon juin 2019.*

Mesquita A. P., (2015), ΕΙ ΕΣΤΙΝ: Des hypothèses d'existence chez Aristote? *Revue de philosophie ancienne,* Éditions Ousia, 2015/2 Tome XXXIII, pp. 129 –172.

Patočka, J., (2011), La science philosophique de la nature chez Aristote (extrait), *Les Études philosophiques,* 98(3), pp. 303–330.

Perroux F., (1973), *Pouvoir et économie,* Bruxelles-Montréal, Ed. BORDAS

Piaget J., (1970), *L'épistémologie génétique,* PUF, 127 p.

Schuhl P. M., (1953), Remarques sur Platon et la technologie, In: *Revue des Études Grecques,* tome 66, fascicule 311–313, Juillet-décembre 1953, pp. 465–472

Tessier P., (2015), Chapitre 6 Définir l'accident: Du concept philosophique à l'événement «malheureux», In: P. Tessier, *Le corps accidenté: Bouleversements identitaires et reconstruction de soi,* pp. 189–216, Paris cedex 14, Presses Universitaires de France.

Van Aubel M., (1963), Accident, catégories et prédicables dans l'œuvre d'Aristote, In: *Revue Philosophique de Louvain,* Troisième série, tome 61, n°71, 1963, pp. 361–401.

Van der Eijk P., (2012), Hippocrate aristotélicien : In: *Comptes rendus des séances de l'Académie des Inscriptions et Belles-Lettres,* 156e année, N° 4, 2012. pp. 1501–1522;

Verbeke G. (1963), Thèmes de la morale aristotélicienne : À propos du Commentaire des Professeurs Gauthier et Jolif sur l'Éthique à Nicomaque, In: *Revue Philosophique de Louvain,* Troisième série, tome 61, n°70, 1963. pp. 185–214.

CHAPTER 105

TRANSFORMING THE MENTAL STRUCTURES OF ORGANIZATIONS

A Clinical Approach to Socio-Economic Intervention

Daniel Bonnet and Emmanuel Beck

ABSTRACT

This chapter puts into perspective the clinical dimension of Socio-Economic Intervention Research. The clinical dimension of the Socio-Economic Intervention-Research allows for an in-depth search for the root causes of the dysfunctions at the origin of Hidden Costs-Performances. Socio-Economic Intervention-Research leads the actors to carry out an intellectual and psychological work to collectively implement the actions of change to be envisaged to "repair" the dysfunctions and convert the hidden costs into value added for the company. In certain contexts, it is a matter of dealing with major problems. The work of the actors is guided by a research device accompanying the transformation of mental structures.

The conduct of the change imposes an intervention on the mental structures of the organization when this one requires to transform in the stable part of the interactions "structures-behaviors" (Savall and Zardet, 1995a). It opens up different questions. This chapter orients the implementation of the clinical device during the Socio-Economic Intervention-Research aiming at orienting the search for solutions.

- How to incorporate a transformation of the mental structures of the functioning and management of the organization?
- What work mechanisms should be put in place?

SEAM Treatise, pages 859–865

The co-construction of problems and solutions is a key factor for leading transformations in situations of strategic rupture or "critical contextuality."

- How to deal with questions of personal or collective strategy, marked by rivalry, for example during mergers or inter-organizational cooperation, or economic recovery?
- In what way does the intervention in socio-economic management include a clinical dimension, which allows to act on mental structures?

Socio-Economic Intervention-Research offers a therapy, but it is more than that, insofar as it allows for an in-depth cleaning up of the quality and efficiency of operations and management. In this respect, it is different from other approaches, including Action Research, Sociological Intervention, Psychosociological Intervention, not to mention coaching and interventions proposing elements of a psychoanalytical approach.

Socio-Economic Intervention-Research integrates a clinical approach to the conditions and modalities of Socio-Economic Approach to Management (SEAM) (Savall, 1974, 1979; Savall & Zardet, 1987, 1996), making it possible to diagnose situations of change management, and then to pilot the processes of in-depth transformation after the implementation of socio-economic action plans. In addition, it allows for effective and rapid intervention in critical development situations (strategic implementation, mergers, restructuring, etc.) or economic and financial recovery. The perspectives proposed by the Socio-Economic Intervention-Research are presented in two sections:

- The framework of the generic issue and subsequent issues (1).
- The clinical positioning of the Socio-Economic Intervention-Research (2)

1 THE FRAMEWORK OF THE GENERIC ISSUE AND SUBSEQUENT ISSUES

Socio-Economic Intervention-Research is positioned around a pivotal problem, known as the generic problem, corresponding to the problem to be addressed in depth to transform, as the investigation progresses. It allows us to establish a hypothesis (Box 1) from which the clinical observation is oriented.

The CCA case (Consortium des Coopératives Agricoles)

The observation allows us to formulate the hypothesis of a conflict of ambivalence that impacts the definition and elaboration of the cooperation strategy, while the actors function in the register of ambiguity. Ambivalence activates opposing emotions. The transformation is structured on the equivocations allowing each of the actors to defend their own strategies, during the collective game. The actors fixate on rivalries in the name of competition rather than on the terms of the quality and the effectiveness of the cooperation. It is a question of the researcher intervening to orient the work in the register of the factual; thus, the mental reconstruction will make it possible to remove the toxic equivocations, i.e., the terms of the social rivalry between them which prevent the elaboration of the regime of governance.

The mental structure of the organization governs its functioning and its management. It organizes the representation of mental activity and is defined about a conceptual apparatus that originates in the fundamental hypothesis of socio-economic analysis and is based on the "structure-behavior" link that is unique to each organization.

1.1 The Socio-Economic Intervention Device Concerning its Clinical Component

During the intervention, the clinical component is built in the peripheral core of the research for the implementation of the clinical work on the cognitive processes and on the psycho-affective processes. This clinical work in the articulations is called the work of enantiosis.

The intervention in the transformation of mental structures refers to the basic conditions of socio-economic management. Their evaluation during the diagnosis crosses the indicators and the components of economic performance (Savall and Zardet, 1995a). In the CCA case, particular attention was paid to the variables of Strategic Implementation and to the basic conditions of strategic change. The clinical component was deployed more specifically on the variable of strategic change and its governance.

1.2 The Work Carried Out by the Actors is Incorporated Into the Deployment Process of Socio-Economic Intervention-Research

The work carried out by the actors introduces, from the start of the intervention, the implementation of the clinical work mechanism. This very early implementation is made possible by the fact that the researcher pilots the intervention with scientific research tools, in particular the construction of a body of hypotheses (Savall and Zardet, 2004). In the CCA, since the problematic is one of ambivalence conflict, the interveners sought to obtain an in-depth knowledge of ambivalent and contradictory productions. Contradictory intersubjectivity is one of the three fundamental principles of the epistemological framework of research (Savall and Zardet, 2004). Within the CCA, work on discriminating variables establishing the constant relationship between conjunctions of opposites was considered. They highlighted the collective play of unconscious defense mechanisms. The research shows the importance of Lewin's work (1951) in this respect, around a notion which is at the origin of the concept of "force field," namely the hodological space (Kaufmann, 1984).

The device makes the actors work on the socio-cognitive conflicts born of the interplay of polarities dividing the process of transformations between rivalry and cooperation. Within the CCA, it was judicious to base this work on the discovery by the actors of psychic conflicts. These conflicts appear to be the deep-rooted causes of cooperation getting bogged down in local rivalry between the cooperatives.

1.3 The Components of Clinical Management and Their Implementation Within the Framework of Socio-Economic Intervention

This aims at the adjustment work of the intervention in the articulation of the cognitive and psycho-affective registers.

This approach allows to consider the work of enantiosis in the register of the latent contents (Bonnet D., 2017, 2019). It allows to approach the transformations of invariants (Bonnet D., 2007), to better know the functioning of the "structure-behavior interactions" to elaborate a strategy of transformations allowing the actors to build a real change. This proactive process of transformation is iterative and is initiated by the will of the actors confronted with the observation of facts. The observations validated by the mirror-effect are the subject of a strategy developed by the actors themselves within a methodological framework elaborated by the researcher-interventionist acting as a catalyst according to the principles of maieutics (Beck, 1981, 1982). Socio-economic tools accompany this iterative process, including the competency grid and the behavior grid to transform the mental structures of the organization.[1]

2 A CLINICAL APPROACH TO SOCIO-ECONOMIC INTERVENTION-RESEARCH: THE GENERAL FRAMEWORK OF APPLICATION CASES

Let us emphasize the diversity of the cases of application: All configurations, which can be companies of all sizes, non-for profit organizations, local authorities, administrations, territories...

The constraints thus identified constitute the basis for tetranormalization (Savall, Zardet, 2005) (technical and environmental, financial, commercial and social standards) to which are added political, linguistic and ethical standards that are not very explicit in organizations.

In all cases, the socio-economic intervention-research (SEIR) is confronted with the transformation of mental structures. The actors of the organization become aware of the mental work at work which determines their own transformation and the collective change, with regard to the problems to be dealt with.

2.1 The Broad Conceptual and Practical Scope of the Issues

The work of 585 ISEOR researchers since 1975 (Savall and Zardet, 1995a) has helped to identify the 4713 types of pathologies from which organizations suffer. These pathologies are codified by means of a nomenclature of six major zetetic themes (table n°1). These works are at the origin of a management clinic for organizations. Dysfunctions, which for the most part become relatively stable elements in the functioning of organizations, are at the origin of hidden costs and performances, the amount of which is very important, since they reach between 20,000 € and 70,000 €/person/year. This amount is an indicator of potential socio-economic productivity. The effect is obviously only sustainable if the company takes the necessary care to maintain the quality and efficiency of the management and operation of the organization. In this respect, socio-economic management is therapeutic.

It should be noted that an intervention in strategic and organizational transformation confronts the subject with the paradoxes and conflicts that govern human behavior. The limit is that management can only intervene in the transformation of organizational behavior. In this respect, socio-economic management fills the gap in current theories of change management. It places transformation in a field in which human operations work towards the continuous, synchronized and chrono-biological transformation of mental structures.

In the new contexts resulting from the deployment of digital transformation, management precipitates the adaptation of behaviors in this respect. The classic distinction between internal and external environments, common in management, is no longer efficient.

We find this problem of hasty behavior in situations of economic recovery and restructuring. Whatever the efforts made by governance and management (information, communication, training), the contextuality of the situated interaction is never well prepared. The result is an exacerbation of criticality. The grip of demands and injunctions generates suffering. This is the perspective proposed by the principle of a clinical approach to the transformation of mental structures, putting into perspective a theoretical and transdisciplinary apparatus (Bonnet D., 2017) to better know the transformations of invariants, as we show in the following part (3.0).

2.2 The CCA Case Study

The CCA (Consortium de Coopératives Agricoles) is made up of 11 regional cooperatives specialized in packaging and marketing fruits and vegetables for their members, about 850 producers (fruits) and 400 (vegetables). It is a Producers' Organization (PO). The actors of this sector of activity are confronted with periodic economic crises and study each time the measures to be taken to face them. The crisis of autumn 2008 was more severe than the previous ones and led to financial losses that reached up to 50% of the turnover of 2009 to produce summer fruits. For stone fruit, the competitive gap with Spanish competition was 0.30 €/kg.

The purpose of the mission was to carry out a *study of the opportunity and feasibility of the merger of the cooperatives*, which led to the development of the project of their merger.

The mission was carried out within the framework of the protocol of the Socio-Economic Intervention. The evaluation of the Hidden Costs-Performances for a value of 0.43 €/kg, showed that the situation could be rectified, of which nearly 50% caught up by the merger and the balance within the framework of the implementation of a mobile five years "marketing plan" having for object a strategic repositioning on the national market. The socio-economic analysis phase assessed the opportunity, while the socio-economic project phase described the feasibility in concrete terms. The managers agreed on the evaluation of the Hidden Costs-Performances, essentially related to the strategic deficit.

What is known to the actors is the reality. They have been struggling with it collectively for more than twenty years and this explains the evolution of cooperatives in a competitive impasse. The fault lies with the salespeople who fight every day in a framework of local rivalry to defend the price and sell short shelf-life products, and especially with the large-scale distribution. The actors would agree enough to consider the commercial merger. But the socio-economic analysis shows that the catching up would only be of 0.05 €/Kg, to be invested in the marketing plan, quickly taken over by the market. This option has the support of the powerful agricultural unions and the Consular Chamber; the representatives of the State are rather reserved because it is necessary to contain the revolt of the producers and although some prescribe the principle of the fusion, nobody sees it clearly, more especially as in other regions, it failed.

The "real," it was the impossible to say and to be said..., it is what is seized and deduced at the limit of the knowledge of the actors (principle of the generic contingency). It is also the crucible of the imaginary, of the creativity, of the emancipation, of the liberation. It is the lie of reference to oneself sent back to the other, with whom it was impossible to "marry" because the other is necessarily less good producer than oneself. It was a question of the "mirror-effect" exposing them to the "reality" of a toxic reality that they thought was healthy. The "real" is what is captured in the unknown part of us, closed off by representations, beliefs, prejudices, ideologies... including closed off by managerial knowledge. Knowledge is not knowledge. Knowledge is something else that comes from hermeneutic experiences. To access it, one must pass through the word given to the other, language. This is the key to transformation. And then, the desire to make this fusion together came. It was another beginning...

The CCA case describes quite precisely the experimental positioning of the clinical approach of socio-economic essence proposed by the Socio-Economic Intervention-Research. You don't need to be a psychoanalyst, but you do need to be very rigorous about the scientific protocol. The Socio-Economic Intervention-Research, a clinical approach of a socio-economic nature, opens perspectives that have not been explored by the management sciences (Savall, Fière, 2014). Its application is integrated into the framework of applications implemented by "Organizational Development." It has allowed in the CCA case to intervene on heavy issues in strategy and organization. In 2020, the regional production is maintained at around 100,000 tons, whereas predictions indicated its disappearance by 2025, because the benefit extends to the sector of activity as a whole insofar as it has contributed to the redefinition of market strategies.

The psychosocial dimension of the case studied is particularly significant in identifying the levers of action and thus transforming "structure-behavior" links, and particularly mental structures. Cross-fertilization with other psychosocial approaches, such as non-violent communication or new forms of governance, organization and management (sociocracy, holacracy . . .), can complete this process of transforming mental structures in organizations.

CONCLUSION

The transformation of mental structures is the pivot of a profound change. It requires a clinical approach that allows the actors to carry out the in-depth, iterative, and contradictory work of transformation. Within the framework of the Socio-Economic Intervention-Research, the actors build together the actions to be implemented and evaluate them. To do this, the system is installed by the Socio-Economic Intervention-Research in the organization's operating and management infrastructures. It allows for the permanent monitoring of the quality of management and its economic and social efficiency.

NOTE

1. The socio-economic tools are presented in various chapters of this Treatise

REFERENCES

Beck E., (1981), *Equilibration formation-emploi et changement de structure des qualifications en milieu industriel,* Thèse de Doctorat ès Sciences de Gestion, sous la direction de Henri Savall, Université Lumière Lyon 2.

Beck E. (1982), Enjeux de l'équilibration formation-emploi dans une firme industrielle, *Revue Française de Gestion,* n° 37, pp. 51–58.

Bonnet D. (2007), Le pilotage de la transformation en environnement de coopération inter-organisationnelle : Essence socio-économique de la transformation et des stratégies de transformation, *Thèse de Doctorat de Sciences de Gestion,* sous la direction d'Henri Savall, Université Jean-Moulin Lyon 3, 749 p.

Bonnet D. (2017), « Énantiologie des transformations et transformation d'invariants. Appareillage théorique et éclairage transdisciplinaires ». *Revue Année de la Recherche en Sciences de l'Éducation. Perspectives pour la transdisciplinarité.* AFIRSE, L'Harmattan, pp. 149–168.

Bonnet D. (2019). « Mettre en œuvre un processus de transformations au sein de organisations. Cinq tableaux pour caractériser une approche énantiologique », *Revue Connexions,* n° 111, Éditions Erès, pp. 219–234.

Chazal G. (2004), *Médiations théoriques,* Champ Vallon, 257 p.

Kaufmann p. (1968), *Kurt Lewin. Une théorie du champ dans les sciences de l'homme,* Vrin, 382 p.

Lewin, K., (1951–1952), *Field theory in social science; selected theoretical papers.* D. Cartwright (Ed.). New York : Harper & Row, 1951, 346p. – Cf. également Éditions du Tavistock (1952).

Piaget J. (1968), *Le structuralisme,* PUF, 125 p.

Sallaberry J.C. (2007), « Représentation et théorie du champ », *Revue Cognitiques,* n° 11, pp. 11–22.

Savall H., Fière D., (2014), « Étude comparative de méthodologies de recherche en médecine et en gestion. Cas de la recherche-intervention socio-économique d'ordre qualimétrique », *Journal de Gestion et d'Économie Médicales,* Vol. 31, n° 5–6, pp.354–370.

Savall H., Zardet V., Bonnet D. (2015), « Gestion des risques psychosociaux au travail. Un impératif à démystifier… », *Revue Connexions,* n° 103, *Les risques psychosociaux en question,* Éditions Eres, pp. 61–74.

This page intentionally left blank.

CHAPTER 106

THE MIRROR-EFFECT

A Self-Image for Change

Éric Davoine

ABSTRACT

This chapter focusses on the mirror-effect session which is a crucial stage in the SEAM approach of the organizational change process. Through the validation of a (dysfunctional) "self-image" of the organization, this stage initiates a learning process that encourages the action of organizational actors. Using conceptual frameworks of Lacan (1949) and Argyris (2004), we analyze the impacts of the mirror (-effect) stage in two audit cases carried out in Switzerland within two industrial firms, and we discuss the contributions of different types of information used during mirror-effect sessions.

In the methodological approach to the socio-economic analysis of the organization (Savall, 1974, 1979), a distinction is made between two stages at the end of the organizational audit and before the organizational change, the mirror-effect and the expert advice sessions (Savall and Zardet, 1987). The sense of this distinction is to separate, on the one hand, a stage of validation by the actors of dysfunctions identified on the basis of information and interviews collected, and, on the other hand, to formulate, after the first stage, an expert-advice session integrating non-organizational knowledge and an interpretation of 'what has not been said by the actors' (Savall and Zardet, 2002). Considering the production of knowledge about the organization with an epistemological perspective, the mirror-effect session is an important step in the validation of hypotheses by organizational actors, making it possible to limit the effects of the intervener's interpretation. In an intervention approach, this stage has two distinct purposes: on the one hand, the validation of a synthetic "self-image" of the organization and its dysfunctions, and on the other hand, the initiation of a learning

SEAM Treatise, pages 867–872

process that encourages the action of organizational actors. We explain these two aims by drawing on Lacan (1949) and Argyris (2004). We illustrate the impacts of the mirror-effect with the help of two audit cases carried out in Switzerland within two industrial firms (Box 106.1), and we discuss the contributions of different types of information used during mirror-effect sessions.

BOX 106.1: PRESENTATION OF THE TWO BUSINESS ILLUSTRATION CASES

Alpha is an industrial company with about 500 employees. We carried out an audit of the personnel turnover following the voluntary departure of 15 technicians and engineers the same year. The audit was carried out using a socio-economic diagnostic approach identifying dysfunctions and estimating hidden costs. It was based on 45 interviews with colleagues and supervisors of the employees leaving the company, documents to estimate costs, and a survey of all employees leaving on their reasons for leaving. The mirror-effect included a summary of the reasons for leaving, an analysis of the impact of the departures on work processes with interview 'fieldnote quotes" and an estimation of hidden costs. In the socio-economic diagnosis method, the fieldnote quotes are illustrative and representative extracts from interviews, selected from the exhaustive notes of interveners-researchers.

Beta is an industrial services company with about 400 employees. We conducted a knowledge management audit based on two empowerment evaluation workshops with the members of the executive committee and the board of directors (17 workshop participants separated into two groups). The mirror-effect included a synthesis of the participant self-assessment scores on the knowledge management performance and an exhaustive list of dysfunctions identified from the recorded discussions of the workshops.

The two audits led to the implementation of a series of measures, including a strengthening of the Human Resources departments in both companies, with the creation of positions for training & development managers. Follow-up interviews after one year confirmed the implementation of measures.

1 THE MIRROR-EFFECT: A "MIRROR STAGE" FOR ORGANIZATIONAL ACTORS?

The first purpose of the mirror-effect is the validation of a synthetic 'self-image' of the organization and its dysfunctions. From an epistemological perspective, this stage is important for testing and confirming the internal validity of the hypotheses formulated on the phenomena observed (Savall and Zardet, 2002, pp. 333–341). From an intervention perspective, it is important to make the actors concerned recognize what they consider to be really problematic and dysfunctional, in the gaps between ortho-functioning and the actual functioning of the organization. For example, in the case of voluntary departures from the Alpha company, several phenomena have been recognized as negative consequences of departures: the productivity of the engineers who leave is lower during the last months of work, the productivity of the new recruits is lower in the first employment months, the learning of the new recruits involves the collective mobilization of supervisors and colleagues, who are then less productive on their own jobs... There are also overwages (Savall and Zardet, 1987), when the supervisors of the departing engineers have to assume the tasks of the departing engineers during the transition.

The mirror-effect has a function of shaping these micro-phenomena systematically to build a complete and synthetic vision of the dysfunctional face of the organization. In the case of the Alpha company, the mirror-effect session began in front of executive committee members who were not convinced of the importance of the departures, because there was no visible negative consequences of personnel turnover on personnel costs. The three directors, with their noses on their screens, checked their e-mailbox when we presented the reasons for departure. When we finally showed the impacts on work processes, the three managers raised their heads to read the testimonials. When the tables estimating hidden costs were displayed for each departure, leading to an estimated overall loss of CHF 2 million for the first year, they asked to review the first slides on the reasons for voluntary departures.

The mirror-effect has the primary purpose of producing an effect of consciousness. What used to be a set of signs or individual experiences within the organization takes on a synthetic meaning when integrated into an all-encompassing concept. The mirror-effect recalls the mirror stage of Lacan (1949), the experience of the mirror for a child who recognizes himself for the first time in a mirror, with a perspective on himself that is the one of other persons looking at him. For Lacan, this Mirror stage is an important stage in the construction of identity and self-awareness, because it poses a unique and external synthetic image of the body (the one reflected in the mirror), where the child had until then an inner experience of a fragmented body, via the multiple sensitive and sensory experiences of the different parts of his body before the consciousness of his unity. In order to understand the experience of the fragmented body, we can mobilize the traditional Indian tale of the six blind men and the elephant (Lacan's fetish animal), to underline that the confrontation of the various perspectives of sensitive experiences (with the trunk, the legs, the ears, the tusks…) is not enough for the six blind men to understand the coherent and conceptual totality of what an elephant is.

In the case of the organization, the mirror-effect makes it possible to create this integral conceptual vision, in a complementary duality of perspectives: that of the external actor (the mirror) and those of the organizational actors and their individual partial experience. The mirror effect also recalls a medical diagnosis situation, in which the physician strives to give overall coherence to a set of reported experiences and signs collected in the anamnesis: the patient's signs are given sense by being transformed into symptoms consistent with one or more referenced pathological profiles (Savall and Fière, 2014). In the example of the Alpha company, the categorization of hidden costs, associated with the information collected, makes it possible to give meaning and to conceive certain organizational practices as consequences of dysfunctions, and thus to conceptualize the audited organization as a dysfunctional organization.

2 THE MIRROR EFFECT: THE FIRST STEP IN A COLLECTIVE LEARNING PROCESS FOR ACTION

Using the example of the elephant, Jacques Lacan (1954, p. 201) illustrates the power of conceptualization and the importance of naming things in order to control or dominate them: thanks to the word "elephant," humans will begin to deliberate on the fate of elephants and to plan the hunt. In the mirror-effect, conceptualization work allows organizational actors to consider the signals of experience with a symptom perspective: naming, categorizing and measuring dysfunctions allows to initiate actions to control those elements in the organization that are considered pathological. The appropriation of a common representation of organizational dysfunctions by the organizational actors facilitates collective action and change.

In the case of the Beta company, the method used for the organizational audit is a method of empowerment evaluation: a rapid evaluation method that proposes to organizational actors to discuss organizational performance by using a grid of pre-established criteria in a workshop lasting a few hours (Davoine and Deitmer, 2009). Each workshop participant is first asked to individually propose a weighting of the criteria and the organization's performance scores for each criterion. Then, a discussion on the differences in weightings and scores is initiated in order to obtain consensus scores. The discussion is recorded and analyzed, in order to highlight divergent perspectives as well as points of convergence within the group. The objective of the workshop is to develop a consensus of performance scores, and above all to collect the comments, ideas and arguments of the participants around these scores. As part of the Beta company's knowledge management assessment, the workshop session with the board of directors identified several dysfunctions. The mirror-effect session presented a spectral diagram of the evaluated performance, with twelve major dysfunctions identified and presented in the form of hypotheses to be validated. The hypotheses are associated with extracted sentences taken from the workshop verbatim, i.e., the transcribed text from the discussion. The twelve hypotheses concerned, for example, insufficient customer knowledge storage practices, the absence of a common training plan process or the insufficient knowledge sharing between subsidiaries.

The mirror-effect of the empowerment evaluation method is based on several principles, very similar to those of the qualimetric method of socio-economic analysis (Savall and Zardet, 2004; Bonnet and Péron, 2014). As in socio-economic diagnosis, empowerment evaluation is based on a principle of contradictory intersubjectivity in the discussion between stakeholders. This principle posits the explicit confrontation of the perspectives and rationales of the organizational stakeholders, thus respecting the polyphony of representations within the organization (Savall and Zardet, 1996). The mirror-effect makes explicit the differences in beliefs and cognition that actors may have about their performance evaluation, before proposing an imperfect common representation that is never presented as objective. Moreover, in accordance with the principle of cognitive interactivity, the mirror-effect stage is a moment of co-construction of the cognitive framing of performance evaluation between the intervener and the organizational actors (Savall and Zardet, 1996). Exchanges with the auditor or researcher-intervener gradually lead to the emergence of a common representation of evaluation criteria and categories, as well as a common representation of the performance—and non-performance—of organizational practices.

The mirror-effect is a lever of reflexivity based on practices, discourses and artifacts, without interpretation of the unsaid and the underlying beliefs or cognitive schemas of organizational actors. The mirror-effect seems to facilitate organizational change by single-loop learning. Single loop learning corresponds to a change in organizational routines that does not question the values and basic assumptions of organizational actors (Argyris, 2004, p. 29). Double-loop learning corresponds to a change in routines preceded by a change in basic values, assumptions and cognitive frames. In order to design double-loop learning process, actors must go beyond the recognition of dysfunctional routines, i.e., they have to understand the values, attitudes, strategies and principles of action that underlie these routines. It is the role of the expert advice session, after the mirror-effect stage, to enable double-loop learning, since it is in the expert advice session that the intervener-researcher interprets and gives a shape to the unsaid, to the beliefs and to the organization's implicit cognitive schemas. However, the mirror-effect remains a key phase that allows organizational actors to change their perspective. By following the analogy with the Lacanian mirror stage, it enables an approach of reflexivity to be initiated among organizational actors and to integrate the external perspective on the Self-image. It allows the organization to understand, accept and integrate an external view on oneself and to begin to reflect differently on what this 'self' is. It is therefore an indispensable prerequisite for expert-advice session and a double loop learning process, because it identifies the subject of the learning process.

3 FUNCTIONS OF THE DATA OF THE MIRROR EFFECT

In the perspective of knowledge production, the diversity of qualitative, quantitative and financial data allows a triangulation of sources in order to ensure a more complete and reliable representation of organizational practices (Savall and Zardet, 2002; Delattre and Zardet, 2014). These three categories of data have specific functions in the mirror-effect session.

On a qualitative level, fieldnote quotes have several functions in the mirror-effect session. First of all, the use of verbatim, i.e., verbatim sentences, gives credibility to the results by referring to the collection of information through interviews: *"this is what has been said."* The presence of fieldnote quotes shows the work of the interviews carried out, the effort of triangulation and qualitative understanding of the organization: it provides detailed and contextualized information (Savall and Zardet, 2002, p. 216). At the same time, it gives a human dimension to the results, an embodied and emotional dimension: the verbatim nature of the fieldnote quotes anchors the things said in an everyday, human language that is not a technocratic audit language, but rather a real life language with humor, syntax errors and opinions: *"this is what people have said."* The verbatim of the fieldnote quotes makes it possible to think about organization beyond the metaphor of the ortho-functional or dysfunctional machine, beyond the abstraction of numbers and economic performance. The organization is thus perceived as a human group. Finally, the verbatim should allow the organizational actors to recognize themselves: *"This is what you have said."* Verbatim sentences transcribe the vernacular of the organization, its terminologies, codes or dialects. The third function of verbatim is to facilitate identification with the results presented. One of the key moments of the mirror-effect is the reaction of organizational actors saying *"yes, it is indeed a good picture of us,"* which recalls the jubilation of the child in the Lacanian mirror stage. For example, in the case of the two companies Alpha and Beta, these are bilingual companies where French and German are spoken fluently in the daily work practices. It was therefore very important to collect information in both languages of the interviewees and to reproduce a mixed verbatim, which could translate better the identity of the organization.

Statistical and quantitative data has complementary functions in the mirror-effect session. Apart from statistics on generic dysfunctions (absenteeism, voluntary departures, breakdowns, non-quality, lower productivity), statistical information is present in mirror-effects through survey results, incident frequencies, weighting percentage, or performance indicators. The figures, their standardized and decontextualized nature, give an appearance of "objectivity" and mathematical veracity to the results. This is their primary function, even when they are produced on the basis of estimates. A second function of quantitative information is to allow a standardized measurement of phenomena, facilitating the monitoring of evolutions as well as intra- and inter-organizational comparisons. This standardized measurement also makes it possible to set thresholds. Finally, a third function of statistical information is to be synthetic. For example, in the case of the Beta company, the spectral diagram of the results, which nevertheless only reflects the consensus of the group's evaluation, provides a synthetic visualization of several performance dimensions.

Financial information, especially hidden costs, introduce another dimension of meaning to the figures, the economic dimension of dysfunctions (Delattre and Zardet, 2014). When we estimated in the Alpha company the average hidden costs of a voluntary departure to more than 100,000 CHF, the number of voluntary departures takes on a completely different meaning for management. Financial information associated with other indicators (absenteeism, non-quality…) can have a serious impact on the basic cognitive frames and beliefs of organizational actors. The economic value associated with dysfunctional events leads to a new understanding of routines. A voluntary departure becomes a major event impacting performance and revealing other organizational dysfunctions. Thanks to the association of hidden costs to their organizational practices, the actors will conceive differently and durably their routines, and can develop a double-loop learning of new routines, since they have new interpretation frameworks. Finally, this financial estimate will have a stimulating effect on the actions and decisions of managers, since it brings the analysis of dysfunctions into resonance with the company's economic and financial objectives.

CONCLUSION

These three types of data are therefore not only useful for producing triangulated knowledge on the organization (Delattre and Zardet, 2016), they are also useful for producing an effect, or rather a set of effects on actors, which are complementary for the mirror-effect session (Savall and Zardet, 2014). The mirror-effect offers actors a reflective and reflexive image of the organization, co-constructed on internal and external perceptions and on diverse data. It is a key moment when organizational actors begin to recognize themselves by integrating an external perspective on their organizational reality. The mirror-effect perspective will bring other grids of interpretation on their organizational reality which will be deepened in the expert advice session with the interpretation of the unsaid, the values and the underlying cognitive frameworks of actors. The mirror-effect session is therefore a pivotal stage in the intervention process that formally concludes the diagnostic phase and constitutes a decisive moment to start the change process.

RÉFÉRENCES

Argyris, Chris (2004). Double-loop learning and implementable validity. In : *Organizations as knowledge systems.* London: Palgrave Macmillan. pp. 29–45.

Davoine, Eric et Deitmer, Ludger. L'évaluation participative et responsabilisante: un instrument de structuration des projets de partenariat public-privé en recherche et développement. *Revue francaise d'administration publique,* 2009, no 2, pp. 275–289.

Davoine, Eric (2003). Building effective innovation networks: Enhancing cooperation in public-private partnerships. *Enhancing inter-firm networks and inter-organizational strategies. Research in Management Consulting. Charlotte, NC: Information Age Publishing,* pp. 187–206.

Delattre, Miguel, and Véronique Zardet (2016). "Combining qualitative and quantitative data: a powerful lever for driving an organizational change process." *Academy of Management Conference–Anaheim–MC Division.* https://hal.archives-ouvertes.fr/hal-01355001/

Lacan, Jacques (1949). Le stade du miroir comme formateur de la fonction du Je, telle qu'elle nous est révélée dans l'expérience psychanalytique. *Revue française de psychanalyse,* 1949, vol. 13, no 4, p. 449–455.

Lacan, Jacques (1954). *Le séminaire, Livre I.* Les écrits techniques de Freud, Paris.

CHAPTER 107

LIFTING THE VEIL OF A MANAGERIAL ILLUSION THROUGH THE CONTRIBUTION OF THE HUMANLY INTEGRATED OPERATIONAL AND FUNCTIONAL INFORMATION SYSTEM

Saying What We Do and Doing What We Say

Miguel Delattre and Rodolphe Ocler

ABSTRACT

Organization and information are inseparable in management science. However, the lack of clarity in the hypotheses used sometimes leads to vagueness about the nature of the link between them, as well as to biased representations for decision-making. The notion of a humanly integrated and stimulating Operational and Functional Information System offers a fruitful perspective to avoid giving in to the ease of an overly normative managerial discourse.

SEAM Treatise, pages 873–879

The generalization of the information society maintains beliefs about the life of organizations, especially that of the primacy of information in the formation of performance.

1 INFORMATION IS ONLY AVAILABLE FROM ACTIVE PEOPLE

The "HISOFIS degree" (Humanly Integrated and Stimulating Operational and Functional Information System) (Zardet, 1985; Savall and Zardet, 1987) is an innovative concept, in that it introduces the psychological and sociological dimensions into the definition of information systems. It refers to the ability of a company or organization to stimulate more effective behaviors among its members through integrated information that leads to action (Savall and Zardet, 1987, 2015, p. 26).

1.1 People in Action

The organization is part of a structural-behavioral representation according to a dynamic of permanent search for balance. The impulse is social. Activities are carried out by actors in constant (re)negotiation within teams. Indeed, human actions can be perceived both as structures (relatively stable) and as their more "moving" dimension: behaviors (Savall, 1979). The actors in the organization do not have places that are solely defined according to the division of labor and a hierarchical position. The design of the management of activities ("who does what") impresses their behavior without locking them into a theater where, if not by convention, a prescribed staging would prevail over the idea that each person would have of his or her role. The organization as a place of collective action is a management situation (Girin 1990; Moisdon, 1997): a collective production subject to the appreciation of internal-external third parties. The quality of a social production is largely a result of the combined action of the actors, particularly the saying and doing.

The identification of each individual with the collective objectives of the organization is often part of convenient models, supported by implicitly normative assumptions (Perroux, 1970). The notion of HISOFIS allows for an explicit recognition of the place of individuals in organizations according to a more anthropological understanding *homo œconomicus* or the work force within a mechanistic framework of execution defined elsewhere; the human relations man or the recognition of the social dimension of the group or team in the levels of performance achieved; *homo sociologicus* or a relative proactivity, limited to a space of room for maneuver within a given system (Crozier and Friedberg, 1977).

Acting that the individual producer in organization does not renounce his other statuses in society, refusing the segmentations traditionally operated with the citizen and the consumer (Savall, 1974–1975; Savall et al., 2015) encourages the understanding of the mechanisms of interaction, of struggle-cooperation within organizations. In the socio-economic theory the HISOFIS is a root cause of the quality of functioning of an organization: it promotes and stimulates a quality of action of the actors with regard to collective objectives.

1.2 Activating Individual and Collective Energies

In the socio-economic theory, the emphasis is on the individual with an individual strategy rather than on the *ex ante* determination of his or her action in an organization. Active unity (Perroux, 1975) allows for the recognition of the active will of actors, endowed with projects in a plastic environment, under the effect of their combined actions. The notion of HISOFIS contributes to structuring a collective space and to going beyond the technical or utilitarian conceptions of information. In the latter, the attributes of scarcity or the characteristics of stimulation too often frame collective action, independently of individuals. The scarcity of information as a means of exercising power is also combined with the proliferation of "umbrella" notes or e-mails, and other practices of hidden copies, where the "political" impulse takes precedence over the recipient who is the bearer of the decision or action.

The activity of actors is observed factually and reveals individual or collective behaviors. The functional and operational dimensions of the information system are justified by the coordination implied by the organizational division and the effective distribution of work: who does what, how and where? The collective dimension refers to the "traditional" structuring of an Information System (IS), requiring the coordination of functions and the creation of conditions for operational collaboration within the framework of a division of labor and the management of activities (operations, tasks, etc.).

Qualifying an Information System as Humanly Integrated reminds us of the need to make a distinction between the management of activities (operations) and the animation of people (management). The management of activities too often favors process approaches (input-throughout-output), providing a feeling of security linked to instrumentation and formalism. For example, the ISO 9001 standard for the implementation of a quality management system is based on a process architecture that sequences the different steps and operations to be carried out to satisfy the customer. This process vision does not take into account, in its implementation, the need to put "oil in the wheels": to mitigate the differential between standardized processes and human behaviors that evolve over time and their methods of expression.

The animation of people is more a matter of finding a balance that must be constantly rebuilt. The cooperation of the actors cannot only be inscribed in the link of subordination supposed in a work contract (unless one believes it), nor in the sole realization of activities (unless one denies the social dimension of their interactions), since their speeches and their actions are impacted by the processes. *"We've been hearing about case management meetings for a long time, but nothing has been done!"* [Surveyor's office][1]

The specificity of "humanly integrated" consists in privileging a point of view focused on the activity support rather than on its design. Man at work, modeled on the notion of the active unit (Perroux, 1975), implies the recognition of room for maneuver and negotiation capacities of the individuals involved. Numerous studies on information systems have shown that, in addition to technical assessment, efficiency also depends on the quality of the coupling with the organization's social system (Tabatoni and Jarniou, 2000). (Tabatoni and Jarniou, 1975; Kalika, 1988; Reix, 1995; Delattre, Saint Léger, 2005).

Stimulating: it is through action and the quality of its deployment that the realities of a collective action can be appreciated. The dysfunctions and differences in the perceptions of the various actors are all "indicators" of "leftovers" to be negotiated in order to strengthen the doing together. *"There are people who refuse to talk to each other. We are forced to act as intermediaries to transmit information and move cases forward."*

In the numerous intervention-researches carried out over the past 25 years, actors frequently emphasize the observed gap between activity flows and actual practices, in the form of a rupture or lack of coherence between the way tasks or operations are carried out (the expected work) and the possibilities of adjusting practices. Performance benchmarks are not sufficiently coupled with arrangements for negotiating the rules of the game. *"We don't have enough information on certain issues. We feel there is a lack of accessibility and we are left a bit in the dark in terms of explanations for dealing with problems encountered on a case."*

The individual perception of doing one's job well is not always a guarantee of doing it well at the team level or with internal-external clients. The "interest in" (illusio, Bourdieu, 1988) of an actor in a team or collective can be developed and nurtured by HISOFIS -type devices that will promote exchanges and interactions. This can result in the adjustment of individual strategies with regard to the implementation of a collective strategy. The activation of individual and collective energies (decision-making and action) is fueled by arbitration and negotiation mechanisms to define or redefine the rules of the game between the different actors, but also new cooperation arrangements or collaborative arrangements to improve the articulation between the individual and collective levels (Delattre, 1998). *"There are increasingly recurrent phenomena of disruptions, people start one file and then another and we can no longer meet the deadlines."*

The managerial illusion: "say what you do and do what you say," is tenacious in the life of organizations. It impresses the representations of the actors and feeds the belief that a lasting alignment of individual strategies would be possible with that of the organization's strategy. The socio-economic intervention mechanism is part of the perspective of a veiled reality to be invested (d'Espagnat, 1979).

2 HISOFIS AND INTERVENTION

The socio-economic intervention protocol corresponds to a global architecture that aims to reactivate the spaces for dialogue between actors within a given perimeter (the micro-space).

2.1 Building a Structured Dialogue Pedagogy

One of the first objectives of an intervention-research is to install more relevant spaces for dialogue. Like a dissonant orchestra, the actors think they are communicating when in fact they are often immersed in a hubbub that is a source of social and economic dysfunction. *"I lack direct exchanges with members of management, with whom communication is limited to technical points."*

Whatever the size of the organization -because it would be an illusion to believe that small structures have better communication than larger ones-, quality dialogue cannot be decreed! Even if they are great professionals, the status of the actors does not durably condition their behavior, in the same way as injunctions, directives, notes, memos, e-mails, etc. *"We don't do any, or very few, updates on the files with our management. When cases are problematic, it is difficult to be accompanied before it is too late."*

The socio-economic intervention contributes, over a given period of time, to structuring links between the actors of a micro-space by making the limits of the perimeter explicit. The space is concretized through the definition of groups of actors constituted according to criteria of hierarchical belonging. For small structures (architects, notaries, private doctors, etc.), the managers are included in an inter-structure mechanism (Savall, 2003), in order to break their isolation and to situate the word of the hierarchical leader in a contradictory dynamic with peers. Time is part of a chronobiology that alternates between individual and collective arrangements.

Personalized individual or sometimes small group assistance is interspersed with collective training and cooperation on tools for the major basic functions of an organization: time management, training-job matching, definition and deployment of a strategy, instrumentation-steering and performance incentives.

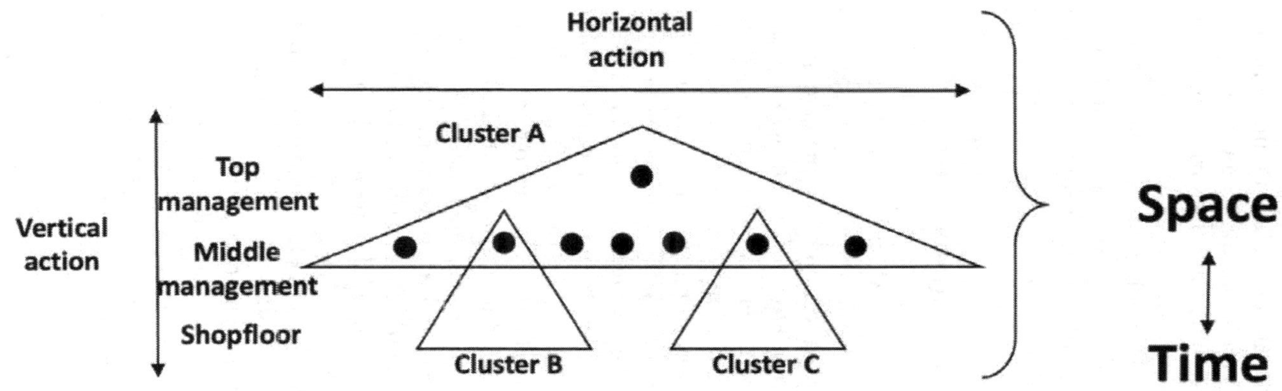

Action / Months	June	July	August	Sept	Oct	Nov	Dec	January	Feb	March
Collaborative training										
Cluster A	1			2	3 4	5	6	7 8	9	10
Clusters B, C…				1 2	3	4 5	6	7	8 9	10
Customized Assistance Cluster A				2		4	6	8	9	10
Customized Assistance Clusters B, C…				2		4	6	8	9	10
Diagnosis				X	X					
Focus Group					X	X X	X	X	X	X
Collaborative training = 10 sessions	N°1 Socio-economic approach to management principles N°2 Competency grids N°3 Presentation of the qualitative diagnosis N°4 Time management N°5 Hidden costs					N°6 Priority Action Plan N°7 Presentation of the quantitative diagnosis N°8 Strategic Piloting Logbook + methodology of project N°9 Periodically Negotiable Activity Contract N°10 Periodically Negotiable Activity Contract				

Figure 107.1 Time and space in the intervention system. *Source:* ISEOR.

This system creates links, more than a link between the actors, by stimulating the motives and contexts of mutual adjustments. The intervention dynamic implies a form of collective implementation discipline: respecting deadlines, but also providing information to affected actors or negotiating implementation resources (time, skills). The interweaving of the different hierarchical levels leads the actors to leave their comfort zones: it is the implementation that is evaluated. Finally, the position to be held by each person has multiple entries: top-down, bottom-up and also transversal. Ultimately, the conditions for achieving a higher degree of "hisofis-genesis" are met at the level of the micro-space and the surrounding services, to create and develop HISOFIS effects: the stimulation of decision-making and of taking action with the help of more stimulating information. The reduction of organizational dysfunctions corresponds, for a given time, to new arrangements between actors on how to work together. The energy input is fed by the production of information with higher added value/that which triggers a decision or an action.

2.2 Creating and Consolidating Spaces for Internal Negotiations

The intervention process is defined by the three axes of the SEAM trihedron (Savall and Zardet, 1987): Process (diagnosis, project, implementation, evaluation), tools (the six tools of socio-economic management) and political decisions (clarification of the management's strategic orientations) contributes to a *participatory humanly integrated operational and functional information system process.* The cross-fertilization of the different axes of the trihedron allows for the development of individual and collective negotiation spaces.

The sharing of dysfunctions improves the contradictory intersubjectivity (Savall and Zardet, 1996, 2004) between the actors. For the management: *"While we ask our employees to be rigorous and self-controlled, we have young people who are not always able to explain the elements of their calculations,"* while the employees are in demand for support and pedagogy: *"The files are placed on the desks and we do not always know what to do: we often ask how to deal with a file."*

The dysfunction identified by the various stakeholders facilitates dialogue to find negotiated solutions. Certain forms of generic contingency (Savall and Zardet, 1996, 2004) are identified in relation to deficits in the transmission of technical and operational information. It is also an opportunity to recall the rules of the game and to confront the strategic compatibility thresholds of the different actors: management's expectation to be able to count on reliable work with explicit results, and employees' demand for greater visibility on the context of the work to be done.

The development of dialogue between the actors, particularly the line managers, is part of the need to clarify expectations about activities by formulating the rules of the game. When the management of an organization defines its strategic ambitions, even if these have been discussed and validated with the employees, the quality of the implementation is not guaranteed. Socio-economic tools and devices are designed as pretexts for structuring the quality of life of an organization and doing things together. Each component is interrelated to the others, since each one integrates at its level a miniaturization of the deployment architecture: a process, an instrumentation as well as a political dimension through the construction of the necessary cooperations.

As an example, the priority action plan illustrates this approach of HISOFIS. The document is synoptic and stimulating. The link between the organization's strategic axes and the contribution of each actor is made: both in terms of expectations and the conditions of realization (in collaboration with whom and within what timeframe?). This tool leads to the improvement of individual and collective conflict-cooperation behaviors. Negotiating upstream a deadline, an hourly volume, and a frequency of reporting on the progress of the task entrusted to us, participates in a more shared process of "hisofis-genesis" which contributes to the fight against "organizational entropy."

CONCLUSION

The indicators of effectiveness and efficiency of an organization's activities are the first building block of a stimulating information system, itself an essential component of the intensity of activity management. Beyond an instrumental approach, the human being constitutes the first active force of organization in management sciences. On the basis of this hypothesis, privileging the tool over the bearer of a human intentionality would be tantamount to believing in the normative force of a managerial discourse. The requirement of quality in collective action consists for each person, in saying and doing together, to "be as imprecise as possible and as precise as necessary" (Arkhipoff, 1984 p.46).

NOTE

1. Fieldnote quotes presented in this chapter are excerpts of an intervention-research carried out in a surveyor'soffice.

REFERENCES

Arkhipoff O. (1984). «La qualité de l'information et sa précision», *in* "*Qualité des informations scientifiques en gestion,*" ISEOR avec le concours de la FNEGE, 285 p., pp. 46 – 67.

Bourdieu P. (1988). «Intérêt et désintéressement», *Cours du Collège de France,* Faculté d'Anthropologie et de sociologie de l'Université Lyon 2, 1 et 8 décembre, Cahiers de recherche n°7: Groupe de Recherche sur la Socialisation UA 893 CNRS.

Crozier M., Friedberg E. (1977). *L'acteur et le système,* Éditions Points Seuil.

Delattre M., Saint Léger G. (2005). «Quelle responsabilité sociale des entreprises dans la mise en œuvre et l'utilisation des ERP?», *3ème Conférence Internationale sur la responsabilité sociale des entreprises co-organisée par l'AOM et l'ADERSE,* octobre 2005, Lyon.

Delattre M. (1998). «Contribution à l'élaboration d'un mode de pilotage de l'organisation à forte composante bénévole—analyse spectrale du pilotage de l'organisation vivante—Cas d'expérimentations», *Thèse de Doctorat,* Université Lyon 2.

Espagnat (d') B. (1979). À la recherche du réel. Le regard d›un physicien, Gauthier-Villars, Bordas

Girin J. (1990). «Analyses empiriques des situations de gestion: éléments de théorie et de méthode» *in Epistémologie et Sciences de Gestion,* Economica, pp. 142–144.

Kalika M. (1988), Structures d'entreprises : réalités, déterminants, performances, Economica, 1988

Moisdon J.-C. (sous la direction de) (1997). Du mode d'existence des outils de gestion. Les instruments de gestion à l'épreuve de l'organisation, Seli Arslan.

Perroux F. (1970). «Les conceptualisations implicitement normatives et limites de la modélisation en économie», Cahiers de l'ISMEA, tome IV, décembre, pp. 2255–2290.

Perroux F., (1975). Unités actives et mathématiques nouvelles, révision de la théorie de l'équilibre économique général, Dunod, 1975.

Reix R. (1995), Savoirs tacites et savoirs formalisés dans l'entreprise, RFG, n°15, pp. 17–29.

Tabatoni P., Jarniou P. (1975), Les systèmes de gestion, PUF, 1975.

CHAPTER 108

INTERVENTION IN SOCIO-ECONOMIC MANAGEMENT

Epistemci and Methodological Elements and Principles of Action

Jean-Michel Plane and Florence Noguera

ABSTRACT

This chapter is devoted to the question of management intervention in organizations. It raises several epistemological, methodological, and axiomatic problems of various kinds. Most of these difficulties are beginning to be well known by the scientific community, and some answers and perspectives for action have been developed for several years now.) The reflections and the works devoted to the methods of intervention in management are certainly structured in an unequal but also constant way.

The intervention in organizational management, although an exciting and sometimes fascinating adventure, is not without problems of different kinds. Most of these difficulties are beginning to be well known by the scientific community and elements of response and per spectives of action have even been constituted for some years now (Buono, Savall, Cappelletti, 2018). The reflections and works dedicated to the methods of intervention in management are certainly structured in an uneven way but also in a constant way. The perception of management intervention is certainly often ambiguous, but it seems to us that academic bodies (such as CNU in France or CAMES...in Africa) have an increasingly positive image of it. Management intervention thus appears to be a fruitful means of generating new knowledge about the functioning of organizations and their strategies. In the field of management sciences and management, we can see the rise of numerous doctoral theses based on one

SEAM Treatise, pages 881–885

or more management interventions that provide a robust methodological framework for the results and the ensuing discussion. An increasing number of current studies aim to find ways to improve the overall performance of organizations, but also the living and working conditions of individuals. Most often, this research aims at analyzing the development processes of the human potential of organizations based on management interventions. But what is a management intervention? To what extent can it be transformed into research with scientific intent? What are the ethical, epistemological, and methodological conditions to be considered in order to distinguish "the wheat from the chaff"? Can we objectify inevitably subjective data, as the late scholar Jacques Girin often said? Under what axiomatic and methodological conditions? What are the deontological and even ethical precautions to take? Basically, the intervention of the management researcher based mainly on "human resources" can be considered as the first possible lever of development. The importance of organizational development based on the activation of these resources is based on the thesis that the intervention process, based on knowledge-producing interactivity, stimulates the introspective and conceptual capacities of the actors, thus contributing to the development of the organization (see Plane's doctoral dissertation, 1994 and more recent works 2000, 2018). The authors have been working for many years based on multiple observation sites in France and abroad (particularly in French-speaking sub-Saharan Africa), and these reflections lead us to reflect on the question of producing actionable knowledge in management science and management based on such an approach. Indeed, an intervention in management is often confronted with scientific and methodological problems. Cognitive dissonance related to the acceptability of the problems to be solved, to the reconciliation of the values held by each of the actors in the organization, to the possible divergences between the scientific intention, the initial project and the operational action are examples of this. The objective of this chapter is to present the questions raised by an intervention approach in management for the construction of actionable and ethically sustainable knowledge.

1 MANAGEMENT INTERVENTION: A COGNITIVE AND AMBIGUOUS PROCESS

The socio-economic management intervention, as we have practiced it, can be a research method that allows intelligible and relevant phenomena to emerge to feed an exploratory research project. According to this perspective, the intervener is both present and an actor in the organization, he interacts, and this intervention has been the subject of a prior negotiation with the management team. This method is preferred to approach the field and management situations. The interest of this approach lies in the production of theoretical knowledge from observation and participatory investigation by one or more people in the field.

Essentially, the approach has several methodological characteristics because the tension between the different positions of the speaker(s) and the practitioner requires confrontation, analysis, and distancing to avoid privileging the scientific viewpoint over the practical viewpoint or vice versa. This balance should be seen rather as a conciliation of objectives that can vary according to time, but in concrete terms the intervention systematically proposes two "deliverables": one managerial, the other research. Firstly, the question of the objective of the research for the researcher and the practitioner constitutes an important clarification upstream of an intervention to enlist, convince and associate professionals. Indeed, the question of divergent interests, scientific production and experimentation for the researchers and improvement of resource management practices for the practitioners, must be asked at the outset to establish the basis for collaboration. As David (2000) points out, if there is cooperation between a researcher and an actor in a company or organization, and if the objective is to produce knowledge that is both scientifically and empirically valid, then it must be admitted that theory and practice are methodologically linked. The intervention may originate from a request for help from the management of a company or organization. In all cases, this request will have to be formalized in a set of precise specifications.[1]

Secondly, the co-production of knowledge generally positions the interventions in the constructivist paradigm since the change and the transformation process of the studied object are not problems for the researcher but research opportunities (Plane, 2000). It is indeed from the variation of the research object (i.e., the organization) that knowledge is extracted. The constructivist posture considers that reality is not given but is constructed by the researcher himself from a given research context. The object of research can be modified according to the interactions between the researcher and the actors of the studied micro-space.[2] The researcher is part of a process of co-construction of knowledge and of the envisaged solution approach. This transformative approach makes it possible to change a situation and to study the effects of these changes on individual, collective and organizational levels and to produce results relating, for example, to the impact of the implementation of a new Human Resources Management policy on remuneration systems.

Finally, the intervention draws its characteristics from its relationship with the field and its vocation to innovate. The researcher can be disruptive, capable of moving the lines and is not only a kind of expert applying a technique, tools, and management models. His or her observation, analysis, confrontation, and reflection produce knowledge, scientific knowledge.

2 ABOUT THE INTERACTIVITY BETWEEN MANAGEMENT PRACTITIONERS AND THE FIELD

The process of management intervention in organizations is complex and subject to strong uncertainties. This approach is a complex management process through which the researcher is simultaneously confronted with two logics that may seem contradictory. On the one hand, it is a question of producing knowledge from interactions carried out in the field, and on the other hand, the researcher actively contributes to the organizational development of the organization that is the subject of his or her investigations. This complexity leads the researcher to try to discuss the conditions of validity of the knowledge produced from work based on experimentation. The chapter developed here aims to recall the nature of the questioning and the quest for knowledge pursued. To what extent and under what methodological conditions can valid knowledge be produced from a highly interactive approach and process? At the epistemological level, how can we try to enter a logic of objectivation from inevitably subjective information? To do this, it is necessary to study the relationships and interactions between researchers and actors. Within the framework of an intervention-research approach, the researcher is involved in a cognitive process in which knowledge is simultaneously created and changed. From this perspective, the contribution of the actors in the organizations to the research itself can take two forms. In some cases, they may do so without knowing it, because the researcher uses the action, he or she is piloting to produce knowledge, but his or her interlocutors in the field are not aware of this. In other cases, the actors actively contribute to the construction of the research process. In this sense, they are considered to hold a share of the knowledge and can implicitly contribute to the evolution of the emerging problem. The interactive method with a transformative aim aims to transform the functioning of the organization to observe its effects. We can consider that such an approach is in line with the logic of knowledge advocated by Lévi-Strauss (1950) who shows that "in a science where the observer is of the same nature as his object, the observer is part of the observation." This epistemological option amounts to discussing the following research question: can valid knowledge be derived from subjective data collected on the spot? Following this logic, the researcher aims to extract knowledge from the field by contextualizing and objectifying it, that is, by relating it to the management situations in which it was produced. Specifically, the phenomena of transfer and counter-transfer—that is, the projections made by the actors of the organization on the researchers and vice versa—are not considered to be disruptive phenomena that must be eliminated or, worse, concealed. On the contrary, under certain ethical and methodological conditions, they can generate knowledge. In an observation field, as soon as there is interaction, there are necessarily expectations, preferences, taboos, unspoken things, etc., the analysis of which can provide a wealth of information regarding the inner workings of the organization under analysis. The researcher therefore confronts his or her own hypotheses with those of the different actors to generate progress in knowledge. Moreover, the question of the place and neutrality of the researcher always arises in the context of a management intervention. From numerous examples taken from various investigations, we have been able to identify that it is illusory to want to occupy a position of neutrality; this is always a utopian aspiration. It seems, in fact, that this position is difficult to hold in the field, insofar as the actors have a need for representation and mental identification of the researchers, and consequently, necessarily situate them in places in the organizational system. However, this system of places is contingent because the researchers can try to construct them from their behavior. This phenomenon constitutes for a researcher what Devereux (1980) calls the observer's anxiety in the face of the richness and diversity of his observations. Many management researchers have been confronted with the difficulty of measuring the distance to be adopted from their field of observation. This complexity posed by the question of the researcher's involvement can be partly resolved by the introspection that any researcher can show. To do this, it is necessary to rely on different methods of distancing oneself (logbook, research meeting, communication at a colloquium, meeting with one's thesis director, etc.). Basically, the interactions between a researcher and his or her field of observation can be set up as instruments of knowledge development (Plane, 2000). For all that, researchers often have a disturbing view of the actors, or at least a disturbing view. These disruptions, instead of constituting obstacles to research, constitute valuable material both for increasing the quality of the services provided and for improving the level of knowledge and therefore of skills of the actors in their environment. The level of distancing also offers researchers the possibility of not exposing themselves too much to the risks of conscious and/or unconscious manipulation of their work by certain actors. Indeed, an outsider to an organization is often considered as an intruder who is always suspected of trying to question certain achievements and of wanting to divulge information that certain actors prefer to keep silent (Plane, 2000). All in all, the involvement and immersion of a management researcher in an organization raises the question of researchers' increased awareness of the scope of the triptych: actions-impacts-effects in the organization.

Finally, we will return to the idea that this methodology of research for action consists of producing knowledge and concepts that make it possible to "think about trajectories" in which companies and organizations could engage (Hatchuel, 1994). Since practice remains one of the two purposes of intervention-research, the knowledge created is also communicated to practitioners in a language that they can use and that can be translated into practice. Of course, research laboratories are responsible for putting in place mechanisms for distancing researchers to stimulate the clarification of tacit knowledge. These distancing devices are more and more numerous and can take several forms: weekly meetings, logbook, participation in research workshops, individual meetings with the research director, PhD or DBA thesis committee, etc.

In the context of an intervention in socio-economic management, the purpose of this paper was to clarify the specificities of such a research project as well as the choices that the researcher must inevitably manage. In the 21st century, it is high time—and even crucial in our eyes—to assert its relevance and potential with its dual project of scientific knowledge and its setting in motion of the organization.

NOTES

1. The terms of reference for an intervention-research specify the essential stages of the intervention process, the timetable, the objectives and methodology of the intervention, the people involved, and the resources required. As a rule, an exploratory phase is necessary to clearly define the problem and to discuss it with the actors of the company or organization. A steering group is also set up with the company's management and HR department to make a point of cooperation at the peak of the intervention.
2. The micro-space is the research perimeter, within which the research work will be carried out. The scope of the intervention-research may concern all the company's employees or only one or several categories of actors.

REFERENCES

Argyris C., (1995). Action science and organizational learning. *Journal of Managerial psychology*, vol 10, issue 6.

Argyris, C., & Schon, D. (1978). *Organizational Learning: A Theory of Action Perspective*, Addison Wesley.

Bueno A.F, Savall H., Cappelletti L. (ed) (2018*), La recherche-intervention dans les entreprises et les organisations. De la conception à la publication*, Caroline du Nord, Information Sage Publishing.

David, A, La recherche-intervention, cadre général pour la recherche en management ? in David, A, Hatchuel, A et Laufer, R, *Les nouvelles fondations des sciences de gestion*, Paris, Vuibert/FNEGE, 2000, p. 193–202.

Girin, Jacques, «L'objectivisation des données subjectives: éléments pour une théorie du dispositif dans la recherche interactive», Paris, *Actes du colloque FNEGE/ISEOR*, Paris, 18–19 novembre 1986.

Hatchuel, A. (1994). «Les savoirs de l'intervention en entreprise». *Entreprise et Histoire*, n°7, pp. 59–75

Miles M., & Huberman A., (2003). *Analyse des données qualitatives – recueil de nouvelles méthodes, Bruxelles, De Boeck Université*

Noguera F (2018), Tools and Devices for Intervention Research: The Case of Intervention in Human Resource Management in *La Recherche-Intervention dans les entreprises et les organisations*, dirigé par Buono A. F, Savall H., and Cappelletti L. North Carolina, Information Age Publishing.

Plane J.M (2000), *Méthodes de recherche-intervention en management*, préface de Roland Pérez, Paris, Le Harmattan.

Plane J.M (2018), From intervention-research to the production of knowledge. A summary of experimentation in *Intervention-Research: From Conceptualization to Publications*, dirigé par Buono A. F., Savall H., and Cappelletti L. Charlotte, North Carolina, Information Age Publishing.

Savall H., Zardet V. (2004), *Recherche en sciences de gestion: approche qualimétrique. Observer l'objet complexe*, préface de David Boje, Paris, Economica, collection «recherche en gestion».

Schein E.H. (1987), *Process Consultation.* Lessons for Managers and Consultants, Vol. II, New York, Addison Wesley, OD series.

This page intentionally left blank.

CHAPTER 109

INTERVENTION-RESEARCH AND TEAM MANAGEMENT

Epistemological Reflections and Proposal of a Heuristic and Transformative Methodological Device

Antoine Masingue

ABSTRACT

This chapter aims to better understand the complexity of intervention-research applied to team management. It questions the epistemological framework of this type of intervention and presents an engineering device likely to help us better understand the functioning of teams to improve their performance.

Teams are particularly important research objects in socio-economic management. Indeed, teams are the basic cells of most organizations. And, even more globally, the processes of inter-individual cooperation seem to be at the heart of what is now called the "collaborative" economy.

Yet, intervention-research applied to teams faces several challenges. First, teams are "complex" objects: they are human systems, governed by homeostasis processes that make them resistant to change. Secondly, they are open systems, with sometimes unpredictable emerging effects. Therefore, implementing a change process, oriented towards improving "socially responsible" performance, is a difficult test, but always rich in lessons for the researcher.

SEAM Treatise, pages 887–893

The aim of this chapter is multiple:

1. to clarify what is meant by "team" and what is expected from a intervention-research.
2. to question the epistemological framework in which intervention-research applied to teams is embedded and to pose methodological precautions.
3. to present an example of a tried and tested, but eminently perfectible, research mechanism.

1 THE TEAM: A COMPLEX RESEARCH OBJECT

It seems essential, as a preliminary step, to clarify what the notion of team covers: more than a restricted group, it is a collective governed by specific logics.

1.1 Notion of a Restricted Group

Social psychologists equate the notion of a small team with that of a restricted group (or primary group).

A classic definition is given by Anzieu and Martin (1968, p.36). A small group, according to them, is characterized by: 1) a limited number of members (3 to 13) allowing the deployment of numerous inter-individual exchanges; 2) the presence of a common goal shared by the members of the group; 3) the constitution of affinity relationships that can become intense (antipathies, sympathies); 4) the existence of strong interdependencies between members, calling for role differentiations; 5) the sharing of a culture (made up of values, norms, beliefs, rituals . . .) allowing for collective cohesion.

1.2 From the Restricted Group to the Notion of Team

Management sciences, and particularly those concerned with Organizational Behavior, readily distinguish the notion of a small group from that of a team.

The team must be understood as a restricted group within which the relational logics that are deployed must lead to the most efficient result possible (optimization logic). And this performance requirement calls for a management need.

Olivier Devillard (2005) distinguishes several relational logics that run through a team:

1. an additive, territorial logic: according to which each person is specialized in one type of task in a given territory (Taylorian approach). This logic calls for coordination.
2. a logic of co-action, of cooperation: it extends the previous one, in the sense that it authorizes team members to leave their territory to invest in that of another when the situation requires it (for example, to replace or help a collaborator with an increased workload). Action is guided not by the team member's function, but by the situation and the performance requirements that accompany it. The responsibility for the final result is, in fact, shared and the team members must assume collective responsibility for it. The logic of cooperation requires the existence of bonds of trust between team members.

3. a logic of synergy: this is the result of a deepening of the two previous logics. It implies that team members know each other very well and that they establish bonds of complicity between them, sometimes very subtle. Each team member is aware of his or her own talents, as well as those of the others, and puts himself or herself at the service of the others when the situation requires it; in the same way, he or she is able to choose the appropriate team members with whom to interact in a given context. In a logic of synergy, the result is much more than the sum of individual actions. And the individuals interact in a subtle and harmonious way (a bit like some jazz bands), in the service of effective action.

2 ELEMENTS OF EPISTEMOLOGY AND METHODOLOGY

2.1 Elements of Epistemology

If it is clear that teams are organizations governed by systemic logic, working on and with teams implies being situated in what Herbert Simon (1996) calls the paradigm of the "sciences of the artificial," which study "the world shaped by men" (as opposed to "natural" sciences such as physics or biology).

This double observation has many implications:

- in a system, causalities are circular (every phenomenon is both a cause and a consequence of the others), which generates interdependencies and games of reciprocal influences (the change of one part affects all the others). From a concrete point of view, this interdependence is the source of resistance to change (one part can block the change of the whole system) and also allows the implementation of homeostatic processes (which allow a system, disturbed by a shock or a change, to return to its initial mode of functioning);
- It is important to use comprehensive "teleological" frameworks, i.e., those that integrate the existence of goals that guide actions.[1] Management is, in essence, teleological, moral and political. It consists, in fact, in directing behavior in a desired direction (objectives, goals). Setting objectives is tantamount to proposing an organizational project: this is the essence of politics. To set objectives implies an appreciation that qualifies them as "good" or "just": this is the essence of moral judgment.
- systems have a capacity for self-organization: they are capable of structuring themselves and becoming more complex, under certain conditions, seeming to contradict the second principle of thermodynamics, which stipulates that the unfolding of time can only lead to disorder, i.e., to destructuring. This contradiction was removed by the Nobel Prize winner (1977) Ilya Prigogine, who asserts that the principle of increasing entropy applies only to closed systems: in systems open to external energy flows, as soon as the intensity of the flows reaches a certain threshold, the organization becomes more complex with the creation of "dissipative structures" that allow for the best possible absorption of incoming energy.

Human systems, because of the numerous interdependencies that drive them and the flows that cross them, are very unpredictable and produce phenomena that are said to be "emergent" and not anticipated. This unpredictability is reinforced by the creative (and innovative) capacity of the human being (being endowed with freedom), as well as by his emotional and passionate reactions (which can be unforeseen). In general, human "reality" is never given once and for all because humans, through their actions (which are themselves the result of their representations and beliefs), constantly modify this reality. Moreover, reality is never external to the observer, who interacts with this reality and thus influences it.

- fundamentally, human systems bring into play representations produced by the actors, which involves interactions. In the constructivist, comprehensive perspective (in the Weberian sense of the term), which is that of intervention-research, it is appropriate to take an interest in the subjective perceptions of the actors: how do they represent the situation? What meaning do they give to their actions?

These representations are shaped by beliefs and cognitive schemas. And these beliefs have very concrete effects since they guide actions, sometimes generating self-fulfilling phenomena (the principle of the "self-fulfilling prophecy").

Finally, the validation of the knowledge produced in the "sciences of the artificial" cannot be the result of an empirico-formal logic, as practiced in the physical sciences (replication of an experiment in the laboratory, by methodically changing the conditions; construction of a mathematically formalized model): it is the result of a process known as "legitimization" and "co-construction" by the actors of the knowledge produced.

2.2 General Elements of Methodology

Based on these initial observations, some general methodological implications can be posed:

1) to approach the study of teams, it is appropriate to use the so-called systemic mode of thought. The latter, whose foundations have been made explicit by the practitioners of the Palo Alto School (see next section) or by authors such as Edgard Morin (1990), is "affixed" (and not "opposed") to the traditional analytical, Cartesian mode of thinking.

In the Cartesian mode of thinking, phenomena must be broken down into elementary units and causal links must be created. Cartesian thought is a causalist thought: every phenomenon finds its cause in another phenomenon and it is up to the scientist to establish causal links, in particular by a work of thought. Faced with a phenomenon, the causalist asks himself the question "what?" and "why? Every problem has a cause: by determining and removing the cause, the problem disappears. The analytical way of thinking is also called "disjunctive" because it is based on the alternative "either/or": a phenomenon is either a cause or a consequence. A proposition is either true or false, according to the logical posture stated by Aristotle (also called "Aristotelian logic of the third party").

This way of thinking is and remains very powerful: it has been at the heart of the great scientific discoveries. Nevertheless, in the face of complexity, the causalist posture is not always adapted, especially in terms of producing change. This calls for the use of systems thinking.

In systems thinking, causalities are circular: some people speak of a "conjunctive" posture based on "and/and": a phenomenon is both cause and consequence. Faced with a phenomenon, the systemicist asks the question of "how": how does the system work? And he questions it in terms of functionality: "what is it for? Faced with a problem, he asks himself: "what is the positive function of this problem? what does it allow to satisfy? To produce change, it is necessary to understand and validate the functions identified and to try to find other alternatives that satisfy the functions or criteria discovered.

2) It is necessary to work on the representations and beliefs of the actors ("constructivist" logic) and therefore to put in place a methodological device that will allow these beliefs to be worked on and updated.

2.3 It is Necessary to Set Up Knowledge Legitimization Systems

The principles developed by ISEOR (principles of "contradictory subjectivity," "cognitive interactivity," "mirror effect," and "expert opinion") seem, in this respect, particularly adapted.

Beyond the (systemic) posture, a difficulty that arises for the researcher: how to approach a team to understand its functioning?

The basic collection instruments are, to use the acronym coined by Savall and Zardet (2004), the EDOs: Interviews, Documents, Observations.

Of course, the idea of participant observation is the one that comes to mind first, but this, advocated by ethnologists, is often difficult to carry out over a long period of time in a company, especially as the researcher rarely has the skills required to become a full-time employee. Thus, as Plane points out (2000, p.48), "this fieldwork approach has limitations such as the difficulties in observing and reporting on phenomena that occur in all micro-spaces. On the other hand, it is a contemplative approach to research that is interesting in sociology, but through which the researcher hides himself, which can harm his credibility and his societal legitimacy.

3 A PROVEN TRANSFORMATIVE PROCESS THE PALO ALTO SCHOOL APPROACH

An intervention carried out within the marketing teams of a large group listed on the CAC 40 (Masingue, 2016) has allowed us to experiment with a research process, which can be eminently improved, and of which we will describe some of the main features here.

To respond to the request for intervention, we had to choose a transformative operational approach compatible with the systemic and constructivist aspects of management intervention-research to structure and solidly anchor our approach. And also with the deeply systemic nature of the objects studied: the teams. The approach chosen was that of the Palo Alto School.

On the other hand, we mobilized heuristic tools and processes aimed at better understanding the functioning of teams and enabling them to change: the use of Golden's Typological Development Inventories (Golden, 2004) and of the belief decoding technique developed by Robert Dilts (1990). These tools were used longitudinally, through individual interviews and group reflection and feedback.

We present here some of the main principles of the transformative approach advocated by the Palo Alto School. We also outline the research protocol used and the type of results produced.

3.1 Guiding Principles of Change According to the Palo Alto School

The Palo Alto School, whose founder is the anthropologist Gregory Bateson, places its transformative approach in a systemic perspective. According to the school, any process of change involves: 1) discovering how the system functions and decoding its resources; 2) clarifying the objective of the change; 3) understanding the dysfunctions observed with regard to the goal pursued; 4) proposing actions for change that are based on the resources of the system; 5) evaluating the results and re-examining the transformation strategy if it does not prove effective (failure is a source of learning).

Change may involve building up resources and skills that require learning. It can also be based on a minimal action ("minimal change") which, through a ripple effect, transforms the whole system.

One of the techniques used extensively by Palo Alto practitioners is that of "reframing": it encourages individuals to examine reality "with new glasses," a new perspective, another interpretative grid, another set of cognitive schemas. This allows them to give another meaning to their lived experience and brings about change.

In the end, the transformative approach advocated by the Palo Alto School fits perfectly into the process of management intervention-research: understanding and decoding representations to make them evolve and to produce actions of change oriented in the desired direction.

3.2 Research Protocol

The system implemented during our research consisted in combining group dynamics and individual interviews, incorporating the use of specific tools. The modus operandi is developed in the previously cited article (Masingue, 2016).

The individual interviews explored the psychological types of the team members (Golden Inventory), collected their perceptions of the team's functioning, and explored some of their cognitive patterns (Dilts' Method).

The group meetings were an opportunity to examine the functioning of the team, using "expert opinion" and "mirror effect." Milestones were marked, allowing each time to evaluate the evolutions and to consider new actions, according to an incremental approach. Training seminars (particularly in the principles of interpersonal communication) were also set up.

3.3 Results

The protocol deployed was a source of numerous discoveries, concerning both the overall dynamics of the teams and the individual operating modes of the employees.

From a qualitative point of view, some relational conflicts were resolved and the team members stated that they came out of the process with the conviction that they knew each other better, which had positive effects on both their professional and private lives. From a "quantitative" point of view, an evaluation tool, in numerical terms, was co-constructed with the managers (with a definition of Units of Work allowing to measure the work related to each file and to make productivity calculations). In all teams, productivity has increased.

In addition, the comparison of teams highlighted the crucial nature of the relational skills of team managers, validating transformational leadership theories (Bennis and Nanus, 1985; Bass, 1985).

In the end, the protocol and the tools used proved to be particularly fruitful in terms of heuristics, comprehension, and transformation.

CONCLUSION

Thus, teams are complex research objects, which allow for a very detailed understanding of the functioning of organizations. The study of teams requires that they be studied within the framework of the paradigm of the "sciences of the artificial" (Simon, 1996) and that appropriate heuristic, comprehensive and transformative processes be put in place. The systemic dimension of the team always remains central. In this respect, the transformative approach developed by the Palo Alto School seems particularly well suited to the process of intervention-research applied to teams: it constitutes a fertile framework, which can be enriched by an instrumental engineering co-constructed by the researcher and the actors in the field, and of which we cite an example in this chapter. Other instrumental devices can of course be imagined: intervention research is a living and creative process. And that is what makes it exciting.

NOTE

1. This notion of "final cause," to use Aristotle's terminology, is discarded in the physical sciences, in which causes can only be "antecedents" of a phenomenon.

REFERENCES

Anzieu, D., Martin, J-Y. (1968). La dynamique des groupes restreints, Paris, Presses Universitaires de France.

Bass, B. M. (1985). Leadership and Performance Beyond Expectations, New York, The Free Press.

Bennis, W. G., & Nanus, B. (1985). Leaders, Collins Business Essentials.

Bateson, G. (1977). Vers une écologie de l'esprit, Paris, Seuil.

Devillard, O. (2005). Dynamiques d'équipes, Paris, Editions d'Organisations.

Dilts, R., Hallbom, T., & Smith, S. (1990). Croyances et Santé, Paris, Desclée de Brouwer.

Golden, J-P. (2004). Inventaire Typologique de Développement, Paris, Editions du Centre de Psychologie Appliquée.

Masingue, A. (2016). «Recherche-intervention et management des petites équipes: proposition d'un outil heuristique et transformatif», Recherches en Sciences de Gestion, 2016/2, (N°113), p. 197–218.

Morin, E. (1990). Introduction à la pensée complexe, Paris, Le Seuil.

Plane, J-M. (2000). Méthodes de recherche-intervention en management, Paris, L'Harmattan.

Prigogine, I. (1971). Structure, stability and fluctuations, Paris, Masson.

Simon, H. (1996). The Sciences of the Artificial, third edition, Cambridge, The MIT Press.

Weber, M. (1971). Economie et société, 1922, Paris, Plon.

This page intentionally left blank.

PART XI

CONNECTIONS: PHILOSOPHICAL, SOCIOLOGICAL, GEOGRAPHICAL

This page intentionally left blank.

CHAPTER 110

SOCIO-ECONOMIC MANAGEMENT OF URBAN SPACES

From Urban Planning to "Urbanology"[1]

Jacques Bonnet and Nathaël Torrès

ABSTRACT

Urban planning reflects society defined by experts and elites. Urbanology is oriented by the society of users. The latter places the question of housing at the heart of its concerns, not as a simple commercial product, but as a center of social life for living together.

The crisis is also a question of behavior, more societal than social in origin. It is necessary to find a social link to give more sense to the collective and individual existence. Individualism, which has been the foundation of Western culture for five or six centuries, has today resulted in a withdrawal into oneself, or at best an "entre-soi" environment. How can we live together in an archipelago society, when generations seem to misunderstand each other, when ideological communities clash violently and when neither families, nor schools, nor churches, nor political parties really contribute?

Housing is at the heart of the debate. The tide of housing estates and large collective complexes are successively indicted. Criticisms that focus on the form of the constructions, when the substance is elsewhere, in the social organization and in the minds.

Whether it is a suburban building or not, social housing—almost half of the rental housing stock in France, a record—is an opportunity to recreate social ties. Social housing has a bad reputation among political actors. It is therefore necessary to reconsider both politics and social housing: on the one hand, empowering residents in the spirit of the common good in the service of social and intergenerational diversity, and on the other hand, engaging in

SEAM Treatise, pages 897–901

a participatory approach and undertaking innovative social engineering by developing user assistance, which implies a consequent evolution of the social landlord's profession

The concept of the neighborhood is thus recast as a meeting place, in the geographical sense of a real territory, i.e., a place of uses and social links. The landlord thus participates in the creation of new centralities in the city. In this way, we move from housing to habitat, from quantitative to qualitative, from simple urbanism to complex urbanology.

1 THE *CHERS VOISINS ASSOCIATION*: EVOLUTION OF THE SOCIAL LANDLORD PROFESSION

The *Chers Voisins association* provides an operational response to the need to promote social diversity and social cohesion. It brings together social landlords, a social engineering and urban planning consultancy, *Récipro-Cité,* and students enrolled as apprentices in a master's degree in geography ("Territorial planning and development"). The University of Lyon has thus contributed a reflection on action-research. National partners followed the experiments in several application areas, in the departments of Rhône, Ain, Savoie, Bouches-du-Rhône, Alpes Maritimes, and finally in Île de France. In all, there are now 13 intergenerational solidarity and participatory housing projects, 32 residences, and nearly 1,400 homes located in some 20 municipalities.

In the field, the action starts with assistance to the owner, to define upstream with the inhabitants the expectations of the local fabric. The *Chers Voisins association* offers tenants of social housing an innovative pact for living together. A charter provides for the assumption of responsibility for routine maintenance by the tenants of the residence, common premises, and green spaces, in exchange for a significant reduction in rental charges. A collective agreement leaves the residents free to participate or not according to three progressive commitment formulas, allowing for increasing savings on charges. A household can thus save the equivalent of one month's rent per year.

The appropriation by the inhabitants of their living space is illustrated above all by a project house, a central place for meetings and exchanges, a reception structure for all the activity clubs, neighborhood clubs (which can be open to outside populations) on a wide variety of themes: do-it-yourself, gardening, sports and gymnastics, walking, childcare, computers, and job hunting. The referent of the employment-economy club gives advice to the inhabitants to find a job. An energy club can help optimize the equipment in the residences and make new reductions in charges.

To support the residents in the field, the landlord finances a full-time position of manager-animator for the first year, half-time the following year, and then quarter-time, before referring users can take over the animation. A total autonomy that has rarely been reached yet.

A workshop of the master proposes to make an assessment 2013–2020 of the first territorial action of *Chers Voisins,* in a popular district of Saint-Germain au Mont d'Or. The questioning concerns the sustainability of this residential support operation. The assessment is underway. Is the observed approach sustainable, reproducible, on what scale?

2 THE TENANT BECOMES AN ACTOR OF HIS/HER HABITAT

"To be oneself, but together" wrote the sociologist Jean Viard (2015). How to live together? How to create a community between different people? The reflection calls upon several social sciences. The *association Chers Voisins,* chaired by a geographer and inspired by geography, places territories at the heart of this reflection. The economist will highlight the recycling of hidden costs (Savall, 1974, 1979; Savall and Zardet, 1987). The landlord has observed a very significant drop in turnover and therefore in the vacancy rate, proof that the inhabitants are well in the premises. Incivilities have decreased significantly. For the local authority, the benefits are also significant. It has been said that the activity clubs could be open to outside populations. These project houses are new centralities that attract and retain residents.

The social and environmental responsibility of all parties takes on a more global meaning here to give a different image of the city. Innovative social engineering, participative approach, collective responsibility, the tenant becoming an actor of his/her housing, rediscovery of the common good, were highlighted during the containment ordered during the epidemic of the virus COVID 19. In the face of the health crisis, acts of solidarity between neighbors have multiplied. In Marseilles, for example, three tenants who are members of the *Chers Voisins association* have mobilized to help the residents who need it most by collecting and distributing food packages. The manager of the local association played an important role in coordinating the actions, ensuring contact with the tenants, and providing the volunteers with the necessary premises for storing the donations and preparing the packages.

There are other equally positive formulas. Nearly 200 active operations have been analyzed by Nathaël Torrès (2020). He found that "the building, housing and development sectors are opening up more and more to services." Housing is becoming a serviced residential product. "Housing exchanges, training, resource and recycling centers, club cards and proto-conciergeries, local exchange systems, etc.: often grouped under the label of social innovation, social housing actors offer a profuse array of services that go far beyond their traditional management functions.

In the private sector, the specifications of the "ZACs" or consultations with the operators of almost all large-scale projects include requirements in terms of services to the residents or the population and state, in addition to standard real estate criteria, ambitions in terms of creating social links, living together, sustainable mobility, home automation, energy savings, etc. In Palaiseau, the developers of the Claudel eco-neighborhood are financing a seven-year neighborhood concierge service for their residents. In Annecy, the developer (*TERACTEM*) of a 200-home eco-neighborhood wants to accompany its project with a neighborhood concierge service to *"create social and intergenerational links and a shared life in the neighborhood."* In Marseille, *Eiffage immobilier* is building a demonstration block (called *Smartelle*) of innovations from its foresight laboratory (*Phosphore*): connected housing (NTIC package, applications, consumption monitoring, intranet platform), neighborhood e-conciergerie, self-service bicycle and electric car stations, entertainment and intergenerational links in shared collective spaces, shared gardens. In Lyon, a developer (*Bouygues immobilier*) is offering its future buyers, in addition to a home on plan, a set of dedicated residential services: a shared garden at the foot of the residence and the support of a gardener-animator made available to residents free of charge for three years, a shared toolbox, a bicycle station, a shared guest room. Housing players, developers, promoters and social landlords, have become familiar or are now familiarizing themselves with more complex setups, adding to their "classic" offer of project owners an ecosystem, or a more or less fleshed-out portfolio of residential services, which are fed by the latest technological and social innovations. "

In most of the experiments identified we find the important role of shared collective gardens. The role of urban agriculture in the appropriation of space and in the development of a more sustainable city seems essential. By participating in the development of collective gardens, the actors of a territory appropriate a space. People's sociability seems to be stimulated when they garden. Gardens allow people to meet, exchange and learn. They can play a major role in popular education by developing practical (manual work), intellectual (classification of plants, biological cycles of plants and animals) and personal (knowing how to be, listening to others, solidarity) learning. Citizenship is also largely put forward in several cases, because making a garden in the city is also becoming aware of one's living space, it is a will to embellish the landscape by the colors of the plants and by the creation of places of creative freedom. From an environmental point of view, we can talk about reducing heat islands, reducing and recovering waste, and preserving biodiversity. The pleasant and self-managed living environments developed by urban gardens also help to calm down violence in the neighborhoods.

3 FROM URBAN PLANNING TO URBANOLOGY

In the city, the soft dominates the hard, the qualitative prevails over the quantitative, the service framework over the material environment. Precisely the opposite of the functional urbanism of the 1960s–1975s. This trend began around 1990, when the question of a living environment for the pleasure of city dwellers was asserted, as shown by the development of public squares and streets for pedestrians to stroll around, the revaluation of public gardens and riverbanks, the development of bicycle paths or the street art fashion. In Lyon, for example, Michel Noir's term of office was marked by the reinforcement of central poles in the City of Light and by the inclusion of the environment in the public policies of Greater Lyon. This took concrete form with the establishment of an Ecology Mission at the same time as the Housing, Transportation and Economic Development Missions, and with the drafting of the urban ecology charter in 1992.

This approach obviously reflects a change in behavior, at least for part of society. The forms of the city also reveal the mutation from a production economy to a society of communication, consumption, and leisure a service economy. There are obviously correspondences between economic modes, social models, and urban territorial forms.

The confinement of metropolitan populations imposed in 2020 by the epidemic (COVID 19) may mark a complementary evolution: the primacy of concern for life, of course, but even more so an awareness of the necessary benefits of community, of places of meeting and exchange: cafés, restaurants, theaters, squares and public gardens, banks and beaches, squares, and shopping streets.

The big city must combine the inhabitants' quest for greenery and green spaces on the one hand—the denser the neighborhood, the greater the demand for nature—and on the other hand the enhancement of meeting places, both space and densification, individual freedom, and neighborhood solidarity. Public and private housing and development actors must propose new forms. Bougrain and Carassus (2004) explain:

> What the economy expects from construction is no longer a massive increase in the stock of buildings and infrastructures (as during the expansion phase of the "30 glorious years"), but an optimization of the service rendered by the structures, existing or to be built, based on a wide use of new information and communication technologies, and satisfying the requirements of sustainable development.

Engineers are thinking about the "smart city," which is increasingly open to services, whether they be connected buildings and approaches to support residents, home automation, neighborhood janitors, or digital neighborhood social networks. N. Torres (2020) emphasizes the rise in social responsibility of low-income housing organizations, the rise of social engineering. Thus, we are moving from urban planning to urbanology.

Innovation implies a multidisciplinary mastery of interactions. The soft is more complex than the hard. The organization of collective interactivities is more difficult than a simple material production. The territory is a meta-organization that cannot be decreed. Social innovation partly escapes political or administrative decision. It imposes a long and indecisive path between experimentation and standardization. Projects in this field always leave room for utopia. Urbanology is a decentralized utopian project that jurists, political actors and especially administrations may have difficulty understanding, but that the populations must impose.

CONCLUSION

The territory is a meta-organization composed of a set of public and private organizations whose governance combines the dimensions of geopolitics and management. The requirements of territorial development, which lead to taking private as well as public actors as references, invite us to put the geographical study of the spatial and territorial behavior of actors (individuals, households, communities) back at the center of the reasoning and practices of planning. At the same time, and paradoxically in a context of decentralization, planning has been the subject for the last twenty years of a very important legislative and regulatory production which makes the approach more and more normative.

NOTE

1. Term borrowed from Michel RAGON (1986) *Histoire de l'architecture et de l'urbanisme modernes* Casterman (second part «les nouvelles approches de l'urbanisme»; chapter 1 «*de l'urbanime à l'urbanologie*»).

REFERENCES

Argoud, D. (2012). L'habitat intergénérationnel: vers une nouvelle forme de mixité ?, *Pouvoirs locaux n°94, 2012*

Bonnet, J. (2021). (sous la direction de): *Aménagement et développement territorial.* Ellipses

Bonnet J., & Vieillard-Baron, H. (2012), *Le logement en France: diversité, complexité, contradictions.* in *Historiens & Géographes n°419–420 «Façons d'habiter les territoires de la ville aujourd'hui».* Dossier du Comité National Français de Géographie pour l'Union Géographique Internationale

Bougrain, F., & Carassus, J. (2003). Bâtiment: de l'innovation de produit à l'innovation de service. Programme de recherche Innover ensemble, PUCA.

Chapon. P. M. (2013). (Sous la direction de). *Bâtir une ville pour tous les âges.* La Documentation Française.

Ragon, M. (1986). *Histoire de l'architecture et de l'urbanisme modernes.* Casterman

Torres, N. (2020). *Mixité sociale et vieillissement de la population -quelles perspectives pour un habitat intergénérationnel durable?* Thèse de doctorat en géographie-aménagement, Université de Lyon.

Viard, J. (2015). *Le triomphe d'une utopie. La révolution des temps libres.* L'Aube.

CHAPTER 111

FROM THE SOCIO-ECONOMIC MODEL TO ORGANIZATIONAL ABILITY

A Human-Centered Path

Consuelo García de La Torre, Osmar Arandia Pérez, and Luis Portales Derbez

ABSTRACT

This chapter analyzes the current organizational ecosystem in which human beings operate. It places the human being at the center of the action, under the assumption that, if he/she works in conditions of trust, freedom to act and is empowered, he/she will become the agent of change that the company needs to face today's challenges. The most important finding is that the socioeconomic management model, as well as organizational agility, are management concepts that are born and developed in volatile, uncertain, complex and ambiguous contexts.

History has shown us that large and rapid contextual changes are not exclusive to the 21st century. In the 1970s, the world was in the throes of social and economic effervescence, caused by social movements all over the planet, and by a sharp fall in oil prices (Erfle & McMillan, 1990; Lounsbury, Ventresca, & Hirsch, 2003; Savall, 2010). Today, at the beginning of the second decade of the 21st century, humanity faces equally complicated challenges: the price war between oil-producing giants and the pandemic caused by Covid–19 are just two examples of the major challenges facing humanity and its organizations.

In such a volatile, uncertain, complex and ambiguous environment, the way in which organizations face their challenges is a significant challenge both socially and economically, where people play a fundamental role as agents of change and developers of solutions. This context forces the organization and people to respond in an agile and efficient way; agility

SEAM Treatise, pages 903–908

being understood as the speed of response, the ability to shape and change behaviors and structures, causing the least possible stress. This ability to respond quickly and flexibly becomes essential.

This chapter compares two management perspectives defined in different eras, but which consider the human being as a fundamental and significant actor in achieving organizational objectives. Both perspectives are based on the human being as an agent of change capable of facing the challenges of the environment, if they are empowered, given freedom, but above all, if they are given the confidence that their actions have a transcendental purpose.

1 THE SOCIO-ECONOMIC MANAGEMENT MODEL AND ITS FOUNDATIONS

When Henri Savall proposed that the economic performance of organizations was strongly linked to the social performance of people, he recognized the importance of human talent as a detonator of value generation for organizations (Savall, 1974; 1979). Its objective is to introduce the economic aspect in an area where labor psychology and sociology were fundamental, and where the inclusion of the economic element helped to comprehensively understand the performance phenomena occurring in organizations (Delors, 1975). The principle of socio-economic approach to management is that the development of companies is based on the development of people's human potential (Savall, 1975).

The socio-economic approach to management is based on the understanding that companies are social organizations formed by human beings who unite their will and capabilities in the search for individual and common welfare (Granovetter, 2010). However, recurrent economic and social crises seem to indicate a mismatch between the desired well-being and the results obtained, which stem from inadequate organizational and social structures, and undesired individual and organizational behaviors.

In this sense, socio-economic management is a proposal that addresses these mismatches by detecting and addressing the dysfunctions that exist within organizations (Savall and Zardet, 1987). These dysfunctions interrelate atrophied behaviors and atrophied structures, in the same proposal, where the testimony of people is of utmost importance to discover and understand the phenomena that occur in organizations. It is presented as a response to organizational and individual challenges, based on the development of the human potential of an organization.

The socio-economic theory is based on three epistemological pillars (Savall and Zardet, 1996, 2004), which are related to human beings and their social interaction with other people in the organization, and with the structures of the organization itself.

The first pillar is called Generic Contingency. It assumes that each case and actor is unique, therefore, it seeks to recognize particularities in each of them to find generalities that allow a broad understanding of the phenomena that occur in the organization from the perspective of the actors, and thus analyze the consequences on their performance.

The second pillar is Contradictory Intersubjectivity, which considers that each actor views the same phenomenon from different perspectives, therefore, the analyses may seem contradictory, however, the fact of organizing interactions between people allows to draw a representation of reality as a mixture of contradictory and convergent opinions.

The third pillar is Cognitive Interactivity. It assumes that the actors, thanks to their interactions, generate knowledge and, therefore, help to solve dysfunctions. From this perspective, no one can reduce dysfunctions in isolation or alone.

The epistemological pillars of the socioeconomic model indicate that the empowerment of people, freedom of action and individual perspectives are the triggers for the potential of organizations. Based on these pillars, it can be understood that the human being is the relevant actor in the development of the entire socioeconomic theory and the management model that follows from it. At the same time, they are relevant actors in the solution of the dysfunctions that afflict the company and therefore have an impact on the company (see Table 111.1).

Socio-economic management is not static, as it recognizes that organizational structures have evolved, knowledge management has become common in organizations worldwide, and companies have sought to improve the work environment and employee satisfaction (Savall and Zardet, 2015). These changes have occurred as a response to the social, economic, institutional and organizational changes that have occurred worldwide, where traditional management is unfeasible, forcing organizations to adopt a management model where people are the agents of change they need to respond to these new contexts and realities. Under this understanding, for socioeconomic management, human beings and their potential are the best response to the challenges posed by such a volatile environment as the one we are living in.

The management model is based on individual and collective suggestions for improvement (generic contingency, cognitive interactivity and contradictory intersubjectivity) to generate potential, reduce dysfunctions and improve not only organizational but also individual performance (Savall, 1977; 1979; Savall and Zardet, 1995).

In the socio-economic management model, the human being is a fundamental element in the generation of value and reduction of dysfunctions in organizations. Based on the actions of people and their interaction with each other, the company reduces its dysfunctions and improves its economic performance by recycling the organization's hidden costs. Change is based on people within the organization, considering their perspectives and empowering them to propose actions that enhance the organization's performance. The

TABLE 111.1 The Relationship of People in Each of the Model's Epistemological Pillars

Epistemological pillar	People and their relationship with the pillar	Impact on the company
Generic contingency	Each person has a different vision and interpretation of the problems afflicting the organization	By understanding the individual interpretation that each person gives to the company's problems, the model assumes that by interviewing each actor, a better understanding of the company's problems can be generated.
Contradictory intersubjectivity	Contradictory intersubjectivity The particularities of each actor, their personal history, and their history in the organization presuppose different visions of the same problem, however, it is in this diversity that a better understanding of the company and its circumstances is generated	Understanding the different perspectives, but above all using the different strengths, helps the company to better face its challenges.
Cognitive interactivity	Cognitive interactivity Knowledge is built through time, thanks to interactions between people, since nobody has THE solution.	Knowledge management in organizations is a source of sustainable competitive advantage if the organization succeeds in managing and documenting knowledge.

Source: Own elaboration.

collective energy and the individual energy of each actor work together in the organization to achieve its strategic objectives. According to Perroux (1975), the level of favorable energy of each individual depends directly on the compatibility between the individual project and the collective strategy of the organization.

2 ORGANIZATIONAL AGILITY AND ITS FUNDAMENTALS

Agility is the successful application of competitive fundamentals such as speed, flexibility, innovation and quality by integrating reconfigurable resources and best practices from a knowledge-rich environment to deliver customer-oriented products and services in a rapidly changing environment (Yussuf et al., 1999). The concept of agility, traditionally comprised characteristics of adaptability and flexibility, representing the evolution of the idea that the organization is able to adapt. The agile organization, under this logic, represents the last stage of development of this idea, since it combines the most important notions of adaptability and flexibility (Sherehiy et al., 2007).

Organizational agility can be understood as a set of dynamically coordinated, collaborative and transactional activities that deliver value to customers (Smith and Fingar, 2003). Such activities are proposed and born from the individual and joint perspective of the organization's collaborators. This type of agility is realized when organizations develop the dynamic capabilities necessary to respond to the challenges of the environment (Teece et al., 1997).

According to Crocitto and Youssef (2003), organizational agility is achieved when people and technological tools are integrated into the organization's processes in an effective and efficient manner. This integration occurs when people, their ideas, motivations and experiences are considered within the organizational dynamics, and technology is visually aligned as an enabler. In this sense, dynamic and agile organizations are those that can deal with chaos, change, adaptability, emergence and innovation, being the capacity of people to adapt and innovate their fundamental characteristic, managing to face the challenges of the environment (Dyer and Shafer, 2003).

In an agile organization, the environment inside the company must favor and develop teamwork, empowerment of people and active collaboration (Muduli, 2017). Therefore, organizations with systems that encourage employee involvement, organizational learning systems and psychological empowerment of employees that develop self-determination, are more likely to become agile organizations, capable of facing changing environments. For example, psychological empowerment is able to promote the agility of human talent, since it is born from the organization's recognition of the particularities of each collaborator, and the effort to involve them in the decision-making process and strategic definition of the organization (Mudili and Pandya, 2018).

In the same vein, in times of organizational agility, traditional work performance indicators must change and become organizational indicators that measure the self-determination capacity of employees and the organization's ability to involve its employees in the strategic decision-making process (Holbeche, 2018).

In summary, organizational agility represents the dynamic capabilities of the organization. It enables it to learn, modify, reconfigure and adapt to highly volatile and uncertain environments. Such agility is achieved by transforming and involving the organization's employees, and by developing their capacity for adaptation and innovation. To achieve employee participation, the company must empower them, listen to them, train them and recognize them; only in this way will the organization become agile and flexible to respond to the challenges of its environment.

3 SIMILARITIES BETWEEN THE SOCIO-ECONOMIC APPROACH TO MANAGEMENT AND ORGANIZATIONAL AGILITY

When analyzing the socio-economic management model and the premises of organizational agility, it is easy to find important similarities with respect to how both perspectives consider the human being and its importance in organizations.

This comparison is not new, as Worley et al. (2015) made an in-depth and at the same time empirical analysis, about the conceptual similarities between organizational agility and the socioeconomic management model. These authors found that agile organizations make effective and efficient changes because organizational members understand, are engaged and feel involved in strategic decisions. This involvement implies a shared understanding and commitment, which helps an organization's collaborators understand what their roles are, and what changes must be made to achieve business objectives. In summary, like the socioeconomic model, organizational agility is born from people, their interpretation of the context, their interaction with other collaborators and their desire to support and participate in organizational challenges.

Another similarity is found in the understanding of employees. In the concept of organizational agility, the empowerment of people, the capacity for self-direction and involvement in strategic decisions are fundamental pillars for developing agility in organizations. On the other hand, in the Socioeconomic Management model, the epistemological pillars are the substantial foundation that stems from the human being and that enables the organization to face the rapid changes that occur in its environment. We thus understand that the actions of people are fundamental in both perspectives, and that they are born and flourish due to the interaction of human beings in organizations.

Among the possible differences, these are at the level of the concepts they use, but not necessarily in terms of the substance of each of them. For example, at the level of practice, we find that the socioeconomic model seeks learning and intersubjectivity as a central part of the way to identify the dysfunctions that need to be addressed, while in the concept of agility the practice focuses on the design of what as a way to solve these problems. At the level of implementation mechanisms, agility focuses on the creation of agile routines, while the socio-economic model seeks strategic decisions and contracts by all levels of the organization. The socio-economic model focuses its continuous improvement process on the tools contained in the triedro, while agility focuses on the creation of differential capabilities.

CONCLUSION

The socio-economic management model, like organizational agility, are management concepts that are born and developed in volatile, uncertain, complex and ambiguous contexts. In both perspectives, the human being plays a fundamental role, since he/she is the relevant actor that generates ideas and perspectives that are born from his/her experience, skills and commitment to the organization.

The epistemological pillars of the socio-economic management model also explain the importance of involving people in the organization in its agile processes, thus facilitating the achievement of organizational objectives and reducing dysfunctions when seeking organizational agility.

In both perspectives, organizational agility and the socioeconomic management model, the learning and knowledge developed and acquired by people are fundamental inputs for the organization to achieve agile adaptation processes in the face of constant and rapid changes in the context. We assume that socioeconomic management is equally useful when the organization seeks agility, i.e., the management tools designed by the ISEOR are extremely useful for the organization that wishes to be agile, and complement perfectly with the tools designed by agility.

REFERENCES

Crocitto, M., & Youssef, M. (2003). *The human side of organizational agility.* Industrial Management & Data Systems.

Delors, J. (1975). Préface in Savall (1974, 1975). *Enrichir le travail humain: l'évaluation économique.* Dunod

Dyer, L., & Shafer, R. A. (2003). *Dynamic organizations: Achieving marketplace and organizational agility with people.* Cornell School.

Erfle, S., & McMillan, H. (1990). Media, political pressure, and the firm: The case of petroleum pricing in the late 1970s. *The Quarterly Journal of Economics,* 105(1), 115–134.

Granovetter, M. (2010). *19 Business Groups and Social Organization. The handbook of economic sociology,* 429.

Holbeche, L. S. (2018). Organizational effectiveness and agility. *Journal of Organizational Effectiveness: People and Performance.*

Lounsbury, M., Ventresca, M., & Hirsch, P. M. (2003). Social movements, field frames and industry emergence: a cultural–political perspective on US recycling. *Socio-economic review,* 1(1), 71–104.

Muduli, A. (2013). Workforce Agility: A Review of Literature. IUP *Journal of Management Research,* 12(3).

Muduli, A. (2017). Workforce agility: Examining the role of organizational practices and psychological empowerment. *Global Business and Organizational Excellence,* 36(5), 46–56.

Muduli, A., & Pandya, G. (2018). Psychological empowerment and workforce agility. *Psychological Studies,* 63(3), 276–285.

Perroux, F. (1975). *Unités actives et mathématiques nouvelles. Révision de l'équilibre économique général.* Paris: Dunod.

Sherehiy, B., Karwowski, W., & Layer, J. K. (2007). A review of enterprise agility: Concepts, frameworks, and attributes. International Journal of industrial ergonomics, 37(5), 445–460.

Teece, D. J., Pisano, G., & Shuen, A. (1997). Dynamic capabilities and strategic management. Strategic management journal, 18(7), 509–533.

Worley, C. G., Zardet, V., Bonnet, M., & Savall, A. (2015). Becoming agile: How the SEAM approach to management builds adaptability. John Wiley & Sons.

Y. Yusuf, M. Sarhadi, A. Gunasekaran (1999) Agile manufacturing: the drivers, concepts and attributes. International Journal of Production Economics, 62 (1–2), pp. 33–43.

CHAPTER 112

THE GOLDEN TRIANGLE OF THE SOCIO-ECONOMIC APPROACH TO MANAGEMENT (SEAM)

Philippe Trouvé

ABSTRACT

Starting from a pictorial triangular representation of the Socio-Economic Management Model, the sides of which represent three of its main dimensions and the inner surface of which represents sustainable socio-economic performance as a general objective, this chapter attempts to show that the approach modeled and tested for nearly five decades by ISEOR provides a radical departure from mainstream management technologies, the most accomplished forms of which in contemporary companies and organizations have today entered into crisis. The game is not won in advance, since the innovations brought about by the socio-economic approach are at odds with the dominant currents, both in business practices and in the academic world.

If we force the line a little, a triangle could represent the main innovative dimensions of the Socio-Economic Management Model. One of its sides would illustrate the managerial instrumentation and its uses, the second, the human potential and its energies of creation of value, and the third side finally the relations of cooperation between the actors on the activity. The successive approach of these three parts highlights, according to us, a significant departure of the Socio-Economic Management Model. from the mainstream forms of contemporary management technologies. The surface of the triangle evokes the product and the purpose of the interactions between these three dimensions, sustainable socio-economic performance, which will not be discussed here.

The first part of the attached proposal shows that, thanks to a refined methodology built up over time, the Socio-Economic Management Model. makes a break with the unmeasured

SEAM Treatise, pages 909–913

extension of control and rationalization tools – known as *managerialism* – disseminated from the 1980s in most organizations. The second part, by focusing on the concept of human potential linked to value creation, underlines the originality and interest of the Socio-Economic Management Model's contribution to a real organizational energy, mobilizing creative forces throughout the organization, instead of control devices imposed exclusively from above. Finally, in the third part, the insistence of the Socio-Economic Management Model. on the forms of cooperation, cohesion and synergy between actors called for by socio-economic innovation questions its capacity to produce the Common where neo-liberal forms of organization and dominant managerial technologies have, on the contrary, led to the dissolution of work collectives and to the individualization of social relations in companies and organizations. It is this sort of "golden triangle" of the Socio-Economic Management Model. that is the subject of this contribution.

1 AVOIDING BOTH HYPERTROPHY AND DEFICIT OF INSTRUMENTATION

For nearly three decades, in a particularly unstable and uncertain macro-economic context, under the combined pressure of, on the one hand, the performance requirements generated by shareholder capitalism or budgetary austerity policies and, on the other hand, the need to mobilize human resources to face these major challenges, the leaders of companies and organizations—specifically the largest ones—have been led to adopt alternately new forms of management, based on two apparently contradictory models. Taken in isolation, these models have revealed their limits and have been the subject of much criticism. The first, the management control or *managerialism* model, characterized by the exclusive search for short-term economic performance, has resulted in an obsession with control and a "procedural delirium" (Dupuy, 2011) marked by the proliferation of standards, rules, procedures and reporting, the effects of which have proven to be counterproductive: bureaucratization of organizations, neglect of customers, distancing of actors from their core business, stifling of strategic decision-making places by the abundance of irrelevant or biased information and, ultimately, loss of value. The second, which could be generically related to the *participatory traditions*, promised an increase in employee commitment and responsibility, thanks to the soft action and shared vision of liberating leaders. In contrast to the previous model, in the absence of robust instrumentation and doctrine, the latter has not yet managed to go beyond the rhetorical stage and somewhat mitigate the centralizing and authoritarian tendencies of French-style management. This is regularly demonstrated by the extensive surveys (notably the Reponse survey) of the DARES (Coutrot, 1998): the development of participative injunctions in managerial discourse coexists with the maintenance of prescription, control and low autonomy felt by employees.

Faced with this persistent dilemma, the Socio-Economic Management Model (SEAM) does not lack arguments. In its initial doctrine and throughout its approach, it posits the compatibility of the social and the economic, where the dominant models of management do not manage or do not seek to reconcile them (Savall, 1974, 1979). This is the case with quantitative and qualitative indicators, co-constructed along the way with operational or managerial staff, which combine immediate results and the creation of potential (Savall and Zardet, 1989) and are not reduced to financial indicators alone, which often generate hidden costs and are usually indifferent to the deterioration of working conditions (Savall et al., 2017). As for its renewed and broadened conception of management control, far from blindly adhering to the generalization and applicability of abstract norms defined by the hierarchical top, it is concerned with the social acceptability of measurement tools, incorporating human and social variables at all times (Savall, Zardet, 2015) and mobilizing operational actors, not only in the diagnostic phases, in the setting of individual and collective objectives, but also in the elaboration of budgets and in the steering of corrective actions at the scale of micro-areas. Unlike the participatory and liberating ideologies conveyed by the new managerial rhetoric, the robustness of the instruments and methodology is not lacking here. But unlike the most widespread forms of management control, the use made of it by the MMSE is conducive to learning and emancipation. Is this not a form of contribution to the democratization of the functioning of companies and organizations?

2 AN ORGANIZATIONAL ENERGY

Beyond the instruments, the Socio-Economic Management Model presupposes the continuous mobilization of creative social forces which, in general, diminish over time. This is the fate of all "innovations" in management and business intervention. Once the initial moment of "social effervescence" (Durkheim) that sociologists have identified in all nascent religious movements has passed, a phase of decline and "cooling" (Weber) of the affects and enthusiasm follows, analogous to the entropy of physical systems, involving new behaviors and aspirations in practitioners and requiring prophets to reorganize the stimulation devices to keep the initial fervor alive, much as maintenance actions keep physical systems in good working order.

It is the merit of the socio-economic approach recommended by ISEOR that it took into account this energetic dimension—one could even say "vitalist" in opposition to traditional mechanists approaches—of organized action very early on, not only in the phase of appropriation of the tools by all of the actors, but also and above all in the maintenance engineering of improvement and innovation actions, thanks in particular to a set of tools focused on the improvement of human potential: for example, skills development grids, integrated training actions, systematic information of actors during the implementation of priority actions, revisions by periodic "cleaning up" of objectives, priority actions, procedures or even the organization of the company (Savall, Zardet, 1989 , 2010). However, we know that in most companies or in intervention practices aimed at managerial innovation, this persistence of action is lacking for the reasons mentioned above, i.e., not because of simple "resistance" on the part of the actors or because of a lack of institutionalization of support mechanisms, but because of a weakening of individual and collective energies.

From a doctrinal point of view, we see that the notion of energy is illustrated in the MSSE by the concept of human potential, "the only active factor in value creation" (Savall et al, 2017). More than that, it is based on the confidence in the capacity of the actors brought into synergy, to self-organize and transform their behaviors and skills through the whole process of socio-economic innovation. This is how this main lever of action to reduce dysfunctions, when sufficiently maintained, guarantees the involvement of individuals and collectives right up to the "recycling of hidden costs," which always requires a surplus of creativity and commitment, to imagine new solutions and adopt new practices.

3 TOWARDS THE REACTIVATION OF WORK COLLECTIVES

The analysis of the effects of the Socio-Economic Management Model 's break with the mainstream of management would not be complete without highlighting its sustained attention to practices of *cooperation, cross-functional synergy, cohesion and synchronization* between hierarchical levels, to the point where we might wonder whether the socio-economic approach might not be conducive, if not to reconstituting work collectives, at least to halting their decline, which began nearly three decades ago at multiple levels: in the micro-spaces of interaction, in the professions, in the corporate culture and project, in the assemblies of stakeholders on a territorial scale…

In fact, the bureaucratization of organizations, which is the product of a generalized control of organizations by managers faced with the uncertainty of the environment and the ever-increasing demands of shareholders, has led to a compartmentalization and hyper specialization of the main functions of companies. According to the Socio-Economic Management Model, this has led to an uncontrolled proliferation of sources of normativity (tetranormalization), which generates *"an intensity of control, particularly on the part of managers at all levels, which is all the greater as this compartmentalization are more rigid"* (Savall et al., 2017) and regulation costs that affect the overall performance of organizations (Hibou, 2013). On the other hand, the new forms of human resource management have led to an extreme individualization of the wage relationship, which has contributed to the deconstruction of work collectives, which industrial sociology had once shown, in addition to their function of supporting professional identities, to be effective in regulating dysfunction (Bernoux, 1981).

By mobilizing the knowledge of actors about their sphere of work instead of the abstract conceptions generally imposed by experts in support services, the Socio-Economic Management Model avoids confusing structures and organization, as is too often the case with corporate practitioners and traditional consultants (Dupuy, 2015). While the former is a matter of ordinary knowledge and strives to change behaviors by adopting new formal rules and procedures, which are ever more constraining and numerous, the latter is mainly interested in how actors use them, how they work and solve their problems, individually and collectively. Hence the importance of the various forms of cooperation experimented with throughout the socio-economic innovation process: for example, collective debates on the hidden costs generated in the spheres of action by dysfunctions, or the setting up of transversal or specialized focus groups whose function is to stimulate exchanges at the interface, which is usually not very solicited, between the various hierarchical or functional entities of the organization. In addition, the progressive nature of the methods used seeks a better integration of the actions undertaken while improving the social acceptability of transformation projects. Finally, based on the idea that the value generated by actions to recycle hidden costs *"is a value that can be shared between the various internal and external stakeholders, as opposed to the usual strategies for reducing costs and, in particular, labor costs"* (Savall, Zardet, 215 : 8), one might ask whether the mobilization of these deposits does not participate, at least partially, in the construction of a Common in the strong sense of the term (Dardot, Laval, 2015) at the very heart of firms.

CONCLUSION

By examining some of the principles of Socio-Economic Management Model around the instruments and their uses, by underlining its singular contribution to an organizational energetics and then by suggesting its potential to reactivate work collectives thanks to the creation of spaces for deliberation and the construction of autonomous rules on real work instead of applying abstract prescriptions, this contribution has endeavored to identify the main gaps that it maintains with today's dominant forms of management in corporate practices. This would largely explain why, despite its high-performance potential, the Socio-Economic Management Model has not been more widely disseminated, both in business practices and in academic training.

REFERENCES

Bernoux Ph. (1981), *Un travail à soi*, Toulouse, Privat.
Coutrot Th. (1998), *L'entreprise néolibérale, nouvelle utopie capitaliste ?* Paris, La Découverte.
Dardot P., Laval C. (2015), *Commun : essai sur la révolution au XIXe siècle*, Paris, La Découverte.
Dupuy F. (2011), *Lost in management 1. La vie quotidienne des entreprises au XXIe siècle*, Paris, Seuil.
Dupuy F. (2015), *La faillite de la pensée managériale. Lost in management 2*, Paris, éd. Du Seuil.
Hibou B. (sous la dir.) (2013), *La bureaucratisation néolibérale*, Paris La Découverte.

This page intentionally left blank.

CHAPTER 113

SOCIALLY RESPONSIBLE CAPITALISM

A Relevant Setting for the Socio-Economic Approach to Management (SEAM)

Henri Savall, Michel Péron (†), Véronique Zardet, and Marc Bonnet

ABSTRACT

Socially Responsible Capitalism (SRC) is based on entrepreneurship, promotes exemplary behavior that is effective, efficient and ethical, and encourages the assumption of social responsibility by companies and organizations, combined with the development of economic empowerment and the legitimate efforts of each citizen, considered as actor in the economy. SRC does not confuse financial capitalism with entrepreneurial capitalism. The former cultivates the creation of fake value that leads to financial bubbles and ruins the real economy. On the contrary, entrepreneurial capitalism creates robust economic value and jobs, justified by production activity that responds to the legitimate needs of citizen-consumers. SRC is not a utopia; it is already part of the history of economic and social facts and covers a set of good practices, described as socio-economic management, which has been successfully experimented.

In times of crisis, capitalism is questioned by its critics or defended by its supporters. There is some confusion about the emergence of the concept of capitalism and what it really means. What kind of capitalism are we talking about? It is not an ideological approach corresponding to the simplistic definition of a market economy system, based on the private ownership of the means of production and exchange with the aim of making a profit. This chapter aims to define the characteristics of the framework that allows socially responsible companies and organizations, whether public or private, to develop and to promote the implementation of a so-called Socio-Economic Approach to Management (SEAM), because it consists in improving the economic performance of the company and its social performance in a

SEAM Treatise, pages 915–921

sustainable way. This framework is that of *socially responsible capitalism* (SRC) based on the entrepreneurial spirit, tending to exemplary behavior, putting forward the social responsibility of companies and organizations, combined with the economic responsibility and ethical efforts of each *citizen-actor* (Savall, Péron, Zardet, Bonnet, 2015).

1 WHAT IS SOCIALLY RESPONSIBLE CAPITALISM (SRC)?

SRC constitutes the theoretical and pragmatic framework of the socio-economic theory of organizational development, reconciling two overly differentiated levels of analysis: the organization and the economic and social environment. ISEOR's contribution is not restricted to the field of social responsibility limited to companies, since the company is only the capitalist microcosm (Perroux, 1948) and sustainability lies in the structures of a territory (Savall, Zardet, 2005).

There is a certain *isomorphism* of the different territorial levels: the interior of an organization, a company and its environment, a profession, or a market, a nation, a region of the world or the space of economic and social globalization (Savall, Zardet, 2005). Isomorphism allows us to understand that the different territorial levels are fields of application of the socio-economic approach to management (Bonnet, 2013). The latter is thus opposed to the monolithic conception of the firm as a self-sufficient entity as presented by Milton Friedman and the ultraliberal school (1962).

We are not making a prognosis on the imminent end of capitalism, as assumed by Joseph Stiglitz (2010), Nobel Prize winner in economics. We are not interested in capitalism as an ideology, but as the *engine of the economy*, over the centuries, and as a *catalyst of human energy* to promote growth and development. We seek to characterize a model of SRC. Our proposals are applicable to the different levels of the economic space, considered both from the perspective of *entrepreneurship* and *intrapreneurship*, acting mainly from within the company or organization, through the relatively consensual approach favored by the *socio-economic approach to management* (SEAM). The distinction between entrepreneurship and intrapreneurship emphasizes respectively the freedom to undertake in the business environment and the freedom to undertake within the organization itself.

It is not surprising to see a debate on liberalism accused of all the evils either for its insufficiencies or for its excesses and the need to make the market regulated and semi-state or, on the contrary, ultraliberal and without regulatory hindrance. Pope Francis also attacks "the ideologies that promote the absolute autonomy of markets and financial speculation, thus denying the right of control to the States" (2013).

The market has always been a primary arena for demonstrating moral responsibility, and in the eighteenth century, many books were replete with discussions of the *moral quality* of the market and its responsibility to the well-being of individuals and society. As early as the Middle Ages, the economic and social organization of the Italian and Rhenish merchant cities (Venice, Genoa, Florence, Bruges, the Hanseatic League) had already been made efficient by entrepreneurial management. Setting up of far-flung expeditions and the development of enterprises and financial instruments would not have been possible without it.

The premises of SRC are to be found in day-to-day or long-term management and not in theoretical discourses. Our conception of SRC does not originate in a sidereal void, but in the evolution of society, of production and exchange, of the gradual transition from a domestic economy to a market economy, of the creation of new financial instruments, sticking to the reality of the field.

Over the centuries, we have thus moved from a policy of impoverishing our neighbors and from pure, hardline protectionism to *laisser-faire*, from the "all-State" to the "less-State," from a so-called ultraliberalism where all blows are permitted, to the application of plethoric and binding international norms and regulations (Savall, Zardet, 2008), leading to a disoriented world where we delocalize in order to relocate, "de-industrialize" in order to then seek to revive industrial activity, as is currently the case.

The study of certain philosophical doctrines in concomitance with the evolution of the liberal approach to the world of economics allows us to better understand what underlies the symbolism of the social contract and the attachment to human values today. This leads to questions about the contribution of CSR to *democracy*, as well as the roles of the *individual and the State*, the place of *technology* and the educational role of *media*.

2 THE SOCIALLY RESPONSIBLE INDIVIDUAL: PRODUCER AND CONSUMER OF VALUE(S)

The *socio-economic approach to management* (SEAM) refuses to see the level of manpower as the inevitable adjustment variable in times of crisis, resulting not only in a reduction in manpower, but also in a reduction in working hours, a reduction in training budgets, or a freeze on salaries. Our experience shows that such a policy can only lead to the demoralization of the surviving staff and their demobilization. The *mismatch* between the supply of jobs and the requirements of the market and job seekers is often rightly attributed to the training offered by specialized institutions. This can be explained by insufficient consideration of the interests of the *individual-producer*, whose needs for accountability are ignored in current managerial and organizational practices, and whose improvement of working conditions remains *wishful thinking* (Beck, 2013).

3 RESPONSIBILITY OF THE INDIVIDUAL CITIZEN-CONSUMER-PRODUCER

In exchange for more participatory behavior, a genuine policy of internal professional training, implemented in close *proximity* to management, really mobilizes the actors in a sustainable way. The SRC recognizes, on the one hand, the need to bring the technical and professional aptitudes required by companies into line with the aspirations and expectations of employees as human beings. We therefore propose a better coupling between the life of the human citizen, "pampered, considered and solicited" (Savall, 1979; Savall, Zardet, 1995), and that of the human producer, relatively neglected and left behind. "Each individual is both a physical-chemical and socio-economic being. He/she therefore has multidimensional needs in four areas: physiology, psychology, sociology and economics" (Savall, Zardet, 2005).

The Socio-Economic Approach to Management encourages initiative and responsibility. To avoid the risk of splitting up the company's teams, it is necessary to build and rebuild an operating consensus zone. Human behavior is the result of a dialectical movement between conflict and cooperation, attraction and repulsion, a scenario well known in theatrical productions (Savall, Zardet, 2005). The outcome, to continue the metaphor, consists in reducing or eliminating the imbalances in the dynamics between conflict and cooperation through the socio-economic approach to management. It is Management's responsibility to know the existing balance between conflict and cooperation at a given moment, in order to take corrective action to re-establish an effective dosage. Many dysfunctions could be avoided by a better appreciation of the unvoiced aspects of communication and the true motivations of each person.

In companies, a multitude of actors intervene, with many facets, dimensions and stakes. When Taylor considered the consumer as the most important individual, he had forgotten the multiplicity of roles of all the people participating in the life of the company, and that the "workhorse" that, in his eyes, the basic worker represents is himself/herself a consumer who feeds the demand on the market.

It is advisable to develop an awareness of the working conditions of a person who produces compared to the person who is a citizen, who has benefited from numerous laws facilitating his/her democratic achievements and his/her development as a responsible actor in political life, or to the person who is a consumer, who is the object of all the solicitude of marketing companies or advertisers who spend considerable sums of money to keep him/her informed (Savall, Zardet, 2001, p. 3; 2005).
The *competency grid* tool meets this need, by highlighting the know-how and qualifications of individuals as sources of competitive advantage, and the *time management self-analysis* tool helps to find a more efficient use of time to develop individual scheduling , in cooperation with the partners in the activity.

The SRC aims to rehabilitate companies. It is necessary to stop considering them as hotbeds of corruption, and to recognize that they are the essential crucible for the creation of healthy value, which can only be guaranteed by the exemplary behavior of individuals (Savall, 2013).

In the context of the principle of strategic vigilance, *each person is a key element,* a true internal sensor of external information and, as such, represents a potential agent of change for the company. This is why it is essential to involve individuals at all levels of responsibility in the *decision-making and action processes,* thus leading to a better recognition of human resources value .

4 WHY DO WE NEED SOCIALLY RESPONSIBLE CAPITALISM (SRC)?

This is a capitalism that needs to be reinvented, filled with the spirit of *creation, innovation* and evolution. We are rethinking capitalism in a different way, forced by the disappearance or bankruptcy of other systems and by the disarray that this causes. Ultra-liberal financial capitalism is the worst enemy of capitalism.

We need an economic system that is sustainable. The notion of *sustainability* is intrinsic to that of *individual and collective responsibility,* which cannot be ephemeral and is maintained by daily practices, in the proximity between actors. Putting people back at the center of action (Bernácer, 1922; Savall, 1975; Perroux, 1975) makes it possible to produce economic *value* and anthropological *values* that are inseparable. This SRC is not a utopia, it has already been inscribed in the history of economic and social facts and is also *viable* in our time.

4.1 To Undertake is to Create

The Socio-Economic Approach to Management (SEAM) scheme started in 1973, but it has not lived in isolation. It has evolved, faithful to its basic leitmotiv: management and administration are synonymous with *change.* The company and the organization are living beings and only a dynamic approach is likely to enlighten us on the path to prosperity, for the greatest number, and to sustainable social and economic performance. The notion of *creation* is intrinsic to business. *To undertake is to create.* A company is also a group of people who produce economic value and *anthropological* values. It is the *crucible* in which socio-economic value is forged and elaborated. An essential motor of economic and social activity is the *project*, the movement, the creation, embodied by the *individual* and his/her capacity to involve other individuals. We adhere to the thought of Perroux (1975) who considers human beings not as a simple subject but a *project* in movement. The company or the organization is the *environment of proximity* which favors the stimulation, the development and the blossoming of the contribution of an individual to the creation of value(s) (Savall, Zardet, 2001).

4.2 Interaction with Democracy

Socially responsible capitalism is at the service of *democracy*, a universally recognized, if not practiced, value. It constitutes an economic system that contributes to *democracy* and is nourished by it. Democracy must not be virtual and intermittent, it is played out every day in the reality of human relations, whether productive or not. It is at this price that the company is exemplary. The socio-economic approach to management proposes the concept of *daily democracy of proximity*, not an electoral democracy in the usual political sense. Daily democracy of proximity contributes precisely to prolonging, rooting and reinforcing each day the practices and devices of political democracy.

4.3 Greatness and Servitude of the State

The State has an irreplaceable role to play through its great missions, where capitalism, even when it is socially responsible, can be neither legitimate, nor effective, nor efficient. These are the great sovereign missions such as education, justice, security and health. The economic mission of the State is to set the rules of the economic and social game, through democratic dialogue, and to take the initiative in piloting and financing *fundamental economic infrastructures*, either with its own public resources or with the help of private partners, within the framework of a singularly efficient mixed economic system (Zardet, Bonnet, 2008). The servitudes of the State are mainly based on the principle of a State that *respects* the individual and decentralized social groups, private, associative and public. Its specifications are to ensure the respect of the freedom of each one, of its *dignity*, of its personal or collective development.

4.4 Eminent Educational Role of the Media

The *media* have played a *historic educational role* in the advent and progress of democracy as well as in the opening to the world. Today, the media are at risk of an "irresponsible" overflow of a certain use of *social networks.* This threat is also an opportunity for the media to recover their educational function of channeling and to assume their responsibilities in this cacophonous concert, by contributing to the growth of democracy. The condition of this renewal of the media is to cultivate the critical spirit of the citizen reader and to avoid the drift towards a kind of clientelism demagogy of bad taste, source of exacerbation of the fights in the society.

4.5 The "Tamed" Technology, Immanent Creation of the Human for the Human

The history of more than two centuries has revealed a phenomenon of *technological idolatry.* This can be seen in the loss of a critical mindset in the face of technological investment decisions, where any purchase of machines appears to be a rational decision that goes in the direction of history. Economic models have never questioned the fact that technology is *not naturally* complementary to human action and that it can be diverted from its purpose. However, technology is a creation of humans, whose legitimacy is proven when it is put at the service of humankind because at the core of its mission. Well mastered technology is a precious tool that has a multiplier effect on economic value and social values. For example, information and communication technologies facilitate access to information and education. Technological investment is rational from a socio-economic point of view, provided that resources are devoted to the integrated training of users, producers and clients, in the form of *intangible investments* in the *qualitative development of human potential.* SRC must promote this mastery of *citizen technology,* the fruit of individual and collective human genius, through debate, dialogue and *reconstructive* criticism.

4.6 Building Instead of Destroying

The resolution of economic and social problems and challenges has historically swung between two diametrically opposed options and recommendations: struggle or recourse to social dialogue based on *negotiation.* Some theories and ideologies have favored struggle in their recommendations. Recent history has shown that their effects are not convincing, as can be seen by observing and analyzing the current state of interminable world crisis since 1973. The constructive path of *creative negotiation* deserves to be better exploited, at all levels of society and at all stages of projects.

Our objective is not to propose small quick remedies in the face of the acuteness of the crisis, but *sustainable* solutions to be invented. It is not a *pro domo* plea but a roadmap for companies, organizations, consultants, teachers and researchers. However, we hope that politicians, journalists and all civil society actors will find in it material and tools for constructive reflection that will bring hope.

REFERENCES

Beck, E. (2013). Le développement de l'homme, producteur et consommateur dans les loisirs. *in* Agir dans un nouveau monde : le développement et les coûts de l'homme. Proceedings of the François Perroux Conference, December 7, 2010. ISEOR publisher.

Bernácer, G. (1922). La teoría de las disponibilidades como interpretación de las crisis y del problema social, *Revista nacional de economía,* n° 40, noviembre-décembre.

Bonnet, M. (2013). Growth and development poles. Cas de la Métropole lyonnaise, in Agir dans un nouveau monde: le développement et les coûts de l'homme. Proceedings of the François Perroux Conference, December 7, 2010. ISEOR Publisher.

Friedman, M. (1962). *Capitalism and Freedom.* Chicago: The University of Chicago Press.

Perroux, F. (1948). *Le capitalisme.* Paris : Presses Universitaires de France.

Perroux, F. (1975). Unités actives et mathématiques nouvelles. Révision de la théorie de l'équilibre économique général (*Active units and new mathematics. Revision of the theory of general economic equilibrium).* Paris: Dunod.

Perroux, F. (1979). L'entreprise, l'équilibre rénové et les coûts cachés», preface to the book Savall, H. *Reconstruire l'entreprise,* Paris: Dunod.

Savall, H. (1973, 1975). *G. Bernácer: l'hétérodoxie en science économique.* Paris : Dalloz, Collection des Grands Économistes.

Savall, H. (1979). *Reconstruire l'entreprise ; analyse socio-économique des conditions de travail.(Reconstructing the firm; socio-economic analysis of working conditions). Paris:* Dunod.

Savall, H. (2013) Individu, entreprise et nation : comment se crée le PIB ? in *Agir dans un nouveau monde : le développement et les coûts de l'homme.* Proceedings of the François Perroux Conference, December 7, 2010. ISEOR Publisher.

Savall, H., Péron, M. (2015) Socially Responsible Capitalism in Buono, A., Savall, H. (eds), *The Socio-Economic Approach to Management revisited: the Evolving Nature of SEAM in the 21st Century.*Charlotte, USA: IAP.

Savall, H., Péron, M., Zardet, V., Bonnet, M. (2015), *Le capitalisme socialement responsable existe,* Caen : EMS.

Savall, H., Zardet, V. (1995), *Ingénierie Stratégique du roseau,* Paris, Economica.

Savall, H., Zardet, V. (2001). Contribution of the socio-economic theory of organizations to the continuation and valorization of the work of François Perroux in the 21st century.. 21–40 In *Humanisme et Travail chez François Perroux.* Paris: Economica.

Savall, H., Zardet, V. (2005). *Défis et dynamique de la tétranormalisation.* Paris: Economica.

Savall, H., Zardet, V. (2008). Tetranormalization and the new rules of the game: contribution of socio-economic theory. In *Comment vivre ensemble : conditions économiques de la démocratie.* P.99–150. Proceedings of the François Perroux Conference, February 12, 2008. ISEOR Publisher.

Stiglitz, J. E. (2010). *Freefall: America, Free Markets, and the Sinking of the World Economy.* New York: Norton & Co.

Zardet, V., Bonnet, M. (2008). Public-private partnerships. In *Comment vivre ensemble: conditions économiques de la démocratie.* P.151–172. Proceedings of the François Perroux Conference, February 12, 2008. ISEOR Publisher.

This page intentionally left blank.

AFTERWORD

R. Murray Lindsay

The Treatise makes a valuable addition to the corpus of writings about SEAM that Savall and his colleagues have produced over the last half century. It leaves me with the following general impressions. First, reading the opening chapter by Savall and Zardet (SZ) reminds me that SEAM is a difficult theory for a novice to comprehend which must certainly contribute to why it is not well known in North America. SEAM consists of a plethora of foreign, non-intuitive concepts (e.g., "generic contingency") that stand as a barrier for appreciating the richness and novelty of this theory because they do not travel well or easily. That being said, SZ's chapter (along with others) will be invaluable to newcomers wanting to learn SEAM and for those writing about it because, in a single source, it provides updated and authoritative definitions, explanations, clarifications, and synthesis of SEAM's key concepts.

Second, SZ's chapter provides the reader with a Lakatosian sense of the *progressiveness* of the research program over time as witnessed by the increasing theoretical content and discovery of new empirical facts that flow from the paradigm's "hard core" which (on my interpretation) reflects the pre-eminence of human potential over capital in the process of creating economic value. This guiding view led early-on to the need to actively manage the chronic resurgence of dysfunction and value destruction giving rise to the key concept of hidden costs. It would be an interesting exercise to formally document the nature of this progressiveness over time in Lakatos' (1970) terms. Doing so might also serve to explain the interconnections among the various concepts and their logic.

Third, several of the chapters reveal how SEAM can be expected to become increasingly relevant in the future because it is equipped to assist organizations in managing challenges and societal expectations involving such matters as "doing good", protecting the environment, providing work-life balance, employee retention, hypercompetition, and the increasing malaise in developed societies. Faced with such issues, SEAM's concepts of

SEAM Treatise, pages 923–926

socially responsible capitalism, sustainable economic performance, and socio-economic performance are needed now more than ever to integrate the expectations of *all* the organization's stakeholders (rather than just shareholders) as the links between business and society become redefined. The key notion introduced by these terms is one of "balance" (Chapter 22 captures this nicely), where SEAM has demonstrated (to my mind) that long run economic sustainability can only be achieved by investing in social and societal performance due to their complementarity because economic value and human value are inseparable; it is not charity or utopian. In addition, SEAM has provided the management tools and calculus for both the motivation and accomplishment of these ideas.

Fourth, the various chapters (and their authors) reveal the breadth of SEAM's application. They show the concepts being applied to for-profit (private or public), not-for-profit, and governmental organizations, both large and small, in a number of different countries and cultures. They also show that the theory covers a wide range of academic disciplines and foci: accounting, cybernetics and general systems theory, economics, human resource management, consultancy, leadership, management, management control, operations, organizational development and change, research methods and their epistemological foundations, social issues in management, sociology, and strategy (both creating and implementing). In addition, SEAM is a highly practical theory in that several of the chapters are written by practitioners describing how they have applied the concepts, which implies a market-based validation of ideas (see Kasanen et al. 1993). Importantly, this breath of application across disciplines, within practice, and across geographic borders suggests that SEAM's concepts possess a degree of "hardness" or invariance that transcends the context of their original formulation – a defining feature of scientific knowledge (Ravetz 1971).

This accomplishment not only demonstrates that acquiring genuine knowledge about organizations is possible, but it also suggests how it is developed in a manner that stands in marked contrast with today's career-oriented science based on accumulating one-off "hits." SEAM's development was based on a 50-year cumulative research program involving more than 2,100 intervention-research projects (referred to as "scientific consultancy" by SZ) that provided researchers with the opportunity to intimately observe organizational phenomena "in vivo" through written documents, discussions with actors, and witnessing behavior. The program was conducted within a spirit of openness to learning and not with a fixed mindset focused on confirmation, seemingly consistent with Popper's (1963) view of science (i.e., conjectures and refutations). More specifically, this approach facilitated acquiring facts (robust empirical generalizations) about organizations and the people within them (e.g., the TFW virus, the five natural characteristics of humans that question the subordination of employees to their superiors, the ongoing dialectic between conflict-cooperation guiding actor behavior) that provides the explanandum to be explained; permitted the client to act as a partner in the co-production of knowledge through their "validation" of researcher observations; and allowed researchers to systematically *experiment* with new ideas. By evaluating client performances periodically and learning from their "failures", and by approaching phenomena with a variety of theoretical lens due to the multi-disciplinary constitution of the ISEOR team, the researchers were in a position to revise their theoretical framework(s) and research procedures based on the accumulated evidence. Finally, the research team focused on abstracting (translating) local findings into higher level generalizations (i.e., what SEAM calls "generic contingency") that are resistant to trivial refutations. The development of SEAM is a splendid example of what Van de Ven (2007) calls "engaged scholarship."

SEAM's emphasis on developing generic contingencies deserves further comment because it has led to a universal theory that any organization can use despite their idiosyncratic nature. SEAM does not tell organizations what to do; instead, it provides a generic change platform (see below), methods, and tools that can be used by organizations to understand and manage their own situation in line with their particular circumstances.

The success described above did not occur by happenstance, which leads to our next and final observation. Savall and colleagues were highly attentive to and reflective on methodological matters and epistemology, and it is useful to draw out the implications of their methodological contributions for managing organizations to better understand SEAM. Specifically, SEAM introduced a number of principles (cognitive interactivity, contradictory intersubjectivity) and practices (qualimetrics, horivert method, the mirror-effect) in response to recognizing that the complexity of understanding organizational reality leads to diverse and parochial interpretations. These innovations reflect that the (philosophically discredited) notion of a simplistic, objective (neutral) reality that underlies the conventional functionalist paradigm—a view that serves to propagate the TFW virus by placing management at the center of rationality—must be abandoned and replaced with the social construction of reality that Gephart (2014) refers to as "deliberative democracy." Together with the importance SEAM attaches to taking a systems view, transparency, the contribution of every individual ("intrapreneurship"), and the proximity principle, this shared construction of reality assists in countering the powerful forces impeding strategic adaptation that Foster and Kaplan (2001) have coined as "cultural lock-in", leads to increased buy-in of decisions, and meets anthropologic needs connected with fulfillment. Further, this crucial idea in combination with the fact (established by ISEOR researchers) that organizations are always in flux and revert to disequilibrium (dysfunction), suggests that SEAM is best viewed, following Hamel and Zanini (2014), as a "change platform" because change is ongoing and should not be initiated and managed from the top (see Cappelletti et al. 2015).

In closing, one can only be in awe of this highly innovative and original overarching theoretical framework of organizations and their management that a reading of the Treatise will serve to convey.

—R. Murray Lindsay
University of Lethbridge
Alberta, Canada
Former President of the Management Accounting Section,
American Accounting Association

REFERENCES

Cappelletti, L., Lindsay, R.M. and Ennajem, C. The Socio-Economic Approach to Management Control. *The Socio-Economic Approach to Management Revisited: The Evolving Nature of SEAM in the 21st Century* (A.F Buono and H. Savall editors). Charlotte, North Carolina: Information Age Publishing, 2015: 75–102.

Foster, R., and Kaplan, S. (2001). *Creative Destruction: Why Companies that are Built to Last Underperform the Market—and How to Successfully Transform Them.* New York: Doubleday.

Gephart, R.P., Jr., Deliberating Cost: Deliberative Practices in Qualimetrics and the Socio-Economic Approach to Management. *In Facilitating the Socio-Economic Approach to Management* (H. Savall, J. Conbere, A. Heorhiadi, et al. eds.), Charlotte, NC: Information Age Publishing, 2014.

Kasanen, E. Lukka, K., & Siitonen, A. (1993). The constructive approach in management accounting research. *Journal of Management Accounting Research, 5*, 243–264.

Lakatos, I. (1970). Falsification and the methodology of scientific research programmes. In *Criticism and the Growth of Knowledge*, edited by I. Lakatos and A. Musgrave. Cambridge: Cambridge University Press, 91–196.

Popper, K. R. (1963). *Conjectures and refutations.* London: Routledge and Kegan Paul.

Ravetz, J. R. (1971). *Scientific knowledge and its social problems.* New York: Oxford University Press.

Van de Ven, A. H. (2007). *Engaged Scholarship: A Guide for Organizational and Social Research.* Oxford, UK: Oxford University Press.

APPENDICIES

This page intentionally left blank.

APPENDIX A

MAIN GENERAL REFERENCES ON THE SOCIO-ECONOMIC APPROACH TO MANAGEMENT (SEAM) THEORY

(in addition to the references found at the end of the chapters)

For a comprehensive bibliography, browse the ISEOR website http://164.132.163.82/SiteIseor/publications.asp

BOOKS

Ansoff, H. I. (1981). Preface to Savall's book *"Work and people; an economic evaluation of job enrichment."* New York: Oxford University Press; 2nd edition Charlotte in 2010., USA: IAP.

Bernácer, G. (1945). *La doctrina funcional del dinero* [The functional doctrine of money]. Aguilar, Madrid.

Bernácer, G. (1955). *Una economía libre sin crisis y sin paro* [A free economy without crisis and unemployment]. Aguilar, Madrid.

Boje, D. (2015). Preface to the book Savall H., Péron M., Zardet V. et Bonnet M., *Socially Responsible Capitalism and Management,* New York: Routledge.

Boje, D. (2004). Preface, in Savall & Zardet, *Recherche en sciences de gestion: approche qualimétrique. Observer l'objet complexe,* Paris: Economica. Translated into English: *Qualimetrics: Observing the complex object,* Charlotte: IAP.

Boje, D.(ed.) (2011). *Storytelling and the Future of Organizations; an Antenarrative Handbook.* New York: Routledge.

Boje, D., Gephart, R., & Thatchenkery, T.J. (1995). *Postmodern Management and Organization Theory.* London: Sage Publications.

Brignone A., Lambert J., Martinet A., & Savall H. (1978), *Encyclopédie de l'économie. Le présent en question,* (*Encyclopedia of Economics. The present in Question*) Larousse, Paris.

Buono A.F., & Savall, H. (eds.) (2007). *Socio-Economic Intervention in Organizations – The intervener-researcher and the SEAM approach to organizational analysis,* Information Age Publishing, Charlotte.

Buono A.F., & Savall, H. (eds.) (2015). *The Socio-Economic Approach to Management Revisited: the Evolving Nature of SEAM in the 21st Century,* Information Age Publishing, Charlotte.

SEAM Treatise, pages 929–934

Buono, A., Savall, H., Cappelletti, L. (2018). *La recherche-intervention. De la conceptualisation à la publication* [Intervention-research: From Conceptualization to Publication]. Charlotte, USA: IAP.

Cappelletti, L., & Hoarau, C. (2013). *Finance & Contrôle au quotidien: 100 fiches.* Avant-propos de René Ricol. (*Finance & Control in everyday life: 100 sheets.* Foreword by René Ricol) Paris: Dunod. https://doi.org/10.3917/dunod.cappe.2013.01

Cappelletti, L., Pigé, B., Zardet, V. (2015). *Dynamique Normative: arbitrer et négocier la place de la norme dans l'organisation* [Normative Dynamics: arbitrating and negotiating the place of norms and standards in the organization]. Caen, France: EMS.

Carré, J.J., Dubois, P., Malinvaud, E. (1972). *La croissance française. Un essai d'analyse économique causale de l'après-guerre* [French growth. An attempt at causal economic analysis of the post-war period]. Paris, France : Seuil.

Conbere, J., Heorhiadi, A. (2018). *Socio-economic Approach to Management: The Steering Organizations Into the Future.* World Scientific Publishing.

Delay-Termoz, R. (1982). La valorisation des résultats de la recherche. L'insertion des résultats de la recherche dans les enseignements de 2e et 3e cycles. In Savall, H. *Gestion socio-économique innovatrice: stratégie des entreprises et évolution des emplois.* (*The valorization of research results. The insertion of research results in graduate and post-graduate courses.* In Savall, H. *Innovative socio-economic management: business strategy and job evolution)* Lyon: ISEOR *éditeur.*

Delay-Termoz, R. (2009). Création de l'ISEOR en 1975 et premiers partenariats. In. H. Savall & V. Zardet (coord.), *Management socio-économique: une approche innovante.(Creation of ISEOR in 1975 and first partnerships.* In. H. Savall & V. Zardet (coord.), *Socio-economic appraoch to management: an innovative approach)* Paris: Economica

Delors, J. (1974–75), Preface to H. Savall's book , *Enrichir le travail humain dans les entreprises et les organisations,* (Preface to the H. Savall's book, *Enriching human work in companies and organizations),* Special Mention of the I.A.E. Management Prize, Paris: Dunod.

Emery, F. E., Trist, E., L. (1960). *Socio-Technical Systems.* Management Sciences.

Ennajem, C., (2011). *Évolution du rôle du contrôleur de gestion* [Evolution of the management controller role]. Sarrebruck, Germany: European University Publishing.

Fayol, H., (1916). *Administration générale et industrielle.* [General and Industrial Administration] Paris: Gauthiers Villars.

Gephart, R. (2018a), Preface to the third edition, Savall, H. *Radical origins to economic crises: Germán Bernácer a visionary precursor.* Palgrave, London: McMillan.

Gephart, R. (2018b), *The Routledge Companion to Risk, Crisis and Emergency Management.* Palgrave, London: McMillan.

ISEOR. (2003). *L'Université citoyenne : progrès, modernisation, exemplarité* [The Citizen University: progress, modernization, exemplarity]. Paris, France: Economica.

Péron, M., (coord.) (1999). Réflexion sur la transdisciplinarité dans la pensée managériale, *Transdisciplinarité: fondement de la pensée managériale anglo-saxonne ? (Reflection on transdisciplinarity in managerial thinking,* In *Transdisciplinarity: foundation of Anglo-Saxon managerial thinking?)* , Paris: Economica.

Perroux, F. (1975). *Unités actives et mathématiques nouvelles* [Active units and new mathematics]. Paris, France: Dunod.

Perroux, F. (1979). L'entreprise, l'équilibre rénové et les coûts «cachés», préface au livre Savall, H. *Reconstruire l'entreprise,* (*The enterprise, the renovated balance and the hidden costs),* preface to the H. Savall's book *Reconstructing the enterprise*) Paris: Dunod.

Piaget, J. (1975). *L'équilibration des structures cognitives, problème central du développement (The balancing of cognitive structures, a central problem in development),* Paris: PUF.

Plane, J-M., (2000). *Méthodes de recherche-intervention en management* [Research-intervention methods in management]. France: L'Harmattan.

Reynaud J-D., (1974). *Rapport remis au Ministre du travail, de l'emploi et de la population: les aspects techniques, économiques et financiers de la valorisation des tâches d'exécution* [Report submitted to the French Minister of Labour, Employment and Population: the technical, economic and financial aspects of the valuation of executive tasks]. Paris.

Savall, H. (1973–1975a), *G. Bernácer: L'hétérodoxie en science économique* (*G. Bernácer: Heterodoxy in economics*), Dalloz, Collection Les Grands Economistes, Paris. Translated into Spanish: *Germán Bernácer: La heterodoxia en la economía* (1983), Editorial Publicaciones del Instituto de Estudios Alicantinos, Spain.

Savall H. (1974–1975b), *Enrichir le travail humain dans les entreprises et les organisations,*(*Enriching human work in companies and organizations*) Special mention of the I.A.E. Management Prize, Paris. Prefaced by Jacques Delors, Paris: Dunod. New expanded edition 1989, Economica, Paris.Translations into Spanish, Dutch, and English: English translation (1981), *Work and People. An economic evaluation of job enrichment,* Prefaced by H. Igor Ansoff, London: Oxford University Press. Translated into Spanish (1977), *Por un trabajo más humano,* Madrid: Tecniban; 2nd edition in 2010, IAP, Charlotte (NC, USA).

Savall H. (1979a), *Reconstruire l'entreprise. Analyse socio-économique des conditions de travail,* Préface de François Perroux (*Reconstructing the company. A socio-economic analysis of working conditions,* Preface by François Perroux), Paris: Dunod. Réédition Savall H., & Zardet V. (2014), Paris: Dunod.

Savall H. (1984), *Méthodologies fondamentales en gestion,* Actes de colloque, (*Fundamental methodologies in management,* conference proceedings) ISEOR-FNEGE-CNRS, France.

Savall H. (1985), *Méthodologies fondamentales en gestion: l'implicite et le normatif dans les modèles,* (*Fundamental methodologies in management, Implicit and normative aspects of models*). Conference proceedings; actes de colloque, ISEOR-FNEGE-CNRS, France.

Savall H. (1986), *Méthodologies fondamentales en gestion. Qualité des informations scientifiques en gestion,* (*Fundamental methodologies in management. Quality of scientific information in management,* Proceedings) Actes de colloque, ISEOR-FNEGE-CNRS, France.

Savall H. (2012), *Origine radicale des crises: Germán Bernácer, précurseur visionnaire.* Information Age Publishing, Charlotte (NC, USA), Translated into English (2018), *Radical origins to economic crises: Germán Bernácer a visionary precursor.* London: Palgrave, McMillan.

Savall, H. (2018). *Radical origins to economic crises: Germán Bernácer a visionary precursor.* Palgrave, London: McMillan.

Savall H., & Fernández Ruvalcaba M. M. (2004). *El modelo de Gestión Socio-Económica en Organizaciones Mexicanas,* (*The Socio-Economic Approach to Management in Mexican Organizations*) Universidad Autonoma Metropolitana, Mexico.

Savall H., Péron M., Zardet V., & Bonnet M. (2015), *Le capitalisme socialement responsable existe,* Caen, France: EMS. Translated into English (2017), *Socially Responsible Capitalism and Management,* New York: Routledge.

Savall H., & Zardet V. (1987), Maîtriser les coûts et les performances cachés. Le contrat d'activité périodiquement négociable, (*Mastering hidden costs and performance: the periodically negotiable activity contract*) Harvard-L'Expansion Award of Strategic Management, Paris: Economica. Translated into English (2008), *Mastering Hidden Costs and Socio-Economic Performance,* Information Age Publishing, Charlotte (NC, USA).

Savall H., & Zardet V. (1992), *Le nouveau contrôle de gestion. Méthode des coûts performances cachés,* (*Innovative Management Control: Hidden Costs and Performance Methodology*). Paris: Éditions Comptables Malesherbes-Eyrolles.

Savall H., & Zardet V. (1995), *Ingénierie stratégique du roseau, souple et enracinée,* Paris: Economica, 2° édition 2005. Translated into Spanish (2009), *Ingeniería estratégica: un enfoque socioeconómico,* Ed. UAM, México. In English (2017), *Strategic Engineering of the Reed, flexible and rooted,* IAP, Charlotte (NC, USA).

Savall H., & Zardet V. (2004), *Recherche en Sciences de Gestion: Approche Qualimétrique: observer l'objet complexe,* Préface de David BOJE, Paris: Economica. Translated into English (2011), *The Qualimetrics approach, observing the complex object,* IAP, Charlotte (NC, USA).

Savall H., & Zardet V. (2005), *Tétranormalisation: défis et dynamiques.* Paris: Economica. Translated into English (2013), *The dynamics and Challenges of Tetranormalization,* IAP, Charlotte (NC, USA).

Savall H., & Zardet V. (2007), *Evaluación de desempeño y gestión socioeconómica,* Gobierno del Estado de Yucatán (México). (*Performance evaluation and Socio-Economic Approach to Management.* Government of the Yucatan State).

Savall, H., Zardet, V. (2021). *Traité du management socio-économique: Théorie et Pratiques.* Caen, France: EMS.

Savall H., Zardet V., & Bonnet M. (2000, 2008), *Releasing the untapped potential of entreprises through socio-economic management,* ILO, Geneva. Spanish version (2000), *Mejorar los desempeños ocultos de las empresas a través de una gestión socioeconómica,* BIT, Genève. In French: *Libérer les performances cachées des entreprises et organisations par un management socio-économique,* Bureau International du Travail (BIT), Genève (2000)

Tabatoni, P., & Jarniou, P. (1975). *Les systèmes de gestion. Politiques et structures.* (*Management systems: policies and structures*) Paris: Presses Universitaires de France.

Taylor, F.W. (1911) *Scientific Management,* New-York: Harpers and Brothers; 2nd French Edition, 1957: *La direction scientifique des entreprises,* Paris: Dunod.

Weber, M., (1924, 1964). *The theory of social and economic organization.* New York: Free Press.

Worley C., Zardet, V., Bonnet M., & Savall A. (2015), *Becoming agile. How the SEAM approach to management builds adaptability.* New Jersey, USA: John Wiley.

ARTICLES AND PAPERS

Bernácer, G. (1922). La teoría de las disponibilidades como interpretación de las crisis y del problema social [The theory of availabilities as an interpretation of crises and of the social problem]. R*evista nacional de economía.*

Boje, D. M., & Rosile, G. A. (2003). Comparison of socio-economic and other transorganizational development methods. *Journal of Organizational Change Management, 16(1), 10–20.*

Buono, A.F. (2003), SEAM-less post-merger integration strategies: a cause for concern, *Journal of Organizational Change Management,* 2003.

Krief N., & Zardet, V. (2013), Analyse de données qualitatives et recherche-intervention [Qualitative data analysis and intervention-research], *Revue Recherches en sciences de gestion- Management Sciences – Ciencias de Gestión* (2), 211–237.

Moisdon, J.-C., (1984). Recherche-intervention et gestion [Intervention-research and management], *Revue française de gestion,* n°47-48, september-october.

Péron, M., & Péron, M. (2003). Postmodernism and the socio-economic approach to organizations. *Journal of Organizational Change Management, 16*(1), 49–55.

Quesada Sánchez, F. J. (2020). El origen radical de las crisis económicas – Germán Bernácer precursor visionario (The radical origin of the economic crises - Germán Bernácer a visionary precursor). *Revue Recherches en sciences de gestion – Management sciences – Ciencias de gestión. 135*: 173–190.

Sardier, M. (1989). Mobiliser les ressources humaines pour libérer la productivité (Mobilizing human resources to unlock productivity). In Maëder, R. (coord.) *Compétences financières pour l'entreprise* (Financial skills for companies). Paris : CEPP.

Savall, H.(1974), Conditions de travail du personnel d'encadrement (*Working conditions of managers*) In *Le Creuset,* supplément 659, 25 mai.

Savall, H. (1977), Propositions en vue de développer la contribution de la formation initiale à l'amélioration des conditions de travail, (*Proposals to develop the contribution of initial training to the improvement of working conditions*), *Revue Enseignement et Gestion,* n° 3.

Savall, H. (1978b), À la recherche des coûts et performances cachés de l'entreprise pour un diagnostic socio-économique de l'entreprise (*In search of the company's hidden costs and performance for a socio-economic diagnosis of the company*) , *Revue Française de Gestion,* n° 18.

Savall, H. (1977, 1978a), Propos d'étape sur la régulation socio-économique de l'entreprise par la recherche de la compatibilité de l'efficience économique et du développement humain (*A step-by-step proposal on the socio-economic regulation of the company through the search for the compatibility of economic efficiency and human development*), *Revue Économie appliquée,* n° 4.

Savall, H. (1979b), La dimension psychologique de l'analyse socio-économique des conditions de vie au travail (*The psychological dimension of the socio-economic approach to working conditions*). *Bulletin de psychologie.* n°344, pp. 443–448.

Savall, H. (1984), Comptabilité et décision (*Accounting and decision-making*), *Colloque de l'Association Française de Comptabilité*, Nice. In Cahiers de l'IAE de Nice, n° 16.

Savall, H. (1985), Le développement socio-économique de l'entreprise et ses enjeux *(The development of companies and its stakes), Revue Française de Gestion,* n° 52.

Savall, H. (1987), Coûts cachés et analyse socio-économique des organisations (*Hidden costs and the socio-economic analysis of organizations*), In *Encyclopédie du management,* 2e éd., Economica.

Savall, H. (1989), Professeur-consultant: le bilan d'une expérience (*Professor-consultant: the results of an experience*) , *Revue Française de Gestion,* n° 76.

Savall, H. (2003b), An update presentation of the socio-economic management model and international dissemination of the socio-economic model, *Journal of Organizational Change Management,* 16(1), 33–48.

Savall, H. (2003a), Socio-Economic Approach to Management, *Journal of Organizational Change Management* (special issue), Emerald.

Savall, H. & Fière, D., (2014), Étude comparative de méthodologies de recherche en médecine et en gestion. Cas de la recherche-intervention socio-économique d'ordre qualimétrique (Comparative study of research methodologies in medicine and management. The case of socio-economic qualimetric intervention-research). *Journal de gestion et d'économie médicales, 32*(5).

Savall, H., & Péron, M. (2007), Raising the curtain on business. Operation theatrics, *Revue Sciences de gestion – Management Sciences – Ciencias de gestión,* n° 58.

Savall, H., Péron, M., & Zardet, V. (2016), Human Potential at the Core Socio-Economic theory (SEAM). In J. Conbere & H. Savall (Eds.), *Decoding the Socio-Economic Approach to Management.* Charlotte: Information Age Publishing.

Savall, H., Savall, A., & Zardet V. (2018), New Trends in Organizational Challenges and Need for Change: The ISEOR Research Programs, *Organization Development Journal.* Winter.

Savall, H., & Zardet, V. (1985), Où va la recherche en sciences de gestion? (*Where is the research in management sciences going?*), *Revue Française de Gestion,* n° 53–54.

Savall H., & Zardet, V. (1986a), Les sciences de gestion en France: tendances actuelles (*Management sciences in France: current trends*), *Le Courrier du CNRS,* n° 64.

Savall, H., & Zardet, V. (1986b), Un regard sur la recherche en sciences de gestion en France dans les années 80 (*A look at management science research in France in the 1980s*) , In *La recherche en sciences économiques et en gestion,* Édition du CNRS.

Savall, H., & Zardet, V. (1996), La dimension cognitive de la recherche-intervention: la production de connaissances par interactivité cognitive (*The cognitive dimension of intervention-research: knowledge production through cognitive interactivity*), *Revue Internationale de Systémique,* 10 (1–2), 157–189.

Savall, H., & Zardet, V. (1997), Vers la "pensée en action" stratégique ou le non-dit dans le discours sur la stratégie. Propositions pour améliorer la qualité scientifique des recherches en stratégie (*Towards strategic «thinking in action» or the unspoken in the discourse on strategy. Proposals for improving the scientific quality of strategy research), Revue Management International.*

Savall, H., & Zardet, V. (2001), Coûts-performances cachés et gestion des ressources humaines (*Hidden costs & performance and HRM*) , In *Encyclopédie des Ressources Humaines.* Paris: Vuibert.

Savall, H., & Zardet, V. (2005a), Améliorer la gouvernance des systèmes complexes: le cas de la filière-territoire «Sortie du Monde Hospitalier et Retour à Domicile» (*Improving the governance of complex systems: the case of the «Discharge from Hospital and Return to Home» network*), *Revue Santé et Systémique.*

Savall, H., & Zardet, V. (2005b), Processus participatif de changement pour une performance socio-économique durable: cas évalués d'entreprises et d'organisations (*Participatory change processes for sustainable socio-economic performance: evaluated cases of companies and organizations), revue Gestion 2000.*

Savall, H., & Zardet, V. (2008), Le concept de coût-valeur des activités. Contribution de la théorie socio-économique des organisations (*The concept of cost-value of activities. Contribution of the socio-economic theory of organizations*), *Revue Sciences de gestion – Management Sciences – Ciencias de gestión.*

Savall, H., & Zardet, V. (2011b, 2013), La RSE, lien entre l'individu, l'organisation et la société: nouvel énoncé de la théorie socio-économique (*The Corporate Social Responsibility as a link between the individual, the organization and the society: new statement of the socio-economic theory*), Congrès ADERSE, Brest. Published in *Management et sciences sociales*, n°14.

Savall, H., & Zardet, V (2011a) Linking individual, organizational and macro-economic performance levels: Hidden costs model , *Academy of Management Conference*, Orlando.

Savall, H., & Zardet, V (2014a), Action research and intervention-research in the French landscape of organizational research. *International Journal of Organizational Analysis*, Vol. 22 ISS 4, 551–572.

Savall, H., & Zardet, V (2014b), La théorie du socle stratégique et l'effet de levier de la cohésion (*The strategic bedrock theory and the leverage effect of cohesion*). *Academy of Management & ISEOR conference.* Lyon.

Savall, H., & Zardet, V (2016), Strategic Bedrock Theory and the Cohesion Leverage Effect, The *Theory and Practice of Socio-Economic Management Journal* (USA). Volume 1, issue 1.

Savall, H., & Zardet, V (2017), The difference between management consultancy and research-intervention. A report on a method, and a study of the advantages and drawbacks for researchers and companies *The Theory and Practice of Socio-Economic Management Journal.* (USA). Volume 1, issue 2 .

Savall, H., Zardet, V., Bonnet, M., & Cappelletti L. (2019), Valorisation de la recherche par l'expérimentation en entreprise. Cas du modèle de management socio-économique (*Valorization of research through experimentation in companies. Case of the socio-economic management model*), *Revue Française de Gestion.* Special issue «La valorisation de la recherche», 7 , n°284.

Savall, H., Zardet, V., Bonnet, M., & Péron, M. (2008), The Emergence of Implicit Criteria Actually Utilized by Reviewers of Qualitative Research Articles: Case of a European Journal, *Organizational Research Methods*, vol 11, issue 3, 510–540.

Savall, H., Zardet, V., Péron, M., & Bonnet, M. (2012), Possible Contributions of Qualimetrics Intervention-Research Methodology to Action Research, *International Journal of Action Research*, Vol 8, Issue 1, 29 p.

Savall, H., Zardet, V., Péron, M., & Bonnet, M. (2014), Potential contribution of the socio-economic approach to management to a better integration of CSR norms and economic standards: Case study of a pastry company. *Society and Business Review, 9* (3), 232–242.

Sorensen, P. F, Yaeger, T. F., Savall, H., Zardet, V., Bonnet, M., & Péron, M. (2012), A Review of Two Major Global and International Approaches to Organizational Change: SEAM and Appreciative Inquiry. *Organization Development Journal, 28*(4), 31–39.

Yanat, Z., Bonnet, M. (coord.) (2021), Responsabilité sociétale des enseignants-chercheurs en management (Social responsibility of management professor-researchers). Special Issue. *Management et sciences sociales, 30,* January–June.

Zardet V.(1985), Des systèmes d'informations vivants: étude des conditions d'efficacité à partir d'expérimentations (*Living information systems: study of the conditions of effectiveness from experiments),* Revue *Sciences de Gestion, Économies et Sociétés*, n° 6.

Zardet V., & Bonnet V. (2018), Henri Savall: Connecting the Dots between OD and Economic Performance, In Szabla D. (Ed.), *The Palgrave Handbook of Organizational Change Thinkers* Palgrave Ed. 1–16.

APPENDIX B

List of Doctoral Dissertations Prepared at the ISEOR Institute, Under the Direction of the Institute's Research Directors, Since 1976

N°	Nom	Prénom	Titre	Année
1	Savall	Henri	Germán Bernácer, économiste espagnol (1883–1965). Une théorie générale de l'emploi, de la rente et de la thésaurisation : Thèse d'État ès sciences économiques, Université Paris 2). *(Germán Bernácer, Spanish economist (1883–1965). A general theory of employment, rent and hoarding: PhD in economics, University of Paris 2)*	1973
2	Savall	Henri	L'enrichissement du travail humain dans les organisations: Thèse complémentaire en sciences de gestion, Université Paris 9-Dauphine. *(The enrichment of human work in organizations: Doctoral thesis in management sciences, University of Paris 9-Dauphine).*	1974
3	Grivel	Michel	L'impact du style de gestion des dirigeants et cadres sur la nature des conditions de vie au travail en milieu informatisé. *(Impact of the management style of company directors and executives on the nature of working conditions in a computerized administrative environment).*	1980
4	Mardonet Rencoret	Gloria Jeannette	Étude de l›application de l›accord national sur les classifications de la métallurgie dans cinq entreprises de la région lyonnaise. *(Study of the application of the national agreement on classifications in the metallurgy industry in five companies in the Lyon region).*	1980
5	Beck	Emmanuel	Équilibration formation-emploi et changement de structure des qualifications en milieu industriel. *(Training-employment matching and change in the structure of qualifications in an industrial environment).*	1980
6	Bonnet	Marc	Transformation du statut de la maîtrise au sein d'un processus de restructuration des emplois dans les ateliers en milieu industriel. *(Transformation of the status of supervisors within a process of job restructuring in industrial workshops).*	1981
7	Thomas	Jean	La prise en compte du mode de vie dans la gestion des ressources humaines: le cas d'une population de «jeunes». *(Taking lifestyle into account in human resources management: the case of a "young" population).*	1981

(continued)

SEAM Treatise, pages 935–952

List of Doctoral Dissertations Prepared at the ISEOR Institute, Under the Direction of the Institute's Research Directors, Since 1976 (continued)

N°	Nom	Prénom	Titre	Année
8	Uzan	Odile	Contribution à l'élaboration d'un modèle opératoire d'évaluation du comportement économique d'une organisation face à l'aléa. L'exemple de l'absence au poste de travail. (*Contribution to the elaboration of an operational model for the evaluation of the economic behavior of an organization in the face of hazards. The example of absenteeism*).	1982
9	Zardet	Véronique	Vers une gestion socio-économique de l'hôpital. *(Towards a socio-economic approach to hospitals management)*.	1982
10	Enríquez-Galván	Oscar	Analyse socio-économique des conséquences sur les conditions de vie au travail des décisions stratégiques de transfert de technologie. Cas d'entreprises mexicaines. (*Socio-economic analysis of the consequences of strategic technology transfer decisions on working conditions. Cases of Mexican companies*).	1982
11	Labaume	Gérard	Nouvelles technologies et gestion socio-économique innovatrice. Étude de convergence stratégique dans des cas d'entreprises industrielles. *(New technologies and innovative socio-economic management. Study of strategic convergence in industrial companies)*.	1983
12	Bartoli	Annie	Actions d'innovation socio-économique dans des entreprises industrielles. Analyse de la phase de généralisation et méthodologie du pilotage. *(Socio-economic innovation actions in industrial companies. Analysis of the generalization phase and piloting methodology)*.	1983
13	Hermel	Philippe	Information et mise en oeuvre stratégique. Étude de cas d'entreprises. *(Information and strategic implementation. Company case studies)*.	1983
14	Fernández-Ruvalcaba	Martha M.	Interactions entre conditions de vie au travail et conditions de vie hors du travail. Applications à des cas d'innovation socio-économique. *(Interactions between work and non-work life conditions. Applications to cases of socio-economic innovation)*.	1984
15	Marques Teixeira	Claudio	Du contenu du travail vers la gestion: analyse critique d'un processus de changement organisationnel dans une entreprise industrielle portugaise. *(From work content to management: critical analysis of an organizational change process in a Portuguese industrial company)*	1984
16	Niktabe	Saied	Vers un modèle socio-économique d'évaluation de la capacité créative de l'atelier de production. Étude de cas de la capacité créative des nouvelles formes d'organisation du travail en milieu industriel. *(Towards a socio-economic model for evaluating the creative capacity of the production workshop. Case study of the creative capacity of new forms of work organization in an industrial environment)*.	1984
17	Feugier	Dominique	De l'interêt d'un département de compensation au sein d'une enterprise industrielle. Essai d'évaluation socio-économique. *(The interest of a compensation department within an industrial company. Essay of socio-economic evaluation)*.	1984

(continued)

List of Doctoral Dissertations Prepared at the ISEOR Institute, Under the Direction of the Institute's Research Directors, Since 1976 (continued)

N°	Nom	Prénom	Titre	Année
18	Zardet	Véronique	Contribution des systèmes d'informations stimulants à l'efficacité de l'entreprise: Thèse d'État. (*Contribution of stimulating information systems to the efficiency of the company: State doctorate thesis*).	1986
19	Bocquillion	Michel	Perspectives nouvelles dans l'évaluation des emplois. L'apport des approches socio-techniques et socio-économiques. *(New perspectives in job evaluation. The contribution of socio-technical and socio-economic approaches)*.	1986
20	Triki	Mohammed	L'informatisation des réseaux financiers. (*The computerization of financial networks*).	1986
21	Bonnet	Marc	Liaisons entre organisation du travail et efficacité socio-économique. Analyse d'expérimentations dans des services de fabrication en milieu industriel: Thèse d'État. (*Links between work organization and socio-economic efficiency. Analysis of experiments in manufacturing departments in an industrial environment: State doctorate thesis*)	1987
22	Merle	Françoise	La gestion des compétences, condition préalable à une formation utile à la stratégie d'entreprise. *(Competence management, a prerequisite for training useful to the company's strategy.)*	1988
23	Guillaume	Yves	Recherches expérimentales sur la gestion hospitalière. Apports de l'analyse socio-économique et de l'analyse psycho-sociale pour débusquer et réduire le mimétisme soignants-soignés. *(Experimental research on hospital management. Contributions of socio-economic analysis and psycho-social analysis to detect and reduce caregiver-patient mimicry)*.	1989
24	Lallé	Béatrice	Changement technique, innovation produit et performance socio-économique en agences bancaires. (*Technical change, product innovation and socio-economic performance in bank branches*).	1989
25	Harbi	Nouria	Système expert en diagnostic d'entreprise. *(Expert system in business diagnosis)*.	1990
26	Amoroso Lima	Marcelo	Qualité d'utilisation des ressources dans l'émergence technologique: recherche-expérimentation, diagnostic et propositions de solutions. *(Quality of resource use in technological emergence: research-experimentation, diagnosis, and proposed solutions)*.	1991
27	Deubel-Hirniak	Christine	Pratiques organisationnelles et de pilotage des cadres: diagnostic, transformation et cas d'expérimentations. *(Organizational and management practices of executives: diagnosis, transformation, and experimental cases)*.	1992
28	Boge	Anne	Gestion innovante des organisations de service public. *(Innovative management of public service organizations)*.	1992
29	Buthion	Valérie	La décentralisation synchronisée: un principe de management moteur pour accroître l'efficacité des organisations. *(Synchronized decentralization: a driving management principle to increase the efficiency of organizations)*.	1993

(continued)

List of Doctoral Dissertations Prepared at the ISEOR Institute, Under the Direction of the Institute's Research Directors, Since 1976 (continued)

N°	Nom	Prénom	Titre	Année
30	Rocher	Odile	Apport d'un modèle dynamique des relations de travail à la connaissance des processus d'innovation. *(Contribution of a dynamic model of work relations to the knowledge of innovation processes).*	1993
31	Boussofara	Sami	Acquisition et maîtrise technologique dans les entreprises tunisiennes. Incidences des structures mentales et apports de la gestion socio-économique. *(Acquisition and technological mastery in Tunisian companies. Impact of mental structures and contributions of socio-economic management).*	1993
32	Nobre	Thierry	La structuration des entreprises en phase post-création et de pré-développement. L'apport de l'intervention socio-économique. *(The structuring of companies in the post-creation and pre-development phase. The contribution of the socio-economic intervention)*.	1993
33	Trigui	Ezzeddine	Dysfonctionnements, comportement vivant au travail et performances socio-économiques: application à des entreprises tunisiennes. *(Dysfunctions, living behavior at work and socio-economic performance: application to Tunisian companies).*	1994
34	Barth	Isabelle	Propositions pour un marketing interne-externe innovant. Éléments théoriques et de mise en œuvre. *(Proposals for an innovative internal-external marketing. Theoretical elements and implementation).*	1994
35	Plane	Jean-Michel	Contribution de l'intervention en management au développement de l'entreprise. *(Contribution of management intervention to the development of the company).*	1994
36	Cornu-Demont	Nathalie	Pour des politiques et des pratiques de gestion des ressources humaines conciliant performance sociale et performance économique. *(For human resources management policies and practices that reconcile social and economic performance).*	1995
37	Walter-Seifart	Rolf	Stratégie commerciale internationale de la firme—Intégration des systèmes experts. *(International business strategy of the firm—Integration of expert systems)*.	1996
38	Faure	Caroline	Le transfert de savoir-faire d'ingénierie en management des cabinets conseils aux entreprises. L'apprentissage organisationnel dans les enterprises. *(The transfer of management engineering know-how from consulting firms to companies. Organizational learning in companies).*	1996
39	Tillet-Bernard	Évelyne	La contribution d'un système de rémunération de la performance à l'efficacité des entreprises et des organisations: un enjeu stratégique. *(The contribution of a pay-for-performance system to the efficiency of companies and organizations: a strategic issue).*	1996
40	N'Kanagu	Gervais	Contribution de la méthode de formation intégrée à l'amélioration des performances des entreprises de l'Afrique Centrale—Cas au Burundi. *(Contribution of the integrated training method to the improvement of the performance of enterprises in Central Africa—Case in Burundi).*	1996

(continued)

List of Doctoral Dissertations Prepared at the ISEOR Institute, Under the Direction of the Institute's Research Directors, Since 1976 (continued)

N°	Nom	Prénom	Titre	Année
41	Benollet	Philippe	Principe de régulation sociale: le rapport structuro-comportemental dialectique-recherche expérimentale. *(Principle of social regulation: the structure-behavior relationship dialectic-experimental research).*	1996
42	Écoto	François	Les critères d'évaluation de la compétitivité et performance d'une entreprise. *(Criteria for evaluating the competitiveness and performance of a company).*	1996
43	Thouverez Giboudot	Chantal	Contribution du management socio-économique dans l'amélioration de la qualité des prestations et du fonctionnement des services hospitaliers. *(Contribution of socio-economic management in improving the quality of services and the operation of hospital services).*	1996
44	Gaschet	René	Vers un management socio-économique des collectivités locales ? Obstacles et réalités. *(Towards a socio-economic management of local authorities ? Obstacles and realities).*	1997
45	Mrabet	Mansour	L'implication modulaire de l'individu dans les processus stratégiques—expérimentation dans les entreprises et les organisations tunisiennes. *(The modular involvement of the individual in strategic processes—experimentation in Tunisian companies and organizations).*	1997
46	Bruneau-Duperron	Nathalie	Contribution à l'amélioration de la qualité des politiques et des pratiques de recrutement. *(Contribution to the improvement of the quality of recruitment policies and practices).*	1997
47	Bensalem	Radouane	Des incidences des coûts cachés sur le système d'information de comptabilité et leurs répercussions sur les décisions stratégiques et opérationnelles des entreprises et des organisations. Cas d'expérimentation. *(The impact of hidden costs on the accounting information system and their impacts on the strategic and operational decisions of companies and organizations. Experimental cases).*	1997
48	Bernadet	Anne Claire	Contribution des pratiques de toilettage à l'amélioration du fonctionnement des organisations. (*Contribution of clean-up practices to the improvement of the functioning of organizations).*	1997
49	Voyant	Olivier	Contribution à l'élaboration d'un système de veille stratégique intégré pour les PME-PMI. *(Contribution to the design of an integrated vigilance strategic system for SMEs).*	1997
50	Roulle	Pascal	L'amélioration du pilotage des frontières de la formation continue. Cas d'expérimentations auprès d'organismes d'enseignement et de service. *(Improvement of the management of the borders of continuous training. Experimentation cases with teaching and service organizations).*	1997
51	Boulanger	Georges	L'usage des systèmes informatiques dans la performance économique et sociale des organisations: contribution méthodologique à l'intégration des systèmes sociaux et des systèmes informatiques. *(The use of computer systems in the economic and social performance of organizations: a methodological contribution to the integration of social systems and computer systems).*	1997

(continued)

List of Doctoral Dissertations Prepared at the ISEOR Institute, Under the Direction of the Institute's Research Directors, Since 1976 (continued)

N°	Nom	Prénom	Titre	Année
52	Tamo	Kianvu	Proposition d'un modèle interprétatif du développement humain susceptible d'améliorer les performances des organisations africaines: applications à l'administration publique angolaise. *(Proposal of an interpretative model of human development likely to improve the performance of African organizations: applications to the Angolan public administration).*	1998
53	Cappelletti	Laurent	L'ingénierie d'audit d'activité d'une entreprise: la production d'intelligence socio-économique. *(Engineering of the audit of a company's activity: the production of socio-economic intelligence).*	1998
54	Garcia	Manuel	Adaptation des méthodes de contrôle de gestion à une conception de la productivité intégrant la dimension qualité. *(Adapting management control methods to a conception of productivity integrating the quality dimension).*	1998
55	Haim	Patrick	Contribution et adaptabilité d'une représentation neuronale de l'intelligence informationnelle à la performance des organisations. *(Contribution and adaptability of a neural representation of informational intelligence to the performance of organizations).*	1998
56	Delattre	Miguel	Contribution à l'élaboration d'un mode de pilotage de l'organisation à forte composante bénévole. Analyse spectrale du pilotage de l'organisation vivante. *(Contribution to the elaboration of a steering mode of the organization with a strong voluntary component. Spectral analysis of the living organization steering).*	1998
57	Kammoun	Hatem	Equilibration du rôle des cadres: un essai de modélisation pour une conduite du changement et du développement de l'efficience de fonctionnement des PME; cas de la Tunisie. *(Balancing the role of managers: an attempt to model for a conduct of change and development of the efficiency of operation of SMEs; case of Tunisia).*	1998
58	Carvalho Da Silva	Rosimeri de Fatima	Management de la qualité totale et les changements du contrôle organisationnel. Le cas d'une usine sidérurgique brésilienne. *(Total quality management and changes in organizational control—The case of a Brazilian steel plant).*	1999
59	Colin	Pascal	Vocation d'entreprise et stratégies innovantes de création d'emplois. *(Business vocation and innovative strategies for job creation).*	1999
60	Drevet-Prunet	Géraldine	Quelle polyvalence développer à l'hôpital pour concilier les objectifs de soins et objectifs socio-économiques. Cas des hôpitaux publics. *(What kind of multi-skilling should be developed in hospitals to reconcile care and socio-economic objectives? The case of public hospitals).*	1999
61	Bousta-Jullien	Yasmine	Vers un management public communal: interactivité structurelle et cognitive, pertinence et efficacité de l'action publique communale. *(Towards a communal public management: structural and cognitive interactivity, relevance, and efficiency of communal public action).*	1999

(continued)

List of Doctoral Dissertations Prepared at the ISEOR Institute, Under the Direction of the Institute's Research Directors, Since 1976 (continued)

N°	Nom	Prénom	Titre	Année
62	Davoine	Éric	Comportements au travail et gestion du temps des managers. Une étude franco-allemande comparée. *(Work behaviors and time management of managers. A comparative Franco-German study).*	1999
63	Krief	Nathalie	Les pratiques stratégiques des organisations sanitaires et sociales de service public. *(Strategic practices of public service health and social organizations).*	1999
64	Leymarie	Stéphane	La gestion des investissements immatériels. Cas d'expérimentation dans des entreprises industrielles. *(The management of intangible investments. Case studies of experiments in industrial companies).*	1999
65	Romero Urrego	Ricardo	Traduction de la démarche stratégique dans le management des hôpitaux publics. Le cas de la Colombie. *(The introduction of the strategic approach to public hospitals management. The case of Colombia).*	2000
66	Bertézène	Sandra	Les démarches qualité dans les hôpitaux français. *(Quality processes in French hospitals).*	2000
67	Chalus-Sauvannet	Marie-Christine	Dynamisation du dispositif de veille stratégique pour la conduite de stratégies proactives dans les secteurs industriels. *(Dynamization of the strategic intelligence system for the conduct of proactive strategies in industrial sectors).*	2000
68	Antoine	Stéphane	Système intégré d'approche du contrôle vers la gouvernance conciliant l'économique et le social. Cas du secteur de l'habitat. *(Social Integrated system of approach from control to governance reconciling the economic and the social. Case of the social housing sector).*	2000
69	Bonhomme	Claude	Contribution au management des processus de construction par l'élaboration d'un système de régulation finalisée de leurs activités élémentaires. *(Contribution to the management of construction processes through the development of a system of finalized regulation of their elementary activities).*	2000
70	Yamurémye	Hercule	Contribution de pratiques de délégation concertée à l'amélioration du fonctionnement des équipes de direction. Cas d'expérimentations innovantes dans des PME burundaises. *(Contribution of concerted delegation practices to the improvement of the functioning of management teams. Case of innovative experiments in Burundian SMEs)*	2001
71	Leckie	Christine	Déterminer les conditions de pertinence de la norme ISO 9001 pour l'assurance de la qualité des soins (*(Determining the conditions of relevance of the ISO 9001 standard for quality assurance of care).*	2001
72	Grijalvo	Christian	Proposition d'un modèle d'évaluation de l'action collective pour un management stratégique des organisations *(Proposal of an evaluation model of collective action for a strategic management of organizations).*	2001
73	Aman	Abdelajid	La formation intégrée, méthode de gestion des compétences: expérimentation dans une administration publique marocaine *(Integrated training, a method for managing skills: experimentation in a Moroccan public administration)*	2001

(continued)

List of Doctoral Dissertations Prepared at the ISEOR Institute, Under the Direction of the Institute's Research Directors, Since 1976 (continued)

N°	Nom	Prénom	Titre	Année
74	Lahlali	Mustapha	Le management des organismes de formation professionnelle au service du pilotage des systèmes de formation. Cas d'expérimentation au Maroc (*The management of vocational training organizations in the service of training system management. Case study in Morocco)*	2001
75	Noguera	Florence	Management stratégique du temps de travail: instrumentation et impacts de l'aménagement-réduction du temps de travail (*Strategic management of working time: instrumentation and impacts of the organization-reduction of working time)*	2002
76	Ocler	Rodolphe	Vers la notion de stratégie pro-active: éléments de définition et de mise en œuvre (*Towards the notion of pro-active strategy: elements of definition and implementation)*	2002
77	Demissy	Benjamin	Étude des impacts des nouvelles technologies d›information et de communication sur les performances *(Study of the impact of new information and communication technologies on performance)*	2002
78	Moulette	Pascal	Contribution à la gestion de la remédiation aux situations d'illettrisme en entreprise *(Contribution to the management of the remediation of illiteracy situations in companies)*	2002
79	Rymeyko	Karine	Enjeux stratégiques des professions libérales réglementées, mutation des pratiques de management et impacts sur la performance. Cas des offices de notaires *(Strategic issues of regulated liberal professions, changes in management practices and impacts on performance. The case of notaries' offices)*	2002
80	Faisant	Jean-Paul	Développement d'une gestion des compétences en contexte de changement organisationnel. Cas d'expérimentation industrielle (*Development of skills management in a context of organizational change. Case of industrial experimentation)*	2003
81	Srajek	Benjamin	Revalorisation du rôle managérial de l'encadrement de proximité (*Revalorization of the managerial role of front line management*	2003
82	Bourcieu	Stéphane	Le développement international des PME par l'action sur l'environnement institutionnel: «La stratégie d'ascendance institutionnelle». Application aux pays en transition. *(The international development of SMEs through action on the institutional environment: "The strategy of institutional ascendancy." Application to countries in transition)*	2004
83	González	Gerardo	Los desafíos para el cambio en organizaciones públicas en México. Dos casos de innovación tecnológica en el sistema de transporte colectivo de la ciudad de México *(Challenges for change in public organizations in Mexico. Two cases of technological innovation in the public transportation system)*	2004
84	Saint Léger	Guy	Quel processus de changement peut permettre une mise en œuvre et une utilisation efficace et efficiente d'un système d'information de type ERP dans les moyennes structures de production de biens et de services ? *(What process of change can enable the effective and efficient implementation and use of an ERP-type information system in medium-sized goods and services production structures?)*	2005

(continued)

List of Doctoral Dissertations Prepared at the ISEOR Institute, Under the Direction of the Institute's Research Directors, Since 1976 (continued)

N°	Nom	Prénom	Titre	Année
85	Looky	Léni	Proposition d'une gestion de type socio-économique pour l'amélioration des performances (*Proposal of a socio-economic type of management for performance improvement*)	2005
86	Martínez Vázquez	Griselda	La contribution du management socio-économique à l'aménagement des performances économiques et sociales. Cas d'expérimentation dans trois petites entreprises mexicaines (*The contribution of socio-economic management to the development of economic and social performance. Case of experimentation in three small Mexican companies*)	2005
87	Kauffman	Xavier Émile	Face aux défis des organisations innovantes du 3ème millénaire: apports de la stratégie d'auteur à la croissance socio-économique (*Facing the challenges of innovative organizations in the 3rd millennium: contributions of the author's strategy to socio-economic growth*)	2005
88	Henriot	Julien	Génération et gestion d'une dynamique coopérative entre intervenants-chercheurs et acteurs praticiens (*Generation and management of a cooperative dynamic between researchers and practitioners*)	2005
89	Moore	Rickie	Évaluation de la performance économique durable des entreprises—Méthodes et pratiques américaines et européennes (*Evaluation of the sustainable economic performance of companies—American and European methods and practices*)	2005
90	Goter	Françoise	Étude du système de sanctions-récompenses en lien avec la performance des organisations de service public (*Study of the sanctions-reward system in relation to the performance of public service organizations*)	2005
91	Tabchoury	Patrick	La mise en œuvre du changement par l'introduction de la démarche socio-économique dans les hôpitaux privés au Liban (*Implementing change by introducing the socio-economic approach in private hospitals in Lebanon*)	2006
92	Hillon	Mark Edward	A comparative analysis of socio-ecological and socio-economic strategic change methodologies	2006
93	El Mekdessi	Selim	La relation entre le management socio-économique et la certification ISO, dans le secteur bancaire libanais (*The relationship between socio-economic management and ISO certification in the Lebanese banking sector*)	2006
94	Chapon	Évelyne	La violence dans les établisements scolaires secondaires: quels changements organisationnels nécessaires? Cas de recherche-intervention dans des lycées professionels publics et privés (*Violence in secondary schools: what organizational changes are needed? Case of intervention-research in public and private vocational high schools*)	2006
95	Peñalva Rosales	Laura Patricia	Inducción al aprendizaje organizacional en la Universidad pública para el desarrollo de estrategias de vinculación con el sector productivo (*Induction to organizational learning in the public university for the development of linkage strategies with the productive sector*)	2006

(continued)

List of Doctoral Dissertations Prepared at the ISEOR Institute, Under the Direction of the Institute's Research Directors, Since 1976 (continued)

N°	Nom	Prénom	Titre	Année
96	Ramírez Alcántara	Hilda	Elementos estructurantes de la confianza y su relación con el desempeño en una universidad pública mexicana *(Structuring elements of trust and its relationship with performance in a Mexican public university).*	2006
97	Lafarge	Hervé	Mesure de la responsabilité sociale des entreprises et des organisations, cas d'évaluation socio-économique d'organisations de l'économie sociale et solidaire (*Measuring the social responsibility of companies and organizations, a case of socio-economic evaluation of organizations in the social and solidarity economy)*	2006
98	Sánchez Trejo	Víctor	Construction d'un processus de prise de décision stratégique dans la PME pour améliorer sa performance globale: recherche-intervention dans une entreprise mexicaine (*Construction of a strategic decision-making process in the SME to improve its global performance: intervention-research in a Mexican company)*	2006
99	González Pérez	Claudia Rocío	L'organisation créatrice de connaissances. L'organisation synaptique *(The knowledge-creating organization. The synaptic organization)*	2006
100	Briones Rodríguez	Brenda Marcela	Les enjeux de l'interaction entre les comportements et les compétences, et son impact sur la coopération entre les individus. Cas de trois PME mexicaines (*The challenges of the interaction between behaviors and skills, and its impact on cooperation between individuals. Case of three Mexican SMEs)*	2006
101	Datry	Frantz	Les performances des projets de conception et de fabrication de décors lyriques. Cas d'expérimentation dans un opéra national (*The performance of design and manufacturing projects for opera sets. Case of experimentation in a national opera)*	2006
102	Brindis Almazán	María de Lourdes	Les structures organisationnelles du développement socio-économique local: Cas de la communauté artisanale au Mexique *(Organizational structures of local socio-economic development: the case of the artisanal community in Mexico)*	2007
103	Pomar Fernández	Silvia	La nature hybride des organisations et le processus de transfert de modèles. Cas des crêches subventionnées au Mexique *(The hybrid nature of organizations and the process of model transfer. The case of subsidized day care centers in Mexico)*	2007
104	Fontanel	Gautier	Les transformations structurelles des clubs sportifs: recherche d'un cadre d'analyse approprié à leur gestion (*Structural transformations of sports clubs: the search for an appropriate analytical framework for their management)*	2007
105	Bonnet	Daniel	Le pilotage de la transformation en environnement de coopération inter-organisationnelle essence socio-économique de la transformation et des stratégies de transformation *(The management of transformation in an environment of inter-organizational cooperation socio-economic essence of transformation and transformation strategies)*	2007
106	Ibarra Cortés	Mario Eduardo	Stratégie et gestion financières. Le cas de la municipalité de San Luis Potosí au Mexique *(Financial strategy and management. The case of the municipality of San Luis Potosí in Mexico)*	2007

(continued)

List of Doctoral Dissertations Prepared at the ISEOR Institute, Under the Direction of the Institute's Research Directors, Since 1976 (continued)				
N°	**Nom**	**Prénom**	**Titre**	**Année**
107	Mousli	Morad	L'efficience du système budgétaire comme conséquence du style de management stratégique des directions générales: cas des sociétés cotées françaises (*The efficiency of the budgetary system as a consequence of the strategic management style of top management: the case of French listed companies*)	2007
108	Amari Cherif	Amina	Gestion des compétences dans les organisations publiques en Tunisie *(Skills management in public organizations in Tunisia*	2007
109	Payre	Sébastien	Analyse du stress dysfonctionnel au travers de la dégradation de la performance socio-économique des moyennes entreprises *(Analysis of dysfunctional stress through the degradation of the socio-economic performance of medium-sized companies)*	2007
110	Rey	Emmanuelle	Manager les comportements au travail inefficaces cas des comportements déviants non violents (*Managing ineffective work behaviors: the case of non-violent deviant behaviors)*	2008
111	Petit	Renaud	Les stratégies de développement du couple attractivité-fidélisation des organisations envers les jeunes entrants sur le marché du travail (*Strategies for developing the attractiveness and loyalty of organizations towards young people entering the job market)*	2008
112	Ozdemir	Adnan	Impacts des styles de management des dirigeants sur les performances de l'organisation de la police. Cas de la Turquie *(Impacts of the management styles of the leaders on the performance of the police organization. The case of Turkey)*	2008
113	Dávila	Andrés	La gestion de la petite entreprise internationale, langage commun de management et compétences interculturelles *(The management of the small international company, common management language and intercultural competencies)*	2009
114	Guillot	Bernard	Contribution à une méthodologie d'évaluation des compétences entrepreneuriales. L'exemple des étudiants des grandes écoles françaises *(Contribution to a methodology for assessing entrepreneurial skills. The example of students from French "Higher schools")*	2009
115	Thiébaut-Bertrand	Anne	Contribution à l'analyse des stratégies de reconfiguration d'activité permettant de préserver et d'améliorer le rapport qualité des prestations-maîtrise des coûts à l'hopital: cas de la transfusion sanguine dans les hôpitaux publics français *(Contribution to the analysis of activity reconfiguration strategies allowing to preserve and improve the quality of services/cost control in hospitals: the case of blood transfusion in French public hospitals)*	2010
116	Pierre	Xavier	Pilotage institutionnel des coopérations interorganisationnelles dans la mise en oeuvre de stratégies territoriales: cas d'acteurs de l'efficacité énergétique et du développement durable *(Institutional management of inter-organizational cooperation in the implementation of territorial strategies: the case of energy efficiency and sustainable development actors)*	2010
117	Bouyoud	Floriane	Le management stratégique de la responsabilité sociale des entreprises *(Strategic management of corporate social responsibility)*	2010

(continued)

List of Doctoral Dissertations Prepared at the ISEOR Institute, Under the Direction of the Institute's Research Directors, Since 1976 (continued)

N°	Nom	Prénom	Titre	Année
118	Thiam	Fatou	Pilotage de la performance socio-économique dans les organisations en réseau dans les pays en voie de développement. Cas de recherche-intervention au Sénégal *(Steering socio-economic performance in networked organizations in developing countries. Case of intervention-research in Senegal)*	2010
119	Dorantes	Patricia	Les stratégies proactives pour l'amélioration de la compétitivité internationale des PME au Mexique *(Proactive strategies for improving the international competitiveness of SMEs in Mexico)*	2010
120	Khenniche	Samia	Contribution à l'étude de la dynamique coopérative intra-organisationnelle: analyse croisée des coopérations transversales, verticales et horizontales *(Contribution to the study of intra-organizational cooperative dynamics: cross-analysis of transversal, vertical and horizontal cooperations)*	2010
121	Ennajem-Savall	Cécile	Évolution du rôle du contrôleur de gestion dans un contexte de contrôle de gestion décentralisé *(Evolution of the role of the management controller in a context of decentralized management control)*	2011
122	Ben Hassen	Noura	Le développement de l'employabilité dans les organisations: une aide à la rénovation des politiques et des pratiques de GRH et à l'accroissement des performances. Cas d'entreprises industrielles tunisiennes (*The development of employability in organizations: an aid to the renovation of HRM policies and practices and to the increase of performance. Case of Tunisian industrial companies)*	2011
123	Sy	Issiaga Thiam	Étude des liens entre l›appropriation des normes IAS/IFRS et les dimensions organisationnelles et managériales des services comptables (*Study of the links between the appropriation of IAS/IFRS standards and the organizational and managerial dimensions of accounting departments)*	2011
124	(Caillat) Horvath	Isabelle	Développement d'outils de management et actes de langage dans les entreprises de spectacle vivant (*Development of management tools and language acts in performing arts companies)*	2011
125	Seghier	Sofiane	Le pilotage des interfaces organisationnelles. Contribution à l'équilibration des processus d'intégration-différenciation des organisations *(Management of organizational interfaces. Contribution to the balancing of integration-differentiation processes in organizations)*	2012
126	Makdessi	Riad	Organisation du travail et qualité de service dans le secteur bancaire libanais: la mise en œuvre du changement par le management socio-économique (*Work organization and service quality in the Lebanese banking sector: the implementation of change through socio-economic management)*	2012
127	Fakhfakh	Hanen	Le management socio-économique et la mise en œuvre d'une démarche de qualité intégrale dans un établissement d'enseignement supérieur en Tunisie *(Socio-economic management and the implementation of an integral quality approach in a higher education institution in Tunisia)*	2012

(continued)

List of Doctoral Dissertations Prepared at the ISEOR Institute, Under the Direction of the Institute's Research Directors, Since 1976 (continued)

N°	Nom	Prénom	Titre	Année
128	Girisit	Hermine	Gérer la résistance au changement: contribution de la mesure des niveaux de résistance des acteurs dans les projets de changement *(Managing resistance to change: the contribution of measuring the level of resistance of actors in change projects)*	2012
132	Gourine	Réda	Enjeux et performance socio-économique d'actions proactives et innovantes de gestion des risques qui s'appuient sur la tradition de solidarité *(Challenges and socio-economic performance of proactive and innovative risk management actions based on the tradition of solidarity)*	2013
130	Roche	Alexis	Reconnaissance et performance: proposition du concept de reconnaissance-activatrice et d'un modèle intégrateur *(Recognition and performance: proposal of the concept of recognition-activation and an integrating model)*	2013
131	Damaj	Kamar	La transformation des organisations publiques au Liban et son impact sur la qualité de service et la satisfaction des usagers *(The transformation of public organizations in Lebanon and its impact on service quality and user satisfaction)*	2013
132	Lassoued	Yousri	L'essaimage stratégique. Cas des entreprises tunisiennes *(Strategic spin-offs. The case of Tunisian companies)*	2013
133	Zakkour-Tabchoury	Donabelle	Développement des compétences managériales comme levier des performances économiques et sociales: cas de l'encadrement infirmier dans les hôpitaux privés du Liban *(Development of managerial skills as a lever for economic and social performance: the case of nursing management in private hospitals in Lebanon)*	2013
134	Drhourhi	Mohamed	Les pratiques du management de la santé et de la sécurité au travail dans les entreprises marocaines *(Occupational health and safety management practices in Moroccan companies)*	2014
135	Desmaison	Gérard	Durabilité des méthodes de management dans les organisations. Cas des projets de management socio-économique *(Sustainability of management methods in organizations. The case of socio-economic management projects)*	2014
136	Foure-Joopen	Helga	La dynamique coopérative inter-organisationnelle dans les réseaux innovants : le facteur confiance dans le cas de deux clusters français *(Inter-organizational cooperative dynamics in innovative networks: the trust factor in the case of two French clusters)*	2014
137	Torres	Arnaud	Pilotage de la transmission des compétences et des savoir-faire par le manager de proximité comme facteur de développement et de performances socio-économiques *(Steering the transfer of skills and know-how by the local manager as a factor of development and socio-economic performance)*	2014
138	Frachette	Marc	Le pilotage médico-pharmaceutique: vers une plus grande légitimité de la pharmacie hospitalière par la coopération avec les services cliniques. Cas de recherches-interventions en hôpital public *(Medical-pharmaceutical management: towards greater legitimacy of hospital pharmacy through cooperation with clinical departments. Cases of intervention-researches in public hospitals)*	2014

(continued)

List of Doctoral Dissertations Prepared at the ISEOR Institute, Under the Direction of the Institute's Research Directors, Since 1976 (continued)

N°	Nom	Prénom	Titre	Année
139	Savall-Zardet	Amandine	Les facteurs endogènes de performance durable de l'internationalisation de l'entreprise familiale: cas longitudinal de recherche-intervention *(The endogenous factors of sustainable performance of the internationalization of the family business: longitudinal case of intervention-research)*	2014
140	Fernandez	Guillaume	Mesure et lisibilité de la performance globale et durable: modélisation d'un tableau de bord de pilotage intégrateur *(Measurement and readability of global and sustainable performance: modelling of an integrative piloting logbook)*	2015
141	Combaudon	Christophe	L'amélioration conjointe des structures et des comportements, facteur de survie-développement des entreprises en phase de création *(The joint improvement of structures and behaviors, a factor of survival and development of companies in the creation phase)*	2015
142	Girard	Stephen	Contribution à l'analyse des pratiques de coopération inter-organisationnelle territorialisée. Le cas de l'insertion par l'activité économique *(Contribution to the analysis of inter-organizational territorialized cooperation practices. The case of integration through economic activity)*	2015
143	Ruat	Thibault	Le management stratégique des coopérations entre parties prenantes d'un projet de construction. Cas d'entreprises de maîtrise d'œuvre du bâtiment *(Strategic management of cooperation between stakeholders in a construction project. The case of construction management companies)*	2016
144	Salmeron	Jérémy	Le processus d'innovation socio-économique: un processus ambidextre? *(The socio-economic innovation process: An ambidextrous process?)*	2016
145	François	Pierre	La conduite d'une stratégie de différenciation dynamique. Recherche-intervention dans une PME hybride *(The conduct of a dynamic differentiation strategy. Intervention-research in a hybrid SME)*	2016
146	Farah	Soleil	Enhancing performance of information systems in healthcare through Socio-Economic Approach to Management. Case of a Private Hospital in Lebanon	2017
147	Saab	Rony	Efficiency improvement through Socio-Economic Approach to supply chain management: A case study on Shipping Lines Companies (SLC)	2017
148	El Haddad	Pierre	Prescriptive management practice between theory and measurable outcomes: improving performance of an international inspection and certification body	2017
149	Kuran	Omaya	SEAM contribution to meet the internal and external challenges in a private Lebanese University	2017
150	El Hajjeh	Maya	The Link between Internal Strategy and Overall Performance. Application of Socio-Economic Approach to management in a multi-activity family business in Kingdom of Saudi Arabia	2017
151	Saba	Habib E.	Sustaining profitability in the marketing industry in Saudi Arabia through SEAM implementation	2017

(continued)

List of Doctoral Dissertations Prepared at the ISEOR Institute, Under the Direction of the Institute's Research Directors, Since 1976 (continued)

N°	Nom	Prénom	Titre	Année
152	Olleik	Adel	Increasing profitability by minimizing hidden costs in hospital inpatient revenue cycle using SEAM	2017
153	Nehme	Ziad N.	Socio-economic contribution to health care strategic planning	2017
154	Al Rabaa	Sally	Classical management vs SEAM impact on hospital operations improvement and accountability program	2017
155	Sawaya	Rana A.	Sketching innovative goals to integrate accreditation standards in higher education institutions through socio-economic approach to management	2017
156	Masry	Jihane	Strategic human resource management on small family business	2017
157	Kobrossi	Jamil	A socio-economic tool for a systematic performance: The case of a Hospital in North Lebanon	2017
158	Mazen	Hazim	Investigating the impact of Socio-Economic Management theory on East Mediterranean healthcare employee performance intervention-research case study	2017
159	Vachon	Marc	Maîtriser les stratégies de décision: positionnement prescriptif, ébauche et test d'un modèle-outil d'aide à la résolution de problèmes pour les dirigeants des organisations *(Mastering decision strategies: prescriptive positioning, drafting, and testing of a problem-solving model-tool for organizational leaders)*	2017
160	Boko	Violette	La professionnalisation managériale des responsables d'établissements scolaires privés au Bénin par le management socio-économique *(The managerial professionalization of private school managers in Benin through socio-economic management)*	2017
161	Rasolofoarisoa	Andry	La transformation des contraintes normatives en opportunités: cas d'organisations du secteur médico-social *(The transformation of normative constraints into opportunities: the case of organizations in the medico-social sector)*	2017
162	Rouveure	Thomas	Vers une performance globale et durable de la micro-entreprise en phase de post-naissance. L'impact des compétences de l'entrepreneur *(Towards a global and sustainable performance of the micro-enterprise in the post-birth phase. The impact of the entrepreneur's skills)*	2017
163	Rateau	Maïté	Contributions des managers d'établissements médico-sociaux au développement d'une fonction commerciale orientée client *(Contributions of managers of medico-social organizations to the development of a customer-oriented sales function)*	2017
164	Holtz	Théo	Les mutations du management dans les «entreprises libérées»: vers un renouveau du leadership? *(Changes in management in "liberated companies": towards a renewal of leadership?)*	2017
165	Barakat	Raghida	Business development of banking sector through SEAM methodology. Case of Lebanese banking	2018
166	Kassab	Jack	How to improve attractiveness and motivation in small businesses?	2018
167	Dabboussy	Habiba	Reducing the costs of diabetes complications through the socio-economic theory	2018

(continued)

List of Doctoral Dissertations Prepared at the ISEOR Institute, Under the Direction of the Institute's Research Directors, Since 1976 (continued)

N°	Nom	Prénom	Titre	Année
168	Moussa	Firas	Linking sales performance to corporate governance in SME's and family businesses in the Middle East: The case of an electric products distributor in Lebanon	2018
169	Bassil	Dolly	Developping public organizations through an innovative change approach: an intervention in Lebanon	2018
170	El Hajjeh	Rim	Overcoming organizational change challenges through SEAM: Construction company in the state of Qatar	2018
171	Al Mallah	Mohamad	Contribution of the Socio-Economic Approach to Management (SEAM) to the information and telecommunication sector	2018
172	Khabbaz	Lara	The SEAM contribution to the management of theatrical performances: the case of Château Trianon - Lebanon	2018
173	Chaanine	Luciana	Applying the socio-economic approach to improve efficiency and employees' performance in NGOS: The case on an autism center	2018
174	El Masri El Shaarani	Abdul Karim	Improving efficiency in startup enterprises; evidence from Lebanon	2018
175	El Mallah	Ali	Contribution of Socio-Economic Approach to Management to the banking industry in Lebanon	2018
176	Akiki	Youssef	The Procurement management: A Trial to Improve its Effectiveness and Efficiency in Private Hospitals	2018
177	Jneid	Viviane	Enseignements retirés de la mise en place d'une démarche de management socio-économique dans un groupe scolaire au Liban *(Lessons learned from the implementation of a socio-economic management approach in a school group in Lebanon)*	2018
178	Yacoub (Abdou)	Imen	Les contradictions de la norme dans la maîtrise des risques bancaires. Résultats d'une recherche-action conduite en position de praticien réflexif dans une banque régionale *(The contradictions of the norm in the control of banking risks. Results of an action-research conducted as a reflective practitioner in a regional bank)*	2018
179	Bousquet	Carole	L'articulation des compétences individuelles et collectives à la stratégie de l'entreprise. Recherche-intervention dans une PME *(The articulation of individual and collective competences to the company's strategy. Intervention-research in an SME)*	2018
180	Saliba	Fabio	L'articulation des compétences individuelles et collectives à la stratégie de l'entreprise. Recherche-intervention dans une PME *(The strategy for reducing resistance to organizational change in creative teams in the communication sector: a Brazilian case study)*	2019
181	Adoumbou	Caroline	L'installation d'une fonction managériale dans les très petites organisations du spectacle vivant: cas de deux recherches-interventions *(The installation of a managerial function in very small performing arts organizations: case of two intervention-researches)*	2019
182	El Othman	Sajida	Impact of long working hours on women's socio-economic empowerment.	2019

(continued)

List of Doctoral Dissertations Prepared at the ISEOR Institute, Under the Direction of the Institute's Research Directors, Since 1976 (continued)

N°	Nom	Prénom	Titre	Année
183	Hamandi	Mohamad Ali	Improving communication-coordination-cooperation (3Cs) among private hospitals in Lebanon: The syndicate of private hospitals as 3Cs agent	2019
184	El-Masri	Majd	Change management in a Lebanese money exchange and money transfer company	2019
185	Daaboul	Mireille	Development of delegation practices to non-family managers and competitiveness in family business	2019
186	Berjaoui	Mahdi	Work organization in family business: a case study of a medium Lebanese textile company	2019
187	Takieddine	Karim	Improving the soundness of a bank's credit granting process	2019
188	El-Ayoubi	Claudia	Improving undergraduate business student satisfaction in a branch of Lebanese higher education sector: Case of University X	2019
189	Yamine	Badawi	The use of SEAM as a potential corporate social responsibility (CSE) tool for SMEs	2019
190	Tannous	Alain	Improving job satisfaction to drop turnover rate. Case of a private school in Dubaï	2019
191	Tang	Ziyuan	Motiver les salariés chinois à mettre en oeuvre le KAIZEN tourné vers l'individu: recherche-intervention dans une entreprise praticienne du LEAN management *(Motivating Chinese employees to implement KAIZEN turned towards the individual: intervention-research in a company practicing LEAN management)*	2019
192	Zidi	Tariq	Le management socio-économique de la responsabilité sociale de l'entreprise (RSE) et la performance globale de l'entreprise: cas d'une PME de service marocaine *(The socio-economic management of corporate social responsibility (CSR) and the overall performance of the company: case of a Moroccan service SME)*	2019
193	Ennajem	Mohammed	Le pilotage de la création et de la répartition de la valeur ajoutée dans les systèmes de coopération inter-organisationnelle *(Managing the creation and distribution of value added in inter-organizational cooperation systems)*	2020
194	Barazi	Rana	Application of SEAM as a project management methodology in non-governmental organizations: an intervention-research in Lebanon	2020
195	Balian	Patrick	Intellectual capital impacts on firm performance: The case of e-commerce firm	2020
196	Khachan	Laura	Reducing dysfunctions in the prescription drug cycle: Intervention-research in a pharmaceutical company	2020
197	Eid	Jocelyne	The Integration of the Control Departments to Manage Complex Norms. The Case of a Lebanese Bank	2020
198	El Rahbani	George	Helping a family business firm become a better SR provider for greater results towards stakeholders	2020
199	Ghaleb	Elias N.	Evaluating IT impacts through Socio-Economic Intervention-Research on Business Performance. The Case of Travel Agence in the Middle East	2020

(continued)

List of Doctoral Dissertations Prepared at the ISEOR Institute, Under the Direction of the Institute's Research Directors, Since 1976 (continued)

N°	Nom	Prénom	Titre	Année
200	Fata	Alan	SEAM and Entrepreneurship: Establishing a New Venture in Lebanon. The Case of PDE Provider SARL	2020
201	Murad	Hanna	A Startuper Ecosystem Strategy, Through The Socio-Economic Approach To Management: The Case of Lebanon	2020
202	Nasrallah	Ahmad	Increasing Efficiency and Boosting Performance through SEAM Intervention-Research: the Case of a Kuwaiti Private Hospital	2020
203	El-Haddad	Pierre	Developing Cooperation among NGOs: Exploratory research in Lebanon	2020
204	Dupouy	Jocelyne	L'équipe de direction et sa performance: une fonction de socle stratégique ? (*The management team and its performance: a strategic "bedrock function"?*)	2020
205	Sanchez	Mélissa	L'intégration raisonnée des mutliples normes exogènes et endogènes pour maintenir la performance socio-économique de l'entreprise (*The reasoned integration of multiple exogenous and endogenous standards and norms to maintain the socio-economic performance of the company*)	2020
206	Buens	Luis	Contribution du renforcement du «socle» managérial au processus d'intégration normative dans les petites entreprises (*Contribution of the strengthening of the managerial "bedrock" to the process of normative integration in the small enterprises*)	2022
207	Biscafé	Benjamin	Contribution de la représentation syndicale de l'encadrement à la performance durable des entreprises—Enseignements d'une recherche-intervention (*Contribution of union representation of management to the sustainable performance of companies—Lessons from an intervention-research*)	2022

ABOUT THE CONTRIBUTORS

Imen ABDOU is a Doctor of Management Sciences specializing in accounting-control-audit. She defended her PhD dissertation in 2018 on the contradictions of the standard and norm in the control of banking risks. Her doctoral work presents the devices put in place by banking institutions to meet regulatory requirements and analyzes the consequences, coherence and stakes of the standards and norms on the control of risks and on the internal organization of the institution. The results of this work underline the interest of the complete and integrated management of standards and norms in this sector of activity. Indeed, the results of the research show that the performance of a retail bank will directly depend on its ability to anticipate and manage the various bodies of standards and norms with which it is faced. She is also a part-time lecturer at the IAE of Lyon and a management controller in the banking sector.

Caroline ADOUMBOU has been an opera singer for 10 years with the status of intermittent performer. In parallel to this musical career, she is at the initiative of the creation of the cultural mediation group "*Brins de Voix l'opéra autrement*" of which she is the administrative and artistic co-director since 2010. In her managerial practice, she is particularly interested in proximity management and in the power of transformation that the contribution of energy from one actor to another can have within an organization. In 2019, she obtained a PhD in Management sciences at the University of Lyon 3 under the supervision of Véronique Zardet for her dissertation entitled: "The installation of a managerial function in very small performing arts organizations." She teaches project management in several structures and continues her research activities within the ISEOR laboratory.

Herman AGUINIS is Professor of Management at The George Washington University School of Business. He has served as President of the Academy of Management (AOM) during 2021–2022, and is now serving as AOM Immediate Past President. Since 2018, Web of Science Highly Cited Researchers Reports has ranked him among the world's 100 most impactful researchers in Economics and Business. His research is interdisciplinary and addresses the deployment of talent in organizations and organizational research methods. Recent projects address corporate social responsibility & business sustainability. His profes-

SEAM Treatise, pages 953–994

sional and life agenda is to have an impact on the academic community, but also on society at large. Herman Aguinis has written 200 articles, 50 book chapters and 11 books including *Performance Management* (5th edition. 2023). He served as Editor-in-Chief of *Organizational Research Methods* and as President of the Iberoamerican Academy of Management. He teaches courses at the MBA, executive, and PhD levels in the areas of organizational behavior. Herman Aguinis has consulted with organizations in the U.S., Europe, and Latin America, including the United Nations, as well as traditional media outlets in the U.S. and abroad including *The Economist, Wall Street Journal, Forbes, Business Week,* among others.

Osmar ARANDIA PÉREZ is director of postgraduate studies in administration at the University of Monterrey (Mexico), previously he worked in the digital transformation teams of the same university, and as academic director of the administration and marketing department. At this university, he teaches classes on Sustainability, Ethics, and Social Responsibility in Business, Sales, and Strategy. Previously, he was vice-rector of strategic development at the Cristóbal Colón de Veracruz University, where he also served as professor of the marketing degrees and postgraduate degrees in business administration, marketing, as well as the doctorate in administrative sciences of said university. He is part of the chair of humanism and management and has participated in various international conferences. He has several publications in academic journals and book chapters.

Alexandre ASSELINEAU, Doctor in Economic Sciences, is Director of CEREN (EA 7477), and Associate Professor at Burgundy School of Business in the Management-Strategy-Entrepreneurship Department. He is also an Associate researcher at ISEOR & Magellan, IAE Lyon 3 Jean-Moulin, where he is preparing an Accreditation to Direct Research (HDR) in Management sciences under the supervision of Prof. Véronique Zardet. After an experience in strategy consulting, he joined the world of management schools in 2004, where he successively held several management positions. His research work, which has led to academic publications, press articles, CCMP case studies and book chapters, focuses on the responsible strategic management of territories and organizations, particularly around the themes of strategic alignment and sustainable transition, "coopetition," and more recently on the societal impact of management research.

Rodolphe BACHAUD has been an intervener-researcher at ISEOR for three years. He obtained a Master's degree in change management from the IAE Lyon – Université Jean Moulin Lyon 3. Each year, he conducts between ten and fifteen interventions in companies and organizations, within professional firms and proximity companies. He is particularly interested in the evolution of human potential as a main factor in the development of organizations and performance. Rodolphe Bachaud also provides professional training in strategic management to company managers and executives.

Miguel Juan BACIC is Full Professor at the Economics Institute of the State University of Campinas (UNICAMP), Brazil; PhD in Administration (UNS, Argentina, 1998). He teaches Cost Management, Business Finance, Business Strategy in undergraduate and graduate courses in economics and in specialization courses. He was the director of 3 doctoral dissertation and 26 master's theses. He develops research works in the areas of management, cost management, strategy, entrepreneurship, local economic development, economics of small and medium enterprises and solidarity economy. He has published two books on costs, 36 chapters, 55 articles in scientific journals and 167 papers in scientific congresses in the area. He was president of the International Institute of Costs (2003–2007) and of the Brazilian Association of Costs (ABC) on two occasions (1996–1998 and 2010–2012).

Charles Richard BAKER is Professor of Accounting at the Willumstad School of Business, Adelphi University, Long Island, New York. His main research interests are focused on the public accounting profession, in particular: the history of the profession, comparative systems of regulation, ethical issues, independence, and legal liability. Professor Baker has published over 120 academic and profession articles in various academic and professional journals such. He has also served on the editorial board of academic and professional journals including: Accounting, Auditing, Auditing and Accountability Journal, Critical Perspectives on Accounting, Accounting Forum, Accounting History, Accounting Historians' Journal, Research on Professional Responsibility and Ethics in Accounting, and The CPA Journal. He received a PhD from the University of California, Los Angeles (UCLA) and he is a Certified Public Accountant (CPA) in New York State.

Rana BARAZI is professor of management at the University of Balamand. She holds a DBA from Université Jean Moulin Lyon 3, a Master of Public Health, and a BSc in Environmental Health from the American University of Beirut. She is a certified Project Management Professional (PMI, USA) and certified in Clinical Research (Tufts New England Medical Center, USA) and a certified Optometrist (MoPH, Lebanon). She is an active member of the Academy of Management and the Project Management Institute. She has multidimensional expertise in academics, management consulting, research, and project management. She is active in research on several themes including business management, project management, public health, and health economics. Her fields of interest include Organizational Development and Change, SEAM, Management Control, NGOs and community development.

Isabelle BARTH is a University Professor of management. After 10 years in business in France and abroad (Africa), she has held numerous teaching, research and management positions in university and private higher education. She was the General Director of the Strasbourg School of Management (2011 to 2016), Director of Research at INSEEC U. and Director of INSEEC Business School (2018–2020). Her expertise is in leadership, inclusion, change management, emerging human, and organizational behavior.

Michaël BASKA, after studying political science and regional planning at the University of Lyon 3, joined the City of Lyon in 1998 in the Urban Social Development Department. He developed the evaluation of public policies to measure their impact in priority neighborhoods, communication actions, training of local actors, and participation of residents accompanying the first generations of city contracts in Lyon. Deputy Director of Territorial Development in Lyon since 2004, he is responsible for the teams in charge of steering territorial projects organizing social and urban changes and transformations in Lyon's priority neighborhoods. The various partnerships developed with the academic world have made it possible to structure over time a foundation of experiments and work aimed at strengthening the functions of observation and evaluation in the service of steering public action.

Dolly BASSIL, MPH, DBA is an experienced international consultant with a public health and development background and a doctorate degree in Socio-Economic Approach to Management. Her expertise revolves around strategies, systems and programs development besides monitoring and evaluation of development programs. She closely collaborates with UN agencies, INGOs, and NGOs besides public and private entities in different regions.

Emmanuel BECK is an Honorary Senior lecturer in Management Sciences. Jean-Moulin Lyon 3 University – IAE of Lyon. Trained as an engineer, he began his professional career in several international industrial groups, notably as a management controller and organization consultant. He defended his doctoral dissertation in Management science in 1981, on the theme of the training-employment balance in an industrial environment and led a career as a teacher-researcher at the University of Lyon, notably as head of the Master's degree in social audit. At the same time, he continued his research in socio-economic management, at ISEOR, in numerous companies and organizations.

Laurent BERTRAND is the General Manager of the Aigues-Vertes Foundation since 2010, after having been active in the management of private Swiss hospitals for 10 years. His first ten years of professional career were spent in the banking sector, in various positions of responsibility. His activity as a life coach for the last 10 years illustrates his strong interest in human understanding, psychology, and personal development. He has also followed the training courses to become a mediator in non-violent communication and a practitioner in individual coaching.

Gilbert BLARDONE (†) economist, was Professor Emeritus of Universities, founder and Honorary President of the Association of Friends of François Perroux. He was a Doctor of Economic Sciences, University of Paris Sorbonne. He had a graduate degree in Roman Law and History of Law. He was Director of La Chronique Sociale de France (1964–1972) and a member of the General Commission of the Semaines Sociales de France (1958 –1990). With Georges Hourdin at the «Publications de La Vie Catholique», he launched the Revue Croissance des Jeunes Nations (1961); in Lyon, the Revue «Informations et Commentaires : Le développement en question» (1972). He was a specialist in economic and financial policies and development analysis, and an international consultant: economic and financial diagnoses in Africa, the Near and Middle East and Latin America. From 1974 onwards, he taught at the International Institute for Labour Studies (IILS) of the International Labour Office (ILO), at the African Institute of Geneva, which later became the Graduate Institute of Development Studies (GIDS), and then at the Graduate Institute of International Studies in Geneva. He remained an emeritus Professor until his retirement. He was also Director of Research at the Institute of Applied Mathematical and Economic Sciences (ISMEA) in Paris and, from 1981, at the Institute for Economic and Social Development Studies (IEDES) directed by François Perroux in Paris.

David M. BOJE has been learning and teaching socioeconomic approach to management (SEAM) with a storytelling method at New Mexico State University, USA. He contributed 27 books and over 150 journals on storytelling, and introduced the now widely-used concept of antenarrative, a prospective sensemaking (foresight) and intuitive-world (the beyond of spirit) in the field of storytelling systems research. His most recent books: True Storytelling (2021, Routledge, Francis & Taylor) with Jens Larsen and Lena Bruun, Doing Conversational Storytelling Interviewing for Your Dissertation (2020, Edward Elgar Publishing Ltd.) with Grace Ann Rosile. David and Grace Ann's work on 'embodied restorying' and their work with veterans and others to get unstuck from problem-saturated narratives of past trauma and develop antenarrative prospective sensemaking of futures of well-being. See publications with online books and articles at https://davidboje.com/vita.

Laura BONDIN, after training at the Institut Paul Bocuse and a management experience within the Bocuse and Ducasse Groups, resumed her studies at the EUGINOV Center, iae-Lyon, Université Jean Moulin, to follow a Master's degree in Socio-economic Management. Since 2018, she has been an intervener-researcher at ISEOR where she pilots and co-pilots interventions within VSEs, SMEs and Intermediate Size Companies (ISCs). Her research work focuses on emotional intelligence.

Michelle BONNARD, after a long professional experience in an industrial company, in various logistics, human resources and quality departments, joined the ISEOR research center in 2005, where she is responsible for the preparation of the annual professional conference, the annual academic conferences as well as the management of the journal *Recherches en sciences de gestion – Management sciences – Ciencias de gestión.*

Daniel BONNET has a PhD in Management sciences and is Accredited to Direct Research (ADR). He is a consultant in strategic and organizational change management. At the same time, he is an Associate researcher at the Institute of Socio-economics of Enterprises and Organizations (ISEOR). As President of the Institut Psychanalyse & Management (I.P&M), he contributes to the development of psychoanalytical research within groups, organizations, and institutions. He has founded the *Revue Psychanalyse & Management* and he is its senior editor. He is the founder of the Management of Organizational Technologies (MTO) conference and co-director of the *Revue Management des Technologies Organisationnelles.*

Jacques BONNET is an honorary professor of geography (University of Lyon), director of the "Environment, City, Society" joint research unit from 1995 to 2006. He has been an Associate researcher at the Magellan Research Center, Jean Moulin University, and at the ISEOR (Institute of Socio-economics of Enterprises and Organizations) since 2007. His PhD dissertation on "*Lyon, place tertiaire. Contribution to a geography of business*" (in 1982) marked an orientation in economic and urban geography. This was followed by a reflection on metropolitan functions in the world with a book on "the great world metropolises" (in 1994). The geography of large companies and the relationships between companies and territories are the themes that qualify a third scientific stage ("Company and territory" in 2009). A final stage concerns territorial management («Aménagement et développement territorial» 2012).

Marc BONNET is Deputy Director of ISEOR and Professor of Management at iaelyon, Université Jean Moulin. He has been with ISEOR since 1978, participating in numerous socio-economic intervention-research projects in companies as well as in societal issues such as the management of insertion and requalification devices for people in illiteracy situations. He has also accompanied projects to disseminate socio-economic approach to management in the United States, particularly within the framework of the Academy of Management. At the University, he has developed work-study programs, from the bachelor's degree to the Doctorate in Business Administration (DBA), which are based on socio-economic management. He was President of the Association Francophone de Gestion des Ressources Humaines (2006–2009) and President of the Management Consulting Division of the Academy of Management.

Carole BOUSQUET is an Associate Professor at IDRAC Business School, specializing in change management, human resources management and strategy. Trained in intervention-research since 2014, she defended her PhD dissertation in 2018 on the articulation between individual and collective competencies to corporate strategy, under the supervision of Professor Véronique Zardet. Today, she is a professor-researcher at IDRAC Business School and a part-time lecturer at Jean Moulin Lyon 3 University. Her academic work is linked to other fields such as marketing, psychology, and sociology.

Pascal BRENOT graduated from Sciences Po Paris in 1987. He has been Director of Territorial Development for the Lyon City Council since 2004, and as such is responsible for the implementation of city policy, local social development (partnership relations with popular education associations), employment and professional integration policy, youth policy and health prevention. After having been posted to Togo for the French Cooperation, he joined the Municipality of Lyon in 1992 as chief of staff to the director general of services before being appointed head of the urban social development department in 1998. Questions of design, steering and evaluation of local public policies have always been at the heart of his professional activity. He is also a member of the National Council of Cities and of the Board of Directors of Labo Cités, a resource center for urban policy in the Auvergne-Rhône-Alpes Region.

Anthony F. BUONO is professor of Management and Sociology and founding director of the Alliance for Ethics and Social Responsibility at Bentley University, USA, which he oversaw from its inception in 2003 through 2013. A former Chair of Bentley's Management Department, Tony's research and teaching interests include organizational change, inter-organizational strategies, management consulting, and ethics and corporate social responsibility. He has written or edited 22 books, including The Human Side of Mergers and Acquisitions, is the founding editor of the Research in Management Consulting book series (Information Age Publishing), and a two-time chair of the Academy of Management's Management Consulting Division. He holds a PhD with a concentration in Industrial and Organizational Sociology from Boston College. He has been actively involved in the UN Global Compact-sponsored PRME and was honored as a PRME Pioneer at the 2017 Global Forum on Responsible Management Education.

Jean CAGHASSI is an engineer, graduated from the Polytechnic Faculty of Alexandria University (Egypt) in 1972 and from the French Institute of Management, Paris, in 1985. After several professional experiences in Spain, Italy, Belgium, and France in the management of industrial projects and in the international commercial field, exercised in the engineering, textile, food-processing, airport or pharmaceutical industries, he turned in 1985 to the management and recovery of activities in difficulty as a consultant or profit center manager. In 1994, he took charge of the turnaround of an industrial bodywork company, which he transformed into a major player in the French and European market until its sale in 2010. Since then, he has been cooperating with ISEOR to contribute to the dissemination of the Socio-Economic Theory of Organizations (SEAM) and has been working as a consultant in the strategic field.

María Elizabeth CANLLO DE MONTOTO, originally from Argentina, is a Certified Public Accountant, founder of Estudio Canllo Montoto, an organization dedicated to professional services in accounting, tax, auditing, management, corporate and bankruptcy. She also acts as partner of Centro de Distribución Parque SRL, dedicated to strategic management, consulting, auditing, tax, and accounting strategy of the firm. She has presented papers in several management and cost management conferences since 2007.

Laurent CAPPELLETTI is a graduate of EDHEC Business School and holds a PhD in Management Sciences. He is a professor at the Conservatoire National des Arts et Métiers, where he holds the chair of Accounting and Management Control and chairs the College of Chairs. He is a researcher at the LIRSA laboratory and program director at the ISEOR Institute. He is also coordinator of the international research network on the management of standards and norms, Tétranormalisation, and an expert with the think tank *Institut Sapiens.* He is also deputy mayor of Mauguio-Carnon, in charge of trade and digital development, and councilor of the county council. He has published more than 200 papers on socio-economic management control, standards and norms management, public policy management and qualimetric intervention-research, twice receiving a "best paper award" from the Academy of Management (USA). He regularly writes columns for the newspapers *Le Monde, Les Echos, Le Figaro* and *l'Opinion.*

Daniel CARRASCO is Professor of public accounting and past director of the Department of Accounting and Management of the University of Málaga (UMA), president of the *Comité científico-academico de OCU,* president of the *Comité de expertos para la Tributación y cálculo de costes del Ayuntamiento de Málaga* and Member of the *Academia Malagueña de Ciencias.* Has formed part of several committees of experts on university costs, local administration, etc. created by the Ministries of Education and Public Administration, Education, Culture and Sports, Spanish Federation of Municipalities and Provinces. President of the *Instituto Internacional de Costos,* Vice-president of the *Fundación Instituto de Estudios de la Hacienda Pública Andaluza* y Vice-rector of A.E. of UMA. He is a member of the board of various national and international journals, has supervised 23 doctoral dissertations, and is the author or coauthor of 112 books, book chapters, and articles in national and international journals, and has participated in 78 national and international conferences.

Graciela CARRILLO GONZÁLEZ holds a PhD in Economics from the University of Barcelona and a Master's degree in Economics and International Politics from the Centro de Investigación y Docencia Económicas, Mexico. She is a full-time research professor at the Universidad Autónoma Metropolitana Xochimilco, where she teaches in the undergraduate program in Management, the Graduate Program in Economics and Innovation Management and the master's Program in Sustainable Societies. She is Head of the research area "Analysis and socioeconomic management of organizations" and editor of the journal *Administración y Organizaciones.* He participates as vice-president of the *Red de investigación y docencia sobre Innovación tecnológica (RIDIT)* and is a member of the *Asociación Latinoamericana de Gestión tecnológica* (ALTEC) and of the *Sociedad Mesoamericana de economía ecológica (SOMEEC)* She is a member of the National System of Researchers and specializes in environmental and innovation issues, related to management in organizations and public policy.

Juan CASTAINGTS TEILLERY is Doctor of State in economic sciences, University of Paris-10 and holds a PhD in Anthropology, École Pratique des Hautes Études de Paris. Professor-researcher in the Department of Economics at the Universidad Autónoma Metropolitana (Mexico). He teaches and supervises dissertations in the doctoral programs of Anthropological Sciences, Organizational Studies, and Economic Sciences at the same university. Appointed Distinguished Professor by the Academic College of the Universidad Autónoma Metropolitana in 1989. President of the Mexican Academy of Political Economy (2011–2012). More than 60 academic articles; author of 9 books. The last three are: *Symbolisms of Money, Anthropos.* UAM-Iztapalapa. Barcelona, Spain 2002; second edition, corrected and enlarged in 2017. *Antropología Simbólica y Neurociencia, Anthropos* and UAM-Iztapalapa. Barcelona, Spain 2011. *Money, Work and Power.* Anthropos and UAM-Iztapalapa. Barcelona, Spain 2015. He wrote weekly for 25 years, the column "Así vamos...," first in the newspaper *Excelsior* and then in *El Financiero.*

Victor CAUMEIL was an intervener-researcher at ISEOR. He graduated from the University of Lyon 1 with a Diploma of Technology in Business Administration, then from the IAE Lyon, University Jean Moulin, where he obtained a Master in Management and Change Management. He wrote a master thesis on the value of management consulting. For the past four years, he has been leading and piloting managerial and organizational transformations in various sectors: mass distribution, sports goods trade, industries, liberal professions... He is particularly interested in the need for proximity management. Victor Caumeil also provides professional training in strategic management to company managers and executives and gives courses in operational management at the IUT, University Claude Bernard Lyon 1.

Geneviève CAUSSE, Professor Emeritus at the University of Paris-Est Créteil and ESCP Europe, is an *Officer of the Légion d'Honneur*, the *Palmes Académiques* and the International Order of the *Palmes Académiques de CAMES*. In addition to her teaching activities, she has participated in the implementation and evaluation of educational engineering projects in many African and Eastern European countries. She has participated in the writing of approximately 40 books and has published numerous articles. Her activities, as well as her publications, place particular emphasis on the need to adapt management methods and tools to the economic, social, and cultural contexts of the countries in which they are implemented.

Jérôme CHABANNE-RIVE is Professor of Management Sciences at the University Jean Moulin Lyon 3 and is currently General Delegate of the European Institute for Advanced Studies in Management in Brussels (EIASM). Previously, he was General Director of iaelyon, and President of the IAE France network. His work focuses on the quality criteria of management schools. He is a member of many audit committees of accreditation of business schools, for EFMD (European Foundation for Management Development). He also teaches human resources management and international management considering cultural specificities.

Marie-Christine CHALUS-SAUVANNET, University Professor at the IAE Lyon School of Management, University Jean Moulin Lyon 3, is responsible for the development of research, the teaching and research center "Strategy, operation, decision," as well as the Executive Doctorate in Business Administration of the Business Science Institute, for the IAE Lyon. She is also the founder and coordinator of CREATE, an applied research team on the "Entrepreneurial Ecosystem" theme, which includes some twenty national and international researchers. She regularly publishes articles and papers on entrepreneurship, management, and strategic intelligence. From 2016 to 2019, she was president of the *Société d'Économie Politique et Sociale de Lyon* (SEPL), a think tank founded in 1866.

René CHARMASSON, is a graduate of the École Supérieure de Commerce de Lyon (EM-Lyon). He held increasing responsibilities at Xerox France, in operations at the Lyon regional office and in marketing at headquarters from 1972 to 1984. From 1985 to 1990, he took an active part in the creation and development of Publiprint – Province N°1. From 1990 to 1995, he broadened his experience in the field of IT services, notably in the CEGID group. Since 1995, he has been one of the pioneers of interim management in France. In 2002, he created the Lyon office of Boyden Interim Management, a leading player in this field, present throughout the world. From 2008 to 2011, when he retired, he was managing all the French activities. From 2011 to 2019, he was a volunteer at the Fondation de France Centre Est, where he contributed to the creation of several foundations, including the "Henri Savall – ISEOR Foundation." He is the General Delegate of this Foundation since October 2020, an Associate member of the IHEDN and Secretary General of Lyon International.

Nylème CHETTIH is a graduate of the EUGINOV center of the IAE of Lyon, Jean Moulin University, in Master of socio-economic management. She is an intervener-researcher at ISEOR where she conducts, since 2019, change management interventions in various companies, especially in professional firms and proximity companies, VSEs (very small companies), SMEs and ETIs (intermediate size companies). She is particularly interested in the analysis and action on dysfunctions and hidden costs-performances, which lead to the development of economic sensitivity and managerial practices.

Bruno COHANIER is Professor of Accounting at EADA Business School in Barcelona, Spain. His 28 years' career in the academic community involved acting as Associate International Relations Director, Chair of the Accounting, Law, Information and Operations Management Department, and Director of the Grande École Program of NEOMA Business School. His main research interest is in international managerial and financial accounting, cross functional performance measurement and sustainability. His research has been published in leading journals and at international conferences such as the American Accounting Association, EAA, AFC. He has taught internationally at undergraduate, graduate and executive education levels for Saint-Gobain, Carrefour, Orange, and led sponsored E&Y projects. Before receiving his PhD from Aston University, Birmingham, U.K., and a research degree from Paris-Dauphine University, he acted as financial manager in the automotive industry in France and Germany.

Christophe COMBAUDON is an intervener-researcher, Associate researcher at the ISEOR research center and manager of Christophe COMBAUDON Consulting & Associés. He holds a PhD in Management science from the University of Clermont-Auvergne. After a career as an executive in the pharmaceutical industry, he has been conducting experimental research in socio-economic innovation for nearly 15 years in a wide variety of sectors: health, industry, services, agri-food, mass distribution, and the indenpendent professions. His research also focuses on business creation. He is also an Associate Professor at the University of Auvergne and teaches in various business and engineering schools about strategic management, management control and entrepreneurship. He is a member and former administrator of the *Réseau Entreprendre Auvergne.*

John CONBERE, MDiv, EdD, is President of SEAM, Inc., and Co-director of the SEAM Institute. For many years, he was Professor and director of the doctoral program in Organization Development at the University of St. Thomas, Minnesota, USA. He has co-authored many articles, chapters and a book about socio-economic theory and practice (see www.seaminstitute.org for details) as well as numerous peer reviewed articles about conflict management and organizational change. Conbere is on the editorial board of the *OD Journal* and has been on several scientific committees for ISEOR conferences and journal.

Eva CONRAUD KOELLNER holds a PhD in Management sciences from the Instituto Politécnico Nacional (Mexico). Professor-researcher at the Guanajuato Campus, University of Guanajuato. Member of the National System of Researchers (level I). With recognition of Desirable Profile PRODEP and responsible for the Academic Body in consolidation "Business Strategies and Competitiveness." Author and co-author of several articles in indexed journals, books and book chapters, national and international. International lecturer. Her lines of research are: sustainable marketing, social responsibility in organizations and business strategies and competitiveness. Reviewer in international scientific journals in Europe, Mexico and Asia. Member of RAITES and RENUTEG research networks.

Thomas G. CUMMINGS is Professor of Management and Organization at the Marshall School of Business, University of Southern California, USA. He is a leading international scholar and consultant on strategic change and high-performance organizations. He was President of the Western Academy of Management, Chair of the Organization Development and Change Division of the Academy of Management, Founding Editor of the *Journal of Management Inquiry*, and the 61st President of the Academy of Management. He has authored over 80 articles and 25 books including the critically acclaimed: *Self-Designing Orga-*

nizations: Learning How to Create High Performance, with Susan Mohrman, and *Organization Development and Change,* 11th Edition, with Christopher Worley.

Frantz DATRY is Program Director at ISEOR where he prepared his PhD dissertation in Management sciences, defended in 2006 under the direction of Professor Véronique Zardet. For the past 20 years, he has conducted several intervention projects per year in France and abroad. He has contributed to numerous organizational transformation projects in various sectors: industry, services, medico-social activities, and artistic organizations. His research work focuses on the development of managerial practices and their impact on the economic responsibility of companies and individuals.

Xavier DAUDÉ holds a *Diplôme supérieur du notariat* from the University of Paris 1 Panthéon Sorbonne, after having obtained a Diplôme d'études approfondies (DEA) in Business Law and a *Diplôme d'enseignement supérieur spécialisé (DESS)* in Asset Management from the University of Lyon 3 as well as a DESS in Notarial Law from the University of Paris 1 Panthéon Sorbonne. After four years as an assistant notary at the Thibierge et associés notary office in Paris, he became Director of Training and Development at the *Conseil Supérieur du Notariat* from 2003 to 2019. Since then, he has been Deputy Director General of the National Institute of Notarial Training in Paris.

Eric DAVOINE is Professor of HRM and Organization at the University of Fribourg (Switzerland) since 2003. He has gained PhD degrees from the University of Freiburg (Germany) and from the University of Lyon (ISEOR). He has been board member of the association of French speaking HRM researchers (AGRH) since 2007, co-director of university executive programs in the fields of HRM and Philosophy for managers. He serves in several editorial and reviewer boards for journals like *Journal of Organizational Effectiveness, International Journal of Organizational Analysis, Career Development International,* and *Recherches en Sciences de Gestion – Management Sciences – Ciencias de Gestión.* His main research topics are International HRM, International mobility and Top management careers. He published several books and about 30 articles, for example in *International Business Review, International Journal of Human Resource Management, European Management Journal, Journal of Global Mobility* and *Research in Sociology of Organizations.*

Miguel DELATTRE is a Senior lecturer at iaelyon, Université Jean-Moulin, Lyon 3, in charge of the Master 2 Management of the development and transmission of small businesses and regulated activities, and a member of the ISEOR and Magellan research centers. For more than 20 years, he has conducted and participated in research and interventions in companies and organizations of various sizes and sectors. His multidisciplinary work focuses on the recognition and contribution of human potential to organizational performance and the development of corporate social responsibility (CSR). Involved in international teaching programs and research projects, he is also an active member of AGRH (*Association de Gestion des Ressources Humaines*) and treasurer of ADERSE (*Association pour le Développement de l'Enseignement et de la Recherche sur la Responsabilité Sociale de l'Entreprise*).

Gérard DESMAISON has been a senior executive in international groups (Danone, Lenôtre, Accor, Ferrero) where he practiced the socio-economic approach to management (SEAM) for 30 years with and without ISEOR. He is a certified coach (2003) by HEC. He has taught SEAM at ISEOR and at the University, he is a Doctor of Management Sciences (PhD) since 2014, and an Associate researcher at ISEOR, member of ADERSE (Association for the Development and Teaching of CSR). He has published numerous papers on CSR, Human Potential, and coaching, and participated in several collective works. He is President of a think-tank " *l'Atelier Du Dirigeant Durable*" (A3D) and has coordinated the book " *Reconciling the Economic and the Human in Business* ". He is a member of the association "60 000 Rebonds," which supports entrepreneurs who have gone through liquidation. He contributed to the creation of 60,000 *Rebonds-Alpes*, which trains sponsors in the Auvergne-Rhône-Alpes region. He is currently the coordinator of the *Observatoire du Rebond*.

Norbert DEVILLE is the General Manager of the Technical Center for Support and Training of Health Examination Centers (CETAF) and a senior manager of the National Health Insurance Fund (CNAM). He has spent 17 years working for CNAM, successively as a management controller, Chief of Staff of the Director of General Administration and Director of Legal Affairs. He is a member of the Supervisory Board of the University Hospital of Saint-Etienne, a member of the *Gerontopole-AURA Region*, a member of the Board of Directors of the *Association Prévention Bucco-dentaire des Seniors*, a member of the Scientific Council of *Seniors Autonomie*, and a member of the *Conférence Nationale de Santé*. He has published in the fields of health (*Revue Regards de l'EN3S* and he has contributed to the book *"Comprendre la santé des aînés,"* Dunod) and management. He teaches occasionally at the *École Nationale de la Santé et de la Sécurité Sociale* (National School of Health and Social Welfare), at the Université Jean-Monnet in Saint-Étienne and at the IAE School of management in Lyon.

Guy DEVILLEBICHOT studied economics at the Sorbonne (Paris). After his two doctoral theses (1964-Paris), he was appointed Professor in Martinique and then in Toulouse (1966–1998). In 1975, he created a university laboratory: the Center for the Study of Productive Organizations (CETOP). A member of the Steering Committee of the French Association of Economic Science (AFSE), he was its General Secretary from 1979 to 1981, based in Toulouse. He translated two books: *Shackle*, 1967, 1961, Dunod, and *Shingo*, (1990, 1987), Éditions d'Organisation), wrote about 40 articles or "working papers" and directed about 40 theses. He claims the filiations of "OST software (Mogensen–1932), Benielli 1956–67, USA/France)," of Shigeo Shingo (1909–1989), Japan and of "Value is created in the Workshop for all products" (White collars and Blue collars).

Dave DOBOSENSKI, MBA, is the President and CEO of St. Croix Regional Medical Center in rural Wisconsin, USA. He started in health care in 1984 as an Industrial Engineer and a Quality Improvement Consultant, followed by almost thirty years of experience as a healthcare executive. He pioneered SEAM interventions in rural healthcare and in his medical center. They carry forward the learning and principles of SEAM today as they continue their organizational transformation.

François DU PENHOAT, with an agricultural background, worked in Africa as an agricultural technician for two years, then studied philosophy-theology-spirituality in Spain and England, and was ordained a priest in 1985. Since then, he has worked as a missionary in Benin for 15 years, vicar general of the *diocese of N'Dali* from 2004 to 2013, also works in Spain for the formation of future priests. To the Provincial Council of France in 2013, Provincial of Lyon since 2016. During these last years, the Provincial Council has sought to renew the presence of the African Missions in France by insisting on the contribution of Africans for a renewal of spirituality and to make the meeting of cultures a means of working for peace in the world and for the blossoming of each culture.

Nicolas DUFOUR holds a PhD in Management science, his dissertation was defended in 2015 on operational risk and the role of standards and norms in banking and insurance. He is also Associate Professor at CNAM, Lirsa and risk manager in the insurance sector.

Yves DUPUY is a former professor at the University of Montpellier. He has chaired the Association Francophone de Comptabilité and the jury of the agrégation d'économie et gestion. He was also editor-in-chief of the journal Comptabilité Contrôle Audit. His work, publications – about a hundred references -, supervisor of nearly sixty PhD dissertations and Accreditations to direct research . The guiding principle of his teaching is a socio-technological understanding of organizations, their limits, the power games that develop within them, and the control mechanisms that are established. Among the themes explored are corporate groups and networks, organizational processes related to the automation of information systems, and the analysis of the meaning and scope of accounting representations, particularly in the context of public organizations.

Jocelyne B. EID, DBA is currently the Operational Risk Manager for Lebanon & Gulf Bank s.a.l. She has more than 20 years of banking experience. She implemented compliance sanctions and anti-money laundering projects, developed policies and procedures related to financial operations, reporting, and internal control. Originally from Lebanon, she holds a Doctorate in Business Administration from University Jean Moulin (Lyon 3) prepared at ISEOR international research center in Lyon, France, and university of Balamand Lebanon in Management science, change management, organizational development, and strategic management control.

Pierre EL HADDAD is professor of management at Saint Joseph University (USJ), Lebanon, chair of RISE Conference, founder, and chair of the Network of Organizational Development Experts (NODE), and president of SEPT NGO in Lebanon. He is also a member of ISEOR research center, Lyon. He holds a PhD and DBA from Université Jean Moulin Lyon 3, MBA in economics and finance from Notre Dame University-Louaize, and civil engineering from *École Supérieure des Ingénieurs de Beyrouth* (ESIB). He is also Hubert H. Humphrey fellow from Maxwell School of Citizenship and Public Affairs, Syracuse University, NY, USA. He has a record of consulting toward the immediate performance improvement and developing the dynamic capabilities of organizations. He is also a researcher on diverse themes such as organizational development, responsible decision-making, performance improvement, and sustainable strategies. His fields of interest include business, NGOs, municipalities, and public affairs.

George N. EL-RAHBANI, originally from Lebanon, holds the Canadian Passport, and a Doctorate in Business Administration (DBA) from University Jean Moulin-Lyon 3, in Lyon, France, in Management science, change management, organizational development, and strategic management control. He is currently the EMBA-Program Director in the University of Balamand. Part-time lecturer in INSEEC–Paris Campus & Vocational Trainer in Bredin College–Edmonton. He has more than 22 years of managerial experience, he implemented change management and re-organization projects, developed processes, and implemented techniques related to operations management in both small and big businesses.

Cécile ENNAJEM is a Doctor of Management Sciences and Associate Professor at IAE Lyon, Université Jean Moulin. She oversees the accounting and management control department at ISEOR and carries out socio-economic research in companies and organizations. Her areas of teaching, professional training and research are management control, accounting, and finance. His main publications, articles, and communications, are: "The construction of new relationships between management controller and operational managers in the context of a decentralized management control" in journal *Recherches en sciences de gestion-Management sciences-Ciencias de gestión* (2019, No. 130); "Measurement and spectral analysis of socio-economic productivity reserves: the hidden costs. 101 cases.15th CII Congress – 4th Transatlantic Congress of Accounting, Auditing, Control and Cost Management, June 2017.

Mohammed ENNAJEM is a Doctor of Management Sciences, after a course of public accounting, at IAE Lyon, Jean Moulin University, at HESAM Paris and a diploma of Consultancy in management engineering, obtained at Lyon 2 University. He is Administrative and Financial Director. He has 21 years of teaching experience at IAE Lyon and Lyon 2 University in the fields of accounting, control, auditing, finance, strategic and organizational management, and socio-economic management. His main publications and communications: "Socio-economic innovation project for the development of citizenship," XXVth ALASS Congress, Granada – Spain (2014); "Construction and implementation of a strategic plan for organizational change of institution taking care of chronic disease," XXIVth ALASS Congress, August, Rennes – France (2013); "Creation and distribution of value added. Tutorat du Grand Sud, June, Grenoble – France (2013).

Christophe FARGIER. At the age of 20, he flied to the United States, with dreams in his pocket and a crazy desire to discover new things. He met Kurt and they fell under the spell of American microbreweries. The two spent months traveling the American continent in search of knowledge and exchange. A few years later, after graduating from the ESC Saint – Étienne, Christophe Fargier decided to implement his project of setting up micro – breweries in France. He learned the brewing trade at the Siebel Institute of Technology in Chicago, and then created the company, the *Ninkasi*, in Lyon in 1997. Beyond brewing beers, he also thought of brewing professions, audiences, talents, styles, cultures, and tastes... He likes to spend time with friends over a beer, a burger, and the sound of a concert. Ninkasi is a clever mix of these moments of sharing.

Daniel FARRÉ is a Certified Public Accountant. In the *Facultad de Ciencias Económicas*, Universidad de Buenos Aires, Argentina, he is professor in charge of the Chair of Costs and coordinates the Commission of Management Processes of the Center for Management and Cost Studies. He teaches postgraduate courses on management subjects at several Argentine universities. Director and former president of IAPUCO (Association of accounting Professors). He was Editorial Director of the magazine *"Costos y Gestión."* Speaker and member of reviewers committees of management congresses in France, Spain, Portugal, Brazil, Argentina, Colombia, and Uruguay. Member of Scientific Committees in indexed journals of Argentina and France. Researcher in business management with 14 published articles. His academic career has focused on topics related to the general theory of costs and managerial processes of decision making and management, under a "Stakeholder" vision and a subjectivist economic conception. In the business world, he is a member of *Paradigma,* a Latin American consulting firm in management and technology.

Sandra FATTORUTTO is currently in charge of the Project Office and the network of internal consultants within the *Société wallonne du crédit social* (SWCS – Belgium) after having evolved in a role of internal consultant in socio-economic management within the *Office wallon de la formation professionnelle et de l'emploi* (FOREM – Belgium) from 2001 to 2009 and certified in socio-economic management (SEAM) in 2007–2008. Within this framework, she carried out 6 vertical diagnoses, 3 thematic diagnoses, 1 transversal diagnosis, 4 evaluations, the animation of project groups as well as more than 600 hours of training on the SEAM tools in direct within teams or with the team of internal consultants. Previously, she was a journalist with the RTL Belgium / Contact group, from 1996 to 2004.

Martha Margarita FERNÁNDEZ RUVALCABA holds a PhD in Management sciences, University Lyon 2, France. She is a Professor-researcher at the Universidad Autónoma Metropolitana, Mexico (UAM). He participated in the design and updating of curricula for the bachelor's degree in Management in a pedagogical system that combines scientific research processes with the solution of professional practice problems. Co-Responsible for two ECOS-Norte, UAM-ISEOR projects related to the socio-economic development of Mexican organizations and pro-active change strategies (1998–2007). Founding member of the journal "*Administración y Organizaciones*" and Director of the journal, 2011–2014. Member of the Scientific Committee of the journal "*Sciences de Gestion–Management Sciences–Ciencias de Gestión*," ISEOR, from 2006 to present. Member of the National System of Researchers, Mexico, 2006–2012; member of the Mexican Network of Researchers in Organizational Studies (REMINEO). In 2015 she received the appointment of "Distinguished Professor" by the UAM.

Denis FIÈRE is a physician and Professor Emeritus at the University of Lyon. After studying medicine and specializing in hematology at the Faculty of Lyon, he became a professor at the University of Lyon and a hospital practitioner specializing in hematology, before taking on the responsibility of Chief Physician of the Hematology Department at the University Hospital Center of Lyon, which he held for some twenty years. He specialized in the treatment of leukemia, created a French research group for the treatment of acute leukemia and developed marrow transplants. He has participated in numerous international research programs and held responsibilities within the European Organization for Research and Treatment of Cancer. In the 2000s, he conducted an experiment in socio-economic approach to management in his hematology department and then actively cooperated in the work of ISEOR, on research methods in medicine and management.

Barbara FILIPPAZZO, is currently business manager of her own traditional restaurant "Cavatello" opened since November 7, 2016, in Corbas (69 960), composed of ten employees. Holder of an international master's degree in hotel and restaurant management at the Institut Paul Bocuse (2010- 2011), preceded by a university course at the IAE of Lyon in team management and quality at EUGINOV (2007–2009), an internal school of the IAE specialized in socio-economic management. Since 2008, she has worked in several catering companies in both operational and management positions. She put socio-economic management into practice during her apprenticeship, followed by four years as operations manager and franchisee network coordinator within a Lyon-based restaurant group that has been practicing socio-economic management for over 15 years.

François FILIPPAZZO is the President and CEO of Soly Import, a company that operates as an importer, ripener and distributor of tropical and off-season fruits and vegetables (bananas, avocados, pears, citrus fruits . . .). In 2001, after studying in a business school, he graduated from Grenoble School of Management and joined the family business at a time of generational transition.

Helga FOURE-JOOPEN is a Professor of management at the ESC-Clermont Business School in Clermont-Ferrand, France. She holds a PhD in management from the University of Lyon, France, and her research focuses on different aspects of management related to the socio-economic management of organizations developed by the ISEOR Research Laboratory of which she is a member. She teaches various management courses in different Master's programs in French and English, and has been a visiting professor in several universities abroad. Her courses and conferences focus on management-related topics such as intercultural management, organizational behavior, knowledge sharing and trust in organizations. After having been responsible for several programs at ESC Clermont, such as several MSc, she is currently very involved in the development of foreign university partnerships.

Michel FOUCART is an industrial electromechanical engineer, graduated in 1968, then acquired a specialization in management at the University UCL- IAG (Louvain-la-Neuve, Belgium), in 1984 and obtained his DEA (*Diplôme d'études approfondies*) in Management sciences at the University Jean Moulin Lyon 3 in 2004. He is President and founder of the Technord group and of the "*Les p'tits soleils*" daycare center (Tournai, Belgium), administrator of a social restaurant "*L'assiette pour tous*," administrator and founder of a citizen movement for the socio-economic development of the "*Wallonie picarde*" territory, the CHOQ association, administrator and founder of the "La Maison de la Formation" association, co-founding member of the *Groupement des chefs d'entreprise du Québec en Belgique*, and a member of the APG in Lille. He was elected "Walloon of the Year" by the Jules Destrée Institute in 1998 and received the distinction of Chevalier du Mérite Wallon in 2018. He was Vice President for 22 years of the Walloon Business Union.

Marc FRACHETTE manages Cap O2, a consulting firm in organizational engineering in the health sector. He develops change management approaches and mobilizes project engineering. He is an Associate researcher at the ISEOR laboratory and at Jean Moulin Lyon 3 University. He holds a PhD and a master's degree in Management science and a master's degree in business engineering. He teaches management in Master 2 CTERSAMS at the IAE of Lyon, at the IFCS-TL and in faculties of medicine-pharmacy. Marc Frachette is a member of various groups: AFAV, ALASS, ARAMOS and co-created " Thank Pharma ".

Sofyane FRIMOUSSE is a Senior lecturer, PhD and Accredited to direct research in Management sciences, University of Corsica, University of Montpellier 3. Associate researcher at ESSEC Business School Paris. He is an Associate researcher at HEC Montreal, a researcher at the Jacques Berque Center in Rabat, a researcher at the GIS Middle East and Muslim Worlds, CNRS and Deputy Editor-in-Chief of the journal *Questions de Management*. His areas of expertise are leadership, alternative management models, innovation, and transformation management. He is a member of the *Association Francophone de Gestion des Ressources Humaines* (AGRH) and of the International Institute of Social Audit (IAS). He contributes to several collective works and numerous French and international academic and professional journals. He is the author of the book *"Innovation and agility in the digital age: Africa, the world's laboratories of tomorrow"* published by Wiley.

Victor FRONTERA is President of VF Finance, the governing body of 8 Intersport franchise stores and a sneaker shop. Following his studies in geological engineering in Canada, he had difficulty finding a professional opportunity in France. So he continued his studies in business school (INSEEC Paris) to complete his resume. In 2014, he put together the following three ideas: his father saying that the future of business was in groups, a similar business group that was selling and limited opportunities on his original degree. Finally, from a lack of professional opportunity, he found another opportunity that allowed him to take up the challenge of taking over the family business, accompanied by strong external growth. Since then, Victor Frontera has been working hard to keep the group and its 180 employees alive.

He believes in the human aspect and in the behavior of everyone as a vector of expansion and quality of the business that his stores offer.

Manuel GARCIA is a graduate in economics and management and a Senior lecturer at the Jean Monnet University. He has been trying to bring together scientific research, technology, and teaching since 1984. Creator of numerous training programs and three professional license programs, he pilots the ACOFI license delocalized in three Moroccan universities, allowing an in-depth reflection shared by ISEOR and CIRPEC (Morocco) on the professionalization of students (conference in Rabat in December 2019 and conference planned in Marrakech in late 2022). Its teaching is structured around measurement in management, costing and finance. In addition to works on the proximities between Plato, Aristotle, and current research, he associates, in a territorialized inter-organizational approach, managerial activities, mutational skills, structures-behaviors and management systems with the measurement of externalities and dysfunctions.

Consuelo GARCÍA-DE-LA-TORRE (†) had a Doctorate in Management from the HEC of the University of Montreal, Canada, a master's degree from the University of Leuven in Belgium. She was a Professor-researcher at UDEM and EGADE Business School, Tecnológico de Monterrey, in Mexico. Member of the National System of Researchers of Mexico, (SNI), Researcher of the Strategic Research Group in Social Innovation, EGADE Business School. International Network of Humanistic & Management. She was a member of the Champions PRME Advisor Committee and received recognition as a Pioneer PRME at the UN. She had diverse publications among books, book chapters and articles in international journals.

Joseph GAUCHARD, self-taught, he started working at the age of 17 (agriculture, trade) before moving on to the public services, National Education, SNCF. In 1962 he joined the French Post Office for its opportunities for social promotion. As a counter clerk, he brilliantly followed all the distance learning courses offered by the Post Office to benefit from internal promotion: in 1969, he became a manager in a post office, and in 1973: Secretary to the Director of the Ille & Vilaine Department. In 1976, he became a senior manager working as a trainer for 6 years, then financial-management manager for 6 years. In 1988 he oversaw communication/quality in a center of 1100 agents. In 1991, he was promoted to Head of Social Relations for the Western Delegation of La Poste and participated in the search for a new management style. In 1993, he was promoted to Functional Status as Director of the Postal Group in Sables d'Olonne in the Vendée and ended his career in 2000. Throughout his career and in addition, he has worked in the Union field and then in the Social Works Committee, helping agents on long term sick leave) and animating the Staff Associations corresponding to his different functions.

Isabelle GÉNIAUX holds a PhD and the Accreditation to Direct Research. She is a Senior lecturer at iaelyon, Jean Moulin University, where she is responsible for the Management and Business Administration program and the General Management program. She is a researcher at ISEOR and at the Magellan Center and holds a PhD in management science. Her research has been in the field of entrepreneurship for more than 30 years, particularly on the creation of new activities by SMEs. She also works on entrepreneurial support and, more particularly, on student entrepreneurship.

Robert P. GEPHART is Professor Emeritus, The University of Alberta School of Business, Edmonton, Canada, and Associate researcher, ISEOR & Magellan, IAE Lyon. He is a Past Chair of the Research Methods Division, Academy of Management and Past Chair, Organizational

Behavior Division, Administrative Sciences Association of Canada. R. Gephart was Associate Editor of the *Organizational Research Methods* journal and as an Editorial Board Member for the *Academy of Management Journal, the Academy of Management Review, Organization Studies, Journal of Management, Journal of Management Inquiry,* and *Management Sciences.* He is the author of *Ethnostatistics: Qualitative Foundations for Qualitative Research,* co-editor of *Postmodern Management and Organization Theory* (Sage, 1996), and lead editor of *The Routledge Companion to Risk, Crisis and Emergency Management* (Sage 2019). Robert Gephart received the Sage/RMD Distinguished Career Achievement Award from the Academy of Management in 2015.

Frédéric GLORO began his career in public accounting in 1992. In 1998, he joined the finance department of a large poultry group in Brittany (Amice Soquet Group). He discovered the medico-social sector in 2002 and joined the finance department of Adapei 22 (now ADAPEI-NOUELLES des Côtes d'Armor) where he became Deputy General Manager in 2013 and then General Manager in 2016. He holds various positions and mandates: General Manager of a SCIC (Habitat Handi Citoyen for the housing of people with disabilities), President since 2020 of the CREAI (Regional Center for Studies of Actions and Information), activist in an association of Côtes d'Armor (Handicap 22), member of the Office of the CTS of Armor, President of the mental health commission, member of the office of the CDA 22 (PH) as Nexem, member of the Piveteau commission on inclusive housing as UNAPEI and member of the CRSA of Brittany.

Claudia Rocío GONZÁLEZ PÉREZ. Full-time tenured research Professor at the Universidad Autónoma Metropolitana (UAM), has a degree in communication sciences and journalism from the UNAM, Faculty of Political and Social Sciences. She has a master's degree in Organizational Studies from the UAM. She holds a PhD in Management Sciences from the University Jean Moulin Lyon 3, France, and a PhD in Organizational Studies from the UAM-Iztapalapa. She has a Diploma in Management of Cultural Enterprises UAM-GRECU. Research professor at UAM-Iztapalapa, professor of the Master in Reuse of built heritage UAM-Xochimilco and in the Doctorate in Sciences and Arts for design in the research line in Heritage Conservation. She is currently working on the research project: *Elementos para la creación de un Sistema regional de patrimonio, Factores determinantes de la creación de valor y capacidades para la construcción de un Sistema nacional de patrimonio histórico Mexicano.* (Elements for the creation of a regional heritage system, Determining factors for the creation of value and capacities for the construction of a national system of Mexican historical heritage).

Françoise GOTER, Senior Lecturer at iaelyon, Université Jean Moulin, teaches team management and public management. She oversees the Master alternating course in Team Management and Quality. Her work focuses on the modernization of management in public service organizations, the economic recovery of companies, the socio-economic performance of very small businesses in the liberal professions, and managerial practices within family businesses. She has conducted some fifty research papers presented in journals and conferences in France and abroad. She is a reviewer for international conferences and academic journals. She oversees a program at ISEOR *(Institut de Socio-Économie des Entreprises et des Organisations)* and leads intervention-research projects conducted within companies and public or private organizations. Elected member of the National Council of Universities (CNU) since 2015.

Yann GOUDY began his career as a professional driver in single-seater car racing, after training in management and marketing. From the 2000s onwards, he followed a "postulant" career path within the *E.Leclerc movement*: department manager, then department manager, then operations manager in various stores. In 2014, he took over the company created by his parents in 1987 and became CEO of E.Leclerc Océanis, in Saint-Gilles Croix de Vie, in the Vendée region, which now employs 220 people and has been implementing socio-economic management for three years. He has been actively promoting this management approach to the leaders of the E.Leclerc Movement, considering that it is perfectly adapted to the values of the company. He also has international responsibilities at the group level, in charge of commercial negotiation for fresh products, and regional responsibilities, in charge of coordinating commercial negotiations and as a member of the board of directors of the Western logistics center.

Réda GOURINE is General Manager of the École des Hautes Études d'Assurances in Algiers. He is also a Professor-researcher in management and has been a scientific consultant for fifteen years. He holds a PhD in Management science from the CNAM, Paris, on the theme of insurance and risk prevention inspired by the practices of a tradition of solidarity: the Twiza. He has a dozen academic and professional publications and has participated in commissions of reflection for the reform of the State. Moreover, Réda Gourine is active in various societal projects such as incubators and academic associations.

Pierrick GOVART assisted a small business manager for a dozen years, before taking the Master 2 in Change Management at the EUGINOV Center at IAE Lyon. He joined the ISEOR research center in 2021, and is currently piloting several interventions in local companies. He is particularly interested in the evolution of the managerial practices of the leaders of small enterprises as a lever of economic and social performance.

Michel GRIVEL, married with 4 children, graduated from EM LYON in 1970. He studied the systemic approach at the IAE of Grenoble and obtained a DEA in Socio-Economic Management at the University of Lyon. He then studied operations research at the University of Texas. He received his PhD in Management science from the University of Lyon in 1980, and was the first doctor trained at ISEOR. After teaching mathematics in Burkina Faso from 1970 onwards, he became a teacher at EM Lyon, and director of the IT department, then, in 1978, director of continuing education and international cooperation. In 1993, he was appointed Associate Professor at the IUT Lumière University of Lyon 2 and in masters, before assuming the presidency of the Board of Directors of this IUT in 2006. At the same time, since 1974, he has created and managed companies. Today, the company Ciril Group includes management software, geomatic software and Cloud-Computing. Since 2016, after passing the company on to two of his children, he has been Chairman of its Supervisory Board. He is President of the Executive Committee and founding member of the "Henri Savall – ISEOR Foundation, under the aegis of the Fondation de France."

Arturo GUERRERO LIZARDI is an industrial engineer at the University of Guadalajara, Mexico. He was trained as a consultant in socio-economic management by Dr. Savall and Dr. Zardet, Franchisee for Mexico of ISEOR with interventions in companies and participation in Colloquiums to disseminate the results achieved. He was a founding consultant of COMPITE (National Committee for Productivity and Technological Innovation, Mexico) making interventions in companies and institutions for more than 15 years and counting by hundreds the work done in areas of manufacturing and management, participant, and coordinator for the development of intervention methodologies. He is currently working as a consultant for companies.

Gilles GUYOT is a Professor of management, Honorary President of the University Jean Moulin Lyon 3, Honorary Director of the IAE Lyon and former President of the IAE network. He has published on the evolution of management schools in the world, including

L'Internationale de l'Intelligence (Éditions L'Harmattan, 2012). He resides in the United States and currently teaches courses on various topics of International, Comparative and European Studies at a major American university, his latest published work is *The Homeland of Human Rights* (2016). His latest publications focus on the critical analysis of research methodologies in Management sciences.

Denis HAMAYON has spent his entire career in the social sector, insertion and medico-social field, he was director of CHRS (Centre d'Hébergement de Réadaptation sociale) for 12 years, then for 15 years General Director of the association les Nouelles and, from 2016, Deputy General Director of the association ADAPEI-NOUELLES Côtes d'Armor. He is a graduate of the École des Hautes Études en Santé Publique (HESP) in Rennes and holds a master's degree from the IAE in Lyon 3 (Management sciences – socio-economic approach). For the past 10 years, he has been a part-time lecturer in the master's degree program in management of health and medico-social units in Lyon 3. He was President of the AFPE, a training association for future professionals in social and medico-social services in Brittany, and Vice-President of URIOPSS Bretagne. He is currently elected Mayor and Vice-President of an agglomeration community in Côtes d'Armor (170,000 inhabitants).

Nouria HARBI is a Senior lecturer at the University Lumière Lyon 2, member of the ERIC laboratory and responsible for the Master 2 OPSIE (Organization and Protection of Information Systems in Enterprises) in cybersecurity. She obtained her PhD from INSA Lyon in 1990. She then joined the ISEOR laboratory, where she worked on information systems. Her research area is particularly focused on the security of business intelligence systems, including access control to data warehouses based on profile management, data integrity and veracity. In addition, she is involved in research activities using data mining techniques for computer security, intrusion detection, and confidentiality and availability of data stored in cloud computing and cryptography.

Tonya HENDERSON is an organization development (OD) scholar-practitioner and aerospace industry professional, USA. She was the 2019 Chair for the Academy of Management's Management Consulting Division and the 2016 Organizer and Curator of TEDx Colorado Springs. Tonya Henderson has provided complexity and OD-informed consulting and problem-solving to a wide range of industry clients and currently works for Torch Technologies developing future system requirements. As a Doctor of Management, a graduate of the US Naval Academy, and a veteran of the consulting and aerospace industries, her work is informed by multi-disciplinary experience, education, and scholarship. She loves exploring how repeated patterns of perception, communications, and group behavior can be leveraged to solve complex problems.

Hervé HENRY holds a master's degree in Mechanics and Robotics and a master's degree from the *École des Mines de Saint-Étienne.* He started his career as a salaried employee for 17 years, first as an automatician and roboticist, then as a project manager, then as a sales manager and finally as a profit center manager in various industrial companies. In 2002, he created the company Sileane (St Étienne), a specialist in Robotics, Vision, and Artificial Intelligence. The robotic systems built by this company are distinguished by their ability to reproduce and adapt gestures in real time in industrial environments with high technological and regulatory requirements (food processing, pharmaceuticals, nuclear, environment, etc.). The company currently employs 85 people and is one of the European leaders in these fields.

Alla HEORHIADI, PhD, EdD, is scholar-practitioner who practices research, and teaches about the socio-economic approach to management (SEAM). Experienced OD consultant and University Professor who have taught OD to doctoral students in the past, shifted her focus primarily to SEAM. She co-directs the national association of socio-economic scholar-practitioners, SEAM Institute (www.seaminstitute.org), and annually organizes conferences of European and North American scholar-practitioners.

Pierre HIDALGO worked for ten years in the private sector as a production manager, then logistics director. In 1974, he was recruited by the United Nations to join the International Labour Office (ILO), where he remained until his retirement in 1998. First as a management expert, then as a project manager and regional advisor, and finally as head of the management development department at the Geneva headquarters. During this experience, he was confronted with the difficult times faced by countries during the implementation of Structural Adjustment Programs, as well as the challenge of transforming millions of jobs in the military-industrial complex in transition countries. He contributed to the joint ILO-ISEOR publication "*Releasing the Untapped Potential Through Socio-Economic Management*" and to the ILO publications "*Introduction to the Study of Work*" and "*Management Consulting.*" He is an Officer of the Order of Merit of Niger, as an UN-ILO expert.

Yue Cai HILLON is a Professor of management at Western Carolina University, USA. She holds a PhD in Strategy from New Mexico State University and has advanced training in management consulting, practical experience that helps her students learn strategic decision-making as a skill-based process. All her courses are built around value-added projects with regional businesses and non-profit organizations, learning that offers students highly relevant career preparation. Her expertise and main research interest is in creating value via management education and improved practice to further regional economic development in Western North Carolina.

Mark E. HILLON has had an eclectic life in civil engineering, international development, sustainable agriculture, strategic planning, and critical management scholarship, in the USA. He holds a PhD in Strategy from New Mexico State University and a PhD in Management Science from ISEOR/Jean Moulin University, a *co-tutelle* Doctorate supervised by David M. Boje and Henri Savall. The Lafayette Institute is his current venture to improve management practice in America.

Isabelle HORVATH holds a PhD in Management Sciences and an Accreditation to Direct Research (HDR) from the IAE of Lyon, Jean Moulin University. She is a Senior lecturer at the University of Haute Alsace. She is a member of CREGO (Centre de Recherche En Gestion des Organisations), an Associate researcher at Magellan, IAE Lyon, and the *Institut de Socio-Économie des Entreprises et des Organisations* (ISEOR). She is interested in organizational and managerial transformations of individual and collective structures in the artistic and cultural field and, more broadly, in the field of creation, as well as in the improvement of inter-actor cooperation modes. Her research work has been the subject of some twenty communications, publications in scientific and professional journals and three book chapters. She co-edited a collective work on entrepreneurship in the art and culture sectors and the conciliation between creative ambition and economic rationale (EMS editions).

Jocelyn HUSSER is a Professor at the Institute of Business Administration, Aix Marseille University, AMGSM-IAE Aix, CERGAM, Aix en Provence, Puyricard, France, where he teaches CSR management, management control and finance. He holds a PhD from the University of

Bordeaux and an Accreditation to Direct Research (HDR) from the University Jean Moulin Lyon 3. He is interested in three different research areas: sustainable development and its impact on financial performance and executive compensation, public hospital management and ethical decision making in purchasing. He was the editor-in-chief of the journal *VSE* (*Vie et Sciences de l'Entreprise*). He is currently President of the Association for the development of teaching and research in corporate social responsibility (ADERSE). He is also the director of the FCC research axis of CERGAM. He has published 2 books and 22 articles, 16 of which are in international journals.

Claude JAMEUX is Professor Emeritus of Management Sciences and has been President of the University of Savoie Mont Blanc (2004–2008), Director of the Institute of Research in Management and Economics (IREGE, 1996–2004), of the doctoral school (2002–2004) and of the IAE (2011–2012) of this university. He has been responsible for degrees in the three training cycles: DUT GEA (1990–1993), MSG (1998–2000), DEA (post-graduate diploma) Management and Technology of Information Systems (1992–2003). At the national level, he was a member of the MSU/DS7/Management Sciences expert group (1998–2002) and of the jury for the second agrégation competition in Management sciences (internal competition, 2001). After the presidency of the USMB, he was scientific delegate at the AERES, section of institutions (2009–2012), then advisor of sites and institutions at the DGESIP, Mission Expertise et Conseil (2012–2017). His work focuses on organizational power, the relationship between strategy and organization and public management. He is a Knight of the Legion of Honor (2008) and Commander in the Order of Academic Palms (2014).

María Ángela JIMÉNEZ MONTAÑÉS holds a PhD in Economics and Business Administration from the University of Castilla La Mancha, she is a Professor and Chartered Accountant. Secretary of the International Institute of Costs and director of the IIR Journal; Assistant of the Editorial Committee. She has published more than 20 works and numerous research articles in accounting, business management and auditing and has contributed to conferences. She has participated in various research projects: Semantic consolidation of economic and business terms in the Pan-Hispanic Dictionary of Economics and Finance of the Royal Academy of Economic and Financial Sciences of Spain; Implementation of Education for Sustainable Development in Legal and Social Degrees; CSR teaching innovation from the classroom; Responsible Business Information Systems: Accounting and non-financial information. Has participated in Masters in Argentina, Cuba, Italy, Portugal, and Spain.

Michel KALIKA is Professor Emeritus at the University Jean Moulin, iaelyon School of Management. He is the director of the BSIS (Business School Impact System) that he developed for the FNEGE & EFMD. To date, this system has been used in more than 50 management schools in 17 countries. Michel Kalika is also President of the Business Science Institute, an international academic network organization that delivers an Executive Doctorate in Business Administration for managers. Previously, he was Dean of EM Strasbourg Business School, where he led the merger of two institutions, Dean of IAE Poitiers, Director of Research at Audencia and Professor at Paris-Dauphine University where he created the international MBA & DBA programs. Michel Kalika is the author or co-author of more than 25 books, including *Strategic Management,* the most reprinted French book in this field. His research focuses on information overload (the *"Millefeuille"* theory) and on the impact of management schools. 40 colleagues have dedicated a book to him in 2019, "*Entrepreneur at the University,*" EMS editions. www.Michelkalika.com.

Lara KHABBAZ is a passionate researcher with a demonstrated history of working in the marketing and communication industry. She has also researched and lectured in topics related to organizational development and change, innovation and entrepreneurship, sustainable development, and corporate social responsibility (CSR), strategic marketing, customer journey and customer-centricity culture, sales techniques, digital transformation, total quality management. She participated in several conferences: Academy of Management (AOM), EURAM, ADERSE, Annual ODC Conferences by ISEOR and IAE Lyon 3, Young SDGs Innovators Program, Lebanese League for Women in Business. Lara Khabbaz is co-founder and managing partner at INSIGHTS' For Consultancy (IFC), a leading multi-disciplinary consultancy firm specializing in a wide array of services dedicated for individuals and corporations in different industries. She is currently occupying the role of Director of marketing at Notre Dame University-Louaize taking care of all that is related to business development and positioning.

Samia KHENNICHE is Senior Lecturer at University Gustave Eiffel and was an Associate Professor at the Conservatoire National des Arts et Métiers in Paris where she teaches management control and change management. Her research focuses on cooperative dynamics, change management, steering, and the performance of public action, and is published in French and international academic journals, as well as in professional journals. She is a partner and co-founder of Akoros Stratégie, along with professors and researchers in political science and Management science. She conducts research and interventions within public organizations to think about and accompany their political, strategic, and managerial evolutions.

Frédéric KLETZ is a professor-researcher at MINES ParisTech, within the Scientific Management Center (CGS) where he oversees the Scientific Management-Organization and Company Performance option and co-leader of the health course. He is a member of the reading committee of the journal Management International (Canada) and author of more than 50 scientific publications. He is developing research on the transformation of the health sector, the organization of hospitals, funding reform, the decompartmentalization of city and hospital, the modernization of public management, and on the cultural sector, particularly mediation. This work is carried out using an intervention-research method. He is responsible for several training programs for hospital doctors, notably in partnership with the *Assistance publique des hôpitaux de Paris (AP-HP)* and the association with the *École des hautes études en santé publique (EHESP)* for the supervision of student directors.

Omaya KURAN is full-time Assistant Professor, Chairperson-Undergraduate Programs and Co-director-DBA Program at the Faculty of Business and Management, University of Balamand, Lebanon. Previously she held the position of Director at the Career Services Center, where she created and organized over 10 students' programs and promoted student employability through various cooperation. Omaya is a double Award winner at the AOM Conference 2017, Winner of Best paper Award of the Management Consulting Division and of the Benedictine University Scholar-Practitioner Collaboration Award. Omaya Kuran holds a Doctorate in Business Administration (DBA) from University Jean Moulin Lyon 3. She holds a Master of Business Administration from the Lebanese American University and a Bachelor of Arts in Economics fron the American University of Beirut.

Philippe LACROIX was the CEO-Managing Director of the BELUX subsidiary, Belgium and Luxembourg, of the *MANPOWER Group worldwide.* The BELUX subsidiary, which he managed, provides human resources solutions for more than 2,500 clients, and employs 600 people in 60 branches. Trained at the EPM and then at the Haute École "*Groupe ICHEC" – ISC*

Saint-Louis," Philippe Lacroix has made his career in human resources where he held various management positions at Adecco and Vedior. He is an expert in the field of employment and socio-economic innovations that transform companies and their environment. He has chaired the federation of HR service providers (FEDERGON).

Philippe LAURIER is a researcher at the IRT SystemX technological research institute on the quantification of computer attack damage. He is responsible for teaching modules at the *École Polytechnique,* the *École des Mines de Paris,* the ENSTA and the Universities of Paris 1 Sorbonne and Paris 9 Dauphine. He is a Senior lecturer at the *École Nationale des Ponts et Chaussées.* Member of the Foundation Committee of the Maurice Allais Foundation. Author of eleven books on economics, money, crises, economic intelligence, and innovation. He is a specialist in innovation, creator of an incubator for young technological companies, and author of several patents.

Muriel LEGENDRE is a consultant specialized in strategic management, ISEOR franchisee since 2013. Graduated from AUDENCIA in 1981, she spent more than 20 years in SMEs and large groups (PPR) in the textile and clothing sector where she held various positions: several research & development-purchasing-production departments, sales manager, project manager. In particular, she has managed the organization or reorganization of the entire value chain of several industrial and commercial companies to develop their efficiency and economic performance. In 2004, she created her own consulting firm, *Objectif Performance,* to support small and medium-sized companies in their strategic thinking. In 2009, she met Henri Savall in a management conference and started her training in the socio-economic management method. In 2013, she became an ISEOR franchisee in addition to her strategy consulting business.

R. Murray LINDSAY is the former Dean and currently Professor of Accounting at the Dhillon School of Business at the University of Lethbridge (Alberta, Canada). His research interests lie in two broad areas. The first involves developing a comprehensive research methodology focused on increasing the relevance of academic research for practice and appropriate to the process nature of management control systems. The second involves performance management, where he studies how management control systems facilitate, or impede, employee empowerment innovation, strategic adaptation, and the unleashing of human potential. A former President of the Management Accounting Section of the American Accounting Association, he is currently on the editorial board of *Contemporary Accounting Research Journal.*

Anne LOUBÈS is a University Professor of Management Sciences at the IAE University of Montpellier, a member of AGRH and the Montpellier Research in Management (MRM) Laboratory. She has conducted numerous research projects on the partnership and territorial dynamics of Human Resources Management (HRM). For more than five years, she has been co-leading the Responsible Management and Ecological Transition transversal axis within the MRM laboratory. She participated in the creation of the thematic research group of the *Association Francophone de Gestion des Ressources Humaines (AGRH): GRH et territoires* (HRM and territories), which she co-directed with Christian Defélix and Isabelle Bories-Azeau for eight years. She is currently director of the IAE of Montpellier

Antoine MASINGUE is University Professor at Polytechnic University of Hauts-de-France and holds a PhD in Management science (Paris 2 – Sorbonne University). He is Accredited to direct research (HDR), specializing in organizational psycho-sociology (Organizational Behavior). He is a Senior lecturer at Sciences Po Paris, School of Management, and Innovation. He is Vice President of AIRMAP (International Association for Research in Public Management) and Director of AGRH (French-speaking Association of Human Resources Management Researchers). He is a member of the scientific committee of the journal *Recherches en sciences de gestion – Management sciences – Ciencias de gestón* and a member of the editorial board of the journal Gestion des Ressources Humaines. He is also a member of the scientific committees of the Academy of Management – ISEOR, and of the international symposiums ADIMAP – HEC Montréal *(École Nationale d'Administration Publique)*. He is also a member of the French Association of Psychological Types.

Susana T. MÁSPERO is a Certified Public Accountant from the Faculty of Economic Sciences, University of Buenos Aires (UBA) in Argentina. She is certified by the *Programa formador de formadores: contabilidad tridimensional* (ICEAC-AIC Network) and has a specialization in the direction and management of micro, small and medium-sized companies of the UBA. She is currently an independent accountant and accountant auditor since 2014 of the association Eccles, CEA San Pedro. Simultaneously, she is currently teaching assistant of the subject Social and Environmental Accounting at the UBA, in Economic Sciences. She participates in the Commission of Studies on Social, Economic and Environmental Sustainability of CPCECABA-Argentina, is moderator of RCyT (CPCECABA) "*Keys to Cost Management on Triple Impact Sustainability*" and lecturer of the course D.A.C. of CPCECABA, "Introduction to the generation of indicators for the adherence, measurement and reporting of the O.D.S. in Argentina organizations and companies."

Rocks MAZRAANY holds a PhD in Management and Mathematics at the Lebanese University, Faculty of Management and Economics. Author of numerous professional and academic publications in the field of data analysis and financial management of public and private organizations. Experienced executive researcher in the public sector for administrative decentralization in local government systems, where he participated in many conferences in France. Experienced researcher in statistical studies and research techniques, tutor of many theses on quality performance and financial improvement. Member of LUTF (Lebanese University task force) for the analysis and organization of prevention measures against the coronavirus.

Robert-Louis MEYNET is a Doctor of State in Economic Sciences, after a university education that allowed him to obtain a master's degree in management control and the Diploma of Advanced Accounting Studies (DECS). He also holds a first year Master's degree in law. Based in Lyon, he has been a Judicial Administrator registered on the national list for many years.

Sylvie MIRA BONNARDEL holds a PhD and the Accreditation to direct research, she is a Senior lecturer at the École Centrale de Lyon, PhD in Management science from the Université Jean Moulin – Lyon 3 and is a graduate of the École de Management de Lyon (EM Lyon). She is a researcher at ISEOR and at the Centre Magellan, iaeLyon, Université Jean Moulin. She teaches strategy and corporate finance at the École Centrale de Lyon. Her research focuses on innovation strategies, particularly in relation to network strategies in the context of open innovation and entrepreneurial dynamics.

Jean-Claude MOISDON was Director of Research and Professor of Management at the *École des Mines de Paris* (now Mines-Paristech) until 2008. He directed the Scientific Management Center between 1976 and 1996. He taught decision mathematics, risk analysis, organizational theory and organizational research methodology. His research has focused on the role of management instrumentation in organizations. He has conducted long-term intervention-researches in many sectors, industrial or service, public or private, including the health system. His most recent work has focused on the effects of new modes of health financing. He has published about 100 articles in refereed journals. He is a member of various scientific committees, including the National Committee of the CNRS and the National Committee of Universities. He has received several distinctions: *Chevalier de la Légion d'honneur, Officier du Mérite National and Commandeur des Palmes Académiques.*

Emmanuel MONOD, PhD, is currently visiting professor at the Research Institute "Artificial Intelligence and Change Management," Shanghai University of International Business and Economics (China), professor at Paris-Dauphine University and visiting researcher at Case Western Reserve University (USA). Emmanuel Monod was previously professor at Shanghai Jiao Tong University and Georgia State University (Atlanta, USA). He was previously Associate editor for ISR, ISJ, Database and ITP, CAIS and JAIS. His publications appear in *EJIS, ISJ, IO, EJM, CAIS.* He was guest editor of a special issue of ISJ and guest Associate editor for MISQ. Overall, he published 14 academic papers including 4 UT Dallas B+ papers and 7 SSCI papers, 2 of them being also SCI. He also published 27 conference papers including 6 at AOM. Two of these papers obtained the best paper award of the AOM MC division at AOM 2020 Conference Vancouver, Canada, and AOM 2019 Boston, USA.

Juan Matías MONTOTO CANLLO from Argentina, is a Certified Public Accountant, Master in socioeconomic management, Partner of Estudio Canllo Montoto, performing socioeconomic consulting services since 2013 and performing socioeconomic interventions in organizations of different industries. Currently dedicated to the strategic management and implementation of sustainable changes in the company Centro de Distribución Parque of which he is part. He has been a paper presenter at scientific congresses on management and cost management since 2011.

Rickie A. MOORE is Professor in entrepreneurship and business innovation at EMLyon Business School, Lyon, France. He is also a strategy advisor, educator and author, and his areas of expertise include new venture creation, intrapreneurship, and economic performance of firms and organizations. Rickie teaches to undergraduate, graduate, and corporate audiences and has designed and delivered executive programs in business innovation, corporate entrepreneurship, and firm performance. He is a strong advocate for experiential and challenge-based learning and is a visiting professor at several institutions around the world. Rickie has received his PhD in Management sciences from the University Jean Moulin Lyon 3 and has twice served as the Chair of the Management Consulting Division of the Academy of Management. He is currently the Director of the MSc in Global innovation and entrepreneurship at EMLyon Business School, one of France's leading academic institutions. His most recent work on Relevant Leadership: the dynamic equilibrium of managing and leading academic departments appears in *'How to lead academic departments successfully'* edited by A. Lindgreen, A. Irwin, F. Poulfelt, and T. U. Thomsen published by Edward Elgar.

Karile MOREL is responsible for the promotion and organization of inter-company professional training courses in French, English and Spanish, at ISEOR research center. After training as a translator and interpreter, Karile Morel worked in the international sales department of a manufacturing company. She then joined the ISEOR research center in 2011. She also assists Frantz Datry in the animation and management of the network of franchisees in socio-economic management throughout the world.

Arnaud MURET is an engineer from EIGSI, graduated from the University of Paris–Dauphine in technology and innovation management and has a PhD in socio-economics of innovation from the *École des Mines de Paris.* He has led changes in various ecosystems, bringing a strategic vision of innovation in environments under strong budgetary and regulatory constraints. He began his professional career at the French Atomic Energy Commission (CEA), and then moved on to work in government agencies, institutions and local authorities undergoing transformation, and in companies, particularly in the social protection sector. He is currently the General Manager of the OPCO-EP (*Opérateur de compétences des entreprises de proximité).*

Gérald NARO is a University Professor in Management Sciences at the Montpellier Management Institute, University of Montpellier, where he is Deputy Director in charge of research. Former director of Montpellier Recherche en Management, he is currently co-director of the Management and Entrepreneurship Chair of the LabEx "*Entreprendre.*" His research and main publications focus on strategic performance management systems, particularly in relation to the issue of Corporate Social Responsibility. In his most recent research work, he is interested in the question of the social responsibility of the professor-researcher in management control and in the sustainability strategies of management schools.

Thierry NOBRE is a University Professor at the Strasbourg School of Management. His work focuses on the performance and transformation of healthcare organizations, with a strong emphasis on interaction with the field through the methodology of intervention-research in numerous healthcare institutions. He held the chair of "management of health organizations" at the *École des hautes études en santé publique* (EHESP) from September 2011 to October 2014 and is president of the ARAMOS association. He has published about twenty articles in scientific journals and three books on this topic. The last one published in October 2020 analyzes the Covid crisis by coordinating the contributions of field actors who had a central role in public and private institutions. He currently oversees the "*Ad Salutem*" series on the theme of management and health at EMS.

Florence NOGUERA is University Professor of Human Resources Management at the University Paul Valéry Montpellier 3. She completed her PhD under the direction of Henri Savall and is Accredited to direct research at the University of Paris 2 Panthéon-Assas. After having been treasurer of the French-speaking Association of Human Resources Management (AGRH) for 9 years, she is President of AGRH. She manages an Executive MBA and an EDBA in France and in China. Her research work focuses on performance measurement and HRM standardization in service activities and public organizations where she conducts intervention-researches in socio-economic management. She is the author of more than 150 publications presented at conferences in France and abroad.

Rodolphe OCLER is Associate Professor at the University of Bedfordshire (UK), Director of Doctoral Admissions, and oversees the research training program for the business school's research center. He oversees an international MBA delivered in four countries and especially the one delivered in Jordan. He manages the undergraduate dissertation unit for the BS in Management, with about 250 students. His research interests include social responsibility, sustainable management, and critical thinking. He has supervised 5 PhD students who have received the title of PhD and is currently supervising 4 others. He is currently working on a video series for Henry Stewart on the methodological approach.

Nathalie OMBELETS is currently General Manager of the Société wallonne du crédit social (SWCS – Belgium) since 2008. The SWCS is a public company that grants loans in the framework of access to housing and its renovation. In her 13 years as General Manager, the company's staff has increased by 65% and the types of loans have greatly diversified from one to four. From 1993 to 2008, she held several positions at the Walloon Office for Professional Training and Employment (FOREM – Belgium). Nathalie Ombelets was certified by ISEOR in socio-economic management (SEAM) for the years 2007–2008 and she was responsible for the network of internal consultants which included about thirty people. She completed the basic SEAM and socio-economic management control modules as well as a series of in-depth modules. She has spoken on several occasions at ISEOR conferences.

Pascal PASQUIER is Chairman and CEO of the Brioche Pasquier Group. In 1977, he joined his four brothers to continue their father's bakery business. He began by taking on a commercial role to establish the Brioche Pasquier brand in Brittany. After this success, he left for Germany to master the language and culture of the country and to develop local commercial relationships. On his return to France, he created the Eastern France zone and became sales and marketing director for the Eastern, Rhône-Alpes and Provence Alpes Côte d'Azur zones. At the beginning of the 90s, he became sales manager for the "Brioche" activity and started exporting. In 2003, he took over the management of this activity. In 2007, he became CEO and accelerated the internationalization strategy by creating the "International" Division. Pascal Pasquier is a founding member of the "Henri Savall-ISEOR Foundation (under the aegis of the Fondation de France)." In 2014, he was awarded the Prix de l'Entrepreneur Région Ouest, in 2017: Winner of the Eponymes Trophy, honoring the leaders of companies whose name is that of a family owner.

Sébastien PAYRE is a Senior lecturer and researcher at the University of Caen Normandy and a member of the NIMEC research team. He is head of the social careers department at the IUT of Caen and co-editor of the journal *Management et Avenir Santé.* He was a research assistant at ISEOR (2004–2009) where he prepared his PhD in Management sciences. His main areas of expertise are human resources management, management and managerial skills, and job forecasting. He is a founding member of the PIMS research group and has written various articles and papers on dysfunctional stress, managers, outplacement, and human resource management skills.

Bertrand PAYSAC is Administrative and Financial Manager of *SLB Médical.* A graduate of the ESSCA School of Management, he joined *SLB Médical* upon graduation in 2017. He is responsible for the management of physical and financial flows, production as well as quality and regulatory affairs.

Laurent PAYSAC is the Director of SLB Médical. He founded the company in 2001 after ten years of experience in the pharmaceutical industry, particularly in international markets. He is a graduate of the Conservatoire National des Arts et Métiers (CNAM) and has a DUA from EM Lyon Business School. Since 2016, the contributions of socio-economic approach to management have led him to pilot a controlled organic growth as well as an external growth operation in 2021. SLB Médical's strategy for the coming years will be to increase its activity on the French market and to commercialize its offer on the German market. Laurent Paysac is a founding member of the "*Fondation Henri SAVALL – ISEOR,*" *under the aegis of the Fondation de France.*"

Georges PEILLON has been an expert in crisis management and communication for fifteen years. He regularly intervenes in companies and institutions on crisis issues and more particularly on the social role of the manager in a conflict situation. He was previously a communications advisor, spokesperson, and press relations officer at the Ministry of Defense. He teaches in various universities (*Grenoble Alpes, Lyon 2, Lyon 3, Université Catholique de Lyon*) and higher education institutions (IMIS, ISEG, IGS). He is also a writer under the name Georges Neyrac and has published six books of stories, novels and short stories.

Laura P. PEÑALVA ROSALES has a degree in Physics and Mathematics from the Instituto Politécnico Nacional (IPN) and a master's degree in Artificial Intelligence from the *Fundación Arturo Rosenblueth,* A.C., in Mexico; a PhD in organizational studies from the Universidad Autónoma Metropolitana (UAM, Mexico) and a PhD in Management sciences from the Université Jean Moulin, Lyon 3, France. She is a full professor and researcher at UAM-Xochimilco, Mexico City. She has been coordinator of the bachelor's degree in Administration, chair of the research area "Analysis and socio-economic management of organizations" and coordinator of postgraduate studies in the Social Sciences and Humanities Division. Participates as a reviewer in editorial committees of national and international magazines. She has more than 60 academic publications and 100 papers in his areas of interest: techniques, methods, and mathematical models for the representation, structuring and management of knowledge; organizational learning; mathematics education; and industry 4.0.

Jean-Claude PÉNICAUD-TESSON holds a master's degree in public law (1982 – University of Poitiers) and was a civil servant in the prefectural administration between 1984 and 1989. He has been an independent manager of a large-scale distribution company, under the *E.Leclerc brand,* since 1998 after having managed two hypermarkets (1989–1997) as an employee. He is looking to implement the socio-economic approach to management in his company in the long term. Jean-Claude Pénicaud-Tesson is a founding member of the *"Henri Savall-ISEOR Foundation (under the aegis of the Fondation de France)."*

Jean-Marie PERETTI is Professor Emeritus at the University of Corsica, Professor at ESSEC Business School Paris, Professor of the ESSEC Chair of Change and the ESSEC Chair of Managerial Innovation. Honorary President of the French-speaking Association of Human Resources Management (AGRH) and of the International Institute of Social Audit (IAS). President of the ASMP, editor-in-chief of *Question(s) de management* journal, he has published about a hundred books and numerous articles in the fields of human resources management (HRM), corporate social responsibility (CSR), social audit and managerial innovation.

Roland PÉREZ is an alumnus of the École Normale Supérieure de Cachan (ENS Cachan) and holds a PhD in economics (Paris I) and Professor of management techniques (1965) then of economics and management (1971). He got successively a position in Lille, Tunis, CNRS Paris, the University of Amiens (where he was President 1973–78), and the University of Montpellier I since 1981. He was, for several years, seconded as Director of the Mediterranean Agronomic Institute of Montpellier. He became Director of the Doctoral School of Economics and Management of Montpellier (1999), then Professor Emeritus (2003). He was President of the French Society of Management – SFM (2006) and of the International Network on Organizations and Sustainable Development (2007-09). Roland PÉREZ has worked successively on corporate finance, industrial analysis, and strategic analysis, then on general questions of management and governance of organizations as well as finalized socio-economic systems.

Éric PERNOUD is President and CEO of *Savoie-Volailles,* which employs more than 120 people. He and his brother took over the reins of the family business. The family business began with the parents who developed, for more than 25 years, a business of selling live poultry. In 1976, the family business stopped and moved to a regional food trade business but kept the name

Savoie Volailles Pernoud. At the head of the company since 1980, he and his brother worked on the progressive opening of new stores and the development of existing stores. Today, the company has five stores in Haute-Savoie as well as a logistics and manufacturing platform for artisanal products. The company is also present in about ten markets and owns orchards.

Gilles PERNOUD is the General Manager of *Savoie Volailles* which employs more than 120 people. He and his brother took over the reins of the family business. The family business started with the parents who developed, for more than 25 years, a business of selling live poultry. In 1976, the family business stopped and moved to a regional food trade business but kept the name *Savoie Volailles Pernoud.* At the head of the company since 1980, he and his brother worked on the progressive opening of new stores and the development of existing stores. Today, the company has five stores in Haute-Savoie as well as a logistics and manufacturing platform for artisanal products. The company is also present in about ten markets and owns orchards.

Michel PÉRON (†) was Professor Emeritus of Anglo-Saxon languages and civilizations at the University of Paris Sorbonne Nouvelle. A lexicographer, he published several English-French dictionaries. He also specialized in the history of economic thought and devoted his PhD dissertation to the study of the work of William Petty. A member of the *Centre d'Études et de Recherche sur la Vie Économique dans les Pays Anglo-Saxons* (CERVEPAS), he also chaired the international scientific committee of ISEOR. Mayor of Saint André la Côte for 24 years, he was involved in the development of this rural commune. Among his numerous publications, we should mention "*Le Robert & Collins du management,*" Édition dictionnaire Le Robert, 1992 (in collaboration) and his coordination of the collective work "*Transdisciplinarity: the foundation of Anglo-Saxon managerial thought*" .Economica, 2002.

Serge PÉRON is an administrator at the Economic, Social and Environmental Council (CESE). He spent the first part of his career as a naval commissioner, where he held administrative, financial, and logistical responsibilities at sea and on land, in the field of officer training and human resources, as well as operational legal functions. He was deputy chief of staff to the President of the Republic Jacques Chirac. After becoming a civilian administrator, he quickly joined the EESC as the secretary of a parliamentary-type committee. He participated in the drafting of numerous reports on subjects related to the three dimensions of sustainable development. He has also been a lecturer on several occasions, notably in maritime law and law of the sea, and has been responsible for training activities for French-speaking economic and social Councils.

Yvon PESQUEUX is Professor Emeritus, holder of the chair "Development of Organizational Systems" at the Conservatoire National des Arts et Métiers (Paris). Doctor of Economics from the University of Paris-Sorbonne and Doctor honoris causa from the University of Galati (Romania). He is the author of numerous scientific articles and several books on organizational theories, such as *Psychological Contract and Organizations – Understanding Written and Unwritten Agreements,* Pearson France, Paris, 2014, (in collaboration with Denise Rousseau, Pascale de Rozario & Rémi Jardat), *Organizational Theory,* Pearson, Paris, 2018 (in coll. with P. de Rozario).

Renaud PETIT is a Senior lecturer at IAE Lyon, Jean Moulin University, pedagogical manager of the Master in Human Resources Management (HRM) – Specialty "Social Audit, Social Responsibility of Stakeholders" since 2016, after three years in position at the IUT of Besançon. He has conducted intervention-researches at ISEOR, for 18 years and is currently

Program Director. He is a member of the Academy of Management, AGRH, ADERSE, IAS. His main areas of research, published in more than 35 articles, book chapters and communications, are the development of the attractiveness/loyalty of organizations and the management of inter-generation. In addition to the management of human resource changes in organizations with complex governance in the health and social sector, his latest work focuses on the impact of the socio-economic performance of very small enterprises (VSEs) and local SMEs as a lever for the vitality of a territory.

Xavier PIERRE is Director of Strategy & Development at the consulting firm PGF (Ottawa, Canada). He holds a PhD in Management science under the direction of Henri Savall. He was trained in and uses the methods developed by ISEOR in his interventions. He has accompanied – in Canada, France, Switzerland, and Belgium – public non-profit organizations such as municipalities, ministries, chambers of commerce, agencies and non-for profit organizations.

Benoît PIGÉ is a University Professor in Management Sciences and teaches at the University of Franche-Comté. He was a visiting professor for more than ten years in Togo and Cameroon. He is the author of the following books : «*Le modèle cybernétique du contrôle de gestion – Vers une anthropologie du contrôle de gestion*», EMS (2020), «*Les normes comptables – Cadre conceptuel et gouvernance*», EMS (2017); «*Audit et contrôle interne – De la conformité au jugement*» 4e éd, EMS (2017); «*Qualité de l'audit*», De Boeck (2012); «*Éthique et Gouvernance des Organisations*», Economica (2010); «*Gouvernance, contrôle et audit des organisations*», Economica (2008).

Jean-Michel PLANE is a University Professor in Management Sciences at the University Paul-Valéry Montpellier 3. He is Director of the CORHIS research unit, which is composed of nearly 80 researchers and professor-researchers. He is responsible for the doctoral program in management within the doctoral school "Territories, Time, Societies and Development." Author of numerous books and scientific articles, he completed his doctoral dissertation under the direction of Henri Savall as well as numerous interventions in socio-economic management in organizations in France and in Africa. He is known worldwide for his work on leadership and organizational theory. He leads management seminars and accompanies leaders in the perspective of capacity building. A recognized specialist in organizational behavior management, he directs the Master of Science in Organizations and Institutions.

Sébastien PODEVYN-MENANT is an Associate Professor at the Gustave Eiffel University, where he teaches political science. His research focuses on conservatism. After nearly 20 years in political collaboration, within local authorities, the two Houses of Parliament and in ministerial cabinets, he is now the General Director of the association France Silver Eco, working for the development of the ageing economy. He is a co-founding partner of Akoros Stratégie, along with professors and researchers in political science and management science. He conducts intervention-researches within public organizations to think about and accompany their political, strategic and managerial evolutions.

Silvia POMAR FERNÁNDEZ is Doctor in management of the Universidad Autónoma Metropolitana (UAM, Mexico City) and Doctor in Management science of the University Jean Moulin Lyon 3, Francia. She is a full-time professor in the Master in Administration and in the postgraduate courses in Administrative Sciences, Economics, Management and Innovation Policy and Organizational Studies at the UAM. She is currently the Academic Secretary of the Division of Social Sciences and Humanities. Research topics: strategy and competitiveness of the micro, small and medium enterprise, organizational change, innovation, industry 4.0, business model. Area of research analysis and socio-economic management of organizations, member of academic networks of organizational studies, the *Association Internationale de Recherche en Entrepreneuriat et PME* and the Latin American Council of Social Sciences. Co-author of three books, author of one book, has written 44 book chapters, 63 articles published in journals and conference proceedings and has participated in more than 100 conferences in several countries.

Luis PORTALES DERBEZ holds a PhD in Social sciences with a specialty in social development from the Instituto Tecnológico de Monterrey (Mexico). He is currently a professor-researcher at the University of Monterrey (UDEM), where he directs the Center for well-being studies and is co-founder of the Social Transformation Laboratory. Since 2013 he has been a member of the National System of Researchers, Level I, and has published more than twenty indexed articles and four books. He has carried out various impact evaluations and documentation of social development processes for municipal governments, civil society organizations, and companies. He is a consultant on issues of ethics, social responsibility, sustainability, social business models for organizations, and impact evaluation.

Joanne C. PRESTON, President and CEO is a full-time international consultant with Joanne C. Preston & Associates, USA and Editor of the *Organization Development Journal.* Currently, she is serving a second term as President of ISODC. She enjoys a multinational involvement with her clients and has worked with companies, as well as governments, in Japan, China, Korea, Mexico, Argentina, Ireland, England, Spain, Germany, Poland, Russia, Zimbabwe, Kenya, United Arab Emirates and South Africa. She has worked at high community levels with President Carter and his Atlanta Project as well as a very visible position in the recovery of New Orleans after hurricane Katrina. Her personal involvement with Lech Walesa and Nelson Mandela during their presidencies included personal coaching of these two recognized leaders. She has received the OD Consultant of the Year Award in 1994 and in 2017 & 2021, she has a chapter about her work in the Great Leaders in OD.

Francisco Javier QUESADA SÁNCHEZ is Professor of Financial Economics and Accounting at the Universidad de Castilla La Mancha and holds a PhD in Business Administration and Management from the Universidad Autónoma de Madrid. He is an insurance actuary by the Universidad Complutense de Madrid, Technical architect in execution of works by the Universidad Politécnica de Madrid, Auditor of accounts of the official Register of Auditors of accounts of Spain. He has supervised more than fifteen doctoral theses, the results of which have been outstanding *cum laude* in all of them. He has published more than thirty books and reprints on accounting, actuarial and economics. He has published more than one hundred and fifty articles in specialized journals and in presentations at national and international congresses. He has given courses for over 13 years in various universities. From the point of view of professional works, he has done more than three hundred works in the actuarial and accounting field.

Agustín RAMÍREZ GARCÍA is the founder and CEO of Grupo Aganova. He has more than 20 years of experience in the analysis and control of water distribution and transportation systems. In addition to being the founder of the two companies of the Aganova Group, he has led the development of the Nautilus system for the detection of water leaks in large diameter pipes, which has been patented in more than 70 countries. Its professional development has been rewarded with various company awards: for the Best use of technology in the area of sustainability, for the Best company track record, and for the company with the Best future prospects.

Pierre-Alain RAPHAN has been a French Member of Parliament since 2017. He holds a master's degree in acoustics and multimedia from the University of Marne La Vallée, a master's degree in Political Science from SciencesPo Paris and a Doctorate in Business Administration from the University of Paul Valéry (CORHIS Laboratory). He began his professional career as a Manager at Accenture and then as a director of consulting firms dedicated to managerial and technological innovations. He has published a book entitled *Intelligence artificielle et démocratie* (Artificial Intelligence and Democracy), published by Librinova (2020). His political mandate led him to be the rapporteur of the law on the financing of research (25 billion €) and rapporteur of the reform of the governance of sports federations. He has proposed various laws on the accompaniment of French people in arbitrary detention, the integration of sustainable development objectives in the French Constitution, a responsible charter for Artificial Intelligence and a regulation of the "attention economy." Holder of the rank "4th dan" of taekwondo and international referee of this discipline, he was decorated with the Medal of Youth, Sports, and Associative Commitment.

María-Ángeles RASTROLLO-HORRILLO is a Professor of Business Organization at the University of Málaga (UMA) since 1993. She has been Deputy Director of International Relations and Cooperation at the UMA. She is currently in charge of the research and consultancy group «Socio-Economic Approach to Management-THE SEAM TEAM" and has been director of the WBU Internationalization Center since 2004. She has participated in numerous research projects at the international level (MED, Tempus and Erasmus+ projects). Her scientific work has been presented at conferences of the stature of the *Academy of Management*, in scientific journals such as *Scandinavian Journal of Management*, *Journal of Sustainable Tourism*, or *Journal of International Entrepreneurship*. She is the author of several books and book chapters. Her research interests include socio-economic management, international business, innovation and business competitiveness. She is a member of the ISEOR Franchisee Network to apply the methodology in Spain, where she disseminates the model and helps companies to implement organizational change processes.

Marisa RASTROLLO-HORRILLO has obtained the diploma of *Social Graduate* of the University of Sevilla in 1991, and the *Labor relations and HR management degree of* the University of Málaga, through the expert adaptation course in 2013. He created his own professional office in 1995, offering consulting on accounting, fiscal and tax matters, labor law and social security, including both administrative management and representation before the Social Court. He is currently a member of the board of directors of the College of Social Graduates of Badajoz (Spain), where she is in charge of training and relations with the members. After completing the specialization course in Socio-Economic Management at ISEOR, she joined the SEAM team and participates in the realization of interventions in Spain.

Maïté RATEAU holds a PhD in management science, whose research has focused on sales development in non-profit organizations. She has been a intervener-researcher at ISEOR since 2013, accompanying organizations of various sizes and sectors, both by conducting socio-economic interventions within organizations and by training professionals from different backgrounds at the research center. She works with the team to disseminate socio-economic management internationally.

Jeannette RENCORET holds a Diploma of Advanced Studies in Business Management from the University of Chile and a PhD in Management Sciences from the University of Lyon 2, under the direction of Professor Henri Savall. As a Senior lecturer at the University of Lyon 2 until 2018, she taught translation, communication, and intercultural negotiation.

She chaired the Pedagogical Commission of the Faculty of Applied Foreign Languages and was responsible for internships in Spain. At the same time, she oversaw studies and development of computer applications for hospital and medical management at the *Hospices Civils de Lyon* (University Hospital Center). She now works as a freelance management consultant and financial auditor (Barcelona, Spain). Since 1976, she has been an Associate researcher at ISEOR. In this context, she has participated in the Regional Program of the Americas organized by the International Labor Office.

René RICOL is a Certified Public Accountant and Auditor, partner of DGR, then Managing Director of Calan-Ramolino. In 1986, he created ACA in Lyon and Ricol Lasteyrie in Paris. He was President of the Compagnie des Commissaires aux Comptes de Paris (Paris Statutory Auditors Association) from 1983 to 1985 and of the Compagnie Nationale (National Auditors Association) from 1985 to 1989, before becoming President of the Conseil Supérieur de l'Ordre des Experts-Comptables (Higher Council of the Order of Chartered Accountants) from 1994 to 1998. Deputy President, then President of the International Federation of Accountants (IFAC) from 2000 to 2004, founding President of Euro-Défi and France-Défi, he created the Compagnie des Conseils et Experts Financiers (Financial Experts Association). René Ricol will carry out several missions for the French government: President of the Observatory of payment deadlines, President of the Agency for Business Creation, President of the Orientation Council of France Investissement, Credit Mediator, General Commissioner for Investment. René Ricol was also a judicial expert before the French Supreme Court.

Martha RÍOS MANRÍQUEZ holds a PhD in accounting and auditing from Universidad Complutense de Madrid (Spain). Professor-researcher at the Celaya-Salvatierra Campus, University of Guanajuato (Mexico). Member of the National System of Researchers (level II), with PRODEP desirable profile recognition and member of the academic body in consolidation "Vulnerable groups and policies for development" recognized by PRODEP. Author and co-author of several articles in indexed journals, books, and book chapters, national and international. Her research interests are new trends in business management, social responsibility in organizations. Her professional experience in general contact and cost administration. Reviewer in international scientific journals in Spain, United States, Brazil, Colombia, Mexico. Editor of the journals *RAITES* and *Acta Universitaria*, President of the international network RENUTEG, Network of Networks of New Management Trends.

Alexis ROCHE is a Senior lecturer at the IAE Lyon School of Management where he is responsible for a Master in management and quality-safety-environment. He has been in charge of programs at ISEOR for more than 12 years and has worked with more than 40 companies and organizations: very small companies, SMEs, large organizations and associations in the fields of industry, services and the medico-social sector. He is developing his research on the link between recognition at work and performance. He is also interested in tools, methods, and effective pedagogies for change management in organizations, particularly in the context of work relations, quality of life at work, rewards and accomplishments at work.

Suzon ROCHE has been an intervener-researcher at ISEOR since 2019. After a bachelor degree in Team Management, Quality and Sustainable Development, she obtained her Master's degree in Management, consulting and change at the IAE in Lyon. For the past three years, she has participated in and piloted change management interventions in businesses with a workforce ranging from 2 to 200 people. Her Master thesis focused on the value of internal consultants in a socio-economic intervention.

Jean-Jacques ROSÉ has shared his activities between business, administration (Ministry of Public Works), teaching (École Nationale de Commerce, then University of Paris IV Sorbonne) and research. He has accompanied companies facing ever more radical changes. Among his publications: with E. Pisani, in *Revue mensuelle Hommes et Citoyens,* (1967–1968) ; *L'Or pour l'Art: de mécène aux sponsors* (1986) ; with A. Chauveau, *L'Entreprise responsable* (2003) ; as coordinator: *Responsabilité sociale de l'entreprise. Pour un nouveau contrat social* (2006) et *RSE. Entre Globalisation et Développement Durable* (2011) ; with F. Lépineux & alii, *RSE, La Responsabilité Sociale des Entreprises. Théories et pratiques,* (2010 – 2016). He is Vice-President of the Association for the Development of Teaching and Research in CSR (ADERSE). Finally, he is completing a PhD dissertation: "Social Sciences and Business – From P. Bourdieu to CSR" (EHESS-CNRS).

Grace Ann ROSILE, PhD, University of Pittsburgh, is Professor Emeritus of Management at New Mexico State University, USA. She studies organizational storytelling, "Ensemble" organizing processes, indigenous ethics, and pedagogy. She has been studying and applying the SEAM method for over 20 years. She is author of numerous academic articles and book chapters, most recently focused on "Ensemble" leadership through "Ensemble" storytelling. She is co-founder (2010, with David Boje) of the New Mexico Quantum Storytelling Conference, co-founder (2020) of the True Storytelling Institute, and founder of HorseSense at Work, offering management development and teamwork training. She also developed 7 educational films and edited a book (2016) on "Tribal Wisdom for Business Ethics.." She is co-author (with Boje) of "*How to do Conversational Storytelling Interviews*" (Elgar Publishing, 2020).

André ROSTAN is an honorary Public Chartered Accountant. He was a chartered accountant, managing partner of a chartered accountancy firm, elected to the Regional Council of the Rhône-Alpes Order of Chartered Accountants (12 years), Departmental Delegate of the Order of Chartered Accountants for the Savoie department (9 years). He also carried out quality control missions for accounting firms and was Censor of the Regional Council of the Rhône-Alpes Order of Chartered Accountants (12 years). He was also an auditor, elected to the *Compagnie des commissaires aux comptes de* Chambéry (Association of Statutory Auditors of Chambéry area) (8 years) and performed quality control functions for accounting firms. He is Vice-president of the association «*Les Anciens de Rawa-Ruska et leurs descendants – Savoie-Dauphiné* «.

Marc ROSTAN is a Public Chartered Accountant and Statutory Auditor. He is a managing partner of an accounting and auditing firm.

Paul ROUSSET has a PhD in economics and a degree in sociology. In 1970, he became an assistant at the University of Lille, then Algiers and Lyon, where he became a Senior lecturer. He was Dean of the Faculty of Economics and Management (1986–1991), before founding and directing the IUT Lumière from 1992 to 2003. He was then the first Rector of the French University in Armenia (2003–2007). His work has focused on development and emigration; work, unemployment, underemployment, and their measurement; the statistical approach to prices and purchasing power; the employment/training relationship; work-study programs and professional integration. He has implemented or participated in the implementation and evaluation of numerous international cooperation projects. Retired from the civil service, he became a training consultant in vocational training engineering and work-study programs (Algeria, Cameroon, Katanga, Haiti, Mauritania, Comoros, Senegal, etc.). He has been a road companion of *Trouver/Créer* since its creation and has been its president since 2015.

Thomas ROUVEURE, PhD in Management science, is a company director and Associate researcher the Magellan Research Center and ISEOR. He assists entrepreneurs in the creation of their projects and the managers of very small companies (VSE) in the survival and development of their companies. He teaches at the University of Lyon and in business schools. He publishes scientific papers and articles, and his research work focuses on entrepreneurial skills and entrepreneurial cognition. He is particularly interested in the impact of entrepreneurial competencies on the overall and sustainable performance of the firm.

Jean RUFFIER is Professor Emeritus and Director of Research at the National Center of Scientific Research (CNRS). He has spent his life studying the functioning of factories around the world. He began working on the rejection of Taylorism and new job design in the 1970s, within the Lyon Group of Industrial Sociology, under the direction of Philippe Bernoux. He then worked mainly within international networks, conducting research on technology transfer and innovation in Europe, Latin America and China. He created and directed a research center at Sun Yatsen University (Canton) dedicated to these themes. He was a member of the board of the International Association of French-speaking Sociologists and is responsible for Latin America for "Academics Without Borders."

Jérémy Clément SALMERON is Program Manager at ISEOR where he has been participating and conducting intervention-researches since 2013. He has a PhD in management science and is a part-time lecturer at the IAE Lyon and in various higher education institutions (ESG Clermont Ferrand, IFBTP). He works with various audiences in continuing education, directors and managers of medico-social establishments, students on work-study programs, etc. He has co-directed with Prs. Zardet and Bonnet several doctoral theses in Business Administration (DBA) within the framework of the partnership between Jean Moulin Lyon 3 University and Balamand University in Lebanon. Active in the international scientific arena, he is currently an elected representative and historian of the Management Consulting Division of the *Academy of Management*. His main research topics are strategic management practices, innovation project management and medical practice management.

Debra SALSI (†) is a scholar-practitioner of Organizational development and change management. She serves as a pedagogic supervisor and external examiner for ISEOR & Magellan, IAE Lyon, Université Jean Moulin in Lyon, France. She has been a business professor and chair for several universities as well as a mentor, visiting evaluator and international reviewer for business school accreditation bodies, including AACSB and ACBSP. As a "protégé" of Dr. David Boje, she became involved with the theory of quantum ontological storytelling, focusing her research interests on the intangible, unheard and unseen aspects of change management and organizational decisions within organizations.

Isaac SANCHEZ has been involved in the avocado business since 2001, founder of branch business unit in 2003, in charge of avocado marketing, packing business unit, from 2003 to 2006, trained in ISEOR-COMPITE pilot test in 2005, involved in socio-economic management since 2005, manager of packing business unit, from 2006 to 2015. Since 2015, he has been CEO of *Sanchez Aguacate Hass* corporate. He was Vice President of the *pro-avocado commission* 2007–2009 and President of the union of *avocado packers* of Periban (Michoacán, Mexico) in 2009–2010.

Mélissa SANCHEZ is an intervener-researcher at ISEOR and holds a PhD in Management Sciences from the University Jean Moulin Lyon 3. Her research areas are standards management, strategic management, and corporate social responsibility (CSR). She is also a part-time lecturer at the IAE of Lyon, Jean Moulin Lyon 3 University. Her recent publications are: "Management decisions and practices to integrate multiple standards and norms," 2021, *Management & Avenir* journal; "Tetranormalization and neo-institutionalism: how to be pro-active on your normative environment," 2019, International Conference organized by the *Academy of Management* and ISEOR.

Daniel SÁNCHEZ TOLEDANO is Director of the Department of Accounting and Management of the University of Malaga (UMA) and Partner-Director of the company *Sistemas de Información Inteligente para la Gestión*. He is Director of the UMA Aytos Berger-Levrault Center for Smart Governance Development, and Head of the Research Group "Public Sector Sustainable Information" SEJ 265. He is coordinator of the Observatory of costs and financing of collective urban transport and member of the Academic Scientific Committee of the Office of University Cooperation (OCU). He has been Vice president of the International Cost Institute. His main research interests include cost analysis, implementation of cost accounting systems, management indicators and BI initiatives in the public sector, auditing, and governance. He has supervised 7 doctoral theses and is the author or co-author of 60 scientific publications (books, book chapters, papers) and 96 communications and conference papers.

Eric J. SANDERS, PhD is a scholar-practitioner in organization development. He is a Senior lecturer in Business and Economics at Elmhurst University (USA) and serves as a guest instructor at Marquette University, Benedictine University, and The Chicago School of Professional Psychology. Sanders has practiced as a consultant since 2004 with clients in financial services, manufacturing, health care, and non-profits, and worked in retail sales and management for 20 years prior to that. His research interests include the characteristics and practices of scholar-practitioners, organizational culture, diversity and inclusion, and change management, with publications in journals including *OD Practitioner, OD Journal, and Journal of Organizational Psychology*, plus multiple book chapters. He currently serves as the Peer Review Editor for the OD Journal and is an active member of the *Academy of Management*, 2020 Chair of the Management Consulting Division.

Raymond SANER is Full Professor at Basle University, Switzerland, Dept. of Economics & Management since 2002 and teaches at the Center for sustainability (CSM) in Lüneburg and taught at Sciences Po, Paris, in the Master of Public Affairs program. His researches focuses on sustainable development (UNDESA), trade and development (UNCTAD/WTO), employment and poverty reduction (ILO), social economy (UNRISD), education (OECD, WTO/GATS), investment and climate change (UNCTAD, UNFCCC), and PPPs (UNECE/WHO). He was member of expert groups that drafted the Global Sustainable Development Report, is co-founder of CSEND (1993), an ECOSOC accredited research organization and co-chair of the OECD Responsible Business Conduct network and member of the UN Task Force on Solidarity and Social Enterprises. His publications are 7 books, 30 co-authored books, 8 book chapters and 34 refereed journal articles. He served on the executive board of *Academy of Management*'s ODC division and chaired its Advisory Council to the Board of Governors.

Philippe SAUVANNET is an honorary administrative magistrate. He has also held responsibilities in the senior civil service as a project manager at the General Inspectorate of the National Education and Research Administration (IGAENR), particularly in the higher education sector. He extended this experience to the Court of Auditors as External Reporter to the 3rd chamber in charge of the education sector and to the Regional Chambers of Auditors, where he worked as a magistrate. Finally, his professional career has led him to work in the prefecture as a sub-prefect of a district.

Amandine SAVALL holds a PhD from the CNAM, Paris in 2014, dedicated to the internationalization strategy of the Brioche Pasquier group. She is an active member of ISEOR: since 2011, she has been conducting intervention-researches on change management in various companies, such as very small companies (VSE), SMEs and mid-sized companies (MSE) in France, Spain, Mexico, Lebanon as well as a company in Belgium, belonging to a global group listed on the New York Stock Exchange. She leads a team of researchers and has published several times in academic journals and books. She is co-author of the book "*Becoming Agile*" (2015). She was an active contributor to the *Academy of Management* from 2015 to 2019 and as Chair of the Management Consulting Division in 2018. She is currently a board member of ISODC, an American association of international consultants and experts in organizational development and change management.

Henri SAVALL is Professor Emeritus at Jean Moulin University. In 1975, he created ISEOR, of which he is now President *www.iseor.com.* After obtaining a PhD in economics in 1973, he decided to focus his research on Management sciences. His complementary doctoral dissertation in Management sciences in 1974 marked the beginning of his work on socio-economic theory: *Enrichir le travail humain; l'évaluation économique* (Enriching human work, economic evaluation), published one year later by Dunod, then in the United States and Spain. For the past 53 years, his research has focused on socio-economic theory and the theory of hidden costs and performance in companies, organizations, and territories. His research focuses on strategic management, sustainable improvement of economic and social performance in companies, public organizations, and non-for profit organizations, as well as qualimetric (qualitative, quantitative, and financial) intervention-research methodology. Author of some 30 books in French, English and Spanish and 300 articles, he has coordinated 43 collective works and directed more than 90 PhD theses and Doctorate in Business Administration (DBA) dissertations. In 2001, he received, jointly with Véronique Zardet, the Rossi Prize from the *Académie des Sciences Morales et Politiques (Institut de France, Paris)* for their work on the integration of social variables in corporate strategies. *Chevalier des Palmes Académiques,* he was named *Chevalier de la Légion d'Honneur* (Knight in the Order of the Legion of Honor) in 2017.

Aline SCOUARNEC is an University Professor of Management at IAE Caen, where she oversees the Human Resources (HR) Master in work-study program. Her field of expertise is the Prospective of jobs and skills. In 2000, she and Luc Boyer created a methodology for analyzing the impact of external and internal changes on the future of jobs, skills, work organizations and managerial practices. She conducts prospective studies on organizations and observatories of branches of activity and leads work in academic and professional associations. Co-founder and co-editor-in-chief of the *Management & Avenir* journal, she has written numerous books and publications, including the founding work *La Prospective des Métiers,* with Luc Boyer (2009). She was President of AGRH (2014 to 2017) and has multiple responsibilities including Vice President of the National Association of HR Masters. Named Knight in the Order of the Legion of Honor in 2017.

Pedro Constantino SOLÍS PÉREZ is Full Professor "C" of the Economics Department of the Universidad Autónoma Metropolitana, Unidad Iztapalapa (Mexico) since 1976. Visiting professor at HEC-Montreal and at the Université Dauphine, Paris. Currently, Head of the research area of organization and society. He holds a B.A. in administration (UNAM), an M.A. in administration (HEC-Paris), and a PhD in organizational studies (UAM). He was president-founder of the Academy of Administrative Sciences (ACACIA-Mexico). His academic positions: Coordinator of the undergraduate program in administration, Head of the Strategic Planning Research Area and the Organizational Studies Area, Head of the Economics Department, Coordinator of the Graduate Program in Organizational Studies. Director of the Division of Social Sciences and Humanities of the UAM-Iztapalapa (2006–2010). Coordinator and founding member of the Graduate program in Administrative Sciences. His current research: Overall Value Framework and Sustainable Development.

Peter F. SORENSEN, PhD is Professor and director of the PhD program in Organization development (OD), and the M.S. Program in management and organizational behavior at Benedictine University. He has authored more than 300 articles, papers and books, including a number of best paper selections. His work has appeared in the *Academy of Management Journal, Group and Organization Studies, Leadership and Organization Development Journal, Journal of Management Studies, and Organization and Administrative Science*, among others. He has been Chair of the ODC Division of Academy of Management, and serves on editorial boards for *OD Journal, the OD Practitioner*, and the French journal, RSDG (*Revue Sciences de Gestion-Management sciences-Ciencias de gestión*).

Patrick TABCHOURY holds a PhD in Management sciences and is the author of several academic and professional publications and book chapters. He is an intervener-researcher mainly in the field of management of health care institutions. He has participated in several international conferences and has conducted several intervention-researches in the United States, Europe, and the Middle East, which have earned him several acknowledgements and certificates of appreciation for outstanding achievements. Patrick Tabchoury has restructured and managed several healthcare institutions and co-founded and co-directed a Doctorate in Business Administration (DBA) program at the University of Lyon. He has trained several hospital executives and has directed several theses in this field. He has been a consultant for the elaboration and implementation of business plans and development plans for several hospitals in the Middle East.

Jean-Simon TABOURNEL, a graduate of Political Science and holder of a PhD in Economic Sciences, is an Honorary Professor at the *École Supérieure de Commerce de Saint-Étienne* and at the *Catholic University of Lyon*, where he was Dean of the Faculty of Law and Economic and Social Sciences. He has also taught at the *Institut Français de Gestion* and at the Université Jean Moulin Lyon 3. He has written numerous articles for the journals «*Chronique Sociale de France*», «*Croissance des Jeunes Nations*», «*Informations et Commentaires*». He is the author of three books: *Nouvel ordre économique international et pouvoir* (2002); *Sociologie politique* (2003) and *32 leçons sur les défis géopolitiques du XXIème siècle, Prométhée contesté* (Éditions Chronique Sociale de France, 2010). Currently Honorary President of the François Perroux Association and lecturer in geopolitics, he works on the various aspects of international restructuring.

Henri TALASZKA (†) was Chairman and CEO of Belin (Nabisco), Chairman of the Board of Directors of Lenôtre, Managing Director of Ferrero, and Chairman and CEO of Pêcheries de Fécamp. He was President of Talaszka Conseils, a firm franchised by ISEOR, which supports companies and organizations in transformation processes aimed at developing their socio-economic performance.

Kianvu TAMO holds a PhD in Management Sciences from the University Lumière Lyon 2, Professor of the Chair of the *University Eleven of November*, Angola; he was Rector of the same university; Regent of the disciplines of management, management of human resources and methodology of research in social sciences; Director of monographs in 3° Cycle and theses in socio-economic management (University Agostinho Neto); author of several books. His experience also includes the functions and missions of President of the Ethics Committee of the public company UNICARGAS and President of the National Council for Education, Research and Development of the Order of Economists of Angola.

Ziyuan TANG holds a PhD in Management Sciences, defended in Lyon in 2019, prepared under the joint supervision of Prof. Marc Bonnet and Prof. Jean Ruffier. Ziyuan Tang is currently a temporary teaching and research Associate at the Faculty of Languages of Jean Moulin Lyon 3 University and an Associate researcher at the ISEOR research center. He has conducted socio-economic intervention-researches in Chinese industrial enterprises of various sizes since 2015. His research activities aim to help Chinese companies to get out of the bidding paradigm and achieve continuous improvement of their overall performance, through the application of socio-economic management. Her work currently focuses on human resource management (HRM) practices that reactivate the motivation of Chinese employees to continuously improve the performance of their company.

Mireille TESSON-PÉNICAUD. Self-taught, Co-manager of a retail company since 1994. In 2010, she piloted the change of her company's brand. In 2018, she joins a new company and commits herself to the deployment of socio-economic management. Mireille Tesson-Pénicaud is a founding member of the "*Henri Savall-ISEOR Foundation* (under the aegis of the Fondation de France)."

Anne THIÉBAUT-BERTRAND. Medical Doctor, hospital practitioner, in clinical hematology since 2001. She has spent her entire career in a University Hospital Center (CHU), initially at the Hospices Civils de Lyon (HCL) and then at the CHU of Grenoble-Alpes (CHUGA). She oversaw hospitalization units in Lyon from 2001 to 2008 and, since January 2021, has been the head of the oncology-blood disease unit of the CHUGA. Her area of expertise is the management of adult patients with acute leukemia, hematopoietic stem cell transplants and infectious complications. During her activity at the HCL, she participated in a socio-economic approach to management intervention undertaken in the hematology department and defended a PhD dissertation in Management sciences in 2011 at the J. Fourier University of Grenoble on the analysis of activity reconfiguration strategies in public hospitals, using the example of blood transfusion. She is co-author of more than 80 articles published in national and international medical journals.

Chantal THOUVEREZ was a nurse and then a teacher in a nursing school before choosing to study at university. After obtaining a master's degree in health and social work at the Lumière University in Lyon, she decided to pursue her career in Switzerland. From 1985 to 1996, she held the position of Director of Care at the Hôpital de Zone de Morges (Vaud), while pursuing doctoral studies in management sciences in Lyon, under the direction of Prof. Henri Savall, PhD dissertation defended in 1996. For four years, she worked as a consultant and then became head of Health Affairs at the Department of Health and Social Action (DSAS) in Lausanne. In 2004, following a decision by the Vaud government, she created the Cantonal Health Mediation Office (BCMS) and oversaw it until 2017, when she retired. In addition to her professional activities, Chantal Thouverez was a municipal councilor in Bavois (Vaud).

Nathaël TORRÈS holds a PhD in Geography and land planning. In December 2020, he defended a dissertation on the intergenerational housing formula. He is the director of the

Auvergne Rhône-Alpes agency of Récipro-Cité, a social and solidarity economy company specialized in social engineering for city and housing actors.

Denis TRAVAILLÉ is University Professor of Management Sciences at iaelyon, Université Jean Moulin Lyon 3, where he is Director of the Finance Department. Former director of the iaelyon Magellan Research Center, he is currently scientific director of the "Sustainable Performance" research team within the Magellan laboratory. His research and main publications focus on the links between management control, logistics and strategic processes. In his most recent research work, he examines the link between management control, management schools and organizational social responsibility (OSR).

Stéphane TRÉBUCQ is a University Professor at the University of Bordeaux, in the *Institut d'Administration des Entreprises,* where he teaches accounting, financial analysis, management control, and overall performance management. He holds a PhD and an Accreditation to direct research from the University of Bordeaux. His research has led him to deal with several successive themes: employee shareholding, societal performance, corporate governance, the "balanced scorecard," the "integrated scorecard," integrated reporting, human capital, environmental accounting. He is co-editor of the journals *Gestion et management public (GMP)* and *Recherche et Cas en sciences de gestion (RCSG)*. He is also in charge of the SME and CSR project, within the IRGO research laboratory, and holds the Human Capital and Overall Performance Chair attached to the Bordeaux University Foundation.

Philippe TROUVÉ holds a PhD in sociology from the École des Hautes Études en Sciences Sociales (EHESS) and is Accredited to direct research (HDR) in management. He was a teacher in organizational behavior and corporate sociology at the European Business School (formerly EAP), then a professor at the *Groupe ESC Clermont,* where he headed the Human Resources Management Department, then the Research Department. In addition, he taught for a long time at the University of Auvergne and at the IAE Lyon. His work focuses on forms of workforce management in SMEs, changes in local management, managerial innovation and experiences of democracy in companies. He was a columnist for the daily newspaper Le Monde from 1988 to 2013. From 1996 to 2001, he was a scientific advisor at the Mission Animation de la Recherche of DARES at the Ministry of Labor, then from 2013 to 2016, he was the National Scientific Director of the CÉREQ. He is currently Scientific Director of the PEOPLE research program at ESC Clermont Business School.

Julien VINAY. After a scientific training in biochemistry, he followed a master's degree in business administration (MAE) in Grenoble. In 1998, he joined the family business of equipment trading, then in full development, at the request of his father to perpetuate the business he had created. He gained his own experience in wholesale trade, moving from one department to another: from the reception of goods to sales at the counter. The transmission of the company "Vinay Matériel" is done in 2008, when he becomes its manager. In 2014, he decided to make socio-economic management his management system. This allows the company to continue its growth and to move to new premises.

Olivier VOYANT is a Senior lecturer at iaelyon, Jean Moulin Lyon 3 University, and is responsible for the Master 2 "Management, Consulting and Change" (MC2). His research and teaching focus on strategic management, on the support of leaders, directors, and managers as well as on the strategic involvement of all employees. For the past 30 years, he has led transformation projects at ISEOR in France and abroad.

Christopher G. WORLEY is the Research Professor of management at Pepperdine University's Graziadio School of Business, and a Research affiliate at USC's Center for effective organizations (CEO), USA. He is a recognized leader in the field of organization agility, organization development, and organization design. Prior to Pepperdine, he was the founding Strategy Director at the Center for leadership and effective organizations at the NEOMA Business School, in France, and served as Director of the Master of science in organization (MSOD) program at Pepperdine University. He received the McGregor Award Best Paper Award from the Journal of Applied Behavioral Science and the Luckman Distinguished Teaching Fellowship. Christopher Worley is co-author of *The Agility Factor, Becoming Agile, Management Reset, Built to Change, Integrated Strategic Change*, and seven editions of *Organization Development and Change*, the leading textbook in the field.

Therese F. YAEGER, PhD, is Professor at Benedictine University, USA, in the PhD-OD, and Ms in Management and organizational behavior programs. Publications include "*Critical Issues in Organization Development: Case Studies for Analysis and Discussion*" with Sorensen and Johnson (2013), "*Global Organization Development: Managing Unprecedented Change*" with Sorensen and Head (2006), and "*Appreciative Inquiry: Foundations in Positive Organization Development,*" with Cooperrider, Sorensen and Whitney (2005). Yaeger is a Past Chair of Management Consulting Division of the *Academy of Management.* She is former President of the Midwest Academy of Management and is a member of the Editorial Boards of *OD Review, Journal of Management Inquiry*, and the French journal, *RSDG (Revue Sciences de Gestion – Management sciences – Ciencias de gestión)*.

Lichia YIU is co-founder and president of the *Center for Socio-Economic Development* (CSEND) based in Geneva since 1993. CSEND promotes inclusive, transparent and participation based on sustainable development. Her research focuses on capacity building for sustainable development within public administration and the private sector. She designed the transformation project of public administration in Slovenia (1993–1996); the modernization of the in-service training system in China (1988–1997), co-designed a business and training platform for CIS countries on behalf of EBRD and leadership development for 3M in the Pacific region. She did her post-doc on organizational development and change (ODC) at Columbia University, teaches ODC, leadership and the SDGs at universities in Asia, Europe and North and South America. She is a long-time member of the *Academy of Management* and of the International Institute of Administrative Sciences and has published 16 books, 29 book chapters, 56 refereed academic journal articles.

Donabelle ZAKKOUR holds a PhD in Management Sciences from the Conservatoire National des Arts et Métiers (CNAM, Paris) and is the author of several academic and professional publications. She is an intervener-researcher and Associate Professor at the *Lebanese University* in the field of management, human resources management and the economic and social performance of companies. She has participated in several international conferences, conducted several intervention-researches in the Middle East and directed several theses in this field. Previously, she held positions in human resources management.

Véronique ZARDET is University Professor of Management at IAE Lyon, Université Jean Moulin (France), where she is responsible for the EUGINOV center (university school of innovative management) and the master's degree in Socio-economic Management. She directs ISEOR, alongside Henri Savall, founding president. Since 2012, she has chaired the academic association ADERSE, which promotes teaching and research in corporate social responsibility. Within ISEOR, she conducts socio-economic intervention-researches in companies of all sectors and health organizations. She has directed 53 PhD dissertations in Management sciences and "Doctorate in Business Administration" (DBA), published 25 books and more than 280 articles and communications. Her last article was published in 2019 in the *Revue Française de Gestion*: Valorisation de la recherche par l'expérimentation en entreprise. Case of the socio-economic management model (Savall, Zardet, Bonnet & Cappelletti). Together with Henri Savall, she was awarded the *Rossi Prize by the French Academy of Moral and Political Sciences* (Institut de France) for their work on the integration of social variables in corporate strategies. (www.iseor.com).

Rhida ZIANI is currently a freelance consultant, developer, and trainer in the field of software engineering and more specifically rich internet applications. He obtained his PhD from the University of Warwick in the UK in 1991 and has since held several positions in research and development in parallel computing.

Tariq ZIDI, PhD in Management Sciences, and researcher at the ISEOR laboratory, is the director of a company operating in new information and communication technologies in Marrakech, Morocco. He was one of the founding members of the *Centre des Jeunes Dirigeants de Marrakech* in 2006 and became its President in 2012–2014, before becoming the National President of the *Centre des Jeunes Dirigeants "CJD Maroc"* for the period 2019–2021 (www.cjd.ma). In 2020, he founded one of the first African incubators and gas pedals of startups, whose mission is to train and support a new generation of entrepreneurs equipped to meet the challenges of Africa's future, advocating innovation through the emergence of new economic and social models. (*www.ibdaa.africa*).

INDEX

SEAM Treatise, pages 995–999

D

F

G

H

I

K

L

M

N

O

P

Q

R

S

T

V

W

The manufacturer's authorised representative in the EU for product
safety is Easy Access System Europe – Mustamäe tee 50, 10621 Tallinn,
Estonia, easproject.com, +372 5696 8939, gpsr.requests@easproject.com

Printed and bound by CPI Group (UK) Ltd, Croydon, CR0 4YY
14/03/2026
02071360-0001